THE MUSHIRUL HASAN OMNIBUS

The Mushirul Hasan Omnibus

COMPRISING

Nationalism and Communal Politics in India,
1885-1930

A Nationalist Conscience:
M.A. Ansari, the Congress and the Raj

Islam in the Subcontinent:
Muslims in a Plural Society

MANOHAR
2006

First published 2006

ISBN 81-7304-686-7

Published by
Ajay Kumar Jain *for*
Manohar Publishers & Distributors
4753/23, Ansari Road, Daryaganj
New Delhi 110 002

Printed at
Lordson Publishers Pvt. Ltd
New Delhi 110 007

Distributed in South Asia by
FOUNDATION BOOKS
4381/4, Ansari Road
Daryaganj, New Delhi 110 002
and its branches at Mumbai, Hyderabad,
Bangalore, Chennai, Kolkata

Foreword to the Omnibus Edition

Professor Mushirul Hasan has honoured me by asking for these few lines to introduce this welcome omnibus volume. Professor Hasan is a scholar of phenomenal energy—whose steady stream of historical writings and edited volumes keeps more than one publisher busy. It is a mark of his scholarly vision that he should ask a sociologist to write this foreword. I am grateful, for it allows me to offer some sociological reflections over his work.

Mushir made his debut among historians with his study of the Khilafat movement, which opens this volume (I).[1] The processes it examined came to a head in the early 1920s. Several key figures in that movement received closer attention later, and his study of M.A. Ansari (II), an important but little remembered figure, is reproduced here. From these beginnings, Mushir has let his interests stretch as far back as the late eighteenth century, to Mirza Abu Taleb Khan, who travelled in Asia, Africa, and Europe between 1797 and 1803; and forward to our own times, as in his comparative essay on India and Pakistan which concludes the collection that rounds this volume off (III). His studies on the late nineteenth century include volumes on Awadh's *Qasbas*, small towns around Lucknow, building a story around the interesting Kidwai clan; and on a remarkable group active in and around Delhi at that time. In addition to all this, we have learned to expect from Mushir a regular flow of edited volumes which recover long forgotten, but historically significant texts, or make archival materials available in print, or assemble papers from the numerous conferences that he has instigated over the years.

At the centre of Mushir's writings is the history of modern India, and the relatively neglected place of Muslims in that history: their social arrangements and political experiences, individually or in groups large or small. Of that large 'space', he has focussed especially on moments when Muslims reached out to the world around them:

to travel extensively, to relate with Westerners like C.F. Andrews in Delhi and with Western forms of knowledge; or to work with their Hindu neighbours, as during Khilafat or in the life of M.A. Ansari. In a moment I shall argue that this 'open', outgoing style has been central to the history of Islam. Mushir's writings—as his many academic and administrative initiatives at Jamia Millia Islamia, where he is now Vice-Chançellor—seek to reinvigorate the outgoing and universalist strands in the Islamic, and the Indic, traditions to which Muslims in India, and in South Asia at large, are heir.

* * *

Civilizations are complex human creations, evolving historically in course of encounters with diverse realities—ecological, social, political, and so forth. Given the array of concerns that bear on their evolution, any civilization learns to nourish multiple, *contrary*, purposes—and concomitant cultural styles and orientations.[2] Think of China, say, in the twelfth century: a gentle, Taoist, contemplation of nature; exceptionally resourceful technological capabilities; bureaucratic traditions which could underwrite some of the largest empires in human experience, able also to organize resistance to potential horse-borne conquerors from the vast northern steppe—all this and much more was part of the Chinese tradition. Diverse cultural styles for coping with the world have found nourishment in the Islamic tradition too.

An open, outgoing, style has been central to Islam's repertoire: large numbers of bearers of the Judaic, Christian, Pahlavi, and other traditions swelled its ranks in its early decades, bringing their older ideas, expectations, and practices with them, making these part of Islam. Arab and Persian merchants had long travelled to the edges of the Indian Ocean, and after the seventh century, they carried the Prophet's message too—to the east African coast on one side, and India's west coast and South-East Asia on the other—relating to local communities everywhere. Sufi mystics related to peoples and religious traditions wherever they went; and numerous Muslim rulers—the Abbasids in the Fertile Crescent, the Umayyad dynasties in southern Spain, the Ottoman Turkish empire, the Mughals in India—drew strength from the social, cultural, and religious diversity of their peoples, and promoted extensive commerce in ideas as well as goods. Hidden here was a key moment in the intellectual history of mankind: Arab thinkers took in large parts of the ancient Greek philosophical tradition in the Byzantium, rendering them into Arabic, and carrying them to the then Arab kingdoms in Spain. There, in the Arab libraries, European scholars, familiar then with only a thin slice of the Greek tradition—whatever had been rendered into Latin by the sixth century—discovered something of the vast, unsuspected parts of the Greek corpus, in the eleventh and twelfth centuries, thanks to the Arabs in Spain. In responding to the challenge presented by this infusion of ancient Greek, and recent Arab thought, scholarship in western Europe took a quantal leap.

Alongside this open, outgoing style, Islam has nurtured a stern, inward looking style too. Shaped by religious scholars, *ulama*, between the eighth and the tenth centuries under the Abbasids in the Islamic heartlands around the Fertile Crescent, this style turned on *sharia*, the Islamic Law, codified by the scholars on the basis of the Koran, which they believed was divinely inspired, and on the basis of the Prophet's sayings and deeds, which too were believed to have been divinely inspired. The *sharia* was a social code for living a worthy life, a life of individual responsibility to God's will, as revealed in the Prophet's words and deeds. The authors of the *sharia* wished to stay aloof from royal courts which embodied organized power, for they believed that those who lived by Islam, following its law, the *sharia*, needed no external power to govern them. In practice, though, the *ulama* have been appreciative of the advantages that accrue from royal patronage of Islamic religious establishments—and, indeed, for advancing the frontiers of Islam.[3]

These two styles, one open and outgoing, the other looking inward, have always been present among Muslims, sometimes opposing each other, and sometimes cooperating, in more or less stable arrangements.[4]

* * *

Underlying the course of modern Indian history are a couple of sociological puzzles. Mushir refers recurrently to Muslims' heterogeneity: Shia / Sunni, Deoband, Barelwi, Ahl-i-Hadith. To these could be added differences of traditional status (Sayyid, Pathan, Sheikh, etc.), of contemporary class, of differential Westernization, and much else. Heterogeneity on the Hindu side would be no less. All this is true. Yet at several points, as in the 1946 elections, the course of events makes sense only if we concede that very large numbers, possibly majorities, were acting as if they were homogeneous, acting with reference to comprehensive categories, Muslim and Hindu, conceived in adversarial terms. The puzzle then is: how did this happen?

Evidence from latter day Haryana and Uttar Pradesh suggests that the key to the puzzle lies in processes beginning in early nineteenth century. One aspect of the political situation had become clear: whatever the formal arrangements, the colonial regime was firmly in control. That, however, settled only the question of the power-in-the-large. Power-in-the-small—the local pecking order everywhere—became available for fresh negotiation as its former guarantors, say the Mughal or the Awadhi state, lost control. Local-level contests for a new order followed. These frequently took the form of gathering crowds to assert control over public spaces, like thoroughfares, since formal institutions for political competition were slow in coming. Consequently, these contests moved in somewhat disorderly ways. The settings were scarcely propitious for envisioning futures of a comprehensive, non-sectarian sort.

Skirmishes began in localities, contextually, here and there, though news of particular incidents would carry by word of mouth along customary channels of communication. Old knowledge, say about Muslim irritation over music near mosques at prayer time, could be used to precipitate an incident. With passing decades and accelerating communications, the contestatory arenas moved to regional levels, around wider issues, like the right to sacrifice kine at Id, or the question of Urdu or Hindi as the language of the law courts in UP.

With growing experience of mobilization, the protagonists of these issues were beginning to work with relatively *general* symbols. That is, symbols not tied to particular, small, groups, as a local deity might be; rather, symbols like the cow or Urdu, not limited to small groups or their interests, which could therefore be invoked for rallying support across differences of *jati*, class, sect, and the like. By the second half of the nineteenth century, symbols and memories from the past—Rajput resistance to Mughals, the Vedas, Ganesha, Shivaji; or, as Hasan notes, 'mosque, *hajj*, sufi shrine' (II, p. 76)—were being invoked and charged emotionally, sometimes as foci for more or less durable movements and organizations. Around such general symbols, emotions may be whipped up to a frenzy, giving the corresponding identity a greater salience, indeed legitimacy, than that of older, more familiar, smaller identities.

Several protagonists were discovering how effective religious and other symbols of wide reach could be in gathering large volumes of support. As distinctive religious consciousness gained intensity, the older shared spaces began to lose their sense of mutuality. Nothing in the memories or experience of their protagonists would have warned them of the likely consequences of heightening such exclusive consciousness—and undermining the shared spaces—especially in the then unforeseeable future milieu of competitive electoral politics. Late nineteenth century activists, it will be remembered, had to manage without the kind of university-based knowledge and understanding that this volume offers us.

* * *

As Mushir notes, during two decades, from 1928 to 1947, numerous seemingly promising constitutional formulae for India's future failed—though agreement often seemed to be close. In shaping a constitutional arrangement, the participants have to take a risk about the uncertain future, assuming that the other participants would act fairly and reasonably, and abide by the formal arrangements. Prerequisite to such arrangements is a level of mutual trust between the participants; and this mutual trust between Muslims and Hindus had been fading for several decades. Why? I shall trace this decline in mutual trust to a process which was spread over more than a century.

At the heart of this process were numerous moments of *social aggression*. The following discussion will distinguish between three modes of social aggression: *symbolic*, whose working we have seen already; *societal*, expressed most tellingly in the drives for conversions from other faiths to one's own; and *physical* violence, witnessed in the recurrent series of communal 'riots'. The importance of social aggression, or even of physical violence, in the widespread hardening of mindsets has not entered our explanations and understanding of the process. At work was a two way process, in which social separativeness and social aggression fed on each other:

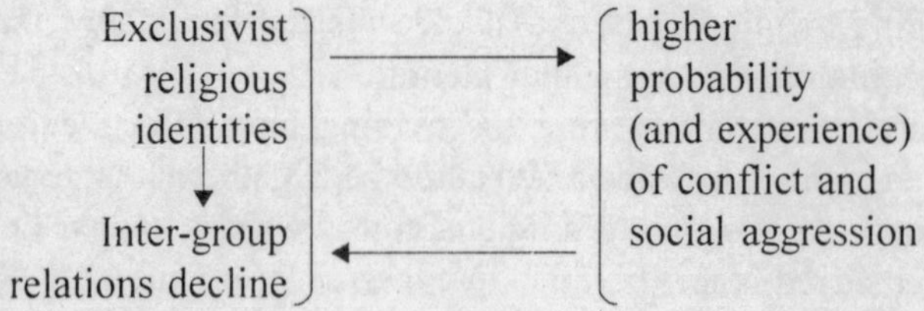

As the sense of mutuality between groups declines, each other's actions and intentions are more likely to be misunderstood. Routine, innocuous moves begin to seem ominous. Conflict becomes more likely. On the other side, the anxiety, or experience, of being threatened helps cement one's commitment to the social entity with whose members one can feel a sense of shared fate: that, then, is one's identity, an island of belongingness and mutual support, against what are seen to be threatening others.[5] Perceived threats can be potent cementers of exclusive identities and, conversely, exclusive identities can be seen to be the more threatening.

Of the three modes of social aggression, we have already seen the beginnings of the first. The earliest studies of locally organized pressure are from latter day UP; its incidence spread out, and scale grew over time. By the 1870s, the separative, indeed adversarial, tendencies were becoming institutionalized, most consequentially in the Arya Samaj of Lahore and the Islamic seminary at Deoband. Arya Samaj arose around Dayananda's invocation of the Vedas, summoning all Hindus, regardless of their caste and other differences; and the founders of Deoband *madrasa* advanced what I have called Islam's second style, urging all Muslims in the far-flung corners of India to re-shape their lives along the lines codified in the *sharia* a thousand years ago. To the extent that these vigorous initiatives were heeded, the older shared spaces weakened, and exclusive religious identities advanced. In contrast, during this period, there was little effort at fostering cross-cutting social networks, networks whose members may intervene to control and defuse situations of conflict, renewing the conditions for mutual trust. 1885 saw the emergence of Indian National Congress; but it began in a leisurely way. By the time Gandhi entered the scene, the separative reconfiguration of the social and political spaces was already settling down, aided by the institution of separate electorates, from 1909 onwards.

Adversarial identities are not a matter merely of attitudes; these have had consequences for social encounters. The more the adversarial assumptions settled into what was emerging as common sense, the less remained of mutual trust and goodwill within local communities, and the easier it became for minor issues to slide into confrontations—each episode helping to renew and aggravate the wider, ongoing process. Rafiuddin Ahmed has examined the scene in rural Bengal in late nineteenth century. In Kushtia in 1897 things got to a point where Muslim villagers had to secure police protection in order to proceed with the customary cow sacrifice at Id festival.[6] For the Bengal of the 1920s, Pradip Datta has documented a variety of incidents—the 1911 Census, the death of a long silent, destitute man of unknown antecedents, some women in rural areas deserting their husbands—arousing anxious comments in newspapers, counterposing the interests of Hindus and Muslims.[7]

Datta's canvas includes the period of the Khilafat and non-Cooperation which, as Mushir's monograph (I) shows us, had witnessed shared public effort in unprecedented measure. Gandhi and a galaxy of *ulama* had mounted that effort despite widespread reservations and expressions of mistrust. One part of the movement had sought to rally mass support around Islamic religious symbols and issues; and when a series of violent incidents persuaded Gandhi to terminate the movement, there was a reaction; the communal situation became more fraught than ever before (II, pp. 153ff).

In a charged milieu, an aggressive act has at times set off a chain of reprisal and counter-reprisal in the subcontinental theatre. As Khilafat gathered steam in 1921, the heightened religious passions found expression in conflict in northern Kerala, which pitched Mapilla Muslim peasants against Hindu landlords—which included some forced conversions of the latter. The two parties here may be seen either as agrarian classes or as communal groups; but the events were interpreted elsewhere as Muslim violence against Hindus.

The riposte came from Swami Shraddhanand, an Arya Samaj leader in north India, who organized a coalition of Hindu groups—

which worked then on the vast numbers who had accepted Islam long ago but had kept their earlier bonds and cultural practices intact. Over a two year period, in the region around Agra and Mathura, some 163,000 were persuaded to 'return' to Hinduism. Such a campaign for conversion has to be seen as societal aggression, directed against the category to which the targetted groups have been seen to belong. The consequent anxieties among some Muslims spurred the activities of Tableeghi Jamaat, aiming to forestall future surprises of this kind. The Jamaat has subsequently worked among the millions throughout the subcontinent who have carried their Islamic identity lightly, urging them to become better Muslims.[8] Somewhat similar anxieties among some Hindus came to be embodied in Rashtriya Swayamsevak Sangh (RSS). The consequent social contestation, now silent, now raucous and violent, continues down to our day.[9]

The rising frequency of episodes of communal violence, between Khilafat and 1947, made for a growth of antagonisms and a hardening of communal identities, as news of each dramatic incident spread through the print media, word of mouth, and rumours, confirming on each side beliefs about its own sense of being threatened, and the dubiousness of the other side's intentions. Communal violence reinforces the identities of groups engaging in that violence; and it drains the reservoirs of mutual trust that have to underlie a sense of community. For Gandhi, of course, non-violence was a core value; but many others on both sides were locked into adversarial mindsets—suspicious of moves from the other side, and anxious to defend, and hopefully secure advantage for, what they saw as 'their' own side.

We face an extraordinary paradox. As 1947 approached, a large bulk of leading *ulama* offerred ideological supports for a single polity in a 'united' India, where Muslims and Hindus could live together amicably. Yet, separative identities on the ground had been hardening since late nineteenth century, aided later by separate electorates, and the recurrent bouts of social aggression in its various forms. When the crunch came, the *ulama*'s vision availed little. The response to the Muslim League's platform was electric, despite the paltriness of its political organization.[10]

* * *

Where do we go from here? Professor Hasan's vision calls for open social arrangements, away from the animosities that loomed large in South Asia during the twentieth century. The Constitution of India provides a framework for such arrangements, though the Hindutva zealots remain to be subdued. At the core of Hasan's scholarship, furthermore, is the effort to recover and reinvigorate the powerful, open, outgoing style in the Islamic repertoire, a style that has been comfortable in living with social differences—participating in the mutual give and take that has marked the historic processes between civilizations.

We in South Asia have the unique advantage of being heirs, not to one, nor to two, but to three civilizations: Indic, Islamic, and European. The last is important: peoples of South Asia have interacted with Europe closely over the past three centuries—for nearly half a millennium in Goa. Indeed the premises of our Constitutions, and of countless other institutions and arrangements, central to our lived realities, are Western much more than either Indic or Islamic. We have the historic right, and the opportunity, to appropriate from all three civilizations whatever will suit our purposes today—especially those of living together in orderly and creative ways.

March 2006 SATISH SABERWAL

NOTES

1. 'I' here refers to the Khilafat study, *Nationalism and Communal Politics in India: 1885-1930* in this volume; 'II' to *A Nationalist Conscience: M.A. Ansari, the Congress and the Raj*; and 'III' to *Islam in the Subcontinent: Muslims in a Plural Society.*
2. By 'cultural style' I mean the distinctive ways of thinking, and of doing things, which come to acquire considerable weight, and to exercise durable influence, in a civilization's historical experience. Illustratively, I think of China's great bureaucratic tradition, of the varied institution-building in western Europe since the thirteenth century, and of the idea and practice of *umma* in Islam, which will concern us later.
3. Here and elsewhere I owe my understanding of the Islamic tradition substantially to Marshall G.S. Hodgson's magisterial *The Venture of Islam: Conscience and History in a World Civilization*, 3 vols., Chicago: University of Chicago Press, 1974 (reprinted Lahore: Vanguard Books, 2004).

4. During its long and eventful history, several other styles also came to be associated with Islam; of these I shall mention only one, which followed from its spread into Central Asia. As the medieval horsemen in the Central Asian and Mongolian steppe upgraded their skills at mounted combat, they generated, recurrently, warriors and war leaders who could mount rather brutal campaigns. Among their best known leaders was the thirteenth century Mongol, Changhez Khan, whose religious inclination was, if anything, to Buddhism. Other Central Asian war leaders, several clusters of Turks, who were more or less recent converts to Islam, were at their devastating worst when they conquered Islam's own heartlands, like Iran. Different Turkish groups went on to found several empires, among them the Safavid in Iran, the Ottoman in Turkey, and the Mughal in India.
5. N. Jayaram and Satish Saberwal, eds., *Social Conflict*, Delhi: Oxford University Press, 1996, reviewed the issues briefly: pp. 19, 514f, esp. fn. 11 there.
6. Rafiuddin Ahmed, *The Bengal Muslims 1871-1906*, Delhi: Oxford University Press, 1981, p. 179.
7. Pradip Kumar Datta, *Carving Blocs: Communal Ideology in Early Twentieth-century Bengal*, Delhi: Oxford University Press, 1999. A little later in March 1931, following Bhagat Singh's execution, Congressmen in Kanpur gave a call for *hartal*. Muslim merchants were not impressed, and the city exploded into murder and rioting. N. Gerald Barrier, ed., *Roots of Communal Politics*, Delhi: Arnold-Heinemann, 1976.
8. Yoginder Sikand, *The Origins and Development of the Tablighi Jamaat (1920-2000)*, Delhi: Orient Longman, 2002, pp. 35ff.
9. Shail Mayaram, *Resisting Regimes: Myth, Memory and the Shaping of a Muslim Identity*, Delhi: Oxford University Press, 1997.
10. Separativeness on the Hindu side was camouflaged politically, as Muslim leaders never tired of pointing out, because numerous assertive Hindu leaders, like Malaviya and Lajpat Rai, were able to steer the Congress towards their preferences. Muslim presence in the Congress peaked during Khilafat—and fell away in its aftermath.

Nationalism and Communal Politics in India, 1885–1930

MUSHIRUL HASAN

For
Francis Robinson
and
Khalid Shamsul Hasan

Contents

List of Tables

Preface

Nationalism and Communal Politics in India was published in 1979. It was based on my Ph.D. thesis submitted at the University of Cambridge. The work was done under the supervision of Anil Seal, though I also had the opportunity of interacting with and benefiting from discussions with a number of historians then based in Cambridge. The late Eric Stokes was a source of much intellectual inspiration. I could also count on the support and friendly advice of Francis Robinson, Chris Bayly and Tom Tomlinson. Over the years they have continued to take an interest in my researches.

My book dealt with the years 1916 to 1928 and covered several important themes which were then largely unexplored. However, since the publication of my book quite a few scholarly works have offered new insights. This has necessitated a thorough revision of *Nationalism and Communal Politics in India*. I have undertaken the task, though I have discovered the hazards of rewriting one's own work after more than a decade.

The introduction, along with chapters two to six, bears little resemblance with what appeared in *Nationalism and Communal Politics in India*. For the first time I have made extensive use of Theodore Beck Papers. This rich collection, which I am editing for publication, illumines several vital facets of the Aligarh movement and sheds new light on the role of Beck and Syed Ahmad Khan, the grand old man of Aligarh.

I have modified chapter seven in the light of recent researches, though the thrust and basic structure of the argument has not been substantially altered. The following two chapters have been completely re-written, with a shift in emphasis as well as interpretation. In the discussion on the Nehru Report, I have offered a reappraisal of M.A. Jinnah's role and argued that, in the light of recent evidence, 1928 can no longer be treated as the 'Parting of Ways'. Quite clearly, Jinnah was then and for many years later still part of the nationalist mainstream. This aspect has also been discussed at length in my *A Nationalist Conscience: M.A. Ansari, the Congress and the Raj* (Manohar: Delhi, 1987).

There are several gaps in this study, though I like to imagine that at least some have been covered by me elsewhere. I have made a conscious attempt not to draw from my earlier writings. Yet, it has not always been possible to do so, for the overall theme of nationalism and communal consciousness figures in much of what I have written.

Over the years, I have received assistance, both financial and academic, from a large number of people and institutions. I am grateful to all of them. My colleagues in the Department of History, Jamia Millia Islamia, have taken a continuing interest in my work over a long period. The staff of Dr Zakir Husain Library at the university has been most helpful. I want to thank, in particular, the Librarian, Mr Shahabuddin Ansari, Mrs Nigar Nomani and Mr Nazar Burney.

A number of scholars have taken the trouble of reading and commenting on my writings. I am grateful to, among others, Ravinder Kumar, S. Gopal, Francis Robinson, Sudhir Chandra, Asim Roy, Gail Minault, Peter Robb, Rajat Ray, Asghar Ali Engineer, Anwar Jamal Kidwai, Simon Commander and Sarah Ansari. Swati Mitra read the final draft of this book and offered useful suggestions.

My principal debt is to Ravinder Kumar who has extended considerable scholarly support. He has sustained my interest in the subject and has offered invaluable advice and comments. My association with the Nehru Memorial Museum and Library, of which he is Director, proved to be fruitful and intellectually rewarding.

Shaaz and Shehzad have been wonderful. They have offered the sort of affection the value of which can hardly be expressed in words.

A final word for Zoya. She has shown much interest in this work and, as always, provided intellectual and emotional support.

I dedicate this book to the memory of my mother who is, alas, no more.

Introduction

In August 1947 a nation-state came into being amid brutal and bloody violence. Its architect, Mohammad Ali Jinnah, had joined the All-India Muslim League in 1913 on the condition that it did not imply any disloyalty to the idea and cause of a united India. Among his lieutenants were those who, not long ago, considered the Pakistan scheme 'chimerical' and 'impracticable'.

So many of those who lived through the trauma of independence and partition were unable to comprehend how a nation, built around certain common symbols and shared ideals, was so easily fragmented. So many more could scarcely understand why their dream of a united and secular India was destroyed by religious fanaticism. Urdu poets like Faiz Ahmad Faiz and Josh Malihabadi captured the mood.[1] So did Saadat Hasan Manto in *Thanda Gosht* (Cold, Like Ice), a short story which appeared soon after the gruesome riots that accompanied the emergence of free India and Pakistan. Elsewhere, he expressed the dilemma of his generation vividly. After his journey to Pakistan in January 1949, he observed:

What my mind could not resolve was the question: what country did we belong to now, India or Pakistan? And whose blood was it that was being mercilessly shed every day? And the bones of the dead, stripped of the flesh of religion, were they being burnt or buried? . . . When I sat down to write, I found my thoughts scattered. Though I tried hard, I could not separate India from Pakistan and Pakistan from India. I

[1] Victor Kiernan, trans., *Poems by Faiz* (London, 1971). Reactions and impressions of some leading writers and poets are examined by a set of scholars in Amit Kumar Gupta (ed.), *Myth and Reality: The Struggle for Freedom in India 1945–47* (Delhi, 1987), especially the contributions of Alok Rai and S. S. Hans. For comments of *Savera*, an organ of the progressive writers, see Muhammad Umar Memon, 'Partition Literature: A Study of Intizar Husain', *Modern Asian Studies* (*MAS*), 1980, vol. 14, 3, pp. 383–86.

would repeatedly ask myself: to whom will now belong what had been written in undivided India? Will that be partitioned too?[2]

Reflecting on the events at the time of independence and partition, social scientists often reiterate the view that the colossal human tragedy in 1947 was the result of British machinations, the culmination of a separatist process initiated by a colonial government to foster its imperial interests.[3] But not all agree with this indictment. Some adhere to the view that Pakistan came into being because Muslims constituted a separate nation and their animus with Hindus started long before the British surfaced on the scene.[4] Hindu-Muslim antagonism, states a proponent of this view, 'was embedded in the historical logic of India. Britain only witnessed it; she did not create or exaggerate it'.[5] The evolution of 'Muslim nationalism', so runs the argument, was linked with an independent demand of a 'nationality' apprehensive of its own political future.[6]

This study will not support either of these polar views. Even if one were to argue that some objective similarities unified Muslims,

[2] Quoted in Khalid Hasan, 'Saadat Hasan Manto: Not of Blessed Memory', *Annual of Urdu Studies*, 1984 (4), pp. 89–90, and by the same author in *Scorecard* (Lahore, 1984), pp. 34–36.

[3] See, for example, Bipan Chandra's view that the government played 'an important role in the promotion, spread and the ultimate partial success of communalism in modern India'. *Communalism in Modern India* (Delhi, 1984), p. 242. For earlier nationalist views on the divide and rule policy, Jawaharlal Nehru, *An Autobiography* (London, 1936), p. 136; Rajendra Prasad, *India Divided* (Bombay, 1946), p. 83.

[4] The best formulation of this argument is in Ishtiaq Husain Qureshi, *The Muslim Community of the Indo-Pakistan Subcontinent, 610–1947* (The Hague, 1962), and K.K. Aziz, *The Making of Pakistan: A Study in Nationalism* (London, 1967), pp. 94–95. Their viewpoint is sometimes echoed, though in slightly different terms, in the writings of some social scientists in India. For example, Satish Saberwal has explained the rise of communalism in relation 'to the long-standing separativeness of religious networks, the acute social distancing expressing a high level of social antagonism between Hindus and Muslims. . . .' *India: The Roots of Crisis* (Delhi, 1986), p. 75.

[5] K.K. Aziz, *Britain and Muslim India: A Study of British Public Opinion vis-a-vis the Development of Muslim Nationalism in India, 1857–1947* (London, 1963), pp. 206–07.

[6] Hafeez Malik, *Sir Sayyid Ahmad Khan and Muslim Modernization in India and Pakistan* (New York, 1980), p. 252.

it would still be inaccurate to treat them as a cohesive group acting in unison and arrayed against other segments of society. The powerful bond of Islam is a fact to be reckoned with; yet, it did not prevent Muslims from pursuing separate and conflicting goals and working out their relationship outside the realm of religion and community. Religious passions were sometimes roused to a feverish pitch and appeals for restoring the unity and solidarity of the followers of Islam went out from the mosques. But such was the divide amongst them that it could not be bridged by the common symbols of Islam. This was evident time and again, when conflicting claims were advanced by men of religion, politics and education to carve out their independent spheres of influence in the bureaucratic and administrative structures created by the raj.

British historians and civil servants turned a blind eye to the wide ranging differences that set Muslim groups apart. They advanced the view, which suited imperial interests and conformed to colonial perceptions of Indian society, that the seventy million Muslims in India were a 'nation', their interests were different from and conflicted with the rest of the population,[7] and that 'the solidarity of Islam is a hard fact against which it is futile to run one's head'.[8] The lieutenant-governor of Bengal, who lived in a province where most Muslims lived, put forward the official view that

> the ethnic pageant which passes across one's vision as one travels over India is made up of many tableaux. There is one such tableau which at once arrests attention because of the many points of contrast which it provides with the rest of the procession. . . . It is the tableau in which we see represented a religion, a civilization and culture, and an outlook differing profoundly in all material respects from those of Hinduism... that of Islam.[9]

Not long afterwards, Jinnah and his followers echoed the same sentiments: the two-nation theory, which they put forward to

[7] T.W. Holderness, *Peoples and Problems of India* (London, 1911), p. 127.

[8] Lawrence, second Marquess of Zetland, *Essayez* (London, 1956), p. 119.

[9] Earl of Ronaldshay, *India: A Birds's-Eye View* (London, 1924), p. 214.

sustain the claim of a separate nation, derived ideological sustenance from the notion of a unified Muslim community with common concerns and shared experiences.

There is more to it than that. The ideologues of the Pakistan movement also harped on the familiar theme of perpetual Hindu-Muslim conflicts, the strength of divisive forces and the contradictions between the 'Islamic' and 'Hindu' traditions.[10] Their views, based on the writings of Henry Elliot and other colonial writers who had reasons to project a distorted image of medieval Indian society, are inconsistent with both the structures and patterns of relationships during that period. Admittedly, a fragmented form of religious consciousness existed but its essential component was hardly ever derived from the notion of a unified 'community' which formed the basis of modern day 'communalism'.[11] In general, integrative and syncretic forces were at work both at the elite and popular levels, though their progress was impeded by stray, localized and sporadic incidence of conflicts over religious symbols.[12] The dominant picture of the eighteenth

[10] According to the late Aziz Ahmad, the history of medieval and modern India 'is to a very considerable extent a history of Hindu-Muslim religio-cultural tensions . . . The divisive forces have proved much more dynamic than the cohesive ones'. *Islamic Culture in the Indian Environment* (Oxford, 1964), p. 74. In his subsequent writings, however, Aziz Ahmad recognized the importance of popular and syncretistic beliefs and practices. For example, *An Intellectual History of Islam* (Edinburgh, 1969), pp. 47–48.

[11] There is no standard definition of communalism. Throughout this book I have used communalism as an ideology and a movement that employs narrow religious loyalty as a basis of collective action, and, in the process, accentuates artificially contrived distinctions and heightens community-oriented consciousness. One is inclined to go along with W.C. Smith who defined communalism as an ideology 'that has emphasized as the social, political, and economic unit the group of adherents of each religion, and has emphasized the distinction, even the antagonism, between such groups; the words 'adherent' and 'religion' being taken in the most nominal sense'. *Modern Islam in India* (London, 1946), p. 157.

[12] Instances of religious conflicts are cited in C.A. Bayly, 'The Pre-History of 'Communalism'? Religious Conflict in India, 1700–1860', *MAS*, 1985, vol. 19, 2, pp. 177–203. Bayly's conclusions are tentative and based on insufficient data. Also, the view that 'by the dawn of the twentieth century, India remained a pluralistic society, fundamentally divided along religious lines'. Stanley A. Wolpert, *Morley and India 1906–1910* (Berkeley, 1967), p. 185.

century is not of the Hindus and the Muslims forming exclusive and antagonistic groups but of their co-operating in cultural life and social affairs.[13] To appreciate the significance of such trends in medieval Indian society, historians anxious to uncover the 'pre-history' of communalism may find it profitable to consider the insights provided by R.P. Tripathi, Tara Chand , K.M. Ashraf, Mohammad Habib, his brother, Mohammad Mujeeb, and son, Irfan Habib.

An effective refutation of the two-nation theory came from writers and publicists in the 1940s. Wedded to the concept of a composite Indian nationality, which was the quintessential feature of the nationalist movement, they emphasized the ongoing process of assimilation and integration throughout Indian history.[14] Some two decades later, this debate was enriched with the aid of newly-developed analytical categories, the introduction of certain unexplored themes and the shift in the focus of analysis from the national to the provincial and district arenas. Social scientists have, in this way, suggested new ways of looking at two of the most important themes in modern India—nationalism and communalism.

In his book *Language, Religion and Politics in North India*, Paul R. Brass has argued that the ideology of Muslim separateness did not flow out of the objective differences between Hindus and Muslims but out of the uses which were made of those differences through a conscious process of symbol selection. Nor was it the consequence of the objective circumstances of Muslims in the United Provinces (UP), who were better placed than Hindus in urbanization, literacy, English education, social communications and government employment.[15] Francis Robinson arrived at similar conclusions, pointing out that it was the threat of becoming backward, rather than backwardness itself, which encouraged UP Muslims to organize themselves separately. Their influence

[13] Satish Chandra, *Parties and Politics at the Mughal Court 1707–1740* (Delhi, 1972 edn.), pp. 261–62.

[14] Asoka Mehta and Achyut Patwardhan, *The Communal Triangle in India* (Allahabad, 1942).

[15] Paul R. Brass, *Language, Religion and Politics in North India* (London, 1974), p. 178 and ff.

in the province helped them to do so with much effect.[16]

More recently, Robinson has extricated himself from the historical traditions of the 'Cambridge School' in trying to establish a 'fundamental' connection between Islam and political separatism. In a lively debate with Brass, he has noted, though without conveying much conviction, the importance of Islamic traditions in the development of Muslim separatism. Siding with the primordialists as against the instrumentalists, Robinson concludes that Islamic ideas had a moulding and, on occasions, a motivating role to play amongst the elites of UP.[17] Acceptance of this bald generalization must await a detailed examination of Islamic ideas and movements. In the meantime, one must delineate the contours and content of Muslim separatism before attributing its growth to those ideas and movements which were supposedly rooted in Islam.

Brass and Robinson have traced the history of Muslim separatism in UP; others have turned to regions outside the Indo-Gangetic belt and have traversed the familiar terrain of elite politics both within and outside the formal imperial structures.[18] In recent years, however, social scientists, drawing heavily on the works of

[16] Francis Robinson, *Separatism Among Indian Muslims: The Politics of the United Provinces Muslims, 1880–1923* (Cambridge, 1975), chapter 1.

[17] Francis Robinson, 'Nation Formation: The Brass Thesis and Muslim Separatism', and Reply by Brass, *Journal of Commonwealth and Comparative Politics*, November 1977, 15, 3, pp. 215–34. Also, Francis Robinson, 'Islam and Muslim Society in South Asia', *Contributions to Indian Sociology*, July-Dec., 1983, vol. 17, 2, pp. 185–203.

[18] Stephen F. Dale, *The Mapillas of Malabar, 1498–1922: Islamic Society on the South Asian Frontier* (Oxford, 1980); K.N. Panikkar, *Against Lord and State: Religion and Peasant Uprisings in Malabar 1836–1921* (Delhi, 1989); Kenneth Mcpherson, *The Muslim Microcosm: Calcutta, 1918–[illegible]5* (Heidelberg, 1974); Rafiuddin Ahmad, *Bengal Muslims, 1871–1906. A Quest for Identity* (Delhi, 1981); Asim Roy, *The Islamic Syncretistic Tradition in Bengal* (Princeton, New Jersey, 1983); Shila Sen, *Muslim Politics in Bengal, 1937–1947* (Delhi, 1976); David Page, *Prelude to Partition: The Indian Muslims and the Imperial System of Control 1920–1932* (Delhi, 1982); Ian Talbot, *Punjab and the Raj 1849–1947* (Delhi, 1988); David Gilmartin, *Empire and Islam: Punjab and the Making of Pakistan* (London, 1988); Farzana Shaikh, *Community and Consensus in Islam: Muslim Representation in Colonial India 1860–1947* (Cambridge, 1989).

Max Weber, Louis Dumont and Clifford Geertz, have shed new light on the structure of the Muslim community, its social perceptions and cultural moorings, moulded by or independently of the colonial impact, and the extent to which these can be regarded as crucial variables in the process of identity formation and the growth of communitarian consciousness. As a result, a number of significant works have appeared on caste and social stratification among Muslims;[19] the bases of authority and codes of behaviour in South Asian Islam;[20] the patterns and strands of nineteenth century movements of reform and revivalism;[21] and the role of various groups, especially the *ulama*, in interpreting the *shariat* and preserving the Islamic way of life.[22] Thus Barbara Metcalf takes a close look at the *ulama* of Deoband, who were engaged in a self-conscious reformulation of their religious thought—a reformulation that involved new emphases and new concerns from *within* the framework of their own received tradition.[23] While work on the Barelwis is in progress, Robinson has unfolded the history of Lucknow's Firangi Mahal family, which played a large part in 'Indian Islamic life' for nearly three hundred years and came to stand for a distinctive style of Indian Islam.[24]

Some of these concerns, coupled with explorations of the nationalist movement and the communal phenomena, are of increasing relevance in a society which is traumatized by periodic outbursts of communal violence and is today engaged in narrowing down areas of conflicts and contradictions.

[19] Imtiaz Ahmad (ed.), *Caste and Social Stratification Among the Muslims* (Delhi, 1973).

[20] Barbara Daly Metcalf (ed.), *Moral Conduct and Authority: The Place of Adab in South Asian Islam* (Berkeley, 1984).

[21] Mujeeb Ashraf, *Muslim Attitudes towards British Rule and Western Culture in India* (Delhi, 1982), and the unpublished Oxford thesis of Farhan Nizami cited in Bayly, op.cit.

[22] Katherine P. Ewing (ed.), *Shariat and Ambiguity in South Asian Islam* (Delhi, 1988).

[23] Barbara Daly Metcalf, *Islamic Revival in British India: Deoband, 1860–1900* (Princeton, New Jersey, 1982).

[24] Francis Robinson, 'Problems in the History of the Firangi Mahall: Family of Learned and Holy Men', *Oxford University Papers on India*, vol. 1, part 2 (Delhi, 1987).

This study offers a reappraisal of some important themes relating to Indian nationalism and the growth of community-oriented formations, which are described in historical literature as 'communal' or 'separatist'. Its central concern, however, is to analyze how various segments among Muslims related to and defined their relationship with the nationalist forces, spearheaded by the Indian National Congress. This exercise is backed by an examination of several vital issues which reflect on the Congress movement, the structure of its support amongst Muslims and the crucial determinants that dictated its strategy towards the communal question. Also discussed is the part played by the colonial government in defining political identities in religious terms and translating them into constitutional arrangements. Some other issues, such as the role of the *ulama* in promoting an 'Islamic ideology', the content and structure of political separatism and the crystallization of communal identities, also figure in the discussion. The aim is to unfold the breakdown of inter-communal networks which had, for so long, kept intact the social fabric of Indian society, and to offer possible explanations to a larger historical question: Why did secular nationalism fail to create a united nation, drawing equally upon the participation of the major communities?

This book concentrates on the national arena, on national organizations and on political leaders who operated at the all-India level. At the same time, the provinces have not been ignored, for the high politics of premier political bodies can be meaningfully explained only by investigating their linkages with their supporters at the provincial and local levels. Besides, the ideological contours of Muslim activists cannot be easily identified without reference to their constituents and their specific regional concerns in the provinces and districts of, say, UP, Bengal and Punjab.

Bengal and Punjab were, so to speak, Muslim-majority provinces. This fact was of little importance as long as franchise was limited and only men of substance could aspire for a berth in legislative councils and local bodies. But once the Montagu-Chelmsford Reforms set in motion the process of distributing power according to the numerical strength of a community, a few Muslim groups were catapulted into prominence in Bengal and

Punjab. Their leaders, who were often castigated for playing second-fiddle to the UP-based leadership, now had the opportunity to exert their influence over the newly-enfranchised Muslim voters.

This change in the political scenario had far-reaching implications. For one, it was no longer possible for the Muslim League stalwarts of Aligarh and Lucknow to ignore, as was done when the Lucknow agreement of December 1916 was being finalized, the claims of Bengali and Punjabi Muslims. Nor could the government do so in its elaborate political arithmetic that was being worked out in Whitehall and Delhi. From the 1920s the great communal debates were, in fact, conducted in Lahore and Calcutta and not so much in UP. Eventually, of course, the political map of India had to be redrawn once Bengal and Punjab lent their fulsome support to the Muslim League campaign. Muslims of these provinces, more than any other group, made the creation of Pakistan possible.

UP Muslims, too, played a pivotal role in moulding political attitudes and in shaping the destiny of their co-religionists. The province was the arena where Syed Ahmad Khan, the genius behind the founding of the Aligarh college, conducted his educational and political activities. The Muslim Educational Conference and the Urdu Defence Associations had their headquarters in UP. The All-India Muslim League, though founded in Dacca, was run from Aligarh and Lucknow. Likewise, the most vociferous pan-Islamists belonged to UP and were at the centre of a massive mobilization campaign over the Khilafat issue. Their allies were the *ulama*, drawn mainly from famous theological centres like Deoband, Nadwa and Firangi Mahal—all located in UP.

II

More Muslims lived in the subcontinent than in any other part of the world. In 1921, they numbered 69 million, or one-fifth of British India's population. Their distribution ranged from 91 per cent in the North-West Frontier Province to less than 7 per cent in Madras. In absolute numbers they were most numerous in Bengal, where Islamic incursions took place in the eigth-ninth centuries through Arab traders and Sufi missions. What needs to be underlined is the predominantly rural character of the Muslim population in Bengal, a fact that stood in significant contrast to the general pattern of Muslim distribution in India and elsewhere. Only in the western districts of Bengal were they proportionately more numerous in urban rather than in rural areas.

In Punjab, which lies on the route by which successive armies entered India, migration and conversion created an Islamic community located predominantly in the western half of the province. Though part of the Ghaznavid Empire in the eleventh century, Punjab acquired greater commercial and strategic significance under the Ghoris. Cities like Lahore, Multan and Uch flourished, drawing large numbers of traders, administrators, soldiers, scholars and creative writers from parts of Central Asia.

Also attracted were the Sufis with their established mystical orders. Though there is evidence of some Sufi activity before 1200, the first and foremost Sufi missionary to reach India was Khwaja Hasan Muinuddin Chishti, who reached Delhi in 1193. Among his illustrious disciples were Bakhtiyar Kaki and Baba Fariduddin Ganj-i Shakar, founder of the Chishti order in Punjab. The Baba settled in Ajodhan and is said to have converted some sixteen backward Hindu tribes in that region. The Suhrawardi order, founded by Bahauddin Zakariya, gained a foothold in Multan. The Qadiris met with success in Uch. Pilgrimage to the shrines of such venerated holy men was of great symbolic value in, what Ernest Gellner describes, as the ritualistic, hierarchical popular religion of the masses as opposed to the puritanical, egalitarian, orthodox Islam of the learned.[25]

Establishment of Turkish rule influenced other parts of north Indian society, especially the area which the British constituted as the North-West Provinces and Oudh or the United Provinces of Agra and Oudh. For one, it ushered in major changes in the structure of medieval economy and gave impetus to, as was elucidated by Mohammad Habib, the growth of new towns.[26]

[25] Ernest Gellner (ed.), *Islamic Dilemmas: Reformers, Nationalists and Industrialization* (Berlin, 1985), and *Saints of the Atlas* (London, 1969).

[26] Mohammad Habib, Introduction to Elliot and Dowson's third volume of 'History of India', reprinted in K.A. Nizami (ed.), *Politics and Society during the early Medieval Period* (Delhi, 1974).

Some developed as centres of trade and industry, while others gained fame as rendezvous of the learned and resorts for artists and creative writers. Jaunpur, capital of the Sharqi Sultans (1394–1500), was the *Shiraaz-i Hind* or the *Dar al-ulum* (abode of learning). Agra, on the other hand, was a premier Mughal city for trade and commerce, with all land routes in north India radiating to and from Agra, rendering it 'the heart of the Empire' or the 'navel of the whole realm'. Lucknow, with its broad expanse of palaces, its groves and gardens, its courts and squares, and its mosques and *imambaras*, also remained a prime city at least until 1856, when Awadh was gobbled up by the British. A correspondent of the London *Times* offered a vivid description of the city. He wrote:

> Not Rome, not Athens, not Constantinople, not any city I have seen appears to me so striking and beautiful as [Lucknow]; and the more I gaze, the more its beauty grows upon me.[27]

Lucknow had a rich cultural life, with the Nawabs liberally adopting secular Hindu mores and folkways and contributing to a Hindu-Muslim cultural synthesis. They participated in Hindu festivals, on occasions even supporting the construction of temples, and freely employed Hindus as senior officers and bankers. The communal riots that shook Lucknow were those between Shias and Sunnis, not Hindus and Muslims.[28]

In the second half of the nineteenth century, the Muslim service and landed classes tried to emulate the traditions of the Nawabs, extended patronage to poets, writers, musicians and dancers, funded schools and colleges and helped to create a distinct cultural and intellectual ethos. Occasionally, they also dabbled in politics. They could be heard fulminating against the Congress,[29] discreetly

[27] W.H. Russell, *My Diary in India, in the year 1858–59* (London, 1860), p. 257. The colonial history of Lucknow is discussed in Rosie Llewellyn-Jones, *A Fatal Friendship: The Nawabs, the British and the City of Lucknow* (Delhi, 1985); Veena Talwar Oldenburg, *The Making of Colonial Lucknow 1856–1877* (Princeton, New Jersey, 1984).

[28] Thomas Metcalf, *Land, Landlords and the Raj: Northern India in the Nineteenth Century* (Berkeley, 1979), p. 37.

[29] Thus the Raja of Mahmudabad presided over an anti-Congress meeting in 1899 and criticized the 'short-sighted, ill-advised and misconceived' Congress propaganda.

lending support to the agitation against the Nagri resolution of April 1900 and preparing the groundwork for the establishment of the Muslim League.

III

It is commonplace to argue that the Indian Muslims, notwithstanding their varied historical experiences and their differentiated socio-economic structures, were united by certain common symbols of Islam. Mohammad Iqbal was the principal exponent of this view in the twentieth century. He laid stress on the egalitarian character of Islam, on congregational prayers and the rite of pilgrimage, which provides the great occasion for the meeting of Muslims from all over the world. The Kaaba, described in most vivid colours in *Rumuz-i Bekhudi*, symbolized the essential unity of the Islamic peoples.[30]

In recent years, social scientists have turned to some of the themes underlined in Iqbal's formulations. Thus Sandra B. Frietag has examined the use of Islamic symbols in Kanpur city—in 1913 and 1931—to highlight important shifts in the ways in which Muslims in north India perceived themselves and the world around them.[31] So has David Gilmartin in his analysis of the Shahidganj mosque agitation.[32] Still others have shown how the use of Islamic symbols during the Khilafat movement provided the rallying point for a massive communitarian response.[33]

Though such interpretations of local situations are useful, they tend to conceal important dimensions, including the inner ideological and socio-economic differences of both an inter and

[30] Annemarie Schimmel, *Gabriel's Wing: A Study into the Religious Ideas of Sir Muhammad Iqbal* (Leiden, 1963), pp. 195–96.

[31] Sandra B. Frietag, 'The Roots of Muslim Separatism in South Asia: Personal Practice and Public Structures in Kanpur and Bombay', Edmund Burke III and Ira M. Lapidus (eds.), *Islam Politics and Social Movements* (Berkeley, 1980), pp. 115–41.

[32] David Gilmartin, 'The Shahidganj Mosque Incident: A Prelude to Pakistan', ibid., pp. 146–68.

[33] Gail Minault, *The Khilafat Movement: Religious Symbolism and Political Mobilization in India* (Delhi, 1982), and the collection of articles in Mushirul Hasan (ed.), *Communal and Pan-Islamic Trends in Colonial India* (Delhi, 1985 edn.).

intra-regional nature. For example, adequate attention is not paid to the deep ideological divide that set Shias and Sunnis apart and to the intense rivalries between various theological schools, such as the Deobandis, the Barelwis and the Ahl-i Hadith. And it is only in recent years that scholars have begun to ask if Muslims have a monolithic perception of their faith and have reached the inescapable conclusion that they do not. Most interpret Quranic injunctions and the sayings of the Prophet in different ways—each according to their historical background and the realities encircling them.[34] Local accretions and bold theological innovations have, in some cases, even altered the basic structure of beliefs.

Doctrinal disputes and sectarian feuds have not just been a fea ure of Indian Islam; Muslim societies elsewhere and in most periods have never ever been free of schisms. What is perhaps unique in India is that sectarianism has hardly ever constituted the basis of political solidarity. Being a Shia or a Sunni, a Barelwi or a Deobandi, a Hanafi or a Shafai was, no doubt, a vital component of one's religious and sometimes social identity. Yet, identification with and loyalty to one or the other 'school' or 'sect' did not generally influence political decisions. Only in exceptional situations did Shias and Sunnis charter an independent political course. Again, only in rare cases did the Barelwis or the Deobandis advance separate political claims. In general, their political options were not constrained by purely sectarian considerations.

What moulded and stimulated a separate and distinct political consciousness was the placement of Muslims in the political and economic structures and their access to the levers of power, authority and influence under colonial rule. Nowhere was this fact in greater evidence than in Bengal, where more than half the population consisted of Muslims who had virtually no access to the resources of the province. And nowhere else was this fact a greater source of communal antipathy.

The impact of colonial rule, though unevenly felt in different parts of the country, affected Muslims of Bengal more than any other section of society. Here the operation of Permanent Settlement resulted in many families, mainly Muslims, losing their land

[34] See the collection of papers in Ewing (ed.), *Shariat*, op. cit.

to a new class of Hindu landlords. The Resumption Proceedings between 1828–1846 impoverished the few families which had survived the Permanent Settlement and destroyed Muslim educational institutions which were entirely run by revenue-free grants.[35] In Tippera, for example, families of Muslim zamindars, covering half the district, lost their land to Hindu landlords.[36] By the end of the nineteenth century, most of the land in Bengal, especially in the eastern districts, was owned by Hindus.

The 'reformist' initiatives of Warren Hastings and Cornwallis reversed the fortunes of those Muslims who had secured commanding positions in revenue, judicial and executive departments. Substitution of English for Persian in 1836 and the novel examination procedures added to their discomfiture. With most Muslims preferring to stay aloof from English schools and colleges, (Table 1.1) the prospects of government and professional employment were inevitably dimmed. Not surprisingly, the number of Muslim pleaders, attorneys, proctors and solicitors dwindled between 1851 and 1869.[37] And where recruitment was by test, as in the judicial and executive branches, Muslims did not have much of a chance. Consequently, when their representatives appeared before the Hunter Commission of 1882–83 and the Aitchison Commission of 1886–87 there was the familiar clamour for nomination as against competitive examinations.

Mayo and Dufferin steered a different course from the one plotted by their predecessors. Though still suspicious of Muslims and distrustful of their intentions, they were nevertheless sensitized to the need to win them over through carefully planned conciliatory gestures. Wherever Dufferin went in India, he let it be known that he was anxious to promote the education of Muslims and to appoint a great number of them in public services. After an official enquiry, the government announced in July 1885 that where Muslims did not have the 'full share of state employment' efforts would be made to 'redress this inequality'.[38] The address presented

[35] W.W. Hunter, *The Indian Mussalmans* (Calcutta, 1945 edn.), pp. 177–79.

[36] *Census*, 1921, Bengal, part I, p. 414.

[37] Hunter, *Indian Mussalmans*, p. 164.

[38] S. Gopal, *British Policy in India 1858–1905* (Cambridge, 1965), p. 158.

to Lytton by the MAO College Fund Committee on 8 January 1877 expressed gratitude to the government 'for having shown so strong a disposition to advance the cause of education amongst our community, and for issuing directions to the provincial governments to adopt special measures to supply our intellectual needs'.[39]

Outside the precincts of the Aligarh college there was little cause to feel contented, for government initiatives neither led to a significant increase in levels of literacy nor a substantial improvement in the Muslim share of government jobs. In 1911, only 12.6 per cent of the Muslim population in Bengal was literate in English. And in 1913 they held only 10.6 per cent of jobs in the executive and judicial departments.[40]

The imbalance between the relative positions of the Hindus and Muslims created the first stirrings of communal consciousness in Bengal, enabling Muslim organizations to make use of the sense of deprivation that gripped so many of their potential supporters and to conduct their mobilization along communitarian lines. Predictably, the more advanced Hindu groups combined to ward off any possible assault on their material interests.

W.W. Hunter's magisterial generalizations hardly made sense in another area of British India—UP—where the Muslim service and professional classes were not so badly off. In the first edition of *Athar al-Sanadid*, a pre-1857 archaeological study of Delhi, Syed Ahmad Khan included a chapter on the most successful and well-known of the traditional intellectual elites.[41] Their presence here and elsewhere in upper India was due, in part, to the fact that the British introduced fewer changes in the administrative machinery, and because there was much less insistence on educational attainment for securing government posts. Recruitment was not always, as Syed Ahmad's career illustrates, on the basis of college degrees but on account of family background and tried loyalty to the raj. Muslims in Punjab, for example, lagged far

[39] C.H. Philips (ed.), *The Evolution of India and Pakistan 1858–1947: Select Documents* (London, 1962), p. 183.

[40] *Census*, Bengal, part II, table VIII B; *Royal Commission on Public Services in India* (hereafter *RCPS*) (London, 1917), appendix V.

[41] Malik, *Sir Sayyid*, p. 38.

TABLE 1.1

Statement Showing the Hindu and Muslim Students who Passed the Entrance and B.A. Examinations at the University of Calcutta, 1876–86

Entrance Examination										
Year	1876	1877	1878	1879	1880	1881	1882	1883	1884	1885–86
Hindu	1,196	980	914	905	1,421	1,170	1,216	1,338	—	1,230
Muslim	66	67	66	59	90	67	92	123	—	91
B.A. Examinations										
Hindu	118	53	81	92	146	99	178	189	114	268
Muslim	7	3	—	4	4	1	6	15	3	8

SOURCE: *Public Service Commission, 1886–87, Report* (Calcutta, 1888), pp. 78–79.

TABLE 1.2

Employment of Muslims in the Provincial Civil Service, Punjab, 1913

	Total	Europeans and Anglo-Indians	Hindus	Muslims	Other Indians	Total Indians	Muslims per cent of Indians
Executive Branch:							
Total	136	14	52	52	18	122	42.6
Posts Rs 1,000 and over	5	1	3	—	1	4	—
Post up to Rs 1,000	131	13	49	52	17	118	44.1
Judicial Branch:							
Total	48	7	18	19	4	41	46.4
Posts Rs 1,000 and over	4	1	1	2	—	3	66.6
Posts up to Rs 1,000	44	6	17	17	4	38	44.7
Total both branches	184	21	70	71	22	163	43.5

SOURCE: *Royal Commission on the Public Services in India. Report of the Commissioners*, Command 8382 (Parliamentary Papers, 1916, VII). Appendices to Report. Appendix VIII.

behind the Hindus in western education, particularly in western districts where they constituted three-quarters of the population. There were only 57 Muslim graduates in the two decades before 1857;[42] yet in 1886–87 there were 127 Muslim officers in the uncovenanted judicial and executive branches, i.e., 41.6 per cent of all Indians.[43] By 1913, their share in the provincial service had increased appreciably: 66 per cent of the posts in the judicial sector, carrying a salary of Rs 1,000 and above, were held by Muslims. (Table 1.2)

Similarly, Muslims retained their position in the services because Urdu remained the medium of education and the language of administration.[44] The *qasbati* elites, though aware of their declining position, managed to adjust to new demands and challenges. Some sought appointment in the princely States of Rampur, Jaora, Bhopal, Arcot and Hyderabad; others like Mohsinul Mulk and Viqarul Mulk went to Aligarh to carve out their place in the expanding educational system.

Muslim landowners also survived the rigours of British rule. In spite of the trauma of 1857, so vividly described by the poet Asadullah Khan Ghalib,[45] they remained a substantial landholding interest in upper India. It is true that their fortunes remained much more stable in Punjab than in UP, where the corrosive action of commercial forces, combined with political change and the rise of monied classes, undermined the position of the traditional landholding class and placed pressures on the qasbah-based

[42] *Report of the Punjab Provincial Committee: Appendix to Education Commission* (Calcutta, 1884), p. 116; *Census*, 1901, Punjab, part II, table VIII, for Muslim literates in English.

[43] *PSC*, appendices, pp. 78–79.

[44] Anil Seal, *The Emergence of Indian Nationalism: Competition and Collaboration in the Later Nineteenth Century* (Cambridge, 1975), pp. 304–6; Robinson, *Separatism*, pp. 18–19.

[45] Ghalib was in Delhi for the entire period between the arrival of the mutineers from Meerut on 11 May 1857 and the successful British assault upon the city on 14 September. The *Dastambu* reflects his mood and that of his brethren in Delhi. 'No light burns in their (Muslims) homes at night, and no smoke rises from them by day. Ghalib, who knows this city, who had a thousand friends to speak with him and none but his shadow to bear him company'. Ralph Russell, *Ghalib: The Poet and his Age* (London, 1977).

'Islamic gentry'.[46] Yet, there was really no substantial decline in their fortunes, especially in the post-1860 period. Most zamindars and taluqdars in Awadh, extolled as the 'ancient, indigenous and cherished leaders of rural society', emerged from the 1857 upheaval with augmented, not diminished, landholdings.[47] In Muzaffarnagar and Meerut districts, a considerable portion of the Syed land, transferred between 1841 and 1861, was acquired by a few Syed families in Jansath. In Aligarh district, one of the principal regions of Muslim disaffection in 1857, a number of recently converted Muslim zamindars increased their holdings between the settlements of 1839 and 1869 from 47,822 acres to 72,218 acres.[48] W.J.D. Burkitt, settlement officer of the district, referred to 'sound business men' steadily increasing their possession.[49] Elsewhere, such men turned British rule to their profit and came to terms more easily with British revenue demands and a commercialized agriculture. Thus in parts of Agra division,

[46] Francis Robinson mentions Kanpur as an example of the rapid passage of land from the traditional to the commercial castes. Chris Bayly refers to the pressure placed on the Islamic gentry by the rise of monied men and the resurgence of Hindu landholding communities. *Rulers, Townsmen and Bazaars: North Indian Society in the Age of British Expansion, 1770–1870* (Cambridge, 1983), p. 355. Eric Stokes, however, did not agree with Robinson's larger argument about the corrosive action of commercial forces on the position of the traditional landholding classes. His conclusion was that the decisive revolution in land control had occurred before 1857, in a pre-commerical era, and was the product of institutional rather than economic change. He noted the stability of the great estates in the post-1860 period. E.T. Stokes, *The Peasant and the Raj: Studies in Agrarian Society and Peasant Rebellion in Colonial India* (Cambridge, 1978), p. 216.

[47] Ibid., p. 180. Bayly notes that the Syeds of Barha in Muzaffarnagar and Meerut districts were able to 'creep back' into some of the villages from which they had earlier been ejected. Op. cit., pp. 190, 355.

[48] Peter Hardy, *The Muslims of British India* (Cambridge, 1972), p. 78; Zoya Hasan, *Dominance and Mobilization: Rural Politics in Western Uttar Pradesh 1930–1980* (Delhi, 1989), p. 35, for land concentration of the great Pathan landlords of Atrauli and the Sherwanis of Bhikampur. Stokes noted that many of the zamindars suffered many vicissitudes and some carried a heavy load of debt and litigation, but they remained the great revenue payers of their districts. Op. cit., p. 217.

[49] Metcalf, *Land, Landlords*, p. 162.

Muslims were a major landholding group. They were dominant in Rohilkhand, owning 33.1 per cent of the land in Bareilly district. The Pathans, in particular, held considerable estates. In 1909 they held 135,289 acres or 13.38 per cent of the land, mainly in the Bareilly tahsil and in the north of the district.[50]

The foregoing survey is intended to serve as a background to the tumultuous decades, covered in this book, which witnessed the rise of nationalism and the rapid growth of unity as well as friction between sections of the Hindu and Muslim populations.

[50] *District Gazetteers of the United Provinces*, Bareilly, vol. 13, pp. 100–05.

Chapter Two

'The Muslim Breakaway'

The Indian National Congress, its development and character has been a major theme in modern Indian historical writings. In recent years, a number of regional and local studies have emphasized that the Congress did not, as had once been supposed, represent just the interests of particular class, caste or interest groups. Anil Seal's argument that the Congress was the party of English-educated and professional men, drawn mainly from the higher literate Hindu castes of the three maritime presidencies, is no longer tenable. It is becoming increasingly clear that the role of the educated in the Congress was that of publicists and spokesmen who represented a much wider range of interests and whose social composition and political aims were, in fact, much more heterogenous than either the British or some historians dominated by the official mind have argued. Moreover, since Congressmen had local roles to play and were often members of the patron-client groups in their own localities, they had a complex relationship with the elites of Indian society, both urban and rural, and with the peasants and workers whom they claimed to represent.

One of the main objectives of the founders of the Congress was to seek legitimacy as the representatives of Indian aspirations. This was necessary in order to unite the scattered and fragmented elements in Indian society and also to impress Calcutta and London that the Congress represented more than a 'microscopic minority' and was not just a 'ramshackle coalition'. Admittedly, its members were drawn from different backgrounds whose interests were not always compatible with each other; yet, pursuit of parochial goals and advancement of careers was not their sole concern. They shared a nationalist vision and were committed to the collective welfare of all Indians. They were conscious of their historic role as architects of an Indian nation; so they dwelt on the theme of 'national opinion' and 'national aspirations' with unfailing regularity. 'It is difficult to conceive', claimed the *Report of the First Indian National Congress*, 'any gathering . . . more thoroughly representative of the entire nation than the Congress'. What, in 1885, was little more than an experiment, the Madras Congress (1887) proudly announced, 'bore every appearance of becoming a national institution'.

In a divided and disparate country like India, it was no less important to proclaim the non-communal character of the Congress. Indeed, the claim of being a national body could only be sustained by transcending, even if only in theory, caste and sectarian boundaries. Besides, a non-communal posture alone could disarm the apprehensions regarding Congress policies and programmes. Thus the Congress in 1887–88 decided not to discuss any subject which either Hindus or Muslims 'unanimously or nearly unanimously' opposed.[1] In the same spirit, the Subjects Committee bowed to mounting pressure from Muslim delegates and dropped the Punjab Alienation Bill discussion from the agenda.[2] Surendranath Banerjea went on to reaffirm the unity of the Congress movement. 'Here', he declared, 'we stand upon a common platform. . . . Here we have all agreed to bury our differences.'[3]

However, such assurances were not always matched by practice: while denying religious identifications and asserting secular orientations, the Congress relied upon Hindu symbols and traditions for its legitimization. Tilak, Aurobindo Ghose and Lajpat Rai maintained that the Hindu masses could only be aroused through the use of religious predispositions, the popularization

[1] The *Tribune* observed: 'After this assurance let us hope our Mohammedan friends will no longer hesitate to join their Hindu fellow subjects. Nothing can be a stronger proof of the good faith of Congress than this resolution'. 23 January, 1889.

[2] John R. McLane, *Indian Nationalism and the Early Congress* (Princeton, New Jersey, 1977), pp. 254–56.

[3] *Speeches and Writings of Surendranath Banerjea* (Madras, n.d.), p. 265. Or, the statement of Ajudhia Nath Kunzru, a leading pleader in Allahabad during the 1880s, that the Congress 'works not for the good of this or that class, nor of this or that province, but for the benefit of the whole nation', *Tribune*, 23 January 1889.

of national historical myths, and the celebration of Hindu festivals and decided to blend Hinduism with nationalism. Tilak invoked the spirit of resurgent Hinduism to mobilize the masses, promoted the Ganapati festival to provide his followers with a recognizable identity, and rehearsed the tale of past Maratha greatness by resuscitating the memory of Shivaji. Though intended to elicit, activate and canalize dormant political energies, Tilak's mobilization strategy had a divisive impact and polarized Maharashtra's urban society around communal lines.[4] Likewise, the Swadeshi movement in Bengal, despite its contribution to the anti-colonial struggle, acquired a certain communal colouring. Worship of the elephant-headed god, Ganesh, and of Bhawani, demonstrative ablutions in the river Ganga, and fervent appeals to the 'grim goddess', Kali, all involved a religious intensity which weakened Muslim enthusiasm for the movement.[5] In fact, the coalition

[4] Bipan Chandra is of a different view. According to him, Tilak's politics, ideology and agitational methods were not communal. His campaigns were organized around political and economic issues and contained little appeal to Hinduism. This interpretation is hard to accept in the light of Tilak's own writings and the researches of a number of historians. While recognizing Tilak's vital contribution to the anti-colonial struggle, it is hard to ignore his role in heightening communal consciousness in western India. It is also no coincidence that most of his lieutenants in that region had purely Hindu concerns and were communal in their political orientation. They were in the forefront of the Mahasabha movement and the chief organizers of *sangathan* bodies. *Communalism in Modern India*, pp. 143–44.

Here it may be useful to emphasize the obvious difference between revivalism and communalism. Yet, the distinction is often blurred in some cases, a fact conveniently overlooked by historians like Bipan Chandra. The Hindu Mahasabha, for example, not only harked back to a romantic past and revelled in religious enthusiasm, but also adopted narrow, sectarian and divisive attitudes. It thus combined elements of both revivalism and communalism.

[5] Sumit Sarkar, *The Swadeshi Movement in Bengal, 1903–1908* (Delhi, 1973), p. 411; for the Hindu concept of Indian nationalism, Amales Tripathi, *The Extremist Challenge: India Between 1890 and 1910* (Delhi, 1967), p. 61; Hiren Mukherjee, 'The Role of Revivalism in the Indian National Movement', in *Essays in Honour of Professor S.C. Sarkar* (Delhi, 1976), pp. 592–93; Barbara Southhard, 'The Political Strategy of Aurobindo Ghosh: The Utilization of Religious Symbolism and the Problem of Political Mobilization in Bengal', *MAS*, 1980, vol. 14, 3, pp. 362–66, 375–76.

between religious conservatism and political extremism hindered their mobilization. A more secular-oriented political front, then and later, had a much greater chance of success in drawing diverse sections of society into the nationalist fold.

The disquieting fact was that so many Congressmen of stature were so closely identified with revivalist tendencies. The cow protectionists in Punjab were 'very generally' Congressmen.[6] The Gaurakshini Sabha in the Central Provinces was backed by Mahratta Brahmin pleaders, the same men who patronized the Congress.[7] In UP, the heartland of Aryavarta, prominent Congressmen, backed by wealthy traders, bankers and landowners, campaigned for the outlawing of cow-slaughter as well as for the recognition of Devanagri as an official script in courts and government offices.[8] Ram Charan Das, who served on three Congress reception committees, was actively involved in the cow protection movement and in all the conferences and societies which culminated in the formation of the Hindu Sabha, and ultimately in the All-India Hindu Mahasabha.[9] His mentor, Madan Mohan Malaviya, was the moving spirit behind the Hindu revitalization movement. He was connected with the Prayag Hindu Samaj, the Sanatan Dharm Mahasammelan and the Shuddhi Sabha, which enabled him to forge close links with those influential groups who shared his undaunting enthusiasm for *shuddhi, sangathan*, Hindi, the cow and the Hindu Sabha. It was on the strength of their support that this orthodox and socially conservative Brahmin wielded considerable influence in local, provincial and national politics.

The Congress mobilization campaign suffered from another serious drawback: the insistence on treating Muslims as a distinct religious community and a homogeneous political entity.[10] This implied a recognition of the government's categorization of

[6] McLane, *Indian Nationalism*, p. 305.

[7] Ibid., p. 306.

[8] C.A. Bayly, 'Patrons and Politics in Northern India', *MAS*, vol. 7, 3, July 1973.

[9] Table I in R. Gordon, 'The Hindu Mahasabha and the Indian National Congress, 1915–1926', *MAS*, vol. 9, 2, April 1975, p. 153.

[10] Addressing the Punjab Political Conference in October 1906, Lala Lajpat Rai said that the 'religious ideals' of Hindus and Muslims were so different that it was 'impossible to expect a complete union of them in the near future'.

Indian society into exclusive religious groups, who also possessed a distinct political identity. In this way the avowed goal of uniting various groups and classes around a common socio-economic programme was trimmed to suit the dictates of political expediency. It suited the early Congress leaders to strike a bargain with 'Muslim' politicians without challenging their status in the community they so boldly claimed to represent and without questioning their exaggerated claims. Even their opposition to separate electorates was feeble, because of the more pressing compulsion to keep the Congress ranks united and to sustain the image of both a popular and representative organization. There was much substance in the observation of the Lucknow writer-essayist, Abdul Halim Sharar,

> . . . whether we support Congress or not, one very sad thing which we do notice about its activities is that it seems to be creating more differences between Hindus and Muslims than existed previously.[11]

However, the Congress strategy did not seem to work to its advantage. By legitimizing the role of self-appointed guardians of the faith, the Congress scuttled its own prospect of courting and nursing a potentially powerful constituency. And by accepting the notion of a politically distinct community, it lent credence to the claims advanced by the Aligarh leaders and their followers in the All-India Muslim League. By the time the Congress strategy was modified in the mid-1930s and its leaders were awakened to the reality of a communal monster, the opportunity of forging independent links with the Muslim masses was lost.

II

In explaining the 'Muslim breakaway' from the Congress—a major theme in studies on Indian nationalism—historians assume the existence of an all-India Muslim consciousness, which found

---

Panjabee, 13 October 1906, quoted in P. Nagar, *Lala Lajpat Rai: The Man and His Ideas* (Delhi, 1977), p. 252. And a more recent view of a Bengali intellectual that Indian Muslims 'constituted a society of their own with a distinct culture, and would never be absorbed in a unified nation which could be called India'. Nirad C. Chaudhuri, *Thy Hand Great Anarch! India 1921–1925* (London, 1987), p. 330.

[11] Abdul Halim Sharar, *Lucknow: The Last Phase of an Oriental Culture*, translated and edited by E.S. Harcourt and Fakhir Hussain (London, 1975), p. 23.

organized and tangible expression in the ideological orientation of Syed Ahmad Khan and his associates at Aligarh. This, however, is a questionable assumption and this section will examine why it is so. It will also try to establish that 'Muslim response' to the Congress did not crystallize at an identifiable level, and that isolated and sporadic reactions of fragmented groups must not form the basis of a highly generalized reconstruction. Bodies like the Central National Mahommedan Association and the United Patriotic Association, with their localized concerns, had no popular following and could not legitimately sustain their claim to represent Muslim interests generally.[12] Consequently, their response to the Congress, as Badruddin Tyabji perceptively pointed out, rested on 'local, special and temporary causes'.[13]

Given their different socio-economic interests there was no likelihood of a monolithic Muslim response to the Congress movement. There was none. The Congress demands affected Muslims of various classes and regions in several different ways; so, their reactions were moulded by local, regional and sometimes class-based interests as opposed to the altruistic concerns for the larger community of Indian Islam.

This section alludes to yet another contentious issue in contemporary historical writings: the part played by Syed Ahmad Khan, who is said to have orchestrated the 'Muslim viewpoint' on political matters with vigour and consistency and whipped up an anti-Congress stir among his followers. While the weight of his arguments against the Congress must be recognized, as also his influence on Muslim society, at the same time, we need to explore how a group of Muslims, imbued with the spirit of nationalism, were beginning to work out an alternative political strategy in the last decade of the nineteenth century. Admittedly, they could not match the intellectual resources of Syed

[12] There is evidence of considerable mutual antipathy between the so-called Muslim leaders. In Bengal, for example, Ameer Ali and Abdul Latif hurled mutual accusations at each other. W.S. Blunt, who was in India in 1883–84, recorded that Latif criticized Ameer Ali for having 'broken with the mass of the community by affecting English dress and ways, and posing as reformers, although they were in no way qualified in a religious sense for such a position'. W.S. Blunt, *India Under Ripon: A Private Diary* (London, 1909), p. 97.

[13] *Hindu*, 16 January 1888.

Ahmad and his disciples at Aligarh. They also did not possess the organizational strength to counter their more influential detractors. But they were not lacking in ideological conviction and consistency, a fact that enabled them to develop and pursue their nationalist aims and spearhead a pro-Congress movement in the early decade of the twentieth century. Thus, our preoccupation with Syed Ahmad's anti-Congress crusade need not lead historians to ignore alternative political currents within the Muslim community.

The mixed and diverse reactions to nationalist forces is evident from the ways in which some of the Congress demands were perceived. Most educated Muslims in Bengal and Punjab were averse to competitive examinations, because they were educationally ill-prepared to compete with the more advanced Hindus. Ameer Ali and Abdul Latif, representing two of Bengal's premier organizations, maintained that the Congress goal of a more open and competitive society, if implemented, would favour educated Hindus and accentuate existing disparities between the religious communities.[14] The same argument was echoed in upper India in order to make a case for nomination. Moreover, there was the familiar clamour for separate representation in public appointments and its extension to representative bodies, especially because many 'respected families' had been left out on account of franchise being confined to those who fulfilled property, wealth and educational qualifications.[15]

In UP, too, the Congress faced stern opposition. Here the main apprehension was of being swamped by the so-called Hindu majority in a prospective popular government—a fear reinforced

[14] *Report of the Public Service Commission, 1886–87* (Calcutta, 1888), vol. 4, pp. 196, 201, 262–68. A common grudge was that Muslims had limited chances of representation on local bodies, because franchise extended only to those who fulfilled property, wealth and educational qualifications. Thus in 1875–76, six of the 25 Indians on local bodies were Muslims. They fared still more poorly in the triennial election to the Calcutta municipality, held in 1897; there were only six Muslims as against 37 Hindus. *Administrative Report on the Municipality of the Suburbs of Calcutta 1875–76* (Calcutta, 1876), p. 6; *Statement Exibiting the Moral and Material Progress of India, 1897–98*, p. 6.

[15] Ibid., vol. 1, p. 162.

by some isolated examples in western UP. When some Muslim candidates were defeated in the municipal board elections held in 1890, the *Najmul Akhbaar* struck an alarming note: 'If the elective principle was extended to the legislative council an entire exclusion of Muslims from the council would follow.'[16] 'This is not an imaginary bugbear presented to scare away Muslims from the Congress camp', wrote a contributor to the *Aligarh Institute Gazette*, 'but a stubborn fact daily illustrated in the proceedings of the district and municipal boards scatterd all over the country.'[17] If anything, this was a reiteration of Syed Ahmad's arguments against the Congress demand for a more representative and popular government.

Though Syed Ahmad's assault on the Congress has been interpreted in several different ways,[18] most explanations are often based on later day ideological predilections. Besides, there is a tendency—more pronounced in the subcontinent than elsewhere—to try and prove or disprove that the genius behind the founding of the Aligarh college was also the progenitor of a 'Muslim nation'. This has distorted perspectives, stimulated, somewhat needlessly, acrimonious controversies, and obscured the more vital aspects of Indian polity and society during Syed Ahmad's lifetime. So far, attempts to establish him as the architect of 'Muslim nationalism' have proved to be as unrewarding as the efforts to discover in him elements of an 'Indian nationalist'.

It is, at first, hard to make sense of Syed Ahmad's fiery denunciation of the Congress. After all, he had the required credentials to be a leading light in any nationalist organization. Hindu-Muslim unity was close to his heart and a constant refrain in his public utterances.[19] Friendship between the two communities, he said, should be a matter of course, for since 'centuries we have been living on the same soil, eating the fruit of the same land . . . brea-

[16] *Najmul Akhbaar* (Etawah), 24 March 1890; *Jubilee Paper* (Lucknow) and *Azad* (Lucknow), 1 April 1890; *Mihir-i Nimroz* (Bijnor), 7 May 1890, Selections from the Native Newspaper Reports (hereafter SNNR), UP, 1890.

[17] *Aligarh Institute Gazette*, 12 September 1896.

[18] For a summary of various interpretations, C.W. Troll, *Sayyid Ahmad Khan: A Reinterpretation of Muslim Theology* (Delhi, 1978).

[19] Maulvi Mohammad Imamuddin (ed.), *Mukammal Majmuah wa Speeches* (Lahore, 1901), pp. 197–98.

thing the air of the same country'.[20] In 1873, he declared that he did not care for religion to be regarded as the badge of nationhood. He advocated separation between matters religious and political. Spiritual and religious matters, he asserted, cannot have any connection with worldly affairs. A true religion only stated cardinal principles comprising ethical values and only incidentally dealt with the problems of the world. When he was a member of the viceroy's legislative council he strove for the welfare of both Hindus and Muslims: so when he toured north India in the eighties he was feted on all sides.[21] In 1884, Syed Ahmad made clear that

> by the word qaum, I mean both Hindus and Muslims. . . . In my opinion it matters not whatever be their religious beliefs, because we cannot see anything of it; but what we see is that all of us, whether Hindus or Muslims, live on one soil, are governed by one and the same ruler, have the same sources of benefits, and equally share the hardships of a famine. . . .[22]

Common territory, in the eyes of Syed Ahmad, thus imposed upon Indians the obligation of mutual co-operation and unity in order to ensure the common good.

The Aligarh reformer was no religious bigot or Hindu baiter. He worked closely with Hindus in the Scientific Society, the Aligarh British Indian Association and the United Patriotic Association;[23] both the vice-president and the secretary of the British Indian Association were Hindus. Communal concerns did not figure in his favourite MAO college project: he sought and secured generous support from Hindu rajas and zamindars.[24]

[20] J.M.S. Baljon, *Reforms and Religious Ideas of Sir Sayyid Ahmad Khan* (Leiden, 1949), p. 36.

[21] Iqbal Ali (ed.), *Sayyid Saheb ka Safarnama-i Punjab* (Lahore, 1979), pp. 140–67.

[22] Hafeez Malik, *Sir Sayyid Ahmad Khan and Muslim Modernization*, p. 240, and Hardy, *Muslims of British India*, p. 136.

[23] S.R. Mehrotra, *The Emergence of the Indian National Congress* (Delhi, 1971), pp. 209–10; Shan Muhammad (ed.), *The Aligarh Movement—Basic Documents 1864–1898* (Meerut, 1978), vol. 2, p. 939.

[24] Among the donors was the Maharaja of Patiala. Syed Ahmad to the Maharaja of Patiala, n.d., Collection Fund, F. No. 1, Aligarh Archives, Aligarh Muslim University, Aligarh (hereafter AMUA). Blunt and Maulvi Samiullah, Syed Ahmad's close friend and colleague, had animated discus-

Hindus were well-represented in the managing committee and among the teachers, while Hindu students even outnumbered Muslims in some of the early years of the college. As a concession to their religious susceptibilities, cow-slaughter was banned on the campus.[25]

In 1888, Syed Hosain Bilgrami pontificated on Hindu-Muslim unity and its value in forging a joint anti-Congress front. 'The interest of the peoples', he wrote to the Syed, 'are one and indivisible . . . and it behoves them both to unite and make common cause against this [Congress] movement.'[26] This was a needless sermon. The Syed should have told him so. But he was too polite to tell Bilgrami that he had been echoing the same feeling well before the Congress came into being, and that it was he who compared India to a pretty bride whose two eyes were the Hindus and the Muslims.

Syed Ahmad's political concerns were no less secular and there was little in his early attitudes to suggest that he wanted separate and favoured treatment for his co-religionists. He was the first to argue that the 1857 upsurge had been caused by the monumental indifference of the East India Company to the economic plight of the masses, and the failure to grant Indians some form of advisory representation in the council. He supported local self-government, the right of Indian judges to try English defendants, wrote in defence of Indians entering the covenanted civil service and revived the British Indian Association at Aligarh to join with Surendranath Banerjea in a campaign to restore the age of entrance for the Civil Service examination from nineteen to twenty-one.[27] Banerjea had attended a meeting at Aligarh in

---

sions on a Hindu-Muslim concordat. The Maulvi explained that 'the proper conduct' for the Muslims was being debated in the college, with some people arguing the case for making common cause with the Hindus. 'All, however, were at heart vexed and angry at what had been done, and recognized in the Ilbert Bill a matter of common interest'. Blunt, *India Under Ripon*, p. 103.

[25] Rajmohan Gandhi, *Understanding the Muslim Mind* (Delhi, 1987), p. 34.

[26] To Syed Ahmad, 20 August 1888, Muhammad (ed.), *The Aligarh Movement*, vol. 3, pp. 100-02.

[27] Seal, *Emergence of Indian Nationalism*, p. 319; David Lelyveld, *Aligarh's First Generation: Muslim Solidarity in British India* (Princeton, 1978),

1877. When he returned to the city in 1884 to start a branch of a new political organization, the National Fund, with Syed Ahmad as president, he was received with 'utmost kindness'. His friendly relations with the Syed continued 'notwithstanding differences of opinion, which the Congress movement subsequently gave rise to'.[28]

With a background so remarkably similar to that of any contemporary Congress leader, Syed Ahmad's December 1887 outburst at Lucknow surprised many. He sharply criticized the application of the principles of representative and parliamentary government in so diverse, so divided and so complex a society. He also raised the spectre of Bengali dominance. 'If you accept', he said at Lucknow and repeated elsewhere, 'that the country should groan under the yoke of Bengali rule and its people lick the Bengali shoes, then, in the name of God, jump into the train, sit down, and be off to Madras.' The Congress demands, he thundered, would hurt the Muslims most. The enlarged councils would have no place for them: it would be dominated by 'Babu-so-and-so Mitter, Babu-so-and-so Ghose and Babu-so-and-so Chuckerburtty.' This was not the language one associated with a man who had once held up the Bengalis as an example to be admired and imitated, and was generally known for his balanced views on so many public issues since the publication of his celebrated *Asbaab-i Baghawat-i Hind* in 1858.

It is doubtful if Syed Ahmad worked out his arguments against the Congress on his own. Though acutely sensitive to the changing climate of opinion in India in the decades after 1857, he was only

---

p. 305. Notice the following comment by a 'Muslim: A Political Observer':

> Do not his writings and his whole political conduct of the pre-Congress days show that he had himself been an advocate of what the Congress demanded later on—the full recognition of our political rights? What was his position with regard to the Ilbert Bill?... Above all, had he not written the 'Causes of the Indian Revolt' in which he traced the origin of the Mutiny to the shortsighted policy (of) the British?... Was he not in one sense the creator of the 'spirit' that found its culmination in the Congress movement?

'The Indian Muhammadans and the National Congress', *Kayastha Samachar* (Allahabad), November 1902, vol. 6, 5 (New Series), p. 392.

[28] S. Banerjea, *A Nation in Making* (Calcutta, 1963: reprint), p. 45.

superficially familiar with the intricacies of the newly-developing institutions of representative government. In such matters he was tutored by British officials in north India, whose active backing he required for his prestigious Aligarh project. The person who influenced him most was the MAO college Principal, Theodore Beck, 'a pretty young man with pink cheeks and blue eyes.' This 24-year old Cambridge undergraduate was the political mentor and ideologue of the grand old man of Aligarh.[29]

Theodore—meaning gift to God—was educated in Quaker schools, University College, London, and Trinity College, Cambridge. He was president of the Cambridge Union in 1882 and was a key figure in the Conversazone Society, better known as the 'Apostles.'[30] In 1883, he was fortuitously chosen Principal of the Aligarh college and travelled to India to assume duties on 1 February 1884. But the college, then and later, remained peripheral to his concerns. His preoccupation with political affairs 'swallowed up' much of his time.[31] He ignored accusations of derilection of duty, took pride in having a 'finger in the political pie'[32] and boasted that there were 'very few Englishmen in the country so well up as myself in the Congress business'.[33]

Beck, says David Lelyveld, was a 'Tory' radical at Cambridge: he stood for Home Rule for Ireland, women's rights and the creation of a classless society. He denounced British rule in India for not fulfilling 'our duty, training the nation and leaving it,

[29]It has been argued that the ideological basis of Syed Ahmad's opposition to Indian nationalism had been clearly articulated well before either Beck or the Congress had appeared on the scene. This view is based on Syed Ahmad's speech on the local self-government bill of the Central Provinces, delivered in January 1833. See Lelyveld, *Aligarh's First Generation*, p. 311, and, Robinson, *Separatism*, p. 110.

[30] Other members were Walter Raleigh, Arthur Strachey and J.K. Stephens, described by Eric Stokes as the political philosopher of the Indian Civil Service. These Cambridge recruits carried to Aligarh a particular subculture of British intellectual life, one that suited the aspirations and priorities that Syed Ahmad considered appropriate to his educational efforts. Lelyveld, op. cit., p. 213.

[31] Beck to his mother, 21 July 1888, Beck Papers, India Office Library and Records (hereafter IOLR).

[32] Ibid., 7 July 1888.

[33] Ibid., 10 September 1888.

when strong enough, to itself.'[34] But Lelyveld does not tell us that the Cambridge interlude did not have a lasting impression on Beck: it was not long afterwards that he changed his views. His faith in British democracy was shaken. 'I believe', he observed on the eve of the 1892 general elections, 'it has no more wisdom in it than the oracle of Delphi had of divine inspiration'.[35] He also abandoned his undergraduate sympathy for Indian nationalism. This was not, as Lelyveld suggests, on account of 'intense indoctrination' from Syed Ahmad's son, Syed Mahmood, notorious for his drunken escapades and intellectually incapable of being anybody's mentor. In any case, Beck was too arrogant and self-righteous an individual to be guided by Syed Mahmood. By training and temperament he was a hardheaded Tory, with a deep distrust for political liberalism. He was averse to Gladstonian liberalism[36] and hostile to British politicians and civil servants who were soft towards Indian aspirations. W.S. Blunt, William Digby, Samuel Smith and John Slagg were 'cranks who unite on India'; W.W. Hunter, Richard Temple, W.C. Plowden, Richard Grath and Charles Turner were 'men of danger' and the 'dupes of every impudent journalistic liar'.[37] He reserved his harshest comments for Hunter, 'a notorious humbug . . . sacrificing both England and India for his advancement.'[38]

Though Beck described himself as one of 'England's adventurers', he reached the Indian shores with a clear sense of mission: to stamp out sedition in order to bolster imperial rule for the good of the Indian people. 'To have a great grievance shop, an anti-government cave of Adullum marching about the country will be

[34] Lelyveld, op. cit., p. 217. In India, Beck stated that he was 'a man who enjoys agitation. Fighting the authorities would be a most congenial task to me. But agitation for the backward and fanatical Muslims in upper India would be disastrous.' Beck to Badruddin Tyabji, 7 May 1888, Tyabji Papers, National Archives of India (hereafter NAI), New Delhi.

[35] Beck to his mother, 28 June 1892, Beck Papers.

[36] He regretted that the 'Gladstonians have got in' but was glad that their majority 'is so small'. To his mother, 19 July 1892, ibid.

[37] Ibid., 15 September 1888.

[38] Beck denounced the articles of Hunter in the *Times*, adding: 'I despise and loathe that man. He is a notorious humbug and all his knowledge of the people is secondhand. He is sacrificing both England and India for his own advancement'. Ibid., 21 June 1888.

bad for the peace of India,'[39] he wrote with reference to the Congress. He was constantly haunted by such apprehensions. Yet he set out to counter the 'evil' influence of the Congress with an evangelical fervour. He assiduously cultivated Muslims to create a 'strong conservative school of thought' and 'complete a breach' between them and the Bengali dominated Congress.[40] He kept his students on a tight leash. The Siddons Union Club, a Cambridge-like institution, debarred discussions on sensitive political affairs. Unlike the Cambridge prototype, the Principal had the veto power over any discussion so as to prevent the Union from becoming a forum for Bengali-style 'sedition'.[41] But Beck's eyes were set on the world beyond the Aligarh college: his aim was to establish an enduring Anglo-Muslim alliance and to stiffen Muslim feelings against the 'incendiary' Congress. 'I am more excited about this blessed Congress,' he wrote to his mother in April 1888, 'than about anything else. . . . It seems likely this Congress will create a great stir in this part of India, and I shouldn't be surprised if some jolly good rows occur. The opposition has got well on its legs. . . .'[42]

With his stature, influence and connections, Syed Ahmad was an invaluable asset to further Beck's ideals. He was, therefore, goaded into taking anti-Congress postures. Beck was dutifully present whenever his 'chief' fired his shots at the Congress. After the Meerut speech, he gleefully recorded: 'We have played off our 81 ton gun against the Congress again.'[43] He encouraged the launching of an anti-Congress newspaper,[44] herded the scattered elements of opposition to the Congress into the United Patriotic Association,[45] prompted some students to congregate at the Delhi Juma Masjid to collect signatures for an anti-Congress petition to Parliament[46] and kept on jogging up the *Pioneer* and

[39] Ibid., 3 May 1888.

[40] Ibid., 28 March and 20 September 1888.

[41] Lelyveld, op. cit., p. 220.

[42] To his mother, 24 April 1888, Beck Papers.

[43] Ibid., 28 March 1888.

[44] Ibid., 28 April 1888.

[45] Beck to Syed Ahmad, 13 February 1890, F.No. 69/10, AMUA. To his mother, 3 June 1888, Beck Papers.

[46] To his mother, 28 August 1888. He also mobilized Syed Ahmad to get

the government with little accounts of Muslim demonstrations against the Congress.[47] Beck's intentions were clear; yet, he was sometimes daunted by the outcome of his endeavours. 'It is a desperate struggle. If we relax our energies they will give us a thrashing. If we stick to it we may possibly—I say possibly, but probably—give them a desperate blow.'[48] He foresaw, thanks to his own initiatives, the emergence of a 'gigantic' Muslim organization in upper India with a distinct political creed. This would naturally suit the government, 'which will have some people to defend it. . . . We shall have a body of men bent on rooting out the fallacies of their [Congress] arguments.'[49]

Syed Ahmad could hardly match the young Principal's boundless energy and passion. Besides, after the initial spurt of activity he was reluctant to prosecute his anti-Congress campaign any further.[50] He bluntly said so to Beck in April 1888, just a few months after his well-publicized Lucknow speech. 'We have I think done enough in opposition to the Congress', he firmly stated.[51] In the same conversation, he recalled how during the turbulent days of 1857 the British employed brute force to crush the revolt—reminiscent of the atrocities perpetrated by Chingiz Khan and Timur. Beck was not pleased with the comparison. 'This little conversation', he noted despondently, 'has put a damper on my politics.'[52] But as one made of sterner stuff, he not only

a petition signed by Muslims against the Braudlaugh's Bill of Indian Councils (1889). To his father, 25 February 1890, Beck Papers.

[47] Beck referred to a meeting with UP's lieutenant-governor at which he discussed the Congress agitation. He was 'immensely flattered' at the reception he received and 'felt myself quite a big man, discussing the affairs of state with the King of the province'. Two years later, he went up to Shimla to meet Lansdowne and discussed the 'official encouragement' given to the Congress in some circles. To his mother, 3 June 1888, 16 June 1890, ibid.

[48] Ibid., 20 September 1888.

[49] Ibid., 10 April 1888.

[50] Beck was alarmed to notice that the Syed was inclined to 'take matters too calmly' and that he was not keen to prosecute the anti-Congress movement. A few month later, he complained to his mother that the Syed did not attach 'sufficient importance to educate the community in sound political thought'. 24 April and 20 September 1888, ibid.

[51] Ibid., 28 April 1888.

[52] Ibid.

kept up the tempo of his activities but also kept the Syed on a tight leash. His perseverance paid off. Constrained by his dependence on government support for the college of his dreams and ingratiated by the honour and approbation he received from the British, the ageing Syed Ahmad relented to the charms of the young Principal and lived up to his expectations of playing the anti-Congress drum loud and clear. Moreover, the rising tide of Hindu revivalism and its links with Indian nationalism reinforced his growing fears that the Congress movement was prejudicial to Muslim interests and that the 'well-being of the people of India, and especially of the Mussalmans, lies in leading a quiet life under the benign rule of the English government'.[53] Beck's aim of bringing the Aligarh reformer to the centre of the political stage was a consummate success.

There is no denying Syed Ahmad's profound impact on north Indian Muslims. He was a visible symbol of Muslim regeneration, a catalyst of social and educational reforms, a 'Notre eminent contemporain,' as Gracin de Tassy called him. His political message also carried weight: hence the Congress overtures to court his support. But his influence was by no means all-pervasive, because his anti-Congress stance did not go down well with *all* his co-religionists.[54] The United Indian Patriotic Association and the Muhammadan Anglo-Oriental Defence Association were tame affairs. They petered out, despite much fanfare, within two years of their lazy existence. Mohamed Ali, an Aligarh graduate, recalled how Syed Ahmad, his British patrons and the college trustees got together to pass a resolution against the Congress and had it published in the *Pioneer* and the *Aligarh Institute Gazette*. 'That was all that the Mussalmans would do in those days in the field of politics.'[55]

[53] *Aligarh Institute Gazette*, 18 September 1897.

[54] For criticizm of his political views in a section of the Urdu press, Prem Narain, *Press and Politics in India, 1885–1905* (Delhi, 1970), pp. 83, 92–94. Speeches of Muslim Congressmen like Maulvi Hidayat Rasul, Nawab Reza Khan, Hamid Ali Khan, Maulvi Syed-Sharfuddin and Shaikh Kadir Buksh are reproduced in A.M. Zaidi (ed.), *The Muslim School of Congress* (Delhi, 1987), pp. 345–50, 358–64.

[55] Mushirul Hasan (ed.), *Mohamed Ali in Indian Politics: Select Writings* (Delhi, 1982), vol. 1, p. 32.

Sustained and organized opposition to the Congress was generally confined to Aligarh and its neighbouring districts; elsewhere, there were enough Muslims who were unmoved by Syed Ahmad's political exhortations. In 1887, seventy Muslims from Awadh attended the Madras Congress. Of the 222 Muslims gathered at the Allahabad Congress a year later, ninety came from Allahabad and Lucknow districts.[56] In 1889, 254 Muslims turned up in Bombay, of whom 125 were from Delhi and UP. At least some of them were inspired by a *fatwa*, signed by over a hundred *ulama*, in support of the Congress and in opposition to the Patriotic Association. The signatories included Rashid Ahmad Gangohi, Mahmud Hasan and several other eminent Deobandi *ulama*.[57] The *fatwa*, published under the title *Nusrat-al Abraar*, received wide publicity. It served as a political manifesto for the succeeding generations of the *ulama* at Deoband.

Aligarh's first generation students, brought up under Syed Ahmad's benign influence and tutored incessantly on the virtues of loyalty to the raj, were not all cut out of the same cloth. His Lucknow and Meerut speeches drew no applause from several Aligarh students, including Syed Nabiullah and Rafique, soon to be a Cambridge graduate after a brief stint with the Lucknow paper, *Advocate*. The Meerut outburst, according to another Aligarh graduate, Inayatullah, 'smacked of flattery'.[58] Rafique was equally forthright in his rebuttal. 'The prospect of a united India', he observed in one of his inspired moods, 'does seem at first utopian and impracticable. But it is an object worth striving for'.[59] In a similar vein, though with greater incisiveness, Mir Mohamed Husain told Beck in April 1888:

As long as you talk to me about the interests of Muslims alone I won't

[56] J.L. Hill, 'Congress and Representative Institutions in the United Provinces 1886–1901' (Unpublished Ph.D. thesis, Duke University, 1969). Tables 1 to 3 are also drawn from this thesis.

[57] Husain Ahmad Madani, *Naqsh-i Hayaat: Khudnawisht Sawaanih* (Karachi, 1979 edn.), pp. 481–82; I.H. Qureshi, *Ulama in Politics* (Karachi, 1974), p. 227. Allan Octavian Hume boasted that in Punjab 'we are sweeping Sir Syed away.... The Ludhiana Maulvis have the absolute command of over 40,000 Muslims'. To Tyabji, 5 November 1888, Tyabji Papers.

[58] Beck to his mother, 3 April 1888, Beck Papers.

[59] Ibid., 10 February 1888.

listen to you. I will only look to the interests of the country. And by the country I mean these 90 per cent of poor peasants who live from hand to mouth. Every effort should be made to improve their condition. How? Not by trying to get more appointments for Muslims, but by trying to improve the material condition of the country—its industry and commerce. If you stir up ill-will between Hindus and Muslims you will ruin the country. . . . The Anglo-Indians don't like two things—union amongst us, and the improvement of our material conditions. . . . We should have joined the Congress and opposed their bad schemes. We should have directed the attention of the Congress on improving the material prosperity of the country and bettering the conditions of these poor peasants.[60]

This was 'subversive' talk by men who, in Beck's assessment, had 'gobbled up the radicalism of England and of Young Bengal.'[61] But neither he nor the sage from Aligarh could quite foresee the course of events which would slowly but steadily lead the young English-educated Muslims, especially those trained at Aligarh, to clamour for a reordering of political priorities and autonomy of political action. The anguished successors of Syed Ahmad watched helplessly as some of Aligarh's brilliant products—Mohamed Ali, Hasrat Mohani, Zafar Ali Khan, Shaukat Ali, Raja Ghulam Husain, Ghulam-us-Saqlain[62] and Wilayat Ali Bambooque[63]—moved into the political arena with a fresh disposition, a distinct style of politics and a new ideological

[60] Beck Papers, 5 March 1888.

[61] Ibid.

[62] He was at the Aligarh college from October 1889 to April 1894, where he developed a keen interest in nationalist affairs. In January 1903 he started the *Asr-i Jadeed* from Meerut, a paper with nationalist concerns. The paper ceased publication in December 1908 on account of the illness of Ghulam-us-Saqlain.

[63] Wilayat Ali was born in 1887 in Masauli village in Barabanki district. He belonged to the Kidwai clan, which traced its descent to Kidwatuddin who came to India in the wake of the Ghorid invasion of north India. He was educated at the Aligarh college and was a contemporary of Syed Mahmud, Khaliquzzaman, Shuaib Qureshi and Raja Ghulam Husain. His humorous sketches were credited with literary excellence. In July 1918, Wilayat Ali, popularly known as 'Bambooque', was stricken with cholera. Dr M.A. Ansari rushed to his bedside in Barabanki but could not save his life.

orientation. The Ali brothers—Mohamed and Shaukat—both graduates of the Aligarh college, villified Beck and his successors[64] and were at pains to establish that the radical temper of their comrades was consistent with the intentions of their mentor, Syed Ahmad. Mohamed Ali announced in an Urdu verse:

It is you who had taught the community all this 'mischief'
If we are its culmination, you are its commencement

III

Out of 1,620 individuals from UP who signed the roll as delegates to the annual Congress sessions from 1885 to 1901, 596, or slightly over one-third, were Muslims from UP (Table 2:1), the province where Syed Ahmad is supposed to have exercized the greatest of influence. Their strength increased steadily from 8 per cent in 1886 to high-points of 42 per cent in 1889 and 55 per cent in 1890.[65] The delegates included members of the dispossessed nawabi elite, newspaper editors like Munshi Sajjad Husain, editor of *Oudh Punch*, and a mixed group of teachers, lawyers, bankers and traders. Connected with secular-oriented organizations like the Rifah-i Am and the Anjuman-i Muhammadi, many of them had close cultural and professional links with Congress leaders in Lucknow and Allahabad. The Rifah-i Am was headed by Shaikh Raza Husain Khan, a close friend of Babu Ganga Prashad Varma, editor of *Hindustani* in Lucknow, and among its patrons was Pandit Ajudhia Nath Kunzru. The Anjuman-i Muhammadi elected over 150 delegates to the Congress session in 1890: its president, Nawab Ali Mohamed Khan, served on the Congress Subjects Committee in 1892 and 1899.

Six-tenths of all Muslim delegates from 1886 to 1901 came from Lucknow, the city where the composite, cross-communal traditions continued to ensure a broad secularity in public life. When the Congress met at Allahabad in 1888 and 1892, Lucknow had more Muslim delegates in attendance than the host city. There were 313 Muslims at the 1899 Congress and 288 came from

[64] Margaret H. Case, 'The Aligarh Era: Muslim Politics in North India 1860–1910' (Unpublished Ph.D. thesis, Chicago, 1970), p. 179.
[65] J.L. Hill, op. cit., p. 41, f.n. 41.

TABLE 2.1

UP Congress Delegates by Religion and Year of Attendance

Year	Jains	Chris-tians	Muslim	Percentage of UP Dele-gation	Hindu	Percentage of UP Dele-gation
1885						
1886	. .	. .	6	8	68	92
1887	. .	. .	7	15	41	85
1888	6	18	151	26	396	68
1989	1	6	113	44	139	53
1890	. .	3	82	55	62	42
1891*	—	—	—	—	—	—
1892	2	4	79	25	235	73
1893	1	1	122	9	117	89
1894	. .	1	1	8	10	77
1895	1	1	1	4	21	88
1896	. .	2	5	8	52	87
1897	. .	1	0	0	9	90
1898	. .	.	1	0	11	100
1899	2	4	304	51	288	48
1900	3	3	1	3	31	80
1901	. .	3	6	7	84	90

* No delegates' lists for this year is available.

Lucknow itself (Tables 2:2–3). It was the largest Muslim attendance at any annual session before 1916.

Next to Lucknow, Allahabad, the 'city with its hoary traditions, inspiring memories, sacred associations [and] high intellectual reputation,'[66] elected one-fifth of the Muslim delegates. They included some small zamindars from Daryabad, poverty-stricken Shia dependents of the old royal house of Awadh and a group of lawyers led by Abdul Majid and Abdur Rauf who were closely tied to Ajudhia Nath Kunzru.[67] In general, however, the Shias were more numerous in the Muslim delegation. It is surprising

[66] MSS.EUR. E.251/3, Hallet Papers, IOLR.

[67] They addressed several public meetings with Kunzru who was their senior colleague at the Allahabad bar. *Tribune*, 22 February 1888.

TABLE 2.2
UP Muslim Delegates from Major Cities by Year of Attendance at the Congress

Year	Lucknow	Allahabad	Banaras	Kanpur	Agra	Aligarh
1885						
1886	3		1	. .	. .	. .
1887	1	.	. .	. .	1	2
1888	42	33	20	13	9	7
1889	32	23	2	11	7	6
1890*	—	—	—	—	—	—
1891*	—	—	—	—	—	—
1892	28	31	.	1	. .	8
1893	2	. .	. .	. .	3	5
1894	. .	. .	. .	. .	. .	1
1895	. .	. .	. .	. .	. .	1
1896	3	. .	. .	. .	. .	1
1897	. .	. .	. .	. .	. .	. .
1898	1	. .	. .	. .	. .	. .
1899	288**	1	2	1	1	3
1900	. .	. .	. .	. .	. .	1
1901	. .	2	1 .	1	. .	. .

*No delegates list available.
**264 of these attended in 1899 only.

that this was so. Their population was small, the level of political consciousness was low and, above all, there was no institutional or organizational structures to sustain their political concerns. Their sudden, active interest in Congress affairs can only be explained in terms of their rift with the Sunnis over the *Madhe Sahaba* issue, which gripped so many cities of UP in the last quarter of the nineteenth century.[68]

Shia leaders in Allahabad and Lucknow turned to the Congress to defend their right to take out *tazia* processions and exercize control over their endowments. They seized the initiative and, in November 1888, a Khoja Muslim from Bombay, Mohammad

[68] Mushirul Hasan, 'Sectarianism in Indian Islam: The Shia-Sunni Divide in the United Provinces', *The Indian Economic and Social History Review*, vol. 27, 2,90; J.R.I. Cole, *Roots of North Indian Shiism in Iran and Iraq: Religion and State in Awadh, 1722–1889* (Delhi, 1989).

TABLE 2.3

Total Number of Muslim Delegates from Each City of the United Provinces, 1886–1901

City	Delegates		City	Delegates	
	Number	Percentage of total Muslim Delegates		Number	Percentage of total Human An Ebyss
Dehra Dun	1	.2	Allahabad	76	13
Saharanpur	1	.2	Azamgarh	5	.8
Muzaffarnagar	2	.3	Mirzapur	6	1
Meerut	6	1	Banaras	24	1
Aligarh	19	3	Ghazipur	4	.7
Naini Tal	2	.3	Basti	1	.2
Almora	3	.5	Lucknow	355	60
Moradabad	5	.8	Barabanki	1	.2
Bareilly	5	.8	Sitapur	1	.2
Shahjahanpur	7	1	Kheri	4	.7
Agra	19	3	Fyzabad	4	.7
Farrukhabad	11	2	Gonda	2	.3
Kanpur	24	4	Rae Bareli	1	.2
Fatehpur	1	.2	Pratapgarh	5	.8
Banda	1	.2			

Ali Bhimji, was invited to address a pro-Congress Shia gathering. Sunni leaders were not to be outmanoeuvred. Maulana Mohamed Husain of the Diara Shah Hujatullah, already won over by the Syed Ahmad–Beck combine, launched a counter-attack.[69] The Congress in UP was caught up in the crossfire between the Shia zealots and the Sunni orthodox opinion. Appearing to be impartial

[69] C.A. Bayly, *The Local Roots of Indian Politics—Allahabad, 1880–1920* (Oxford, 1975), p. 130. Beck noted that the Maulvi, 'a man of great learning and piety' was drawn into the anti-Congress movement by Syed Ahmad's speeches and by the agitation against cow slaughter. Expressing satisfaction at Maulvi Mohamed Husain's presence at an anti-Congress rally in Allahabad, Beck observed: 'I think the National Congress is doing the Muslims a lot of good. These meetings are infusing spirit into the community and inducing it to shake off its fatal stagnation'. To his mother, 2 March 1888, Beck Papers.

in the deepening sectarian controversies was the only way to ensure the balance of its support. Increasingly, however, Shia-Sunni conflicts, which erupted in the years 1937 to 1939, imposed severe strains on Congress' ability to maintain an equilibrium in its relationship with the two rival sects.

The social profile of Muslim Congressmen in Bengal and Punjab[70] was no different from other regions of British India. They were urban-based and connected with various professions, such as journalism and law. Shared professional experience, besides removing mutual prejudices which often stemmed from social distancing, provided the stimulus for acting in unison on contemporary political issues. This is illustrated by the career of Abdul Rasul, a prominent Congress leader in Bengal. He went to St. John's College, Oxford, and was called to the Bar from the Middle Temple. On his return to India, he enrolled himself as a barrister of the Calcutta High Court, where he came in contact with leading lawyers like W.C. Bonnerjee and Lal Mohan Ghose and was much inspired by their political activities. Likewise, the social background of Abdul Halim Ghuznavi and Abdul Kaseem, founder of *Mussalman*, was decidedly important in the making

[70] Some of the important Congressmen in Punjab were: Muharram Ali Chishti, Syed Nadir Ali Shah, Hakim Ahmad Ali and Munshi Nabi Baksh, editors of *Rafiq-i Hind*, *Rehbar-i Hind*, *Takmilul Hikmat* and *Koh-i Noor*, respectively. Among the prominent lawyers associated with the organization were Shaikh Umar Baksh and his brother Nabi Baksh. They headed the district Congress committees of Hoshiarpur and Gurdaspur. See *Tribune*, 14 October, 25 November, and 13 December 1893. In general, however, there was not much enthusiasm for the Congress in Punjab. K.W. Jones has explained why this was so. In the case of some groups, such as the militant Arya Samajists, the Congress appeared pro-Muslim. This impression was confirmed when the Congress Subjects Committee decided to drop the di cussion on the Punjab Alienation Act from the agenda as a concession to the feelings of Punjabi Muslims. Soon thereafter, plans were set afoot to organize an exclusively 'Hindu' body. According to Jones, the provincial world appeared far more real and relevant than the wider sphere of the Congress and national issues. Instead of national politics, factional struggles and communal competition commanded far greater attention. K.W. Jones, *Arya Dharm: Hindu Consciousness in 19th Century Punjab* (Berkeley, 1976); pp. 241–50, 254–55; N.G. Barrier, 'The Arya Samaj and Congress Politics in the Punjab 1894–1908', *Journal of Asian Studies*, vol. 26, May 1967.

of their ideological orientation. It helps to understand why they, along with Liakat Hossain, Hassan Jan and other Muslims, marched with the opponents of the partition of Bengal and joined heart and soul in the swadeshi *tehrik*.[71]

In western India, Badruddin Tyabji, a Sulaimani Bohra, was the prized trophy of the Congress. His father Tyab Ali was not born with a silver spoon but made a neat fortune through his matrimonial links with an affluent trading family. He did not have the benefit of studying in an English school or college but saw the advantage of educating his sons in England. That is how Badruddin became the first Muslim to qualify at the London Bar (1867) and to be enrolled as an advocate of the Bombay High Court. His brother, Camruddin, was the first Muslim to be trained as a solicitor in England and the first Muslim Indian to be admitted to the profession in that country. In this way, Tyab Ali 'triumphed in founding a family that, endowed by him with self-sufficiency, imbued with his ideals of work . . . continued to make a mark on Indian national life for over a century and a half'.[72]

Tyab Ali was a devout Muslim, though not one to harp on Hindu-Muslim differences. Badruddin Tyabji was no different. His association with the London Indian Society and the East Indian Association provide enough clues to his cosmopolitan outlook and political inclinations.[73] In 1882 he was given a place on the legislative council to represent graduates and lawyers and not simply the Muslims. And in 1885 Badruddin became one of the founders of the Bombay Presidency Association which that December played host to the first Congress. Here, as elsewhere, he worked, along with two other members of the 'trio'—Pherozeshah Mehta and K.T. Telang—'not as Hindus, Mahomedans and Parsis but as soldiers in the public cause.'[74]

Given his background and concerns, Badruddin Tyabji was the obvious person to spearhead the Congress movement. It is,

[71] Sarkar, *Swadeshi Movement*, pp. 426–35; Jayanti Maitra, *Muslim Politics in Bengal 1885-1906: Collaboration and Confrontation* (Calcutta, 1984), pp. 244–46, 249–50.

[72] Badr-ud-din Tyabji, *Memoirs of an Egoist* (Delhi, 1988), p. 7.

[73] In London, Tyabji was among those who rallied round Dadabhai Naoroji to found the London India Society.

[74] A.G. Noorani, *Badruddin Tyabji* (Delhi, 1969), p. 132.

therefore, not surprising that W.C. Bonnerjee insisted that his friend from student days in England occupy the presidential chair at the Second Congress, and the Congress Standing Committee unhesitatingly declared in November 1887 that Badruddin was 'not only the best, but the only possible man for the post.'[75] What was surprising was how quickly his election provoked a counter-reaction. Syed Ahmad was angered. He chose the occasion of Badruddin's presidency to come out publicly against the Congress.

Badruddin rebutted the views of Syed Ahmad. The Congress, he said, should be allowed to play the major role in aggregating the Muslims' articulated interests and that Muslims could by united action confine Congress to such issues as they deemed safe for discussion. On 18 February 1888 he wrote:

> My policy, therefore, would be to act from *within* rather than from *without*. . . . We should thus advance the general progress of India, and at the same time safeguard our own interests.[76]

Many Muslims, Badruddin claimed, recognized this and supported the Congress. Those who did not was because of 'certain special, local and temporary causes', which applied 'only to a particular part of India.'[77]

Syed Ahmad Khan did not think so. There was no such thing as 'the general progress of India' or 'India as one nation'. The different castes and creeds, he told Badruddin in January 1888, did not belong to a nation and their aims and aspirations were also not the same. 'You regard', he continued, 'the doings of the misnamed National Congress as beneficial to India, but I am sorry to say that I regard them as not only injurious to our own community but also to India at large.'[78] Small but significant gatherings of Muslims in Bombay endorsed Syed Ahmad's line of reasoning rather than Badruddin's plea for Muslim participation in Congress.[79] In October 1888, a dejected Badruddin suggested

[75] Hume to Tyabji, 3 December 1887, Tyabji Papers.
[76] Tyabji to Ameer Ali, 3 December 1887, ibid.
[77] *Report of the Indian National Congress*, 1887, p. 72.
[78] Syed Ahmad to Tyabji, 24 January 1888, Tyabji Papers.
[79] *Rast Goftar* and *Kaside Mumbai*, 12 August 1888; *Parsi Punch*, 19 August 1888, SNNR, Bombay.

that the Congress activities be suspended for five years because 'an overwhelming majority of Mohammedans is against the [Congress] movement'.[80] Nobody took the suggestion seriously. And nobody ever agreed with Badruddin's assessment of Muslim hostility. For once the future judge of the Bombay High Court had spoken too soon.

IV

It is worth reiterating the several different ways in which Muslims related themselves to developments around their immediate and distant surroundings. Admittedly, there was some talk of 'Muslim solidarity' and some half-hearted endeavours to steer the political discourse around religious lines, but neither Syed Ahmad nor his compatriots could translate their objectives in any tangible form. Diverse regional and local concerns, conflicting class interests and sectarian animus sharpened cleavages and impeded the growth of an all-India Muslim political consciousness. In fact, no amount of pious exhortations could bridge the wide gulf that separated, say, the East Bengal Muslim peasant from the Muslim taluqdar in Awadh. By the end of the nineteenth century, all attempts to bring about 'some degree of solidarity among the disintegrated masses of Mahomedan society' failed to achieve any measure of success.

No summing up of late-nineteenth century trends can, however, be complete without reference to the spurt in cow-protection activity and the strident demand for securing recognition of the Nagri script in government and law courts.[81] These were not isolated assertions of militant, religio-revivalist tendencies but

[80] Tyabji to Hume, 27 October 1888, Tyabji Papers.

[81] McLane, *Indian Nationalism*, pp. 271–331, for an insightful account of the cow-protection movement. See Robinson, *Separatism*, pp. 66–78, for a sensitive portrayal of Hindu revivalist tendencies, including the development of the Hindi-Urdu conflict and the campaign for Hindi. The Hindi-Urdu controversy is also discussed in: Aziz Ahmad, *Islamic Culture in the Indian Environment*, pp. 259–62, Brass, *Language, Religion and Politics*, pp. 127–138, and Jyotirindra Das Gupta, *Language Conflict and National Development: Group Politics and National Language Policy in India* (Berkeley, 1970), chapter four.

were outward manifestations of the new and burgeoning sense of Hindu consciousness. There were similar trends among Muslims. The Graeco-Turkish War of 1897 stimulated pan-Islamic feelings.[82] Islamization in Bengal and parts of upper India, inspired by the Waliullahi traditions and bolstered by the success of the Faraizi ideology, was an equally important force. Insistence on a revitalized Islamic consciousness and identity, with its corresponding denigration of Islam's local roots, was beginning to erode the syncretistic traditions and undermine inter-religious peace and understanding.[83] The massive communal rioting in the summer of 1893 was a grim reminder to the nationalists that the fabric of Hindu-Muslim unity was too fragile to withstand the onslaught of various revitalization movements. 'If the smouldering fire of religious enmity . . . is not put out', warned an observer, 'it will before long be kindled into a mighty flame and destroy the noble edifice which the Congress has built up with so much pains.'[84]

The prophecy did not come true. Though relations between Hindus and Muslims were sometimes strained, their deterioration was neither deep nor irreversible. 'Nothing strikes the intelligent traveller in India more forcibly', observed a senior police official, 'than the friendly and peaceable attitude of all castes and classes towards each other.'[85] He was right. Communal friction was not ordinarily a major source of civil disturbance in the last quarter

[82] Subscriptions were raised at Kanpur in aid of Turkey, prayers were offered at Jhansi and Agra for the success of the Khalifa, who was commonly described as the *Khalifat al-Muslimeen* in contemporary newspapers. An indication of the depth of Muslim feelings is reflected in the bitter criticizm of Syed Ahmad's views on pan-Islamism. *Zamanah* (Kanpur), 13 May 1897, *Nasim-i Agra* (Agra), 22 May 1897, *Akhbaar-i Islam* (Agra), 23 May 1897, *Azad* (Lucknow), 4 June 1897, *Shahna-i Hind*, 1 July 1897, *Riaz al-Akhbaar*, 4 July 1897, *Naiyar-i Azam* (Moradabad), 5 February 1900, *Jami al-ulum* (Moradabad), 14 February 1900, SNNR, UP.

[83] Roy, *Islamic Syncretism*, p. 251, and Ahmad, *The Bengal Muslims*, p. 184; S.M. Ikram, *Muslim Civilization in India* (London, 1964), pp. 282-86.

[84] *Al-Waqt* (Gorakhpur), 21/26 February 1894, SNNR, UP.

[85] T.C. Arthur, *Reminiscences of an Indian Police Official* (London, 1894), p. 145. English and Indian witnesses before the Public Service Commission testified to the harmonious relations between the Hindus and Muslims and took serious note of the cross-communal links. *PSC*, NWP & O Sub-Commission (Calcutta, 1888), pp. 15, 26, 23.

of the nineteenth cenutry. During the quinquennium, 1889–1894, there was no communal violence in Bengal, except one in Calcutta and its suburbs.[86] Such sporadic outbursts did not signify, as some writers are wont to suggest, the fragmentation of Indian society along communal lines. Intercommunity tensions and conflicts were counterposed to the quiet, commonplace routines in which Hindus and Muslims intermingled without notice or incident and could still be found involved in a range of 'religiously promiscuous' practices. In 1909, the *Imperial Gazetteer of India* stated that 'it was, until recently, the regular practice of low-class Muhammadans to join in the Durga Puja and other festivals'; it mentioned Muslim consultation of Hindu almanacs, worship of Sithala and Manasa, use of vermilion, and joint offerings to village deities before the sowing or transplanting of rice seedlings.[87] Another inspiring legitimation of the more mundane expressions of peaceful coexistence came daily in the sounds of Muslim *shahnai* players joining in the *arti* at Hindu temples, including the *arti* at the most sacred Vishwanath temple in Banaras.[88]

Contemporary writings took note of cordial Hindu-Muslim relations, highlighting the ongoing process of social and cultural fusion.[89] The poet Mohammad Iqbal shared the vision of a united India—one that was free of both alien domination and inner dissensions. In 'Sayyid's Tomb', he called his land of birth as a garden, and the people inhabiting it as members of a *qaum* (nation), with the two circles of Islam and *watan* intersecting and at several places coalescing into a coherent whole. *Himala*, the first poem

[86] Rajat Kanta Ray, *Social Conflict and Political Unrest in Bengal 1875–1927* (Delhi, 1984), p. 121. The Commissioner of Dacca noted the 'extraordinary fact' that in five years 'not a single riot of any description should have occurred'.

[87] *Imperial Gazetteer of India*, pp. 48–49.

[88] Judy F. Pugh, 'Divination and Ideology in the Banaras Muslim Community', Ewing (ed.), *Shariat and Ambiguity*, p. 289.

[89] For instance, Syed Ahmad Dehlavi, *Rasum-i Delhi* (Delhi, 1905), pp. 37–41, and for comments and reactions of Asadullah Khan Ghalib, see Percival Spear, 'Ghalib's Delhi', Ralph Russell (ed.), *Ghalib: The Poet and His Age* (London, 1977), p. 49. Again, for Hindu-Muslim relations in Delhi, see C.F. Andrews, *Zakaullah of Delhi* (Cambridge, n.d.), pp. 11, 15–17.

in *Bang-i Dara*, was inspired by the beauty of the land of his birth, while *Hindustani Bachhon ka Qaumi Geet* (National Anthem of Indian Children) and the *Tarana-i Hindi* (The Song of India) were refined, buoyant and non-communal expressions of patriotic sentiments.[90] In *Naya Shiwala* (New Temple), he chided both Hindus and Muslims for their narrow mental horizon,[91] and appealed to the keepers of the temple and the mosque to foster mutual goodwill and understanding.[92] Indeed, Iqbal echoed, in large measure, the ideology of secular nationalism.

Akbar Allahabadi, a merciless satirist equipped with an irrepressible sense of humour, had similar concerns. He subjected to ridicule, to scathing criticizm or damning exposure the social and political strategy of imperialism and Syed Ahmad's policy of loyal co-operation with the government.[93] And, like Iqbal, he championed Hindu-Muslim unity. Both Hindus and Muslims, he said, have to bear the blows of those who wield the rod of worldly power, but they should respond by being like water, on which the blows of a rod have only a momentary effect.[94]

Iqbal and Akbar were stating the obvious. They recognized, as indeed did others, that the direction in which patronage

[90] See the collection of essays in Hafeez Malik (ed.), *Iqbal: Poet-Philosopher of Pakistan* (Columbia University Press, 1971).

[91] I'll tell you the truth, Oh Brahmin, if I may make so bold!
Those idols in your temples—these idols have grown old;
To hate your fellow-mortals is all they teach you, while
Our God too sets his preachers to scold and revile;
Sickened, from both your temple and our shrine I have seen,
Alike our preachers' sermons and your fond myths I shun.
In every garden image you fancied God: I see
In every speck of my country's poor dust, divinity.

V.G. Kiernan, *Poems from Iqbal*, p. 8.

[92] Come, let us remove all that causes estrangement,
Let us reconcile those that have turned away from
each other, remove all signs of division.
Desolation has reigned for long in the
habitation of my heart—
Come, let us build a new temple in our land.

M. Mujeeb, *The Indian Muslims* (London, 1967), p. 485.

[93] Ibid., p. 477.

[94] I say the same to Hindus and to Muslims:

economic welfare and authority flowed in everyday life indicated the continuing importance of cross-communal networks.[95] Syed Ahmad's Aligarh project was backed by Hindus and Muslims alike.[96] He encouraged, despite his misgivings over the Nagri agitation, a Hindu-Muslim *entente* in cultural and religious matters. His contemporary, Ajudhia Nath Kunzru, owed his fortunes as much to the wealthy Muslim landholders as to his extensive banking and commission agencies.[97] In east UP and Awadh generally, the dominant factor in the politics of the towns tended to be an Urdu-speaking elite connection based on landed interests. Communal matters did not always foul the path of politics.[98]

The competing units in early municipal politics were multi-factions, not antagonistic communal groups. In the composition of early municipal factions, conflicting caste and communal considerations played a secondary role to personal rivalries and connections. A Muslim lawyer, Maulvi Serajul Islam, was elected from Chittagong to the Bengal legislative council, largely on the Hindu vote. Surendranath Banerjea, on the other hand, was backed by Muslims for a seat on the prestigious Calcutta Corporation.[99] Around the same time, a similar move was afoot in UP, where the Congress backed Hamid Ali Khan for a seat in the council.

Nor did communal divisions last long after they had been politicized. Soon after the violent eruptions in 1893, tempers began to cool everywhere and there was much display of 'mutual love and affection' in the riot-torn cities of UP.[100] Public statements

---

Be good, each as your faith would have you be.
The world's a rod? Then *you* become as water.
Clash like the waves, but still remain one wave.

Ralph Russell and Khurshidul Islam, 'The Satirical verse of Akbar Illahabadi (1846–1921)', *MAS*, 1974, vol. 8, 1, pp. 44-46.

[95] D.A. Washbrook, *The Emergence of Provincial Politics. The Madras Presidency, 1870–1920* (Cambridge, 1976), pp. 143–44, 262.

[96] For example, one Sita Narain, a barrister at Rajkot, donated Rs 45,000 to the Aligarh college and Rs 16,000 to the Central Hindu College at Banaras. *Al-Bashir*, 24 February 1901. SNNR, UP.

[97] Henry Sender, *The Kashmiri Pandits: A Study of Cultural Choice in North India* (Delhi, 1988), p. 244.

[98] Robinson, *Separatism*, p. 79.

[99] Ray, *Social Conflict*, pp. 41, 131–32.

[100] The years 1897 to 1900 may well be regarded as a period of exceptionally

and newspaper editorials on national unity and the commonality of Hindu-Muslim interests were matched by strenuous efforts of local reconciliation committees to resolve and diffuse tensions.[101] When asked how the 'upper classes' of the two communities behaved when riots occur, the Assistant Magistrate of Gorakhpur replied:

> By taking leading Hindus and Muslims into confidence, matters are satisfactorily arranged.... In Aligarh, we left the whole matter to leading Hindus and Muhammadans and everything went off without hitch.[102]

Such was the pattern everywhere, reinforcing the view that, by the end of the nineteenth century, there was no sign of Hindus and Muslims going their separate ways. If anything, the lines of cleavages in north India were more sharply drawn between the Sunnis and the Shias rather than Hindus and Muslims.[103] Though expressed in exaggerated terms, there is merit in the observations of W.S. Blunt and Henry Cotton that Hindu-Muslim animus was accentuated only after the government decided to pursue the principle of divide and rule with vigour.[104]

---

cordial Hindu-Muslim relations in most parts of the country. This was, in part, attributed to the combination of the two communities against plague measures. 'Let the people', stated the *Jami al-ulum* (Moradabad) of 21 March 1897, 'welcome the return of the plague to India a thousand times, were it for the purpose of effecting a union among them. The government was alarmed by the combination. Elgin's private secretary apprehended that 'if Hindus and Muslims were forced into active opposition (against the plague measures), the combination between them might be perpetuated and might assume a dangerous form'. Quoted in Ray, op. cit., p. 118.

[101] For example, *Riaz al-Akhbaar* (Gorakhpur), 8 January 1894; *Nagari Nirad* (Hindi weekly: Mirzapur), 8 February 1894; *Mehr-i Nimroz* (Urdu weekly: Bijnor), 7 February 1894, and *Hindustani* (Lucknow), 19 December 1894. For references to local reconciliation committees and to public meetings on Hindu-Muslim amity in UP and Punjab, see *Hindustani*, 8 June 1898, *Oudh Punch*, 9 June 1898; *Akhbaar-i Alam* (Meerut), 13 June 1898, *Riaz al-Akhbaar*, 1 November 1898, *Anis-i Hind* (Meerut), 2 November 1898, SNNR, UP.

[102] *PSC*, NWP & O, Evidence, p. 158.

[103] See Mushirul Hasan, 'Sectarianism in Indian Islam: The Shia-Sunni Divide in the United Provinces', op. cit; Cole, op. cit.

[104] Henry Cotton, *India and Home Memoirs* (London, 1911), p. 317; Blunt, *India Under Ripon*, p. 94.

Chapter Three

In Search of an Alternative

Nineteenth century orientalists sensitized western opinion to the idea of political religion, to a structure in which religion and politics combine to make Islam an aggressive, hostile and explosive force. Official opinion in India was no different. Moulded by the experience of the Faraizi movement, the 'Wahabi conspiracy' and the large Muslim presence among the 1857 'mutineers', the government began to see Muslims as a potential threat, a subversive element and a conservative force. The familiar clamour in the aftermath of the 1857 revolt was to humble them, to reduce them to nothingness and to destroy their religious and cultural symbols.

The spectre of a 'Muslim uprising' continued to haunt a section in officialdom, though less so in the 1870s when distrust of and hostility towards the Muslims was much less pronounced. Mayo's note of 26 June 1871 would have been inconceivable a generation earlier. Then, W.W. Hunter's celebrated book helped to dispel many of the impressions which had dominated official thinking. 'I cannot see any sign of disaffection (unusual) or of any belief in a struggle at hand', he wrote to contradict fears of a Muslim conspiracy. He sought sympathy and understanding for the rising generation of Muslims which would be tempered with the 'sober and genial knowledge of the West'.[1] W.S. Blunt, who toured India in the winter of 1883–84, pleaded vigorously for the advancement of Muslim education, their encouragement in commercial and industrial pursuits and protection of their religious interests outside India. 'The neglect of these things', warned Blunt, 'will secure beyond redemption their disloyalty'.[2] John Strachey played the same tune. He believed that

[1] Hunter, *Indian Mussalmans,* p. 123.

[2] Blunt, *India Under Ripon,* p. 296.

the fears that are sometimes expressed that we may see in India a general outburst of Mohammedan fanaticism, and a simultaneous rising of millions of Mohammedans against our power, seem to me....not only groundless but absurd.... The better classes of Mohammadans are already a source to us of strength and not of weakness, and a continuously wise policy might, I believe, make them strong and important supporters of our power.[3]

Mayo, Dufferin and Ripon recognized the importance of winning the confidence of the Muslims, arguing that unless conciliated they would remain the most dangerous class in the raj.

One man who chose to ignore such warnings was Anthony MacDonnell, who assumed charge as UP's lieutenant-governor in 1894. He, more than any other civil servant in UP, was uneasy with the Muslims, their interest in pan-Islamism, their position in government service and the professions,[4] and their inclination to take positions against the government. He was indifferent to the cause of Urdu, hostile to the Nadwat al-ulama which he regarded as 'an association of narrow-minded bigoted and conservative Mussalmans' and unsympathetic to the Muslim point of view over the cow-protection movement in north India. 'Taking his administration in general', wrote the ***Al-Bashir,*** an otherwise pro-government newspaper from Etawah, 'Sir Anthony MacDonnell has sowed the seeds of discord between the Hindus and Muslims...and caused general unrest and distrust in the province'.[5]

MacDonnell assumed that all Muslims were getting organized to overthrow British rule, and proceeded to clip their wings through a series of administrative and bureaucratic measures. He first fixed a communal quota for Muslims in public service: in other words, there were to be three Muslims to every five Hindus. He then placed the Devanagri script on an equal footing with Urdu, provided for its optional use in court documents and made the knowledge of both forms of writing necessary for

[3] John Strachey, *India* (London, 1888), p. 225.

[4] An instance of his hostility was when the list of candidates for tahsildarship and deputy-collectorship was rejected on the ground that the number of Muslims was too large. *Al-Bashir*, 25 December 1901, SNNR, UP.

[5] Ibid., 28 November 1901

ministerial appointments. These decisions engendered widespread disaffection amongst Muslims, undermined the basis of the Anglo-Muslim alliance, and stimulated, much to everybody's surprise, political radicalism. There were strong objections to the course adopted by MacDonnell—to the 'undoing of all that the late Syed Ahmad did...in the way of removing doubts from the minds of the authorities regarding the loyalty of Mussalmans'.[6] Altaf Husain Hali, Syed Ahmad's close friend and associate, bemoaned:

> *Woh din gaye ke nazaan thi qaum saltanat par*
> *Ab qaum ko khuda ka ya apna aasraa hai*
>
> Gone are the days when Muslims were proud of the Empire
> Now, they rely on themselves and their hopes rest with God.

Resentment centred around the April 1900 Resolution, which threatened Muslims, because unlike Hindus, they did not learn the Devanagri script in their normal course of education. Consequently, they saw the grim prospect of losing their privileged position in public service and in the liberal professions.[7] They argued in vain that material interests alone did not concern them, but that they were concerned for the effect it would have on the composite cultural ethos of the Indo-Gangetic plain. Urdu was not spoken only by Muslims; the Kayasths and the Kashmir Pandits were equally fluent in the language. It was the language of the *qasbati* elites, the language of refinement and culture, a symbol of Hindu-Muslim integration which MacDonnell was striving to destroy. Even in cases where the language of both Hindus and Muslims was entered as Urdu in the census schedule, as in Marehra in Etah district, the entries were altered at the instance of the district magistrate.[8] The language of all Hindus was shown to be Hindi and that of Muslims to be Urdu. The *Al-Bashir* regretted that this was so, for there was no real distinction between Urdu and Hindi: they were names of

[6] Maulvi Mushtaq Husain and Mohsinul Mulk in *Aligarh Institute Gazette*, 22 August and 17 October 1901.

[7] *Liberal* (Azamgarh), 10 April 1900; *Naiyar-i Azam*, 19 January 1901, SNNR, UP.

[8] *Al-Bashir*, 11 March 1901; *Shararah* (Moradabad), 21 January 1901, ibid.

one and the same language, there being slight dialectic differences between the language spoken in villages and that spoken in towns.[9] In the *mushairas* that were held in Lahore until the early decades of the twentieth century, Hindus and Muslims participated and there was no trace of the Hindi-Urdu controversy that developed in Punjab soon thereafter.[10]

The agitation against the Nagri resolution started with public meetings all over UP and the setting up of Urdu Defence Associations in Aligarh, Gorakhpur, Lucknow and Allahabad. Support from the associations came from all quarters—from Mohsinul Mulk who reorganized the Urdu Defence Association at Aligarh; from Syed Raza Ali who was present at the mammoth public gathering at Lucknow in August 1900; from Hamid Ali Khan, a Congress supporter and the moving spirit behind the Lucknow meeting; and from lawyers, pleaders and barristers in Allahabad, Moradabad, Aligarh and Gorakhpur.[11]

The protest movement, masterminded by Mohsinul Mulk, started off with great vigour but petered out within no time as MacDonnell acted tough and threatened to withdraw government support from the Aligarh college. Mohsinul Mulk was tamed. Lutf Ali Khan, president of the Urdu Defence Association, could not withstand the official wrath.[12] He, along with seven other rais of Aligarh district, ensured the decline of the Urdu movement in their area. By 1901, the lieutenant-governor had isolated the tall poppies from the Urdu agitation only to leave them discredited in the eyes of their followers. The *Azad* commented:

[9] *Al-Bashir,* 21 January 1901, SNNR, UP.

[10] Mohammad Abdullah Qureshi, 'Lahore ke mushaire aur Iqbal', *Iqbal,* October 1955, vol. 4, 2, pp. 72–77.

[11] *Rohilkhand Gazette* (Bareilly), 1 May 1900; *Azad,* 8 May 1900; *Mufid-i Aam* (Agra), 20 May 1900; *Riazul Akhbaar,* 20 May 1900; *Oudh Akhbaar,* 23 May 1900; *Jaam-i Jamshed* (Moradabad), 27 May 1900. Report of a meeting of barristers and *ulama* at Gorakhpur to found an Urdu Defence Association is mentioned in *Riazul Akhbaar,* 16 August 1900, SNNR, UP. An account of the agitation is in Syed Raza Ali, *Aamal Naama* (Delhi, 1943), pp. 88–89.

[12] *Oudh Akhbaar,* 17 September and *Riazul Akhbaar,* 24 September 1901, SNNR, UP; Rais Ahmad Jafri, *Kaarawaan-i Gumgushta* (Karachi, 1971).

By his abrupt secession from the Urdu Defence Association [Mohsinul Mulk] has shown himself to be a great coward and utterly unfit to be a leader. It was sheer cunningness, hypocrisy and deceitfulness on his part to decoy a people into a trap, and then quickly withdraw from it.[13]

The Aligarh leaders, brought up in an atmosphere of official 'billying and cooing' were at a loss as soon as they found themselves deprived of official support. 'They flinched, they faltered, and they fell, and great indeed has been their fall'.[14]

MacDonnell used the big stick to quieten senior Aligarh leaders and the first game of the match was easily won. But the next round with a group of radical Muslims turned out to be tough. Vociferous in their criticizm of government, they exposed the inadequacy of mendicant tactics[15] and expressed preference for a political forum that would be representative in its composition and democratic in its functioning.[16] The editor of *Al-Bashir* observed that the policies of the lieutenant-governor, more than anything else, led to persistent demands for an organized political association.[17] Its absence, commented the *Asr-i Jadeed,* edited by a former Aligarh graduate, was why Muslim interests were being trampled underfoot.[18]

These were muted expressions of an aggrieved group. A more strident demand—one that was destined to alter the tenor and

[13] *Azad,* 22 October 1901, SNNR, UP.

[14] By a Hindu Nationalist, 'Sir Syed as a Factor in Indian Progress', *Kayastha Samachar,* December 1902, vol. 6, 6, p. 516.

[15] *Riazul Akhbaar,* 24 September and *Oudh Akhbaar,* 17 September 1900, SNNR, UP.

[16] In October 1901, a meeting held at the home of Hamid Ali Khan resolved to launch a political organization. Lucknow and not Aligarh was chosen as the headquarter so that the college officials were not suspected of encouraging and spreading political agitation. *Hindustan,* 30 October, *Al-Bashir,* 29 October, and *Advocate,* 31 October 1901, ibid.

[17] *Al-Bashir,* 12 August 1903, ibid., Jafri, *Kaarawaan-i Gumgushta,* p. 155.

[18] *Asr-i Jadeed,* May 1903. In its issue of February 1903, the paper welcomed the initiative taken by the Lucknow meeting and reiterated its plea for an organization that would defend the political interests of Muslims. It wanted the rais and zamindars to be kept at a distance; otherwise, the new body would meet 'the same fate as the Urdu Defence Association and its President No. 1'.

content of 'Muslim politics' over the next two decades—was to make common cause with the Congress.[19] What was, after all, the difference between the 'interests' of the Muslims and the demands of the Congress? None, stated a 'Muslim Political Observer', in his contribution to the *Kayastha Samachar*. He went on to add:

> Ahmad and Abdullah have received the same education and their minds have been fed on the same strong pabulum of English literature and English History and Political Philosophy as those of Banerjea's and Bose's. Both are governed by the same laws and are suffering from the same legal and political disabilities.[20]

Quite true. The *Asr-i Jadeed* believed that it was desirable for Muslims to co-operate with the Congress on issues of common concern—the reduction of salt duty, the raising of the minimum limit of taxable income and greater employment of educated Indians in the commissioned ranks of the army.[21] Shaikh Abdullah, a vakil at Aligarh, argued that it was time for Muslims to strike out the word silence [*sukuut*] in their dictionary. He maintained that 'to refrain from public agitation simply because the Congress has adopted it, is as absurd as not to use boots for no better reason than that they are used by Christians'.[22] After all, the reasons which had led Syed Ahmad to keep his co-religionists away from the Congress did not hold good anymore.[23] In fact, his own son, the mercurial Syed Mahmood, considered presiding over the Congress session and expressed

[19] Prominent amongst those who advocated this position were: Ghulam-us-Saqlain, Hasrat and Ahmad Hasan Shaukat, editors of *Asr-i Jadeed, Urdu-i Moalla* and *Shahna-i Hind,* published from Meerut. Jamal Ahmad, 'Mussalman aur Politics', *Asr-i Jadeed,* May 1903; *Shahna-i Hind,* 24 June, 1 July 1899 and 1 November 1901; Haider Ali Qureshi, 'Muhammadans and Politics', *Hindustan Review* and *Kayastha Samachar,* October 1904, vol. 10, 4, p. 398.

[20] By a Muslim: A Political Observer, 'The Indian Muhammadans and the National Congress', *Kayastha Samachar,* November 1902, vol. 6, 5, p. 398. Similar views were expressed in *Tufrih* (Lucknow), 14 January, and *Israar-ul Alam* (Allahabad), 21 February 1907, SNNR, UP

[21] *Asr-i Jadeed,* March 1903.

[22] *Al-Bashir,* 27 June 1903, SNNR, UP.

[23] *Kayastha Samachar,* op. cit., p. 397.

sympathy for the organization.[24] In 1903, Badruddin Tyabji chaired the Muslim Educational Conference with Nawab Syed Mohamed as chairman of the reception committee. This would have been unthinkable a few years ago, for the conference had served as a platform for giving vent to anti-Congress sentiments. Tyabji was present on the occasion, because the Conference was no longer hostile to the Congress; otherwise, he would have stayed away from any forum which 'had the slightest trace of being hostile or antagonistic to the Congress'.

These were ominous pro-Congress tendencies. Senior Aligarh leaders moved quickly to counter them. Haji Musa Khan, a rais of Datauli in Aligarh district, floated the idea of a UP-based organization which would preserve Syed Ahmad's political legacy.[25] Mohsinul Mulk mooted the revival of the MAO College Defence Association,[26] but he had lost face after the collapse of the Urdu Defence Association.[27] He approached Archbold, Principal of the Aligarh college, with the idea of presenting a memorial to the viceroy.[28] The idea found favour and, on 1 October 1906, thirty-five Muslims, mainly from UP, submitted their first major political statement to the viceroy. Minto's response, its tone, as well as the promises it carried, was clearly partial to the aspirations of the memorialists.

Although Mohsinul Mulk and his club wrested the initiative from the 'young gentlemen' in organizing the Simla deputation and in founding the Muslim League at Dacca in December 1906, their glory was short-lived. They were under attack in Aligarh college, where the radical mood of some students led to a strike in February 1907.[29] A year later, news from the campus attracted

[24] S.C. Banerji, 'Syed Mahmood: Recollections and Reflections', ibid., May 1903, vol. 7, 5, p. 442.

[25] *Jami-ul-ulum,* 14 August 1900, SNNR, UP.

[26] *Aligarh Institute Gazette,* 17 October 1903.

[27] *Uruuj* (Bijnor) 14 July and *Oudh Akhbaar,* 10 December 1903; *Riazul Akhbaar,* 1 February 1905, SNNR, UP.

[28] Mohsinul Mulk to Archbold, 4 August 1906, quoted in Raza Wasti, *Lord Minto and the Indian Nationalist Movement 1905–1910* (Oxford, 1964), p. 63; Robinson, *Separatism,* pp. 143–46.

[29] Trouble was sparked off by an incident at the exhibition ground which led to the rustication of Raja Ghulam Husain. Students at the Aligarh

public notice once again. An article on 'The Educational Policy of the English in Egypt', published in Hasrat Mohani's *Urdu-i Moalla,* caused a furore. The government sentenced the editor to two years' of imprisonment while the college authorities expelled the author, a graduate student. In the ensuing controversy, which was symptomatic of the divide between the Indian and the European staff, Viqarul Mulk defended the right of the student to express his views. How could he not 'when the very atmosphere of the country seems to be surcharged with politics'. Under the circumstances, he added, it would be futile to try to keep students beyond the pale of contagion'.[30] Around the same time, a district official had prophesied that

> Aligarh is destined to be the focus of all Muhammadan intelligence and activity in India. Begun as a defensive move, it is already acquiring an offensive character.... It has already lost its reliance on Englishmen and its trust in English methods and ideals. The danger I foresee is that if it is indulged and uncontrolled it will develop rapidly on undecidedly anti-English lines.[31]

---

college were angered by the decision of the authorities. They chose to go on strike, the first in the history of the college. Contemporaries commented that their action was in reaction to their long-standing grouse on several issues: the predominance of the European staff on the Board of Trustees and the insensitive attitude of Archbold, the Principal, towards their problems. Some were of the opinion that Gokhale's visit to Aligarh in February 1907 stimulated political action on the campus. Newspaper articles demanded that the rustication orders be rescinded and the demands of the students considered sympathetically, 'for the nation has no love for the college building, the secretary or the Principal, but it has certainly love for students who are the ornaments not only of the college but of the nation as well'. *Israar-i Alam* (Moradabad), 7 March 1907. For reactions to and analysis of the causes of Ghulam Husain's expulsion see *Naiyar-i Azam,* 26 February 1907, *Nizam-ul-Mulk,* 28 February 1907, *Indian People,* (Allahabad), 7 March, *Shahna-i Hind,* 8 March 1907, SNNR, UP. Choudhry Khaliquzzaman, *Pathway to Pakistan* (Lahore, 1961 edn.), p. 17.

[30] *Aligarh Institute Gazette*, 29 July 1908. Viqarul Mulk's article was welcomed by, among others, the *Riazul Akhbaar*, 4 August 1908, SNNR, UP.

[31] Quoted in Irene A. Gilbert, 'Autonomy and Consensus under the Raj: Presidency (Calcutta); Muir (Allahabad); M.A.O. (Aligarh)', S.H.

The prophecy of William Marris came true a few years later when an extraordinary convergence of forces generated strong anti-government feelings and heightened nationalist consciousness.[32] There was, for example, the annulment of Bengal's partition, a decision that hurt Muslims of East Bengal most. 'Agitate and you will get what you want; remain calm and you will have your heads chopped. This is the moral we are given', observed a correspondent in the *Mussalman,* a Calcutta paper with nationalist commitments.[33] Then, the Turko-Italian War caused deep anguish, because the view gained credence that Britain acquiesced in the Italian attack on Tripoli and concluded treaties with Russia and France to partition the Ottoman Empire. 'There is a great agitation in Muslim circles', reported the viceroy, 'over the war in the Balkans, and a general feeling that the Christians are combining to thrust the Muslims out of Europe'.[34] In December 1912, Mukhtar Ahmad Ansari, an Edinburgh-trained surgeon, headed a medical mission to Constantinople.[35] In May 1913, the Anjuman-i Khuddam-i Kaaba came into being in Lucknow. Its main architect was Maulvi Abdul Bari, a renowned *alim* of Firangi Mahal. His main associates in this enterprise were Shaukat Ali, an Aligarh graduate who had quit his government post in the opium department to lend a helping hand to his younger brother, Mohamed Ali; and Mushir Husain Kidwai, a taluqdar from Gadia in Barabanki district and author of *Islam and Socialism,* a book which sought to prove that Islam was the first religion to establish a state on the principles of socialism and communism.

Both the medical mission and the Anjuman-i Khuddam-i Kaaba symbolized the growing Muslim anxiety over the future of

---

Rudolph & L.I. Rudolph (eds.), *Education and Politics in India* (Delhi, 1972), pp. 198–99.

[32] See, for example, the impressions of E.M. Forster, quoted in Mushirul Hasan, *A Nationalist Conscience: M.A. Ansari, the Congress and the Raj* (Delhi, 1987), p. 36.

[33] *Mussalman,* 12 January 1912.

[34] Hardinge to Chirol, 22 October 1912. For Bengal and Punjab, see Carmichael to Hardinge, 6 September 1914, and O'Dwyer to Hardinge 11 August 1913, Hardinge Papers (84/88), IOLR.

[35] Hasan, *A Nationalist Conscience,* pp. 42–45.

Turkey and the sanctity of the Holy Places. Nobody expressed the anguish more vividly than Shibli Nomani, a distinguished scholar of Islamic history and literature and founder of the prestigious Nadwat al-ulama. In a poem that was widely read and recited at poetry sessions [*mushairas*], Shibli, probably inspired by Hali's *Mussaddas,* lamented:

When decline has set in over political power, the
name and banner will stand—how long?
The smoke from the burnt candle of a vanished
assembly will rise—how long?
Gone is Morocco, gone is Persia. We have now to see
this helpless 'sick man of Turkey' will live—how long?
This tide of woe which is advancing from the Balkans,
the sighs of the oppressed will stem—how long?
Shibli: should you long to migrate, where can you go now?
Syria or Najd or Cyrene are sanctuaries—how long?

Likewise, the poems of Iqbal did the rounds. According to Mohamed Ali, who wrote his incomplete autobiographical account in mid-summer 1923, 'the modest, shy and retiring barrister of the Punjab' was the poet of Islam's reawakening in India and was a household word throughout the Urdu-speaking world. 'We loved Iqbal the Revolutionary', recorded Khaliquzzaman, 'calling upon his people to rise to action, the Iqbal who introduced Muslim heroes in their true glory, the Iqbal who by his own new interpretation of Quranic injunctions put life into what had been stale by philosophical ponderings'.[36] And Salim Ali, the celebrated ornithologist, recalled how Shuaib Qureshi entertained him with the 'moving, patriotic and pro Islamic verses' of Iqbal. 'One of his recitations, the beauty and sonorousness of which still rings in my ears, is the touching *shikwa* of the vicissitudes of the island of Sicily, once an important Muslim stronghold in Europe'.[37]

The belligerence of the European powers, combined with the

[36] Khaliquzzaman *Pathway to Pakistan,* p. 38; Mohamed Ali, *My Life A Fragment: An Autobiographical Sketch,* ed. Afzal Iqbal (Lahore, 1944). Also, see Abu Salman Shahjahanpuri, *Allama Iqbal aur Maulana Mohamed Ali* (Karachi, 1984).

[37] Salim Ali, *The Fall of a Sparrow* (Delhi, 1985), p. 50.

rejection of the Aligarh university scheme and the inept handling of the Kanpur mosque affair, caused uneasiness and hostility towards the government. In the words of Mohamed Ali, the key figure in organizing the protest movement on these issues, 'the Mussalmans felt themselves to be betrayed both in India and abroad'.[38] However, they were unable to give organizational expression to their resentment. The Muslim League, dominated by men who were wary of agitational methods, was a tame affair. So, when a group of lawyers, journalists and *ulama* stepped into the political space created by reckless government policies and the moderate stance of the Muslim League, there was much relief at the prospect of getting heard. Hopes were aroused to a feverish pitch as energetic and enthusiastic young leaders, mostly educated at Aligarh, went around the country imbued with a sense of mission and commitment.

People turned to the Oxford-educated Mohamed Ali, 'the centre and inspiration of the pan-Islamic movement'.[39] What he wrote was avidly read; what he spoke was listened to with rapt attention. 'Meeting the Ali Brothers was like drinking wine; it made us fresh and lively'.[40] In Punjab, Zafar Ali Khan created quite a stir. As soon as copies of *Zamindar* were brought into the bazaar, large crowds of people surrounded the news-shops and bought copies: its circulation rose from 5,000 to over 25,000 copies in less than a month.[41] Like some of his contemporaries at

[38] Mohamed Ali, *My life,* p. 35. Some years later, he wrote to the viceroy, Chelmsford:

> Muslim loyalty and support has so often been assured to government in our generation, and even Muslim contentment was so often unduly taken for granted, that other communities had with some justice made our attitude towards government almost a matter of reproach. It was strange for all this loyalty and support that, without any effective protest...blow after blow was aimed at the temporal power of Islam.

To Chelmsford, 24 April 1919, Mushirul Hasan (ed.), *Mohamed Ali in Indian Politics: Select Writings* (Delhi, 1983), vol. 2, p. 226.

[39] Mushirul Hasan, *Mohamed Ali: Ideology and Politics* (Delhi, 1981), and *A Nationalist Conscience*, pp. 37-40, for the role of Mohamed Ali in the early phase of the pan-Islamic agitation.

[40] Khaliquzzaman, *Pathway to Pakistan,* p. 33.

[41] FR (Punjab), 28 January 1915, Home Poll. A. F.No. 173, May 1916,

Aligarh, Zafar Ali Khan was moved by Shibli's poems on the evils inflicted upon Islam and inspired by his articles published in the *Muslim Gazette* in support of the Congress.[42] He was also influenced by the editor of *Al-Hilal*, Abul Kalam Azad, who denounced British imperialism in no uncertain terms and advocated communal unity and co-operation. It is no exaggeration to assert that never before did such talented men agree on so many issues of common concern. And never before did so few exercise so great an influence on so many in their community.

The second rank leadership was no less impressive. There was, for example, the fiery journalist-poet Hasrat Mohani, editor of *Urdu-i Moalla,* who was imprisoned as early as 1908 for an article on British education policy in Egypt.[43] No less important was a group of lawyers—Khaliquzzaman, Shuaib

---

NAI. Harcourt Butler, *India Insistent* (London, 1931), p. 27. Zafar Ali Khan studied at Aligarh before joining the Hyderabad Civil Service. In 1912, he visited Constantinople to present to the Grand Vizièr a part of the money raised from the sale of Turkish bond. He was in Turkey again the next year where he furthered a proposal to provide a colony in Anatolia for Muslim refugees. In January, the Punjab government forfeited the security of his paper for publishing an article entitled 'Come Over Macedonia and Help Us'. For biographical information, see Shorish Kashmiri, 'Zafar Ali Khan', *Nuqqush* [*Shakhsiaat* Number], January 1955, p. 597. In English, the only perceptive account of Zafar Ali's role is in Ravinder Kumar, *Essays in the Social History of Modern India* (Delhi, 1983), pp. 182–85. The chapter is a reprint of his contribution in *Essays on Gandhian Politics: The Rowlatt Satyagraha of 1919* (Oxford, 1971).

[42] Shibli's articles were first published in *Muslim Gazette* before being printed in volume eight of *Maqalaat-i Shibli* (Azamgarh, 1938). The editor of this Lucknow paper was Wahiduddin Salim. He had worked as Syed Ahmad's literary assistant before founding the *Maarif.* He edited the *Aligarh Institute Gazette* from April 1907 to June 1909 and the *Muslim Gazette* until August 1913. He resigned from the *Muslim Gazette* because of his criticizm of government policies and its clumsy handling of the Kanpur mosque affair. Manzar Abbas Naqvi, *Wahiduddin Salim: Hayaat aur Adabi Khidmaat* (Aligarh, 1969).

[43] Known as the *Rais al-Ahrar,* Hasrat Mohani obtained his B.A. degree from the Aligarh college in 1903. His family was attached to Shaikh Abdur Razzak of Firangi Mahal. He was himself a *murid* of Abdul Wahhab and received *Khilafat* from Maulana Abdul Bari. He was a man with varied interests and concerns. He edited the *Urdu-i Moalla* from July 1903 to

Qureshi and Syed Mahmud—all graduates of Aligarh and devoted to Mohamed Ali and Ansari. Their followers included Raja Ghulam Husain, editor of the *New Era* from Lucknow; Sajjad Husain, editor of *Oudh Punch;* writers like Sajjad Haider Yaldaram, Abdur Rahman Bijnori and Abdul Majid Daryabadi. And, of course, there was Wilayat Ali, born in 1887 in Masauli in Barabanki district. He belonged to a movement with serious intents, but while his friends and contemporaries held forth from agitational platforms or indulged in denunciatory political writings in the press, Wilayat Ali laughed at British rule and made fun of it. Writing humorous and satirical sketches under his pen name—Bambooque—this young Aligarh graduate became the centre of a lively group of wits, wags and radical intellectuals.[44]

The Bambooque house lived from one political excitement to the other. He was so thrilled by the Young Turk Revolution that he gave his young sons and nephews the names of Turkish

---

June 1913 [except from May 1908 to September 1909 when he was interned by the government], plunged into the swadeshi movement with a high sense of duty and identified himself with Tilak and the 'extremist' wing of the Congress. He also had considerable poetic talent and is ranked among the front rank Urdu poets. He possessed boundless energy which he used to promote the cause of swaraj; in fact, he was the first to demand complete independence in 1921 and parted with Motilal Nehru over the issue of Dominion Status.

In 1917, he gave poetic expression to his passions in a verse:

How can I instil in others a passion like my own?
I've grown weary of my fellow-travellers' lack of spirit

After 1924, however, the flames of Hasrat's poetry began to dim, though his attachment to various causes was not affected. The only biographical study of Hasrat in English is by K.H. Qadiri, *Hasrat Mohani* (Delhi, 1985). The translation of the above verse is from Saleem Ahmad, 'The Ghazal: A Muffler, and India', *Annual of Urdu Studies,* vol. 2, 1982.

[44] In the gallery of carricatures is the England-returned barrister desperately aping the Sahibs manners and speech and pretending to have forgotten his native tongue during his brief stay in England. There are, then, the specimens of the Babu culture in India from the patwari to the deputy-collector; comic both in their servility to their white superiors and their arrogance towards the common people.

generals. During the Balkan War he would recite Iqbal's *Shikwah* and *Jawaab-i Shikwah*, with tears dripping from his face. During World War I, the Bambooque circle watched the ebb and flow of German fortunes with intense anxiety, elated by German victories and depressed by German setbacks. The circle was small and consisted of young men who combined feudal graces with modern education.[45] They would meet in Masauli, eighteen kilometres from Lucknow, indulge in endless political arguments, draw up resolutions or memoranda for forthcoming Congress and Muslim League meetings, plot their future political course, and then relax in easy chairs, pulling leisurely at long hubble bubbles, filling the air with the smoke of scented tobacco, bandying Urdu or Persian verses and reciting or reading the compositions in verse or prose. Behind them hovered a short, plump, shy boy, doing the chores of the host, or running errands between the *zenana* and the men's part of the *haveli*. Little did the company suspect that he was to be their fellow traveller on the road to India's freedom and plod on to the journey's end even when some of them were to fall by the wayside or stray from the path. He was Rafi Ahmad Kidwai.

The young men of Bambooque's generation had many heroes. Their political guru was Mohamed Ali, though Azad did much to stimulate their radical consciousness. They also derived inspiration from Akbar Allahabadi, Hali and Iqbal. They admired Akbar's outspokenness in condemning western imperialism, his criticizm of government machinations in keeping Hindus and Muslims apart and his indignation at the exploitation of India's material resources.[46] They also turned to the writings of Hali, the poet-writer from Panipat, who had the distinction of being close to two outstanding intellectuals in the second-half of the nineteenth century—Syed Ahmad and Asadullah Khan Ghalib. One of Hali's earliest poems was on nationalism and pat-

[45] It included Khaliquzzaman, Shuaib Qureshi, Raja Ghulam Husain, Sajjad Husain and M.A. Ansari who was drawn to the circle through his cousin Aziz Ansari, a member of the medical mission to Turkey.

[46] See Muhammad Sadiq, 'Understanding Akbar Allahabadi', *Iqbal*, January 1968, vol. 16, 3, p. 42; Ralph Russell and Khurshidul Islam, 'The Satirical Verses of Akbar Illahabadi'.

riotism—themes that were echoed at the fourth session of the Muslim Educational Conference held at Aligarh in 1899. Such was his commitment to these causes that he told Abdul Halim Sharar in 1904 that the spread of education would make people recognize the value of national unity and 'national integration'.[47]

Nobody expressed such ideas with greater passion, eloquence and coherence than Iqbal. He was therefore the favourite poet in his days. His poems *Tarana-i Hindi* (India's Anthem), *Naya Shiwala* (The New Temple), and *Tasvir-i Dar* (Picture of Grief) swayed the imagination of young Indian Muslims. His message was simple. He stood for the repudiation of differences based on religion. He saw God 'in each speck of my country's poor dust' and wanted to build a new altar where the votaries of motherland would gather together and sing songs of love. His mission was summed up in the verse:

> Let us remove once again the curtain of otherness;
> bring together those divided (by religion) and wipe out
> the stamp of estrangement.

Such ideas, backed by leading intellectuals and publicists, altered the course of political currents among Muslims. As the premier Muslim organization, the Muslim League was the first to feel the pinch. The influx of radical ideas overwhelmed the conservative diehards, who were lampooned in the *Oudh Punch, New Era, Comrade* and *Maloomaat.* Their world turned topsy-turvy as they helplessly witnessed the passing of an era and the decline of their prestige and authority. Everywhere, complained Haji Ishaq Khan, the 'moderate men' had lost ground with the public and were afraid of being ridiculed.[48] The Nawab of Rampur, finding the political climate in Aligarh too oppressive, resigned from the visitorship.[49] Aligarh was an inhospitable place for the protagonists of Syed Ahmad's political message of subservience to the raj. The Aga Khan, whose support for the reunification of Bengal made him a target of bitter attack,

[47] Shaikh Mohammad Ismail (ed.), *Makatib-i Hali* (Karachi, 1950), p. 54.

[48] To Meston, 21 August and 20 November 1913, Meston Papers, F.No. 136 (6), IOLR.

[49] To Ishaq Khan, 15 November 1913, ibid. (4).

suddenly bolted and relinquished the Muslim League presidential chair which he had occupied since its inception.[50] 'The time has come', wrote the Khoja leader, 'when the community must wake up and reorganize the League on a popular basis....'[51]

Change in leadership led to changes in policies. The League, having lived up to the traditions of Syed Ahmad and Nawab Salimullah, underwent a gradual transformation so as to reflect the new mood of the bulk of its supporters. The headquarter was moved from Aligarh, a decision of considerable symbolic significance. The constitution was amended at the instance of, among others, Mohammad Ali Jinnah. The League began to meet in the same city as the Congress and affirmed its goal of self-government year after year. The Congress was being increasingly seen as a national body, which was motivated to advance the interest of the country and was willing, as was evident during the debate over the Punjab Alienation Act, to accommodate sectional claims. The success in organizing the Swadeshi movement lent Congress the legitimacy it had lacked for so many years and brought home its potential as an instrument for introducing vital changes in Indian polity. Hali shared this thought.[52] So did Iqbal, already famous for his patriotic poems. In May 1906, he observed:

> If this movement [swadeshi] helps to foster unity of purpose among Muslims and Hindus and strengthens this feeling [of unity] gradually, then nothing else is needed. The fate of India will definitely change for the better and the name of my country would be written in gold letters among the countries of the world.[53]

Some years later, the Bihar lawyer, Mazharul Haq declared:

[50] The Governor of Bombay observed: 'I imagine that the Aga Khan is dead as a leader, and from what he told me I think he realizes that his power is gone. Anyhow he suddenly bolted, some weeks before he originally intended'. Sydenham to Hardinge, 18 March 1913, Hardinge Papers (85).

[51] To Wazir Hasan, 3 November 1913, Crewe Papers, I/14 (2), Cambridge University Library; To Harcourt Butler, 3 March 1913, Butler Papers, F. No. 116 (71), IOLR.

[52] *Maqalaat-i Hali* (Delhi, 1934), vol. 1, p. 308.

[53] *Zamaanah* (Kanpur), May 1906.

...there were no political questions in which the interests of both communities were not equally involved, or with regard to which they differed. As far as he himself was concerned, he would much rather be represented on the council by his friend Gokhale than by anyone else. Our interests are practically identical.[54]

Mazharul Haq was not speaking out of turn. He was stating what had become an article of faith with so many educated Muslims of his generation.[55] This was testified to by an official who was horrified to learn that most western-educated Muslims he had met in north India were in favour of combining with the 'Hindu Congress party'. The viceroy, too, grudgingly conceded that he could, alas, not count on the loyalty of Muslims, because they were inclined to make common cause with any other faction in order to express their antipathy to the government.[56] 'In mutual help and co-operation', observed Khuda Bukhsh, the well-known writer and philanthropist, 'lies our hope, in division and dissension our feebleness and death'.

II

The men who plotted this course for their community were drawn from a mixed background. They included the *ulama*, especially those based at Deoband: prominent amongst them were the Shaikh al-Hind Maulana Mahmud Hasan and his disciple, Ubaid-Allah Sindhi, two of the principal figures involved in the 'Silk Letter Conspiracy'. They played a singularly important role in heightening anti-colonial consciousness among their followers and travelled to distant lands to stir up an agitation against British rule.[57] Under their influence, institutions like the Dar

[54] *Bombay Chronicle,* 20 June 1914. His views were also quoted in *Tribune,* 21 January 1911 and *Bengalee,* 27 December 1912.

[55] WRDCI, 4 July 1912, Home Poll. B, August 1912, NAI. To Crewe, 14 August 1913, Hardinge Papers (86).

[56] *Essays on Indian and Islamic* (London, 1911), p. 267.

[57] For official versions, see P.C. Bamford, *Histories of the Non-Co-operation and Khilafat Movements* (Delhi, 1975: reprint), and the report by B. Lindsay and A. Rauf, 11 December 1918, in Hasan (ed.), *Mohamed Ali in Indian Politics,* vol. 2. Accounts sympathetic to the *mujahidin* are by: H.A. Madani, *Naqsh-i Hayaat: Khudnawisht Sawaanih* (Karachi, 1979),

al-ulum, Firangi Mahal and the Nadwat al-ulama were also politicized. Abdul Bari, once engaged only in scholarly pursuits, became the rallying point of the pan-Islamic upsurge. The Anjuman-i Khuddam-i Kaaba was his brainchild and Ansari's medical mission had his backing. In fact, many of those involved in these enterprises—the Ali Brothers, Ansari and Hasrat Mohani—were his *murids*. The influence of these men also spread to Nadwat al-ulama in Lucknow, where students went on strike in March 1914 to protest against government policies which culminated in the tragedy at Macchli Bazaar in Kanpur,[58] and later to the Dar al-Mussannifin, an institution founded in 1914 by Shibli. The Commissioner of the Gorakhpur division reported 'that the Shibli Academy is no longer what its founder intended it to be, but has become 'an extremist political institution' under the leadership of Syed Sulaiman Nadwi, Shibli's disciple and biographer.[59]

The western-educated Muslims were much more strident in criticizing government policies and much more vocal in espousing the Congress cause. They were not a monolithic group, nor did they always act in unison. Yet they shared a vision and a commitment to the welfare of all their countrymen without being indifferent to the affairs of their co-religionists. This was because of their training, their social and educational background: most belonged to petty landed families or to the service class and possessed the means and the opportunity to study in Indian or British colleges and universities. Here they came into contact with students from other communities who belonged essentially to the same economic background. Interaction at this stage and level helped to narrow down religious and cultural differences and remove mutual prejudices. Wazir Hasan, having studied in the cosmopolitan ethos of the Muir Central College in

---

and Jafri, *Kaarawaan-i Gumgushta,* pp. 498–536. For a recent analysis, see K.H. Ansari, 'Pan-Islam and the Making of the Early Indian Muslim Socialists', *MAS*, 1986, vol. 20, 3, pp. 509–537.

[58] Note by P. Biggane, 30 October 1914, General Administration Department (GAD), F.No. 79, 1914, UP State Archives, Lucknow (UPSA).

[59] Gracey to Lambert, 8 January 1920, GAD, F. No. 1921, UPSA.

Allahabad, could well appreciate how education on similar lines had fostered Hindu-Muslim understanding and enabled young graduates to recognize a common destiny above the 'existence of separate entities and the din of communal claims'.[60]

Notice, for example, how Saifuddin Kitchlew, the hero of the Rowlatt Satyagraha in Punjab, Syed Mahmud, Abdul Majid Khwaja, and Tassaduq Ahmad Khan Sherwani—all contemporaries of Jawaharlal Nehru at Cambridge—returned home with a broad vision and a liberal outlook. They rose to fame in the Congress movement and were rarely, if ever, moved by the communal claptrap. There are other instances too—of the Ali Brothers, of Zafar Ali Khan, Shuaib Qureshi, Khaliquzzaman, Abdur Rahman Siddiqi, Raja Ghulam Husain, Wilayat Ali and Hasrat Mohani, all products of the Aligarh college. Then, there was Mohammad Ali Jinnah, liberal and secular to the core before he spearheaded the Muslim League campaign in the 1940s. He was in London, where thanks to Dadabhai Naoroji's inspiring example, he entered politics as a liberal nationalist, joining Congress soon after he returned to India. Fazlul Haq in Bengal followed the same course. He studied Law and Mathematics at the Calcutta University, joined Ashutosh Mookerjee at the High Court in 1900, and some years later began to play a pivotal part in the Bengal Congress.

Henry Cotton, a keen sympathizer of nationalist aspirations, noted in 1914 that political co-operation between such men and their 'Hindu' counterparts was the result of a common educational background. As he explained in the *Asiatic Review*:

> 'Unity of ideas due to uniformity of training and the ideal which was present in Syed Ahmad's mind when he founded the Aligarh college—but was incapable of realization—is at last attained. Mutual trust, a desire for the achievement of common ends and objects, nationalism and self-government—these are the inspiration of the rising generation not less of Mohammedans than of Hindus.[61]

Mohamed Ali and Azad were ideal representatives of this 'rising generation', because their concerns mirrored the two

[60] *India*, 17 October 1913.

[61] 'India: Old and New', *Asiatic Review*, July 1914.

most powerful strands among Indian Muslims—pan-Islamism and sympathy for nationalist forces. Both burst on the national scene around the same time, achieved fame through journalism, and voiced, with equal vehemence, the anguish of their brethren over the Balkan issue, the Kanpur mosque and the Muslim university at Aligarh. They also spearheaded the pan-Islamic campaign, with Azad as the ideologue and Mohamed Ali its effective propagator. When the British government put them in gaol time and time again, they reflected on their role with a sense of pride, deriving comfort from the fact of occupying centre stage and influencing the course of history.[62] Azad saw himself in the same role as that of Jesus, a victim of unjust courts:

> At all events, how strange and glorious a place is this prisoner's deck where both the greatest and the best of men are made to stand! For even so great a being as He, this was no inappropriate place.[63]

Mohamed Ali wrote from the Chhindwara jail: 'Such sufferings and privations as ours have only too often been the lot of mankind in all ages and climes...'.[64] The trial, he said at Karachi on 26 October 1922, was not 'Mohamed Ali and six others *versus* the Crown', but 'God *versus* man'. And the question was: 'Should God dominate over man or shall man dominate over God?'

Mohiuddin Ahmad, better known as Azad, was not the product of the Aligarh college. He studied at Mecca and, in 1898, when the family returned to India, he was tutored by his father Maulana Khairuddin Ahmad in the Islamic Sciences. Later, he came into contact with Shibli and was exposed to the liberal, reformist writings of Egyptian scholars—Mohammad Abduh

[62] In response to a suggestion to write a historical monograph, Mohamed Ali stated: 'This is not the time for historical writing. This is the moment to create history'. The implicit suggestion in this remark is obvious. Mohamed Ali to Abdul Majid Daryabadi, 1916, quoted in I. Askari, 'Mohamed Ali: Ek Sadaa-i Shikast. Saaz', *Aligarh Magazine,* 1960–61, and A.M. Daryabadi, *Mohamed Ali: Zaati Diary ke chand Auraaq* (Hyderabad, 1943), p. 14.

[63] Quoted in Ian Henderson Douglas, *Abul Kalam Azad: An Intellectual Biography* (Delhi, 1988), p. 130.

[64] To James DuBoulay, 18 February 1919, Hasan (ed.), *Mohamed Ali in Indian Politics,* vol. 2, p. 193.

and Rashid Rida. In later years, his ideological discourse was influenced by his knowledge of and his interaction with Islamic societies while his political praxis was determined by the specificity of the colonial experience in India. At the same time, he was not easily swayed by a unified stream of thought or a monolithic ideology. Though Islam was central to his worldview, his thought processes were constantly at work in a critical evaluation of established notions. 'There is no conviction in my heart', he wrote, 'which the thorns of doubt have failed to pierce: there is no faith in my soul which has not been subjected to all the conspiracies of disbelief'.[65] Moreover, allegiance to his intellectual mentors, ranging from Syed Ahmad to Shibli, also shifted from time to time as he traversed the rough terrain of religion, politics and philosophy. 'I am under no obligation', he claimed, 'for guidance to any man's hand or tongue, nor to any syllabus of education. All the guidance I have received has been from the Divine Throne'.[66] In the end, he emerged from the darkness of his inner strivings a very independent man.

The same spirit of independence was the hallmark of Azad's political career. He was nobody's follower, not even Gandhi's. Even though religion and moral fervour bound the Mahatma and the Maulana in a common quest for swaraj, their perspective on and outlook towards socio-political issues had little in common. Azad's relationship with other Congress stalwarts was ambivalent. He respected some and admired others, but rarely did he follow their dictates. This was because his political survival was never ever dependent on his paying obeisance to a Gandhi or a Nehru or his alignment with or opposition to any of the factions in the Congress. His political stature and charismatic appeal rested on his unimpeachable loyalty to the Congress, his interest in India's independence and his antipathy to communal forces in the country.

Azad's political career began in Calcutta, then in the throes of the Swadeshi agitation against the partition of Bengal. He was impressed by the revolutionaries and claimed to have joined one

[65] Cited in Kenneth Cragg, *Counsels in Contemporary Islam* (Edinburgh, 1965), pp. 132–33; Abdur Razzaq Malihabadi, *Zikr-i Azad* (Calcutta, 1960), p. 251, quoted in Douglas, op. cit., p. 29.

[66] Ibid., p. 134.

of their groups through the mediation of Shyam Sunder Chakrabarty, an associate of Aurobindo Ghose.[67] From 1910 until his imprisonment in 1921, he was closely connected with several political movements for which he was often sent to gaol. He toiled in and out of prison over a monumental *Tarjuman al-Quran*—the theological credo of Azad—and put forward the view of the transcendental oneness of all faiths and the theology of multi-religious co-operation. In the final phase of his life, he returned to the front rank of politics as the Congress' leading Muslim president from 1939 to 1946, and as the symbol of those Muslims who worked for a united India. During the last years of the freedom struggle he opposed partition heart and soul. His speeches echoed the themes of his earlier life and writings: communal harmony, religious broad-mindedness and cultural cosmopolitanism.

Mohamed Ali was born at Rampur, scion of 'a fairly prosperous and educated Indian Muslim family'. His early career followed a familiar graph—degrees obtained at Aligarh and Oxford, and an unsuccessful attempt to join the ranks of 'heaven born' in the Civil Service, followed by jobs in the princely states of Rampur and Baroda. While in service, he turned to political issues and expressed his ideas in 'Thoughts on the Present Discontent', which appeared in the *Times of India* and the *Indian Spectator* in 1907. He lectured on the contemporary political scene; took part in the foundation of the Muslim League and was *en rapport* with leading nationalists at various levels. By the time the *Comrade* was launched on 14 January 1911, Mohamed Ali—yet to acquire the prefix 'Maulana' before his name—had won many hearts and gained a substantial following in his alumni, the MAO college. Around this time, Azad was busy planning his journalistic assault in Calcutta, where the echoes of the Swadeshi movement continued to reverberate in many circles.

When the *Comrade* and *Al-Hilal* appeared, they bore the unmistakable style of their editors. Azad was a consummate

[67] For a revealing account of Azad's early political life, see Rajat K. Ray, 'Revolutionaries, Pan-Islamists and Bolsheviks: Maulana Abul Kalam Azad and the Political Underworld in Calcutta, 1905–1925', Hasan (ed.), *Communal and Pan-Islamic Trends in Colonial India*, pp. 101–24.

stylist. He wrote authoritatively. His discourse was subtle, complex and incisive. His style was often fierce and combative and was akin to the Egyptian journal *Al-Urwa al wuthqa* rather than the simple mode of expression adopted by Syed Ahmad, Shibli, Hali and Hasrat. He marshalled a wide variety of scriptural and rational arguments and assaulted the positions of his opponents generally with great effectiveness, pausing only to regret occasionally the necessity of dealing with noisome adversaries. He spoke in the language of a 'high-souled prophet', reminiscent of the pontification of Shah Waliullah of Delhi. He appealed to his community's religious passions, awakened their dormant spirits by the use of Islamic symbols and altered the language and tenor of discourse amongst the *ulama*. He envisaged leading the Muslims at the head of a 'Party of God' [*Hizbullah*], which would unite all Indians in ousting the British. He also founded the Dar al-Irshad in order to enact a radical reform in the teaching methods used in religious institutions, encourage independent thinking and make plain to the students the social applicability of what they were studying. Such activity was not only a necessary preliminary to Azad's emergence as a powerful political force, but was also a means for changing the intellectual and political attitudes moulded by Syed Ahmad and for training a whole generation of *ulama* who went forth to play a leading role in the events leading to the Khilafat movement.

Azad took educated Muslims by storm with his eloquence and fervour when he began the publication of *Al-Hilal*. 'The Muslims were set on fire by his passionate words', recalled Sulaiman Nadwi, who worked with Azad on the staff of *Al-Hilal* for a time in 1913.[68] The demand for the paper was so great that, within three months all the old issues had to be reprinted as every new subscriber wanted the entire set. At one stage the circulation exceeded 25,000.

Mohamed Ali had an equally meteoric rise in the world of

[68] Quoted in Douglas, op. cit., p. 100. And the comment of Hasrat Mohani:
From the time that I saw Abul Kalam's prose,
Even the beauty of Hasrat's poetry
faded before my eyes.

journalism. But, unlike Azad, he was neither an ideologue nor a theorist. His concern was not for historical accuracy but for the emotional effect. He was a crusader—one who sought to undo the 'wrongs' done to his community by the forces inimical to Islam. That is why he took to journalism, 'the only avenue through which I could reach a place in which I could prove of any appreciable use to it....' Though his style was verbose, pedestrian, rambling and repetitive, he moulded public opinion to an appreciable degree. The UP government thought that 'no paper has so much influence with the students as the *Comrade,* and no individual has the authority over them which is exercised by Mohamed Ali'.[69] When, at the beginning of his internment, Mohamed Ali wanted to stop the *Hamdard,* he was implored not to do so. 'I don't approve of your decision and I don't think many will', observed Wilayat Ali Bambooque, 'You can't imagine what the loss of *Hamdard* will mean to us—the Mussalmans'.[70] Wilayat Ali was not alone in recognizing the contribution of *Comrade* and *Hamdard* to a general awakening of educated Muslims. Numerous Muslims throughout the country responded with warmth and enthusiasm to the writings of Mohamed Ali.

Though Islam as expressed in Mohamed Ali's life was different from Islam as expressed in Azad's life, it was still, in both cases, a vital component in defining their identity and the main source of inspiration. The early religious training of Mohamed Ali involved but a superficial acquaintance with the rudiments of Islam and the concomitant ritual. Family influences, too, do not appear to have been such as to have either inclined him in favour of dogmatic theology, or fostered in him independence of thought and a spirit of rebellion against prevailing religious beliefs. His mother's gentle influence, to which Mohamed Ali owed so much in life, was exerted more in the direction of promoting his educational career than in creating around him a religious atmosphere.

In *My Life,* Mohamed Ali laments that he did not have the benefit of acquiring the traditional Muslim education. 'It is not

[69] Home Poll. D., F.No. 31, December 1914, NAI.

[70] Wilayat Ali to Mohamed Ali, 20 August 1915, Mohamed Ali Papers, Jamia Millia Islamia, New Delhi.

without a feeling of deep shame that I have to confess, we boys and girls born and bred in Muslim households were taught far less of our religion than most English boys and girls of our age and position'.[71] He regretted that Aligarh 'furnished' students with 'little equipment in the matter of knowledge of faith'.[72] Though he attended Shibli's lectures on the Quran, referring to the 'exquisite elation of sitting in the Principal's Hall attending [his] lectures on the Quran with all the dignity of a quasi-'Undergrad',[73] the Quran still 'practically remained a closed book to us, and the traditions of the Prophet was no more than a name'.[74]

Mohamed Ali's *Life* is a document of deep religious feeling: it serves to illuminate his inner self-awareness of Islam. He became, as he put it, intoxicated with the force and grandeur of the Quran, which he read in Maulvi Nazir Ahmad's Urdu translation. After years of ignorance of his Islamic heritage, he discovered that the Quran was a 'perennial of truth', and offered a 'complete scheme of life, a perfect code of conduct and a comprehensive social policy....'[75] *Tauhid* grew upon him as a personal reality, man in the dignity of his 'service' as viceregent of God, and himself as part of this great strength. 'This was my unique discovery in that small volume revealed some thirteen centuries ago to an Arab of the desert whose name I bore'.[76]

In this way the enforced leisure at Chhindwara, Lansdowne and Betul jails enabled Mohamed Ali to steep himself afresh in his Islamic heritage and turn to the study of his religion—charting out an unfamiliar subject, getting at its rudiments and exploring its nuances. Again, it was during those years of internment at Chhindwara and Landsowne that he read the *Sihah-i Sitah,* a compilation of the traditions [*Hadith*] of the Prophet Mohammad, and the works of Imam Ghazali, Jalaluddin Rumi and

[71] Mohamed Ali, *My Life*, p. 2.
[72] Ibid., p. 22.
[73] Ibid., p. 27.
[74] Ibid., p. 23.
[75] Ibid., p. 37 and Afzal Iqbal (ed.), *Selected Writings and Speeches of Mohamed Ali* (Lahore, 1946), p. 170.
[76] *My Life*, p. 96.

Iqbal. The reading of *Asraar-i Khudi* [Secrets of Self] was an enthralling experience. 'I experienced an exquisite thrill of delight', he wrote, 'when I found the Poet and Philosopher was, in his own inimitable fashion, giving expression to the same basic truth of Islam, which I had in a blundering sort of way discovered for myself'.[77] And on turning to the study of Islamic history, Mohamed Ali saw its great men as figures to whom he could talk, and its crises as guides to action in current affairs.[78] Studying Islam was not uncommon; in fact, people like Syed Ahmad, Shibli and Azad studied it with greater scholarship, but none with a greater personal need.[79] To Gandhi, he wrote:

> Whatever else my internment may or may not have done, it has I believe set the soul free...What I could dimly perceive before I now realize with distinctness, and it is this, that the whole aim and end of life is to serve God and obey His Commandments..I confess I had never before grasped this truth in all its fullness....Internment made us seek refuge in the Holy Quran, and for the first time, I have to confess it, I read it through and with new eyes. It was then that this truth dawned upon me and gave me coherence and a unity to a thousand vague aspirations to do good to my people, my country and women in general.[80]

The experience was, in some ways, similar to that of Azad. His three-and-a-half year internment in Ranchi kindled his Islam into warmth and fervour. He began writing the *Tarjuman al-Quran,* with his commentary on the opening *Sura, Al-Fatiha,* and its themes—Divine Providence, benevolence, justice, unity and guidance, *rububiyya, rahma, adala, tauhid* and *hidaya.*

The authors of *Tazkirah* and *My Life* asserted their faith in the transcendental truth of Islam, which offered 'a way of life, a moral code and social polity'.[81] They felt the rightness of the Islamic ideals—a complete way of life for an organized commun-

[77] Ibid., p. 127.

[78] Daryabadi, *Zaati Diary,* p. 14; to Daryabadi, 22 May and 25 July 1916, Hasan (ed.), *Mohamed Ali in Indian Politics,* vol. 1, pp. 269–76.

[79] Mohamed Ali, *My Life,* p. 18.

[80] To Gandhi, 20 February 1918, *Mohamed Ali in Indian Politics,* vol. 1, p. 240.

[81] *Al-Hilal,* 23 October 1912.

ity living out Allah's plan under the kind of government which had prevailed in the days of the Prophet. At the same time, they affirmed that the basic principles of Islam were perfectly compatible with reason or science. This was the central argument of Mohamed Ali's article, 'The Future of Islam' and of Azad's essays published in the first three issues of *Al-Hilal*. Alone among his contemporaries in the religious institutions, Azad conceived for Islam a vital socio-political role that went against the apparently triumphant secularizing tendencies of the age and conveyed first to his associates and pupils and then to Indian society at large the vibrant and comprehensive vision of Islam that had first begun to animate his being in youth.

Azad's rationalism was not only an element in his modernist, intellectual explorations, but also—and primarily—an integral part of his traditional scholastic training. Mohamed Ali, on the other hand, propounded neo-intellectual modernism. And like Azad, he was *en rapport* with Syed Ahmad and the Egyptian reformers in his appeal for cultivating scientific disciplines and rejecting *taqlid*.'I have as much right to interpret God's message as any other man', he declared in *My Life*, a personal credo from gaol. 'Formal renunciation of a 'mildewed scholasticism' will set Islam 'right with the progressive world of science' and 'right with itself'.[82] Azad echoed similar views in his inimitable scholarly manner. 'The shopkeepers of religion have given the name of 'religion' to ignorance and *taqlid*, to prejudice and indulgence', he wrote in *Al-Hilal*. Many years later, he commented:

> The greatest hindrance to human intellectual progress is unquestioning acceptance of traditional beliefs . . . the first thorn of doubt which pricked my heart was against this very *taqlid*.... The foundation of belief should be knowledge, why on *taqlid* and inheritance.[83]

The underlying rationalist strain in the thought processes of Azad and Mohamed Ali found tangible expression in their ability to reconcile their passionate attachment to Islam and pan-Islamism with the ideological underpinnings of Indian nationalism. Their Islamic heritage, combined with their Indian experiences, led

[82] Mohamed Ali, *My Life*, pp. 163–64.
[83] Cited in Douglas, op. cit., p. 76.

them to reject Syed Ahmad Khan's plea for an Anglo-Muslim alliance and to pay heed to the exhortations of Jamaluddin Afghani and Mohammad Abduh on cultivating brotherly relations with fellow-Indians in the struggle against colonial rule. In addition, they received stimulus from those groups and individuals who were beginning to clamour for concerted action in support of the rising tide of Indian nationalism and in opposition to the raj. Hasrat Mohani was among the first to say so. Known as the *Rais al-Ahrar,* he plotted, quite early in his public life, a radical course for himself and joined Tilak after the split in 1907. Shibli, agonized over the Balkan War and the Kanpur mosque incident, also came round to supporting the Congress. His essays, published in the *Muslim Gazette,* may well have motivated Azad to speak at the Congress meeting in December 1913 on Hindu-Muslim unity and in praise of Congress policies.

Mohamed Ali's first editorial was a plea for Hindu-Muslim friendship. It was his firm belief 'that if the Muslims or the Hindus attempt to achieve success in opposition to or even without the co-operation of one another, they will not only fail but fail ignonimously'.[84] In fact the *Comrade* was intended to prepare Muslims to 'contribute to territorial patriotism without abating a jot of the fervour of their extra-territorial sympathies which is the quintessence of Islam'.[85] Whatever misgivings he had about the Congress were removed in Chhindwara when he had the leisure to reflect on the role of Tilak[86] and came into contact with Gandhi, whom he had first met at Aligarh in 1915. Soon thereafter, Mohamed Ali came under the Mahatma's spell. He wrote to Saifuddin Kitchlew:

> It is Gandhi, Gandhi, Gandhi, that has got to be dinned into the people's ear, because he means Hindu-Muslim unity, non-co-operation, *swadharma* and *swaraja,* while the rest are after petty communal or local bodies, most of them tinged with personal ambition.[87]

[84] *Comrade* (Calcutta), 14 January 1911.

[85] Mohamed Ali, *My Life,* p. 46.

[86] To Tilak, 12 November 1916, *Mohamed Ali in Indian Politics,* vol. 1; p. 292.

[87] Quoted in Afzal Iqbal, *Life and Times of Mohamed Ali* (Delhi, 1978: reprint), p. 308. See, Chintamani's assessment of Mohamed Ali in 1924.

Equally noteworthy is the fact that Azad and Mohamed Ali perceived no contradiction between their nationalist concerns and their communitarian interests, such as the Khilafat issue. Asserting that pan-Islamism and nationalism were compatible ideologies, they sought to establish that their community's anguish over the future of Turkey deepened their involvement in the anti-colonial struggle and brought them closer to the Congress under Gandhi's leadership. In fact, Azad, more than Mohamed Ali, was able to draw upon the Quran and the *Hadith* to advocate Hindu-Muslim amity and to strengthen the case for non-co-operation against the British. Following closely the views of Abduh who, in answer to inquiries from India, had endorsed inter-religious co-operation, Azad reiterated, with all the religious fervour he could command, that Muslims should be up in front, fighting for freedom.

The moves towards communal unity and Congress-Muslim League co-operation were stimulated by the ideas and activities of men like Azad and Mohamed Ali. Khuda Bukhsh's comments on such developments concluded with the prayer:

> The laurel, the palm and the paen to
> thee, O Khwaja (Muinuddin Chishti),
> for having, at least in Ajmer, effected
> an enduring reconciliation between these
> two communities, and united them in the
> silken bonds of brotherly love and esteem.[88]

He wrote to his Liberal Party colleague, Srinivasa Sastri: ' I had seen the latter (Mohamed Ali) more than a decade ago. How completely he has been transformed. Great I believe has been the Gandhian influence over him.' Chintamani to Sastri, 6 October 1924, T.N. Jagadisan (ed.), *Letters of V.S. Srinivasa Sastri,* 2nd edn. (Asia Publishing House, 1963), pp. 139–40.

[88] Bukhsh, *Essays on Indian and Islamic,* p. 269. Also, the comment of C.F. Andrews about Maulvi Zakaullah's 'profound' and 'mystical faith' in Hindu-Muslim unity. 'That was his own ideal, and it coloured all his actions. In that faith he lived, and in that faith he died.' Andrews, *Zakaullah of Delhi,* pp. xxix–xxx.

Chapter Four

Congress-League Rapprochement: The Lucknow Pact

The setting for the Congress-Muslim League meeting in the Christmas week of 1916 was perfect. The Raja of Mahmudabad, a sympathizer of nationalist aspirations, was acting host. Qaiser Bagh, the nerve centre of political activity during the Home Rule movement, was the venue. The leaders met every morning to hammer out the details of an accord, they dispersed early when faced with contentious issues; otherwise the deliberations went on till late afternoon when it was time to enjoy the Raja's hospitality. The exercise, interspersed with *mushairas* and elaborate luncheons and dinners, continued for three days until the final details of the Lucknow Pact were made public.

The Lucknow accord took place at an opportune moment. After years of fruitless negotiations the Congress and the League leadership recognized the need to set their own house in order before embarking on a quest for constitutional concessions.[1] The League made its intention known through changes in its constitution and in its leadership. The Congress was also in an accommodating mood, seeking to lend legitimacy to nationalist elements in the Muslim League. Consequently, a series of Congress-League meetings were held between 1909 and 1915 to achieve a workable political consensus.[2] The Lucknow gathering

[1] Such initiatives were backed by contemporary writings and the speeches of leading nationalists. See, for example, *Speeches of Gokhale at Lahore* (Lahore, 1907); *Speeches of B.C. Pal* (Madras, 1907), p. 43; S.M. Mitra, *Hindu-Muslim Entente Cordiale* (London, 1909); Yatindranatha Choudhri, *Observations on the Present Situation* (Calcutta, 1907), p. 36, IOLR Tracts (1025, 1050).

[2] The first important meeting was held at Allahabad from 31 December

placed its seal of approval on all such initiatives.

There was, however, an immediate and pressing need for the sort of agreement that took place in 1916. It was occasioned by the outbreak of World War I and the expectation, aroused by official statements, that the Allies who were fighting for the cause of freedom and liberty would themselves advance the cause of self-government.[3] 'The old regime *must* change', remarked the viceroy in July 1915, 'and the people must have more to say in their administration'.[4] Reginald Craddock, his home member, submitted concrete reform proposals in recognition of India's contribution to the war efforts. The demand for political concessions, he stated, would be vigorously pressed by the political sections of the educated classes and would receive a hearing in England.[5]

Such views heightened hopes of reforms and led Indian nationalists to prepare their schedule of demands in the light of the inadequacies of the Act of 1909. Gokhale did so in February 1915, ten days before he died. Wazir Hasan, the Muslim League secretary, gave advance notice of his party's proposals and spoke of the 'shifting horizon and broadening political outlook' on Indian affairs.[6] Annie Besant and Surendranath Banerjea, hero of the Swadeshi movement, also set forth their ideas. Soon these leaders moved uneasily towards the goal of achieving unanimity

1910 to 1 January 1911. It was attended by, among others, Gokhale, Surendranath Banerjea, the Aga Khan, Mazharul Haq, Bhupendranath Basu, Motilal Nehru, Jinnah, Tej Bahadur Sapru, Mohamed Ali, Mohammad Shafi, Viqarul Mulk and Wazir Hasan. *Tribune* of 22 January 1912 described the meeting as 'memorable', 'historical' and 'epoch-making'.

[3] 'During the war we Indians were looking forward to a great advance in self-government at its end...Nationalism received a needed lift from talk of what was to come'. Nirad C. Chaudhuri, *The Autobiography of an Unknown Indian* (London, 1951), p. 399.

[4] Hardinge to Walter Lawrence, 29 July 1915, Hardinge Papers (94).

[5] To Hardinge, 25 March 1915, ibid. (89). Non-official opinion was more vocal on the issue. Henry Cotton was one of those who vigorously pleaded for the grant of provincial autonomy to India and its gradual admission into the Federation of the Empire. 'India: Now and After', *Contemporary Review*, February 1915, pp. 195, 200.

[6] FR (UP), Home Poll. D, F. No. 56, March 1915, NAI.

on certain basic but potentially divisive issues concerning India's constitution.

Discussions between the Congress and the League started in early October 1915. Reporting on their progress, the editor of *Leader*, C.Y. Chintamani, informed Mohamed Ali in Chhindwara jail:

> ...We are making satisfactory progress...and it is my earnest prayer that nothing may happen to bring back the old days of strife. Even on the question of representation we are most anxious to arrive at an understanding and I am hopeful that we shall succeed.[7]

Mohamed Ali was kept posted with developments, because he had pressed the Muslim League council to take a series of momentous decisions, including the holding of the League meeting in Bombay to confer with the Congress which was also going to assemble in the same city and to work

> shoulder to shoulder with the sister communities of India for securing the recognition of all the legitimate claims of India as a whole, while safeguarding at the same time all the legitimate rights and interests of the Muslim community.[8]

The much-publicized League meeting was held in Bombay in December 1915 with Jinnah as the star performer. He moved a resolution, seconded by Azad and Fazlul Haq, appointing a committee to prepare a reform scheme in consultation with the Congress. Hindu-Muslim unity was the theme of his lectures then and later. Azad, too, commended the Muslim League meeting that resulted in a 'clear and effective step...in the direction of Hindu-Muslim national unity.'[9]

The spirit of unity that Jinnah had spoken of prevailed at the joint Congress-League conclaves. To begin with, the contentious issue of separate electorates was resolved smoothly, with most Congress leaders grudgingly accepting a principle which, in their judgement, had sowed the seeds of communal dissensions. Compromise was also reached on the proportion of Muslim rep-

[7] 27 October 1915, Mohamed Ali Papers, JMI.

[8] To Wazir Hasan, 26 September 1915, cited in Hasan (ed.), *Mohamed Ali in Indian Politics*, vol. 1, pp. 225–26.

[9] Douglas, *Abul Kalam Azad*, p. 145. For a fuller analysis of Jinnah's role, see Stanley Wolpert, *Jinnah of Pakistan* (New York, 1984), chapter 4.

resentation in the councils. In some provinces, such as Bihar, Bombay, Madras and the Central Provinces, they secured seats over and above their population. In return, their seats in Punjab were reduced from 55 per cent, to which they were entitled to by their population, to just 50 per cent.

Still, the joint conference, reconvened in the last week of December 1916, was left with the daunting task of fixing the proportion of Muslim seats in UP and Bengal. After some hard and prolonged bargaining, their share was fixed at 40 per cent in Bengal. But the deadlock over UP remained. Chintamani and Malaviya agreed to only 25 per cent as against the 35 per cent seats claimed by the League representatives.[10] Bhupendranath Basu, then, suggested the figure of 30 per cent which was reluctantly accepted on both sides.

The *Tribune*: 'There must be satisfaction all over the country that the question [of Muslim representation in the councils] has set at rest any further discussion in haggling...and that the scheme of post-war reforms prepared by the joint conference can now go to government.'[11]

Discussion on all other issues went off smoothly. In the end, the Congress-League scheme postulated representative government and dominion status, with the provision that India would be an equal partner in the empire as a self-governing dominion. The councils in the provinces would consist of four-fifths elected and only one-fifth of nominated members, and the elected members, so the scheme envisaged, would be returned on as broad a franchise as possible.

How did all this come about? Why did the Congress accept separate electorates after its sanctimonious opposition for so long? Who were the architects of the Lucknow agreement? And what were its implications on future political developments?

In 1909-10, Congress leaders had denounced the Morley-Minto Reforms for introducing separate electorates. Their arguments dwelt on the identity of Hindu-Muslim interests, the danger of Muslims securing more seats than they were entitled to

[10] GAD, F.No. 140, 1917, UPSA; FR (UP), 6 January 1917, Home Poll. F.No. 5, NAI.

[11] *Tribune*, 29 December 1916.

and the grave risks involved in introducing 'unjust invidious and humiliating distinctions' between Hindus and Muslims.'[12] The climax to their opposition came in June 1911, when the secretary of UP, Richard Burn, sought the opinion of his divisional commissioners on:

1. The introduction of separate electorates in local boards.
2. The proportion of seats to be allotted to Muslims under separate electorates.
3. The laying down of special qualifications for Muslim voters and candidates.
4. Participation of Muslims in general electorates.

There was much hue and cry in the press over the infamous Burn circular. It would lead to, stated the *Advocate,* the exclusion of Hindus from the council:

> [It was] only by a majority of one vote that the municipalities and the district boards in the Bareilly division could send a Hindu to the council, under the present condition. If the proposed changes come into effect, the Bareilly division will have the privilege of being represented by Muslims both from separate and joint electorates. Such also might be the fate of six out of the eight large cities in UP. The Hindu middle class representation, meagre as it is in the council, will be reduced to nullity.[13]

Opposition to the Burn circular was followed by an agitation over the UP Municipalities Bill, which acknowledged the principle of separate representation. Based on a compromise between Motilal Nehru, Jagat Narain Mulla, Tej Bahadur Sapru and the Muslim councillors,[14] Muslims secured a large representation in

[12] *Tribune,* 4 March 1910.

[13] *Advocate,* 18 June 1911. 'If Mohamedans have more than proportional representation, Hindus will *ipso facto* have less than their proportional representation...If, in addition, Mohamedans are empowered to get into local bodies through the general electorates, will not the less than proportional representation allowed to Hindus become less? Hindus very naturally and very properly resent this differential treatment which operates entirely to their detriment and it is against this that their agitation will be principally directed.' *Leader,* 29 June 1911.

[14] Robinson, *Separatism,* p. 247: Sender, *The Kashmiri Pandits,* pp. 270–72.

areas where they were more numerous as well in areas where they were in a minority.[15] In consequence, Hindus were placed in a minority on municipal boards even in places where they outnumbered the Muslims. Malaviya, who organized the protest against the Bill, summed up his powerful indictment:

Though the Hindus were convinced that separate communal representation on municipal boards was fraught with evil, they were willing to consent that Muslims should have separate representation. But they could not agree that they should have an excessive representation too. If there were 70 per cent of Hindus in a town and 30 per cent of Muslims it was utterly unfair that Muslims should have nearly the same representation as Hindus, and yet that was what the Act will bring about. The 30 per cent of Muslims of Allahabad would be entitled to appoint eight out of twenty-one elected representatives on the municipal boards, while the 70 per cent of Hindus would have only ten such representatives.[16]

This outcry, supported by massive protest meetings, posed a serious threat to the Congress-League negotiations which were well underway. But the Kashmiri triumvirate of Motilal, Sapru and Jagat Narain Mulla diffused the tension by securing the endorsement of the Jahangirabad amendment, introduced in the council in March 1916. Their principal interest in doing so was to keep intact the Congress-League alliance. In any case, they had come round to accepting separate electorates as a 'necessary evil', because Muslim leaders were insistent on having them. 'In order to make it possible for the Muslim community to co-operate with us', Sapru declared in the UP council, 'and in order to remove at least one of the several causes of friction, I should not grudge separate representation to the Muslims'. A satisfactory adjustment of inter-communal relations, according to Sapru, was a necessary condition for India's political evolution.[17]

Outside UP, the expediency of accepting separate electorates had been recognized much earlier. Gokhale explained in 1909

[15] Under sections 11-12 of the Act, Muslims were given 30 per cent of seats if they formed less than 25 per cent of the population; 38 per cent if their population stood between 25 to 38 per cent. Above 38 per cent, they were to receive seats in accordance with their numerical strength.

[16] *Amrita Bazar Patrika*, 21 July 1916.

[17] Quoted in Sender, op. cit., pp. 272–73.

that separate electorates would minimize friction and ensure the representation of minorities;[18] so did R.N. Mudholkar, Congress president in 1912.[19] Tilak's line of thought flowed in the same direction as Gokhale's. At the Lucknow meet in December 1916, he prevailed upon the intransigent Malaviya to reach an understanding rather than wreck the prospect of a Congress-League *entente*. He said:

> There is a feeling among Hindus that too much has been given to the Muslims. As a Hindu I have no objection to making this concession.... We cannot rise from our intolerable position without the aid of the Muslims. So in order to gain the desired end there is no objection to giving a percentage, a greater percentage, to the Muslims.[20]

Mohamed Ali, pleased with Tilak's role, wrote from Chhindwara:

> I must confess I had long been a prey to grave misgivings about the catholicity of your political and social ideals....I confess this all the more readily today because long before today I learnt to regret those misgivings and have already offered my apologies to you in spirit if not in flesh.[21]

Mohamed Ali was echoing the sentiments expressed long ago by Hasrat Mohani who wrote poems in praise of the Maharashtrian leader.[22]

II

In the opinion of the government, the main architects of the Congress-League *entente* were 'ignorant and self-seeking men', whose motives were 'love of notoriety and the lust of gain'. Thus

[18] *Tribune,* 16 July 1909.

[19] *INC.*, 1912, p. 19.

[20] D.V. Tahmankar, *Lokmanya Tilak: Father of Indian Unrest and Maker of Modern India* (London, 1956), p. 244; Stanley Wolpert, *Tilak and Gokhale: Revolution and Reform in the Making of Modern India* (Berkeley and Los Angeles, 1962), pp. 282–83.

[21] To Tilak, 12 November 1916, cited in *Mohamed Ali in Indian Politics,* vol. 1, pp. 292–93.

[22] Qadiri, *Hasrat Mohani,* pp. 156–57.

Mohamad Ali was a 'mischievous agitator' and Wazir Hasan a 'born intriguer'. Their patron, the Raja of Mahmudabad, was considered 'vain and unbalanced' by James Meston and Harcourt Butler.[23] What angered these officials was that the Raja backed the activities of young Muslims who were active in the Congress-led nationalist campaigns. They were the men of Nai Raushani' [New Light] and protagonists of 'new ideals' and 'new forces'.[24] As champions of 'democracy against oligarchy...freedom against convention...idealism against opportunism...and faith against cynicism and compromise,'[25] they were fierce in their denunciation of British colonialism and its allies. Wilayat Ali did so with candidness. So did Raja Ghulam Husain, the great crusader against the 'old race of patriots'. He summed up the ideological orientation of his group in an editorial published in *New Era* on 26 May 1917:

> A community of about 70 millions...has to work out its political destiny in close and active co-operation with the rest of the Indian people. Any other alternative...is unthinkable. Any self-respecting Muslim who knows what political freedom means for the self-realization of individuals as well as communities, can feel no enthusiasm for a political creed that does not aim at a free and united India.

Such views did not go uncontested. In Punjab, Mian Shah Din, the first Punjabi Muslim to go to England for legal studies, and his cousin, Mian [later Sir] Mohammad Shafi, were arrayed against the nationalist stream represented by Fazli Husain and Zafar Ali Khan. Of the two, Shafi was more prominent as founder of the Punjab Muslim League in 1907, member of the legislative council and patron of Anjuman-i Islamia and the Anjuman-i Himayat-i Islam, organizations where Iqbal first recited his patriotic songs. While the Morley-Minto Reforms were being formulated, the Baghabanpura Mian followed the line which the

[23] Sydennam to Hardinge, 18 March 1913, Hardinge Papers (86); FR (Delhi), 16 August 1914, Home Poll. A, September 1914, F.No. 1–3, NAI; Butler to Allan, 6 April 1913, Butler Papers (71); Meston to Chelmsford, 20 August 1917, Meston Papers (1).

[24] Mohamed Ali, *My Life*, p. 39; Mazharul Haq, quoted in *Bombay Chronicle*, 27 January 1916.

[25] *New Era*, 14 April 1917.

government was pleased to endorse. Muslims, he told Dunlop Smith, were 'the most important minority in the country' and their political importance was much more than their numerical strength. Moreover, 'they constitue a distinct community having, in part, interests of their own, which while in line with those of their rulers, are separate from and often antagonistic to those of the majority'.[26] Shafi assured Dunlop Smith that the government could safely rely on the loyalty of his community which was 'a stable element in the political atmosphere of this country'. His attachment to British rule was above reproach. As a follower of the 'Anglo-Mohammedan school of politics', he would never ever 'take part in anything calculated, in the slightest degree, to injure British interests and to weaken the stability and permanence of British rule in India.'[27]

Shafi's main political rival in Punjab was Mian Fazli Husain. Their differences first surfaced in the Anjuman-i Himayat-i Islam, though they were temporarily resolved by Nawab Fateh Ali Qizilbash, a landowner with large estates in Lahore and the Awadh district of Bahraich.[28] The final rupture took place in mid-1915, when Shafi opposed the holding of the Muslim League session in Bombay. Soon thereafter, the Punjab Muslim League, of which he was secretary, was disaffiliated by the League council and Fazli Husain was placed at the helm of affairs. Shafi had to swallow another bitter pill when his attempts to chair the Muslim Educational Conference, a prestigious forum set up by Syed Ahmad Khan, were thwarted by his detractors.[29] As his star faded, the editors of *Zamindar, New Era, Muslim Observer,* backed by Wazir Hasan and the Raja of Mahmudabad, triumphantly recorded the advance of nationalist forces in Punjab.[30]

[26] Shafi to Dunlop Smith, 18 June 1909, Dunlop Smith Papers, MSS. EUR. F. No. 166 (13), IOLR.

[27] To Dunlop Smith, 11 January, 13 April and 8 June 1909, ibid.

[28] *Tribune,* April 1910.

[29] FR (Punjab), Home Poll. Deposit, February 1917, F. No. 49, NAI. FR (UP), Home Poll. Deposit, January 1917, F. No. 42, NAI.

[30] For example, the *New Era* wrote a strongly-worded editorial against Shafi. 'He is trying', the paper wrote, 'to arrogate to himself the right to speak on behalf of the Mussalmans, and he intends in this garb to play the

In Bengal, the Nawab of Dacca and his proteges called the shots from the time the Muslim League came into being. But the annulment of Bengal's partition placed the leadership on the defensive. The death of the Nawab in 1915 was the last straw. It marked the end of an era in which the landlord-government servants combination had successfully resisted the growth of political radicalism. Reflecting on the changes ushered in by the decline of the old-style leadership, the *Mussalman,* an organ of nationalist opinion, observed:

> In every age, in every clime, and in every country there are reactionaries. Whenever any progressive movement is set on foot, they stand in the way. But they have never been able to block the way; they only place temporary difficulties in the path of progress.[31]

After the Nawab, Fazlul Haq emerged as a potential leader of a new kind. Born in 1873 in a family of Barisal lawyers, Fazlul Haq studied in Calcutta University and worked with Ashutosh Mookerjee as an articled clerk in the High Court. His involvement in politics began in 1906, when he attended the Muslim Educational Conference at Dacca and was entrusted with the task of drafting the Muslim League constitution. This was the time when he began to drift apart from his patron, the Nawab of Dacca, who had helped him secure an important position in the Rural Co-operative Societies and a seat in the legislative council. Restless with the Nawab's policy of collaboration with government and opposition to the Congress, he decided to adopt an independent course in politics. As a first step he gained control of the League in Bengal and began to marshal his resources in order to operate from a position of a strength. He was able to do so with much effect, because unlike the traditional Muslim leaders—of the Ameer Ali and Abdul Latif kind — Fazlul Haq had made his

---

traitor and bring everlasting disgrace on his community. It is the duty of every true and honest citizen in this country to expose him and take the sting out of his action by demonstrating that he represents his own views and has absolutely no right to speak on behalf of this community or country. It appears to be the old game of the separatists by trying to set the Mussalmans against the Hindus and in the end ruin both.' *New Era,* 15 and 22 September 1917.

[31] *Mussalman,* 23 January 1917.

way up the political ladder by personal ability. His education, combined with his wide professional experience, set him apart from his predecessors in the Muslim League. He excelled in organizational work and was dynamic, forward-looking and cosmopolitan in outlook.

Fazlul Haq's political views were defined by the experience of the annulment of Bengal's partition. He realized, as did so many young Muslim leaders of his generation, that the government could no longer be relied upon for the redressal of Muslim grievances. It was not even willing to consider their submissions. Such was, after all, the experience of Mohamed Ali and Wazir Hasan, who undertook a journey to England in September 1913 to explain the 'Indian Muslims' point of view' to the British government.[32] But they were snubbed: Montagu did not grant them an interview. The secretary of state did not want to meet them, because it would be misunderstood by 'those of your co-religionists with whom you are not in accord, who claim equally with you to represent the political attitude and temper of the Mussalman community'.[33] The secretary of state should have known better, for nobody represented the political temper of his co-religionists more than Mohamed Ali and his associates. Mohamed Ali returned home with the conviction that an agitational course was the only option that remained with his aggrieved community. As he reported to Shaukat Ali:

> It may be that government organs here may give us *darwaza band* [but] we cannot be effectively gagged. Besides, if we are gagged here, we would not be gagged in India and I appealed to Sir James Dunlop Smith to consider the likely effect of our going back to India and telling our people, whether in a loud voice from the public platform or in whispers to our closets, that if the smallest official is unjust to you in this country there is no house of redress except by our taking the law into our hands.[34]

Mohamed Ali and his comrades chose the public platform,

[32] *Mohamed Ali in Indian Politics*, vol. 1, pp. 164–65.

[33] Holderness to Wazir Hasan and Mohamed Ali, 11 November 1913, Crewe Papers, F. No. 1/14 (2).

[34] To Shaukat Ali, 24 October 1913, *Mohamed Ali in Indian Politics*, vol 1, p. 167.

which they often shared with the Congress leaders, to mount a sustained agitation against the government.

III

The Lucknow Pact enhanced the value of India's constitutional demands and bridged the gulf that separated the Congress and the League. It was masterminded by Jinnah whose nationalist credentials were beyond reproach. 'Young India ought to be proud', observed a correspondent, 'that in the Hon'ble Mr. Jinnah it has found a leader who labours under no illusions as to what United India ought to have.'[35]

But not all agreed with the fairness of the accord. Hindu Sabhas, forerunners of the All-Hindu Mahasabha, were most vocal in denouncing separate electorates and communal representation. The feeling was strongest in UP, where Muslims were allowed 30 per cent of seats in the council though their population did not exceed 14 per cent. Hindus and Sikhs in Punjab, on the other hand, were allowed only a small amount of weightage. In places like Lucknow, Allahabad, Banaras and Kanpur there were loud and angry protests over the arbitrary distribution of seats proposed by the Congress-League scheme.[36]

Among Muslims there were cranks like an *alim* from Madras who told Montagu, the secretary of state, that there was no sanction in the Quran for an alliance with non-Muslims.[37] There were others who were alarmed at the growing nationalist tide among Muslims and were dismayed by their Congress leanings. 'The stereotyped Congress slogans', observed Syed Hosain Bilgrami, once member of the Imperial Legislative Council and tied to the court in Hyderabad, 'are a threat to our very existence'.[38]

[35] *Amrita Bazar Patrika*, 6 December 1916; *Bengalee*, 4 January 1917; *Young India*, 3 January 1917.

[36] FR (UP), 1 January 1917, Home Poll. Deposit, F.No. 26, February 1917, NAI; *Leader*, 30 December 1916.

[37] Quoted in H.F. Owen, 'Negotiating the Lucknow Pact', *Journal of Asian Studies*, vol. 31, May 1972, p. 581.

[38] To Mohamed Ali, 12 June 1915, Mohamed Ali Papers. Bilgrami told

Nobody perceived the threat more seriously than the rajas, zamindars and taluqdars, who were brought up in the traditions of sturdy loyalty to the raj whose 'salt they had eaten' and were nursed through successive legislations, such as the Taluqdari Succession Law (1869) and the Encumbered Estates Act (1870). 'We must preserve and develop', stated Harcourt Butler, 'a landed aristocracy, and work through it if we wish to keep an absolute foot in India ... I do not see how we can carry on without it'.[39]

Encouraged by their patrons, the landed classes and their allies launched a well-orchestrated campaign against the Congress-League alliance. As early as 1913, Fateh Ali Khan, acting at the behest of James Meston, UP's lieutenant-governor, condemned the resolution on self-government adopted by the League and made an abortive bid to have it rescinded.[40] A year later, he floated the scheme of a Shia College in Lucknow, a move intended to divide the Aligarh university movement.[41] This project also had Meston's backing. But it failed to take off because the Raja of Mahmudabad, himself a staunch Shia, did not extend his patronage to a scheme which, he feared, would estrange Shia-Sunni relations.

Another abortive move came in the form of an attempt to prevent the League from holding its meeting in 1915 at Bombay, also the venue of the Congress session.[42] A group of traders, merchants and government servants, having first agreed to host the session, developed cold feet and aired their opposition to the Jinnah-Wazir Hasan combine. Urdu newspapers began an acrimonious vilification campaign. Prominent amongst them were the *Al-Bashir*, the *Aligarh Institute Gazette*, *Al-Mizan*,

---

Meston that he did not want to be 'ruled by men like Mr. Jinnah, Mr. Malaviya, or even the Raja of Mahmudabad.' He described Jinnah as a man of very low birth'. To Meston, 14 November 1917, Meston Papers (4).

[39] To H.E. Richards, 16 September 1906, Butler Papers (65).

[40] To Meston, 21 August 1913, Meston Papers (6).

[41] The aim was 'to produce an educated class with which will be associated every kind of healthy progress and which will produce members who will readily constitute a pious community of loyal subjects.'

[42] For details, see Owen, op.cit., pp. 571–72; Robinson, *Separatism*, pp. 242–45.

Mashriq and *Zul Qarnain*.[43] Jinnah offered a powerful rebuttal to the charges levelled against him. In a rejoinder to an editorial comment in the *Times of India,* he stated:

Surely the Mahomedans who have shown the greatest self-restraint and control throughout these grave and momentous crisis may be trusted to formulate their demands along with their Hindu leaders. Can there be a better opportunity than this that the Congress and the League should meet in one place and confer together as to the future of India?...May I say that it is not the energies of the few members of the League that has put the Mahomedan community in rather an awkward position but it is the 'wire-pullers' and 'Jo-hukams' who are responsible for all this. I still venture to say that all the thinking Mahomedans all over India are in favour of holding the next session of the League in Bombay.[44]

The League session was eventually held amid much fanfare, with Jinnah, Mazharul Haq, Wazir Hasan and Fazlul Haq as the main performers.[45] Those who stayed away felt humbled and isolated. Suleman Cassim Mitha, Fazulbhoy Currimbhoy and Maulvi Rafiuddin, chief detractors of Jinnah, lost face with the government whose interests they were trying to promote. Meston took note of their sliding fortunes and insisted on devising a new political strategy in the light of the waning influence of the 'conservative' Muslims. In a note to the viceroy, he sorrowfully reflected :

In deciding either on the strategy of its post-bellum policy or to handle the Home Rule agitation, the Government of India will no doubt have

[43] *Al-Bashir,* 8 June 1915; *Al-Mizan,* 12 June 1915; *Medina,* 22 October 1916; *Mashriq,* 19 December 1916, SNNR, UP.

[44] Syed Sharifuddin Pirzada (ed.), *The Collected Works of Quaid-e-Azam Mohammad Ali Jinnah* (Karachi, 1984), vol. 1, p. 135.

[45] The Governor of Bombay played a key role in uniting the different factions and made it easier for the League session to be held in the city. But Meston was unhappy with his role. He believed that Willingdon had given the 'Lucknow gang an inflated sense of their own importance'. He was of the opinion that 'the small clique, which Wazir Hasan organizes and Mahmudabad feeds, are in no sense representative of the Muslims of north India', but that a 'triumph of this coterie will be taken as a triumph for Mohamed Ali and his followers'. To Hardinge, 23 December 1915, Hardinge Papers (90).

regard to the strength of the Nationalist feeling in India at the present moment. It is unquestionably greater than it has ever been in our time. The Christmas meetings at Lucknow caught up and consolidated popular sentiment as few political events have done. Extremists and Moderates have united after years of misunderstanding; and, greatest marvel of all, the Mahomedans also had come into the fold. A few Moderates may grumble here and there; and a few conservative Mahomedans may urge that the League does not represent their community. But they do nothing. They are voiceless in public; they do not hold meetings; they have completely lost command of the Press. For all practical purposes they have, for the time at least, disappeared as a separate party. The resultant union of all voices has filled educated India with a pride and a feeling of nationality which it is impossible to ignore.[46]

Meston was making this observation just when a powerful agitation was being mounted against the Lucknow Pact in Bengal and Punjab.[47] While Muslims of UP and Bihar were jubilant that their representatives had extracted both separate electorates and weightages, reactions in Bengal and Punjab were much less subdued. Fazlul Haq and Fazli Husain, having backed the Congress-League *entente cordiale,* were now bitter that the claims of their constituents were sacrificed in the course of the hard bargaining that preceded the Lucknow Congress. In late November 1916, Fazlul Haq had sounded a warning. In a letter to Mohamed Ali, he had written:

To me it seems that that there is no hope for the Muslim community in Bengal and it would indeed be a miracle if, at some future date, the Bengali Muslims can be so fortunate as to attain a position on account of which they might be recognized as any living community in India.... May God have mercy upon us to see better days.[48]

Placed on the defensive by mounting criticizm, the principal negotiators of the Lucknow Pact, including Fazlul Haq, tried to retrieve their position by insisting on having 50 per cent of seats

[46] 7 February 1917, Meston Papers (17).

[47] *Paisa Akhbaar,* 17 and 19 July 1917, 22 December 1918, SNNR, Punjab; *Moslem Hitaishi,* 5 January 1917, SNNR, Bengal; *Searchlight,* 1 September 1918.

[48] To Mohamed Ali, 23 November 1916, Hasan (ed.), *Mohamed Ali in Indian Politics,* vol. 1, p. 307.

in the council and half the positions in public services. But they were still not able to win over their lost following. Accused of a sellout, they remained the target of attack in the press. The Lucknow Pact, stated the *Resalat,* would place Muslims under the 'thumb of the Hindus'. Communal riots in Bihar in September 1917 hardened attitudes. The *Resalat's* warning to 'learn a lesson from the universal ruin of their brethren in Bihar' struck a sympathetic chord in many circles.

> Those who apprehend that the Muslims will suffer political death if they do not unite with the Hindus are greatly mistaken. We have already stood alone for 1300 years. What is wanted is that we should firmly abide by our religious laws and not become faint-hearted.[49]

This was the *Moslem Hitaishi* giving vent to its anger against the Lucknow Pact.

Taking advantage of such feelings, the Central National Mohammadan Association and the Indian Muslim Association staked their respective claims to represent their community in Bengal. They demanded 52 per cent of seats as against the 40 per cent allotted by the Lucknow Pact. In a memorial submitted to Montagu and Chelmsford, they argued that as the trend of government policy was towards granting autonomous administration to various provinces and towards reduction of the British element, it was essential 'to have the rights of Muslims...placed upon a firm...basis'. The spirit of the address was characterized by the concluding section:

> For England now to place the Indian Muslims, without proper, definite and ample safeguards, under the heels of a hostile non-Muslim majority, would, your humble memorialists venture respectfully to submit, be a cruel act of breach of faith and violation of trust.[50]

W.H. Vincent, a member of the governor-general's executive council, endorsed the demands of the various associations. But the Southborough Committee (Franchise) was willing to recommend only 54 per cent of the territorial seats. The Bengal

[49] *Resalat,* 2, 7 and 17 December 1917, *Mohammadi,* 14 December 1917, *Moslem Hitaishi,* 10 August 1917, SNNR, Bengal.

[50] Addresses presented at Calcutta, Montagu Papers (34).

government was willing to go only this far.[51] In the end, the efforts of the Bengal Muslim leaders to nullify the effects of the Congress-League scheme and to secure major concessions from Montagu and Chelmsford proved unsuccessful. Nawab Ali Chaudhuri, the main architect of the Indian Muslim Association, failed to impress and belied all hopes that had been aroused by his activities. The Montagu-Chelmsford Report, much to the dismay of educated Muslims in Bengal, recognized the Congress-League compact as 'the most complete and authoritative settlement between the claims of the majority and the minority' and as an 'accomplished fact and a landmark in Indian politics'. Moreover, the image of Nawab Ali and his associates was tarnished because of their complicity in the September riots in 1918.[52] Having lost face with the public, the Nawab withdrew into the safety of the council chamber.

In UP and Punjab, opposition to the Lucknow Pact was initiated and sustained by the landlords. In 1917, they were advised to advance their claims before Montagu and Chelmsford so that the Congress-League scheme was undermined and the professional groups were prevented from dominating the councils. Michael O'Dwyer made his intentions known. He was committed to defending the interests of the landed gentry in Punjab, who 'were in close touch with the rural masses...the recognized leaders and an invaluable support to the administration'. This was the class to which the Punjab government 'has looked and never looked in vain in times of stress and difficulty'.[53] Meston followed a similar course in UP, urging the Nawab of Rampur to throw his weight behind the UP Muslim Defence Association, organized at his instance by Nawab Fateh Ali Khan, Nawab Muzammilullah Khan, a zamindar with large estates in Aligarh and Etah districts, Syed Abdur Rauf, member of UP legislative council from 1913 to 1916, and Ibni Ahmed, a petty zamindar of Budaun and a practising lawyer at the Allahabad High Court. His advice to the Nawab was:

[51] J.H. Broomfield, *Elite Conflict in a Plural Society: Twentieth Century Bengal* (Berkeley and Los Angeles, 1968), pp. 126–29.

[52] Broomfield, op. cit., pp. 192–93.

[53] *The Political Situation in India* (Calcutta, 1917), p. 47.

It is assuredly time to stop a great deal of the nonsense that is preached by the leaders. You will remember my parting prayer to you the other day, and my earnest entreaty that you should come forward and take your right position at the head of your community. I never give advice which is likely to be embarrassing, and even if I give it, I never resent it being rejected. But I do ask Your Highness to think over this opportunity of taking a brilliant and dominant part in organizing wise and moderate and orthodox Moslem opinion in India.[54]

The Defence Association got into the act of presenting an address to the secretary of state and the viceroy. Quite familiar views were orchestrated. For example, any 'large measure of self-government which might curtail the moderating and adjusting influence of the British government would be nothing short of cataclysm'. A number of demands flowed from this formulation, but they were completely out of tune with the realities of contemporary political life. With British influence gradually being curtailed in legislative bodies, there was no chance of the demands of the Association being accepted. And with the agitation against the Montagu-Chelmsford proposals gathering momentum, the Defence Association was left with no *raison d'etre:* it petered out after a brief and lazy existence.

IV

The Lucknow accord ushered in an era of Congress-League co-operation on vital political and constitutional issues. In August 1918, the League followed the Congress line in rejecting the Montagu-Chelmsford reforms. Both protested against the insinuation contained therein that the Indian people were unfit for responsible government, reaffirmed their ideas on self-government [adopted at their annual sessions in Lucknow and Calcutta], and emphasized that self-government within the Empire alone would satisfy Indian aspirations.[55] On several other issues, such as the Rowlatt Bills and the ghastly happenings at Jallianwala Bagh, the Congress and the League spoke and acted in unison.[56]

[54] To Hamid Ali Khan, 12 November 1917, Meston Papers (4).

[55] *Tribune,* 5 September 1918.

[56] 'It is impossible to go through the proceedings of the session (Muslim League) without being struck by the fact that the national inspiration is as

The distinction between the two organizations was blurred, at least for the time being. The concurrent sessions of the Congress and the League became a convention over the next five years and provided Gandhi and his Khilafat allies with an enlarged arena for mounting their campaigns.[57]

Unity between the Congress and the League created a climate for inter-community fraternization. It was common for leaders of different religious persuasions to visit temples and mosques and to exhort on the virtues of communal unity. Such sentiments were echoed at the Nakhoda mosque in Calcutta, the Juma Masjid in Delhi and the Sonepur mosque in Bombay. Elsewhere, there were dramatic scenes of Hindus and Muslims joining in each other's festival and removing the irritants in their otherwise harmonious relationship. Allahabad, Agra, Azamgarh, scenes of communal rioting in earlier years, were, in 1917-18, examples of Hindu-Muslim amity.[58] At some of these places, local Congress committees and Home Rule Leagues organized and conducted religious processions which, in the past, were sources of discord. In Bengal, Hindus and Muslims of Patnakhali joined each others prayer meetings and resolved to attain Home Rule. Such instances, recorded in official reports, can be cited from other areas as well. In sum, they held out hopes of a stable and durable resolution of communal disputes which were occasioned by local feuds over processions, cow-slaughter and music before mosques. Gandhi was able to capitalize on the existing goodwill to cement the bonds of Hindu-Muslim friendship during the Rowlatt

---

strong, as deep and as universal in the League as in the Congress and the country.' Ibid., 13 January 1918.

[57] See essays in Ravinder Kumar (ed.), *Essays on Gandhian Politics,* and J.M. Brown, *Gandhi's Rise to Power: Indian Politics 1915–1922* (Cambridge, 1974).

[58] *Leader,* 18 September, 4 and 15 November 1917; *Tribune,* 21 and 30 November 1917. J.C. Smith, the Collector and magistrate of Azamgarh, issued the following statement on 2 November: 'The district of Azamgarh is to be congratulated on the fact that the Dasehra and Muharram ceremonies passed off without disturbances of any kind. For more three years past the government have been anxious regarding this matter and it is highly creditable to the people that at so critical a period there has been no sign of hostility between the different communities'. *Leader,* 15 November 1917.

satyagraha and the Khilafat movement. The editor of *Amrita Bazar Patrika* wrote : 'Though the Rowlatt Act sits like a dread nightmare on our breasts, it has united both Hindus and Mussalmans in a way which has never been witnessed.'[59]

In the years following the Lucknow Pact, a number of younger Muslims were drawn into the Congress movement and played a leading part in the Home Rule movement and the Rowlatt satyagraha. The Bihar Congress, for example, was dominated by Mazharul Haq, Hasan Imam, Mohammad Shafi and Sarfaraz Husain Khan. In UP and Delhi nationalist feeling was in full flow with Ansari, Ajmal Khan, Hasrat Mohani, Wazir Hasan, Shuaib Qureshi and the Ali Brothers in the forefront of the Congress and Home Rule movements. They had a large following of young Muslims, graduates from British and Indian universities, trained in the professions of journalism and law. They included Asaf Ali, who rose to prominence in Delhi during the Rowlatt satyagraha; Abdul Majid Khwaja, Jawaharlal's contemporary at Cambridge and founder of the Home Rule League in Aligarh; Zahur Ahmad, Kamaluddin Jafri, Manzar Ali Sokhta and Wahid Yar Khan, all connected with the Nehru household in Allahabad; Shuaib Qureshi, Khaliquzzaman, Raja Ghulam Husain and Abdur Rahman Siddiqi—Aligarh graduates bound to Ansari and Mohamed Ali by personal and political loyalty.[60] According to Meston, this 'clique of noisy and aggressive Muslims', patronized by the Raja of Mahmudabad, 'make the Raja's house their headquarters and live and agitate at his expense.'[61] He was alarmed that both the 'extremists' and the 'moderates' in his province had combined in the Home Rule agitation; and, the 'greatest marvel of all, the Muhammadans had also come into the fold'.[62] The same process was underway in other areas, such as in Bombay where Jinnah, Omar Sobhani and Syed Abdullah Brelvi were involved in nationalist agitations. M.C. Chagla recalled: 'When I left India in 1919, Jinnah was the uncrowned King of Bombay. He was the idol of the youth. His personality

[59] Motilal Ghose to Mohamed Ali, 14 April 1919, Mohamed Ali Papers, JMI.
[60] For a fuller discussion, see Hasan, *A Nationalist Conscience*, pp. 25–30.
[61] To Chelmsford, 20 August 1917, Meston Papers (1).
[62] Home Poll. Deposit, May 1917, File No. 3, NAI.

and his sturdy independence appealed to the best elements in the city. He was the President of the Home Rule League, and had made stirring speeches in Shantaram Chawl, which was then the venue of political meetings.'[63]

A few general conclusions flow out of our analysis of the Lucknow Pact. The first relates to the different ways in which Muslims reacted to its provisions and the several different ways in which they sought to promote their interests in the power structures envisaged by Montagu and Chelmsford. Political activists in UP were mainly interested in securing separate electorates and weightages in order to retain their advantages in the council and local bodies. Their counterparts in Bengal, on the other hand, were much more concerned with representation on the basis of population rather than separate electorates.

Religious associations, small and large, had their own ideas. Sometimes they reflected local concerns, as did the Anjuman-i Islam of Bombay which approved the Congress-League scheme but demanded a larger share for Muslims in the legislative council. Often, their concerns were limited to religious affairs. The *ulama* of Deoband, for example, wanted a berth for an *alim* in the councils. They wanted *auqafs* and mosques to be placed under the charge of a Shaikhul Islam and called for a strict application of the Islamic Personal Law, which was divine and immutuable.[64]

Religious groups were not always united in putting forward their views. One group of Ahmadiyas, 'a body of about 50 persons' was sympathetic to the Lucknow accord but the other was not.[65] Similarly, the Barelwis were averse to extending any support to the demands of the Deobandis. The Anjuman-i Islam in Saharanpur decided to strike a somewhat different chord. It regarded the political implications of the Lucknow agreement 'ruinous' and announced:

[63] M.C. Chagla, *Roses in December: An Autobiography* (Bombay 1973), p. 78.

[64] Maulvi Mohammad Ahmad to Sheweth, 30 October 1917, Meston Papers (19).

[65] Memorial submitted by the Anjuman-i Ahmadiya Ishaat-i Islam, Lahore, Montagu Papers (35).

our instinct of self-preservation compels us to always keep at a safe distance from them [Hindus] in politics.... We are fully convinced that without *equal* strength, we are not for one minute safe with them in the political arena, because their interests happen to be so diametrically opposed to ours and their angle of vision so irreconcilably different.[66]

This manifesto was not consistent with the political mood of the *ulama,* especially those based at Firangi Mahal, Nadwa and Deoband. It also did not reflect the radical temper of large sections of Muslims who, for a variety of reasons, hitched their fortunes with the nationalist struggles.

With such glaring differences it was not surprising that Montagu and Chelmsford received not one but forty-four representations from 'Muslim' bodies—each one of them purporting to represent the community. And each one posed as the defender of the faith and the custodian of 'Muslim interests'. These were dubious claims. No organization, not even the Muslim League, had acquired the status of a truly national and representative body in the first quarter of the twentieth century. Moreover, given the multiplicity of interests at different levels it was not easy for anyone to identify the so-called Muslim interests and to then formulate a set of coherent and unified demands. Montagu knew it. He recognized that the communal categories imposed by the raj made no sense and that it was not right to treat Muslims as a distinct political interest. But he could not reverse a process initiated long ago. Likewise, he was averse to communal representation, regarding their introduction as 'a great mistake in the history of India and as more harmful perhaps in its consequences than the permanent settlement of Bengal or the partition of that province'.[67] Yet, for all the nobility of principles displayed by such

[66] Meston Papers (19).

[67] E. Montagu, *An Indian Diary,* vol. 2, p. 62, Montagu Papers (39). The *Report* observed that 'division by creeds and classes means the creation of political camps organized against each other, and teaches men to think as partisans and not as citizens; and it is difficult to see how the change from this system to national representation is ever to occur. The British Government is often accused of dividing men in order to govern them. But if it unnecessarily divides them at the very moment when it proposes to start them on the road to governing themselves, it will find it difficult to meet the charge of being hypocritical or shortsighted.' *Report on Indian Constitutional Reforms* (London, 1918), Cd. 9109, p. 187.

statements, no attempt was made in 1919 to abolish the system. On the contrary, it was expanded to include Sikhs in the Punjab and Eurasians elsewhere. The reasons in 1919 were the 'settled facts' of Minto's promise of 1906, the Act of 1909 and the belief that Muslim regarded separate representation and communal electorates as their only adequate safeguards.

One final point. By negotiating the Lucknow Pact on the questionable terms of communal representation, the Congress legitimized what were later derided as 'separatist' and 'communal' demands. By allowing itself to be dictated by narrow regional and sectarian causes, the Congress created a space within which such concerns had to be accommodated even at the risk of destroying the democratic and secular structures it was striving to build. Instead of curbing divisive tendencies through a concerted ideological campaign, the Congress settled for hastily concluded agreements for immediate political benefits. Consequently, it lost the moral authority and the political conviction to challenge the assumptions that went into the making of the Montagu-Chelmsford Reforms. The British translated their assumptions into concrete legislative proposals and, in the process, created a separate and distinct political identity for the Muslims. The Congress, caught up in its own contradictions, woke up to this painful reality only after the Khilafat and Non-Co-operation movements had petered out. By then, the contours of Indian politics had changed. So had the terms of discourse.

Chapter Five

Islam, Khilafat and Nationalism-I

Sambhlo ke wo zindaan goonj utha, jhapto ke wo qaidi choot gaye
Utho ke wo baitheen deewaren, dauro ke wo tooti zanjeeren

(Josh Malihabadi)

Take heed,
the prison-house reverberates
Spring forward,
the prisoners are free;
Arise,
the walls are collapsing
Surge ahead, the chains
have snapped asunder

Between 1919 and 1921 India experienced an unprecedented political upheaval, 'a magnificent struggle', characterized by mass involvement and by messianic ambitions on the part of some of its leaders.[1] In scholarly literature, however, the Khilafat upsurge is often treated as an artifact, a compound of material fears topped up by a dash of ideological whipped cream by the 'Young Party' Muslims,[2] as a movement 'devoid of

[1] Shahid Amin, 'Gandhi as Mahatma: Gorakhpur District, Eastern UP, 1921–2', Ranajit Guha (ed.), *Subaltern Studies III: Writings on South Asian History and Society* (Delhi, 1984).

[2] For example, Robinson argued that the professional politicians had 'continually to manufacture issues and to whip up agitations to keep their newspapers going, their organizations active and their coffers full.... The issues were religious, usually pan-Islamic: these were the only sure sources of the money they needed.' *Separatism,* p. 354. This interpretation is not shared by, among others, Gail Minault. She has tried to analyze the different meanings of the Khilafat symbol in the Indian context and examine how certain leaders attempted to create a self-conscious and unified Indian Muslim

constructive thought...purely negative in its aims, methods and policy'.[3] Its disintegration is attributed to an ideology that was romantic and out of touch with actualities,[4] to the religious fervour heightened by reactionary political forces,[5] to the apocalyptic spirit in which the movement was conducted, and to its being out of tune with the political realities in West Asia.

I propose to read existing historical accounts 'against the grain' so as to bring ideology to the centre of my analysis. I will argue that there was always a significant group of Muslims who could find in their tradition the ideological resources which would enable them to bridge their sense of 'difference' and the nationalist movement, which would enable them to be both good Muslims and ardent supporters of India's plural nationhood. In short, the object of this chapter and the one to follow is to describe and analyze both the Islamic and nationalist components of the Khilafat movement.

II

It is not commonly recognized that the Muslim intelligentsia in India has taken much pride in fostering its fraternal links with fellow-Muslims in other societies. It has followed the history of the lands from the *huertas* [irrigated lands] of Andalusia, to the oasis of the Maghrib, to the valley of the Nile, the Sawad of Iraq, and all the way to Farghana.[6] Iqbal explained why this was so.

---

constituency. This quest, according to Minault, grew out of Islamic cultural and educational reform movements of the nineteenth century. *The Khilafat Movement,* p. 208.

[3] Hardy, *Muslims of British India,* p. 196.

[4] Smith, *Modern Islam in India,* p. 240.

[5] Bipan Chandra, *Communalism in Modern India,* p. 172.

[6] One of the most eloquent instances of this nostalgia for the departed glory of Muslims is in Hali's famous poem 'The Flow and Ebb of Islam', composed in 1879. So great was its influence that Syed Ahmad Khan is reported to have said that if he was asked about his good deeds on the Day of Judgement, he would say: 'I got Hali to write his *Mussadas*'. See Table 5:1 as illustrative of the interest in the political, social and cultural history of Muslim countries. Of course, the list of publications is by no means exhaustive.

The record of the past, he observed in *Rumuz-i Bekhudi,* 'illuminates the conscience of a People, memory of the past achievements makes it self-aware;...the present thrusts its head up from the past, and from thy present shall thy future stem'.[7]

When Islam fell on evil days in the nineteenth and twentieth centuries, the heritage of the past stood forth as a symbol of community pride and distinction. [Table 5:1] Some eloquent instances of nostalgia for the departed glory was expressed in Hali's 'The Ebb and Flow of Islam,[8] in Shibli's pan-Islamic anguish and in Iqbal's ode to once-Arab Sicily.[9] Iqbal also wrote *Bilaad-i Islamia* (Muslim Cities) to express his deep emotional loyalty to the world of Islam——to Delhi, Baghdad, Cordova—'the light of Muslim's eye,' Constantinople and Medina—the *watan* of all Muslims, their centre and refuge. All these places had fine, grand and sublime achievements to their credit. Mohamed Ali told his readers that

[7] A.J. Arberry, *The Mystery of Selflessness* (London, 1953), p. 97.

[8] For example,

Would anyone see humiliation transgressing her limits?
Let him look at Islam, not lifting her head after falling.
That high tide follows low tide, he would never admit,
Who would watch the ebbing wave of this ocean of ours.

G.E. Ward and C.S. Tute, *The Quatrains of Hali* (Oxford University Press, 1932), p. 65.

[9] The poem read:

Once thou wast the cradle of the civilization of this race
The fire of whose glance was world captivating beauty
The nightingales of Shiraz wailed over Baghdad;
And Dagh wept tears of blood over Delhi

To sing the dirge of ruin was to fall to my lot;
This torture—yea, self-torture was reserved for me,
Tell me of thy anguish; I am too full of pain;
I am the dust raised by that caravan which once broke its journey here.
Paint me that picture of the old,
Rouse me by telling the tale of bygone days;
And I shall carry thy gift to India,
And make others weep as I weep now.

S.A. Latif, *The Influence of English Literature on Urdu Literature* (London, 1924), pp. 111–13.

the Indian Mussalman's heart throbs in unison with the Moor of Fez, who sees his country passing into alien hands, with the Persian of Tehran who feels the grip of the Russian Cossack on his throat, and with the Turk of Stamboul who has to watch an act of shameless brigandage with impotent rage.[10]

There was more to it than just that. Muslims were asked to seek inspiration from their own *Islamic* heritage and turn to the Quranic and *Sunna* ideal paradigm as a blueprint to confront colonial aggression and exploitation. Syed Ahmad in India and Mohammad Abduh in Egypt sought a reformed, revitalized Islam that would neither be beholden to western trends nor weighed down by age-old accretions. They insisted that a reformed Islam, with its supportive values of brotherhood, community and union and its proven ability to express the poetry of collective life, could co-exist with western ideas, accept their challenges and replace the imitation, either of Europe or of antiquated tradition, with a dynamic and innovative culture such as distinguished Islam at the time of first generation of *salaf*. Thus the *salafiya* doctrine in Egypt came to be associated with attacks on mysticism, saint-veneration, and specifically the sufi doctrines, just as it was embedded in programmes for modern education that emphasized reason and rational sciences.

As the modernist-reformist ideas of Abduh and Jamaluddin Afghani gained adherents in countries under colonial domination, Islam became an ever more frequent symbol of and channel for nationalists protests. In fact, pan-Islamism—a multifaceted, often opaque search for an Islamic meaning in the modern world—was the vehicle through which radical and nationalist ideas were conveyed. Thus Tan Malaka, representing Indonesia at the fourth Congress of the Comintern in 1922, maintained that pan-Islamism meant 'the national struggle for freedom'.[11] Transposed into Islamic terms, it signified the unity and solidarity of all Muslims against the common threat of western empires which had penetrated into the heartlands of the Muslim world. A

[10] *Comrade,* 14 October 1911.

[11] R.V. Niel, 'From Netherlands East Indies to Republic of Indonesia 1900–1945', Harry Eveling (ed.), *The Development of Indonesian Society* (Queensland, 1979), pp. 112, 120.

TABLE 5.1
Published writings on some Muslim countries

Author	Title Year/Place of Publication
Maulvi Mohammad Inshaullah	*Saltanat-i Usmania ke Maujooda Halaat* (Amritsar, 1897).
Sirajuddin	*Hayaat-i Salauddin* (Amritsar, 1897).
Author not known	*Musafir-i Damishqi* (Lucknow, 1899).
Author not known	*Ayyam-i Arab* (Lucknow, 1899).
Syed Sha ı Kabir	*Tazkirat al-Ikraam: Tarikh-i Arab wa Islam* (Kanpur, 1900).
Author not known	*Tarikh-i Turkaan-i Rum* (Moradabad, 1889), vol. 1.
Mirza Hairat	*Khilafat-i Usmania* (Delhi, 1901).
Mohammad Farhatullah	*Tarikh-i Ref* (Bijnor, 1901). History of Morocco.
Aghlab Mohani (Mohammad Husain)	*Nairang-i Afghan: Qaumi aur Mulki Tarikh Afghanistan* (Lucknow, 1904).
Hakim Abdullah Rashid	*Mauritius aur Islam* (Bombay, 1906).
Mau na Shibli Nomani	*Safar Nama-i Rum wa Misr-o-Shaam* (Azamgarh, 1340 A.H.) and his multi-volume history of Persian literature.
Mohammd Abdullah	*Damishq* (Amritsar, 1911).
Sajjad Hyder Yaldaram	*Lehra: Ek Turkish novel ka tarjuma* (Aligarh, n.d.).
Abdul Halim Sharar	*Shaheed-i Wafa* (Lahore, 1920). Account of the social and cultural life of the Muslims in Spain.
Wajahat Husain	*Anwar Pasha* (Lahore, 1921).
A.R. Bulandshahari	*Seerat-i Ghazi Mustafa Kamal Pasha* (Bijnor, 1921).
Ameer Ali	*Short History of the Saracens* (London, 1921).
Abdul Wahid Ibn-i Ali	*Khilafat-i Muwahidda* (Madras, 1922). Translated from the Arabic—a history of Morocco and Spain.
Asghar Ali Nizami	*Shaan-i Islam aur Turki Talwaar* (Lahore, 1923).
S. Khuda Bukhsh	*Contributions to the History of Islamic Civilization* (Calcutta, 1929). 2 vols.

Abdul Rab	*Sair-i Undalus* (Allahabad, 1934). Historical novel on the Muslims in Spain.
Abdur Rahman Shauq	*Hayaat-i Khalid bin Walid* (Lahore, 1936).
Mohammad Aslam Jairajpuri	*Tarikh-i Millat* (Delhi, in 10 vols.)
Qazi Abdul Ghaffar	*Aasaar-i Jamaluddin* (Delhi, 1940).
Maulana Saeed Ahmad	*Mussalmanon ka Urooj-o-Zawaal* (Delhi, 1942).

renewed commitment to faith and action, individual or collective, private or public, was understood by the ideologues of the pan-Islamic idea not only as an act of defense against the intellectual and cultural imperialism of the West, but as the pre-condition for the building of a strong, united Islam as the only road of salvation for the world.

India was not the only country swept by the pan-Islamic tide. Abdul Hamid II, who reigned from 1876 to 1908, attracted allegiance from many African Muslims who acknowledged Turkey as the only remaining Islamic power in a world of aggressive Christian States. Thus the Sultan had been addressed by and replied to the Muslims in Lagos in 1894 on the importance of western education. From the 1870s there were close contacts between Istanbul and Cape Town Muslims. The Sultan of Zanzibar was entertained by Abdul Hamid, and as late as 1910 Friday prayers in the capital were still being said in the name of the Ottoman Sultan. At the outbreak of World War I, the Ottoman call for a *jehad* against the Allied powers was widely distributed in North Africa. It surfaced also in East and Central Africa, where, in 1915, the British arrest in Nyasaland of a Muslim from Mozambique uncovered Swahili tracts bearing Istanbul's call for holy war against the English. Likewise, pan-Islamic sympathies came to the fore in Sudan. That it did not develop greatly was on account of special efforts to counteract the pan-Islamic propaganda and on account of the fact that the Mahdi's revolt had been directed against the Turko-Egyptian regime. One of its aims was to reject the Khalifa at Istanbul as the representative of the Muslim world. The position had not changed when World War I broke out and there was no reason for the Mahdists to co-operate with the Turks in the name of Islam.[12]

In Indonesia, pan-Islamism constituted a danger to the political *status quo*. So also the modernist Islamic ideas being taught in Cairo, in particular those stemming from the teachings of Abduh.[13] Snouck Hugronje, the Dutch authority on Islam,

[12] C.C. Stewart, 'Islam', A.D. Roberts (ed.), *The Cambridge History of Africa* (Cambridge, 1986), pp. 199–200.

[13] See Daniel Noer, *The Modernist Muslim Movement in Indonesia 1900–1942* (Oxford, 1973).

observed that Indonesians then studying in the international Islamic milieu of Mecca were absorbing pan-Islamic notions 'which can make their disposition towards the European administration of their fatherland unfavourable'. But he altered the government policy of restricting pilgrimage to Mecca on the grounds that as a religious doctrine Islam should be free of interference, although as a political force it should be destroyed.[14] During the 1880s, some 2,000 pilgrims were counted annually as leaving the Dutch provinces for Mecca. After the opening of the Suez Canal in 1869, the number grew steadily each year until, by the late 1890s, the figure was fluctuating from more than 11,000 in 1895 (a 'Great Pilgrimage' year) to 7,000 in 1900.[15]

C. Poenson, a nineteenth century missionary in Central Java, noted the profound influence of *Haj* in heightening anti-imperialist consciousness.[16] More recently, William R. Roff has described the impact of even brief exposure to a wholly Muslim environment in which the universality of the faith was demonstrated by a congregation of pilgrims of all races, all levels of society. Returning to the Indies, to the towns and villages, the mosques and religious schools, they took with them not only a renewed zeal for purification of action and belief but a certain readiness to reject the colonial *status quo* if the occasion should present itself.[17]

[14] George McTurnan Kahin, *Nationalism and Revolution in Indonesia* (Cornell, 1952), pp. 44–48.

[15] William R. Roff, 'South-East Asian Islam in the Nineteenth Century', in P.M. Holt, Ann K.S. Lambton, Bernard Lewis (eds.), *Cambridge History of Islam* (Cambridge, 1970), vol. 2, pp. 180–81. In India, too, an average of just over 12,000 pilgrims sailed from Bombay from 1882 to 1893. The numbers increased as the government initiated several measures, including the formation of *Haj* committees, to make the journey less painful. See UP Government (GAD), Poll. F.No. 89, 1894 and F.No. 142, 1913, UPSA. Also, see J.A. Rahim, *Report of the Special Haj Enquiry,* in Public and Judicial Department, F.No. 8/758, IOLR.

[16] He noted that Arabia was not just the 'uniting centre' for devoted pilgrims, but that the *Haj* provided both the occasion and an opportunity for political leaders to devise future plans. Quoted in Noer, op. cit., pp. 25–26. Like many of his contemporaries, Poenson was haunted by the spectre of a pan-Islamic conspiracy being hatched annually at Mecca.

[17] Roff, op.cit., p. 172. Again, this was also the point made by Iqbal and

III

Among Sunni Muslims, who formed the overwhelming majority of the Muslim population, Turkey's Sultan was the *Amir al-Mumineen* (Commander of the Faithful) or the *Khilafat al-Muslimeen.*[18] The Khilafat was the viceroyalty of the Prophet of Islam, ordained by Divine Law for the perpetuation of Islam and the continued observance of the *Shariat.* In addition, the Khalifa was the defender of the Holy Places of Islam *(Jazirat al-Arab),* which at one time extended—from Aden to the Mountains of Syria—and the sea coast to the agricultural lowlands of Iraq.[19] The *Jazirat al-Arab* included Constantinople,[20]

---

several other writers in India. For Iqbal, see Schimmel, *Gabriel's Wing,* pp. 195–96. Also, Meer Hasan Ali, *Observations on the Mussulmans of India* (Reprint of 1834 edn., Oxford, 1974), pp. 112–13; Mushir Hosain Kidwai, *Pan-Islamism and Bolshevism* (London, 1937), pp. 224–26.

[18] The *Sadiq al-Akhbaar* of Lahore commented on 24 February 1904 that whenever the Turkish Sultan is in danger, the Muslims in India offer prayers and observe fast for his well being. Quoted in I.A. Malik, *Punjab Muslim Press and the Muslim World 1885–1911* (Lahore, 1974). Likewise, the secretary of state for India was surprised to learn that Muslims 'pray weekly for the Sultan.' Austen Chamberlain to Chelmsford, 29 August 1916, Home Poll. Deposit, December 1916, F.No. 20, NAI.

[19] Mohamed Ali reiterated time and again that the mandate of *Jazirat al-Arab* 'has been given to us by the Prophet'. Mazharul Haq stated that the areas located therein 'touched the deepest religious sentiment of the followers of Islam' and that it 'must remain under the suzerainty of the Muslim Khalifa'. *Motherland,* 19 January 1922, quoted in Qeyamuddin Ahmad and J.S. Jha, *Mazharul Haque* (Delhi, 1976), p. 91. Obviously, the prospect of the areas in *Jazirat al-Arab* falling under non-Muslim control caused much consternation. So also the widely circulated rumours of the sacred precincts being desecrated. Circulated through vernacular pamphlets, such rumours were clearly intended to rouse religious passions. See, for example, S. Ghafoor Shah, *Khoon-i Khirman aur sada-i intiqaam;* Munshi Wali Mohammad, *Islam ki Faryaad* (Delhi, 1971); Majid Ahmad, *Dard-i Khilafat* (Aligarh, n.d.). Proscribed Publications (8, 44, 142), IOLR. Notice the following verse:

Ae barq aaj shola-fishaan kyon nahin hai tu
Ae abr aaj girya kunaan kyon nahin hai tu
Darya-i qahr aaj rawaan kyon nahin hai tu
Islam aaj kufr ke narghe men aa gaya
Baadal siyah rang ka Kaaba pe chaa gaya

Jerusalem, Medina, and, above all, Mecca with its *Baitullah,* the focal point of daily prayers and the annual *Haj.*[21] Mohamed Ali announced in London :

We, who consider ourselves to be the spiritual heirs of Abraham, Moses and Jesus, consider that this is a land apart and consecrated in a peculiar degree and reserved for us. We are charged with the duty of maintaining its sanctity inviolate, of keeping it peaceful and tranquil, a sanctuary for the faithful, and safe for theocracy. In order to preserve that sanctity and peace and tranquillity which we desire, it is necessary that it should remain with us. It would be a sad day indeed for us when any part of it goes out of the hands of the Muslims, for then we would have betrayed a divine trust. Muslims will never acquiesce in any arrangement that permitted any form of control being exercized by a non-Muslim power over any part of the *Jazirat al-Arab.*[22]

O the thunderbolt why dost not thou scatter flames?
O the lightning why thou wailest not?
O the clouds why weepest not thou?
Why is the river of curse a frozen puddle and flows not?
Islam has been swamped and overwhelmed by the Unbelief
And the Kaaba has been engulfed by darkness.
Proscribed Publications (8), IOLR.

[20] Constantinople was one of the holy cities, ranked next only to Mecca, Medina and Jerusalem. It was identified with the past glories of Islam and regarded as a 'relic of a great national and religious value by the whole Muslim world'. Yaqub Hasan to Lloyd George, 1 July 1919, Foreign and Political Dept., External B, F.No. 361–68, October 1920, NAI; Home Poll. A, F.No. 363–68, May 1919, NAI.

[21] The number of Muslims who undertook the arduous journey, so vividly described by Meer Hasan Ali, an English woman married to a Shia official in Lucknow, was quite considerable. The numbers increased in the first decade of the twentieth century (Table 5.2) for the reasons indicated above.

TABLE 5.2

Number of Pilgrims from British India, 1907–8 to 1913–14

1907–8	1908–9	1909–10	1910–11	1911–12	1912–13	1913–14
21,648	15,947	20,901	17,884	22,995	15,555	15,186

Source : *Statistical Abstract for British India, 1916–17* (Calcutta, 1919), vol. 4, p. 129.

[22] See Hasan (ed.), *Mohamed Ali in Indian Politics,* vol. 2, pp. 231–32, vol. 3, pp. 65, 79, 125–26.

For these reasons, interest in Turkey's welfare continued: each time it was involved in hostilities, like the Russo-Turkish war of 1877–78 or the Greco-Turkish war of 1897, Indian Muslims took up the cudgels for Turkey and reaffirmed their attachment to and prayed for the well-being of its Sultan. 'If the Muhammadans of the world were compared to the human body', commented the *Akhbaar-i Am,* 'the Sultan would be the heart and brain'.[23] Anthony MacDonnell, lieutenant-governor of UP, quoted to the viceroy a leaflet describing the Ottoman Sultan as *Amir al-Mumineen* and *Padshah-i Mussalmanan* and reported the 'great sympathy' for him 'partly due to incitement from outside India and partly spontaneous'. Many more people, he was told, had taken to wearing the Turkish *fez.* This, he concluded, 'is perhaps the straw indicating how the wind is beginning to blow'.[24]

The incitement from outside came from two distinct sources. In the first place, the British government exploited pro-Turkish sensibilities in order to secure Indian Muslim loyalty, as in 1857, and to protect their imperial interests from Russian encroachments by bolstering 'the sick man of Europe', as they did from the Crimean war of 1853-56 onwards. Then, the Sultan of Turkey, Abdul Hamid II, sent his agents to India, as to other lands, to rally support and enthusiasm for his feeble regime which was threatened by external aggression and internal strife, caused by nationalist movements sprung up among his Christian Balkan subjects [American, Greek, Romanian and Bulgarian] in southeast Europe.

Syed Ahmad was the only prominent Muslim to dispute Abdul Hamid's pretensions. The pan-Islamic surge threatened to wreck his effort to prop up the Anglo-Muslim alliance in India; so he wanted to cut the silver cord which tied

[23] *Akhbar-i Am,* 14 March 1895, SNNR, Punjab.

[24] Hardy, *Muslims of British India,* p. 177. Blunt was told on the eve of his visit to India that he should not say anything against the Sultan of Turkey, because his name 'was now venerated in India as it has not formerly been'. Blunt, *India Under Ripon,* p. 13. Also, see Yusuf Husain Khan, 'Indian Muslims and the Caliphate', S.T. Lokhandwalla (ed.), *India and Contemporary Islam* (Indian Institute for Advanced Study: Shimla, 1971), pp. 168–174.

Muslims to the international fraternity of 'all believers', personified in the Khilafat. He spoke against the Turcophilia among his co-religionists, arguing that they were legally bound to obey the writ not of an external Muslim Khalifa but of the British Indian government. In 1900, one of Syed Ahmad's associates suggested that Muslims should refrain from printing the Crescent on their book on the ground that it may be mistaken as a sign of their leaning towards the Turkish government. But such endeavours to sever the Muslim attachment to the Turkish Khilafat were greeted with suspicion and distrust. Nawab Mohsinul Mulk, one of Syed Ahmad's most distinguished successors at the Aligarh college, learnt his lesson the hard way. When he expressed unhappiness over the ever-increasing pan-Islamic meetings on campus, he was castigated as a 'downright sycophant'.[25]

The most bitter criticizm of Syed Ahmad's views came from that celebrated roving reformer, teacher and political agitator, Jamaluddin al-Asadabadi 'al-Afghani'. He regarded the Aligarh reformer's religious views and his educational programme as ancillaries to his political servitude to the British and chided him for relying on them instead of joining hands with the Indian nationalists. Afghani considered Syed Ahmad as his main adversary in India, opposed to pan-Islamism, isolating Indian Muslims from the rest of *Dar al-Islam,* especially from the Turks, and hostile to the conception of a universal Muslim Khilafat. According to him, the reassertion of Muslim identity and solidarity were prerequisites for restoring political and cultural independence, and unity and solidarity were essential at both levels.[26]

[25] *Jasus* (Agra), 14 July 1906; *Al-Aziz* (Agra), 28 July 1906, SNNR, UP.

[26] Afghani was in India between 1857 and 1865. He came again in 1879 and spent three years travelling to places like Bombay, Hyderabad, Bhopal and Calcutta. The purpose of his visit was to

> meet with all the *navvabs* and princes and *ulama* and grandees of that land and to explain to them one by one the results that are manifested from unity and solidarity in the whole world and the injuries that have appeared from division and disunity; and to caress their ears with the mystery of the *hadith;* ...and to express inspiring and prudent words and to attract the friendship and co-operation of the learned and the eloquent; and to breathe into them the new spirit of love of nationality and to rend the curtain of their neglect

The Muslims were to be united as the Germans and Italians were united, and Afghani passed his life in search for a Muslim monarch to whom he could be a Bismarck or a Cavour. The enemy from which Islam needed to be saved was Europe, and especially Britain, the imperial power in India and Egypt. Afghani therefore spent the greater part of his life travelling from one country to the other as the chief exponent of pan-Islamism. His efforts did not go unrewarded: his pan-Islamic vision inspired various activist groups in different lands and lives on patiently, if amorphously, in the aspirations of many Muslims.[27] It is also curious and relevant that the only instance where his political programme of combined radicalism, modernism, nationalism and pan-Islamism ever became a serious political agenda of a vibrant and spirited opposition was in the Khilafat agitation in India, years after his death.[28]

---

to explain to them the place of the luminous Sultanate in the world of Islam; and to reveal and make manifest to this group the fact that the perpetuation of religion depends on the perpetuation of this government. And in all the mosques of the famous cities I shall light a flame in their inner hearth by means of appealing sermons and *hadith* of the Best of the Prophets, and I shall together burn out their patience and long-suffering.

Quoted in Nikkie R. Keddie, *Sayyid Jamal ad-Din "al-Afghani": A Political Biography* (Los Angeles, 1972), p. 130.

[27] See Keddie, op.cit., p. 167; Fazlur Rahman, *Islam* (London, 1966, p.277; Albert Hourani, *Arabic Thought in the Liberal Age 1798–1939* (Oxford, 1970), pp. 118–19; Anwar Moazzam, *Jamal al-Din al-Afghani: A Muslim Intellectual* (Delhi, 1983), p. xiii, points out that Afghani's main contribution was to provide a 'broad intellectual framework for redefining the relationship between Islam and the changing world'.

[28] It is often argued that Afghani's reputation and influence was to a large extent posthumous and the work of disciples, or else of academic writers and publicists 'eager to discover trends and precursors' to magnify the importance of their subject. Elie Kedourie, *Afghani and Abduh: An Essay on Religious Unbelief and Political Activism in Modern Islam* (London, 1966), p. 3, and Keddie, op. cit., p. 26. Apart from the fact that contemporarary writers like Blunt point to Afghani's influence on a section of Muslims, it must also be borne in mind that Afghani's ideas gave moral support to the 'instinctive and natural tendency' among many Muslims to see western military and political domination, as enemy number one. It has been rightly suggested that 'even if this was only the initial phase of the various

The power of Afghani's appeal was felt generally in the first decade of the twentieth century, when he became a symbol of the pan-Islamic enterprise. Among those who came under his spell was Shibli who visited Istanbul in 1893, received a medal from Abdul Hamid, and parleyed with Afghani's co-worker and disciple, Mohammad Abduh.[29] His pan-Islamic ideas were echoed in Hali's *Musaddas.* His strong advocacy of the co-existence of diverse religious faiths was in accord with Mohamed Ali's idea, expressed in 1923, of the 'Federation of Faiths'. And his view of a natural solidarity beyond the nation: that which binds together all the peoples of the East threatened by the West, was developed by Ansari, who led the medical mission to Constantinople and was a key figure in the Khilafat agitation. At the All-India Khilafat Conference, the Edinburgh-trained physician-surgeon spoke of an Asiatic Federation that would promote solidarity among the peoples and countries of Asia and rescue them from the political and economic bondage of Europe.[30] Such suggestions were, to an appreciable degree, inspired by the anti-colonial concerns of Afghani.

Afghani also influenced Iqbal and Azad. The future *Shaair-i Mashriq* acknowledged that 'the man whose deep insights into the inner meaning of the history of Muslim thought and life, combined with a broad vision engendered by his wide experience of man and manners, would have made him a link between the past and the future, was Jamal-ud-Din Afghani'.[31] He was

national independence movements which later, for the most part, almost ceased to appeal to Islam, this form of 'Islamic protest' had a direct and more lasting effect in the spheres of culture and religion'. Jacques Waardenburg, 'Islam as a Vehicle of Protest', Ernest Gellner (ed.), *Islamic Dilemmas: Reformers, Nationalists and Industrialization* (Berlin, 1985) p. 28.

[29] Shibli Nomani, *Safarnama-i Rum wa Misr-o-Shaam* (Azamgarh, 1921); Ahmad, *Islamic Modernism,* p. 129.

[30] *The Indian Annual Register,* 1923, vol 1, p.921.

[31] Mohammad Iqbal, *The Reconstruction of Religious Thought in Islam* (Delhi, 1974: reprint), p. 97. In fact, Iqbal admired Afghani who 'never claimed to be a prophet; yet no other man in our time has stirred the soul of Islam more deeply than he'. He was of the view that 'if somebody deserves to be called renewer after Abdul Wahab—the founder of the Wahabi movement—it is Jamaluddin Afghani'. Quoted in Schimmel, *Gabriel's*

interested most of all in Afghani's endeavour to find in Islam a means of unification in resisting the domination of the West, and shared his desire to express unity on the religious basis of Muslims as a supra class and a supra-national entity. Iqbal, who was still composing and reciting his patriotic songs on the eve of and during World War I, tied his hopes for liberation from colonial dependency to pan-Islamic solidarity. This was reflected in the poem *Shama Aur Shaair* (The Candle and the Poet), written in 1912. In his reply to the *Shikwa* (Complaint of God), he struck the same note :

The trouble that is raging in the Balkans
Is a message of awakening to the forgetful
Thou may'st think it the means of vexing thy heart
But in reality it is a test of thy self-sacrifice and self-reliance[32]

It is not sufficiently recognized that Azad's leadership of the Khilafat movement, far from being a sudden or accidental phenomenon, was the outcome of several years of diligent political, ideological and organizational work. Nor is it adequately appreciated that when he began his public career in 1911–12, he had behind him nearly a decade of close and dedicated involvement in the affairs of the nation and the community, of study, writing and reflection, and—not least—of concerned observation of the state of Islamic societies.

Afghani's influence on Azad can be seen from the time of his stay in Constantinople and Cairo, when he first developed close relations with the *Al-Manar* [The Lighthouse] group of Syrian and Egyptain scholars.[33] This is when the young Azad may have

---

Wing, p. 21, and L.R. Gorden-Polonskya, 'Ideology of Muslim Nationalism,' in Hafeez Malik (ed.), *Iqbal: Poet Philosopher of Pakistan,* pp. 115-16.

[32] Latif, *The Influence of English Literature on Urdu Literature,* pp. 111-12.

[33] Aziz Ahmad, *Islamic Culture,* p. 67. For Afghani's influence on one of Azad's devoted followers, see Abdul Ghaffar, *Aasar-i Jamaluddin* (Delhi, 1940). Ghaffar claimed that he was inspired by Ajmal Khan and Ansari to undertake the work. Also, see Amin Afghani, *Syed Jamaluddin Afghani* (Amritsar, 1940). For a different version, see Douglas, *Abul Kalam Azad,* pp. 82-83.

evolved a distinctive vision of Islam, embracing its spiritual, intellectual, social and political dimensions, to which he held fast for more than half a century. He developed, sometime around 1909–10, the nationalist and anti-imperialist thrust of Afghani's ideas in the *Al-Hilal,* inspired by the *Al-Urwa al-wuthqa* [The Indissoluble Link], an anti-imperialist journal published by Afghani in collaboration with Abduh. He also tried to galvanize Muslims into strong pan-Islamic fervour and action. Political fidelity, according to Azad, was due to the Ottoman Khalifa and compliance with his wishes was binding on the faithful.[34] He went on to argue, as did Jamaluddin Afghani, that *jehad* was imperative against those who had occupied even a part of the *Dar al-Islam.*[35]

Azad provided greater ideological coherence to the concerns of fellow-Muslims who had come to terms with Indian nationalism and its ideal of a unified anti-colonial struggle. In addition to his symbolic use of Islam in heightening anti-colonial consciousness, he emphasized the need for a powerful inter-communal union; in fact he cited the Hudaybiyya Treaty of 628 as a valid historical precedent for a Hindu-Muslim alliance. He asserted that uniting with one category of non-Muslims, the Hindus, against another category of non-Muslims, the British, was obligatory.[36] In a similar vein, Ansari, in December 1920, quoted the *Sura-i Mumtahanah* [60:8–9] to argue that Muslims should behave 'righteously, affectionately and in a friendly manner towards all those non-Muslims who are neither at war with Muslims nor are they assailants intending to invade or occupy their territories.[37] Earlier, both Azad and Ansari had commended the Muslim League meeting at Bombay in 1915 that resulted in 'a clear and effective step...in the direction of Hindu-Muslim

[34] Azad tried to legitimize the institution of Khilafat on the ground that the Ottoman Empire provided the 'political centre' (*Siyaasi Markaz),* so essential for the survival of a community and a nation.

[35] He wrote that so long as the world of Islam did not come together in an 'international and universal alliance' the future of Muslims everywhere would be in jeopardy. Quoted in S.M. Ikram, *Modern Muslim India and the Birth of Pakistan* (London, 1965), p. 146.

[36] Hardy, *Partners in Freedom,* pp. 22, 28-29.

[37] Quoted in Hasan, *A Nationalist Conscience,* p. 82.

national unity', and lent their approval to the Lucknow Pact a year later.[38]

This emphasis on a peaceful *modus vivendi* with the Hindus reflected the viewpoint of Afghani and Abduh who, in answer to inquiries from India, had endorsed inter-religious co-operation.[39] Afghani, in particular, advocated inter-communal oneness and defied any breach in the anti-British front. In his articles published in the Hyderabad journal, *Muallim-i Shafiq,* he evoked not only the universal Islamic but also national aspirations with special emphasis on the affinity of Hindu-Muslim interests. And just as he helped awaken Egyptian nationalism by alluding to the ancient glories of the past, so in India, even when talking to a primarily Muslim audience, he harped on the glory of ancient India.[40] His appeal to take pride in that epoch of India's past was no different from his earlier exhortation to Egyptian Muslims to seek inspiration from pre-Islamic Egyptian greatness. In both cases Afghani appealed to an effective basis for solidarity against the foreigner.[41] His message inspired, among others, Azad. He was one of those Muslims who pioneered the pan-Islamic movement in the first decade of the twentieth century and later piloted the Khilafat campaign in all its tumultuous phases.

Azad never ever wavered in his conviction that Indian Muslims should be up in front fighting for freedom.[42]Nor was his commitment to Hindu-Muslim unity ever in question. 'Not only is our national freedom impossible without it', he declared as Congress president in 1923, 'we cannot create without it principles of humanity within ourselves'. He continued:

> If today an angel descending from the clouds were to declare from the top of the Qutb Minar in Delhi, 'Discard Hindu-Muslim unity and

[38] Douglas, op.cit.

[39] Hourani, op.cit., p. 118.

[40] Keddie, op.cit., pp. 155, 159–60.

[41] Ibid., p. 160, and by the same author, *Islamic Response to Imperialism: Political and Religious Writings of Sayyid Jamal al-Din "Al-Afghani"* (California University Press, 1968), p. 59.

[42] Azad proclaimed that it was God's wish that Muslims should stand up for the freedom of India and it was His Pleasure *(marzi-i Khudawandi)* that they should give new life to the forgotten duty of *jehad (farz-i Jehad)* Hardy, *Partners in Freedom,* p. 22.

within twenty-four hours swaraj is yours', I would prefer to sacrifice swaraj rather than Hindu-Muslim unity. For delay in the attainment of swaraj will be a loss to India alone, but if our unity disappears, it will be lost to the whole world of humanity.[43]

The influence of Afghani is also evident in the exercise—one that has scarcely received scholarly attention—to reconcile pan-Islamic sentiments with nationalistic aims and to remove the widespread conception that the essence of pan-Islamism implied a break with territorial nationalism. The ideologues of the Khilafat movement insisted that the sum and substance of pan-Islamism was to remove foreign domination; so their activities, bound with the concept of an emerging Indian nation, had an obvious nationalist dimension. They also pointed out that, in spite of their pan-Islamic ambition, or fantasy as some preferred to call it, they had their own Indian community clearly in mind and were not oblivious to its trials and tribulations. The emblem used on the Khilafat delegation stationery, which was made up of twin circles of equal size and overlapping, with the word 'Khilafat' on one and the word 'India' on the other, was symbolic of their loyalties and their vision of a free India and the liberation of Muslim countries from the yoke of colonial rule. Ansari linked colonial policies in India with the larger interests of the West in exploiting the weaker nations of the East and in perpetuating 'the bondage and slavery of Asiatic people'. To him it was not only a question of India's honour and freedom, but of a great struggle for emancipating all the enslaved people from the thraldom of the West.[44]

It has been argued that such notions of independence from foreign rule were advanced to restore a single Islamic state under a revived Khilafat, that the call for *jehad* had a strong traditional basis, and that the anti-colonial rhetoric was merely eyewash, a clever device for achieving sectarian ends. It is also pointed out that the Muslim alliance with nationalist forces was of an 'ephemeral and opportunistic' nature, because they were moved only by loyalty to the invisible theocracy of which God was the

[43] Douglas, op.cit., pp. 193–94.
[44] Quoted in Hasan, *A Nationalist Conscience*, p. 83.

ruler, and that they had developed a nationalism of their own which was Islamic in tone and content.

I have tried to question some of these formulations by arguing that the Khilafat agitation, in fact, served an objective need of mobilizing large segments of Indian society against colonial authority, and, in the process, made them more conscious than even before of forging and strengthening inter-communal links. Muslims, in particular, were at the head of this mobilization. This was a singularly important feat. It was also an unprecedented one. What deserves equal consideration is that the Khilafat movement, despite its pan-Islamic bias, merged into a general political struggle far outstripping its original limitations.

The relationship between the Indians and the Turks was in the nature of a compact, because both Turkey and India were subjected to colonial rule. Azad observed that the agitation in India had, at first, been directed towards the salvation of the Khalifa and the Ottoman Empire, but later it became an integral part of the issue of British imperialism. Khilafat workers must win India's liberty by means of non-co-operation; only then would they be able to save the Khalifa. In the presidential addresses delivered before the Khilafat Committee from 1921 to 1925, Azad was very careful not to let his audience divert its attention from the Indian scene and used pan-Islamic sentiments to generate enthusiasm for India's swaraj. Mohamed Ali's advice was the same: Muslims must fight for swaraj with their non-Muslim brethren, for only in this way would it be possible to achieve the Khilafat aim. He also tried to show the consistency between pan-Islamism and nationalism and to establish that his community's reactions to events in Turkey deepened their involvement in the anti-colonial struggle in India and brought them closer to the Congress under Gandhi's leadership.[45] That, according to him, was the reason why Muslims were able to easily swing back and forth between pan-Islamic and local nationalist appeals; depending upon which was a more appropriate anti-imperialist weapon in a specific Indian situation.

It is a lesser known fact of modern Indian history that the

[45] See chapter three above, and Mohamed Ali to the Sultan of Turkey, 28 May 1920, Hasan (ed.), *Mohamed Ali in Indian Politics*, vol. 3, p. 88.

Khilafat committees were often indistinguishable from local Congress bodies, volunteer groups, Kisan Sabhas and Home Rule Leagues in their composition and political objectives. 'There is nothing to choose locally', commented an official, 'between a gathering under the auspices of the Kisan Sabha or of the Khilafat Committee. Both movements appear to have been completely captured by the non-co-operation party...'[46]. This was not just a joyful demonstration of the newly-found sense of solidarity, but an awareness of the 'extraordinary stiffening-up' of a demoralized, backward, and broken-up people taking part in disciplined, joint action on a countrywide scale.[47]

In several areas of UP peasant unrest was not just tacked on to the Khilafat and non-co-operation programme, but Khilafat committees and Kisan Sabhas provided a tangible sign of acting in unison in attacking their common identifiable enemy, the landlord, who was perceived as an ally of the government. Here lay the danger in governments' assessment, a fact referred to when the secretary of the Rae Bareli Khilafat Committee spoke at a Kisan Sabha meeting on 6 February. 'What might have been in its way a harmless and beneficent movement', observed an official, 'is in danger of being rapidly perverted into a vehicle for virulent abuse of and violent agitation against the Government'.[48] Evidence of the potentially dangerous alliance came from other areas as well. A Kisan Sabha rally at Fyzabad, held on 20-21 December 1920, was probably organized by Khilafat workers.[49] Local Khilafat leaders, Lal Mohammad and Maulvi Riasat Husain, addressed a similar gathering at village Salethu in Maharajganj on 2 February 1921; the meeting at village Balla in the same police station area a week earlier was organized by Amid Syed, a local Khilafat agitator.

A notable feature of such meetings was the attempt to establish

[46] S.R. Mayers to A.G. Shireff, deputy-commissioner, 25 February 1921, UP Government (GAD), F.No. 50, 1921, Box No. 135, UPSA. All subsequent references are drawn from the same file.

[47] Nehru, *An Autobiography*, p. 76.

[48] Note on Rae Bareli disturbances, op.cit.

[49] M.H. Siddiqi, *Agrarian Unrest in North India: The United Provinces 1918–22* (Delhi, 1978), p. 149; Kapil Kumar, *Peasants in Revolt: Tenants, Landlords, Congress and the Raj in Oudh* (Delhi, 1984), pp. 146, 165.

a definite link between the demands of the Kisans and the Khilafatists, on the one hand, and the attainment of swaraj, on the other; in fact, words like 'Khilafat', 'kisan ekta', 'swaraj', 'Gandhi' were all intended to conjure up in the minds of the people a picture of bringing about a better world under the direction of better leaders.[50] Peasants in many places believed that the promised swaraj was coming soon and their economic salvation lay in the preservation of their faith, the Khilafat and the interests of the Muslim world outside India.[51] Thus Maulvi Salamatullah, associated with Abdul Bari, assured a Kisan Sabha gathering that the peasant interests would be protected only after the dignity and prestige of the Khalifa was restored. Kamaluddin Jafri, the Allahabad-based lawyer, linked the redressal of their grievances with the attainment of swaraj under the Congress directives. This view, expressed at a Kisan Sabha meeting at Akbarpur in Fyzabad district on 27 January 1921, was endorsed by Hafiz Alam and Mohammad Nabi of Tanda, important Khilafatists in eastern UP.[52] Jawaharlal Nehru was among those present at the conference.

The collaboration between the Khilafatists and groups of

[50] The idea was summed up in the following verses of Mohammad Haider, a school teacher in Pilibhit:
Jamaa do Qaum ka sikka bajaa do deen ka danka
Mohamed, Shaukat-o-Gandhi ke pairokar ho jao
Swadeshi se karo raghbat bidesi se karo nafrat
Ki jis se muflisee ho door aur zardaar ho jaao
Let the respect for the nation be restored
And the trumpet of the faith heralded
Follow Mohamed (Ali), Shaukat and Gandhi
Adopt swadeshism and shun all that is from outside
So that poverty is removed and self-reliance is achieved.
Proscribed Publications (43), IOLR.

[51] Jawaharlal Nehru noted that 'even in remote bazaars the common folk talked of the Congress and Swaraj, and what had happened in the Panjab, and the Khilafat—but the word 'Khilafat' bore a strange meaning in most of the rural areas. People thought it came from *khilaf,* an Urdu word meaning 'against' or 'opposed to', and so they took it to mean: opposed to Government!'. *An Autobiography,* p. 69.

[52] UP Government (Police Dept.), F.No. 51–N, 1921, UPSA. Note by Lakhte Husain and Jagannath, 28 February 1921, op.cit.

peasants and workers was equally pronounced in Bengal, where the joint Hindu-Muslim command under C.R. Das, Maulana Akram Khan, Ashrafuddin Choudhury, J.M. Sengupta and other leaders of the province emphasized the economic and political rather than the religious aspects of the Khilafat protest, and where the agitation, according to some government sources, 'was entirely Muhammadan but not religious'.[53] Facilitated by the failure of harvests between 1918 and 1922, the rise in prices, the fall in the price of jute and the influenza and cholera epidemics, the common slogans centred around the attainment of swaraj rather than the restoration of the Khilafat.

In Punjab the North Western Railway strike, initially called at the end of April 1920 for the improvement of the workers' material conditions, subsequently coalesced with the Khilafat agitation as the strikers began to perceive it as a movement against a 'tyrannical and exploitative' government.[54]

In assessing such strands in the Khilafat agitation, it is also worth taking note of the Congress-Khilafat-League *entente*. These organizations met in the same city and around the same time; often, Khilafat Committees and the Muslim League took their political cue from the Congress and endorsed its decisions. The 1918 League session did so, and, as in the Congress, so in the League, wrote an intelligence officer, 'the moderate have lost all control'. The same spirit prevailed a year later, though speeches made at the League platform 'were more violent in their language and defiant in their general attitude than the extremist Hindus at the meetings of the Congress'. Anti-British spirit 'reigned supreme'.[55] In July 1920, the League insisted that the Congress

[53] Tajul Hashmi, 'Peasants and Politics in East Bengal 1920–1974' (Unpublished Ph.D. thesis, University of Western Australia, 1986), p. 72.

[54] Khizar Humayun Ansari, 'The Emergence of Muslim Socialists and their Ideas in India between 1917–1974' (Unpublished Ph.D. thesis, University of London, 1985), pp. 83–85.

[55] Home Poll. B, F.No. 160–3, January 1919, NAI, WRDCI (January 1920), Home Poll. Deposit, F.No. 52, February 1920, NAI. Notice the comment of Jawaharlal Nehru that 'the political and the Khilafat movements developed side by side during the year 1920, both going in the same direction...'. *An Autobiography*, p. 46.

meet first so that it could recommend and decide the course of action for the Muslims.[56]

Such demonstrations of political unity were matched by spontaneous expressions of communal harmony. When O.M. Martin visited Noakhali in December 1921, he was struck by the 'curious spectacle of Muslims and Hindus spinning cotton thread as enjoined by Mahatma Gandhi, as a symbolic act indicating Hindu-Muslim unity in the attempt to drive the British from India'.[57] It is not without significance that communal violence was a rare occurrence, and that frictions over cow-slaughter and music before mosques were settled amicably. Such was the role of Prem Sabhas and Anjuman-i Islam in Delhi and Punjab.[58] The spirit of the time was captured by Zafar Ali Khan in the verse:

Aaee hain Aasman se chal kar woh quwaten
Jo Muslim-o-Hunood ko Sheer-o-shakar karen

Heavenly forces have helped to forge the bonds of friendship between the Hindus and the Muslims.
Or, by Agha Hashr:

Ho gaeen bikhri huee eenten baham tameer ki
Mil gaee har ek kari tooti huee zanjeer ki
But-shikan wahdat-parast ek jism ek jaan ho gaye
Ghul hua duniya me phir kafir Musalman ho gaye

The disjointed pieces have been put in order again
The links of the broken chain have been discerned
The idol-worshippers and the iconoclast have joined hands
There is a dinning clamour that the kafirs have again embraced Islam.

Short-lived as this unity was, the fact that it was accomplished

[56] Zahur Ahmad to G.N. Misra, 26 July 1920, All India Congress Committee [AICC] Papers, Supplementary, NMML. In distant Malabar every mosque became a centre of Congress-Khilafat activity. Taluqa and district level leaders toured the Muslim centres with Muslim colleagues, organizations and Khilafat volunteers. E.M.S. Namboodiripad, *How I became a Communist* (Trivandrum, 1976), p. 35.

[57] 'Memoirs of O.M. Martin', p. 113, O.M. Martin Papers, Centre for South Asian Studies, Cambridge.

[58] *Tribune,* 13 October 1919; *Fateh* (Delhi), 1 July 1920; Swami Shraddhanand, *Inside Congress* (Bombay, 1946), p. 37.

was a sufficient indication of the strength and fervour of the nationalistic spirit of which it was the outward expression. The secretary of the Bengal Khilafat Committee recalled:

> The scenes that were enacted before my eyes made me feel that the artificial barriers that had long been preventing the two major communities of the country to come together, had been miraculously swept away by the onrush of the all-embracing non-co-operation movement.[59]

IV

Shaikhji tum ko mubarak Rum-o-Reh
Hum to kehte hai ke Gandhiji ki jai

The Shaikh is welcome to think of Constantinople and Persia
I prefer to say, victory to Gandhism

(Akbar Allahabadi)

The architect of Hindu-Muslim unity during the Khilafat and non-co-operation days was no other than Mohandas Karamchand Gandhi. The cause was dear to him in South Africa, where he was convinced that his doctrine of Ahimsa would be put to its severest test on the issue of Hindu-Muslim unity.[60] The conviction was still there after his return to India in 1915. He sought and secured the friendship of leading Muslims in the Congress and the Muslim League, because he was eager to understand the 'Mussalman mind'.[61] He prized his contact with, among others,

[59] Abul Hayat, *Mussalmans of Bengal* (Calcutta, 1966), p. 37.

[60] Nanda, *Gandhi, Pan-Islamism, Imperialism and Nationalism,* pp. 198–9; Judith M. Brown, *Gandhi's Rise to Power: Indian Politics 1915–1922* (Cambridge, 1972), pp. 151–154.

[61] In his autobiography, Gandhi noted: 'I was seeking the friendship of good Mussalmans, and was eager to understand the Mussalman mind through contact with their purest and most patriotic representatives'. *An Autobiography or the Story of My Experiments with Truth* (Ahmedabad, 1958: reprint), p. 325. On another occasion he told a Khilafat meeting that his desire of meeting 'good' Muslim leaders was satisfied after meeting the Ali Brothers. 'It was a question of love at first sight between us', he said. His circle of friends widened after he had met Ansari and Abdul Bari. Speech on Khilafat, Bombay, 9 May 1919, *CWMG,* vol. 15, p. 295.

the Ali Brothers and mounted a campaign for their release. He assured Mohamed Ali: 'I need hardly say that you are never out of my mind, although we may not for some time come to meet face to face'.[62] He added that his interest in Mohamed Ali's release was quite selfish—to utilize his services to achieve a 'common goal'. In the proper solution of the 'Mohammeden question lies the realization of Swaraj'.[63]

The 'Mohammedan question' that concerned the Mahatma was the future of Khilafat, an issue that was, in his judgement, more important than the repeal of the Rowlatt Act.[64] It was so as it affected the religious susceptibilities of some of his countrymen. Moreover, in helping Muslims in 'the hour of their peril', he hoped to cement the bonds of communal unity'—a thousand times more valuable than...our connection with the British', and secure their much needed support for the nationalist struggle. He made it clear in *Young India:*

> It goes without saying that it is the bounden duty of the Hindus...to associate themselves with their Mohammedan brethren. It is the surest and simplest method of bringing about the Hindu-Mohammedan unity. It is the privilege of friendship to extend the hand of fellowship, and adversity is the crucible in which friendship is tested. Let millions of Hindus show to the Mohammedans that they are one with them in sorrow.[65]

Again, he observed in May 1920:

> If I kept aloof from the Khilafat question I would consider myself as having lost all my worth. That work is my dharma par excellence. It is through the Khilafat that I am doing the triple duty of showing to the world what ahimsa means, of uniting Hindus and Muslims, and of coming in contact with one and all...[66]

From May 1919 onwards, Gandhi was busy exhorting the *ulama* to mobilize their constituency and urged his co-religionists to join Muslims in fasting, prayer and hartal and thus 'put a sacred seal on the Hindu-Mohammedan bond'.[67] 'It is impossible', he

[62] 29 June 1919, ibid., p. 404.

[63] 18 November 1918, ibid., p. 64.

[64] Speech on Khilafat, Bombay, 9 May 1919, ibid., p. 297.

[65] To Mangalbhai, 3 May 1920, Mahadev Desai (ed.), *Day-To-Day with Gandhi* (Varanasi, 1968), vol. 2, pp. 154.

[66] Ibid.

noted in *Navajivan*, 'that one of the four limbs of the nation be wounded and the rest of the nation remains unconcerned. We cannot be called one nation, we cannot be a single body, if such a wound has no effect on us'.[68] At the same time, he assured his Muslim audience: 'You are my neighbours and my countrymen. It is my duty to share your sorrows. I cannot talk about Hindu-Muslim unity and fail in giving effect to the idea when the test comes'.[69] This assurance was a proclamation of Gandhi's intent and an appeal to Congressmen to follow his lead.

The All-India Muslim Conference in September and the All-India Khilafat Conference in September 1919 confirmed Gandhi's overall dominance of the Khilafat agitation. He settled its tone and tenor. At the Khilafat Conference, for example, he firmly opposed the resolution on the boycott of British goods.[70] So, consensus was reached only on the boycott of Peace Celebrations. The extent of Gandhi's influence is further apparent from the Muslim League session in December 1919. In deference to his wishes, the League resolved to prohibit cow-slaughter on *Bakr Id*, a concession never ever offered by any Muslim organization. Moreover, gratitude was expressed to the King for the spirit in which the Royal Proclamation was issued. In this resolution, too, the Mahatma's influence is noticeable, for he was at the same time carrying a similar motion through the Congress amidst strong opposition.[71]

[67] Letter to the Press, 10 October 1919, *CWMG*. vol. 16, p. 227.

[68] Ibid., p. 104. And his speech at the Khilafat Conference on 24 November 1919, p. 308.

[69] Speech on Khilafat, 9 May 1919, ibid., p. 297.

[70] Speech at Khilafat Conference, 23 November 1919, ibid., p. 307. While opposing Hasrat's resolution on boycott of foreign goods, Gandhi stated on 24 November that 'there is a world of difference between withdrawal of co-operation and boycott. It is a man's privilege to withhold co-operation when he likes, but we must have regard for the opinion of the world before adopting any political step. What we intend to do cannot be effected through boycott'. Ibid., p. 310. Gandhi's speech was in response to Hasrat's insistence that 'we want something that will produce an immediate effect on the British. Let your boycott of foreign cloth stand, we do not mind it, but give us something quicker, and speedier in addition'. Quoted in D.G. Tendulkar, *Mahatma: Life of Mohandas Karamchand Gandhi* (Publications Division: Delhi, 1969: Reprint), vol. 1, p. 274.

[71] Brown, op.cit., p. 188.

The Khilafat protest reached a new level of intensity in early 1920 on account of Gandhi's involvement, and also because of vigorous campaigning by Azad, the Ali Brothers and Zafar Ali Khan, all of whom were released from prison at the end of 1919.[72] Inspired by Gandhi's initiatives, they set out to secure wider support for the Khilafat agitation, particularly in Sind and the North-West Frontier Province which had, for the most part, remained politically inert. The Aligarh students were mobilized for the purpose: they addressed meetings in Kohat and Peshawar and raised Rs. 23,000 for the Khilafat Fund. In February the renowned *alim* of Firangi Mahal, Abdul Bari, Azad and Shaukat Ali were busy in Sind, where they spoke at largely attended Khilafat meetings.[73] This was followed by a tour of eastern Bengal. In addition, several missions were active in UP and Punjab. The campaign was in full swing and was well orchestrated through mosques and madrasas.

In most parts of the country the *ulama*, with some exceptions, were the most vehement advocates of non-co-operation. Inspired by the militant stance of Azad and Abdul Bari, they made fiery speeches, as at Hyderabad on 4/5 January 1920, and clamoured for *jehad* against the enemies of Islam. At the Bengal Khilafat Conference on 28 February, they decided to boycott British goods in spite of Gandhi's reservations, expressed just a few months earlier. On this occasion, however, Gandhi went along with Abdul Bari and his more militant followers, including the Ali Brothers, Hasrat Mohani and Azad Sobhani. In view of the popular excitement which had been mounting steadily since the observance of the first 'Khilafat Day' on 17 October,[74] Gandhi tailored his strategy to suit the mood of his more vocal Khilafat

[72] Hasan, *A Nationalist Conscience,* pp. 95–96; Minault, *Khilafat Movement,* pp. 84–86.

[73] *Amrita Bazar Patrika,* 18 February, 15 March 1920.

[74] The decision to observe Khilafat Day was taken at the All-India Muslim Conference on 21 September. Held at the Aminabad Park in Lucknow, the Conference was attended by over 5,000 delegates, including a large number of *ulama. Tribune,* 27 September 1919, and Robinson, *Separatism.*, pp. 295–96. For details on the success of the first Khilafat Day, see the first edition of my *Nationalism and Communal Politics in India,* pp. 152–55, and Minault, *Khilafat Movement,* pp. 76–78.

friends. In fact, a week after the Bengal Conference, his own mainfestò advocated non-co-operation with the British more vigorously than ever before. The intention was to keep up his alliance with the 'extremists' who, since the Muslim League session in December 1919, were demanding action instead of words.

The decisions of the Bengal Conference, backed by Gandhi, were adopted by, among others, the UP Ulama Association. In the Subjects Committee, with Abdul Bari in chair, it was planned to depute students to preach *jehad* in mofussil towns. In March 1920, the Punjab Khilafat Committee recognized the need to boycott British goods. This was enthusiastically backed by nearly ten thousand *ulama* present at the meeting.[75] Never before did so many of them gather at one place, on one platform and for a single cause. It was a striking demonstration of how religion had roused the *ulama* from their slumber and an indication of their gaining control of Khilafat committees and their policy decisions.

The second Khilafat Day on 19 March 1920 was quite a success. Its effect, as in October 1919, was felt throughout the country. Hartal was widely observed in Bombay presidency and there was a 'complete cessation' of business in Bombay city, particularly in Mahim, Dadar and Bandra areas.[76] In Sind, four honorary magistrates resigned in protest against the government's anti-Islamic policies. There were a spate of meetings, with the Pirs occupying centre-stage.[77] In Bengal, the Khilafat Committees sustained their agitation with meticulous care. In Calcutta there was much enthusiasm, with the famous Hogg market, which had remained open even during the Swadeshi movement, 'barred, padlocked and guarded'. In Dacca, Mymensingh and Chittagong public meetings endorsed the decisions of the Bengal Khilafat Conference.[78]

Hartal, fasting and prayer were the general features of Khilafat day in Punjab, while public meetings at Amritsar, Lahore. Multan, Sialkot and Peshawar demanded the settlement

[75] *Amrita Bazar Patrika,* 5 March 1920.
[76] *Bombay Chronicle,* 20 March 1920.
[77] *Mahratta,* 21 March 1920.
[78] *Amrita Bazar Patrika,* 20 and 22 March 1920.

of the Turkish question in consonance with Muslim sentiments and ideals.[79] In neighbouring Delhi, there was an impressive religious service at the Juma Masjid, and the suspension of all business. 'A very complete hartal was observed', reported an intelligence officer, 'with Muslim League and other volunteers posted in most of the bazaars and were insistent and almost aggressive in discouraging the collection of even the smallest crowd'.[80] In UP, prayers were widely offered for the Khalifa. A meeting at Allahabad was attended, among a great many others, by Zahur Ahmad, Hyder Mehdi, Kamaluddin Jafri, Maulvi Wilayat Husain, Jawaharlal Nehru and Purshotamdas Tandon.[81] In Mainpuri, a resolution was carried sentencing to religious ostracism any one who did not observe the rules of Khilafat day. A government report noted :

> By means of violent declarations that the Powers meant to obliterate Islam, emissaries from the big cities worked on the feelings of their brethren in outlying places and on the actual day it became apparent that an increased number of small towns had been affected. Hartal was carried out as generally as on the 6th April 1919.[82]

The publication of Turkish peace terms on 14 May heightened Muslim resentment and lent depth to their relentless campaign against the government.[83] Gandhi was quick to sense their anger and disappointment and offered a powerful indictment of the peace terms. He declared non-co-operation as the 'only effective remedy...for healing the wounds inflicted on Mohammedan opinion',[84] and informed the Viceroy: 'I consider that as a

[79] *Tribune*, 21 March 1920.

[80] Home Poll. Deposit, F. No. 4, April 1920, NAI.

[81] *Leader*, 21 March 1920.

[82] 'The Khilafat Movement in the United Provinces 1919–1924' [Printed], UPSA.

[83] The terms were described by the *Moslem Outlook* [20 May 1920], a weekly newspaper published by the London-based Islamic Information Bureau, 'as a monument of hypocrisy and the blackest breach of faith'. The *Mohammadi* declared that Muslims 'vow in God's name never to accept these terms'. 2 April 1920, SNNR, Bengal.

[84] Press Statement on Turkish Peace Terms, *CWMG*, vol. 17, pp. 426–27. Incidentally, Gandhi had already committed himself to non-co-operation on 7 March 1920 as 'the only remedy left to us' and the

staunch Hindu wishing to live on terms of the closest friendship with my Mussalman countrymen, I should be an unworthy son of India if I did not stand by them in their hour of trial'.[85]

But not everybody shared Gandhi's enthusiasm. The Liberal leader, Srinivasa Sastri, was alarmed at the prospect of Muslims 'breaking out here and there in futile demonstrations'.[86] Others were wary of Muslim influence in Congress affairs[87] and the possible outbreak of widespread violence.[88] Such apprehensions were echoed in May 1920, when Gandhi first explained his non-co-operation programme to the All India Congress Committee, and also on 1–3 June at the Central Khilafat Committee meeting in Allahabad.[89] Tej Bahadur Sapru, Annie Besant and Jamnadas Dwarkadas voiced their dissent.[90] So did Motilal Nehru, Madan Mohan Malaviya and Lajpat Rai. But Gandhi ignored their defiance and hastily appointed a sub-committee to

---

Central Khilafat Committee had endorsed his decision at its meeting held on 14 March. This was reaffirmed in early June when a committee was formed, with Gandhi as chairman, to give practical effect to the non-co-operation programme. On 22 June, Muslims informed Reading that they would withdraw co-operation from the government from 1 August 1920 if their demands were not fulfilled. Gandhi wrote to the viceroy separately, informing him that he was advising Muslims to adopt non-co-operation, because the peace terms violated ministerial pledges and disregarded Muslim sentiments.

[85] To viceroy, 22 June 1920, *CWMG,* vol. 17, p. 503.

[86] To Sivaswamy Aiyer, 13 April 1920, quoted in Kanji Dwarkadas, *India's Fight for Freedom* (Bombay, 1966), p. 146.

[87] For example, it was observed that the adoption of non-co-operation would mean that the Congress would gradually become 'a part and parcel' of the Muslim League and the Khilafat Committee and 'its predominant Hindu influence would be lost'. *Nayak,* 8 September 1920, SNNR, Bengal.

[88] Ibid., 8 March 1920. The *New India* had announced on the eve of the first Khilafat Day: 'Madras does not want Hartal ... and Mahatma Gandhi's name must not be used to ask Madras to do that which it is unwise for it to do, and which might disturb rather than cement the good relations hitherto subsisting between the two communities'. *New India,* 15 October 1919.

[89] Home Poll. B, F.No. 109, 1920, NAI.

[90] Dwarkadas described Gandhi's programme 'as an unnecessarily circuitous method of dislocating the functions of the State and paralyzing Government to the detriment of public safety and peace'. *Bombay Chronicle,* 7 June 1920.

give practical effect to non-co-operation. And when the work of the committee was hampered by certain elements in the Congress, he adopted a course unforeseen in Congress history—launching of the non-co-operation movement a month before the special session of the Congress was to meet in Calcutta.[91] This extraordinary step was calculated to take the sting out of the mounting campaign against non-co-operation and give himself and his allies enough time to garner support well before the Calcutta Congress, where he expected stiff opposition.

By December 1920, Gandhi had outmanoeuvred his opponents, with most leading politicians marshalled on the side of non-co-operation. In September his plan had already been approved in the Subjects Committee and at the open Congress session in Calcutta. Lajpat Rai, who held different ideas at the All India Congress Committee meeting in May 1920, was converted to the Mahatma's credo.[92] Motilal Nehru, once in search of a constituency for the UP legislative council, tailored his political stance to suit the mood in Calcutta.[93] The picture was no different in Nagpur, where the opponents of Gandhi were humbled one by one.[94] The Chief Commissioner of Central Povinces wrote :

[91] Gandhi defended his decision of not consulting colleagues in the following words: 'In my humble opinion it is no Congressman's duty to consult the Congress before taking an action in a matter in which he has no doubts...'. *Young India*, 4 August 1920, *GWMG*, vol. 18, p. 112.

[92] Robinson, *Separatism*, p. 318, f.n. 1.

[93] Nehru, *An Autobiography*, pp. 64-65. On Motilal's conversion to non-co-operation, see Ravinder Kumar, *The Making of a Nation: Essays in Indian History and Politics* (Delhi, 1989), pp. 108–10.

[94] C.R. Das, for example, made the dramatic announcement that he would move the main resolution in support of non-co-operation. He is said to have changed his earlier stance, because the boycott of legislatures, to which he was chiefly opposed, was no longer an issue as the elections had already taken place. S.C. Bose, *The Indian Struggle 1920–1942* (London, 1964), p. 44. For the view that it was Das's programme which won at Nagpur, not Gandhi's, see Rajat Ray, *Social Conflict and Political Unrest in Bengal*, pp. 262–63. Of course, the man who was clearly humbled at Nagpur was Jinnah. His opposition to the non-co-operation resolution was howled down with cries of 'shame, shame'. For details, see Wolpert, *Jinnah*, pp. 71-72.

> The outstanding feature of the Congress has been the personal domination of Gandhi over all political leaders and followers alike. He has carried through the policy that he had decided for this Congress without any material modification...The moderates of Nagpur were not heard; the extremist opponents under Khaparde and Moonje were brushed aside; Pandit Madan Mohan Malaviya's efforts were negatory; Jinnah carried no influence; Lajpat Rai wobbled and then became silent.[95]

The Chief Commissioner should have added that Gandhi's triumph at Nagpur was largely due to the overwhelming Muslim support of those who had flocked to the Congress session in large numbers. As in Calcutta where Muslim delegates 'swamped the rest',[96] the Congress pandal in Nagpur was packed with Muslims; they constituted nearly 72 per cent of the total number of delegates.[97]

V

Idhar taaid bari hai udhar taaleem Gandhi hai
Dar-i Uumeed ko khole khuda himmat to baandhi hai

With divine assistance, on the one hand, and the teachings of Gandhi, on the other
May God open the promised door, we have now gird up our loins

(Akbar Allahabadi)

With non-co-operation gaining such overwhelming support,

[95] F. Sly to Chelmsford, 1 January 1921, Chelmsford Papers (26).

[96] Willingdon to Montagu, 15 September 1920, Montagu Papers (20); *Bombay Chronicle* and *Amrita Bazar Patrika,* 10 September 1920. Of the 217 Bombay-based delegates who voted for Gandhi's resolution on 9 September , 43 were Muslims. Of the 161 delegates from Madras 125 voted for non-co-operation. *Bombay Chronicle,* 9 and 10 September 1920; *Hindu,* 16 September 1920. Out of the 57 persons from the Central Provinces who attended the Calcutta Conference and voted for the non-co-operation resolution, 16 were Muslims, including Samiullah Khan, a leading Khilafatist in the province. 'History of the Khilafat Movement in the Central Provinces and Berar' (Printed), p. 2. This report was made available to me by Dr D.E.U. Baker of St. Stephen's College, Delhi.

[97] See Gopal Krishna, 'The Development of the Indian National Congres as a Mass Organization', *Journal of Asian Studies,* May 1966, vol. 25, p. 418.

the Khilafatists, especially the *ulama,* pursued their concerns with renewed zeal and vigour. The Shaikh al-Hind, Maulana Mahmud Hasan, now returned to India after his wartime imprisonment in Malta, called for a total boycott of government-administered educational institutions.[98] So did other Deobandi *ulama* like Maulvi Mohammad Idris Kandholwi and Maulana Shabbir Ahmad Usmani.[99] The sweet-tongued Maulana Abdul Majid of Budaun extolled the virtues of those who surrendered titles and honours,[100] while Abdul Bari issued a *fatwa,* which was endorsed by five hundred *ulama*, in support of non-co-operation.[101] A *fatwa* on similar lines emanated from the *Pirs* of Almohar in Sialkot district and from Sail Sharif in Hoshiarpur.[102] The *Pirs* of Sind were also swept by the pan-Islamic tide. It was reported that they had joined hands with the *ulama* in spreading the 'infection of religious enthusiasm among many classes of the inhabitants of Sind', and that the excitement caused by non-co-operation was 'growing in intensity among all classes of educated Muhammadans'.[103]

No less touching were reports of Muslims resigning from government, surrendering titles and suspending their legal

[98] Address read out at the foundation laying ceremony of the National Muslim University, Aligarh (Jamia Millia Islamia), 29 October 1920, and Bashir Ahmad, *Tark-i Mavalaat* (Deoband, 1920), Proscribed Publications (53–54), IOLR.

[99] In *Al Ahkaam al-Quraniya Mavalaat al-Burtaniya* (Delhi, 1920) the author cited the *fatawa* of Shah Abdul Aziz and Maulvi Abdul Haye to establish the validity of non-co-operation. Assisting the enemies of Islam *(Ahl-i Harb)* through trade or employment was unlawful while an alliance with the *Ahl-i Sulah,* i.e., the Hindus, was lawful. Shabbir Ahmad Usmani made a similar plea at the Jamiyat al-ulama conference in Delhi, though he cautioned Muslims against the tendency to place Gandhi on a spiritual pedestal. See *Tark-i Mavalaat par zabardast taqreer* (Delhi, 1920), pp. 17, 22, 24–25

[100] See *Fazle-al Khitaab* (Delhi, n.d.), and 'Khilafat ka Paighaam Mussalmanon ke naam', pp. 17–18.

[101] For a collection of the most important *fatawa* on the Khilafat issue, see Rais Ahmad Jafri (ed.), *Auraaq-i Gumgushta* (Lahore, 1968).

[102] Home Poll. F.No. 459, 1922, NAI.

[103] WR (Sind), 12 and 26 November 1921, J.C. Curry Papers, Centre for South Asian Studies, Cambridge.

practice. In November 1920, twenty-two out of the forty-four lawyers who gave up practice were Muslims.[104] By November 1921, the number of Muslim policemen who had resigned was thirty-one, forty and seventeen in UP, Bengal and Bombay.[105] Among those who renounced their titles were Hakim Ajmal Khan, Syed Ali Nàbi and Maulana Badruddin of Phulwari.[106]

The legislative council elections, which took place on the eve of the Nagpur Congress, were also boycotted, particularly in the Muslim constituencies. Similarly, in Madras only six of the provincial council seats were contested by Muslims, and only a small number of enfranchised Muslims voted—6.6 per cent of those eligible.[107] In C.P. 'the boycott of the Councils was more successful...than was thought to be probable'.[108] In UP, only 7 per cent votes were polled in the Muslim urban constituencies as compared to 14 per cent in the non-Muslim urban constituencies, and in many areas groups of *ulama* and students prevented voters from going to the polling booths.[109] In eastern and northern parts of Bengal, there was a dearth of candidates and little polling was reported from most areas. In Rajshahi and Dinajpur the

[104] F.No. 5, 1920, AICC Papers.

[105] Brown, op.cit., p. 309. For the Central Provinces and Berar, see D.E.U. Baker, 'The Muslim Concern for Security: The Central Provinces and Berar, 1919–1947', in Hasan (ed.), *Communal and Pan-Islamic Trends,* pp. 221–243.

[106] *Mussalman,* 6 August 1920. While renouncing his government titles, Hakim Ajmal Khan stated: 'As a humble Muslim, I have decided to relieve myself of all honours conferred upon me by the Government and I return herewith the gold medal of Kaiser-i-Hind together with the two silver medals of the Coronation Darbar of England and India, and, henceforward, I give up the title of Haziq-ul-Mulk'. Quoted in Tendulkar, *Mahatma,* vol. 1, p. 287.

[107] Kenneth Mcpherson, 'The Political Development of the Urdu and Tamil-speaking Muslims of the Madras Presidency 1901–1937' (Unpublished M.A. thesis, University of Western Australia, 1968), p. 127.

[108] 'History of the Khilafat Movement in the Central Provinces and Berar', p. 3.

[109] Valentine Chirol happened to be in Allahabad on the election day and made round of the polling booths. At one rural polling station, about fifteen miles from Allahabad city, he found that not a single voter had appeared. Nehru, *An Autobiography,* p. 67.

bulk of educated men, including pleaders, refrained from voting Almost all Muslims from Rangpur town abstained, as did large numbers of Muslims in Gaibandha sub-division of Rangpur district. In Bakarganj, very few Muslims voted and, in Mania, not a single voter, Hindu or Muslim, appeared.[110]

Among those who resigned their seats from the councils or withdrew their candidature from Muslim constituencies were Nur Mohammad, Kader Baksh, Kazi Azimuddin, Sheriff Deoji Kanji, Mohammad Arif Mulla and Salembhoy Karamji from Bombay; M.A. Wasim, Maulvi Wahid Husain, Mandud Rahman, Mazharul Haq, Mahbubul Haq, Maulvi Nadir Ali, Mazharul Anwar, Hasan Suhrawardy, Abdul Karim, Fazlul Haq, Syed Sultan Ali, Azizul Haque, Maulvi Shamsuddin, Maulvi Tamizuddin Ahmad, Maulvi Mohammad Daud, Maulvi Saidullah, Maulvi Ikramul Haque, Nuruddin Ahmad, Fazlur Rahman Adil, Abdur Rashid Khan, Abdul Halim, Abdul Jabbar and Maulvi Abdul Halim from Bihar and Bengal; and Kamaluddin Jafri, Sheikh Zahur Ahmad, Hafiz Alam, Zahuruddin, Syed Zahur Ahmad, Syed Hyder Mehdi and Aziz Ahmad Khan from UP. These names give a clue to the varied background of at least some non-co-operators. They included rich merchants from Bombay, petty landowners like Abdul Jabbar from Bengal and successful lawyers like Kamaluddin Jafri and Syed Zahur Ahmad from Allahabad. Most non-co-operators were Sunnis but there were some notable Shias as well. They shared the view that non-co-operation was the only way to defend the Holy Places.[111]

[110] Rajat K. Ray, 'Masses in Politics: The Non-co-operation Movement in Bengal 1920–22', *The Indian Economic and Social History Review*, December 1974, vol. 2, 4, p. 362; Hashmi, 'Peasants and Politics', p. 80.

[111] The Shias consider the first three Khalifas, recognized by the Sunnis, as 'usurpers' of the rights of Ali since, according to them, the Prophet of Islam acting under divine guidance designated Ali, his son-in-law and cousin, and his descendants to a continuing authority. Yet, the Shias were closely associated with the Khilafat movement in India. According to a report from Sind, they were sympathetic to the Angora government 'in spite of their different religious standpoint as regards the Khilafat'. WR (Sind), 11 June and 26 November 1921, Curry Papers. For more details, see *Comrade,* 7 October 1911, *Paisa Akhbaar,* 22 June 1920, SNNR, Punjab,

Students and teachers responded to the non-co-operation call with equal enthusiasm.[112] This is best illustrated by the turn of events at the Aligarh Muslim University, where pan-Islamic sentiments coalesced with patriotic and nationalist feelings in good measure and generated a powerful anti-colonial movement.[113]

The M.A.O. college of Syed Ahmad Khan's days followed an ardent and sustained pro-British policy and steered clear of political movements. It was hard to be otherwise. The founder considered education as the sole means for the regeneration of his community and regarded Anglo-Muslim rapprochement as a necessary condition for its upliftment. The *raison d'etre* of the college was, thus, to make Muslims 'worthy and useful subjects of the Crown', to groom students to go on to British universities, and to train them for government employment. These expectations were fulfilled during Syed Ahmad Khan's lifetime. Students cultivated English habits and tastes; expressed loyalty to the Crown by decorating their rooms with portraits of Queen Victoria and the Prince of Wales, and paid heed to repeated admonitions to avoid political discussions. The campaign against the Congress, launched by Syed Ahmad Khan, struck a favourable chord in Aligarh circles.

In the early years of the twentieth century this most 'benighted' and conservative of institutions suddenly exploded into political

---

Bombay Chronicle, 7 May 1921, and Minault, *Khilafat Movement*, pp. 129–30.

[112] Minault, op. cit., pp. 118–19. There were reports of strikes at the Calcutta Madrasa and the Government College, Lahore. In Amritsar the Anjuman-i Islam refused to accept a government grant. The overall situation in various educational centres was summed up by H. Sharp, secretary to the government of India. According to him, 'within the last few weeks, strikes of students have occurred upon a considerable scale in Bengal and it appears that in other provinces, where the trouble seemed to have been scotched, it has now attained a new lease of life'. Home Poll. B, F.No. 259, 1921, NAI.

[113] The account on Aligarh is based on my *A Nationalist Conscience*, pp. 98–108, *Mohamed Ali: Ideology and Politics*, pp. 17–20, and 'Nationalist and Separatist Trends in Aligarh 1915–1947', in Gupta (ed.), *Myth and Reality: The Struggle for Freedom in India 1945–47* (Delhi, 1987), pp. 116–151.

activity confronting the British with the most serious Muslim movement of dissidence they had faced since the 1857 revolt. The agitation against the Nagri resolution of 18 April 1900, followed by the students' strike of February 1907, represented a new trend in Aligarh politics—a trend to steer the Muslim community on a course different from that plotted by Syed Ahmad Khan. Though this strain in Aligarh politics reflected the changes taking place at other levels of Muslim society, contemporaries were never tired of pointing out how, just a few years before the new trend appeared, there was not the slightest sign of its imminence. This earlier quiescence, attributed to Syed Ahmad Khan's influence and to the predominance of landed interests on the Board of Trustees, was gradually replaced by a position in favour of the Congress and in opposition to the government. In so doing, the Aligarh students threw to the winds all the caution that had been enjoined upon them by Syed Ahmad Khan.

Inspired by the poems of Shibli Nomani, Hasrat Mohani, and Hashmi Faridabadi and the exalted prose of Mohamed Ali, Azad, and Zafar Ali Khan, political activity on the campus was sustained during the course of World War I. Students raised funds for beleagured Turkey, offered prayers for the success of Turkish armies, and took a deep interest in the Anjuman-i Khuddam-i Kaaba. Four Aligarh graduates joined Ansari's medical mission to Constantinople and at least one Aligarh Old Boy—Mahendra Pratap—was part of the 'Silk Letter Conspiracy,' and headed the Provisional Government in Kabul. This was not all. The themes of capitalist exploitation, class conflicts, of revolt against imperialism, of nationalism, and of socialism figured in the works of important writers and poets at Aligarh, including Hasrat Mohani, Sajjad Hyder Yaldaram, Wilayat Ali Bambooque, Qazi Abdul Ghaffar and Abdur Rahman Bijnori. The Progressive Writers' Association, formed in the mid-1930s, represented the continuation and development of the literary and political trends set by writers who were either in or closely connected with Aligarh. Its activities gave Urdu literature a vital stimulus, a new vigour and a liberating consciousness.

Encouraged by reports of nationalist activity on the campus, Gandhi and his Khilafatist allies turned to Aligarh to muster support for the non-co-operation programme, adopted by the

Congress in September 1920. Gandhi fired the first shot. He reached Aligarh on 11 October in the company of Ansari, Azad, Ajmal Khan and the Ali Brothers, and addressed a students' meeting the same evening. According to an eye-witness account, he spoke haltingly in Hindustani, trying to find the right words but his accent seemed droll to his 'pseudo-sophisticated' audience who did not agree with him because their political and economic background and affiliations did not predispose them to accept his radically new doctrines of non-co-operation. The first shot had clearly misfired. He then appealed to the trustees

> to decline any further Government grant, disaffiliate the great institution of which you are the trustees and reject the charter of the Moslem University. The least that the Aligarh boys can do, if you fail to respond to the call of Islam and India, is to wash their hands clean of an institution acknowledging the aegis of Government that has forfeited all the title to the allegiance of Islam and India and to bring into being, a larger, nobler and purer Aligarh that would carry out the inmost wishes of its great founder.

The trustees were not impressed. They had unanimously decided, much before Gandhi's letter of 24 October reached them, to run the institution on 'old established lines' and reiterated that the college aimed to make Indian Muslims 'worthy and useful subjects of the British Crown'. Sir Akbar Hydari, a trustee, commented:

> After my personal experience of the doings and sayings of Mr. Mohamed Ali and his student-following in Aligarh, I am firmly convinced that it is in the highest degree necessary...to get them not only outside the precincts of the college, but to absolutely prevented (sic) them from establishing what they are pleased to call a National Muslim University in Aligarh, but what is really...an instrument for seducing students from collegiate study and working them up to a pitch of religious frenzy and hatred.[114]

After repeated failures to counter Mohamed Ali's influence, who meddled in Aligarh affairs brazenly, the trustees at last had

[114] Akbar Hydari to Muhammad Ali, 17 November 1920. Also M. Habibur Rahman Khan and S.R. Masood to Muhammad Ali, 17, 18 November 1920, UP Government (Education Dept.), F.No. 40, 1918, UPSA.

their taste of revenge. The doyen of agitational politics was able to muster the support of only 10 members; the rest rallied round the loyalist Principal, Ziauddin Ahmad, who consistently warned students against being swept away by forces outside the college and had introduced an official ban on their joining the Anjuman-i Khuddam-i Kaaba.

Undeterred by this rebuff, Ansari, Azad Sobhani, Azad and the Ali Brothers returned to Aligarh on 23 October and addressed numerous meetings with a small group of students led by Zakir Huṣain, a graduate in economics, and Kunwar Mohammad Ashraf, a Meo Muslim from Alwar State who rose to political prominence in the 1930s. On this occasion there was a change of heart. A graduate student wrote defiantly that he had his

> doubts removed within the last four or five days, and I am now a strong supporter of non-co-operation. I can and will read in your college only in the case it is nationalized [sic], otherwise I am ready to face the doom awaiting my non-co-operating brothers. I consider it my duty to intimate you of these views, so that I may not be considered a double game player.

One Nurul Hasan of Azamgarh, impressed by Azad and Azad Sobhani, gave up his studies to join the growing band of non-co-operators. Amidst fiery and passionate speeches, resolutions, promises and assurances, many more students responded—estimates range from 200 to 700—to the call of non-co-operation and enrolled themselves with the newly founded Jamia Millia Islamia. Mohamed Ali thus scored a major victory; the college authorities were humbled. The pan-Islamic fervour, combined with the nationalist upsurge, swept the campus and Syed Ahmad Khan's vision of sustaining the Anglo-Muslim rapprochement through the M.A.O. college was all but shattered.

In the late 1920s, Aligarh remained an advanced centre of political activity. K.G. Saiyadain, who joined the Teachers' Training College on his return from the University of Leeds in 1925, recalled his participation in the Jubilee Debate in 1926, when his fellow-students endorsed a policy of united nationalism. He argued, in the presence of luminaries like the Aga Khan, Jinnah and Ali Imam, that Indian Muslims should not organize themselves on communal lines but must work, together with nationalist forces, for the freedom and progress of the country. The message was well taken. A few years later the vice-president of the Students' Union spoke of Aligarh's role in the freedom struggle and exhorted his audience to

> turn ourselves into the biggest, the most disciplined, the most educated and the most united army that India possesses, to fight against the evils that have made India the laughing stock of the world and let nobody say that Aligarh lagged behind anybody in India's battle of freedom ...To be indifferent towards anything that happens in a depressed country like India is criminal. To be ignorant of one's own political status is far worse than death. And not to think of and dream of a brilliant future for one's own country is a state which will reduce one to a lifeless mass of flesh.

Such pronounced nationalist sentiments were echoed because political activity on the campus was not inspired by communal concerns. In 1931 Tofail Ahmad Manglori, one of Aligarh's distinguished Old Boys, wrote a powerful critique of the Muslim demand for separate electorates, arguing that the real cause for the communal tangle was the recognition of special interests 'which appears to have dimmed the national outlook.' His view was an article of faith with many comrades in Aligarh who spurned leaders with communal proclivities and followed instead, T.A.K. Sherwani, Khaliquzzaman, Shuaib Qureshi, and A.M. Khwaja—all graduates of Aligarh and closely associated with Jawaharlal Nehru and the Congress movement in UP. All of them were members of the most powerful university body—the University Court. Likewise, most office-bearers of the influential Students' Union belonged to the radical *alumni* circles, anti-British and pro-Congress; the widely circulated *Aligarh Magazine* retained its pro-Congress bias, and the theme of national unity and communal harmony evoked a ready response.

Equally important was the influence of socialism and communism which, though feeble in the early 1920s, was more pronounced in the 1930s. Syed Mohammad Tonki, who was actively involved in the non-co-operation movement and who later turned to 'Islamic Socialism' under the influence of Hasrat Mohani, recalled receiving M.N. Roy's writings 'which discussed the Russian revolution, the reality of the socialist system, and the weakening of the big empires as a result of capitalist and imperialist exploitation.' He and Kunwar Mohammad Ashraf often discussed 'what a socialist system might achieve in India'.

It is noteworthy that Muslims like Ashraf were initiated into the political mainstream during the Khilafat excitement and imbibed the nationalistic spirit and fervour which gripped large segments of Indian society during the years 1919 to 1922. Even thereafter,their interest in and association with nationalist forces continued, though regional and local compulsions sometimes distorted their perspective. What is equally important is the degree to which the top brass of the Khilafat leadership, tutored in the virtues of patriotism and anti-colonialism, eventually moved away from the Khilafat cause either in response to the spurt in communal activity or simply in search of new solutions to new problems.

The strength of the Khilafat movement lay in its proven ability to express the poetry of collective life: not the frenzy stirred by modern-style demagogues, but the intensity of earnest moments. Caught up in their millenium-seeking exhilaration, its leaders lived in a kind of intoxication during the years 1919–22—full of excitement, optimism and buoyant optimism. Even after their hopes were shattered and the bottled-up energy of their followers found an outlet in communal clashes, the principal Khilafat leaders remained convinced that, not long before, an immense event had taken place, that there had been a moment of power in the history of their country, a moment so close that it was almost within their grasp.

Chapter Six

Islam, Khilafat and Nationalism-II

The *ulama** were at the heart of the Muslim concern over Turkey and the Holy Places. They galvanized their followers in dedication to the Khilafat idea, foisted the flag of 'pure Islam' to carry it into battle against external and internal enemies and deployed the cultural and intellectual resources of Islam in an attempt to mobilize and legitimize anti-colonial aspirations. Their passionate commitment and fervour helps us to see more clearly the roles Islam has played in politics, as well as sensitizing us to the many

*The role of the *ulama* in modern Indian politics has received considerable scholarly interest. Some well known writings on the subject are: W.C. Smith, 'The Ulama in Indian Politics', C.H. Philips (ed.), *Politics and Society in India* (London, 1963), pp. 39–51 and his *Modern Islam in India;* Ishtiaq Husain Qureshi, *Ulema in Politics: A Study Relating to the Political Activities of the Ulema in the South-Asian Subcontinent from 1556 to 1947* (Karachi, 1974 edn); Hardy, *Partners in Freedom,* and his *Muslims of British India.* The history and role of the Dar al-Ulum, Deoband, is covered in the works of: Sayyid Mahboob Rizvi, *History of the Dar al-Ulum Deoband* (Deoband, 1980); Metcalf, *Islamic Revival;* Z.H. Faruqi, *The Deoband School and the Demand for Pakistan* (Bombay, 1963); Mushirul Haq, *Muslim Politics in Modern India 1857–1947* (Delhi, 1970). For the role of the Deobandi *Ulama* and the Jamiyat al-ulama during the Khilafat and non-co-operation movements, see Minault, *The Khilafat Movement,* pp. 103–07, 121–22, and her 'Islam and Mass Politics: The Indian Ulama and the Khilafat Movement', Donald E. Smith (ed.), *Religion and Political Modernization* (Yale University Press, 1974), pp. 168–82; Robinson, *Separatism,* chapter seven; M. Naeem Qureshi, 'The Ulama of British India and the Hijrat', *MAS,* 1979, vol. 13, i, pp. 41–59. Aseer Adrdai, *Tarikh-i Jamiyat al-ulama-i Hind* (Deoband, 1960) and Parween Rozeena (ed.), *Jamiyat al-ulama-i Hind: Dastaaveez 1919–1945* (Islamabad), in two volumes; Mohammad Miyan, *Ulama-i Haq aur unke kaarname* (Deoband, 1972 edn.).

ways the cultural norms and social precepts of Islam were invoked in the early twenties.

It is well known that Islam did not provide for a priesthood or a comparable religious institution. Gradually, however, a body of men developed to perform specialized religious functions—chiefly readers and reciters of the Quran and experts in recording and interpreting the sayings and doings of the Prophet of Islam. These were the *ulama,* literally those who possessed knowledge (*ilm*). They formed an 'unnumbered aggregate of academicians of all degrees of learning and intelligence'. Still, the hallmark of an *alim* was his learning in subjects like *Ilm-i Hadith* (science of Prophetic Tradition), *Tafsir* (Quranic exegesis), *Fiqh* (Jurisprudence) and *Ilm-i Kalaam* (Theology).[1] According to Fakhr-i Mudabbir, a fourteenth century chronicler at the Delhi court, the *ulama* owed their special status to their knowledge. He observed:

> All people know that after the apostles and prophets rank the truthful persons, martyrs and scholars. The scholars are included in the category of siddiqis and have preference over the martyrs. The Prophet has said: 'The ulama are the heirs of the prophets'. The world exists on account of the piety of the learned. The laws of shariat...are enforced by them... and things illegal and not sanctioned by the shariat are suppressed by them.[2]

Again, the *ulama* are described as those

> who will stand higher than the martyrs on the Day of Judgement. It is because of their learning, probity and piety that the world is

[1] Hardy, *Partners in Freedom,* p. 11. The following observation of Mohamed Ali is useful:

> Had I belonged to one of the families that specialize in religious training, I would, no doubt, have spent half a lifetime in the study of the Quran and its *tafsir* or exegesis, or *Hadith*.... or *Fiqh*.... and *Aqaid* and *Kalaam* or dogmatics and dialectics, which form the scholastic philosophy of the Musalmans regarding their creed....As a necessary preliminary to these religious studies, I would have had to receive instruction for a number of years in Arabic grammar and along with it in some secular Arabic literature. Mohamed Ali, *My Life,* pp. 2–3.

[2] K.A. Nizami, *Some Aspects of Religion and Politics in India during the Thirteenth Century* (Bombay, 1961), p. 150.

replenished. It is up to them to see that the commands of the Shariat are observed and good work is performed. Under their spiritual influence vices diminish and recede into lurking places....[3]

Such a glorified image was not entirely a product of Fakhr-i Mudabbir's fantasy but was, indeed, grounded in Muslim ethics; it helps to explain why the *ulama* occupied such a privileged position in Muslim societies.

The *ulama* were a powerful group in medieval India. They dominated the upper echelons of religious hierarchy, manned the judicial and ecclesiastical services, and wherever there was a mosque—and every Muslim locality had one—the *imam,* the *khatib,* the *muhtasib* and the *muftis* represented an interest which received State recognition. Some simply acquiesced in the *status quo,* repeated the utterances of the State and gave the deeds of rulers religious sanction and cover. But their functions were not restricted to legitimizing authority. They also performed regulatory functions in social and economic life, and the more prominent amongst them derived, not only social prestige, but also wealth from the performance of these functions. As a result, the *ulama* prospered: they acquired property, accumulated respectable fortunes, established matrimonial alliances with ruling houses, and emulated the *umara* in lavish expenditure. Criticizm and denunciation of their life-style and involvement in the politics and revolutions of the palace came only from the sufis and other men of religion, who led an abstemious life of pious devotion to religious learning and often eschewed entanglement in materialistic pursuits and political affairs.[4]

The medieval rulers needed the intellectual, administrative and educational services of the *ulama.* They also secured the one important element of authority which force alone could not command—legitimacy.[5] As quasi-officials of the State, they upheld the dominant political viewpoint, capitulated before the whims of even the 'impious' rulers, quoted scriptures and used it

[3] *Tarikh-i Fakhruddin Mubarak Shahi,* quoted in Agha Mahdi Husain, *Tughlaq Dynasty* (Allahabad, 1960), p. 361

[4] Nizami, op. cit., p. 152.

[5] See K.M. Ashraf, *Life and Conditions of the People of Hindustan* (Delhi, 1970 edn: reprint), p. 44.

against their 'enemies', and, above all, taught the faithful a dull stagnation in matters of belief and the acceptance of political autocracy, knowing all the time that almost everything the Sultans did as persons and as rulers was repugnant to the *shariat.*[6] They did all this in order to retain their control over the religious structure which was almost entirely dependent on State patronage. But opportunism does not explain everything, for the ideology of the *ulama* was also at work: the fear of chaos, disunity, and fragmentation of the ordered practice of religious duties. This attitude is illuminated by a writer from a different culture in a passage that applies here very well:

> Better that thousands should suffer than that a people should become a disintegrated mass, helpless like dust in the wind. Obscurantism is better than the light of incendiary torches. The seed germinates in the night. Out of the dark soil springs the perfect plant. But a volcanic eruption is sterile, the ruin of the fertile ground![7]

The establishment of British supremacy, however, led in the long run to the undermining of the position of the *ulama* in society. They were apprehensive of and opposed to clear breaches of Islamic traditions in education, the removal of important sections of law from under the jurisdiction of the *qazis,* the growth of local governments and the gradual secularization of some sections of Indian society. In his address to the first Congress of Nadwat al-ulama in April 1894, Shibli lamented:

> Gentlemen: In the days of the Muslim rule the worldly as well as the religious affairs of the Muslims were in the hands of the ulama...the reins of the affairs of the community relating to both this and the next world were in the hands of the ulama. Now that things have changed, and worldly affairs have come under the authority of [the British] government, we have to see what relationship the ulama have with the community.[8]

[6] In the nineteenth century, the traditional idea of a partnership between the rulers and the *ulama* was brought up to date by, among others, Rafi Al-Tahtawi (1801–73) of Egypt. See Hourani, *Arabic Thought in the Liberal Age,* p. 76.

[7] This is drawn from a secondary source, but I am unable to locate the reference.

[8] Quoted in Robinson, *Separatism,* p. 275; Shaikh Mohammad Ikram, *Mauj-i Kausar* (Lahore, 1970), p. 233.

The *ulama* instinctively distrusted government's trespassing on their turf and reinterpreting their age-old doctrines. Asserting the pre-eminent position of the *shariat*, they advanced their sole right to interpret its meaning for all groups and classes,[9] initiated steps to prevent the influx of subversive ideas from the religiously alien and 'morally inferior' British, and, as behind-the-scenes propagandists, discouraged unorthodox thought and learning, which was calculated to undermine their position amongst Muslims. Thus Shibli declared that the purpose of Nadwa was to defend Islam against contemporary times.[10] He held the view that through such institutions the *ulama* would be able to determine what was true or desirable in the light of the Quran and *Hadith* and thus maintain uniformity in belief and practice. Likewise, the objectives of the Dar al-Ulum at Deoband, as envisaged by Mohammad Qasim Nanotawi and Rashid Ahmad Gangohi, were to renew and establish contact between the *alim* and the average Muslims and to reorientate the community to its 'original' cultural and religious identity.[11]

Traditionally, madrasas formed the basis of Muslim education.[12]

[9] Thus Shibli insisted that the Muslim community could not develop unless the *ulama* had undisputed control over its secular and religious life: *Mauj-i Kausar,* p. 233. Shibli also organized a memorial against the Privy Council decision of 1894, which had set aside the law of *waqf-ul alal-aulaad.* Some decades later, the *ulama* of Firangi Mahal demanded special treatment in judicial matters, such as the establishment of special courts presided over by Muslim judges. Note by W.S. Marris, 17 November 1918, Meston Papers (34).

[10] *Makaatib-i Shibli* (Azamgarh, 1928), vol. 1, p. 329. Also, see *Rudaad-i Nadwat al-ulama,* 22–24 April 1894 (Kanpur, n.d.), vol. 1, pp. 22–24.

[11] The Dar al-Ulum, stated the 'official' historian of the institution, 'is not only a religious teaching institution but is also...an effective and active movement. This movement, cleansing the Muslims' beliefs and action of all the rubbish and trashery, acquainted them with pure and unalloyed Islam, liberated them from polytheism and superstitions...'See Rizvi, *History of the Dar al-Ulum Deoband,* p. 107, and pp. 108–10 for its aims and objectives. Also, Ahmad, *Islamic Modernism,* p. 104; Faruqi, *Deoband School,* p. 27.

[12] The earliest known madrasas were established by Iltutmish (1211–1236) and Balban (1266–1286) in the thirteenth century. Under Mohammad bin Tughlaq (1325–1351), Delhi alone had over a thousand madrasas. Jaunpur had at least thirty. A sixteenth century English traveller

Their curriculum, which remained largely unchanged over the centuries, included the study of Arabic and Persian language and literature, logic, philosophy, *Shariat, Hadith* and commentaries on the Quran. Aurangzeb, the last of the great Mughal emperors, reprimanded his former teacher for having taught him Arabic, grammar and philosophy, rather than subjects more practical for a future ruler of an empire.[13] But his pungent criticizm was of no avail. In the eighteenth century, Mulla Nizamuddin Sihalawi introduced the Dars-i Nizamia, which was regarded as the most comprehensive form of education and was therefore adopted as the basis for instruction in several institutions.[14] In this system, the curriculum was largely confined to purely religious sciences (*maqulaat*), with a bit of grammar and literature thrown in. The core areas of study included *Hadith, Fiqh, Kalaam* and *Tafsir,* with the Quran being at the heart of the curriculum and its memorization the highest scholastic attainment.

Maktabs were usually of two kinds: the first, of a purely religious character in which the rituals and tenets of Islam were taught, and the second, of a more secular type in which a good measure of Persian literature was also taught.[15] The most important of the

---

visiting Thata—now a picturesque ruin near Karachi (Pakistan)—reported 400 large and small madrasas. See Rizvi, op. cit., pp. 52–64.

[13] Shaikh Mohammad Ikram, *Ruud-i Kausar* (Karachi, 1958), pp. 424–26. Syed Ahmad Khan held that the Muslim schools of the old sort were 'altogether useless', because their syllabus and books 'deceive and teach men to veil their meaning...to describe things wrongly...and in irrelevant terms....and to relate facts like tales and stories. All these things are quite unsuited to the present age and to the spirit of the time, and thus instead of doing good they do much harm to the Muhammadans'. Quoted in Philips (ed.), *The Evolution of India and Pakistan,* p. 174. And Syed Ahmad to Mohsinul Mulk, 11 February 1872, quoted in Shan Muhammad, *Sir Syed Ahmad Khan: A Political Biography* (Meerut, 1969), p. 59.

[14] Details of the *Dars-i Nizamia* are outlined in Mujeeb, *Indian Muslims,* pp. 407–8. Some of the famous madrasas in UP were: Madrasa-i Kalaan in Sandila, Madrasa-i Chashma-i Rahmat in Ghazipur and the madrasa of Haji Imam Bukhsh in Jaunpur. In Bengal, such madrasas flourished in Murshidabad, Birbhum and Burdwan. The famous Jalaliya Madrasa was established by Munshi Sadruddin at Burdwan. Maulana Khairuddin Ahmad, *Tazkirat al-ulama* (Calcutta, 1934), pp. 13–14.

[15] In Punjab, besides the Quran and the *Kanzul-i Mussali,* a book of

first type, which later developed into a Dar al-Ulum [institution of high learning], was founded in a sleepy village of Deoband in 1867. As a protagonist of the Hanafi doctrines, the Dar al-Ulum achieved much fame and distinction as a theological seminary. Its goal was clear: to train well-educated *ulama* who, as prayer-leaders, writers, preachers and teachers, would tenaciously maintain the religious identity of the believers. A traditionalist course of studies was planned to the exclusion of modern sciences, because it was believed that the 'perfection' of the community lay in conserving its traditional heritage and in preventing the unprecedented and precipitous decline of Muslim traditional sciences (*manqulat*).[16] There was actual opposition, led by Gangohi, to the teaching of logic, philosophy and jurisprudence.[17]

The Nadwa, founded in 1894 as a middle of the road institution between the extremes of Aligarh's 'secularism' and Deoband's 'rigid conservatism', failed to combine both religious and secular types of education because of the attachment to the narrow curriculum of Nizamuddin.[18] The institution developed conservative contours and there was not much to choose between their theological and intellectual outlook and that of Deoband.[19]

---

prayers in verse, several works on rituals and the Islamic tenets were prescribed. These included the *Rah-i Najaat, Risaala- Namaazaan, Masaail-i Hindi, Nasihat Nama, Subha ka Sitara,* and *Masaail-i Subnaani.* H.S. Reid, *Report on Indigenous Education and Vernacular Schools* (Agra, 1852); R. Nathan, *Progress of Education in India 1896–77 to 1901–2* (Calcutta, 1904), vol 1, p. 375. In 1916–17, the enrolment to government-aided maktabs in UP was nearly nine thousand. By 1926–27, the figure rose to 43,973. This was a fair indication of the popularity of maktabs. *Report,* UP, 1921–28, vol. 2, p. 140.

[16] Ahmad, *Islamic Modernism,* p. 104. Nanotawi is reported to have said in 1874 that it was proper and desirable to pay attention to only traditional sciences and 'harmful beyond the capacity of students to be trained simultaneously in too diversified and too many a discipline'. Quoted in Faruqi, *Deoband School,* p. 30.

[17] Metcalf, *Islamic Revival,* p. 101.

[18] This was the time when scholars like Rafi al-Tahtawi in Egypt and Khayr al-Din (1810–1889) in Tunis urged the *ulama* to come to terms with the new learning and be in touch with the spirit of the times. See Hourani, op. cit., pp. 92–93.

[19] Ahmad, *Islamic Modernism,* p. 112.

Shibli's attempt to work out a new theology, a new *Ilmul Kalaam*, was widely attacked as heretical.[20] A government report noted:

> Generally, it would appear that Shibli's ideal in the early days of his connection with Nadwa was the adoption of a system of education not markedly progressive like that of Aligarh, but possessing (*sic*) as a medium of correction to the old maktab system a measure of western education. [But] he failed to influence the maktabs, and though the Nadwa can point to logic, history, mathematics and geography classes, the internal dissensions which have been such a marked feature of its history in recent years...would appear to militate against efficiency.[21]

Both the Dar al-ulum and Nadwa were attempts to make Muslims aware of their Islamic identity, to maintain the charismatic or divinely-instituted nature of the community and to warn the government that the *ulama* would brook no intrusion in their special field of religious interpretation and instruction. There were shared paradigms of religious renewal, rooted in the Quran. The basic concern of the *ulama* was to eliminate 'false accretions' derived from the Sufis or the Shias—on a detailed Islamization of every aspect of religious and everyday life. Their visions were meant to be a challenge to the world in general—and the West in particular—and as such had become powerful beacons for large numbers of backward and impoverished Muslims living in a cruel and uncertain world.

But not everybody was enthused by their role. This was because the *ulama*, in general, clung to the vestiges of their religious identity with a desperate vigour, zealously guarded their theological strongholds, treated the scriptures as if they were fossilized, scholastic parchments rather than inspirations for a dynamic world outlook, and presented an Islam that was static and lacking the dimension of internal evolution.[22] Their turbans and flowing gowns made them stand out as symbols of conservatism, especially at a time when the modernists or reformists proclaimed Islam to be a flexible, dynamic system that was and should

[20] Police Dept., F.No. 79, 1908, UPSA.

[21] Metcalf, *Islamic Revival*, p. 339.

[22] For a powerful criticizm of the role of the *ulama* on these lines, see *Asr-i Jadeed*, December 1908, p. 460.

always be interpreted and moulded from within to accommodate the social and political changes of the times.

Hali in his *Musaddas* and Akbar Allahabadi in his numerous poems lamented that most *ulama* concerned themselves with minutiae of ritual and in fruitless disputes, excelled in denouncing each other, and dubbing the adherents of other schools of thought as ignorant, irreligious and atheistic.[23] A religion which was once the fountainhead of ethics had become a rigid jumble of ritual and prayer in the hands of those who regarded their own traditional interpretations more as authoritative than the simple word of God or of His Prophet.[24] Azad, too, spoke out against the *ulama* demanding *taqlid* from their congregations, retaining a monopoly over religious texts, and preventing the believers from gaining access to true Islam.[25] Iqbal, on the other hand, attacked them for their conservatism, clumsy bookish wisdom and lifeless traditionalism. *Mulla* is for him the representative of the traditional way of those who learnt by heart texts which they themselves did not understand and who imposed upon people innumerable religious and ritual prescriptions without knowing their inner meaning. The theological hair-splitting in which they indulged was nothing but a welcome opportunity for the devil to blindfold the power of Islam.[26]

Such criticizm did not, however, undermine the position of the *ulama*. Though some failed to rise to any heights and performed a variety of roles without attracting notice, others, whose

[23] See, for example, M. Manzar and R.A. Khan, *Deoband aur Bareilly ikhtilaaf par Nazaa aur faislakun Munaazara* (Sambhal, 1966). For debates between the Ahl-i Hadith and the Hanafis, see *Rafi al-Akhbaar,* 8 July 1901, SNNR, UP. The Ahl-i Hadith have been the target of sharp criticizm from the same quarter. They were charged with 'betraying' Muslims in the 1857 revolt and supporting the British. Maulvi Nazir Husain of Delhi, Nawab Siddiq Husain Khan (1832–1890), a leading exponent of Ahl-i Hadith thought, and Maulana Mohammad Husain Butalwi were derided and accused of collusion with the British. Bashir Ahmad Qadiri, *Ahl-i Hadith aur Angrez* (Abu Hanifa Academy: Karachi, 1979), pp. 28–29, 55, 71–72, 104–5.

[24] Ahmad, *Islamic Modernism,* p. 99.

[25] Douglas, *Abul Kalam Azad,* pp. 76, 166–67, 273.

[26] Schimmel, *Gabriel's Wing,* pp. 75–76.

authority became more firmly held and more generally conceded by the public opinion, represented the Muslim community in matters relating to faith and law. They not only continued to make their presence felt through mosques and shrines, maktab and madrasas, but also endeared themselves for their ceaseless efforts to preserve, maintain and renew the unity, continuity and the divine guidance of the *Ummat an-Nabi,* the community of the Prophet. Above all, they played a variety of roles as guardians, transmitters and authorized interpreters of the *shariat,* which comprehends Muslim beliefs, rituals, public and personal law. They clarified controversial points of the doctrine and expressed views on subjects as wide-ranging as divorce, inheritance and disputes over property. That is how the Deobandi *ulama* issued 1,47,851 *fatawa* from 1911 to 1951, with Rashid Ahmad Gangohi, giving rulings that it was lawful to learn English if there was no danger to religion, that it was unlawful to take interest from a Christian, to use money-orders and bills of exchange in which the element of interest enters, and to wear a cross or a *topi*.[27] Such rulings were rarely flouted, at least not openly. The *ulama* were becoming, in the Gramscian sense, traditional intellectuals, enunciating an ideology that was powerful and favoured by the majority.

How did the *ulama* fit into an individual's daily life? One can begin to answer by imagining what kind of contact an average Muslim had with them. As a young boy he would attend a maktab, where he would be taught to recite some portions of the Quran from memory and to read and write. He may then go on for higher education at the madrasa which, like the maktab, was staffed by the *ulama.* In this way they exercized a near-monopoly over learning, sanctity and, consequently, moral authority.

The *ulama* had the greatest influence in regulating religious life. On Friday, the average Muslim would perform the *namaaz* and listen to the weekly sermon by the *khatib,* who was usually the prayer leader (*imam*). Here the *ulama* would come into contact with all classes and groups of people. Likewise, an *alim* or two would be drawn to conduct the marriage ceremony as well as the

[27] Hardy, *Muslims of British India,* p. 171; Ahmad, *Islamic Modernism,* p. 105.

funeral service. There were numerous other occasions when the *ulama* entered the 'private' domain and the 'public' sphere of individuals and groups to lend their name and legitimacy to religious rituals and social obligations.

Thus the *ulama* served as an important link between various Muslim groups, commanded considerable resources and the loyalties of diverse groups of people. It is, therefore, not surprising that, in small towns and villages, where the Muslim population was more susceptible to religious exhortations through local mosques and madrasas, the men of religion provided the inspiration behind a burst of Khilafat activity. They were successful in doing so because of their dominant religious hegemony which transcended class and caste divisions, enabling them to develop an extensive network of social connections which ranged from the Oudh taluqdar to the impoverished Muslim peasant in East Bengal.

It is true that in the realm of earthly politics the men of religion were frequently attacked for their conservatism and, as often, blamed for the backwardness of the Muslim people. Yet, even in a world turned upside down, their support was continually sought by, for example, the promoters of the Aligarh Muslim University. A conciliatory attitude towards the Muslim divines was intended to allay their fears about the future character of the institution and convince the government that the university movement was backed by influential Muslim groups. Likewise, the Muslim League leaders needed powerful allies to rally public opinion around their brand of agitational politics;[28] so they wooed the *ulama* and tried to remove their fears about the *la-dini* (religionless) character of the League. For the time being, the dividing line between the Western-educated and the orthodox

[28] The *Nai Roshni* of Allahabad, edited by Wahid Yar Khan, stressed the need to draw the *ulama* into the struggle against the repressive policies of the government. Likewise, the *Mohammadi* of Calcutta thought that the *ulama* should be encouraged to take the lead in making the masses conscious of the impending danger to the world of Islam. 'Let the alim', stated the paper, 'betake themselves to work. Let the first steps in this great national work be begun in the mofussil and let it be explained from each village mosque'. *Nai Roshni,* 23 December 1917, *Intikhab* (Gujranwala), 10 January 1920, SNNR, Punjab; *Mohammadi,* 23 April 1920, SNNR, Bengal.

was gradually blurred, almost obliterated, and with it were buried their bitter doctrinal feuds. The younger Muslims, observed the lieutenant-governor of UP, 'try to work with the priests, hoping through them to influence the mob. For the time being, however, it would be idle to deny that they have attained success'.[29]

In March 1915, Meston tried to explain why this was so. According to him, young educated Muslims were 'restless', 'dissatisfied' with the world around them and in search of a 'cause', a call, something that they could be proud of. 'This he finds in his religion. It gives him a link with great traditions'. Meston concluded:

> At this point he comes into touch with the priest of the arrogant domineering type, whose ambition lies in swaying the passions of the tolerant masses. Hence arises Pan-Islamism, the idea of the Muslim 'nation' and many of the fantasies generated from.[30]

Meston missed out a crucial aspect in his analysis—the ways in which the revocation of Bengal's partition, the Turko-Italian War, the furore over the Kanpur mosque affair, and the rejection of the Muslim University scheme added thrust to the converging courses in politics of the modern and the traditionally-educated.

The *ulama* responded favourably to these overtures, mainly because they were politically unorganized and indeed unaccustomed to political life. Moreover, their bitter doctrinal disputes and mutual rivalries created fissures in the apparent solid phalanx of orthodoxy and prevented them from moving in unison.[31] By 1911, however, they were rudely awakened by the growing threat to Islam—an awakening which coincided with, and was also to a certain extent caused by, the political upheaval in Turkey. They were conscious that they must now be active in addressing themselves to the current anxieties—political, social and religious—of Indian Muslims, or else see true Islam as they understood it, and their own claims to guide the community go by default. Such a realization led some *ulama* to cultivate the

[29] Meston to Hardinge, 25 March 1915, Hardinge Papers (89).
[30] Ibid.
[31] Robinson, *Separatism*, pp. 268–71.

modern-educated Muslims who had some experience of conducting constitutional politics and, in the words of Mohamed Ali, 'to pocket their pride and in a way even accept the lead of men whom they had but a generation ago finally consigned to perdition'.[32] An early move in this direction was initiated by Maulana Mahmud Hasan, who was convinced of the need to further greater fraternity between the alumni of Deoband and Aligarh.[33] The Jalsa i-Dastarbandi, convened in 1910 and attended by a delegation from Aligarh led by Aftab Ahmad Khan and the Jamiyat al-Ansar, founded by Ubaid-Allah Sindhi, was the fruition of such endeavours.

These initiatives were followed by the establishment of the Anjuman-i Khuddam-i Kaaba in May 1912. This was the beginning of the formal participation of the *ulama* in Indian politics in their capacity as religious leaders. Above all, the Anjuman provided the basis for an alliance between leading *ulama* of all shades of opinion and the modern-educated. This was of great significance because it illustrated that, on purely religious issues, the *alim* and the modernized Muslim could strive together for common ends. The orthodox and the anglicized 'were drawn together and as in a flash of lightning, saw that after all they were not so unlike each other as they had imagined'. Mohamed Ali wrote optimistically:

> Once more Muslim society in India presented a level of uniformity and the bitterest opponents of a generation ago stood shoulder to shoulder.... If even a decade previously anyone had ventured to foretell such a result, he would have been laughed at for such a fantastic prophesy.[34]

Having gained the trust and confidence of some leading *deendars,* the men of 'New Light' or 'Nai Raushani' began to use the existing networks of religious organizations and institutions to propagate pan-Islamism. In March 1914, Mohamed Ali, Ajmal Khan and Ghulam-us-Saqlain, editor of *Asr-i Jadeed,* were asked to enquire into the affairs of Nadwa. Mukhtar Ahmad Ansari was elected president of the Anjuman-i Islamia, Ghazipur, a position which had always been occupied by the local maulvis. In December 1918, Ansari and Shuaib Qureshi,

[32] Mohamed Ali, *My Life,* p. 43.
[33] Faruqi, *The Deoband School,* pp. 56–57.
[34] Mohamed Ali, op. cit., p. 43.

son-in-law of Mohamed Ali, addressed a meeting at Juma Masjid, Delhi, where they spoke in support of the Muslim League. In return for such concessions, the *ulama* expected the League leadership to orchestrate their specific religious demands.[35] For the same reason, leading *alim* like Abdul Bari rallied round Gandhi, submitted to his leadership because he was the only guarantor of Congress support, and accepted non-violence with all its implications. It was not easy for the *ulama* to grasp the idea of non-violence. But they accepted it, making it clear that they did so as a policy only and not as a creed, for their religion did not prohibit the use of violence in a righteous cause.[36] Writing to Gandhi in November 1920, Abdul Bari observed: 'I have accepted his [Gandhi] support in getting our aims fulfilled and for that purpose I think it is necessary to follow his advice.... I know that the strength of Islam lies in association with him.[37]

The same sentiment was echoed by his *murid,* Mohamed Ali. In July 1921 he wrote:

> When the Congress was adopting for the first time the Khilafat programme of non-violent non-co-operation, the essential thing was the unity of Hindus and Muslims and even if Muslims had been ready for violence, which they were not, they couldn't have succeeded without Hindu goodwill.... Long before we were free we had made up our minds to bring about a complete entente between Hindus and Muslims...and the best man among the Hindus to deal with was Mahatma Gandhi, a peace-loving and non-violent patriot who was intensely religious without a fury of a theologian and whose honesty all could rely upon. He found us to be equally religious and equally without a fury of a theologian, and as Muslims we could not pledge ourselves to remain non-violent in all circumstances, he found that we too regarded force at present to be futile, and above all he could trust our word as much as we trusted him. Even if we ourselves wished to use force immediately, which we did not and could not, we would have lost his support and thus have lost the chance of bringing about the Hindu-Muslim entente and of bringing the government to its senses.[38]

[35] See, for instance, Maulvi Mohammad Ahmad to Sheweth, 30 October 1917, Meston Papers (19).

[36] Nehru, *An Autobiography,* pp. 45–46.

[37] Home Poll. Deposit, F.No. 4, 1921, NAI; WRDCI, March 1919, Home Poll. B, F.No. 148–52, 1919, NAI.

[38] Quoted in Brown, *Gandhi's Rise to Power,* pp. 330–31; Also,

Such a subservient posture was distasteful to, among others, Syed Ahmad Raza Khan of Bareilly who was hostile to non-co-operation and to Gandhi's domination of the Khilafat movement.[39] But such men were few and wielded limited influence during the popular pan-Islamic upsurge. Most *ulama* favoured accommodation with Congress and political co-operation with Hindus because of the vital necessity of enlisting their support for the Khilafat campaign. For this reason alone they found Gandhi's leadership very welcome.

II

The principal shibboleth of the 'fundamentalists' in both Sunni and Shia Islam is that Islam is an all-encompassing way of life in which there can be no distinction between religion and politics. During the first decade of the twentieth century, Shibli and Azad insisted that 'a very large part of the national life is in the *ulama* right of ownership (*haqq-i-malkiat*) and they alone have or can have absolute sway (*mutlaq-al anaan*) over it'.[40] In his address to the first Congress of Nadwat al-ulama, Shibli berated the *ulama* for being lackadaisical and urged them to combine and organize themselves to offer an enlightened interpretation of religion, to reorganize Arabic and Persian studies, to exert pressure on the government for a revision of its legal policy, and to control and efficiently administer *waqfs*.[41] All this entailed, so he argued, active and vigorous involvement in politics. In 1912, his distinguished disciple, Azad, summed up his political ideology in an attempt to provide guidance to the *ulama*.

> The question whether political discussion should be separated from religious education is very important. But you must know that this is the foundation on which we intend to build the whole edifice of Al-Hilal. If

---

Mohamed Ali to Chelmsford, 24 April 1919, quoted in my *A Nationalist Conscience*, p. 70.

[39] Syed Jamaluddin, 'The Barelwis and the Khilafat Movement', in Hasan (ed.), *Communal and Pan-Islamic Trends*, pp. 400–13.

[40] *Khutbaat-i Shibli*, pp. 29–33, quoted in Shaikh Mohammad Ikram, *Modern Muslim India and the Birth of Pakistan, 1858–1951* (Lahore, 1965 edn.).

[41] Ahmad, *Islamic Modernism*, pp. 109–10; Smith, *Modern Islam*, p. 39.

you say that the arch is not beautiful we may try to alter its shape, but if you wish that the key-stone should be removed, then we cannot accede to your wishes. There will be nothing left with us if we separate politics from religion.[42]

This was common talk in the early 1920s, when the theological weight of Indian Islam was fully behind the Khilafat movement. Maulana Abul Muhsin Mohammad Sajjad, *Naib Amir-i Shariat* and *Nazim* of Jamiyat al-ulama, suggested to Abdul Bari that the *ulama* should 'take the reins of politics in their own hands and cross their voices with those in authority' in order to establish their religious supremacy and to fulfil their higher aim of protecting Islam from Western imperialism.[43] Maulvi Kifayatullah of Madrasa-i Aminia in Delhi, founder of the Jamiyat and its president from 1920 to 1939, echoed similar sentiments at the Muslim League meeting in December 1918. He declared:

In Islam religion and politics are not two separate things. For a long time they were together, but probably those who have received modern education think that they are separate from one another. This, however, is a wrong concept: they think that they should monopolize politics and leave religion for the *ulama*.[44]

Words were soon translated into deeds. The *ulama* thronged to the Muslim League session to determine the temper of the meeting, assert the voice of orthodoxy, assume leadership of the Khilafat agitation and contribute to its radical development. Soon after, they called upon the believers to wage *jehad* against the government, boycott foreign goods, and migrate (*hijrat*) to the *dar al-Islam*. They exercized their right to issue *fatawa* freely, using the Quran and the *Hadith* as powerful weapons to gain the adherence of the masses who accepted them as infallible. Abdul Bari, the chief ideologue of the *ulama*, did so on many occasions. He was among the signatories to the famous *fatwa* on non-co-operation. So was Azad. He was also the author of the *fatwa* on

42 *Al-Hilal*, 8 September 1912, quoted in Mushirul Haq, *Muslim Politics in Modern India*, p. 72.

43 A.M.M. Sajjad to Abdul Bari, 4 December 1918, *Nuqqush* (Lahore), 1918, p. 91.

44 Cited in Qazi Abdul Ghaffar, *Hayaat-i Ajmal*, P. 185.

hijrat.[45] The lesser known *ulama* did not lag behind. The maulvis of Sukkur in Sind, inspired by Abdul Bari's *istifta* [questionnaire] of January 1919, issued a *fatwa* declaring the Jazirat al-Arab as a sacred place 'wherein non-Muslims cannot rule or remain in possession'.[46] Twenty-six *ulama* issued a *fatwa* in Bengal forbidding Muslim participation in the Peace Celebrations.[47] In legitimizing the local leaders and exhorting the hesitant to take up arms for *jehad,* Abdul Bari and Azad bestowed unity—however temporarily—on fragile alliances, because they used religion as a language with its own potent meanings and universal symbols.

There were strong objections to such outbursts from some quarters. The *istifta* was opposed, among others, by the *ulama* of Deoband. The *Muttaffiqa fatwa,* which made non-co-operation mandatory on all Muslims, was rejected by Maulana Ashraf Ali Thanwi, Ahmad Raza Khan and the Bahr al-ulum Party of Firangi Mahal.[48] Others like Maulvi Mohammad Ikramullah of Nadwa supported non-co-operation but not the boycott of educational institutions.[49] The *Pirs* of Sind were equally divided. The *Pir* of Kingri, for instance, not only opposed non-co-operation but also advised his followers to rally round the government. Rashidullah, another influential *Pir,* held aloof from the non-co-operation campaign as it was 'initiated and controlled by Hindus'.[50]

However, such opposition, often inspired by cynical government officials, failed to stem the pan-Islamic tide. As Ishtiaq Husain Qureshi observed:

> The stand taken up by the supporters of Non-co-operation found overwhelming support. Hardly any one examined the reasoning behind

[45] Azad declared that for the Indian Muslims there was no *shariat* alternative to *hijrat*. 'Before the Great War *hijrat* was commendable but now it was mandatory.' The exact date of this *fatwa* is not known, though it is said to have been issued in April or early May 1920. Qureshi, 'The Ulama of British India', op.cit., p. 51

[46] *Tribune*, 21 March 1919.

[47] *Mohammadi*, 12 December 1919, SNNR, Bengal.

[48] Qureshi, *Ulema in Politics*, p. 270.

[49] Maulvi Mohammad Ikramullah, *Masla-i Taaleem aur Tark-i Mavalaat* (Aligarh, 1920), pp. 34, 36.

[50] WR (Sind), 9 April 1921, Curry Papers.

the pro-Non-co-operation *fatwa*. The general feeling was that the British and their allies were out to destroy Islam as a force in international affairs, hence they were the enemies of Islam, therefore, non-co-operation against them must be right.... The Muslims supported the movement with rare abandon.[51]

The *ulama* were not content with sheafs of *fatwa*, but wandered from rural areas to cities and other rural areas in order to mobilize their followers through a well-modulated campaign. The governor of Bengal nervously reported that they were busy travelling all over eastern Bengal enjoining the faithful to perform *jehad*.[52] The Ahl-i Hadith group was particularly active in Dinajpur, western Rangpur, northern Rajshahi and north-western Bogra. So strong was its impact in parts of Rangpur district that a swaraj *thana* was established by one Ghyasuddin Ahmad, popularly known as 'Gandhi-darogha'. In some areas 'free villages' were organized under the aegis of local Anjuman-i Islamia's.[53] This was not all. The Majlis-i Ulama of Madras toured the presidency to incite Muslim emotions on the Khilafat issue, and, in May 1920, the United Provinces' Ulama Association sent students to preach *jehad* in the mofussil. A few months earlier, Abdul Bari and Shaukat Ali toured Gujarat together, preaching the sanctity of the Khilafat and Hindu-Muslim unity; later, they were joined by Azad for a tour of Sind.[54]

The *ulama* quickened the tempo of their agitation, establishing *shariat* tribunals in a few places and national schools in parts of the North West Frontier Province.[55] In Bengal, the *ulama* 'who had formerly held aloof from politics' were drawn into the boycott movement.[56] In UP, the homeland of most vociferous pan-Islamists, educational centres like the Nadwat al-ulama and the Dar al-Musaniffin became the main foci of agitations.[57] The

[51] Qureshi, *Ulema in Politics*, pp. 271–72.

[52] 16 May 1919, Diary of Ronaldshay, Ronaldshay Papers, MSS.EUR. F. No. D 609 (1), IOLR.

[53] Tajul Islam Hashmi, 'Peasants and Politics in East Bengal', pp. 74–75.

[54] For details, see Brown, *Gandhi's Rise to Power*, pp. 224–25.

[55] Bamford, *Histories*, p. 151.

[56] FR (Bengal), November 1921, Home Poll. Deposit, December 1921, F. No. 18, NAI.

[57] After leaving Nadwa in 1913, Shibli went to Azamgarh where he

pan-Islamic ferment at Nadwa, generated by Shibli's poems on the Balkan,[58] the Indian Medical Mission to Constantinople, and the Kanpur mosque incident, culminated in the effective students' demand in November 1920 to refuse the grant, sanctioned by J.P. Hewett in 1908.[59] At the Dar al-Musaniffin, Syed Sulaiman, one of Shibli's favourite pupils at Nadwa and member of the 1920 Khilafat delegation to Europe, urged Muslims to sacrifice their lives in defence of the Holy Places and insisted that the political emancipation of India was a 'religious duty'. If Muslims wanted to liberate Kaaba, he told Abdul Bari, they would have to liberate India first.[60]

Masud Ali, founder of a Khilafat Committee (in April 1920) and its branch committees in the Azamgarh district, was a leading non-co-operator. According to the Commissioner of Gorakhpur,

---

collected a small band of followers to carry on his literary activities and especially to assist him in the compilation of the life of the Prophet. In this way the Dar al-Musaniffin came into being. After the death of Shibli in November 1914, the society was registered in Lucknow on 4 July 1915 and secured grants from Hyderabad and Bhopal. Though formed as a literary society, the Dar al-Musaniffin, or the Shibli Academy, soon became 'the centre of the political activities in Azamgarh district'. Its press printed and distributed pamphlets on the Khilafat issue. A government report added : 'There is no doubt that the Shibli Academy is no longer what its founder intended it to be, but has become an extremist political institution of a class with which I feel sure that neither...the Nizam nor...the Begum of Bhopal would wish to support'. H.R. Gracey to G.B. Lambert, 8 January 1921, Police Dept., 1921, F.No. 1, UPSA.

[58] The Nadwa came under suspicion for its pan-Islamic leanings due to Anthony MacDonnell who regarded its founder, Shibli, as disloyal to the government. However, Hewett did not share this view. At Shibli's request, he sanctioned an initial grant of Rs 6000 and laid the foundation of the Nadwa building on 28 November 1908. Education Dept., 1908, F.No. 79, UPSA. In 1911–12, Shibli's involvement in the pan-Islamic movement was again discussed when the question of giving him an award was considered by the government officials. The matter was deferred on the grounds that he was already a *Shams al-ulama*, 'which seems a sufficient distinction for a gentlemen whose most praise-worthy quality is that he is a good writer of Urdu prose'. L. Porter to DuBoulay, 25 July 1911, Hardinge Papers (50).

[59] The strike was called off following the intervention of Aftab Ahmad Khan, Ajmal Khan and Nawab Mohammad Ishaq Khan. C.F. De La Fosse to O'Donnell, 8 February 1914, 1908, F.No. 79, UPSA.

[60] Gracey to Lambert, 8 January 1926, GAD, 1921, F.No. 1074, UPSA.

his activities turned the Dar al-Musaniffin into 'an extremist political institution' and a centre of radical politics in Azamgarh. His influence extended to small towns in the region, such as Mau, Sarai Mir and Pharuja. In Mau, which was predominantly inhabited by Muslim *julahas,* Abdul Aziz, a barber, Maulvis Mohammad Sabir, Abdullah and Zamir pushed the honorary magistrates into resigning and persuaded the local Islamia College to renounce its government aid. 'Mau, in short', noted an official, 'is the danger point in the district and wants watching'. In Sarai Mir, Khilafat activities were centred around the Arabic school. The manager, M. Hamiduddin, the staff and students were found busy explaining the significance of the *fatawa* issued by Abdul Bari and Azad. 'These mullahs', observed an alarmed official, 'are ignorant and fanatical and will believe anything if they believe their religion to be in danger. They get worked up to the boiling point by itinerant, professional agitators, who are in my opinion the most dangerous class now'.[61]

Such organized activity, supported by the rapid circulation of a variety of opinions and images, was a priceless asset and the key to the extraordinary vigour of the Khilafat agitation. Jawaharlal Nehru aptly summed up the position of the *ulama* during this period.

> Owing to the prominence given to the Khilafat movement in 1921, a large number of Moulvis and Muslim religious leaders took a prominent part in the political struggle. They gave a definite religious tinge to the movement, and Muslims generally were influenced by it. Many a Westernized Muslim, who was not of a particularly religious turn of mind, began to grow a beard and otherwise conform to the tenets of orthodoxy. The influence and prestige of the Moulvis, which had been gradually declining owing to new ideas and a progressive Westernization, began to grow again and dominate the Muslim community.[62]

III

'Take great care', the *Independent* of Allahabad warned its readers on 3 June 1920, 'that the control of the Khilafat movement does not fall entirely within the hands of theologians and

[61] Note by Bigg Wither, 7 December 1921, Police Dept., 1921, F.No. 1074, UPSA.

[62] Nehru, *An Autobiography*, pp. 71–72.

divines'.[63] But nobody paid heed to the warnings of those who stressed the necessity, or at least the desirability, of minimizing the intrusion of religion in political life. By early 1921, however, it was clear that the *ulama* were no longer an asset but a liability. This was indicated at the Meerut Khilafat Conference in April 1921, when some hot-headed elements objected to the Hindu involvement in the Khilafat movement and demanded its scope to be defined according to the *shariat*.[64] This was followed by Abdul Bari's warning that Muslims were ready to adopt violent methods to redress their grievances. Words were soon translated into deeds.[65] In May 1921, *Darul Qaza* courts (House of Justice) were set up in parts of Bihar and the North-West Frontier Provinces, and talk of *jehad* filled the air in the countryside.[66] The Jamiyat al-ulama, founded in November 1919 mainly on Abdul Bari's initiative, took a momentous decision in March 1921: it was declared *haraam* [sinful] for a Muslim soldier to serve in the army.[67] The Karachi Khilafat Conference in July 1921 simply endorsed this resolution which was introduced by Maulana Husain Ahmad Madani and supported by the Ali Brothers, Pir Ghulam Mujadid, a Sindhi follower of Abdul Bari, and Maulana Nisar Ahmad of Deoband.

Gandhi supported the Karachi resolution. But he was nervous about the growing militant posture which threatened to destroy

[63] A number of writers, mostly in Pakistan, have argued that involving the *ulama* in the political agitations of the day was a mistake. For example, Abdul Hamid, *Muslim Separatism in India : A Brief Survey 1858–1947* (Lahore, 1971 : reprint), pp. 151–52; Mohammad Noman, *Rise and Growth of the All-India Muslim League* (Allahabad, 1942), pp. 213–14.

[64] WRDCI, 11 April 1921, Home Poll. Deposit, June 1921, F.No. 54, NAI.

[65] Abdul Bari said in June 1921 that Muslims held non-violent non-co-operation as 'a useful weapon to get our grievances redressed' but that they were not committed to 'always adhere to this principle'. Home Poll. 1921, F.No. 45, NAI. Reporting the deliberations of the Provincial Conference held sometime in November 1921, Jawaharlal Nehru reported to Gandhi that its president, Hasrat Mohani, expressed dissatisfaction with the creed of non-violence. 'Several other speakers used violent language and apparently looked forward to a time when violence would have full play. All this took place on the Karachi Resolution. S. Gopal (ed.), *Selected Works of Jawaharlal Nehru* (Delhi, 1972), vol. 1, p. 201.

[66] Bamford, op.cit., pp. 168–69.

[67] *Dastaaveez*, op. cit., vol. 1, pp. 129–30.

the credibility of his non-violent non-co-operation technique. He was aware of the discontent amongst some of his Congress comrades, particularly after the Moplah riots in August 1921, and was anxious that they should not be alienated any further. But the hard-liners were not easy to tame. They flocked to various national gatherings in December 1921 and demanded the immediate adoption of civil disobedience. Their enthusiasm was temporarily curbed by Ansari, Azad and Ajmal Khan.

The showdown came soon thereafter, when the poet-politician, Hasrat Mohani, representing the more militant *ulama,* proposed that the Congress and Muslim League should strive to attain 'complete independence' and declared that if martial law was imposed Muslims would either have to abandon non-co-operation or face the bullets and bayonets. In the latter event, violence was the natural course to adopt in self-defence. This was symptomatic of the tensions between Gandhi's ideal of satyagraha and the Khilafat leaders' adoption of it as a political technique, a fact which remained a constant feature of the Khilafat movement. Gandhi himself created this tension, despite his laments about Muslim motives, by making non-violence the pre-condition of his support. His hopes of transmuting the pan-Islamic sentiments of the Muslims into a nationalist movement seem to have failed, because some Khilafatists, notably the *ulama,* were not willing to go along with him in the realization of his ideals. They merely extended grudging support to the non-violent non-co-operation programme as a price for securing Gandhi's adherence to the Khilafat cause.

Gandhi threw his weight against Hasrat's resolution, arguing that complete independence could not be incorporated in the Congress creed unless and until Hindu-Muslim unity was completely accomplished.[68] This was another way of saying that

[68] He said : 'Let us understand our limitation. Let Hindus and Muslims have absolute, indissoluble unity. Who is here who can say with confidence : Yes, Hindu-Muslim unity has become an indissoluble factor of Indian Nationalism?' *Young India,* 19 January 1922, *CWMG,* vol. 22, p. 108. Writing to Montagu within a few days of the close of the Ahmedabad meeting, Reading observed that the discussion...must be regarded as very serious, not only because of the language used but also because the defeat of Hazrat (*sic*) Mohani's motion was really on grounds of inexpediency'. The Marquess

the idea of complete independence was premature, as it was unlikely to find favour with a section in the Congress. Congress finally backed Gandhi rather than Hasrat Mohani, as did the Subjects Committee of the Muslim League on 30 December. Hasrat's resolution, opposed by Ajmal Khan, Ansari and Syed Raza Ali, was rejected by thirty-six votes to twenty-three.

The *ulama* were enraged. Having first mooted the idea of complete independence in March 1921, the Jamiyat al-ulama felt cheated by these attempts to curb the militant instincts of its followers. Consequently, some harsh words were exchanged, which reflected the rift between the Mahatma and the Muslim priests. Hopes of a reconciliation were dimmed in the absence of the Ali Brothers who, having acted as mediators between Gandhi and the *ulama,* were languishing in British jails. By the end of 1921, the Khilafat movement was beginning to slip out of Gandhi's control. The viceroy had rightly assessed in 1921 that Mohamed Ali was a 'real factor in the situation' and a 'link' between the Congress and the Muslims. His view, vindicated by later day events, was that any strains in Gandhi-Mohamed Ali relations would lead to 'the collapse of the bridge over the gulf' that separated Hindus and Muslims.[69]

There was some distancing between the Khilafatists and a group of Hindu politicians as well. It started from Mohamed Ali's statement in April 1921 that, in the event of an Afghan invasion of India, India's Muslims would stand by them against the British.[70] This unrestrained commitment to anti-colonialism was widely misunderstood and raised quite a few eyebrows. There was talk of Islamic hegemony being established in India and of Hindus 'raising their heads' to thwart all such attempts.[71]

---

of Reading, *Rufus Isaccs First Marquess of Reading, By his son,* (London, 1945) pp. 242–245.

[69] The Marquess of Reading, ibid., p. 199.

[70] P. Parasram to the Ali Brothers, 8 July 1921, Mohamed Ali Papers, JMI; Brij Narain Chakbast to Sapru, Sapru Papers, National Library Calcutta, and the comments of Lajpat Rai in V.C. Joshi (ed.), *Lala Lajpat Rai : Writings and Speeches* (Delhi, 1966), vol. 1, p. 203.

[71] Moonje to Shankaracharya of Puri, n.d. (Report), Moonje Papers (35).

This distrust and imaginary fears were reinforced by the Moplah riots along the Malabar coast of South India.

Stirred by the pan-Islamic euphoria, the Moplahs directed their long suppressed anger against the Hindus, desecrated temples and resorted to forcible conversions. Reports of such happenings, often distorted and exaggerated, widened the breach in the Hindu-Muslim front. Congress leaders, in general, adopted a partisan attitude, accusing each other of instigating violence and speaking for and on behalf of their respective communities in Malabar. Some argued that oppression and exactions on the part of 'Hindu' landlords were at the root of the trouble denying that fanaticism entered into the picture at all. Hasrat Mohani said to the Congress Subjects Committee that the Moplahs suspected Hindus of collusion with government and were, therefore, justified in 'presenting the Quran to the Hindus. And if the Hindus became Mussalmans to save themselves from death, it was a voluntary change of faith and not forcible conversion'.[72] Syed Mahmud told Gandhi that there were no forced conversions; Abdul Bari accused government of circulating false rumours in order to drive a wedge between Hindus and Muslims. But Malaviya, Lajpat Rai, Moonjc and Shraddhanand were not satisfied with these explanations, arguing that fanaticism was used as an instrument by pan-Islamists to excite Muslims against the Hindus. They demanded that the Hindus should be united, integrated and consolidated in defence against any such future occurrence. Moonje, the aggressively anti-Muslim leader from Nagpur, mooted the idea of providing the settlement of 'our warlike races, such as the Marathas, Rajputs, Sikhs etc., in Malabar which alone, I think, can solve the problem of Moplah terrorism over the meek and helpless Hindus'.[73] This was in preparation of launching the *sangathan* movement, which greatly embittered Hindu-Muslim relations throughout the country.

Amid such heated controversies, Gandhi dropped a bombshell by suspending civil disobedience. 'The whole conception of

[72] Quoted in Ram Gopal, *Indian Muslims : A Political History 1858–1947* (Bombay, 1959), p. 157.

[73] Moonje Papers (13).

civil disobedience', Gandhi informed the Congress Working Committee, 'is based upon the assumption that it works in and through its non-violent character... I personally can never be a party to a movement half violent and half non-violent'.[74] Two other reasons might have also influenced Gandhi's decision. First, its patchy success in some areas,[75] and secondly, the growing strains in his alliance with the Khilafatists and his inability to curb their militant activities. The Karachi resolutions of July 1921 were intemperate enough to alarm Gandhi and the violent and xenophobic speeches of the *ulama* confirmed fears of an outbreak of violence. He was also aware of the effects of the Moplah riots on Hindus. He tried to soothe their feelings, but reached the inescapable conclusion that Hindus were becoming increasingly apathetic to the Khilafat cause and were anxious to extricate themselves from the travail of non-co-operation. Having read the danger signal, Gandhi recognized the political necessity of withdrawing civil disobedience.

For Muslims, however, the future of Khilafat and the Holy Places was still very much a live issue. As a consequence, Gandhi's arbitrary call in the summer of 1922 was received with anger, dismay and disappointment. 'Abandon Mr Gandhi's remedy of non-co-operation', stated Maulvi Mohammad Kazim Ali at the Bengal Provincial Conference in April, 'and find another path and follow it'. 'It is proper', added another speaker, 'that there should be assaults and bloodshed', and that 'he who is your enemy should be met with the sword'.[76] Hasrat Mohani rejected the Bardoli programme.[77] So did his political mentor, Abdul Bari, when he attacked Gandhi and the Bardoli resolution at the Jamiyat al-ulama conference held in Ajmer.[78]

After the suspension of civil disobedience, Muslims had

[74] To members of the Congress Working Committee, 8 February 1922, *CWMG*, vol. 22, pp. 350–51.

[75] Brown, *Gandhi's Rise to Power*, chapter 9.

[76] 'History of the Khilafat Movement in Bengal', p. 4, *Tarikh-i Jamiyat*, op.cit., pp. 61–62. And the later day verdict of A.B. Rajput and Ziauddin Suleri, quoted in Sayeed, *Pakistan : The Formative Phase*, p. 60.

[77] Home Poll. February 1922, F.No. 18, NAI.

[78] According to a report, his speech was 'wild, impolitic and full of destructive programme'. Home Poll. February 1922, F.No. 501, NAI.

another surprise in store. On 21 November, 1922, the Turkish National Assembly at Ankara decided to separate the Khilafat from the sultanate. And since the maintenance of the temporal power of the Khalifa was one of the main objects of the Khilafat movement, this action by a purely Muslim body completely took the wind out of its sails. In March 1924, the final blow was struck by Mustafa Kamal Pasha who burst the bubble of the Khilafat. Its immediate result was the disruption of the Khilafat Party. From 1918 to 1922, religious zeal and the overwhelming anti-British bias had united various groups amongst Indian Muslims. But once the initial euphoria had worn thin, the inherent contradictions in the alliance destroyed the appearance of unity and brought to surface the division among the ranks of the *ulama*, as among Muslims in general. The Jamiyat al-ulama was divided with Nisar Ahmad of Kanpur and Abdul Majid Budauni joining the *tanzim* movement and also founding a parallel ogranization in Kanpur.[79] The rapprochement between the political and religious wings of the Khilafat movement was also unable to sustain itself because international developments had undermined its *raison d'etre* and because there was no sound basis for permanent adjustments of diversified and, in some cases, conflicting interests.

One of the immediate consequences of such developments was the disappearance of Muslim divines from the national scene. They had gained in confidence from the time of the Muslim League session in 1918, but the unexpected setback shattered many of their plans and reduced their growing influence in national politics. The result was bewilderment, confusion, and even inactivity. Having once mobilized new groups, roused their religious fervour and articulated their grievances, the *ulama* were now like a contrary jack-in-box refusing to retire, out to seek new outlets for their energy, and to build something positive out of the Khilafat experience. Some doggedly kept the Khilafat movement gasping, some capitulated to the communalist camp, and some, including the *ulama* of Deoband, entered the arena of religious controversies and organized the *tabligh* and *tanzim* societies as a counterpart to *shuddhi* and *sangathan*.

[79] Qureshi, *Ulema in Politics*, p. 302.

The Khilafat agitation provided the *ulama* with a distinct enemy and goals; when the enemy and goals proved elusive other whipping boys and solutions had to be found. Much of their interests, geared to religious goals, remained, because they seemed to be the hope for the Muslim community. In consequence, many of the *ulama* who participated in the Khilafat movement reverted to their former religious preoccupations. For the time being, the Jamiyat al-ulama, despite its nationalist sympathies, moved along a course parallel to that of the nationalist Muslim political leadership. It was mainly concerned to secure safeguards against interference with the *shariat* and guarantees for its preparation and implementation. At Calcutta in March 1926, the Jamiyat directed its members to educate in the proper requirements of the *shariat* those Muslims who were following customary laws of inheritance. The Jamiyat also demanded the setting up of qazi courts for the settlement of disputes over marriages, divorce, inheritance and *auqaf*.[80]

The *ulama* of Firangi Mahal, too, were marginalized. Abdul Bari, the chief architect of the alliance between the *ulama* and the Congress, felt despondent, isolated and alienated from the Congress. In August 1923, he complained: 'The position of the Muslims has been rendered very awkward. Those who pretended to be our friends at one time and made a catspaw of the *ulama* now seem anxious to get rid of them'.[81] Abdul Bari was right. The *ulama* had been brought into political life because of their influence in the countryside and their ability to gather various groups under their own banner. But in the aftermath of civil disobedience and the Khilafat fiasco, their services were no longer required. They were bluntly told not to dabble in politics. Men like Abdul Bari were remembered merely as 'interesting' and 'esteemable representatives of the good old days' and as a 'distinguished figure out of the fast disappearing galaxy of that ancient culture which is still dear to us'.[82]

The widespread confusion in the ranks of various influential

[80] Hardy, *Partners in Freedom*, p. 35.

[81] Statement to the Press, Abdul Bari Papers.

[82] Maulvi Mohammad Yaqub, UP Provincial Muslim League, Annual Session, 24 April 1926 (Moradabad, n.d.).

Muslim groups, including the *ulama,* was best summed up by Khaliquzzaman:

The history of the next sixteen years of Muslim India is a mass of confusion and a chapter of political benightedness. The disruption of the Khilafat organization was like a breach in the embankment of the flowing stream of Muslim mass emotion, which diverted it into several petty streams, some leading to desert lands there to dry up, some flowing by zig-zag routes to meet the original bed in their headlong march and some others rushing towards the mighty ocean to drown themselves. To try to find any consistency, sound reasoning or logical method in Muslim politics during that period would be utterly futile. We were divided between ourselves.[83]

IV

Events following the Khilafat and Non-Co-operation movements have been a subject of much historical research. Yet, it may still be useful, before we cover them in some detail in subsequent chapters, to offer a corrective to certain established notions on the state of communal relations.

There can be no doubt that Hindu-Muslim relations worsened during 1922-1926 and the edifice of inter-communal unity began to crumble in a way that was unforeseen by the architects of the Khilafat and Non-co-operation agitations. Still, it would be misleading to draw the conclusion, tempting though it is, that the two communities were arrayed against each other or that Indian society came to be hopelessly polarized along communal lines. Notwithstanding mounting religious and communal tensions, most people continued to lead, as they had always done, a life of harmonious co-existence. In fact, bonds of socio-economic interests and centuries of common historical experiences were strong enough to withstand the communal onslaught. The pan-Islamic euphoria, which had caused so much excitement in the subcontinent, did not take much time to disappear as the Turkish nationalists began to rewrite their political agenda without a Khalifa/Sultan. Faced with this reality, unpleasant though it was to the more committed pan-Islamists, there was an unmistakable reordering of priorities. From now on, Islam was once more firmly rooted in the Indian soil and

[83] Khaliquzzaman, *Pathway to Pakistan*, p. 76.

the interests of its followers were seen to be more closely linked with the people they lived with and the society they were born in. It is sheer romanticism to suggest that 'the ideal of the Islamic community shaped and shapes their [Muslim] apprehensions of what is legitimate, desirable and satisfactory political action'.[84]

The *ulama* based at Deoband and those connected with the Jamiyat al-ulama were vocal champions of composite nationalism and firmly attached to the nationalist forces. It is fair to uncover their motives but it is no less important to assess their objective role in heightening anti-colonial consciousness. After all, their track record was enviable, for time and time again they rallied round the Congress-led agitations. In 1928-29, they sided with the Congress in boycotting the Simon Commission and adopted complete independence as their political creed. And in 1930-31, they took a prominent part in the civil disobedience campaigns.[85] The meeting at Amroha where some of these vital decisions were taken echoed their unmistakable commitment to the political radicalization of the nationalist struggle.[86] Some like Maulana Anwar Shah declared that the country's liberation from foreign domination was consistent with the Hanafi code.[87] Others like Maulana Shah Muhiuddin Ahmad of Phulwari insisted that Muslims should join Gandhi's Dandi March and defy government laws.[88] There were still others—Hafiz Mohammad Said, Mufti Kifayatullah and Ataullah Shah Bukhari—who languished in jails for organizing local civil disobedience campaigns.[89]

[84] Francis Robinson, 'Islam and Muslim Separatism', in Hasan (ed.), *Communal and Pan-Islamic Trends in Colonial India*, p. 373.

[85] Hasan, *A Nationalist Conscience*, pp. 182–83. A number of leading *ulama* appealed to Muslims in the name of Islam to join civil disobedience. The occasion for the appeal was the unfurling of the national flag on New Year's day. *Bombay Chronicle*, 31 March 1930.

[86] See Hasan, *Mohamed Ali: Ideology and Politics*, p. 105.

[87] *Medina*, for the week ending 5 April 1930, SNNR, UP.

[88] *Hamdam*, for the week ending 26 April 1930. Syed Shah Muhiuddin issued a manifesto, which was endorsed by the Bihar branch of the Jamiyat al-ulama, endorsing the decisions of the Amroha conference. *Rozana Akhbaar* and *Medina*, for the week ending 12 and 19 July 1930, SNNR, UP.

[89] *Amir-i Shariat* Ataullah Shah Bukhari made a vigorous plea at the

It was by no means easy for such men to maintain this degree of consistency, especially in periods of intense communal conflicts, and to face the wrath of some *ulama* from among their own ranks.[90] Though Husain Ahmad Madani and his band of followers were condemned and villified in the press and at public platforms,[91] they remained true to their ideals. In 1938 the Jamiyat al-ulama president, Madani, delineated the broad contours of his theory of composite nationalism in his letters to Iqbal. He pointed out that regardless of religion, common habitat or race the word *qaum* (community) was applicable to any collective group and that it did not have the same meaning as *millat,* which refers to a collectivity with a *shariat* or *din*. Indian Muslims, though separate from others in religion, were fellow-nationals with other communities and groups in India. They were therefore advised to join in a collective endeavour to achieve freedom and independence.[92] In independence thus gained Muslims and non-Muslims would be co-partners in creating a society and an administration which, though not modelled entirely on the

---

Amroha meeting for adopting civil disobedience and was a key figure in promoting the movement in Punjab. For details of his role, see Jaanbaaz Mirza, *Hayaat-i Amir Shariat* (Lahore, 1970). Bukhari was also involved in organizing meetings in support of Bhagat Singh. One such meeting—attended by over 1,500 Muslims and addressed by Zafar Ali Khan—was held in Delhi on 19 March 1931. Tegart Papers, Centre for South Asian Studies, Cambridge.

[90] Prominent amongst them were Shabbir Ahmad Usmani and Ashraf Ali Thanwi. See Munshi Abdur Rahman, *Maimaaraan-i Pakistan* (Lahore, 1976), and Mohammad Sadiq Qasuri, *Akaabir Tehrik-i Pakistan* (Lahore, 1979 edn.).

[91] Maulana Razi, *Mutahidda Qaumiyat aur Islam* (Lahore, 1967 edn.) was a powerful rebuttal of Madani's ideas on composite Indian nationalism. Asrarul Haq Siddiqi, *Congressi Ulama Ki Siyasi Karwaten* (Delhi, n.d.), was a sharp criticizm of Madani's presidential address at the Saharanpur session of the Jamiyat al-ulama. While such pamphlets were being written, the *Inqilab* of Lahore was carrying on a vicious campaign against the leaders of the Jamiyat. See its editorial comments on 11 September 1937, 19 May 1938, 6 January 1939, 5 March 1939, 15 March 1939. Also, see Choudhry Habib Ahmad, *Tehrik-i Pakistan aur Nationalist Ulama* (Lahore, 1966).

[92] Ahmad, *Islamic Modernism,* pp. 192–93; Hardy, *Muslims of British India,* pp. 227–28. For Madani's presidential address at the June 1940 Jamiyat al-ulama conference, see Faruqi, *The Deoband School,* pp. 103–4.

conception of an Islamic State, would comprise effective and influential Muslim elements in it.[93]

Inspired by this elucidation in *Mutahhidah Qaumiyat aur Islam* (Composite Nationalism and Islam), the Jamiyat al-ulama joined the Congress in a common endeavour to rid the subcontinent of its British masters rather than set a course for the partition of the region.[94] The creation of an 'Islamic State' was therefore not the work of the *ulama* but rather the determined effort by informed, western-educated Muslims who developed the capacity to whip up a massive agitation in support of their claim for a separate nation.[95]

Some of these aspects must await a detailed examination. But two general conclusions flow from the literature available to us. First, the *ulama* can no longer be regarded merely as standard-bearers of orthodoxy whose concerns, according to popular understanding, were limited to regulating the religious and educational life of the Muslims. They were not, as Ishtiaq Husain Qureshi once suggested, ignorant of politics or of the forces working in the world of today'.[96] Such a view ignores their wide range of interests and their involvement in organizing, conducting and leading several political campaigns.

The ideological basis of the politics of the *ulama* also needs to be re-examined as a corrective to the oft-repeated notion that their concerns were mainly communitarian and their anti-colonial stance, grounded in Islamic theology, was not consistent with the secular thrust of Indian nationalism.

It is true that the future of Muslims and of Islam were central to the concerns of the *ulama*. Given their position and their role in Muslim society, it could not have been otherwise. In fact, at

[93] Ibid., p. 191.

[94] See Faruqi, op. cit., pp. 96–101.

[95] Lawrence Ziring, *Pakistan The Enigma of Political Development* (Dawson : Westview, 1980), p. 24.

[96] In *The Future Development of Islamic Polity* (Pakistan Literature Series No. 8 : Lahore, 1946), Qureshi opined that the *ulama* 'have neither the training nor the vision to be of any use' and that 'the work of the reconstruction of political thought in Islam cannot be left in the hands of the *ulama*, because they have no knowledge either of politics or of the forces working in the world of today'. pp. 11–12.

the dawn of the twentieth century and with the beginning of organized politics, the concerns of the *ulama* were restricted to the religious domain and to issues which impinged on the *shariat.* Their political intervention, on the other hand, was of a varied and complex nature. Yet, it must be said that an important section of the *ulama* did not always see their role solely in relation to their community. They developed, as was the case with Maulana Mahmud Hasan, Ubaid-Allah Sindhi, Azad, Mufti Kifayatullah and Husain Ahmad Madani, a theory of composite Indian nationalism and intervened in political affairs to effect an integrated alliance with other groups and communities. The Prophet's covenant with the people of Medina, including Jews and pagans, still retained, in Azad's view, validity as a precedent for other situations and in other lands in the subsequent history of Islam, and was especially pertinent in India.[97] The use of such religious idioms and Islamic symbols served the secular objective of rallying the Muslims around the nationalist struggle.

[97] Ahmad, *Islamic Modernism*, p. 189; Douglas, *Abul Kalam Azad*, pp. 249–250.

Chapter Seven

The Communal Breach

The 37th Annual Session of the National Congress at Gaya marked the close of an historic period in our struggle for liberation.... Non-Co-operation as a political force is dead, that is, that orthodox brand of Non-Co-operation which makes religion out of politics and has turned the traditional organ of national struggle into a prayer-hall and conclave of theologians.*

M.N. Roy, 15 February 1923.

In short conditions in India have never ever been worse. The reaction of the N.C.O. movement which set in in 1922–23 has since been slowly but surely undermining all public activity. There is not much of it left now but the rot is still proceeding—at a quicker pace now than before. The only education the masses are getting is in communal hatred .... The older people among the nationalists have given way to despair. The younger men are taking greater interest in their own advancement by whatever means and however reprehensible in their opinion of 2 years ago. Imagine Congressmen in the Assembly & the Councils tumbling over each other to shake hands with officials, stealthily attending functions after taking care that their names are not reported to the press, actually applying for invitations to such functions....**

Motilal Nehru to Jawaharlal Nehru, 30 March 1927.

By 1922–23 the edifice of communal unity, so assiduously built by the Mahatma, lay in a state of fragile vulnerability, the Non-Co-operation campaign was brought to a halt by Gandhi, the struggle for establishing swaraj was thrown into the

*'Open Letter to C.R. Das', 3 February 1923, Sibnarayan Ray (ed.), *Selected Works of M.N. Roy* (Delhi, 1988), vol. 1, p. 77.

**Jawaharlal Nehru Papers, part 1, vol. 1, p. xix.

background and the nationalist fervour, which had been aroused to a high pitch against Pax Brittanica, petered out. India's secretary of state sensed the mood when he observed:

> The greatest thing is to have got the co-operation of the people without whose co-operation government would after all be bound sooner or later to break down; the advanced thinkers, the suspects of 1910 are the co-operators of today; some of them active and strenous participators in the work of government.[1]

The changed political scenario is most commonly attributed to Gandhi's abrupt decision to suspend civil disobedience.[2] The argument of the early communist ideologues was that the bottled-up energy of the people, unleashed during the non-co-operation days, found an outlet in communal clashes. Jawaharlal Nehru agreed. Reflecting on the events of the period, he observed:

> The drift to sporadic and futile violence in the political struggle was

[1] Montagu to Ronaldshay, 23 February 1922, Ronaldshay Papers, MSS.EUR. D. 609 (5–A), 1, IOLR. Only a few years later, Surendranath Banerjea, the most persistent and outspoken among living Indian agitators, recorded the change. 'Our angle of vision', he wrote, 'has changed with closer contact [with the European community] and with better knowledge. In public work and in helping the Reforms, we have become colleagues, and the feeling between European and Indian leaders is being gradually transformed into one of mutual esteem and respect'. Banerjea, *A Nation in Making*, p. 311.

[2] R.P. Dutt and other left-wing writers regarded Gandhi's decision as a 'betrayal' and a concession to the capitalists, landlords and other propertied classes who felt threatened by the ever-increasing militancy and radicalization of the Non-Co-operation movement. The question, observed Dutt, was not that of violence or non-violence, but of 'class interest in opposition to the mass movement, which was the breaking point of the national struggle in 1922'. *India Today* (Bombay, 1947), p. 353. This interpretation is no longer accepted as an authoritative Marxist formulation. See, for example, Sumit Sarkar, *Modern India* (Delhi, 1983), pp. 225–26, and Bipan Chandra, Mridula Mukherjee, Aditya Mukherjee, Sucheta Mahajan, K.N. Panikkar, *India's Struggle for Independence 1857–1947* (Delhi, 1987), pp. 192–95. The Gandhian motive for calling off civil disobedience is also discussed by Ravinder Kumar in his introduction to *A Centenary History of the Indian National Congress* (Delhi, 1985), vol. 2, pp. 18–20, and by Nanda, *Gandhi, Pan-Islamism, Imperialism and Nationalism*, pp. 350–56.

stopped, but the suppressed violence had to find a way out, and in the following years this perhaps aggravated the communal trouble. The communalists of various denominations, mostly political reactionaries, had been forced to lie low because of the overwhelming mass support for non-co-operation and civil disobedience movement. They emerged now from their retirement.... *It is just possible that if civil resistance had not been stopped and the movement had been crushed by Government, there would have been less communal bitterness and less superfluous energy left for the subsequent communal riots* [emphasis added].[3]

Gandhi was also held guilty for introducing religion into politics through his support of the Khilafat movement,[4] which was the precursor of the 'worst form of denationalizing [*sic*]...movement of communalism, pure and simple'.[5] His alliance with the pan-Islamists, so runs the argument, was 'built on the unreliable foundations of religious sentimentalism'[6] and encouraged 'the most retrogade form of Islamic group consciousness'.[7] In fact, M.R. Jayakar, member of the Bombay legislative council and a leading light in the Hindu Mahasabha movement, attributed the rise of communalism to

> Gandhi's policy during the last four years, which aimed at a most artificial and unreal unity between Hindus and Muslims, awakening sentiments and impulses in the latter community which, like the Frankenstein, it is now very difficult to allay. It makes me very sad to think that so great a patriot should have on this issue bungled so easily.[8]

Recent historical writings have hinted at some additional reasons which served to heighten communal consciousness, such as the 'methods' adopted by the Congress leaders during the Non-Co-

[3] Nehru, *An Autobiography*, pp. 86–87.

[4] This view was widely shared, though it was forcefully expressed in the writings of M.N. Roy. See, G. Adhikari (ed.), *Documents of the History of the Communist Party of India, 1923–1925* (Delhi, 1974), vol. 2, p. 210.

[5] *Mahratta*, 4 July 1927; *Leader*, 2 January 1927.

[6] G. Adhikari (ed.), op.cit., p. 211. Nehru spoke—some thirty years after the event—about 'the artificial unity Gandhi had forged out of diverse discontents'. Quoted in A.C. Niemeijer, *The Khilafat Movement in India 1919–1924* (The Hague, 1972), p. 93.

[7] N.C. Chaudhuri, *Thy Hand Great Anarch! India 1921–1952* (London, 1987), p. 39.

[8] To Lajpat Rai, 8 September 1925, F.No. 405, Jayakar Papers, NAI.

operation movement and in subsequent electoral and agitational campaigns.[9] There is, then, the baldly stated view of Bipan Chandra that communalism in the twenties or thereafter had no objective reality; if anything, it symbolized 'a distorted or perverse reflection of reality.' In the absence of a 'real conflict' between communities, the use of religion as a vehicle of political organization and mobilization was an aspect of 'false consciousness.'[10]

These explanations have no doubt enriched scholarly discourse, but they fail to come to grips with the intense and complex nature of communal antipathies at the regional and local levels. This is in large measure due to the inadequate attention paid to the impact of the Montagu-Chelmsford Reforms, more so in the provinces of British India.[11] It will not do to minimize this vital aspect, for the operation of the Act of 1919 quite perceptibly altered the tenor of relationships between dominant classes, especially in the Muslim-majority provinces, stimulated sectional concerns all around, and sharpened mutual rivalries in areas with scarce resources.

II

It is not uncommon to trace the roots of conflicts to the Act of 1909 which, for the first time, provided institutional legitimation to the notion of a distinct, separate Muslim political identity. Introducing separate electorates was a clever and novel British device to create a sense of communitarian solidarity and to then watch the spectacle of alignments being forged on the basis of religious affiliations. The measure of success in achieving such goals is, in part, reflected in the arguments marshalled to advance and sustain sectional claims. Muslim groups, in particular, not only

[9] Gyanendra Pandey, *The Ascendancy of the Congress in Uttar Pradesh 1926–34: A Study in Imperfect Mobilization* (Delhi, 1978), p. 115.

[10] Bipan Chandra, *Communalism in Modern India*, p. 23.

[11] This does not apply to the works of J.H. Broomfield, *Elite Conflict in a Plural Society: Twentieth Century Bengal* (Berkeley: Los Angeles, 1968); R.J. Moore, *The Crisis of Indian Unity 1917–1940* (Delhi, 1974); David Page, *Prelude to Partition*.

discovered a new vocabulary to articulate their aspirations but also insisted on being heard as representatives of their community. Their claims were dubious, for they were, in effect, pleading on behalf of dominant classes, both in urban and rural areas, for a share in the new power structures created first by the Act of 1909 and, a decade later, by the Montagu-Chelmsford Reforms.

Such claims went uncontested in official circles, for it suited the British, more than any other group, to turn a blind eye to the limited following and concerns of the so-called 'Muslim' organizations. Time and again they were propped up, rescued from oblivion and used to counterbalance the nationalist forces.

The Act of 1919 enlarged the scope of communal politics. The franchise was extended,[12] the elected and non-official members were represented in much greater strength in enlarged legislatures (Table 7:1), and, above all, they received some degree of authority, at least in the 'transferred' departments. Moreover, local bodies experienced vital structural changes as a result of wide ranging reforms, including the extension of the principle of election.[13] In 1920–21, the elective system was in force in all but five of the 116 municipalities in Bengal.[14] In Punjab, at least 75 per cent of elected members were, by 1922–23, directly returned from a much broader franchise.[15] Likewise, the UP District

[12] The number of electors to the pre-reform legislative council was only 2,774, of whom 2,306 were Muslims and landholders, who returned six members by direct election, and the remaining 468 were members of district and municipal boards who returned thirteen members. According to the first electoral roll drawn up in 1920, the number of voters stood at 1,347,922. By the time of the second election in 1923, the 'disqualification' clause that was applied to women was dropped. So the size of the electorate rose to 1,509,127, of whom 49,067 were women. *Report on the Working of the System of Government: United Provinces of Agra and Oudh* (henceforth *Report*, UP) (Allahabad, 1928), p. 175.

[13] A private bill introduced in the UP legislative council, which was adopted in 1922, reduced certain categories of municipal qualifications to the level of those required of electors to the legislative council. Ibid., p. 190.

[14] *Resolution Reviewing the Reports on the Working of Municipalities in Bengal* (Calcutta, 1922), p. 1.

[15] *Report on the Working of the Municipalities in the Punjab, 1922–23* (Lahore, 1923), p. 1.

Boards Act of 1922 incorporated important provisions: the official element disappeared, franchise was extended and the number of elected members went up.[16] 'Real local self-government in the rural areas of the United Provinces may with some justice be claimed to have been born in 1923', wrote the governor of the province.[17]

These changes meant that, for the first time, Indian ministers began to exercize some degree of control over education, local self-government, public works, public health and sanitation. It also meant that they could provide jobs, give out contracts for public works undertakings and grant permission to organize and regulate bazaars, melas and religious processions. As chairman of the Allahabad municipal board, Jawaharlal Nehru was 'pestered with the applicants for appointments...chits and recommendations have been brought to me from friends and attempts have been made to influence me in favour of various applications.'[18] With the scope and functions of local institutions enlarged, there was a corresponding increase in their power and sphere of influence.[19] This was an added incentive for influential groups to contend for a seat on local bodies and for their allies to take a keen interest in the electoral process.[20]

[16] *Report,* UP, vol. 2, p. 230.

[17] *Indian Statutory Commission: Memorandum submitted by the Government of the United Provinces to the Indian Statutory Commission* (London, 1930), vol. ix, p. 481.

[18] S. Gopal (ed.), *Selected Works of Jawaharlal Nehru,* vol. 2, p. 7.

[19] This was, of course, related to increases in both the income and expenditure of local bodies. Municipal incomes in Bombay, for example, rose by 40 per cent between 1918 and 1922. The increase there and elsewhere was a reflection of the post-war boom following the rise in property taxes and increases in octroi and other levies on trade. One of the areas which benefited most from these increases was education. There was a consequent expansion of schools and an increase in expenditure from 12.48 lakhs in 1920 to 17.60 lakhs in 1922. Hugh Tinker, *The Foundations of Local Self-Government in India, Pakistan and Burma* (London, 1968), pp. 121–24.

[20] In the 1925–26 elections in Bengal, 61.3 per cent of the electorate voted in Dacca, over 70 per cent in the seven wards of Rajshahi division and about 75 per cent in the four wards of Commilla division. *Bengal Municipalities 1925–26,* appendix B, pp. 73–76. For Bombay municipal elections, see Tinker, op.cit., p. 132.

TABLE 7.1

Composition of the Provincial Legislative Councils Established under the Montagu-Chelmsford Reforms

Province	NOMINATED				ELECTED														
						BY SPECIAL ELECTORATES				BY COMMUNCAL ELECTORATES						BY GENERAL ELECTORATES			
	Total (*ex-officio*, nominated and elected).	Total (nominated and *ex-officio*).	Officials (nominated and *ex-officio*).	Non-officials.	Total (elected).	Total	University.	Landholders.	Commerce and Industry including mining and planting.	Total	Urban Muslims.	Rural Muslims.	Europeans.	Anglo-Indians.	Indian Christians.	Sikhs.	Total.	Rural. Non-Muslims.	Urban. Non-Muslims.
1. Madras	127	29	23	6	98	13	1	6	6	20	11	2	1	1	5	..	65	56	9
2. Bombay	111	25	20	5	86	11	1	3	7	29	22	5	2	..	..	..	46	35	11
3. Bengal	139	26	20	6	113	21	1	5	15	46	33	6	5	2	..	..	46	35	11
4. United Provinces	123	23	18	5	100	10	1	6	3	30	25	4	1	..	..	..	60	52	8
5. Punjab	93	22	16	6	71	7	1	4	2	44	27	5	..	..	..	12	20	13	7
6. Bihar and Orissa	103	27	20	7	76	9	1	5	3	19	15	3	1	..	..	..	48	42	6
7. Central Provinces	70	16	10	6	54	7	1	3	3	7	6	1	..	..	..	..	40	31	9
8. Assam	53	14	9	5	39	6	..	..	6	12	12	..	..	...	..	..	21	20	1

SOURCE : *Statement Exhibiting the Moral and Material Progress and Condition of India* (London, 1921), Cmd. 202, p. 249.

The implications of the Reforms were not felt at the height of the Non-Co-operation movement, when provincial elections in 1920 were generally boycotted. But once that phase was over, the writing on the wall was clear. In 1922, a powerful lobby of Punjab-based traders, merchants and moneylenders resorted to the boycott of municipalities to protest against the provision of separate representation for the Muslims.[21] In another region, the Calcutta-based Hindu commercial and professional men were up in arms when Surendranath Banerjea, the first minister for local self-government in Bengal, conceded separate electorates in the 1923 Calcutta Municipal Bill.[22] 'How can he [Banerjea] face a non-Muslim constituency with this fatal record of pro-Muslim activities?', wrote the *Amrita Bazar Patrika* in its campaign against Banerjea's election to the council.[23] Its outcry was reminiscent of the furore over the Jahangirabad Amendment Act of March 1916, when a spate of loud and angry protests led to the boycott of and resignation from the municipal boards in UP.

The divisive effects of devolution of power were mostly felt in Bengal where Muslims were economically and politically weak and were therefore less well represented within the councils and, for that reason, less capable of utilizing the Reforms to their advantage.[24] This was why the more vocal educated Bengali

[21] For background studies, see N.G. Barrier, 'The Punjab Government and Communal Politics', *JAS*, vol. 27, May 1968, P. 529; Jones, *Arya Dharm*, p. 286; *Reports on the Working of Municipalities in the Punjab, 1896–97.*

[22] In November 1921, Banerjea proposed the abolition of separate electorate in a bill introduced in the council. But such was the intensity of Muslim opposition in Bengal that Banerjea accepted a compromise: provision for separate electorates was made for the first ten years, after which Muslims were to have reserved seats in general electorates. Leonard A. Gordon, *Bengal: The Nationalist Movement 1876–1940* (Delhi, 1979), p. 204. Banerjea did not mention this fact in his account. While chiding the swarajists for extending the 'communal system', he self-righteously procclaimed: 'In the meantime I remain unconvinced and prefer to tread the old path of obstinate opposition to the communal system in the constitution of our local bodies'. Banerjea, *A Nation in Making*, p. 340.

[23] *Amrita Bazar Patrika*, 1 December 1923.

[24] In 1921, Muslims were nearly 54.6 per cent of the population in the

Muslims, already aggrieved by the terms of the Lucknow Pact, insisted on securing the benefit of their majority position. Maulvi Abdul Karim observed:

> Theoretically it is all very well to say that communal representation stands in the way of the building up of a national state. But in India, which is a land of many communities, many creeds, many cultures and many traditions, it is not possible to have a thorough national fusion, completely separating the religious and socio-religious concerns of life from the economic and political interests. For the present the interests and aspirations of different communities must be separately considered and satisfied....[25]

Karim was stating what was then and later an article of faith with educated Muslims in Bengal and elsewhere. At the same time, they were wary of the fact that those who controlled the levers of power in urban and rural areas would resist sharing it with others on an equitable basis. A keen and bitter contest was therefore unavoidable, especially in Bengal and Punjab. We focus on these provinces of British India because of the intense communal competition, and because nowhere else was the interplay of religion and politics as stark and as ominous.

The exclusion of UP from the discussion is because the standard political explanation for the growth of communalism in Bengal and Punjab will not fit the facts in the province. In UP, the landholders constituted the largest single group in the council and held their position not as representatives of Hindus or Muslims but as spokemen of landed interests.[26] The Zamindar Party, founded by the Nawab of Chattari in 1921, was only marginally involved in communal controversies. Its primary function was to consolidate the gains that accrued to the landlords in the 1919

---

electoral area but were allowed only 39 seats. Hindus, on the other hand, had 46 seats against their population of nearly 45 per cent.

[25] Maulvi Abdul Karim, *Letters on Hindu-Muslim Pact* (Calcutta, 1924), p. 21.

[26] Though communal issues figured in the council, Hindu and Muslim landlords spoke with one voice and acted in unison on most issues that concerned their class. Thus the resolution to increase the representation of the zamindars of the Agra province was introduced by the Nawab of Chattari and supported by Thakur Jagannath Bakhsh Singh and D.R. Ranjit Singh. *Proceedings of the UP Legislative Council*, March 1923, vol. xii, pp. 160–69.

Act and to maintain their rural dominance, which was threatened by the spurt in peasant activity in several parts of UP. Shaikh Habibullah of Barabanki conveyed this concern to Harcourt Butler, an ardent champion of the UP landed aristocracy. He stated: 'Formerly it was the tenants who were in need of protection, now it is the landlords who need the protection of government'.[27]

The Oudh Rent Act [1921] and the District Boards Bill, introduced the same year, heightened the feeling of insecurity. Both pieces of legislation were stoutly resisted by the landlords, even though Harcourt Butler was able to secure their passage. But they sensed the impending threat to their prestige and power. 'The landless agitator is out for the destruction of the landholders', warned the Raja of Jahangirabad. He criticized the 'self constituted champions of the oppressed' for inciting the peasantry and pleaded with his audience at the UP Landholders' Conference to play a greater part in 'moulding public opinion'. Raja Durga Narain Singh of Tirwa [Farrukhabad district] harped on the same theme.[28]

Such pleas gave a semblance of unity to the Zamindar Party. Winning as many as 58 of the 77 rural seats, the landholders emerged as the largest single group in the 1923 council. Yet, they could not consolidate their gains. Divided and disorganized, they were unwilling to subordinate their personal interests or beliefs to those of the Zamindar Party. 'It is very distressing to me', wrote Harcourt Butler, 'to feel that the landowners are so divided among themselves and allow personal feelings to come before personal interests.'[29] Clumsy, naive and self-seeking, the Zamindar Party remained fragmented and out of touch with the realities of Indian politics.

[27] Habibullah to Butler, 6 March 1921, Butler Papers (80).

[28] Speech on 14 July 1922, ibid.

[29] Butler to the Nawab of Chattari, 20 December 1923, Chattari Papers, NMML. Earlier, Butler's predecessor, James Meston, had expressed his deep anguish over the disunity that plagued the group of landlords. On the eve of Montagu's mission to India, he made strenuous efforts to organize them and to 'stir them up to realize the magnitude of the occasion'. To Willingdon, 22 August 1917, Meston Papers (17).

III

By the end of 1922, the Civil Disobedience Enquiry Committee found the country unprepared for civil disobedience. But this judgement did not settle the controversy between those who favoured the continued boycott of the new councils and those who urged the reversal of Gandhi's ban on council entry. When the 'No-Changers' turned down the plea for council entry at the Gaya Congress in December 1922, the dissidents constituted themselves into the Congress-Khilafat-Swaraj Party, headed by C.R. Das and Motilal Nehru. Throughout the summer of 1923, the swarajists steadily gained ground. The tide finally turned in their favour in September of that year, when the Congress approved the modification of the boycott in favour of council entry and made it possible for them to breach the 'citadel of bureaucracy' both from inside and outside the councils. In the elections, the swarajists did quite well except in Punjab, Bihar, Orissa and Madras. They won a clear majority in the Central Provinces. In Bengal, they represented the strongest individual group. In UP and Bombay, they did not secure the majority of votes but were returned in considerable numbers.

The only way to bring the bureaucracy to its knees was to command the weight of united public opinion, to count upon the undivided support of the legislative council members. Nowhere was this need greater than in Bengal, where one-third of the members happened to be Muslims. Hence the suggestion of a pact—the condition precedent to concerted action within and outside the council walls.[30] The terms, worked out by Das with a section of the Khilafat leadership, were:

[30] Khuda Bukhsh referred to a meeting at his residence—5 Elliot Road—where the details of the proposed Bengal pact were hammered out. He noted that throughout the discussion Das showed a 'spirit of charity and compromise' and was willing to give any undertaking that would satisfy Muslims of his good faith. *Studies: Indian and Islamic,* p. 259. Maulvi Abdul Karim mentioned that a draft of the proposed pact, drawn up in consultation with Azad, Maulvis Nasim Ali and Waheed Husain, was discussed with Das on 9 December 1923. It was approved by the swarajist members of the council on 16 December. *Letters on Hindu-Muslim Pact,* p. 3.

1 For the provincial council—representation on a population basis with separate electorates for Muslims.

2 For the local bodies—representation in district boards and municipalities in the proportion of 60 to 40 in every district : 60 to the majority community and 40 to the minority. The question of separate electorates was kept open.

3 For government appointments—55 per cent seats were fixed for Muslims and the remaining 45 per cent were for other communities.

4 To ensure religious tolerance and communal harmony, music was to be prohibited before the mosques and Muslims were to enjoy the freedom to perform cow-killing for religious purposes *[Qurbani]*.

Das held out an olive branch, pleaded for reconciliation and an end to religious feuds. The Muslim leadership in Bengal reciprocated warmly. They swelled the ranks of the swarajists and helped turn the party into an effective political force. 'Mr Das', announced a Muslim councillor, 'was the only man in Bengal who was trying to bring about the unity of the communities', while Bose was 'the second man in Bengal who was trying to improve the position of the Muslim community'.[31] He was, in the words of Khuda Bukhsh, a principal negotiator of the pact, 'the healer of many festering wounds, the composer of the many apparently unadjustable differences, the man of the occasion'.[32]

The detractors of the pact, on the other hand, had no reason to eulogize its author. According to them, he betrayed the 'Hindu' cause[33] by entering into an 'unholy', 'unauthorized' alliance with Muslims.[34] Though they used nationalistic arguments and voiced patriotic sentiments to denounce the pact, it was apparent that

[31] For appreciation of Das's role and his contribution to the cause of communal amity, see Sisir K. Bose (ed.), *Subhash Chandra Bose Netaji: Collected Works* (Calcutta, 1981), vol. 2, p. 129; Kenneth Mcpherson, *The Muslim Microcosm*, p. 77; Gordon, *Bengal: The Nationalist Movement*, pp. 219, 220; Rajat Ray, *Social Conflict and Political Unrest in Bengal*, pp. 135–16, 322.

[32] *Studies: Indian and Islamic*, p. 269.

[33] *Amrita Bazar Patrika*, 17, 19, 22 December 1923.

[34] 'It seems strange', wrote the *Amrita Bazar Patrika*, 'that these gentlemen should meet in a secret enclave and enter into a contract with one another in matters affecting the rights and liberties of more than four million of the people'. 23 December 1923.

they were alarmed by the prospect of losing their political and economic hegemony to a relatively new class of Muslim professional men and up-country merchants. From all sides rang stridently vocal shouts—'Down with the pact; down, down with it'.

To begin with, the hue and cry was on account of the Muslim seats raised in the council from 40 per cent, as provided by the Lucknow agreement of 1916, to 55 per cent. In local bodies, too, the principle of 60:40 representation upset the balance of power in favour of Muslims, more so in areas where they were numerically strong [Table 7:2]. This was so in places like Dacca where a substantial increase in Muslim representation led to a corresponding fall in the share of Hindus—from 72 per cent to only 40 per cent. The most obvious fall out of such an arrangement was that some Muslims in certain areas had the opportunity, denied to them by the Lucknow concord and the Act of 1919, to wrest control of local bodies and of local patronage from Hindu zamindars and their clients.[35]

Das was not unduly perturbed by these implications of the pact, for he insisted that Muslims had not received more than their share. But the fairness of the arrangement was hardly an issue at stake. The detractors of Das, notably Surendranath Banrerjea and his group who were smarting under the crushing defeat they suffered at the polls, were eager to pick up any stick with which to beat the swarajists.[36] Their assault was reinforced by Lajpat Rai, Malaviya, Jayakar, Moonje and N.C. Kelkar, some of whom exerted pressure on the 1923 Kakinada Congress to scuttle the pact. Das was furious:

> You may delete the Bengal National Pact from the resolution, but I

[35] John Gallagher, 'Congress in Decline: Bengal 1930 to 1939,' in John Gallagher, Gordon Johnson and Anil Seal (eds.), *Locality, Province and Nation: Essays on Indian Politics 1870 to 1940* (Cambridge, 1973). Notice the Swaraj party campaign in 1925 against the extension of Union Boards in Noakhali. It was feared that the Village Self-Government Act would give more power to the Muslim peasant and relax the hold of the urban Hindu lawyer class over the villages, on which the party relied for mobilizing support. Rajat Ray, *Social Conflict*, p. 337.

[36] *Amrita Bazar Patrika*, 25, 29 December 1923 and 23 December 1925. For general criticizm of the pact, see Mcpherson, *The Muslim Microcosm*, pp. 78–79.

TABLE 7.2:
Representation of Hindus and Muslims on local and district boards in Bengal districts (excluding Darjeeling), 1923 [Percentages]

Name of Districts	Population		Local Boards		District Boards	
	Hindus	Muslims	Hindus	Muslims	Hindus	Muslims
Burdwan	78.0	18.5	88.1	11.11	79.5	19.05
Birbhum	68.1	25.1	81.3	18.7	75.0	25.0
Bankura	86.3	4.6	91.7	8.3	86.7	13.3
Midnapur	88.2	6.8	91.7	8.3	94.1	5.9
Hooghly	81.9	16.4	84.7	15.3	81.3	15.38
Howrah	79.3	20.3	94.4	5.5	87.5	12.5
24 Parganas	64.2	34.6	76.7	23.3	63.5	36.5
Nadia	39.1	60.2	80.0	20.0	71.3	28.7
Murshidabad	45.1	53.6	55.6	44.4	50.8	49.2
Jessore	38.1	61.8	83.4	.16.6	66.7	33.3
Khulna	50.0	49.8	81.3	18.7	62.1	37.9
Dacca	34.2	55.4	72.8	27.2	70.2	29.8
Mymensingh	24.3	74.9	54.2	45.8	39.0	61.0
Faridpur	26.3	63.5	58.4	41.6	54.6	45.4
Bakargunj	28.8	70.6	50.0	50.0	43.6	56.4
Chittagong	22.6	72.8	50.0	50.0	43.3	56.4
Tippera	25.8	74.1	46.7	53.3	34.0	65.6
Noakhali	22.4	76.6	29.2	70.8	31.2	68.8
Rajshahi	21.4	76.5	45.5	54.5	33.4	66.6
Dinajpur	44.1	49.1	66.7	33.3	60.0	40.0
Jalpaiguri	55.0	24.8	85.7	14.3	88.9	11.0
Rangpur	31.6	68.0	55.6	44.4	46.3	53.7
Bogra	16.6	82.5	50.0	50.0	40.7	59.3
Pabna	24.1	75.8	58.4	41.6	52.8	47.2
Malda	40.6	51.5	66.7	33.3	—	—
(Province)	43.7	53.6	67.0	33.0	60.8	29.2

SOURCE: *Census*, 1921, *Resolution Reviewing the Reports on the Working of the District Boards in Bengal, 1923–24* (Calcutta, 1925).

assure you, you cannot delete Bengal from the Indian National Congress or from the history of India. Bengal demands the right of having her suggestions considered.... She is an integral part of the constitution of the Indian National Congress. And she is intimately associated with the history of all political agitations from the commencement of this Congress down to the present day.[37]

Das warded off the attack against him by prevailing upon the Bengal Provincial Conference to ratify the pact in May 1924. His successor, J.M. Sengupta, kept it alive in order to retain Muslim votes in the November 1926 elections. But the 'Big Five' were not prepared to let go.[38] They were of the view that if the Congress, already bedeviled by factionalism, was to maintain its ascendancy in Bengal it was necessary to correct the popular image of being favourably disposed towards Muslims. Otherwise, the new mass of Hindu electorate would seek refuge in communal organizations, such as the Hindu Mahasabha, and other militant expressions of Hindu resurgence, including the Cow Preservation League, presided over by the vice-chancellor of the Calcutta university, Ashutosh Mukherjee, and patronized by rich Marwaris.[39]

Given the political climate in Bengal, it was not surprising that the pact, pushed too hard and too fast by its author, was thrown to the winds at the earliest. In this way, 'an immense funeral pyre was set up at Krishnanagar town and preparations were made to burn up the movement of swaraj...on that pyre'.[40] 'Two-fold is our debt to Mr Das', commented Khuda Bukhsh. 'We are beholden to him for his liberal-mindedness and we are beholden to him, far more, for opening our eyes to the true Hindu feeling and attitude towards us'. He added:

The pact is at an end, but this little episode is not without a lesson and a warning. What Swaraj would be like, who can say? But one thing is

[37] Quoted in Gordon, *Bengal,* p. 197.

[38] See *Forward,* 25 June 1926.

[39] Rajat Ray, op. cit., pp. 333–34. In June 1926, Madan Mohan Burman and Jatindra Mohan Das Gupta of the Bengal Hindu Sabha convened a conference to safeguard 'Hindu interests'. *Forward,* 8 June 1926.

[40] *Mohammadi,* 28 May 1926. For reactions to the rejection of the pact, see *Asr-i Jadeed* and *Hanafi,* 23 May 1926, SNNR, Bengal.

beyond doubt—it would be a paradise where the followers of the Prophet would have no milk or honey. It is idle, then, to look to Swaraj for the cure of our present ills. And equally idle is to look to it for a reign of right or righteousness.[41]

These fears, though expressed in exaggerated terms, reflected the strong sense of anger and disappointment at the drift of events in Bengal politics. Most educated Muslims wanted to know what went wrong. After all, they had stood by the Congress through thick and thin, even though the rank and file of the party firmly resisted the few concessions and constitutional safeguards given to them.[42] But the repudiation of the pact was too bitter a pill to swallow. The view gained wide credence that 'neither in terms of the Muslim interest nor of the *proja* interest, was it possible to rely any longer on the Congress.'[43]

This perception was reinforced by instances, cited daily in the 'Muslim press', of discrimination against Muslims in the employment market and their exploitation by Hindu zamindars and mahajans. The 'Hindu' swarajists, most of whom were zamindars, were taken to task for their pro-landlord position in the council. Abdur Rahim lambasted them for obstructing the Tenancy Bill beneficial to the 'dumb millions of cultivators of whom the majority are Muslims.'[44] Kazi Nazrul Islam, the revolutionary

[41] *Studies: Indian and Islamic*. pp. 269–70. And the following comment in the *Moslem Chronicle* of 18 June 1926:

We confess we were never enamoured by the artificial alliance which Das's instinct of self-preservation prompted him to conclude with the Muslim community.....We know that the Hindu politicians were playing a foul game, and when the pact was put to test within a few months of its birth, the astuteness of Hindu politics was quite apparent.

[42] Mcpherson, op. cit., pp. 84–86. Also, resistance to concessions was echoed by *Dainik Basumati*, 3 January 1926 and *Desher Vani* (Noakhali), 29 December 1925.

[43] Quoted in Partha Chatterjee, 'Agrarian Relations and Communalism in Bengal, 1926–1935', Ranajit Guha (ed.), *Subaltern Studies I: Writings on South Asian History and Society* (Delhi, 1982), p. 10.

[44] Sharifuddin Pirzada (ed.), *Foundations of Pakistan*, vol. 2, pp. 56–57; Broomfield, *Elite Conflict*, p. 274.

poet, denounced the vested interests in the council which had conspired to betray the people's cause.[45]

Once the political honeymoon with the swarajists ended, a number of Muslim groups, including Congressmen of long-standing, changed their political course.[46] In the 1926 elections, of the 39 Muslims elected, only one was a swarajist. The remaining thirty-eight members searched for a role in other political groupings.

Not long ago the swarajist movement seemed to hold the Bengali Muslims in thrall. Now, they hoped against hope that some spark would relight the flame that was snuffed out by short-sighted and hot-headed swarajists. The hope lay, according to some, in carrying on

> C.R. Das's work to its consummation. Let us hush our differences. Let us prove ourselves worthy of the torch handed over to us by him—a torch which he held with heroic steadfastness.[47]

IV

Writing in the context of the bloody Calcutta riots, M.N. Roy referred to the 'office-hunting intelligentsia' as the spokemen of communal interests.[48] In this apt description, two individuals fit in quite well—the Barisal lawyer, Fazlul Haq, and the Madras High Court judge, Abdur Rahim. They stand out as champions of interests, which were defined, elaborated and articulated within a strictly communal framework.

Fazlul Haq was the most prominent Muslim in the Bengal Congress during the all too brief honeymoon of Hindu-Muslim

[45] Rajat Ray, op. cit., p. 338. Even the *Ananda Bazar Patrika* complained that the Congress was apathetic towards the cultivators and that many of its pious resolutions were not put into action. 'There is no wonder then that this sham-campaign of swaraj will come to nothing like a bewildered traveller in the desert'. 29 April 1927, SNNR, Bengal.

[46] *Mussalman*, 10 September 1926.

[47] Khuda Bukhsh, op. cit., p. 260.

[48] 'The Calcutta Riot', Sibnarayan Ray (ed.), *Selected Works of M.N. Røy*, vol. 2, p. 436.

relations. He was one of the principal negotiators of the Lucknow Pact, leaving behind the political legacy of his one-time mentor, the Nawab of Dacca. But he split from the Congress over the non-co-operation programme. 'You know very well', he stated in response to an invitation to join a Congress meeting, 'that between me on one side and those representing the present-day politics of the Congress, there is a gulf of difference which no worldly diplomacy can possibly bridge over. Your ideals and mine are different. You have adopted an ideal in the Congress to which I cannot subscribe.'[49]

Fazlul Haq's defection was a blow to the Congress in Bengal, for he was a leader with considerable mass appeal and organizational flair. In losing his support the Congress lost an important spokeman of its cause among Muslims.

The offer of a ministerial berth in 1924 marked the fulfilment of Fazlul Haq's political ambitions. But his luck ran out—the ministry was overthrown by the swarajists within six months of its being in office. During this period of heady confrontation, Fazlul Haq and his colleagues gave up all scruples to stay in office. The cat was let out of the bag when word spread that a greedy council member had agreed to abstain from voting for the swarajists after accepting a bribe of Rs 3000.[50] It was also known that Fazlul Haq worked behind the scenes trying to convince the governor to induct Rai Bahadur Pyarelal into the ministry, because he commanded the votes of Bhusan Roy and Allabux.[51]

Along with these efforts, Fazlul Haq raised the cry that the Hindus, as it were, hatched a conspiracy to overthrow a 'Muslim Ministry'. This was the trump card. But this was not all. Khan Bahadur Musharraf Husain was pressed into service to demand the recruitment of a certain percentage of Muslims in government service. The motive was to embarrass the swarajists, create communal schisms in their rank, and weaken their opposition to the ministry. But the move led to no immediate gains. When the

[49] To S.C. Bose, 22 February 1921, quoted in A. Rab, *A.K. Fazlul Haq*, p. 56.

[50] To Lytton, 9 July 1924, Lytton Papers, MSS. EUR. F. No. 16 (46), IOLR.

[51] 4 August 1924, ibid.

demand for ministerial salaries was rejected for the second time on 26 August, the ministers resigned and the governor promptly suspended the constitution. Fazlul Haq, who had masterminded the communal strategy, was crestfallen. With his political ambitions thwarted, he now bitterly complained of 'having fallen a victim to the vilest conspiracy' of the Hindus.[52] The accusation was false, for the ministry was overthrown by the combined opposition of the swarajists. Out of thirty-seven elected Muslims voting in the council, the majority—nineteen—voted against the ministers. The significance of this fact was not lost on Mujibur Rahman, always mature and sober in his judgements. He rejected Fazlul Haq's claim to stand for the so-called Muslim interests. To say that the Muslim ministers held on to their posts to serve the cause of Islam and to protect Muslim interests was to palm off a gigantic fraud upon the entire community.[53]

By the end of 1925, Fazlul Haq's image in Bengal politics was tarnished. The Swaraj party made great play of the fact that he offered bribes to several councillors to buy their votes. In his own words, it 'had the effect of weaning away the sympathy of some of my best friends and supporters'.[54] His credibility with the government was also low; his claims were ignored when a new ministry was constituted in 1926. Bitter and sullen, he told Lytton:

> I sacrificed a position of assured success at the Bar to take to politics [more with a view to serve my community than anything else], and politics has given me but a poor return.[55]

Though shaken by his fluctuating political fortunes, Fazlul Haq was aware of his charismatic appeal in the Bengal countryside, especially among the Muslim peasantry, and was conscious of his organizational skills. Determined to regain the position he had once occupied in Bengal, he chose the easiest political course available to him—to merge with the swelling ranks of Muslim political formations in Bengal and emerge as their sole spokesman. His aim was to create a strong and unified Muslim party which

[52] 2 September 1924, (18).
[53] Rajat Ray, op.cit., p. 323.
[54] To Lytton, 11 March 1925, Lytton Papers.
[55] 25 November 1925, ibid.

would provide him with a strong base to negotiate with the Bengal Congress and the provincial government.

Fazlul Haq launched himself in this new role on the eve of the provincial elections in November 1926. As a first step, he founded the Bengal Council Party with the help of Husain Suhrawardy, former deputy mayor of the Calcutta Corporation, Mujibur Rahman, editor of *Mussalman,* Haji Abdur Rashid Khan, Calcutta Corporation's deputy executive officer and Maulana Akram Khan, lawyer and defector from the Non-Co-operation movement. The organ of the new party wrote:

> We have, after all, realized that the Congress is a Hindu organization and Muslims have no chance of holding its leading strings. They are welcome within the ranks of Congress as long as they prefer to remain as the henchmen of Hindu leaders and slaves to their cunningly planned intrigues to keep Muslims out of real power.[56]

This was the voice of aggrieved politicians. Having failed to make much profit out of the so-called Hindu-dominated council, they were now busy fanning communal passions. They were playing with fire.

Abdur Rahim, a zamindar of Midnapur and a former judge of the Madras High Court, moved into the political arena after the expiry of his term on the executive council. His first act was to address the Muslim League session in December 1925 at Aligarh, where he spoke against the Congress to create a constituency among the Urdu-speaking Muslims of Bengal. By mid-April 1926, he had garnered enough sympathy for his newly-formed Bengal Muslim Party. Its manifesto stated:.

> The experience of the last three years has shown how time after time the Muslim members of the council belonging to the swaraj or nationalist parties, which are organizations controlled by astute Hindu politicians who supply the brains and the funds of the parties, had to sacrifice, at their behest, the clear interests of the Muslim electorate and the Muslim community.[57]

[56] See *Moslem Chronicle,* 20 August and 24 September 1926.

[57] *Indian Quarterly Register,* January-June 1926, vol. 1, p. 67.

The Bengal Muslim Party promised to remove the 'considerable disabilities and difficulties' faced by Muslims. It proposed to achieve this by ensuring their representation—56 per cent in the council, local bodies, public services, universities and other professions. In other words, everything was to be organized along communal lines and Muslims *per se* were to have power and influence in proportion to their population.

With this distinctly communal platform, Rahim plunged into the election fray in November 1926. Everything worked in his favour. He exploited to the full the bitter legacy of the Calcutta riots in April 1926 and went to the electors with a simple religious appeal: 'Mussalman! who are you going to vote for? For the servants of Rahim or for the slaves of Rama?'[58] Most Bengali Muslim voters fell in behind Rahim, giving his party a majority of seats in the council. Rahim's own popularity reached commanding heights: he secured 641 of the 648 votes in the North Calcutta seat.

Rahim was invited to form a ministry in January 1927 but was unable to recommend a Hindu member willing to co-operate with him.[59] He tried to win over the Muslim MLCs by representing the intransigence of Hindus as a gross insult to the Muslim community. He said:

> There can be no doubt that this [the willingness of the Hindus to cooperate with him] is the result of a combination among B. Chakravarti and P.C. Mitter and some other Hindu gentlemen of their ways of thinking to prevent me from forming a ministry. For some time past politicians of this class have been carrying on a ceaseless campaign against me simply because I sought to unite the representative men of my community in order to protect and safeguard its just interests.[60]

Suhrawardy and A.K. Ghuznavi, who were themselves

[58] Quoted in Broomfield, op. cit., p. 280.

[59] He was described as the 'high priest of communalism'. The *Amrita Bazar Patrika,* an arch critic of Abdur Rahim, was of the view that Abdur Rahim's association with the ministry plunged Bengal 'into the vortex of communal strife'. *Amrita Bazar Patrika,* 23 January 1927. Page, *Prelude to Partition,* p. 45, and Mcpherson, op.cit., p. 98 discuss the role of Abdur Rahim.

[60] Ibid., 27 January 1927.

jockeying for a position in the ministry, refused to oblige. The governor approached Ghuznavi, who formed a ministry by weaning away some of Rahim's own supporters. Ghuznavi also won over a few dissident swarajists, led by Byomkesh Chakravarti. In this way the political initiative in Bengal still rested with communally-oriented leaders.

Bengal, after all, provided an ideal setting for them to exploit communal tendencies. With most Muslims, especially in the eastern region, nursing a long-standing grievance against the landlord-moneylender combination and the 4,22,000 enfranchised rural voters being susceptible to religious and communal exhortations, men like Rahim, Ghuznavi and Suhrawardy found an excellent target for attack in the dominant Hindu community to which belonged the landholders and their agents, the moneylenders, the lawyers, the tax collectors, and other government officials with whom every Bengali Muslim, rural and urban, was obliged to have dealings. To charge this group with tyranny and to call for united backing to break its stranglehold was one way of arousing popular enthusiasm. What lent weight to this appeal was that the symbols of Islam—mosques, shrines and religious festivals—often cut across the dividing lines of caste and class and simplified the task of mass communication.[61]

V

The balance of forces in Punjab was strikingly different from that of Bengal where educated Muslims had to settle their claims only with Hindus. In upper India, the Sikhs, too, demanded their due share in the distribution of seats. Although their population was less than 14 per cent, they claimed a far higher proportion of

[61] Broomfield, op. cit., p. 328. Some folk writings in Bengal were full of venomous remarks against the usurious mahajans and the exacting Hindu zamindars. Villifying them and their agents, a Muslim bard wrote:
I think....of the great zamindar, who does not recite the name of Allah even once in a month.
The raja, the zamindar and all their *amla* (staff) suck the *proja* like jackals and dogs.
Quoted in Tajul Islam Hashmi, 'Peasants and Politics in East Bengal', p. 125.

seats—about 30 per cent—on the grounds that they were the former rulers of the province and formed a large proportion of the army. Added to this was their belief that Sikhs possessed a 'separate identity as a community given to us by our Gurus' and their insistence that 'we will not be prepared to merge it into any other community'.[62]

Certain Muslim groups in Punjab were relatively better placed than their co-religionists in Bengal. This was so in government services.[63] Moreover, Punjab had a well-entrenched Muslim aristocracy which was nursed over the decades by the British government and was, consequently, a strong pillar of the imperial edifice. It owned vast tracts of land in Gujrat, Jhang, Jhelum and Attock, and also in eastern districts where the Hindu and Sikh landowning position was much stronger.[64] To the west of Lahore, Muslims were the main landholding group: in the districts opened up by irrigation projects, notably Gujranwala, Lyallpur and Montgomery, they shared this dominance with the Sikhs, but further west, in the districts where Muslims constituted more than 80 per cent of the population, their pre-eminence was unqualified.[65]

The fortunes of the landed aristocrats in Punjab were indissolubly linked with the raj. Both had equal stakes in maintaining the *status quo*. The British bolstered their interests and accommodated their claims in constitutional arrangements, because they were the chief source of recruitment to the army, made substantial financial contributions to the imperial coffers, and served as the

[62] R.M. Sahni, 'Communal Representation,' *Tribune*, 19 September 1924; Rajiv Kapur, *Sikh Separatism: The Politics of Faith* (London, 1986), chapter six.

[63] While Muslims were not employed in the higher echelons of government in numbers proportionate to their share of the population, their proportion was much higher than the level of literacy. In the Police department, for example, they held 25 per cent of appointments and held nearly 50 per cent of the posts in the scale of Rs 200 to Rs 300. The Sikhs and the Hindus, on the other hand, jointly held just over 16 per cent of the positions. *PSC*, 1913, vol. 12, appendix 15, pp. 156–158.

[64] See Talbot, *Punjab and the Raj*, p. 20.

[65] Page, *Prelude to Partition*, p. 48.

instrument through which the *sarkar* exercized its authority in far-flung areas.

Thus the chief beneficiaries of the 1919 Reforms were members of the Punjab Muslim Association and the Punjab Central Association, the latter representing the Sikhs and Jats. Influential Muslims who dominated the council were the Nuns and Tiwanas who exercized social authority in the north-western parts of the canal colonies and whose services had proved to be of special value for the supply of recruits and other contributions to the war effort.[66] Umar Hayat Khan Tiwana served first in the council of state from 1920 to 1929 and then on the secretary of state's council during the crucial period when the Act of 1935 was being framed. Feroz Khan Nun, who represented Shahpur West from 1920 to 1923 and Shahpur East from 1926 to 1936, was minister for local self-government in 1927 and minister for education in 1931.[67] The Daulatanas, too, figured as a major force in Punjab politics. Ahmad Yar Khan Daulatana had an estate of 45,000 acres and was elected to the council from east Multan in 1920 and 1926 and from the Muslim landholders constituency in 1930. In the mid-twenties, they added to their already vast riches when their private canal, the Daulatwah, was amalgamated into the Sutlej valley project. The government gave them handsome compensation in the form of further grants of canal colony land.[68]

The first Punjab Council comprised, besides 23 nominated officials and non-officials, 71 elected members. Out of them 35 were Muslims, 15 Sikhs and the rest were Hindus. As in UP, these members were neither loyal to any communal formation nor were they obsessively concerned with the claims of their community. Generally, their formation, as Fazli Husain suggested:

> has taken the line of the 'have-gots', and 'have-nots', with the result that there is a party existing of most of the Muslims and some of the landholding Hindus and Sikhs, because these are the communities which have been more or less excluded by the 'have gots' who had

[66] Imran Ali, *The Punjab under Imperialism 1885–1947* (Princeton, 1988), p. 82.

[67] For details, see Page, op. cit., pp. 61–63.

[68] Imran Ali, op. cit., p. 83.

enjoyed the monopoly of the public services under the pre-reform administration.[69]

Landlords belonging to all religious denominations, including the emerging class of rich Jat farmers like Lal Chand and Chhotu Ram, formed the core group in what is commonly designated as the agriculturist party. The aim of the Punjab Unionist Party, outlined in its 1923 election manifesto, was to advance the interests of the backward classes and communities, irrespective of their caste or creed.[70] Thus the move to repeal the Punjab Alienation Act of 1901 was stoutly resisted, for it was seen as an assault on the rural dominance of the Unionist Party members.[71] The response to the increasing criticizm of the Act was to stiffen the resolve of the 'agricultural class' to stand by 'the Magna Carta of their political and economic life'.[72] They also pinned their hopes on other legislative enactments, such as the Moneylenders Registration Bill, The Punjab Courts Fees [Amendment] Bill and the Punjab [Urban Property] Rent Regulation Bill.

These measures evoked sharp criticizm from moneylenders, traders, merchants and the Lahore-based professional groups. But they were most strident in denouncing the policies of Fazli Husain who, as minister of education, doled out patronage to Muslim educational institutions, offered grants, where none had been available, to existing schools and colleges,[73] and aided the

[69] Azim Husain, *Fazli Husain*, p. 152.

[70] The programme of the Unionists was to attain dominion status within the British Commonwealth of Nations, secure a fair distribution of taxes on rural and urban areas, prevent the exploitation of economically backward classes and support the Punjab Alienation Act.

Serious research on the Unionist Party has been undertaken only in recent years. In addition to Azim Husain's biography of his father and Ashiq Husain Butalvi's *Iqbal ke aakhri do Saal* (Karachi, 1961) which covers the early history of the Unionist Party, there are now quite a few scholarly works. Notable amongst them are the writings of David Page, Imran Ali, Ian Talbot and David Gilmartin. Prem Chowdhry, *Punjab Politics: The Role of Sir Chhotu Ram* (Delhi, 1984) highlights the role of a key figure in Punjab politics.

[71] *Punjab Administration Report 1922–1923* (Lahore, 1924), p. 17.

[72] Gilmartin, *Empire and Islam*, p. 38.

[73] By the close of the nineteenth century, Punjab had a large number of

setting up of new ones.[74] He founded three intermediate colleges in Gujrat and Campbellpur for the large Muslim population in western Punjab,[75] and distributed seats at the Lahore Government and Medical Colleges amongst Hindus, Muslims and Sikhs in the ratio of 40:20:20. He introduced separate electorates in municipalities and district boards and apportioned elected seats in proportion to the population of communities. Between 1917 and 1920, the Punjab government increased the number of municipalities with communal electorates; so the percentage of Muslim seats rose from 40 to 44 per cent. Fazli Husain's new formula bolstered their position all around,[76] with Muslims controlling over 53 per cent of district boards. (Table 7:3)

Such concessions impinged on the socio-economic position of

---

special Muslim schools which were mostly under private management. In places like Lahore, Multan and Sialkot there were local *anjumans* whose main function was to further the cause of education in local community, and they maintained a college as well as a number of high, middle or primary schools. The Anjuman-i-Himayat-i Islam, for example, was entirely supported by private subscriptions and donations, and it maintained a college, a high school and a primary school for boys and girls. Other institutions were the M.A.O. High School, Amritsar, and Mamuje High School, Rawalpindi.

[74] In justification of his policy of giving financial aid to Muslim schools and colleges, Fazli Husain argued that there was an unequal distribution of grants to government-aided institutions. He provided the following figures for 1921–22 to illustrate his point. These figures set out the amount of grants sanctioned [in Rupees] to government-aided schools in five districts.

	Hindus	Muslims	Sikhs	Christians	Total
Ambala	55,245	15,800	8,698	20.887	.100,430
Jullundur	52,396	13,741	30,943	27,287	123,367
Lahore	97,413	61,954	88,189	117,224	364,780
Rawalpindi	46,220	37,015	60,039	40,253	183,527
Multan	35,287	30,249	17,073	250	83,333
Total	286,561	158,929	204,942	205,901	856,333

SOURCE: *Punjab Legislative Council Debates,* 5 March 1924 (Lahore, 1924), vol. 6, no. 8, p. 315.

[75] Ibid., 18 November 1924, vol. 7, no. 7, p. 470.

[76] Muslims formed 53 per cent of the municipal population; from 1920 to 1923 the proportion of Muslims was increased from 44 to 49 per cent.

TABLE 7:3
Composition of the District Boards, 1925

District Boards	Population			Number of Members Elected or Nominated		
	Muslims	Sikhs	Hindus and Others	Muslims	Sikhs	Hindus
Hissar	18,571	42,956	487,620	11	—	27
Rohtak	91,854	432	604,291	5	—	34
Gurgaon	189,119	846	420,933	16	—	24
Karnal	235,618	12,280	580,828	11	3	26
Ambala	157,388	95,155	311,122	9	—	27
Kangra	38,197	1,830	722,600	1	—	37
Hoshiarpur	279,450	132,250	495,326	13	12	18
Jullundur	303,427	199,923	202,347	15	21	3
Ludhiana	147,336	230,777	111,519	10	24	1
Ferozepur	437,462	291,788	251,580	14	22	7
Lahore	227,198	90,684	88,599	20	17	4
Amritsar	343,073	262,067	144,887	12	22	2
Gurdaspur	385,661	133,892	269,259	15	15	12
Sialkot	580,532	74,939	282,352	20	12	5
Gujranwala	387,152	45,027	99,782	21	10	4
Sheikhupura	357,797	85,253	110,023	19	7	4
Jhelum	422,979	18,626	35,463	25	3	2
Rawalpindi	214,070	10,819	11,254	24	4	2
Attock	436,418	14,631	15,840	32	2	2
Mianwali	288,451	2,242	33,281	25	—	5
Montgomery	497,945	93,297	91,827	17	5	6
Lyallpur	515,122	145,063	177,868	27	11	3
Jhang	475,388	9,376	85,795	24	1	5
Multan	671,307	16,342	105,432	29	3	4
Muzaffargarh	482,134	4,530	57,697	24	1	5
Dera Ghazi Khan	385,104	670	39,577	29	3	4
Shahpur	552,014	24,490	65,692	32	3	1
Gujrat	670,340	47,105	50,609	35	2	2

Source: *Punjab Legislative Council Debates,* 30 November, 1925, vol.8, no. 26, p. 1319.

the Punjabi Hindu elite. Hence the hue and cry. Fazli Husain was maligned as the apostle of communalism and the high priest of separatism. The minister rebutted the charge in the council: 'If there is any one man who can claim to have brought Hindu-Muslim unity, I claim, Sir, that I am that man'. But he was not heard. Amar Nath Chopra, a High Court vakil in Lahore, lamented that Fazli Husain was 'out to relegate Hindus to an insignificant position in the Punjab'.[77] The Municipal Amendment Bill evoked a similar reaction. Lala Duni Chand, member of the legislative assembly, and Lala Ganga Ram, member of the Punjab legislative council, persuaded Hindu voters and candidates to withdraw from the municipal elections (held on 17 December 1923) in protest against increased Muslim representation on municipal boards.[78] In Lahore, Rawalpindi and Ferozepur, where Muslims gained control of the municipalities, Hindu members resigned.[79] They did not do so in places like Gojra, Hissar and Rohtak, where their dominance was intact. The Sikhs also joined in the boycott to press for separate representation instead of representation by election jointly with the Hindus.[80]

Communal controversies further deepened in the council chamber. The Moneylenders Registration Bill,[81] a progressive piece of legislation, was given a communal colour simply

---

Tinker, *Foundations of Local Self-Government*, p. 135. See, Page, *Prelude to Partition*, p. 71.

[77] *Tribune*, 28 December 1923.

[78] The municipality of Ambala had an equal number of Hindus and Muslims. But, in pursuance of Fazli Husain's reforms, the number of Muslims increased from six to eight. The number of Hindus remained at six. *Punjab Legislative Council Debates*, 29 February 1924, vol. 7, no. 1, p. 89.

[79] FR (Punjab), 1 July 1923, Home Poll. F.No 125, 1923, NAI.

[80] *Legislative Council Debates*, 29 February 1924, vol. 6, no. 5, p. 205.

[81] Most moneylenders in Punjab, especially in the western districts, belonged to the Agarwal, Khatri and Arora castes. The debtors, on the other hand, happened to be Muslims. The extent to which indebtedness had grown amongst them is illustrated by the case of western Dera Ismail Khan district where approximately 86,000 [8 per cent] of cultivable land was transferred from 1880 to 1885. S.S. Thorburn and M.L. Darling were alarmed by the growing indebtedness of Muslim cultivators and the transfer of landed property by mortgage and sale to the urban moneylenders. The

because it was to benefit the Muslim peasantry more than any other group.[82] Pandit Nanak Chand, representing the non-Muslim rural constituency of Hoshiarpur and with extensive trading and banking connections, declared it as 'a Muhammadan measure because in the Quran people are asked not to lend money on interest'.[83] Ram Singh of Kangra was equally vehement in his denunciation.[84] A legislative measure, wrote M.N. Roy in 1924, 'checking the flagrant abuse of the Hindu usurers is not taken on its merit, but made a butt of communal antagonism'.[85]

Irrespective of the nature of issues, the dominant Hindu groups arrayed themselves against Fazli Husain in a bid to oust him.[86] In March 1923, Raja Narendranath, president of the Punjab Hindu Sabha, introduced a vote of censure against Fazli Husain. He charged that the Hindus had received insufficient weightage in the Panchayat Act, the Municipal Act and the District Board Act, and that communal representation in the services had led to 'competent' Hindus being replaced by 'incompetent' Muslims.[87] Chhotu Ram, Fazli Husain's chief ally in the Unionist

---

government intervened to pass the Punjab Land Alienation Act which prevented a professional moneylender from dispossessing an agriculturist who had cultivated his land for more than twenty years. Besides, the peasant could neither be evicted nor arrested for debt; his plough, cattle, implements and seeds could not be attached for the redemption of his debt. The Moneylenders Registration Bill was intended to remove some of the loopholes in the Punjab Alienation Act. Moneylenders were, for example, required to register themselves with the government so that their accounts could be checked and monitored.

[82] *Tribune*, 25 October 1924, M.N. Roy in Ray (ed.), *Selected Works*, vol. 2, pp. 439, 441–42.

[83] *Punjab Legislative Council Debates*, 18 November 1924, vol. 7, p. 514.

[84] Ibid., p. 523.

[85] Ray (ed.), *Selected Works of M.N. Roy*, vol. 2, pp. 442–443.

[86] See speech of Lala Sevak Ram, *Punjab Legislative Council Debates*, 14 March 1925, vol. 8, no. 2, p. 559.

[87] For the role of Raja Narendranath, see Bruce Cleghorn, 'Religion and Politics: The Leadership of the All-India Hindu Mahasabha in Punjab and Saurashtra,' B.N. Pandey (ed.), *Leadership in South Asia* (Delhi, 1977). In June 1926, the Raja told C.Y. Chintamani that he could not join any party that did not protect the 'just' and 'legitimate' rights of the Punjab Hindus. His ideal was to attain swaraj with justice to the Hindu minority in the province. 7 June 1926, Chintamani Papers, NMML.

Party, echoed the same view while endorsing the censure motion.[88]

Significantly enough, the motion against Fazli Husain was backed by elected Hindu and Sikh members: the only non-Muslims who opposed it were L.K. Rallia Ram, a nominated Christian, and Harkishen Lal and Sunder Singh Majithia, both of whom held official posts. The minister was able to save his skin on account of the timely support of Muslims and British officials. In this way, a beleagured Fazli Husain, deserted even by his Jat allies, not only relied more and more on the Muslim bloc but became their chief spokesman, especially after his appointment to the viceroy's executive council in 1930. From this position, he played a critical behind-the-scenes role in the early 1930s 'as informal strategist and director of Muslim policy during the great constitutional reappraisals of these years'.[89] Fazli Husain's major goal was to protect Muslim interests—interests he identified with those of Punjab's Muslims.[90]

The mud-slinging that accompanied the introduction of Narendranath's censure motion was not just a setback to Fazli Husain's political career in Punjab but also a bad omen for communal relations in the province. A sober politician, with years of close association with the Congress and a firm commitment to Hindu-Muslim unity, was needlessly pushed into the All-India Muslim Conference, a body consisting of political reactionaries and obscurantists. Fazli Husain was not spared even after he was moved to the viceroy's council in the summer of 1925. The *Tribune* gleefully recorded:

> The disappearance of Sir Fazli Husain from the stage of Punjab politics, even though temporary, will undoubtedly make many people heave a sigh of relief.... The tide of communalism among the educated and politically-minded Muslims of Punjab, thanks largely to Fazli Husain's policy, has been so high during the last four years, that it is no easy thing for any individual or group...to go against the tide.[91]

[88] Chowdhry, *Punjab Politics*, p. 171.

[89] Ayesha Jalal and Anil Seal, 'Alternative to Partition: Muslim Politics Between the Wars', *Modern Asian Studies*, vol. 15, no. 3, 1981, p. 433.

[90] See Gilmartin, *Empire and Islam*, p. 111

[91] *Tribune*, 26 August 1925.

VI

When a group of leading Congressmen visited Punjab in March 1923, they were appalled to discover that 'each community had practically arrayed itself in an armed camp against each other'. They found that almost the whole of the province was divided along communal lines, though not always for the same reasons. 'The reasons which apply to the so-called educated classes are entirely different from those which apply to the masses and we feel constrained to say that the latter have to no small extent been exploited by interested parties among the former for their own selfish purposes'.[92] In such a fragmented and communally-polarized society, it was easy for revivalist tendencies to gain a firm foothold and for communal bodies to secure recruits. The revival and resurgence of the Hindu Sabha and the Arya Samaj can be seen in this light.

The Hindu Sabha was not new to Punjab.[93] It was founded in 1907, almost immediately after the Muslim League came into being in December 1906, and attracted notice in 1909 by its condemnation of the Punjab Alienation Act and the 'extravagant and unwarranted', Muslim demands for representation in the councils.[94] 'The Hindus', stated the *Indian Patriot,* 'have organized themselves into a separate body in the belief that by such separate organizations alone can they safeguard the interests of their community'.[95] The issues raised by the Sabha provided topics for excited discussions as its followers hoped for a better future—one in which they could maintain their status and prevent further governmental action against their interests.[96]

On the eve of and during the Khilafat and non-co-operation agitations, the Punjab Hindu Sabha maintained a low profile. Thereafter, a vigorous ideological crusade was set afoot, drawing upon the sympathy of those who were anxious to thwart Fazli

[92] F.No. 3, All-India Congress Committee (AICC) Papers, NMML.
[93] See Jones, *Arya Dharm*, pp. 288–290, 294–299.
[94] *Tribune*, 6 April and 3 November 1909.
[95] Quoted in ibid., 3 November 1909.
[96] Jones, op. cit., p. 291.

Husain's belligerence. There was the familiar cry of 'A Dying Race', of the imminent disintegration of the Hindu community through conversion and more rapid growth rates among Muslims, and of discrimination against Hindus in government service.

'Many a Congressman', stated the younger Nehru in his autobiography, 'was a communalist under his nationalist cloak'.[97] One person he must have had in mind was the rustic, narrow-minded and bigoted Lala Lajpat Rai. In Jawaharlal's judgement, he did not have a good enough 'intellectual or cultural background'; hence his 'peculiar behaviour' in public life'.[98] He was conservative in political matters with pronounced communal proclivities.[99] Such a person spearheaded the Hindu Sabha movement in Punjab.

There is no denying Lajpat Rai's influence in his home province.[100] He had the image of a relentless crusader, a tough bargainer and a symbol of Punjabi Hindu identity. He was active in cow-protection societies and the Arya Samaj, which, in his own words, taught the 'true and genuine Hinduism of the Vedas', worked to serve the Hindus and defended them from the 'onslaught of alien religions'.[101] *Shuddhi* [102] and *sangathan* were

[97] Nehru, *An Autobiography*, p. 136.

[98] Gopal (ed.), *Selected Works of Jawaharlal Nehru*, vol. 2, p. 255.

[99] Nehru, *An Autobiography*, p. 158.

[100] According to the *Tribune* [7 December 1923]: 'In the Punjab and at the present time the Congress and Lala Lajpat Rai are inseparable terms. His influence, authority and prestige are the influence and authority of the Congress itself'. Although this is an exaggerated assessment, it gives some idea of Lajpat Rai's influence in Punjab.

[101] Lajpat Rai, *A History of the Arya Samaj* (Bombay, 1967), p. 183.

[102] *Shuddhi* means purification. In religious terminology it was applied to (1) conversion to Hinduism of persons belonging to 'foreign religions'; (2) reconversion of those who adopted one of the 'foreign religions', (3) reclamation, i.e., raising the status of the depressed classes. The *shuddhi* movement received direct inspiration from the Arya Samaj movement, launched by Dayanand Saraswati in 1875. The proselytizing work of the Samaj was effected largely by a branch of the Arya Pratinidhi Sabha which was established in 1909. Later, other organizations, such as the Hindu Ashrams, the Hindu Sabhas, the Rajput Shuddhi Sabha and the All-India Khatri Sabha, also joined in.

his other passions. 'The principle of *shuddhi*',[103] he observed, 'has now been accepted by the Hindu Sabha, and I am free to confess that the idea at the back of this decision is partly political, partly communal, and partly humanitarian'.[104]

Acting as a spokesman of Punjabi Hindus, Lajpat Rai's aim was to unite Hindus against communal representation and, in co-operation with their brethren in other provinces, to 'arrange for a permanent machinery to clarify and crystallize Hindu public opinion on all political questions'.[105] For this reason, he pleaded with his community to set aside differences and unite under the flag of the Hindu Mahasabha, which would shape the destiny of the 'Hindu Nation' in all its social, political and cultural aspects.[106]

The Punjab Hindu Sabha served as a rallying point for a multitude of revivalist groups: the Shuddhi Sabha, the Arya Samaj and the Sanathan Dharma Sabhas. A prominent leader of the Shuddhi Sabha was Mahatma Munshi Ram, known as Swami Shraddhanand, who came under the influence of the Arya Samaj leader, Dayanand Saraswati, early in his life. In the 1890s, he was associated with the Antaranga Sabha, a branch of the Shuddhi Sabha, before renouncing his legal career to conduct a *gurukul,* an educational institution, with the aim of reviving ancient Indian philosophy, history and literature.[107] During the Rowlatt Satyagraha, he followed in the footsteps of the Mahatma to

[103] The *sangathan* movement aimed at consolidating and uniting the Hindus. Moreover, it sought to efface the image of a Hindu as a *dhoti*-wearing coward and to replace it with the image of a militant Hindu willing to maintain his honour and that of his community. G.R. Thursby, *Hindu-Muslim Relations in British India* (Leiden, 1975), p. 159.

[104] Lajpat Rai, 'Hindu-Muslim Problem', *Tribune,* 13 December 1924.

[105] Lajpat Rai to Purshotamdas Thakurdas, 13 December 1924, Thakurdas Papers, NMML.

[106] *India Quarterly Register,* January-June 1925, vol. 1, pp. 378–80. From April to December 1925, the Lala was busy enlisting support for the Hindu Sabhas and the *sangathan* movement. He presided over the Calcutta session of the All-India Hindu Mahasabha, visited Assam, Burma and Sind to organize *sangathan* and local Hindu Sabhas, and chaired a meeting of the Bombay Hindu Conference in Bombay.

[107] See M.R. Jambunathan (ed.), *Swami Shraddhanand* (Bombay, 1961).

emerge, along with M.A. Ansari, as a front-rank satyagrahi in Delhi. He was a symbol of communal amity when invited to preach to the Friday congregation at the Juma Masjid, and was part of the Khilafat deputation to the viceroy. But the Swami's fascination for Gandhi faded and his enthusiasm for the Khilafat cause dampened. He developed a dislike for the militancy of the Khilafatists and lost faith in the efficacy of the Gandhian methods. His interests lay elsewhere: in the *shuddhi* movement, which was conceived by him as an essential part of a broader movement for Hindu solidarity, or *sangathan*. He was present at the first ceremony of reclamation of Malkanas to Hinduism at Raibana, near Agra.[108] Within the first months five thousand Malkanas were reclaimed, and by the end of the year the total had risen to about thirty thousand. Shraddhanand and his Arya Samaj collaborators were the acknowledged leaders of this initial push. But, in the process, they strained the already fragile communal equations in north India. Iqbal expressed his fears in 1923:

> It is a pity that in the Punjab the jealousy, no, rather enmity of Hindus and Muslims is growing. If it remains like that, then life will become difficult for both the communities during the next 30 years.[109]

The fears of the poet proved prophetic.

[108] The Malkana Rajputs were converted under the Afghans and settled as military colonies in the Jumna tract in the neighbourhood of Agra and Delhi. Their origin, however, is not clear. Malkanas—a title and not a clan name—were probably Jadon Rajputs formerly, some were Jats and others were Agarwal *banias,* Many Malkana Rajputs in the Mathura district were descendants of Tarkar Brahmans.

[109] Schimmel, *Gabriel's Wing*, p. 131.

Chapter Eight

Competing Symbols, Revivalism and Mobilization

Interested persons who were disappointed during the balmy days of non-co-operation, now that it has lost the charm of novelty, have found their opportunity and are trading upon the religious bigotry or the selfishness of both the communities. The result is written in the history of the feuds of the past two years. Religion has been traversed. Trifles have been dignified by the name of religious tenets. ... Economic and political causes have been brought into play for the sake of fomenting trouble.*

M.K. Gandhi, 26 December 1924.

It is always difficult to calculate the dynamics of rioting; one observes all the signs and the portents, but it is not easy to determine the exact temperature at which feelings will boil over. The atmosphere may continue surcharged for prolonged periods without an outburst, unless some chance spark produces a sudden blaze.**

Malcolm Hailey, 7 May 1927

The record of Hindu-Muslim riots dates back to 1800, but in no other period were they so bloody, so gruesome and so widespread as in the mid-twenties.[1] In 1923–24, most parts of UP and Punjab were thoroughly inflamed. The fire of communal hatred even engulfed Delhi and Kohat which had an impressive record of communal amity. Gandhi was shaken by the happenings. He

* *CWMG*, vol. 25, p. 477.

** To Alexander Muddiman, 7 May 1927, F. No. 10 (B), Hailey Papers.

[1] See table 7 in Page, *Prelude to Partition*, p. 74, and for UP table 5:1 in Pandey, *The Ascendancy of the Congress in Uttar Pradesh*, p. 116.

began a fast——'the final plunge'—to do 'penance...for sins unwittingly committed'.[2] A Unity Conference ensued.[3] But platitudinous resolutions could not stem the tide of violence. Gandhi himself expressed his disappointment. The resolutions, he said, were 'inadequate; those attending it were imperfect; hence the beginning too has been deficient'.[4]

The Mahatma was agonized and started to despair. The Hindu-Muslim problem, he announced in March 1925, was an 'insoluble puzzle' and so he would keep out of it.[5] At public meetings in Madras and Calcutta he talked of a 'hopeless tangle' being 'put away in my cupboard'. He felt that in the prevailing 'surcharged atmosphere' and 'mutual distrust' he would not be able to persuade either the Hindus or the Muslims to accept his solution.[6]

In the following year—1926—the *Young India* dwelt on the Hindu-Muslim problem only twice: when Shraddhanand was assassinated by a Muslim fanatic[7] and when Syed Mahmud pleaded with Gandhi to resolve the communal tangle by bringing to an end his self-imposed political exile.[8] But the Mahatma was not convinced. He told the Bihar lawyer that 'my meddling at this juncture, I am convinced, can only do harm'.[9] Like the War of Roses in England, in India, too, 'order must come out of present chaos'. Unity, he emphasized in an unprophetic statement, will not precede but will succeed freedom.[10]

Gandhi's refusal to be drawn into the communal controversies of the day made no sense. His admission of 'defeat' also came a bit too soon. It is true that his political credibility among Muslims was low, but he alone could still command their allegiance. Muslim Congressmen, in particular, still gathered around him and turned to him for guidance and leadership. But they were

2 'All About the Fast', 22 September 1924, *CWMG,* vol. 24, pp. 199-200.
3 See *Indian Quarterly Register,* vol. 2, pp. 149-160.
4 *CWMG,* vol. 24, p. 263.
5 Interview to the Press, 5 March 1925, ibid., vol. 26, p. 233.
6 Speech at public meeting, Madras, 7 March 1925, ibid., p. 244.
7 *Young India,* 30 December 1926, ibid., p. 473.
8 9 September 1926, ibid., vol. 38, p. 316.
9 Ibid.
10 Ibid.

disappointed by his intransigence and his reluctance to thwart the mounting pressure of Hindu communalists in the Congress and to censure their chief spokesmen—Malaviya and Lajpat Rai. It was commonly felt then and later that a sulking Mahatma, with his studious silence and self-imposed inactivity, could not have boosted the morale of those engaged in fighting the demon of communalism. He pursued his other 'hobbies'—charkha, removal of untouchability and cow-protection—while the country experienced communal riots all around.

Neither Gandhi nor his Congress colleagues made a serious attempt to analyze the factors behind the sudden eruption of Hindu-Muslim violence. There were generalized contemporary assessments, most notably by Jawaharlal Nehru and his Marxist comrades, who saw riots as a 'special product of British rule' [11] and as the end result of British economic policies which created arenas of conflict and competition.[12] There was, then, the favourite official view with its emphasis on the long-standing antagonism between the followers of Hinduism and Islam which were intensified by social segregation, separate religious rituals and practices.[13] But this interpretation did not answer why communal disturbances occurred more frequently and with greater intensity in the mid-twenties and not earlier.[14]

In the end, one will have to explore both the immediate causes

[11] See, for example, Nehru's presidential address at the Bundelkhand conference, 13 June 1921, Gopal (ed.), *Selected Works of Jawaharlal Nehru,* p. 185. And the comments of M.N. Roy, quoted in Ray (ed.), *Selected Works of M.N. Roy,* vol. 2, pp. 537-38.

[12] Palme Dutt, *India Today,* p. 445.

[13] *Report of the Indian Statutory Commission: Survey,* Cmd. 3568 (London, 1930), vol. 1, p. 27. Zetland, governor of Bengal and later secretary of state for India, detailed the differences. According to him, the Hindu-Muslim divisions were not only due to religious belief and practice 'but to a profoundly different outlook on life resulting in social systems which are the very antithesis of one another'. This being so, it was, in Zetland's judgement, 'inevitable that an artificial...system such as that of communal electorates, should encourage the fissiparous tendencies already existing'. Lawrence, Second Marquess of Zetland, *Essayez* (London, 1956), pp. 119-120.

[14] There were 88 recorded riots during the years 1923 to 1927. The casualty list was high—400 dead and 5,000 injured.

of Hindu-Muslim friction as well as the subtle institutional and socio-economic processes, set in motion by the colonial government, which engendered various forms of caste, communal and regional conflicts.

II

In general, the communal pot was kept boiling by disputes over music before mosques, cow-protection and routes of religious processions. There were a few more irritants—the process of conversion and reconversion, conducted under the aegis of *tabligh* and *shuddhi* societies, and the constant flow of polemical literature designed to heighten and offend religious sensibilities.[15]

Routes of religious processions and the playing of music before mosques were among the principal reasons of discord. This was not so in earlier decades when Hindus and Muslims took part in each others festivals and religious processions. Rajendra Prasad recalled how in the Zaradei village of Bihar there was mutual celebration of Holi and how the *tazias* of prosperous Hindus were bigger and brighter than those of Muslims.[16] This was no longer the case in the mid-twenties. Even places like Delhi and Lucknow, which had an excellent record of communal cordiality and were regarded as symbols of India's rich, composite life, were overwhelmed by the communal tide.[17] Given the prominence accorded to religion and religiosity in public life, it was common for religio-cultural formations to stake claims which came in conflict with the beliefs or practices of others. Thus the Hindus refused to entertain any suggestion of

[15] G.R. Thursby, *Hindu-Muslim Relations in British India,* chapter one.

[16] Rajendra Prasad, *Autobiography* (Delhi, 1957), pp. 13-14. Also see Blunt, *India Under Ripon,* p. 72 and W. Crooke, *The North-Western Provinces of India: Their History, Ethnology and Administration* (London, 1897), p. 263, for Shia-Sunni and Hindu-Muslim participation in Muharram observances. And for examples drawn from Bombay, see Jim Masselos, 'Change and Custom in the Format of the Bombay Muharram during the Nineteenth and Twentieth Centuries', *South Asia,* December 1982, pp. 54, 57.

[17] Home Poll. F.No. 249/x, 1924, NAI.

banning music before the mosques, arguing that both rituals and social customs required processions, accompanied with music, to pass thoroughfares.[18]

It was quite common in the past for religious processions to go through crowded streets and for music to be played around mosques. The only notable difference then was that wherever disagreements arose, one could hope for their resolution through existing local mechanisms, which were evolved in almost every locality through centuries of corporate living. It was possible to turn to mohalla committees, voluntary associations and civic bodies for sane advice and sober judgement. But with the rise in communal temperature and the consequent hardening of attitudes the local command structures collapsed and there was hardly an initiative to take recourse to traditional institutions for resolving localized differences. Militant groups could now be seen to take pride in flouting the few general rules or norms that regulated religious processions. Having tasted 'victory' in one area they could stridently move elsewhere to test their muscle power. This was the pattern everywhere—at Lucknow and Allahabad in September 1924, at Dehradun in 1925, at Rawalpindi in 1926 and at Bettiah in August 1927.[19]

By far the worst incident, caused by a drummer in an Arya Samaj procession passing by a mosque, took place at Calcutta on 2 April 1926. The casualty list was high and the damage to property considerable.[20] The rioters were drawn from many sections of society, though the 'goonda' elements, brought to Calcutta by rich Marwari traders and merchants to guard their homes and property, were principally involved in looting and arson. They

[18] See Home Poll. F.No. 166, 1927, NAI.

[19] Thursby, *Hindu-Muslim Relations*, pp. 90-94.

[20] From April 2 to 12, 44 persons were killed with 584 injured. During the first four days 151 cases of fire were reported. Besides, 8 temples, 3 gurudwaras and 10 mosques were destroyed. The areas worst affected were Harrison Road, College Street and Raja Bazaar near the Sealdah Railway Station. For official accounts, see The Earl of Lytton, *Pundits and Elephants: Being the Experiences of Five Years as Governor of an Indian Province* (London, 1942), pp. 167-73. And *Report of the Calcutta Riots of April 1926*, Lytton Papers, F.No. 160 (46).

were doing more than protecting their employees; they were committing assaults as well.[21]

Cow-slaughter was another issue that undermined the traditional fabric of corporate social life. As is well-known, Islam enjoins upon the faithful to offer animal sacrifices at the *Id al-Zuha* or, as it is called in India, the *Bakr Id*. It also lays down that, while the minimum obligatory offering for a Muslim is a sheep or a goat, the offering of a camel, cow or buffalo is equivalent to seven sheeps or goats, and by such a single offering seven persons can participate in the sacrifice. And because horned cattle were numerous and cheap in India it was economical to use one of them for *qurbani* (sacrifice) rather than to provide the equivalent number of sheeps or goats. These were the reasons, stated the two *fatawa* issued by the Anjuman-i Zahirin Ala Haq, Jabalpur, and the Anjuman-i Islamia, Panipat, why Muslims preferred the sacrifice of cows. The timing of these religious decrees was significant: they were issued and circulated in the aftermath of bloody riots during *Bakr Id*.[22]

The sanctity of the cow was recognized in pre-British days; in fact a number of medieval Sultans, including Zainul Abidin of Kashmir and Zahiruddin Babur, founder of the Mughal Empire, imposed a ban on cow-slaughter. But the first recorded society for the protection of the cow was formed in 1882 by Dayanand Saraswati before its branches spread to Bengal, Maharashtra, Punjab and UP. In 1893 and in September-October 1917, the cow issue was the spark which ignited widespread riots in eastern UP[23] and in the Shahbad district of Bihar—at Piro Bazaar, 25 miles from Arrah on the Sassaram road, Bhagalpur, Milki and Ibrahimpur. A mob of nearly ten thousand went on a rampage killing Muslims and burning and looting their property. Those

[21] Memoirs of O.M. Martin, p. 149, Centre for South Asian Studies, Cambridge.

[22] See *Adaalat Gaushala Parasthan* (Jabalpur, 1922). *Mussalmanan-i Panipat ki Bipta aur Afsaana* (Delhi, 1926). Also, see A. Raoof, *Submission About the Qurbani Question* (Calcutta, 1911), IOLR Tracts (1084).

[23] McLane, *Indian Nationalism*, pp. 273, 326-27; Thursby, *Hindu-Muslim Relations*, pp. 76-88; Gyan Pandey, 'Rallying Round the Cow: Sectarian Strife in the Bhojpur Region, c. 1888-1917', Ranajit Guha (ed.), *Subaltern Studies II: Writings on South Asian History and Society* (Delhi, 1983).

found guilty were high-caste Hindus, supported by Ahirs, Kurmis and Telis. Among the 37 charged with offences of dacoity and rioting were 8 Brahmans, 5 Rajputs, 9 Bhumihars and 3 Kayasths. In Katar, situated east of the Sassaram-Arrah Road, high-caste Hindus were the principal offenders. Among the 105 accused were 40 Rajputs and a leading zamindar family from the neighbouring district. So also in Mauna village, located in the Nasirganj police station. The assault, led by the Brahmin-Rajput-Bhumihar combination, 'is a grim and moving story, the isolated position of this Muslim village surrounded by big Hindu villages,...the determination of the Muslims to resist, the erection of barricades, the five hour battle in the course of which thousands of Hindus were more than once repulsed by the defenders, with fatal results'.[24]

In his judgement, H.L.L. Allanson commented that such events 'went far beyond a riot to stop *qurbani*' and opined that they were the result of a deliberately engineered conspiracy to stir up religious passions against the Muslims. He went on to add:

> The thousands of rioters did not content themselves with merely preventing the *qurbani* taking place on that day [i.e., 28 September] but looted and damaged the property of the Muslims in those three villages, forced the women to give up their ornaments and outraged their religious feeling by entering and damaging the mosque and destroying the Quran.[25]

Disputes over land, indebtedness and non-payment of dues lent a local specificity to such organized assaults.[26] At the same time, Bihar and its neighbouring districts in UP had a long and consistent record of violence over the cow question. The Gaurakshini Sabhas, financed by the Rajas of Banaras and Darbhanga, had been active in the region. And for nearly two decades the cow symbol remained an integral part of nationalist mobilization and was linked with militant assertions of 'Hindu identity'. In the creation and articulation of this identity,

[24] 'In the Court of Commissioner of the Special Tribunal of Arrah', 18 January 1918, p. 5, H.L.L. Allanson Papers, Centre for South Asian Studies, Cambridge.

[25] 20 November 1917, p. 6, ibid.

[26] 18 January 1918, p. 7, ibid.

high-caste Hindus discovered in the cow a powerful symbol of common identification. Its utility in defining the broad contours of 'Hindu identity' provided the *raison d'etre* for its protection.

In 1893, the government was sensitized to the strength of the Gaurakshini movement in Bihar and the neighbouring districts. Pamphlets on and appeals for cow-protection were in circulation. Zealous preachers, despatched by the Arya Samaj Leagues in UP and Punjab, lectured in Champaran district. They spoke with passion and fervour. Such was their influence that, in certain villages Muslims were not even allowed to draw water from the wells.[27] These were ominous signs in the wake of large-scale rioting that engulfed Ballia, Ghazipur and Azamgarh and had even spread to distant Bombay, Poona and Yeola in August 1893.[28] A government report had predicted in July 1893:

> I do not feel satisfied that we enjoy immunity from an inroad of riotous Hindus, and if it takes place, there will be terrible bloodshed. The excitement among Hindus here is so great and the League [Cow Preservation] so widespread that the material for an uprising is among us even without external excitement.[29]

The happenings in Shahbad and other districts of Bihar in 1917–18 followed a predictable course. By and large the structure of the riots was the same. The organizers and participants were, as in the past, drawn from the same high-caste Hindus. And the victims in most places were Muslims. In fact, one can draw a striking parallel between the events of 1893 and 1917–18. The following account of the 1893 riots by M.L. Ferrar, commissioner of Gorakhpur division, could well have been written in 1917–18:

> Our rule was practically at an end for some time in certain parts of the district, and the Muhammadans were at the mercy of their enemies, having in most places saved their lives or their property, or both, by being forced to sign a document *[Iqraarnaama]* that they would not sacrifice cows. The Hindus have so far won all along the line, slaying the

[27] W. Hoey to Ferrar, 9 June 1893, UP Government (General Administration Dept), F.No. 730 (B), Box No. 44, 1893, UPSA.

[28] S. Krishnaswamy, '1893: A Year of Unrest in India', *Quarterly Review of Historical Studies,* vol. 4, no. 3, 1966-1967, p. 155.

[29] Hoey to LaTouche, 16 July 1893, op.cit.

Mussalmans, looting them, forcing them to go against their religion, terrifying the lives out of them, and riding roughshod over them in every way.[30]

If this was the price to be paid for cow-protection, it is hard to understand why so many Congress leaders, claiming to be ardent champions of Hindu-Muslim amity, so readily promoted movements connected with it. Tilak made the cow symbol an integral part of the Shivaji festival and assumed a leading role in Poona's Cow-Preservation Society. Others venerated and worshipped the cow and shared a life-long passion for its protection. Gandhi was one of them. He regarded the cow with the same veneration as his mother, declaring that its protection was 'a central fact of Hinduism' and was 'dearer to [him] than anything else'.[31] With the protection of cow, he wrote in *Young India,* 'is bound up not merely the welfare of the cattle of all India and the good name of Hinduism, but, also to a very large extent, the economic welfare of the people'.[32] He presided over a cow-protection conference at Belgaum, attended its meetings in Delhi and Bombay to draft a constitution and worked in close co-operation with Malaviya, Lajpat Rai, Shraddhanand and Moonje.[33] All the time he seemed keen to assure his readers that the work of cow-protection 'does not come to a standstill even for a single moment. I keep all the time thinking of it and also discuss it'.[34] And when Mohamed Ali presented him with a cow to be sent to a *pinjrapole,* the Mahatma was delighted. He wrote:

You are more than a brother to me. I have seen the cow. My bed was lifted to enable me to see her. What love that has prompted the act! May the bond between you twins [Shaukat and Mohamed] and me fructify into an indissoluble bond between Hindus and Mussalmans for the good of

[30] Ferrar to LaTouche, 28 June 1893, ibid.

[31] *Young India,* 29 January 1924, *CWMG,* vol. 24, p. 150, and *Navajivan,* 3 May 1925, vol. 27, p. 18. For arguments in support of cow-protection, see F.No. 12, 1922-23, AICC Papers.

[32] *Young India,* 3 September 1925, *CWMG,* vol. 28, p. 145.

[33] See vol. 25, pp. 512-22. and vol. 26, pp. 35-36 for the draft constitution of the Conference.

[34] *Navajivan,* 1 November 1925, ibid., vol. 28, pp. 404.

our respective faiths, for the good of our country and for the good of humanity. Yes, God is great. He can work wonders.[35]

The Mahatma hoped that as a reciprocal gesture Muslims would voluntarily renounce cow-slaughter during the Khilafat movement. Though firmly opposed to a bargain, he believed that 'the best and the only way to save the cow is to save the Khilafat'.[36] That is why, he said, 'I have [therefore] called Khilafat our Kamadhenu'.[37] In 1925, he recalled:

I gave all the help that I could for the Khilafat, because I wanted to enlist the sympathy in the matter of cow-protection.[38]

Gandhi's expectations were not belied. Muslims of Phulwari Sharif in Bihar renounced eating beef. Abdul Bari assured Gandhi that Muslims in Lucknow would avoid cow-slaughter at *Bakr Id*. The Muslim League passed a cow-protection resolution in December 1919. The Ali Brothers gave up eating beef, and Seth Chotani, president of the Central Khilafat Committee, saved hundreds of cows in Bombay during *Bakr Id*.[39]

But the cow-Khilafat formula did not enthuse everybody. In Gaya, Maulvi Mohammad Sajjad, Naib Amir-i Shariat, refused to follow the Muslim League directive; in fact, Rajendra Prasad and Abul Kalam Azad were deputed by the Congress to prevail upon the Maulvi not to destroy the Hindu-Muslim accord. In August 1921, the Bihar government noticed the tension brewing and was wary of the activities of the militant followers of Maulvi Sajjad, Swami Biswanand and Kripa Baba of Chapra.[40] Yet it was possible then for national leaders to keep the firebrands in

[35] To Mohamed Ali, 8 October 1924, ibid., vol. 25, p. 226.

[36] Speech on Khilafat, 26 January 1921, ibid., vol. 19, p. 283.

[37] U.A. Rao (ed.), *The Way to Communal Harmony*, p. 90.

[38] Speech at the All-India Cow-Protection Conference, Bombay, 28 April 1925, ibid., vol. 26, p. 557.

[39] Mohibbul Hasan, 'Mahatma Gandhi and the Indian Muslims', in S.C. Biswas (ed.), *Gandhi: Theory and Practice, Social Impact and Contemporary Relevance* (Indian Institute of Advanced Study: Shimla, 1969), p. 140. Abdul Bari's position on the subject emerges from his statements and correspondence quoted in Jafri (ed.), *Karawaan-i Gumgushta*, pp. 173-181.

[40] Home Poll. F.No. 18, 1921, NAI; *Hamdam*, 24 August 1920, quoted in ibid., p. 181.

check and to curb their religious zeal in the larger interest of promoting a joint Hindu-Muslim struggle against colonial rule. But there was much less of a chance for such initiatives to succeed in the aftermath of the Khilafat and Non-Co-operation campaigns.[41] The political linkages established by all-India leaders with their constituents in the provinces and localities had snapped and enthusiasm for Hindu-Muslim unity dampened.

Take the case of the Jamiyat al-ulama, a close political ally of the Congress, which commanded considerable influence during the Khilafat agitation and could thus secure strict adherence to its policy on cow-slaughter. But once the influence of the Jamiyat leaders waned, their followers began to take independent positions. In some places the old arrangement continued, but in most areas Muslims began to assert their right to sacrifice cows.[42] In Delhi, they decided to use the Pahari Dhiraj route for taking cows to the slaughter house in violation of a previous agreement.[43] Mohamed Ali commented: 'This was so unlike the spirit of 1920–21 that the contrast was shocking'.[44]

Mohamed Ali explained why the mood had changed. One of the reasons he referred to was the apprehension that, if Muslims accepted the principle of cow-protection, they would then have to give in on other contentious religious issues. In the words of Mohamed Ali: 'Today it was the Pahari Dhiraj; tomorrow it would be something else, and instead of leaving it to us to consider genuine Hindu susceptibilities, the Hindu majority will be more and more aggressive as every day passes in imposing its will upon us and in insisting that Muslims should live on its sufferance in Aryavarta'.[45]

Mohamed Ali also took the opportunity to comment on the

[41] There were, of course, some notable exceptions as in Nagpur where, in October 1924, the citizens heeded to the admonitions of Motilal Nehru and Maulana Azad and resolved their differences amicably. F.No. 50, 1921–25, AICC Papers.

[42] *Akhbaar-i Aam* (Lahore), 21 February 1923, SNNR, Punjab.

[43] *Comrade,* 17 July 1925, and Abdur Rahman to Ansari, 1 July 1925, Hasan (ed.), *Muslims and the Congress,* pp. 13–14.

[44] *Comrade,* 17 July 1925.

[45] Ibid.

petty-mindedness and bigotry of the 'pseudo nationalists'. He added:

> They talk and write as nationalists and run down communals [*sic*]; but only in the use of counters and catchwords of Nationalism are they nationalists for their hearts are narrow and they can conceive of no future for India except to be one of Hindu dominance and the existence of Mussalmans as a minority living on the sufferance of the Hindu majority.... It is my sad conviction that not one of these pseudo-Nationalists would have talked so glibly of Nationalism, majority rule and mixed electorates, if his own community had not been in the safe position of an overwhelming majority. It is they who are the real culprits as narrow communalists, but since the position of their community is safe enough they mouth all the fine phrases of nationalism and parade themselves as nationalists. *The Cow question provides the best topic for the exposure of their pseudo-nationalism, for in the name of nationalism they make demands on their fellow-countrymen so absurd that none has ever heard of them in any other country or nation in the world, and it is time that their nationalism was fully exposed* [emphasis added].[46]

These were harsh sentiments expressed in strong language. But they reflect the social and political perceptions of an influential Muslim and his lack of conviction in the nationalist discourse. Furthermore, Mohamed Ali's remarks reveal the emotional intensity with which the cow question was being debated in the subcontinent.

III

Areas of Hindu-Muslim strife extended far beyond disputations over music before mosque and cow-protection. In a society of unequal opportunities and disparities, economic impulses and motivations raised possibilities of conflict and competition. Sometimes, the tension between the exploiting classes and the exploited took the form of class struggles which were manifested in organized kisan and trade union movements. But more often they tended to acquire a communal colour, with different classes articulating their interests through religious symbols and

[46] Ibid.

idioms.[47] Recent works of K.N. Panikkar on Malabar, of Tanika Sarkar and Tajul Islam Hashmi on Bengal and of Chitra Joshi on the Kanpur labour force illustrate how agrarian conflicts and working-class movements had a marked tendency to correspond to the contours of a communal fracas.[48] Let us first take a cursory look at the roots of agrarian conflicts in Bengal.

Without elaborating on the structure of Bengal agrarian society and the subtle differentiation in the Muslim peasantry, aspects covered by a number of distinguished scholars, one can state the obvious fact that the peasantry in Bengal, largely Muslim, was subservient to groups or classes who happened to be predominantly Hindus: To the Hindus belonged the land and the capital. Magistrates and judges to whom the peasants submitted their cases, police officers who investigated them and lawyers who represented them in law courts were all Hindus. Mymensingh's district magistrate found 'universal complaints among the poorer Muslims of oppression and intimidation by pleaders, mukhtars, backed by the authority of the zamindar's *amala*.[49] Circumstances such as these proved conducive for communal antipathies to take roots in the countryside.

Agrarian discontent was the chief cause of rioting in Mymensingh, for in no other district was the domination of the landlord over the tenant so blatant.[50] The Tenancy Act of 1885 was a dead-letter, while the excesses of landlords, such as enhanced rents, unauthorized cesses and tampering with occupancy rights, were

[47] See, for example, S.B. Chaudhuri, *Civil Disturbances in India,* pp. 75–77; K.K. Sengupta, 'The Agrarian League of Pabna, 1873', *Indian Economic and Social History Review,* vol. 7, 1970, pp. 253–268.

[48] Tanika Sarkar, *Bengal 1928–1934: The Politics of Protest* (Delhi, 1987), p. 106, and *Communal and Pan-Islamic Trends in Colonial India,* pp. 302–319.

[49] Report by R. Nathan, Home Poll. A, F.No. 57–63, December 1907, NAI. Mymensingh was the largest district in the Bengal Presidency in terms of area and population. Nearly three quarters of its population (4,526,422, in 1911) were Muslims. F.A. Sachse, *Bengal District Gazetteer: Mymensingh* (Calcutta, 1917).

[50] Sugata Bose, 'The Roots of Communal Violence in Bengal: A Study of the Kishoreganj Riots, 1930', *Modern Asian Studies,* vol. 16, no. 3, 1982; Sumit Sarkar, *Swadeshi Movement,* pp. 444–449.

facts to be reckoned with. An added irritant was the *Ishwar Britti.* Muslims resented paying this subscription for the upkeep of Hindu idols. In 1907, therefore, rioting at Bakshiganj and Dewanganj began by an attack on the idol erected with the *Ishwar Britti.* This was the pattern in many places—the Kishoreganj subdivision, Pabna, Madaripur and Barisal.[51] 'Discontent always prevails', noted a peasant leader, amongst those who are exploited and the discontent finds vent in class struggles'.[52]

The root cause of the Moplah 'uprisings' in Malabar was economic. Descendants of Arab traders and of converts to Islam, the predominant Muslim peasantry had a long-standing grudge against the Namboodri landlords and Nayar moneylenders. Reduced to insecure tenancy, vulnerable to rack-renting and eviction at the hands of landlords who were sustained by British Indian courts, the Moplahs responded with a series of attacks on the landed castes which 'represented a continuation of the Mapilla challenge to the economic and social power of the upper castes'. These attacks were carried out as ritual acts in which the Moplahs sought martyrdom. Stephen Dale emphasizes that they were not just religious expressions of socio-economic grievances but on occasions the expression of religious drive alone. MacGregor, district collector of Malabar in the 1880s, placed the emphasis elsewhere, arguing that the 'outrages' had an agrarian basis and that 'fanaticism is merely the instrument through which the terrorism of the landed classes is aimed at'.[53] While arriving at similar conclusions in 1881, the Logan Commission proposed changes, which were never ever put into practice, in Malabar's land tenure to mitigate the long-standing plight of the Moplahs. As late as 1900, the region continued to suffer under an oppressive system of subinfeudation. South Malabar, in particular, earned the 'unenviable reputation of being the most rack-rented country on the face of this earth'.[54]

[51] Report by Nathan, op.cit.

[52] *Ganavani,* 28 April 1927, SNNR, Bengal; *Mussalman,* 2 August 1927.

[53] E. Thurston, *Castes and Tribes of Southern India* (Madras, 1909), vol. 4, p. 478.

[54] Quoted in Robert L. Hardgrave Jr., 'The Mapilla Rebellion, 1921:

IV

Sometimes agrarian discontent, as in eastern Bengal and Malabar, found expression in or derived sustenance from the forces of revivalism or fundamentalism, as it is called in recent decades.

There is no standard definition of what constitutes revivalism or fundamentalism. Yet, one can generally comment on its central role which is to modify or transform social, religious and cultural experiences in accordance with 'basic' and 'fundamental' religious tenets. In the second-half of the nineteenth century, stress was laid on the need to reform Indian Islam by purging it of Hindu customs and practices. Restoring the puritanical spirit of early Islam, i.e., the days of the Prophet and the four Khalifas, was thus the cry of the movements conducted in different regions by Shah Abdul Aziz and Haji Shariat Allah. With their grassroots connections and ashraf-jotedar patronage, they were instrumental in raising the levels of religious consciousness outside the well-established composite framework of religious discourse. Islamization, as Asim Roy has so ably demonstrated, became a major component of peasant consciousness.[55] This was equally true of the Meos in Mewat and the Malkanas in Agra district.

In the second-half of the twentieth century, a number of theological seminaries were established with a specific purpose—to reorganize the traditional system of education in order to meet the challenge of the West and of Hindu resurgence, such as the Arya Samaj in Punjab, to raise the levels of Islamic consciousness and to *redefine* the relationship of the Muslim community with others.[56] Their network was extensive and their ideological

Peasant Revolt in Malabar', *Modern Asian Studies,* vol. 2, 1, February 1977, p. 65.

[55] S. Abul Hasan Ali Nadwi, *Life and Mission of Maulana Mohammad Ilyas* (Lucknow, 2nd edn., 1983), chapters two and three.

[56] Among the principal movements which aimed either to defend the faith or to renew the pristine purity of Islam were the Ahmadiya movement in Punjab, founded by Mirza Ghulam Ahmad (1883–1908). Its aim was to revitalize the Islamic tradition and counter the polemical writings of Christian missionaries against Islam. The Ahmadiyas were also involved in a bitter and acrimonious debate with some Arya Samaj leaders. See S. Lavan, *The Ahmadiyah Movement: A History and Perspective* (Delhi, 1975).

cohesion was, as and when in evidence, impressive. Of course, the most important of these organizations were the reputed Firangi Mahal in Lucknow, the Dar al-ulum at Deoband and the Nadwat al-ulama in Lucknow. Besides, there was the Madrasa-i Aliya in Kanpur, the Anjuman-i Taleem,[57] the Anjuman-i Ittehad wa Taraqqi,[58] the Anjuman-i Islamia and the Anjuman-i Himayat-i Islam in Lahore,[59] and a chain of institutions run by the Barelwis. Their interests covered education, proselytization and countering the ideological assault of Christian missionaries and Arya Samaj propagandists.[60] But even in the pursuit of such diverse concerns, they altered, in varying degrees, the tenor of discourse, sharpened religious cleavages and stimulated among their followers the feeling of being separate and distinct from others. Islam became a tool for political manipulation, a kind of bogeyman conjured up by turns against the Hindus and Indian nationalism, just as it could be used for the goals of political and social conservatism. All sorts of popularizers of Islam never ceased to emphasize its collective mobilizing powers under the well-worn heading of *umma*.

Hindu revivalism expressed itself in several different ways,

[57] It was founded by Mohammad Shafi and Nawab Fateh Ali Khan Qizilbash in 1910. *Tribune,* 6 May 1911.

[58] Ibid., 30 April 1911.

[59] This was founded at Lahore in 1885. Its aim was to disseminate western learning along with religious education and to improve the 'social, moral and intellectual condition of the Muslims'. By 1905, the Anjuman had established a number of schools in different parts of the Punjab, including one in Lahore which had 1,582 students on the rolls. Its income also increased from Rs 758 in 1885 to Rs 1,10,546 in 1905. In 1910, a Provincial Muslim Educational Conference was organized under the auspices of the Anjuman and was attended by many leading Muslim politicians, including Fazli Husain, Ibid, 10 July 1906, 1 April 1910.

[60] The activities of some Arya Samaj leaders contributed greatly to the growth of communal tension in Punjab. In the 1880s, Pandit Lekh Ram (1858–1897), a devoted follower of Dayanand Saraswati (1824–1883), used his paper, *Arya Gazette,* as a vehicle for venting his wrath against Islam, particularly the Ahmadiyas. He was also the chief spokesman on the issues of cow-protection and the promotion of Hindi in government departments. See Lavan, *Ahmadiyah Movement,* pp. 76–82; Jones, *Arya Samaj,* pp. 149–51.

though its main contours were defined by the cow-protection agitation, the crusade for Hindi, and the *sangathan* of a caste-ridden society. From mid-1884 onwards, the Arya Samaj, the chief vehicle of social and religious transformation in Punjab,[61] sponsored and gradually came to perform ceremonies of readmission to Hinduism. Although individual reconversions had little impact on the general standing of Hindus in relation to other communities, they possessed great symbolic value. They offered hope and signified a new world in which Hindus could fight to maintain themselves and their religion.[62] Har Dayal, an exiled revolutionary, believed that India's future rested on Hindu *sangathan,* Hindu Raj and *shuddhi.* The *shuddhi* of the Muslims and Christians was required 'just as one removes foreign matter from the eye'.[63] He was reiterating the proclaimed ideals of All-India Shuddhi Sabha, established in 1909 by the Arya Samaj in Punjab.

Both Hindu and Muslim revivalist movements initially emerged as a reaction to Christian missionaries and the western system of education. Both assumed the infallibility of their religious beliefs and pinned their hopes in the revival of the idyllic past, when Islam or Hinduism flourished in its pure and pristine form. 'Islam', wrote the *Mohammadi* of Calcutta, 'will again raise its head, and, by dispelling the abhorrent darkness of trinity, scepticism and idolatry she will again illumine the whole world with her radiance'.[64] The Tabligh al-Jamaat had the same message. Its leader, Mohammad Ilyas, exhorted his followers to eschew politics altogether, concentrate on prayers (*ibaadat*), and on the dissemination of the message of Islam with the same spirit that characterized the activities of the Companions of the Prophet Mohammad.[65]

[61] There is considerable historical literature on the Arya Samaj. For example, Jones, *Arya Dharm;* J.T.F. Jordens, *Dayananda Saraswati: His Life and Ideas* (Delhi, 1978) and his biography of *Swami Shraddhananda: His Life and Causes* (Delhi, 1981). And the essays of Arvind Sharma and Kenneth Jones in Robert D. Baird (ed.), *Religion in Modern India* (Delhi, 2nd revised edn. 1989).

[62] Quoted in Emily Brown, *Har Dayal* (Tueson, 1975), pp. 233–34.

[63] See Jones, *Arya Dharm,* p. 231.

[64] *Mohammadi,* 11 February 1927, SNNR, Bengal.

[65] Nadwi, *Life and Mission of Maulana Mohammad Ilyas,* p.89.

Religion was not the only source of revivalism. In a society where the appropriation of separate symbols became a common feature, there was a tendency to elevate, through a conscious, selective process, *some* historical figures on a higher pedestal and to magnify the achievements of *certain* dynasties. There was thus a marked tendency to dwell on the glories of 'Muslim rule' and to harp on the contribution of medieval rulers. The *Hanafi* of Calcutta urged its readers to celebrate the conquests of Mohammad bin Qasim and Bakhtiyar Khalji 'to bring to mind the brilliant achievements attained by our forefathers'.[66]

Hindu revivalists, on the other hand, sought legitimacy by contrasting the oppressive character of medieval rule with the assimilative capacity of the Hindus, their record of tolerance and their rich religious and cultural heritage. Seeing no virtue in any of the medieval sultans, they idolized Prithvi Raj Chauhan, Rana Pratap and Shivaji, who was used by Tilak as a symbol for stimulating resurgent Maratha nationalism for resisting Muslim aggression.[67] In this way, a handful of petty, feudal chiefs with territorial ambitions were appropriated as symbols of both revivalism and nationalism.

The dominant images of the Muslim presence in major literary works of the nineteenth and twentieth centuries are concerned with the degradation of Hindus under 'Muslim rule'. The noted Hindi poet, Bharatendu Harishchandra (1850–1885), hailed the

[66] *Hanafi,* 21 February 1927 and *Dainik Soltan,* 21 February 1927, SNNR, Bengal.

[67] This view was encouraged by the writings of some British historians in the nineteenth and the first quarter of the twentieth centuries. Their aim was to emphasize that the British did more 'for the substantial benefit of the people than the 'despotic', 'intolerant' and 'cruel' medieval Sultans. Henry Elliot, one of the leading British historians of the medieval period, referred to 'the few glimpses we have, even among this single volume, of Hindus slain for disputing with Muhammadans, of general prohibitions against processions, worship and ablution, of other intolerant measures, of idols mutilated, of temples razed, of forcible conversions and marriages ...' His purpose, as he confessed frankly, was to make 'our native subjects more sensitive of the immense advantages' of British rule. See R. Thapar, H. Mukhia, B. Chandra, *Communalism and the Writing of Indian History* (Delhi, 1969).

supplanting of 'Muslim rule' by the British as the termination of centuries of oppression. He referred to the 'wounds in the heart' that were kept green by the sight of the mosque that stood besides the sacred temple of Vishwanath in Varanasi. In another poem, written in 1878, he talked of the Muslims who had taken away the religion, wealth and women of the Hindus.[68] Similar images figure in the works of Marathi writers like Gopal Hari Deshmukh (1823–1892), better known as Lokahitawadi, and Gopal Ganesh Agarkar (1856–1895). In the writings of Tilak there is use of the same images related to 'Muslim' domination as were common in the earlier periods. He, too, referred to the destruction of the Somnath temple by Mahmud of Ghazna, Timur's carnage, Aurangzeb's aggression in Maharashtra, and Ahmad Shah Abdali's raids.[69]

In nineteenth-century Bengali literature the Muslims were referred to under the contemptuous epithet of Yavana. The writings of Bankim Chandra Chatterji, 'positively and fiercely anti-Muslim', and of Romesh Chandra Dutt glorified 'Hindu' rebellion against the medieval Sultans and showed the Muslims in a correspondingly poor light.[70] The *Hanafi* made the point that writers like Bankim caricatured Muslims and depicted them as defilers of Hindu temples and destroyers of Hinduism. In this way, the paper added, the mind of the Hindus was being systematically 'vitiated' against the Muslims.[71]

Nirad C. Chaudhuri, who shares the Bengali bhadralok antipathy towards Islam and its followers,[72] pointed out that

[68] Sudhir Chandra, 'Communal Consciousness in Late 19th Century Hindi Literature', Hasan (ed.), *Communal and Pan-Islamic Trends*, pp. 180–195.

[69] B.G. Gokhale, 'Hindu Responses to the Muslim Presence in Maharashtra', Yohananan Friedman (ed.), *Islam in Asia: South Asia* (Jerusalem, 1984), vol. 1, pp. 162–65.

[70] The comment on Bankim is that of Nirad Chaudhuri, *The Autobiography of an Unknown Indian*, p. 226. And for an analysis of R.C. Dutt's writings, see Sudhir Chandra, 'The Lengthening Shadow: Secular and Communal Consciousness', in Bidyut Chakrabarty (ed.), *Secularism and Indian Polity* (Delhi, 1990).

[71] 12 December 1927, SNNR, Bengal.

[72] Notice Nirad Chaudhuri's observation that while living in Calcutta he

Bengali thinkers and reformers of modern India—from Ram Mohun Roy to Rabindranath Tagore—based their life-work on the formula of a synthesis, by which they understood a synthesis of Hindu and European currents. 'Islamic trends and consciousness did not touch even the arc of their consciousness'. Thus the new Indian culture of the nineteenth century

> built a perimeter of its own and put specifically Muslim influences and aspirations beyond the pale. In relation to it the Muslims stood outside as an external proletariat, and if the Muslims wanted to come into its world they could come only after giving up all their Islamic values and traditions.[73]

Again,

> nothing was more natural for us than to feel about the Muslims in the way we did. Even before we could read we had been told that the Muslims had once ruled and oppressed us, that they had spread their religion in India with the Koran in one hand and the sword in another, that the Muslim rulers had abducted our women, destroyed our temples, polluted our sacred places. As we grow older we read about the wars of the Rajputs, the Marathas, and the Sikhs against the Muslims, and of the intolerance and oppressions of Aurangzeb.[74]

Such sentiments were nurtured more easily in urban areas, which were the foci of revivalist activities. Towards the end of the nineteenth century, in particular, the growth of revivalism, both in its overt and latent forms, took place in cities and towns where cow-protection societies, Hindi Pracharini Sabhas, *tab-*

---

had 'an arrogant contempt for the Muslims and a deep-seated hostility towards them'. From the end of 1906–7, 'we became conscious of a new kind of hatred for the Muslims'. *The Autobiography*, pp. 227-28. In his latest book, too, the author writes in a similar strain. To quote his own words, he was 'strongly anti-Muslim in 1920' and was 'repelled' by the 'idea of living under Muslim social and cultural domination'. In his opinion, Indian Muslims constituted a society of their own with a distinctive culture and could not be absorbed in a unified Indian nation. For this reason, 'no historical argument was too false or too foolish to be trotted out by the Hindus to contest the demand of the Indian Muslims to have their own way of life'. *Thy Hand Great Anarch!*, pp. 38, 330.

[73] *The Autobiography*, pp. 227–28

[74] Ibid., p. 226.

ligh and *tanzim* anjumans and *shuddhi* and *sangathan* groups received material support from their rich patrons. It is, therefore, not surprising that communal riots in the mid-twenties took place with much greater intensity in urban rather than in rural areas.[75] The most serious outburst in UP occurred in Agra, Shahjahanpur and Saharanpur in 1923; at Allahabad and Lucknow in 1926; and at Bareilly, Kanpur and Dehradun in 1927. Calcutta had the largest share of riots in Bengal, while Multan, Lahore and Amritsar figured as rioting centres in Punjab. Western India was relatively quiet, except for some outbursts in Bombay, Pune and Sholapur. Hindu-Muslim relations in South India were generally cordial. The massive rioting in Malabar was more of an exception than a rule. So were the incidents of rioting in Madras city, Vellore and Bangalore.

It would thus seem that Hindu-Muslim riots in the twenties occurred mainly in the Indo-Gangetic belt. There were several reasons why this was so. First, the growth of newspapers in this region[76] and improved systems of travel and communication

[75] There appears to be a consensus on this point in the case of Bengal. It has been recently suggested that apart from localized violence in rural areas during the Swadeshi days, Hindu-Muslim rioting had been an urban phenomenon. Sugata Bose, 'The Roots of Communal Violence in Rural Bengal', op.cit., p.464.

[76] Both British-owned and Indian newspapers played a key part in keeping communal issues alive. The nationalist newspapers were no exception, for they, too, pandered to religious passions and prejudices, jumped on to the communal bandwagon and legitimized Hindu militancy or Muslim communalism. Yet they appeared in the garb of nationalism, justifying their position in terms which carried some measure of credibility. They could thus lend support to the Congress as well as the Hindu Mahasabha. Thus the *Amrita Bazar Patrika* made the distinction between the Congress as a political party with an all-India perspective and concerns, and the Hindu Mahasabha imbued with the mission to revitalize Hinduism and to turn it into 'a new living force, both defensive and even militant if necessary'. *Amrita Bazar Patrika,* 15, 17, 18, 19 August 1923 and editorial comments, 8 and 15 September 1923. Moonje's suggestion of organizing the lathi-wielding Hindus was endorsed by the paper, because 'the Hindus find themselves weak and emasculated, unable to defend their hearth and home, the sanctity of their temples and the honour of their women'. 4 January 1923 and 1 May 1927. Similar views were expressed in the columns of *Tribune,* 11 January

enabled men of religion and politics of all shades to reach out to a wider audience and influence their thinking and modes of expression. Secondly, the eruption of violence in certain areas was linked with two inter-related processes—the communalization of Indian politics, an aspect covered in the previous chapter of this book, and the levels of sectarian feelings generated by powerful currents of religious revivalism. It is noticeable that communal squabbles and controversies figured mostly in Bengal and in the heartland of Aryavarta which were also the strongholds of the Arya Samaj, cow-protection societies, *tabligh* and *tanzim* societies and *shuddhi* and *sangathan* sabhas.

The organizers of *tabligh* and *tanzim* groups defined their identity in explicitly religious terms and asserted their Muslimness through a neatly organized ideological campaign. They heightened the sense of community solidarity and religiosity by exhorting their followers to imbibe the letter and spirit of the Quran, follow the standards of an ideal life set by the Prophet and his Companions *(Ashaab)* and work towards the realization of an Islamic ideal. 'The real ailment of the Muslims', stated Maulana Mohammad Ilyas (1885–1944), chief architect of the *tabligh* movement, 'is that their hearts are devoid of religious consciousness and no eagerness is found in them for seeking the knowledge of Faith. If religious inclination and appreciation of the importance of the Faith is produced in their hearts, Islamism will be revived in them in no time'.[77] This was the inspiration behind the *tabligh* venture.

Tabligh groups had surfaced earlier. The Ahmadiyas, headquartered in Punjab, despatched preachers to thwart the aggressive designs of the Arya Samaj.[78] Murray T. Titus referred to the Jamiyat-i Tabligh al-Islam, with headquarters in Ambala, as a 'strong, growing organization of India-wide character', with

---

1923 and *Leader,* 2 January 1923. For role of the press in fanning the fires of communal animus, see Home Poll. and K.W. F.No. 236, 1926, NAI.

[77] S. Abul Hasan Ali Nadwi, *Life and Mission of Maulana Mohammad Ilyas*. Translated from Urdu by Asif Kidwai (Lucknow, 1983), p. 163.

[78] 'Note on the Tabligh Movement', p. 18, Home Poll. F.No. 6/IX, 1924, NAI.

provincial and district branches.[79] According to the claims of its founder, Syed Ghulam Bhik Nairang, 370 volunteers conducted extensive tours from 1923 to 1928, sponsored 16,000 meetings and converted or 'readmitted' 25,000 people to the Islamic fold.[80]

The Barelwis, with their large following among skilled workers and entrepreneurial groups, also took to *tabligh*. They worked amongst the Malkana Rajputs of Agra district who were converted and reconverted to Islam in rapid succession.[81] The Mazahir-i Ulum in Saharanpur, which in size and influence was second only to Deoband in the subcontinent, was not lacking in proselytical spirit.[82] In April 1923, a local Tabligh al-Islam was established at Aligarh.[83] And in Delhi, the sufi-politician, Hasan Nizami, produced pamphlets on *tabligh* and sought public subscriptions

[79] Murray T. Titus, *Indian Islam* (Delhi, 1979: reprint), p. 201.

[80] Besides, a newspaper, *Tabligh*, was started which came out until the end of 1925 and was resumed as a monthly journal in 1927. *Jamiyat-i Markaziya Tabligh-al Islam Ambala shehar ki satra saala khidmaat ka khulaasa*. (Organization of Tabligh, Ambala: Resume of its activities during the first seventeen years) (Ambala, 1940).

[81] In 1926 when the *shuddhi* and *tabligh* movements were at their height it was common for the Malkanas to be converted and reconverted to Hinduism in rapid succession. It was said that many of them made quite a lot of money out of their conversion and reconversion. *Census of India*, 1931, UP of Agra and Oudh (Allahabad, 1931), p. 499. It was amongst this group that the Barelwis carried out their missionary activity. At the All-India Sunni Conference at Moradabad on 17–19 March 1925, Syed Jamaat Ali Shah detailed some of the work done by the Barelwis and claimed much success for the Anjuman-i Khuddam Al-Sufia and the Ahl-i Sunnat al-Jamaat in establishing madrasas and mosques. While launching a blistering attack on the Ahmadiyas and the Deobandis, i.e., the 'Wahabis', and ruling out the possibility of uniting with them, the Shah called for religious reforms [*deeni islaah*], adherence [*taqlid*] to the fundamentals of Islam and rejection of un-Islamic practices [*rusoomat-i biddat*]. *Filbadiya Khutba-i Sadaarat* (Extempore Presidential Address) (Lahore, n.d.), pp. 15–16, 43–66.

[82] Metcalf, *Islamic Revival*, pp. 132–33.

[83] Its chief organizer was Kunwar Abdul Wahab Khan, who was himself a Muslim Rajput. He was associated with the Jamiyat-i Tabligh of Ambala. Home Poll. F.No. 6/ix, 1924.

for his project of translating the Quran in the Nagri script so as to make it accessible to the common people.[84]

Close to Hasan Nizami's headquarters and Nizamuddin Auliya's *dargah* in Nizamuddin east is the historic Banglewali masjid where Maulana Mohammad Ismail, a descendant of Shah Waliullah, had done the spadework for his son, Mohammad Ilyas, to launch an ideological assault in the region of Mewat in south-west Delhi, now in the state of Haryana. The area was inhabited by the Meos who, even after conversion, adhered to many of their 'Hindu' beliefs and retained their social customs. Some had purely Hindu names or tagged on *Khan* to a Hindu name. They celebrated Diwali, Dussehra and Janmashtami, the birthday of Krishna, and worshipped the *salar*, or banner, of one Salar Masud Ghazi, believed to be one of the generals of Sultan Mahmud of Ghazna. The Meos, like the Hindus, did not marry within the *gotra* and their daughters were not entitled to inherit.[85]

As a representative of the great Waliullahi tradition, Mohammad Ilyas was repelled by the distortions that had crept into the belief structures of the Meos. He launched a crusade against the 'unislamic' practices and sought to draw the Meos into the Islamic fold. He worked amongst the masses after his return to India in September 1925 and was the first Muslim reformer to conceive of an elaborate mass contact programme to spread the meaning of Quran and highlight the virtues of *salaat* (prayer). He established educational centres, founded charitable institutions, and, above all, organized *Jamaats* (groups). Its disciplined members, trained and tutored under a common roof, were fired with religious fervour and a missionary zeal. They travelled far and wide 'acquiring and imparting [of] Islamic knowledge, inviting the attention of the people towards Islamic practices, spreading the message of Allah, hymning his glory and sanctity and offering

[84] For example, *Tabligh Ishtihaaron ka Majmua* [Pamphlets on *Tabligh*] (Delhi, 1925); *Juma wa Idain ke Urdu Khutba at* [Urdu Sermons delivered at Friday prayers and on Id] (Delhi, 1926); *Dalail-i Islam* (Delhi, 1927).

[85] Mujeeb, *Indian Muslims*, pp. 10–11.

prayers and supplication at every step'.[86] The following description is useful :

> Anyone who saw the *Tabligh* parties of Mewat, travelling on foot, with blankets thrown on their shoulders, the *Siparaas* tucked under the arms and parched grain or bread tied in a corner of the mantle, their tongues engaged in *Zikr,* eyes showing the signs of nightly vigil and the mark of *Sajda* on the foreheads would have been reminded of the martyred Companions of the Bir Maona who were killed while going on the mission of teaching the Quran and imparting the knowledge of the commandments of the Shariat on the orders of the Holy Prophet.[87]

These men, formally constituted into the Tabligh al-Jamaat, were eulogized for their piety, simplicity, dedication and missionary spirit. Their impact was considerable, for they revived the faith by introducing the 'real' or 'true' spirit of Islam and translated into reality the Islamic ideal of Muslim brotherhood. Syed Abul Hasan Ali of Nadwat al-ulama reflects on the changes that took place in Mewat. 'Within a few years', he observes, 'the whole region emerged from darkness into light'. According to him,

> the gains of irreligiousness began to appear in Mewat which would not have, otherwise, been possible even after long years of struggle. Thousands of mosques were built where not one was to be seen for miles, and innumerable maktabs and Arabic madrasahs were established... A dislike for Hinduized garments was created and people began to dress themselves according to the specifications of the Shariat. Bracelets got removed from the arms and rings from the ears of men. Beards were grown freely and without compulsion. Polytheistic ceremonies that had become a part of marriage began to be discarded... Religious indifference and innovations and lewd and profane habits and customs started to wither away in the new climate of faith and piety.[88]

The *tanzim* societies, also started in the mid-twenties, could

[86] See Nadwi, op.cit., chapter four, and Maulana Wahiduddin Khan, *Tablighi Tehrik* (Delhi, 1985); C.W. Troll, 'Five Letters of Maulana Ilyas', in Troll (ed.), *Islam in India: Studies and Commentaries* (Delhi, 1985), vol. 2, pp. 138–150 for biographical details and the ideology behind *Tabligh.* Troll's account, however, is entirely based on Nadwi's work.

[87] Nadwi, op.cit., pp. 39–40.

[88] Ibid, p. 40.

not stake any such claims. Its founder was not a traditional *alim* but the Cambridge-educated graduate, Saifuddin Kitchlew, who rose to fame during the Rowlatt Satyagraha and was the principal mobilizer of the Khilafat cause in Punjab. Following his differences with the Congress and his rift with a section of the Khilafat leadership, Kitchlew outlined his *tanzim* scheme at the Belgaum Khilafat Conference in December 1924 and at a Muslim meeting in Amritsar in July 1925. He proposed the formation of Muslim *jathas* [volunteer corps], establishment of primary schools in mosques, Muslim banks, co-operative societies and technical institutes and the proper utilization of the incomes from *auqaf* for the educational and economic progress of the Muslim community.[89] He started a newspaper called *Tanzim,* formed the Jamiyat-i Tanzim and secured the support of a mixed group of journalists, publicists and a few *ulama*. They included Malik Barkat Ali of Lahore, Jalib Dehlawi, editor of the Lucknow paper *Hamdam,* Choudhry Afzal Haq, leader of the Ahrars, Maulana Mazharuddin, editor of the Delhi paper, *Al-Amaan,* Zafar Ali Khan, editor of *Zamindar*, Maulana Abdul Majid of Budaun, Raja Ghazanfar Ali Khan and Mohammad Shafi.[90]

Though launched amid much fanfare, Saifuddin Kitchlew's various projects failed to take off. The *ulama* were the first to raise the banner of revolt. They had weakened the *tabligh* movement through their constant ideological bickerings and were now set to undermine Kitchlew's grandiose plans. The Faridkot-born leader was an 'outsider' and his reformist aspirations could not be legitimized by men of religion, i.e., the *ulama*. More importantly, his scheme to control mosques and *auqafs* posed a serious threat to their own authority, an encroachment on their own sphere of influence. Many Barelwi *ulama* were closely tied to Punjab's *pirs* and to shrine-based structures of

[89] Toufique Kitchlew, *Saifuddin Kitchlew: Hero of Jallianwala Bagh* (National Book Trust: Delhi, 1987) pp. 51–52. Some of Kitchlew's ideas, such as the setting up of co-operative societies, stores and mortgage banks, were incorporated in a resolution adopted by the Muslim League in December 1925. Pirzada (ed.), *Foundations of Pakistan,* vol. 2, pp. 73–74.

[90] *Jamiyat-i Markazia Tanzim ka Dastur al-Amal* [Constitution of the Organization for Tanzim] (Amritsar, 1925), pp. 15–16.

mediation. To organize a scheme like Kitchlew's, a network of local organization independent of the structures of imperial influence, proved extremely difficult.[91] The Muslim League president lamented in 1926:

> It is a pity that the *Tanzim* has not made the progress that was expected of it, because people are not sufficiently trained to appreciate quiet and solid work and because Dr Kitchlew has been practically single-handed in his efforts. And many of those who were enthusiastic about him when he was advocating the process of revolution left his side when he began to press evolution.[91a]

The protagonists of *shuddhi* and *sangathan* conducted a more effective and ideologically cohesive campaign. Founded by Pandit Bhoj Dutt Sharma in 1907, *shuddhi* sabhas functioned under the aegis of several socio-religious organizations in northern India and could thus count on the existing networks to reach out to a wider audience. Their initial success was facilitated by the Kshatriya Upakarini Sabha, the movement for interclan unity among the Rajputs, and the association of Rampal Singh and Raja Durga Narayan Singh of Tirwa.[92] In 1907, the Rajputs in Agra division flocked to the *shuddhi* sabhas and the Arya Samaj in an attempt to reconvert the Muslim Rajputs.[93] In the wake of the Moplah riots, they gained more recruits. Chief among them was Shraddhanand, who was mainly responsibile for reconverting

[91] Gilmartin, *Empire and Islam*, p. 82; Page, *Prelude to Partition*, pp. 101–104; Thursby, *Hindu-Muslim Relations*. pp. 153–54, 171. Following was the government's assessment:

> The organization...as the word Tanzim signifies, is full of potentialities, but it is still in its infancy and unless some new pretext is found to excite public feeling against the Government, it is not likely to be a source of danger to the Government at the present time. If perfected, it is capable of being directed against both the Government as well as the Hindus, as it may suit the needs of the organizer.

Home Poll. F. No. 6/ix, 1925, NAI.

[91a] Pirzada (ed.), *Foundations of Pakistan*, vol. 2, p. 91.

[92] R. Gordon, 'The Hindu Mahasabha and the Indian National Congress 1915 to 1926', *Modern Asian Studies*, vol. 9, 2, April 1975, p. 172.

[93] The society claimed to have converted 1,052 Muslim Rajputs from 1907 to 1910. Lajpat Rai, *History of the Arya Samaj*, p. 121.

many of the Malkana Rajputs and for bringing in eighty-four 'non-Hindu villages' into the Hindu fold.[94] When the *shuddhi* campaign was officially included in the programme of the All-India Hindu Mahasabha in August 1923, it had the unqualified backing of leading Congress stalwarts, such as Malaviya, Lajpat Rai and Moonje.[95]

Moonje was described by the *Mahratta* as a 'staunch Hindu, committed to restoring Hinduism in its proper place'.[96] As Tilak's lieutenant in the Central Provinces, he popularized Ganapati and Shivaji festivals and organized the first Kirtan Conference. As a leading swarajist in the Central Provinces, he spearheaded the *sangathan* movement—the panacea for the ills of the Hindus and the perfect answer to ward off Muslim 'aggression' in Malabar, Kohat and Multan.[97] 'I am glad to tell you', he informed one of his friends, 'that I have been able to organize the Hindus of Nagpur for self-defence. It was a sight for Gods to see when well-built Hindus about 5,000 strong with big lathis in their hands paraded the streets of Nagpur.... I am sure you will be delighted to hear of the Hindu sangathan of Nagpur which is of a purely defensive character'.[98]

Moonje's basic concern was to revive martial traditions so that Hindus could confront a 'bully and savagely aggressive' Muslim community on equal terms. He told a group of Maharashtrians that young Maratha men must always remember

> their national and historical peculiarity which consisted in fighting the Muslims to success. I cannot contemplate a situation with equanimity where along with others even the Maratha youngmen are broken down to submission by Muslims. Therefore I said taste should be cultivated in young men of Maharashtra for wrestling and lathi plays so that they may as readily come out in streets with lathis in hand as Muslim goondas.[99]

[94] *Forward,* 6 January 1927.

[95] For the views of Lajpat Rai, see *Tribune,* 13 December 1924.

[96] Quoted in R.I. Cashman, *The Myth of the Lokamanya: Tilak and Mass Politics in Maharashtra* (California University Press, 1975), p. 189.

[97] 18 December 1923, Moonje Dossier (19), Moonje Papers, National Library, Calcutta.

[98] Ibid.

[99] 20 April 1926, Diary (1).

The Nagpur-based eye surgeon had a two-fold mission: to liberate the country from British rule and to bring some sense into the 'rowdy' and aggressive Muslims. In this respect, the fight for swaraj 'was merely a continuation of the struggle initiated by Prithviraj Chauhan when the Hindu Raj, culture and religion was first assailed under the Mughal impact'.[100] It was no good harping on non-violence as a political creed, for Gandhi's philosophy of Ahimsa had caused 'irreparable' harm to the Hindus alone. Moonje declared:

> In one word I have been saying to Gandhi's followers that I consider my mission in life now to do everything possible so that the teachings of love and Ahimsa, of which we have been saturated since Buddha's and Jaina's time, may not take root at least in Maharashtra... I believe [Gandhi's] philosophy will lead to destruction and extermination of the Hindus from the face of world.[101]

To convince Hindus of the validity of his position and beliefs, Moonje reached out to many sections of society. He appealed to the Raja of Darbhanga and the landlords in the region to recruit their tenantry from the 'martial races'—the Gurkhas, Rajputs and Marathas.[102] He approached and secured the patronage of wealthy Bhatias and other Hindu merchants in Bombay.[103] Such veteran politicians like Khaparde, Kelkar and Jayakar were already playing to his tune in the region. The Amils of Sind, anxious to thwart the Muslim League demand to separate Sind from Bombay Presidency, hitched their fortunes with the Moonje bandwagon. Moonje also secured a footing in Bengal, where he was anxious to 'rouse the latent Hindu mentality'.[104] He even established contact with Rabindranath Tagore, who, according to Moonje's version, approved of his ideas and his rabidly communal Patna speech. The poet is reported to have told Moonje that 'all those bitterness between the Hindus and Muslims is the result of the bungling of Gandhi and [that] he had warned him in time'. Moonje asked Tagore to issue a message to

[100] 3 May 1926, ibid.
[101] 13 July 1926, ibid.
[102] 18 July 1926, ibid.
[103] To Jayakar, 2 June 1925, Jayakar Papers (405).
[104] 17 February 1927, Diary (2).

the Hindus on the occasion of the Shivaji festival. 'It may, I said, inspire the young men of Bengal to come out to carry on the mission of the Hindu Sabha in Bengal. He replied in a way which appeared to be hopeful'.[105]

Such antagonism towards the Muslims, though not generally shared by his swarajist colleagues, was indicative of an ideological strand in the nationalist movement which could be curbed through a sustained ideological campaign and not by setting up peace committees and drawing up paper pacts. The Congress leadership, in general, settled for a soft option by accommodating the various cross-currents even if they undermined its principles and avowed goals. This is further evident from the way in which some of the key Congress figures were allowed to occupy prominent positions in the Hindu Mahasabha and disseminate its pronounced anti-Muslim ideology.

Founded in 1915 to safeguard the 'separate and distinct interests of the Hindu community', the Mahasabha lent a common platform to orthodox groups, patronized by rich bankers, landowners and professional men. The executive committee of the UP Hindu Sabha contained twelve lawyers, three zamindars who were also lawyers, and six commercial and landed magnates. They belonged to the large trading centres, with extensive linkages in local bodies and provincial organizations.[106] In Bihar,

[105] 28 April 1927, Diary (1). Tagore did not require much persuasion, for he had already expressed himself in favour of unity among Hindus 'to counteract the mentality which engenderd fanatical outrages [such as Shraddhanand's murder] and riots'. *Forward*, 29 December 1927.

[106] While the All-India Hindu Mahasabha was founded in April 1915, provincial Hindu Sabhas were already active in Punjab and Bihar since 1907, and at UP since 1914. CP and Berar, Bombay and Bengal had their branches in 1923–24 and Sind in 1926. It is significant, however, that outside UP, Punjab and Central Provinces, the Mahasabha had limited support. It was strongest in the Central Provinces, where as an immigrant community the Brahmins in 1924 and 1925 rallied round it in preference to the Congress as a means of counteracting the non-Brahman movement which was wresting control of local bodies. See Home Poll. F. Nos. 25 and 112, 1924, 1925, NAI. The history of the Sabhas and their activities are covered in: Kenneth W. Jones, 'Politicized Hinduism: The Ideology and Program of the Hindu Mahasabha', Baird (ed.), *Religion in Modern India,* pp. 239–74; and for

the Hindu Sabha was founded by the Maharaja of Darbhanga in 1907 and popularized by two leading lawyers—Parmeshwar and Sachidanand Sinha.[107] In Punjab, the Sabha comprised of, among others, the Lahore bankers and traders, journalists like Gulshan Rai, landowners like Raja Narendranath, and all-India politicians like Lajpat Rai.

The spate of protest meetings against the Lucknow Pact gave impetus to the Hindu Mahasabha. Its prestige was further enhanced soon after the Non-Co-operation movement came to a halt. Spirits were high at the Hindu Mahasabha conference in December 1922, which was held in the Congress pandal at Gaya. A 'Hindu Relief Committee' and the Hindu Raksha Mandal were launched.[108] In August 1923 the Mahasabha listed the *shuddhi* campaign on its agenda. This lent a more specifically religious emphasis to its platform. From now on *shuddhi* was to be conducted by the Mahasabha as well as the All-India Shuddhi Sabha, attached to the Arya Samaj.

The man who occupied a pivotal position in reviving the Mahasabha and in pushing through the *shuddhi* resolution was Madan Mohan Malaviya. His position was of truly special importance, for he had been a key figure in Congress politics since 1886 and exercized a profound influence on Hindu revivalism in UP. His achievements were impressive. He founded one of India's most well-known English dailies—the *Leader*—and also a Hindi newspaper—*Abhyudaya*. He conceived and carried out, with remarkable tenacity and devotion, the project of a Hindu university at Banaras. He was a protagonist of Hindi and the protection of the cow. As the chief ideologue of

---

background information, see Walder K. Andersen and Shridhar D. Damle, *The Brotherhood in Saffron: The Rashtriya Swayamsevak Sangh and Hindu Revivalism* (Delhi, 1987).

[107] J.S. Jha, 'An Unpublished Correspondence relating to the Bihar Hindu Sabha', *Journal of the Bihar Research Society,* January-December 1968, pp. 339–44.

[108] Among the members were Malaviya, Raja Rampal Singh, Lala Hansraj, Shraddhanand, Khaparde, C. Vijayaraghavachariar, former Congress president, S. Satyamurti, Kelkar, Moonje, Jamnalal Bajaj and K. Natrajan, editor of *Indian Social Reformer*. See Gordon, 'The Hindu Mahasabha', pp. 168–69.

Hindu resurgence and revivalism and as patron of the Prayag Hindu Samaj, the Sanatan Dharm Mahasammelan and the UP Hindu Sabha, Malaviya developed wide-ranging linkages with rulers of princely states, prosperous landowners, commercial magnates and professional men. It was on the strength of their support that he built his political base. He proved that there was no contemporary politician in Allahabad who could match his enthusiasm for the causes associated with Hinduism, his astuteness and his immense organizing capacity. He was a master tactician, adept in the art of political temporizing.

In his address to the Hindu Sabha meet in Gaya, Malaviya dwelt on his community's 'disintegration' and the need to arrest the process through the Hindu Mahasabha.[109] At his behest, *shuddhi*, too, became an integral component of the Mahasabha programme. In December 1925, he urged his audience at Kanpur to establish local branches of the Hindu Sabhas and *akharas* in every village, and thus bring about complete *sangathan*.[110] Following the Mahasabha's decision to contest the provincial elections in November 1926, he used communal slogans against his arch swarajist rivals, especially Motilal Nehru, and incited communal unrest, particularly in Allahabad.[111] 'The real reason', noted a government report, 'why Hindu-Muslim relations are worse in Allahabad is because of Malaviya family and their followers, who constitute the Hindu Sabha. This body with its doctrine of *sangathan* has aroused an aggressive spirit, which has spread into the small towns and villages'.[112] This was not all. A

[110] He stated in his presidential address at the Mahasabha session in Varanasi: 'Friendship could exist only between equals. If the Hindus made themselves strong and the rowdy section among the Muslims could not rob or dishonour Hindus, Hindu-Muslim unity would be established on a stable basis'. *Leader,* 22 August 1923.

[111] 'Note on the Activities of Malaviya', Home Poll. F.No. 187, 1926, NAI. See, Pandey, *The Ascendancy of the Congress,* 119–20, and Page, *Prelude to Partition,* pp. 127–28.

[112] Ibid. And 'Note by Alexander Muddiman', 21 September, F.No. 368, 1925, NAI, for the role of Malaviya's family.

correspondent from Bijnor reported that Malaviya and Bhai Parmanand were busy trying to 'create and fan the communal fire among the electorate'.[113]

Motilal's endeavours to keep the Swaraj party firm against the communal blitzkrieg were thwarted; such was the communal hatred aroused that he considered retiring from public life. During the election campaign he was berated for his anti-Hindu views and pro-Muslim proclivities. Word was spread that he was in league with the Muslims to legalize cow-slaughter.[114]

The election results in UP marked the triumph of the communal forces, headed by Malaviya and financed by G.D. Birla.[115] The swarajists, despite having made concessions to communal sentiments, fought on a non-communal plank but were reduced in size—from 31 in 1923 to 16 members in 1926. The erosion of their base among Muslims was substantial.[116] Not only was their enthusiasm for the Swaraj party dwindling but they were slowly but steadily drifting towards organized communalist formations.

V

British officials, in general, attributed Hindu-Muslim animus to the reforms of 1919. The growing antipathy, observed the governor of Bengal, 'was one of the fruits of the Reforms'.[117] This view is echoed, though with sophistication and scholarly rigour, in the writings of Francis Robinson, G.R. Thursby, David Page and

[113] F.No. 21 (part 2), 1926, AICC Papers, NMML.

[114] Motilal Nehru to Jawaharlal, 2 December 1926, *A Bunch of Old Letters* (Delhi, 1958), pp. 51–52.

[115] In the elections Swami Shraddhanand openly canvassed for Birla, 'one of those very few persons who were eager to do as much as they could for every good cause and in the interest of Hindus particularly'. Shraddhanand, quoted in Jordens, *Swami Shraddhananda*, p. 166. Motilal referred to the 'Malaviya-Lala gang' which was being aided by Birla's money to capture the Congress.

[116] See Page, op.cit., pp. 136–38.

[117] Lytton, *Pundits and Elephants*, pp. 165–66; J. Coatman, *India in 1926–27* (Calcutta, 1928), p. 19; R. Coupland, *The Indian Problem, 1833–1935* (Oxford, 1942).

Ian Talbot.[118] Page was among the first historians to detail the profoundly divisive effects of the Montagu-Chelmsford Reforms. Communal antagonism, he argued, became a 'permanent feature' of provincial politics, political interests began to be consolidated around communal issues, and 'Muslim attitudes' were formed towards the emergence of provincial autonomy and towards the eventual withdrawal of imperial control.[119]

The nationalists analyzed communalism in terms of either the 'one mighty economic force' which divided people 'horizontally into two homogeneous parts' or as a fall-out of government policy which stoked the fires of communal unrest through a collusion with feudal, semi-feudal and reactionary elements.[120] They were able to show how 'British governments in the past and the present have based their policy on creating divisions in our ranks',[121] nursed sectional groups and their leaders, and rewarded them with seats in legislatures, high-sounding titles and honours. Communalism was an acceptable corrective to nationalist zeal provided it did not lead to a community's alienation from government or to political chaos from which the opponents of the raj might benefit.[122]

[118] Thursby, *Hindu-Muslim Relations,* pp. 134–35; Page, op.cit., 260. Talbot is of the view that British officials were 'anxious to limit communal violence rather than to risk encouraging it by dividing and ruling'. *Punjab and the Raj,* p. 4. Francis Robinson maintains that while British policy *played* the main part in establishing a separate Muslim identity in Indian politics and contributed to the development of Muslim separatism, it was not *intended* to do so. The fact was that the British feared the Muslims and sought to pacify them through special concessions. These were aimed not at setting Muslims against Hindus, but at reconciling them to British rule. Robinson concludes: 'There was no deliberate attempt to foster communal hostility; indeed the aim was to avoid it'. *Separatism Among Muslims,* pp. 131–32, 348–49.

[119] Page, op.cit., p. 259.

[120] This was M.N. Roy's classic formulation. Among other writers who endorsed this view were: K.B. Krishna, *The Problem of Minorities or Communal Representation in India* (London, 1939), and Asoka Mehta and Achyut Patwardhan, *The Communal Triangle in India* (Allahabad, 1942).

[121] Jawaharlal Nehru's speech at the Brussells Congress, 10 February 1927, *Selected Works of Jawaharlal Nehru,* vol. 2, p. 275.

[122] Page, op.cit., p. 91.

It is evident from the large mass of archival material that the raj was unabashedly partisan in pitting one community against the other to serve its imperial interests.[123] When repressive measures failed, as in the early 1920s, hopes were pinned 'upon the eternity of the communal situation'. Clandestine means were employed to organize Muslim opposition. This policy was pursued during the civil disobedience movement. Muslims were told to conduct local campaigns, itinerant preachers were financed by the UP government, and Shaukat Ali was pressed into service to revive the *tanzim* movement.[124] 'We have even gone so far', wrote Hailey, 'as to pay from Secret Service Funds the travelling expenses of some...preachers. It is our intention to watch [the] progress [of *tanzim*], and so long as its activity is directed mainly towards countering civil disobedience, to continue to give it moral support'.[125]

In Bengal, the divide and rule policy was put into operation to break the stranglehold of the swarajists and to draw a wedge amongst its supporters. An attempt to sow the seeds of dissension was first made in March 1924, when a Muslim councillor from Malda sought to corner Das by insisting on the implementation of certain provisions of the Bengal pact. Das was able to foil the move. Then, when the demand for ministerial salaries was rejected, Lytton and his aides made much of the fact that the two ministers—Fazlul Haq and A.K. Ghuznavi—were Muslims. The vote of the official and non-official blocs in the council was thrown in to prop up the shaky ministries, who were built up as an effective political counterforce.[126]

The situation in Punjab was different. The presence of well-entrenched landed and commercial classes and their anxiety to be accommodated in the constitutional structures imposed constraints on the administration's options in augmenting its support base. It was easy to play up one sectional group against

[123] For Bengal, see Broomfield, *Elite Conflict,* p. 272; Rajat Ray, *Social Conflict and Political Unrest,* pp. 354–56; Tanika Sarkar, *Bengal,* p. 105.

[124] Hailey to Irwin, 9 June 1930, F. No. 18 (B), Hailey Papers.

[125] Hailey to J. Crerar. Home Member, 25 September 1930, F.No. 19 (B), Hailey Papers.

[126] Broomfield, op.cit., pp. 252–62; Rajat Ray, op. cit., pp. 352–55.

the other and to take advantage of the controversies which beleagured Fazli Husain's ministry. But this strategy could only be partially successful in Punjab, where the lines of cleavages were not always defined in purely communal terms. So, besides inducting communally-oriented groups into positions of power, Edward Maclagan and his successor, Malcolm Hailey, relied heavily upon the 'agriculturists' and their chosen leaders—Fazli Husain, Chhotu Ram and Lal Chand—against the urban-based trading and commercial classes.

Hailey did not undervalue Muslim support but warned against making wholesale concessions in their favour. When it became clear that the swarajists were losing ground and that the body politic was being divided along communal lines, he started wooing the urban Hindus with political concessions to hold 'the balance between the parties'.[127] 'To have carried on with the old arrangement', he observed, 'would have meant that the Hindu party as such was to be permanently excluded; it would have driven them back on opposition and ultimately to swaraj'.[128] This rethinking on Hailey's part adversely affected the fortunes of the Unionists, especially its Muslim constituents. The Registration of Moneylenders Bill was vetoed and the passage of the Land Revenue [Amendment] Bill was obstructed. Fazli Husain's wings were also clipped. While he was relegated to the reserved half of the government, his arch-critic Manohar Lal occupied the ministerial berth. In this way, Hailey divided ministerial offices among the communities and thereby divided the legislative council into communal blocs.[129]

The ministerial reshuffle achieved its immediate goal of encouraging the urban Hindus to turn more whole-heartedly to government and curbing the political ambitions of Fazli Husain and his allies. Hailey commented on its outcome in more general terms and indicated the drift of his policies. 'In the political world', he informed the viceroy,

[127] See Page, op.cit., p. 91.

[128] Hailey to Alexander Muddiman, January 1927, F. No. 10 (A), Hailey Papers.

[129] Azim Husain, *Fazli Husain*, p. 161.

the balance between Muhammadans on the one hand and Sikhs and Hindus on the other created a situation which, if on occasions led to communal troubles embarrassing the government, on the other placed government in a strong situation as holding the balance between the parties. As a consequence, the politically-minded Hindus found themselves unable to maintain a consistent opposition to government and, at all events, during the last three years came definitely to the view that they would have to depend on government if they were to maintain their position vis-a-vis the Muslims.[130]

Hailey was an old hand. He played his cards well. Yet, he was obliged in the last resort to throw his weight behind the Muslim bloc. And when he moved from Lahore to Lucknow, he soon turned into a spokesman of 'Muslim interests'.[131] He advised the viceroy on Muslim representation at the Round Table Conference, sought explicit assurances on the preservation of 'Muslim rights' and insisted on an official pronouncement on the communal question. He believed, as did many of his British contemporaries, that if the decision was 'moderately satisfactory to Muslims', it would be possible to keep the 'great mass of moderate Muslims on our side, and there would be far less tendency on their part to drift into opposition to Government'.[132] Any amount of sophisticated jugglery could not obscure the sinister design behind Hailey's advocacy.

130 Hailey to Irwin, 16 October 1928, F.No. 14 (A), Hailey Papers.
131 Page, op.cit., 92–93.
132 Hailey to viceroy, 7 April 1932, F.No. 23 (B), Hailey Papers.

Chapter Nine

Illusions of Insecurity: The Nehru Report

Some of the issues which polarized political opinion in India came to the fore in 1928 when the All-Parties Conference, stung by Birkenhead's challenge, met to draw up a constitution—one that would represent a consensus as well as reflect the fears and aspirations of variegated groups and parties. Was India to adopt a unitary or a federal model? What will be the position of minorities in either system? Would they be entitled to 'safeguards', such as separate electorates and community-wise representation? If so, were seats to be distributed according to the Lucknow Pact or the newly-formulated Delhi Proposals of March 1927?[1]

The Nehru Committee Report—the swan song of the Congress—faced some of these issues and suggested ways of giving the 'finishing kick to communalism'. But its recommendations, as was predicted, evoked angry protests, generated heated debates, and created fissures in the Congress. This chapter seeks to understand why this was so and suggests new ways of looking at the communal controversies that raged during the years 1927 to 1929. In doing so, the first step is to take note of the Delhi Proposals, which haunted the leading lights at All-Parties meetings.

[1] *Hindustan Times* [20 May 1928] summed up the problems: 'When one thinks of the numerous differences, political as well as communal, that separate the various parties in the country, one is almost overwhelmed with a feeling of despair. Dominion Status or independence, music before mosques, cow-slaughter, separation of Sind, joint electorates or separate electorates, reform for the Frontier Province, representation of minorities in the legislature and services, are all baffling problems, and have, each one of them, proved a stumbling block in the way of the success of past conferences'.

II

Thirty prominent Muslims congregated in Delhi on a common platform to surrender their long-cherished preference for separate electorates. But their offer was conditional. They insisted on the acceptance of four proposals—Muslim representation in the Bengal and Punjab legislative councils in proportion to their population; one-third of reserved Muslim seats in the central legislature; creation of Sind as an independent province; and introduction of reforms in the North-West Frontier Province. 'It is for the other party', stated Mohammad Yaqub, a participant at the Delhi meet, 'to clasp the hand of friendship which the Muslims have extended'.[2]

Predictably, there was reluctance in certain quarters to 'clasp the hand of friendship'. The Provincial Congress Committees in Maharashtra and Berar shared this reluctance.[3] So did Congressmen loyal to the Hindu Mahasabha. Backed by the 'nationalist' press, they denounced the Delhi offer at the AICC meeting on 5 May. But the views of the Nehrus, Srinivasa Iyengar and the Congress Muslims prevailed. Jayakar was won over. Lajpat Rai and Malaviya were silenced for the time being by Motilal Nehru. With Gandhi's backing, he secured the AICC's acquiescence of the Delhi Proposals.[4] 'The Congress', wrote an indignant newspaper editor, 'has become a handmaid of Motilal Nehru and the sole function of the AICC is to register his decrees. It was therefore a foregone conclusion that his views in the matter would prevail'.[5]

Spirited opposition to the Delhi Proposals and to their endorsement by the Congress coincided, much to everybody's relief, with a momentous development—the appointment of an all-British Statutory Commission on 8 November 1927.

[2] To M.C. Chagla, 20 March 1927, M.C. Chagla Papers, NMML.

[3] *Leader*, 9 and 10 April 1927; *Mahratta*, 10 April 1927.

[4] See Mushirul Hasan, 'The Communal Divide: A Study of the Delhi Proposals', in Hasan (ed.), *Communal and Pan-Islamic Trends*, pp. 289–91.

[5] *Surya*, 4 June 1927, SNNR, UP; Moonje to M.R. Jayakar, 10 June 1927, M.R. Jayakar Papers; *Basumati*, 9 May 1927; *Hitavada*, 10 June 1927; SNNR, Bengal.

Archbold, who had served under Minto and was the prime organizer of the 1906 Simla Deputation, had warned Birkenkead only two days earlier that 'there will be no end of a row in India'.[6] He was right, because the composition of the Simon Commission—'an awful political blunder'[7]—was widely denounced in India. It could not have been otherwise. 'Jallianwala Bagh was a physical butchery, the Simon Commission is a butchery of our souls', declared an indignant Jinnah.[8] Sapru, the Liberal leader, was enraged. The Simon Commission, he said, 'must start its work with the very serious handicap that it will not carry with it Indian confidence and support'.[9] Declared Ansari, the Congress president: 'We can have no part or lot in a Commission which has been appointed in direct defiance of the declared will of the people', a line that brought an approving roar from the public in the Congress pandal.[10] The Madras Congress, therefore, voted to boycott the Commission, proclaimed independence as its goal and resolved to draft India's future constitution. The All-India Khilafat Conference, the Jamiyat al-ulama and the Muslim League took their cue from the Congress and adopted the same course of action.

Birkenhead's challenge could be met only if the various political combinations put their heads together to sustain the boycott of the Simon Commission.[11] As Congress president, Ansari gave the lead, appealing for unity and the sinking of differences.[12]

[6] 6 November 1927, L/PO/6/32, IOLR.

[7] Archbold to Hailey, 29 January 1930, ibid.

[8] Quoted in Wolpert, *Jinnah of Pakistan*, p. 91.

[9] *Pioneer Mail*, 24 June 1927, L/PO/100 (iii), IOLR. In his note, John Simon noticed that even the 'Responsivists' went helter skelter into the swarajist camp. 'It is the adherence of these moderate politicians to the policy of boycott which has been the unexpected and disturbing element in the Indian parliamentary situation'. Baldwin Papers, vol. 102, University Library, Cambridge.

[10] Hasan, *A Nationalist Conscience*, pp. 164–65.

[11] 1 December 1927, Hasan (ed.), *Muslims and the Congress*, p. 24.

[12] Notice the comment: 'Now that the talk of boycotting the Simon Commission is swaying the public mind, it is high time for the advanced Hindus to come to an understanding with the Muslims'. *Soltan*, SNNR, Bengal.

The response was impressive. Some leading Khilafatists, estranged from the Congress for one reason or the other, buried their differences and responded to Ansari's pleadings.[13] Jinnah, too, was moved. 'For [to] me, this offer is more valuable than any concession which the British government can make. Let us then grasp the hand of fellowship. This is indeed a bright day; and for achieving this unity, thanks are due to Lord Birkenhead'.[14]

Jinnah had spoken too soon, for bitter feuds and seemingly endless wranglings marred the All-Parties Conference in February 1928. After ten days of it, the strain was so great for Jawaharlal Nehru that he 'fled to avoid riot and insurrection'.[15] When he returned to the conference table, he was 'thoroughly fed up' by 'extremists' on either side—Jinnah, Mohamed Ali and Hasrat Mohani on one side and Lajpat Rai, Moonje and Jairamdas Daulatram, on the other.[16] The deadlock was over the future of Sind.[17] This was expected, for the Hindu Mahasabha's position was well publicized on the eve of the conference. Their intransigence over reservation of Muslim seats in the Punjab and Bengal councils was also known. What irked Jinnah and his group was that Motilal, having pushed through the Delhi Proposal at the AICC meeting, was now soft-pedalling on reservation of seats for Muslims in Bengal and Punjab. Incensed by Motilal's *volte face,* the Muslim League stayed away from the rest of the deliberations.[18] The

[13] Hasan, *A Nationalist Conscience,* pp. 162–64.

[14] Jinnah took the initiative to convene an all-parties conference so as to evolve 'a policy of common and concerted action' to meet the challenge posed by the Statutory Commission. He stressed that 'the principle and the policy underlying the exclusion of Indians from the Commission are proved to be more objectionable than ever'. To Mohamed Ali, 30 November 1927, Mohamed Ali Papers, Jamia Millia Islamia, reproduced in Hasan, *Mohamed Ali: Ideology and Politics,* p. 157.

[15] To Gandhi, 23 February 1928, *Selected Works of Jawaharlal Nehru (SWJN),* vol. 3, p. 36.

[16] To Syed Mahmud, 17 March 1928, ibid., p. 37.

[17] See Hasan, 'The Communal Divide', op. cit., pp. 282–86.

[18] Rejecting the invitation to attend the conference, Mohammad Yaqub stated: 'The strength of opposition on the part of these (Hindu Mahasabha) cannot be overlooked and it seems nearly impossible to obtain support of majority organizations to a reasonable plan providing safeguards for all interests'. *Hindustan Times,* 16 May 1928.

Mahasabha went a step further: its Jabalpur meeting in April rejected the Delhi Proposals. There was, thus, not even a remote chance of a reconciliation. The younger Nehru told the Congress Working Committee:

> It is too much to be hoped that these conflicting viewpoints will be able to accommodate themselves and will agree to a common formula. We are therefore to prepare ourselves for this conflict and to decide on our course of action.[19]

So they did. After the failure of the February and May meetings, the Nehrus, backed by Ansari, Sapru, Annie Besant and Iyengar, garnered their forces to overcome opposition. Some sort of consensus was pushed through—one that was 'neither complete nor of the genuine type but something we can stand for both in All-Parties Conference and the country at large'.[19a] A committee was put together to draw up India's future constitution.[20]

III

The deliberations and decisions of the committee bore the stamp of two of its members—Motilal and Sapru. The Mahatma paid his compliments to Motilal, 'without whose effort there would have been no Committee, there would have been no unanimity, and there would have been no report.'[20a] Irwin, the viceroy, referred to the report as the 'Nehru-Sapru constitution'.[21]

Motilal Nehru and Tej Bahadur Sapru had much in common. Both were lawyers of distinction in Allahabad. Both were Kashmiri Pandits, having grown up in an 'Indo-Persian cultural atmosphere' which was the legacy of the Mughal court in north

[19] 3 May 1928, *SWJN*, vol. 3, p. 38.

[19a] Motilal Nehru to Gandhi, 11 June 1928, F.No G/1, Motilal Nehru Papers, NMML. All future references, unless otherwise stated, are drawn from the same file.

[20] Of the ten members of the committee, Jayakar conveyed his inability to serve on it, N.M. Joshi did not show up at a single meeting, while Ali Imam and G.R. Pradhan attended just a few meetings. Motilal to Gandhi, 27 June 1928, Motilal Nehru Papers.

[20a] *CWMG*, vol. 21, p. 212; Bose, *Collected Works*, p. 165.

[21] Irwin to Birkenhead, 6 September 1928, Irwin Papers, MSS. EUR. C 152/4, IOLR.

India. They were proficient in Persian and Urdu and enjoyed reading and reciting the poetry of Shaikh Sadi, Hafiz Shirazi, Maulana Jalaluddin Rum, Mir Taqi Mir and Ghalib. Motilal's first teacher was Kazi Sadruddin, an oriental scholar attached to the princely court of Khetri. 'In the days of my boyhood', recalled Motilal, 'my earliest impressions were received at the feet of Muslim professors and teachers and the more than half a century that has since elapsed has not in the least blunted the effect which those first impressions produced upon my young mind'.[22] Sapru had a similar background. He was unmoved by the language controversy and remained a consistent protagonist of Urdu, the language which symbolized the composite and syncretic culture of north India.[23] The *Kashmiri Darpan,* published from 1903 to 1906, was an Urdu monthly. 'Let not the language in which Atash, Insha, Wazir...wrote', he stated, 'be despised; let it not perish or even languish....Cultivate the language and develop it'.[24]

In public affairs, Motilal and Sapru evinced a breadth of vision and freedom from a sectarian approach. Secular and broad-minded in their outlook and approach, they wanted to separate religion from politics. Both were uncomfortable with Gandhi's emphasis on religion and spirituality and only reluctantly did Motilal endorse his support to the Khilafat cause. Religion, according to the elder Nehru, signified bigotry, intolerance and narrow-mindedness. Its association with politics, he observed at the Calcutta Congress in 1928, 'has been to the good of neither. Religion has been degraded and politics has sunk into the mire. Complete divorce of one from the other is the only remedy'.[25] This was the thinking which went into the making of the Nehru report.

[22] *Legislative Assembly Debates,* February 1924, vol. 4, 14, p. 784.

[23] Sapru stated: 'I believe the growth of Urdu in the seventeenth and eighteenth century was a natural sequence of comingling of the Hindus and Muslims in north India. It toned down differences and enabled the Hindus to understand the Muslims and the Muslims to understand the Hindus'. Quoted in Sender, *The Kashmiri Pandits,* p. 252. And Sapru's speeches on Urdu in *Hamaari Qaumi Zabaan* (Delhi, 1941).

[24] K.N. Raina (ed.), *Welding the Nation: Academic Addresses and Selected Writings* (Bombay, 1974), p. 13.

[25] *Congress Presidential Addresses, 1911-1934* (New Series), p. 864.

The communal phenomena was an anathema to these stalwarts of Allahabad, a threat to their vision of a secular society. Yet, they recognized the need for an equitable settlement of inter-communal claims. Such was the political climate created by the raj that it was no longer possible to ignore the demands of minorities—the Muslims and the Sikhs in Punjab. Even though Motilal was not directly involved in the negotiations which led to the Lucknow Pact, there is evidence to suggest that the wider agreement between Hindus and Muslims, 'of which the Lucknow Pact was a part,....[was] hammered out at a meeting' in Anand Bhawan in Allahabad.[26]

Motilal and Sapru pronounced separate electorates as a pernicious principle in public life. But there was no doing away with it. Motilal stated in the UP legislative council:

> Over a question like this my motto is peace at any price....Whatever my personal views on the merits of the question may be, there is no doubt that, practically speaking, we cannot be preaching these principles, keep off the actual separate representation of Muhammadans for any length of time. It must come. It has come already in the elections to the Councils and it must go on and filter down to.....the lowest rungs of the ladder of public life.'[27]

Sapru also recognized separate electorates as a 'necessary evil'. Participating in the debate on the UP Municipalities Bill, he said:

> Unfortunately we do not live in a world of perfection, every day of our life we realize the imperfections of our surroundings and we realize that compromise is of the very essence of politics...Having regard to the circumstances which exist at present, the only solution lies in providing separate representation to the Muslim community. Separate representation ...is a necessary evil in our present social and political condition.[28]

These were not popular views; in fact, Motilal and Sapru were

[26] B.R. Nanda, *Gokhale, Gandhi and the Nehrus: Studies in Indian Nationalism* (London, 1974), p. 126.

[27] *Proceedings of the United Provinces Legislative Council, 1916. The United Provinces Municipalities Bill, 1915* (henceforth *Proceedings)*, p. 227.

[28] Ibid., p. 218

castigated then and later as *Addha* [half] Mussalmans and accused of 'selling out' Hindu interests. Sapru came to be distrusted by his own Liberal colleagues, including C.Y.. Chintamani and Srinivasa Sastri.[29] 'I have never been looked upon as a good Hindu in any sense of the term', Sapru lamented in August 1932.[30] Motilal was denounced by the 'Malaviya-Lala gang' for his pro-Muslim proclivities. The communalists, aided by Birla money, ganged up against him in the 1926 election campaign.[31] They included Shraddhanand, the high priest of the *shuddhi* movement, who canvassed for men like Birla, 'one of those very few persons who were eager to do as much as they could for every good cause and in the interest of Hindus particularly'.[32] With such forces arrayed against him, Motilal fretted and fumed, and felt that his voice 'will be a cry in the wilderness'. Not quite so. The All-Parties Conference gave him opportunity to have his say.

IV

The Nehru Committee Report, published on 15 August 1928, covered a variety of constitutional issues—an exercise never ever attempted by any representative body in India. A case was made out for dominion status,[33] much to the annoyance of

[29] V.S. Srinivasan to D.V. Gundappa, 15 December 1930, in Jagadisan (ed.), *Letters of Srinivasa Sastri*, p. 203.

[30] Sapru to E. Thompson, 22 August 1932, Sapru Papers, vol. 37, p. 113, National Library, Calcutta.

[31] This was the year, i.e., July 1926, when Motilal and Sapru took the lead in forming the 'Indian National Union', which aimed at creating a 'national consciousness and a national atmosphere in which religious and communal conflicts will be relegated to a subordinate plane'. Other members of the Union were Abul Kalam Azad, Srinivasa Sastri, Hakim Ajmal Khan, Sarojini Naidu and the Raja of Mahmudabad. *Indian Quarterly Register* (henceforth *IQR*), 1926, vol. 2, pp. 90–95.

[32] See f.n. 115, chapter 8 above.

[33] There was an obvious difference in the nationalist and colonial perceptions of dominion status. In an interesting note in the Baldwin Papers it was stated: 'When an Englishman speaks of Dominion Status, he means a constitutional state enjoyed within the Empire by a political entity over which the His Majesty's Government retains no right of supervisory

Jawaharlal Nehru and Bose.[34] Three chapters tried to come to grips with Hindu-Muslim discord. The final recommendations, which bore the impress of considerable labour and thought, dwelt on reservation of seats, form of electorate, and the future status of Sind and the North-West Frontier Province. Also incorporated was a Declaration of Rights guaranteeing religious liberty and cultural autonomy. This was done to 'prevent the harassment and exploitation of any individual and group by another'.[35]

The Committee agreed to Sind's separation from Bombay and its elevation, in company with the North-West Frontier Province, to the status of an independent province. M.S. Aney and Mangal Singh acquiesced grudgingly.[36] But they had the satisfaction of securing a major gain—the rejection of the demand, incorporated in the Delhi Proposals, for reservations in Bengal and Punjab.[37]

---

interference'. Indians, however, were not so much concerned with the *achieved constitutional state* as they were with the 'indeafeasible assurance of such achievement. They were keen to fashion a constitution which would contain within itself the seed of full Dominion Status, growing naturally to its full development in accordance with the particular circumstances of India'. Thus, 'what is to the Englishmen an accomplished process, is to the Indian rather a declaration of right, from which future and complete enjoyment of Dominion privilege will spring'. Baldwin Papers, vol. 103.

[34] Sarvepalli Gopal, *Jawaharlal Nehru: A Biography* (Delhi, 1975), vol. 2, p. 121; Bose, *Collected Works*, p. 169.

[35] *All-Parties Conference 1928: Report of the Committee Appointed by the Conference to determine the Principles of the Constitution for India* (henceforth *All-Parties Conference)* (Allahabad, 1928), p. 29.

[36] Motilal to Gandhi, 27 June 1928, Motilal Nehru Papers.

[37] Jawaharlal Nehru was one of the signatories to the AICC resolution against reservation of seats. See *SWJN*, vol. 3, p. 52. Shuaib Qureshi, however, argued that the Muslim population in Bengal and Punjab should be reflected in the legislatures. In his minute of dissent, he referred to the Congress resolutions passed at Bombay and Madras in May and December 1927 and asked: 'Is it open to Congress to denounce an agreement while the other party to it, the League, stands by it and specially when it has driven one section of it out of its fold on that particular issue? I maintain that it is too late in the day for political explorers to equip expeditions to pick holes in the agreement'. See Page, *Prelude to Partition*, pp. 171–172, and Motilal to members of the All-Parties Conference Committee, 20 July 1927, Hasan

A laboured exercise by Jawaharlal and Bose convinced the authors of the report that Muslims in those provinces did not require any 'adventitious aid' or 'artificial protection'.[38] Such was their distribution of population [Table 9:1] that they were sure of securing effective representation in councils and local bodies.[39] Election results of the Bengal district board were marshalled to lend weight to the argument [Table 9:2].

Muslim candidates did well in elections, even though the electorate was mixed and electoral rolls were based on property or tax-paying qualifications. They won all the seats in Mymensingh[40] and Chittagong districts and fifteen of the sixteen seats in Jessore.[41] Elsewhere, they often managed to bag seats in excess to their population. So, the fear, based on the superior economic and educational standards of the Hindus, was largely imaginary. 'We have seen', observed the report, 'that this superiority has not helped the Hindus of Bengal at the District Board elections and we are sure that the result of Council elections will be even more strikingly in favour of Muslims', especially if they forged electoral alliances with the Congress and with regional parties.[42]

Punjab was no different. Here, as in Bengal, adult suffrage would have a levelling effect and the minorities in both the provinces would cease to have an advantage in voting registers.[43]

The Nehru report identified three natural belts or areas in Punjab: the predominantly Muslim area, the neutral area but

(ed.), *Muslims and the Congress*, pp. 58–62. The circular reflects the serious differences over the principle of reserving seats for the 'majorities' and 'minorities'.

[38] Jawaharlal to Syed Mahmud, 30 June 1928, *SWJN*, p. 51. Bose claimed that 'the greatest achievement of the Nehru Committee was the settlement of the question of Hindu-Muslim-Sikh representation in the Legislatures under the proposed Constitution'. *Collected Works*, p. 167.

[39] Sharif al Mujahid has argued that the conclusions drawn from the aggregate figures are misleading. 'Jinnah and the Congress Party', in D.A. Low (ed.), *The Indian National Congress: Centenary Hindsights* (Delhi, 1988), pp. 221–222.

[40] Bose to Motilal, 12 July 1928, F.No. 2, AICC Papers.

[41] *All-Parties Conference*, p. 47.

[42] Ibid., p. 48.

[43] For a different view, see Mujahid, op. cit., p. 222.

TABLE 9:1

Hindu and Muslim populations in Bengal, 1931

District		Population	Hindu	Per cent.	Muslim	Per cent.
Burdwan	...	15,75,699	12,38,872	78%	2,92,471	19%
Birbhum	...	9,47,554	6,36,425	67%	2,52,908	27%
Bankura	...	11,11,721	10,11,654	91%	51,012	5%
Midnapur	...	27,99,093	24,92,989	89%	2,12,473	8%
Hooghly	...	11,14,255	9,24,061	83%	1,80,217	16%
Howrah	...	10,98,874	8,60,448	78%	2,33,608	21%
24-Parganas	...	27,13,874	17,42,387	65%	9,13,233	34%
Calcutta	...	11,96,734	8,22,293	69%	3,11,155	26%
Nadia	...	15,29,632	5,74,046	38%	9,44,915	62%
Murshidabad	...	13,70,677	5,89,551	43%	7,61,582	56%
Jessore	...	16,71,164	6,34,230	38%	10,35,371	62%
Khulna	...	16,26,148	8,16,620	50%	8,04,909	50%
Rajshahi	...	14,29,018	3,26,018	23%	10,83,105	76%
Dinajpur	...	17,55,432	7,93,832	45%	8,86,723	51%
Jalpaiguri	...	9,83,357	6,64,015	68%	2,35,951	24%
Darjeeling	...	3,19,635	2,36,913	74%	8,391	3%
Rangpur	...	25,94,785	7,46,546	28%	18,36,840	71%
Bogra	...	10,86,419	1,77,629	17%	9,05,638	83%
Pabna	...	14,45,654	3,32,367	23%	11,11,712	77%
Malda	...	10,53,766	4,44,406	43%	5,71,943	54%
Dacca	...	34,32,577	11,24,893	33%	22,93,396	67%
Mymensingh	...	51,30,262	11,74,328	23%	39,27,552	77%
Faridpur	...	23,62,215	8,47,064	36%	15,07,157	64%
Bakarganj	...	29,39,050	8,12,585	27%	21,05,184	72%
Tippera	...	31,09,735	7,50,724	24%	23,56,609	76%
Noakhali	...	17,06,719	3,66,391	22%	13,39,055	78%
Chittagong	...	17,97,038	3,92,352	22%	13,26,208	74%
DIVISIONS						
Burdwan	...	86,47,189	71,64,741	83%	12,22,779	14%
Presidency	...	1,01,08,229	51,79,117	51%	47,71,165	47%
Rajshahi	...	1,06,68,066	29,27,896	27%	57,60,580	54%
Dacca	...	1,38,64,104	39,58,870	21%	98,33,289	71%
Chittagong	...	68,26,414	15,46,243	23%	50,30,088	74%

• Excluding Cooch Bihar State, Chittagong H.T. and Tripura State.

Source: Issued by R.G. Ghose, 148, Manicktolla Street, Calcutta.

TABLE 9:2

Statement about elected members of the District Boards in Bengal, 1927-8

Districts	Total no. of seats	No. of Hindu members	No. of Muslim members
24 Parganas	20	16(64.2)	4(34.6)
Bogra	15	4(16.6)	11(82.5)
Bakarganj	20	5(28.7)	15(70.6)
Midnapur	22	1(88.2)	1(6.8)
Rajshahi	18	7(21.3)	11(76.6)
Rangpur	18	7(31.5)	11(68.1)
Khulna	16	11(50.0)	5(49.8)
Hooghly	20	17(81.9)	3(16.0)
Mymensingh	22	Nil(24.3)	22(74.9)
Pabna	16	3(24.1)	13(75.8)
Noakhali	16	6(22.3)	10(77.6)
Jalpaiguri	16	14(50.0)	2(24.8)
Tippera	19	13(25.8)	6(74.1)
Nadia	20	15(39.1)	5(60.2)
Burdwan	16	14(78.0)	2(18.5)
Murshidabad	15	7(45.1)	8(53.6)
Faridpur	20	8(36.3)	12(63.5)
Malda	15	8(40.6)	7(51.6)
Howrah	12	10(79.3)	2(20.3)
Birbhum	16	15(68.1)	1(25.1)
Bankura	10	9(86.3)	1(4.6)
Jessore	16	1(38.2)	15(61.7)
Dacca	22	16(34.2)	6(65.4)
Chittagong	20	Nil(22.6)	20(72.8)
Dinajpur	18	4(44.1)	14(49.1)

N.B. The figures given in brackets are ratios to the total population.
Source: *All-Parties Conference,* appendix c, pp. 154-5.

with a Muslim majority, and the Hindu-Sikh area. In the north and north-west, no other community could encroach on the 'Muslim reserve'.[44] In the 'Hindu-Sikh area' in the south the two communities were evenly matched.[45] Between these two zones there was a third area where Muslims were predominant, such as Lahore and Gurdaspur districts, though not so in the north and north-west. The inference drawn was that while Muslims would capture 47.3 per cent of the legislative council seats from the 'overwhelmingly Muslim zone', the Hindus and Sikhs would jointly capture nearly 30 per cent. The remaining seats lay in either a predominantly Muslim area or in zones where Muslims were numerically strong. 'Allowing for every contingency', ran the report, 'we cannot conceive of Muslims not capturing enough seats in this area to give them a clear majority in the provincial legislature.[46]

All this made some sense. At least, Muslim groups in Bengal and Punjab thought so. By September 1928, 'barring a few die-hards of the Shafi school, the great bulk of the Mussalmans' had given their nod to the Nehru report.[47] Ansari, whose role in the All-Parties Conference was generously commended by Gandhi and others, was jubilant. The Punjab Khilafatists, led by Saifuddin Kitchlew and Zafar Ali Khan[48] and supported by Sardar Habibullah Khan, deputy-president of the council, and Mohammad Alam Khan,[49] leader of the Nationalist Party, 'have almost overwhelmed the forces of reaction'.[50] The picture was

[44] The districts included in the overwhelmingly Muslim zone were: Gujrat (86.2%), Shahpur (82.8%), Jhelum (99.7%), Rawalpindi (82.6%), Attock (90.9%), Miawali (86.3%), Montgomery (71.8%), Lyallpur (60.8%), Jhang (83.3%), Multan (82.6%), Muzaffargarh (86.8%), Dera Ghazi Khan (88.3%), Sialkot (61.9%), Gujranwala (71.9%) and Sheikpura (63.3%). Figures given in brackets are ratios to the total population.

[45] This zone included the districts of Hissar, Rohtak, Gurgaon, Karnal, Ambala, Shimla, Kangra, Hoshiarpur and Ludhiana.

[46] *All-Parties Conference*, pp. 44–5.

[47] Motilal to Annie Besant, 30 September 1928, *Bunch of Old Letters*, p. 65.

[48] He introduced the resolution in support of the Nehru report at the Delhi Provincial Conference in October 1928. *IQR*, 1928, vol. 2, p. 437.

[49] *Tribune*, 21 and 28 August 1928.

[50] Ansari to Motilal, 19 September 1928, F. No. 105, supplementary, AICC Papers.

no different in Bengal, where Azad was deputed to canvas support for the report. The Bengal Provincial League and the Khilafat Committee were satisfied, particularly after their bitter experience with the Lucknow Pact which had disregarded the interests of their constituents with contempt.[51] So was Abdur Rahim, once a vocal advocate of separate electorates. Rejection of the report, he said, would be a 'political blunder'.[52]

Motilal's spirits were bolstered notwithstanding the powerful dissent, led by his own son, over dominion status. With Bengal and Punjab in his pocket he had no fear from other quarters, who were to be 'easily settled by throwing a few crumbs here and there'. This was sheer arrogance. More was to follow. The UP Muslims need to be told, he wrote to Gandhi who had kept aloof from the All-Parties Conference and had refrained from expressing his views on the Nehru report, that their co-religionists in Bengal and Punjab 'do not need the other provinces to champion their cause'.[53] The storm in UP was brewing when Motilal wrote these lines.

The anger in UP was because the Nehru report postulated the ideal of dominion status. Hasrat Mohani did not approve of it.[54] A unitary central government was also an anathema, because the Muslim League demand was for a decentralized federal government in which residuary powers would be vested in the component provinces.[55] What irked political activists most was that the Nehru report proposed the abolition of separate electorates, discarded weightages and did not agree to reserving one-third of the seats in the legislature for Muslims. Shuaib

[51] *Mussalman*, 2 October 1928; *Khadem*, 22 August 1928; *Mohammadi*, 23 August 1928; *Soltan*, 7 September 1928; SNNR, Bengal.

[52] *IQR*, 1928, vol.2, p. 148. In the resolution moved in the Bengal legislative council, Rahim dropped both communal electorates and reservation of seats and voted against Fazlul Haq's amendment for separate electorates. Motilal to Jinnah, 2 August 1928, Pirzada (ed.), *The Collected Works of Quaid–e–Azam Mohammad Ali Jinnah*, vol. 3, p. 302.

[53] 24 November 1928, Motilal Nehru Papers.

[54] Hasrat had stated his position in 1924 when he announced that the 'real Muslim feeling is for independence'. *Hindustan Times*, 14 November 1924.

[55] *IQR*, vol. 2, p. 404; *Haqiqat, Sada-i Muslim, Mansur, Mashriq, Aligarh Mail*, for the week ending 8 and 15 September, 1928, SNNR, UP.

Qureshi protested but was silenced. The principle of weightage, so argued his detractors, had no place in joint or mixed electorates. The report observed:

It is of course not physically impossible to reserve a larger proportion of seats for Muslim minorities than their population would justify, but, apart from the obvious injustice of such a course not only to the majorities but to the minorities as well, it will in our opinion be harmful to the development of Muslims themselves on national lines. We have allowed them their full share on the population basis by reservation and anything over and above that share they must win by their own effort. We do not propose to impose any restrictions on their right to contest a larger number of seats than those reserved for them.[56]

Mohamed Ali was not convinced and declared angrily:

You make compromises in your constitution, with false doctrines, immoral conceptions and wrong ideas, but you make no compromises with our communalists—with separate electorates and reserve seats. Twenty-five per cent is our proportion of the population and yet you will not give us 33 per cent in the Assembly. You are a Jew, a bania.[57]

Equally powerful was his indictment of joint electorates. He and others assumed that non-Muslim voters in most constituencies would hardly ever vote for Muslim candidates. Such was the mutual antipathy that separate electorates had become vital to 'our political existence as our experience...has convinced us that Muslims will disappear from all legislative bodies unless separate electorates is guaranteed to us'.[58]

Equally emphatic was the plea for weightage, which was justified in terms of the 'historical and political importance' of the UP Muslims and was accepted by the Lucknow Pact.[59] Without weightage, Hindus would establish a 'legalized tyranny of

[56] *All-Parties Conference,* p. 52.

[57] Speech at the All-India Khilafat Conference, Calcutta, 25 December 1928, *IQR,* vol. 2, p. 403.

[58] 'Memorandum submitted by the Muslims of the United Provinces', *Indian Statutory Commission: Selection from Memoranda and Oral Evidence by Non-Officials* (henceforth *ISC*), vol. 6, part 1, p. 338.

[59] *Representation of the Muslims of the UP to the Indian Statutory Commission* (Allahabad, 1928), p. 172. Also, H.A. Haroon, *The Constitution of the Future Commonwealth and the Rights of the Muslim Minority: A Representation* (Karachi, 1928).

numbers' and usher in a 'Brahmin or Kayasth domination'.[60] This was an exaggerated fear and did not quite reflect the objective position of certain segments of Muslim society in UP.

Those Muslims who chose to be in government employment had little cause to complain, for they invariably held on to their position because the government secured, either by a rule or by convention, a proportion of Muslims. This was fixed at 30 per cent. For instance, one-third of the vacancies filled by competitive examinations in the Civil Service [Executive] were reserved for Muslims. Similarly, under the rules regulating appointments to the Police Service, the Governor-in-Council was empowered to announce, with a view to preventing the preponderance of any community, vacancies reserved for particular communities. This power was often used to favour Muslims. The bias in their favour extended to the Subordinate Revenue Service: it was laid down that not less than two Muslims would be appointed for every five Hindus. In the Subordinate Educational Service, on the other hand, 30 per cent of the appointments were, by convention, reserved for Muslims.[61] The result of this preference is reflected in Table 9:3, which sets out the proportion of Hindus and Muslims in some services.

TABLE 9.3

Proportion of Hindus and Muslims Appointed to certain Services, 1918-23

Name of Service	Hindus	Muslims
Listed Posts of Collectors	—	1
Deputy Collectors	75	55
Tahsildars	87	87
Naib-tahsildars	104	73
Inspectors of Police	25	32
Sub-Inspectors of Police	333	238
Registrars of Cooperatives	37	23

Source: *Proceedings of the UP Legislative Council, February and March 1923*, vols. 12 and 14, p. 30 and p. 420.

[60] Mohamed Ali, quoted in R.A. Jafri (ed.), *Nigarishaat-i Mohamed Ali* (Hyderabad, 1944), vol. 2, p. 23; 'Representation of the Muslims', p. 149; *Moslem Outlook*, 19 August 1928.

[61] Note by T. Sloan, 10 December 1928, *ISC*, vol. 6, part 1, pp. 346–47.

Figures on representation to elected local bodies tell the same story. In 1925-26, one-fourth of the 1,408 elected district board members were Muslims.[62] In March 1928, 66 out of 240 members of Notified Area Committees[63] were Muslims.[64] So were 391 out of 935 members of municipal boards. Likewise, 30 per cent of those who served on the legislative council were Muslims. This was in addition to those nominated by the government. The Nehru Committee was right in arguing that Muslims stood to gain under its proposed arrangement, because in several urban towns they were in a majority while in others they were a strong and influential minority.[65] But several Muslim groups in UP pointed out that, as a minority in every district, they would not have a chance of winning a 'fair proportion' of seats with joint electorates. Even if the electoral unit was smaller than the district, they would still not fare any better, because in districts where Muslims were most numerous, such as Budaun and Moradabad, their proportion in rural areas was so low that they had no chance of gaining seats in a system of straight voting with mixed electorates.[66]

Government servants and landowners had their own reasons to join the anti-Nehru report bandwagon. Having gained their position in the councils either through nomination or through separate electorates, their strategy was to work in close co-operation

[62] *Report*, UP., vol. 2, p. 231.

[63] The Municipalities Act of 1900 for the first time recognized non-municipal urban areas as distinct units of local self-government. They were designated 'notified areas' and their status was, with many important reservations, modelled on that of municipalities. The question whether a town would be set up as a notified area was decided on a combination of factors—population, industrial development, importance for commerce, or as junctions for railways or roads. By 1928, UP had 54 notified areas, and each notified area committee consisted of four elected and one nominated member. Ibid., p. 224.

[64] Brass, *Religion and Politics*, p. 172.

[65] Muslims were in a majority in fourteen municipalities, including Deoband, Najibabad, Bijnor, Chandpur, Saharanpur, Moradabad, Budaun, Sambhal and Amroha. The large towns in which they formed nearly 50 per cent of the population were Meerut, Aligarh, Bareilly and Lucknow. For district-wise distribution of Muslim population, see Robinson, *Separatism*, pp. 12–13.

[66] For details, see *Report*, UP, vol. 3, pp. 6–7.

with the government and press for the retention of separate electorates. When a Muslim Conference agreed to forego separate electorates in March 1927, these legislators were the first to protest. Joint electorates, they said in one voice, were detrimental to the 'political advancement of the Muslim community'.[67] This was another way of saying that their own prospect of getting elected was endangered. There was another danger. Adult suffrage, in effect, meant the disappearance of reserved seats and the enfranchisement of over fifteen million voters, mainly tenants. The landlords, therefore, faced the prospect of being ousted from general constituencies as well. Hailey informed John Simon:

> Curiously enough, the Nehru Committee's Report is likely to work in our favour for the landowners are not unnaturally perturbed at the prospect of adult suffrage and the abolition of reserve seats they now hold.[68]

In November 1928, these concerns were voiced in a memorandum submitted to the Statutory Commission by Nawab Jamshed Ali Khan, president, Muzaffarnagar Zamindar Association, Munshi Ihtisham Ali, president, UP Muslim League, and the Raja of Jahangirabad, an affluent landlord of Barabanki.[69] They claimed to speak on behalf of the 'Muslims of the United Provinces', though they were primarily concerned to defend their own class interests. That is why they opposed all forms of self-governing schemes and were aggrieved that the Nehru report proposed the abolition of the nominated elements and of special constituencies. They appealed to their British patrons to incorporate separate electorates and weightage in their recommendations and added a few more demands to appear more representative. These were: effective Muslim representation on all autonomous institutions created by legislatures, safeguards for Urdu and for the exercise of religious rights, and an adequate share in services.

The All-Parties Muslim Conference was more emphatic in its

[67] *Leader*, 29, 30 March and 11 May 1927, and *Searchlight*, 3, 8 April, 1927.
[68] Hailey to Simon, 28 August 1928, F. No. 13–B, Hailey Papers.
[69] *ISC*, vol. 6, part 1, pp. 338–39.

preference for a federal system, with complete autonomy and residuary powers in the constituent provinces. In fact, the Conference served as a platform through which organized Muslim political opinion was expressed in the early nineteen-thirties.

The Ali Brothers were not just the principal spokesmen of the Muslim Conference but were most vocal in the cacophony of protest orchestrated against the Nehru report.[70] They were angry that the Congress, having accepted the Delhi offer, now advanced certain propositions which would make their community subservient everywhere. Its leaders, complained the Ali Brothers, buckled under pressure from the Hindu Mahasabha. Wrote Shaukat Ali:

> I know the present Hindu mentality well. They do not want our friendship; they want our allegiance and God-willing, they will never get that. For any honourable peace and pact we are always ready but not for the slavery of the Hindus; just as we do want to remain slaves of the English.... It is no good to exasperate us. Our record is there now, and the future will show how we serve Islam and the motherland.[71]

The impetuous Shaukat was forthright in his condemnation of Ansari, indicting him for his 'blind adherence to Motilal Nehru and other Hindus' and accusing him of 'betraying' his community. He charged:

> Non-co-operation was ruined by these people, chances for Hindu-Muslim friendship have been throttled.. ., Swaraj Party dismembered and now you see what is being done to kill the Congress, which has ceased to be National now. It has become an adjunct of the Hindu Mahasabha and will soon be a seeker of favours at the door of the English.[72]

Again,

> It is you [Ansari] who has changed while the Central Khilafat Committee and I stand where we were, not in a spirit of obstinacy but because we consider that Motilal and his Committee have intentionally or uninten-

[70] I have discussed their angry response to the Nehru report in *Mohamed Ali: Ideology and Politics,* pp. 94–101, and *A Nationalist Conscience*, pp. 170-74.

[71] To Ansari, 19 May 1929, Hasan (ed.), *Muslims and the Congress,* p. 70.

[72] Ibid.

tionally treated the Muslim point of view with undeserved contempt.... It is so easy to play the generous liberal-minded patriot at the expense of one's own people. For the time being it pays and gains the applause and I congratulate Azad on the part he played in the affair.[73]

These words were matched by an aggressive campaign, launched by the Ali Brothers in the company of Haji Abdullah Haroon of Sind and Maulvi Shafi Daudi of Bihar. But their efforts were rewarded in Bombay alone. Bihar, Bengal and Punjab did not waver in their commitment to the Nehru report. In UP, too, the Muslim League was divided. This became evident when the Raja of Mahmudabad, an enthusiastic supporter of the Nehru report, trounced Mohamed Ali, the hero of the Khilafat days, in the contest for the League presidency. Mohamed Ali's unexpected defeat may well be interpreted as a verdict against his political stance.

It was hard to swallow this bitter pill. So, towards the end of December 1928, the Ali Brothers made a desperate bid to turn the table on their opponents. In co-operation with Shafi Daudi, they disrupted meetings of the All-India Khilafat Committee and the Central Khilafat Committee and adopted dilatory tactics. They were noisy and abrasive, with the senior Ali— Shaukat— hurling abuses at his detractors. Amid the pandemonium, a group of Khilafatists, led by Tasadduq Ahmad Khan Sherwani, Mohammad Alam and Maulvi Mujibur Rahman, resigned from the executive committee. Over forty signatories condemned the 'methods of obstruction and procrastination adopted by the representatives of the other party'. They met separately to endorse the Nehru report and boycotted the Khilafat Conference which met under Mohamed Ali's presidentship.[74]

The Khilafat Conference turned out to be a tame affair. The Ali Brothers were humbled. The splintered factions they had united were in complete disarray after the Calcutta meeting. They sought refuge in the All-Parties Muslim Conference, a command performance initiated by the redoubtable Aga Khan.

[73] 6 September, F. No. 105, AICC Papers.
[74] *IQR*, 1928, vol. 2, pp. 405–7.

It was now Ansari's turn to fire his guns at Shaukat Ali. Chiding him for his conduct in Calcutta, he said:

After seeing how partisan spirit had utterly blinded you and how under its influence you had acted unfairly, unjustly, and in a manner I could never have dreamt you capable of acting, my faith in your righteousness and fair play completely broke down.... I had been a loyal co-worker of yours for the last 18 years, who had idolized you, worshipped the very ground on which you trod, [and] had given you such friendship, love and loyalty....But when I saw the clay feet of my idol I felt as if the world had turned topsy-turvy and that I could never, in future, trust any one whoever it might be....

Ansari added that his political convictions were at variance with the Ali Brothers and that he could not 'be the same with you [Shaukat] as I have been before'. He was sad that the life-long bond of friendship had to be severed. 'At our age', he wrote, 'new friendship and new attachments are difficult.... Life in future would be the less fuller, the less richer for want of such friends as you and I have been'. But, then, 'I bow to the inexorable march of events and have fortified myself against whatever the future may have in store, and have prepared myself to go on working in the service of my faith and my country, in the best manner that I can do'.[75]

The Ansari-Shaukat differences could not be resolved through the mediation of friends. This was no less true of the gulf that separated Mohamed Ali and Gandhi, the two men who symbolized Hindu-Muslim friendship during the Khilafat and Non-Co-operation movements. Gandhi admitted that the Ali Brothers had 'a fairly heavy list of complaints' against him and that he could not make an 'impression on them as they distrusted the role of my associates'.[76] One of them was that the Mahatma 'had defeated all Muslim attempts for a compromise' and was 'giving free reins to the communalism of the majority'.[77]

There was thus no basis for a reconciliation. The Mahatma was

[75] To Shaukat Ali, 14 May 1929, Hasan (ed.), *Muslims and the Congress*, pp. 64-66.

[76] To Motilal Nehru, 12 August 1928, Motilal Nehru Papers.

[77] Mohamed Ali's statement, quoted in Hasan, *Mohamed Ali: Ideology and Politics*, p. 101.

no longer interested in an amicable settlement of the 'Muslim claims', while the Congress was seen as a mere tool in the hands of the Hindu Mahasabha. So, the brothers—Shaukat and Mohamed—appealed to the British for the redressal of their grievances, something they had not done before in the course of their public life. Mohamed Ali rushed to London to attend the Round Table Conference before lampooning Gandhi for his ill-timed civil disobedience movement. Instead of civil disobedience, he advised his co-religionists to press their demand for freedom in London. But he soon realized the futility of his own advice, for neither the Indian delegates at the Round Table Conference could agree on a unified set of demands nor was the British government inclined to come to terms with nationalist aspirations in India. In fact, Mohamed Ali knew, much before he left the Indian shores for what turned out to be his final journey, that his mission was condemned as traitorous by those very people with whom he had worked in the past. And in London, the Maulana felt that his 'real place was in the fight in India, not in the futile conference chamber in London'.[78] In Oxford, where he had once studied Modern History, he addressed the students in their tail coats, talked cricket and made them laugh. But he made

> little or no impression and quite failed to put across the case for the Muslims to a youthful but intelligent audience who were to provide a fair number of the nations' political leaders in later years.[79]

Shaukat Ali was also a spent force, isolated from the mainstream of nationalist politics and spurrned by a section of his own community for his proximity with British officials. His pension— Rs 150 per month—was restored from 1 October 1930, 'that date being fixed as the time when he went to the Round Table Conference and may be regarded as having publicly abandoned his previous subversive activities'.[80] The viceroy found this 'difficult and shifty customer' in 'the most amazing frame of

[78] Nehru, *An Autobiography*, p. 120.

[79] Box No. 2, Benthall Papers, Centre for South Asian Studies, Cambridge.

[80] Haig to Hailey, 20 December 1933, F. No. 27/A, Hailey Papers.

mind',[81] an impression confirmed later when Shaukat told Hailey in December 1933 that he would not accept any settlement with the Congress which did not 'embrace peace with the Government'. At the same time, he insisted on being rewarded for his loyalty and betrayed considerable pique at the neglect by the government of 'one who has smashed Gandhi'.[82]

Shaukat Ali was taken to task by the Congress Muslims for his views on dominion status, his stance on the Ahrar agitation in Kashmir,[83] and his pro-British pronouncements at the Round Table Conference. The *Medina* of Bijnor was unsparing in its criticizm.[84] The *Hamdam* of Lucknow was aghast at his London speech which reflected his 'slave mentality'.[85] In its editorial on 6 February 1932, the paper observed:

> He who was yesterday trying to dig the foundations of Englishmen in India is today their best friend and is trying his utmost to injure the national movement.... When a man who has always subsisted on public subscriptions is invited to lunch by Viceroys and Governors, it is not strange that he should abandon his past beliefs and rub his forehead on the threshold of Government.[86]

This was an uncharitable comment from a colleague who had for years worked in close co-operation with the Ali Brothers. Shaukat Ali knew it. He had no defence to offer except to argue that he was still devoted to the 'Muslim cause', which the Nehru Committee had summarily dismissed. Around the same time, another prominent leader—Mohammad Ali Jinnah—was echoing the same sentiment, the same sense of disillusionment with the Congress strategy of dealing with the communal problem.

[81] Irwin to Samuel Hoare, 15 February 1932, MSS. EUR. E. 240, F. No. 5, Samuel Hoare Papers, IOLR.

[82] Hailey to Haig, 15 December 1933, F. No. 27/A, Hailey Papers.

[83] *Medina,* for the week ending 12 March 1932, SNNR, UP.

[84] Ibid., for the week ending 17 October 1931.

[85] *Hamdam* (Lucknow), for the week ending 7 November 1931.

[86] Ibid. Shaukat Ali visited Mysore in July 1931 and expressed preference for dominion status within the British Empire. In another speech he stated that there could be no peace for India except within the British Empire. L/P and S/, F. No. 13, IOLR. Compare this with Shaukat Ali's views on dominion status quoted in *Hamdard,* 23 August 1928.

Jinnah's views were, of course, of much greater consequence in determining the future course of India's history. It need not have been so had the fateful meeting of the All-Parties National Convention in December 1928 been more sober and sympathetic in meeting his viewpoint.

IV

M.A. JINNAH: 'Are you an Indian first, or a Muslim'?
THE RAJA OF MAHMUDABAD: I happened to say that I was a Muslim first and an Indian afterwards. So he didn't agree with me'.
JINNAH: 'No, you are an Indian first'.
THE RAJA OF MAHMUDABAD: 'And he said it with such violence in his voice that tears rolled down my cheek'.[87]

Sarojini Naidu's ambassador of Hindu-Muslim unity lived up to his reputation for several decades. He radicalized the Muslim League in 1913, presided over the affairs of the Bombay Home Rule League, and brought the Congress and the League closer to each other. He was, as is well known, the architect of the Lucknow Pact and a consistent protagonist of Hindu-Muslim unity. What attracted the young M.C. Chagla to Jinnah was 'his sterling nationalism and patriotism'. As a brilliant lawyer and a fearless critic of the government, he sustained his reputation all over the country. Such was the goodwill he enjoyed in his own city that the people built a Hall, which they named after him.[88]

Though marginalized in the early 1920s and rebuffed by the Gandhian leadership, Jinnah was unrepentant in his indifference to the pan-Islamic euphoria and irreconciled to the mixing up of religion with politics. His nationalistic credentials were, as always, impeccable. Though distanced from the common people, he made his presence felt in the Central Assembly as leader of the Independent Party.[89] He was *en rapport* with the swarajists, particularly its leader Motilal Nehru. He opposed the

[87] Typescript of a B.B.C. (British Broadcasting Corporation) interview with Jeremy Bennet. The Raja of Mahmudabad was eleven years old and addressed Jinnah then and later as 'uncle'.

[88] Chagla, *Roses in December*, p. 78.

[89] For Jinnah's role in the Assembly, see Wolpert, *Jinnah of Pakistan*, pp. 80-83, and Mujahid, op. cit., pp. 217–19.

formation of a 'Muslim Party', refused to sign the 'Majority Report' of the Reforms Enquiry Committee, blessed the Indian National Union, floated by Motilal and Azad,[90] and stayed away from the unhappy communal wranglings. The Delhi offer of March 1927 was his brainchild. This was the first time that Muslims had agreed to have joint electorates, and, in the judgement of some, 'the chance of a lifetime, a rare unexpected opportunity for a new start on a real national political life'.[91]

Though never ever tied to the Congress, Jinnah's political concerns were no different from many of its leaders. The cause of India's freedom and of communal amity were close to his heart—a passion he shared in equal measure with Azad, Ajmal Khan and Ansari. No wonder, his leaving India in May 1928 caused anxiety in Congress circles.[92] Jinnah's absence from the country, Motilal told Purshotamdas Thakurdas, 'is most disappointing. I can think of no other responsible Muslim to take his place'.[93] Ansari was equally upset, because Jinnah was, in his judgement, 'the only man to deliver the goods on behalf of the Muslim League'.[94] So, when Jinnah returned to India in October, Motilal was delighted. He confided in Thakurdas again:

> So much depends on Jinnah that I have a mind to go to Bombay to receive him. If I have the necessary funds within the next few days I hope to create a strong opinion amongst the Mussalmans to greet Jinnah on his arrival. Therefore please lose no time to raise as much money as you can for this great enterprise.[95]

Jinnah did not disappoint. He was unhappy that the Nehru Committee repudiated two of his favourite schemes—the Lucknow Pact and the Delhi Proposals. But he was neither bitter nor indignant. Though troubled by Ruttie's serious illness and by

[90] Chagla, op. cit., p. 91.

[91] Ibid., p. 93.

[92] There was talk of postponing the All-Parties Conference until Jinnah's return from Europe but Jawaharlal Nehru was not agreeable to the suggestion. See Page, *Prelude to Partition*, pp. 166–67.

[93] Motilal to Purshotamdas, 28 April 1928, F. No. 40, Thakurdas Papers.

[94] Ansari to Jawaharlal Nehru, 29 March 1928, F. No. G 60, AICC Papers.

[95] 28 April 1928, Thakurdas Papers.

the anti-Nehru report crusade in UP, Jinnah kept his cool and, as always, appeared unruffled. With meticulous care, he took charge of the Muslim League and negotiated with Motilal and other Congress leaders with his usual skill and aplomb. The one time disciple of Dadabhai Naoroji faced the Congress-dominated All-Parties National Convention in a spirit of compromise. Little did he anticipate the belligerent mood of those who had turned up in full strength at Calcutta in the festive Christmas week.

Jinnah proposed three amendments to the Nehru report: first, that one-third of the central legislature should consist of Muslims; secondly, in the event of adult suffrage not coming into effect, the Bengali and Punjabi Muslims should have reserved seats for ten years; and finally, residuary powers must vest in the provinces. He pleaded for statesmanship and cited constitutional precedents from other countries where, he said, political adjustments were made not on a population basis but on principles of equity. 'We are here, as I understand, for the purpose of entering into a solemn contract.... What we want is that Hindus and Muslims should march together until our object is attained'. He emphasized the need for mutual adjustments and co-operation not as a 'naughty' or 'spoilt' child but as the country's well-wisher. In a speech reminiscent of his earlier pronouncements, Jinnah said:

> We are all sons of this land. We have to live together and whatever our differences may be, let us at any rate not create more bad blood. If we cannot agree, let us at any rate agree to differ, but let us part as friends. Believe me there is no progress of India until the Mussalmans and Hindus are united, and let no logic, philosophy or squabble stand in the way of coming to a compromise and nothing will make me more happy than to see a Hindu-Muslim union.[96]

The last line may have been borrowed from his own evidence before the Parliamentary Select Committee in 1919. When asked whether he wished to see complete elimination of political distinctions between Muslims and Hindus, his answer was: 'Yes, nothing will please me more when that day comes'.

The Hindu Mahasabha and Sikh delegates were in no mood to listen to Jinnah at the Convention. They refused to accept 33 per cent Muslim representation at the Centre. The Liberals, along

[96] Quoted in Wolpert, op. cit., p. 101.

with the Hindu communalists, stood firmly against vesting residuary powers in the provinces. Jayakar warned the delegates that, having once restrained his supporters from rebelling against the Nehru report, it would be impossible for him to persuade them to accept further concessions. They listened to his admonition rather than take note of Jinnah's pleading. Jinnah was mocked, rebuffed and rejected by a hostile gathering. He was never ever going to return to such an unfriendly assembly.

Soon after the December Convention, Jinnah found himself in the company of the Aga Khan, Mohammad Shafi, Ibrahim Rahimtoola, Maulvi Shafi Daudi, Haji Abdullah Haroon, Shaukat Ali and other politically reactionary leaders from UP, Bengal and Punjab. He had no ideological affinity with them, no common ground on which to build the edifice of national unity and integration. Yet, he was there because neither the Congress nor the Calcutta Convention paid heed to his warnings.

Those who listened to him at the Muslim conference saw merit in the amendments which, on the one hand, encapsulated the long-standing demands of their organization and, on the other, reconciled their conflicting regional claims. In this way, delegates from UP were satisfied.[97] So were representatives from Bengal and Punjab, who were told that reservations were absolutely essential, because the voting strength of the Muslims was far below their population.[98] They were won over by Jinnah's insistence that, in the event of adult suffrage not being introduced, the Convention should reserve seats for Muslim majorities in accordance with their population. Jinnah had, at last, vindicated his claim that the amendments embodied the 'united will of the

[97] 'The heavens would not have fallen if a few amendments that were proposed had been generously accepted and the sad chapter of communal bickering and disharmony closed. The short-sightedness of Hindu politicians on this occasion could not be surpassed', declared Khaliquzzaman from the vantage point of Pakistan. *Pathway to Pakistan,* p. 98. Chagla's statement quoted in Uma Kaura, *Muslims and Indian Nationalism: The Emergence of the demand for India's Partition* (Delhi, 1977), p. 40.

[98] Notice the version of Mohammad Azizul Haque, one of the Muslim League delegates who participated in the All-Parties National Convention. Quoted in Sayeed, *Pakistan: The Formative Phase,* pp. 70–71.

Muslim community'. So what if the Convention questioned his credentials? After all, Muslim leaders in different provinces, having ignored Jinnah for nearly a decade, were now trickling into his camp to lend legitimacy and stature to his leadership. In this way, 'failure' at the Convention brought unexpected rewards to Jinnah, unforeseen by his band of admirers less than a decade ago when he refused to be swept by the pan-Islamic tide and chose, instead, to pursue his concerns in an unobtrusive manner.

In 1929-30, Jinnah was estranged from the Congress but the rejection of his stand at the Calcutta Convention did not mark the 'parting of ways'. He was in a defiant mood; yet, he was not averse to sorting out his differences with the Congress leadership. He parleyed with his *bete noire,* Gandhi, conducted talks with Malaviya and backed various initiatives to resolve the communal deadlock.[99] His stand was unambiguous. The Hindu-Muslim question must be tackled as a 'national problem' and not just as a 'communal dispute'. 'Unless the majority community and the leaders grasp that elementary principle and deal with it in that spirit', he told Chagla who had parted company with his political mentor over the 'Fourteen Points', 'it will not be possible to get the minority community into line with any national progamme'.[100] This is what he said to Sapru as well. Ignoring Sapru's indiscretion and outburst at the Convention, Jinnah wrote to the Liberal leader in a conciliatory mood:

> I have always counted upon your support and I know that if we could sit together the settlement can be arrived at in ten minutes, because I know that you look upon this question as a Nationalist and an Indian and, believe me, so do I. It is the duty of every Nationalist who wants self-government for India to take with him seventy millions of Mussalmans and other communities, and any reasonable concessions, though not logical, that can secure the whole-hearted support and co-operation of such a large body of people in our country is...essential.

[99] The viceroy, too, found evidence to indicate that Jinnah was keen on a rapprochement. The only hurdle was the Hindu Mahasabha, which 'seems to be stiffening in its attitude towards Muslim claims'. Irwin to Peel, 21 March 1929, L/PO/F.No. 6/42, IOLR.

[100] Chagla, op. cit., p. 97.

After all, are the proposals of the Mussalmans so very radical? Even the fifteen points,...if accepted, I cannot see how they can seriously prejudice the Hindu interest in the future constitution...

Jinnah concluded with the comment that the settlement of the Hindu-Muslim question was a national problem and had to be dealt with accordingly.

I have no hesitation in saying that it is obvious for every nationalist to do his utmost to find a solution without which there is no hope for any real advancement on the part of India towards Dominion Status, responsible government or self-government, or by whatever name you may describe the goal for which we have been working.[101]

Jinnah wrote this lengthy letter from his home. The address—Mount Pleasant Road, Malabar Hill, Bombay. It was despatched on 14 December. The year was 1929, nearly a year after he is supposed to have told one of his friends of his irrevocable break with the nationalist forces. The 'parting of ways' had yet to take place.

V

Some important points stand out in the discussion on the Nehru report. The first relates to the view, advanced by I.H. Qureshi, Aziz Ahmad, Khalid bin Sayeed, K.K. Aziz and other historians of Pakistan, that the Muslim community's rejection of the report was 'swift, unmistakable and unqualified'.[102] Such an interpretation stands refuted, for it has been shown that leaders from Bengal and Punjab saw the Nehru proposals in a favourable light and that they went over to the Muslim Conference only after the National Convention. Political opinion was divided in UP, with the Congress Muslims, led by Ansari, Azad and the Raja of Mahmudabad, being vocal supporters of the Nehru report.

The second issue concerns the approach of the Nehru Committee to the communal issue. The underlying strain of its argument was that abolishing separate electorates and communal representation was a panacea of all ills and their disappearance would, in

[101] 5 December 1928, vol. 31, pp. 389–90, Sapru Papers.

[102] Aziz, *Britain and Muslim India*, p. 92.

particular, encourage people to think in terms of larger political and economic problems. 'We shall then find Hindus and Muslims and Sikhs in one party acting together and opposing another party which also consists of Hindus and Muslims'.[103] This prophecy stemmed from Jawaharlal Nehru's simplistic analysis of communalism and his view that 'we must...begin to think of and act on common economic issues. If we do so, the myth of communalism will automatically disappear. Conflict there may be, but it will be between different classes and not different religions'.[104] Nothing of the sort happened.

The development of parties on non-communal lines did not take place because the Congress strategy of mass mobilization was flawed from the outset. Instead of emphasizing the commonality of Hindu-Muslim interests, the Congress sought a following sometimes by exploiting religious issues and more often by concluding pacts for immediate political gains. Believing, as Jawaharlal did, that communalism was not 'such a power as it is made out to be',[105] it was considered both convenient and expedient to mollify the 'educated classes in search of office and employment'. This was attempted in the Lucknow compact [1916], the Ansari-Lajpat Rai proposals [1923][106] and the much-maligned Bengal Pact.

The ostensible logic behind these formal proposals was that Muslims—always treated as a monolith entity in Congress literature —required some measure of safeguards because their interests were somehow different from others. This was, quite evidently, a questionable assumption. The concern for securing 'safeguards' was restricted to professional Muslims, government servants and the landowning class. Outside these circles, there

[103] *All-Parties Conference*, p. 49.

[104] Presidential Address at Punjab Political Conference, Amritsar, 11 April 1928, *SWJN*, vol. 3, pp. 225–26. Or, his view that 'representation by economic units will not only ensure real and effective legislatures representing the life of the country or every interest therein, but will also automatically do away with the problem of communal representation'. Statement at All-Parties Conference, 8 March 1928, *SWJN*, vol. 3, p. 37.

[105] Address at the Punjåb Political Conference, op. cit.

[106] I have discussed the Ansari-Lajpat Pact or the Indian National Pact in *A Nationalist Conscience*, pp. 116–18.

was no all-India consciousness of a unified Muslim community, with the same set of demands and concerns. There was none. What was, after all, common between western-educated professional Muslims and their less privileged brethren in the countryside? How could they agree to press a common cause and unite on the same platform? They did not until the early nineteen-forties.[107]

In its anxiety to keep divisive forces in check and maintain togetherness in the face of the communal onslaught, the Congress perpetuated the communal categories created by the raj and fostered, despite protestations to the contrary, a climate and an ethos in which the rank and file of the party thought and acted as 'Muslims', 'Hindus' and 'Sikhs'. At the same time, by legitimizing the status of sectarian leaders, the Congress willy-nilly encouraged alignments which did not cut across caste, community and regional barriers. Having done so, it was futile to expect those Muslims who had extracted major concessions under the Act of 1919, to be easily swayed by the sanctimonious arguments of the Nehru Committee. They were not. The organizers of the Muslim Conference spurned Congress overtures for reconciliation and appealed to their overlords in Delhi and London to save them from the unhappy prospect of 'Hindu domination'.

Jawaharlal Nehru argued in February 1928 that communalism had 'feet of clay', that it was a 'myth with no connection with reality' and that it would not 'endure'.[108] He was mistaken in his beliefs. On other occasions, he and his father took serious note of heightened communal consciousness in the country, hardening of attitudes, and the tendency to judge most contemporary issues from a community-oriented standpoint. This was reflected in the painful discourse at the Congress-sponsored confabulations in 1927 and 1928. Both father and son found the atmosphere nauseating. They were no less alarmed by the steadily increasing influence of communal forces in Congress. Motilal had a taste of

[107] Notice the comment of the governor of Bengal. He was exasperated by the fact that Muslims were 'so hopelessly divided amongst themselves...(that) there seems no possibility of getting them together as a party....' Stanley Jackson to Irwin, 19 April 1929, F. No. 23, Irwin Papers.

[108] Presidential Address at the Punjab Conference, op. cit.

it during the 1926 election and, again, at the National Convention.[109]

There can be little doubt that the Hindu Mahasabha, in alliance with a motley of Sikh factions, jeopardized the prospect of a Congress-League reunion. Lajpat Rai's speech delivered from a Hindu Mahasabha platform was widely circulated at the Convention as his last will and testament.[110] He had earlier warned Gandhi and Motilal neither to negotiate with Jinnah nor to soften their stand on communal representation.[111] Moonje, Malaviya, Kelkar and Jayakar said the same. 'You should tell Mahatmaji,' Moonje wrote to Malaviya, 'that if he were to yield on these points [Jinnah's amendments], you would be painfully obliged to lead the opposition on behalf of the Hindus even against him, Jinnah and Motilal combined'.[112] Muslims must know, Moonje told the Mahatma, 'that no compromise is possible for the purpose of tampering nationalism with communalism.'[113] They met in August 1929, soon after the Gandhi-Jinnah talks. The following is the recorded conversation of their meeting:

MOONJE: What do you advise us to do Mahatmaji in regard to the negotiations you have opened with Jinnah for the amendment of the Nehru report [and] in acceptance of the 14 points of Jinnah?

GANDHI: You are not well informed. I did not open negotiations with Jinnah. [Sarojini] Naidu pressed me to meet Jinnah and you do not mean to say that I should not have gone to see Jinnah when he had expressed a desire that I should see him.

MOONJE: [By travelling from Sabarmati to Bombay in weak health] you have thus endowed him [Jinnah] with an amount of

[109] Motilal wrote: 'The silly resolution which the Hindu Sabha passed at Surat just before the Calcutta Convention was in a great measure responsible for the deadlock that ensued'. To Gandhi, 14 September 1929, Motilal Papers.

[110] Ibid.

[111] To Motilal, n.d., F. No. 108, supplementary, AICC Papers. A letter signed by Kelkar, Jayakar, Moonje and K.M. Munshi warned Gandhi that 'if any terms are settled by you without consulting the leaders of Hindu opinion in the country, it will not be acceptable to the Hindu community'. F. No. 437, Jayakar Papers.

[112] To Malaviya, 31 July 1928, ibid.

[113] To Gandhi, 5 August 1929, ibid.

importance and greatness which proves most embarrassing to or rather as an obstacle in the way of the Hindus to bring around the Muslims to an understanding with the Hindus....

GANDHI: ....I simply heard Jinnah fully and came away expressing no opinion of my own. I do not represent anybody and do not want to say anything on behalf of anybody.[114]

The Mahatma was not obliged to offer an explanation. He also had no reason to sound defensive. But, then, such was the hegemonic influence of the Hindu Mahasabha in the late nineteen-twenties that even the secular-oriented Congress leadership often succumbed to its ideological pressures.[115] Notice, for example, how the Malaviya-Lajpat Rai combination used a communal platform as a means of rallying public support from 1922 onwards and made concessions to communal feelings which were already running high. Yet, they and their allies adorned the Swarajist benches and occupied important positions in the Congress heirarchy. Malaviya represented the Mahasabha point of view at the 1931 Round Table Conference and was immediately rewarded with a presidential chair at the 1932 Congress. In this way, the most communally-minded leader could assume the nationalist garb and freely sail between the Mahasabha and the Congress.[116] No attempt was ever made to curb this trend.

[114] Diary, 22 August 1929, Moonje Papers.

[115] In July 1926, Sri Prakasa, a swarajist candidate for the Banaras-Gorakhpur Assembly seat, urged Motilal Nehru not to put forward Sapru's suggestion [that the constituencies in which riots occurred should be disfranchised. Motilal agreed and went further in suggesting (a) that recipients of honours belonging to riot-ridden districts would have their names removed, and (b) exclusion from public service of anybody belonging to the area] regarding the Hindu-Muslim *entente* 'as a plank of our platform. It is too dreadful'. F. No. 1? 1, AICC Papers.

[116] Jawaharlal Nehru, *Recent Essays and Writings* (Allahabad, 1934), and *An Autobiography*, p. 136. During the debate on the extension of reforms to the Frontier Province, Syed Murtaza, a swarajist from Madras, observed that the most communally-minded Hindu can pose as a nationalist and pretend that he asks for the abolition of communal representation and of separate electorates only because their existence is incompatible with nationalism'. *The Frontier Question in the Assembly* (Delhi, 1926), pp. 26–27.

The Congress Muslims were the first to criticize their party for its failure to curb the influence of the Mahasabha and to come to terms with Jinnah and his group. Azad, Khaliquzzaman and Chagla, enthusiastic supporters of the Nehru report, expressed their indignation.[117] So did Ansari who, in his correspondence with Gandhi and Motilal, voiced his anguish over the Congress response to the Delhi Proposals and the developments thereafter. He observed with uncharacteristic candidness:

> I have not the slightest doubt that if we had stuck to [the Delhi proposals] we would have gradually overcome the opposition of the Hindu Mahasabha and Hindu-Muslim unity would have been an accomplished fact by now. But, we wanted to be just and fair and in our effort to do justice and bring greater harmony and unity in the shape of the Nehru Constitution, I am afraid we lost at Lucknow what we had gained at Madras.

Ansari then commented on how at the Calcutta Convention, 'it was the Hindu Mahasabha which completely did the work of destruction, and how Jayakar, Malaviya, Moonje and 'Hindu Mahasabha friends destroyed all chances of understanding'. He added:

> After that the communalist Muslims got the chance and the Muslim attitude hardened as shown by the absurd resolutions passed at the All-Parties Conference at Delhi and subsequently the Fourteen Points of Mr. Jinnah.[118]

[117] The reactions of the Congress Muslims is examined in: *A Nationalist Conscience*, chapter eight.

[118] Ansari to Gandhi, 13 February 1930, Hasan (ed.), *Muslims and the Congress*, pp. 95–96. This letter along with the replies of Gandhi (from Sabarmati), Motilal and Jawaharlal reached the viceroy through the Nawab of Bhopal who, in turn, had received the correspondence from Ansari. Irwin's comment was: 'The general impression of the three replies to Ansari seems that the writers felt they had to do something, had burnt their boats and hoped, without being sanguine, for the best'. Irwin to Wedgwood Benn, 27 February 1930, L/PO/6/16, IOLR.

Chapter Ten

Reflections

Who killed India? Was it the work of an insane individual, a stab in the back as in a communal riot; or a diabolical conspiracy of a gang? Was it a case of slow poisoning? Or, as it might be, was it a mere cunning master plan, in which the victim himself was hypnotically induced to commit suicide....

That an imperialist power planned the dismemberment of our country is not surprising. The wonder, and the tragedy is that India should have been killed by the children of India....

Khwaja Ahmad Abbas, 'The Last Page', 1947*

This study has tried to argue that, notwithstanding common religious experiences and shared symbols, the followers of Islam in India did not constitute a monolith entity. The diversity of responses to the early Congress movement and the mixed reactions to the Lucknow Pact and the Nehru report illustrate both the range and depth of intra-community and intra-regional divisions that set Muslims apart and laid to rest the notion of a unified community. In 1918, India's secretary of state was met by a cascade of not one, but forty-four deputations from Muslim groups and organizations. Each one of them played a separate tune. And each one of them made the patently hollow claim of representing its community. Likewise, the Simon Commission was innundated with numerous representations and petitions from several quarters. Their demands were not always the same. At the Round Table Conferences in London, too, 'Muslim' delegates, reflecting different shades of opinion and interests,

K.A. Abbas, *I am not an Island: An Experiment in Autobiography* Delhi, 1977), pp.280.

staked certain claims which were at variance and in conflict with each other.

The Muslim League's success in the 1940s does not alter the basic thrust of our argument. Nor does it vindicate or legitimize the ideological underpinnings of Jinnah's two-nation theory, for the birth of Pakistan in August 1947 was neither imminent nor historically inevitable. It was more of an aberration, a historical accident, caused by a complex configuration of forces at a particular juncture. Indian nationalists of all shades, including the socialists and communists, failed to grasp this reality. As a result, they bowed to the mounting pressure of the Muslim League and, though for different reasons, acquiesced in India's partition.

Nobody can deny that the Muslim League enjoyed considerable popular support. Yet, the birth of Pakistan symbolized, more than anything else, Jinnah's personal triumph, his answer to the obdurate Congress leadership which had persistenly refused to treat him on equal terms. It also reflected the effectiveness of his political strategy which was coolly worked out with active government support. Most British officials in India were at first averse to dealing with Jinnah.[1] But they could not forever rebuff his

[1] Some official and 'non-official' impressions at the Round Table Conference are illustrative. Malcolm Hailey thought that in the plenary session Jinnah was always 'the perfect bounder and as slippery as the eels which his forefathers purveyed in the Bombay market'. The secretary of state recalled in 1934: 'Of all the Indians I have met I think I have disliked Jinnah the most. Throughout the Round Table Conference discussions he invariably behaved like a snake, and no one seemed to trust him'. Benth found Jinnah's speech 'clever' and 'offensive' and found him 'thoroughly disloyal and purely out for his own ends'. Hailey to Irwin, 14 November 1920, F.No. 34, Hailey Papers; Hoare to viceroy, 5 April 1934, F.No. 4 Hoare Papers; 9 January 1931, Diaries, Box 12, Benthall Papers. The Raja of Mahmudabad recalled a luncheon meeting at the governor's house in 1936, the year he joined the Muslim League. The host asked him if he knew that the estate was a gift from the British sovereign, 'adding after I had nodded in assent, that I held it at his pleasure'. The governor then asked the Raja to dissociate himself from one whom he called 'the arch enemy of the British Raj'. 'After a few minutes of conversation I realized that this 'arch enemy' was none other than M.A. Jinnah. On my asking what I was expected to do, he ordered that I should join the National Agriculturist party and made it clear that the British government had no intention of letting the activities of

initiatives. The future Quaid demanded a price for supporting the war efforts; the government grudgingly agreed to his terms. In his interview with Jinnah on 27 June 1940, the viceroy, Linlithgow, 'gave proof of our determination to have full regard to Muslim opinion and to the legitimate rights of so large a minority of the people of India'. He made clear to Whitehall that, in order to enlist Jinnah's support 'at this stage', it was 'essential that any declaration that might be made should not preclude a fair and unprejudiced hearing for the Muslim League's proposal for the creation of two India's'.[2]

In the behind-the-scenes negotiations that took place then and later, there was no attempt to ascertain the views or the wishes of the people, both Hindus and Muslims. The predictable collapse of the interim ministry and the fire of violence in Bihar and Bengal, which nobody tried to extinguish, offered an opportunity and an excuse to the Congress and League leaders to hammer out the modalities of transferring power to two separate nations. Mountbatten, the impetuous representative of the Crown, was anxious to hasten the process and preside over the liquidation of an Empire which had already lost its *raison d'etre*. Asking the people to sit in judgement on an issue that had already been settled was an act of deception, a monumental fraud. Those privileged to vote in the 1946 elections, under a restricted franchise, did so in an atmosphere vitiated by communalism. The die was cast and they could not, even if they wanted to, reverse a process that was well underway.

Jinnah and his party continue and that I would have to watch my steps in future'. Raja of Mahmudabad, 'Some Memories', C.H. Philips and D.A. Wainright (eds.), *The Partition of India: Policies and Perspectives, 1935-1947* (London, 1970), p. 384.

[2] L/PJ/8/507. This was a reiteration of the viceroy's earlier position, when he told the secretary of state that while there was 'danger' in 'leaning too heavily on the Muslim Community or attaching undue weight to the more exaggerated claims, it would be as foolish to underrate the importance of their support to us'. He added: 'It would be short-sighted and unfair to all not to give the fullest consideration to its [Muslim community's] legitimate claims'. Linlithgow to secretary of state, 28 November 1939, L/PO/258 (iii), IOLR. For a perceptive and sensitive description and analysis of Jinnah's political role and his relationship with the government, see Ayesha Jalal, *The Sole Spokesman: Jinnah, the Muslim League and the Demand for Pakistan* (Cambridge, 1985).

II

Those who lived through the nineteen-twenties could have hardly predicted the collapse of the imperial edifice in their lifetime. Likewise, they could have barely visualized that Hindu-Muslim strife would, in the end, culminate in the vivisection of the country. The period covered in this book cannot therefore be treated, except with the benefit of hindsight, as the 'Prelude to Partition'.

There can be no doubt that Hindu-Muslim cleavages widened in the aftermath of the Khilafat and Non-Co-operation agitations. The Khilafat movement itself was bogged down in religious issues instead of concentrating on the consolidation and integration of anti-colonial forces. In consequence, a popular political movement, a gift of history, was a great opportunity absurdly wasted. The Congress, caught up in its factional struggles and hemmed in by diverse ideological positions, was unable to steer its ship through the rough currents of communalism. Gandhi, who had once piloted a remarkable Hindu-Muslim alliance, developed cold feet in dealing with the communal monster and thereby lost much of the political initiative he commanded from the days of the Rowlatt Satyagraha. His political heir, Jawaharlal Nehru, understood communalism in very different terms. He was no doubt troubled by the country being 'caught in a whirlpool of mutual hatred', but like the Mahatma he could find no way out of the 'impenetrable darkness'. His remedy was to 'scotch our so-called religion and secularize our own intelligenstia'.[3] He cited the example of Europe which had got rid of religion by mass education and argued that religion would not be able to stand the test of large-scale education. This process, he stated, 'is bound to be repeated in India'.[4] Noble thought, yes, but quite out of tune with the realities of Indian social and political life.

[3] To Syed Mahmud, 25 May 1926, *SWJN*, vol. 2, p. 235.

[4] To Syed Mahmud, 14 July 1927, ibid., p. 329. Or, his view expressed in January 1940. 'If we have adult franchise, it is just possible that we might get over this separatist tendency as the masses will think more along economic lines. That is why adult franchise is essential and that is why Jinnah is opposing a Constituent Assembly generally and adult franchise specially ....'. To S. Satyamurti, 23 January 1940, Satyamurti Papers, NMML.

The nationalistic discourse on communalism was, in general, flawed by such formulations.

At the same time, there was one aspect of the Gandhi-Nehru discourse which is beyond reproach. This is related to their view, which was sadly not aired as frequently as it should have been, that communal rivalries alone should not be projected as *the* Indian reality but that notice should be taken of large areas of mutual co-operation and tangible expressions of inter-communal understanding. After all, the governor of Bengal, where Hindu-Muslim conflicts were almost endemic, commented on how the 'rank and file' of the communities co-operated with each other in all 'daily business of life', and that it was 'only at rare intervals, when religious feelings became inflamed, that they treat each other as enemies and clashes occur'.[5] O.M. Martin, who served in the province from 1915 to 1926, observed the same. Hindu-Muslim unity, he added, was not a temporary occurrence but an old and cherished tradition'.[6]

Most people, Hindus and Muslims alike, clung to their inherited ideas, traditions and customs. This was so in the case of, for example, the Meos, the Malkana Rajputs, the Khojas, Bohras and Memons in western India, and the Moplahs in Malabar. Given their long, uninterrupted history of social mingling and cultural fusion, it is hard to think of a different scenario. Similar trends, syncretic and composite, were at work elsewhere. Islam in Punjab provided a 'repertoire' of concepts and styles in authority which had served to encompass potentially competing values, including the values of tribal kinship, within a common Islamic idiom.[7] Islam in Bengal took many forms and assimilated values and symbols not always in conformity with Quranic ideals and precepts. Cultural idioms of Islam underwent a rapid transformation, giving birth to a set of popular beliefs and practices which, in essence, represented the popular culture of rural Bengal rooted in the pre-Islamic past.[8]

[5] Lytton, *Pundits and Elephants*, p. 172.

[6] 'Memoirs of O.M. Martin' [Typescript], Centre for South Asian Studies, Cambridge.

[7] David Gilmartin, 'Customary Law and *Shariat* in Punjab', in Ewing (ed.), *Shariat and Ambiguity*, p. 44.

[8] Rafiuddin Ahmad, 'Conflict and Contradictions in Bengali Islam: Problems of Change and Adjustment', in ibid., p. 115.

In most parts of the country and in most periods of Indian history, Hindus and Muslims identified themselves with certain common cultural and religious symbols. It was thus common for Hindus to observe Muharram with solemnity[9] and to gather around shrines of the sufis and other venerated holy men and seek their intercession to avert calamities, cure diseases, procure children for the childless, or even improve the circumstances of the dead. Frederick Graham Cracknell, magistrate and collector of Etawah and Kanpur, reported that the *mela* commemorating Badiuddin or Shah Madaar, who settled in Makanpur in Bilhaur tahsil in the fifteenth century, was attended by 50,000 people, mostly Hindus. In 1931, Hindus and Muslims flocked to the shrine in equal numbers despite a Hindu-Muslim clash in the area.[10]

The extent to which narrow religious barriers were transcended and strict codes of behaviour transgressed is evident from Bahraich in eastern UP, where the outbreak of cholera in 1930 prompted Muslims to join the Hindus in great force to worship the goddess Bhawani to induce her to remove the pestilence.[11] In the Bengal countryside, pre-Islamic ceremonies relating to birth, marriage and death continued to be observed. As a concession to the 'reformist' movements, the 'outer labels' were discarded to make the rituals and practices look 'Islamic'.[12] The *Census* report of 1921 summed up the situation as:

> There are...communities among the Muslim population, chiefly among converts from Hinduism, whose religious ritual and exercises

[9] *Census of India*, 1931, UP of Agra and Oudh, vol. 1, appendix e, p. 515.

[10] Cracknell Papers, Centre for South Asian Studies, Cambridge. Or, the later day experience of Mohammad Mujeeb of the Jamia Millia Islamia, Delhi: 'I remember that shortly after the orgy of violence in Bihar I visited the grave of a sufi on the banks of the Ganges. The Muslims living in the *dargah* had fled and the place looked desolate. But soon a group of Hindu women appeared. They performed circumambulations and prostrations, as if nothing had happened that affected their sentiments of veneration for the tomb of a Muslim saint'. M. Mujeeb, 'The Partition of India in Retrospect', Philips and Wainright (eds.), *The Partition of India*, p. 407.

[11] *Census of India*, 1931, p. 515.

[12] Rafiuddin Ahmad, op. cit., p. 134.

have a very strong tinge of Hinduism and who retain caste and observe Hindu festivals and ceremonies along with those of their own religion.... The rigidity of intolerance of view, which is a marked feature of the religion of Islam in its purer form, does not extend to the masses, who are quite willing to recognize and assist the efforts of their neighbours to keep on peaceful terms with the unknown powers.[13]

It is not intended to portray an idyllic picture as such but to highlight a certain facet of communal relations which tends to be overlooked in the face of stark and irrefutable evidence on Hindu-Muslim antagonism. Harping on conflicts alone and turning a blind eye to instances of Hindu-Muslim co-operation and fraternization has not just distorted our perspective but has strained India's fragile social fabric. To discover elements of communal tensions, even if one is thrown back into India's pre-colonial past, is a legitimate historical exercise in so far as it does not offer a one-sided view.

III

An important conclusion that flows from this study is that political developments until the early 1930s were not necessarily leading towards a communal impasse. In reaching this conclusion, I have neither ignored the powerful communal currents sweeping across the country nor minimized the importance of the heated debates at the Round Table Conferences and in the wake of the Communal Award.[14] What is being suggested is that the India of the early 1930s, despite its contradictions and fractious polity, can hardly be characterized as a communally polarized society. I have shown elsewhere the presence of Muslims in the Congress,[15] their joining the ranks of satyagrahis during the civil disobedience campaign [Table10:1], their identification with

[13] *Census of India*, 1921, vol. 1, p. 115.

[14] I have discussed these controversies in *A Nationalist Conscience*, chapter nine. See Bidyut Chakrabarty, 'The Communal Award of 1932 and its Implications in Bengal', *Modern Asian Studies*, vol. 23, 3, 1989.

[15] 'Congress Muslims and Indian Nationalism: Dilemma and Decline', in Jim Masselos (ed.), *Struggling and Ruling : Indian National Congress 1885-1985* (Delhi, 1987).

progressive and radical literary and political movements,[16] and their responding to the Muslim Mass Contact Campaign, launched by Jawaharlal Nehru in 1937.[17]

But this was not all. One of the unstated facts of twentieth century Indian history is that, until the mid-thirties, there was no worthwhile organization which could legitimately claim to represent the large Muslim constituency. The Muslim League, in political wilderness during the Khilafat movement, was needlessly treated by the Congress as its political adversary. It was, as one contemporary stated, a 'souless' body, devoid of any programme.[18] Its ranks were in disarray, with splits taking place one after the other. In 1927, the League's membership plummeted to 1,330.[19] Provincial branches fared no better. The Bombay branch could boast of only 71 members in 1928.[20] They included men like Syed Abdullah Brelvi, Abbas Tyabji and M.C. Chagla whose heart was with the Congress rather than the League.

Such was the apathy that the 1929 session was adjourned for lack of a quorum. The adjourned meeting, held four months

[16] Ralph Russell, 'Leadership in the All-India Progressive Writers Movement, 1935-1947', in Pandey (ed.), *Leadership in South Asia,* and my 'Nationalist and Separatist Trends in Aligarh, 1920-1947', Gupta (ed.), *Myth and Reality*. In 1932, a group of young men—Sajjad Zaheer, Ahmed Ali, Rashid Jahan and Mahmuduzzafar—produced a collection of short stories, *Angare,* which was symptomatic of the radical political trends amongst some Muslims. The stories were 'a declaration of war by the youth of the middle class' against the prevailing social norms, political values, and religious institutions. Sajjad Zaheer, son of Wazir Hasan, and his group were the forerunners of the All-India Progressive Writer's Association, which met for the first time in Lucknow on 9-10 April 1936, coinciding with the Congress meeting in that city at the same time. This summary is based on Carlo Coppola, 'The Angare Group: The Enfants Terribles of Urdu Literature', *Annual of Urdu Studies,* vol. 1. 1981.

[17] Mushirul Hasan, 'The Muslim Mass Contacts Campaign: Analysis of a Strategy of Political Mobilization', in Richard Sisson and Stanley Wolpert (eds.), *Congress and Indian Nationalism: The Pre-Independence Phase* (Berkeley, 1988).

[18] *Jiddat* (Lucknow), for the week ending 9 December 1933, SNNR, UP. And the editorial comments of *Mussalman,* 3 July 1930.

[19] Chagla Papers, NMML.

[20] Sayeed, *Pakistan: The Formative Phase,* p. 176.

later in Delhi, ended in a fiasco.[21] When Iqbal presented his address at Allahabad in 1930 demanding the establishment of a Muslim state in north-western India, the meeting did not have its quorum of 75 members.[22] Even after the annual subscription was reduced from Rs 6 to Re 1, the organizers of the 1933 session in Delhi had a busy time filling up the empty hall with students of the Anglo-Arabic College.[23] A split at this juncture was the last straw, with Mian Abdul Aziz of Peshawar and Haji Hidayat Husain of Kanpur heading rival factions.[24] 'A little oversight or a little expression of inactivity', warned one of League's office-bearers, 'means life-long suffering and probably bondage'.[25]

The leadership, which had lost much of its political initiative to the All-Parties Muslim Conference,[26] was divided, disorganized and lacking in imagination. Jinnah was nursing his political wounds at his home in Hampstead. Liaquat Ali Khan, who is credited with having persuaded Jinnah to return to India, was himself angling for a High Commissionership in London.[27] The Aga Khan, exhausted after his hectic lobbying at the Round Table Conferences, was left with no political options. He was attracted to the idea of acquiring a sort of Vatican in the territory of a protected ruler either in India or in the Persian Gulf.[28] In 1934, the year of Jinnah's return to India, Hailey commented:

[21] *Mussalman,* 3 July 1930.

[22] Mukhtar Zaman, 'Duaazda Manzil se Manzil-i Pakistan', *Nuqqush* [Iqbal Number], September 1977, p. 501. Notice the comments of Sayeed, pp. 176-77 and Khaliquzzaman, *Pathway to Pakistan,* pp. 108-9. For a recent analysis of 'Muslim Politics' during this period, see Mukul Kesavan, '1937 as a landmark in the course of communal politics in the UP', Occasional Papers on History and Society, second series, no. xi, NMML.

[23] *Sarfaraz* (Lucknow), for the week ending 9 December 1933, SNNR, UP.

[24] Wolpert, *Jinnah of Pakistan,* pp. 134-35.

[25] *Annual Report of the All-India Muslim League for the Years 1932 [up to 15 November]* (Delhi, n.d.), p. 2.

[26] This was admitted by Mohammad Yaqub. He stated that the Muslim Conference 'has devided [*sic*] our energies and caused a great deat of harm to the All-India Muslim League'. *Annual Report of the All-India Muslim League for the Year 1931* (Delhi, n.d.), p. 4.

[27] Liaquat Ali Khan to Willingdon, 14 September 1934, F.No. 4. Hoare Papers.

[28] Hoare to Willingdon, 8 March 1935, Hoare Papers.

TABLE 10:1

List of Convicted and Imprisoned in District Jail, Fyzabad.

		Place of Birth	Occupation	Period of Conviction	Duration
1	Maulana Ziman Khan	Gonda	Teacher	Not Known	Not Known
2	Niyaz Ahmad	Etah	"	"	"
3	Shaikh Mohammad Fakhir	Allahabad	Sufi pir	Six months	from 27 September 1930
4	Maulana Mohammad Miyan	Muzaffarnagar	Teacher, Arabic madrasa	One year	" 9 October 1930
5	Maulana Rashid Husain	Deoband	Teacher	"	"
6	Manzar Ali Sokhta	Allahabad	Lawyer	One Month	" November 1930
7	Maulana Murtaza Husain	Barabanki	Not Known	Six Months	" 17 September 1930
8	Sadiq Ali	Allahabad	Student	"	" 6 November 1930
9	Maulana Ghulam Husain	Fyzabad	Lawyer	"	" 15 May 1930
10	Maulana Manzoor Ali	Allahabad	Lawyer	Three Months	" 14 August 1930
11	Abdul Hakeem	Lucknow	Lawyer	Six Months	" 3 August 1930
12	Idris Khan Lodi, (President, Badaun district Congress Committee)	Budaun	Lawyer	Six Months	" 20 November 1930
13	Maulana Manzoor Nabi	Saharanpur	Lawyer	One year	Not known
14	Maulana Ahamad Zamman Khan	Gonda	Lawyer	Not known	"

•This list is merely illustrative. Details from other jail records may help to give a more rounded picture.

Source: *Aseeran-i Watan* (Lucknow, 1931), Part 1, pp. 65-86, PIB 6/18, IOLR.

It is a fatality of the Muslims at present that they have too many third class leaders. A community only shows real solidarity when it is in serious danger, and the fact that the Muslims have gained a great deal of their demands by the Communal Award removes some of that sense of danger and prevents reunion under a strong leadership.[29]

If the League did not represent the Muslims, who did? Nobody. The Muslim Conference, cobbled together by the Khilafatists or the Leaguers, was a splintered structure. It petered out after a brief and lazy existence. The All-India Nationalist Muslim Party, founded in July 1929 by Ansari and other Congress Muslims, also collapsed within a few years.[30] The only organization to have survived and kept up its elan as a national entity was the Jamiyat al-ulama-i Hindi. There were, then, the Khudai Khidmatgars in the North-West Frontier Province, the Ahrars in Punjab and Kashmir, the All-India Momin Conference in eastern UP and Bihar, and the Khaksars in upper India.[31] Although their area of operation was limited, these groups were led by charismatic figures who were able to introduce a level of ideological cohesion among their followers. More importantly, they had a much greater degree of affinity with the Congress whose policies and programmes they endorsed.

It is thus clear that until the mid-thirties there existed neither a sharp communal political polarization between Hindus and Muslims nor any significant solidarity in the Muslim 'community'. Communal and divisive forces were strong, but not strong enough to destroy the social fabric of Indian society. It was still possible, despite the dismal prophecy of contemporary analysts, to curb communal instincts and to integrate estranged groups and factions into a broadbased nationalist alliance.[32] Jinnah had

[29] Hailey to the Nawab of Chhatari, 15 February 1934, F.No 27-A, Hailey Papers.

[30] Hasan, *A Nationalist Conscience*, pp. 202-210

[31] Praveen Saberwal, 'The Role of the Nationalist Muslims in Indian Politics, '1923-1947' (Unpublished Ph.D. thesis, Jamia Millia Islamia, 1990: forthcoming)

[32] Notice the comment of *Mussalman* which was echoed in different ways by the Muslim intelligentsia in the twentieth century. 'We believe', wrote the Calcutta paper, 'that Hindus and Muslims must unite, that they will

pleaded for such an approach at the All Parties National Convention in December 1928, and, again, during his talks with Rajendra Prasad in 1935.[33] But the Congress could not break the Hindu Mahasabha stranglehold and found itself trapped in the cross-fire between communalists of all shades. It considered the Muslim League as its political adversary, though certain elements within its own ranks, backed by the Hindu Mahasabha and Rashtriya Swayamsevak Sangh (RSS), were, in fact, out to wreck all prospects of a Hindu-Muslim rapprochement.

The Congress had repeatedly sworn by the principles of national integration and secularism. But when the occasion came to oppose partition and stand by proclaimed ideals and goals, its top leadership readily accepted the partition plan. Only one man, who was unfairly and unjustly condemned and ridiculed by Muslim League leaders, was irreconciled to his party's decision and stayed aloof from the festivities that accompanied independence. He was Mohandas Karamchand Gandhi. The dawn of freedom had arrived, but at what cost. Partition symbolized his personal tragedy, the defeat and negation of all that he had stood for, just as it reflected the failure of the Congress to keep the country united. He trudged on and on in riot-ravaged Bihar and Bengal to provide the healing touch. Here was the Mahatma in body and spirit.

---

contribute their diverse culture, tradition and history in order to build up a new wondrous type of nationality—a nationality not simple and unitary, but strange, complex and multi-fold, like a jewel with many facets each iridescent with the gleam of latent fire'. *Mussalman,* 29 January 1926.

[33] Hasan, *A Nationalist Conscience,* pp. 238-39.

Biographical Notes

ALI, AMEER [1849–1928]: played an important part in two Muslim political organizations that began in Bengal, the Central National Mohammedan Association, founded in 1876, and the Muslim League. From 1908 to 1913, he and the Aga Khan were instrumental in setting up and running a London branch of the Muslim League. He resigned in 1913 because the League, in his view, had been taken over by 'extremists'. During the visit of Mohamed Ali and Wazir Hasan to London, Ameer Ali sought the permission of the Lord Chancellor to attend the proposed controversial dinner. He was advised not to attend.

ALI, ASAF [1888–1953]: educated at St. Stephen's College, Delhi; called to the Bar in London, 1912; returned to India at the outbreak of War and joined the Home Rule League; participated in Khilafat activities and gave up his practice during Non-Co-operation movement; general secretary, Indian National Congress, 1927, and working committee member, 1930; member, legislative assembly, 1934–46; arrested in August 1942, and released in May 1945; minister of transport and railways in interim government, formed in August 1946.

ALI, MOHAMED [1878–1931]: educated at M.A.O. College, Aligarh, and Lincoln College, Oxford, from 1898 to 1902. On his return, joined the Rampur education department and the Baroda service. Launched the *Comrade* on 11 January 1911, which was hailed as the 'new star in the firmament of Indian journalism'. From 1911 to May 1915, he was active in the Kanpur mosque agitation, the pan-Islamic movement and the Aligarh Muslim university movement; interned with Shaukat Ali, May 1915 to December 1919; led a Khilafat deputation to Europe, January-September, 1920; imprisoned, 1921–23; president, Indian National Congress, 1923; joined campaign against the Nehru Report, 1928; urged Muslims to remain aloof from civil disobedience movement; attended Round Table Conference, 1930–31.

ALI, SHAUKAT [1873–1938]: born into a family associated with the court of Rampur. His father died while he was seven years old. His mother, Begum Abadi Bano, later known as 'Bi Amma', sent Shaukat to Aligarh college in 1888; sub-deputy opium agent till 1912; organized Muslim university fund collections; founded with Abdul Bari and M.H. Kidwai the Anjuman-i Khuddam-i Kaaba, 1913; interned with his younger brother, Mohamed Ali, May 1915 to December 1919; secretary, Central Khilafat Committee till interned with his brother in September 1921; president, Khilafat Conference at Kakinada, 1923; became estranged from Congress after 1923 and campaigned against the Nehru Report; one of the organizers of the All-India Muslim Conference, 1929–31; attended the Round Table Conference, 1931; member, legislative assembly, 1935. Halide Edib described him as 'a very big man in every sense...He has a flowing beard, a shock of picturesque grey hair, and eyes which twinkle like those of a mischievous boy. His dress is suggestive of the vagueness of his politics. He wears a long shirt over tight Indian trousers and leggings; and a loose Arab *Mashlak* (mantle) with a Turkish *Kalpak* (fur cap) in the fashion of about sixteen years ago. His attire is reminiscent of a combination of Indian, Muslim, Arab and Turk; in a word, it is a reflection of Pan-Islamism...In carricatures he is represented as a big baby to whom the King gives a pretty doll so as to keep him quiet'.

ANSARI, MUKHTAR AHMAD [1880–1936]: educated at Queen's College, Banaras, Muir Central College, Allahabad, Nizam College, Hyderabad; went to England in 1901 where he was the first Indian house surgeon in the Charing Cross Hospital, London; began practice at Delhi in 1910; led the Indian Medical Mission to Turkey, 1912–13, for which he received a special award from the Ottoman consul-general. According to Meston, 'in Moslem circles he [Ansari] commands considerable respect.... His work in the Medical Mission during the last Turkish War is a matter of pride to them...'; founded the Home Rule League at Delhi, 1917, and was elected its president; chairman, reception committee, Muslim League, Delhi, 1918; played a leading part in the Khilafat movement; president, Muslim League, Nagpur, 1920, and All-India Khilafat Conference, Gaya, 1922; member, Congress Civil Disobedience Enquiry Committee, 1922, and opposed Council entry till mid-1923; chairman, reception committee, Special Congress, Delhi, September, 1923; drafted a National Pact with Lajpat Rai for improving Hindu-Muslim relations, 1923; president, Congress, 1927; founder of the All-India Muslim Nationalist Party, July 1929;

opposed Gandhi's civil disobedience movement in 1930, but said or did nothing against the Congress policy 'because of my loyalty and my deep attachment to the Congress and to those who have got its reins in their hands'; president, Congress Parliamentary Board, 1934.

AZAD, ABUL KALAM [1888–1958]: son of Maulana Khairuddin Ahmad (d. 1909), who worked in Calcutta under the patronage of a wealthy Surati merchant, Haji Zachariah; travelled to Egypt and Turkey where Azad came into contact with Iranian revolutionaries and the Young Turks. Azad was associated with several journals and magazines. He wrote for the *Ahsan al-Akhbaar*, a Calcutta journal, and started a literary journal, *Lisan al-Sidq*, in 1904. On Shibli's suggestion, he edited the *Al-Nadwa* and then joined the *Vakil* of Amritsar, an Urdu newspaper. On 12 July 1912, Azad launched *Al-Hilal* under the patronage and financial support of Haji Nur Mohammad, son of a wealthy merchant who had brought Azad's father, Maulana Khairuddin Ahmad, to Calcutta. For the next four years, through *Al-Hilal* and *Al-Balagh*, Azad expressed his ideas on religious reforms, education and politics. In July 1914, he started a society known as the Jamiyat-i Hizbullah. Its object, according to the *Al-Hilal* of 8 July 1914, was 'to send preachers to stay in cities, towns and villages where the religious condition of Muslims may be deplorable; where superstition and intrigues are prevalent and where brotherhood and sympathy for the misfortunes of Islam and zeal for communal work are forgotten.' But the 'Party of God' remained restricted in size and gained nothing like the publicity enjoyed by the Anjuman-i Khuddam-i Kaaba. In August 1915, Azad launched the Dar al-Irshaad (College of Divinity) with practically the same objects as those of the Jamiyat-i Hizbullah. But this organization also failed to secure any widespread support. By this time the career of *Al-Hilal* had ended (in November 1914), when its security deposit was forfeited by the Bengal government. In November 1915, Azad launched the *Al-Balagh*, but that too was closed in March 1916. Soon afterwards he was interned in Ranchi in Bihar, where he remained until January 1920.

BANERJEA, SURENDRANATH [1848–1925]: educated at Doveton College, Calcutta; founder, Indian Association, 1876; proprietor, *Bengalee*, 1878; editor, 1877; member Bengal legislative council, 1893–1901; president, Indian National Congress, 1895, 1902; played a leading part in the agitation against the partition of Bengal in 1905 and the swadeshi and boycott movements which followed; left Congress in 1918 following differences over the Montagu-Chelmsford Reforms; minister in Bengal government, 1921–23; defeated in the elections to the Bengal legislative council, 1923.

BARI, ABDUL [1876–1926]: *alim* of Firangi Mahal, Lucknow, and *pir* of the Ali Brothers, M.M. Chotani, and of the wife and sister of Abdul Majid Khwaja; one of the founders of the Anjuman-i Khuddam-i Kaaba; took a leading part in the Kanpur mosque agitation and the Khilafat movement; president, Jamiyat al ulama-i Hind, December 1919; after 1923, he was estranged from the Congress and complained that 'those who pretended to be our friends at one time and made a catspaw of the *ulama* now seem anxious to get rid of them'.

BILGRAMI, SYED HOSAIN [1844–1926]: was first private secretary to Salar Jung and then to the Nizam himself; director of Public Instruction Hyderabad State, 1887–1902, and member of the universities in commission; member of the secretary of state's council 1907–1909; elected trustee of Aligarh College in 1886. His brother Syed Ali Bilgrami (1851–1911) was author of several important works and held high positions in the Nizam's service; his half-brother, Major Syed Hasan (d. 1915) was secretary of the Muslim League, 1908–10.

BUTLER, SPENCER HARCOURT [1869–1938]: was deputy-commissioner, Lucknow, 1906–7; secretary to the foreign department, 1908–10; council of the governor general, 1910–15; lieutenant-governor, 1918–20, and governor of UP, 1920–23. He was a supporter of the Muslim university movement and considered it politically expedient for government to lead the educational movement and encourage denominational universities, which would provide religious instruction and inevitably tend to keep 'alive the Hindu-Muslim feelings'. Later, when the Foundation Committee rejected the government's terms for the university in July 1913, Butler tried to persuade the Raja of Mahmudabad to avoid political agitation on the question and urged the Aga Khan to exert his influence in restraining his co-religionists from political agitation. On the other hand, he was disappointed with the decision of the India Council. 'It makes one wonder', he wrote to Lovat Fraser, 'for the future of the Empire when an arrangement of this kind, worked out by the Government of India in communication with the Muslim leaders, is upset by men of the calibre of Morison and LaTouche'. Butler's assessment of some Muslim leaders was: 'Aga Khan is clever but a weather cock. Mahmudabad is weak as water; so is Rampur and unreliable to boot. The Nawab of Dacca hates Aligarh and all its works as much as he hates the Aga Khan...Wazir Hasan is a born intriguer and a mischievous fellow. He is a Shia and plays on Mahmudabad's religious weakness'.

CHAGLA, MOHAMED CURRIM [b. 1900]: educated at St. Xavier's High School and College, Bombay, and Lincoln College, Oxford; president of the Oxford Indian Majlis, 1922; professor of constitutional law, Government Law College, Bombay, 1927–30; wrote articles and addressed public meetings in favour of the Nehru Report, August-December 1928; secretary of the Bombay Muslim League, but resigned over the Nehru Report controversy; vice-chancellor of Bombay University, 1946–47; judge of the Bombay High Court 1941–47.

CHELMSFORD, 3rd Baron & 1st Viscount [1868–1933]: called to the Bar, 1893; governor of Queensland, 1905–09; governor of New South Wales, 1909–13; viceroy of India, 1916–21; first lord of admiralty, 1924.

CHINTAMANI, CHIRRAVOORI YAJNESWARA [1880–1941]: editor of *Leader* (Allahabad), 1909–23 and 1926–1941; member, UP legislative council, 1916–23; general secretary, National Liberal Federation of India, 1918–20 and 1923–29; Minister of education and industries, UP, 1921–23; member, UP legislative council, 1927–36.

DAS, CHITTA RANJAN [1870–1925]: son of a reputed solicitor of the Calcutta High Court; joined legal profession after his return to India in 1894; came into prominence as counsel for defence in the trial of Aurobindo Ghose; joined the Congress in 1906; came to the forefront of national politics in 1917 when invited to preside over the Bengal provincial conference; member, non-official Jallianwala Bagh enquiry committee; allied with Gandhi, 1920, and became leader of Non-Co-operation in Bengal; president, Indian National Congress, 1922; organized the Swaraj Party with Motilal Nehru and succeeded in having his policy of Council entry accepted by the

Congress; elected to the Bengal legislative council, 1923; mayor, Calcutta corporation, 1924–25; chief architect of the 'Bengal Pact'.

FAZLI HUSAIN [1877–1936]: educated at Government College, Lahore, and Christ College, Cambridge; began practice in Sialkot, 1901–08 and later in Punjab High Court, Lahore, 1905–20; elected to the Punjab legislative council, 1920; appointed minister of education in 1921; returned unopposed to Punjab legislative council, 1923; re-appointed minister of education, 1924; appointed revenue member in 1926.

HARDINGE, BARON, Hardinge of Penshurst [1858–1944]: was viceroy of India 1910–16, and witness to many important developments among Muslims. The annulment of Bengal's partition, the rejection of the Muslim university scheme and the Kanpur mosque affair all happened during his viceroyalty. He was on the best of terms with Ajmal Khan, Ansari and Mohamed Ali and extended support to the Indian Medical Mission to Constantinople. But relations turned sour around 1913. The viceroy urged the secretary of state not to encourage the 'self-imposed mission' of Mohamed Ali and Wazir Hasan to London. He described the former as a 'mischievous agitator' and the latter as a 'man of no importance'.

'HALI', ALTAF HUSAIN [1837–1914]: author of *Hayaat-i-Javed,* a biography of Syed Ahmad Khan, and of a famous epic poem—*Mussadas,* a comment on the history of Islam, highlighting Muslim achievements in conquest, literature and sciences and contrasting it with the decay and backwardness in his times. The *Mussadas* is often characterized as 'the Bible of the new movement', because its contribution in creating a widespread awakening among Muslims was 'next only to that of the Aligarh college and the Muslim Educational Conference'.

HAQ, FAZLUL [1873–1962]: educated in Calcutta University; joined government service as a deputy-registrar, 1906; resigned and joined the Bar in 1912; entered Bengal legislative council, 1913; secretary, Bengal Presidency Muslim League, 1913–16, and from 1916–21 president of the All-India Muslim League; took a leading part in Congress-League negotiations, 1916; joint-secretary, Congress, 1917; secretary, Congress, 1918–19; resigned from the Congress after acceptance of non-co-operation resolution; minister of education in Bengal government, 1924; represented Muslims at the Round Table Conferences, 1930-32; founded the Krishak Praja Party in 1927; mayor of Calcutta, 1935–36; chief minister of Bengal, 1 April 1937–38 to March 1943.

HAQ, MAZHARUL [1866–1930]: educated in Patna and in England; called to the Bar, 1891; attended the Muslim Convention at Dacca in 1906 and was one of the founders of the All-India Muslim League; president, All-India Muslim League, Bombay, 1915; instrumental in bringing about accord at Lucknow in December 1916; supported Gandhi in Champaran, 1917; became a non-co-operator at Gandhi's call in 1920; launched the *Motherland*, an English weekly on 30 September 1921; opposed Council entry; elected first Indian chairman of the Saran district board, 1924–27; defeated in the election to the Bihar legislative council in 1926; retired from public life after 1927.

HASAN, MAHMUD [1851–1920]: graduated from Deoband in 1873 and joined the staff there; principal of the Dar al-ulum, 1890; launched an anti-British campaign in favour of Turkey, 1911; moved to the Hejaz with his associates to avoid arrest, 1915; arrested by the British in 1916, and was interned at Malta, 1917-20; returned to India in June 1920 and joined the Khilafat movement.

HASAN, WAZIR [1874–1947]: educated at Muir Central College, Allahabad; began legal practice in Jaunpur, moving later to Pratapgarh and then to Lucknow; one of the founder members of the All-India Muslim League and its assistant secretary, 1910–12, and secretary, 1912–19; member, AICC, 1919; dominated Muslim League politics, 1913–16, when he played an important role in Congress-League rapprochment; member, UP legislative council, 1916–19; resigned from the Muslim League in 1919; appointed second judicial commissioner, 1921; one of the Puisne Judges of the chief court after its inauguration in 1925; received knighthood in 1934.

HUSAIN, RAJA GHULAM [1882–1917]: commenced public career as the associate of Mohamed Ali and sub-editor of *Comrade*. His was a 'sobering influence on the brave enthusiast of the Muslim cause, Mohamed Ali, whose generous impulses proved more profitable when allied with the 'sweetness and light' of his admirable colleague'. [*New Era,* 1 Sept 1917]. After *Comrade* ceased publication Ghulam Husain joined the *Indian Daily Telegraph* before launching the *New Era* on 7 April 1917. He was a supporter of the Sultania College scheme, launched in May 1917 by Syed Husain Bilgrami, Abdur Rahim of Bengal, Ajmal Khan, Ali Imam and the Nawab of Bhopal. The scheme aimed to bring the best educational facilities within the reach of middle class Muslims, and to offer 'adequate outlet to the suppressed spirit of devotion and service'. This, according to the *New Era* [5 May 1917], would 'rescue modern education among Muslims from the taint of commercialism and lift it to a high plain of duty and patriotic endeavour'. When the University Foundation Committee [8 April 1917] resolved to accept the university on the lines of the Banaras Hindu University, the *New Era* [14 April 1917] described it as a 'surrender' and explained it in terms of 'expediency, partisan differences, threats of revolt, vague fears of possible injury to Muslim educational interests, a growing sense of futility of all further efforts, intellectual fogginess....'

IQBAL, MOHAMMAD [1876–1938]: educated at the Scotch Mission College, Sialkot, Government College, Lahore, Cambridge and Munich; returned from Europe in July 1908; associated with the Anjuman-i Himayat-i Islam of Lahore and with Punjab Muslim League; secretary of the Punjab Khilafat Committee in 1919; resigned from both the Muslim League and the Khilafat Committee after the non-co-operation resolution was passed in September 1920; attended the Calcutta Unity Conference, October 1927; one of the few Muslims in Punjab who opposed the Nehru Report; presided over the annual session of the All-India Muslim League in 1930 and called for the establishment of an autonomous state in the north-west of British India. Iqbal's fame rests on his collection of Urdu and Persian poems and his lectures on the reconstruction of the religious thought of Islam. He is regarded as one of the greatest Urdu poets of the twentieth century.

JAYAKAR, MUKUND RAMRAO [1873–1959]: educated at Elphinstone School and St. Xavier's College, Bombay; called to the Bar in London in 1905; practised as a barrister in Bombay High Court; member, Bombay legislative council, 1923, and was leader of the Swaraj Party in the council, 1923–25; member, legislative assembly, 1926–30, and deputy leader of the Nationalist Party;

attended Round Table Conference in London and was member of the Federal Structure Committee; closely associated with the All-India Hindu Mahasabha and the *sangathan* movement.

KHALIQUZZAMAN, CHOUDHRY [1889–1973]: educated at M.A.O. College, Aligarh, 1907–16; joined Congress in 1916 acting as a member of the reception committee; took a leading part in the Home Rule movement, 1917–18; elected president of the Lucknow Congress Committee in March 1920; gave up practice during the Non-Co-operation movement; joined the swarajists, January 1923; chairman, Lucknow municipal board, 1923; a leading Muslim politician in the 1930s and 1940s; after Independence, governor of East Pakistan.

KHAN, AGA [1875–1958]: assumed spiritual headship of the Ismailis in August 1885; member of the imperial legislative council, 1902–4; led the Simla Deputation to Minto, 1906; president, All-India Muslim League, 1907–13; resigned because he found it impossible to lead the Muslims 'for my advise will be loyalty of the kind that means trust and confidence and that trust and confidence the Muslims are not now giving to government; president of the All-Parties Muslim Conference at Delhi, December 1928; chairman of the British Indian delegation to the Round Table Conference 1930, 1931; led the Indian delegation to the League of Nations, 1932, 1934–47; president of the League of Nations, 1937.

KHAN, HAKIM AJMAL [1863–1927]: family came from Kashgar, Turkestan and held important positions under the Mughal emperor, Babur; produced a long line of physicians of which the most famous was Hakim Sharif Khan, Ajmal's grandfather; educated in the Islamic branches of learning and learnt medicine from his father, Haji Mahmud Khan and his brother; founder member of the All-India Muslim League; board of management of the Nadwat al-ulama; chairman, reception committee, All-India Muslim League, 1910; trustee of Aligarh college; visited Europe 1911; became involved in active politics on his return; president, Muslim League, 1919; took part in the Khilafat agitation and was the first to renounce his title in April 1920; chancellor, Jamia Millia Islamia, November 1920; president, Indian National Congress and All-India Khilafat Conference, Ahmedabad, December 1921; member, Congress civil disobedience enquiry committee and voted in favour of Council entry; joined the swarajists, January 1923; retired from politics in 1925 because of ill-health. He was described by C.F. Andrews as 'quiet, humble, modest, with all the dignity of a man of character, learning and religious sincerity. ...' As a 'moderate' leader, he had little in common with Mohamed Ali and his colleagues, though their differences never came to the fore except during the Khilafat movement when they disagreed over the conduct of the agitation. In the estimate of Hardinge, Ajmal was 'much respected generally throughout India, and as far as I know absolutely loyal in every way. I used to see him a good deal at Delhi and often talked to him of Muslim affairs, especially in connection with the war'.

KHWAJA, ABDUL MAJID [1885–1962]: educated at M.A.O. College, Aligarh, and Christ College, Cambridge; on his return to India set up practice first at Aligarh and then at Patna; elected trustee of Aligarh, 1912; succeeded Shaukat Ali as secretary of the Aligarh Old Boys' Association, 1915; organized the Home Rule League at Aligarh; gave up practice during the Non-Co-operation movement; principal, Jamia Millia Islamia, 1922; secretary, Congress working committee, 1923; chairman, Aligarh municipal board, 1923; member of the Muslim Nationalist Party, founded by Ansari and Azad.

KIDWAI, MUSHIR HUSAIN [b. 1878]: belonged to a petty zamindar family of Gadia in Barabanki district; one of the founders of the Anjuman-i Khuddam-i Kaaba; president, Oudh Khilafat Conference, May 1920; joined the swarajists, 1923; president of the socialist group of legislative assembly members formed in March 1924.

KHAN, ZAFAR ALI [1873–1956]: educated at M.A.O. College, Aligarh, from where he graduated in 1895; joined the service of the Nizam of Hyderabad; took over as editor of the *Zamindar*, formerly edited by his father, Sirajuddin Ahmad; visited Turkey in 1912 to deliver the purse collected by the Indian Muslims through the Indian Crescent Mission; one of the leading figures in the Khilafat movement, and went to England, Paris and the Middle East as member of the Khilafat delegation, 1925; joined the Ahrar Party in 1929; member, Punjab legislative council, 1937–46.

KIFAYATULLAH [1875–1952]: prominent *alim* of the Ahl-i Hadith school and head of the Aminiya Madrasa, Delhi: first president of the Jamiyat al-ulama, 1919; took leading part in the Khilafat movement and went to prison.

KITCHLEW, SAIFUDDIN [1884–1963]: educated in India, England and Germany; started legal practice at Rawalpindi in 1913; moved to Amritsar in 1915, where he took prominent part in the Rowlatt Satyagraha; sentenced to life imprisonment but was released under amnesty December 1919; took a leading part in the Khilafat movement and gave up practice in 1920; member, Non-Co-operation Committee of the Central Khilafat Committee, 1920–21; interned for supporting the Karachi resolutions; conducted the *tanzim* campaign during 1924–27.

MADANI, HUSAIN AHMAD [1879–1957]: educated at Deoband, 1892–99; joined its teaching staff on graduation and was principal of the Dar al-ulum from 1926 to 1957; joined Mahmud Hasan in his pan-Islamic schemes, 1915–16; arrested along with his leader and three other associates, 1916; interned at Malta by the British, 1917–20; joined the Khilafat movement and interned for supporting the Karachi resolutions, 1921–23.

MALAVIYA, MADAN MOHAN [1861–1946]: educated in Hindi and Sanskrit at the Dharmjyan Updeshak Pathsala, the English district school and Muir Central College, Allahabad; edited the *Hindustan*, 1887–89; *Indian Union*, 1889–92; *Abhyudaya,* 1907–09; member, UP legislative council, 1902–12; president, Indian National Congress, 1909 and 1918; member, imperial legislative council, 1910–19; founded Banaras Hindu university, 1916; president, All-India Hindu Mahasabha, 1923–25.

MESTON, JAMES SCORGIE [1865–1943]: educated at Aberdeen Grammar School, Aberdeen University, Balliol College, Oxford; entered ICS, 1885; assistant magistrate and collector of Saharanpur, Basti, Moradabad, Pratapgarh, 1885–89; served as assistant commissioner and as settlement officer before becoming third secretary to UP government, 1899–1903; secretary to the government of India, finance department, 1906–12; lieutenant-governor, UP, 1912–18.

MOHAMMAD ALI MOHAMMAD, Raja of Mahmudabad [1889–1931]: descendant of Qazi Nasrullah, a Siddiqi Sheikh of Baghdad, who came to India in the thirteenth century; Mahmudabad's ancestors settlled at Mahmudabad in the sixteenth century and greatly increased their estate in the eighteenth century; member, UP legislative council, 1908–9; governor-general's council, 1907–20; played a leading role in the Kanpur mosque agitation and the Muslim University movement; supported the Home Rule movement 'with a clique of noisy and aggressive Muslims of the young party, who make the Raja's house their headquarters and live and agitate at his expense'; president, All-India Muslim League, 1915–19; Home Member, UP government, 1920–25; president, British Indian Association, 1817–21, 1930–31; vice-chancellor, Aligharh Muslim univeristy 1920–23; encouraged boycott of Simon Commission, 1927; supported the Nehru Report, 1928; president, Muslim League, 1928.

MOHANI, HASRAT [1877–1951]: leading journalist, poet, and politician; founded the *Urdu-i Moalla* in 1903 which was published intermittently until the 1930s; attended the Surat Congress in 1907 and joined the 'extremist' group of Tilak; was in the forefront of the Kanpur mosque affair, the 'Silk Letter Conspiracy', and the Khilafat Conference at Delhi, November 1919; demanded complete independence for India at the Khilafat Conference and the Congress at Ahmedabad, December 1921; president, All-India Muslim League at Ahmedabad, 1921; imprisoned in 1922; joined Shaukat Ali in the campaign against the Nehru Report.

MOHSINUL MULK, NAWAB MEHDI ALI HASAN [1837–1907]: settled in Aligarh in 1893; secretary, Aligarh College, 1898–1907; main organizer of the Urdu Defence Association in 1900 in response to MacDonnell's Hindi resolution; but was forced to retrace his steps by the lieutenant-governor; played a leading role in organizing the Muslim memorial, deputation and League of 1906 and, in the words of Khaliquzzaman, 'the greatest boon that [he] conferred on his people was the securing of separate electorates'.

MONTAGU, EDWIN SAMUEL [1879–1924]: educated at Clifton, City of London School and Trinity College, Cambridge; Liberal M.P., 1906–22; parliamentary under-secretary of state for India, 1910–14; secretary of state for India, 1917–22.

MOONJE, BALKRISHNA SHEORAM [1872–1948]: educated in Hislop College, Nagpur, and Grant Medical College, Bombay, 1894–98; started practice as an eye specialist in Nagpur, 1901; attended Congress session in 1904, and helped organize the Central Provinces' Conference in 1905; joined 'extremists' after the Surat split in 1907; took part in the Home Rule League; member, swaraj party, and responsive co-operation party and the Hindu Mahasabha; president, All-India Hindu Mahasabha, Patna, 16 April 1927; founder of *sangathan* and was accused by Muslims of fomenting communal trouble throughout India; closely associated with the *shuddhi* movement; bitterly opposed to the Delhi proposals and to any negotiations with Jinnah after the All-Parties National Convention.

NOON, FIROZ KHAN [b. 1893]: belonged to one of the important landowning families of Punjab; graduated from Oxford in 1917; member, Punjab legislative council, 1920; minister for local self-government, 1927–31, and later minister for education, 1931–36; high commissioner for India in Great Britain, 1936–41; labour member, viceroy's executive council, July 1942-September 1945.

PHULWARI, SHAH MOHAMMAD SULAIMAN [1859–1935]: leading Qadiriya *pir* and pan-Islamist *alim* from Phulwari and a close associate of Abdul Bari; educated at Firangi Mahal, Lucknow, and the Hejaz (1885–86); took a leading part in the Khilafat and Non-Co-operation movements.

NADVI, SYED SULAIMAN [1884–1953]: educated at Phulwari Sharif, Madrasa Imdadiyya, Darbhanga, and Nadwat al-ulama, Lucknow; edited *Al-Nadwa*, 1912; one of the founders of *Dar al-Musannifin*, Azamgarh, 1914; member, Khilafat delegation to Europe, 1920, and of delegation to the Hejaz 1924–25.

NARENDRANATH, (Raja) [1864–1945]: educated in Calcutta and Lahore; appointed assistant commissioner of Gurdaspur in 1887, deputy commissioner of Montgomery in 1895, and promoted to officiate as commissioner for the Lahore division in 1911; represented the landholder's constituency in the Punjab legislative council, 1921–37; president, All-India Hindu Mahasabha Conference, 1927, and for many years president of the Punjab provincial

Hindu Sabha; attended the Round Table Conference, 1930–31. After 1931, he emerged as a champion of the interests of Hindu commercial and professional classes. 'I for one', he wrote in June 1926, 'cannot whole-heartedly join any political party unless that party undertakes to protect the just and legitimate rights of the Hindus of the Punjab'.

RAHIM, ABDUR [1867–1947]: called to the Bar [Middle Temple], 1890; practised as Advocate at the Calcutta magistracy, 1900–03; member, royal commission on public services, 1913–15; officiated as chief justice, Madras, July-October 1916 and July-October 1919; member, executive council of the governor of Bengal, 1920–25; elected to central legislative assembly in 1931 and was its president, from 1935 to 1945.

RAI, LALA LAJPAT [1865–1928]: educated at the Lahore College, 1890; passed the Law examination in 1886; practised first at Hissar and later at Lahore; joined Congress in 1888; seconded a resolution on the boycott of British cloth at the Congress in 1905; deported to Burma in 1907; went to England in 1908 and delivered lectures on Indian political situation; established the Indian Home Rule League in the United States on 15 October 1916; arrested in 1921 while presiding over the Punjab provincial political conference; president of the Special Congress session, Calcutta, September 1920, and opposed Gandhi's non-co-operation resolution; supported non-co-operation at Nagpur; joined swaraj party; founded an Urdu daily, *Bande Matram* and an English weekly, *The People;* president of the Agra provincial Hindu conference, Etawah, 27 October 1928, where he supported the Nehru Report; closely associated with the Hindu Sabha, the *shuddhi* and *sangathan* movements.

RAM, CHHOTU [1881–1945]: born in a poor Jat family; served as private secretary to Raja Rampal Singh of Kalakankar; president, district Congress committee, Rohtak, 1917–20; editor of the *Jat Gazette*; resigned from Congress over non-co-operation; one of the founders of the Unionist Party and its leader in the Punjab legislative council, 1926–36; minister in the Punjab government, 1924–45.

READING, RUFUS DANIEL ISAACS, 1st Marquess of [1860–1935]: educated at University College, London, and Brussels and Hanover; M.P., 1904–13; solicitor-general, 1910; attorney-general, 1910–13; lord chief justice of England, 1913–21; viceroy of India, 1921–26.

SAPRU, TEJ BAHADUR [1875–1949]: advocate, Allahabad High Court, 1896–1926; member, UP legislative council, 1913–16; member, imperial legislative council, 1916–20; member, AICC, 1906–1917; president, UP Liberal League, 1918–20: member, Reforms Enquiry Committee, 1924; played a leading role in the making of the Nehru Report, 1928; delegate to the Round Table Conferences, 1930–32. 'It has been a very hum–drum sort of life' Sapru said on his 70th birthday, 'punctuated in private spheres by occasional moments of happiness and more by sorrow than anything else. In public life there has been nothing remarkable except that I have represented a school of thought which is on the wane'.

SHERWANI, TASSADUQ AHMAD KHAN [d. 1935]: member of the Bilona branch of the Sherwani Pathan family; one brother, Nisar Ahmad Khan, became a superintendent of post offices, resigning his post in the Non-Co-operation movement, and another, Fida Ahmad Khan, managed a sugar factory in Etah; educated in Aligarh and at Cambridge where he was a contemporary of Jawaharlal Nehru; a close friend of Ansari and Mohamed Ali and followed them in the Aligarh Muslim University movement and the Home Rule League. 'He had a genial personality', wrote Khaliquzzaman, 'and was loved and respected by his friends and foes alike'.

SEN GUPTA, JATINDRA MOHAN [1885–1933]: associated with political movements in Bengal since 1919; vice-president, Bengal provincial Congress committee; member, Congress working committee, 1922; elected mayor of Calcutta corporation for the first time in 1925 after the death of C.R. Das. At the same time, he was elected president of the Bengal Congress committee and also the leader of the Congress party in the legislative council.

SHAFI, MOHAMMAD [1869–1932]: president, All-India Muslim League, 1913; president, All-India Muslim Educational Conference, 1916; member, provincial and imperial legislative councils, 1909–19; education member, government of India, 1919–22; law member, government of India, 1922–24; led the campaign in Punjab against the boycott of Simon Commission.

SHRADDHANAND [1856–1926]: educated at Queen's College, Banaras, and University College, Lahore; started legal practice in 1885; took an active interest in the Arya Samaj and emerged leader of its Gurukul section in 1893; founded the Gurukul at Hardwar in 1902; organized the Rowlatt Satyagraha in Delhi and was invited by the Muslims to address them in Juma Masjid, Delhi; chairman of the reception committee of Congress, Amritsar, December 1919; launched the *shuddhi* movement towards the end of 1922 and reconverted many Malkana Rajputs to Hinduism; killed by a Muslim fanatic, Abdur Rashid.

SMITH, JAMES ROBERT DUNLOP. held several important positions in Punjab before joining Minto as his private secretary. He was the key figure in the negotiations surrounding the Simla deputation and provided Minto with the notes from which he began to draft his reply. He knew many Muslims, including Mohamed Ali. exchanged letters on a wide range of issues. He also tried to secure a government appointment for Mohamed Ali.

SUBHANI, AZAD [b. 1873]: rose to prominence during the pan-Islamic agitations of 1913–14; leading local agitator during the Kanpur mosque agitation; joined the Anjuman-i Khuddam-i Kaaba; president, All-India Khilafat Conference, September 1920; introduced resolution demanding complete independence at the Muslim League session in January 1922. After the Khilafat movement, he became associated with the labour movement in Kanpur.

SUHRAWARDY, HUSAIN SHAHEED [1893–1963]: son of Zahid Suhrawardy, judge of the Calcutta High Court; educated at St. Xavier's College, Calcutta, and Oxford university; member, Bengal legislative council, 1921, and was deputy mayor of Calcutta for three successive years; minister, Bengal government, 1927-43, chief minister 1946.

TYABJI, BADRUDDIN [1844–1906]: educated in England; called to the Bar [Middle Temple], 1867; leading Bombay barrister; member, Bombay legislative council; founder member, Bombay Presidency Association, 1885; president of the Indian National Congress 1887; Judge of the Bombay High Court.

TILAK, BAL GANGADHAR [1856–1920]: born in an orthodox Chitpavan Brahmin family of petty landowners; studied Sanskrit, Law and Mathematics in Poona; one of the founders of the Deccan Education Society and the Fergusson college in 1885; imprisoned for 'sedition' on 14 September 1897, and in July 1908; released on

17 June 1914; launched the Home Rule agitation 1916, and rejoined the Congress; played a leading part in the Congress-Muslim League negotiations, and supported the Lucknow Pact. 'There is a feeling among the Hindus', he said, 'that too much has been given to the Muslims. As a Hindu I have no objection to making this concession.... We cannot rise from our present intolerable condition without the aid of the Muslims. So in order to gain the desired end there is no objection to give a percentage, a greater percentage, to the Muslims.'

VIQARUL MULK, NAWAB MUSHTAQ HUSAIN [1841–1917]: put forward the scheme for the formation of a Muslim political association; member, Simla Deputation, and chairman, League's foundation session at Dacca; secretary, Aligarh College, 1907-1913. He was spokesman for those who opposed an increase in British authority at Aligarh and came into conflict with Archbold, Morison's successor. In 1909, Hewett was forced to intervene amid widespread criticizm. Hewett was compelled to retreat and Archbold resigned. Viqarul Mulk was also unhappy with the government proposal for a Muslim university and, at the Foundation Committee's meeting on 26 December 1912, joined Mohamed Ali and Azad in denouncing the leadership of the movement.

Bibliography

PRIVATE PAPERS

Aligarh Muslim University Archives, Aligarh [AMUA]
- Syed Ahmad Khan Papers
- Papers relating to the Non-Co-operation movement at the M.A.O. College, Aligarh

India Office Library and Records, London [IOLR]
- Beck Papers
- Chelmsford Papers
- Dunlop Smith Papers
- Hailey Papers
- Harcourt Butler Papers
- Hardinge Papers
- Irwin Papers
- Lytton Papers
- Meston Papers
- Montagu Papers
- Reading Papers
- Ronaldshay Papers

National Archives of India, New Delhi [NAI]
- Jayakar Papers
- Tyabji Papers

National Library, Calcutta
- Moonje Papers
- Sapru Papers

Nehru Memorial Museum and Library [NMML]
- All-India Congress Committee Papers
- Chagla Papers
- Chhatari Papers
- Chintamani Papers
- Daryabadi Papers
- Khwaja Papers

Motilal Nehru Papers
Satyamurti Papers
Thakurdas Papers

University Library, Cambridge
Baldwin Papers
Crewe Papers
Hardinge Papers

Jamia Millia Islamia, New Delhi [JMI]
Mohamed Ali Papers

Centre for South Asian Studies, Cambridge
Allanson Papers
Benthall Papers
Curry Papers
Hume Papers
Martin Papers
Tegart Papers

GOVERNMENT RECORDS

National Archives of India, New Delhi [NAI]

Records of the Home Department of the Government of India, filed as Home Political. Home Political files are divided into A, B and D (Deposit) categories.

The Uttar Pradesh State Archives, Lucknow [UPSA]
Records of the UP government in the General Administration, Education and Police Departments.

OFFICIAL PUBLICATIONS

Census of India, 1921, vol. xv. *Punjab and Delhi,* part I. (Lahore, 1923).
Census of India, 1921, vol. xvi. *United Provinces of Agra and Oudh,* part I. (Allahabad, 1923).
Census of India, 1921, vol. xv. *Punjab and Delhi,* part II. (Lahore, 1923).
Census of India, 1921, vol. v. *Bengal,* part I. (Calcutta, 1923).
Census of India, 1921, vol. v. *Bengal,* part II. (Calcutta, 1923).
Census of India, 1931, vol. v. *Bengal,* part II. (Calcutta, 1933).
District Gazetteer of the United Provinces of Agra and Oudh, Aligarh, vol. vi.
District Gazetteer of the United Provinces of Agra and Oudh, Agra, vol. xiii.

District Gazetteer of the United Provinces of Agra and Outh, Bareilly, vol. xiii.

District Gazetteer of the United Provinces of Agra and Oudh, Lucknow, vol. xxxvii.

District Gazetteer of the Bengal Presidency, Mymensingh, (Calcutta, 1917).

Government of India, *India in 1917-18* to *India in 1927-28,* reports prepared annually for presentation to Parliament.

Nathan, R. *Progress of Education in India 1887-88 to 1891-92. Fourth Quinquennial Review* (Calcutta, 1893).

Proceedings of the United Provinces Legislative Council, 1916 (Allahabad, 1917)

Proceedings of the United Provinces Legislative Council, 1923 (Allahabad, 1924)

Punjab Administration Report, 1922-23 (Lahore, 1924)

Punjab Administration Report, 1924-25 (Lahore, 1926)

Punjab Legislative Council Debates, 1923-26

Report of the Working of the System of Government, United Provinces of Agra and Oudh, in three vols. (Allahabad, 1928)

Report on the Working of Municipalities in the Punjab (Lahore, 1924)

Report on the Working of Municipal Politics in the Punjab, 1922-23 (Lahore, 1924)

Report on the Administration of Bengal, 1889-90 (Calcutta, 1890)

Report on the Administration of Bengal, 1918-19 (Calcutta, 1921)

Report on the Administration of Bengal, 1920-21 (Calcutta, 1923)

Report on the Administration of Bengal, 1921-23 (Calcutta, 1923)

Report of the Municipality of the Suburbs of Calcutta, 1875-76 (Calcutta, 1876)

Resolution Reviewing the Reports of the Working of Municipalities in East Bengal and Assam, 1906-7 (Shillong, 1908)

Resolution Reviewing the Reports on the Working of Municipalities in Bengal, 1920-21 (Calcutta, 1922)

Resolution Reviewing the Reports on the Working of Municipalities in Bengal, 1925-26 (Calcutta, 1927)

Resolution Reviewing the Reports on the Working of Districts Boards in Bengal, 1923-24 (Calcutta, 1925)

PARLIAMENTARY PAPERS

Year	Command Number	Short Title
1888	5327	*Report of the Public Service Commission*, 1886-7, with appendices (Calcutta, 1888).
1914	8382	*Royal Commission on the Public Services in India*. vol. I, Report.
1914	7293	*Royal Commission on the Public Services in India*. vols. II to XI, Appendices to the Reports.
1918	9109	*Report on Indian Constitutional Reforms*.
1918	9178	*Addresses Presented to His Excellency the Viceroy and the Right Honourable the Secretary of State for India*.
1925	2361	*Views of Local Governments on the Working of Reforms, 1923*.
1925	2362	*Views of Local Governments on the Working of Reforms, 1924*.
1930	3568	*Report of the Indian Statutory Commission*, vol. I, *Survey*.
1930	3569	*Report of the Indian Statutory Commission*, vol. II, *Recommendations*.

NEWSPAPERS AND JOURNALS

Aligarh Institute Gazette (Aligarh)
Amrita Bazar Patrika (Calcutta)
Asr-i Jadeed (Meerut)
Bombay Chronicle (Bombay)
Comrade (Calcutta, Delhi)
Forward (Calcutta)
Inqilaab (Lahore) [1937–39]
Kayastha Samachar (Allahabad)
Leader (Allahabad)
Mahratta (Poona)
Mussalman (Calcutta)
Moslem Chronicle (Calcutta)
Moslem Outlook (Calcutta)
Searchlight (Patna)
Tribune (Lahore)

and

Reports on or Selections from Native Newspapers [SNNR] from Punjab, UP, and Bengal, [NAI] and [IOLR].

PUBLISHED BOOKS AND UNPUBLISHED THESES

Abbas, K.A. *I am not an Island: An Experiment in Autobiography* (Delhi, 1977)

Adhikari, G. (ed.), *Documents of the History of the Communist Party of India*, vol. III–B (Delhi, 1979)

Ahmad, A. *Islamic Modernism in India and Pakistan 1857–1946* (London, 1967)

————*Studies in Islamic Culture in the Indian Environment* (Oxford, 1964)

————*An Intellectual History of Islam* (Edinburgh, 1969)

Ahmad, I. (ed.), *Caste and Social Stratification Among the Muslims* (Delhi, 1973).

Ahmad, Q. and Jha, J.A. *Mazharul Haque* (Delhi, 1976)

Ahmad, R. *Bengal Muslims 1871–1906: A Quest for Identity* (Delhi, 1981)

Ali, I. *The Punjab Under Imperialism, 1885–1947* (Princeton University Press. 1988)

Ali, H M. *Observations on the Mussulmans of India* (London, 1917 edn.)

Ali, Mohamed. *My Life a Fragment: An Autobiographical Sketch of Maulana Mohamed Ali* (Lahore, 1966 edn.)

Ali, Salim. *The Fall of A Sparrow* (Delhi, 1985)

All-Parties Conference, 1928: Report of the Committee appointed by the Conference to determine the principles of the Constitution for India (Allahabad, 1928)

Andrews, C.F. *Zakaullah of Delhi* (Cambridge, n.d.)

Ansari, K.H. 'The Emergence of Muslim Socialists and their Ideas in India between 1917 and 1947' (Unpublished Ph.D. thesis, University of London, 1985)

Arthur, T.C. *Reminiscences of an Indian Police Official* (London, 1894)

Ashraf, M. *Muslim Attitudes towards British Rule and Western Culture in India* (Delhi, 1982)

Aziz, K.K. *Britain and Muslim India* (London, 1968)

Baird, R.D. (ed.), *Religion in Modern India* (Delhi, 2nd rev. edn., 1989)

Banerjea, S. *Speeches and Writings of Surendranath Banerjea* (Madras, 1912)

———— *A Nation in Making* (Calcutta: reprint, 1963)

Baljon, J.M.S. *Reforms and Religious Ideas of Sir Sayyid Ahmad Khan* (Leiden, 1949)

Bayly, C.A. *The Local Roots of Indian Politics—Allahabad 1880–1920* (Oxford, 1975)

———— *Rulers and Townsmen and Bazaars: North Indian Society in the Age of British Expansion 1770–1870* (Cambridge, 1983)

Blunt, W.S. *India Under Ripon: A Private Diary* (London, 1909)

Bose, S.K. (ed.), *Subhash Chandra Bose Netaji: Collected Works,* vol. 1, (Calcutta, 1981)

Brass, P. *Language, Religion and Politics in North India* (Cambridge, 1974)

Broomfield, J.H. *Elite Conflict in a Plural Society: Twentieth Century Bengal* (University of California Press, 1968)

Brown, E. *Har Dayal: Hindu Revolutionary and Rationalist* (Tueson, 1975)

Brown, J.M. *Gandhi's Rise to Power: Indian Politics 1915–1922* (Cambridge, 1972)

Bukhsh, K. *Studies: Indian and Islamic* (London, 1927)

Burke, E. and Lapidus, I.M. (eds.), *Islam Politics and Social Movements* (University of California Press, 1988)

Case, M.H. 'The Aligarh Era: Muslim Politics in North India 1860–1910' (Unpublished Ph.D. thesis, Chicago, 1970)

Cashman, R.I. *The Myth of the Lokamanya: Tilak and Mass Politics in Maharashtra* (University of California Press, 1975)

Chagla, M.C. *Roses in December: An Autobiography* (Bombay, 1977)

Chandra, B. *Communalism in Modern India* (Delhi, 1984)

———— *et al. India's Struggle for Independence* (Delhi, 1987)

Chaudhuri, N.C. *The Autobiography of an Unknown Indian* (London, 1951)

———— *Thy Hand Great Anarch! India 1921-52* (London, 1987)

Choudhry, P. *Punjab Politics: The Role of Sir Chhotu Ram* (Delhi, 1984)

Cole, J.R.I. *Roots of North Indian Shiism in Iran and Iraq: Religion and State in Awadh 1722-1859* (Delhi, 1989)

Cotton, H. *India and Home Memoirs* (London, 1911)

Coupland, R. *The Indian Problem, 1833-1935* (New York, 1944)

Cragg, K. *Counsels in Contemporary Islam* (Edinburgh, 1963)

Dale, S.F. *The Islamic Society on the South Asian Frontier: The Mapillas of Malabar, 1498-1922* (London, 1980)

Datta, V.N. *Maulana Azad* (Delhi, 1990)

——— and Cleghorn, B.E. (eds.) *A Nationalist Muslim and Indian Politics* (Delhi, 1974)

Douglas, I.H. *Abul Kalam Azad: An Intellectual and Religious Biography,* eds. Gail Minault and C.W. Troll (Delhi, 1988)

Dutt, R.P. *India Today* (Bombay, 1949 edn.)

Dwarkadas, K. *India's Fight For Freedom* (Bombay, 1966)

Eveling, H. (ed.), *The Development of Indonesian Society* (Queensland, 1979)

Ewing, K.P. (ed.). *Shariat and Ambiguity in South Asian Islam* (Delhi, 1988)

Farquhar, J.N. *Modern Religious Movements in India* (Delhi, 1967 edn.)

Faruqi, Z.H. *The Deoband School and the Demand for Pakistan* (Delhi, 1967)

Gallagher, J. Johnson, G. and Seal, A. (eds.), *Locality, Province and Nation: Essays on Indian Politics 1870–1940* (Cambridge, 1973)

Gandhi, M.K. *The Collected Works of Mahatma Gandhi* (Delhi, in process of publication)

——— *An Autobiography or the Story of My Experiments with Truth* (Ahmedabad: reprint, 1958)

Gandhi, Rajmohan. *Understanding the Muslim Mind* (Delhi, 1987)

Gellner, E. (ed.), *Islamic Dilemmas: Reformers, Nationalists and Industrialization* (Berlin, 1985)

Gordon, L.A. *Bengal: The Nationalist Movement 1876–1940* (New York, 1974)

Gilmartin, D. *Empire and Islam: Punjab and the Making of Pakistan* (London, 1988)

Gopal, S. (ed.), *British Policy in India 1858–1905* (Cambridge, 1965)

——— *Jawaharlal Nehru—A Biography, 1889–1947,* vol. 1 (Delhi, 1975)

——— (ed.), *Selected Works of Jawaharlal Nehru* (Delhi, in process of publication)

Gupta, A.K. (ed.), *Myth and Reality: The Struggle for Freedom in India 1945–47* (Delhi, 1987)

Hamid, A. *Muslim Separatism in India: A Brief Survey 1858–1947* (Lahore, 1971)

Hardy, P. *The Muslims of British India* (Cambridge, 1972)

——— *Partners in Freedom—and True Muslims: The Political Thought of some Muslim Scholars in British India* (Lund: Studentlitteratur, 1971)

Hasan, Khalid, 'Saadat Hasan Manto: Not of Blessed Memory', *Annual of Urdu Studies,* vol. 4. 1984
Hasan, Khalid. *Scoreboard* (Lahore, 1984)
Hasan, Mushirul. *Nationalism and Communal Politics in India, 1916–1928* (Delhi, 1979)
——— *Mohamed Ali: Ideology and Politics* (Delhi, 1981)
——— *A Nationalist Conscience: M.A. Ansari, the Congress and the Raj* (Delhi, 1987)
——— (ed.) *Communal and Pan-Islamic Trends in Colonial India* (Delhi: 2nd rev. edn. 1985)
——— (ed.) *Muslims and the Congress: Select Correspondence of Dr. M.A. Ansari 1912–1935* (Delhi, 1979)
——— (ed.) *Mohamed in Indian Politics: Select Writings* (Delhi: in three volumes)
Hasan, Z. *Dominance and Mobilization: Rural Politics in Uttar Pradesh, 1930–1980* (Delhi, 1989)
Hashmi, T.I. 'Peasants and Politics in East Bengal, 1920–1947' (Unpublished Ph.D. thesis, University of Western Australia, 1986)
Hayat, A. *Mussalmans of Bengal* (Calcutta, 1966)
Hill, J.L. 'Congress and Representative Institutions in the United Provinces 1886–1901' (Unpublished Ph.D. thesis, Duke University, 1966)
Holderness, T.W. *Peoples and Problems of India* (London, 1911)
Holt, P. M. *et al. The Cambridge History of Islam: The Central Islamic Lands,* vol. 1 (Cambridge, 1970)
Hourani, A. *Arabic Thought in the Liberal Age, 1798–1939* (Oxford, 1970)
Hunter, W.W. *Indian Mussalman: Are They Bound in Conscience to Rebel against the Queen* (Calcutta, 1945 edn.)
Husain, A. *Fazli Husain: A Political Biography* (Bombay, 1936)
Ikram, S.M. *History of Muslim Civilization in India and Pakistan* (Lahore, 1961)
——— *Modern Muslim India and the Birth of Pakistan* (London, 1965)
Iqbal, A. *Life and Times of Maulana Mohamed Ali* (Delhi: reprint, 1978)
——— (ed., *Selected Speeches and Writings of Maulana Mohamed Ali* (Lahore, 1944)
Iqbal, M. *Reconstruction of Religious Thought in Islam* (London, 1934)
Jagadisan, M.R. (ed.), *Letters of Srinivasa Sastri* (Asia Publishing House, 1963 edn.)
Jalal, A. *The Sole Spokesman: Jinnah, The Muslim League and the Demand for Pakistan* (Cambridge, 1985)

Jones, K.W. *Arya Dharm: Hindu Consciousness in 19th–Century Punjab* (University of California Press, 1976)

Jones, R.L. *A Fatal Friendship: The Nawabs, the British and the City of Lucknow* (Delhi, 1985)

Jordens, J.T.F. *Dayananda Saraswati: His Life and Ideas* (Delhi, 1978)

——— *Swami Shraddhananda: His Life and Causes* (Delhi, 1981)

Joshi, V.C. (ed.), *Lala Lajpat Rai: Writings and Speeches,* vol. 1, (Delhi, 1966)

Kahin, G.M. *Nationalism and Revolution in Indonesia* (Cornell, 1952)

Kapur, Rajiv. *Sikh Separatism: The Politics of Faith* (London, 1986)

Karim, A. *Letters on Hindu-Muslim Pact* (Calcutta, 1924)

Kaura, U. *Muslims and Indian Nationalism: The Emergence of the Demand for India's Partition 1928–1940* (Delhi, 1977)

Keddie, N.R. *Sayyid Jamal-ad Din "al-Afghani": A Political Biography* (University of California Press, 1972)

——— *Islamic Response to Imperialism: Political and Religious Writings of Sayyid Jamal ad-Din "al-Afghani"* (University of California Press, 1968)

Kedourie, E. *Afghani and Abduh: An Essay on Religious Unbelief and Political Activism in Modern Islam* (London, 1966)

Khaliquzzaman, C. *Pathway to Pakistan* (Lahore, 1961)

Kidwai, M.H. *Pan-Islamism and Bolshevism* (London, 1937)

Kiernan, V.G. trans, *Poems from Iqbal* (London, 1955 edn.)

——— trans. *Poems by Faiz* (London, 1971)

Kitchlew, T. *Saifuddin Kitchlew: Hero of Jallianwala Bagh* (Delhi, 1987)

Kumar, R. *Essays in the Social History of Modern India* (Delhi, 1983)

——— *The Making of a Nation: Essays in Indian History and Politics* (Delhi, 1989)

——— (ed.), *Essays on Gandhian Politics: The Rowlatt Satyagraha of 1919* (London, 1971)

Latif, S.A. *The Influence of English Literature on Urdu Literature* (London, 1925)

Lavan, S. *The Ahmadiyah Movement: A History and Perspective* (Delhi, 1974)

Lawrence, second Marquess of Zetland. *Essayez* (London, 1956)

Lelyveld, D. *Aligarh's First Generation: Muslim Solidarity in British India* (Princeton University Press, 1978)

Low, D.A. (ed.), *Soundings in Modern South Asian History* (University of California Press, 1968)

——— (ed.), *The Indian National Congress: Centenary Hindsights* (Delhi, 1988)

Lytton, Earl of. *Pundits and Elephants. Being the experience of five years as Governor of an Indian Province* (London, 1942)

Malik, H. *Sir Sayyid Ahmad Khan and Muslim Modernization in India and Pakistan* (New York, 1980)

——— (ed.), *Iqbal: Poet-Philosopher of Pakistan* (New York, 1971)

McLane, J.R. *Indian Nationalism and the Early Congress* (Princeton University Press, 1987)

Mcpherson, K. *The Muslim Microcosm: Calcutta, 1918 to 1935* (Heidelberg, 1974)

Mehrotra, S.R. *The Emergence of the Indian National Congress* (Delhi, 1971)

Mehta, A. and Patwardhan, A. *The Communal Triangle in India* (Allahabad, 1942)

Menon, M.U. 'Partition Literature: A Study of Intizar Husain', *MAS*, vol. 14, no. 3, 1980

Metcalf, B.D. *Islamic Revival in British India: Deoband, 1860–1900* (Princeton University Press, 1982)

——— (ed.), *Moral Conduct and Authority: The Place of Adab in Islam* (California University Press, 1984)

Metcalf, T.R. *Land, Landlords and the Raj: Northern India in the Nineteenth Century* (California University Press, 1979)

Minault, G. *The Khilafat Movement: Religious Symbolism and Political Mobilization in India* (Columbia University Press, 1982)

Mitra, H.N. (ed.), *Indian Annual Register* (later *Indian Quarterly Register*) (Calcutta, 1919 onwards)

Moore, R.J. *The Crisis of Indian Unity 1917–1940* (Delhi, 1974)

Muhammad, S. (ed.), *The Aligarh Movement: Basic Documents 1864–1898* (Meerut, 1978)

——— *Sir Syed Ahmad Khan: A Political Biography* (Meerut, 1969)

Mujeeb, M. *The Indian Muslims* (London, 1967)

Nadwi, A.H.A. *Life and Mission of Maulana Mohammad Ilyas* (Lucknow, 1983)

——— *Muslims in India* (Lucknow, 1980)

Nagar, P. *Lala Lajpat Rai: The Man and his Ideas* (Delhi, 1977)

Nanda, B.R. *Gandhi, Pan-Islamism, Imperialism and Nationalism* (Delhi, 1989)

Nehru, J. *A Bunch of Old Letters* (Bombay, 2nd edn. 1966)

——— *An Autobiography* (London, 1936)

Niemeijer, A.C. *The Khilafat Movement in India, 1919–1924* (The Hague, 1972)

Nizami, K.A. *Religion and Politics in India during the Thirteenth Century* (Bombay, 1961)

Noer, D. *The Modernist Muslim Movement in Indonesia 1900–1942* (Oxford, 1973)

Noman, M. *Rise and Growth of the Muslim League* (Allahabad, 1942)

Noorani, A.G. *Badruddin Tyabji* (Delhi, 1969)

Oldenburg, V.T. *The Making of Colonial Lucknow, 1856–1877* (Princeton University Press, 1984)

Page, D. *Prelude to Partition: The Indian Muslims and the Imperial System of Control, 1920–1932* (Delhi, 1982)

Pande, B.N. (ed.), *A Centenary History of the Indian National Congress*, in three volumes (Delhi, 1985)

Pandey, G. *The Ascendancy of the Congress in Uttar Pradesh 1926–1934 A Study in Imperfect Mobilization* (Delhi, 1985)

Panikkar, K.N. *Against Lord and State: Religion and Peasant Uprisings in Malabar 1836–1921* (Delhi, 1989)

Philips, C.H. (ed.), *The Evolution of India and Pakistan 1859–1947: Select Documents* (London, 1962)

Pirzada, S. (ed.), *The Collected Works of Quaid-e-Azam Mohammed Ali Jinnah*, vol. 1 (Karachi, 1984)

——————— (ed.), *Foundations of Pakistan: All India Muslim League Documents 1906–1947*, in two volumes (Karachi, 1970)

Prasad, R. *India Divided* (Bombay, 1946)

——————— *An Autobiography* (Asia Publishing House, 1957)

Qadiri, K.H. *Hasrat Mohani* (Delhi, 1985)

Qureshi, I.H. *The Muslim Community of the Indo-Pakistan Subcontinent 610–1947* (The Hague, 1962)

——————— *Ulema in Politics: A Study Relating to the Political Activities of the Ulema in the South-Asian Subcontinent from 1556 to 1947* (Karachi, 1974)

Rab, A.S.M. *A.K. Fazlul Haq: Life and Achievements* (Lahore, n.d.)

Rahman, F. *Islam* (London, 1966)

Rai, Lajpat. *A History of the Arya Samaj* (Bombay, 1967)

Raina, K.M. *Welding the Nation: Academic Addresses and Selected Writings* (Bombay, 1974)

Ray, R.K. *Social Conflict and Political Unrest in Bengal 1875–1927* (Delhi, 1984)

Ray, S. (ed.), *Selected Works of M.N. Roy*, in two vols. (Delhi, 1988)

Reading, Rufus Isaccs. *First Marquess of Reading, by his son, 1914–1935* (London, 1945)

Reeves, P.D. 'The Landlords' response to Political Change in the United Provinces of Agra and Oudh, India, 1921–1937' (Unpublished Ph.D. thesis, Australia National University, 1963)

Rizvi, S.A.A. *Shah Abdul Aziz: Puritanism, Sectarian Polemics, and*

Jihad (Canberra, 1982)
——— *Shah Wali Allah and His Times* (Canberra, 1980)
Rizvi, S.M. *History of the Dar al-Ulum Deoband,* in two volumes (Deoband, n.d.)
Robinson, F. *Separatism Among Indian Muslims: The Politics of United Provinces' Muslims, 1860–1923* (Cambridge, 1975)
Ronaldshay, Earl of. *India: A Bird's-Eye View* (London, 1924)
Roy, A. *The Islamic Syncretistic Tradition in Bengal* (Princeton University Press, 1983)
Russell, R. *Ghalib: The Poet and His Age* (London, 1977)
Saberwal, S. *India: The Roots of Crisis* (Delhi, 1986)
Shaikh, Farzana. *Community and Consensus in Islam: Muslim Representation in Colonial India* (Cambridge, 1989)
Sharar, A.H. *Lucknow: The Last Phase of an Oriental Culture.* Translated and edited by E.S. Harcourt and Fakhir Hussain (London, 1975)
Sarkar, S. *The Swadeshi Movement in Bengal, 1903–1908* (Delhi, 1973)
——— *Modern India, 1885–1947* (Delhi, 1983)
Sarkar, T. *Bengal, 1928–1934: The Politics of Protest* (Delhi, 1987)
Sayeed, K.B. *Pakistan: The Formative Phase 1857–1948* (Karachi, 1968 edn.)
Schimmel. A. *Gabriel's Wing: A Study into the Religious Ideas of Sir Muhammad Iqbal* (Leiden, 1963)
Seal, A. *The Emergence of Indian Nationalism: Competition and Collaboration in the Later Nineteenth Century* (Cambridge, 1968)
Sender, H. *The Kashmiri Pandits: A Study of Cultural Choice in India* (Delhi, 1988)
Sisson, R. and Wolpert, S. (ed.), *Congress and Indian Nationalism: The Pre-Independence Phase* (University of California Press, 1988)
Smith, D.E. (ed.), *Religion and Political Modernization* (Yale University Press, 1974)
Smith, W.C. *Modern Islam in India* (Lahore, 1947)
Stokes, E.T. *Peasants and the Raj: Studies in Agrarian Society and Peasant Rebellion in Colonial India* (Cambridge, 1978)
Stratchey, J. *India* (London, 1888)
Talbot, I. *Punjab and the Raj, 1849–1947* (Delhi, 1988)
Tendulkar, D.G. *Mahatma: Life of Mohandas Karamchand Gandhi,* vol. 1, (Delhi, reprint, 1969)
Thursby, G.R. *Hindu-Muslim Relations in British India* (Leiden, 1975)
Tinker, H. *The Foundations of Local Self-Government in India, Pakistan and Burma* (London, 1968)

Titus, M.T. *Indian Islam: The Religious Quest of India* (Delhi, 1979 edn.)

Troll, C.W. *Sayyid Ahmad Khan: A Reinterpretation of Muslim Theology* (Delhi, 1978)

———— (ed.), *Islam in India: Studies and Commentaries*, vol. 1 (Delhi, 1982)

Tyabji, B. *Memoirs of an Egoist* (Delhi, 1988)

Washbrook, D. *The Emergence of Provincial Politics. The Madras Presidency, 1870–1920* (Cambridge, 1976)

Wasti, S.R. *Lord Minto and the Indian Nationalist Movement 1905 to 1910* (Oxford, 1964)

Wolpert, S. *Tilak and Gokhale: Revolution and Reform in the Making of Modern India* (University of California Press, 1962)

———— *Jinnah of Pakistan* (New York, 1984)

———— *Morley and India, 1906–1910* (University of California Press, 1967)

Zaidi, A.M. (ed.), *The Muslim School of Congress* (Delhi, 1987)

———— (ed.), *The Evolution of Muslim Political Thought in India*, vol. 4 (Delhi, 1980)

Ziring, L. *Pakistan: The Enigma of Political Development* (Dawson: Westview, 1980)

ARTICLES

Amin, Shahid. 'Gandhi as Mahatma; Gorakhpur District, Eastern UP, 1921–2', in Ranajit Guha (ed.), *Subaltern Studies III: Writings on South Asian History and Society* (Delhi, 1984)

Barrier, N.G. 'The Arya Samaj and Congress Politics in the Punjab, 1848–1908', *Journal of Asian Studies*, 27 May 1967

Bayly, C.A. 'The Pre-History of 'Communalism'? Religious Conflict in India 1700–1860', *Modern Asian Studies (MAS,)* 19, 2, 1985

———— 'Patrons and Politics in Northern India', *MAS*, 7, 3, 1973

Bose, S. 'The Roots of 'Communal' Violence in Rural Bengal: A study of the Kishoreganj Riots, 1930', *MAS*, 16, 3, 1982

Brass, P. 'Elite Groups, Symbol Manipulation, and Ethnic Identity among the Muslims of South Asia', in David Taylor and Malcolm Yapp (eds.), *Political Identity in South Asia* (London, 1979)

Brennan, L. 'The Illusions of Security: The Background to Muslim Separatism in the United Provinces', *MAS*, 18, 2, 1984

Broomfield, J.H. 'Four Lives: History as Biography', *South Asia*, August 1971

Chandra, S. 'Communal Consciousness in Late 19th Century Hindi Literature', in Mushirul Hasan (ed.), *Communal and Pan-Islamic Trends in Colonial India* (Delhi, 1985)

——— 'The Lengthening Shadow: Secular and Communal Consciousness', in Bidyut Chakrabarti (ed.), *Secularism and Indian Polity* (Delhi, 1990)

Chatterjee, P. 'Agrarian Relations and Communalism in Bengal, 1926–1935', in Ranajit Guha (ed.), *Subaltern Studies I: Writings on South Asian History and Society* (Delhi, 1982)

Cleghorn, B. 'Religion and Politics: The Leadership of the All-India Hindu Mahasabha, Punjab and Maharashtra, 1920–1939', in B.N. Pandey (ed.), *Leadership in South Asia* (Delhi, 1977)

Cotton, H. 'India Old and New', *Asiatic Review,* July 1914

——— 'India Now and After', *Contemporary Review,* February 1915

Gilbert, I.A. 'Autonomy and Consensus under the Raj: Presidency (Calcutta), Muir (Allahabad); M.A.O. (Aligarh)', in S.H. Rudolph and I.I. Rudolph (eds.), *Education and Politics in India: Studies in Organization, Society and Polity* (Delhi, 1972)

Gordon, R.A. 'The Hindu Mahasabha and the Indian National Congress 1915–1926', *MAS,* 9,2, 1975

——— 'Non-Cooperation and Council Entry 1919–1920', *MAS,* 7, 3, July 1973

Gupta, K.K.S. 'The Agrarian League of Pabna, 1873', *The Indian Economic and Social History Review,* 7, 1970

Hardgrave R.L. Jr. 'The Mapilla Rebellion, 1921: Peasant Revolt in Malabar,' *MAS,* 2, 1, 1977

Hasan, M. 'Mahatma Gandhi and the Indian Muslims', S.C. Biswas (ed.), *Gandhi Theory and Practice: Social Impact and Contemporary Relevance* (Shimla, 1969)

Hasan, Mushirul. 'The Communal Divide: A Study of the Delhi Proposals', in *Communal and Pan-Islamic Trends*

——— 'Nationalist and Separatist Trends in Aligarh, 1920–1947', in A.K. Gupta (ed.), *Myth and Reality: The Struggle for Freedom in India 1945–47* (Delhi, 1987)

——— 'Communal and Revivalist Trends in Congress', in *Communal and Pan-Islamic Trends*

——— 'Sectarianism in Indian Islam: The Shia-Sunni Divide in the United Provinces', *The Indian Economic and Social History Review,* 27, 2, 1990

——— 'Congress Muslims: Dilemma and Decline, 1928–1934', in Jim Masselos (ed.), *Struggling and Ruling: Indian National Congress 1885-1947* (Delhi, 1986)

———— 'The Muslim Mass Contacts Campaign: Analysis of a Strategy of Political Mobilization', in Richard Sisson and Stanley Wolpert (eds.) *Congress and Indian Nationalism: The Pre-Independence Phase* (University of California Press, 1988)

Jalal, A. and Seal, A. 'Alternative to Partition: Muslim Politics Between the Wars', *MAS*, 15, 3, 1981

Krishna, G. 'The Development of the Indian National Congress as a Mass Organization 1918–1923', *Journal of Asian Studies*, 25, 3, May 1966

Masselos, J. 'Change and Custom in the Format of the Bombay Muharram during the Nineteenth and Twentieth Centuries', *South Asia*, December 1982

Mujahid, Sharif Al. 'Jinnah and the Congress Party', in D.A. Low (ed.), *The Indian National Congress: Centenary Hindsights* (Delhi, 1988)

Owen, H.F. 'Negotiating the Lucknow Pact', *Journal of Asian Studies*, 31, 3, May 1972

Pandey, G. 'Rallying Round the Cow: Sectarian Strife in the Bhojpur Region c. 1888–1917,' in Ranajit Guha (ed.), *Subaltern Studies II: Writings on South Asian History and Society* (Delhi, 1983)

Qureshi, M.N. 'The Ulama of British India and the Hijrat', *MAS*, 13, i, 1979

Ray, R.K. 'Revolutionaries, Pan-Islamists and Bolsheviks: Maulana Abul Kalam Azad and the Political Underworld in Calcutta, 1905–1925', in *Communal and Pan-Islamic Trends*

———— 'Masses in Politics: The Non-Cooperation Movement in Bengal 1920–23', *The Indian Economic and Social History Review*, 11, December 1974

Roff, W.R. 'South-East Asian Islam in the Nineteenth Century', in P.M. Holt, Ann K.S. Lambton, Bernard Lewis (eds.), *Cambridge History of Islam*, vol. 2 (Cambridge, 1970)

Robinson, F. 'Islam and Muslim Separatism', in David Taylor and Malcolm Yapp (eds.), *Political Identity in South Asia* (London, 1979). Revised version in *Communal and Pan-Islamic Trends*

———— 'Islam and Muslim Society in South Asia', *Contributions to Indian Sociology*, 17, 2, 1983

———— 'Problems in the History of the Firangi Mahall: Family of Learned and Holy Men', in *Oxford University Papers on India*, vol 2 (Delhi, 1987)

———— 'Municipal Government and Muslim Separatism in the United Provinces 1883–1916', *MAS*, 7, 3, 1973

Sarkar, Tanika. 'Communal Riots in Bengal', in *Communal and Pan-Islamic Trends*

Stewart, C.C. 'Islam', in A.D. Roberts (ed.), *The Cambridge History of Africa* (Cambridge, 1986)

URDU BOOKS, ARTICLES AND PROSCRIBED LITERATURE [PP: IOLR]

Afghani, A. *Syed Jamaluddin Afghani* (Amritsar, 1940)
Ahmad, B. *Tark-i Mavalaat* (Deoband, 1920), PP. 53–54.
Ahmad, C.H. *Tehrik-i Pakistan aur Nationalist Ulama* (Lahore, 1966)
Ahmad, K. *Tazkirat-al ulama* (Calcutta, 1934)
Ahmad, M. *Dard-i Khilafat* (Aligarh, n.d.), PP. 142
Adalat Gaushala Parastaan (Jabalpur, 1922)
Al Akhaam al-Quraniya Mavalaat al-Burtaniya (Delhi, 1920)
Bulbulaan-i Hurriyat ke Taraane (Jaunpur, 1920), PP. 47
Butalawi, A.H. *Iqbal ke Aakhri do Saal* (Karachi, 1961)
Daryabadi, A.M. *Mohamed Ali: Diary ke Chand Auraaq* (Hyderabad, 1943)
Fazl-al Khitaab (Delhi. n.d.)
Fiil Badiya Khutba-i Sadarat (Lahore, n.d.)
Ghaffar, A. *Aasaar-i Jamaluddin* (Delhi, 1940)
——— *Hayaat-i Ajmal* (Aligarh, 1950)
Hasan, Maḥmud. *Tark-i Mavalaat* (Bijnor, 1919)
Inayatullah, M.M. *Masla-i Taleem aur Tark-i Mavalaat* (Aligarh, 1920)
Ikram, S.M. *Mauj-i Kausar* (Lahore, 1970)
——— *Ruud-i Kausar* (Karachi, 1958)
Ismail, S.M. (ed.), *Makaatib-i Hali* (Karachi, 1950)
Islam, M. *Taraana-i Khilafat* (Deoband, 1914), PP. 43
Jafri, R.A. *Auraaq-i Gumgushta* (Lahore, 1968)
Jamiyat-i Markazia Tanzim Ka Mujawaza Dastur-al'Amal (Amritsar, 1925)
Kashmiri, S. 'Zafar Ali Khan', *Nuqqush (Shakhsiaat Number)*, January 1955.
Khan, R.A. and Manzar, M. *Deoband aur Bareilly ikhtilaaf par nazaa aur faislakun Munaazara* (Sambhal, 1966)
Madani, H.A. *Naqsh-i Hayaat: Khudnawisht Sawanah* (Karachi, 1979 edn.)
Maqalaat-i Hali, vol. 1, (Delhi, 1934)
Mirza, J. *Hayaat-i Amir Shariat* (Lahore, 1970)
Miyan, M. *Ulama-i Haq aur unke Mujahidaana Kaarname* (Delhi, 1946)
Mohammad, M.W. *Islam ki Faryaad*, PP. 44 (Delhi, 1971)
Naqvi, M. A. *Wahiduddin Salim: Hayaat aur Adabi Khidmaat* (Aligarh, 1969).

Nomani, Shibli. *Makaatib-i Shibli* (Azamgarh, 1928)
——— *Maqalaat-i Shibli* (Azamgarh, 1938)
——— *Safarnama-i Rum wa Misr-o-Shaam* (Azamgarh, 1921)
Qadiri, B.A. *Ahl-i Hadith aur Angrez* (Karachi, 1967)
Qasuri, M.S. *Akaabir Tehrik-i Pakistan* (Lahore, 1979 edn.)
Rahman, M.A. *Maimaaraan-i Pakistan* (Lahore, 1976 edn.)
Razi, Maulana. *Mutahidda Qaumiyat aur Islam* (Lahore, 1967 edn.)
Rozeena, P. *Jamiyat al-ulama-i Hind: Dastaaveez Markazi Ijlaas, 1919–1945,* in two volumes (Islamabad, 1980)
Rudaad-i Nadwat al-ulama, 22–24 April 1984, vol. 1 (Kanpur, n.d.)
Shah, S.G. *Khoon-i Khirman aur sada-i intiqaam,* PP. 8.
Shahjahanpuri, A.S. *Allama Iqbal aur Maulana Mohamed Ali* (Karachi, 1984)
Siddiqi, A.H. *Congress i ulama ki siyasi karwaten* (Delhi, n.d.)
Usmani, S.A. *Tark-i Mavalaat par zabardast taqreer* (Delhi, 1339 A.H.)

Index

A Nationalist Conscience

M.A. ANSARI, THE CONGRESS AND THE RAJ

MUSHIRUL HASAN

To the memory of
my brother

NAJMUL HASAN

Thandi thi jis ki chaaon woh deewaar gir gaai

Contents

List of Tables

Foreword

It gives me great pleasure to say a few words about this scholarly work, entitled *A Nationalist Conscience: M.A. Ansari, the Congress and the Raj*, which Professor Mushirul Hasan has placed before the community of historians. Over the years, Mushir has earned for himself an enviable position among scholars through his writings on the role played by the Muslim community in the freedom struggle, and its relationship with the Indian National Congress, on the one hand, and with the Muslim League, which initiated the partition of the subcontinent in 1947, on the other. His scholarly writings are characterized by a liberal and secular vision, and behind his exploration lies a seminal question: Why did secular nationalism in India fail in creating a united nation, resting equally upon Hindu and Muslim participation, in 1947?

In the present volume, Mushir explores this theme through reflecting upon the political career of Mukhtar Ahmad Ansari, one of the most distinguished nationalist Muslims in the country. Ansari hailed from a section of the Muslim landed gentry in the United Provinces (as it was then known) which was turning increasingly to the liberal professions for sustenance, and which played a leading role in public life in the first half of the 20th century. In portraying Ansari's stance on the great issues of the times, Mushir illumines the history of an entire class; though it would be wrong to assume that all its members possessed the professional eminence or the flawless integrity of Mukhtar Ahmad. Be that as it may, this scholarly work looks upon the social underpinnings of political behaviour with sensitivity and skill, and in doing so, it throws a flood of illuminating light upon a seminal area of nationalist politics in the period under review.

Perhaps the first decade of the 20th century was a crucial period for men like Ansari as they struggled to define afresh the position of their community within the framework of political society in India. This position, it needs to be stressed, was radically different from that of the Hindu community. So far as the latter was concerned, powerful elites drawn from the landed classes, or from the commerical and professional bourgeoisie, had already organized themselves under the aegis of the Congress against British imperialism. But the Muslim community found itself in a quandary and the nationalist stance was no easy stance for a Muslim leader. Like the Hindus, nationalism came to the Muslim elites through a heightened consciousness of their religious identity. For this very reason, it was difficult for the Muslim leaders, or for the rank and file of the community, to relate their identity to the resurgence of nationalism; more particularly, because the victory of nationalism could possibly result in a political society in which the numerical strength of a community played a crucial part in determining its access to power. In other words, the triumph of nationalism in India could pave the way for a democratic polity in which the Hindus, through sheer weight of numbers, could dominate those who subscribed to other religious worldviews.

Ansari's entry into nationalist politics sensitively highlighted the dilemmas confronting Muslim leaders in the opening decades of the century. The strategy to which Syed Ahmad Khan and his followers had given currency earlier, namely, that it was inadvisable for the Muslims to associate themselves with the freedom struggle, had become somewhat discredited by this time. A new generation of Muslims—related as much to the land as to the liberal professions—were drawn increasingly to political action in the cause of nationalism. Behind this transformation lay a bitter realization of the humiliation which British imperialism had inflicted upon Islam within India as well as in the world community. The British assault upon the Turkish Empire in the 19th and 20th centuries triggered off a powerful wave of anti-imperialism among young Muslims of Ansari's generation, and the growth of this sentiment lay behind the medical delegation which he led to Turkey with the objective of expressing the solidarity of the Indian Muslims with the international community of Islam. On his return from Turkey, Ansari suddenly found himself in a position of prominence within his community, and the pan-Islamic sentiment which he spearheaded and reinforced became the basis of a radical transformation of Muslim opinion within India. This was reflected in a change in the constitution of the Muslim League just as it was also reflected in the creation of a united front with the Hindus in the struggle against British imperialism.

The metamorphosis of anti-imperialism and pan-Islamic values into a national consciousness was a complex process bedevilled by serious inconsistences and tensions. Mushir illumines this process with commendable skill through pursuing the career of Mukhtar Ahmad Ansari and other leaders like Maulanas Abul Kalam Azad and Abdul Bari, or the Brothers Shaukat and Mohamed Ali. Behind this transformation lay a crucial alliance between the Muslim professional classes and the landed gentry, on the one hand, and the clerical classes, led by the Deoband *ulama* and the religious leaders of Firangi Mahal, on the other. This alliance of nationalist Muslims and pan-Islamists in turn reached out to a wider leadership, prominent among them Mahatma Gandhi, in a bid to liberate India from British rule. Mushir portrays both the strengths and the weaknesses of such a nationalist consolidation which brought Hindus and Muslims together in a way they had never been united before. The popular character of non-cooperation during the years 1920-22 was largely the result of such a consummation. Yet from the very outset this alliance carried within itself the most serious contradictions. The sentiment of nationalism which non-cooperation conjured into existence among its supporters was a sentiment which drew heavily upon religion as a mediator between the citizen and the nation. Small wonder, then, that whatever be the short-term gains of such an alliance, in the long run it was designed to heighten the cohesiveness of religious communities at the cost of national solidarity. Indeed, the evidence which Mushir brings to light bears ample witness to the fragility of Hindu-Muslim unity which had been conjured into existence during the heyday of the non-cooperation movement. His perception of the reasons behind the breakdown of this alliance, more particularly, of the tensions which developed between the two communities in the course of the anti-imperialist struggle, is equally significant. Perhaps there was a fatal flaw here upon which we shall dwel. some more later.

Whatever be the reasons behind a growing religious cleavage in the 1920s, men like Ansari, who stood true to the cause of Hindu-Muslim unity, as they also stood true to the cause of nationalism, found themselves increasingly out of touch with the sentiments in the Muslim community. Indeed, the consequences of the political strategy adopted by Mahatma Gandhi during 1920–22 became manifest towards the end of the decade, when the nationalist leaders, young and old, radicals and conservatives, sought to bring different religious groups together in a movement which sought to achieve *purna swaraj*. The constitutional bargaining between Hindu and Muslim leaders, at this juncture, vividly reflects the extent to which communal and religious identities had hardened with the passage of time. Of course, the imperialist tactic of creating divisions among different classes and communities played a crucial role in all this; witness Birkenhead's taunt that the nationalist leaders were incapable of producing a constitution acceptable to everyone in the subcontinent. Nevertheless, it cannot be denied that the strategy of divide and rule was successful, to some extent, because of the religious cleavages within Indian society, which provided a backdrop to the confrontation between nationalism and imperialism. Ansari remained true to the vision of a united India, in which Hindus and Muslims would live as partners and equals, long after this ideal had been betrayed by men like the Ali Brothers, or Jinnah, who had entered politics as a staunch nationalist. Perhaps the stirring call which he gave for national unity, at the annual session of the Indian National Congress in 1927, over which he presided, provides a sensitive clue to the role which he sought to play at this juncture. Yet Ansari found himself utterly isolated at the fateful session of the Congress in Lahore, in December 1929, where a decision was taken to embark upon civil disobedience in order to achieve *purna swaraj*. As he pointed out to both the senior generation of leaders, represented by Mahatma Gandhi and Motilal Nehru, and the younger generation, represented by Jawaharlal Nehru and Subhas Chandra Bose, to embark upon a struggle against the British Government without ensuring unity between Hindus and Muslims was to take a step that could lead to the most fateful consequences. That Ansari's warning was prophetic is vindicated by subsequent events. Yet his tragedy lay in the lonesomeness of his position in 1930. As Mushir observes, even the staunch supporters of Ansari, like Mahatma Gandhi and Jawaharlal Nehru, turned a deaf ear to his warnings at this juncture. Yet there was a fearful price to pay for such indifference.

Although Ansari found himself isolated on the eve of the civil disobedience movement, this did not prevent him from attempting to put across the secular viewpoint to his co-religionists shortly afterwards. The All-India Nationalist Muslim Party, which he created in 1929 was his last and potentially most significant contribution to politics. Here was a heroic attempt to mobilize all Muslims, rich or poor, landlords or peasants, merchants or professionals, the *ulama* or the artisanate, on a common nationalist platform. Mushir pursues the fate of this gallant effort by Ansari in considerable detail. His assessment of the strengths and weaknesses of Ansari's leadership, who despite high-mindedness and sterling integrity was unable to reach out to the Muslim masses or provide them with a vision of the 'good society' with which they could identify, constitutes the finest section of this scholarly book and holds out a perceptive account of Muslim politics. It is difficult to fault Mushir's conclusion that Ansari fell between two stools; on the one hand, the indifference of the Muslim leaders and their followers to the nationalist position; and on the other, the pressures which even secular Hindu politicians experienced from their co-religionists. If Mushir's account of nationalist politics in the 1930s adds up to a depressing story, we have only to turn to communalism, as a divisive factor (and worse) within Indian politcs, in our own times, to realize the validity of his perception.

What then (we may finally ask ourselves) was the solution to the communal problem in the 1930s? Or, for that matter, how can it be resolved in our own times? These are questions with which we may have to wrestle for quite some time in the future. Perhaps the solution to the communal problem lies in a total refusal to be drawn into any political dialogue along religious lines. This is not to deny the existence of a religious sensibility among different classes or communities; historically or contemporaneously. This is merely to argue that the only way of handling communalism is to banish it altogether from the domain of politics. The creation of a secular society is an ideal to which responsible Indians are as firmly committed today as they were during the course of the freedom struggle. Furthermore, it is obvious that secularism in India cannot replicate secularism in western societies, where this term implies the displacement of the religious sensibility from the psyche of the citizen. Nevertheless, it is possible to work for a secular order in which religion is absent from the public domain, although it may exercise a powerful influence in the private domain. The creation of such a secular society calls for a vigorous effort by all concerned to devise a language of politics wherein religion occupies no place at all. No such solution to the communal problem was even attempted in the decades reviewed by Mushir in this scholarly work. Yet a refusal to be marginalized by the idiom of religious politics offers the only way out of a dilemma which has haunted India for a century and more. Indeed, this dilemma shall continue to bedevil politics in the subcontinent unless the people of India launch a bold assault upon the virus of communalism in the body politic.

Professor Ravinder Kumar
Director, Nehru Memorial Museum and Library,
New Delhi

Preface

This book embodies elements of research and study done over more than a decade, beginning with my Ph.D. dissertation submitted at the University of Cambridge in 1977 and continuing until today. Following the publication of my book *Nationalism and Communal Politics in India, 1916–1928* I chose to take a closer look at some of the chief exponents of these tendencies among Indian Muslims. In 1981 I wrote a monograph on Mohamed Ali's ideology and politics. This was followed by the publication of his correspondence and speeches. Three of the proposed six volumes have appeared in print.

The present work is part of the same endeavour—an exploration into the many facets of the nationalist struggle and an examination of the ideas and movements which concerned certain influential groups among Muslims. I have chosen Mukhtar Ahmad Ansari because he symbolized and represented a powerful nationalist strand during the epic struggles of the 1920s and the 1930s.

During the course of researching and writing this book I have incurred innumerable debts of gratitude. I am indebted, first and foremost, to the family and relatives of the man who forms the subject of this study: to Begum Zohra Ansari and Professor Azhar Ansari.

I have used a great number of libraries and archives in India, Pakistan and the United Kingdom. Without exception their librarians and archivists have been unfailingly helpful. Of the many people in Pakistan who have helped make my stay there a pleasure, I must mention at least two: Khalid Shamsul Hasan and Sharif al-Mujahid. The staff of the Nehru Memorial Museum and Library in Delhi rendered all possible assistance to me. I am grateful, in particular, to Hari Dev Sharma, A.K. Awasthi, S.K. Bhatnagar, N.C. Mahajan, Umesh C. Mandal and Deepak Vashisht.

I owe a considerable debt to the Governing Council of the Nehru Memorial Museum and Library which offered me a Professorial Fellowship for three years during which most of this book was written. My greatest debt is to Ravinder Kumar who read the whole text with care, offered suggestions for improvements, and agreed to write a thoughtful foreword to this book. His insights have done much to help my understanding of Indian nationalism and the communal question, though he cannot, of course, be held responsible for anything I have written here.

A special debt of gratitude is owed to a number of persons who read chapters in the state of their first creation. I am especially indebted to: S. Gopal, Azhar Ansari, Francis Robinson, V.C. Bhutani, Hari Dev Sharma, Muzaffar Alam and Shahid Amin. Zoya offered invaluable suggestions on style and content and provided much support to my modest scholarly endeavours. My father, Professor Mohibbul Hasan, has always been a source of inspiration to me. His thorough and insightful scholarship, combined with his professional integrity, has long set me a worthy standard.

Many other people have assisted by passing on references and other helpful information, provided hospitality during the course of my research, or taken time off their own work to seek out material for me. I would particularly like to thank the following: Khalid Shamsul Hasan, Arif Husain, Praveen Saberwal, Rewa Pathak and Abu Salman Shahjahanpuri.

A suitable title eluded everyone—except my friend Simon Commander, who came up with a balanced title/sub-title. I also enjoyed his hospitality during my stay in London.

The Indian Council of Historical Research offered me a modest study grant. Dr T.R. Sareen and S.M. Mishra were kind enough to have it sanctioned.

By an unwritten convention authors seldom venture to thank their publishers. I wish to depart from this custom by recording here my sincere appreciation of Ramesh C. Jain. His professional skill and integrity has won him many friends. I am privileged to be one of them.

I hope Barbara, Shaaz and Shehzad would derive some comfort from the fact that this book is dedicated to the loving memory of

Sonny (Najmul Hasan) who is, alas, no more. His memory will always remain part of us. My feelings as a younger brother are summed up by Faiz Ahmad Faiz:

Mujh ko shikwa hai mere Bhai ki tum jaate hue
Legaye saath meri umr-i guzashta ki kitaab
Is men to meri bahut qeemti tasweeren theen
Is men bachpan tha mera aur mera ahd-i shabaab
Is ke badle mujhe tum degaye jaate jaate
Apne gham ka yeh damakta hua khoon-rang gulaab
Aake le jaao tum apna yeh damakta hua phool
Mujh ko lauta do meri umr-i guzashta ki kitaab

Jamia Millia Islamia M.H.
October 1986

Introduction

On 14 May 1936 Asaf Ali suggested to Gandhi that an appropriate memorial be raised in memory of Mukhtar Ahmad Ansari who dedicated his life to the cause of the Indian nationalist movement. His idea was to associate Ansari's name with rural medical aid all over India in the form of 'Ansari Medical Corps' or 'Ansari Travelling Dispensary'.[1] But neither then nor later did such suggestions receive consideration.[2] The 'Ansari Road' in Delhi is the only reminder of Ansari's long-standing association with the city as a physician-surgeon, political activist and educationist. Close to it is the now dilapidated house of Ansari—*Dar-us-Salam*—once the venue of Congress meetings and the focal point of much political activity in the capital of British India.[3] But not many in the neighbourhood are familiar with its significance or have heard of its previous occupant.

Sometime in 1934-35, Mohammad Mujeeb, then a teacher at the Jamia Millia Islamia, undertook to write Ansari's biography with the aid of a rich collection of papers which included letters, press clippings, pamphlets and books.[4] But the biography was never written.[5] The papers were promptly transferred to a basement in the Jamia Library, and were retrieved in the early

[1]Asaf Ali to Gandhi, 14 May 1936, F. No. G-21, 1936, All India Congress Committee Papers [AICC], Nehru Memorial Museum and Library [NMML].

[2]It was sold in 1946 by Shaukatullah Ansari and is now owned by a Jain trust. Zohra Ansari, Oral History Transcript, NMML.

[3]'I remember, of course, that nothing of the kind (Memorial Fund) has yet been done about Hakim Saheb, my father and Ansari. It is not for me to move in this matter and I suppose it is rather late now to take any step.' Jawaharlal Nehru to M.K. Gandhi, 9 February 1947, S. Gopal (ed.), *Selected Works of Jawaharlal Nehru* [SWJ], second series, Vol. 3 (Delhi, 1985), pp. 496-7.

[4]Ansari transferred a large collection of his books, journals and magazines to the Jamia Millia Islamia. I have come across a list of 534 books which were donated by Begum Ansari in memory of her husband. But the Jamia Library has not preserved this collection.

[5]Mujeeb noted in his preliminary draft of Ansari's unfinished biography that he was 'quite lost' because Ansari had little time to spare for interviews. He wrote a small section of chapter one—'The Lights and Shades'—but was unable to complete it. Draft, Mujeeb Collection, Dr. Zakir Husain Library, Jamia Millia Islamia [JMI].

1960s. In the meantime, part of the collection, especially Ansari's correspondence from 1912 to 1925, was destroyed. Today, little is known of Ansari in the Jamia—an institution he nursed from the time of its inception in October 1920. A 'Health Centre' housed in three small rooms, is Jamia's modest tribute to its founder and *Amir-i Jamia* (Chancellor).

Ironically, some historians in England, America and Australia have taken adequate notice of Ansari's involvement in political agitations, his commitment to the cause of inter-communal unity, his efforts in drawing Muslims into the freedom struggle, and his effective role as a mediator between his community and the Congress movement. Judith M. Brown, D.W. Ferrel, Francis Robinson, Gail Minault, David Page and B.R. Tomlinson have shed light on these facets of his personality within the context of political processes in the larger national arena.

Historians in the subcontinent, however, have ignored Ansari's active political life which spanned over two decades of a tumultuous phase in India's struggle for liberation from colonial domination.[6] It is easy to explain this omission in Pakistan, where scholars are hard-pressed to discern a separatist strain in Ansari's political concerns which were steeped in the essentially secular, democratic ethos of the nationalist struggle. As one wedded to the Congress ideals in the tradition of many of his predecessors and contemporaries—Badruddin Tyabji, R.M. Sayani, Hasrat Mohani, the Raja of Mahmudabad, Mazharul Haq, Umar Subhani, Saifuddin Kitchlew, Abul Kalam Azad, Hakim Ajmal Khan, Ali Imam, Professor Abdul Bari, Rafi Ahmad Kidwai, Abdul Majid Khwaja, Mujibur Rahman, Khan Abdul Ghaffar Khan, Syed Mahmud, Asaf Ali and Tassaduq Ahmad Khan Sherwani—he would have poured scorn on the idea of a separate Pakistan as unequivocally as he opposed the potentially divisive tendencies during his lifetime. The two-nation theory would have been as much an anathema to him as was the notion of granting separate electorates and communal representation to the Muslims. He envisaged a democratic, secular and federal polity for the future independent

[6]The omission is surprising in the accounts of those writers who were associated with Ansari and followed his activities closely. See, for example, Mohammad Mujeeb, *The Indian Muslims* (London, 1967) which has no reference to Ansari; also, Abid Husain, *The Destiny of the Indian Muslims* (Delhi, 1970); Swaliha Abid Husain, *Jaane Waalon Ki Yaad Aati Rahi* (Delhi, 1974); K.G. Saiyidan, *Andhi me Chiragh* (Delhi, 1962); Imdad Sabri, *Dehli ki Yaadgar Hastiyaan* (Delhi, 1972).

India and his vision in this respect was similar to that of Gandhi and his political heir, Jawaharlal Nehru. He was neither a theorist nor a creative thinker, but he certainly had a vision of a just society, a civilized and harmonious whole, a society in which there would be no friction on account of caste, regional, linguistic and religious diversities.[7] 'I consider the brotherhood of man as the only tie,' he declared, 'and partition based on race or religion are, to my mind, artificial and arbitrary.'

Ansari is not the only leader to escape attention in India. After independence, there has been a stream of biographical literature on Gandhi and Jawaharlal who played so central a part in the shaping of modern India. Scholarly interest has also extended to such other leaders who possessed a distinct cultural, religious, or regional identity and have therefore inspired the particularist tendencies of certain castes, communities and regions. This is true of C.R. Das and S.C. Bose in Bengal, C. Rajagopalachari in Tamilnad, Madan Mohan Malaviya in UP and Lala Lajpat Rai in the Punjab—all identified with a particular region where they are eulogized and placed in the category of 'heroes'. Other leaders bearing no specific affinity to a region or a religious group have not received much notice. Ansari is among them. Cut off from his home state—UP—he chose to live in Delhi in a composite cultural environment and followed a political course which did not reflect the interests and aspirations of any particular region or community. In consequence, his role is not only obscure but he also appears much less charismatic and influential than many of his contemporaries like Mohamed Ali. In contrast with Ansari, the popular hero of the Khilafat days is *en rapport* with many Muslims in India and Pakistan today; they see in him a vocal champion of certain causes which were dear to the community then and are no less important now.

Another reason for ignoring the Congress Muslims must be located in the popular perception of their supposed failure to counter the two-nation theory, their inability to present a viable enough alternative to the Muslim League and to rally their community around the Congress banner. 'The collapse and elimination of the Nationalist Muslims as a group,' wrote Jawaharlal,

[7]See, for instance, his presidential address at the All-Karnatak Hindi Prachar Sabha held at Mysore in 1929 and his address at the Bengal Nationalist Muslims Conference held at Faridpur in July 1931.

'forms a pitiful story.'[8] Even if we accept this judgement, a historian is still called upon to analyse the *process* through which the Congress Muslims were marginalized and the *reasons* why they ceased to be an effective force in Indian politics. To uncover this aspect is an important enough subject for investigation, for 'success' stories alone do not form the core of a historian's concern. As an important component of the nationalist stream and as representative of a particular ideological strand, the emergence of the Congress Muslim group and their subsequent 'decline' and 'disintegration' deserves critical appraisal in order to understand certain vital dimensions of the nationalist and separatist political processes.

The present work is an attempt to focus on the political career of one such person—Ansari—who put forward the point of view of the Congress Muslims with clarity, consistency and conviction and furthered an ideological position which he and his band of followers adhered to with remarkable tenacity. He succeeded—where others failed—in reconciling his community's concerns with what he perceived as the nation's interests and remained true to all that Indian nationalism stood for. Above all, he articulated a line of action which inspired many of his comrades to stay clear of communal proclivities and left behind a legacy and a tradition which was pursued relentlessly by many of those associated with the All-India Nationalist Muslim Party, an organization he founded in July 1929. One of the purposes of this book is to uncover this essential but neglected aspect of India's nationalist history.

It is indeed tempting to exaggerate the importance of such a leader and to extol his virtues. This study, however, is not meant to serve that purpose. The aim throughout has been to reveal Ansari as what he undoubtedly was—one of the most important figures in Indian politics—to delineate his principal political interests, to explore his ideological predilections and to draw a portrait that captures his flaws as well as his strong points, his failures as well as his successes. Wherever possible, the endeavour has been to analyse his responses and attitudes in the larger historical context provided by colonial rule in India. Various influences on the style and content of his politics have been alluded to, if not always given their full historical weight.

[8]Jawaharlal Nehru, *An Autobiography: With musings on Recent Events in India* (London, 1936), p. 139.

This is not all. An attempt is also made, with the aid of much fresh literature, to examine political developments from 1912 to 1936—the years covered in some detail in this study—, to look afresh at the nature and character of the pan-Islamic movement in India and to review some of the existing notions on what is usually described as the communal question. In so doing, I hope not only to throw light on certain important and unstudied dimensions of modern Indian history, but also to suggest that the role of the Congress Muslims in general provides a useful entree for understanding many facets of nationalism and communalism in India.

1

Ghazipur to Delhi

FOUNDED IN AD 1330, Ghazipur gained much importance in the sixteenth century as a seat of government and as capital of a *sarkar* in the *suba* of Allahabad. In December 1763, the East India Company acquired control of Ghazipur with the collector of Banaras as its administrator. This arrangement continued until 1818 when Ghazipur was constituted as a district.

In the revolt of 1857 Ghazipur figured prominently when the bulk of the people, led by some zamindars who were aggrieved at their ejection by auction-purchasers, joined in the massive upsurge and pillaged government offices and treasury. Reported an official: 'On all sides of the District, itself always most troublesome, were disturbances real or reported.'[1] In Zamaniah, one of the four *tahsils*, 'every building belonging to Government or Europeans was plundered and burnt'. HR Nevill's account reveals the distinct popular character of the revolt. It also highlights the repressive measures adopted by government to quell the disturbances.[2]

Muslims of Ghazipur figured prominently in the revolt. It was strange that this was so, for they formed just over 9 per cent of the population and were unevenly distributed in four *tahsils* (Table I:1)—Ghazipur; Zamaniah, which derives its name from Ali Quli Khan, Khan Zaman, who expelled the Afghans from Ghazipur in 1560 and was governor of Jaunpur in the reign of Akbar (1556-1605); Muhammadabad, an old Muslim settlement dating from the days of the Lodi Sultans (1451-1526),

[1] *Narrative of Events and the Restoration of Authority in the Division of Benares in 1857-1858*, UP State Archives (UPSA), Lucknow, Box No. 1.

[2] H.R. Nevill, *Ghazipur: A Gazetteer*, Vol. XXIX (Allahabad, 1909), pp. 171-4.

[3] Passing through Ghazipur on 31 August 1824, Bishop Heber observed: 'The population is great, and the mosques, and Mussulmans in the shops and streets are so numerous, and there are so few pagodas of any importance visible, that I thought I had bidden adieu for the present to the followers of Brahma.

TABLE 1.1

POPULATION BY TAHSIL 1911

Tahsil	*Total*	*Hindus*	*Muslims*	*Others*
Ghazipur	246,861	226,539	20,052	260
Muhammadabad	197,428	177,474	19,716	238
Zamaniah	216,756	191,665	24,945	146
Saidpur	178,690	166,757	11,842	85

SOURCE: *Ghazipur Supplementary notes and statistics to vol. xxxix of the District Gazetteer of the UP of Agra and Oudh* (Allahabad, 1915), appendix i.

and Saidpur.[4] Most Muslims in these areas were *Julahas* or weavers, supporting themselves by weaving either in their own villages or in the mills of Calcutta, Kanpur and Bombay where they went to work for short periods. The *District Gazetteer* described them as 'the most bigoted of all Mussalmans' and as 'a turbulent and lawless race',[5] an assessment formed in the aftermath of the 1857 revolt and quite obviously influenced by their active participation in the revolt.

The Syeds were small in number and relatively uninfluential in the district. The Sheikhs, on the other hand, formed 15.8 per cent of the Muslim population. They claimed to be the descendants of the companions of the Prophet Mohammad (570-632), distinguishing themselves from one another by adding prefixes such as Ansari, Siddiqui and Qureshi. They were followed by the Pathans who traced their origin to Afghan settlers of the days of Aurangzeb (1658-1707), when a powerful colony established itself in Mahaich and another occupied the *tahsil* of Zamaniah.[6]

Mr Melville, however assured me, to my surprise, that it was in the large towns only that the Mussulmans were numerous, and that, taking the whole province together, they were barely an eleventh part of the population, among the remainder of whom Hindooism existed in all its strength and bigotry.' M.A. Laird (ed.), *Bishop Heber in Northern India. Selection from Heber's Journal* (Cambridge, 1971), p. 126.

[4]According to the 1911 Census the Hindus constituted 90.7 per cent of the population and the Muslims 9.11 per cent. 'This is the smallest proportion of Musalmans on record, and is partly accounted for by their greater susceptibility to plague, partly perhaps by the fact that, the Ghazipur Muslims are mainly in poor circumstances. It has never been the experience of this district that Muslims increase more rapidly than Hindus.' *Ghazipur. Supplementary notes and statistics to volume xxxix of the District Gazetteer of the United Provinces of Agra and Oudh* (Allahabad, 1915), appendix i.

[5]*Ghazipur. A Gazetteer*, p. 90.

[6]Ibid., p. 91.

Most Pathans were engaged either in trade or in service, though some had small landholdings as well.

Muslims in Ghazipur owned 148,610 acres, or 17 per cent of the land, a remarkably large proportion for a district containing a comparatively small Muslim population. The principal land-owning families were the Syeds of Nonahra who traced their ancestry to Syed Masud Ghazi, the reputed founder of Ghazipur; the Siddiqui Sheikhs of Pahatia and the Usmani Sheikhs of Salempur, whose estate paid Rs 3,868 as land revenue.

A family of great eminence in Ghazipur district was that of the Ansaris, but they preferred not to use the prefix in order to distinguish themselves from the *Julahas* who also claimed to be the descendants of those *Ansars* (aiders) of Medina who rendered assistance to Prophet Mohammad when he migrated (*hijrat*) from Mecca. The Ansaris, in general, traced their descent from Abu Ayyub Ansari (d. 672), a close companion of the Prophet, his host at Medina, a warrior and a venturous conqueror who, when fighting across the Bosphorus at the age of ninety or more, was killed and had requested to be buried in Constantinople. Direct descent was through the three sons of Khwaja Hamiduddin who came from Arabia in the fourteenth century and settled in Shiraz from where his sons migrated to Delhi. One of them was appointed *Qazi* by Muhammad bin Tughlaq (1325-51) and was succeeded by his nephew who founded Yusufpur.[7] The office of *Qazi* continued to be held by members of the family even after the British acquired control of the area and introduced basic changes in the judicial structure which, as in the case of Bengal, displaced many Muslims from the judicial department and added to their impoverishment. Some members of the Ansari family were also employed in government service which enabled them to purchase property in and around Ghazipur. There were others who either acquired land by purchasing the estates of the old families brought to ruin by the mismanagement or by the unsympathetic revenue administration, or retained their ancestral lands, as in the case of Bhitri which was given to the Ansaris by the Mughal emperor, Akbar. The *District Gazetter* noted: 'There are numerous members of the family and they hold a fair amount of land in the neighbourhood, including Yusufpur itself, which is 327 acres in extent and is assessed at Rs 712, the tenure being *bighadam*.'

[7] *Ghazipur: A Gazetteer*, p. 99

With Mukhtar Ahmad [hereafter referred to as Ansari], the youngest of the four sons of Haji Abdul Rahman, the Ansaris came into prominence: they emerged from the position of an old Ghazipur family into national eminence. From the early 1920s, some of his close relatives—Aziz Ansari (1889-1985), Faridul Haq Ansari (1895-1966) and Shaukatullah Ansari (1908-1972)—played an important part in political affairs. None succeeded in scaling the heights achieved by their political mentor, but they consistently championed his secular ideals and remained loyal to the nationalist movement. Aziz joined the Indian Medical Mission to Constantinople and went to jail during both the non-cooperation and the civil disobedience agitations: Farid was member of the All-India Congress Committee (AICC) from 1927 to 1948, secretary of the Delhi Pradesh Congress Committee in 1929-30 and one of the founders of the Congress Socialist Party; Shaukatullah, a nephew of Ansari and married to his adopted daughter, Zohra (b. 1913), floated various organizations, especially in the mid-1940s, in support of the Congress. Notable amongst them were the Azad Muslim Board and the All-India Muslim Majlis. In 1940 he was elected general secretary of the All-India Azad Muslim Conference and in 1944 he published a powerful indictment of the two-nation theory. Partition, he concluded, 'would throw back India back to something like the state she was in after the Mogul Empire had collapsed and before the British Raj replaced it. For, once the frame of unity was broken, once the process of disruption had begun, it would not be likely to stop at the separation of a Moslem State or States from Hindu India.'[8]

Born on 25 December 1880 in Yusufpur, Ansari had a quiet but deep pride in his ancestry, and it pleased him to think that his roots lay deep in the soil of Arabia and that he belonged to a distinguished family with branches in different parts of the country. Mohammad Mujeeb (1902-1985), then a teacher at the Jamia Millia Islamia in Delhi, records an interview in which he quotes Ansari as saying: 'My family originates from the Ansari. But then he stopped, then laughed. Why should one imagine that Ansaris are particularly few. There are as many as have been destined to be.'[9]

[8]Shaukatullah Ansari, *Pakistan The Problem of India* (Lahore, 1944), p. 103.

[9]Draft note, Mujeeb Collection, JMI; M. Mujeeb, 'Dr Ansari: Chand Yaaden baaten', *Aaj Kal* (Delhi), Ansari Number, January 1981, pp. 12-13.

The Ansaris enjoyed considerable respect in their area but they were not men of wealth or influence as their fortunes were substantially reduced in the second half of the nineteenth century. They held on to their small landholdings but were unable to make much out of them. Forced by circumstances they took to government service, a distasteful choice for those who were not yet reconciled to the reality of British rule in India.

Ansari's father—Abdul Rahman—was an *Amin* at Rasara in Ballia district. His fame in the region rested on the loyal service he rendered to the British in the 1857 revolt for which he received a small estate near Yusufpur, was granted exemption from the Arms Act and eventually prospered in a modest way.[10] He was not the only one to do so. Kadir Baksh, who made a fortune as a contractor to the commissariat department, was another well-known loyalist in Ghazipur. He was rewarded with a land grant in Jamaluddinpur in Jaunpur district.

Rahman, a devout Muslim who went on the arduous pilgrimage (*Haj*) to Mecca, did not leave behind any great fortune for his sons to inherit, a fact which explains why soon after his death in 1902 the male members of the family moved out of Ghazipur in search of a career. But he took a close and guiding interest in his sons' education. This was a great asset. Few middle class families, particularly in eastern UP, paid as much attention to the education of their children as Rahman did.

Abdul Wahhab (d. 1946), the eldest son, was educated in the Islamic branches of learning, specializing in the *Yunani* system of medicine at the renowned Tibbia school in Delhi, run by *Haziq-ul Mulk* Hakim Abdul Majid Khan (d. 1901). He also went to the *Dar al-ulum* at Deoband, the famous religious seminary born in the throes of the 1857 revolt and was a *murid* of its founder, Rashid Ahmad Gangohi (1828-1905). In his days, his intellect was feared, his character praised and his almost legendary reputation as Hakim *Nabina* (for he was blind) spread to different parts of the country. He practised in Hyderabad, Poona, Bombay and Delhi. where Khwaja Hasan Nizami

[10]Rahman was the son of Sheikh Mohammad Baksh who had two other sons—Mohammad Sadiq and Abdul Ghaffar. Sadiq (d. 1907/8) became an inspector of police in the Punjab. One of his daughters was married to Ansari's brother Abdur Razzaq; the other to Maulvi Mohammad Talib of Ghazipur. Statement of Abdur Razzaq Ansari, J.C. Curry Papers, Centre of South Asian Studies, Cambridge. All subsequent references to Razzaq are drawn from the same statement.

(1878-1957) called him *Lukman-ul Mulk.*[11] Mujeeb went to his house on the western side of the historic Juma Masjid area and found that he had 'an old, established system of preparing medicaments for the needs of the poor as well as the rich'.

Abdur Razzaq (1868-1930) was also a renowned Hakim, though he never attained the reputation of his elder brother. He spent many years in the Nizam's court at Hyderabad and was primarily responsible for drawing several members of his family to the Deccan. 'We soon began to practice apart,' stated Razzaq, 'and lived in separate houses. We both had considerable success there and got large fees.' Although both the brothers invited the wrath of the Nizam for their part in the perpetual court intrigues and were consequently exiled from Hyderabad, they left an indelible mark on the city's social and cultural life. Decades after their forced exile, their family members continued to enjoy the patronage of several nobles who cherished their association with the two eminent hakims.

Apart from their common professional interests, Wahhab and Razzaq were equal in their devotion to the *ulama* of Deoband. Wahhab was a *murid* of Rashid Ahmad Gangohi; Razzaq of Mahmud Hasan (1851-1920), principal of the *Dar al-ulum.* Razzaq described his own initiation:

> I had great respect for the Maulana and had determined to become his *murid*; so I went to Deoband and told him that both I and my mother wished to become his *murids*, but my mother was too old to travel. After some persuasion the Maulana agreed to break his usual rule and came to Delhi where my mother and I both became his *murids.* Dr Ansari became his *murid* at the same time.

These family connections with Muslim divines proved advantageous when they were pressed into service to provide depth to the massive Khilafat agitation in India. Razzaq, influenced by Mahmud Hasan, was drawn into the 'Silk Letter Conspiracy'. Ansari, also a *murid* of the renowned Deoband *alim* and of Hafiz Muhammad Ali of Gorakhpur, acted as an effective link between the *ulama* and the western-educated Muslims and greatly helped to strengthen their alliance in 1919-1922.[12] His

[11] Zia Ahmad Barni, *Azmat-i Rafta* (Karachi, 1961), p. 263.

[12] Ansari kept the *Shaikh-ul-Hind* informed of the government moves against him and his movement, and paid for his travel expenses to the Hejaz. Both he and his brother, Razzaq, provided funds to support his activities. H.A. Madani.

wife, on the other hand, was a *murid* of Hafiz Ahmad Khan, *Mohtasim* of Deoband, and corresponded with him to secure the release of Mahmud Hasan, interned in Malta for his part in the 'Silk Letter Conspiracy'.[13] When Ansari went to Edinburgh for higher studies, he took with him two firmly established family traditions: a vocational commitment to medicine and a religious commitment to the *ulama* of Deoband.

In spite of their brief forays into the political arena, Wahhab and Razzaq lived in a world divorced from politics. Both were deeply steeped in the Islamic heritage, frequenting *dargahs* of *pirs* and *madrasas* of many a well-known *alim* to seek enlightenment, spiritual solace and guidance. Next to this, *hikmat* remained their main concern. Their astonishing success in the practice of *Yunani tibb* was matched only by the almost legendary popularity of Hakim Ajmal Khan (1863-1927), whose house and hospital were filled day by day with the sick and dying and who would minister to them, taking no fees from the poor of Delhi.[14] Exceedingly generous, they earned vast sums of money and spent most of it on their family. Abdur Razzaq supported Ansari and his cousin Mohammad Asghar while they were in London, and later helped his brother in setting up his practice in Delhi. 'I had to set him [Ansari] up in Delhi and sent him several thousand rupees for this, but he soon started well and I had no more need to send him money.' He was able to do so because of the patronage extended by wealthy rajas and nawabs who almost of necessity maintained a retinue of hakims along with poets, writers and dancers. The extent to which such patronage proved rewarding is evident from the fact that Ajmal Khan, according to one of his biographers, had a yearly income of Rs 50,000.[15] It was considerably reduced in later years because of his preoccupation with politics and because some of his clients among the rajas and nawabs were wary of being treated by a political activist with avowedly anti-government views.

The younger brothers—Mohammad Raza (d. 1935)[16] and

Naqsh-i Hayat: Khudnawisht Sawaanah (Karachi, 1979 edn.), p. 620.

[13]'Tehrik-i Azadi ka ek Khamosh Kaarkun: Abdul Ali Khan ke khudnawisht halaat-i zindagi', *Jung* (Rawalpindi), 9 June 1964.

[14]C.F. Andrews, *Zakaullah of Delhi* (Cambridge, n.d.), p. xxiii.

[15]Rasheed Ahmad Khan, *Hayat-i Ajmal* (Delhi, 1931), p. 130.

[16]On his death, Ansari wrote: 'My brother was a brother as well as a friend and his parting has been a great wrench. He was the most popular, the most respected and the most beloved state official in Hyderabad. His was a model

Ansari—were cast in a different mould. This had much to do with their education in schools and colleges organized on Western lines, a fact which helped them to pursue careers different from their relations. While many students of their background preferred the Aligarh College, Rahman did not disdain to send his sons to the Muir Central College at Allahabad, established in 1872 by private subscription of wealthy landowners, bankers and pleaders of the city. Here Ansari studied English, Mathematics, Deductive Logic, Trignometry and Geometrical and Conic Sections, Elementary Physics and Chemistry. The education imparted at the college was valuable. In fact it was this early association with Hindus and the composite environment of life in Allahabad that shaped Ansari's attitude to Hindus in particular and the communal problem in general. Wazir Hasan (1874-1947), who attended the same college and rose to become an important figure in both the Congress and the Muslim League organizations, observed that Western education helped to promote greater understanding among the Hindus and Muslims of each other's problem, enabled them to recognize their common destiny above the 'existence of separate entities and the din of communal claims', and 'form conceptions of a broader obligation and wider responsibilities to their country as a whole'.[18] Likewise, Henry Cotton attributed Hindu-Muslim cooperation on political questions to a common educational background. 'Unity of ideas,' he wrote in July 1914, 'is due to uniformity of training, and the ideal which was present in Sir Syed's mind when he founded Aligarh College—but then was incapable of realization—is at last attained. Mutual trust, a desire for the achievement of common ends and objects, nationalism and self-government—these are the inspiration of the rising generation not less of Mohammedans than of Hindus.'[19]

life of service and dedication to the people in his charge. When he retired from service last year some ten or 15 thousand people gathered to bid him farewell and the poor and suffering people of Aurangabad raised a tearful wail when he left them. He was a truly pious and truly generous hearted man. He was equally respected by his colleagues and his superiors. In him, as I have said before, I lose a brother, a comrade and a true friend. I feel lonely and lost without him.' Ansari to S.A. Brelvi, 13 May 1935, Brelvi Papers, NMML.

[†] For the early history of the college, see Irene A. Gilbert, 'Autonomy and Consensus under the Raj: Presidency (Calcutta); Muir (Allahabad); M.A.O. (Aligarh)', S.H. Rudolph and L.I. Rudolph (eds.), *Education and Politics in India: Studies in Organization, Society, and Policy* (Delhi, 1972), pp. 178-82.

[18] *India*, 17 October 1913.

[19] 'India: Old and New', *Asiatic Review*, July 1914.

The choice of the college was dictated in part because it was one of the premier educational institutions in northern India and in part because the mother who doted upon Ansari wanted him to remain close to the family in Ghazipur. For the same reason, when Razzaq decided to move with his mother to Hyderabad in 1898, Ansari had no choice but to accompany them. There is little doubt that during his childhood and early youth he was the focus of a comfortable and loving family. In the future, the quiet solidity of the family home was to provide a necessary haven to which he could retreat from the rigours of an unexpectedly hectic political life.

Ansari passed his intermediate examination from the Muir College in 1896.[20] He then went up to Nizam College, an institution aided by its founder-patron, the Nizam. Soon after, he was married to Shamsunnisa (d. 1938). She was a pliant wife and a good housekeeper. Visitors to Ansari's household, as Halide Edib (1884-1964), the Turkish author, remembered her as 'very pious, very charitable.'[21] What is perhaps not known is that the Begum did much public work, was associated with the *Anjuman-i-Khuddam-i Kaaba*, leading the appeal for moral and financial support along with the mother of the Ali Brothers and the wife of Mohamed Ali (1878-1931), headed the Delhi branch of the Women's Khilafat Committee[22] and attended Congress sessions regularly; the only one she missed was the one at Belgaum (1925) owing to a motor accident. Confined as she was to the domestic role expected of a woman of her time and station, Shamsunnisa found an outlet for her interests and energy in the political career of her husband.

Ansari graduated from the Nizam College in 1900. He did not do well in his examinations but impressed his teachers with his diligence and earnestness.[23] His potential was recognized and, in 1899, he received the state scholarship to study medicine in Great Britain. This was a dream come true, for men of Ansari's background yearned for an opportunity to obtain a degree from

[20] *University of Allahabad Calendar 1896-97* (Allahabad, 1896), p. 547; *University of Madras: The Calendar for 1917* (Madras, 1917), Vols. 1-2, p. 372.

[21] Halide Edib, *Inside India* (London, 1936), p. 31; Zohra Ansari, 'Shamsunnisa awr Dr Ansari', *Aaj Kal*, January 1981, p. 14.

[22] Gail Minault, *The Khilafat Movement: Religious Symbolism and Political Mobilization in India* (Delhi, 1982), pp. 36, 150.

[23] Zohra Ansari, Oral History transcript.

a British university which was a valuable asset and a passport to joining the 'heaven born'.

At the age of twenty-one, Ansari sailed for London, being the first member of the family to cross the seas; he was followed by a cousin, Mohammad Asghar, who studied law in London. Reporting himself to the educational adviser in London at 21 Cromwell Road and spending a couple of weeks in the accomodation provided for new arrivals, Ansari went to Edinburgh to join the Medical College. By sheer talent and a capacity for prolonged and concentrated work, he secured the degree of Doctor of Medicine and Master of Surgery in 1908. Soon after, he moved to London to serve as resident medical officer in the Charing Cross Hospital and as clinical assistant at the Lock Hospital. He was the first Indian to achieve such a distinction. This caused quite a furore in the local press. An evening newspaper published a leading story entitled 'Grave Injustice to British Doctors' with unmistakable racist overtones. But the Governing Council of the Charing Cross Hospital stoutly defended Ansari's appointment. His selection, stated the Council, 'has been made purely on the basis of merit, and it will be disastrous for British hospitals if any other criterion was employed for appointment purposes.'[24]

This incident gained widespread publicity. It was a matter of pride for many Indians that one of them had established his professional competence and ability in the face of a hostile and racially arrogant section of the British press. Among Muslims, in particular, he became known as among the few in the community who opted for the 'modern method' as opposed to the more commonly practised *Yunani tibb.* There are many others now who have done the same, but Ansari was the first to lead the way.

The youngman's stay in Britain, which lasted from 1901 to 1910, is the least known period of his life. Not a single letter from these years survives, either written or received by Ansari, and it is only from isolated comments contained in a few contemporary accounts that one can tentatively reconstruct in a very limited way the society in which he lived. We know, for instance, that he did indeed work hard, but also found time to be sociable,[25] to act in plays[26] and to make some lively and

[24]Barni, *Azmat-i Rafta*, p. 106.

[25]Zohra Ansari, Oral History transcript.

[26]A photograph at the NMML shows Ansari playing the part of Othello in

intelligent friends. Although an entertaining and at times a fascinating companion when he was in the right mood, with a great store of anecdotes and Urdu *ghazals* on which to draw, he was not by nature very gregarious or sociable. Even in later years he did not easily admit those he met to his confidence or allow them to penetrate the warmth and humanity which lay behind his formidable defences.

Most people who met Ansari in London found him relaxed by temperament, highly cultivated and generous. According to Mujeeb's description in his unfinished biography, Ansari was 'a distinctive figure of average height, broad pleasing looks, openness, of a voice somewhat musical, emotions gushing and effusive, but what struck people at once were his attractive eyes, his pompous moustache and profusive eye-brows'. He exuded the charm which swiftly won friends. Most of the friendships he formed in London lasted until his death; many were to play significant parts in his professional or political life. There was Jawaharlal Nehru (1889-1964) who took to him at once and described meeting 'a smart and clever young man with a record of brilliant academic achievement behind him'.[27] Their association developed into a lifelong friendship which was cemented by a shared political outlook. It was to him and his father that Ansari most readily confided his plans and his feelings, and it was to their home in Allahabad that he liked best to go when he had a holiday. It was a relationship so central to Ansari's life and which he took so much for granted, that he never felt the need to comment on it.

There was also Ajmal Khan, the scion of a family of physicians who had long served the Mughal court and, after their decline, the courts of regional princes. The two first met in London and found each other's company congenial; Ansari had the ability to spark off enthusiasm among those he met. Their friendship ripened after Ansari's return to India when they worked together in the Rowlatt satyagraha. There were few secrets between these two men through the long unbroken years of friendship and few griefs in which they could not solace each other.

All who met Ajmal Khan succumbed to his irresistible spell. Tolerant, human and broad-minded, he was a counsellor to whom people turned instinctively for guidance and political leadership

Edinburgh.

[27]Nehru, *An Autobiography*, p. 17

He was extraordinary in many ways, but in every way the product of the finest Indian Muslim cultural traditions and ideals. His belief in Hindu-Muslim unity was not a matter of policy, it was a part of his heritage; it was in his blood and the substance of his everyday life. He was loved and honoured, and most of all by those who themselves had high ideals of integrity, commitment and refinement.[28] C.F. Andrews (1871 1940) spoke of 'an ever deepening friendship' with Ajmal Khan and revered him for his integrity and dedication.[29] 'Quiet, humble, modest, with all the dignity of a man of character, learning and religious sincerity', wrote Andrews, Ajmal Khan was the one recognized head in Delhi who, all acknowledged as their moral leader, for his character and character alone.[30] Many years later Jawaharlal summed up his many qualities:

> As an ex-president of the Congress he was one of its elder statesmen; but he was something more also, and he occupied a unique place in the Congress leadership. Brought up as he was, entirely in the old conservative way, with no touch of modernism in it. and steeped in the culture of imperial Delhi of Moghal days, it was a delight to watch his fine courtesy and hear his unhurried voice and listen to his dry humour. He was, in his manners, a typical aristocrat of the old order, with princely look and princely ways. and even his face bore a marked resemblance to the miniatures of the Moghal sovereigns. Such a person would not ordinarily take to the rough-and-tumble of politics.... But even during the latter part of the War events, and the influence of his old friend and colleague, Dr M.A. Ansari, were driving him to the Congress; and subsequent happenings—Martial Law in the Punjab and the Khilafat question—moved him deeply, and he turned with

[28]Mujeeb, *The Indian Muslims*, p. 536; for a more recent appreciation of Ajmal Khan's role, see Barbara D. Metcalf, 'Nationalist Muslims in British India: The Case of Hakim Ajmal Khan', *Modern Asian Studies*, 19, I, 1985, pp. 1-28.

[29]C.F Andrews, 'Hakim Ajmal Khan', in *Eminent Mussalmans* (Madras, 1926), p. 287

[30]*Modern Review*, 31, 6 June 1922, p. 686. Hardinge recalled that Ajmal Khan was 'much respected throughout India' and found him loyal in every way. He saw him a good deal at Delhi and often discussed Muslim affairs, especially in connection with the war. Hardinge to Chelmsford, 23 August 1916, MSS. EUR. E. 264 (15) Chelmsford Papers, IOL. Also, Ansari's account quoted in Abdul Ghaffar, *Hayat-i Ajmal* (Delhi, 1950), pp. 110-11. The memoirs of Ansari, quoted at length by Ghaffar, are not traceable.

> approval to the new Gandhian technique of non-cooperation. He brought a rare quality and precious gifts to the Congress—he became a link between the old order and the new, and gave the support of the former to the national movement.... He brought the Hindus and Muslims much nearer to each other, for both honoured him and were influenced by his example. To Gandhiji he became a trusted friend, whose advice in regard to Hindu-Muslim matters was the final word for him My father and Hakimji had naturally taken to each other.[31]

Such was the man Ansari met in London.

Another person of vigorous and independent mind Ansari met in London was Mohammad Iqbal (1876-1938). Iqbal was already well known through his Urdu poetry and his poems like *nala-i-yatim* (Complaint of the Orphan) which he had recited in 1899 at Lahore, were well received. In 1905 Iqbal left for Europe. He studied at Trinity College, Cambridge, read German at Heidelberg and submitted his doctorate dissertation at the University of Munich. Atiya Begum Fyzee, who belonged to an aristocratic family of Bombay and was a cousin of Sir Akbar Hydari (1869-1942), described the young brilliant student of those days; she met Iqbal first in London and later in Germany where he went in June 1907. She has recorded the details of a party at her house on 23 June 1907. 'Dr. Ansari,' she noted, 'entertained us with songs, Lord Sinha's daughters... with music, and Iqbal with extempore compositions of clever and witty verses referring to almost every important guest present by making exaggerated remarks about their peculiarities, sending us all into roars of laughter.'[32] A brief reference to a meeting with Ansari is also available in the account of Atiya's sister-in-law, Rufiah Sultan Nazli Begum.[33]

Such social gatherings were frequently organized to recreate the north Indian culture of the elite in an alien cultural milieu and were often attended by British civil servants and educationists who had served in India. Thus we have references to Ansari, Mohamed Ali and Fazl-i-Husain (1877-1936) attending parties hosted by the families of Theodore Beck (1859-1899), the principal of the Aligarh College in Syed Ahmad Khan's (1817-1898)

[31]Nehru, *An Autobiography*, pp. 168-9.

[32]Atiya Fyzee, *Iqbal* (Bombay, 1947). I owe this reference to the late Mr Atiq Siddiqi.

[33]Nazli Begum of Jangira, *Sair-i Europe* (Lahore, n.d.), p. 26.

lifetime and T.W. Arnold (b. 1864), who joined the institution in 1888 and authored several works on Islam and the history of Muslims.[34] On 21 September 1898 Ansari was in the company of Mohamed Ali and Fazl-i-Husain at 82 Brondesbury Villas in Kilburn, the home of Miss Beck. 'We passed an exceedingly pleasant evening,' recorded Fazl-i-Husain in his diary, 'talked literature, philosophy, politics, and what not'.[35]

In the course of such social interaction people came to share each other's impressions and experiences. Their meetings often generated much lively discussions, providing clues to their political predilections.[36] But there is no evidence to indicate Ansari's involvement in any political debate or his association with any Indian student group, such as the Majlis in Cambridge, the Oxford Islamic Society, or the *Anjuman-i Islamia*, later called the Pan-Islamic Society.[37] Some of his contemporaries —Abdul Majid Khwaja (1885-1962), Haroon Khan Sherwani (1891-1980) and Syed Mahmud (1889-1971)—were deeply influenced by the writings of W.S. Blunt (1840-1922) and Professor E.G. Browne (1862-1926) of Cambridge and were active in organizing Muslim students in Britain in support of pan-Islamism and the nationalist movements in West Asia. Available evidence does not disclose whether Ansari made the acquaintance of either of them at this time, though it is certain that during his stay in London he devoted very little thought to politics, Indian or other. Indeed it was not until the political ferment in his community towards the end of 1911 and, more particularly, until the outbreak of the Turko-Italian War, that he began to take an interest in public affairs.

Ansari returned to India in 1910 and was offered the principalship of the Lahore Medical College But he was unable to

[34]Azim Husain, *Fazl-i Husain: A Political Biography* (Bombay, 1936), p. 20; Afzal Iqbal, *Life and Times of Mohamed Ali* (Delhi, 1978), reprint, pp. 31-2.

[35] MSS. EUR. E. 352 (2), Fazl-i-Husain Papers, IOL.

[36]Notice Fazl-i-Husain's noting on 23 September 1898: 'In the evening we had a very hot discussion. Really we had not fixed upon the topic, the subject under discussion was quite vague and all the more vague because the branch of knowledge to which it belongs is far from precision. We were talking about Religion, Blind belief etc.' Ibid.

[37]There was an Islamic Society in London, an Oxford University Indian Club and the Oxford Islamic Society. Haroon Khan Sherwani, then a student at Jesus College, Oxford, was president of the Oxford Islamic Society. Others associated with it were H. Fyzee, K. C. Tayebji, H.M. Shairani, father of the Urdu poet, Akhtar Shairani, Haroon Khan Sherwani Papers, NMML.

accept the offer because the terms of the scholarship on which he went to Edinburgh stipulated that he would serve Hyderabad State for some years. He waited in vain for six months to be placed in one of the medical institutions. He then toyed with the idea of moving to Calcutta, but two of his patrons—the Raja of Mahmudabad (1879-1931) and Ali Imam (1869-1932), a lawyer and member of the governor general's council at that time—thought otherwise. They saw a bright future for the young brilliant doctor in Delhi, the new capital of British India, and advised him accordingly. Ansari agreed. Delhi was not only the imperial capital but also one of the main centres of the Urdu-speaking world, the home of Urdu prose and poetry; the home of Mir Taqi Mir (1733-1814) and Asadullah Khan Ghalib (1797-1869). In Ansari's own words, it was the 'cradle of Islamic civilization in India' and 'the city of Muslim memories'. 'Time has not yet effaced the landmarks of Islam in the history of this country,' he observed, 'nor has the dust of centuries buried the footprints of our ancestors.'[38] The decision to settle in Delhi was final. From this moment Ansari planned his life with a method rare among young men and adhered to his own rules with inflexible self-discipline. He had every reason to feel satisfied and some excuse for being self-satisfied. He had been successful and popular at the medical schools in London and faced the future with a confident belief in his ability to make the most of it.

Ansari's clinic was for several years housed in a portion of the Fatehpuri mosque in the old city, a mosque sold by the British to a Hindu banker after the 1857 revolt and returned to the Muslims by the viceroy, Lytton (1831-1891). Here and later in Daryaganj he continued to practise and was perhaps among the few famous doctors of India. Many leading Congress-men, princes, rajas and nawabs were among his patients.[39] Also the poor. There were certain hours he gave to the poor daily, no matter what profit he could have made from those hours. The cases were almost all non-Muslim; the needing Muslims were generally treated free directly or through relatives.[40]

[38]Speech at the All-India Muslim League Session, Delhi, 1918, Mushirul Hasan (ed.), *Muslims and the Congress: Select Correspondence of Dr M.A. Ansari, 1912-1935* (Delhi, 1979), p. 264.

[39]He would charge Rs 500 to Rs 1,000 a day from the Nawab of Rampur and the Begum of Bhopal. His consultation fee in the early 1930s was Rs 32. But he treated most Congress leaders free of charge. Motilal Nehru was his patient for long and Ansari was extremely solicitous of his health.

[40]Zohra recalls some of Ansari's acts of generosity. See Oral History transcript.

Ansari's private house—*Behisht* (Paradise)—was by the old city walls, near the Mori Gate. It was in this house that Andrews and Mohamed Ali lectured on the sufferings of Indians in South Africa.[41] The distinguished English novelist E.M. Forster (1879-1970) and his companion Syed Ross Masud (1889-1937) stayed at the *Behisht* during their visit in late October 1912. Forster described his host as 'a most charming Doctor' and was impressed with his hospitality.[42] 'I sit in the verandah of the house.... with now a chicken running past and now a squirrel, and listen to the doves and green parrots making conversation in the garden.... Both garden and house are small, and it is a great kindness on Ansari's part to have put me up. Though a youngman, he has already a large practice.... He seems as competent as he is charming, and I think I would as soon rely on him as on certain paler skins at home....'[43]

The *Behisht* was thronged by unexplained visitors—sitting cross-legged on the beds or on the luggage. There seemed to be no set meal times, but whenever Forster crossed the threshold, tea and poached eggs would appear and Ansari's wife, who observed *purdah*, would send cigarettes, betel nut and *itr* (scent).[44] 'I am in the middle of a very queer life,' he wrote to a friend on 2 November 1912, 'whether typically Oriental I have no means of knowing, but it isn't English.'[45]

Forster also described 'a very homely and pleasant' evening at a *nautch*, or party with dancing girls, arranged by Ansari. He admired the leading performer, a girl 'with a queer but very charming face and delightful manners' and was regaled by her dancing.[46] 'Emotion came to me through the harsh voice and music, so that I enjoyed myself', he wrote. 'When the singer sank down in our midst, with her scarlet and golden robes spread round us, and sang love songs, I realized what a *nautch*

[41]Barni, *Azmat-i Rafta*, pp. 107-8. For Andrews on South Africa, Hugh Tinker, *The Ordeal of Love: C.F. Andrews and India* (Delhi, 1979), chapter five; Andrews to Tagore, 15 November 1913, *Andrews' Papers: Bunch of Letters to Rabindranath Tagore and M.K. Gandhi* (Deshbandhu Andrews Centenary Committee, n.d.).

[42]To Mary Aylward, 30 October 1912, Mary Lago and P.N. Furbank (eds.), *Selected Letters of E.M. Forster, 1879-1920* (London, 1983), Vol. I, p. 141.

[43]To Laury Mary Forster, 31 October 1912; ibid., p. 144.

[44]P.N. Furbank, *E.M. Forster: A Life: The growth of the Novelist 1879-1914* (London, 1978), p. 228.

[45]To Florence Barger, 2 November 1912, *Selected Letters*, p. 144.

[46]To Alice Clara Forster, 6 November 1912, ibid., p. 149.

must be to Indians.'[47] Forster spent the evening in the company of, among others, Mohamed Ali, the volatile editor of the *Comrade* who was much troubled by the affairs in Turkey and even contemplated suicide as the message reached him that the Bulgarians were only 25 miles from Constantinople—'a name that had for five centuries been sacred to every Muslim as the centre of his highest hopes.'[48] Mohamed Ali was indiscreet to share his experience at the *nautch* with a fellow-journalist, and not long afterwards, there appeared in the London *Times* a report of how a leading Muslim, on the eve of Turkey's defeat in the Balkan war, had spent his evening at an 'orgy'.[49]

In 1928 Ansari set up his clinic within the walled city in Daryaganj which remained a sparsely-built up area until 1908 when the British troops stationed there were evacuated to the new cantonment on the Ridge. Gradually, however, some new houses were constructed by some successful lawyers and doctors. Ansari moved into one of them. Apart from the fact that for some years he shared with Dr H.C. Sen the distinction of being the only Indian in Delhi to own motor cars,[50] he soon became the proud owner of an elegant octagonal building, overlooking a square lawn, bought from Lala Sultan Singh at the rather high price of Rs 50,000.[51] It was aptly called the *Dar-us-Salam*,

[47]Quoted in Furbank, *E.M. Forster: A Life*, p. 229.

[48]Mohamed Ali wrote: 'To return to that autumn night in 1912, I was saved a trial of my courage as well as cowardice by the unexpected appearance of a Muslim friend [Ross Masud] who had graduated from Oxford not long before and was on the occasion accompanied by an English fellow-graduate of that University [E.M. Forster] who was his guest and had expressed a desire to see an Indian *nautch*. Arrangements had been made *sub rosa* and the place selected was the house of a barrister who was my next door neighbour. My friend insisted on my company and hard as I pleaded the excuse of a busy editor.... my friend would not take any denial and almost bodily lifted me from the editorial sanctum and carried me by main force to the private *nautch* party next door.' Afzal Iqbal (ed.), *My Life a Fragment: An Autobiographical Sketch of Maulana Mohamed Ali* (Delhi, 1979 edn.), p. 38.

[49]Furbank, *E.M. Forster: A Life*, p. 229; Mohamed Ali wrote: 'Thus it was that instead of being a horror of broken b es and bleeding body supposed to have accidentally fallen down from a third storey, there I was "assisting" at the "orgy" that had been arranged by my young friend to gratify the curiosity of a brother Oxonian. Ibid., pp. 38-9

[50]Narayani Gupta, *Delhi Between Two Empires, 1803-1931: Society, Government and Urban Growth* (Delhi, 1981), p. 58.

[51]'Tehrik-i Azaadi ka ek Khamosh Kaarkun', op. cit.

abode of peace. In the early 1930s, it was the venue of many important meetings and conferences: a counterpart of Motilal Nehru's (1861-1931) Allahabad residence, Anand Bhawan. Halide Edib stayed in *Dar-us-Salam* for two months in 1935 and described it as 'an historical place where the ancient, the medieval, and the modern came together: the ideas and aspirations of divergent personalities meet, coalesce, and the personalities disperse to set in motion new trends elsewhere'. 'In the free India of the future,' she prophesized, 'that house will be one of the principal landmarks in its marking.'[52]

Edib's account also offers a glimpse of Ansari's family. In the left wing of the house lived Shamsunnisa who saw no men other than her relatives, except Gandhi. She lived there with her personal servants and spent her leisure in reading the Quran, the *Gulistan* (Rose Garden: 1258) and *Bustaan* (Fruit Garden: 1257) of the Persian poet, Saadi (1184-1291) and Urdu short stories and poetry. Her attitude towards servants reminded Edib of old Turkey. 'I would often hear young girls taking lessons from different teachers on the verandah behind the curtain. They were as free and as natural as the daughter of the house. There was no trace of class feeling.'[53] Presumably, the lessons were in Quran and the *Hadith*.

Ansari's niece and adopted daughter, Zohra, also lived in *Dar-us-Salam*. Her life, according to the Turkish author, 'seemed to be an Indian version of my life of thirty-five years ago in Turkey. She was too individualistic to fit into a fixed group whether inside or outside of Purdah.'[54] She described Zohra's interest in history and literature:

> She knew her country's history exceedingly well... she did not feel Muslims to be an alien race, a minority grafted on Indian soil, and doomed to remain as such. She was Indian to the core. Asoka was part of her past history just as much as Humayun.... She both humanized and dramatized for me the great monumental edifices which would otherwise have been only heaps of stones more or less artistically arranged. She knew all the legends around the lives of those who had lived in those ruins.[55]

[52]Edib, *Inside India*, p. 27.
[53]Ibid., p. 32.
[54]Ibid., p. 33.
[55]Ibid.

It has been necessary to dwell in some detail upon these impressions because they reveal Ansari's profound influence on the young Zohra who continued the legacy of her father's broad-mindedness and catholic outlook. What is however not brought out, though Edib hints at this in her account, is that children were a constant pleasure and interest to Ansari and the most delightful aspects of his character were aroused by parenthood. He reserved his affection and care for Zohra, his letters to her sparkling with tenderness, humour and affection.[56] In her years spent at *Dar-us-Salam* Zohra proved to be a woman of strong character and intelligence who understood her father as no one else did; and in return Ansari confided everything to her, as he did to no one else, not even his wife. He found in Zohra the intellectual companionship and supportive admiration he needed.

[56]See, for example, Ansari to Shaukatullah Ansari, 21 May 1934. Hasan (ed.), *Muslims and the Congress*, p. 155.

The Political Milieu, 1910-1917

> Delhi, inspite of her newly-conferred dignity, is still dominated by her past which broods over the lives and activities of the living as well as the smouldering remains of the dead. An ever present sense of her tragic history has created in her people a cynical disregard for her needs, the joys and sorrows of the present. She has rarely felt the new enthusiasms which render the lives of the modern cities so absorbing and fruitful and have made them the nerve-centres of the common life of the country. Her biggest sons would seem to an outside observer to be engaged in an incessant personal struggle to keep their heads above the water-line. Their horizon almost exactly resembles that of any out-of-the-way mofussil town whose entire consciousness is filled with the enormous figure of the District Magistrate.
>
> *Comrade*, 12 July 1913.

THE INDIA TO which Ansari came in 1912, at the age of thirty-two, was a land of relative tranquility. The flames which had fired the Swadeshi movement in Bengal had been extinguished with the annulment of Bengal's partition in 1911, and for the time being, a major irritant in government's relationship with the Indian National Congress was removed. The 'moderates', epitomized by men like G.K. Gokhale (1866-1915), Pherozeshah Mehta (1848-1915) and Surendranath Banerjea (1848-1925), now came to dominate Congress affairs after having been eclipsed by the rapid rise of extremist nationalism in Maharashtra, Bengal and the Punjab. The 'extremists', on the other hand, were scattered by British repression, but their hopes of an ultimate victory were kept alive by the outcome of the Russo-Japanese war of 1904-5 and by another inspiring example, that of Mohandas Karamchand Gandhi (1869-1948) who led successful passive resistance struggles in South Africa between 1906 and 1914. The defeat of the Russian army and navy at the hands of a much smaller Asian country than India led the 'extremists' and their revolutionary allies to believe that if Japan could thwart an occidental giant like Russia, then India, a much larger country, could do the same to an insular power like Britain. This thinking gave impetus to the demand for swaraj which became the battle-cry for the Indian nationalists. Such sentiments were echoed in different parts of the country, including Delhi which became the Imperial capital on 1 October 1912.

Delhi remained a political backwater until February 1917 when a branch of the Home Rule League was opened, a fact alluded to by Ansari in his evidence before the Hunter Commission. This marked 'the entry of prominent local men', as the chief commissioner of Delhi put it, 'into the all-India political arena',[1] and led to a sudden flurry of political activity: the Indraprastha Sewak Mandli was formed in May 1917 in response to Annie Besant's (1847-1933) advocacy of boy scouts' organization and a League Volunteer Corps—with Ansari, Ajmal Khan and Asaf Ali (1888-1953)[2] on the management committee—was raised in early 1918.[3] Contemporaries noticed the consequent heightening

[1]*The Disorders Inquiry Committee* [hereafter DIC], Vol. I, *Delhi* (Calcutta, 1920), p. 123. For a background of political developments, Gupta, *Delhi Between Two Empires*, pp. 196-200; Donald W. Ferrel, 'The Rowlatt Satyagraha in Delhi', Ravinder Kumar (ed.), *Essays on Gandhian Politics: The Rowlatt Satyagraha of 1919* (London, 1971), pp. 192-8.

[2]Asaf Ali was in England from 1911 to 1914 and returned to India as a barrister in December 1914. His first public appearance in political affairs was as member of the Home Rule League which he joined in March 1917. Later, he took a prominent part in the Rowlatt satyagraha and the Khilafat and non-cooperation movements. He led a strike in the Government Press, Delhi, and gave up his practice in August 1920. He opposed council elections, 'practiced general intimidation through his volunteers at polling stations, and organized a partial social boycott of candidates'. In November 1921 he led volunteers to picket shops of cloth dealers and was soon put in jail. Home Poll. F. No. 366 1930, NAI. Some of these details are missing in Sudhir Pant, *Asaf Ali Patriot and Humanist* (Delhi, 1984).

[3]The first recorded volunteer organization in Delhi was the Muslim League Volunteer Corps, founded in November 1918. By the end of 1920, there were five more: the *Askar-i Islamia* (literally the Army of Islam), the Khilafat Volunteer Corps, the *Khuddam-i Watan* (Servants of the Nation), the Khilafat Workers Association, established in March 1919, and the Muslim Razakar Volunteer Corps. The chief commissioner of Delhi reported that these bodies were in practice indistinguishable, for 'they execute the decision of the local Khilafat Committee and act in perfect cooperation'. They were subsequently declared 'unlawful' for being a 'serious menace to the social life and public liberties of peaceful and law-abiding citizens'. Home Poll. F. No. 35, 1920; Home Poll. Deposit, February

of political consciousness, manifested in anti-government rumblings of these organizations and suggested the not so unfamiliar remedy of educating the 'public mind on imperial lines'.[4]

Ansari, already known for his good work as leader of the Indian Medical Mission to Constantinople, was a key figure in Delhi's Home Rule movement. As its president he organized an intermittent but comprehensive scheme of propaganda, declared that liberty of thought and speech was the birth-right of every citizen and urged the people to condemn the arrest of Annie Besant. 'It is a matter which concerns not simply an individual community or province, but is an all-India question and touches the liberty and the rights of every Indian. Hence silence at a time like this is cowardly and disloyal to one's own people and to one's self.'[5]

Apart from local men like Asaf Ali, Shiv Narain Haksar, Abdur Rahman (b. 1888), R.S. Piyare Lal and Abdul Aziz (b. 1907), Ansari who already had the nucleus of a small political following, persuaded a number of his younger Muslim friends from UP to attend meetings of the League, hosted their visits to Delhi and initiated them into the Home Rule crusade. Among those he influenced most was Khaliquzzaman (1889-1973), an Aligarh graduate. and Tassaduq Ahmad Khan Sherwani (1889-1935), a contemporary of Jawaharlal at Cambridge who emerged as Ansari's principal lieutenant in subsequent political struggles. The identification of such men threatened to disturb the placid life of Delhi and involve its citizens in an agitation of serious proportions.

In its historical sequence, the Home Rule agitation raised the general level of political consciousness, served as an instrument of mass mobilization and brought to the fore the organizing and leadership qualities of several fresh recruits to the nationalist

1921, F. No. 77, 1921, NAI. It is noteworthy that there was also a general extension of the volunteer movement in UP. When a rough statement of its strength was prepared in November 1921, it was found that there were Khilafat volunteers in some 35 out of 41 districts from which reports had been received. The largest number of volunteers were drawn from Azamgarh (1,423), Saharanpur (926), Gorakhpur (405), Moradabad (400) and Aligarh (387). Muzaffarnagar returned 258 volunteers, Meerut 250, Budaun 200 and Gorakhpur 189. Numbers in Bulandshahr, Mainpuri, Etah, Ballia, Unnao and Gonda also ran into three figures. GAD, F. No. 604, 1920, UPSA.

[4]History of the Non-Cooperation and Khilafat Movements in Delhi (Printed), Delhi State Archives, Delhi. Mrs Rewa Pathak was kind enough to make this report available to me.

[5]*New Era* (Lucknow), 30 June 1917.

movement. Among them were Mohammad Ali Jinnah (1876-1948), Jamnadas Dwarkadas, Shankarlal Banker (1889-1895) and Umar Subhani (d. 1926) in Bombay; Jawaharlal, Harkaran Nath Misra (b. 1890), Khaliquzzaman, Khwaja and Sherwani in UP; Ansari, Ajmal Khan and Asaf Ali in Delhi. Most of them were to occupy a prominent position in the shaping of the country's destiny, but gained their first experience of agitational politics during the Home Rule campaign. Jawaharlal recalled how 'the atmosphere became electric' in those days with the younger men expecting 'big things to happen in the near future' and how Annie Besant's internment added to the excitement of the intelligentsia and vitalized the Home Rule movement all over the country.

The Leagues attracted the old 'Extremists' who had been kept out of the Congress since 1907, as well as large numbers of newcomers from the middle classes.[6] The *New Era*, an organ of the politically radical Muslim group, noticed how Annie Besant's incarceration 'unwittingly accomplished the purpose of an organized agitation and propaganda in a single day', led to 'a fresh stirring in public life' and a 'stiffening of public resolve'.[7] Ansari, too, referred to its impact in Delhi, where 'the recent events have produced a great deal of feeling and people who were not Home Rule Leaguers have either joined the League or are thinking of joining it soon. Even some of the most conservative people have changed their views [and], have come to look upon the actions of some of the local Governments as highly unconstitutional and unwise'.[8]

Ideologically, the Home Rule Leagues were dominated by Hindu theosophical ideas and many of its organizers in some areas had close connections with Hindu revivalist bodies. But, in general, they operated on a supra-communal network and pursued a non-communal programme, a fact which encouraged many Muslims to swell the ranks of Annie Besant's adherents. For instance, Abdul Majid Khwaja, a successful lawyer and a contemporary of Jawaharlal at Cambridge, set up a Home Rule League branch in Aligarh with the backing of Haji Musa Khan, a leading rais of Datauli and one of the stalwarts at the Aligarh College. Some young lawyers and journalists, close to Motilal Nehru, did the same in Allahabad. Prominent among them were:

[6]Nehru, *An Autobiography*, pp. 31-2.

[7]*New Era*, 23 June 1917.

[8]Ibid., 30 June 1917

Sheikh Zahur Ahmad, an Aligarh graduate; Manzar Ali Sokhta, whose father was manager of the Nehru household; Kamaluddin Jafri (d. 1933), a lawyer with close connections with the Congress in Allahabad; Wahid Yar Khan, editor of *Nai Roshni*, a pro-Congress paper published from 1916 to 1918. In Agra the Home Rule League was led by Syed Ali Nabi (d. 1927), member of the UP legislative council from 1909 to 1912 and chairman of the reception committee of the Muslim League in 1913. In Lucknow its main adherents were several prominent lawyers and journalists: Raja Ghulam Husain (1882-1917), editor of *Comrade* and the *New Era*; Syed Jalib Dehlavi (d. 1930), editor of Lucknow's Urdu daily *Hamdam*; Hakim Abdul Wali (b. 1884), proprietor of the *Al-Bayan*, an Arabic-Urdu monthly of Lucknow, and owner of the famous Asi Press; Shuaib Qureshi, Khaliquzzaman and Abdur Rahman Siddiqi (1887-1953), graduates of Aligarh and members of Ansari's medical mission to Turkey.

Some indication of their mood and their political preferences can be gauged from their support to Annie Besant's election as Congress president in 1917, as opposed to their patron, the Raja of Mahmudabad. The *New Era* insisted that 'the dictates of patriotism and national self-interest as well as the sense of national gratitude demand that Mrs Besant should be elected president of the national assembly this year' and appealed to the Raja to withdraw from the contest because 'no other choice, whether of a Hindu or Muslim public man, would symbolize more effectively the faith and will of educated India or express the strength of the national resolve in a more decisive form'.[9] In a note submitted to the viceroy on 7 February 1917, James Meston (1865-1943), lieutenant-governor of UP, summed up the strength of nationalist feelings among such Muslims, noted their sympathy for the Home Rule and Congress movements, and lamented the declining influence of their detractors, especially those allied to the government. He observed with uncharacteristic frankness:

> In deciding either on the strategy of its *post-bellum* policy or to handle the Home Rule agitation, the Government of India will no doubt have regard to the strength of the Nationalist feeling in India at the present moment. It is unquestionably greater than it has ever been in our time. The Christmas meetings at Lucknow caught up and consolidated

[9] *New Era*, 11 August 1917.

> popular sentiment as few political events have done. Extremists and moderates have united after years of misunderstanding; and, greatest marvel of all, the Mohammedans also had come into the fold. A few Moderates may grumble here and there; and a few conservative Mohammedans may urge that the League does not represent their community. But they *do* nothing. They are voiceless in public; they do not hold meetings; they have completely lost command of the Press. For all practical purposes they have, for the time at least, disappeared as a separate party. *The resultant union of all voices has filled educated Indians with a pride and a feeling of nationality which is impossible to ignore* [italics mine].[10]

The growth of political radicalism among Muslims was in reaction to the quickening tempo of events—the annulment of Bengal's partition and British machinations in Turkey. Paradoxical as it may seem, their 'extra-territorial patriotism' served to hasten the development of their territorial patriotism also. The aggression of Western powers hastened their disillusionment with the policy of traditional reliance on the government, and the rejection of the Muslim university scheme and the Kanpur mosque incident made it clear that Muslim interests at home were of no greater consequence to their rulers than their sentiments with regard to their brethren abroad. The effect of the Balkan wars, observed the chief secretary to the Punjab government, helped to unify Muslim sentiment, extend the pan-Islamic idea, stimulate the cry of 'Islam in Danger' and afford the 'hot-headed literati editors, schoolmasters and journalists' to conduct their anti-government agitation.[11] In these years the rhetoric of Muslim political language moved from an emphasis on the preservation of elite interests to more emotive, populist, public symbols of Muslim corporate identity.[12]

[10]Note for the viceroy by Meston, 7 February 1917, MSS. EUR. F. 36 (6), Meston Papers, IOL. The League, according to the lieutenant-governor, had collapsed and was merely doing the bidding of the Congress. 'I am not sure that this state of affairs can last; but we have to accept the fact, for the time being, that on paper the Mahomedans have now come into the Nationalist camp.' Meston to Chelmsford, 11 January 1917, MSS. EUR. E. 264 (18), Chelmsford Papers, IOL.

[11]To Secretary, Home Department, 11 October 1913, Hardinge Papers (86), Cambridge University Library, Cambridge. Also, 'Note on Serious Disturbances and Political Troubles in India from 1907 to 1917', Home Poll. Deposit, February 1918, 31, NAI.

[12]Metcalf, 'Nationalist Muslims in British India', op.cit., p. 19.

Government officials, though keen on retaining Muslim loyalty, were wary of projecting their traditional pro-Muslim policies too openly for fear of alienating those who resented the preferential treatment accorded to the Muslims in the distribution of jobs and in representation to various legislative bodies. Indeed, the opponents of Bengal's partition and the detractors of separate electorates and communal representation, granted by the Act of 1909, had to be mollified in order to stem the anti-government tide.

It was left to Hardinge (1858-1944) to heal some of the wounds left by that deep gash in the body of India—the partition of Bengal. He did so by revoking the partition, a decision which caused much disaffection among Muslims. The viceroy was also unable to meet their demand relating to the Muslim university scheme. The great project, conceived by the successors of Syed Ahmad Khan, juddered to a halt because the secretary of state for India and his council objected to both the term 'Muslim' in the nomenclature of the university and to the scheme to affiliate colleges outside the province. And in dealing with the pan-Islamic ferment in India, Hardinge was constrained by the dictates of European diplomacy and by the anti-Turkish strain of the British government's policy. He tried in vain to impress London with the strength of pan-Islamic feelings in India over the Italian attack upon Tripoli. Remote from contact with the Indian scene, it was difficult for the India Office to feel the feverishly rising pulse of pan-Islamism. Hardinge told the secretary of state for India that the Foreign Office did not sufficiently appreciate the difficulties which the government of India were having with the Indian Muslims over Turkey. Some years later, Montagu told Chelmsford that their 'resentment appears so remote from the minds of my colleagues'.[13]

The unmistakable shift in government policy profoundly altered the tenor of Muslim League politics. To begin with, the politics of collaboration, pursued by its politically conservative leadership, was effectively questioned by an influential group of lawyers, journalists and a section of the *ulama*. Shibli Nomani (1857-1914), Abul Kalam Azad (1888-1958), Hasrat Mohani (1877-1951), Zafar Ali Khan (1873-1956), Mohamed Ali and many of their followers were decisively against the political methods of the first generation of Aligarh Muslim leaders, affirmed their commitment to agitational methods and believed in working out the political destiny of

[13]Montagu to Chelmsford, 31 March 1919, Chelmsford Papers (5).

their compatriots in unison with the rest of the Indian people. Instead of being haunted by the spectre of Hindu domination, they regarded the Congress in a favourable light and endorsed its political creed. Stressing this fact, the *New Era* wrote:

> A community of about 70 million... has to work out its political destiny in close and active cooperation with the rest of the Indian people. Any other alternative to a policy of trust resolutely striving for the complete unity of the Indian races is unthinkable. Any self-respecting Muslim who knows what political freedom means for the self-realization of individuals as well as communities can feel no enthusiasm for a political creed that does not aim at a free and united India.[14]

Shibli Nomani was among the most influential exponents of the idea of cooperation and accomodation with the Hindus in general and the Congress, in particular. In a series of perceptive essays, published in 1912, he berated the reactionary political methods of the Muslim League and exposed the short-sightedness of its leadership. The League, in contrast to the Congress which pursued a comprehensive and constructive economic and political programme, was merely interested in a larger share for Muslims in government services and extension of separate electorates to municipalities and district boards. Pursuit of sectional interests could not be rewarding because politics, according to Shibli, made sense only with organized political parties under forward-looking leaders. In drawing yet another point of contrast, he pointed out that the Congress had not drawn its leaders from the titled and landed gentry, whereas the League was completely in the hands of such people, who could never be courageous enough to sacrifice their selfish and material interests by taking a firm stand against government. Above all, the eminent *alim* of Nadwa believed in a concerted Hindu-Muslim effort to achieve common political objectives. He reminded Muslims of the bonds of unity which had prevailed between the two communities during medieval rule in India. This was an old story, he wrote, 'but even today go to the villages and see for yourself the brotherly feelings that exist between Hindus and Muslims, and the two communities participate in each other's functions as if they were related to each other by family ties'.[15]

[14] *New Era*, 26 May 1917.

[15] *Maqalat-i Shibli* (Azamgarh, 1938), Vol. 6, pp 161-90; also summary in

Expressed by a highly respected and reputed scholar who had impeccable credentials with his community, these ideas received deserved consideration. This was particularly so because of the League's passive role and its preoccupation with constitutional issues. Khaliquzzaman recalled the dominance of 'the titled gentry, Nawabs, Landlords and *Jee Huzoors*' who served the 'Muslim cause' only so far as it did not affect their position either socially or in government quarters. The League activities were confined to 'indoor political shows' and its annual sessions were held either in well-decorated *pandals* or in big halls where a few honourable members were allowed by special cards.[16]

Changes in the League, both in terms of its class composition and in the nature of its demands, began to occur around 1911. The first noticeable development was the transfer of its office (January 1910) from Aligarh to Lucknow, the home of a fairly substantial Muslim professional group and the storm centre of an overtly anti-government movement against the Nagri resolution of April 1900. The League at Aligarh was an adjunct of a college dominated by those who learnt their lesson of loyalty to government and opposition to Congress at the feet of Syed Ahmad Khan. But with the initiative passing into the hands of the politically advanced Lucknow-based leaders, the newly vitalized organization came to reflect, slowly but steadily, the radical temper of Muslim groups represented by Shibli, Azad, Mohamed Ali, Wazir Hasan, Zafar Ali Khan and Mazharul Haq (1866-1930). Described by their contemporaries as the 'younger men' and seen by themselves as standard-bearers of 'new ideals', 'new forces' and *nai raushni*, these men secured their major victory in 1913 when a new clause proclaiming the aim of the League to work with other groups for 'a system of self-government suitable to India' was incorporated in the revised constitution. It was hard to miss the message conveyed in this clause. But the old school of politicians could hardly swallow the bitter pill. They launched a counter attack.[17] Aided and abetted by the provincial governments, Mohammad Shafi (1869-1932) in

K.B. Sayeed, *Pakistan: The Formative Phase, 1857-1948* (Karachi, 1968 edn.), pp. 36-7.

[16]Choudhry Khaliquzzaman, *Pathway to Pakistan* (Lahore, 1961), pp. 137-8.

[17]I have discussed the background to these developments in *Nationalism and Communal Politics in India, 1916-1928* (Delhi, 1979). Also, Francis Robinson, *Separatism Among Indian Muslims: The Politics of the United Provinces' Muslims 1860-1923* (Cambridge, 1974).

the Punjab, Nawab Ali Chaudhuri (d. 1921) in Bengal and Fateh Ali Khan Qizilbash (b. 1862) in UP denounced the resolution on self-government on the ground that it would irk Anglo-Muslim relations and irretrievably damage Muslim interests. Outraged, Fateh Ali Khan advocated a policy of 'cautious advance' and exhorted members of the League: 'Its calamitous character is too obvious and before years add to its sanctity, Muslims must join in undoing the fair but deceptive foundations which they have dug.'[18]

Such warnings, backed by calculated moves to weaken the 'Young Party', were ill-timed. The politics of Fateh Ali Khan and his counterparts in Bengal and the Punjab was quite clearly divorced from reality. Insensitive to the changing mood and temper of their community and unable to comprehend its aspirations, they were gradually isolated from the mainstream of Muslim political life. 'I am far from being out of sympathy with the young party,' wrote Meston, 'because I believe that it was an inevitable reaction against the dignified inefficiency of the old-fashioned Muslims.'[19] Meston should have added that proximity to the Raj contributed to their waning political influence and eventual ouster from the premier Muslim organization.

The Aga Khan (1875-1958), who presided over the League's destiny from 1906 to 1913, was among the first to sense the mood of his community. Ridiculed for his political opportunism in lending support to the reunification of Bengal, the Aga Khan suddenly bolted and resigned on 3 November 1913. Replying to Harcourt Butler (1869-1938), who was constantly urging him

[18]To members of the All-India and Provincial Muslim League, 7 July 1913 enclosure in Fateh Ali Khan to Meston, 24 August 1913, Meston Papers (6).

[19]To Chelmsford, 11 January 1917, ibid., (1). Earlier assessments of Hardinge and Butler also deserve mention. According to the viceroy, the Muslim League was 'like a sheep without a shepherd' and its leadership 'want to do something, but they do not know what to do or how to do it.... The Aga Khan is finished as a leader, and we must hope for and look forward to some moderate men to come to the front and assume the leadership.' Butler's estimate of the leaders was: 'Aga Khan is clever but a weather cock. Mahmudabad is weak as water, so is Rampur, and unreliable to boot. The Nawab of Dacca hates Aligarh and all its works as much as he hates Aga Khan. The Secretary of the Muslim League, Wazir Hasan, is a born intriguer and a mischievous fellow. He is a Shia and plays on Mahmudabad's religious weakness and at present has great influence with him.' Hardinge to Sydenham, 27 March 1913, Hardinge Papers (85); Butler to Allan, 6 April 1913, Butler to Lovat Fraser, 8 April 1913, Butler Papers, MSS. EUR. E. 116 (71), IOL.

to lead the Muslims who 'are as sheep without a shepherd', the Ismaili leader conceded that he was unable to provide the leadership 'for my first advice will be loyalty of the kind that means trust and confidence and that trust and confidence the Muslims are not now giving to Government'.[20]

Heads also began to roll in the Aligarh College, once regarded as the most loyal of institutions. 'Things have been going very badly in Aligarh,' reported Meston, 'Aligarh is suffering from the ferment, like every other institution of its kind. The young party would be glad to see the European element entirely rejected and the whole place handed over to their own theories of education, which at present would be nothing short of a calamity. The older people are beginning to jib at the noisy domination of the younger clique, but have no constructive policy to set up against them.'[21] In August 1913 Ishaq Khan (1860-1918), its honorary secretary, admitted that the moderate men had lost ground with the public and were afraid of being ridiculed. Hamid Ali Khan (1875-1930), the Nawab of Rampur, resigned from the visitorship of the college in disgust;[22] others found their position insecure because of Mohamed Ali, who, according to the panic-stricken viceroy, turned the college into 'a hot-bed of sedition'.

[20]To Harcourt Butler, 3 March 1913, Butler Papers (71). For the resignation letters of Ameer Ali and the Aga Khan, see Mushirul Hasan (ed.), *Mohamed Ali in Indian Politics: Select Writings* (Delhi, 1982), Vol. I, pp. 188-94. His attitude towards the Aligarh Muslim university question and the annulment of Bengal's partition was linked with his attempts to have his status defined by the British government. Complaining that he often faced embarrassing and painful situations, as in Zanzibar where he received no formal recognition owing to the 'ambiguity' of his position, the Aga Khan urged the viceroy to recommend four more guns as an entirely personal distinction, in addition to the 11 which would mark his status, 'for I am regarded by the Indian public as more respected a person than many different gun chiefs'. The Aga Khan to Hardinge, 11 December 1915, L/PS/10/58, IOL.

[21]Meston to Ramsay MacDonald, 11 September 1913, Meston Papers (3). Also, W.S. Marris informed the lieutenant-governor: 'I do not want to trouble you with Aligarh affairs: but things are going decidedly bad at the College.... I don't think the sleeping days can be let lie much longer.' To Meston, 11 December 1913, Meston Papers (6). Compare his earlier assessment of the Aligarh situation, quoted in Gilbert, 'Autonomy and Consensus', op. cit., pp. 198-203.

[22]To Meston, 21 August 1913, and resignation of the Nawab of Rampur in enclosure, Ishaq Khan to Meston, 20 November 1913, Meston Papers (6). Also, the comment of the Governor of Bombay that the 'moderate men are nowhere' and ignorant and self-seeking youngermen—some of them products of Aligarh —were giving dangerous counsels'. Sydenham to Hardinge, 18 March 1913, Hardinge Papers (85).

Forster, who visited Aligarh in October 1912, sensed the drift of things. 'Life at Aligarh shows many seams', he noted in his diary on 25 October 1912:

> The English staff complained that they were not trusted to give the help they had hoped to give, but would be turned adrift as soon as the Mahammedans cd. stand without them: they could make some way with the students—not much, owing to the influence of *The Comrade*, a forward Islamic paper 'which told lies';—and none at all with the government body. The Mahammedans had an air of desperation, which may be habitual, but was impressive; why should Sir Edward Grey have been the *first* to recognize Italian rule in Tripoli (By the Peace of Ouchy in 15 October 1912, Turkery recognized the Italian occupation of Tripoli, its erstwhile province), they asked, and pertinently.[23]

Changes in Aligarh and other areas of northern India had no real impact on Delhi where Muslims had no organized political life of their own. The All-India Muslim League had a branch with a limited membership of 1,316; the rest were educational and religious bodies, such as the All-India *Ahl-i Hadis Conference*, founded in 1912, the *Anjuman-i Ahmadia*, formed in 1880, and the *Anjuman-i Hidayatul Islam*, established in 1906 to propagate Islamic education in the countryside through the setting up of *madrasas*. Their activities were centred round the Juma Masjid, the Fatehpuri mosque and the famous *madrasas* which had retained their hold despite the growing influence of more renowned seminaries like the *Dar al-Ulum* at Deoband and the *Nadvat al-Ulama* in Lucknow. But there was little talk of politics in Delhi generally and among Muslims particularly. Many were still wary of associating themselves with political issues because they could recount the trauma of 1857 when their co-religionists had to pay a heavy price for taking part in the revolt.

The general apathy towards politics could not be allowed to continue for long by leaders of other regions who were out to extend their sphere of influence in the newly-created capital of British India. In order to generate some interest, the Muslim League held its annual session in Delhi in 1910. But this move proved abortive because the Delhi Muslims did not take an active part in its deliberations. Irked by what was considered a

[23] Furbank, *E.M. Forster: A Life*, p. 227.

rebuff, the League stalwarts decided not to include any Delhi Muslim among the office-bearers.

News of the Turko-Italian war, however, transformed the political scene in and around Delhi. Much religious fervour was generated by a sudden burst of political activity, a steady rise in the publication and circulation of newspapers and the mushroom growth of organizations formed to befriend the beleagured Turkey. A weekly report of the Director of Intelligence observed

> that the war is now the one topic of conversation among Muhammadans, who are daily growing more and more excited over the wrongs suffered by Turkey. Passengers in the Durbar Railway trains also are seen eagerly reaching and discussing the latest newspaper war supplements, and even Khansamahs and other Muhammadan servants employed in various camps are said to be taking an extra-ordinary interest in the War news. The sober treatment of the subject that first characterized the utterances of leading Muslim journals is fast disappearing, and is giving way to denunciation of European Christian Powers in general and of Italy in particular.[24]

The diffuse sentiment that arose against the tyranny of the Christian countries found focus and leadership in the activities of Mohamed Ali. It was officially recorded that pan-Islamism had little footing in India till 1912 when Mohamed Ali removed the *Comrade* to Delhi.[25] Soon after, the paper was joined by the *Hamdard*, in Urdu. These journalistic ventures received unprecedented popularity. The energy, skill and buoyancy that Mohamed Ali brought to his enterprises would have probably ensured this anyway; but the fact that they caught the tide of Muslim public opinion at the turn and expressed pungently and clearly what many Muslims were vaguely thinking, proved to be an added asset. In more specific terms, the *Comrade* and the *Hamdard* offered a framework for the uneasiness and dissatisfaction of important Muslim groups, moulded their attitudes towards government and, above all, focussed on the news from the Balkan front which unfolded the story of Turkey's military reverses, and raised the spectre of European forces advancing into the heartlands of the Islamic world.

[24]Home Poll. B, January 1912, 121-3, NAI.

[25]Note by S.H. Fremantle, December 1917, Meston Papers (15).

Mohamed Ali's influence was unrivalled in his days. His every move was followed avidly and with overwhelming approval by most Muslims. He acted as guide and counsellor of many, including Ansari who rarely acted against his advice. It is easy to understand why this was so. Since the foundation of the All-India Muslim League in December 1906, Mohamed Ali was the very model of a leader on the move—bold, outspoken to the point of brashness and confident as reformer and social radical, as crusader for the Turkish cause and as champion of Muslim political interests.[26] And one other thing: he did not shun the limelight. He was always an activist, always restless, always eager and always imbued with a profound sense of playing the leading part in a great drama. He took centre stage so quickly and so dramatically that his detractors often suspected him of being in the middle of one conspiracy and on the fringe of another. But there was nothing of the conspiratorial or the surreptitious about his interests or actions. In nearly everything he said and wrote his overriding concern was to foster his community's interests in India and abroad. But this is not how all contemporaries viewed his role. Cynical and ill-informed government officials—his *bete noire* for long—attributed motives of money and publicity to denigrate him and pooh-poohed the causes he so vociferously championed.

Mohamed Ali's personality was as many-faceted as his political accomplishments. He was a highly emotional man, easily touched to tears and profoundly stirred by glamorous and ardent actions. He combined insatiable curiosity with a reluctance to dwell on anything that did not serve his political concerns; reticence with sociability, elaborate courtesy with moody neglect; a yearning for attention with a demand for privacy. He had a flair for the unorthodox, a freedom of thought and behaviour, and a personal dynamism that evoked a widespread response. His great asset was that he possessed to the full the resources of traditional oratory and journalism. Few among his contemporaries could match his combination of qualities: his range of articulate emotions, his capacity for analytical argument, his pathos, fantasy and wit and his power to marshal all these, through a command over the resources of the language, towards ends clearly discerned and passionately desired. He also had considerable poetic talent,

[26] I have examined his ideology and politics in *Mohamed Ali Ideology and Politics* (Delhi, 1981)

which combined with his fervour and the desperate situation in which Turkey found herself after the war, to create in him a feeling of impending martyrdom. In a scarcely veiled reference to the government's repressive policies, he wrote from Chhindwara: 'Such sufferings and privations as ours have only too often been the lot of mankind, in all ages and climes, and even today so many of our own countrymen and co-religionists have had to bear far worse things than have yet fallen to our share.'[27]

Mohamed Ali, at this period, was primarily a mass-appeal man. Party ties meant little to him; he preferred the role of a lone wolf outside the pack, neither subordinating himself to a group nor subordinating a group to himself except by the force of tongue. He did not allow others to equivocate: they were either for him or against him. For all his self-confidence, he was highly sensitive to criticism, quick to resent opposition and to take it as a personal attack. He therefore made no effort to conceal his scorn for those who disagreed with him and cared little whom he offended by plain speaking. This was true of dissenting comrades during the Muslim university and the Khilafat movements; if, however, they reverted to his orthodoxy he welcomed them back. Likewise, he was not much interested in following the 'correct' line in relation to the Khilafat movement which he pursued with optimistic persistence. He often disregarded Gandhi's admonishment and considered violence a legitimate, indeed a preferred method, and advocated it coldly. The end hallowed all means. Money and other forms of aid could not be tainted by their source, the cause purified them.

The extent of Mohamed Ali's influence is evident from the fact that two of his favourite projects—the medical mission and the *Anjuman-i-Khuddam-i Kaaba*—struck the most respondent chord in the hearts of the Delhi Muslims. The mission was generously funded by traders, merchants and weavers. The *Anjuman*, on the other hand, increased its membership from 900 to 2,000 in June 1914 owing to the active and enthusiastic backing of the hide and shoe merchants, the butchers, the artisans of the city and the students of the *madrasas*, including

[27]To James DuBoulay, 18 February 1919, Hasan (ed.), *Mohamed Ali in Indian Politics*, Vol. 2, p. 193. His political rhetoric is the subject of a study by Gregory C. Kozlowski, 'The Power of Language and the Language of Power: A Study on Mawlana Mohammad Ali's Political Rhetoric', *South Asia*, Vol. 5, 1, June 1982.

those from the *Nazarat al Maarif al Quraniya*, an institution founded in 1913 by Maulana Ubaidullah Sindhi (1872-1944) of Deoband to extend the teaching of the Quran and Islamic theology to members of the 'new Muslim party' Many of these activities owed much to Mohamed Ali's initiative. The troubles, observed H.C. Beadon, deputy commissioner of Delhi, began in 1912-1913 when Mohamed Ali started his two newspapers and launched the *Anjuman-i-Khuddam-i Kaaba*. He thus boomed the Turkish connection and seized the opportunity of the Balkan wars to excite Muslim feelings.[28] All this made it inevitable that the Khilafat question, when it was to become a political issue in 1919, had its supporters in Delhi already organized.

Ansari, fresh from his professional success in England, entered into Delhi's political scene unobtrusively.

[28]*DIC*, p. 134. Also, Aparna Basu, 'Mohamed Ali in Delhi: The Comrade Phase, 1912-1915', Mushirul Hasan (ed.), *Communal and Pan-Islamic Trends in Colonial India* (Delhi, 1985 edn.); Ferrel, op.cit.

3

Pan-Islamism at Home and Abroad

> How long this provoking hurricane of injustice and trouble?
> This delight at wailing and crying—how long?
> How long will ye take vengeance for the victor of Ayyub?
> You will show us the sight of the crusaders—how long?
>
> [Shibli Nomani]

> Dr Ansari was the head of the Mission and, to me, the most representative Indian Muslim. Externally he has not changed much. The same small moustache, the brooding mouth... black and energetic eyebrows stretched over his deep-set eyes. They were purposeful eyes, very kind in spite of the unwavering determination in their depths. His clothes had that masculine elegance which one associated with London. He talked very little, but always to the point and said next to nothing about India. Barring a distinct individuality he was not different from our own eminent physicians.
>
> Edib, *Inside India*, p. 17.

THOUGH IT IS only a guess, it is a fair and legitimate guess that Ansari watched with close attention the political developments around. It was under the influence of Mohamed Ali, for whom he retained a deep and lasting veneration in spite of subsequent political differences, that he was drawn into the vortex of public life and developed an interest in the troubled affairs of the Muslim community. He embraced politics less for ambition than from a sense of duty. He strove for power not for the sake of material rewards or personal prestige, but because he knew that he possessed talents and wanted to use them to do some good—by which he meant promoting the interests of the country and the community he belonged to. But, then, he had his own way to make in the world. Unlike many of his London friends, he had no family wealth or connections to hoist him into a ready-made political niche.

Events in the Balkans, which turned out to be a prelude to the final dismantling of the Ottoman empire, influenced Ansari most. As news of the unprincipled Italian invasion of Tripoli trickled through the columns of the *Comrade*, he discerned clear signs of a conspiracy to destroy and annex the few remaining Muslim states. He was disturbed by Britain's role, for as the Balkan wars progressed it became evident that much water had flown since Britain fought side by side with Turkey against Russia half a century ago. The view gained credence, not unjustifiably, that Britain had acquiesced in the Italian assault upon Tripoli. This triggered off a reaction of serious proportions and virtually guaranteed new spates of headlines in the newly emboldened Urdu press. 'There is a great agitation,' reported the viceroy, 'in Muslim circles over the war in the Balkans, and a general feeling that the Christians are combining to thrust the Muslims out of Europe.' The government of India, which had hitherto regarded the events in the Balkans with cool disdain, was forced to say that it could no longer cover up British culpability.

Indian Muslims conceived a number of projects to voice their concern. The *Anjuman-i-Khuddam-i Kaaba* was one; the medical mission to Turkey was another. Ansari's active association with the mission was a turning point in his public life and his political ideas were affected strongly by his experience in 1912 and 1913. Of all his life, these were the most formative years.

News of the medical mission first appeared in the *Comrade* on 19 October 1912: 'Those who know Dr Ansari's greatest ability as physician and surgeon will hail the idea of a relief mission under his direction with delight.' Ansari's own views appeared in the *Comrade* of 26 October. The Turk, he wrote,

> has been fighting ever since he established his empire on the shores of the Bosphorus and has so far survived the deadliest of struggles. Yet never before in the annals of the Ottoman empire had he to face a situation so critical in nature, so difficult to handle and so dangerous in consequences as he has now before him. It is perfectly obvious that the very existence of the Turkish nation depends upon the issue of this war Firstly, the medical service in the Turkish army has been very recently organized and as such will be unable to cope with the requirements of such a deadly war. Secondly, Turkey's foes are already receiving, on a very large scale,

> medical...help from all parts of Europe; and the poor Turk is left entirely to his own limited resources. What we can do to lighten his burden is to provide an efficient field-hospital where a fair number of the sick and wounded can be accommodated.

He concluded with an appeal for public subscriptions. This met with an immediate and overwhelming response; by the end of November 1912, the total contribution for the Turkish Relief Fund reached Rs 1,18,762.[1] The Red Crescent Society of Delhi and other Muslims of the city raised Rs 32,000. Contributions also came from the ladies of Hyderabad, from the *dargah* at Ajmer and from the *Sajjadanashin* of Fatehgarh and Sassaram.[2] The mission received government support as well. Ansari noted, just before it set out: 'So far the Government of India have not in any way shown any dislike for our human(e) Mission, nor should I think they are likely to do so. My own impression has been that they have been very fair to us and have given every legitimate help and support.'[3]

Ansari claimed that his mission was 'truly All-India' as it included representatives from every province of British India. 'It is gratifying to notice,' he continued, 'that the men who have joined the Mission are from the cultured middle and higher class families, representing the flower of Muhammadan youth, who are fully alive to the responsibilities and nature of the work with which they are entrusted.'[4] The mission was formed of five doctors,[5] seven dressers,[6] and ten male nurses and ambulance bearers.[7] The Old Boys of the Aligarh College were well repre-

[1] *Comrade*, 16 November 1912; Ghaffar, *Hayat-i Ajmal*, p. 122.

[2] *Comrade*, 9 November 1912.

[3] To Mohamed Ali, 29 November 1912, Hasan (ed.), *Muslims and the Congress*, p. 1. It is rather surprising that contemporary accounts of Turkey make no mention of Ansari's medical mission. Mary Poynter, for instance, merely refers to other missions: the British Red Crescent Hospital, to the work of Lady Lowther, the wife of the British Ambassador and to the hospital of Major Doughty-Wylie. See Mary A. Poynter, *When Turkey was Turkey: in and around Constantinople* (London, 1921).

[4] *Comrade*, 30 November 1912.

[5] M.A. Ansari, Ali Azhar H. Fyzee (Bombay), Mohammad Naim Ansari (Jaunpur), Mahmudullah (Calcutta) and Shamsul-Bary (Gaya)—all professional doctors.

[6] Ghulam Ahmad Khan (Lahore), M. Nurul Hasan (Meerut), Mohammad Chiraghuddin (Delhi), Syed Tawangar Husain (Karnal), Hamid Rasul (Chapra), Abdul Waheed Khan (Mirzapur) and Husain Raza Beg.

[7] Abdur Rahman Siddiqi, Shuaib Qureshi, Aziz Ansari, Khaliquzzaman, Abdur

sented, no less than eight of the twenty-one proceeding from India had studied for some time at and, in some cases, graduated from Aligarh. Among them were Abdur Rahman Siddiqi, Shuaib Qureshi and Khaliquzzaman, all bound to Ansari by deep personal loyalty and affection. Khaliquzzaman, who met Ansari on 13 November 1912 at Aligarh where the students had given up their weekly *piece de resistance* of *pulau, zarda* and *firnee* to raise Rs 6,500 for the Turkish Relief Fund, recorded his meeting:

> News was received which spread like wildfire in the College of an attack of the Balkan powers on Turkey. We had already decided to give up meat diet during the Tripoli war agitation and now we took steps to collect funds between ourselves and sent the savings to the Red Crescent Society in Turkey.... One day while I was playing tennis in front of my room... I was introduced as the football captain of my College eleven to Dr Ansari. I expressed my joy and admiration for him for having undertaken the responsibility of leading the Medical Mission. He told me that he had come to Aligarh to find some youngmen to go with him to help him in the discharge of his duties. I said, 'I am not a doctor'. He replied, 'You can do managerial work as well as some nursing', after which he left me seriously cogitating over the matter. By the evening I had made up my mind to join the Mission.[8]

The idea of a medical mission found favour because it carried to Muslims in Turkey a message of deep sympathy and goodwill from their co-religionists in India; Viqar-ul-Mulk (1841-1917), secretary of the Aligarh College, said so in his letter of 29 June 1913.[9] In Delhi alone, 15,000 Muslims accompanied the members of the mission all the way from Juma Masjid to the railway station to bid them farewell.[10] Mohamed Ali was jubilant: 'In joy and in grief the heart of Islam beats in unison, but this is the first time in the history of Indian Mussalmans that their sympathy had taken shape as a humane and beneficent measure to relieve the sufferings of their brethren abroad who lie torn and bleeding. The moral value of this fact can hardly be

Rahman, Qazi Bashiruddin Ahmad, Manzoor Ali—all educated in or connected with the Aligarh College. Besides, there were Yusuf Ansari (Gangoh: district Saharanpur), Ismail Husain Shirazi (Sirajganj: Bengal) and Tafazzul Husain.

[8] Khaliquzzaman, *Pathway to Pakistan*, p. 21.

[9] R.A. Jafri, *Karawan-i Gumgushta* (Karachi, 1971), pp. 333–4.

[10] *Comrade*, 9 August 1912.

over-estimated.'[11] Ansari might have recognized the throng on the railway platform. The viceroy had sent a representative; Ajmal Khan was on the platform with his beard and animated gestures, leaning on his walking stick with its silver band and braced for a parting of poignant significance. Several Muslim divines were there too, so that the *ulama* might be associated with this departure of the mission and their blessings bestowed upon it. They were probably inspired by the example of Shibli Nomani who touched Ansari's feet at the Lucknow railway station in a touching demonstration of his affection for the leader of the medical mission.[12] Mohamed Ali was there of course, because he had much to do both with the choice of Ansari as leader of the mission and with the setting of this scene.

Ansari seemed a trifle overawed by the circumstances of his departure. His short speech was diffident. Habitually modest, he took care to emphasize that this send-off was not a tribute to himself but to the efforts of the people who helped organize the mission.

The mission sailed from Bombay on 15 December 1912, reaching Constantinople on 1 January. The story of its work and experience was told with a minute exactitude in Ansari's letters, published in the *Comrade,* which were the longest and most descriptive he ever wrote. They present his experiences, embellished as a theatrical panorama, with himself a figure in centre stage. They reveal the unflagging interest in Turkey which never left him and further indicate that his experiences in that country set him on the path of strong opposition to British imperial rule in India which characterized so much of his life.

When Ansari reached Turkey the long night of Hamidian despotism was long over and the dawn of freedom had come in July 1908 when the constitution had once again been proclaimed and elections ordered. The Young Turk Revolution, led by the Committee of Union and Progress, achieved many of its objectives and its three important leaders—Enver Bey (1881-1922), Talat Bey (1872-1926) and Kemal Bey (1840-1888)—remained in effective control. But it was not all smooth sailing, as Ansari's despatches were to reveal. There were dissenters both within and outside the Party, many of whom merged to form the Liberal Union *(Hurriyat wa Itilaf)* on 21

[11]*Comrade*, 14 December 1912; Ghaffar, *Hayat-i Ajmal*, pp. 122–3

[12]Sulaiman Nadvi, *Hayat-i Shibli*, p. 595; Jafri, *Karawan-i Gumgushta*, pp. 315–6.

November 1911. What deepened the political crisis was the 'big stick election' in April 1912, the subsequent repressive policies of the Unionists against their opponents, reports of setbacks at the war front against Italy and internal revolts in many of the provinces, notably in Salonika. In the midst of such troubles, a group of 'Saviour Officers', formed in May-June 1912, went into action and forced Said Pasha (1863-1921) and his Cabinet to resign. But the new Cabinet, headed by Ghazi Ahmed Mukhtar Pasha (1839-1918), was short-lived. Taking advantage of their preoccupation with the Italian war and the attack of the Balkan allies in October 1912, the Unionists launched their surprise assault on the Sublime Porte on 23 January 1913. Led by Enver Bey, a small party of officers forced their way into the Cabinet room, shooting the Minister of War and forcing the aged Kamil Pasha to write out his resignation. From then until 1919 Turkey was governed by a virtual military dictatorship, dominated by Enver, Talat and Kemal Pashas. Their rule ended only with the defeat of Turkey in 1918, when the Committee of Union and Progress disbanded itself, its leaders fled abroad and the liberal spokesmen emerged from exile, concealment or insignificance to preside over the dissolution of the Ottoman empire.[13]

Ansari was fascinated by the activities of the Young Turks, baffled by the machinations of European Powers and aghast at the 'inhuman deeds done by the Balkan armies during the occupation of Salonica and Kavalla'. What he witnessed and experienced strengthened his determination 'to do all that lay in our power to lessen the sufferings, to sympathize with and soothe the bleeding hearts of our fellow-Muslims in Turkey'.[14] But the going was often tough. Members of the mission had to set up hospitals, build bridges and pitch tents in the 'teeth of a most bitterly cold wind and the mud almost knee-deep'.[15] There were moments of frustration as well. 'I cannot tell you what difficulties are placed in our way here in arranging a small matter,' complained Ansari. 'Our things have all arrived last week, and in any other country but Turkey everything would have been arranged in a day or two.'[16] He went on to utter a cry of absolute despair: 'My men and myself have been driven to

[13]This paragraph is based on Bernard Lewis, *The Emergence of Modern Turkey* (London, 1961), p. 222.

[14]*Comrade*, 25 January 1913.

[15]Ibid., 22 February 1913.

[16]Ibid., 15 February 1913.

eating nothing but cheese and bread for three days, owing to the box containing our provisions having been stolen by someone.'[17] Such hardships did not dampen Ansari's enthusiasm. He and his comrades worked with characteristic energy to alleviate the plight and sufferings of the Turks. 'We have all been working terribly hard,' he reported on 22 February 1913. 'I may tell you that our field-hospital, if not the best, is second to none in Turkey. Not only are our wards, dispensary, operating theatre and general provision most excellent, but every member of the Mission has got the zeal and energy of ten persons and a most excellent *espirit de corps* exists among them, of which I naturally feel very proud.'

There can be no doubt that Ansari was entranced by Turkey which was the last vestige of Islamic activity and impressed with its military prowess both in the past and in his own times. He was carried away by the ruins of the fortress in Vienna which was captured by the Turks under Suleiman (1496-1566). His imagination was fired by brilliant scenes of the past, almost as if he had lived it and he recalled with pride the glories of the Turkish empire extended over three continents: from Baghdad to Budapest and from Cairo to the boundaries of Morocco. 'It had been a remarkable career of achievements', he wrote in 1925, many years after Turkish military prestige had declined and the myth of the invincibility of Turkish troops shattered. Ansari continued: 'Probably in no other dynasty in the world's history has there ever been a succession of such brilliant rulers.... The Turk may well take immense pride in his glorious military heritage.'[18]

In 1912-13, Ansari identified Turkish military prowess with the Young Turks who had salvaged Turkey's waning prestige. This is borne out by his description of the *coup d'etat* engineered by Enver Bey on 23 January 1913. Commenting on the coup and on Enver Bey's success, Ansari opined: 'It is obvious that the Young Turks have saved the prestige of Turkey and mean to die honourably, if death *must* come. It is impossible even for an adversary to abstain from admiring their pluck, although it still remains to be seen whether this pluck is going to save Turkey.'[19]

[17] *Comrade*, 22 February 1913.
[18] Ansari to Mohamed Ali, 25 July 1925, *Comrade*, 18 September 1925.
[19] *Comrade*, 22 February 1913.

Ansari also admired some leading Turkish nationalists he met. Among those who impressed him most was Enver Bey, 'a youngman of about 35, exceedingly handsome, with most expressive eyes full of determination [and] with a demeanour of a very strong man, chastened with hardships and sufferings'.[20] He and Zafar Ali Khan had several meetings with him. After one such *tete-a tete*, Ansari wrote that Enver Bey 'believed in working loyally for his God and country' and was sure that Turkey would rise soon to 'its full glory and power'. Recently, Ansari informed Mohamed Ali, 'he has had a narrow escape from death by drowning; but he is destined to perform greater work for his nation and God saved him'.[21] Ansari also got together with Halide Edib, 'one of the leading lights of the Party of Union and Progress, a silent, though very effective power working behind the scenes';[22] Khalil Beg 'a gallant soldier' who performed invaluable service against the Bulgarian regiment with his band of volunteers from Crete, Arabia and Anatolia; Talat Bey, with whom Ansari discussed the proposal for the sale of Turkish bonds in India; and Sheikh Abdul Aziz Chawish, 'a very impressive man who chooses every word before uttering it'.[23]

To provide medical relief was not Ansari's sole concern. He was equally active in promoting schemes which would render moral and material support to the Turks and help reaffirm his countrymen's solidarity with their struggle; in fact he indicated in some of his speeches that he thought less of the medical work he had done than of the political results between Turkey and the Indian Muslims and that in doing so he was no ideologue but a patient, open-minded and resourceful pragmatist.

The sale of Turkish bonds, originating in a discussion with Talat Bey, was one of Ansari's favourite schemes. So great was his enthusiasm that he planned an extensive tour to popularize it in India. 'I would deal in my lectures,' he wrote to Mohamed Ali, 'with Turkey, its people, its institutions, its government, the

[20]*Comrade*, 15 February 1913.

[21]Ibid.

[22]Ibid., 8 February 1913. 'The picture of Halide Hanoum,' wrote one of her admirers, 'confronts us on all sides throughout Anatolia. Among the heroes of the revolution, the Turks reverence her as their Joan of Arc. No history of the Nationalist movement can ever be attempted or thought of without a full record of her courageous loyalty and untiring patriotism'. Grace Ellison, *An Englishwoman in Angora* (London, 1923), p. 214.

[23]*Comrade*, 8 February 1913.

war and its results..., the future of Turkey and the way in which the Mussalmans of India can best help the Turks and themselves... I wish to start in Bombay, go to Hyderabad, Bhopal, Lucknow, Rampur, Aligarh and Delhi. And then later on I will go to Lahore, Meerut, Allahabad, Banaras, Bankipur and Calcutta.'[24] He also planned the setting up of a Muslim Bank, a Cooperative Society and a university at Medina. Ansari and Zafar Ali Khan were members of the Constitution Committee. Urging Mohamed Ali to discuss the much canvassed university scheme with Shibli and Iqbal, Ansari wrote: 'We have sent you a cable and hope you will not spare any pains in preparing the constitution and curriculum for the University of Medina on the lines of the Aligarh University.'[25] Then, there was the colonization scheme for refugees in Anatolia "to sow the seeds of greater things'. 'We have had several meetings of the Colonization Society,' Ansari reported to Mohamed Ali on 27 May 1913,

> and a definite plan of work has been decided. Tomorrow a committee consisting of five persons [Ansari, Zafar Ali Khan, Agah Bey (representing Ottoman Red Crescent), Saleh Bey, an agricultural expert and Ahmed Foad] is going to Anatolia to see the tracts of the land the government is willing to place at the disposal of the Society.... The Committee has been given every facility by the government to inspect these tracts. The members are going first to Angora to see 65,000 acres of land in Qara Ilias, then to Konia and Oulihishla by train and from there by carriages to Adana, where 45,000 acres of land near Jabali—Barakat are available. The exact location of the two villages would be decided after the completion of the tour.[26]

Many of these hastily-conceived projects failed to take off and were ignored in Turkey and forgotten in India. But the sincere and devoted work of the mission received wide acclaim in both countries. The scenes of leave-taking at Hindia and Sanjak Tepi

[24] *Comrade*, 17 May and 7 June 1913.

[25] Ibid., 31 May 1913.

[26] Ansari to Mohamed Ali, 27 May 1913, Ansari Collection, NMML. Also, see report submitted by B. Lindsay and Abdur Rauf on the internment of the Ali Brothers. Hasan (ed.), *Mohamed Ali in Indian Politics*, Vol. 2, pp. 145, 159–61. The scheme of colonization was supported by the *Comrade* in a series of articles contributed by Abdur Rahman Siddiqi. See Bamford, *Histories*, p. 113. Urdu extract of Ansari's letters are quoted in Jafri, *Karawan-i Gumgushta*, pp. 326–8.

where the two hospitals were established, were 'most touching and will remain in our memory'.[27] Ansari would have felt the same way when he and his men reached Bombay on the first part of their journey on 4 July 1913. Arriving at the Ballard Pier, leaning on the arm of Mohamed Ali and looking pale and worn out but in good spirits, Ansari and his comrades were greeted by Fazulbhoy Currimbhoy (D. 1872) and Umar Subhani and by cheering crowds bearing banners with hospitable inscriptions and carrying garlands and flowers.[28] A similar welcome awaited them in Delhi on the evening of 10 July. The *Comrade* reported:

> Long before the time of arrival large crowds of people had begun to assemble on the platform and along the approaches to the railway station.... As the train moved slowly in, the air was rent with glad shouts of welcome. Thousands on the platform pressed forward to catch a glimpse of the man and his lieutenants, who had rendered good services to Islam, to kiss their hands and offer them flowers and garlands....
>
> As the party entered the vast courtyard of the mosque [Juma Masjid] it was greeted by thousands of Muslims of Delhi.... They were all inspired by a single sentiment and filled with a single aim—to do honour to the men who had made sacrifices in the cause of Islam.... After the Maghrib prayers the procession was formed again and it started along a different route for the Fatehpuri Mosque.... The entire Muslim Delhi seemed to have turned out for the occasion, [and] nothing but surging masses of humanity were visible in unbroken waves as far as the eye could reach in either direction.... Every now and then loud and irresistible voices called Dr Ansari to stand up and show himself and he could not but obey the call. And one can never forget the emotion of the moment as the hero of the occasion raised himself bashfully from his seat and in his characteristically modest way acknowledged the vociferous greetings of thousands of his admiring brethren—the lusty cheers of the youth, the applause of the grown-up men and the blessings of the aged. It was amidst such thrilling scenes that the long route was slowly traversed

[27]Ansari to Mohamed Ali, 27 May 1913, Ansari Collection, NMML; *Comrade*, 31 June 1913.

[28]*Comrade*, 5 July 1913; Jafri, *Karawan-i Gumgushta*, p. 337.

and the procession reached its destination.... Such remarkable tributes of love and admiration are ample rewards for men who serve a noble cause and prove themselves of some use to their fellow-beings.[29]

Soon after his return from Turkey, Ansari got mixed up in the Kanpur mosque episode—an episode sparked off by the sacrilege committed by the municipality in demolishing a portion of the Machli Bazar mosque as part of the city improvement scheme. But his part in the agitation, whipped up by the irrepressible Mohamed Ali, did not extend beyond accompanying Ajmal Khan on his weekly visits to Kanpur to treat those wounded in the police firing of 3 August.[30] His role in the Muslim university movement was also limited. Though a member of the Foundation Committee and of several deputations, his own links with the college at Aligarh were tenuous. Not being an 'Old Boy' he could hardly be expected to share the enthusiasm of the Ali Brothers, Abdur Rahman Siddiqi, Shuaib Qureshi and Khaliquzzaman. Supporting the university cause was dictated by personal and political considerations: loyalty to Mohamed Ali combined with the need to remain in the mainstream of Muslim political life.[31] At the same time his political interests were widening and he was not only learning rapidly but growing in stature all the time. To compare Ansari of 1912-13, at the time of the medical mission, with Ansari at the time of the Muslim League session in 1918, is to see at once the distance he had travelled

[29]*Comrade*, 12 July 1913.

[30]Ghaffar, *Hayat-i Ajmal*, pp. 136–7.

[31]In 1917 Ansari took the lead in founding the 'Central Bureau for the release of Muslim Internees' and was the chief campaigner, besides Gandhi, for the release of the Ali Brothers from internment. The Raja of Mahmudabad was the president of the Bureau, Ansari and Syed Abdul Rahman of Delhi its secretaries, and Ajmal Khan the treasurer. *New Era*, 24 November 1917. In September 1917 Ansari reaffirmed his loyalty to Mohamed Ali by canvassing for his election to the presidentship of the Muslim League. 'It is imperative,' he wrote to Abdul Majid Khwaja, 'to hold public meetings where popular voice should with all force and unanimity declare him to be the only person fit for this honour'. He and Mazharul Haq wrote a joint letter to the members of the Muslim League in a similar vein. They referred to his 'noble services rendered at the most psychological moment in the history of the community to which he belongs' and which 'mark him out as one of the most potent factors in the formation of the Indian nation' Ansari to Khwaja, 3 September 1917; Circular letter, 3

and the confidence he had gained. The same determination and ability were there, but tempered by a maturing of powers, a deepening of character and experience.

Ansari's heart was in several pan-Islamic schemes. Notable amongst them were the *Anjuman-i-Khuddam-i Kaaba* and the *Nazarat al-Ma'arif al Quraniya*, set up in the Fatehpuri mosque not far from Ansari's consulting chambers. He was one of the patrons of this Quranic school, having helped to raise financial support from the Nawab of Rampur, the Begum of Bhopal and a number of wealthy Muslim traders from Bombay and Karachi. This is testified to by Khaliquzzaman. 'My cousin', he wrote in *Pathway to Pakistan*,

> Istafa Karim, who, after graduating from Aligarh had joined the Arabic institution *Nazaratul Ma'arif* started by Maulana Ubaidullah Sindhi at Delhi, asked me to meet the Maulana in the Fatehpuri Mosque. I found the Maulana as full of anti-British sentiments as myself. In his talk he argued and tried to convince me that the time for Jihad had arrived.... He was a pupil of Maulana Mahmud Hasan of Deoband, who was in close touch with Dr Ansari, the Ali Brothers and Hakim Ajmal Khan. Money was collected in different centres to feed the revolutionary activities but the principal centre was at Delhi where Hakim Ajmal Khan and Dr Ansari with their great influence on the Nawab of Rampur, Begum of Bhopal and the titled gentry, big and small, all over India, were exerting every nerve not to allow the movement to suffer from lack of funds....[32]

Ansari also helped to bring about close relations between the *ulama* and a section of Western-educated Muslims. He was in an ideal position to do so because of his family connections with Deoband. He introduced Ubaidullah Sindhi to Mohamed Ali and Azad.[33] He came into contact with Abdul Bari (1878-1926), the distinguished *alim* of Firangi Mahal, Lucknow, when the Maulana and his *madrasa* students travelled in UP collecting money for Turkish relief and for the Red Crescent Medical

September 1917, Abdul Majid Khwaja Papers.

[32]Khaliquzzaman, op.cit., pp. 31–2; Minault, *The Khilafat Movement*, p. 30; Ghaffar, *Hayat-i Ajmal*, pp. 129–30.

[33]Ubaidullah Sindhi, *Khutbat-i Sindhi*, p. 28, quoted in Minault, *The Khilafat Movement*, p. 30.

Mission. The scheme to set up the *Nazarat al-Ma'arif*, mooted by Mahmud Hasan, Ansari and Ajmal Khan, was intended to reconcile the Deoband and Aligarh traditions of education and provide the necessary thrust to the converging courses in politics of the modern and the traditionally educated. Likewise, the *Jalsa-i Dastarbandi*, convened in 1910 and attended by a delegation from Aligarh led by Aftab Ahmad Khan (1867-1930), the *Jamiyat al-Ansar*, founded by Ubaidullah Sindhi and the *Anjuman-i-Khuddam-i Kaaba*, established in May 1912, were positive efforts to bridge the gulf that separated the modern and the traditionally-educated Muslims. Such initiatives were both timely and rewarding because of the mutual recognition that a unified effort was the only effective way of building a powerful movement in defence of Muslim interests in India and abroad. The 'orthodox' and the 'anglicised' were drawn together and 'saw that after all they were not so unlike each other as they had imagined'. 'Once more,' declared Mohamed Ali, 'Muslim society in India presented a level of uniformity and the bitterest opponents of a generation ago stood shoulder to shoulder.... If even a decade previously anyone had ventured to foretell such a result, he would have been laughed at for such a fantastic prophesy.'[34]

The Muslim League session of December 1918 provided the most striking evidence of the growing fraternization between the 'orthodox' and the 'anglicised' Muslims. A large number of *ulama*, drawn from different regions and representing various theological schools, were present. They had never done so before. What was equally unusual was that they asserted their right to speak and be consulted on both the political and the religious issues concerning their community. This, too, they had not done before. Politics to them had become all of a sudden a necessary part of their faith, which explains why they not only appeared at all subsequent conferences organized by the League and the Khilafat Committee, but also influenced major policy decisions. Having perceived the growing threat to Islam, they realized that they must now be active in addressing themselves to the current anxieties—political, social and religious—of Indian Muslims, or else see true Islam as they understood it and their own claims to guide the community go by default.

[34] Afzal Iqbal (ed.), *My Life: A Fragment*, p. 44.

The presence of the *ulama* was largely due to Ansari's effort. He invited them in order to add weight to the Khilafat protest, assured them a prominent place on the platform and sang peans of praise in their honour. He was also the star performer as chairman of the reception committee, delivered a powerful speech, later proscribed by the Punjab government. His address, according to a government report,

> resembled the sermon of a fanatic more than the address of a politician and amounts to a condemnation to death of the King of the Hejaz and an exhortation to Jehad if Mesopotamia, Arabia and Palestine are not handed back to Turkey. It accuses Great Britain of breaking her promise to respect the sanctity of the holy places and demands the independence of the Muslims of North Africa and Central Asia. Dr Ansari's demands were supported throughout by quotations from the Quran and the Hadis, and the speech... had an extraordinary effect on the audience. The Muslim League of that period regularly took its cue from the Congress and the methods employed to stampede opinion into the ultra extremist camp met with as great success as in the Congress pandal. As they dispersed, members were heard cursing the destroyers of Islam, and strong anti-British feeling was evident.[35]

Interspersed with extensive quotations from the Quran and the *Hadith*, Ansari tried to reassure the *ulama* and allay their fears about the *la-dini* (religion-less) character of the League.

[35] *History* (Delhi), p. 3. Hasrat Mohani made an interesting reference to Ansari's address in one of his poems. The message was not lost on his readers. He wrote:

Khutba-i League hai kafaara gunah-gaari ka
ab hamen shikwa nahin Doctor Ansari ka
kaash samjhen ise ashaab-i hukumat ki nahin
dakhl is pairu-e sidq men ghaddari ka
khud hi insaaf se kahye ki uthaa rakhha hai
aap ne koi daqeeqa bhi dil-aazaari ka
Hasrat is khutbe se naalaan hon na kiyon ahl-e fareb
raaz makhfi na rahaa un ki gunah-gaari ka

The address at the League is an atonement for [its past] sins: now we have no complaint against Dr Ansari.

Would the government realize that there is nothing treacherous in following the path of righteousness.

Judge for yourself, have you left any stone unturned to bring distress to our hearts?

Setting out his ideas with an eloquence and personal feeling that were rare to his time, he echoed the pan-Islamic concerns of his community and articulated the religious demands of the *ulama*, which had so far been ignored by the League. Ansari's manner was direct, his language simple. What he said could scarcely ever be misrepresented; where he stood none could mistake. With his frank, serious look he attracted attention in any crowd by the firmness of his views and the force of his personality.

Ansari was now a recognized leader of the north Indian Muslims and had reached the moment when honours began to fall on him like the leaves of autumn—public receptions, the acclaim of his community and the second class of the Usmanieh Order, conferred by the Sultan of Turkey in recognition of his services.[36] The *Anjuman-i Islamia* of Bombay gave him a welcome. Here he spoke of the success of the medical mission, a 'wonderful conception on the part of Indian Muslims.[37] The Begum of Bhopal feted him and showered words of praise for his sense of devotion.[38] He was specially invited to the Friday congregation at the Delhi Juma Masjid on 11 July 1913 where he described the struggle of the Turks against the Christian powers 'who are bent upon wiping Islam from the face of the earth';[39] for obvious reasons he tried to smother their deficiencies under a flood of eloquence about their patriotic cause. A day later, he lectured amidst a rousing reception at the Aligarh College, where he had raised Rs 45,000 for the medical mission on his last visit. Here he assured his audience that the spirit of the Turkish nation was not dead and boasted that the most important result of his trip was the fusion of a union between Turkey and India.[40] On 29-30 November he spoke on the colonization scheme in Amritsar and gave an illustrated account of his work at the two hospitals, one near Chetalja at Hindia

O Hasrat! how should the deceivers not be annoyed at this 'address'?
The secret of their sins is no longer hidden.

Khalid Hasan Qadiri, *Hasrat Mohani* (Delhi, 1985), pp. 204–5.

[36]Ansari to Secretary, Government of India, Foreign and Political Department, 28 February 1914, Home Poll. Deposit, July 1914, 17, NAI.

[37]*Comrade*, 5 July 1913.

[38]Ibid.

[39]Bamford, *Histories*, p. 113.

[40]Ibid.

and the other at Chanak Qela, near Dardanelles.[41] Everybody was impressed. Mohamed Ali 'privately' suggested to Meston to honour Ansari by making him the viceroy's surgeon and to grant him and other members of the mission the Kaiser-i Hind medal.[42] Shibli Nomani sang paeans of praise and expressed the gratitude of the Muslims in a poem which came to be recited in the towns of northern India.[43] This must have surely gladdened Ansari. To him the trip to Turkey was a novel experience and, coming on top of the impressions left by his journey around the world, it had a powerful effect in crystallizing his ideas. His journey in 1913 provided the experience he needed to fire his imagination and opened a new world to him. He returned to India intellectually stimulated, full of ideas and with the energy to put them across.

When the intelligence department secured some letters implicating Ansari in a pan-Islamic conspiracy, Meston declared that he was not the stuff of which conspirators were made.[44] His professional character 'stands high, unlike that of some of the other men who have recently been interned. Quite moderate men think well of him and regard him as a capable professional man, distinguished by his friendships abroad and reasonably

[41] *Comrade*, 20 December 1913.

[42] Mohamed Ali to Meston, 30 June 1913, Hardinge Papers (85).

[43] *Adaa karte hai hum shukr janaab-i- hazrat-i baari*
ke khairiyat se aaye membaraan-i waafd-i Ansari
yehi tha dard-i Islami yehi thi rasm-i gham khwaari
hazaaron kos jaa kar bhaaiyon ki tum ne khidmat ki
tumhara naaz uthaayen ahl-i millat jis qadar kam hai
ke tum ne ghaaziyaan-i deen ki, ki hai naaz bardaari

We thank the Almighty for the safe return of the members of the Ansari mission. You've served your brethern thousands of miles away. This was consistent with the spirit of Islamic compassion and the tradition of sharing mutual grief and sorrow.

Your deeds surely deserve glorification,
for you have heightened the morale of the conquerors in the way of the Faith.

[44] 'On the other hand', he continued, 'the more respectable Mahomedans have considerable regard for him; they are rather proud of the part that he took in organizing and taking out a medical mission to Turkey during the last Balkan War. Since his return his prestige has been considerable; he has a large medical practice of a thoroughly reputable character; and I believe he has taken to the ordinary duties of intelligent citizenship in Delhi'. Meston to Chelmsford, 7 September 1916, Chelmsford Papers (17).

interested in Muhammadan politics generally, without committing himself in any way, so far as they know, to extreme views.'[45] Opposing the move to arrest Ansari, the lieutenant-governor reiterated that his participation in a conspiracy was unlikely. He concluded:

> In Moslem circles he commands considerable respect and moderate men regard him much more highly than, for example, Muhammad Ali or those who have been more recently interned. His work in the Mission during the last Turkish War is a matter of pride to them, as well as the professional position which he occupies in India; a firebrand is not what he is generally regarded as being.[46]

[46]Meston to Charles Cleveland, 6 September 1916, Meston Papers (4).

[45]Note on Ansari's arrest, 6 September 1916, Meston Papers (1). The viceroy agreed and the proposal to arrest Ansari was dropped. Chelmsford to Meston, 16/17 September 1916, Chelmsford Papers (17).

4

Among the Satyagrahis

> Until the transfer of the capital from Calcutta, Delhi was practically free from agitation. But the seditionist has already invaded its precincts and achieved considerable success in converting the minds of the inhabitants of Delhi, who loved peace and pleasure even to a fault.... I have no hesitation in saying that no other city in India can claim the unenviable notoriety that Delhi enjoys for simmering popular discontent and even active contempt for British institutions and the British point of view. The result is that *within a few years of the change of capital the people of Delhi have become adept in organizing demonstrations and using strong language from the pulpit and in the press* [emphasis added]. Once Delhi decided to assume an hostile attitude, the suggestion was taken up by other towns connected with Delhi by railway and postal communications.
>
> Home Department, F. No. 36, 1920,
> Delhi Archives.

THE COUNTRYWIDE agitation against the Rowlatt Bills, enacted by the government and foisted on the country with scant regard for public opinion, offered Ansari an opportunity to plunge into national politics. By 1919, this shy and youthful doctor with limited experience of public life moved to the epicentre of the Rowlatt satyagraha.

Though Ansari's political exertions in his early years were inspired by Mohamed Ali, he was equally captivated by the charisma, prestige and personal authority of Gandhi. He had not worked with the Mahatma before, but had admired him from afar and was won to him by personal contact in the course of the agitation for Mohamed Ali's release from internment. He was so moved by his initiatives that, at the 1918 Muslim League session, he lionized and extolled Gandhi as the 'acknowledged intrepid leader of India who is never afraid to speak out the truth and who has, by his noble actions, endeared himself as

1. Ansari as an actor in Othello staged in Edinburgh

7. A view of *Dar-us-Salam*.

much to the Mussalmans as to the Hindus'.[1] The strength of his charisma and the extent to which his appeal had aroused sentiments against the Rowlatt Bills, impressed itself forcibly upon Ansari and he plunged into the Rowlatt satyagraha as the Mahatma's chief lieutenant in Delhi.

The Rowlatt Bills, rushed through the imperial legislative council in the teeth of opposition from all Indian members, evoked widespread indignation in India. The country's rage and revulsion was articulated by Gandhi, the hero of Champaran, Kaira and Ahmedabad. From his sick bed, he condemned the 'devilish legislation' which was not just 'a stray example of lapse of righteousness and justice' but 'evidence of a determined policy of repression'. When his repeated appeals to the viceroy to withhold his assent from the 'black bills' failed, he decided on satyagraha, a weapon he had effectively put to use in South Africa. The man who had made common cause with the British in the war and conducted a personal recruitment campaign now advocated satyagraha as 'a process of self-purification' in the 'sacred fight' against the Raj. 'I think the growing generation will not be satisfied with petitions etc.,' he wrote to Dinshaw E. Wacha (1844-1936) on 25 February 1919, 'we must give them something effective. Satyagraha is the only way, it seems to me, to stop terrorism.' In major cities and provincial towns alike people went up against the new legislative provisions and there was excitement all round at the outcome of Gandhi's first ever confrontation with the Raj. The young Jawaharlal was 'afire with enthusiasm' because Gandhi offered at last 'a way out of the tangle, a method of action which was straight and open and possibly effective'.[2]

Various historical accounts have described the upswell of sentiment in favour of the Gandhian movement, delineated the process which enabled divergent groups, often with dissimilar and contradictory interests, to coalesce in a most vigorous assault on government authority, and revealed how the social and economic dislocation caused by the First World War and the Muslim frustration over the indeterminate future of the Khilafat sparked off a serious confrontation with the Raj.[3] In such circumstances, the Rowlatt Act provided the catalyst and Gandhi the

[1]Hasan (ed.), *Muslims and the Congress*, p. 274.

[2]Nehru, *An Autobiography*, p. 41.

[3]See contributions in Kumar (ed.), *Essays on Gandhian Politics*.

spark for ventilating the anger and resentment of aggrieved classes and communities. The Mahatma's ingenuity lay in canalizing their grievances, both latent and active in form, into a massive protest movement.[4]

The quickening pulse of political life in the country, following Gandhi's intervention, had an appreciable impact on Delhi society. Those who earlier noted the apparent quiescence of political life, suddenly became acutely aware of the perceptibly broadened political outlook of the people in Delhi. The capital was now regarded as the centre from which disturbances in the Punjab and in parts of UP were promoted. 'Delhi is radiating sedition [and] is the principal source of inspiration for local agitations in the districts around,' exclaimed an official.[5] Agitators from Delhi stirred up trouble in the Meerut division, going 'in motors as far as Garhmukteswar, and are devoting special attention to Hapur, which is always a difficult place to control'.[6] In Moradabad and Bareilly districts the Delhi traders refused to restock the shops of their clients on the ground that they had not followed up their movement.[7] J.P. Thompson, chief secretary to the Punjab government, disclosed on 28 April 1919 that in distant Multan 'people are watching Delhi—which is important not only as the historic *and present* capital, but as the centre of the present disturbances'.[8]

The 'fissiparous' tendencies, noticed by government, were attributed to the spirited local organizations like the Indraprastha Sewak Mandli, Boy Scouts, the Home Rule League, the Muslim Volunteers and the Delhi Volunteer Corps; to the virulent campaign of newspapers—the *Qaum*, the *Inqilab*, the *Congress* and the *Vijaya*; and to the role of politicians from other provinces, notably, Swami Shraddhanand (1856-1926), who 'played a prominent part in stirring up trouble over the Rowlatt Bills and in fomenting unrest'.[9] Beadon, the unpopular deputy commissioner of Delhi, gave his estimate of Delhi's transition from a mofussil

[4]Ravinder Kumar, *Essays in the Social History of Modern India* (Delhi, 1983), pp. 21–3; Fe el, 'The Rowlatt Satyagraha in Delhi', op. cit.; Gupta, *Delhi Between Two Empires*, pp. 204–5.

[5]Home Poll. A, May 1919, 19–20, NAI.

[6]C.L. Alexander to W. Raw, 17 April 1919, General Administration Department [GAD], F. No. 262, 1919, Box 131, UPSA.

[7]Ibid.

[8]Ibid.; Home Dept. to the Chief Commissioner, Delhi, 20 April 1919; *DIC*, p. 209.

[9]Home Poll. B, January 1910, 160–3, NAI; *History*, (Delhi), op. cit.

town to a centre of political turbulence. 'It will I imagine be readily recognized,' he put down on 20 May 1919

> that before the Delhi Durbar Delhi was a simple mofussil town, with little knowledge on politics, with no political agitations beyond a few anarchists...[and] with no indigenous press...Since Delhi became the capital all this had changed, for the place has been flooded with agitators and politicians from all parts of India and has been the scene of countless political demonstrations and meetings.[10]

Beadon's lengthy exposition fell short of pointing out that a series of government policies, such as the wartime clampdown and the stagnation of political advance, had accentuated 'fissiparous' trends, given rise to disaffection, perked up nationalist sensitivities and enabled Gandhi's campaign against the Rowlatt Act to gain a firm foothold in Delhi and elsewhere.

Ansari played a principal part in organizing strikes, protest gatherings and demonstrations which occurred in Delhi from February onwards. He was Delhi's most prominent satyagrahi, the first president of the Satyagraha Sabha, formed on 24 February 1919 and also the first to take the Satyagraha vow when Gandhi visited the city on 7 March.[11] His house was the venue of many momentous meetings and his voice in support of satyagraha was heard from many platforms, as, on 24 March, when he declared that satyagraha was adopted by the Prophet Mohammad himself. He urged all Muslims to take the vow.[12] He also influenced Ajmal Khan, Hasrat Mohani, Asaf Ali, Abdur Rahman, Arif Husain Hasvi (1888-1936) and Shuaib Qureshi to join the Rowlatt satyagraha and to align themselves with the Mahatma. In general, his yeoman service during the months of February to April proved crucial in ensuring popular enthusiasm for the Gandhian movement in Delhi. That is why some officials considered putting him in jail; others preferred deportation. The idea was eventually dropped on the grounds that either of these stringent measures would help foster Hindu-Muslim unity and affect government's credibility.[13]

[10]Home Poll. B, May 1919, 119–20, NAI.
[11]Home Poll. B, May 1919. 268–73. ibid.
[12]Home Poll. B, May 1919, 141–7, ibid.
[13]Home Poll. B, May 1919, 119–20, ibid.

Some clues to Ansari's role and political disposition are offered in his evidence before the Hunter Commission. From his written statement, submitted on 3 November 1919, we can guage his commitment to the principles of satyagraha and to the element which Gandhi stressed most strongly, non-violence. We are told:

> India's share in the war had largely contributed to the entertainment of high aspirations by Indians, which, however, turned out to be extravagant in view of the later development of government's policy. The introduction of the Rowlatt legislation led to unprecedented agitation throughout India. But government enacted the objectionable measure in the teeth of universal opposition, causing profound disappointment and resentment. This naturally led to the adoption of passive resistance in the form of *satyagraha*, i.e., insistence on truth and negation of all violence.
>
> At such a time Mahatma Gandhi had a message of hope to the people of India, *satyagraha* or passive resistance against the Rowlatt Bills was inaugurated at a meeting held at the Ashram of Mahatma Gandhi at Ahmedabad on Friday, the 24th February 1919. He advocated the only remaining and the most effective constitutional method of agitation against the unjust measures, by practising *satyagraha* or civil resistance. The Mahatma had given to the matter his serious consideration and it was with the sense of full responsibility that he started the *satyagraha* campaign. His own words show the amount of concern and care with which he took this step....
>
> It has been alleged in certain quarters that *satyagraha* was the cause of all disorders during March and April last. This is an absolutely baseless assertion, as can be proved by facts. The principles advocated by *satyagraha*, as described above, had been strictly observed by all *satyagrahis*. Not a single *satyagrahi* has been convicted of any violence. On the contrary, *satyagraha sabha* and *satyagrahis* have always scrupulously observed non-violence and have helped the authorities in restoring order. In Delhi, Ahmedabad, Bombay, concrete instances can be shown to prove this assertion.[14]

Ansari argued that there was nothing new, ominous or threaening in the hartals, which, in connection with the satyagraha

[14] *DIC*, pp. 201–2.

observance, were enjoined as a sign of general protest on the passing of the Rowlatt Act. He pointed out that:

> *Hartal* or the suspension of all business is not a new thing in this country. From olden times it has been practised at various special occasions to express the general sorrow or trouble. In Delhi as in many other towns all business was suspended and shops were closed on receiving the news of the death of Queen Victoria and King Edward the VII, in recent years.... There is nothing, therefore, new or ominous and threatening in *hartal*, as has been stated recently by some persons, in England, as showing the disposition of the people to disorder.[15]

And finally, he spelt out Gandhi's success in terms of the amorphous but widespread discontent against the government which was channelized by the Mahatma into a popular stir through the use of so effective and powerful a weapon as satyagraha. The burden of his argument, quite convincingly proved by recent historical researches, was that the tinder of unrest had been drying for months and Gandhi's satyagraha was merely the spark which started the conflagration. According to him, satyagraha appealed to the masses because India was essentially a religious country and in the mind of the masses any religious creed could easily gain legitimacy and a strong hold. 'Satyagraha as such is a creed and I think the masses follow it most extraordinarily implicitly.'

Fearful of violence, Ansari's task was to ward off a possible direct confrontation with the local authorities. But his labours proved fruitless when, during his absence from Delhi from 26 March to 2 April, there were violent and bloody clashes on 30 March. This spelt danger to the passive resistance movement. So, on his return he tried, along with Shraddhanand and Ajmal Khan, to prevent another round of hartal which was planned on 6 April as a day of 'humiliation and prayers'. On the strength of Gandhi's statement of 3 April that violence was inconsistent with satyagraha, he was able to persuade the Satyagraha Sabha to give up hartal.[16] He recounted: 'It became clear in the morning that :

[15] *DIC*, p. 202.
[16] Ibid., p. 102.

> *hartal* had taken place and an informal consultation of the leading citizens of Delhi took place in my consulting rooms at Fatehpuri to devise means to divert the people from collecting in the Chandni Chowk and the central places of the town. Some two hundred volunteers were sent out to help the preservation of order in the town. A large crowd of people were taken to Fatehpuri mosque to attend the *Fateha* of those who had died of wounds. Permission was obtained from the deputy commissioner to hold a public meeting soon after the *Fateha* was over in Edward Park in order to divert the crowd from the Chandni Chowk and with the same purpose another mass meeting was held at Daryaganj, right away in the outskirts of the town. The day passed off quietly and on the next day, the 7th April and the following days, 8th and 9th, business was resumed all over the town and everything was normal.[17]

It is not surprising that Ansari failed in his efforts. The police firing on 30 March had inflamed passions to such an extent that support for a radical course of action gained momentum at a rapid pace; the flames of revolt rose high and every funeral of the victims of police firing occasioned more deaths.[18] At the same time, it needs to be recognized that Ansari's mediatory role, as indeed that of Ajmal Khan, ensured the peaceful observance on 10 April when the news of Gandhi's arrest spread like wild fire and led to a complete hartal in Delhi. The hartal continued until 19 April and led to fierce clashes between the police and the satyagrahis, and to the mob assuming control of the agitation. While Ansari and Ajmal Khan were unable to control the multitude, they could still persuade local authorities, with whom they were *en rapport*, to exercise restraint in dealing with the outburst.[19] If anything, their success in this respect minimized the loss of lives and diffused the growing tension in the city.

Ansari's mediatory role did not go down well with the pan-Islamists among the *ulama*, who were keen on intensifying the agitation even at the risk of violence. Their spokesman was the firebrand *Sahban-ul-Hind* Maulvi Ahmad Said (1888-1959) of

[17]*DIC*, p. 202.
[18]Ferrel, op. cit.
[19]*DIC*, pp. 202–3.

Madrasa-i Aminia who led the local pressure to extremism even before the full development of the Khilafat movement. In early 1919, he launched forth a tirade about the difficulties in dealing with the British and upbraided Muslims who were not prepared to die for the Khilafat and who by doing good to the Europeans did harm and evil to their country. He was backed by Qazi Abbas Husain, editor of the *Qaum* and Arif Husain Hasvi, editor of the *Congress*. These papers, along with the *Inqilab*, highlighted government's repression during the satyagraha and commended Asaf Ali's suggestion to call the place round the Clock Tower as *Khuni Chauraha* to perpetuate the memory of the Delhi martyrs just as the *Khuni Darwaza* reminded the people of the 1857 revolt.[20] 'These two rags,' an angry official had written, 'are mushroom growths and yet a month old and I doubt whether the sediment of political excitement left by the Congress and Muslim League meetings will furnish sufficient soil to nourish them through six months of existence.'[21] He was wrong. These newspapers flourished and encouraged anti-government rumblings in Delhi throughout the Rowlatt satyagraha.

Ansari had little sympathy with such over-zealous satyagrahis and responded to their outburst with commendable firmness. As one committed to non-violence, he was not favourably disposed to prosecuting the satyagraha on purely agitational lines. Yet, he was prudent enough not to ventilate his views publicly. He worked quietly, often unobtrusively, to pacify his militant colleagues and warned them of the hazards of violence. When his endeavours came to naught he resigned from the Satyagraha Sabha. Writing to Mohamed Ali, who was still interned in Chhindwara, Ansari questioned the purposefulness and efficacy of the satyagraha movement. The letter, intercepted by the deputy commissioner of Chhindwara, illuminates an important facet of Ansari's personality: his ability to take an independent

[20] *DIC*, pp. 145–6.

[21] FR, second half of February 1919, Home Poll. Deposit, March 1919, 17, NAI. In Delhi the main newspapers with a pan-Islamic outlook were: *Congress, Fateh, Fatehmand, Khilafat, Hurriyat and Sabah*. Their combined circulation was just over 6,000, but they fared better than the literary and commercial journals which, according to a government report, 'last a few months, perish and are replaced....' *Annual Report of the Newspapers Published in the Delhi Province, 1920*, Home Poll. F. No. 4, 1921, NAI; *Annual Report of the Newspapers Published in the Delhi Province, 1921*, Home Poll. B, F. No. 12, 1922, NAI.

position on political issues and pursue it even if it involved estranging friends and comrades. He wrote:

> You must have learnt of my differences of opinion from Shaukat Bhai. Then I was against Hijrat (migration) only, but I was entirely in favour of Satyagraha. In Delhi, I have had ample experience of Satyagraha. Though on the 30th March I was not in Delhi, but from the 1st of April, to its end whole day and night I spent all my time in observing the movement of satyagraha with its result and in allaying the excitement and uneasiness that was then common in the public mind and eventually I came to the conclusion that it was possible to carry on the satyagraha on the principles on which its originator M. Gandhi wishes it to be carried on in the present circumstances. There are many causes for its failure and some of those causes are such that we have, if not absolutely none, very little control over them.
>
> In these circumstances I consider the satyagraha movement to be practically impossible and wholly unprofitable and severed my connection with the Satyagraha Sabha. This is my opinion about Indians generally except some selected people I consider Mussalmans generally absolutely unfit to act on the principles of satyagraha. In my humble opinion satyagraha is an impracticable movement, of course, under the direct supervision of M. Gandhi this movement may perhaps succeed to a certain extent.[22]

Such an attitude was anathema to Asaf Ali, Ahmad Said and Arif Husain Hasvi. Besides, Ansari's letter to the organizers of the meeting, held in Delhi on 13 May, to express loyalty to the government in view of the threatened Afghan invasion,[23] and

[22]Home Poll. A, September 1919, 406-28, NAI; Hasan (ed.), *Mohamed Ali in Indian Politics*, Vol. I, pp. 253–4.

[23]Ansari wrote: 'At a time when there is danger of foreign invasion on our motherland, it is the imperative duty of all true and patriotic Indians whether Hindus or Muslims to sink all their differences with the Government and give it their whole-hearted support. Even if we put aside all the higher patriotic and ethical considerations, our self interest demands that we should make common cause with our rulers at this juncture. For, we must bear in mind that "Home Rule", "Responsible Government" and all our highly cherished ideals of constitutional rights and personal liberties could be gained only when there is perfect tranquility inside the country and no apprehension of an attack from outside.' Home Poll. A, May 1919, 119-20, NAI.

his joining a gathering to thank the authorities for their handling of the situation in April caused quite a flutter,[24] and gave rise to all sorts of speculations. Much was also made out of his resignation from the Satyagraha Sabha. According to one source, he quit because 'his views regarding the practicability of the passive resistance movement had changed when he saw excesses to which it led'. It was also rumoured that Ansari suggested that the signatories to the vow in Delhi be given an opportunity of saying whether, in the light of the incidents since 7 March, they still wished to be considered satyagrahis. 'Presumably reckoning on a general recantation,' concluded an intelligence report,'the Committee decided instead to abolish the Sabha and proceeded to burn the list of adherents and the papers on which they had signed the vow'.[25]

It is easy to discern a slight vacillation in Ansari's disposition, but this should not be construed as 'betrayal', as implicitly suggested in government circles. There was also no sign of a shift in his commitment to the satyagraha movement though he demurred at its reckless course in Delhi. There was also no wavering in his devotion to Gandhi as he continued to believe that the movement could still succeed under his 'direct supervision'. Besides, he was genuinely captivated by his personality, his idealism, his concern for the poor and the down-trodden and by his leadership qualities. From now on, the Mahatma was his unquestioned leader; he was to idolize him, follow him and assist him in future political crusades. He enjoyed both his friendship and confidence which at that time was the biggest political asset he could have.

Ansari was not the only Muslim to be influenced by Gandhi; others fell in behind the Mahatma's programme in 1919 without having either worked with him or, in some cases, even having met him. He endeared himself to Ansari's younger colleagues—Shuaib Qureshi and Abdur Rahman Siddiqi—because of the asceticism of his style of life and his moves towards communal unity on the basis of championing specifically Muslim grievances, such as the future of the Khilafat and the Holy Places of

[24]*History* (Delhi), op. cit., p. 5. Home Poll. A, September 1919, 406-28, NAI; Bamford, *Histories*, p. 142.

[25]FR, first half of May 1919, Home Poll. Deposit, July 1919, 49, NAI.

Islam.[26] Oddly enough, they looked up to Gandhi for counsel and leadership on this overtly religious issue.

Gandhi was initially unsure of his own strategy, though his early contacts with Muslims had enabled him to comprehend the import of religious institutions and symbols in Indian Islam. He could therefore appreciate and partake in Muslim anxiety over the Khilafat question. No Hindu Congressman before him had made such an endeavour—which may, perhaps, explain why no other Hindu before Gandhi was so well thought of and earned so much popularity among Muslims. The early Congress leaders were either insensitive to or disdainful of Muslim religious susceptibilities and interposed Hindu symbols and rituals in their political campaigns. Gandhi avoided doing so. With his sharp political acumen, he played up the Khilafat issue so as to transmute the parochial sentiments of the Muslims into the nationalist cause.

Gandhi had worked with Muslims in South Africa and, after his return to India, forged friendly links with some influential Muslims. He met the Ali Brothers in Aligarh and Delhi in 1915, and early in 1916. His circle of Muslim friends widened after he met Ansari and Abdul Bari;[27] with his vigour, charm and obvious organizational flair, Ansari seemed a suitable ally. The Mahatma tried to see the Ali Brothers in the Chhindwara prison, but was refused permission by the government. But he was unflinching in his resolve to secure their release. He told delegates at the 1917 Muslim League session that Hindus were with them to a man in their just struggle for the Ali Brothers' release, pleaded with the viceroy to release them, arguing that they were loyal to the Raj and that their internment irritated both Hindus and Muslims, and sought definite assurance for Turkey's future before endorsing the loyalty resolution of the Delhi War Conference. When the viceroy ignored his pleadings, the Mahatma announced his decision to engage the government in a duel.[28] The fight for Mohamed Ali's release, though a 'crushing burden', had to be borne.[29] He went on to assure Bi Amma—Mataji—that he was leaving no stone unturned to secure their quick but

[26]Hasan, *Nationalism and Communal Politics in India*, pp. 114-5.

[27]Speech on Khilafat, Bombay, 9 May 1919, *The Collected Works of Mahatma Gandhi* [*CWG*], Vol. 15, p. 295.

[28]Gandhi to Maffey, 12 July 1918, Chelmsford Papers (21).

[29]11 April 1918, Mahadev Desai (ed.), *Day-To-Day with Gandhi* (Varanasi, 1968), Vol. I, p. 93.

perfectly honourable release.[30] Gandhi's motives were not quite as high-minded as they seemed, because he believed that his own political advancement lay through an alliance with Mohamed Ali and other weighty Muslims.

Gandhi attached great significance to his relations with Mohamed Ali because he wanted to secure his collaboration in advancing Hindu-Muslim unity, having made it an essential part of his mission to India. '*My interest in your release*', he told Mohamed Ali, '*is quite selfish. We have a common goal and I want to utilize your services to the uttermost in order to reach that goal. In the proper solution of Mohammedan question lies the realization of Swaraj*' [emphasis added].[31] Convinced that self-government could only be achieved if Hindus and Muslims worked hand in glove, he tried to secure 'permanent unity' between them.[32] The Khilafat issue gave him a unique opportunity of doing so—a chance that would not arise in a hundred years.[33] His inner voice told him that the two communities would stand shoulder to shoulder one day because there was no other course open to them but to be brothers.[34] The Khilafat agitation was 'the great churning process of the ocean that India is. Why should we worry as to what will come out (poison or nectar) from the movement? Is it not enough if we are certain that that activity is pure and righteous'.

Gandhi assumed that Mohamed Ali was a representative of Muslim opinion and therefore an ideal instrument for creating Hindu-Muslim comradeship with the aim of obtaining swaraj. Because to Gandhi swaraj meant not just political Home Rule but a state of communal harmony, Mohamed Ali was valuable to him both as an issue on which to cement an inter-communal combination and also because he thought that he was a splendid example of that mingling of Hindu and Muslim culture which had occurred in UP.[35]

Mohamed Ali reciprocated. He was full of admiration for and

[30] 6 August 1918, ibid., p. 211; also, To Shuaib Qureshi, 24 September 1918, pp. 256–7

[31] Gandhi to Mohamed Ali, 18 November 1918, Hasan (ed.), *Mohamed Ali in Indian Politics*, Vol. 2, p. 117.

[32] *CWG*, Vol. 15, p. 296.

[33] Ibid.

[34] *Day-To-Day with Gandhi*, Vol. 1, p. 56.

[35] J.M. Brown, *Gandhi's Rise to Power: Indian Politics 1915-1922* (Cambridge, 1972), p. 152.

placed his entire confidence in the Mahatma. He subscribed to the non-violent programme against the Rowlatt Act which, in his words, were 'enacted in the most tyrannical manner,' ending 'the reign of law'and substituting 'a reign of terror in its place'.[36] While in Chhindwara, he corresponded with Gandhi regularly, exchanged views on various theological questions and appreciated his efforts to secure his release.[37] When released from internment at the end of 1919, he promptly reaffirmed his solidarity with Gandhi. He said:

> Long before we were free we had made up our minds to bring about a complete entente between Hindus and Muslims...and the best man among the Hindus to deal with was Mahatma Gandhi, a peace-loving and non-violent patriot who was intensely religious without the fury of a theologian and whose honesty all could rely upon. He found us to be equally religious and equally without the fury of the theologian, and as Muslims we could not pledge ourselves to remain non-violent in all circumstances, he found that we too regarded force at present to be futile, and above all he could trust our word as much as we trusted him. Even if we ourselves wished to use force immediately, which we did not and could not, we would have lost his support and thus have lost the chance of bringing about the Hindu-Muslim entente and of bringing the government to its senses.[38]

Such a subservient posture was no doubt distasteful to some *ulama*, particularly to Syed Ahmed Raza Khan (1856–1921) of Bareilly and to the *Bahr al-ulum ulama* of Firangi Mahal who took offense to Gandhi's domination of the Khilafat movement. But such men were few and wielded limited influence during the popular pan-Islamic upsurge. Most *ulama* favoured accommodation with Congress and making common cause with Hindus because of the vital necessity of enlisting their support for the Khilafat cause. For this reason alone they cast in their lot with Gandhi and hitched their fortunes to the Congress star.

Another important adherent to the Gandhian movement was Abdul Bari, the spiritual preceptor of Ansari and the *Pir* of the

[36] Mohamed Ali to Chelmsford, 24 April 1919, Hasan (ed.), *Mohamed Ali in Indian Politics*, Vol. 2, pp. 232-3.

[37] For example, Mohamed Ali to Gandhi, 20 February 1919, ibid., pp. 239-41.

[38] Quoted in Brown, op. cit., p. 331.

Ali Brothers. The Mahatma and the Maulana first met at the Lucknow Congress in December 1916. They saw each other again in February/March 1918 at Ansari's home in Delhi and then in March 1919. As a result of the second meeting, Abdul Bari was persuaded to follow the lead of Gandhi during the satyagraha. His motive was simple: the Mahatma was the only guarantor of Congress support to the Khilafat demands. 'I have accepted his [Gandhi's] support in getting our aims fulfilled,' he wrote in November 1920, 'and for that purpose I think it is necessary to follow his advice.... *I know that the strength of Islam lies in association with him*' [emphasis added].[39] In appreciation of his espousal of the Khilafat claims and in deference to his wishes (though Gandhi did not make the abandonment of cow-slaughter a condition of his support), Abdul Bari decided not to sacrifice cows in future and appealed to his co-religionists to do the same. To him, as indeed to many others who paid heed to his exhortation, giving up cow-slaughter was a symbolic gesture of camaraderie and goodwill towards the Mahatma who venerated the cow; in the early 1920s, such well-thought-of gestures were important for sustaining the Hindu-Muslim rapprochement. Khwaja Hasan Nizami also favoured such a move. The Prophet Mohammad, he stated, slaughtered a cow only once in his lifetime, that the Quran did not enjoin upon the faithful to slaughter cows specially and the same religious, cultural and economic compulsions which prompted Hindus to save the cow must apply to the Muslims as well.[40] He was also converted to the principles of satyagraha and non-violence. 'I have decided to adhere to the principles (*tariqa*) laid down by Mahatma Gandhi'.[41]

Muslim artisans, merchants, mill-workers and weavers also rallied round Gandhi and took part in the hartal on 6 April. His

[39]Home Poll. Deposit, 1921, 4, NAI; WRDCI, March 1919, Home Poll. B, April 1919, 148-52, NAI.

[40]Hasan Nizami, *Tark-i Gayekushi* (Delhi, 1920), pp. 6-7, 16. Abdul Bari thanked Gandhi for the success of the Day of Prayer and conveyed Maulana Sulaiman of Phulwari's message that the Hindus of the city, acting on Gandhi's instructions, 'have made us so much obliged that we ourselves have determined not to sacrifice cow in future'. Abdul Bari to Gandhi, n.d., Abdul Bari Papers, Firangi Mahal, Lucknow.

[41]Hasan Nizami, *Government awr Khilafat* (Gurdaspur, 1922 edn.). The pamphlet was first published in 1920.

success in securing their adherence was due to the consummate skill with which he capitalized on the indignation against the government's policy towards Turkey as well as the fear that the Rowlatt Bills were intended to enable officials to coerce the Muslims and 'prevent them from giving trouble so as to facilitate the dismemberment of Turkey'. Secondly, the steadily growing resentment against British domination was fanned by the economic distress flowing from World War I. During and after the war there was a sharp increase in the prices of basic commodities such as rice, wheat, salt and cooking oil. In UP foodgrain production fell sharply because of lack of rain and large areas were hit by famine or scarcity. The province, like other regions of India, was afflicted by the great influenza which caused the death of at least five to six million people. Gandhi's genius lay in canalizing these discontents into a spectacular movement of popular protest against the raj.

An equally important feature of the Gandhian satyagraha was that it ushered in an uprecedented phase of Hindu-Muslim comradeship. 'Though the Rowlatt Act sits like a dread night-mare on our breasts,' wrote the editor of *Amrita Bazar Patrika*, 'it has united both Hindus and Mussalmans in a way which has never been witnessed'.[42] There were reports of a satyagraha movement in Muzaffarnagar and of meetings to harmonize Hindu-Muslim relations. The Muslims went so far as to allow *chandan* to be put on their forehead and promised to abstain from killing any cows at the next *Id*.[43] The commissioner of Banaras division took note of the harmonious spirit and of certain Maulvis of Jaunpur preaching friendship and forfeiting their right to sacrifice cows at the next *Id*.[44] At Delhi this was a common occurrence after the happenings of 30 March. In conformity with the fraternization and unity of purpose, both before and after the hartal on 30 March, Shraddhanand was invited to address the Friday congregation at the Juma Masjid. This was followed by sadhus addressing from pulpits and Muslim divines addressing mixed audiences in Hindu temples in all parts of the country.

The nationalists were no doubt carried away by such dramatic

[42]M.L. Ghose to Mohamed Ali, 14 April 1919, Hasan (ed.), *Mohamed Ali in Indian Politics*, Vol. 2, p. 220.

[43]P.W. Marsh to W. Raw, 27 April 1919, GAD, F. No. 262, 1919, UPSA.

[44]Commissioner of Banaras Division to A.C. Chatterji, chief secretary to UP government, 29 April 1919, ibid.

spectacles of unity and, consequently, tended to simplify the nature of the communal tangle. At the same time, few could deny that a nationalist struggle, free from a sectarian bias, had the potential of embracing many Muslims within its fold. This was later reinforced by the strength of Gandhi's appeal during the Khilafat and Non-cooperation movements.

The message was not lost on Ansari who remained committed to the cause of communal amity. Over the years he tried to wean away Muslims from communal bodies and wanted the Congress to avoid Hindu revivalist rhetoric and stay clear of those issues of discord which would alienate Muslims and create fissures in the nationalist movement. The experience of the Rowlatt satyagraha convinced him that there were many issues which concerned Hindus and Muslims equally; consequently, there were objective reasons for them to coalesce in advancing the country's interests generally. Unity between the Hindus and the Muslims was therefore not only desirable but a necessary condition for the success of the nationalist movement. It is with this conviction that he decided to devote himself whole-heartedly to cementing their bonds of friendship. This was an hazardous task as Ansari was to discover soon, but he responded to the challenge with remarkable tenacity and determination.

Up to 1919, Ansari had given convincing proof of his ability as a man of action, as advocate, negotiator and organizer. In the years that followed, he was to reveal other and rarer gifts as a leader and policy-maker which hitherto had not been brought fully into play.

5

The Khilafat Experience

> It is difficult for anyone not an Indian Moslem to realize what Pan-Islamism means to the Indian Moslems.... It is a sentiment of which the prayers for Turkish success in the Tripolitan and Balkan wars, the Relief Fund, the Medical Mission and even Khilafat movement were weak but faltering expressions. It is not a sentiment inspired by interest, policy or worldly wisdom: it has no practical end in view [M.A. Ansari].
>
> Introduction to Halide Edib, *Conflict of East and West in Turkey* (Delhi, n.d.), pp. iv-v.

> Husain ibn-i Ali Aao Khilafat chheeni jaati hai
> Madad kije khudara ab dam-i mushkil kushai hai
> [Mohammad Haider of Pilibhit]
>
> Proscribed Publications (43), IOL.

THIS CHAPTER SEEKS to examine certain aspects of the Khilafat movement in India, its influence on Ansari and the reasons why men of his social background and political outlook were swept by the pan-Islamic tide.

The Indian Muslims, as is commonly known, share certain religious beliefs and practices with their brethren elsewhere and are often conscious of their fraternal links with them. Some have been following the history and culture of Muslim countries, deriving comfort in their accomplishments and lamenting their slow but steady decline. By the nineteenth and twentieth centuries, in particular, when Islam seemed to fall on evil days because of the European imperial penetration into the heartlands of the Muslim world extending from Morocco to Indonesia, the heritage of the past stood forth as a symbol of community pride and distinction; in fact, everywhere Muslims were told to look to their own glorious Islamic past as the source for their inspiration, identity and unity. This was expressed in the adventurist and revivalist movements led by Mohammad ibn Abdul Wahhab

(1703-92) in Arabia, Syed Ahmad Barelvi (1786-1831) in India, Mohammad Ali ibn al-Sanusi (1787-1859) in Nigeria and Mohammad Ahmad (1848-85), the Mahdi of the Sudan. All of them reemphasized the belief that the socio-moral revival of Islamic society required political action, an activism epitomized by *jehad*, the exertion to realize God's will through moral self-discipline and, when necessary, military combat or warfare. At another level, Islam was defended from the polemical and hostile attacks of nineteenth century Western orientalists and against the intellectual and moral imperialism of the West. Stress was laid on the original message of Islam which had provided the ideal pattern for traditional Muslim society and remained eternally valid, and on the fact that Muslims were fully equipped to respond to the political, cultural and scientific challenge of the West. Syed Ahmad Khan, a major catalyst for reform and change in India, and his contemporary, Mohammad Abduh (1845-1905) in Egypt, tried to show the compatibility of Islam with modern ideas and institutions.

Such currents, which gripped the Muslim countries from North Africa to South-East Asia, left their mark on an influential section of the Indian Muslim intelligentsia. They were most clearly reflected in Altaf Husain Hali's (1837-1914) lamenting the 'ebb' of Islam in the famous *Musaddas*, in Shibli Nomani's pan-Islamic anguish in the topical poem on the 'Trouble in the Balkans' and in Mohammad Iqbal's nostalgic ode to once-Arab Sicily. One may also turn to the works of Shibli and Ameer Ali (1849-1928) to discern the ideological underpinnings of such concerns and reflect on the passion with which the pan-Islamists espoused Turkey's cause in the first quarter of the twentieth century, singling out the Europeans Powers as enemies of Islam.

Elsewhere, there were similar reactions against the aggression of Western empires, which were being felt from the 1870s and which culminated in the French occupation of Tunisia in 1871, the British possession of Egypt in 1882, the Russian conquest of Merv in 1884, the Italian seizure of Tripoli in 1911 and the Balkan war of 1912-13. Muslim responses to these developments ranged from rejection to adaptation, from withdrawal to acculturation and reform. Most notably, however, the examples of German and Italian unifications suggested the potency of movements for unity of divided territories behind a single government.[1] This

[1] Nikkie R. Keddie, *Sayyid Jamal ad-Din "al-Afghani": A Political Biography* (Los Angeles, 1972), p. 130.

idea formed the basis of the pan-Islamic euphoria which swept parts of the Muslim world in the last quarter of the nineteenth century.

For most Indian Muslims, the overriding consideration in their upsurge was that Turkey's Sultan was the custodian and defender of the Holy Places in the area known as *Jazirat al-Arab*. With the sanctuaries and symbols of Islam—central to Muslim belief and practice—exposed to danger,[2] the faithful were impelled to demand that the *Jazirat al-Arab* remain under Muslim sovereignty (according to the injunctions of the Prophet) with the Khalifa as its warden. The protection of the Holy Places thus provided the rallying point for virtually all sections of the Muslim community. Money and ornaments poured into the Khilafat fund, thousands flocked to the Khilafat meetings and some even left the fields and factories to migrate to the *Dar al-Islam* in response to a call for *hijrat*. Students quit their studies and joined the swelling ranks of non-cooperators, while many of their elders gave up their lucrative jobs and high-sounding titles. Never before did so many Muslims unite on a common platform to fight a common cause. This unique example of religious fervour and solidarity merits serious consideration.

In explaining this outburst one must take into account the strength of the unifying powers of religious symbols in Indian Islam. Some of these symbols—mosque, *hajj*, sufi shrine—fostered a sense of belonging to a common fraternity of Islam and thus made it easier for the pan-Islamic notion to permeate Muslim consciousness. Equally, historians will do well to reckon with the theme of 'Muslim unity' which ran through nineteenth century religio-revivalist movements and was echoed by the

[2]It was exemplified, for instance, in the following poem:

Ae barq aaj shola-fishan kyon nahin hai tu
Ae raad aaj garm fughaan kyon nahin hai tu
Ae abr aaj girya kunaan kyon nahin hai tu
Darya-i qahr aaj rawaan kyon nahin hai tu
Islam aaj kufr ke narghe men aa gaya
Baadal siyah rang ka Kaaba pe chhaa gaya

O the thunderbolt why doesn't you scatter flames?
O the lightening why thou wailest not?
O the clouds why weepest not thou?
Why is it that the river of curse is a frozen puddle and flows not?
Islam has been swamped and overwhelmed by the unbelief
And the Kaaba has been engulfed by darkness.

Proscribed Publications (8), IOL. Also, see (142, 152, 153).

ulama of Firangi Mahal, Deoband and the *Nadvat al-ulama*. The concept of a unified Islamic community eventually merged into the stream of pan-Islamic consciousness.

Among Sunni Muslims, who formed the overwhelming majority of the Muslim population, Turkey's Sultan was the *Amir al-Muminin* (Commander of the Faithful) and the protector of the Holy Places. The Khilafat was the viceroyalty of the Prophet of Islam, ordained by Divine Law for the perpetuation of Islam and the continued observance of its *Sharia* (Islamic law) and the Khalifa (derived from the word 'Khalafa'—to leave behind) was both a spiritual and temporal head. Allegiance to him was obligatory which explains why some Sultans of Delhi bore the names of Khalifa on their coins and often received investitures as legal sanction for their rule. The name of the Abbasid Khalifa, Al-Mustasim, continued on the coins for about 40 years after the sack of Baghdad at the hands of the Mongols. It was probably an expression of the sentiment: 'The Khalifa is dead, long live the Khalifa.' The Mughal Emperors as well as some independent Muslim rulers in the eighteenth century often turned towards the Ottoman Khalifa as a source of strength. In 1785 Tipu Sultan sent an embassy to the Ottoman Sultan and his emissaries secured for him letters of investiture which allowed him to assume the title of an independent ruler.[3]

Interest in Turkey's welfare continued: each time it was involved in hostilities—the Russo-Turkish war of 1877-78 or the Greco-Turkish war of 1897—Indian Muslims took up the cudgels for Turkey, reaffirmed their attachment to its Sultan and prayed for his well-being. 'If the Muhammadans of the world were compared to the human body,' wrote the *Akhbar-i Am*, 'the Sultan would be the heart and brain.'[4] Antony Macdonnell (1844-1919), lieutenant-governor of UP, quoted to the viceroy, Elgin (1849-1919), a leaflet describing the Ottoman Sultan as *Amir al-Muminin* and *Padshah-i Mussalmanan* and noted the sympathy with Turkey partly due to incitement from outside India and partly spontaneous—a feeling which, according to him, was fostered by Muslim schools and was more widespread than before. He was told by the commissioner of Agra that many

[3] R.P. Tripathi, *Some Aspects of Muslim Administration in India* (Allahabad, 1936), p. 37; Mohibbul Hasan (ed.), *Waqai-i Manazil-i Rum: diary of a journey to Constantinople* (Delhi, 1968).

[4] *Akhbar-i Am*, 14 March 1895, Punjab Native Newspaper Reports.

more people had taken to wearing the Turkish *fez* and that was perhaps the straw indicating how the wind was beginning to blow.[5]

The 'incitement from outside', referred to by Macdonnell, came from two distinct sources. In the first place, the British government exploited pro-Turkish sensibilities in order to secure Indian Muslim loyalty, as in 1857, and to protect their imperial interests from Russian encroachments by bolstering 'the sick man of Europe', as they did from the Crimean war of 1853-56 onwards. Then, the Sultan of Turkey, Abdul Hamid II (1842-1918), sent his agents to India, as other lands, to rally Muslim support and enthusiasm for his feeble regime threatened by external aggression and internal strife, caused by nationalist movements sprung up among his Christian Balkan subjects (Armenian, Greek, Romanian, Bulgarian) in southeast Europe.

Syed Ahmad Khan disputed Abdul Hamid's pretensions. The pan-Islamic surge threatened to wreck his effort to prop up the Anglo-Muslim alliance in India; so he spoke against the Turcophilia among his co-religionists, arguing that they were legally bound to obey the writ not of an external Muslim Khalifa but of the British Indian government. Such exhortations fell on inattentive ears as the fellow-feeling for Turkey extended to far-flung parts of northern India. Nawab Mohsin-ul-Mulk (1837-1907), one of Syed Ahmad Khan's most distinguished successors at the Aligarh College, learnt his lesson the hard way. When he opposed the holding of pan-Islamic meetings on the campus, he was everywhere maligned and castigated as a 'downright sycophant'.[6]

The most bitter criticism of Syed Ahmad Khan's views came from an unexpected quarter—from that celebrated roving reformer,teacher and political agitator, Jamaluddin al-Asadabadi 'al-Afghani' (1839-1897).[7] He regarded the Aligarh reformer's

[5]Quoted in Peter Hardy, *The Muslims of British India* (Cambridge, 1972), p. 177. W.S. Blunt was told on the eve of his visit to India that he should not say anything against the Sultan of Turkey because his name 'was now venerated in India as it has not formerly been'. W.S. Blunt, *India Under Ripon: A Private Diary* (London, 1909), p. 13. Halil Halid was told by an Englishman who had followed the Prince of Wales during his tour around the colonies that the further one went from Turkey the greater was the influence of the Sultan among Muslims. Halil Halid, *The Diary of a Turk* (London, 1903) and, *The Crescent Versus the Cross* (London, 1907).

[6]*Jasus* (Agra), 14 July 1906; *Al-Aziz* (Agra), 28 July 1906, United Provinces Newspaper Reports.

[7]Afghani was in India from 1857 to 1865. He came again in 1879 to spend three years in Bombay, Hyderabad, Bhopal and Calcutta. The purpose of his

religious views and his educational programme as ancillaries to his political servitude to British interests and chided him for relying on the British instead of joining hands with the Indian nationalists. Afghani considered Syed Ahmad Khan as his main adversary in India, opposed to pan-Islamism, isolating the Indian Muslims from the rest of *Dar al-Islam*, especially from the Turks, and hostile to the conception of a universal Muslim Khilafat. According to him, the reassertion of Muslim identity and solidarity were prerequisites for the restoration of political and cultural independence, and unity and solidarity were essential at both levels.[8]

Afghani spent the greater part of his life travelling from one country to the other (Afghanistan, India, Iran, Egypt and the Ottoman Empire) as the chief exponent of pan-Islamism. His life, one of endless wanderings, touched and deeply affected Muslims in the last quarter of the nineteenth century; his pan-Islamic vision inspired various activist groups in different lands and lives on patiently, if amorphously, in the aspirations of many Muslims.[9] It is also curious and relevant that the only instance where his political programme of combined radicalism, modernism, nationalism and pan-Islamism ever became a serious political agenda of a vibrant and spirited opposition was in the Khilafat agitation in India, years after his death.[10]

visit was to meet with all the *navvabs* and princes and *ulama* and grandees of that land and to explain to them one by one the results that are manifested from unity and solidarity in the whole world and the injuries that have appeared from division and disunity; and to caress their ears with the mystery of the *hadith*, the faithful are brothers; and to express inspiring and prudent words and to attract the friendship and cooperation of the learned and the eloquent; and to breathe into them the new spirit of love of nationality and to rend the curtain of their neglect to explain to them the place of the luminous Sultanate in the world of Islam; and to reveal and make manifest to this group the fact that the perpetuation of religion depends on the perpetuation of this government. And in all the mosques of the famous cities I shall light a flame in their inner hearth by means of appealing sermons and *hadiths* of the Best of the Prophets, and I shall together burn out their patience and long-suffering.

Keddie, op. cit., pp. 134-5.

[8]Aziz Ahmad, *Studies in Islamic Culture in the Indian Environment* (London, 1964), pp. 55-6; Keddie, op. cit., p. 167.

[9]Fazlur Rahman, *Islam* (London, 1966), p. 227; Anwar Moazzam, *Jamal al-Din al-Afghani A Muslim Intellectual* (Delhi, 1983), p. xiii. His main contribution, according to Moazzam, was in providing a 'broad intellectual framework' for redefining the relationship between Islam and the changing world.

[10]Keddie, op. cit., p. 26. Elie Kedourie has argued that Afghani's reputation

The power of Afghani's appeal was felt generally in the first decade of the twentieth century when he became a symbol of the pan-Islamic enterprise. Among those who came under his spell was Shibli Nomani who visited Istanbul in 1893, received a medal from Abdul Hamid and parleyed with Afghani's co-worker and disciple, Mohammad Abduh.[11] His pan-Islamic ideas were echoed in Hali's *Musaddas* while his strong advocacy of the coexistence of diverse religious faiths was in accord with Mohamed Ali's idea, expressed in his Congress presidential address in 1923, of the 'Federation of Faiths'. His view of a natural solidarity beyond the nation: that which binds together all the peoples of the East threatened by the West, was developed by Ansari.[12] At the All-India Khilafat Conference held on 27 December 1922, Ansari referred to the need for an Asiatic Federation to promote solidarity among the peoples and countries of Asia with a view to rescuing them from the political and economic bondage of Europe.[13] This idea was first advocated by Afghani and was known to his contemporaries two decades earlier.

Afghani also influenced Iqbal and Azad. The former became interested most of all in Afghani's endeavour to find in Islam a means of unification for resisting the domination of the West and shared his desire to express unity on the religious basis of Muslims as a supra class and a supra-national entity. On the eve

was to a large extent posthumous and was the work of disciples, or else of academic writers and publicists 'eager to discover trends and precursors' to magnify the importance of their subjects. Elie Kedourie, *Afghani and Abduh: An Essay on Religious Unbelief and Political Activism in Modern Islam* (London, 1966), p. 3. This is not right, for there is adequate evidence to indicate his charisma on his contemporaries and greater evidence of his impact on subsequent political and intellectual movements in Muslim countries. Aziz Ahmad and Keddie also write of Afghani's limited hold. According to them, the people he met exercised no political or religious influence among Muslims, and his articles, published in an obscure journal of Hyderabad, did not cause any stir at the time. But their own evidence does not warrant this conclusion; in fact, the works of Wilfred Scawen Blunt (1840-1922) point to Afghani's influence. Kedourie's cynical view of Afghani becoming a 'British agent' is typical of his attempt to denigrate him and to underplay the role of ideology in politics.

[11]Shibli Nomani, *Safarnamah-i Misr-o-Shaam* (Agra, 1894), pp. 129-32. Aziz Ahmad, *Islamic Modernism in India and Pakistan 1857-1964* (London, 1967), p. 129.

[12]Albert Hourani, *Arabic Thought in the Liberal Age 1798-1939* (Oxford, 1970), pp. 118-19.

[13]H.N. Mitra (ed.), *The Indian Annual Register (IAR)*, January-July 1923, Vol. I, p. 921.

of and during World War I, Iqbal tied his hopes for liberation from colonial dependency to pan-Islamic solidarity. This was reflected, in particular, in his poem *Shama Awr Shair* (The Candle and the Poet), written in 1912.[14] In his reply to the *Shikwa* (Complaint of God) he struck the same note:

> The trouble that is raging in the Balkans
> Is a message of awakening to the forgetful
> Thou may'st think it the means of vexing thy heart
> But in reality it is a test of thy self-sacrifice and self-reliance.

As for Azad, Afghani's influence can be seen from the time of his stay in Constantinople and Cairo when he developed close relations with the *Al-Manar* (The Lighthouse) group of Syrian and Egyptian scholars. He developed the nationalist and anti-imperialist thrust of Afghani's ideas in the *Al-Hilal*, inspired by the *Al-Urwa al-wuthqa* (The Indissoluble Link), an anti-imperialist journal published by Afghani in collaboration with Abduh. He, too, bitterly attacked Syed Ahmad Khan's attitude to the Turkish Khilafat and urged on the authority of the Quran that *jehad* was imperative against those who had occupied even a part of the *Dar al-Islam*. Political fidelity was due to the Ottoman Khalifa. Obedience to him and compliance with his wishes was binding on the faithful.[15]

Azad provided greater ideological coherence to the zestful concerns of those Muslims who were beginning to come to terms with the objective reality of Indian nationalism and its ideal of a unified and powerful anti-colonial struggle. He stood strongly for inter-communal union, citing the Prophet Mohammad's covenant with some Jews as a valid historical precedent for an integrated alliance with the Hindus. He asserted that uniting with one category of non-Muslims, the Hindus, against another category of non-Muslims, the British, was obligatory. Mohammad Idris Qandhari, an *alim* of Deoband, argued

[14]L.R. Gordon-Polonskya, 'Ideology of Muslim Nationalism', Hafeez Malik (ed.), *Iqbal: Poet Philosopher of Pakistan* (New York, 1971), pp. 115-16. For Afghani's influence, see Muhammad Iqbal, *The Reconstruction of Religious Thought in Islam*, p. 92, quoted in Ahmad, *Islamic Modernism*, pp. 129, 136.

[15]Ahmad, *Studies in Islamic Culture*, p. 67 and his *Islamic Modernism*, pp. 129, 136. For Afghani's influence on Qazi Abdul Ghaffar, one of Azad's devoted followers, see Abdul Ghaffar, *Jamaluddin Afghani*, in Urdu (Delhi, 1941). Afghani's stay in India is referred to on pp. 12-13, 16-17, 35-7. Also, Annemarie Schimmel, *Gabriel's Wing: A Study into the religious ideas of Sir Muhammad Iqbal* (London, 1963), p. 21.

on similar lines and justified the alliance with the Hindus on the ground that they were *Ahl-i Sulah* as opposed to *Ahl-i Harb* (enemies of Islam). In a similar vein, Ansari, in December 1920, quoted the *Sura-i-Mumtahanah* (60: 8-9) from the Quran to argue that Indian Muslims should behave 'righteously, affectionately and in a friendly manner towards all those non-Muslims who are neither at war with Muslims nor are they assailants intending to invade or occupy their territories'.[16]

This emphasis on a peaceful *modus vivendi* with the Hindus reflected Afghani's viewpoint that a religious link did not exclude national links with men of different faiths; in fact he had called upon his Indian Muslim audience to make common cause with the Hindus in what pertained to national interests.[17] Far from advocating a split between the two communities, as is commonly believed, Afghani advocated inter-communal oneness and defied any breach in the anti-British front. In his articles published in the Hyderabad journal, *Muallim-i Shafiq*, he evoked not only the universal Islamic but also national aspirations with special emphasis on the affinity of Hindu-Muslim interests. And just as he helped awaken Egyptian nationalism by alluding to the ancient glories of the past, so in India, even when talking to a primarily Muslim audience, he harped on the glory of the Indian Hindu past.[18] His appeal to take pride in the Hindu past was no different from his earlier exhortation to Egyptian Muslims to seek inspiration from pre-Islamic Egyptian greatness. In both cases Afghani appealed to an effective basis for solidarity against the foreigner.[19] His message inspired those Muslims who pioneered the pan-Islamic movement in the first decade of the twentieth century and later piloted the Khilafat campaign in all its tumultuous phases.

Afghani's attempt to reconcile pan-Islamism with nationalism carried conviction. Various theories were therefore worked out to resolve their apparent dichotomy and to remove the widespread conception that the essence of pan-Islamism implied a break with territorial nationalism. The ideologues of the Khilafat movement insisted that the sum and substance of pan-Islamism was to remove foreign domination; so their activities had an obvious

[16]*Al-Ahkamul Quraniya mavalat-al Burtaniya* (Delhi, n.d.), p. 15; Pirzada (ed.), *Foundations of Pakistan*, Vol. I, p. 547.

[17]Hourani, op. cit., p. 118.

[18]Keddie, op. cit., pp. 155, 159-60.

[19]Ibid., p. 160; N.R. Keddie, *Islamic Response to Imperialism: Political and Religious Writings of Sayyid Jamal al-Din "Al-Afghani"* (California, 1968), p. 59.

nationalist dimension and were inextricably bound with the concept of an emerging Indian nation. They pointed out that, in spite of their pan-Islamic ambition, or fantasy as some preferred to call it, they always had their own Indian community most clearly in mind and were not oblivious to its trials and tribulations. The emblem used on the Khilafat delegation stationery—made up of twin circles of equal size and overlapping, with the word 'Khilafat' on one and the word 'India' on the other—was symbolic of their patriotism and illustrative of their perceived link between their vision of a free India and the liberation of the Muslim countries from the yoke of colonial rule. Ansari, for instance, established the connection between British colonial policies in India and the larger interests of the West in exploiting the weaker nations of the East and in perpetuating 'the bondage and slavery of Asiatic people'. To him it was not only a question of India's honour and freedom, but of a great struggle for emancipating all the enslaved people from the thraldom of the West.[20]

It has been argued that men like Ansari extended their concept of independence from foreign rule to all Islamic countries in order to restore a single Islamic state under a revived Khilafat, that their call for *jehad* had a strong traditional basis and their anti-colonial rhetoric was merely an eyewash—a clever device for achieving narrow sectarian ends. We have tried to show that this was not the case. Whatever may have been the unstated objectives of the Khilafat campaign, it served an objective need of mobilizing large numbers of people against the government and, in the process, made them conscious of the importance of a harmonious communal coexistence. Muslims, in particular, were in the forefront of this mobilization. This had never been the case before.

As for the relationship between the Indians and the Turks, it was in the nature of a compact, because both Turkey and India were subjected to colonial rule. For this reason Azad observed that the agitation in India had at first been directed towards the salvation of the Khalifa and the Ottoman empire, but now it was plain that the problem of the Khalifa was part of the larger issue of British imperialism. Khilafat workers must win India's liberty by means of non-cooperation; only then would they be able to save the Khalifa.[21] Mohamed Ali offered the

[20]Pirzada (ed.), op. cit., pp 545-6.

[21]W.I. Watson, 'Muhammad Ali and the Khilafat Movement' (unpublished M.A.

same advice: Muslims must fight for swaraj with their non-Muslim brethren, for only in this way would it be possible to achieve the Khilafat aim.[22]

Mohamed Ali made the most passionate and detailed attempt to demonstrate that pan-Islamism and nationalism were compatible, arguing that Western aggression against Muslim states hastened Muslim disillusionment with their traditional reliance on the British government and thereby contributed greatly to Indian unity.[23] His intention was to prove that, objectively speaking, his community's reactions to events in Turkey deepened their involvement in the anti-colonial struggle in India and brought them closer to the Congress under Gandhi's leadership.

Mohamed Ali further stated that the Muslims have had a pre-eminent sense of community in their *Weltanschauung* and especially so in India, where their adherence to Islam made them unique and gave them their 'communal consciousness'. 'I have a culture, a polity, an outlook on life—a complete synthesis which is Islam,' he said at the Round Table Conference in 1930. He did not, however, believe that being a Muslim he was any less an Indian. His religious beliefs, as indeed his commitment to nationalism, never appeared to him to be incompatible.[24] He could—and must—be true to both Islam and India. To further prove the compatibility of his loyalty to Islam and to his country, he took pains to explain that 'where India is concerned, where India's freedom is concerned, where the welfare of India is concerned, I am an Indian first, an Indian second and nothing but an Indian'.[25] There is little doubt that this conviction was shared by many Muslims who were able to easily swing back and forth between pan-Islamic and local nationalist appeals, depending upon which was a more appropriate anti-imperialist weapon in a specific Indian situation.

The Khilafat movement has often been denounced as unrealistic on the grounds that its emphasis on extra-Indian loyalties stood in the way of genuine unity. It has also been pointed out that those Muslims who joined the Congress and accepted Gandhi's leadership during the Khilafat campaign were motivated by religious considerations and that their alliance with nationalist

thesis, 1955, Mcgill University), p. 64.

[22]Muhammad Ali, *His Life, Service and Trial* (Madras, n.d.), p. 151.

[23]*IQR*, July-December 1923, p. 30.

[24]Mushirul Hasan, *Mohamed Ali Ideology and Politics* (Delhi, 1982), p. 115.

[25]Ibid., p. 115

forces was of an ephemeral and opportunistic nature. The roots of this assumption lay in the unexpressed postulate that Muslims were unpatriotic because they were moved only by loyalty to the invisible theocracy of which God was the ruler and that they had developed a nationalism of their own which was Islamic in tone and content. 'Under the circumstances,' observed the Congress and Hindu Mahasabha leader B.S. Moonje, 'how can peace and amity now grow between the Hindus and the Muslims unless either the Hindus surrender and become a consenting party to the Islamic Mission or if they are equally determined to preserve their essentially scientific identity separate from the one-sided Nationalism of the Muslims.'[27]

The debate centred round the supposed contradiction between Indian nationalism and 'Islamic nationalism' can be disregarded, for its implications, if any, were hardly discernible in the political trends of the early 1920s. What deserves consideration, however, is how the Khilafat movement, despite its pan-Islamic bias, was merged into a general political struggle far outstripping its original limitations.

It is a lesser known fact of modern Indian history that the Khilafat committees in some areas were often indistinguishable from local Congress bodies, volunteer groups, Kisan Sabhas and Home Rule Leagues in their composition and political objectives. This imparted a purposeful political dimension to their activities. 'There is nothing to choose locally,' commented an official, 'between a gathering under the auspices of the Kisan Sabha or of the Khilafat Committee. Both movements appear to have been completely captured by the non-cooperation party.'[27] This was not just a joyful demonstration of the newly-found sense of solidarity, but an awareness of the 'extraordinary stiffening-up' of a demoralized, backward and broken-up people taking part in disciplined, joint action on a countrywide scale.[28]

In several areas of agrarian unrest in UP peasant unrest was not just tacked on to the Khilafat and non-cooperation programme, but the Khilafat Committees and the Kisan Sabhas provided a tangible sign of acting in unison in attacking their common

[26]7 August 1926, Moonje Dossier, Pad No. 35, National Library, Calcutta.

[27]S.R. Mayers to A.G. Shirreff, deputy commissioner, 25 February 1921, GAD, F. No. 50, 1921, Box No. 135, UPSA. All subsequent references, unless otherwise stated, are drawn from the same file.

[28]Nehru, *An Autobiography*, p. 76.

identifiable enemy—the landlord—who was rightly perceived as the government's ally. Herein lay the danger in official assessment, a fact referred to when the secretary of the Rae Bareli Khilafat Committee spoke at a Kisan Sabha meeting on 6 February. 'What might have been in its way a harmful and beneficent movement,' observed an official, 'is in danger of being rapidly perverted into a vehicle for virulent abuse of and violent agitation against the Government.'[29] Evidence of the potentially dangerous alliance came from other areas as well. A Kisan Sabha rally at Fyzabad, held on 20-21 December 1920, was probably organized by Khilafat workers.[30] Local Khilafat leaders—Lal Mohammad and Maulvi Riasat Husain—addressed a similar gathering at village Salethu in Maharajganj on 2 February 1921; the meeting at village Balla in the same police station area a week earlier was organized by Amid Syed, a local Khilafat agitator.

A notable feature of many such meetings was the attempt to establish a definite link between the demands of the Kisans and the Khilafatists, on the one hand, and the attainment of 'swaraj', on the other; in fact, words like 'Khilafat', 'Kisan ekta', 'swaraj', 'Gandhi' were all intended to conjure up in the minds of the people a picture of bringing about a better world under the direction of better leaders.[31] Thus Maulvi Salamatullah, associated with Maulana Abdul Bari, declared at a Kisan Sabha gathering that the peasant interests would be protected only after the dignity and prestige of the Khalifa was restored. Kamaluddin

[29]Note on Rae Bareli disturbances, op. cit.

[30]M.H. Siddiqi, *Agrarian Unrest in North India: The United Provinces 1918-22* (Delhi, 1978), p. 149; Kapil Kumar, *Peasants in Revolt: Tenants, Landlords, Congress and the Raj in Oudh* (Delhi, 1984), pp. 146, 165.

[31]This idea was beautifully summed up in the verses of Mohammad Haider, a school teacher in Pilibhit. He wrote:

Jamaa do qaum ka sikka bajaa do deen ka danka
Mohamed, Shaukat-o-Gandhi ke pairokaar ho jaao
Swadeshi se karo raghbat bidesi se karo nafrat
Ki jis se muflisee ho door aur zardaar ho jaao

Let the respect for the nation be restored
And the trumpet of the faith heralded
Follow Mohamed (Ali), Shaukat and Gandhi
Adopt all that is swadeshi and shun that which is from outside
So that you may remove poverty and achieve self-reliance.

Proscribed Publications (43). Also, see the collection of poems in *Bulbulan-i Hurriyat* in Proscribed Publication (47). The collection was published by the Khilafat Committee in Jaunpur.

Jafri, the Allahabad-based lawyer, linked the redressal of their grievances with the attainment of swaraj under the Congress directives. This view was expressed at a Kisan Sabha conference at Akbarpur in Fyzabad district and was endorsed by Hafiz Alam and Mohammad Nabi of Tanda, important Khilafatists in eastern UP.[32]

The collaboration between the Khilafatists and groups of peasants and workers was equally pronounced in Bengal and the Punjab. In Bengal this was facilitated by the failure of harvests between 1918 and 1922, the rise in prices, the fall in the prices of jute and the influenza and cholera epidemics. In the Punjab, on the other hand, the North Western Railway strike which was initially called at the end of April 1920 for the improvement of the workers' material conditions, subsequently began to coalesce with the Khilafat agitation as the strikers began to perceive it as a movement against a 'tyrannical and exploitative' government.[33]

In assessing such strands in the Khilafat agitation, it is also worth taking note of the Congress-Khilafat-League *entente*. These organizations met in the same city and around the same time; often the Khilafat Committee and the Muslim League took their political cue from the Congress and endorsed its decisions. The 1918 League session, for instance, did so and, as in the Congress, so in the League, wrote an intelligence officer, 'the moderates have lost all control'. The same spirit prevailed a year later, though speeches made at the League platform 'were more violent in their language and defiant in their general attitude than the extremist Hindus at the meetings of the Congress'. Anti-British spirit, emphasized the government report, 'reigned supreme'.[34] In July 1920, the League insisted that the Congress met first so that it could recommend and decide the course of action for the Muslims.[35]

[32]Police Dept., F. No. 51-N, 1921, UPSA: Note by Lakhte Husain and Jagannath, 28 January 1921, op. cit.

[33]Khizar Humayun Ansari, 'The Emergence of Muslim Socialists and their ideas in India between 1917 and 1947' (Ph.D. thesis, University of London, 1985), pp. 83-5.

[34]Home Poll. B, January 1919, 160-3, NAI; WRDCI (January 1920), Home Poll. Deposit, February 1920, 52, NAI.

[35]Zahur Ahmad to G.N. Misra, 26 July 1920, F. No. 18, 1920, AICC Papers (Suppl.), NMML. In distant Malabar every mosque became a centre of Congress-Khilafat activity. Taluq and district level leaders toured the Muslim centres with Muslim colleagues, organization and Khilafat volunteers. E.M.S. Namboodripad, *How I became a Communist* (Trivandrum, 1976), p. 35.

Such demonstrations of political unity were matched by spontaneous expressions of communal harmony. It is noteworthy that most parts of the country were free of communal violence and that existing disputes over cow-slaughter and music before mosques were settled amicably. In Delhi and the Punjab, in particular, the Prem Sabhas and *Anjuman-i Islam* worked strenuously to ensure the peaceful observance of religious festivals.[36] The spirit of the time was captured by Zafar Ali Khan in the verse:

Aaee hain Aasman se chal kar woh quwaten
Jo Muslim-o-Hunood ko sheer-o-shakar karen

Heavenly forces have helped to forge the bonds of friendship between the Hindus and the Muslims.

Or, by Agha Hashr:

Ho gaeen bikhri huee eenten baham tameer ki
Mil gaee har ek kari tooti huee zanjeer ki
But-shikari wahdast-parast ek jism ek jaan ho gaye
Ghul hua duniya me phir kafir Mussalman ho gaye

The disjointed pieces have been put in order again
The links of the broken chain have been discerned
The idol-worshippers and the iconoclast have joined hands
There is a dinning clamour that the *kafirs* have again embraced Islam.

Short-lived as this unity was, the fact that it was accomplished was a sufficient indication of the strength and fervour of the nationalistic spirit of which it was the outward expression. 'The scenes that were enacted before my eyes,' wrote the Secretary of the Bengal Khilafat Committee, 'made me feel that the artificial barriers that had long been preventing the two major communities of the country to come together, had been miraculously swept away by the onrush of the all-embracing non-cooperation movement.'[37]

Ansari and the Khilafat Protest

Historians have chartered the course and development of the Khilafat ferment in India. The following account is therefore limited to an examination of those aspects which place Ansari's

[36] *Tribune*, 13 October 1919; *Fateh* (Delhi), 1 July 1920; Shraddhanand, *Inside Congress* (Bombay, 1946), pp. 68-70.

[37] Abul Hayat, *Mussalmans of Bengal* (Calcutta. 1966), p. 37.

role in perspective as well as illuminate some facets of the Khilafat protest in India. The main focus is on Delhi, though the national context is not lost sight of because Ansari's sphere of activity extended far beyond the confines of the capital. Admittedly, he had no regional political base; yet this did not limit his influence. He had a large following in different regions and in different groups and was known to and well thought of by every major politician in the country, including Gandhi who solicited his advice.

It is a lesser known fact that Ansari was the first to voice the growing disquiet over the future of Turkey and the Holy Places from an organized political platform—the All-India Muslim League session in December 1918. He was also the first prominent leader to highlight the pan-Islamic dimension of the Khilafat excitement and established its correlation with the political aspirations of the Indian people at large. He thus attempted to prove that the Khilafat movement was not just organically linked with Indian nationalism, but that its collapse would spell danger to the Congress movement and its ideal of attaining swaraj.

First, he concentrated on the dismemberment of Muslim states because of the 'avarice and greed of the Chancellories of Europe' and warned that his community would not remain indifferent to the fate of 40 million Muslims in the world. He stressed that the integrity and independence of the present Muslim states be maintained intact, the wrongs done to the Arabs of North Africa and the Tartars and Turks of Central Asia be redressed and they should be given a free chance to choose their own government.

Next he turned to the relationship between the government and the Muslims, describing it as 'one varying from bias against them to that of antipathy, suspicion, mistrust and even dislike', and went on to give forceful expression to the disillusionment, the sense of having been tricked, which Muslims felt from the time of the annulment of Bengal's partition. Now, he pointed out, the secretary of state and the viceroy were against separate electorates and communal representation, 'the life and soul of all our activities of the present day'.[38] He also referred to the

[38]In the *Report on Indian Constitutional Reforms* (1918), communal representation was condemned on the ground that it perpetuated class distinctions, stereotyped existing relations, and constituted a serious hindrance to the development of the self-governing principle. Speech by Ansari at the All-India Muslim League, December 1918, Home Poll. A, March 1919, 251-9, NAI.

interference with religious liberty, guaranteed under the proclamation of 1858, 'the fundamental basis of [Muslim] allegiance to the Crown', the internment of Mahmud Hasan, Azad and the Ali Brothers and the strangulation of newspapers like the *Comrade*, the *Hamdard*, the *Al-Hilal* and the *Zamindar*. Ansari had come to believe, slowly, but with growing conviction, that those who clung to the doctrine of *force majeure* in India advocated an imperial philosophy whose vigour was already spent and which was no longer a solution for the problems of the day. 'Had it not been that our rulers were engaged in a struggle of life and death,' he observed, 'the Mussalmans would have taken such constitutional measures as would have compelled action.'

The rest of the speech was a plea for the burying of mistrust and a new spirit of Hindu-Muslim partnership. Ansari reiterated his faith in the Lucknow Pact, hammered out in December 1916, and in the making of which he played a major part.[39] On Hindu-Muslim *entente*, ushered in by the pact, he contended:

> The Mussalmans have fought the battle of India shoulder to shoulder with their Hindu brethren, their political programme has come in line with that of the Hindus, the Hindu-Muslim rapprochement entered into at Lucknow has, year after year, gained strength and vitality and I believe that as time goes on we shall understand each other better and any causes of friction that remain shall cease to exist. It is my firm conviction that a true Mussalman is always a good Nationalist.

Ansari concluded on the note that the exclusion of India from the application of Woodrow Wilson's (1856-1924) fourteen points was inexcusable in the light of its contributions and sacrifices during the War. It seemed to him a ridiculous paradox that India alone should escape from a movement of political thought that was affecting every other part of the British empire. Making a strong plea for self-determination, he set forth:

> Out of the welter and blood of the Armageddon have emerged certain definite principles on which will be based the foundations of a new and better world.... They have been

[39]The pact was concluded between the representatives of the Congress and the Muslim League. The Congress agreed to separate electorates, to the principle of Muslim representation in the legislative councils and to weightage of seats to Muslims in excess of their proportion of the population in areas where they were in a minority

repeated, explained and amplified time after time, until no doubt has been left in the minds of men that their application will be universal and not confined to the geographical limits of a country or continent nor will they be circumscribed by the prejudices of race, colour or creed. To my mind there is but one single doctrine in which is focussed the entire thought of the whole human race. This doctrine, Gentlemen, is the doctrine of self-determination.[40]

Ansari's address had a profound impression on the Muslim League session, on the city and on Muslims throughout northern India. Contemporaries took serious cognizance of his articulation of political demands, his avouchment of his community's commitment to the Lucknow Pact and his faith in a viable communal accord. His pronouncement brightened up the prospects of closer Congress-Muslim League cooperation and offered hopes of narrowing down the wide gulf that already yawned between the Hindus and Muslims.

Muslims in northern India paid much heed to Ansari's address as it summed up their fears and frustrations which arose out of British policies both in India and in Turkey. In fact, Ansari's effort to stir them out of their torpor was rewarded by a slow but steady surge of resentment against the government and those who served it. 'There is no doubt', reported an intelligence officer,

> that the masses were grieved to hear of the Sultan's defeat.... Now Dr Ansari's address with its quotations from the Quran and the support of the ulamas (*sic*) is producing anger and hate among them. The address has been widely read and by now every Mussalman knows that the Holy Places are going out of the hands of the Mussalmans sovereign and that the English are responsible.[41]

Fresh from his success at Delhi, Ansari devoted the next three years spreading the Khilafat message. In January 1919, he helped to distribute an *istifta* (questionnaire) issued by Abdul Bari in order to obtain an authoritative pronouncement from leading *ulama* in support of the views expressed by Ansari at the historic Muslim League session. He led the Khilafat delegation which met the viceroy on 19 January 1920 and was a member of the second deputation which reached London in February

[40]Quoted in Ferrel, op.cit., p. 201.
[41]Ibid.

1921. He submitted a report of its activities and suggested that the Central Khilafat Committee depute knowledgeable people to Europe to remain in touch with the situation there as well as with 'Near Eastern affairs'. In early 1922, Ansari, Ajmal Khan, Seth Chotani (1873-1932), Syed Mahmud (1889-1971) and A.H.S. Khatri issued a fairly comprehensive statement setting out the Khilafat claims. They also laid out a scheme of political activity for their Muslim brethren with emphasis on attainment of swaraj under Gandhi's leadership. This was followed by an Ansari-Ajmal Khan manifesto, issued in March 1922. It demanded the restoration of the Turkish portion of the Ottoman empire to Turkey with full sovereign rights, the liberation of the Arabic-speaking areas—Palestine, Syria, Mesopotamia and Hejaz—from non-Muslim control and the maintenance of the Sultan's authority over the Holy Places.

The manifesto of early 1922 enunciated the Khilafat demands explicitly and linked them with the overall national struggle against British *imperium*. The world of Islam, its authors stated:

> has grown wise in adversity. We are no longer easily duped by specious pretences. Turkey and the Khalifa of Islam have too often been betrayed by European Powers for us to trust in their good faith today. Only by genuine actions can Europe again win the friendship of the Islamic world. The settlement with Turkey must include the release of the *Jazirat-ul-Arab* from all suggestion of control by a non-Muslim Power and the Khalifa's authority over the administrations of the Holy Places must be recognized. It must include the complete independence of the Khalifa in his own capital. It must include the granting to the Muslims of Syria, of Palestine, of Iraq and of Egypt the common right of determination. No other statement will bring peace. These are the only terms on which Islam can with self-respect admit the Powers to friendship. If these terms are refused today they will be offered tomorrow, since Truth must prevail and the Federation of the Islamic peoples of the world grows stronger every day. Let the recent speech of His Majesty the Amir of Afghanistan warn the Powers of Europe that in sympathy Islam is one and undivided as it is in the Faith. Muslims demand only freedom for Islam—freedom to develop the civilization and the culture we know to be true and beautiful. This freedom is our God-given right and we can be content with nothing less. Islamic civilization cannot develop and thrive if it is in bondage, even if the bonds are called Mandates.

To the Muslims of India, we workers then in the Khilafat cause, appeal that they show an unshaken front. *Our Hindu brothers are with us in our struggle. Their numbers give us confidence in our strength and they are our brothers in all truth for the Holy Quran teaches that the friends of the Faith are our brothers* [emphasis added]. In all mankind it is only enemies of the Faith who are not brothers to true Muslims. Our Hindu brothers are doubly so for they love our country as we do, the country is their's as well as our's to love. *And they suffer with us and for us in the common cause Indians have made to win freedom by non-violent Non-cooperation. Together we will win Swaraj—a Swaraj that will enable us to secure justice for Islam* [emphasis added]. Our enemies seek daily to divide us but let us not fear their intrigues. We have given final proof of our brotherhood in that the Muslims have loyally accepted the dictatorship of that great saint and thinker—Mahatma Gandhi—in our struggle for freedom. Henceforth Hindu-Muslim unity will prevail. We Muslims are called the Army of the Faithful the world over. At this crisis in the history of Islam let us merit the description. Let us remain faithful in thought, word and deed, faithful to our cause, to our country, to the leader we have chosen—Mahatma Gandhi. Though the powers of Europe may seek to deceive us again in the matter of the Khilafat claims, let us have no doubt but that truth will prevail. Making our voice heard and our demands known, let us work loyally for freedom and Swaraj through non-violent non-cooperation. Let us above all remain the Army of the Faithful. India's Muslims have achieved and suffered a great deal for the Faith. Perhaps they believe their suffering has been in vain. But the truth is that through suffering they have grown stronger far more than formerly. And much more remains to be done—much more must be suffered—before we win complete victory—complete freedom for Islam and India. The immediate work before us is that we must—

(1) Collect fifty lakhs for the Angora Fund.
(2) Be prepared to fill the gaols of British India when our Dictator Mahatma Gandhi bids us.
(3) Preserve non-violence at all costs because success depends on this.
(4) Preserve inviolate the sacred spirit of Hindu-Muslim unity.

(5) And last but not least follow Mahatma Gandhi unflinchingly.[42]

This was not all. Ansari presided over district, provincial and all-India gatherings enlisting popular support for the Khilafat and the Congress movements. He took the lead in convening the All-India Muslim Conference held in Lucknow on 21 September, persuaded the Muslim divines to attend in large numbers and when the conference decided to observe 17 October as 'Khilafat Day'—a day of mourning and protest—he ensured its success in Delhi. He was at the head of the Anti-Peace Celebration Committee, the main financier of the innumerable Khilafat volunteer corps in the capital and the chief architect of the local Khilafat committee.

The Delhi Khilafat committee was established on 5 November 1919 at Ajmal Khan's residence, some months after the Central Khilafat Committee came into being in Bombay. Headed by Ansari, Ajmal Khan and Asaf Ali, it included journalists, *ulama*, lawyers and a few petty traders who had earlier patronized the *Anjuman-i-Khuddam-i Kaaba*. The *ulama*, who were at the heart of Muslim concern over Turkey, were represented by Maulvis Kifayatullah, Ahmad Said and Nur Muhammad—all of them had played an active part in the Rowlatt satyagraha. Among the journalists were Abbas Husain, Arif Husain Hasvi, Abdul Ghaffar and Tajuddin who were also catapulted to the fore during the Rowlatt satyagraha.

This unique combination of the Western and the traditionally-educated Muslims helped to turn the once benign imperial capital into a stormy centre of anti-government and the focus of vigorous Khilafat activities. The first fortnight of December 1919, reported the government, 'has only been remarkable in Delhi on account of the Khilafat agitation and the anti-peace celebration campaigns'.[43] In November 1919 the Delhi Khilafat Committee convened and hosted an All-India Khilafat Conference—attended by, among others, Gandhi and Shraddhanand. Its decisions—to boycott the peace celebrations planned by government for 13 December and to withhold cooperation with the government unless the Khilafat issue was settled in accordance with Muslim wishes—radicalized the course of the Khilafat movement in Delhi and elsewhere. The other resolution which

[42] Bamford, *Histories*, pp 186-7, 194-5.

[43] Home Poll. D, January 1920, 44, NAI.

proposed the boycott of British goods did not find favour with Gandhi. His reactions had to be taken into account, for he had come to play an increasingly vital role in Khilafat affairs since his first major pronouncement in May 1919 that the Khilafat question was 'the greatest of all, greater even than that of the repeal of the Rowlatt Act, for it affects the religious susceptibilities of millions of Muslims'. His view prevailed at the conference. So the only resolutions passed thanked him and other Hindus for their support and proposed a boycott of peace celebrations.

The extent of Gandhi's influence was also apparent at the Muslim League session in Amritsar in December 1919. In deference to his wishes and as a reciprocal gesture of goodwill towards the Hindus, the League agreed to substitute the slaughter of other animals in place of cows on the occasion of *Baqr Id*. It is noteworthy that Ansari introduced this resolution. Gratitude was also expressed to the Crown for the spirit in which the royal proclamation was issued. Here again Gandhi's influence is noticeable, for he was at the same time carrying a similar motion through the Congress.

From January to March 1920 the Khilafat protest in Delhi, as elsewhere, reached a new level of intensity owing to hectic campaigning by the *ulama* and the Khilafat volunteer corps, and the release of Mohamed Ali and Shaukat Ali as a result of the amnesty which accompanied the royal proclamation of the Montagu-Chelmsford reforms. The Ali Brothers made their first triumphal entry into Delhi on 9 January. In Ansari's open motor car, they were driven through the main streets of old Delhi decorated with garlands, crescent-emblazoned flags and archways at the various intersections. Khilafat volunteers, stated a government report,

> turned out for their first mass operations on the occasion of the triumphal arrival in Delhi of the Ali Brothers.... They took complete charge of the Chandni Chowk and endeavoured violently but unsuccessfully to control the assembled crowds.[44]

Mohamed Ali returned to the city on 16 January and asked Muslims to sacrifice their 'health, wealth and life in the name of God'. Azad said on the same occasion that the proposed Khilafat deputation to the viceroy had no request to make, but

[44] *History of the Non-Cooperation and Khilafat movements in Delhi*, p. 10
Minault, *The Khilafat Movement*, p. 85.

would simply inform him of the Islamic obligations.

Ansari accompanied the Ali Brothers on their extensive tours and was wholly behind the drive to implement non-cooperation. On 10 September he spoke at the Gora Bazar in Ghazipur on non-cooperation.[45] Towards the end of the year 1920, he presided over the 13th Muslim League session and dwelt at length on *tark-i mawalat*, or the abandonment of friendship with those who were enemies of and at war with Islam and Muslim countries. He said that a government could only survive with the active cooperation or passive acquiescence of the people, but if it was unjust and disregarded the rights of the people the only way of reforming it was to cease cooperation. The principle of *tark-i mawalat*, he emphasized, was not a new idea; rather it was a clear and definite injunction of the *Sharia* which Muslims had consigned to oblivion. But Gandhi's 'far-sighted mind' saw in this Muslim religious principle an effective method of wide application, well-suited to the political requirements of the country and in conformity with the principles of satyagraha. Ansari took the opportunity of reminding his Muslim audience that non-cooperation was not only a political and moral necessity but a religious obligation; hence they had a greater responsibility in carrying it out.

The boycott of government-aided educational institutions, envisaged in the non-cooperation programme, appealed to Ansari a great deal. He accompanied Jawaharlal to Banaras and helped organize a students non-cooperation committee at the university. He did the same in Allahabad, Aligarh and Agra. At the Muslim League session he referred to the substantial and encouraging response of students and made special mention of the 'marvellous patience and fortitude' of those students who left the Aligarh College to join the National Muslim University, familiarly known as the Jamia Millia Islamia. What was unstated was Ansari's own critical role in founding the institution and nursing it from its very inception. Jamia was Ansari's lifelong passion and he devoted himself to its development. For this reason we must examine

[45] Ansari's speech 'clearly has attempted to bring into hatred or contempt or attempted to excite disaffection towards the Govt.... His purpose admittedly is to paralyse the Govt. And he says that no Govt. can carry on its operations when the inhabitants decide to give it no assistance and he preaches that no assistance should be given.' The official proposed Ansari's prosecution. Note on 2 October 1920, Home Police, F. No. 16/7, Box No. 58, UPSA.

its history more closely. We do so for another reason. Jamia's fortunes were inextricably linked with the state of communal relations in the country. It flourished at a time when political unity between the Hindus and Muslims reached its high watermark; it faced the prospect of closure in a less favourable climate.

NON-COOPERATION AT ALIGARH AND THE FOUNDATION OF JAMIA MILLIA ISLAMIA

Addressing a students' gathering at Ahmedabad on 28 September 1920, Gandhi said:

> If [however] all government schools are left empty I promise that you will see the face of India changed within a month. Nothing else will have the same impact on the public and our rulers as that produced by every student leaving his or her school or college forthwith in a day.[46]

This call to national service and self-sacrifice elicited a ready response among diverse types of students; in fact statistics for the boycott of schools and colleges were far more impressive than for boycott of courts or resignation from government service. The Congress Civil Disobedience Enquiry Committee noted that the ranks of Congress workers was swelled by 'the more ardent young men whose patriotism and enthusiasm have greatly advanced the cause of the country.'[47] This was true of, among other places, the M.A.O. College at Aligarh where non-cooperation was a spectacular success.

The college of Syed Ahmad Khan's days was ardently pro-British and steered clear of political entanglements. It was hard to be otherwise. Its founder considered education as the sole means for regenerating his community and regarded Anglo-Muslim rapprochement as a necessary condition for its upliftment. The *raison d'etre* of his college was to make Muslims 'worthy and useful subjects of the Crown', to groom students to go on to British universities, and to train them for government employment so that they could join the 'heaven born'. Such expectations were fulfilled during Syed Ahmad Khan's lifetime. Students cultivated English habits and tastes, expressed loyalty to the Crown by decorating their rooms with portraits of Queen Victoria and the Prince of Wales and paid heed to repeated admonitions to

[46] *CWG*, Vol. 18, pp. 297, 280.
[47] *IQR*, 1922-23, Vol. I, p. 84.

avoid getting enmeshed in politics. Syed Ahmad's crusade against the Congress also made sense and struck a favourable chord in Aligarh circles.

In the early years of the twentieth century, however, this most 'benighted' and conservative of academic centres suddenly exploded into political activity confronting the British with the most serious Muslim movement of dissidence which they had faced since the 1857 revolt. The agitation against the Nagri resolution of 18 April 1900, followed by the students' strike of February 1907, represented extremely new trends in Aligarh politics—a trend to steer the Muslim community on a course different from that plotted by Syed Ahmad Khan. Although this mirrored the changes taking place at other levels of Muslim society, contemporaries were never tired of pointing out how, just a few years before they appeared, there was not the slightest sign of their imminence in Aligarh. This earlier quiescence, attributed to Syed Ahmad Khan's influence and to the predominance of landed interests in the board of trustees, was gradually replaced by a posture favourable to the Congress and antagonistic to government. The Aligarh students threw to the winds all the caution they had learnt at the feet of the grand old man.

Inspired by the emotionally charged poems of Shibli Nomani and Hasrat Mohani and by the exalted prose of Mohamed Ali's *Comrade*, Azad's *Al-Hilal*, and Zafar Ali Khan's *Zamindar*, political rumpus on the campus was sustained during the course of World War I. Students raised funds for beleagured Turkey, prayed for the success of its armies in the Balkan Wars, and were enthused by the *Anjuman-i-Khuddam-i Kaaba*. Four Aligarh graduates were part of Ansari's medical mission and at least one Aligarh Old Boy—Mahendra Pratap—was involved in the 'Silk Letter Conspirarcy' and at the head of the 'Provisional Government' set up in Kabul. This was not all. The themes of capitalist exploitation, of class conflict, of revolt against imperialism, and of socialism figured in the prose of Sajjad Hyder Yaldaram (1880-1943), Vilayat Ali 'Bambooq' (1885-1918), Abdul Ghaffar, and Abdur Rahman Bijnori (d. 1918) and in the inspiring *ghazals* of Hasrat Mohani and other younger poets at Aligarh. The Progressive Writers' Association, formed in the early 1930s, represented the continuation and development of the literary and political trends set by writers who were either in or closely connected with Aligarh. Some of its leading lights gave Urdu literature a vital stimulus, a new vigour and liberating consciousness.

There was another trend in Aligarh politics which, though feeble in the early 1920s, came to dominate university life in the early 1930s. This was the influence of socialism. More specifically, the Bolshevik revolution of 1917 had a favourable impression on students. Syed Mohammad Tonki, a leading non-cooperator who later turned to 'Islamic socialism' under the influence of Hasrat Mohani, recalled receiving M.N. Roy's (1887-1954) writings 'which discussed the Russian revolution, the reality of the socialist system, and the weakening of big empires as a result of capitalist and imperialist exploitation' He and Kunwar Mohammad Ashraf (1903-62), a Meo Muslim from Alwar State who rose to political eminence in the 1930s, often discussed 'what a socialist system might achieve in India'.[48]

Amidst this flurry of activity, the adoption of the non-cooperation programme in September 1920 offered a rallying point for the radical elements in Aligarh circles.[49] Encouraged by reports of nationalist ebullience on the campus, Gandhi and his Khilafatist allies turned to Aligarh to muster support. Gandhi fired the first shot. He reached Aligarh on 11 October with Ansari, Azad, Ajmal Khan and the Ali Brothers and addressed a students' meeting. He spoke haltingly in Hindustani, trying to find the right words but his accent seemed droll to his 'pseudo-sophisticated' audience who did not agree with him because their political and economic background and affiliations did not predispose them to accept his radically new doctrine of non-cooperation.[50] The first shot had misfired. He then appealed to the trustees

> to decline any further Government grant, disaffiliate the great institution of which you are the trustees and reject the charter of the Moslem University. The least that the Aligarh boys can do, if you fail to respond to the call of Islam and India, is to wash their hands clean of an institution acknowledging the aegis of Government that has forfeited all title to the allegiance

[48]Syed Mohammad Tonki, in Horst Kruger (ed.), *Kunwar Mohammad Ashraf: An Indian Scholar and Revolutionary 1903-1962* (Berlin, 1966), p. 344.

[49]K M. Ashraf on Himself, in ibid., p. 391.

[50]This is based on K.G. Saiyidain's memory of Gandhi's visit. He came into personal contact with the Mahatma in 1937 at the First National Education Conference in Sevagram. See *Gandhian Ideas on Education: Their Relevance to our Times* (New Delhi, n.d.), pp. 6-7.

> of Islam and India and to bring into being a larger, nobler and purer Aligarh that would carry out the most wishes of its great founder.[51]

The trustees were not impressed either. They had unanimously decided, much before Gandhi's letter of 24 October reached them, to run the institution on 'old established lines' and 'to make the Mussalmans of India worthy and useful subjects of the British Crown'. After repeated failures to counter Mohamed Ali's influence who meddled into Aligarh affairs brazenly, the trustees at last had their taste of revenge. The doyen of agitational politics was able to activate only ten members; the remaining 48 present at the meeting rallied round the loyalist principal, Ziauddin Ahmad (1878-1947), a Cambridge Wrangler who wasted his talents in administration and petty politicking.

Unruffled by this rebuff, Ansari, Azad Subhani ('1873-1926), Azad and the Ali Brothers reappeared in Aligarh on 23 October with a small group of students led by Zakir Husain (1897-1969), a student-lecturer in economics, and Ashraf, who had already left college and joined the non-cooperators. On this occasion there was a change of heart among students. K.G. Saiyidain (1904-71) responded, together with Zakir Husain, to Gandhi's call to leave educational institutions aided by the foreign government. 'The tumultuous scene at the Students' Union Hall,' recalled one of his contemporaries, 'dwells vividly in one's memory and the din of acclaim that greeted Dr Saiyidain(s) gesture rings in one's ears to this day.'[52] Equally defiant was Mohammad Abid Husain, a graduate student. 'Respectfully I beg to inform you,' he wrote to the principal,

> that I have got my doubts removed within the last four or five days, and I am now strong supporter of non-cooperation.

[51] *CWG*, Vol. 18, p. 369.

[52] S. Bashiruddin, 'Dr K.G. Saiyidain: An Appraisal of Personality and Ideals' and K.A. Abbas, 'Thanks, Bhaijan!', in S. Abid Husain, Abdur Rashid (eds.), *Commemoration Volume* (Delhi, n.d.), pp. 45, 65. Referring to the speech made by Saiyidain on the occasion, his brother Khwaja Ahmad Abbas recalled: 'The impact of that speech must have left a deep impression on my sub-conscious because since then, even as a boy, I could not be swayed by the passion-filled arguments of the communalists. If the secular and humanistic concept of life has remained an integral part of my own personal credo, I owe it first of all to that speech.' Also, K.A. Abbas, *I am not an Island: An Experiment in Autobiography* (Delhi, 1977), pp. 50-1.

> The application which I sent to you a few days ago, informing you of my intention to appear at the Allahabad University examination for B.A. degree should be considered as withdrawn. I can and will read in your college only in the case it is nationalized (*sic*), otherwise I am ready to face the doom awaiting my non-cooperating brothers. I consider it my duty to intimate you of these views, so that I may not be considered a double game player.[53]

One Nurul Hasan of Azamgarh was so enthralled by the speeches of Azad and Azad Subhani that he joined the growing number of non-cooperators.[54] Amidst fiery and passionate speeches, resolutions, promises and assurances, many more students responded—estimates range from 200 to 700—to the call of non-cooperation and enrolled themselves with the newly-founded Jamia Millia Islamia. Mohamed Ali thus scored a major victory; the college authorities were humbled. The pan-Islamic fervour, combined with the nationalist tide, swept the campus and Syed Ahmad Khan's vision of sustaining the Anglo-Muslim combination through the M.A.O. College was all but shattered.

Carried on the crest of the nationalist tide, the Jamia Millia Islamia was founded in Aligarh in those days of 'unlimited dreams, fervent determination and enthusiastic nationalism'.[55] At the opening ceremony (29 October 1920) performed by that consistent anti-imperialist *alim* of Deoband, Mahmud Hasan [his address was read in his absence], it was explained that Jamia's *raison d'etre* was to keep Muslim education free from external control so that 'we may be perfectly immune from pernicious alien influences in our ideas and beliefs, our morals and actions, our character and conduct'. Consequently, it was to remain independent of government aid and control and evolve a philosophy of education which would be in keeping with national characteristics and in consonance with the Islamic spirit.[56] The founders of

[53]M.A. Husain to Ziauddin, 24 October 1920, Sir Syed Academy, Aligarh Muslim University, Aligarh. For details, see Mushirul Hasan, 'Nationalist and Separatist Trends in Aligarh, 1915-1947,' *The Social and Economic History Review*, January-March 1985.

[54]Nurul Hasan to Ziauddin Ahmad, n.d., ibid.

[55]W.C. Smith, *Modern Islam in India* (Lahore, 1943), p. 150. Jamia's history is traced by one of its teachers, Abdul Ghaffar Mudholi, *Jamia ki Kahani*, in two volumes (Delhi, 1965).

[56]*Jamia Millia Prospectus 1924-25* (Aligarh, n.d.), pp. 1-2.

Jamia believed that communal peace and religious understanding were the fruit of true education and sought by their course of study to end religious discord between all faiths, while teaching students to be good Muslims.[57] Halide Edib observed in 1935 that Jamia's general aim was to create a harmonious nationhood without Muslims losing their Islamic identity and that in its aim, if not always in its procedure, it was nearer to the Gandhian movement than any other Muslim institution she had come across.[58] Ansari presided over the destiny of such an institution until his death in 1936.

A noticeable, though hitherto unknown, contribution of the architects of Jamia was to familiarize the youth with their own cultural heritage without rejecting what was true and useful in the culture of others and to evolve an organic synthesis of traditional and modern education. In this way they hoped to create both a good Muslim in the traditional sense and a good citizen of an independent India. Recalled Mohammad Mujeeb, one of Jamia's prized acquisitions in 1926:

> We agreed that Muslim or non-Muslim, our student should learn to represent the values of his religion, of his moral and cultural tradition, that he should make himself a useful citizen by being cultured, modest, thoughtful and competent. The forms in which these qualities were to express themselves were those of the Indo-Muslim culture of the 19th and 20th century. This was the common culture of the region.[59]

This was consistent with the spirit of the Khilafat and non-cooperation days. Gandhi, one of Jamia's chief benefactors, went a step further. He hoped that it would interpret Muslim culture in a manner consonant with truth and the requirements of a people, diverse in culture, striving to achieve political unity, and that Jamia would produce good Muslims who would be men of refinement and character living according to the highest moral standards and serving the people with devotion and sincerity.[60]

[57]Zakir Husain, quoted in Abid Raza Bedar, *Mata-i Faqir* (Delhi, 1969); Sheila McDonough, 'The Spirit of the Jamia Millia Islamia as Exemplified in the writings of S. Abid Husain', R.D. Baird (ed.), *Religion in Modern India* (Delhi, 1981); Freeland Abbot, *Islam and Pakistan* (New York, 1968), pp. 135-6. 145.

[58]Edib, *Inside India*, p. 95.

[59]*The Jamia College: Its history and significance* (Delhi, n.d.), p. 7.

[60]Ibid., pp. 1-2. As its first *Amir-i Jamia*, Ajmal Khan wanted the students to know each other's culture: 'the firm foundation of a united Indian nationhood depends on this mutual understanding.' Cited in Metcalf, op.cit., p. 25.

Jamia was also expected to be a Muslim stronghold of the national movement and its cultural and educational ethos was to reflect the composite and integrated development of Indian society. The *Nation* of Lahore opined on 11 February 1925:

> Al-Azhar in Egypt was the birth place of Egyptian nationalism and is today the sternest opponent of all that Lord Allenby stands for and we trust and believe that the National Muslim University at Aligarh...will prove to be the Al-Azhar of India.

Such expectations were adequately fulfilled: Jamia developed as an antithesis of the Aligarh Muslim University in the domain of politics. Its students and teachers went around the country spreading the gospel of Gandhi during the non-cooperation days and urged their limited band of followers to popularize the constructive programme, outlined in the Bardoli resolution. According to the *Swarajya* of Madras, Jamia trained more than 200 propagandists to keep alive the torch of national idealism.[61] Even afterwards, Jamia stood by the Congress and steadfastly opposed the polemical two-nation theory. And when Delhi was torn by communal strife in 1946-48, it remained one of the few islands of peace and sanity. In November 1946 the vice-chancellor, Zakir Husain, addressing an unusual gathering of Congress and Muslim League leaders, spoke of the fire of mutual hatred which was ablaze in the country and pleaded with them to put their heads together and extinguish the fire. 'This is not the time,' he said, 'to investigate and determine as to who lighted the fire, how it was lighted. The fire is blazing; it has to be put out.'[62]

Jamia's nationalist stance was distasteful to many, including a group of Muslims who called themselves *Khadim-i Millat* (servants of the community). In a lengthy memorandum they indicted their *bete noire*, Ansari and Zakir Husain, for turning Jamia into a Hindu stronghold, pointed out that the syllabi as well as magazines, such as *Payam-i Taleem*, stressed patriotism to the exclusion of Islamic worship (*ibaadat*) and concluded that the orientation of the institution was prejudicial to Islam and its followers in India.[63] Such criticism, voiced particularly after the

[61] 23 January, quoted in *Prospectus 1924-25*, p. 55.

[62] M. Mujeeb, 'Dr Zakir Husain and the Jamia Millia Islamia', V.S. Mathur (ed.), *Zakir Husain: Educationist and Teacher* (Delhi, 1969), p. 45.

[63] *Millat-i Islamia awr Jamia Millia Islamia, Delhi* (Calcutta, 1941), Quaid-e-Azam Academy, Karachi.

Wardha scheme of education was formulated by Zakir Husain and put into practice in the Jamia school, was brushed aside. Zakir Husain and his colleagues were proud of their close links with the national, secular and democratic movement of the Congress.

Devotion to lofty ideals was not enough to keep an institution going for long. Dependent on public subscriptions, Jamia managed its affairs in the initial spate of enthusiasm. But its existence was in jeopardy soon thereafter. Many students, drawn in the expectation of a political revolution or bright career prospects, drifted elsewhere; some staff members also deserted, thinking that they had performed their proper share of national service. 'With the receding tide,' observed the *Comrade* of 7 August 1925,

> the little bark was grounded into the shifting sands of ephemeral politics. Tossed now here, now there, it knew not where it was drifting. The helmsman stood aghast not knowing whether it was wise to flee from his post or to stick on where he was and painfully watch the slow but seemingly sure wreck of his little ship.

The college also suffered owing to the neglect of its first principal, Mohamed Ali. Jamia was too small a place for the fulfilment of his political ambitions. With his eyes fixed on Aligarh he was of the view that it had outlived its usefulness.[64] He became increasingly averse to Jamia's nationalist orientation as he gradually developed narrow communitarian concerns.

Jamia's existence was, in actual fact, threatened by acute paucity of funds. Though initially propped up by public contributions and by a monthly grant from the Central Khilafat Committee, these sources gradually dried up and Jamia was hard pressed to pay salaries to its teachers and provide the minimum of facilities to the 225 students in 1923. Yet the enthusiasm of a group of diehards was not dampened. Determined to make Jamia an example and an inspiration in educational renaissance they were out to convince themselves as well as others that they were

[64]Mohamed Ali is reported to have said in September 1923: 'I never conceived of the Jamia's growth and permanence at all. The Jamia's existence today is rather like that of the refugees and the Prophet's helpers at Medina who were lying in wait for the conquest of Mecca. Our real objective is Aligarh which some day we shall conquer.' Quoted in A.G. Noorani, *President Zakir Husain: A quest for excellence* (Bombay, 1967), p. 25. On this point, see Mujeeb, Oral History transcript (407), p. 35, NMML.

part of a free national establishment and the symbol of a novel experiment in education.[65]

Sometime during 1925 Ansari and Ajmal Khan, while in Europe, prevailed on three brilliant students in Germany—Zakir Husain, Abid Husain (1896-1978) and Mujeeb—to join the teaching faculty. 'We asked several questions,' recalled Abdul Hamied (1898-1972), a nephew of A.M. Khwaja, 'about the Jamia and we pledged our loyalty to these great leaders and thanked them to have kept Jamia alive.'[66] In January 1926 they left the shores of Europe with impeccable academic credentials to join an institution with an uncertain future. Zakir Husain, a Pathan from Qaimganj, taught Economics at Aligarh before joining the Berlin university where he wrote a thesis on the agrarian policies of the British in India; Abid Husain studied at the same University and researched on the educational philosophy of Herbert Spencer (1820-1903); in Jamia he was a teacher, administrator and the chief exponent of India's composite cultural traditions;[67] Mujeeb, cousin of Khaliquzzaman and son of a successful Lucknow barrister, Mohammad Naseem, studied History at Oxford and printing in Germany (1922-1924). Halide Edib met him and Zakir Husain at Munich in 1923. 'With this austere young man [Zakir Husain], so obviously mature,' she reminiscenced, 'was another young student, Mujeeb by name. He was utterly different from Zakir Husain, with a delicate physique, refined features, thoughtful, tortured eyes. A temperament of artistic nature was written all over him. But outwardly he had the same quiet way, the same determined look as his companion. These were the

[65]M. Mujeeb, *Dr Zakir Husain: A Biography* (Delhi, 1972), p. 40. Details of initial financial support and later difficulties are discussed in *Jamia Millia Islamia: Some Appreciations* (Aligarh Millia Press, 1923), p. 1; Mujeeb, 'Dr Zakir Husain and the Jamia Millia', Mathur (ed.), op.cit., p. 38; FR, first half of February 1923, Home Poll. F. No. 25. 1923, NAI.

[66]K.A. Hamied, *An Autobiography: A life to remember* (Bombay, 1972), pp. 45-6. Mujeeb, Oral History transcript, pp. 30-1.

[67]His scholarly pursuits were impressive. He translated a large number of German, English and French works into Urdu. These included Gandhi's *An Experiment with Truth*, Nehru's *Autobiography, Glimpses of World History* and *Discovery of India*, Immanuel Kant's *Critique for Pure Reason*, Bernard Shaw's *St. Joan*, Edward Spangler's *Psychology of Youth*, and Goethe's *Faust*. For an appreciation of his role in Jamia and the list of his publications, see *Abid Husain Felicitation Volume* (Delhi, 1974), pp. 11–12; McDonough, op. cit.

first young Indians to make me wonder whether the talkative, versatile Indian students I had hitherto met, with their emphatic and passionate reactions, were really typical: certainly they were as different from these taciturn young men as Nordics and Latins.'[68]

Back home a group of selfless teachers, led by Shafiqur Rahman Kidwai (1901-1953), A.G. Kellat (1871-1951), Aslam Jairajpuri (1882-1955), Hafiz Fayyaz Ahmad (1897-1964), Saeed Ansari (1904-1984) and Irshadul Haq (1901-1974) signed a pledge to serve Jamia for at least twenty years on a monthly salary of not more than Rs 150. They did not have money and worked amidst and through poverty. They did not even have the shelter of houses; so they pegged away in tents and under the open sky. Yet they cheerfully faced the hard trials 'in an atmosphere of freedom, enthusiasm and an indestructible optimism,' setting high standards of idealism, self-sacrifice and devotion. Zakir Husain remembered those years of deprivation as 'days of joy'. There was a longing to build, he said, 'and nothing to build with. There were no resources, only the will to achieve. In the eyes of every child who came to us we saw the image of freedom. Every child seemed to give us all that we had been deprived of by political enslavement.'[69] Some financial assistance came from outside, but it was not enough. In January 1928 Gandhi gave assurances of putting Jamia on a sound financial basis,[70] and lent his name to a fund drive in memory of Ajmal Khan

[68]Edib, *Inside India*, p. 97. Gandhi described Mujeeb as 'one of the purest minded young men whom I have the pleasure of knowing'. To Mohammad Naseem, November 1929, *CWG*, Vol. XLII, p. 117.

[69]*Jamia Silver Jubilee*, op.cit., pp. 2-3; also, Saiyidain's convocation address at Jamia, 10 November 1965, quoted in Malik Ram, Abid Raza Bedar (eds.), *Afkar-i Saiyidain* (Delhi, 1978), pp. 12-15. In 1923 a number of distinguished scholars served on the teaching faculty. Khwaja Abdul Hai gave lessons in *tafsir*, Aslam Jairajpuri taught *seerat* and Islamic history, Abdul Majid Khwaja taught law, Zakir Husain lectured on economics, while Jwala Prasad Singhal, S.M. Tonki and Moazzam Ali taught Hindu ethics, Urdu and History/Political Science, respectively. The Syndicate of Jamia comprised, among others, Ajmal Khan, Ansari, the Ali Brothers, Khwaja, Sherwani—also the Secretary (*Nazim*), Moazzam, H.M. Hayat who was also the Registrar (*Musajjil*), Nawab Ismail Khan, Syed Mahmud, Hasrat Mohani, Azad Subhani, Syed Sulaiman Nadwi, Abdul Majid of Budaun and Amir Mustafa Khan. See Mudholi, *Jamia ki Kahani*, appendix and K.G. Saiyidain, Oral History transcript. (3), NMML.

[70]Message to Jamia Millia Islamia, 9 January 1928; telegram to M.M. Malaviya, 9 January, 1928, *CWG*, Vol 35, p. 449.

and for putting Jamia on a firm footing.[71] For the purpose, he wanted to draw a 'substantial amount' from G.D. Birla's (1894-1984) 'gift' of Rs 75,000.[72]

In its years of grinding poverty, Ansari was Jamia's saviour. Succeeding Ajmal Khan as *Amir-i Jamia* (Chancellor), he devoted many years to its development. He led a delegation to raise funds in March 1923, desired part of the Khilafat funds to be diverted to Jamia,[73] and made a passionate plea for rescuing Jamia from a serious financial crisis at the Gaya Khilafat Conference the same year. But the response was far from encouraging. The Aga Khan, a patron of the Aligarh College, offered a modest annual grant of Rs 1,200; Jamnalal Bajaj (1889-1942) donated Rs 10,000; Birla grudgingly gave Rs 50,000;[74] others merely

[71] In his appeal, Gandhi wrote:

In my humble opinion, it is the duty of Hindus and Mussalmans who believe in unity to perpetuate Hakim Saheb's memory in the tangible form proposed. It is their duty to ensure the stability of the Jamia, for it was a creation of the times when it was thought that the two communities were united for ever. And if the non-cooperating national colleges do not stand for, work for and finally ensure unity, nothing else can or will. I hope, therefore, that all the lovers of unity will liberally subscribe to the Fund.

There are today two hundred students studying in the central institution and seventy-four in the city branch. There are moreover two night-schools which draw nearly two hundred students. The Jamia has a staff of twenty-three workers. The highest salary being paid is Rs 265, the lowest being Rs 35. The idea constantly before the Principal is to have volunteers who would draw just enough for their wants. The salaries amount in all to Rs 2,300 per month, the house rent is Rs 425 per month. The total monthly expenditure is Rs 4,800. The regular income, including boarding fees Rs 1,300, is Rs 2,700. There is thus a deficit of Rs 2,100. This was somehow met whilst Hakim Saheb was alive. Before the teachers create for themselves a name and a prestige enough to command help, the deficit must be met by the public. And the memorial cannot be considered lasting till the Jamia has a building of its own. The subscribers will, therefore, in deciding the amount of donation bear in mind what is required.

Young India, 19 January 1928, ibid., p. 4.

[72]Gandhi to Birla, 7 February 1928, G.D. Birla, *Bapu: A Unique Association* (Bombay, 1977), Vol 1, pp. 85-6; also Gandhi to Birla, 21 February 1925, G.D. Birla; *In the Shadow of the Mahatma: A Personal Memoir* (Calcutta, 1953), pp. 8-9.

[73]Appeal (with Shafee Daoodi), August 1928, Habibur Rahman Ludhianvi Papers, NMML.

[74]Birla was pestered by Gandhi to give away the money. His own impression of Jamia was less favourable. He felt that it was 'more a communal institution than a national one.... Everywhere you smell nothing but Muslim culture.' But he allowed Gandhi to 'pay any sum which he decides as a suitable amount from all points of view'. Birla to Mahadev Desai, 17 March 1928, *Bapu*, Vol. 1, p. 90.

conveyed their best wishes. The nawabs and taluqdars of UP, who were otherwise the main benefactors of some Muslim educational centres, were not keen on helping a Congress-backed institution. Aiding it was a risk they could ill-afford. Other affluent groups, on the other hand, considered Jamia an improvized rival to the more established university at Aligarh. They pinned their hopes on the 'Muslim Oxford' at Aligarh where a degree could still be a passport to government service. Jamia merely deserved respect rather than recognition.

Ignored by the Muslims and only marginally backed by the Congress, Jamia was again confronted with the prospect of closure in the early 1930s. Yet Ansari did not despair. He was a doer. Instead of worrying he worked. Nothing was more characteristic of him than his tenacity, the refusal to let go of a problem until he could hit on a way of solving it. With a begging bowl he went around the country collecting funds and explained the importance of his mission. He possessed prodigious energy and spent it prodigally as if he knew he would not be there long. In May 1933, he wrote to Abdul Majid Khwaja, principal of the Jamia College, in a state of anguish:

> You are fully aware of the tremendous difficulties and the untold hardships which the Jamia has gone through since 1930 after my going to jail. The Hyderabad grant which was just about to be started was stopped and the grant from Bhopal was also stopped.... You can imagine in the absence of even the meagre allowances given to the teachers of Jamia how poor and destitute and half-starved they must be. It is really pitiable to see their plight and yet like brave fellows, they are going on. Now, however, there is a chance of re-starting both the Hyderabad and Bhopal grants if only we would put in all our best efforts.[75]

Ansari's efforts bore fruit; generous donations poured in from Bhopal, Hyderabad, Rampur and Madras, more in response to Ansari's appeal than in recognition of Jamia's importance. Ansari was now in a position to strengthen Jamia's educational programmes, organize lectures of leading Indian educationists and invite outstanding representatives from Turkey to 'promote cultural

[75] Ansari to Khwaja, 2 May 1933, Hasan (ed.), *Muslims and the Congress*, p. 138.

friendship and understanding between different peoples and to keep Indians actively interested in great movements of the outside world'. Though he never pretended to be an intellectual, he respected men of intellect, whatever their backgrounds and knew how to make the best use of their brains. Thus Rauf Bey, the Turkish soldier and statesman, Dr Behdgt Wahby, the scientist, and Halide Edib, the educationist, novelist and historian of the national revival in Turkey, came at Ansari's invitation to deliver lectures at Jamia. Edib, whom Ansari met at Constantinople in 1913, impressed most. Her eight lectures, delivered in January-February 1935, had a marked impact on her audience. Ansari extolled her virtues as a novelist, a social philosopher and an educationist. He continued:

> she has worn military uniforms and served at the headquarters of the nationalist army, with the din and the smoke of a grim battle around her. She has also been a rebel against customs and traditions that fettered life...she has loved and served her people, but with a large heartedness that could look beyond them to the greater human family; she has thrown herself heart and soul into the struggle of her nation for life and liberty, but never ceased to be aware of the world-wide moral and cultural conflicts of which it formed a part. She speaks, therefore, with greater authority than any person living on the fundamental problems on whose solution will depend the future of the East.[76]

This adulatory note offers clues to Ansari's own commitment to certain ideals which he appreciated most in the personality of Edib. Very often what people admire in others reflects their own world view, their own set of values and their desire to emulate what they appreciate in their heroes.

It is easy to explain Ansari's abiding interest in Jamia, though it is hard to understand its absence in others close to him. Ansari's devotion was, in the main, due to his attachment to Jamia's secular and composite ideology. He was keen to keep it going as a living symbol of the Khilafat and non-cooperation days and the high points of both the anti-colonial struggle and Hindu-Muslim fraternization. To him the college was much more than an experiment in basic education; it represented the national

[76] *Conflict of East and West in Turkey*, p. iii.

urge of a section of Muslim intelligentsia to participate in the larger educational and political processes of the country and contribute to the intellectual awakening of the less privileged sections of society. Its steady decline was disconcerting because it jeopardized Ansari's plan of building a model Muslim educational centre which would be a hub of nationalist activities and serve his ideal of promoting Hindu-Muslim integration.

Ansari's efforts were not wasted. Much of his work has proved enduring. Jamia survives in Delhi and remains true to at least some of the goals set by its benefactors. Led by Zakir Husain and ably aided by his two comrades—Mujeeb and Abid Husain—it chartered a course which was consistent with Ansari's vision. In the 1930s and the 1940s, they accepted Gandhi's guidance in working for an institution entirely free of British control, accepted him as their leader and guide in politics and promoted his constructive programme without being lured by office, power and authority. And when Delhi was tormented by bloody communal riots, Jamia teachers and students organized relief for the victims and helped heal the communal wounds.[77] Ansari had done the same during his eventful public life; his successors at Jamia followed the example set by their chief benefactor. This was truly an apt tribute to his memory.

The Khilafatists in India gave the impression of being a cohesive group inspired by a common cause and motivated by mutually shared ideals. The deliberations of the Khilafat Conferences, however, reveal their personal feuds and ideological wranglings. The *ulama*, for instance, were at odds with each other exposing the fissures in their apparently solid phalanx of orthodoxy. Though leading *ulama* of Firangi Mahal and Deoband buried their differences temporarily to keep up the semblance of unity, their zealous followers conducted their bitter doctrinal debates unabashedly. Likewise, their alliance with the modern-educated allies was ruptured on the method and strategy of conducting the Khilafat movement. Most *ulama* resented Gandhi's domination of the Khilafat campaign and were critical of the subservient posture adopted by Ansari and the Ali Brothers towards him

Begum Anis Kidwai, *Aazaadi Ki Chaaon me* (Delhi, 1980), pp. 44, 47, 53-5, 61. This is an excellent account of the communal holocaust in the aftermath of the partition of India.

and the Congress. Many Western-educated Muslims, on the other hand, were not just uneasy with the presence of Muslim divines in their midst but were wary of their growing political ascendancy.

Yet the initial enthusiasm kept the combination intact. Gradually, however, the rift widened. Gandhi's relationship with the Khilafatists, in particular, was under severe pressure. Ansari was caught up in many of the controversies which strained and eventually brought to an end the Congress-Khilafat honeymoon in Indian politics.

The first potential threat to the alliance surfaced early in 1921 when differences cropped up over the future course of the non-cooperation movement. Was it to be conducted on the familiar lines of non-violence, as advocated by Gandhi? Or, was the use of force a viable method for pressurizing the government? Earlier, the general consensus was to follow Gandhi's ideal of satyagraha because he was the only guarantor of Congress support to the Khilafat cause. But, in the summer of 1921, the efficacy of the Gandhian methods was questioned. Some hot-headed *ulama* expressed dissatisfaction with the limited vigour with which the Mahatma prosecuted the Khilafat agitation and wanted its scope to be defined and extended according to the *Sharia*. At the Central Khilafat Committee and the *Jamiyat al-ulama* meetings held on 21-22 December 1921, considerable friction occurred before Ansari, Azad and Ajmal Khan persuaded the *ulama* to accept that Gandhi, 'the recognized leader of all Indians' considered that the time was not yet ripe for civil disobedience. The *ulama* were mollified for the time being. But the showdown came at the end of the year when the poet-politician, Hasrat Mohani, put up a plucky fight in favour of adopting the 'complete independence' resolution. Gandhi threw his weight against this move, arguing that it could not be incorporated in the Congress creed unless and until Hindu-Muslim unity was completely accomplished. The *ulama*, who had mooted the idea of complete independence as early as March 1921, were enraged. But they were out-voted. The Congress finally backed Gandhi, as did the Muslim League Subjects Committee. Hasrat's resolution, opposed by Ansari and Azad, was rejected by thirty-six votes to twenty-three.[78]

[78]The preceding paragraphs in the conclusion are based on my *Nationalism and Communal Politics in India*. The process is also discussed in Minault, *The Khilafat Movement*, pp. 186-8, Robinson, *Separatism*, chapter nine.

In the course of such debates, Ansari provided the healing touch and softened the acerbities that embittered politics and made for divisions and strife in the Congress-Khilafatist axis. Anxious to maintain at least a semblance of unity and cohesion, he strived to reconcile conflicting positions and often succeeded in resolving personal and ideological dissensions among his colleagues. Often, he acted as an intermediary between the *ulama* and the Westernized Muslims on the one hand and between the Congress and the Khilafatists, on the other; his impeccable credentials enabled him to do so from a position of strength. He enjoyed the respect of the *ulama* because, after all, he was mainly responsible for drawing them into the first important all-India Khilafat Conference. He earned the admiration of other Khilafatists for his organizational flair and received Gandhi's trust and confidence for his deep involvement in Congress affairs. But when matters came to a head necessitating a clear cut preference, Ansari came on the side of Gandhi and the Congress. He realized that if Muslim religious enthusiasm got out of hand, the ensuing violence would not only be turned against the British, but could also have communal repercussions. Their carefully structured alliance would crumble for good and with it Muslim hopes of saving the Khilafat and the Holy Places. Thus when the volatile Mohamed Ali raised the spectre of an Afghan invasion in early 1921, Ansari was quick to dispel the fears raised by some Hindus. Again, when Abdul Bari delivered an intemperate and overtly communal speech on 3 March 1922, he spoke out against the Maulana, calling him 'brainless, insincere and a notoriety hunter'. He did so in order to check the religious frenzy of the Maulana and his followers which threatened to destroy his aim of building bridges between pan-Islamism and nationalism, a lesson he had learnt from the writings of Jamaluddin Afghani and his disciples in India. The causes of Islam and India, according to him, had to go hand-in-hand and Muslims had therefore to continue to work for India's freedom, which was essential if they were to secure justice for Islam. The goal of redressing the Khilafat grievance was by no means enough; Ansari's sights, as always, were centred on India.[79]

On the complex and divisive issue of council entry Ansari followed Gandhi in the continued pursuit of non-cooperation

[79]Minault, op.cit., p. 180.

outside the legislature and refused to join the Congress-Swaraj-Khilafat party, under the leadership of C.R. Das (1870-1925) and Motilal Nehru. His reasons, as indeed those of Rajagopalachari (1879-1972) and K.R. Iyengar (1859-1923), were set out in the 'Report of the Congress Civil Disobedience Enquiry Committee (1922)'. They argued against entry into councils on the grounds that it involved a violation of the principle of non-cooperation, that the people were opposed to any change in the Congress programme, that entry into councils would be futile and that entering them with the avowed purpose of obstructing all measures whether good or bad and of wrecking the reforms was 'obnoxious' to the principle and the spirit of the movement as conceived by Gandhi.[80]

In November 1922 Ansari vigorously challenged, in spite of pressures from Ajmal Khan, Khaliquzzaman and Sherwani, Motilal Nehru's motion in favour of council entry and took the lead in securing an adjournment of the discussion until the Gaya Congress in December. Working hand-in-hand with Gandhi, he continued to favour the no-change party and worked to prevent party divisions from becoming deeper. This was the refrain of his speech at the special Congress session on 15 September 1923. While reaffirming his opposition to council entry, he pleaded for unity in the Congress camp. 'It is a truism,' he said, 'but would bear repetition that no work, which requires our united energies and single-minded efforts, is possible unless we first remove other pre-occupying differences among ourselves.'[81]

[80]Ravinder Kumar and D.N. Panigrahi (eds.), ***Selected Works of Motilal Nehru*** (Delhi, 1984), Vol. 3, pp. 56-8, 61-2.

[81]F. No. 9, 1923, AICC Papers.

6

The Healing Touch

Hindu-Muslim unity. We have talked of it for years. The unity, so rich in aspiration, is still poor in practical life.... It must be confessed Hindu-Muslim unity is not strong enough, not deep enough, yet.

New Times (Bombay), 14 April 1923

It has to be mournfully confessed that at no time in our national history the sapling of Hindu-Muslim unity wore a more sickly or anaemic look than it does now.

Young India, 10 May 1923, p. 159

THE YEAR 1921 was one of feverish political activity. The non-cooperation campaign, launched under the aegis of the Congress-Khilafat Committee combine, generated unprecedented enthusiasm in most parts of the country. In the joyful din of bold and determined opposition to government, the forces of unity and cohesion acquired much strength, a fact which enabled the non-cooperators to achieve greater support for their campaign. But, by the end of 1922, this powerful and unique anti-colonial struggle showed signs of petering out. The suspension of civil disobedience in February 1922, followed by widespread Hindu-Muslim rioting, destroyed the edifice of communal unity built in the aftermath of the Lucknow Pact of December 1916. The over-inflated bubble of popular expectation suddenly burst and the disappointment was as overwhelming as the previous optimism had been exaggerated. 'Complete Hindu-Muslim unity which ought to have been a settled fact today,' lamented Ansari in September 1923, 'is conspicous by its absence. Years of hard work in various fields have failed not only to make unity a permanent and solid factor of civic life but even to check the present recrudescence of communal discord, the neglected disease which now threatens the very existence of Indian Nationalism.'[1]

[1]F. No. 9, 1923, AICC Papers.

In 1923-24, the communal holocaust swept through many parts of northern India. When Das, Motilal, Sarojini Naidu (1879-1949), Azad and Ajmal Khan visited the Punjab in March 1923 they found the situation there virtually beyond hope. They noticed that the relations between the two communities, both educated and uneducated, were so greatly strained that each community had practically arrayed itself in an armed camp against the other.[2] Trouble had blown up again at Multan during Muharram in April 1923 as a sequel to a violent outburst a year earlier.[3] The citizens of Panipat experienced a riot in July and those of Amritsar in April and May. 'It was a cruel irony of fate,' wrote the *Servant of India*, 'that the fourth anniversary of the Jallianwala Bagh, where four years ago common aspirations and common sufferings brought the Hindus and Mussulmans closer together than ever before, Amritsar should have witnessed a serious Hindu-Muslim riot and that British soldiers should have been called in to protect members of each community against the hooligans of the other.'[4] Delhi, the home of two well known apostles of Hindu-Muslim unity—Ansari and Ajmal Khan—was also plunged into scenes of bloodshed and strife on 11–12 July 1924. On 9–10 September a major outbreak took place at Kohat in the North-West Frontier Province.[5]

Gandhi reacted to these and other communal conflagrations by going on a 21-day fast on 18 September 1924. But his efforts to induce his countrymen to work together once more yielded no results. The Congress, too, tried to arrest the trend towards violence. Meetings were held to draw up plans to renew the Hindu-Muslim *entente* and pious resolutions on communal harmony were proposed and adopted even by those who were not entirely unstained by communal blots.

The first of such meetings was the special Congress session, held at Delhi in September 1923, hosted by Ansari and presided over by Azad. The outcome was the formation of a committee, with Ansari and Lajpat Rai (1865-1928) as its members, to prepare a draft of a 'National Pact'. These two individuals, representing two very different strands in the nationalist movement

[2]Quoted in Page, *Prelude to Partition*, p. 85.

[3]Commenting on the Multan riots in 1922, C. Rajagopalachari wrote: 'These terrible events remind us of how much ignorance, false religion and brute passion yet remains to be purged and how much watchful care on the part of leaders is necessary'. *Young India*, 21 September 1922, p. 381.

[4]19 April 1923, Selection from Newspapers in Bombay, 1923, p. 389.

[5]For details and analysis of communal riots between 1922 and 1928, see *Report on the working of the system of Government, U.P. of Agra and Oudh 1921-28* (Allahabad, 1928); *Indian Statutory Commission*, Vol. 1, p. 27.

and united only by common loyalty to the Congress, set out to do so. What follows, then, is an analysis of 'The Indian National Pact', Ansari's part in its making and the result of his early initiatives to resolve the communal deadlock. Also analysed is his role in Indian Muslim and Congress politics in the aftermath of a momentous development—the abolition of the Khilafat. His reactions and responses are located in the broad context of developments taking place in India and in the Islamic world, especially in Turkey.

Attainment of complete swaraj, establishment of a federal and democratic government and full religious liberty—of belief, worship, propaganda, association and education—were some of the features of the draft pact prepared by Ansari and Lajpat Rai. Provision was also made for joint electorates with reservation of seats for the minorities in proportion to their population in the constituencies. On three major issues of communal discord, namely, cow-slaughter, the playing of music before mosques and the route of religious processions, it was proposed that Muslims give up cow-slaughter except on the occasion of *Baqr Id*, that music in front of places of public worship be forbidden and the route and time of religious processions, in case of dispute, be determined by local mixed conciliatory boards.[6]

In marked contrast to these provisions—many of which formed part of the 1916 Congress-Muslim League scheme—Das, with a generosity that seemed extravagant, made large promises to the Muslims in Bengal.[7] While Ansari and Lajpat Rai proposed communal representation in the legislatures alone, Das extended it to local bodies and appointments to government posts. Das' terms relating to cow-slaughter and music before mosques were also more favourable to Muslims.

The Das pact, concluded with the obvious intention of buying Muslim support at the ballot box and in the Bengal legislative council, impinged on the interests of the Hindu landed, commercial and professional classes who faced the cheerless prospect of losing their advantages to a relatively new class of Muslim professional men and up-country merchants.[8] Its author's eloquent pleading that he did not concede to Muslims 'more than they

[6]F. No. 25, 1924, AICC Papers.

[7]Hasan, *Nationalism and Communal Politics*, p. 212.

[8]I have examined the implications of the Das Pact in ibid., pp. 213-16; for Hindu opposition, see press clippings in Home Poll. K.W. II to 66, 1924, NAI.

were entitled to get in fairness and justice', failed to convince most Bengali Hindus. Indignant at this one-sided bargain, they not only launched a massive agitation but also brought their grievance to the Congress session in Kakinada (1923) which found reasons to reject the Das pact.

Das warded off the attacks against him by prevailing upon the Bengal Provincial Conference to ratify that pact in May 1924. But the Swaraj party repudiated it soon after his death a year later. Its decision to do so was in deference to its Hindu supporters who had consistently opposed any concessions to Muslim pressures, especially over tenancy legislation, the opening of Islamia colleges and schools and the appointment of Muslims in the Calcutta corporation.[9] It did not need any great degree of perception to understand that if the Swarajists were to maintain their ascendancy in Bengal politics, they would have to stop pandering to the Muslims. Any attempt to enforce the Bengal pact in the spirit of Das was bound to drive the new mass Hindu electorate into communal organizations.

The draft submitted by Ansari and Lajpat Rai was 'eclipsed' by the bitter and acrimonious debate generated by the Bengal pact. 'Public view' was so 'befogged', lamented its authors, that the draft failed to evoke the balanced appraisal it deserved.[10] In general, provincial and local Congress Committees were averse to it[11] and took strong exception to the clauses relating to cow-slaughter and communal representation.[12] Muslim organizations, such as the Khilafat Committees at Gujranwala and Sialkot in the Punjab and Noakhali and Calcutta in Bengal, regarded

[9] K. Mcpherson, *The Muslim Microcosm: Calcutta 1918-35* (Heidelberg, 1974), pp. 84-6.

[10] F. No. 25, 1924, AICC Papers. Ansari stated that there was much misunderstanding about the two pacts. If the principle of the National Pact was applied to any of the Muslim-majority provinces, the implications would be the same as in the Das Pact. He said: 'I do not see what the trouble is and where lies the unfitness of the Bengal Provincial Congress Committee Pact. If you are not prepared to concede the just rights of whatever community they may be... I assure you that you can never come to any agreement, there can never be peace, there can never be unity and I am afraid there will never be swaraj'. *Report of the Thirty-eighth Indian National Congress held at Coconada, 28-31 December 1923 and 1st January 1924* (Coconada, 1924), pp. 112-14.

[11] For example, the Bihar and Maharashtra Provincial Congress Committees.

[12] Shraddhanand to Ansari, 13 December 1923, F. No. 10, 1924, AICC Papers; Resolution of the Hindu Dharma Sangha of Calcutta in enclosure to Ansari, 27 February 1924, F. No. 25, 1924, AICC Papers.

the pact as an infringement of their political, religious and economic interests.[13] The Punjab Muslim League produced its own 'pact',[14] while the All-India Muslim League, the Khilafat Conference and the *Jamiyat al-ulama* preferred the Bengal pact.[15] 'The Mussalmans,' observed Ansari and Lajpat Rai in their report submitted to the AICC, 'have been quite needlessly alarmed by some of its provisions and have allowed their judgements to be influenced by passing events.'[16] What they failed to point out was that the vested interests among Muslims, especially the beneficiaries of the Montagu-Chelmsford reforms, were not prepared to accept anything short of what was conceded to them in the Act of 1919. Besides, given the history of Congress' political understanding with the Muslim League on the basis of separate electorates, weightage and communal representation, a political 'settlement' was only possible within a self-perpetuating communal framework. In effect, therefore, the Ansari-Lajpat pact could neither satisfy the political aspirations of the dominant Muslim groups nor contain the vociferous Hindu opponents of communal representation. Likewise, suggestions relating to local religious disputes lapsed into insignificance. In consequence, the divide over cow-slaughter, music before mosques and the route of religious processions persisted, causing incalculable damage to Hindu-Muslim relations.

The Congress, wallowing in its seemingly eternal dissensions, made familiar noises as the violent conflagration reached serious proportions in the Punjab, UP and Bengal. But apart from Gandhi whose personal anguish was reflected in his decision to go on a 21-day fast, most of its leaders were either apathetic to the resolution of the communal problem or remained tuned to the idea of joint parleys with Muslim bodies. New political conclaves, such as the 'Unity Conference' at Delhi and the 'All-Parties Conference', were the outcome.

The 'Unity Conference' held in Delhi on 26 September 1924 was convened by Ansari, Ajmal Khan and Mohamed Ali in order to 'decide immediately what we can do in these 21 days to retrieve the situation and relieve the Mahatma's agony of distress'.

[13]F. No. 10, 1924, AICC Papers; Home Poll. K.W. II to 66, 1924, NAI.

[14]*Tribune*, 27 January 1924, Home Poll. K.W. II to 66, 1924, NAI.

[15]Ibid., 8 January 1924; *IQR*, July-December 1923, p. 193 for *Jamiyat al-ulama*; and p. 188 for Khilafat Conference.

[16]F. No. 25, 1924, AICC Papers.

But after all the ballyhoo things ran their course much as they did before. Some pious resolutions were passed, but the basic malady, as Jawaharlal retrospectively observed, could not be cured by conferences. A solution could not be reached by a majority of votes but by virtual unanimity and there were always 'extremists' of various groups present whose idea of a solution was a complete submission of all others to their views.[17] The smiles and handclasp of Delhi faded ingloriously into oblivion.

In November of the same year Gandhi initiated discussions to tackle the Hindu-Muslim problem despite the hemming and hawing of the hard-liners. This led to a conference at Delhi on 23 January 1925. He suggested the formation of a sub-committee which would move on beyond the propagandistic mudslinging and the barren exercises of the past few years. But Madan Mohan Malaviya (1861-1946), Lajpat Rai and Shraddhanand were not willing to oblige. And when the committee was eventually formed at the instance of Jawaharlal and Annie Besant, its deliberations were marred by mutual bickerings, with Gandhi being accused of partiality towards the Muslims in conducting the proceedings. Trouble started when Lajpat Rai took the line that the sub-committee's decisions would remain tentative without the Hindu Mahasabha's acquiescence. Reference was also made to a 'Muslim conspiracy' for bringing about an invasion of India. All this was disconcerting to Ansari, who played a leading part in the conference. 'His own feeling was one of utter disgust so much so that he felt like retiring from public life altogether.'[18]

The meeting was adjourned on 28 January: Motilal announced that 'we were not able to reach final conclusions'. When the committee reassembled in February-March, it accomplished nothing; if anything, bitterness between the participants increased. The All-Parties Conference, its committees and sub-committees, wrote a distraught Jawaharlal in February, 'have not been a success so far. The discussions were painful to listen to. I am afraid the time has not yet come for an agreement which satisfies all parties.'[19] The final session on 1 March was attended by only fourteen of the fifty-three members of the committee, including

[17]Nehru, *An Autobiography*, pp. 139-40. For proceedings of the Conference, see *IQR*, July-December 1925, pp. 149-60.

[18]F. No. 13, 1925, AICC Papers.

[19]Nehru to Syed Mahmud, 3 February 1925, in V.N. Datta and B.E. Cleghorn (eds.), *A Nationalist Muslim and Indian Politics* (Delhi, 1974), p. 32.

Gandhi, the Nehrus, the Ali Brothers, Jinnah, Shraddhanand, Mohammad Yaqub (1879-1942) of Moradabad and N.C. Kelkar (1872-1947). If Ansari had been more experienced and less enthusiastic, he might have realized that there was very little that he—or, for that matter, Gandhi and Motilal could do to rescue the conference from being wrecked. Neither side felt there was much chance of achieving an agreement but each thought, for different reasons, that they ought to go through the motions of trying.

The failure of the January conference, together with the growing incidents of riots, led Gandhi to declare that he saw no daylight out of the impenetrable darkness.[20] Later, he admitted his own imperfection as an instrument for bringing about communal peace,[21] and in despair said: 'I have learnt more and more to resign myself utterly to His grace.' Such a frank admission by the country's most consistent proponent of Hindu-Muslim amity augured ill for the unity of a nation in the making.

The 'Indian National Pact', the Unity conclaves and the All-Parties Conference revealed Congress' strategy in relation to the communal problem: to reach a political accord with 'leading representatives' and 'influential persons' of the Muslim community for immediate political gains. 'The idea of a National Pact,' wrote the *Young India* of 3 January 1924, 'is sound and from a purely political point of view necessary.' 'Precedents in pact making,' it continued, 'for the protection of sectional interests may be lacking, but that fact need not bother us.' The communal issue was thus much too frequently considered from the standpoint of the early attainment of swaraj rather than that of nation-building and there was a far greater desire to work for a patch-up unity than to work towards a long-term and enduring solution. The flurry of stop-gap measures were never bolstered by carefully calibrated long term policies. Centrality was accorded to 'Unity' and 'All-Parties' gatherings and much effort went in the drawing up of manifestos, declarations and resolutions, directed less to the reconciliation of rival policies than to the maintenance of

[20] Cited in Mohibbul Hasan, 'Mahatma Gandhi and the Indian Muslims', in S.C. Biswas (ed.), *Gandhi Theory and Practice: Social Impact and Contemporary Relevance* (Simla, 1969), p. 143.

[21] 'I can understand all about the Hindu-Muslim question, but have been reduced to a state of helplessness.' Gandhi to G.D. Birla, 23 May 1926, G.D. Birla, *In the Shadow of the Mahatma; A Personal Memoir* (Calcutta, 1953), p. 16.

an outward unity on some working formula of compromise. Devoid of any ideological content and lacking in the appreciation of the complex nature of the communal phenomena, such endeavours came to naught in reconciling the conflicting claims of various groups and in furthering Congress' objective of developing a united and powerful nationalist movement. The want of clear ideals and objectives in our struggle for freedom, commented Jawaharlal, undoubtedly helped the spread of communalism.[22]

Ansari did not think differently. He pinned his hopes on an enduring political accommodation with Muslim groups which, he optimistically believed, would help to reduce communal acrimony. On the basis of his presence in and association with the 'Unity' and 'All-Parties' gatherings it is possible to argue that his perspective on the communal question in the 1920s was akin to many of his leading Congress comrades. He, too, saw its resolution in terms of political accommodation and adjustment with representatives of various Muslim groups. A detailed appraisal of his attitude is attempted in the following chapters.

Chaak kar di Turk-i naadan ne Khilafat ki qaba [Iqbal]

Events in Turkey, meanwhile, went their own way. In August and September of 1922, Mustafa Kamal (1880-1938) routed the Greeks, completed the reconquest of Anatolia and wrested a new treaty from the European powers which established complete and undivided Turkish sovereignty in almost all the territory included in the present-day Turkish Republic. Indian Muslims were jubilant. 'Muslims throughout the country,' noted the viceroy, 'have been profoundly stirred and much pleased by the news of the Kamalist victories.'[23] Buoyed up by optimistic misinformation about the situation in Turkey, they failed to see the implications of the Grand National Assembly's momentous decision, adopted on 1 November 1922, to separate the offices of Sultan and Khalifa, divesting the latter of his temporal powers and making him into a symbolic 'pontiff' without even the aura of nominal suzerainty. The general disposition in India was to view deposition with equanimity and to believe in Mustafa Kamal

[22]Nehru, *An Autobiography*, p. 137.

[23]Home Poll. 197-I, 1923., NAI; Mohammad Sadiq, *The Turkish Revolution and the Indian Freedom Movement* (Delhi, 1983), pp. 10-19.

as a proud saviour of his country and champion of Islam.[24] A manifesto issued by Ansari and Ajmal Khan stated that the selection of a new Khalifa by the Turkish National Assembly was a return to the great tradition of elected Khalifas, which would strengthen and not weaken his hand. As president of the Khilafat Conference held in December 1922, Ansari argued that the Turks had not really separated the Khalifa's spiritual and temporal powers, but had only made the Sultan a constitutional monarch. The Khilafat Conference expressed pleasure at the restoration of the ancient practice of electing the Khalifa. Mustafa Kamal was given the title of *Saif al-Islam* (The Sword of Islam), a term used in the past for conquering sultans.[25]

In the meantime, Ameer Ali (1849-1928), a Shia with close links with the government and the Aga Khan, leader of the Ismaili community, wrote to Turkey's prime minister, Ismet Pasha, inviting his attention to the 'very disturbing effects the present uncertain position of the Khalifa-Imam is exercising among the vast populations who belong to the Sunni communion'. They felt that any diminution in the prestige of the Khalifa or his elimination as a religious factor from the Turkish body politic would mean the disintegration of Islam and its practical disappearance as a moral force in the world; so they emphasized the 'imminent necessity for maintaining the religious and moral solidarity of Islam by placing the Khalifa-Imamate on a basis which would command the confidence and esteem of the Moslem nations and thus impart to the Turkish state unique strength and dignity'.[26]

This letter alarmed the Turkish government;[27] it was actually insinuated at Angora—though not officially—that Ameer Ali and the Aga Khan had acted at the instigation of the British government.[28] The fateful letter, according to some historians, influenced

[24]*Pioneer*, 4 January 1924, quoted in Foreign and Poll. Dept., 228 (3)-X, 1923, pp. 64-5. Also, see statements issued by prominent Khilafatists in Home Poll. 721-II, 1922, NAI.

[25]Home Poll. 60, 1923, NAI; Minault, *Khilafat Movement*, p. 202.

[26]24 November 1923, Foreign & Poll. Dept., 228(3)-X, 1923, NAI.

[27]Ismet Pasha is reported to have said that these two Shia leaders had no right to make 'suggestions' and 'observations' in the name of Sunnis. Also, that they did not have 'the right knowledge and experience' to express views on the 'fundamental law of Turkey from a religious point of view'. *Pioneer*, 31 December 1923, quoted in ibid.

[28]The Aga Khan denied the charge in a letter to *The Times*. 'The essential unity of Islam,' he stated, 'is of far greater importance than any sectarian

and possibly precipitated the decision to do away with the Khilafat.[29] Any serious explanation, however, must take into account the fact that Mustafa Kamal realized that as long as the traditional foundations remained intact and their symbol, the Khalifa, maintained his position, it would be difficult to establish a modern national state and a Turkish nation. The Khalifa, still supported by a group of loyal followers, was ready to take part with any strong power to turn against his own people and render the idea of a modern republic meaningless.[30] His presence was a disturbing factor in the foreign and internal political union of Turkey and a constant source of 'strife and duplicity'.[31] 'There had been cruel and corrupt Sultans in Turkey,' wrote Halide Edib, 'there had been imbeciles and drunkards in its history, but never before had a son of Osman fallen so low as to maneuver *(sic)* for the subjugation of Turkey so that he might live comfortably'.[31a]

After a preliminary preparation the Khilafat was abolished on 3 March 1924. This was followed by the closure of the Ministry of *Shariat* and of the religious courts and by unification of the judicial system. Traditional institutions which had governed society and government for centuries were liquidated and the way was opened to a new mode of life.[32]

The Indian Muslims had another surprise in store. Two days after the trauma of seeing the Khilafat disappear, the pretentious Hashemite ruler of the Hejaz, King (formerly Sharif) Husain, proclaimed himself Khalifa. With the exception of Abdul Bari,

differences. For this reason I have advocated the establishment of a strong Khilafat above parties and politics.' *Pioneer*, 19 December 1923, quoted in ibid; Minault, op. cit., p. 203.

29 Ahmad, *Islamic Modernisn*, p. 138; Minault, op. cit., p. 203.

30 P.M. Holt, A.K.S. Lambton and Lewis (eds.), *The Cambridge History of Islam: The Central Islamic Lands* (Cambridge, 1970), Vol. I, part IV, p. 533; Lewis, *Emergence of Modern Turkey*, p. 258.

31 The High Commissioner of Constantinople to the Foreign Office, 6 February 1924, Foreign and Poll. Dept., 34-X, 1924, p. 3.

31a Halide Edib, *The Turkish Ordeal* (London, 1928), p. 12.

32 Soon after the abolition of the Khilafat, a movement arose among the *ulama* of Al-Azhar of reviving the Khilafat in Cairo and vesting that office in the person of the King of Egypt. The *Lujnatual-Khilafat-ul-Azhar* was formed to convene an Islamic world congress in March 1925. And when little enthusiasm was shown by Muslim countries, the proposed congress was postponed to May 1926 on the plea of unsettled conditions obtaining in Egypt and the necessity of carrying out preliminary propaganda'. *Cambridge History of Islam*, pp. 533-4.

leading Khilafatists in general rejected his claim because he was an imperial stooge and a traitor to the Turks and therefore to pan-Islamic solidarity. Then, in late 1924, Abdul Aziz b. Saud, the Wahabi chieftain of Nejd, attacked the Hejaz, captured Mecca and Medina and destroyed a number of tombs and shrines in the holy cities. This caused a split in the Khilafat party with Abdul Bari and other leading *ulama* supporting the Hashemite claim and denouncing the Wahabi ruler for his 'profanity', his religious insensitivity and his territorial aggrandizement. Mohamed Ali, on the other hand, favoured negotiations with Saud, regarding him as a helpful coadjutor in realizing his own ultimate goal—resuscitation of the Khilafat. The two most important factions, headed by the *pir* Abdul Bari and his *murid* Mohamed Ali reached a parting of ways. This was symbolic of the disintegration of the alliance between the religious and the political wings of the Khilafat party.

Efforts to recreate the Khilafat of the classical theorists misfired because Turkey had rejected pan-Islamism and because Muslims in other countries were busy establishing national states independent of external ties of domination: Mustafa Kamal emerged as the symbol of Turkish nationalism, Zaghlul Pasha as the spearhead of the emerging national consciousness of Egypt and the King of Hejaz as the rallying centre of so many Arab aspirations. The Khilafat leadership in India, however, remained ignorant of the potent force of Arab nationalism and the widespread enthusiasm and idealism which expressed itself in movements to eliminate completely Anglo-French domination and attain unconditional independence. The 'Muslim World' which was a relatively closely woven whole during the pre-war days was no longer the same and territorial nationalism, clamant race movements and socialist ferments worked as solvents in the blood of pan-Islamic unity. But the Khilafat leaders in India clung to the symbol of Islamic solidarity—the Khalifa—knowing full well that he was thoroughly discredited in the eyes of most Turks because he had used his religious powers to stamp out the nationalist movement and thus sanctioned indirectly the foreign occupation of Turkey in violation of his basic religious obligation to defend the community against outside invaders. They also failed to recognize that the Khilafat was too remote and exalted an institution to mean much to, say, an average Anatolian peasant. That is why the Turks allowed an age-old institution to disappear with utter calm and indifference.[33] 'The absence of any reaction among the people is noteworthy', observed Halide Edib,

> for it proved beyond doubt that the Caliphate no longer commanded the allegiance of the Turkish people .... As a force of inter-Islamic unity within the Turkish Empire the Caliphate had proved itself ineffective. Abdul Hamid's policy of using it as a political bogey to frighten the West produced disastrous results. The "Jihad" proclamation during the Great War was a farce. Further Vahideddine's (*sic*) troops, fighting under the name of the Caliphate army against the people who are defending their honour and their existence smothered whatever respect and love for the institution still remained in the minds of the people.[34]

Even so, the Khilafat agitation in the subcontinent showed no signs of having run its course. Its protagonists continued to believe that the institution they were trying to defend was 'with all its weaknesses, anti-Islamic trends and digression into pure imperialism ... had served as a symbol of Muslim political unity and a powerful inspiration for the Muslim mind in India to retain its international character'.[35] There was a feeling of despondent bewilderment mingled with indignation towards the National Assembly whose drastic action weakened and isolated the one state on whose revival high hopes were set. It was mournfully recorded that an institution hallowed with traditions of thirteen centuries passed away 'as if in a twinkling of an eye' and the 'edifice which looked as firm as a rock and promised to last as long as the world would last, was swept away by the flood of phenomena'.[36]

In marked contrast with the boisterous elation of the closing months of 1922, when, on the morrow of the Kamalist military successes, no voice was raised, whatever misgivings were secretly felt, to challenge the abolition of the Sultanate and its inevitable sequel—the expulsion of the Khalifa from Turkey—the reforms

[33]It is one of the ironies of history, notes an author, that although the Turks scarcely lifted a finger to preserve the Khilafat, many of them fought doggedly against the new law, introduced by the Kamalist Republic, compelling all male citizens to wear hats instead of the *fez*. So grave were the disturbances in the north-east that a cruiser was ordered to Rize, in the Black Sea and the Independent Tribunals went in action. G.L. Lewis, *Turkey* (London, 1955), p. 92.

[34]Edib, *Conflict of East and West in Turkey*, p. 118; Edib, *Turkish Ordeal*, p. 104.

[35]Khaliquzzaman, op. cit., p. 74.

[36]Mohammad Barkatullah, *The Khilafat* (London, 1924), p. 1.

introduced by the Angora Assembly were now regarded as a calculated system of 'moral disintegration'. Mustafa Kamal, a name to conjure with twelve months ago, was in 1924 an 'Unbeliever' and a 'Salonica Renegade'. 'Is it not our bitter experience,' asked the indignant editor of the widely-circulated *Tarjuman* of Calcutta, 'that when the Turks required our moral and financial support, they exploited our feelings of fraternity, but as soon as they were able to stand on their own legs, they repudiated our assistance and abolished the Khilafat without consulting us?'[37] It seemed, after all, that Mustafa Kamal was not the idol which he was represented to be and that the ideal of pan-Islamism did not appeal to him so much as to his co-religionists in India. Shaukat Ali was bluntly told by Ismet Pasha that his government's action was a purely domestic concern of the Turkish people, for whom the Khilafat had been a cause of embarrassment and trouble in both internal affairs and foreign relations.[38]

Mustafa Kamal's decision to burst the Khilafat bubble had a profound impact on the alliances forged on the Khilafat issue and sustained by an intense anti-government mood. The rapprochement between various Muslim groups, in particular, came to a steady end in the absence of a sound basis for permanent adjustments of diversified and, in some cases, conflicting interests.[39] Once the Khilafat euphoria had worn thin, the inherent contradictions in the hastily concluded alliances and the dissensions in the Khilafat leadership, which were so far kept under

[37] *Tarjuman* (Calcutta) 16 February 1926, Native Newspaper Reports (Bengal), 27 February 1926, p. 109.

[38] Foreign and Poll. Dept., 34-X, 1924, p. 21.

[39] Khaliquzzaman aptly summed up the widespread confusion that prevailed in Indian Muslim circles. 'As a result of this catastrophe,' he wrote:

> For practically one decade they [Muslims] suffered from deep inertia and pessimism and were incapable of any organised mass action either for the freedom of India or for the protection of their own Muslim interests in the country. Khilafat Commitee continued for a few years more but it ceased to have a mass appeal or backing.... As time went on their energy also began to be misdirected and found its escape in fighting for offices in the organisation or for the formation of new parties with new names but no programmes. The Khilafatists who were once known as Khilafat-Congressmen became Congress-Khilafatists and some, after some time, purely Congressmen. Others remained nothing but Khilafatists with no work. The history of the next sixteen years of Muslim India is a mass of confusion and a chapter of political benightedness.

Khaliquzzaman, op. cit., p. 74.

control, came to the fore. Clearly, Islam served as a focal point of unity in the face of a commonly perceived danger, but its utility in sustaining it in the absence of a religious cause was limited. Once the Khilafat issue lost its relevance, a wide range of material and political interests gained primacy over other considerations. The main thrust of Muslim organizations was to promote those interests, a fact which contributed to the growth of both inter-community and intra-community antagonisms.

The collapse of the Khilafat movement affected the Muslim divines most. Rebuffed and ignored by their comrades on the issue of council entry and continuing civil disobedience, they now found themselves isolated, confused and even inactive. Having once mobilized new groups, roused their religious fervour, and articulated their grievances, they were now like a contrary jack-in-box refusing to retire, to seek new outlets for their energy and to build something out of their political experience. Some doggedly kept the Khilafat movement gasping, some capitulated to the communalist camp, but most, including the *ulama* of Deoband, entered the arena of religious controversies and organized the *tabligh* and *tanzim* societies as a counterpart to *shuddhi* and *sangathan*. The *Jamiyat al-ulama*, founded in the throes of the Khilafat movement, was split into factions with Nisar Ahmad of Kanpur and Abdul Majid of Budaun founding a parallel organization of *Jamiyat al-ulama-i Hind* in Kanpur. Abdul Bari, the erstwhile apostle of Hindu-Muslim unity, spoke the language of a zealot, urging Muslims to sacrifice cows without regard for Hindu religious susceptibilities. Addressing the All-India Sunni Conference (*Ahl-i Sunnat wal Jamaat*) in Moradabad on 17-19 March 1925, Syed Jamaat Ali Shah condemned those Muslims who were still associated with the Hindus and called for a rejection of all un-Islamic practices (*rusumat-i bida*), subservience to Prophet Mohammad and adherence to the fundamentals of Islam.[40]

The Khilafat agitation provided the *ulama* with distinct enemy and goals; when the enemy and goals proved elusive other whipping boys and solutions had to be found. Much of their concerns, geared to religious goals, remained, because they seemed to be the hope of the Muslim community. In consequence many of them reverted to their former religious preoccupations.

[40]*Fil Badih Khutba-i Sadarat* (Lahore, n.d.), pp. 43-66.

The *Jamiyat al-ulama*, despite its nationalist sympathies, moved along a course parallel to that of the Congress Muslim political leadership: its chief obsession was to secure safeguards against interference with the *Sharia* and guarantees for its propagation and implementation. In 1940, however, a section of the *Jamiyat* became the nucleus of various nationalist organizations. The Congress, which was otherwise vociferous about the secularization of politics, was ever ready to exploit this reserve of influence to counteract the Muslim League.[41]

Consistent with the widespread disillusionment caused by the Khilafat and non-cooperation fiasco, a group of Muslims parted company with the Congress and founded, organized and led the socialist and communist movements, especially in Bengal. Others, however, became enmeshed in sectarian causes and chose to be the defenders of the faith. In the Punjab, Saifuddin Kitchlew launched the *Jamiyat-i Tanzim* which, in accordance with its constitution of August 1925, organized and consolidated various aspects of Muslim religious, cultural and educational life,[42] while the *Anjuman-i Khuddam-i Al-Sufia*, founded by the followers of Ahmad Reza Khan, sought to counter the activities of the *shuddhi* and Arya Samaj bodies by establishing *madrasas* and mosques in different parts of the country. Of the 40 *madrasas*, two each were built in Kashmir, Jammu, and Baroda and the remaining 24 in Agra, Mathura, Delhi, Etah, Bulandshahr, Gurgaon, Aligarh, Farrukhabad and other parts of northern India.[43] In Delhi and parts of UP Syed Abdul Hai started the *Jamiyat-i Tablighal Islam*. From 1923 to 1928, this organization, formed as a counterpart to the *shuddhi* sabhas, made rapid progress. Over 370 workers toured different parts of the country, converted 15,000 to Islam and reportedly 're-admitted' 10,000 to the Islamic fold.[44]

[41]For a brief outline of the role of the *ulama*, see Mushirul Hasan, 'Religion and Politics: The Ulama and the Khilafat Movement', *Economic and Political Weekly*, 15 May 1981.

[42]*Jamiyat-i Markaziya Tanzim ka Mujawaza Dastur-ul Amal* (Amritsar, 1925), p. 7. Among the members of the All-India Tanzim Committee were: Maulvi Rahim Baksh (Karachi), Malik Barkat Ali (Lahore), Abdul Talib of Delhi, Mohammad Shafi, Zafar Ali Khan and Raja Ghazanfar Ali Khan of Lahore, Nawab Mohammad Ismail Khan of Meerut, Maulana Mazharuddin, editor of the Delhi weekly *Al-Aman* and Zahur Ahmad of Lucknow.

[43]*Fil Badih*, op. cit., pp. 15-16.

[44]Syed Ghulam Bhik Nairang, *Jamiyat-i Markaziya Tablighal Islam Ambala shehar ki Satarsala khidmat ka khulasa* (Ambala, 1940), pp. 4-5.

The doyen of the group estranged from the Congress was Mohamed Ali who faced the inescapable dilemma of either operating within the framework of the Congress organization, as was the case during the Khilafat agitation, or relying upon existing Muslim bodies as instruments for advancing the commonly perceived 'Muslim interests'. The resurgence of communal violence and the squabbles over separate *versus* joint electorates and reservation of seats in legislative bodies and public services offered Mohamed Ali an opportunity to indict the Congress for its failure to settle the 'Muslim claims' and to denounce some of its leading figures for fomenting communal violence. He reached the conclusion that Gandhi in particular and the Congress in general was soft on people like Malaviya and Lajpat Rai who were communal in their orientation and outlook and were therefore opposed to any fair or just agreement with the Muslims. 'It is my sad conviction,' wrote the Maulana in the *Comrade* of 17 July 1925, 'that not one of these pseudo-Nationalists would have talked so glibly of Nationalism, majority rule and mixed electorates, if his own community had not been in the safe position of an overwhelming majority. It is they who are the real culprits as narrow communalists, but since the position of the community is safe enough they mouth all the fine phrases of nationalism and parade themselves as nationalists. The Cow question provides the best topic for the exposure of their pseudo-nationalism, for in the name of nationalism they make demands on their fellow-countrymen that none has ever heard of them in any country or nation in the world'. In the circumstances, the Khilafat Committees alone could advance 'Muslim interests' in India and abroad. Buoyed up by ill-founded expectations of what could be achieved, Mohamed Ali assured his readers that the Khilafat bodies were keen to bring about a truly Islamic rule in the Holy Land and he outlined what the Indian Muslims should do; first of all, they should form a party around the nucleus of Khilafat group. They should attempt to persuade other Islamic peoples to their way of thinking and thus achieve a united Muslim voice. They should contribute money, time, technical assistance, moral support to the Hejaz and make regular religious visits. Above all, they should devote themselves whole-heartedly to the reformation of the centres of Islam and thus earn the good requital in both worlds.[45]

[45]Watson, op. cit., pp. 88-9.

Mohamed Ali's powerful indictment of the Congress leadership was viewed with scepticism by some of his comrades. So was his plea for retaining the Khilafat Committees, which had ceased to have a mass appeal and backing and were confined to a section of people who were struggling to retain the name of the organization rather than to achieve its purpose.[46] This was the view of Mushir Husain Kidwai (1878-1937), one of the founders of the *Anjuman-i-Khuddam-i Kaaba* and vice-president of the Oudh Provincial Khilafat Committee. The Khilafat question, he said, was 'no longer one which should cause anxiety to Indian Muslims'.[47] Equally important was Iqbal's reaction. He had regarded the Khilafat movement, which gave so much fervour to his community, as a means for strengthening the cause of Islam; it unfolded later on aspects in which 'no sincere Muslim could join for a single minute'. Instead of denouncing Mustafa Kamal and his policies, as was the case with Mohamed Ali, Iqbal approved of his experiments. Turkey, in his estimate, was the first Muslim country to shake off the fetters of medieval mentality and had found a way of life of her own.[48]

In marked contrast to his erstwhile political guru, Mohamed Ali, Ansari viewed Congress' role in a favourable light, severed his links with the much maligned Khilafat Committees, stayed clear of the communal processes at work, joined hands with the nationalist forces in the fight for swaraj and combined with Congress, as in the making of the 'Indian National Pact', in breaking the communal impasse. In reaching such crucial decisions with a conviction rare among his contemporaries in the mid-1920s, Ansari was influenced by Congress' historic role in the nationalist struggle and the commitment of its leaders to communal amity and Hindu-Muslim integration. Guided by the belief that it was, in spite of its heterogeneous character, a non-communal body, he saw the fortunes of his community, as indeed of other communities, inextricably linked with the Congress movement. According to Ansari the Khilafat Committees and their newly found allies in the Muslim League played the Khilafat game needlessly, orchestrated sectional interests with divisive overtones and adopted a political strategy which suited

[46]Khaliquzzaman, op. cit., p. 74.

[47]*Kaiser-i Hind*, 1 July 1923, Native Newspapers Report, Bombay, 1923, p. 626.

[48]Cited in Annemarie Schimmel, *Gabriel's Wing: A Study into the Religious ideas of Sir Mohamed Iqbal* (Leiden, 1963), pp. 47-8.

the interests of the government and its collaborators in the landed, business and service classes. He found himself increasingly at variance with their purpose and methods and was unable to reconcile his nationalist concerns with the sectarian bias of the Khilafat bodies. Ansari, much to his credit, stuck to his guns and was finally driven to take the painful but irrevocable decision of resigning from the Central Khilafat Committee of which he had been a member for many years. 'On my return from England in June', he wrote to Shaukat Ali on 16 July 1926.

> I found that communal passions had run amuck.... I therefore felt impelled to ... fight the demon of communalism which was devastating the country and was breaking asunder strong ties formed between the Hindus and Muslims after centuries of intimate associations and common sufferings and sacrifice. As an Indian owing allegiance first to the motherland, I feel I must sever my connections with all communal or sectional political organizations.[49]

Ansari and the Ali Brothers were old comrades, but circumstances had now driven them into opposing camps and into conflict which left unhealed wounds.

Ansari's reactions to events in Turkey, formed after his visit to that country in the summer of 1925, were also refreshingly different from many of his Khilafat colleagues. Uninfluenced by accounts of Turkey's 'decay' and 'decline' he sent regular reports of the country's material progress accomplished by the Kamalist Republic.[50] He was impressed by what he saw and admired the many achievements of the Turks in a period of turbulence and change. It was indeed a novel and worthwhile experience, for Turkey in 1925 was very different from what Ansari saw on his last visit in 1912. The country was then in the throes of a crisis, internally divided and externally besieged by enemy powers. But it was now engaged in the stupendous task of national reconstruction and on its way to achieving rapid socio-economic progress. Ansari was impressed. He was also impressed by the people he met. Then he added a sweetener for the Angora people. They were not quite as difficult or dreadful; in fact they were quite the reverse. Ansari found them willing to discuss every aspect of a question, anxious to clear misunderstanding,

[49] Ansari to Shaukat Ali, 16 July 1926, Hasan (ed.), *Muslims and the Congress*, p. 19.

[50] These were published in the *Comrade*.

keen on placing their point of view, appreciating to the full the opposite viewpoint and amenable to reasonable suggestions.[51] He rebutted the charge of widespread irreligiousness and impiety and observed:

> I have not seen a more baseless and hollow charge .... There are a number of free-thinkers, agnostics or atheists, as there are in all Eastern countries .... But is this phenomenon new, or peculiar to Turkey? I have talked to people of different strata of society; I have visited mosques and public places of worship at all odd hours and I am convinced that in spite of the high priests of free-thinking modernism and laocity (*sic*), the Turk is today as good a Muslim as he was ever before and more true to his faith than the Indian, the Syrian, the Palestinian or the Egyptian.[52]

Ansari's studied and balanced response is also reflected in his introduction to Halide Edib's *Conflict of East and West in Turkey.* He offered an appraisal of the pan-Islamic sentiment in India, explained why his community placed on the Turks 'the burden not only of defending their heart and home, but the honour of Islam and Muslim peoples as well' and lamented that the Turks did not appreciate their 'quaint romanticism' and 'chivalry' or endure their 'oppressive affection'. If the Turks had known what pan-Islamism meant to the Indian Muslims and why the 'pan-Islamist sentiment' was their 'most sacred and exalted passions' (*sic*), they would have understood their frustration over the collapse of the Khilafat. Ansari observed philosophically that time

> has no doubt healed their wounds and they do not now reflect on the matter in the light of sentiment alone. But their world is still bleak and desolate and the wrecks of their dreams lie around them. The pan-Islamism that was once an ideal is now a vague grievance; what was once a hope and an inspiration is now a sorrow. God is still in heaven, but the world has apparently lost its balance. For the hero of the Islamic community has now become the Prodigal Son.[53]

Having dwelt on the pan-Islamic debacle, Ansari conceded

[51] *Comrade*, 18 September 1925.

[52] Ibid.

[53] Introduction, *Conflict of East and West in Turkey*, pp. v-vi. All subsequent references are from the introduction.

that the abolition of the Khilafat was a matter of 'sound policy' because it involved the Turks in pretensions which gave them a certain prestige but which also exposed them to the jealous wrath of their enemies and the shiftiness of selfish friends. The Indian Muslims did not appreciate this because their perspective on the Kamalist Republic was 'faulty'. They tended to identify belief, manners and customs with the prescriptions of faith. Religion and social life were no doubt inseparable and a society that altogether overlooked the religious element was sure to drift from one vicious whirlpool to another. They were also, according to Ansari, unable to distinguish between conservatism and stagnation; so they were ignorant of the good done by Mustafa Kamal. In a tone uncharacteristic of a professional surgeon and with a clarity and frankness rare among many of his Khilafat colleagues, Ansari not only justified Turkish reforms but also made out a case for a liberal interpretation of religious decrees in India. He wrote:

> Religion is the permanent basis of life, but the true religious spirit does not seek to shackle life in order to preserve a theoretical consistency between fact and belief. It endeavours rather to discover fresh sources of inspiration, which are really nothing more than fresh points of contact between the personality of the founder of a religion and of the follower across the gulf of time and altered social conditions. *Rigid conformity to the latter... may be as injurious to society as frivolous disregard for truth. There can thus be need for reform even when the law is all written down* [emphasis added].

The essence of Ansari's belief was that religion and politics no longer formed an indissoluble unity: they were separate realms concerned with different issues and functions, decided and performed by different experts

Journey to Constantinople

Ansari sailed from the Bombay harbour on 10 April 1925 in the company of his ailing friend, Ajmal Khan, who was to receive medical treatment in Paris and London. This voyage was different from his previous two. He first went to England as a student; later, he travelled to Constantinople as a relatively unknown doctor. But it was not the same on this occasion, for his reputation both as a professional surgeon and a statesman with much political acumen was firmly established in the countries he planned to visit. Ansari could have well anticipated the welcome that awaited him.

Ansari's first port of halt was Port Said where he and Ajmal Khan were enchanted by the reception extended by some distinguished Egyptians. He wrote: 'The crowding of the main deck by long-robed officials, the warmth of their welcome, the flow of eloquent and sonorous Arabic in high-pitched voices, accompanied by even more eloquent gestures, though it warmed our hearts greatly, caused a little flutter in official dovecotes'.[54] The reference was to the viceroy of India, Reading (1860-1935), who was on his way to London.

Paris was the next stop. Judging from their letters home, both Ansari and Ajmal Khan were quite ecstatic to be in the French capital and to see much that was new, such as the mosque and the Muslim Institute, situated on the same side of the river Seine as the University of Sorbonne and the Quartier Latin.[55] They were also introduced to the *savants* of the Sorbonne and the University of Paris, received as officials of the Jamia Millia Islamia at a gathering of the *Rapprochement Universitaire*: and feted and lionized by the Carnegie Foundation, a melange of poets, artists, writers and rich young hangers-on. They lectured at the Societe de Sociologie de Paris and the Ligue du Droit de l'Homme et du Citoyen, on the non-cooperation movement, conducted discussions with several prominent Indians which convinced them that India's salvation lay in Gandhi's non-violent non-cooperation programme[56] and were able to keep up with the rapid, esoteric chatter that swirled around them. They were even quicker at becoming adept at the nightly partying. Ansari, in particular, looked every inch the polished performer.

After a month long stay in Paris, the doctor and the hakim spent six weeks in Lausanne where 'at last we have got that complete rest and peace which has done us a world of good'. The trip was all sweetness and light. Vienna was their next halt. Here they saw the Medical Exhibition and purchased pathology specimens, charts and maps for the Ayurvedic and *Yunani* Tibbia College at Delhi. They also went sight-seeing though Ansari was

[54] *Comrade*, 10 July 1925; Ghaffar, *Hayat-i Ajmal*, p. 336.

[55] Ibid., 17 July 1925.

[56] Ibid., 30 June, 24 July 1925.

depressed that the 'magnificent capital of the old dual monarchy looked like a ghost of its former self'. The chateaux, palaces, monuments, public buildings, squares and boulevards in Vienna 'stand today quite neglected, reminding one of their past splendour. The Austrians can hardly keep them in repairs'.[57]

Ansari's stay in Europe was rewarding. He made a round of the hospitals and clinics where work on the regenerative methods of treatment was done, watched with care the technique of different workers and discussed their results with them. He visited Paris, Lucerne and Vienna specially and saw the work of Eugene Steinach, Robert Lichtenstern, a urologist, and S. Voronoff. He gained much in practical and clinical knowledge which was reflected in his paper presented at the Delhi Medical Association in October 1925.

Ansari parted company with Ajmal Khan in Vienna. While the hakim left for Marseilles, Ansari boarded the Orient Express on its journey to Constantinople. He reached the historic city on the morning of 19 July 1925. But it was a city with a difference. On 13 October 1923 the National Assembly had voted that Angora (old Ancyra), founded by the Phrygian king Midas in the seventh century BC and once a great centre from which caravan roads led off into Persia, Syria and Armenia, be the seat of government. The decision to move the capital from Constantinople (Istanbul) into central Anatolia was in recognition of the fact that Anatolia now was in Turkey, unencumbered by European, Arab or African provinces. The shift to Ankara also symbolized a clean break with the Ottoman past.[58] Ansari noticed the change. He reported in the columns of *Comrade* that Constantinople did not show the same 'bustle and activity' as in the days of the Ottoman empire. He found large buildings, military barracks, depots and arsenals empty and bare. Caught up in post-war lethargy and weariness, the people were hungry, taxes were heavy and food scarce. Ansari wrote of 'a vast number of poor, ill-clad, starving humanity begging in the streets'.[59] He

[57]Ibid., 18 September 1925.

[58]Lewis, *Turkey*, p. 76; Poynter, *When Turkey was Turkey*, p. 138. For an account of the state of affairs in Angora by an English writer—the first to visit the city after the Kamalist revolution—see Grace Ellison, *An Englishwoman in Angora*, pp. 135-6. See Edib, *Turkish Ordeal*, p. 49, for an extract from Mustafa Kamal's letter in which he advocated the necessity of transferring the seat of Parliament to Anatolia.

[59]*Comrade*, 18 September 1925.

also referred to the uphill task of making a 'civilized' nation out of nothing, though he was acutely aware of the futility and superficiality of certain reforms, such as the "Hat Law", being part of the much-advertised modernism. Meeting old friends and comrades convinced him that, despite external threats and internal feuds, Turkey was surging ahead on the road to progress.[60]

In relation to India generally and the Muslims in particular, Ansari commended the views of Turkish officials to the judicious and careful consideration of his people. According to his assessment, the Turks were sympathetic to the national ideals and aspirations of the Indians and believed that the greatest service India could render to world peace was to attain freedom speedily. Their message to the pan-Islamists in India was equally significant. In the first place, it was made plain that Turkey was beset with great external and internal difficulties and could not therefore participate in 'any movement involving fresh responsibilities'. Secondly, the Muslim peoples should work towards their educational, social and economic advancement, 'should not even think of electing a Khalifa' and *on no account lend themselves to perpetuate autocracy of an individual or a dynasty in any guise or shape'* [emphasis added].

And finally, Ansari informed the readers of the *Comrade* that the Turkish officials 'are cognisant of the differences in their point of view and ours regarding the question of Khilafat'. But they maintained that it was better to have no Khalifa rather than to have one who would be 'ineffective' and even 'injurious'.[61] The Turkish government could not have disavowed its remaining links with the pan-Islamists in India in a more forthright and categorical manner. Ansari's impressions, published in the *Comrade* of 18 September, sealed the fate of those intransigent pan-Islamists who hoped to make political capital out of the situation prevalent in Turkey. In fact, when Ansari returned to India at the end of 1925 he found the Khilafatists deep in the hot cauldron of party quarrels because their movement had lost its *raison d'etre*. The Khilafat party was split into factions and the factions into fractions.

[60]Ansari's account is similar to that of the British writer Ellison, who was equally appreciative of Mustafa Kamal's contribution in the building up of a strong and united Turkey. See Grace Ellison, *Turkey To-day* (London, 1928).

[61]*Comrade*, 18 September 1925.

Annexure 1

The Draft Indian National Pact

WHEREAS INDIA being a dependency of the British Government has been deprived of all the rights and privileges of a free country and Indians are denied even full citizenship rights in several parts of the British Empire and the present foreign government does not use and in the nature of things cannot be expected to use all its resources to uphold the dignity and protect the elementary rights of Indians; whereas it is essential for the free and full moral and material development of her citizens and the enforcement of due respect for their human rights and their liberties in all parts of the globe that Indians should before all else possess in India the rights and privileges that the free nations of the world enjoy in their respective countries; whereas it is necessary that all the peoples of India, of whatever religion, race or colour should unite together and apply all their resources, moral, mental and material, for the attainment of Swaraj and the only obstacle is the want of cooperation among the different communities due to misunderstanding and mutual suspicion about each other's aims and intentions and whereas a joint declaration by all communities of the goal which they seek to attain and the rights which they wish to secure for the people, which a Swaraj Government will be pledged to guarantee and safeguard, will be beneficial to the creating of that confidence and toleration, which are absolutely essential for a common endeavour.

It is hereby resolved that all the communities and committees represented by the signatories to this document shall enter into an agreement in terms of the following resolutions which shall be known as the Indian National Pact:

In pursuance thereof it is hereby resolved:

and local boards. Lala Lajpat Rai does not agree to this. As an alternative Lalaji proposes that a time limit may be fixed during which communal representation will be enforced and at the expiry of which it will be abolished altogether).

Such representation shall throughout the country be in proportion to the numerical strength of each community in the constituencies (Lala Lajpat Rai wants that special provision shall be made for the small minority such as Christians and Parsis, etc. Dr Ansari suggests that large minorities such as Sikhs and Christians may be given special representation in the Federal Legislatures but only very small minorities such as Parsis should be given special representation both in the Federal and State Legislatures). But the electorate in all cases will be joint.

There shall be no communal or colour or caste distinction in public services and in the educational institutions.

8. In order to achieve national unity and out of regard for the religious feelings of their Hindu compatriots the Mussalmans of India do hereby by a solemn self-denying ordinance bind themselves to give up cow-slaughter except in connection with Id-i-Azha when it will be done, in such a manner as will not injure the feelings of Hindus.
9. In order to secure and preserve a calm atmosphere for public worship it is hereby declared that no music shall be allowed in front of places of public worship at such time as may be fixed by local mixed conciliatory boards.
10. Religious processions of different denominations when falling on one and the same date shall follow such different routes or be fixed for such different times as may be determined by local mixed conciliatory boards.
11. In order to prevent friction and settle all questions giving rise to differences and conflicts between different religious communities, e.g., on the occasion of Dusehra, Muharram, Rath Yatra procession, Sikh Divans, etc., etc. provincial and local joint boards will be appointed to act as conciliatory and arbitration boards.
12. While cherishing feelings of the most friendly nature towards all the nations of the world at large it is further resolved that the people of India should participate in the formation of a Federation of Eastern countries to be established for purposes of mutual help in trade and commerce and the emancipation of the East from economic exploitation and

1. It shall be the firm and unalterable object of the communities represented by the signatories to this pact to secure complete Swaraj for India, that is to say, the Swaraj which will secure and guarantee to Indians the same status, rights and privileges in India as every free and independent nation enjoys in its country.
2. The form of Government under Swaraj shall be democratic and of the federal type; but the exact nature of this Government shall be fixed and determined hereafter by a National Convention consisting of representatives of all communities and all shades of political opinion.
3. Hindustani shall be the national language of India. It shall be permissible to write it in either script Urdu or Devanagri.
4. Full religious liberty, i.e., liberty of belief, worship, propaganda, association and education, is hereby guaranteed to all the communities forming the Indian Nation and shall form a constitutional right which it shall never be lawful for any government to annul, modify, suspend or otherwise the aforementioned liberties shall, however, be exercised subject to such disciplinary rules and regulations as may be found necessary to preserve peace and order and to eliminate force or compulsion by any one party in derogation of the rights of others.
5. To prevent any particular religious denomination being given undue preference over any other, no government funds or funds collected by local bodies from public revenue and public taxes including cesses shall be devoted to the promotion and furtherance of any denominational institutions or purposes.
6. When once the Swaraj has been achieved it shall be the sacred duty of every Indian, be he Hindu, Mussalman, Sikh, Parsi, Christian or of any other denomination to defend it against all attack—external or internal.
7. In view of the present state of feeling prevailing in the different communities and in view of the insufficient development of political sense and responsibility in them, it is necessary for sometime to afford adequate protection to the interests of minorities. It is therefore hereby agreed that the various communities shall have separate representation in the Legislatures, both State and Federal.

(NOTE: Dr Ansari wishes to extend this principle to municipalities domination by Europe and with a view to encourage and support Oriental culture and generally to maintain good and friendly relations between the various nationalities all over the East.

(Dr Ansari wishes to incorporate in the National Pact provision 2 to clause 4 of the Lucknow Pact also which runs as follows: "Further that no bill, nor any clause thereof, nor a resolution affecting any community, which question is to be determined by the members of that community in the Legislature concerned, shall be proceeded with, if three-fourths of the members of that community in the particular Legislature, Federal or State, oppose the bill or any clause thereof or resolution." But as there is no time to get Lala Lajpat Rai's opinion it is submitted with his recommendation only).

LAJPAT RAI
M.A. ANSARI

Report of the Committee

Preamble & Clauses I & II. The preamble and the first 2 clauses of the draft pact appear to have evoked no criticism or only of an insignificant nature except in one or two prominent cases, where doubts are expressed as regards the form of government adumbrated in our draft, otherwise they have been generally accepted.

Clause III. The third clause relating to a common national language has called forth varying opinions; Mussalmans, in general, favouring "Urdu" against "Hindustani", while some political and denominational opinions are in substantial agreement that Hindustani (in both Urdu and Devanagri script) should be the *lingua franca* of India, but each province should retain and use its own vernacular.

Clause IV. Clause IV has again called forth differing opinions. But some Hindus would discourage "Propaganda and proselytization". Others regard this clause as one of the most salutary provisions and one, at least, calls it a constitutional right, which must be made inviolable by any government. There is an overwhelming consensus of opinion in favour of its retention and such amendments as are proposed are verbal and insignificant.

Clause V. This too is upheld by a considerable majority. But some gentlemen would see this provision restricted to future arrangements only and two or three others would relax it in favour of some denominational institutions which may be engaged in social work also....

Clause VI. This is almost unanimously agreed to by all.

Clause VII. Clause VII has evoked the largest quantity of comment and criticism. While opinions are more or less equally divided as regards Dr Ansari and Lala Lajpat Rai's notes to this clause, there seems to be a fair consensus on the point of "separate representation" for the present, i.e., with a time limit. But Mussalman opinion does not favour joint electorates though enlightened Muslim opinion is almost unanimously for common electorates in regard to municipalities and local boards as a necessary step towards the extension of the principle in regard to Federal and State legislatures, when the time may be ripe for such a change and when minorities themselves may ask for it. Nearly all Hindu opinion is for a time limit for "separate representation". As regards the question of public services, again, Hindu and Mussalman opinion is sharply divided. The former condemn (though not unanimously) proportionate distribution of posts according to numerical strength and the latter unanimously insist on it, only some individual Mussalmans accept departments where expert knowledge is essential. By far the most controversial part of the whole draft is article 7, which has been made the subject of keen and earnest comment by individuals, associations and the press alike.

Clause VIII. Clause VIII again has evoked earnest comment. Some Hindus have urged its abrogation as redundant, and some others including some prominent public men, have insisted on the omission of Id-i-Azha also as an exception. Similarly a majority of Mussalmans have emphatically condemned it as subversive of "freedom of action", while a few have endorsed it subject to the condition that the Hindus should leave the matter entirely to the good sense of the Muhammadans—an opinion shared by the Bihar Provincial Congress Committee. One or two Mussalmans hope that it will not be regarded a "bargain" but a voluntary concession to Hindu susceptibilities.

Clause IX. With reference to the playing of bands before places of public worship also, there is some difference of opinion. Some prominent Hindus would stop "music", "uproar of processions" before all places of public worship at all times of day and one or two would restrict the operation of this clause to only "Moslem places of worship" and yet there are others who think that genuine worship ought not to be disturbed by any noises. But the balance of opinion, we think, is in favour of the provision.

Clause X & XI. Clauses X and XI are almost unanimously agreed upon by all parties.

Clause XII. Clause XII has aroused quite unnecessary suspicion and opposition in many persons. Some of them (both Hindus and Mussalmans) regard it wholly premature. They do not feel sure that the time has yet arrived for us to think of an Asiatic Federation. One critic condemns the ideas as "Western" and advises the country to rise above any cramped ideas of Asiatic Federations and expects a development, by India, of the idea of international brotherhood. But the sting of the suspicion we fear seems to lie (at least in the objections of some of the critics) in the erroneous notion that the said federation is meant to provide an opportunity for a certain important minority in India to enter into relations with Afghanistan and Turkey! One critic goes to the extent of saying that none but China and India are the victims of Europe's policy of "economic exploitation of the East" and, therefore, no league with other Asiatic countries is necessary. And yet there are others who think that the object of the federation would be "the emancipation" of Asia from the economic exploitation of Europe, America or Japan.

The sum and substance of the entire criticism of this clause seems to be that its scope and real object have been wholly missed or imperfectly realized by those who have viewed it with distrust and therefore pronounced it premature.

Last Note. Dr Ansari's last note has been almost generally endorsed by all.

In our opinion, however, our draft-pact has quite unjustifiably suffered by contrast with other documents on the same subject, which came into existence since its publication It has not been made the subject of calm and considered judgement by either Hindus or the Mussalmans—although the Christians, the Sikhs and the Parsis seem to have treated it seriously. The attention of the former has been very largely and we feel unduly absorbed by other documents referred to above and they have not accorded to our draft, the thought and consideration which it deserved at their hands; and, again, the Mussalmans have been quite needlessly alarmed by some of its provisions and have allowed their judgements to be influenced by passing events.

Of the omissions pointed out we have noted three.

(1) It is said that we should have treated the interests of "labour", the Sikh and the Parsi communities specifically in separate clauses. But that is taking us too far. In so far, as the adjustment of the "causes of conflict" are concerned, we have, we think, comprehensively dealt with them in this pact—including the principles of special representation. But we do not think that we were required to go further than the settlement of the elementary principles. The deduction of details concerning the allotment of representation (which would include the interests of "Labour" no less than "Capital", "Landholders" and "Tenants") is left to the *National Convention*, which is to draft the constitution of our Federal or State Legislatures.

(2) It is urged that the actual Pact to be subscribed by the representatives of various communities should be written in *Hindustani*. The suggestion is premature, but, we regard it with the *same* respect which it deserves.

(3) Supplementary clauses (of which a notable example is furnished by Maulvi Mohammad Sajjad of Phulwari) are suggested mostly pertaining to the procedure to be followed, but some are more or less irrelevant to the terms of the reference made for us. But when the Pact enters upon its final stages, some of these suggestions, particularly those just pointed out, will be found to form a good basis for discussion.

In conclusion we are of opinion that:

(1) The necessity for a National Pact as fully borne out by the opinions received is urgent as ever; but

(2) Our draft has not so far received the attention which it deserves and, therefore,

(3) We strongly recommend that a gathering of the representatives of all classes of interests, both secular and communal, be convened at the earliest opportunity to consider and settle the terms of the Pact we now submit for the consideration of the All-India Congress Committee with the analysis of opinions, selected so far.

We are still of the opinion that the final adoption and promulgation of a Pact such as the one we submit for the All-India Congress Committee's approval is one of the immediate needs of our present political life.

Annexure 11

RESOLUTIONS
Passed at the Delhi
UNITY CONFERENCE
26 September to 2 October 1924

RESOLUTION NO 1

THIS CONFERENCE places on record its deep grief and concern at the fast which Mahatma Gandhi has undertaken. This Conference is emphatically of opinion that the utmost freedom of conscience and religion is essential and condemns any desecration of places of worship to whatsoever faith they may belong and any persecution or punishment of any person for adopting or reverting to any faith and further condemns any attempt by compulsion to convert people to one's faith or to enforce one's own religious observances at the cost of the rights of others.

The members of the Conference assure Mahatma Gandhi and pledge themselves to use their utmost endeavours to enforce these principles and to condemn any deviation from them even under provocation. This Conference further authorizes the President to convey personally to Mahatma Gandhi the united wish of this Conference that Mahatma Gandhi should immediately break his fast in order to permit this Conference to have the benefit of his cooperation, advice and guidance in deciding upon the speediest means of effectively checking the evil which is fast spreading over the country.

RESOLUTION NO 2

This Conference deplores the dissensions and quarrels that are now going on between Hindus and Muslims in several places in India resulting in loss of life, burning and plunder of property and desecration of temples. The Conference regards them as barbarous and contrary to religion. This Conference is of opinion that it is unlawful and irreligious for any person to take the law into his own hands by way of retaliation or punishment. The Conference is of opinion that all differences, no matter of what nature should be referred to arbitration and if that be impossible even to a court of law.

RESOLUTION NO 3

There shall be a Central National Panchayat of not more than 15 persons, with power to organize and appoint local Panchayats in consultation with the local representatives of the different communities to enquire into and settle all disputes and differences including recent occurrences, where necessary and desirable. The said National Panchayat shall have power to frame rules and regulations for carrying out this resolution.

The Conference appoints the following to act as the Central National Panchayat with power to add to their number up to 15 and co-opt local representatives as additional members:

1. Mahatma Gandhi (Chairman and Convenor)
2. Hakim Ajmal Khan
3. Lala Lajpat Rai
4. Mr K.F. Nariman
5. Dr S.K. Datta
6. Master Sunder Singh of Lyallpur.

RESOLUTION NO 4

With a view to give effect to the general principles for promoting better relations between the various communities of India laid down in Resolution 1 and to secure full toleration of all faiths, beliefs and religious practices this Conference records its opinion:

(*a*) That every individual or group shall have full liberty to hold and give expression to his or their beliefs and follow any religious practice with due regard to the feelings of others and without interfering with their rights. In no case may such individual or group revile the founders, holy persons or tenets of any other faith.

(*b*) That all places of worship, of whatever faith or religion, shall be considered sacred and inviolable and shall on no account be attacked or desecrated whether as a result of provocation or by way of retaliation for sacrilege of the same nature. It shall be the duty of every citizen, of whatever faith or religion, to prevent such attack or desecration as far as possible and where such attack or desecration has taken place it shall always be promptly condemned.

(*c*) (i) That Hindus must not expect that the exercise of the right of cow-slaughter by Muslims can or will be stopped by the use of force, resolution of a local body, act of legislature or order of court but only by mutual consent and must trust to the good sense of Muslims and the establishment of better relations between the two communities to create deeper respect for their feelings.

(ii) Nothing stated in the above clause shall unsettle or affect any local custom or agreement between the two communities already in existence, nor will it authorize cow-slaughter in a place where it has not taken place before; any dispute on facts should be settled by the National Panchayat formed under resolution No 3.

(iii) Cow-slaughter shall not take place in a way offensive to the religious sentiments of the Hindus.

(iv) The Muslim members of the Conference hereby call upon their co-religionists to do everything in their power to reduce cow-slaughter.

(*d*) (i) That Muslims must not expect to stop Hindu music near or in front of mosques by force, resolution of a local body, act of legislature or order of court except by mutual consent but must rely upon the good sense of Hindus to respect their feelings.

(ii) Nothing stated in the above clause shall unsettle or affect any local custom or agreement between the two communities already in existence nor shall it authorize the playing of music in front of mosques where it has not been played before. Any dispute with regard to the latter shall be referred for settlement to the National Panchayat formed under Resolution No. 3.

(iii) The Hindu members of this Conference call upon their co-religionists to avoid playing music before mosques in such a manner as to disturb congregational prayers.

(*e*) (i) That Muslims must not expect to stop by force, resolution of a local body, act of legislature or order of court, except by mutual consent, the performance of *arti* or the playing of music including the blowing of *shankhs* by Hindus during worship and on other occasions in their houses or temples or public places at any time even if the house or temple or place in question is situated in close proximity to a mosque; but they should trust to the good sense of the Hindus to accommodate them.

(ii) Nothing stated in the above clause shall unsettle or affect any local custom or agreement between the two communities already in existence; any dispute on facts should be settled by the National Panchayat formed under Resolution No. 3.

(*f*) That Muslims are at liberty to chant *Azan* or offer prayers in their own houses or in any mosque or public place not set apart for the religious observance of any other community.

(*g*) (i) Where the slaughter of an animal or sale of meat is permissible on other grounds, no objection shall be taken to the method of slaughter, whether by *Jhatka, Bali* or *Zibah.*

(ii) Wherever there is any dispute regarding the sale of any kind of meat in a particular locality or quarter it shall be referred for settlement to the local Panchayat formed under Resolution No. 3.

(*h*) That every individual is at liberty to follow any faith and to change it whenever he so wills and shall not by reason of such change of faith render himself liable to any punishment or persecution at the hands of the followers of the faith renounced by him.

(*i*) That every individual or group is at liberty to convert or reconvert another by argument or persuasion but must not attempt to do so or prevent its being done by force, fraud or other unfair means, such as the offering of material inducement. Persons under 16 years of age should not be converted unless it be along with their parents or guardians. If any person under 16 years of age is found stranded without his parent or guardian by a person of another faith, he should be promptly handed over to persons of his own faith. There must be no secrecy about any conversion or reconversion.

(j) That no community should attempt to stop by force the construction of a new place of worship by a member of another community on his own land but such new place of worship should be built at a reasonable distance from an existing place of worship of any other community.

RESOLUTION NO 5

This Conference is of opinion that a section of the press, specially in the North, is responsible for increasing the tension between different communities by publishing wild exaggerations, reviling each other's religion and by every means fomenting prejudice and condemns such writings and appeals to the public to stop patronage of such newspapers and pamphlets and advises central and local panchayats to supervise such writings and from time to time to publish correct version.

RESOLUTION NO 6

It having been represented to this Conference that in certain places acts of impropriety have been committed in relation to mosques the Hindu members of this Conference condemn such acts wherever committed.

RESOLUTION NO 7

The Hindu and Muslim members of this Conference call upon their co-religionists to extend full tolerance to the minor communities of India and to deal with them in all questions of communal intercourse with justice and generosity.

RESOLUTION NO 8

This Conference is of opinion that attempts on behalf of members of one community to boycott members of any other community and to stop social or commercial relations with them made in certain parts of the country are reprehensible and are an effective bar to the promotion of good relations between the various communities in India. The Conference therefore appeals to all communities to avoid any such boycotts and exhibitions of ill-will.

RESOLUTION NO 9

This Conference calls upon men and women of all communities throughout the country to offer daily prayers during the last critical week of Mahatmaji's fast and to organize mass meetings on the EIGHTH of OCTOBER in every town and village to express the nation's thankfulness to the Almighty and to pray that the spirit of goodwill and brotherliness may pervade and unite all the communities of India and that the principles of full religious toleration and mutual goodwill declared in this Conference may be adopted and given effect to by members of all communities in India.

DELHI,
2 October 1924.

SHUAIB QURESHI
JAWAHARLAL NEHRU
Secretaries of the Conference

Leading the Congress

The Council-splendour has dazzled me in vain.
Oh! take me to the lowly thatched cottage again.
The village-man will love me and come to my call.
His service my Swaraj dearer than all.

Basumati (Calcutta), 7 September 1927

ON HIS RETURN to India in July 1926 Ansari noticed the changes on the Indian political horizon. The Congress, much to his dismay, was riven with dissension and its prestige had sunk to a low ebb. The Swaraj Party was in disarray because the 'Responsivists', supported by Malaviya and Lajpat Rai, were in open revolt. Having defeated Motilal Nehru's Swarajist alliance in the local elections held in 1925, the Malaviya group organized the Independent Congress Party. In the build up to the provincial and central assembly elections Hindu communal concerns provided most of the ammunition for the assault on the Swaraj Party. Motilal was accused of being a beef-eater, the Congress was stigmatized as a prostitute of Muslim India and such was the communal hatred aroused that Motilal afterwards considered retiring from public life.[1] Gandhi, who had himself withdrawn from the hurly-burly of active politics and had at the beginning of 1926 imposed upon himself a year of silence on political matters, advised the dispirited Motilal to let the evil forces of communalism play themselves out and in the meantime to 'wait, watch and pray'.[2]

The storm of inter-communal antagonism was blowing with fury in the summer of 1926 and no voices could make themselves heard against the clamour of the rival partisans. Though explanations for the rise in the communal temperature ranged from the government's divide and rule policy to the militancy of the

[1]Page, *Prelude to Partition*, pp. 134-5; Gyanendra Pandey, *The Ascendancy of the Congress in Uttar Pradesh 1926-34* (Delhi, 1978), pp. 121-4; C.A. Bayly, *The Local Roots of Indian Politics—Allahabad 1880-1920* (Oxford, 1975).

[2]B.N. Pandey, *Nehru* (Delhi, 1976), p. 119.

Khilafat Committees and the Hindu Mahasabha,[3] there were few systematic attempts to curb violent eruptions. The festival of Ramlila occasioned widespread tension even in areas where Congress exercised much influence; its celebration at Aligarh in September was marked by one of the worst riots of the year. Delhi was transformed into something like an armed camp during the *Id* celebrations; yet a minor incident—the scare created by a bolting horse—left three persons killed and sixty injured. Violence was also rampant in Calcutta from June to October 1926. Inter-communal relations in several other parts of the country were generally strained. There was hardly any development of importance in politics, observed Coatman, other than the slow and steady resurgence of Hindu-Muslim fracas and its establishment on new, wider and deeper foundations.[4] The vision of swaraj, stated Srinivasa Iyengar (1874-1941), the Congress president in 1926, 'has somewhat dimmed in the dust of internal strife'.

Ansari's response to such developments was predictable: it exemplified his national idealism, his antipathy to the mixing of religion with politics and the democratic and secular thrust of his concerns. He pinned his hopes, as always, in the Congress which enjoyed a special national status as the spokesman for India's diverse peoples. Other organizations, in his judgement, had neither the will nor the ideological coherence to rally popular support. The Muslim League and the Khilafat Committee, for instance, were enmeshed in narrow and sectarian politics and had therefore become peripheral to the nationalist mainstream. For this reason, he resigned from these bodies on 16 July 1926, stating explicitly that he owed allegiance to the Congress alone. Jawaharlal approved of his decision. Writing to Syed Mahmud from Geneva, he observed, 'I can see no way out of our difficulties except by prodding on—more or less secular lines in politics'.[5] Addressing a conference in Lucknow a few months later Ansari exhorted Muslims not to have any truck with communalism and

[3]Hasan, *Nationalism and Communal Politics*, ch. 5 and 6.

[4]J. Coatman, *India in 1926-1927*, p. 3; Page, op. cit., ch. 2. The only detailed study of communal and revivalist movements in the 1920s and of communal riots is by G.R. Thursby, *Hindu-Muslim Relations in British India* (Leiden, 1975); J. Coatman, *Years of Destiny-India, 1926-1932* (London, 1932), p. 117.

[5]11 August 1926, S. Gopal (ed.), *Selected Works of Jawaharlal Nehru [SWJ]* Vol. 2, p. 241.

join others in liberating the country from the clutches of foreign rule.[6]

On 20 March 1927 Ansari attended a conference at Delhi where a group of Muslim politicians, led by Jinnah, agreed to forego separate electorates if their four demands were met by the Congress *in toto.* The first of these was that the Bengali and Punjabi Muslims should be represented in the legislative council in proportion to their population; the second was that one-third of the seats in the central legislature be reserved for the Muslims. Also that Sind be separated from the Bombay Presidency and constituted as an independent province and finally, reforms be extended to the North-West Frontier Province. 'We have after all succeeded,' Mohammad Yaqub wrote triumphantly, 'in finding out a formula on which there was a unanimity of Muslim opinion and which has shifted the burden of proof on the other party; it is for them [Hindus] to clasp the hand of friendship which the Muslims have extended'.[8]

When these proposals were placed before the AICC, Ansari, Motilal and Srinivasa Iyengar pressed for their acceptance as a basis for a political accord with the League. Their view prevailed. The only concessions offered to dissenters like Malaviya, Lajpat Rai and Moonje was that reforms for the North-West Frontier Province became conditional on the provisions of a suitable judiciary and the separation of Sind conditional on the separation of Andhra. Neither of these conditions militated against the spirit of the four proposals and both Ansari and Mohamed Ali were happy to swallow them.

Such a conciliatory response paved the way for a short-term rapprochement between the Congress and the League. But the spate of communal riots continued unabated. Between the beginning of April and the end of September 1927, twenty-five riots were reported: ten in UP, six in Bombay Presidency, two each in the Punjab, the CP, Bengal, Bihar and Orissa and one in Delhi (Table 7.1). During the seventeen months that the viceroy, Irwin (1881-1959), had been in India, the whole landscape was overshadowed by the lowering clouds of communal tension,

[6] *IAR*, January-June 1927, p. 424.

[7] Mushirul Hasan, 'The Delhi Proposals: A Study in Communal Politics', *The Indian Economic and Social History Review*, Vol. 17, no. 4.

[8] *Leader*, 27 March 1927.

[9] Hasan, 'The Delhi Proposals', pp. 389-91.

TABLE 7.1

COMMUNAL RIOTS IN INDIA—APRIL 1926 TO AUGUST 1927

Province	*No. of communal riots*	*Dead*	*Injured*
Punjab	3	61	380
UP	8	3	131
Delhi	3	4	116
Bengal	12	181	1,512
Bihar	7	14	114
CP	1	Nil	7
Bombay	9	4	253
Madras	1	1	7

SOURCE: Home Poll. F. No. 10/16, 1931 & K.W., NAI.

which repeatedly discharged their thunderbolts, spreading their devastating havoc throughout the country.[10]

Irwin proposed a conference of Indian leaders to address themselves to the problem of growing Hindu-Muslim strife. But those who responded to the viceroy's offer, including Ansari, discovered that such summits offered no magic or quick solutions. The discussions were essentially a dialogue of the deaf, with Muslim delegates—Mohamed Ali, Zafar Ali Khan, Shaukat Ali and Mohammad Yaqub—insisting on tackling the political disputes first, while Malaviya, Lajpat Rai, Moonje and Raja Narendranath (1864-1945) were only prepared to discuss issues of social and religious discord.[11] The recalcitrance on both sides led to a stalemate. The conference floundered without making any progress towards its avowed goal. In the end violent and scurrilous charges were bandied about, with the spokesman of each community blaming the other for its break up. The tendency of Muslim leaders to bargain for political concessions 'under cover of a settlement of what has been admitted to be religious differences was hardly calculated to create an atmosphere favourable to harmony and settlement', pontificated the ***Amrita Bazar Patrika***.[12] The *Mohammadi*, on the other hand, reproached

[10]Speech on 29 August 1927, *India in 1927-28*, p. 17.

[11]See press clippings in Ansari Papers, JMI.

[12]25 September 1927; *Ananda Bazar Patrika*, 26 September 1927, Native Newspaper Reports (NNR), Bengal, 1927; *Abhyudaya*, Note on the Press, United Provinces of Agra and Oudh, for the week ending 1 October 1927, microfilm, NMML.

the 'Hindu members' for their uncompromising attitude. They 'have indirectly said that no true unity should be established unless and until the Mussalmans agree to live in this country as a race of slaves like the *Sudras* and other untouchables'.[13]

Undeterred by this ill-fated conference the AICC, inspired partly by the necessity of maintaining some semblance of solidarity in the Congress and partly by the genuine alarm at the growing Hindu-Muslim clashes, decided to discuss afresh the all-absorbing theme of communal relations. The outcome was a unity conference on 27 October 1927.[14] Ansari was a key figure at the conference. He set the tone early on with an eloquent appeal for unity, spent hours in delicate negotiations and pleaded with Hindus and Muslims to create an atmosphere of non-violence. But such implorings did not carry matters very much further and the fundamentally irreconcilable aims of certain groups present ended in open rupture. The problem at hand was left precisely where it had been before the conference met. Though consensus was reached on conversion, cow-slaughter and music near mosques—issues on which Ansari made a detailed statement—its effect was blunted because the Mahasabha and League delegates had boycotted the conference.[15] Besides, the agreement was more in the nature of an appeal to each side to avoid offending the other. 'Who is going to restrain the enthusiasts and fanatics if they deviate from civilized methods of conversion by persuasion and argument and to take them to task for doing so?', enquired the *Leader* of Allahabad. At the same time, a dispute over, say, music before mosques, could not be solved by means of a formula which assumed tolerance and reasonableness on either side, 'which unfortunately has not been much in evidence in recent times'.[16]

The failure of the unity conferences was a foregone conclusion: there was never much chance of reconciling the claims of certain groups in the Congress, the League and the Mahasabha who had a vested interest in perpetuating communalism. They were afraid of giving away anything and felt it incumbent on them to stick to their demands. They were like parties in a law-suit who thought the more extravagant their claims the more likely were

[13]7 October 1927, NNR, Bengal, 1927.

[14]*Leader*, Note on the Press, UP, 22 October 1927

[15]Ibid., 22 October 1927.

[16]Ibid., 5 November 1927; *Ananda Bazar Patrika*, 29 October, NNR, Bengal, 1927.

they to secure a judgement in their favour.[17] More importantly, an understanding on the immediate causes of conflict, such as the one attempted at Simla and Calcutta, could potentially undercut their support base and render them politically ineffectual. They made good in politics by acting as defenders and custodians of what they perceived as their community's interests in a region or in the country as a whole, a role they could perform either by exploiting religious sentiments or by keeping communal tensions alive. During the 1926 riots in Bengal, for instance, important Hindu and Muslim leaders remained provocatively silent, their attitude being interpreted as tacit approval of mob outrages and murders. Their favourite rhetorical device was to accuse the British of being the instigators of Hindu-Muslim discord.[18]

Ansari was frustrated by repeated failures to counter the communal blitzkrieg; there seemed to be some malign fate attending unity conferences, for every one that was held since September 1924 had no other result than to drive the two communities still farther apart. But Ansari's own doggedness in negotiating a viable settlement did not go unnoticed;[19] it was a commitment that never wavered. Contemporaries acclaimed this fact. They were further impressed by his loyalty to the Congress movement, especially when many of his comrades were, in the words of Motilal, 'tumbling over each other to shake hands with officials' and were afflicted by fear, prejudice and lust for power and wealth. It was easy for him to amass a fortune by concentrating on what was, in the early 1920s, a flourishing practice. But he chose to spend much of his time in politics and whatever he earned—his earnings were substantial because among his clients were some wealthy rajas and nawabs of northern and central India—was placed at the disposal of the Delhi Congress Committee. His house in Daryaganj was virtually a Congress headquarter where meetings of the AICC and the Congress Working Committee were held. His clinic in Fatehpuri was frequented mostly by Congress workers who were treated

[17]The Earl of Lytton, *Pundits and Elephants: Being the Experiences of Five Years as Governor of an Indian Province* (London, 1942), p. 172.

[18]*Madras Mail*, 23 May 1926.

[19]*Swarajya* (Urdu), 10 September 1927; *Hamdard* (Urdu), 9 September 1927; *Khilafat* (Urdu), 9 September 1927, Ansari Papers, JMI; also see Home Poll. 32, 1927, NAI.

free of charge. To his clinic in Daryaganj came the sick and the needy who lined up every morning to receive the attention of one of India's most reputed physician-surgeons.

With his record of service, the choice of Ansari as president of the 1927 Congress was no surprise. But he was not the only one to be considered. Sarojini Naidu, egged on by Jinnah and the Maharaja of Mahmudabad, pressed the claim of Motilal.[20] But, as usual, Gandhi called the shots from the sidelines. 'There are many forces just now working against Motilalji', he wrote to Sarojini Naidu. He did not either favour the younger Nehru, who, in any case, took himself out of the running. Gandhi wrote:

> Things, as they are shaping in the Congress, confirm the opinion that it is not yet time for Jawaharlal to shoulder the burden. He is too high-souled to stand the anarchy and hooliganism that seems to be growing in the Congress and it would be cruel to expect him to evolve order all of a sudden out of chaos .... For the present, we should press Dr Ansari to take the reins. He won't control the hooligans. He will let them have their way; but he may specialise in the Hindu-Muslim question and do something in th matter.[21]

Ansari's own preference was for Jawaharlal who, he believed, would match the 'clever' and 'astute' leadership of the League and the Mahasabha. Motilal, according to Ansari's reckoning, was unlikely to be backed by most PCC's, especially those which were 'over-run by Mahasabhites'.[22]

Gandhi wanted Ansari to wear the Congress crown. His reasons were quite simple: the doctor would be able to pilot a Hindu-Muslim pact through the Congress, his choice would command general acceptance, and his selection by a 'national association containing a preponderating majority of Hindus' was likely to foster Hindu-Muslim friendship.[23] Gandhi lauded Ansari's efforts to promote 'union' and pointed out how if he, Sarojini Naidu and Iyengar had not been pitchforked into the presidency of the Congress at the last three sessions, Ansari would have been

[20]Gandhi to Motilal Nehru, 2 June 1927; to Jawaharlal Nehru, 20 June 1927, *CWG*, Vol. 34, p. 87 and f.n. 2, p. 207.

[21]To Sarojini Naidu, 25 June 1927, ibid., p. 57; to Motilal Nehru, 19 June 1927, ibid., p. 31.

[22]Ansari to Sarojini Naidu, 26 June 1927, Hasan (ed.), *Muslims and the Congress*, p. 20.

[23]*Young India*, 21 July 1927, *CWG*, Vol. 34, p. 214.

elected on any of those occasions. His claim was postponed for 'special reasons', though his name was on everybody's lips when elections took place.[24]

With Gandhi's backing Ansari was in the running for the presidency: his election was a foregone conclusion. Yet he took the unusual, indeed unpopular, step of setting forth his views on Indian politics so that those who disagreed with him would have the opportunity of opposing his candidature. His views and the controversy they generated require explanation.[25]

In his statement of 17 August 1927 Ansari admitted that non-cooperation was dead, even though he believed 'as firmly today as I did in 1920–21 in non-cooperation', and that the policy of blind obstruction within the councils had failed. He assailed Swarajist policies in the legislatures and advocated direct action as was done in the non-cooperation days. While appealing to those who agreed with his assessment to keep away from the central and provincial legislatures, he urged others who still desired to go to the councils to confess that they were cooperators, to sink their differences and compose their quarrels, and form a people's party constituting the opposition.

The country, proceeded Ansari, was a vast camp of warring communal factions bent on destroying each other, 'and appealing to the authorities to protect them from the murderous onslaught of one another'. It was therefore necessary for the Congress to accord the highest priority to the communal malaise in its future programme. His own mission was to weld the various communities into a 'single solid nation'. He wanted others to do the same. He enumerated three lines of activity which would minimize friction: extensive propaganda by leaders of both the communities for communal amity, and establishment of safety bureaus and conciliatory boards in every city and town. With the help of a Hindu and a Muslim journalist the safety bureau would scrutinize and, if necessary, contradict writings and news items calculated to incite communal passions. At the same time, Congress leaders would tour riot prone areas and settle, if possible, issues of discord on the spot.

Ansari's panacea was a tried one. Public safety boards were started as a sequel to the decision arrived at the Unity Conference held in Delhi on 26 September 1924, but they were ineffectual.

[24] *Young India*, 21 July 1927, *CWG*, Vol. 34, p. 214.

[25] For Ansari's statement, see *Times of India*, 19 August 1927.

Also, it was not for want of propaganda that the communal chasm persisted, for Congress resolutions and speeches of Indian nationalists extolled the virtues of Hindu-Muslim unity and comradeship with unfailing regularity. Further, the immediate causes of friction were more often symptoms of a deep rooted socio-economic malady. The slaughter of a cow, the beating of a drum, the reception of a convert into one fold or the other, or the publication of something like *Rangila Rasul* acted as sparks which fired the powder and produced an explosion. The weakness in Ansari's analysis and the limitations of his remedial measures lay in his inability to grapple with the socio-economic roots of communalism.

Ansari's statement on the communal problem, though lacking in depth and analysis, had the merit of being non-controversial. But his views on other issues did not go uncontested. His criticism of the Swaraj Party, for instance, was bitterly attacked. The *Sainik* commented that his fine words and phrases were borrowed from the vocabulary of 'defeated' and 'downtrodden' people and that his sentiments and ideas were 'inopportune' and 'impracticable'.[26] Criticism came from another unexpected quarter. The Communists charged that Ansari—'the die-hard gandhist—would lead the peace-making process with British imperialism. Such an action, though seemingly incongruous with his 'cult', would actually be the 'logical outcome of the cult of gandhism'. In a pointedly ideological attack, the *Masses of India* stated:

> The Swaraj Party whole-heartedly stuck to the bankrupt tactics of parliamentary obstruction in order to satisfy the restlessness of the petty-bourgeois intelligentsia. Now one of the stalwarts [Ansari] of gandhism comes forward to declare that the petty-bourgeois intelligentsia no longer insist upon these tactics for they have become detrimental to capitalist interests. Ansari has proved that petty-bourgeois reaction (gandhism), just as the petty-bourgeois radicalism of the Swaraj Party, only serves the interests of capitalism.[26a]

[26]Note on the Press, UP, for the week ending 3 September 1927. The statement was, however, welcomed by a section of the Muslim press in UP. See *Oudh Akhbar, Aligarh Mail, Sadaqat* and *Medina*. Note on the Press, UP, 27 August 1927; also, Home Poll. 32, 1927, NAI.

[26a]G. Adhikari (ed.), *Documents of the History of the Communist Party of India* (Delhi, 1979), Vol. III-B, pp. 283-4

Motilal was equally harsh in repudiating Ansari's criticism of the Swaraj Party. He ridiculed the suggestion to 'obliterate the last vestiges of the tattered aims of non-cooperation' and pointedly belittled Anṣari by saying that he did not have any political programme of his own.[27]

Though Motilal's rejoinder and his defence of Swarajist policies was feeble, Gandhi chose to defend him and indict Ansari for his draft statement, a 'bomb-shell'. He bombarded him with long letters full of admonition and advice, to which Ansari replied either not at all or briefly and dryly. In trying to persuade him to keep his views to himself and not to publish them, Gandhi wrote:

> I [therefore] ask you to tear your statement to pieces. Keep that opinion to yourself, accept the election with grace, dignity and thankfulness, and announce that you have no political policy of your own to place before the country, that so far as that is concerned, you will take up a strictly judicial and impartial attitude and act merely as chairman of meetings guiding deliberations, keeping order and enforcing decision of majorities, that you have accepted the election with the sole intention of guiding the country during your year of office, by all the power at your command, to domestic peace. For, you owe it to the country as a Mussalman and a staunch nationalist to vindicate the religion of the Prophet and the honour of the country by giving all the talents you have for securing a domestic peace honourable to all parties. *Nobody expects more of you. And, if you meddle in anything else, you will be travelling outside your province....you dare not refuse the crown of thorns that is offered to you by a grateful country and you dare not publish your statement, however precious your views are* [emphasis added]. If you wish to place them before a few friends gathered together in a drawing-room enjoying hookah, you may certainly enliven the company with your views. But beyond the four walls of such a drawing-room, your views may not travel.[28]

Ansari's response to this patronizing—some said offensive—tone of the letter is not known. What is known is his stout refusal to comply with the command. He was not cowed into silence and the statement was promptly released to the press on 15

[27] *Tribune*, 24 August 1927; *Times of India*, 23 August 1927.
[28] Gandhi to Ansari, 10 August 1927, *CWG*, Vol. 34, p. 305.

August. Indignant at this act of defiance, Gandhi suggested 'spontaneous retirement' on the part of Ansari. He changed his mind soon thereafter, but insisted that Ansari should clarify that he would not impose his views upon the Congress and would concentrate on fostering communal unity.[29] Ansari agreed to stay in the running for the presidency but did not respond to the one-sided harangues of Gandhi. He probably felt that as a leader of long-standing he had the freedom to hold and the right to express his views.

If Gandhi had the choice he would have probably promoted somebody else for the presidential *gaddi*. But he was not prepared to risk alienating the Congress Muslims and causing embarrassment to the High Command which had, in principle, endorsed the choice of Ansari. So, he announced that Ansari's election should stand. He assured the Provincial Congress Committees [PCC], somewhat arbitrarily, that Ansari would not use the presidential office to enforce his political views through the Congress. 'His integrity is the surest guarantee of his guiding the deliberations of the Congress as an absolutely impartial chairman and of his giving full effect to any agreement that may be arrived at by the various parties in the Congress.'[30]

The Congress reception committee, as was the practice, elected Ansari as its forty-second president on 4 September. Fourteen out of the seventeen PCC's voted for him; the only other nominee was Kelkar who had been nominated by three PCC's including his home constituency. Wrote the *Hindustan Times*:

> The nation is to be congratulated on the singular sobriety of judgement displayed at a crucial period of its history. A fitter recipient than Dr Ansari for the highest honour in its power could not have been found at the present juncture. His election at the crucial period of our history when the country is groaning under communal antagonism appears...to constitute a valuable national asset.[31]

Similar comments, coming from opposite party standpoints, show what a reputation he had at the time and how broadly it was based.

[29]Gandhi to Ansari, 26 August 1927, Hasan (ed.), *Muslims and the Congress*, p. 22.

[30]Statement, n.d., ibid., p. 23. Also, speech at Madras, see *Hamdard*, 9 September 1927.

[31]*Hindustan Times*, 7 September 1927; *Basumati*, 13 September, Ansari Papers. JMI.

Elevated to the presidency, Ansari followed the time-honoured tradition of inviting prominent Indian leaders, Hindu and Muslim, cooperator and non-cooperator, to attend the Congress at Madras. Referring to the disastrous results of divided counsel and disunion, he made the plea for reuniting nationalist forces. Divisions in the body politic were merely over details: on matters of principle there was virtual unanimity. The reception accorded to Birkenhead's (1872-1930) 'lily white list', the all-British Statutory Commission, was a case in point. It provided an occasion to reunite those who were slowly drifting apart. 'If we can take advantage of the opportunity thus presented to us to organize public opinion and focus it on the speedy attainment of our goal, we shall have created a force in our political life which shall be irresistible'.[32]

Ansari received a number of encouraging replies, some from unexpected quarters. Annie Besant, T.B. Sapru (1875-1949), and B.C. Pal (1858-1932) found the atmosphere favourable for teamwork and suggested the getting together of various parties to draw up a constitution on the lines of the 1916 Congress-Muslim League scheme. Hasan Imam (1871-1933) and the Raja of Mahmudabad were for boycotting the Simon Commission; Mohammad Yaqub agreed that a large number of Muslims should attend the Congress; Abdur Rahim (1867-1952), though unprepared to meet other leaders on the Congress platform, wished to make plans for concerted action; Ibrahim Rahimtoola (1862-1942) affirmed that political progress could only be advanced by pulling together.[33]

Among those who introduced a discordant note was the Home Rule Leaguer, Joseph Baptista (1864-1931), who argued that the boycott of the Statutory Commission would give a pretext to the British government to 'restore autocracy on the ruins of dyarchy'. G.S. Khaparde (1854-1938), once a close lieutenant of Tilak, doubted the effectiveness of the boycott plan. The two Arya Samaj leaders—Bhai Parmanand (1874-1947) and Lala Hansraj

[32]Hasan (ed.), *Muslims and the Congress*, p. 24. M.N. Roy wrongly believed that Ansari desired peace with British imperialism. In a statement published in the *Times of India* on 10 November 1927, Ansari had already stated that the difference between the government and the people of India was so great and fundamental that 'they would be considered self-sufficient for the people to stand aside and abstain from any participation in the work of the commission'. See Adhikari (ed.), *Documents*, op. cit., p. 103.

[33]Ibid., pp. 25-42.

(1860-1938)—on the other hand, expressed disdain for manifestos containing either platitudes on unity or schemes of compromises which found little favour with most groups. Hindu-Muslim differences, observed Parmanand, were based on fundamental principles and the two communities were so far wide apart that cooperation on a common platform was neither desirable nor possible.[34] In a similar strain Haji Hidayet Hosain (1881-1935) of Kanpur indulged in outspoken criticism. He expressed his misgivings, shared by some of his contemporaries, in response to Ansari's circular to attend the Congress. The Haji wrote:

> It is admitted on all hands that no political advancement is possible till the Hindus and the Muslims unite; what have even the Congressmen done to secure this unity. Indeed some of the Congress workers have been the worst offenders in this respect. Has the Congress even as a body attempted to go to the root cause of the Hindu-Muslim riots? Have you realized that it is only since 1923, when the *shuddhi* and *sangathan* were started, that these riots began to repeat themselves with such frequent obstinacy? Nobody has got a right to take exception to these movements but if the object of the *shuddhi* were merely political and pursued by physical force, threat, violence and fraud in order to reduce the numerical strength of the Muslims, then I think these movements can secure no other purpose except the creation of an unbridgeable gulf between the two communities...
>
> Mere honeyed phrases and appeals couched in eloquent and winsome phraseology to the communities to live in amity and grace has never proved to be of any avail. You cry in the wilderness every year and this year you repeat the same process over again. It may do your soul some good, but it does nothing to us. The Congress does not represent the Hindus now, it has never represented the Muslims. You are then a group of men, well meaning, well intentioned, honest and sincere, but all the same afraid to look at things at their face, incapable of tapping the root cause of differences and therefore impotent to devise effective means of cure.[35]

This was strong language. The Haji knew this. He confessed that he was being impertinent. But he was stating, as well as

[34] *Hindustan Times*, 15 December 1927.

[35] 12 December 1927, Hasan (ed.), *Muslims and the Congress*, pp. 41-2.

it was possible for a contemporary, unendowed with the advantage of hindsight, the tangled state of communal prejudices that seemed to inspire people either with cynicism or with woolly idealism.

If the composition of Ansari's entourage for the Madras Congress was any indication, his initiatives certainly bore fruit. It included politicians of the old Delhi-Aligarh axis: Khaliquzzaman, Shuaib Qureshi, Abdur Rahman Siddiqi, Aziz Ansari, the Ali Brothers, Faridul Haq Ansari and Zakir Husain. For the time being party rancour was buried, differences eschewed and political rivalries set aside. All Madras, in fact, seemed awash in enthusiasm for Ansari, who won nearly unanimous applause for being in the national spotlight.[36] Ansari's appeal seemed to work and party unity—on the surface, at least—was achieved against heavy odds.

Flanked on either side by Congress stalwarts and amidst cries of *Bande Mataram, Mahatma Gandhi ki jai ho* and *Hindu-Muslim bhai bhai*, the forty-second president of the Congress strode to the podium to deliver his address: that may have been Ansari's best political moment ever.

In his hour and a half long presidential pronouncement, Ansari, as was to be expected of him, stressed unity—unity among communities, among political parties, among Congressmen and among legislators. Minor political irritants need not stand in the way of purposeful cooperation to thwart the sinister designs of the common adversary. And crucially, given his image as an apostle of Hindu-Muslim unity, Ansari insisted that Hindus and Muslims sink their differences and abide by the agreement reached at the Calcutta Unity Conference.

Ansari devoted a substantial part of his speech to the Statutory Commission. The high-handed manner in which government disregarded the wishes of the Indian people must serve as an eye-opener even to the most confirmed optimist. The enemy was thus met head on, at least rhetorically, and the thematics of the campaign against the Commission were set forth with precision and daring. 'No sane or self-respecting Indian,' he continued, 'can ever admit the claim of Great Britain to be the sole judge of the measure and time of India's political advance. We alone know our needs and requirements best and ours must be the decisive voice in the determination of our future. It is

[36]*Hindu*, 23 December 1927, *Daily Express*, 24 December 1927; *Justice*, 24 December 1927, Ansari Papers, JML.

our inherent and inalienable right.' He therefore announced: 'We can have no part or lot in a Commission which has been appointed in direct defiance of the declared will of the people of India'—a line that brought an approving roar from those present at the Congress session.

Quite understandably, Ansari's major concern was the 'ubiquitous microbe' which had infected every sphere of national activity. A nation trying to shake off foreign domination could not afford to carry on an internecine struggle, that freedom and communalism were incompatible and both self-respect and self-interest required looking beyond momentary and sectional advantage to the lasting national gain. He detailed the history of Congress efforts to resolve the political and religious differences, urged Congressmen to explain and popularize them and called upon Hindus and Muslims to exorcise the demon of communal and political discord.

The speech was logical, moralistic, intense and humourless. It was clear and forceful and as good-natured as the man himself. Ansari was not expected to suggest a radical or even a substantial change in the Congress programme; he was only expected, in view of the need for both political and communal unity, to make a forceful plea to all sections and communities to join the Congress and make it a strong national organization and articulate his vision of the national future. The *Tribune* complimented him on his speech, adding: 'It was exactly the kind of lead to the Congress and the country that one had a right to expect from a man called upon to take up the national leadership at this supreme crisis'.[37] He did not play to the gallery, avoided the use of catchwords calculated to confuse and mislead and refrained from suggesting heroic and spectacular methods for attaining swaraj.[38] The policies he suggested were endorsed by most Indian nationalists and his message, commented the *Indian Daily Telegraph*, was not 'one of retrogression or stagnation, of depression or despair, but one of unflinching determination and unswerving faith in India's great destiny'.[39] The speech as a whole was admired and praised across party lines.

The Madras Congress adopted three vital decisions which had

[37]*Tribune*, 26 December 1927. For comments on Ansari's presidential address, see Ansari Papers, JMI.

[38]*Leader*, Note on the Press, UP, for the week ending 7 January 1928, ibid.

[39]Ibid.; *Bombay Chronicle*, 27 December 1928.

formed the main burden of Ansari's presidential address. In the first place, consensus was reached on the communal question; the 'Unity Resolution' adopted was on the lines suggested by Ansari. The second resolution called for an effective boycott of the Statutory Commission 'at every stage and in every form'; the lead in this respect was also given by Ansari first in his letter of 1 December 1927 and later in his presidential speech. And finally, the Congress committed itself to complete national independence at the insistence of Jawaharlal. On 27 December, he moved the resolution that 'this Congress declares the goal of the Indian people to be complete National Independence'. Gandhi thought that the resolution was 'hastily conceived and thoughtlessly passed'. Right-wing Congressmen agreed. Privately, the Mahatma rebuked Jawaharlal for encouraging 'mischief mongers and hooligans' and for not thinking out the whole situation and the resolutions which might be appropriate.[40]

The significance of the Madras Congress was best summed up by the *Leader*:

> The Madras Congress session has been the most remarkable and successful one since the waning of the non-cooperation movement. The Presidential address was also unique of its kind, breathed a spirit of unity and harmony, and was characteristically outspoken. The complete independence resolution betokens the high moral courage of the Congress and is a necessary corollary of the dictum that Swaraj is the birth-right of the people. The boycott resolution has placed a practical programme before the country and the unity resolution marks the culminating point of the success of the last session of the Congress.[41]

The Nehru Report and its Aftermath

From the early days of their entry into the legislative councils, the Swarajists had pressed for revising the Montagu-Chelmsford reforms. Motilal, leader of the Swaraj Party in the legislative assembly, called for dismantling the half-way houses of dyarchy

[40]Pandey, *Nehru*, p. 129; Judith M. Brown, *Gandhi and Civil Disobedience: The Mahatma in Indian Politics 1928-1934* (Cambridge, 1977), p. 22.

[41]Note on the Press, UP, for the week ending 14 January 1928; Adhikari (ed.), *Documents*, op.cit., p. 313.

and the setting up of full provincial autonomy. When the report of the Muddiman Committee was considered by the assembly in September 1925, he proposed fundamental changes in the constitutional machinery. His motion was adopted. In November of that year the government announced the appointment of a Statutory Commission, and from April 1926 to November 1927 the viceroy and the secretary of state worked out the form, the terms of reference, and the composition of the Commission. On 8 November the British Government appointed a Statutory or Parliamentary Commission, known from its chairman's name as the Simon Commission, two years before the time laid down by the Act of 1919.

The exclusion of Indians from the commission caused quite a consternation. When its members reached Bombay's port, its years of projected labour were already doomed, torpedoed before it got underway, by the pig-headedness of a narrow-minded coterie of imperial managers who put their selfish interests above the needs, aspirations and just demands of most humankind. The Muslim League, led by Jinnah and the *Jamiyat al-ulama* declared emphatically that the commission and the procedure, as announced, were unacceptable. Jinnah declared on 30 December 1927: 'Jallianwala Bagh was a physical butchery, the Simon Commission is a butchery of our souls'.[42]

When the Congress met at Madras at the end of the year, it voted to boycott the commission, proclaimed independence as its goal and resolved to draft a constitution of its own. Earlier, representatives of all parties, including the Liberal Federation, Muslim League, Hindu Mahasabha, held their first meeting on 12 February 1928 to respond to the British challenge that Indians could not produce a constitution of their own. Motilal and Jawaharlal were there, as were Jinnah, Lajpat Rai, Malaviya, Jayakar and most of the other leaders of political India.

From February to July 1928 Ansari was engrossed in the deliberations of the All-Parties Conference, advising its members on matters small and large and providing a welcome leavening influence within the buttoned-up Motilal entourage. As president, at a time of deepening crisis against the government and its allies in India, Ansari was more stretched, with more work and more responsibility, than ever before. It was the kind of situation

[42]Stanley Wolpert, *Jinnah of Pakistan* (Oxford University Press, New York, 1984), p. 90.

in which he throve and which brought out the best in him. He spent long hours in negotiations and manoeuvres that were as obscure and confused at the time as they remain in retrospect. On 18 May he chaired a crucial meeting which took the momentous decision of appointing a committee, headed by Motilal, to draft a nationalist constitution.

Ansari's troubles did not end here. When the Nehru Committee Report was published on 15 August, he emerged as its foremost campaigner. In so doing, he made many enemies as a group of Muslims, mainly from UP, hammered away at the recommendations of the Nehru Report: the abolition of separate electorates, abandonment of reservation of seats for Muslim majorities in Bengal and the Punjab and of weightage in those provinces where Muslims were in a minority. And during the All-Parties Conference and the All-Parties National Convention, he found himself in a series of prickly exchanges, one involving Shaukat Ali who reproached Ansari for treating the 'Muslim viewpoint' with contempt and betraying the community's interest.[43]

Though he occasionally displayed flashes of toughness, Ansari appeared determined to maintain a statesmanlike reserve. He tried hard to set the fears at rest, pursuing his task against a running barrage of ridicule, but without success. In the end he concluded pityingly that Muslim opposition was based on ignorance and confusion of the rights of minorities with the principle of representation. 'I have been writing and sending telegrams to Muslim friends all over India,' he informed Motilal, 'to start an organized campaign in support of the constitution and against the senseless and unreasoned opposition started by Shaukat Ali and his party along with his henchmen, the Muslim reactionaries.'[44] The report, according to him, provided more 'real' and 'solid' safeguards to the Muslims than the League of Nations to racial minorities of the newly-constituted states of Europe. The value

[43]The recommendations of the Nehru Report have been discussed and analyzed at length by me in *Nationalism and Communal Politics*, ch. 8. For Shaukat Ali's criticism, see *Hamdard*, 3 September 1928. Ansari, however, issued a general statement answering criticisms levelled against him by Shaukat Ali and a section of the Urdu press. He denied the charge that Muslim speakers were not allowed to express their views. Ansari to Motilal, 9 September 1928, F. No. 105, 1928, AICC Papers (Suppl.); Also, *Hamdard*, 5 September 1928.

[44]Ansari to Motilal, 19 September 1928, ibid. For Ansari's speech at the All-Parties National Convention, Hasan (ed.), *Muslims and the Congress*, pp. 306-10.

of constitutional safeguards, in any case, was questionable, for they were 'bounties on inefficiency' 'The more a minority has of them,' he said, 'the more it will need and protected from the bracing spirit of free competition by charitable provisions of constitution, it will sink deeper and deeper into ignorance, fanaticism and sloth to be stifled ultimately by the very cords which had appeared to offer it a partial support.'

The Nehru Report, stated Ansari, 'heralded the dawn of a brighter day'. At the Calcutta Convention he warned the delegates of an alien government and its attempts to widen the religious divide and the communalists who were 'inspired by the gospel of more bread and butter'. At the same time, there was no reason to fear the communalists whose 'days are numbered'. 'Already a new generation is coming to the front,' announced Ansari, 'to which differences between Hindus and Mussalmans are unknown and which will not and cannot think in communal terms'. How unprophetic was this view is borne out by the future history of the Indian subcontinent! Ansari's well-meaning statement failed to recognize the intensity of communal feelings and was devoid of any appreciation of how, over the years, the political demands of certain Muslim groups had stiffened and that it was no longer possible to either ignore them or to dismiss them lightly. There was no escape from a recognition of this painful reality. To deny, as Ansari did, the deep communal divide in the country and to brush opposition aside or smother it with ridicule or vituperation served no purpose. If anything, it led to the belief in some Muslim circles that the Congress was unwilling to come to terms with the political demands embodied in the Delhi proposals and in various Muslim League resolutions passed from time to time. This was the burden of Jinnah's speech at the Calcutta Convention where he staked several issues. But his arguments carried no conviction with his audience which, according to one of his recent biographers, marked an even sharper veering off from the road of the Congress than Nagpur had been in December 1920. Nagpur had ended Act One. Calcutta finished Act Two. 'This time there would be a larger intermission.'[45]

Ansari's defence of the Nehru Report was disapproved. Shaukat Ali, delighted at Ansari's discomfiture, burst forth in his best

[45]Wolpert, op.cit., pp. 101-2.

denunciatory vein, chiding Ansari for playing the 'generous liberal minded patriot at the expense of one's people' and for supporting a report which 'intentionally treated the Muslim point of view with undeserved contempt'.[46] 'I know the present Hindu mentality well,' he told Ansari, adding that 'they do not want our friendship; they want our allegiance and God-willing, they will never get that.' He charged that

> in your blind adherence to Motilal Nehru and other Hindus, you betrayed Muslims and your co-workers and we both are free now to take our lines of action. Non-cooperation was ruined by these people, chances for Hindu-Muslim friendship have been throttled, an understanding between princes and people thwarted, Swaraj Party dismembered and now you yourself see what is being done to kill Congress, which has ceased to be National now. It has become an adjunct of the Hindu Mahasabha and will soon be a seeker of favours at the door of the English.[47]

Mohamed Ali, fresh from his trip to Europe, echoed the same feelings, pillorying Ansari in his public speeches; indeed the Nehru Report ushered in a new phase of personal bitterness between the two men. The report, he said, would establish 'a legalized tyranny of numbers', jeopardize Muslim interests everywhere, and lead to the ascendancy of the Hindu Mahasabha.[48] Ansari had actually warned Motilal in mid-September that 'it would be a hard fight as it is, but if Jinnah and Mohamed Ali both go against us the tussle will be harder still'. Mohamed Ali's outburst confirmed his worst fears. At the same time it did not come as a surprise. Over the years, he had developed a point of view from which everything said or done by any Hindu or Congress Muslim was attributed to the Mahasabha influence.

Mohamed Ali, the man with a caustic tongue, seized the opportunity at the Khilafat Committee meeting—convened on 21 December 1928 to elect delegates for the forthcoming All-India Khilafat Conference—to snuff out opposition. With the connivance of Shafee Daoodi, the hot-headed Shaukat Ali and Haji Abdullah Haroon of Sind, he disrupted the proceedings, upbraided those who stood by the Nehru Report and had his

[46]To Ansari, 6 September 1929, F. No. 105, AICC Papers.

[47]To Ansari, 19 May 1929, Hasan (ed.), *Muslims and the Congress*, p. 70.

[48]For details see Hasan, *Mohamed Ali Ideology and Politics*, pp. 94-7.

list of delegates adopted. He caused a similar uproar at the Central Khilafat Committee meeting because he could rouse the partisans behind him but had not the touch to carry his appeal to the groups other than his own. In consequence, about forty-five prominent members of the Central Khilafat Committee, including Ansari, T.A.K. Sherwani and Mujibur Rahman, walked out and decided to boycott the Khilafat Conference.[49] A few days later, Mohamed Ali attended the All-Parties Muslim Conference at Delhi, convened by the pro-government lobby and their allies in the assembly and the legislative councils.

Caught up in the melee, Ansari was disgusted by the rough and overbearing attitude of the Ali Brothers. He found Shaukat Ali, in particular, opinionated and conceited, a dictator who shouted down his opponents and treated those who disagreed with him as if they were trying to start a breakaway body. Having idolized him for the last eighteen years, 'worshipped the very ground on which you trod, [and] had given you such friendship, love and loyalty', he was no longer willing to follow him. 'When I saw the clay feet of my idol,' he wrote some months after the incident, 'I felt as if the world had turned topsy-turvy and that I could never, in future, trust anyone whoever it might be.' He painfully added that friendship with the robust Maulana would never be the same. 'At an age,' he wrote,

> new friendship and new attachments are difficult, if not impossible to make. Therefore, life in future would be the less fuller, the less richer for want of such friends as you and I have been. I, however, bow to the inexorable march of events and have fortified myself against whatever the future may have in store, and have prepared myself to go on working in the service of my faith and my country, in the best manner that I can do.[50]

Ansari and the Ali Brothers were old comrades who had worked together in several political movements from the time of the Medical Mission to Constantinople. But they drifted apart on the issue of the Nehru Report. The Ali Brothers' extremely fragile relationship with the Congress was also disrupted for the

[49] An interesting analysis of the Muslim Conference has been attempted by David Page. I am not aware of any other study on the subject.

[50] 14 June 1929, Hasan (ed.), *Muslims and the Congress*, pp. 65-6.

same reason and they gravitated towards the politically conservative All-Parties Muslim Conference. Writing to Mazharul Haq about them in the most scathingly critical terms, Ansari referred to their association with the 'Aga Khan & Co' whose only 'distinction is that they have always been reactionary both to Indian and Muslim affairs'. He added that their differences which initially concerned a few provisions of the Nehru Report 'have now grown into a conflict of the very outlook.'[51]

Ansari was unfairly accused of political apostasy and opportunism. He could hardly be expected to allow his political views to be permanently governed by the friendships of his youth. At some stage—probably after the Khilafat movement had petered out—he weighed the wisdom of following Mohamed Ali and found it wanting; references to him in Ansari's private letters were at best equivocal and sometimes derogatory. He realized that he could not take the views of anyone, however distinguished, on trust; he had to work out his own views for himself.

Not only were the political methods of Ansari and the Ali Brothers different—sometimes embarrassingly different—but also their perception of the Congress and its role in Indian society. Ansari was among those who refused to become the drift-wood of the communal tide and who during the worst period of communal animus did not allow his broad national outlook to be perverted. He adhered to the Congress movement which, according to his firm belief, served the larger interests of the country and derived legitimacy from its impressive record of launching countrywide crusades against the raj. The Ali Brothers held the same view until the mid-1920s. The Congress, wrote Mohamed Ali in 1925, 'is and must remain the only national political organization.... Let the Muslim League and the Hindu Mahasabha both perish, let the Congress and the nation survive.'[52] In 1928-1930, however, this opinion was drastically altered. The Congress, the hero of the Khilafat days came to believe, was no longer a national organization but a Hindu one, unprepared to condemn those Hindus who were perpetuating communal discord and unprepared to work towards the creation of an India in which all communities could live in harmony. The Nehru constitution was the 'legalised tyranny of numbers', for it threatened to subject the minority province Muslims to a

[51]To Mazharul Haq, 7 September 1929, ibid., pp. 86-7.
[52]*Comrade*, 9 January 1925.

communal Hindu majority. Those Muslims who supported such a constitution, chief among whom was Ansari, were Congress stooges.

Mohamed Ali's relationship with Gandhi also reached a breaking point. There was no sign of this happening until the mid-1920s when the Maulana venerated the Mahatma and held him in great esteem.[53] 'There is none more free from selfish motives, from jealousy and personal ambitions,' observed Mohamed Ali.[54] He also reaffirmed that he held certain views 'with regard to the way in which India can win her freedom, which for the most part I share with Gandhi, whom I am proud to regard as my chief.'[55] But in the midst of the Nehru Report controversy Mohamed Ali quoted from Gandhi's writings of 1924 and 1925 to show that his erstwhile chief was now converted to a different creed, was striving for different goals, had defeated all Muslim attempts for a compromise and was 'giving free reins to the communalism of the majority'.[56]

The gulf that separated Gandhi and Mohamed Ali seemed unbridgeable; in fact Gandhi conceded that the Ali Brothers 'had a fairly heavy list of complaints' against him and that he could not make an impression on them as they distrusted the role of his associates. This was confirmed by Mohamed Ali's outburst in April 1930 at the Muslim Conference. 'We refuse to join Mr Gandhi,' stated the Mahatma's lieutenant during the Khilafat and non-cooperation days, 'because his movement [civil disobedience] is not a movement for complete independence of India but of making the seventy millions of Indian Muslims dependent on the Hindu Mahasabha.' Symbolic of the collapse of the old alliance on which Gandhi had built non-cooperation was Mohamed Ali's appeal to Muslims not to join civil disobedience because its goal was Hindu raj.[57]

The vehemence of Mohamed Ali's attack, while certain to alienate many of his political friends as Ansari, was not certain to attract new support; in fact its immediate effect seems to

[53]'I regard and call my 'Bapu' more than a political chief and more than a brother'. *Comrade*, 9 January 1925.

[54]Ibid., 1 May 1925; *Hamdard*, 24 August 1926.

[55]Ibid., 16 October 1925. Also, see Afzal Iqbal (ed.), *Select speeches and writings of Maulana Mohamed Ali* (Lahore, 1944), pp. 331-2, 337.

[56]Hasan, *Mohamed Ali Ideology and Politics*, p. 191.

[57]Ibid., pp. 101-2.

have been even to increase his unpopularity. And it could not have helped his uneasy frame of mind to know—as he must have done—that his reputation, both personal and political, had not been improved by his outburst against Gandhi and the Congress. Cooperation requires give-and-take, but there was no give in Mohamed Ali's politics. He became a political isolationist and preferred ploughing a lone furrow. Many of his erstwhile comrades who had been the butt of his ridicule, his satirical verses and cutting epigrams were glad to find an opportunity or an excuse to turn against him and to think and speak ill of him.

It has been necessary to dwell at some length on Mohamed Ali's role because, in the years to come, Ansari had to counteract his influence through the All-India Nationalist Muslim Party. Mohamed Ali represented a stream in Indian Muslim politics which threatened to destroy Ansari's vision of a secular polity, free from communal prejudice and animosity. Though Mohamed Ali died in 1931, he left behind a legacy which was potentially divisive. Ansari's task was to stem this process and to weld the two communities into a coherent whole.

8. Ansari's car

9. Ansari with members of the family.

10. Members of the Congress Working Committee at *Dar-us-Salam* during Gandhi-Irwin negotiations.

11. At the inauguration of the Congress Hospital at Allahabad. In the front row (from left except the third) Mahadev Desai, Rajendra Prasad, Vallabhbhai Patel, M.A. Ansari, Jawaharlal Nehru, M.M. Malaviya, J.M. Sengupta, Perinben Captain and Maniben Patel. *Behind* Malaviya and Abul Kalam Azad are Purshottamdas Tandon and C. Rajagopalchari. In back row fifth from left, is Rafi Ahmad Kidwai and third from right is Asaf Ali.

12. Zohra Ansari, M.A. Ansari, Halide Edib and Sarojini Naidu

13. With Tej Bahadur Sapru

WANTED CAREFUL DRIVING

A certain section of No-changers in the United Provinces is reported to be firmly against the Council-entry Programme.

14. 'Wanted Careful Driving'. Cartoon from the *Hindustan Times*, 31 March 1934.

DANGER OF RELEASING THE GENII

In the Arabian Nights, there is a queer story of the "Fisherman and the Genie."

15. 'Danger of Releasing the Geni'. Cartoon from the *Hindustan Times* 22 April 1934.

"WITHER INDIA?"

Nationalist Leaders are taking counsel together in Delhi on future policy as to the direction in which they should next proceed.

16. 'Wither India'

8

Leading the Congress Muslims

> Communalism is too harmful to be left to itself in the hope that it will ..e a natural death some day in the definite future.... Your first duty, therefore, is to carry on a relentless crusade against communalism as an active guiding principle of Indian political life [M.A. Ansari in 1929]
>
> *Modern Review*, July 1929, p. 104.

IN THE AFTERMATH of the Nehru Report controversy, the Congress had to reckon with the crystallization of Muslim political demands, embodied in Jinnah's 'Fourteen Points' and articulated by the All-Parties Muslim Conference. It also had to allay Muslim fears arising out of the Nehru Report which were echoed at the Khilafat and Muslim League meetings held in the Christmas week of 1928. Gandhi tried to soothe suspicions with assurances that swaraj did not mean Hindu raj and held discussions with Jinnah in February and August 1929 to explore possible avenues to peace. But, as on previous occasions, his endeavours were thwarted by Lajpat Rai, Malaviya, Jayakar, Moonje, working president of the Hindu Mahasabha (1927-35), and Kelkar who urged the Mahatma not to reach a solution outside the terms of the Nehru Report.[1] Lajpat Rai refused to accept any modification,[2] while Jayakar pressured Gandhi not to yield to the Muslim demands on the ground that the government, as in 1919, would deliberately make any concessions part of a constitution.[3] Caught

[1]Jayakar to Gandhi, 23 August 1929, Jayakar Papers (437), NAI. In his reply, Gandhi assured Jayakar that he had not 'found anybody' because he had no representative capacity. 'I simply listened to Mr Jinnah's exposition of his position. Similarly with the Ali Brothers too, I heard what they had to say. With the latter the talk turned upon their grievance against me for my reticence.' Gandhi to Jayakar, 24 August 1929, *CWG*, Vol. XLI, pp. 289-319.

[2]Lajpat Rai to Motilal Nehru, n.d., F. No. 108 (Suppl.), AICC Papers; also, see Moonje to Malaviya, 31 July 1928, Moonje to Gandhi, 5 August 1929, Jayakar Papers (437).

[3]Quoted in Uma Kaura, *Muslims and Indian Nationalism: The Emergence of the Demand for India's Partition* (Delhi, 1977), p. 50; R. J. Moore, *The Crisis of Indian Unity 1917-1940* (Delhi, 1974), p. 101.

up in the cross fire between the Muslim League and the Hindu Mahasabha, Gandhi wrote to Motilal in anguish: 'How that can be done [resolving the communal deadlock] or whether it should be done, you know best. My mind is in a whirl in this matter. The atmosphere is too foggy for me to see clearly'.[4]

Since the Gandhi-Jinnah talks were not leading to tangible results and the crusade against the Nehru Report was gaining momentum, the Lahore Congress prudently decided to let the Nehru Report lápse. To woo the Sikhs and Muslims it was resolved not to accept any solution of the communal problem without the concurrence of the minorities concerned.[5] Gandhi hoped that the two momentous decisions arrived at Lahore—declaration of complete independence and the launching of civil disobedience—would enable leaders of various shades of opinion to draw their followers into the anti-colonial struggle. He wrote in *Navajivan:* 'If we have true freedom we will shed communal fear. Hindus and Muslims will cease to fear one another'.[6]

To soothe Muslim feelings was not enough. The issue was how to arrest their growing alienation from the Congress. The process had begun soon after the Khilafat movement came to a halt and was attributed to a wide range of factors, including the supposed hegemony of the Hindu Mahasabha, Congress' inability to curb assertive and militant expressions of Hindu revivalism, and its reluctance to recognize Muslim political aspirations. Such had been the burden of Abdur Rahim's highly inflammatory presidential address at the Muslim League session in December 1925.[7]

The charges levelled against the Congress were often flimsy, exaggerated and misleading. But because of its low credibility in certain areas it was possible for Muslim publicists and propagandists, aided and abetted by the government, to convince their followers that the Congress would jettison their interests in any future scheme of swaraj and that their 'salvation' lay in either forging an alliance with the government or in pursuing independent political action. An index of the success of Abdur Rahim

[4]Kaura, op. cit., p. 51.

[5]Resolution on the communal problem passed by the CWC, July 1931, F. No. G-37/1931, AICC Papers; *IQR*, July-December 1929, pp. 310-11; Motilal to secretary, reception committee, *Jamiyat al-ulama*, 29 April 1930, Motilal Nehru Papers.

[6]9 January 1930, *CWG*, Vol. XLVII, p. 381.

[7]Pirzada (ed.), *Foundations of Pakistan*, Vol. 2, pp. 42-4.

in Bengal and Mohammad Shafi in the Punjab was the steady communalization of politics as well as the gradual decline in Muslim participation at annual Congress sessions and their representation in national, provincial and district Congress committees.

Table 1 indicates the attendance of Muslim delegates at Congress sessions from 1918 to 1923. Though complete figures for later years are not available, the number of Muslims gradually dwindled from a few hundred to less than a score. Likewise, Muslim representation in the AICC was impressive, showing an increase from 11.1 per cent in 1919 to 24.5 per cent in 1923 (Table 2). In 1922-23, 84 of the 338 AICC members were Muslims. By 1928, their number was reduced to 54 out of 332.[8] Provincial and district Congress committees also had very few Muslim members. In UP only seven Muslims served on various district committees: one each in Gonda, Allahabad, Jhansi, Moradabad, Fyzabad, Azamgarh, and two in Barabanki.[9]

The desertion of Muslims from the Swaraj party was linked with their alienation from Congress. In 1922-23 Motilal built his support among an influential group of Lucknow and Allahabad based professional men in UP: Sherwani, Rafi Ahmad Kidwai, Khaliquzzaman and M.H. Kidwai.[10] In Bengal Das forged an opportunistic alliance with several leading Khilafatists and lured them into supporting the Swaraj party by offering a set of extravagant concessions. In consequence, his party swept the November 1923 polls, capturing an overall majority of seats, including half the Muslim seats. Muslim support was strongest in the eastern division of Chittagong and the northern division of Rajshahi, the storm centres of the Khilafat movement in Bengal. Likewise, the Swarajists won 10 of the 15 Muslim seats in the Calcutta Corporation elections held in April 1928. Here

[8]F. No. G/59, 1928, AICC Papers.

[9]F. No. 11, 1926, ibid.

[10]Motilal was a patron of such men, as indeed of other Muslims, whom he helped to find jobs. See, for instance, the case of Hakim Wali who was recommended for the post of executive officer in Banaras municipality. Motilal to T.A.K. Sherwani, 29 July 1928, F. No. 60 (Suppl.), 1925-26, ibid. Motilal also ensured that the PCC's found Muslims of Congress and Swarajist views to elect candidates for elections. In a directive to the Sind PCC he insisted that 'the PCC even though constituted wholly by Hindus must rise above communalism and show that it makes no distinction between Nationalists whether they are Hindus or Muslims'. F. No. 76 (Suppl.), 1928, ibid.

TABLE 8.1

ATTENDANCE OF MUSLIM DELEGATES AT THE SESSIONS OF THE INDIAN NATIONAL CONGRESS, 1918-23

Year	*Total no. of delegates*	*No. of Muslim delegates*
1918	3,975	205
1919	6,717	314
1920	13,532	1,050
1921	4,201	521
1922	NA	NA
1923	1,550	111

SOURCE: Compiled from Reports of the Annual Sessions of the Indian National Congress.

TABLE 8.2

COMPOSITION OF THE AICC, 1919-1923

Religion	*1919 (161 members)*	*1920*	*1921*	*1922*	*1923*
		(163 members)		*(338 members)*	
Hindus	139	133	124	242	248
Muslims	18	21	33	84	83
Sikhs	—	2	2	9	8
Parsees	3	4	2	—	—
Christians	1	2	2	3	2

SOURCE: Gopal Krishna, 'The Indian National Congress, 1918-1923' (D.Phil thesis, Oxford, 1960), p. 747.

the Muslim vote was strongest in central mercantile wards of the city where the electorate consisted of up-country, Urdu speaking merchants, property owners and artisans who had formed the backbone of the Khilafat movement and who now chose pro-nationalist and anti-British candidates in 10 of the 11 wards in which they voted.[11]

This impressive support was steadily eroded after the Bengal Congress repudiated the Das pact. There were 15 Muslim Swarajists in 1923: there were none in 1926. The *Mussalman* charged that the party was inimically disposed towards its erstwhile allies, while the *Satyagrahi* (16 February), *Taraqqee* (4 May) and the *Soltan* (29 June) believed that the Bengal Congress was converted into a platform for preaching *shuddhi*

[11] Mcpherson, *The Muslim Microcosm*, p. 80.

and *sangathan.*[12] Husayn Suhrawardy (1893-1963) and Abdul Karim (1863-1943), leading negotiators of the Das Pact, quit the Swarajist group and led their community in Calcutta deeper into the labyrinth of distinctly communal politics.[13] The picture was the same in UP.[14] As against 11 Muslims nominated and 4 elected in 1923, 6 were renominated in 1926 and only 1 returned. So widespread was the feeling of insecurity that some Muslims who had, in the recent past, contributed to Congress' popularity were now arrayed among its enemies.[15]

The same mood was reflected elsewhere. Of the eight Swarajist Muslims returned in 1923 to the Central Assembly, only 3 were elected in 1926. Many of them were irked by Motilal's attitude towards reforms in the North-West Frontier Province. Syed Murtaza, a Swarajist from Madras, was one of them. He accused Motilal of sacrificing the Frontier Muslims in order to woo Lajpat Rai on the eve of the 1926 elections.[16] Equally harsh was Mohammad Shafee Daoodi's indictment. 'Temporary success in your political endeavours has got greater value for you than the more enduring rapprochement of the two great communities of India'. He charged that the Congress had been gradually drifting towards the Mahasabha since 1923 and that it had now reduced itself to being its tool.[17] Both Murtaza and Daoodi resigned from the Swaraj Party in 1926.

In the midst of such mutual acrimony, the silver lining from the Congress point of view was that political activity among Muslims was sporadic and fragmented and the polarization of communities along religious lines had yet to occur. Conflicting regional, local and class interests—a consequence of the uneven development of the Muslims in different parts of the country—deepened the fissures within a supposedly 'Muslim party' and exposed the hollowness of the League's claim to represent all Muslims. The formal split in that body between the Jinnah and

[12] *Mussalman*, 27 April 1926. Report on Native Newspapers, Bengal, January-December 1927, pp. 127, 204, 271.

[13] Mcpherson. op. cit., sections 5 and 6 in chapter 5.

[14] Pandey, *The Ascendancy of the Congress*, section 5 in chapter 5.

[15] Quoted in ibid., p. 145.

[16] Page, op. cit., pp. 132-3.

[17] Shafee Daoodi to Motilal Nehru, 26 March 1929, F. No. 96, Motilal Nehru Papers. Also, see *The Frontier Question in the Assembly, being the statements of Pandit Motilal Nehru, MLA, Maulvi Shafi Daudi, MLA, and Syed Murtaza, MLA* (Delhi, 1926).

the Shafi factions in 1927 was symptomatic of the deep-rooted divisions in the so-called monolithic Muslim polity. Any new party, whether cobbled together by the Khilafatists or the Leaguers, promised to be a splintered structure that could collapse at any moment. Such was the fate of the Muslim Conference after 1932. The organizers, like the Dutch army, were all generals but no soldiers. Most belonged to the landowning class and none of them was prepared to spearhead the movement or to follow the other.[18]

Equally noteworthy was the fact that, while Muslims were moving away from the Congress, they were not necessarily swelling the ranks of the League which was still a highly disorganized, inefficient and unrepresentative body. Jinnah's brave attempts to infuse some life into it were poorly rewarded; the Leagues' total membership rose from a mere 1,093 in 1922 to a mere 1,330 in 1927.[19] Provincial Leagues did not fare any better; the branch in the Bombay presidency had 71 members in 1928.[20] The 1929 session was adjourned for lack of a quorum. The adjourned meeting, held four months later in Delhi, ended in a fiasco.[21] When Iqbal presented his historic address in 1930 demanding the establishment of a Muslim state in north-western India, the meeting at Allahabad did not even have its quorum of 75 members.[22] The only connection, wrote the *Mussalman* angrily, an ordinary member had with the League was to be visited with a V.P.P. for his membership fee. 'It appears that nowadays there are very few who honour those V.P.P.s as the members have been disgusted with the Muslim League on account of its culpable inactivity. The provincial Leagues have imbibed

[18]Khaliquzzaman, op. cit., p. 117.

[19]The membership of the All-India Muslim League was 1,093 in 1922, 1,097 in 1923 and 1,184 in 1924. *Annual Report of the All-India Muslim League* (Lucknow, n.d.), Chagla Papers, NMML.

[20]Sayeed, *Pakistan*, p. 176.

[21]*Mussalman*, 3 July 1930.

[22]Sayeed, op. cit., pp. 176-7. 'It is a wonder that when this clarion call was made from the Muslim League platform (Iqbal's demand) no one took any notice of it and no one moved any resolution in the session approving the scheme enunciated at Allahabad.' Khaliquzzaman, op. cit., pp. 108-9. The total attendance, according to Fakhrul Islam, was between 400 and 500, including a large number of students. It is noteworthy that Iqbal's address was not even taken note of by the *Leader* of Allahabad. Mukhtar Zaman, 'Duaazda Manzil se Manzil-i Pakistan tak', *Nuqush* (Iqbal Number), September 1977, Vol. 121, p. 501.

the inactivity and the character of the parent body'.[23]

Thus the challenge to the Congress did not quite emanate from the League, but from local and regional expressions of what is variously described as 'Muslim communalism', 'Muslim separatism' and 'Muslim nationalism'.[24] At the same time, it was a comforting thought that within the Congress ranks were a number of important Muslim groups, 'most distinguished and trusted leaders and counsellors'.[25] It was a different matter that Congress neither recognized their potential nor utilized their services in full to extend its political base among other segments of Muslim society.

Most 'Nationalist Muslims' were associated with the nationalist movement from the days of the Rowlatt satyagraha, though the expression became current in the mid-1920s to draw a distinction between Ansari and his comrades, on the one hand, and the Ali Brothers, Mohammad Shafi, Shafee Daoodi and others connected with the Muslim Conference, on the other—all portrayed in the nationalist press as detractors of the Congress and allies of the government. 'They are men,' said Ansari, 'to whom the freedom of the country from alien rule comes merely as a bad second to communal privileges'

The label 'Nationalist Muslim' aptly describes the ideology and politics of those committed to Indian nationalism, but its exclusive application to Muslims conjures a false image of a community largely communally-oriented with only a handful integrated with the dominant nationalist trend. (Notice that the expression 'Nationalist Hindu' has never been used to distinguish the activities of Gandhi, Nehru, Das and Bose from those of Lajpat Rai, Malaviya, Jayakar and Kelkar.) It also needs to be emphasized that the dividing line between a professed nationalist and a

[23]*Mussalman*, 3 July 1930. The League, observed its honorary secretary in his 1931 annual report, was unable to perform its functions effectively because of the Muslim Conference 'which has divided our energies and caused a great deal of harm to the All-India Muslim League'. The situation remained unchanged in 1932-1933 when the joint secretary warned that 'a little oversight or a little expression of inactivity on the part of Muslims today means lifelong suffering and bondage'. In order to gain members, the annual subscription was reduced from Rs 6 to Rs 1 and the admission fee was abolished. *Annual Report of the All-India Muslim League for the year 1931* (Delhi, n.d.), pp. 1, 4; *Annual Report of the All-India Muslim League for the years 1932 and 1933 (upto November)* (Delhi, n.d.), pp. 2-3.

[24]For Bengal, see Mcpherson, op. cit.

[25]Jawaharlal to S. Mohamed Husain, 1 July 1931, F. No. G-37/1931, AICC Papers.

so-called communalist was often blurred. It is thus not easy to place Mohamed Ali in this supposed dichotomous framework. Though a relentless critic of the Congress during the Nehru Report controversy and a stout champion of Muslim interests, he adhered to his unswerving commitment to swaraj. This was amply borne out by his famous speech at the Round Table Conference and his 'Last Letter' to the British prime minister. Ansari, too, conceded that despite being led into the 'camp of national reaction', the Ali Brothers had not 'surrendered their loyalty to the fundamental principle of Indian politics, freedom from foreign domination'.[26]

How, then, does one describe Muslim groups connected with the Congress movement at various levels? It is convenient for descriptive purposes to identify them as Congress Muslims. Admittedly, this term does not quite encompass the range of their activities in the social and educational spheres, but it unmistakably indicates the pro-Congress thrust of their political concerns both in relation to the community and the country at large.

There were two main sources of inspiration for the Congress Muslims. Some like Azad and Husain Ahmad Madani (1879-1957), head of the *Dar al-ulum* at Deoband, derived their nationalist ardour from their interpretation of Islam as a religion of freedom and equality, of justice, of cooperation with, and respect for, all mankind.[27] In May 1930, leading members of the *Jamiyat al-ulama* came around to accepting Gandhi's leadership in the civil disobedience movement; their conference at Amroha called upon Muslims to join Congress and appointed a committee to prepare a programme of action for attaining freedom; the rival conference—*Anjuman-i Tausi-i Islam*—set up by government and encouraged by the Nawab of Chhatari (1889-1982) and the Ali Brothers was a fiasco. By mid-June the *Jamiyat* was able to enrol 15,000 volunteers and over 100 of its leading members were in jail; in Delhi its volunteers went around securing pledges from Muslims that they would discard the use of foreign cloth. Kifayatullah, president of the *Jamiyat*, and Ahmad Said, its secretary and director of the 'War Council', were arrested on 11 October 1930 and sentenced to six months'

[26]*Modern Review*, July 1929, p. 104.
[27]Smith, *Modern Islam*, p. 251.

imprisonment. In the mid-1930s Madani defended full and individual Muslim participation in the freedom struggle by advancing a theory of territorial nationhood for India rather than by appealing to concepts of safeguards and community confederation. His ideas were expressed in a public controversy with Iqbal shortly before the latter's death in 1938.[28]

The Western-educated Muslims had one basic thing in common: a shared perception of nationalism as a legitimate expression of most Indians to achieve swaraj. Without a firm nationalist tradition, stated Ali Imam, the Bihar lawyer-politician, it was impossible to visualize a free India.[29] Likewise, they believed that the Congress ideology and programme symbolized the popular aspirations, and it was therefore the largest, the most important and the most representative organization. It alone could act as a vehicle for bringing about the much-awaited political, social and economic transformation—one which would rescue the people from colonial bondage and exploitation. By joining the Congress in large numbers, stated Mujibur Rahman (d. 1940) at the Bakarganj District Muslim Conference in May 1931, Muslims of Bengal would take a greater share in suffering and sacrifice and a greater part in the freedom struggle.[30] The Frontier leader, Khan Abdul Ghaffar Khan (b. 1890), said at a public meeting in December 1931 that the Congress alone would free the country, feed the hungry and clothe the naked.[31] The *Jirgah* of India, he reaffirmed elsewhere, was called Congress—a common *Jirgah* of all the communities of India. Justifying his alliance with Congress, he said: 'In order to save himself from the enemies did not the Holy Prophet make alliance with the Jews and the politheists (*sic*)?'[32] His audience beamed approvingly.

[28]Peter Hardy, *Partners in Freedom—and True Muslim: The political thought of some Muslim scholars in British India 1912-1947* (Lund, 1971), p. 37. For the support of the *ulama* attached to the *Jamiyat*, see *Bombay Chronicle*, 2, 5, 8, 10, 13, 15 May 1930; F. No. G-94/II, 1930, AICC Papers.

[29]*Mussalman*, 16 April 1931. Mahmudullah, secretary of the UP Nationalist Muslim Party, explained that the Congress Muslims did not seek communal safeguards which would be a negation of a free constitution. 'We do not stand for the division of India into "Hindu India" and "Muslim India". We do not stand for an isolated political existence in the Federated India.' *Bombay Chronicle*, 9 November 1931.

[30]*Liberty*, 1 June 1931, quoted in Bhola Chatterji, *Aspects of Bengal Politics in the early Nineteen Thirties* (Calcutta, 1969), pp. 14-5.

[31]Home Poll. F. No. 5/72, 1932, NAI.

[32]Ibid., F. No. 5/54, 1932, NAI.

The principal Muslim groups, besides the *Jamiyat al-ulama*, which acted in unison with the Congress in the late 1920s, spanned several provinces of British India. In the Frontier province, the Khudai Khidmatgars (Servants of God), led by the charismatic figure of Ghaffar Khan, were at the head of a nationalist and socially progressive movement. Their presence on the all-India political scene was first noticed at the Lahore Congress in 1929 and within two years of its creation the Khudai Khidmatgar Party claimed a membership of 200,000.[33] Quotations from the Quran against slavery served as rallying points for nationalist enthusiasm and the struggle to liberate the country from foreign rule became the Holy War of the Khudai Khidmatgars. 'No section of India,' observed W.C. Smith in 1943, 'has been more thoroughly nationalist'.[34]

During civil disobedience in 1930-31 Khudai Khidmatgar activities were linked with the general Congress movement—the connection being strengthened in August 1931 when the Afghan *Jirga* merged with the PCC. The local *Jirgas* became local Congress committees, while 'Red Shirt' volunteers became part of the Congress at various levels. The whole movement was to be conducted in accordance with the Congress constitution and the flag to be used was to be the Congress flag. The architect of this alliance, Ghaffar Khan, explained in November 1931:

> People complain against me for having joined the Congress by selling my nation. The Congress is a national and not a Hindu body. It is a jirga composed of Hindus, Jews, Sikhs, Parsis and Muslims. The Congress as a body is working against the British. The British nation is the enemy of the Congress and of the Pathans. I have therefore joined it and made common cause with the Congress to get rid of the British.[35]

The intensity of civil disobedience in the Frontier province, so obviously overlooked by some historians, was reflected in the number of those prosecuted and convicted. Until September 1932, the figure was 5,557 in a total population of twenty-five lacs. In neighbouring Punjab, on the other hand, the number was 1,620, though the population was more than eight times that of the NWFP.[36] Convictions in NWFP were also higher than

[33]D.G. Tendulkar, *Abdul Ghaffar Khan* (Varanasi, 1969), p. 116.
[34]Smith, op. cit., pp. 266-7.
[35]Home Poll. F. No. 5/54, 1932, NAI.
[36]Home Poll. F. No. 5/72, 1932, NAI.

the Bombay Presidency [See Table 8.3].

TABLE 8.3

	Convictions in Jan.-Feb. 1932	*Convictions in Mar.-Sept. 1932*	*Total*
Bombay	5,165	6,311	11,476
NWFP	4,318	1,239	5,557

SOURCE: Home Poll. F. No. S/72, 1932, NAI.

Towards the end of 1932, out of 1,500 civil disobedience prisoners in the Peshawar jail, 5 were Hindus, 2 Sikhs, the rest being Muslims. In the Haripur central jail there were 1,938 Muslims and 24 Hindus. In the province as a whole over 90 per cent of the civil disobedience prisoners were Muslims.[37]

Clearly Ghaffar Khan's message struck a favourable chord in an area which had remained relatively tranquil during non-cooperation and was not fully exposed to either the institutional or agitational politics of most other parts of British India. Ghaffar Khan's motto 'We are Pakhtuns but until we attain freedom we do not deserve to be called Pakhtuns'[38] remained the rallying slogan of the politics of the Frontier province in the decades before the partition of India.

The Majlis-i-Ahrar-i Islam, organized in 1929 by a group of Punjabi Muslims who had seceded from the Khilafat committees, was based on the well-to-do peasantry and the lower-middle classes. Its followers combined economic grievances and religious passions to formulate their militant policies.[39] They expressed something of the old Khilafat movement tradition: an ardent and explicit enthusiasm for Indian freedom. Like the Khudai Khidmatgars, they steadily, fervently and inspiredly plunged into the civil disobedience movement and went to jail in large numbers.[40] In Delhi, they combined with the *Jamiyat al-ulama* in organizing processions and picketing liquor shops, leading to the arrest of Azad, Kifayatullah and twenty-five Ahrars in early March 1932. Reminiscent of scenes during the Rowlatt satyagraha was a

[37]Home Poll. F. No. 3/7, 1934, NAI.

[38]Home Poll. F. No. 5/54, 1932, NAI.

[39]Humayun Kabir, *Muslim Politics 1906-47 and other essays* (Calcutta, 1969), p. 22.

[40]Smith, op. cit., pp. 270-1.

mammoth meeting at Fatehpuri mosque where 4,500–5,000 Muslims pledged their cooperation with Gandhi's civil disobedience movement.[41]

The Ahrars were active in Kashmir where they agitated against the Dogra ruler, Maharaja Hari Singh, to seek redressal of the grievances of the Muslim subjects of that state.[42] These were set out in the memorial submitted to the Maharaja on 19 October 1931,[43] and taken note of by B.J. Glancy who headed a commission to enquire into the demands of the memorialists.[44] Led by Mazhar Ali, Habibur Rahman of Ludhiana (1892-1956), Abdur Rahman Ghazi and Ataullah Shah Bukhari (1891-1967), the Ahrars sent *jathas* of red-uniformed *razakaars* (volunteers) from different parts of the Punjab, especially Sialkot, to Kashmir in order to bear pressure on the Maharaja to meet the demands of his Muslim 'subjects'.[45] The outcome was large-scale rioting in Jammu on 2 November 1931 and violent clashes at Mirpur between the *jathas* and the state forces. British troops were pressed into service to quell the disturbances.

The spur in political activity, combined with several factors, strengthened nationalist and progressive forces among the Kashmiri masses, more than three quarters of whom were Muslims. The Jammu and Kashmir Muslim Conference, founded in 1932, was a symbol of their aspirations. The Conference, stated its founder Shaikh Mohammad Abdullah (1905-1982), though Muslim in name was 'in spirit national and was concerned with the welfare of all communities'.[46] He declared in 1931 and, again in 1935, that the country's progress depended on

[41]Home Poll. F. No. 4/46, 1932, NAI.

[42]Malik Afzal Husain, *Kashmir awr Dogra Raj, 1848-1931* (Delhi, 1970 edn.).

[43]Among the demands listed were representation in ministries and in all grades of services in proportion to the Muslim population, religious freedom, the right to hold public meetings and the freedom of speech and press. In other areas, such as Mirpur *tahsil*, Major-General R.G. Finlayson took note of the common grievance relating to high grazing tax and high rent assessments which were double of what they were in neighbouring Punjab, inadequate representation in civil administration, insufficient resources being spent on the development of the *tahsil* and rampant corruption, inefficiency and maladministration. Home Poll. F. No. 10/28, 1932; Home Poll. F. No. 5/2, 1933, NAI.

[44]P.N.K. Bamzai, *A History of Kashmir* (Delhi, 1962), pp. 660-1.

[45]Home Poll. F. No. 13/23, 1931, NAI.

[46]Foreword by S.M. Abdullah in *New Kashmir* (New Delhi, n.d.), p. 6.

harmonious communal relations[47] and his fight was for the emancipation of the country. 'Let us all rise above petty communal bickerings and work jointly for the welfare of the masses,' he said.[48] In the years to come, the economic programme of the Muslim Conference, embodied in the 'New Kashmir' Plan, and its political orientation was akin to that of the Congress. Abdullah repudiated the two-nation theory and hitched the fortunes of his people with Indian nationalism.

In Bombay, Syed Abdullah Brelvi (1891-1949), editor of the *Bombay Chronicle*, launched the Congress Muslim Party on 8 July 1929 in an attempt to induce Muslims to join the Congress.[49] His chief support lay among urban-based politicians, such as Yusuf Meharally (1903-1950), editor of the English weekly *Vanguard*, Abbas Tyabji (1854-1936), a lawyer with long-standing associations with the Congress movement, and M.C. Chagla (1900-1982), also a lawyer who came to the forefront as a vociferous champion of the Nehru Report. Gandhi blessed the Congress Muslim Party with the message: 'If it is fully supported and does not go to sleep, it may prove a tower of strength to the Congress and an instrument of real service to India generally and to Mussalmans in particular'.[50]

The Congress Muslim Party, in spite of stiff opposition from Shaukat Ali and his followers among the Urdu-speaking Muslims, established its hold in Bombay city. Brelvi, backed by several Muslim mercantile associations in Bombay, led a mile-long procession on 2 June 1930 and presided over a meeting of about 10,000, including a large number of Hindus, which called on Muslims to cooperate in the civil disobedience movement.[51] 'Conspicuous amongst organizers of procession and speakers at meeting,' noted a government report, 'were certain Maulanas and Muslim propagandists from other provinces. To this extent, [the] procession must be regarded as success of Congress propaganda and it must be admitted that during the last fortnight many Muhammadans have been gathered into the Congress fold'.[52]

[47]Cited in Bamzai, op. cit., p. 661; M. Ishaq Khan, *Perspectives on Kashmir: Historical Dimensions* (Srinagar, 1983), pp. 146-7.

[48]*New Kashmir*, op. cit., p. 6.

[49]*IQR*, July-December 1928, pp. 405-7.

[50]Ibid., p. 351.

[51]Brown, op. cit., p. 137.

[52]Viceroy to secretary of state, 18 January 1930, Home Poll. F. No. 257/V, 1930, NAI. The *Bombay Chronicle* commented optimistically: 'Mussalmans have

Such examples provide a corrective to the impression, created by government officials and perpetuated by historians of Indian nationalism, of the Muslim community being arrayed against civil disobedience.[53] This is not to deny that, compared to 1920-21, their enthusiasm was much less. But to compare their response in these years to the civil disobedience days, and, then to draw evidence of their indifference or hostility is quite misleading. The religious passions evoked by the Khilafat question were both unique and unprecedented: there was no such issue in the early 1930s to evince the same degree of interest.

The All-India Nationalist Muslim Party

Among the Congress Muslim groups in the late 1920s, the All-India Nationalist Muslim Party (NMP) acquired greater significance because it mirrored local and regional manifestations of nationalist aspirations among Muslims. Such trends remained either dormant in a party of Congress' size or were not adequately projected for fear of inviting the wrath of Muslim communal elements. But they found adequate expression in the making of the NMP and soon became part of, and eventually merged into, the broad stream represented by the newly-formed party and its ideology.

The NMP occupied a vital position both in terms of its influence in urban areas as well as in articulating the views of Congress Muslims. For the first time, they could address themselves exclusively to issues concerning their community either in relation to or independently of the party to which they owed

returned to the old fold to take their place side by side with their Hindu, Sikh and Parsi brethren ...and all talk of minority suspicions is merely a clumsy justification of *Divide and Rule.*' *Bombay Chronicle*, 5 June 1930.

[53]882 persons were convicted in Delhi from 1 April to 15 November 1930. Of these, 88 were Muslims. This is by no means an inconsiderable figure and should at least help historians to qualify their judgement on Muslim aloofness or hostility to civil disobedience in all parts of the country. Home Poll. F. No. 23/26, 1931, NAI. In the Punjab, reported the Provincial Congress Committee, 'among the leaders (Muslim) there are a good number in Jail. Among the volunteers there is a fairly decent number, probably about 600 or 700 out of the total. The Muslim public is apathetic, but not exactly hostile.' F. No. 40, 1931 AICC Papers. Also, see S.L. Malhotra, *From Civil Disobedience to Quit India* (Chandigarh, 1979), pp. 6, 9, 10; Jagdish Chandra, *Gandhiji and Haryana* (Delhi, 1977), p. 86.

allegiance and express themselves freely and frankly. The NMP offered a platform which ideally suited their political objectives.

Formed on 27-28 July 1929, after the AICC at Allahabad discussed the question of forming a new party to organize Muslim support for the Congress in general, and the Nehru Report in particular, the resolution adopted for forming the NMP stated:

> The political struggle started in 1919 is being gradually weakened by inter-communal conflicts and repeated attempts are being made in different quarters to wean Muslims away from political activities. The present disruption among political-minded Muslims and the consequent apathy of the mass of the Muslim community towards the problem of Indian freedom are due to a confused appreciation of the political obligations implicit in the fact of the community being a part of the Indian nation. Muslim political activity is now confined under the auspices of the existing Muslim institutions, to winning political responsibility as the main objective and with freedom for the country as merely incidental thereto. Hence the need for the new party. The formal objects of it are to promote among Muslims a spirit of nationalism, to develop a mentality above communalism and to inspire into them greater confidence in Indian national ideas, to induce Muslims to take their proper share in the national struggle and to create such relations between the majority and minority communities as would lead the former to consider the rights of the latter in a spirit of broad-minded patriotism.[54]

Khaliquzzaman claimed to have founded the NMP. 'As there was nobody of opinion inside or outside the Congress for ventilating organized nationalist view frankly and honestly,' he wrote in his autobiography, 'I hoped that the establishment of this organization might serve to arrest such an undisciplined exhibition of loyalty to Congress, misleading its leaders and dragging it into dark alleys. I talked to Ansari about my views'.[55] This claim is not supported by existing historical evidence which points to Ansari as the architect of the NMP, the man who also held it together by resisting the particularist tendencies of the various constituents. Others closely associated with him were

[54]Khaliquzzaman, op. cit., pp. 101-2: *IQR*, July-December 1929, p. 350.
[55]Khaliquzzaman, op. cit., p. 102.

Rafi Ahmad Kidwai, Sherwani, Azad, Ghaffar Khan, Khaliquzzaman, Brelvi, Khwaja, Mujibur Rahman, Kitchlew and Abdul Bari (d. 1947) of Bihar. The *ulama* support came from Kifayatullah Mohammad Sajjad and Ahmad Said—all of the *Jamiyat al-ulama* and from Qutubuddin Wali of Firangi Mahal in Lucknow.[56]

At its first meeting held at Sherwani's house in Allahabad on 27 July 1929, a central body was constituted: 28 members were elected from Bengal, 27 from the Punjab, 3 from the Frontier, 24 from UP, 14 from Delhi, 17 from Bihar and 10 from Bombay and Sind. Seven provincial and seventy-one district branches were established. District branches in UP were set up in Lucknow, Rae Bareli, Allahabad, Banaras, Fyzabad, Hardoi, Bijnor, Saharanpur, Bareilly, Meerut, Aligarh and Shahjahanpur.[57] In the Punjab, there were NMP committees in eight districts. There were ten of them in Bihar and at least four in Bengal—Calcutta, Dacca, Bogra and Faridpur. The Dacca committee was headed by Shamsul Huda and Ghulam Qadri, the Calcutta committee by Mujibur Rahman, Akram Khan, K. Nooruddin and Abdur Razzack (both Calcutta Corporation councillors), while the local branches in Bogra and Faridpur were controlled by a scattering of others who had been active in the Khilafat and non-cooperation movements.[58]

On the strength of this wide network built in a relatively short time, the NMP claimed to represent the 'entire Muslim

[56]For list of those present at the Allahabad Conference, see *IQR*, July-December 1929, p. 350; for *Jamiyat al-ulama*, see *Leader*, 19 April 1931.

[57]Funds for their support came from several sources, including the Raja of Mahmudabad. He was much active in nationalist campaigns, leading the boycott of the Statutory Commission in Lucknow, presiding over the All-Parties Conference in Lucknow in September 1928, and lending his name to the list of those who endorsed the Nehru Report. He also proposed launching a newspaper and invited Syed Abdullah Brelvi to join as editor. 'In view of the importance of the political situation and also in view of the Nehru Committee Report it is most necessary to start propaganda in right earnest to educate the people and get the report ratified by all recognized institutions.' To Brelvi, 8 September 1928, Brelvi Papers. Earlier, the Raja had supported similar journalistic ventures in support of nationalist causes. The *Comrade*, the *New Era* (Lucknow) and the *Hamdam* (Lucknow) were among them. Both James Meston and Harcourt Butler tried unsuccessfully to persuade the Raja to withdraw his patronage from such 'extremist' papers. See, for instance, Butler to the Raja of Mahmudabad, 4 September 1920, Mahmudabad Papers, NMML.

[58]*Mussalman*, 21 March 1931; for Punjab, see *Bombay Chronicle*, 4 July 1931; also, statement of secretary, UPNMP, *Bombay Chronicle*, 9 November 1931.

intelligentsia' and consisted of people not wedded to the scheme of separatism.[59] Ansari declared that its strength was derived from the intelligentsia, backed by the Muslim masses, and that no other single group of Muslims was as representative as the NMP. Elements that went in the making of the Muslim Conference 'defy definition and if you remove the members of All-India Muslim League, the Central Khilafat Committee, you would find that the real men who go by this name are an unknown quantity'. He scoffed at the League, pointing out that it had long ceased to be a reality, while the Khilafat committees, once so powerful in the country, 'were now but a shadow of its former self. He concluded with the assertion that the NMP was the 'real representative group of the Mussalmans of India today'[60]

These were highly exaggerated claims. Yet, there can be no doubt that the NMP, in spite of its limited political base, had the *potential* of being a powerful force among Indian Muslims.[61] The first warning signal to the government and its Muslim collaborators came when Ansari and his comrades, with Congress backing, staked their claim to represent Muslims at the Round Table Conference in London. Gandhi insisted on taking Ansari with him to demonstrate Congress' representative position[62] and

[59]Ibid., 27 June 1931; for Syed Mahmud's claims, see *Bombay Chronicle*, 20 April 1931.

[60]*Modern Review*, May 1931, p. 611; A.Z. Zaidi (ed.), *The Evolution of Muslim Political Thought in India* (Delhi, 1980), Vol. 4, p. 476. Also, Gandhi's interview to *New Leader*, 25 November 1931, *CWG*, Vol. XLVIII, p. 333 and Ansari's statement in Bombay on the NMP's support in Bengal, *Bombay Chronicle*, 8 July 1931.

[61]'The Muslim members have chosen,' observed Shaikh Mohammad Abdullah (1878-1965) of Aligarh, 'a most psychological moment for launching their campaign and if they succeed in controlling the situation, there is a chance for them to rally the Mussalmans in large numbers.' Letter to the Editor, 15 April 1931, *Leader*, 19 April 1931.

[62]The Raja of Mahmudabad emphatically stated that the list of delegates for the first Round Table Conference was not 'balanced' because the 'Muslim separatists and communalists' predominated. He believed that the 'Muslim Nationalists have larger followings than the authors of the Muslim All-Parties Conference and if Muslim Nationalists are to be invited...their numbers should be in accordance with the volume of nationalistic views to be found among Muslims' The Raja of Mahmudabad to T.B. Sapru, 8 July 1931, Sapru Papers, National Library, Calcutta. According to M.C. Chagla, the only reason why the government was trying to keep the Congress Muslim out of the Round Table Conference was to 'impress upon British public opinion that Mussalmans are determined

told the viceroy that without him he would be 'perfectly helpless' in Hindu-Muslim negotiations.[63] But the viceroy did not acquiesce. The Mahatma said in an interview in London that whoever prevented Ansari from being selected as a delegate committed a 'fatal blunder'.[64]

Ansari's exclusion from Gandhi's party was secured by Fazl-i-Husain who, as member of the Viceroy's Council, influenced official policy on Hindu-Muslim relations. Backed by his allies in the Muslim Conference and a section of the Urdu press, the Punjab leader first opposed the inclusion of Ali Imam and the Raja of Mahmudabad[64a] and then sought to prove the hollowness of Ansari's claim to represent the Muslims. The Muslim press had stated, he wrote in July 1931, 'that Ali Imam and Ansari should not go as representatives of Muslims. This is the right line to take and if it is right there is no reason why it should not succeed'. He expressed admiration for Ansari's character and his motives, adding, however, how 'during the last few weeks he [Ansari] seems to have done his best to convince all his friends and admirers that [his] partisanship of the Congress had deprived him of any sense of fair-play and propriety'.[65] Fazl-i-Husain reserved his harsh comments for Gandhi. 'To confuse the issues,

and united upon the retention of separate electorates.' He said that if the government wished 'to escape the accusation of having always followed the policy of "Divide et Impera" and of always profiting by communal dissensions and differences there is still time to do what is only fair and just.' *Bombay Chronicle*, 8 July 1931.

[63] Gandhi to Irwin (telegram), 20 July 1931, Gandhi to viceroy, 29 August 1931, *CWG*, Vol. XLVII, p. 156.

[64] Interview to *Bombay Chronicle*, 14 September 1931, p. 12, Gandhi to Ansari, cable, 14 October 1931, *CWG*, Vol. XLVIII, p. 148.

[64a] To E.C. Mievell, 27 July 1931, Fazl-i-Husain Papers (10); and earlier, M.H. Kidwai to Fazl-i-Husain, 18 May 1930, Fazl-i-Husain Papers (12).

[65] 'Indian Muslims do not believe that Gandhi is serious in the matter of Muslim rights. His desire to have Ansari in London is only a continuation of his tactics at Delhi to demonstrate the existence of cleavage in Muslim opinion, while, as a matter of fact, it does not exist.' To Shafaat Ahmad Khan, 28 July 1931, Fazl-i-Husain Papers (12). Shafee Daoodi also protested to the viceroy, arguing that the inclusion of Ansari and Ali Imam would be regarded as an attempt to create division in the Muslim delegation and an endorsement of the Congress formula on the communal question. He warned that Muslims would start an agitation and reconsider their attitude towards further participation in the Round Table Conference. *Bombay Chronicle*, 25 July 1931. Also, Home Poll. F. No. 18/7, 1931, NAI.

to indulge in irrelevance and to begin to talk of Muslim demands, and then talk of Congress Muslims, of Dr Ansari and so on', he told friends in October 1931:

> are all devices with which Hindus as well as Muslims are quite familiar. Gandhi's insistence upon Dr Ansari's inclusion and his parading readiness for complete surrender in case complete unity is forthcoming have nothing new about them. They are the very old devices which the Congress, Gandhi and the Indian Hindus have been condemning in the British Government and the British statesmen. They are doing now exactly what they alleged Lord Birkenhead was doing––asking for complete unanimity and resorting to the well-known principle of Divide and Rule; but Gandhi should know that the people are not so unsophisticated today as they used to be and that the game he is now indulging in is one which has been played out for some time.[66]

Ansari did not enjoy being drawn into the controversy. The Mahatma, he reported on 28 September, 'is harking back on me and wanting me even at this eleventh hour to be invited.... It is like a baby crying for his wetnurse'.[67] Convinced that government would not give in, he stated:

> I am positive that the government has deliberately left the Nationalist Muslim Party unrepresented... because they do not want the Hindu-Muslim question to be settled without their intervention. And they know that if there is any party in India which can bring about Hindu-Muslim unity it is the Nationalist Muslim Party. It is, therefore, against their interest to have the representatives of that party at the Round Table Conference, for they would be able to cement the unity of the various parties in India and thus deprive the government from playing

[66]Waheed Ahmad (ed.), *Diary and Notes of Mian Fazl-i-Husain*, p. 228. In February 1932 he told Sarojini Naidu of the 'big mistakes' committed by Gandhi—'mistakes of a nature which are associated with shady politics'. In consequence, Gandhi stood lower in public estimation—'at war with all minorities and in his cabinet a strong body of Hindu Mahasabha and strong body of extremists, the former supporting the latter and the latter supporting the former in their anti-Muslim policy'. 22 February 1932, Diary, Fazl-i-Husain Papers (6).

[67]To Shaukatullah Ansari, 28 September 1931, Hasan (ed.), *Muslims and the Congress*, p. 129

> their trump card against the representatives of India who are pressing hard for complete freedom from the British tutelage.[68]

He also began to feel that Gandhi should not insist on his inclusion but was dissuaded by Jawaharlal not to be 'so rash as to cable him to do what he chooses'.[69] In early October, Gandhi agreed to drop his insistence on Ansari's presence on the ground that 'he will be of no use unless the Muslim Delegation desires or approves of his selection as a delegate'.[70]

The exclusion of Ansari did not end the worries of the organizers of the Muslim Conference who faced the cheerless prospect of losing some of their supporters to the NMP. After all, the NMP was gaining ground with the help of some influential Muslims who had built their reputation through years of selfless political work. Its meetings at Lucknow (18-19 April 1931), Faridpur (27-28 June 1931) and Lahore (24 October 1931) were well-attended, and its policies had a favourable impression on Muslims in the NWFP, Punjab, UP and Bombay.[71] One of the most gratifying signs of the times,' commented the *Leader*,

[68]To Shaukatullah Ansari, 29 September 1931, ibid. An emergency meeting of the NMP was convened on 6 October by Ansari to consider the questions arising from the Round Table Conference and to discuss the future of the party. Ansari, according to the government report, was made a virtual 'dictator' of the party 'to deal with the rapidly changing situation. He is believed to be unwilling to proceed to England even if he were summoned'. Home Poll. F. No. 18/10, 1931, NAI.

[69]To Ansari, 4 October 1931, *SWJ*, Vol. 5, p. 98. Devdas Gandhi (1900-1957) reported from London how difficult it had been for Bapu to discuss the possibility of Ansari coming to London and that he could 'no longer press with dignity for Dr Ansari'. The first argument was that the proceedings of the Minorities Committee could not be held up merelv for Ansari's sake and the second objection was that he would make a settlement impossible by prevailing upon Gandhi not to accede to the Muslim demands. 'Mr Shafee Daoodi quite openly admitted that he had been instrumental in keeping Dr Ansari out and others were eager to share the responsibility with Shafee Daoodi. The whole discussion was sordid.' B.N. Pandey (ed.), *The Indian Nationalist Movement 1885-1947: Select Documents* (London, 1979), p. 71.

[70]Statement to press, 14 October 1931, *CWG*, Vol. XLVIII, p. 150; Devdas Gandhi to Jawaharlal, 2 October 1931, *SWJ*, Vol. 5, p. 48, f.n. 3.

[71]See draft note on the success of Punjab Nationalist Muslims, n.d., Brelvi Papers. 'Lucknow seldom had a bigger gathering of Mussalmans than one seen yesterday in connection with Muslim Nationalists' Conference,' reported the *Tribune* of 23 July 1930, and *Indian Daily Mail*, 24 July 1930, Ansari Collection, NMML.

'is the rapid growth of nationalism among Indian Muslims. The opponents of Indian progress and their allies, the Muslim communalists, will not be willing to admit this fact. But the impressive gathering of the nationalist Muslims at Lucknow from all parts of the country tells its own tale'.[72] The editor of the *Indian Annual Register* hoped that an influential party of nationalist Muslims would 'in the fullness of time, dominate the vast bulk of Indian Mohammedan opinion'.[73]

Encouraged by the NMP conferences, Ansari worked feverishly to weld together the various Muslim factions and tried to persuade them to accept his party's proposals on joint electorates and adult suffrage;[74] on other issues there was no fundamental difference between Jinnah's 'fourteen points' and the main resolution passed at the NMP meeting on 18-19 April 1931.[75] On the question of electorates the NMP reiterated the Nehru Report recommendation, considering separate electorates a negation of nationalism. Political problems, argued Ali Imam, president of the Lucknow conference, were a reflex of social forces. 'If you erect an iron wall between community and community in their politics, you destroy the social fabric.... Nationalism can never evolve from division and dissension'.[76] Ansari, too, refused to countenance separate electorates. The measure and method of representation in the federal and provincial legislatures should be settled, he said, on the basis of joint electorates and adult suffrage, and any constitution which did not contain these provisions would be wholly unacceptable to the Muslims. And he proposed a round table conference of Muslim organizations to iron out their differences.[78]

This statement seemed to conjure up a mood of reconciliation and set the stage for the real business at hand: ongoing talks between representatives of the NMP and the Muslim Conference. On 10-12 May they met at Bhopal. Discussion centred round the vexed issue of joint *versus* separate electorates. Ansari, aided

[72]Note on the Press, UP, for the week ending 23 April 1931.

[73]*IAR*, January-June 1931, p. 80.

[74]For resolutions adopted on these issues at the meetings on 15-17 April, see *Leader*, 19 April 1931, *Mussalman*, 16 April 1931.

[75]*Mussalman*, 23 April 1931.

[76]Ibid., 16 April 1931.

[77]*Bombay Chronicle*, 27 April 1931.

[78]*Leader*, 19, 20, 22, 23 April 1931, Page, op. cit., p. 238.

by Khaliquzzaman and Sherwani, insisted on joint electorates for the first ten years with a provision for a referendum thereafter. Alternatively, fifty per cent of the seats were to be contested on the basis of joint and the other half on the basis of separate electorates in the first general election. The arrangement was to change in the second election when two-thirds of the seats were to be contested by joint electorates. Thereafter, joint electorates with adult suffrage, as proposed in the Nehru Report, would be introduced.

Iqbal, Shafi, Shaukat Ali and Nawab Ismail Khan (1884-1958), taking their cue from Fazl-i-Husain, pressed for joint electorates and adult suffrage after ten years, though with the provision that they could be introduced earlier if a majority of legislators so desired. Their other proposal provided for five years of separate electorates with a referendum on joint electorates at the beginning of the fifth year.[79]

The discussions at Bhopal, announced Ansari with characteristic over-optimism, raised the prospect of a settlement.[80] But his hopes were soon belied by the intransigence of delegates from both sides,[81] combined with Fazl-i-Husain's stout refusal to endorse a compromise.[82] When talks resumed in Simla on 21 June 1931, the Punjab leader reignited the controversy by insisting on separate electorates and wanting Congress to state its position on weightage and reservation of seats for the Muslim majorities in Bengal and the Punjab.[83] Ansari found the atmosphere at Simla 'very inauspicious' for any compromise.[84] The conference there managed to accomplish little more than to restate a daunting agenda of continuing problems and differences.

Much of the blame for the failure of the Bhopal and Simla

[79]Brelvi Papers; Iqbal to Fazl-i-Husain, 14 May 1931, *Letters of Mian Fazl-i-Husain*, p. 143.

[80]*IAR*, January-June 1931, p. 304.

[81]Syed Mahmud to Jawaharlal Nehru, 27 June 1931, V.N. Datta and B. Cleghorn (eds.), *A Nationalist Muslim and Indian Politics* (Delhi, 1974), pp. 115-6.

[82]*IAR*, January-June 1931, pp. 303-6; K.K. Aziz (ed.), *The All-India Muslim Conference 1928-1935* (Karachi, 1972), pp. 75-8.

[83]*Mussalman*, 25 June 1931; Page, op. cit., pp. 238-40; Moore, *The Crisis of Indian Unity*, p. 190, Fazl-i-Husain to Shafee Daoodi, 16 May 1931, Fazl-i-Husain to Iqbal, 30 May 1931, *Letters of Mian Fazl-i-Husain*, pp. 144-8; *Bombay Chronicle*, 23 June 1931.

[84]*Mussalman*, 25 June 1931; *Bombay Chronicle*, 24 June 1931.

meetings was put on Ansari and his colleagues, and a well-orchestrated campaign was launched to deride the NMP[85] Their policies, stated Shafaat Ahmad Khan (1893-1947), were 'like the bloom on the peach; you touch it and it is gone. Where is the party now? Nowhere! The exact, minute and detailed account of its branches and activities may be found in the secretariat of the Indian National Congress, but so far as Muslims of India are concerned they exist only on paper'.[86] Shafee Daoodi repeated the charge: Rafi Ahmad Kidwai replied that the number of Muslims in Congress exceeded the combined strength of all provincial Muslim Leagues and Khilafat committees.[87] Others excoriated the NMP for selling out the community's interest and the interest of Islam.[88] Ansari stoutly refuted the allegation: 'We are surely not worse Mussalmans because we refuse to turn our faith into a greedy superstition or an ignoble exercise in political hide and seek.... Our nationalism is part of our loyalty to our faith and not a betrayal or an infidelity'.[89] Shaukat Ali, who had no pretensions to detachment and only the flimsiest to moderation, made no effort to disguise his hostility. 'I consider you all to be weak men,' he told Syed Mahmud, 'and renegades, and, yielding to the open threats of the Hindus, [to] have chosen to live at their mercy'.[90] This was an ill-chosen way to dramatize his contention that the Congress Muslims had 'sold out' to the Hindus. Ansari found Shaukat Ali's attitude both unintelligible and unreasonable, but tried to convince him that religion and faith were private matters, not symbols to be exploited by partisan politicians. But the Maulana persisted with his barrage of ridicule, causing much distress to Ansari who was a man with strong feelings and a deep instinct of loyalty. He attached importance to keeping his word and observing obligations. The

[85]Home Poll. F. No. 18/6, 1931, NAI; The Nawab of Chhatari to Fazl-i-Husain, 3 July 1931, *Letters of Mian Fazl-i-Husain*, p. 158. Fazl-i-Husain, who did much to undermine the possibility of a settlement, wrote that there were no Muslims in the Congress strong enough to persuade that body to act in a 'just' and 'righteous' manner. To Umar Hayat Khan Tiwana, 20 June 1931, ibid., p. 152.

[86]*IAR*, July-December 1931, p. 225.

[87]*Leader*, 19 April 1931. For Ansari's response, see *Bombay Chronicle*, 6 July 1931.

[88]Speech of Shaukat Ali at the UP Muslim Conference, 8 August 1931, *IAR*, July-December 1931, p. 228.

[89]*Bombay Chronicle*, 21 April 1931.

[90]26 April 1929, Datta and Cleghorn (eds.), *A Nationalist Muslim*, p. 94.

unforgivable crime, in his eyes, was treachery: once he suspected anyone of not playing straight, he could be implacable, and once his confidence was lost, as in the case of Shaukat Ali, it was almost impossible to recover.

The Hindu Mahasabha did not spare Ansari. Moonje was convinced that some Muslims, masquerading as nationalists, were trying to infiltrate the Congress in large numbers in order to exert pressure from within.[91] In substance, he thought, there was no difference between the demands of the communalist and the nationalist Muslims.[92] C. Vijaraghavachariar (1852-1944), president of the Hindu Mahasabha in 1931, believed that the NMP resolutions, adopted at Faridpur, were 'subject to all the infirmities of the proposals of the other section of Muslims to which Mr Jinnah's fourteen points give expression'.[93]

The Hindu Mahasabha adopted a two-pronged strategy: to compare the NMP favourably with the Muslim League and the Muslim Conference, on the one hand, and to prevent the party from extracting any concessions from the Congress, on the other. This was demonstrated during the Gandhi-Jinnah talks in 1929 and later when Sapru tried to reach a communal concordat with representatives of various non-Congress groups. Moonje was morbidly apprehensive of any move that might conciliate the Muslims, while Jayakar and Kelkar insisted that the Liberals declare themselves on the communal question and state the limits beyond which they would not go in negotiating with the Muslims.[94] Disheartened by such an outburst, Sapru considered calling off the conference. But some of his Liberal friends urged him not to do so. 'If you abandon the calling of the conference,' wrote C.H. Setalvad (1901-1971), 'you at once make them dictators and give them a new importance'.[95] Ramaswamy Aiyar

[91]22 August 1929, Moonje Diaries, National Library, Calcutta; Moonje to Jayakar, 31 July 1926, Jayakar Papers (437).

[92]Speech at the Bengal Provincial Hindu Conference, *IAR*, July-December 1931, pp. 260-1.

[93]Speech at Akola, 8 August 1931, ibid., pp. 252-3.

[94]Jayakar to Sapru, 26 January 1930; Kelkar to Sapru, 27 January 1930; Sapru to Aiyar, 21/23 January 1930. Referring to his meeting with Malaviya, Sapru wrote: 'When I raised the Hindu-Muslim question with him frankly I did not find his attitude to be very satisfactory. It was theatrical and academic and did not seem to take note of the reality of the situation.' To Aiyar, 8 January 1930, Sapru Papers.

[95]Setalvad to Sapru, 22 January, 6 February 1930, ibid

(1890-1950) was no less disgusted. 'Under the guise of communalism,' he pointed out, 'the Sabha is perhaps the most aggressive communal body in India and any day one would choose to work with the Raja of Mahmudabad, Jinnah and Ali Imam rather than with Moonje, Kelkar and Co.'[96] The conference was eventually held in March and the Hindu Mahasabha participated uneasily. The preliminary meeting decided to meet in May before the delegates to the Round Table Conference proceeded to London. While the Liberals and the Muslims held to this agreement, the Mahasabhites backed out.[97]

This was not all. In July 1931, a committee consisting of Ansari, Malaviya and Sardar Sardul Singh (b. 1886) recommended, and the Congress Working Committee adopted, a scheme based on 'undiluted communalism and undiluted nationalism'. Its main features were: joint electorates and adult suffrage, with reservation for minorities of less than twenty-five per cent. The NWFP and Baluchistan would have the same form of government and administration as other provinces, Sind would form a separate province provided its people were prepared to bear the financial burden of the separated province, and in the future federal constitution residuary powers would rest with the provinces unless found prejudicial to the country's interests. Gandhi commended these proposals and made special mention of Ansari's incessant labours. 'I have never known Dr Ansari so identified and absorbed in anything,' he wrote in *Young India*, 'as he has been about the communal question'.[98] But the Muslim Conference was unimpressed. Its organ, the *Star*, remarked that despite the 'hotchpotching' by the Ansari-Azad group the substance of the Muslim demands were not met.[99] The Mahasabha's rejection was equally unequivocal and was carried at its annual session and at the Bengal Provincial Hindu Conference 'without a stinge of dissension from any quarter'. The Congress formula, stated the *Abhyudaya*, 'had laid itself open to the charge of having deviated from the path of nationalism, and that it sought to benefit the

[96]Aiyar to Sapru, 18 January 1930, Sapru Papers.

[97]Moore, *The Crisis of Indian Unity*, p. 106.

[98]*Young India*, 16 July 1931, *CWG*, Vol. XLVII, p. 141; *Bombay Chronicle*, 13 July 1931.

[99]Note on the Press, UP, for the week ending 25 July 1931. Also, see Page, op. cit., pp. 241-2.

minority at the expense of the majority community'.[100]

Ansari reacted angrily. The nationalism of the Mahasabha, he said, was merely a cloak for its aggressive communalism—an assessment shared by Jawaharlal in his autobiography. Even with the issue squarely placed in the context of the country's interest—which is where Ansari thought it ought to be—the Mahasabha was anything but enthusiastic.

Ansari watched helplessly as his initiatives were rejected and his overtures fell on stony ground. Though incensed by the Muslim Conference, he was equally critical of some of his fellow Congressmen who, in spite of their communal predilections, wielded considerable influence in decision-making processes. This was true of Malaviya who formed a breakaway group on the issue of Communal Award and was opposed to any agreement with Muslim groups. Yet, he could return to the Congress platform and give lessons on Hindu-Muslim unity, a cause which was never close to his heart. The role of such men distressed Ansari and he poured out his anger and frustration in a stream of letters to his friends.

Meanwhile, Ansari was dogged by persistent ill-health. With a dilated and diseased heart he had been carrying a tremendous load of work and responsibility and pushed himself very hard. He therefore toyed with plans for going to Bad Neuheim (Germany) for treatment and a prolonged period of rest in Europe. He planned to be away some time in January 1930, but was caught up by the turn of political events in the country, and in domestic chores. In May he was involved in arranging the wedding of his friend and political comrade, Shuaib Qureshi; in August he lost his brother Abdur Razzaq; and in the same month (28 August) he was sentenced to six months' imprisonment in Central Jail, Delhi, for organizing civil disobedience in Delhi. He was transferred the following day to the Gujarat Special Jail where, according to Ghaffar Khan, 'under the guidance of Dr Ansari we had formed a parliament of our own to train us to run our government which, we thought, was in the offing'.[101]

Ansari was out of jail at the end of January 1931 but was

[100]Note on the Press, for the week ending 25 July 1931. For the position of the Hindu Mahasabha, see *IAR*, July-December 1931, p. 254, and for the Bengal Provincial Hindu Sabha Conference, see p. 261.

[101]Tendulkar, *Ghaffar Khan*, p. 211.

constantly kept in a 'whirlpool of excitement'. He finally sailed on board the S.S. Victoria at 11 A.M. on 11 August 1932 in the company of Sherwani. There were others as well, but few of them possessed Ansari's practical experience of men and politics and it was this, unfolded in a series of rich anecdotes and drawn upon at every turn in support of his arguments, which fascinated his fellow travellers.

Ansari was treated for his heart trouble at Bad Neuheim. He, then, spent an educative week in Vienna where he was welcomed in the select Viennese society of professors, literary, scientific and artistic people. His next halt was in Ouchy-Lausanne. Here he felt lonely as he did not have a friend or acquaintance. But he enjoyed the unaccustomed peace and quiet of his surroundings and kept himself busy writing letters to Aziz Ansari and Shaukatullah, reading books, sightseeing and making arrangements for sending his son, Ahmad Harold, born from his second marriage and now a medical practitioner settled in England, to an English public school.[102] From Lausanne he travelled to Paris in November and then to London where he stayed till 13 December. This was one of his many visits to Europe and all his old joy in scenery and open air was reawakened.

Ansari returned to Delhi on 14 January and went up to see Jawaharlal at the Naini Central Prison in Dehradun. Jawaharlal noted in his prison diary on 17 February:

> Ansari suddenly turned up without any previous warning... Freshly returned from Europe full of stories of common friends and memories of old haunts in Switzerland and elsewhere. He looked much better than when he came in July. But his heart still gives trouble. He has wandered all over Europe while I sat and fed and slept in this same old little cell.[103]

[102]To Shaukatullah Ansari (Shaukoo), 28 September 1931; to Sherwani, 30 October 1931; to Aziz Ansari (Ajjoo), 10 November 1931, Hasan (ed.), *Muslims and the Congress*, pp. 129-30. Ansari married for the second time to a Christian lady whose name and background is obscure. A son was born soon after the marriage, but 'the family never accepted him' or his mother who lived mostly in Dehradun or Mussoorie. The son—Ahmad Harold—studied medicine in England, settled in that country and is now a consultant. Based on Zohra Ansari, Oral History transcript.

[103]*SWJ*, Vol. 5, p. 458; Ansari to Latif, 26 January 1933, Abdul Latif Bijnori, *Latif Ki Kahani* (Bijnor, 1967), p. 278.

Ansari reached India in a thoroughly gloomy frame of mind. The old communal spectre, far from withering away, was assuming a new and more malignant guise. But what distressed him most was the disintegration of the NMP, of which he was the chief architect. As he sensed the threat of its imminent break-up, he felt powerless, frustrated and increasingly unhappy. Khaliquzzaman, no longer inhibited by fear of Ansari's disapproval, signed the NMP's death warrant in UP by associating with the Muslim Conference in founding the Muslim Unity Board. In the Punjab the NMP was unable to make much headway because of Fazl-i-Husain and the Unionists and in Bengal it lost out to Fazlul Haq and the United Muslim Party. The new Muslim Majlis, formed in UP and Bengal to join hands with progressive and nationalist elements, made no dent on the growing alignment of communal forces. Abdur Rahman Siddiqi, another of Ansari's favourites and founder of the Bengal New Muslim Majlis, joined with Husayn Suhrawardy, while Mujibur Rahman found it difficult to cope with the confusing plethora of groups among Muslims.[104] By 1934, the NMP was split into various factions and the Congress Muslims stood 'divested of every shred of principle or practice on the basis of which they formed their group and which they had proudly nailed to their masthead—of everything, all, except their name!'[105] By its very nature, observed Khaliquzzaman many years later, the NMP could not make much progress. Under its name, several conferences were held, but it had no rules or regulations, no separate membership and no office. 'Being backed by the Hindu Sabha Press it lived in the newspapers all right but beyond that it had no positive existence. My idea that it might serve to bring about discipline in Nationalist Muslim ranks did not materialize because the remedy was not potent enough to eradicate the evil'.[106]

Explanations for the NMP's decline already exist. Jawaharlal attributed it to the upper middle class background of its members, the absence of 'dynamic personalities' amongst them and their method of drawing-room meetings and mutual arrangements and pacts. At this game, he argued, the communal leaders were greater adepts and they

[104] Mcpherson, op. cit., pp. 111, 121-2.
[105] Nehru, *An Autobiography*, p. 139.
[106] Khaliquzzaman, op. cit., p. 102.

drove the Nationalist Muslims from one position to another, made them give up, one by one, the principles for which they stood. Always the Nationalist Muslims tried to ward off further retreat and to consolidate their position by adopting the policy of the 'lesser evil', but always this led to another retreat and another choice of the 'lesser evil'. There came a time when they had nothing left to call their own, no fundamental principle on which they stood except one, and that had been the very sheet-anchor of their group: joint electorates. But again the policy of the lesser evil presented the fatal choice to them and they emerged from the ordeal minus that sheet-anchor.[107]

To Jawaharlal's perceptive explanation, one must add the strong opposition of the Hindu Mahasabha and the Muslim Conference. The NMP also had to contend with powerful local and regional groups. Working under severe constraints, it could not, for instance, replace the Unionists in Punjab and the Praja Krishak Party in Bengal. Its resources were inadequate, the political experience of its leaders was limited and the support extended by their community was at best lukewarm and half-hearted. The NMP was a platform for nationalist groups—the *Jamiyat al-ulama*, the Khudai Khidmatgars, the All-India Momin Conference and the Ahrars—but it lacked the cohesion and the ideological thrust to serve as an alternative party to either the Muslim Conference or the League. It was therefore reduced to arbitrating between the Congress and communally-inclined parties—a role Ansari played in the early 1930s. At the same time, there were serious difficulties in playing this role effectively and sustaining it for long. That is why while such constituents of the NMP as the Khudai Khidmatgars, the *Jamiyat al-ulama* and the Ahrars retained their individuality, Ansari and his compatriots went their separate ways. Consequently, the NMP lost its *raison d'etre* as an independent political entity.

The Congress Muslims suffered from another drawback. With their image indissolubly linked with the Hindus, they were pictured as renegades and accused of a sell-out. The *Himmat*, the *Al-Khalil, Mansur* and the *Aligarh Mail*—newspapers published in UP—denounced the NMP and its leader, Ansari, for sacrificing the community's interests at the altar of the Nehru

[107] Nehru, *An Autobiography*, p. 139. Also K.M. Munshi, *Pilgrimage to Freedom*, Vol. 1 (Bombay, 1967), p. 29.

Report. The *Al-Khalil,* quite uncharitably, dubbed them as 'traitors' and 'mercenary agents' of Motilal and other Hindus.[108] It was not surprising that such charges were bandied about, for the NMP could only be discredited in this manner in the eyes of the Muslim masses. Its leaders, therefore, should have anticipated the nature of the assault and adjusted their strategy accordingly. But they did nothing of the sort. What was equally disconcerting was the absence of any desire to remove this false impression. Ansari persevered doggedly, for he had a greater awareness of the need to respond to the pressures for change than a great many of his Muslim contemporaries. He also had the courage and the conviction to assert his political will and faced the daunting challenge posed by both the Hindu and Muslim communalists with tenacity. He had often to meet criticism and at times bitter attacks, but he never hesitated to carry the issue to the floor and fight it out with his critics. This was so during the communal bickerings over the Nehru Report. But his lieutenants in the NMP were weak, disorganized and unwilling to solve their problems of tactics, coordination or leadership; in fact Ansari soon became aware of how wayward were the elements he was seeking to fuse into one. Used to playing second fiddle—first to Mohamed Ali and later to Ansari—some NMP members gradually succumbed to communal pressures; others chose to be defensive, sulking when faced with the combined assault of the Muslim Conference, the Muslim League and a section of the *ulama.* This was true of Syed Mahmud, Khaliquzzaman, Shuaib Qureshi and Abdur Rahman Siddiqi, all bound to Ansari by personal rather than political loyalty. Jawaharlal's experience with such leaders led him to observe in April 1937:

> Our experience of the Nationalist Muslim Party in the past was not a happy one. Such half-way groupings confuse the issue and the masses are perplexed.... Those who agree (with the Congress) should not stand on the doorstep; they should enter the nation's chamber and take full share in shaping the nation's policy.[109]

The failure of Congress Muslims to face the ideologues of the Muslim Conference and the League can be attributed to their inability to formulate a coherent ideological programme

[108]Note on the Press, UP, for the week ending 29 June, 6, 20, 27 July, 17 August 1929.

[109]Statement to the Press, 25 April 1937, *SWJ*, Vol. 8, p. 128.

and to place their support for the Congress movement in a framework acceptable to the politically conscious sections of the Muslim community. A section of the *ulama*, especially those connected with the *Jamiyat al-ulama*, were able to do so because they worked out a theory of Islamic nationalism *versus* imperialism—one which was grounded in the basic tenets of Islam. Their opposition to communal politics, as conducted by the League, was also based on a neat set of ideas which were rooted in Islamic beliefs and ideology. The future of Islam, as indeed of its followers in India, lay in combining with the forces of nationalism in opposition to the Raj. This was not all. The All-India Momin Conference and the Khudai Khidmatgars, though confined to certain regions, carved out their sphere of influence by reconciling their nationalism with the specific demands and distinct interests of their constituents. The Congress Muslims made no such endeavour.

The weakness of the Congress Muslims' position stemmed from their narrow and unstable political base. The NMP was composed of a small number of professional men—lawyers, doctors and journalists—who did not operate in politics from a position they could claim their own. They were mainly dependent on the goodwill of leading Congressmen who, in turn, patronized them so as to lend credence to their own claim of representing all Indians. There was nothing wrong in relying on Congress; in fact it was consistent with NMP's political objectives. What proved detrimental to its progress and eventual collapse was the absence of any systematic endeavour to extend the political base outside the Congress circles. This was largely due to the rather limited concerns of the Congress Muslims. From the time of the Nehru Report they were caught up in constitutional issues and were involved, somewhat obsessively, in matters concerning joint *versus* separate electorates and reservation of seats. Ansari was closely associated with the All-Parties Conference, Shuaib Qureshi served as a member of the Nehru Committee and Khaliquzzaman, Syed Mahmud, Sherwani and Khwaja were enmeshed in constitutional controversies which raged from the time of the first Round Table Conference and culminated in the squabbles over the Communal Award. So was Ansari. But such preoccupation led to no tangible results: given the alignment of forces, the capacity of such men to negotiate a compromise was, in any case, limited. They could neither bargain for nor on behalf of their co-religionists. In consequence, they operated on the fringes of Indian politics and were made, in the words of Shaukat Ali, a cat's paw by their Congress co-workers. Their fate was similar to that of the Liberals.

The limited interests and concerns of the Congress Muslims are further reflected in their indifference towards the socio-economic problems of the country and the community they claimed to represent, a fact which made them out of touch with the complex interplay of forces in Indian society. Admittedly, there was much identification with the Kisan movements in UP during the Khilafat and non-cooperation movements, while Ansari touched on the problems of the working class in his statement of August 1927. But beyond such expressions of sympathy and concern, the Congress Muslims did not address themselves to issues outside the realm of constitutional politics. They had no role in the working class movement in Bombay and made no contribution to the debate on agrarian issues in UP, Bihar and Bengal. Their speeches and manifestos, though useful and important in relation to the communal phenomena, were devoid of any socio-economic content because they only dimly understood the economic and social changes that were taking place around them. This would probably explain why their perspective on and analysis of communalism was lacking in political depth, comprehension and wisdom. Viewing it largely in the context of the struggle for power, influence and authority, they demonstrated no awareness of the complex historical process and the contemporary socio-economic structures which engendered various forms of tensions and animosities, including Hindu-Muslim rivalries. It would also explain why their political base did not extend beyond the urban-based professional groups. Their disintegration as a cohesive and independent political entity was imminent.

The position of Congress Muslims was also weakened by the apathy of their comrades in Congress. Admittedly, they formed a constituency the Congress assiduously courted in the 1920s to deepen its support. They were flattered and cajoled by Gandhi during the Khilafat campaign. Ansari and Ajmal Khan, for instance, were adroitly used to follow a middle-of-the-road policy and to exercise restraint on the militant Khilafatists led by the Ali Brothers. Later, they formed valuable allies in dealing with estranged communal relations, projecting Congress policies among

Muslims and securing their electoral support.[110] Motilal made special efforts to woo Ansari, Shuaib Qureshi and Khaliquzzaman from the time of the All-Parties Conference in early 1928 till the National Convention in December of that year. Gandhi did the same, making laudatory references to their fervent commitment to Hindu-Muslim unity and insisting on Ansari's participation in the Round Table Conference.

Such symbolic gestures did not help Congress Muslims in their struggle against the communalists. Faced with the combined opposition of the Mahasabha and the Muslim Conference Ansari and the NMP required strong ideological and political backing. This was not forthcoming. They were merely used on occasions, given decorative positions in the Congress hierarchy and loudly proclaimed as selfless and devoted leaders. At the same time, they were wilfully ignored in crucial negotiations and their point of view was often disregarded with undeserved contempt.[111] This was so at the Lahore Congress in 1929. It was a situation which left Ansari restless and frustrated, conscious of his abilities as an organizer and seeing the job that needed to be done, without the chance to take a hand in it. 'We found the atmosphere in Lahore,' wrote Khaliquzzaman,

> very secretive and when in private talks the leading Congressmen decided to throw the Nehru Report into the Ravi, even Dr Ansari was not consulted... Dr Ansari, Tasadduq and myself were leaving Lahore in the evening for our destinations, humbled, disappointed and angry... At the station we had enough time to decide between ourselves that the Nehru Report having been drowned in the Ravi, we could not take the responsibility of shouldering the burden of fighting for

[110]Thus in 1926 Ansari, Ajmal Khan, Azad, Mazharul Haq and Shafee Daoodi issued an appeal to the Muslim electorate of the Madras presidency 'to stand by the Congress and to vote solidly for the Muslim candidates who stand under the banner of the Congress which is the sole common national organization of India'. F. No. G-66, 1926, AICC Papers.

[111]Notice Shaukat Ali's comment at the UP Muslim Conference, Allahabad, *IAR*, July-December 1931; p. 228, and the complaint of the Ahrar leader, Habibur Rahman that those Muslims, expecially over 1,000 workers in the Punjab, who made sacrifices during the civil disobedience movement, were ignored by the Congress. To Abul Kalam Azad, 31 August 1946, in Urdu, Habibur Rahman Ludhianvi Papers.

> the independence of India, for the Muslims were bound to consider it to be a purely Hindu fight.[112]

Assuming, somewhat prematurely, that the Congress Muslims had no large following, the Congress preferred to negotiate with their rivals and was willing to compromise on their terms. They at best were bargaining counters; when not so, they could easily be stored in the deep freeze.[113] This placed Ansari and his friends in a quandary and damaged their credibility in the eyes of their followers. Thus when Gandhi conveyed his readiness to compromise on separate electorates, Khwaja reacted angrily: 'It means,' he wrote indignantly, 'that you are prepared to surrender the Congress Muslims who have fought the battles of the country side by side with you to those Mussalmans who have done nothing except for themselves, their seats, their posts, their salaries and their lunches and dinners at the Government Houses... So far they [Congress Muslims] have fought against the Government and against the self-seekers of their own community... If now they are thrown overboard by the Congress or by you, they must either clear out of the field altogether or must henceforth fight against the Congress. Khwaja opposed both separate electorates and communal representation as he felt that the 'salvation of the Muslims lies in the salvation of the motherland and the salvation of the motherland in its turn lies in the mutual trust and goodwill of the two great communities'.[114]

Ansari's correspondence with Gandhi and Motilal in the summer of 1930 illustrates his disenchantment with the Congress strategy of popular mobilization pursued during civil disobedience. Equally revealing is how the constraints imposed by the Congress limited his political options and that of his comrades, and consequently reduced their effectiveness in propagating the gospel of nationalism among Muslims. This was aptly summed up by Ansari in early January 1930—soon after his criticism of the Lahore Congress resolutions was ignored. Writing to Sherwani in a touchy and despondent frame of mind, he summed up the guidelines of his political conduct in the following terms:

> We must not leave the Congress, nor must we do anything

[112]Khaliquzzaman, op. cit., p. 104.

[113]Chatterji, *Aspects of Bengal Politics*, p. 73.

[114]Khwaja to Gandhi, 12 March 1931, A.M. Khwaja Papers; *Bombay Chronicle*, 21 April 1931.

> to weaken the Congress. After all the will of the majority must prevail, that is the only guide for any democratic institution... To leave the Congress would be to commit political suicide, to oppose the Congress would be a crime. Therefore we must remain in the Congress and let those who believe in the present policy and programme carry on.

Again

> as...for joining the Liberals or the communalists it is unthinkable for you and me. The Liberals will never do anything, even though they are kicked out of the Round Table Conference... As regards the Muslim communalists, we have...extricated ourselves from them. We have formed the 'Nationalist Muslim Party" and it would be the height of unwisdom to leave that party or to cease working for its objects. *To my mind, that is the only avenue left for our political activities* [emphasis added]. We must put all our mind to it and carry on a vigorous campaign to wean the Muslims away from the influence of communalists and reactionary leaders and think and act in terms of "nationalism". *That is the only channel left for our political activities* [emphasis added].[115]

It is perhaps surprising to find such a sober, commonsense approach in a man who combined strict standards of political honesty and political obligation with a passionate emotional involvement in what he was doing. This is not to argue that Ansari was right—that is a question of opinion which every historian of Indian nationalism will answer for himself: only that in opposing Gandhi, Ansari and others who shared his views acted from conviction and in their own opinion would have been false to the principles which brought them into the Congress movement if they had acted otherwise.

[115]Ansari to Sherwani, 6 January 1930, Hasan (ed.), *Muslims and the Congress*, pp. 90-1.

9

The Final Act: Civil Disobedience and After

> I want to declare that we, the Nationalist Muslims, have never been before, nor are we at present, nor shall we be any time hereafter, communalists. We are Congressmen and we never intend leaving the Congress at any time. Our aim is to convert the communalist Muslim to the nationalist viewpoint and make them think on national lines [M.A. Ansari].
>
> *Bombay Chronicle*, 8 October 1935.

THE DECISION OF the Congress to launch civil disobedience created a breach between Ansari and his mentors and led to his isolation, at least for the time being, from the humdrum of political life. In view of the serious nature of the rift, Ansari promptly relinquished the positions he held in Congress and became 'only an ordinary member'.[1] This was a painful decision for one who had occupied so central a position in its hierarchy for nearly two decades. But given Ansari's sense of propriety it was not a surprising course of action. He had done the same in 1926 following his differences with the Central Khilafat Committee which, much to his distaste, had begun to spearhead communal causes.

In 1930 Ansari's estrangement with the Congress was over the efficacy of starting civil disobedience, an issue on which he had a greater degree of agreement with the Liberals than with his partymen. He was unable to attend the Congress Working Committee meeting on 14-16 February where plans for defying British authority were laid out, but had earlier warned Gandhi not to be carried away by the popular response to Independence Day, which was observed on 26 January. It was easy to join

[1]To Brelvi, 2 April 1930, Brelvi Papers. Ansari refused election to the Congress Working Committee and as a general secretary. He resigned from the presidentship of the PCC of Delhi, as well as membership of the Working Committee of the Delhi province and district.

processions, he had written, but quite difficult to face hardships and withstand repression.[2] This was followed by an impassioned appeal from Jaora. Ansari's reasoning was that the country was not prepared for civil disobedience because political conditions were quite the reverse of what they were in 1920, Hindu-Muslim-Sikh unity was wanting and there was danger of the non-violent campaign being submerged by the breaking out of violence.[3] Civil disobedience would therefore be a reckless course and cause 'incalculable damage'. The Congress should thus retrace its steps and, among things, concentrate on the uphill task of restoring communal amity which was not only one of the basic items in the Congress programme, but according to Ansari's conviction, '*the one and only* basic thing'.[4] In a subsequent communication, he pleaded with the Mahatma to reconsider his decision and warned that his politics of confrontation would not appeal to most sections of the population. 'Your movement,' he wrote,

> would thus fail to fructify and all the sacrifices made by you and those who would follow you would be wasted. This is

[2] To Gandhi, 10 February 1930, Hasan (ed.), *Muslims and the Congress*, p. 93. Also, Khaliquzzaman to Jawaharlal, 1 February 1930, Ansari Papers, JMI.

[3] Statement, 6 July 1930, ibid., p. 115.

[4] He compared the situation in the following manner:

(1920)	(1930)
1. Great dissatisfaction against the Govt. owing to wartime promises not having been kept. Dissatisfaction against Rowlatt Act, Martial Law and Khilafat wrongs.	1. Large number of people believe in the goodwill of the Labour Govt. and sincerity of the Viceroy, rightly or wrongly.
2. Highest watermark reached in Hindu-Muslim unity.	2. Lowest watermark reached in Hindu-Muslim unity.
3. Sikhs entirely with the Congress.	3. Sikhs almost entirely against the Congress.
4. Complete unity inside the Congress. Great enthusiasm among the workers and the rank and file.	4. Disunity in the Congress, diversity of purpose, complete lack of enthusiasm amongst the workers. Lukewarmness amongst the rank and file.
5 Complete non-violent atmosphere and yet breaking of violence in Chauri Chaura.	5. Obvious existence of violence, even large number of leading Congressmen believing in it and the certainty of violence breaking out.

Ansari to Gandhi, 13 February 1930, ibid., pp. 99-100. This letter is also published in *CWG*, Vol. XLII, pp. 518-22.

> how I have visualized the whole movement. Believe me, if I saw it as you do, I would have taken the marching orders and had been with you in the thick of the fight and not merely giving my blessing to the movement by mere words. You have that without asking for it.[5]

Ansari's position was easily misunderstood. He was suspected of having gone over to the side of the Ali Brothers and betrayed his leader Gandhi who valued and solicited his support. Ansari was quick to repudiate such allegations. He had no sympathy with Shaukat Ali's distorted view that civil disobedience was aimed against the Muslims, for his perspective on the contemporary political situation was not dictated by sectarian or communal considerations. His charge was 'a piece of monstrous falsehood and unworthy of any Mussalman'.[6]

Gandhi agreed with Ansari that the Hindu-Muslim tangle was the 'problem of problems', but felt that it had to be approached differently. Political adjustment between the two communities, according to him, was possible only after the 'evil' British power was removed and not before; 'there will be no charter of independence before the Hindus and the Muslims have met but there can be virtual independence before the charter is received.'[7] Motilal was sharp in his rebuttal:

> You say the country is not ready for civil disobedience. If so, when and how are you going to make it ready? Do you believe that in the present temper of the so-called leaders of the two communities it is possible to arrive at any formula? Even if it were possible which I seriously doubt how will the existence of that formula on paper carry us in our conflict with the foreign Government?.... I have definitely come to hold the opinion that ***no amount of formulae based upon mutual concessions which those making them have no right to make will bring us nearer Hindu-Muslim unity than we are at present*** [emphasis added].

He concluded by claiming credit for 'realizing what it means to me and mine

[5]The first page of this letter is missing, but it was obviously written by Ansari to Gandhi soon after 3 March 1930. See Ansari Collection, NMML.

[6]To Brelvi, 2 April 1930, Brelvi Papers.

[7]Gandhi to Ansari, 16 February 1930, Hasan (ed.), *Muslims and the Congress*, pp. 101-2; also, *CWG*, Vol. XLII, pp. 510-11.

to throw in my lot with Gandhiji in the coming struggle. Nothing but a deep conviction that the time for the greatest effort and the greatest sacrifice has come would have induced me to expose myself at my age and with my family obligations to the tremendous risks I am incurring. I hear the clarion call of the country and I obey.[8]

This manifesto marked a significant shift from the earlier position, one which was not easily discernible to most of Motilal's contemporaries. The resolution of communal conflicts was one of Congress' main concerns in the 1920s. It was no longer so. Realizing its vexed nature and constrained by the dictates of political expediency, the Mahatma-Motilal axis was now willing, though reluctantly, to let matters drift. Such was the perception of some contemporary observers.[9] Ansari felt that the Congress had not done enough to achieve unity and regretted that Gandhi and Motilal were not so 'persuasive, so active, or so masterful as the great importance of this question required'. 'Perhaps you were not very confident of yourselves,' he told Gandhi, 'or perhaps you felt you could not succeed in bringing about a communal settlement by means of conferences. Whatever the causes that is how it struck me and many others.'[10] Others, on the other hand, disapproved of some of Gandhi's pronouncements during this period, such as his speech in Delhi on 7 March and

[8]Motilal Nehru to Ansari, 17 February 1930, ibid., pp. 103-4.

[9]It seems to us that Gandhi has not so far tried so much as he ought to have done to bring about a Hindu-Muslim settlement...[and] has not yet made any sustained efforts to make the Hindus as a community to take up an attitude that may make for a settlement.' *Mussalman*, 20 June 1931. This assertion was true to a certain extent but was not supported by the impression of other contemporaries. Sapru, for instance, found him anxious for a Hindu-Muslim settlement and felt, quite rightly, that it was unfair to judge Gandhi's intentions by his public statements or by what some of his followers said. Earlier, Gandhi had written to Sapru that he was 'trying in my own way to reach a solution of the communal tangle. If there is no success I would not have the heart to go to London. I said as much to Irwin.' Sapru to Sankey, 24 May 1931, Gandhi to Sapru. 22 April 1931, Sapru Papers (23).

[10]Ansari to Gandhi, n.d., Ansari Collection, NMML. It is noteworthy that Ansari did not change his view until 1934 when he again complained of Gandhi not doing enough to restore communal amity. Gandhi wrote in reply: 'If you entertain this fear I would like to disabuse you of the fear. My views are just as strong as they were on the necessity of this unity. But I have come to the conclusion that this is the time for real lovers of unity to sit still and simply pray showing in their individual action what a living unity of hearts can mean. Do you not

at the *Jamiyat al-ulama* session on 1 April 1931.[11] The *Mussalman* took strong exception to his remark that Hindus should not 'return blow for blow but treat the Muslims as brethren, even if the Muslims are wrong' and contested the implicit notion of an 'aggressive' Muslim versus a 'defensive' Hindu community. Communalists were among both the communities. The only difference was that the Hindus, being in a majority, had the advantage of palming off their communalism as nationalism or altruism.[12]

The point was overstated. It was wrong to assume a communal bias on the part of Gandhi or Motilal and, then, to expect them to produce a magic formula which would resolve the issue altogether. What deserved reflection was their insistence that a successful anti-colonial struggle would cement bonds of unity and minimize Hindu-Muslim friction. Gandhi told Ansari that a meeting of minds could only be accomplished through fighting for common causes and wanted him to recognize the new orientation he had given to the civil disobedience campaign.[13] This assumption, though questionable in the light of subsequent happenings, was based on Gandhi's experiences in dealing with the communal divide. Having failed to heal the communal wound through his own methods, he reached the inescapable conclusion that independence would precede and not succeed the resolution of the communal question.[14] Ansari did not share this view. He felt that Gandhi's way of bringing about unity had already proved ineffective when conditions for joint action were ideal and reiterated his faith in mutual adjustments through dialogue and discussion, a method considered ineffectual by Motilal and the Mahatma. In a candid and perceptive elaboration of this argument—one which illustrates Ansari's differences with Gandhi as well as offers clues to his way of dealing with the communal tangle—Ansari observed:

> Immediately after the setback of the N.C.O. movement, there was a reaction which, instead of keeping the Hindus and

meet in your practice with boils which grow worse with teasing? I find communal discord such a boil. The more you tease it the worse it becomes. It needs a rest cure.' Gandhi to Ansari, 18 March 1934, Hasan (ed.), *Muslims and the Congress*, p. 145.

[11] *Mussalman*, 10 March, 4 July 1931.

[12] Ibid., 4 April 1931

[13] Gandhi to Ansari, 3 March 1930, Hasan (ed.), *Muslims and the Congress*, p. 118.

[14] This was the essence of Gandhi's letter of 16 February to Ansari.

> Muslims together, made them fight each other as they had never done before. Unity patched up to fight a common foe always breaks down as soon as the fight ceases. Unity during a deluge or in the face of any elemental force is brought about by common danger and lasts till the danger lasts. Unity to be lasting should be achieved during normal and peace time after careful thought and based on collective judgement. The parties should have occasion to fully weigh the gains and losses and should accept them with open eyes and full knowledge. *This is possible only through conferences, as in the present pressing circumstances led by a great urge* [emphasis added]. This is how other countries have achieved it. I believe that urge is felt today by the contending parties. Along with the Liberals, the imprimatur of the Congress would have aided much to help them onwards.
>
> *I have all along pinned my faith in mutual adjustments through formal and informal conversations* [emphasis added].[15]

Gandhi's high-minded sentiments did not inspire most members of the NMP. Ansari's letter and Gandhi's reply created doubts in Syed Mahmud's mind and he sought advice, torn between loyalty to Jawaharlal and dislike of the Lahore resolution, reinforced by his need to earn a living at the Bar.[16] Sherwani was disappointed because the Mahatma's reply showed utter indifference to the feelings of those Muslims who stood by him in his movement just like soldiers.[17] Khaliquzzaman wondered about the future of the Congress Muslims. If they were to accept Gandhi's order of priorities and time scale, they would, in effect, proclaim to their co-religionists to find their leaders in people who played the communal game unabashedly. Khaliquzzaman did not want this to happen. He wanted to form a group committed to the creed of independence and, at the same time, insistent on Hindu-Muslim unity as a cardinal basis for India's progress. The future protagonist of Pakistan discerned widespread support for this view and hoped that many Muslims who left the NMP on the issue of the Nehru Report would return to its fold in sheer disgust with the aggressive attitude of Jinnah and Shafi.[18]

nsari to Gandhi, n.d., Ansari Collection, NMML.

Syed Mahmud to Ansari, n.d., Hasan (ed.), *Muslims and the Congress*, pp. 106-7.

7Sherwani to Ansari, 3 March 1930, ibid., p. 113.

18Khaliquzzaman to Ansari, 1 March 1930, ibid., pp. 110-11.

It was all very well to feel aggrieved and nurse grandiose plans of future political strategy. But the Congress Muslims realized, more than anybody else, that they could not afford to defy their party and stay aloof from civil disobedience. They recognized, as Ansari did, that their political fortunes were inextricably linked with the Congress and they could only stay with it by following the dictates of the brute majority. Exhorting Sherwani not to do anything drastic, Ansari stated the obvious: 'to leave the Congress would be to commit political suicide'.[19] His heart was not in civil disobedience,[20] but he ultimately joined the Congress bandwagon partly because of his personal loyalty to Gandhi and partly because of his desire to remain in the political mainstream. Thus when Vallabhbhai Patel (1875-1950) appealed for his return to the Working Committee in July 1930 after the arrest of the two Nehrus,[21] he was quick to respond. He issued a press statement which was prompted by the government's stern counter measures, the 'unparalleled fidelity of a people to the principles of non-violence' and the shockingly retrograde recommendations of the Statutory Commission report.[22] He rejoined the Working Committee in August as he could neither 'view with equanimity the policy of ruthless suppression' nor allow government to 'kill the paramount national organization of India, loyalty to which has been my lifelong creed'.[23]

He succeeded Azad as Congress 'dictator' and was arrested

[19]Ansari to Sherwani, 6 January 1930, ibid., pp. 90-1.

[20]He put it somewhat differently in his letter to Gandhi. 'My heart,' he wrote, 'is with you but my brain is not, in spite of all the bias in your favour.' To Gandhi, n.d., Ansari Collection, NMML. Also, Ansari to V.J. Patel, 29 May 1930, Hasan (ed.), *Muslims and the Congress*, p. 123.

[21]Vallabhbhai Patel to Ansari, 13 July 1930, ibid., p. 126.

[22]Ansari to Brelvi, 2 April 1930, Brelvi Papers; press statement by Ansari, 7 July 1930, Hasan (ed.), *Muslims and the Congress*, pp. 123-4. For further details, see *Bombay Chronicle*, 7 July 1930, and *IQR*, July-December 1930, p. 331.

[23]Ibid., 13 August 1930; Home Poll. F. No. 5/46, 1932, NAI. Writing to the *Manchester Guardian* soon after Ansari's death, Horace Alexander recalled his meeting with the departed leader during civil disobedience. 'He had disapproved Mr Gandhi's starting of civil disobedience and was eager for peace. On my visiting him, he admitted that he had been opposed to civil disobedience, but as the weeks had passed by, with daily lathi beatings of unarmed peaceful men and women and other brutalities, he had felt unable to stand aside any longer. On that very day, as a result of the arrest of another Congress leader, he had become acting president of the Congress.' *Manchester Guardian*, 13 May 1936, Nehru Papers, Vol. 45.

on 27 August 1930 while the Working Committee meeting was on at *Dar-us-Salam* in defiance of the official ban.[24] He served another term in prison. Succeeding Rajendra Prasad (1884-1963) as Congress president, he was arrested in Delhi on 8 January 1932 and was sentenced to six months' imprisonment. The man who was a reluctant participant joined civil disobedience in the larger interest of the country and languished behind British jails.

Ansari's NMP comrades followed their leader once Gandhi was arrested on 5 May. Syed Mahmud was arrested on 30 June for being secretary of the 'unlawful' Working Committee, Sherwani was convicted in Bombay in connection with the "Tilak Day" procession on 2 August, Azad, acting president, was sent to gaol on 21 August, Khaliquzzaman served for a while as Congress 'dictator' and Hasrat Mohani, Saifuddin Kitchlew, Rafi Ahmad Kidwai, Khwaja and Brelvi were incarcerated more than once for defying government ordinances. The Congress Muslims everywhere were now in the forefront of a movement they had joined with extreme reluctance. The NMP conference in July, chaired by Ansari, supported mass action, such as general strike and movement of non-cooperation, especially because all resources to protest by means of representation, press, platform and public demonstration had been exhausted.[25] Ansari chose the occasion to repudiate the charge that Muslims, particularly those connected with the NMP, were wary of joining civil disobedience.

> We had to stop this misrepresentation of the community by parties and persons who would exploit the Muslim community to serve ends that are neither Indian nor Indian Muslim. We had to give the direct lie to libellers so that future generations

[24]Wrote Azad: 'Before I was arrested, I nominated Dr Ansari as my successor. At first he was not willing to join the movement but I was able to persuade him.' *India Wins Freedom* (Delhi, 1959), reprint, p. 11. Horace Alexander and his companion were in *Dar-us-Salam* when 'it was surrounded by the police, who had come to arrest the whole committee. In the midst of all this anxiety Dr Ansari came out on the balcony and smilingly said: "Well, you see how it is. I apologize for receiving you in this manner. I hope to be able to offer you better hospitality at some future time when we are free." ... Then the members of the Congress Committee were carried off in police cars; last of all, the police superintendent himself drove his own car, containing Dr Ansari, the Muslim president, and the veteran Hindu leader Pandit Malaviya. As they passed us in the Drive Dr Ansari and Malaviya waved to us as if they were schoolboys off for a holiday.' Ibid.

[25]*IQR*, July-December 1930, p. 331.

might not point their finger of scorn at the supposed indifference of Mussalmans in their country's hour of trial.[26]

Much of the drive behind this enthusiasm followed the crucial decision of the *Jamiyat al-ulama*, arrived after much deliberation, to participate in Gandhi's movement of civil disobedience.[27] If the *ulama* could do so, so ran the argument, the Congress Muslims had no reason to distance themselves. Furthermore, they could not risk being found in the company of the Ali Brothers and their credibility, as indeed their political survival, depended on their ability to retrace their steps and choose the one course which made them part of the national mainstream. With the *ulama* and the Congress Muslims of the NMP behind the Congress, Ansari's claim that large segments of the Muslim community backed civil disobedience carried weight.

The rigours of a hectic political life, combined with his stint in British jails, damaged Ansari's health. He went to Europe for treatment—in October 1932, August 1933 and May 1934—but his heart condition did not improve. He complained of hard work and heavy responsibilities. 'I don't think I would last long

[26] *Bombay Chronicle,* 24 July 1930.

[27] After three days of strenuous discussion on the question whether Muslims should participate in the struggle for independence, the *Jamiyat* at its session at Amroha resolved: '(a) Whereas the Indian National Congress has adopted complete independence as its political goal which has so long been the creed of the *Jamiyat,* and whereas it has nullified the Nehru Report and has resolved that no constitution will be acceptable to the Congress unless it gives full satisfaction to the minorities concerned, this session of the *Jamiyat* considers that under the present circumstances there is no reason why Muslims should keep themselves aloof from the Congress. (b) In view of the religious and national interest of Muslims, this session of the *Jamiyat* wants to make it clear that any future programme of the Congress will not be regarded as the final word for Muslims, unless the *Jamiyat* accepts it. (c) Whereas the Sarda Act is an open interference with Islam and is an outrage upon the Islamic personal law and whereas the Government, in spite of widespread agitation and protest, has not exempted Muslims from it; (d) Whereas complete freedom of the country and the nation from British domination is the only means to put a stop to all this mischief and to safeguard the honour of Islam, this session of the *Jamiyat* appeals to Muslims that for the sake of the freedom of the country and to protect from the outrage the Islamic personal law, they should, in cooperation with the Congress, carry on the non-violent struggle for freedom with courage, zeal and determination. (e) This session of *Jamiyat* appoints a Committee, consisting of Maulana Kifayatullah, Maulana Ataullah Shah Bukhari and Maulana Muhammad Naeem to prepare a programme of action on the following lines for the attainment of freedom and the protection of personal

at this rate,' he wrote in December 1933.[28] He informed Jawaharlal around the same time that he was unable to stand the rigours of political life and apologized in advance for his inability to attend meetings and conferences.[29] But, then, a politician of his stature and reputation could not quit that easily. He was pressed into service just when he contemplated resigning from the Congress bodies. In fact Ansari's last major intervention in Indian politics—one which greatly enhanced his political prestige—was in the revival of the Swaraj Party. He returned to active politics and in the form which most suited him. He became the go-between, the man who tried to arrange compromise between the contending political parties.

The Making of the Swaraj Party

The opportunity of playing a major political role was provided by the slackening of the civil disobedience movement and the feeling among Congress leaders outside jail that its momentum could not be maintained any longer.[30] By mid-1933 there were open demands for revising the Congress strategy as civil disobedience had outlived its usefulness as a method and devising a

law and invites Muslims to execute it:—(i) Publication of proscribed *Fatwa* and other literatures. (ii) Picketing of liquor shops. (iii) Boycott of British cloth and to carry on a propaganda in favour of British goods and specially British goods and cloth made in India. (iv) The *Jamiyat* expects that, if the Congress makes an attempt to remove the doubts and suspicions of some of the Muslims who are not yet satisfied with its attitude, prompt success is bound to come through the united actions of the Muslims.' *IQR*, January-June, p. 43.

[28]To Shaukatullah Ansari, 9 December 1933, Hasan (ed.), *Muslims and the Congress*, p. 141. He had earlier written to Jawaharlal to say that there was an acceptable improvement in his heart condition. A week before sailing for India he wrote from France: 'A week in London was enough to make me run away from there. I am here for this week before taking my boat on 26th. One at least sees the sun here.' To Jawaharlal, 19 October 1933, Nehru Papers (3).

[29]To Jawaharlal, 20 December 1933, Nehru Papers (3); Ansari to A.L. Bijnori, 19 October 1934, Bijnori, *Latif Ki Kahani*, pp. 280–1. Horace Alexander met Ansari at London in 1933 and remembered how his health had been broken by his imprisonment, and 'he had become an old man'. Nehru Papers (3).

[30]There is much useful secondary literature on the subject. I have mainly relied on: Brown, *Gandhi and Civil Disobedience*, chapter 7, section 2; B.R. Tomlinson, *The Indian National Congress and the Raj 1929-1942: The Penultimate Phase* (London, 1976), pp. 37-9; B.B. Misra, *The Indian Political Parties* (Delhi, 1976), pp. 299-307. Some of the essays in D.A. Low (ed.), *Congress and the Raj: Facets of the Indian Struggle 1917-47* (London, 1977) revise some of the existing notions on civil disobedience.

practical plan to turn the energies of the nation into 'channels of fruitful activity'.[31] Such views, when voiced at the Poona Conference on 12-14 July 1933, met with Gandhi's strong opposition. Yet, the Mahatma, with his unmatched political skill which he used to his advantage, agreed to a compromise on his own terms: civil disobedience would not be unconditionally withdrawn but would take the form of individual civil disobedience. As Congress had been unable to communicate the essence of satyagraha to the masses it was now to be conveyed to them by the example of individuals acting in a true 'spirit of resistance'.[32]

Ansari sensed the political mood in Congress circles on his return to India in early November. S. Satyamurti (1887-1943) founded a provincial Swarajya Party a month earlier to contest elections to the local boards and legislatures and chalked out plans for holding a conference to launch a party at the all-India level.[33] K.F. Nariman (1883-1948), a Working Committee member, declared his intentions of restoring the Congress 'from the wrong track to which...it was drifting'. But Satyamurti and Nariman did not tread warily and their initiatives were thwarted by Gandhi and the Congress. Nariman tried in vain to seek a referendum on revoking, modifying, or retaining the civil disobedience movement started in 1932.[34]

Soon thereafter, Ansari and B.C. Roy (1882-1962) entered the scene to carry on Nariman's unfinished work. They met in Bombay in late December, conferred with Azad, Sarojini Naidu and K.M. Munshi (1887-1971),[35] and then drafted a letter, after consultations with Gandhi, inviting forty prominent Congressmen to draw up a scheme to implement the constructive programme outlined in the Poona Conference and later amplified in Gandhi's statement.[36] Plans were then set afoot to convene a meeting in March. Ansari hoped that it would lead to the revival of the

[31] *Hindu*, 19 August 1933, *A Hundred Years of the Hindu: The Epic Story of Indian Nationalism* (Madras, n.d.), pp. 438-9.

[32] The process has been described by Tendulkar, Nanda and Brown. I have tried to keep the details to the minimum. Also, the chronological order of events has not been followed in the subsequent narrative.

[33] Satyamurti to Ansari, 11 November 1933, Home Poll. F. No. 4/19, 1933, NAI.

[34] Nariman to Ansari, 11 December 1933, Hasan (ed.), *Muslims and the Congress*, pp. 142-4.

[35] Roy to Ansari, 8 January 1934, B.C. Roy Papers, NMML; Ansari to Brelvi, 1 February 1934, Brelvi Papers.

[36] Ansari and Roy to Munshi, 10 January 1934, *Pilgrimage to Freedom*, Vol. 1, pp. 358-9, and enclosure in Roy to Ansari, 8 January 1934, Roy Papers.

Swaraj Party and the formulation of a political programme.[37] He had an excellent reason to entertain such a desire. Opposed to civil disobedience even in 1930, he wanted a change realizing that Muslim seats in the legislatures would all go to the communalists unless Congress could rehabilitate itself in his co-religionists' eyes.[38] Besides, with the communal situation deteriorating steadily and civil disobedience proceeding haltingly, he and his NMP colleagues felt demoralized and searched for a way out of the growing impasse. Jawaharlal learnt of the 'demoralization ousdide' which had afflicted Ansari, Sherwani and Khaliquzzaman, though he was surprised and a bit disheartened that Rafi Ahmad Kidwai was also part of the same flock.[39]

The initial move to hold a conference ran into trouble, but Roy's meeting with Gandhi on 17 March straightened matters. The latter informed Ansari the next day that he would not stand in the way of a Council entry party because of his belief that the paralysis of the intelligentsia had to be removed. He would therefore welcome a party of Congressmen prosecuting the programme rather than remaining sullen, discontented and inactive.[40]

The conference that followed Gandhi's signal was held at *Dar-us-Salam*, with Ansari as the star performer. Many of those present already belonged to provincial parties that had formed themselves on the ruin of the Congress Party machine and had taken Council entry as their avowed or tacit objective. 'For God sake,' he implored, 'end this deadly political paralysis that is slowly creeping on the nation and has resulted in a political lethargy and blankness that may ultimately lead to disaster.' 'Believe me,' he assured his detractors, 'that I am still as staunch a Non-changer as before and I have been compelled to adopt this course as the only possible alternative to end the present deadlock.'[41] He gave assurance of Gandhi's support and spoke effectively and convincingly; in fact, an hour's forceful oration gave the final touch to the proceedings and made a unanimous decision on the revival of the Swaraj Party possible.[42] Two days

[37]Ansari to Brelvi, 1 February 1934, Brelvi Papers.
[38]Brown, op. cit., p. 368.
[39]Prison Diary, 23 June 1933, *SWJ*, Vol. 5, p. 485.
[40]Gandhi to Ansari, 18 March 1934, Home Poll. F. No. 3/6, 1934, NAI.
[41]*IAR*, January-June 1934, pp. 261-3, for a summary of the proceedings.
[42]*Bombay Chronicle*, 3 April 1934.

earlier, Ansari had gathered that government intended to hold assembly elections in the autumn. He seized on this 'God-sent opportunity' as a handle for a new programme which would enable a challenge to government but would side-step the thorny question of withdrawing civil disobedience and making an immediate decision on the new legislatures.[43] He put his argument to Brelvi, who, having condemned the council entry policy as divisive in November 1933,[44] now extended his cooperation to Ansari's endeavours:

> I know that you would stand by me realizing fully well that what I have done is entirely conceived in the interest of the country and solely with a view to remove the paralysis and death-like inertia...as a result of complete inactivity on the part of Congress workers.... I admit that the scheme has many drawbacks and is far from perfect, but I want you to see what other schemes would have been devised which would be dynamic, would catch the imagination of the people, would offer a challenge to the Government and would at the same time be fighting the government on constitutional lines.... You would also see that, as it confines itself to the election of the Assembly, it would be possible for the Swarajya Party to send the most outstanding men to contest the elections and thus ensure not only their return but the raising of the opposition in the Assembly and all Congressmen in the country.... The Swarajya Party after its campaign for the assembly elections would have reached the electorate and familiarized the people to its aims and ideals and therefore it would be in a position to stand up in opposition to the forces of bureaucracy, of reaction, of capital and of communal organizations, which you may rest assured would all combine against the Congressmen.

Ansari concluded on a cautious note, making it clear that he had no delusions regarding the limited scope of the assembly work. But in the existing state of 'deadlock and paralysis' there was no alternative to the plans chalked out at the Delhi gathering.[45]

Ansari's optimism, reflected in his Delhi speech, was not

[43]Ansari to Brelvi, 10 April 1934, Brelvi Papers; Brown, op. cit., p. 364.
[44]Brelvi to Satyamurti, 12 November 1933, quoted in Brown, op. cit., p. 364.
[45]Ansari to Brelvi, 10 April 1934, Brelvi Papers.

misplaced. When he and Roy met Gandhi at Patna in early April they had no difficulty in convincing him that the Swaraj Party's revival was a political necessity and that many Congressmen were reticent to go to jail in pursuance of individual civil disobedience.[46] Gandhi agreed and pledged his support to the revival of the party.[47] He, then, suspended civil disobedience, a decision which agonized, among others, Jawaharlal. Gandhi's statement of 7 April withdrawing civil disobedience, the reasons given and the general outlook displayed seemed to Jawaharlal an insult to the nation and to the Congress. He felt with a stab of pain that the chords of allegiance that had bound him to the Mahatma for many years had snapped.[48] The Congress Socialist Party, inaugurated at Patna on 17 May 1934, was no less indignant. Abandonment of civil disobedience and the decision to enter the Delhi assembly was a clear violation of the 1929 Lahore resolution which had called for boycotting legislatures and had demanded nothing less than complete independence. The new policy, pursued under Gandhi's leadership, was further proof that the national movement was drifting inevitably towards constitutionalism and accommodation with the British.[49] Jayaprakash Narayan (1902-1979), writing in 1936 in *Why Socialism*, characterized Gandhism as a mixture of 'timid economic analysis, good intentions and ineffective moralizing'. To socialists like him Gandhi was a 'reformist', who offered only palliatives for India's chronic and grievous social ills, when a purgative was required.[50]

[46] *IAR*, January-June 1934, Vol. 1, pp. 262-3.

[47] Gandhi to Ansari, 5 April 1934, Hasan (ed.), *Muslims and the Congress*, p. 147. The journalist Durga Das concluded after his discussions with Gandhi that he had realized that 'whereas the Swarajists counted on his movement as a sanction for their fight within the legislatures, hereafter the constructive programme for which he stood could receive an impetus through the power that the coming Reforms Act would place in the hands of popularly chosen Ministers in the province'. Durga Das, *India From Curzon to Nehru and After* (London, 1969), p. 164.

[48] *SWJ*, Vol. 6, p. 272; Gopal, *Jawaharlal Nehru*, Vol. 1, pp. 186-7; Pandey, *Nehru*, pp. 178-9.

[49] *IQR*, January-June 1930, pp. 340-4. J.P. Haithcox, 'Left Wing Unity and the Indian Nationalist Movement: M.N. Roy and the CSP', *Modern Asian Studies*, Vol. 3, I, 1969, pp. 19, 21; Minoo Masani, *Bliss was it in that Dawn: A Political Memoir Upto Independence* (Bombay, 1977), pp. 46-50. For reactions to socialist pronouncements, see Tomlinson, op. cit., pp. 52-5.

[50] For a recent study, see Bimal Prasad, *Gandhi, Nehru and J.P.: Studies in Leadership* (Delhi, 1985).

Such criticism was of limited value, for neither Jawaharlal nor his socialist followers could influence Gandhi's decision or desert the Congress ranks. Acharya Narendra Deva (1889-1956) summed up his party's strategy succintly: 'Howsoever one may criticize and denounce the Congress, it is the only broad platform of anti-imperialist struggle in India and it is the only centre today from which such a struggle can be conducted.'[51]

The Swarajists were unmoved by the criticism. Amidst scenes of enthusiasm, nearly a hundred of them met in Ranchi on 2 May to implement the Delhi conference decisions. Being unanimously voted to the chair, Ansari again occupied the centre stage. He detailed the history of the efforts which went into the making of the Swaraj Party and concluded with the plea to accept Gandhi's definition of satyagraha and civil resistance and to abide by his advice.[52] At the AICC meeting on 18-19 May, he placed the Swarajist view, moved the all important resolution for suspending civil disobedience and shrugged socialist opposition by pointing out that most of their demands were contained in the Karachi Congress National Demand.[53] 'We have achieved in six weeks,' he proudly announced,

> what the most sanguine amongst us could not have expected in six months or a year and we have achieved what to us is the most priceless of all the assets: the recognition, the moral and political support of the greatest Indian National organization, the Indian National Congress.[54]

The wheel had taken full circle. The 'no-changer' of 1922-23 was now a vocal champion of the council entry programme. Though ridiculed by some for executing a *volte face*, Ansari brushed aside criticism with disdain. He enjoyed being at the centre of a controversy and heard with pleasure the words of praise showered on his dynamic leadership. He had not received such compliments before and relished them in his final hour of glory. His role in reviving the Swaraj Party was widely commended and he received credit for that 'great and wonderful miracle'—the conversion of the author of non-cooperation 'into a silent blesser

[51] *Bombay Chronicle*, 24 May 1934.
[52] *IAR*, January-June 1934, pp. 271-2.
[53] Ibid.
[54] *Bombay Chronicle*, 25 May 1935 (editorial comment)

of parliamentary methods'.[55] Nariman, elected mayor of Bombay in April 1935, commented that the Mahatma's assent was entirely due to Ansari's 'advocacy of such transparent sincerity and honesty'.[56] The praise did not end here. As president of the Congress Parliamentary Board, an honour he greatly valued, there were more kudos for the man who emerged as the chief election campaigner—issuing policy statements, settling factional feuds, raising funds and laying down guidelines for candidates. It was a position of prominence Ansari greatly welcomed. Such was the goodwill he earned that, on the eve of his departure for Europe on 24 May, he was specially feted in Bombay.[57] Both Gandhi and Jawaharlal kept him informed of political developments at home and solicited his advice. On his return to Bombay on 5 October, Patel eulogized his contribution at a massive public meeting held at the Chowpatty sands.[58] This was Ansari's hour of triumph as he gazed at the massive gathering which applauded at the mention of his name.

Ansari was drawn into the fray immediately after returning from Europe. He opened the assembly election campaign on 6 October in Bombay.[59] This was followed by an assurance to the electorate that the Swaraj Party would press for self-determination and pursue its task of national reconstruction. 'Every voter,' stated the appeal, 'must look upon himself as the custodian of the country's honour and of both collective and personal interests and therefore he should not waste his vote on small or subsidiary issues or allow it to be exploited by candidates who are not supported by the most powerful party of the country.'[60]

The Congress did well in the assembly elections, winning 44 of the 88 elected seats. Brelvi, for one, felt no surprise; 'there is not the least doubt that during the last few years the Congress had a tremendous hold over the people'.[61] Rajendra Prasad attributed Congress' success to the faith and confidence of the people who were impressed by the party's record of sacrifice

[55]Ibid., 11 April 1935, and editorial comment, 6 April 1935.

[56]Ibid., 7 October 1934.

[57]Ibid., 25 May 1934.

[58]Ibid., 6 October 1934.

[59]Ibid., 7 October 1934.

[60]Hasan (ed.), *Muslims and the Congress*, pp. 165-7.

[61]Brelvi to Ansari, 24 November 1934, Hasan (ed.), *Muslims and the Congress*, p. 192.

and service.[62] Later, he talked of the party's hold on the masses and their respect 'not for the individual but for the institutions'. He had earlier felt that the large gatherings at public meetings were due to Gandhi's charismatic personality and did not necessarily represent interest in Congress or swaraj. But he found the same kind of response in his tours throughout the country, indicating the depth of support for the Congress and its policies.[63]

What Rajendra Prasad ignored was the singularly important contribution of Ansari in organizing the election campaign with imagination, purposefulness and efficiency. He minimized friction within the Congress, sorted out the all important problem of raising funds and ensured, much to everybody's satisfaction, its proper distribution. His personal contribution to the election expenses, raised through a private loan, was substantial and entailed quite a burden to pay it off; 'the result has been that I have had to go on grinding day after day and month by month without taking any rest or holiday,' he wrote to B.C. Roy in October 1935.[64] But this was scarcely recognized, a fact which seemingly distressed Ansari. This would probably explain why some of his statements, issued soon after the assembly elections, were muted and underlined his disappointment.[65] What added to his irritation was the irresponsible criticism of his statement of 16 October: his critics charged that his views were 'calculated to bring down the dignity of the Congress'.[66] B.C. Roy came to his defence,[67] but Ansari's feelings were not assuaged. In disgust, he contemplated resigning from the Congress Parliamentary Board.[68]

The Communal Divide

Ansari had little cause to complain, for his political trajectory

[62]Rajendra Prasad to Ansari, 26 December 1934, Hasan (ed.), *Muslims and the Congress*, p. 227.

[63]Rajendra Prasad to Sri Prakasa, 11 December 1935, Sri Prakasa Papers, NMML.

[64]Ansari to B.C. Roy, 10 October 1935, Roy Papers.

[65]Statement of 26 November 1934 and letter to Congress members of the Legislative Assembly, 11 December 1934, Hasan (ed.), *Muslims and the Congress*, pp. 196-7, 213-4.

[66]*Bombay Chronicle*, 7 January 1935.

[67]Ibid.

[68]Ansari to G.B. Pant, October 1934 (telegram), Hasan (ed.), *Muslims and the Congress*, p. 167.

had worked out quite well from 1930 to 1935. There were of course some failures and setbacks but they were a necessary part of a politician's life. He was disappointed with the performance of the NMP which lingered on but had long ceased to be an effective force. He was equally concerned at deteriorating communal relations and his desire to bring the two major communities closer seemed a distant dream. But he was not willing to abandon his efforts and persevered doggedly to find a basis for a Hindu-Muslim *entente*.

The spate of Hindu-Muslim riots had subsided after 1926-27. But the failure of the Round Table Conferences, followed by the announcement of the Communal Award on 16 August 1932, created a climate of intense communal friction.[69] Those present at the London conferences noticed the unmistakable polarization of Indian delegates on communal lines. On the one side were the self-proclaimed spokesmen of the Muslim community, standing on the platform of the Delhi resolutions of January 1929, seeking assurance of statutory majorities in Bengal and the Punjab, veto to such legislation which appeared inimical to Muslim religious interests, an elected 33 per cent representation in the central legislature and a loose centre with full administrative and financial autonomy resting in the provinces. On the other side was the group under the Mahasabha's influence arrayed against most of these demands. Representatives of other minorities were equally anxious to defend themselves against majority domination. The Sikhs, in particular, were vigilant with regard to their interests in the Punjab.

The Congress was not represented at the opening session in November 1930, as it was conducting the civil disobedience campaign against the government's refusal to accept dominion status as the presupposition of all discussions at the Round Table

[69]For official and semi-official accounts of the Round Table Conference, see Reginald Coupland, *India: A Re-Statement* (Oxford, 1945), pp. 137-41; William Roy Smith, *Nationalism and Reform in India* (Yale University Press, 1938) follows the official version closely. The communal question is discussed by Brown, Moore and Uma Kaura. The role of Sapru is examined by D.A. Low in *Soundings in Modern South Asian History* (University of California Press, 1968), though his account does not shed much light on the communal issue at the Round Table Conference. Moore, *The Crisis of Indian Unity*, pp. 218-23; also, Aga Khan, *The Memoirs of Aga Khan: World Enough and Time*, pp. 214-22, 228-31, is an account of one who was closely involved in the negotiations. His suite in Hotel Ritz was the venue of several informal discussions.

Conference. After the Gandhi-Irwin talks in February and March 1931, ending in the Gandhi-Irwin 'pact', the Mahatma attended the second session of the conference, held between 14 September and 1 December 1931, as Congress' sole representative. 'I happened to be in Delhi,' recalled Khaliquzzaman, 'when Gandhiji was staying at Dr Ansari's house [during his talks with the viceroy] and to my great surprise I used to see many inveterate enemies of Congress and well-known supporters of the British raj, both Hindus and Muslims, hovering round Dr Ansari's residence.'[70]

Gandhi brought with him the Congress plan which proposed, among other things, separate representation on the basis of joint electorates for both Hindus and Muslims in provinces where they were less than 25 per cent of the population, with the provision to contest additional seats. He made it clear in the Federal Structure Committee that adult suffrage was an essential feature of the plan and that its adoption would enable him to satisfy the reasonable aspirations of the Muslims, the so-called Untouchables, the Christians and all kinds of 'classes'. As negotiations went on, the Mahatma, with his customary flair, conveyed his readiness to modify some of his proposals.[71] But most Muslim delegates, following the directives of Fazl-i-Husain, stuck to their demands.[72] Shafi and Shafaat Ahmad Khan, confident of government backing, insisted on a statutory majority in Bengal and the Punjab and 33 per cent representation in the central legislature.[73] Neither the Sikhs nor the Hindus, led by Raja Narendranath, Malaviya, Moonje and Jayakar, were willing to submit to the

[70]Khaliquzzaman, op. cit., p. 111.

[71]For a detailed discussion, see Note by P. Stewart, 4 November 1931, appendix I, Templewood collection, MSS. EUR. E. 240 (65). IOL. Appendix II is Moonje's memorandum on the Congress formula, while the demands of the Sikhs are set out in the memorandum submitted by Ujjal Singh and Sampuran Singh. This is included as appendix IV. For secondary accounts of Gandhi's role, see B.R. Nanda, *Mahatma Gandhi: A Biography* (London, 1958), pp. 313-5; Tendulkar, *Mahatma*, Vol. 3.

[72]Fazl-i-Husain to Shafaat Ahmad Khan, 6 November 1930, Fazl-i-Husain to Mohammad Shafi, 6 November, 1 December 1930, Fazl-i-Husain to Shafaat Ahmad Khan, 7 September 1931, Waheed Ahmad (ed.), *Letters of Mian Fazl-i-Husain*, pp. 106-9, p. 190.

[73]*Indian Round Table Conference 12th November, 1930–19th January 1931. Proceedings of Sub-Committees (Part II) (Sub-Committees II-IX)* (London, 1931), pp. 98-9; and, *Proceedings of Sub-Committees (7 September–1 December 1931)*, (London, 1932), p. 4.

Muslim claims. As time went on there emerged a series of contradictory and irreconcilable claims and counter-claims, the hair-splitting became finer and finer and the arguments more and more abstract. 'The sum total of all our work,' wrote the Aga Khan, 'was a vast array of statistics and data, a great many speeches and little or no positive understanding.'[74]

By 25 October, negotiations between various parties came to a standstill. Gandhi tried his best to break the impasse, but 'with deep sorrow and deeper humiliation' he announced 'utter failure to secure an agreed solution of the communal question'. Even after their return to India, a representative body of delegates to the Round Table Conference continued their efforts to reach a consensus, but failed. Not long after the conference ended, the Congress resumed civil disobedience. 'The first Round Table Conference was as round as a circle, the second one was rounder still and when the third round table conference ended it became a well round zero.'[75] Ramsay MacDonald (1866-1937), the British prime minister, announced that since there could be no constitutional progress without settling the issue of communal representation, he would decide the competing claims. The infamous Communal Award was the outcome.

The Award smacked of the government's divide and rule policy and was designed to deepen Hindu-Muslim fissures. It prolonged the system of separate electorates for Hindus, Muslims and Sikhs and extended the system to those described as the Depressed Classes. The Act of 1909 was the beginning and the Communal Award the culmination of the government's strategy of leaning heavily on the Muslims and giving them a distinct political identity which they did not actually possess. The British played

[74]Aga Khan, *The Memoirs of Aga Khan*, p. 232. For the Aga Khan's role, see Mihir Bose, *The Aga Khans* (London, 1984), pp. 241-3.

[75]Speech by Jamnadas Mehta, *Free Press Journal*, 10 February 1933, Sapru Papers (30). There was much bitter controversy at the outcome of the conference. The *Pratap* and the *Abhyudaya* blamed the Muslim delegates—'hirelings of the British Government'—for the deadlock over the communal question. The *Himmat, Hamdam* and the *Naiyar-i Azam*, on the other hand, attributed the failure of the talks to the obstinacy of the Hindu and Sikh delegates. They even disputed Gandhi's claim that the Congress represented all communities, classes and creeds and asserted that it was a purely Hindu organization which the Muslims had abandoned long ago. This was a typical example of the scurrilous and irresponsible writings in a section of the vernacular press. Charges were bandied about without any realization of its implications on communal relations.

their cards well, but in the process widened existing cleavages and virtually undermined the possibility of a Hindu-Muslim front in the long and arduous fight for independence. Said Jayakar: 'The Lucknow Pact divided India into Hindus and Muslims. This Award will divide it further into Hindu versus Muslim women, Europeans versus Anglo-Indians, white Christians versus coloured Christians, high castes versus Depressed classes and, eventually, north India versus south India.'[76]

The effects of the Award were apparent soon after its publication. The Working Committee of the Hindu Mahasabha denounced it on the grounds that it gave the Muslims control of Bengal and the Punjab, that it denied to the Hindus in those provinces representation in proportion to their population, that it granted too much weightage to Muslims in the Hindu-majority provinces and that it implied the formation of Sind as a separate province.[77] The Sikhs were equally embittered because the Award did not give them and the Hindus together a majority of the seats in the Punjab. Muslims alone had reasons to feel satisfied. It is true that their main demand—statutory majorities in the Punjab and Bengal legislatures—was not conceded, but in both the provinces they retained not only their separate electorates but they were also given more seats than any other community in the provincial assemblies. (Table 9:1). Provincial autonomy was now a pleasing prospect for Muslims in Bengal and the Punjab and also for Muslims in the newly-created province of Sind as well as the NWFP, which was to be elevated to the status of a Governor's province.[78] For these reasons, except for Bengal, where Fazlul Haq and his

[76]Statement on the Communal Award, Sapru Papers (29). Sapru agreed that the Award had 'ugly features', though he added that 'we never seized the opportunity of settling it [Hindu-Muslim problem] ourselves'. To Jayakar, 23 August 1932, Sapru Papers.

[77]*IAR*, January-June 1933, p. 420; and presidential address of Bhai Parmanand at the Ajmer session of the Hindu Mahasabha on 14 October 1935. *IAR*, July-December 1933, p. 204.

[78]Fazlul Haq moved a resolution at the 1933 Muslim League session which, while welcoming the Award, recorded dissatisfaction that one-third of the seats were not guaranteed to the Muslims in the central legislature and Bengali Muslims were not given the number of seats to which they were entitled by virtue of their strength in population. Pirzada (ed.), *Foundations of Pakistan*, Vol. 2, p. 203. For details of reactions in Bengal, *IAR*, July-December 1933, pp. 212-3, 217-8; Mcpherson, *The Muslim Microcosm*, pp. 117-8, 120; John Gallagher, 'Congress in decline: Bengal 1930 to 1939', *Modern Asian Studies*, Vol. 7, 3, July 1973, pp. 615-25.

Province	General	Depressed Class	Representatives from Back ward Areas	Sikh	Muhammadan	Indian Christian	Anglo Indian	European	Commerce and Industry, Mining and Planting, Special	Landholders, Special	University, Special	Labour, Special	Total
Madras	134 (including 6 women)	18	1	0	29 (including 1 woman)	9 (inc. 1 woman)	2	3	6	6	1	6	215
Bombay (including Sind)	97 (including 5 women)	10	1	0	63 (including 1 woman)	3	2	4	8	3	1	8	200
Bengal	80. (including 2 women)		0	0	119 (including 2 women)	2	4 (including 1 woman)	11	19	5	2	8	250
United Provinces (including	132 (including 4 women)	12	0	0	66 (including 2 women)	2	1	2	3	6	1	3	228
Punjab	43 (including 1 woman)	0	0	32 (including 1 woman)	86 (including 2 women)	2	1	1	1	5	1	3	175
Bihar and Orissa	99 (including 3 women)	7	8	0	42 (including 1 woman)	2	1	2	4	5	1	4	175
Central Provinces (including Berar)	77 (including 3 women)	10	1	0	14	0	1	1	2	3	1	2	112
Assam	44 (including 1 woman)	4	9	0	34	1	0	1	11	0	0	4	108
North-West Frontier Province.	9	0	0	3	36	0	0	0	0	2	0	0	50
Bombay (without Sind)	109 including 5 women)	10	1	0	30 (including 1 woman)	3	2	3	7	2	1	–	175
Sind	19 (including 1 woman)	0	0	0	34 (including 1 woman)	0	0	2	2	2	0	1	60

As explained in paragraph 9 of the statement, the number of special Depressed Class seats in Bengal—which will not exceed 10—has yet been fixed. The number of General seats will be 80, less the number of special Depressed Class seats.

SOURCE: *East India (Constitutional Reforms), Communal Decision*, pp. 1931-2. XVIII, Cmd. 4147.

followers made some noises and proposed modifications,[79] the Award was welcomed by most Muslim organizations, including the Muslim League.[79] 'In the provinces,' wrote Azim Husain, the biographer of his father Fazl-i-Husain, 'the Muslims now woke up from somnolence and for every meeting held by the Hindu Mahasabha asking for joint electorates a meeting was held by the local branch of the Muslim Conference to approve of the Award.'[80] Thus government's design of setting one group against the other worked with a fair measure of success. New areas of conflict were created which, as intended, kept on enlarging in the years to come.

The Congress was placed in a dilemma, for it could neither acquiesce in the Award nor reject it without causing a serious rift within its own ranks and driving the Muslims further into the communalist camp.[81] At first, civil disobedience postponed the dilemma. Gandhi and the other leaders were in gaol and the Mahatma, who was not released until August 1933, advised his followers to keep mum.[82] But the issue could not be deferred for long, specially after the formation of the Swaraj Party and its decision to fight the elections to the assembly. At this stage, the Congress Working Committee, meeting on 17-18 June 1934, adopted the course of neither accepting nor rejecting the Award.[83] It was an extraordinary decision, yet it could hardly be very different. It was the inevitable outcome of the past neutral and

[79]On this point, see Kaura, op. cit., pp. 86-7. For its implications in the Punjab, see Page, op. cit., pp. 253-8 and Ayesha Jalal and Anil Seal, 'Alternative to Partition: Muslim Politics Between the Wars', *Modern Asian Studies*, Vol. 15, 3, 1981, p. 443. It was noted that the Award gave Muslims of Bengal and the Punjab 'considerable opportunities to win a clear majority for themselves'. If they were able to capture 2 out of the 10 special seats in the Punjab and 7 out of 10 special seats in Bengal, they were to obtain a majority over all other communities combined. 'And this should not be an impossible or even a difficult task if they are able properly to organize themselves'. Reforms Dept., F. No. 86, Box No. 3, UPSA. Also, see Ayesha Jalal, *The Sole Spokesman: Jinnah, the Muslim League and the Demand for Pakistan* (Cambridge, 1985), p. 13.

[80]Husain, *Fazl-i-Husain*, p. 263; *IAR*, July-December 1933, pp. 9, 11, 15, 20.

[81]Notice the comment of Rajendra Prasad, Congress president-elect. *Bombay Chronicle*, 3 August 1934.

[82]Gandhi to Birla, 21 January 1933, quoted in Gallagher, op. cit., p. 621.

[83]The Working Committee resolution laid down that the 'Congress claims to represent equally all communities composing the Indian Nation and therefore, in view of the division of opinion, can neither accept nor reject the award so long as the division of opinion lasts'.

feeble policy of the Congress. A strong line adopted at an earlier stage and followed regardless of short-term consequences would have enabled it to resist all forms of communal demands. But, as it had been unwilling to do so, there was no other course open except the one it took.[84]

Congress' neutral—some said ambivalent—position raised a storm of protest in different circles. For once its own structure, built on the principle of 'consensus', was under severe strain, particularly after Malaviya, Aney and their followers broke away to form the Congress Nationalist Party on a programme of total opposition to the Communal Award. When they began marshalling their forces at the Anti-Communal Award Conferences on 23-24 February and 25 October 1934, most of the old faces from the Mahasabha breakaway of 1926 were to be seen. Predictably, the Congress attitude to the Award was castigated as 'a virtual acquiescence in the decision'.[85]

There were loud protests from other quarters as well. Shadi Ram Sharma, member of the Hoshiarpur Congress Committee, spoke of his party's anomalous position. 'Blowing hot and cold in the same breath the Congress says: "*We are Nationalists, we oppose communalism, we reject it.*"' But after a pause when called upon to declare their policy on the Communal Award they say, "*We neither reject it nor accept it.*" Congressmen, he wrote, 'are expectant that these clouds of uncertainty and dubiousness will be blown off and blown away by a clear-cut declaration by the President of the Indian National Congress and the AICC against the Communal Award in the near future.'[86] This demand was most vigorously made in Bengal where educated Bengali Hindus, aggrieved by the denial of their claims to weightage, were up in arms. Besides organizing public meetings,

[84]Nehru, *An Autobiography*, pp. 575-6.

[85]'*The Communal Award'? Examined and Criticised* [with a foreword by C.Y. Chintamani] (Allahabad, 1934). 'The entire outlook from which the problem of communal award is approached,' wrote Aney in his letter of resignation from the Congress Working Committee, 'is in my opinion opposed to the very fundamental principles of nationalism and at variance with the policy of the Indian National Congress pursued during the last fifty years.' 18 June, 29 July 1934; and Malaviya and Aney to Gandhi and the members of the Congress Working Committee, F. No. G-24, 1934-36, AICC Papers.

[86]Sharma to Jawaharlal, n.d., F. No. G-24, 1934-36, ibid. Jawaharlal expressed surprise at the association of some Congressmen and 'even persons calling themselves socialists' with the Anti-Communal Award Conference at Lahore. 'The socialism that prevails amongst some quarters in the Punjab is of a peculiar variety'. Jawaharlal to Satyapal, 10 July 1936, *SWJ*, Vol. 7, pp. 366-7.

they drew up a memorial, signed by all Hindu members of the legislative council, by twenty-three chairmen of municipalities, by eight chairmen of district boards and by thirty-six 'representative Hindu leaders' urging London to amend the Communal Award by order in council. The signatories included Ramanand Chatterji (1865-1943), editor of the *Modern Review*, and the Nobel laureate Rabindranath Tagore (1861-1941).[87]

The Bengal Congress, beleaguered by numerous factions, was one in opposing the Communal Award.[88] This would probably explain its defiance of the AICC resolution on the Award. When censured by Gandhi, Patel and Nehru, Sarat Chandra Bose (1889-1950) drew attention to the popular opinion against the Award, attributed Congress' defeat in the assembly elections to its ambivalence on such a vital issue and warned Jawaharlal that the Hindu electorate in Bengal was impatient with the party's uncertain and equivocal stance. 'To ignore that fact would be to court defeat at the coming elections and we shudder to think what the effect of such a defeat would be on the Congress organization as a whole.'[89]

Gandhi and Nehru did not relent. The thrust of the Mahatma's argument was that the Congress, claiming to stand for all the communities, should do nothing which would make Muslims feel that it had departed from that position. He said that it would be a betrayal of the Muslims to oppose their view of the Communal Award.[90] 'The more I think about it,' he wrote to Aney, 'the clearer I become that the Working Committee resolution is faultless. Non-committal is the only position the Congress can take up. We must not tease the communal boil. The more we tease it, the worse it becomes.'[91] He made it

[87]See *Bengal Anti-Communal Award Movement: A Report* (Calcutta, 1939). For a fairly perceptive account of the anti-Communal Award movement in Bengal, see Gallagher, op. cit., pp. 615-25.

[88]Gallagher, ibid., pp. 618-9.

[89]Bose to Jawaharlal, 19 September 1936, F. No. G-24, part I, AICC Papers.

[90]Speech at the Congress Parliamentary Board on 16 June 1934. Gandhi reiterated this view in his interviews to provincial Congress leaders (13 July 1934), Akali and Khalsa Durbar deputation (15 July) and the deputation of Punjabi Hindus and Sikhs (15 July). *CWG*, Vol. LVIII, pp. 83, 181, 191-2.

[91]27 July 1934, ibid., p. 253. Yet the Mahatma took the extraordinary stand that in the elections to the central assembly, the Congress should 'unreservedly' vote for Aney as opposed to the non-Congress candidate. To V.G. Joshi, 20 October 1934, ibid., Vol. LIX, p. 204.

clear to the Calcutta Congressmen that everybody condemned the Award, 'but a Congressman, because he is a Congressman, can neither accept it nor reject it because if he did one or the other he would be taking sides and therefore not represent the whole nation'.[92]

Jawaharlal agreed that the Award was dangerous, but took pains to explain that an agitation against it was not central to Congress' order of priorities. The main issue was of independence and the real question was not one of principle but of methods to be employed to give effect to that principle. He hoped that those who thought in terms of political freedom and economic issues would some day see the Communal Award in perspective and join hands in fighting it.[93] This was a highly romantic view, one which glossed over the context in which opinions on the Award were shaped and crystallized. Expecting any of the parties to dilute their demands or soften their attitudes in the years 1932-35 reflected Jawaharlal's failure to recognize the historical currents which were inescapably moving towards a greater degree of communal polarization and a hardening of attitudes. Arresting the process was a stupendous task, though by no means a hopeless one. Jawaharlal was aware of this, but he never addressed himself to the complexity of the communal phenomena and their ramifications. His analysis was based on assumptions which took no account of the intensity of the communal differences. This is most clearly evident in his statements on the Communal Award which reflected an inadequate and somewhat simplistic understanding of the communal divide. Addressing the All-India Trade Union Congress on 18 May 1936, he said:

[92] 19 August 1934, ibid., p. 234. The lack of any consistency in the Gandhi-Jawaharlal advice to Congressmen in the assembly was indicative of the general confusion in Congress circles. Gandhi directed that Congressmen must vote against a resolution or amendment accepting the Award. 'And since they cannot vote for rejection, naturally they must abstain from voting in regard to a resolution or amendment rejecting the Award'. Gandhi to B.C. Roy, 25 August 1934, ibid., p. 365. Jawaharlal, on the other hand, believed that the Congress members must 'inevitably' give their opinion against the Award 'but they will add that it must be changed by agreement'. Jawaharlal to Habibur Rahman, 13 December 1936, *SWJ*, Vol. 7, p. 403; also, *Bombay Chronicle*, 15 February 1935.

[93] *SWJ*, Vol. 7, p. 37; Jawaharlal to Jagatnarainlal, 30 September 1936, F. No. G-24, part I, AICC Papers; Jawaharlal to S.C. Majumdar, 6 August 1936, *SWJ*, Vol. 7, p. 273.

> I consider the Communal Award to be a dangerous thing.... But everyone should seriously engage himself in the major problem of achieving freedom for the country and then the *communal question will automatically be solved* [emphasis added].[94]

Again, speaking at Amritsar on 31 May 1936, Jawaharlal stated:

> The issue of the Communal Award, important as it is, is not the main issue before the country. *The day on which India achieves her freedom, communal differences and jealousies will get solved of themselves* [emphasis added].[95]

These were comforting thoughts but they did not reflect a recognition of the painful realities of Indian political life in the 1930s.

Ansari learnt his lesson the hard way. Experience of conducting parleys with the Muslim Conference and later with Shaukat Ali and Jinnah demonstrated, though somewhat belatedly, that make-show attempts at achieving reconciliation widened existing rifts. Such was the fate of his initiatives as leader of the NMP and of the Unity Conference at Allahabad, held towards the end of the year 1932, where Indian politicians turned real conflicts into bland unrealities. Ansari's intervention in the Communal Award controversy and the Rajendra Prasad-Jinnah talks in January 1935 pointed to him the difficulties in evolving a formula which would be acceptable to various groups whose interests and perceptions were not the same. Memories of the Lucknow Pact (1916) were no doubt fresh, but it was equally clear to Ansari that the Congress-League concordat happened in somewhat exceptional circumstances, created by an unusual configuration of forces. It was therefore not easy, though he did not say so, to achieve the same agreement in the mid-1930s for reasons which were linked with either British policies or connected with the historical experiences and perceptions of large segments of the Hindu and Muslim communities in the aftermath of the Khilafat and non-cooperation movements.

Ansari's own views on the Communal Award were unmistakably clear, forthright, and consistent with the objectives of the NMP. He characterized the Award as a vicious document based on

[94] *SWJ*, Vol. 7, p. 268; also, speech at Lahore, 29 May 1936, p. 268.
[95] Speech at Amritsar, 31 May 1936, ibid., p. 270.

the principle of divide and rule.[96] Reaffirming, along with Azad and Sherwani, the NMP's position that joint electorates with adult suffrage constituted the only acceptable basis for India's constitution, he asserted that the Award would create fresh communal groups and interests and impede future prospects of Hindu-Muslim cooperation. In a statement issued from Freiburg in Germany, he said: 'Rescue our common motherland out of chaos and extricate ourselves from the most humiliating position and fervently hope that the Award will open the eyes of both the communities and an era of sense of goodwill will be ushered'.[97] Given the choice, Ansari would have campaigned against the Award and rallied his band of followers in the NMP, who seemed uncertain and confused, on to his side. But Congress' strategy to play it safe clipped his wings and offered him little scope for manoeuvre. In the end, he performed the role expected of him: to explain and defend Congress' policy. He did so in a press statement on 21 May 1934:

> The Congress knows that while a large number of Hindus and Sikhs have taken strong exception to the Communal Award, a considerable section of Mussalmans, Harijans and Christians have accepted it for so long as an agreed substitute is found. The Congress will always strive to find a national solution of the question, but in my opinion such a solution of the question cannot be found except by a Constituent Assembly convened to frame a national constitution. Until then, the question of acceptance or rejection of the mode or proportion of representation as contained in the Award does not arise. It would not be dignified for any self-respecting people to ask any outsider to decide what is purely a domestic matter, nor would any such decision succeed in satisfying all.[98]

Soon thereafter, Ansari turned to Jinnah, re-elected that October by the Muslims of Bombay City to represent them in the central assembly. He sought an exchange of views and, as president of the Parliamentary Board, wanted to know the basis on which most elected members of the assembly could cooperate.[99] They

[96] Interview to the *Bombay Chronicle, The Communal 'Award'*, op. cit., pp. 16-7.
[97] Ibid., p. 73.
[98] *IAR*, January-June 1934, p. 296.
[99] Ansari to Jinnah, 30 December 1934, Hasan (ed.), *Muslims and the Congress*, p. 235.

had met earlier—in April 1934—when Jinnah offered a formula for a compromise: acceptance of the Communal Award for the time being on the understanding that joint electorates would be substituted for separate electorates after a specified period. Though Ansari, Bhulabhai Desai and B.C. Roy, who were confronted with what seemed a reasonable offer, remained non-committal because of the constraints imposed by the Congress Working Committee mandate,[100] Jinnah's proposal opened up the prospect for yet another round of negotiations.

Jinnah reacted favourably to Ansari's suggestion,[101] for his strategy at this point was to turn back towards the Congress to see if its leadership was prepared to concede all that the Communal Award had promised to Muslims, thus clearing the way for Hindus and Muslims to join forces in a common front against the White Paper, presented by Samuel Hoare (1880-1950) to parliament in March 1933.[102] He hoped the time was ripe for communal peace and was ready to launch a new series of talks aimed at weaning Congress from its dependence upon the Hindu Mahasabha position. He made his offer in plain terms:

> I have nothing in common with the Aga Khan. He is a British agent. I am devoted to my old policy and programme.... If the Congress can support the Muslims on the question of the Communal Award, I would be able to get all the Muslim members except 7 or 8.... As things stand, the practical way would be for just a few leaders of political thought to combine for the purpose of preparing a formula which both the communities might accept. The Congress I admit would have to change its attitude in some respects, but looking to the great interests at stake Congress leaders should not flinch. I think the future is with the Congress Party and not with me or the Aga Khan.[103]

These were not empty words. In the assembly, Jinnah and the Muslim Independents were able to cooperate with Congress members on several issues. The "Ambassador of Hindu-Muslim Unity" secured their backing for three resolutions of his own,

[100] *IAR*, July-December, 1934.

[101] To Ansari, 3 January 1935, Hasan (ed.), *Muslims and the Congress*, p. 235.

[102] Wolpert, *Jinnah of Pakistan*, pp. 135-6.

[103] 'Summary of conversation between Mr Jinnah and myself', Vallabhbhai Patel Papers, quoted in Gallagher, op. cit., p. 628.

the first acquiescing in the Communal Award pending an alternative settlement by the communities themselves, the second criticizing the provincial part of the Act of 1935 but not condemning it outright, the third denouncing the federal part as 'fundamentally bad and totally unacceptable' and demanding the prompt establishment of full responsible government in a federated British India. This alliance was more or less consistently maintained. In 1935 and again in 1936 it brought about the rejection of the budget and forced the governor-general to 'certify' it. 'Never before,' wrote the official British historian, 'had the nationalist opposition pressed the Government so hard as it did in this period of Hindu-Muslim cooperation.'[104] This augured well for the talks between Jinnah and the Congress president, Rajendra Prasad, held at Delhi in January 1935.

Discussions between Prasad and Jinnah started in *Dar-us-Salam* on 23 January and continued until the end of February at 13 Asoka Road. After protracted deliberations they agreed on the following as a basis for further discussion:

1. Franchise to be framed and adjusted to reflect the proportion of population of the various communities in the electoral rolls for the province as well as the centre. For that purpose differential franchise would be adopted wherever necessary.

2. There would be no overlapping of electorates or constituencies.

3. The Sikhs in Punjab would choose the number of constituencies for the seats allotted to them in the Communal Award. Thereafter, the Hindus would have the choice to fix on such constituencies as they might desire for the number allotted to them. The remaining constituencies would go to the Muslims in accordance with the provision in the Award, excluding the seats given to Europeans, Anglo-Indians, Indian Christians and special constituencies.

4. In Bengal if any seats were obtained from Europeans they would be divided between Hindus and Muslims in proportion to their population. However, seats reserved for the Muslims under the Award would stay, excluding the seats given to Europeans, Anglo-Indians, Indian Christians and special constituencies.

5. In other provinces and in the central legislature, the number

[104]Coupland, *India: A Re-statement*, p. 151

of seats reserved for the Muslims would be the same as in the Award.

6. On this basis it was agreed that joint electorates would replace separate electorates in all the provinces and in the centre.[105]

Bhulabhai Desai (1877-1946), Patel and the Congress president accepted this formula.[106] Gandhi, too, nodded in approval.[107] Serious opposition, however, was mounting in other quarters, particularly among the Sikhs in the Punjab and a section of urban Hindus in Bengal. The Sikhs rejected the Punjab formula.[108] The Hindu Mahasabha denounced the Bengal formula. So did C.Y. Chintamani (1880-1941), president of the Anti-Communal Award Conference,[109] and Malaviya, the voice of Hindu orthodoxy in north India.[110] Yet, Prasad and Patel, impressed by the accomodating spirit displayed by Jinnah and the Muslim League and their acceptance of joint electorates, were willing to ignore the dissenters.[111] When Prasad met Jinnah on 27 February he suggested confining the agreement to the Congress and the

[105]Notes of Conversation held between Jinnah and Prasad on 13-14 February 1935, AICC Papers.

[106]Prasad to Patel, 14 February 1935, Rajendra Prasad Papers, NAI; also, Gallagher, op. cit., pp. 630-1.

[107]'If the kind of compromise you have outlined in your letter can be brought about, I would love it.' Gandhi to Prasad, 7 February 1935, Valmiki Choudhary (ed.), *Dr Rajendra Prasad Correspondence and Select Documents*, Vol. 1 (Delhi, 1984), p. 6. Again, he informed Rajendra Prasad: 'As I am willing to do everything, why would I be averse to the joint electorate? If Muslims can accept even this and if Sikhs and Hindus agree, I have no doubt it will be extremely good. To bring around Malaviyaji appears to be a difficult proposition, but he would put up no opposition if Sikhs could be persuaded.' Gandhi to Rajendra Prasad, 28 February 1935, *CWG*, Vol. LX, p. 266.

[108]See Birla to Gandhi, 25/26 February 1935, *Bapu*, Vol. 1, p. 35.

[109]The Anti-Communal Award Conference, held on 23-24 February 1935 and presided over by Chintamani, coincided with the Jinnah-Prasad talks in the same city. Rajendra Prasad noted on 23 February that Chintamani had expressed scepticism over the outcome of the negotiations, for 'his experience had been that on every occasion when settlement had been talked about, the demand of Mussalmans had increased and on Hindus failing to agree, the Mussalmans and some Hindus also had blamed the Hindu leaders'.

[110]'Panditji (Malaviyaji) is here and he has turned down Jinnah and Rajendra Babu's formula'. Birla to Mahadev Desai, 21 February 1935, *Bapu*, Vol. 2, p. 33.

[111]Gallagher, op. cit., pp. 630-1. The Muslim League Council had declared JPC Report as reactionary and agreed to cooperate with any community or party to secure a constitution satisfactory to the people. *Bombay Chronicle*, 28 January 1935.

League, leaving aside the more intransigent bodies. Jinnah refused. The Congress president's own notes described Jinnah's position:

> As regards future procedure he [Jinnah] said that Mussalmans had told him that on several previous occasions the question had been discussed and ended in no agreement. They wanted to know whether the Hindu Sabha leaders and Sikh leaders were agreeable and particularly what was Pandit Malaviya's attitude. If I could get the signatures of these people he hoped to carry it through so far as the Mussalmans were concerned. I asked him if resolutions of Provincial Legislators and the Assembly would do. He said they might as mere expressions of opinion but the Government might insist on resolutions of communal organizations and signatures of individual leaders. I told him that organizations might be easier to tackle than some individuals and perhaps legislature could be managed best. He said an individual like Malaviyaji could in no case be ignored. He pointed out that with propaganda being carried on his position was becoming very difficult and even negotiations were made very difficult.[112]

The Congress president was unable to accept the conditions laid down by Jinnah and their talks came to an 'infructuous end'. His own version reflects his disappointment at the outcome of the talks and places the controversy about its failure in perspective.

> In the conversations which I had with Mr Jinnah in 1935 we were able to evolve a formula. I accepted it not only in my personal capacity but as President of the Congress and offered to have it ratified by the Congress. I was keeping in touch with prominent Congressmen while the conversations were going on and had received universal support for it from them. There were several members of the Congress Working Committee at Delhi at the time and were in full agreement with me. There was absolutely no difference among Congressmen and I was successful in obtaining the support of the leaders of the Hindu Mahasabha of the Punjab also. But Mr Jinnah insisted on having the signature of Pandit Madan Mohan Malaviya and other leaders of the Hindu Mahasabha. This I

[112]Daily Notes taken by Rajendra Prasad, 20 February 1935, Rajendra Prasad Papers.

was unable to secure and the matter had to be dropped. It was not dropped because Congressmen were not agreeable but because those leaders of the Hindu Mahasabha on whose signature Mr Jinnah insisted were not agreeable.... I had gone further and had told Mr Jinnah that the Congress and the League should accept the formula and the Congress would fight those Hindus who were opposed to it, as it had fought them during the recent Assembly elections quite successfully in most Provinces. But this was not considered enough by Mr Jinnah and as it was impossible to fulfil his demand that Hindu Mahasabha should also join, the matter had to be dropped.[113]

It would thus appear that as far as Prasad and Jinnah were concerned, the negotiations brought about a substantial measure of agreement and left to themselves, they would have reached a settlement which, they had every hope, would have been endorsed by the Congress and the League.[114] But the president's attempt to make others outside the Congress agree to the terms had no chance of success. To expect Moonje, Parmanand and H.N. Dutt, president of the Bengal Provincial Hindu Conference, to come to terms with the Muslim leaders implied an ideological reorientation in the Hindu Mahasabha which could not conceivably happen. The Mahasabha was blatantly anti-Muslim and it derived support and sustenance from such a posture which was the hallmark of all its social, cultural and political activities. It had opposed all previous attempts to reach a meaningful agreement between the Congress and League leaders and had no reason to act differently in January-February 1935. 'How is it that Moonje, Jagatnarainlal can be better Hindus than Vallabhbhai, Rajendra Babu and others?' enquired Birla who was much concerned with the failure of the talks. He continued:

> Have not we ourselves given them undue importance and so by unanimous votes, they are the real leaders so far as communal matters go? I fear that in any constructive work that you may do in future, these false prophets would put obstructions in your way.[115]

[113]Statement of 6 July 1937, F. No. G-65, AICC Papers.

[114]Birla to Mahadev Desai, 28 February 1935, *Bapu*, Vol. 2, p. 38.

[115]Birla had advised Rajendra Prasad to accept the formula and was hopeful of persuading the 'Hindu masses' to do the same. 'I am quite optimistic about

Thus, once again, the fate of helpless millions was sealed by a few stubborn leaders who refused to stretch that extra inch of representational concession to close the gap dividing India's pluralistic society and keeping it constitutionally fragmented. Jinnah, who was the only Muslim leader capable of reining his community into harness with Congress' bullock team, was alienated and driven to the position of obduracy and belligerence towards the Congress.[116]

Ansari not only keenly followed the Jinnah-Prasad talks which started in *Dar-us-Salam*, but was in 'constant attendance'. After all, he had prepared the ground for their meeting and had coaxed the Congress president into inviting Jinnah for discussions. But he could not sustain his active interest owing to the poor state of his health. Strained by his involvement in the launching of the Parliamentary Board and the subsequent election campaign, his health was in a 'chronic state of deterioration'. For two months he travelled all over the country, hosted meetings of the Working Committee and the Board at his residence and remained closely in touch with the day-to-day developments in the Jinnah-Prasad parleys. 'Are you surprised that with all this care and responsibility, my damaged health has completely broken down and I find myself totally unable to go any further?' he wrote to Brelvi in April 1935.[117]

In early March 1935 Ansari dropped a bombshell by deciding to quit public life 'under great compulsion of pressing personal and private necessity'.[118] This was followed by his resignation from the Working Committee and the Parliamentary Board, a move which caught many by surprise.[119] Some thought that it was in consequence of his feuds with members of the Parliamentary Board, particularly Bhulabhai Desai and Malaviya who made his

---

the results,' he wrote, '*if only the Congress will take up a definite attitude* [emphasis added]. Even the Hindu Sabha could ratify the formula in its session provided the Congress would work for it. I hope Bapu would approve of such a move.' Birla to Mahadev Desai, 21 February 1935, ibid., p. 33.

[116]Wolpert, op. cit., p. 137; Rajendra Prasad, *India Divided* (Bombay, 1946), p. 134; Khaliquzzaman, op. cit., p. 139

[117]Ansari to Brelvi, 15 April 1935, Brelvi Papers; Ansari to Jawaharlal, 11 October 1935, Nehru Papers (35).

[118]Ansari to Rajendra Prasad, 23 March 1935, Hasan (ed.), *Muslims and the Congress*, pp. 253-4.

[119]Ibid., p. 255.

effective functioning difficult.[120] Both Ansari and Desai contradicted such reports.[121] The *Bombay Chronicle* found it necessary to print in bold letters that Ansari's retirement was due solely to reasons of health and speculation as to other possible reasons were without any foundation.[122]

Not many had reasons to rejoice at Ansari's decision. Gandhi, who cared for Ansari more than anybody outside his close and inner circle of friends and followers, insisted that he should not desert the Board or the Committee.[123] Others pleaded with him to give up the idea. Nariman was one of them. He wanted Ansari's association with the Parliamentary Board because he occupied

> a peculiar and unique position, both in Congress and the country. His unassailable nationalism and his uncompromising anti-communalism give a peculiar value to his association to all political organizations in general and to the Congress Parliamentary Board in particular. With him at the helm, none dare charge the Board with communalist tendencies.... He is a strong link between the two great communities and his nationalism and cosmopolitanism serve as an inspiring example to young political India...and also as an effective check to the canker of communalism. To remove both this inspiration and check at a time when both are most needed would be a suicidal and retrograde step.

Nariman concluded by pointing out that 'a general has no right to retire till the fight is over and the rank and file can demand at least his association, if not active service, so long as the objective is not reached'.[124]

Unmoved by such earnest pleas Ansari quickly withdrew into the quiet surroundings of *Dar-us-Salam*. He was occasionally

[120] *Bombay Chronicle*, 5 April 1935; on differences between Ansari and Malaviya, see Tomlinson, op. cit., pp. 39-40; *IAR*, January-June 1934, pp. 281-4.

[121] *Bombay Chronicle*, 18 April 1935.

[122] Ibid.

[123] 'I hope you will not desert the Board or the Committee. You need not take any great active part requiring much strain. But your counsel cannot be dispensed with'. Gandhi to Ansari, 16 February 1935, *CWG*, Vol. LX, p. 237. Later, of course, Gandhi acceded to Ansari's request. 'I shall not strive with you but plead with Rajenbabu to release you,' he wrote. To Ansari, 8 March 1935, Hasan (ed.), *Muslims and the Congress*, p. 253, and *CWG*, Vol LX, p. 285.

[124] *Bombay Chronicle*, 12 April 1935. Also, editorial comment of 6 April 1935.

consulted, as in the case of electing the Congress president for the 1935 session,[125] but was generally reticent to dabblle in public affairs.[126] 'Now that I am free from all responsibilities for the future,' he wrote to B.C. Roy, 'I shall breathe freely and feel my own master, a luxury which I have not enjoyed all these years owing to my intimate connection with the Congress.'[127] He had been engaged in writing his book on *Regeneration in Man* and was happy to see it through the press. Published in early 1935, this extremely readable work gave a historical retrospect and a review of the advances in the knowledge of the endocrinal activity of the sex glands.[128] There were words of praise and appreciation from several quarters. Gandhi was among those who read it with great interest, though he refrained from offering any comments.

Ansari's main interest lay in nursing the Jamia Millia which had suffered years of neglect. His appeal for funds, issued in mid-February,[129] met with a favourable response and funds came

[125]Ansari expressed his preference for Rajagopalachari, 'the best suited man to occupy the responsible post'. As regards Jawaharlal, Ansari wrote: 'He is undoubtedly the idol of the people and specially of Congressmen. Whether he is elected to the Congress Presidentship or not, his place in the hearts of the people and of Congress is ensured forever.... I feel that owing to Jawahar's domestic condition and his prolonged incarceration, it would be cruelty on our part to put him at once to the yoke without giving any respite....' Ansari to Rajendra Prasad, 6 October 1935, Rajendra Prasad Papers. He reiterated the same to Jawaharlal. 'I have felt all along that all of those who are responsible for your election this year are very very thoughtless and unkind to you both from the point of view of your domestic difficulties and from the public point of view. I do not think that in the present condition of things even your dynamic personality would be able to do much during your year of Presidentship. And if nothing is achieved at the end, the fact that one of our very best men have failed to achieve something would produce a great set-back'. Ansari to Jawaharlal, 11 February 1936, Nehru Papers (3).

[126]'And having retired from active politics, I consider it presumptuous and uncalled for to be always writing about current events to those who are responsible for guiding the policy of the Congress. If they seek my private advice, it would be gladly given. But, without any desire on their part, I feel I should abstain from doing so.' Ansari to Brelvi, 25 July 1935, Brelvi Papers.

[127]Ansari to B.C. Roy, 6 October 1935, Roy Papers.

[128]Mohammad Amin, *'Adaa-i Shabab' (Regeneration in Man)* in Malik Ram (ed.), *Nazr-i-Hameed* (Delhi, 1981), pp. 525-32; Shahabuddin Ansari, 'Dr Ansari ki Kitaab: Regeneration in Man', *Jamia* (special number), July 1981, pp 65-8.

[129]He said: 'I believe what counts as the most remarkable contribution of the Jamia to our national life is that it has carried on a constructive educational and cultural enterprise...without seeking any aid from the government. And the fifteen years of its life are a proof that cannot be challenged that there is no

pouring in from different quarters.[130] This enabled him to organize the foundation ceremony of a new building at a site in Okhla, now in South Delhi, where 100 acres of land was acquired for Rs 10,000. Performed by the youngest child in Jamia[131] and amidst much pomp and show, the ceremony was witnessed by luminaries like Rajendra Prasad, Patel, Sarojini Naidu, Bhulabhai Desai and the Turkish guest, Halide Edib. The *Amir-i Jamia* said on the occasion: 'We desire to build an institution which, while being Islamic in its traditions, will be national in its outlook.'[132] His dreams were partially fulfilled, but he was not destined to be associated with Jamia's slow but steady progress for long. In April he entrusted the work for raising contributions for the Jamia building fund to Shafiqur Rahman Kidwai and Zakir Husain[133] and thereafter did little beyond performing his minimal duties as *Amir-i Jamia.*

So ended a distinguished public life which spanned over two decades and encompassed some of the most tumultuous years in India's fight for freedom. Some still hoped that he would be restored to his normal health and take his place 'in the political life of the country to which few living men have made a more disinterested, glorious and invaluable contribution'.[134] But such hopes did not come true. While returning from Mussoorie where he had gone to attend on the Nawab of Rampur, Ansari suffered a heart attack near Jainpur Saun station and died a little after 12.30 A.M. on 10 May 1936. 'Few deaths leave me disconsolate as this has done,' wrote Gandhi in his tribute to the man he admired and respected. 'Quite wrongly, I know, but I had pictured Dr Ansari as one destined to finish his century. When therefore I got the Press wire, I could not believe at first. He had become part of the lives of many.'[135]

lack of idealism, patience and organizing capacity.' *Bombay Chronicle*, 19 February 1935.

[130]Jinnah, Shaukat Ali, Fazlul Haq and Asaf Ali were among those who associated themselves with Ansari's appeal. Ibid., 26 February 1935.

[131]Gandhi welcomed the idea and congratulated the *Shaikhul Jamia*, Zakir Husain, on the 'originality of the conception'. He thought that Jamia had a 'great future' and through it he expected the 'seed of Hindu-Muslim union to grow into a majestic tree'. Gandhi to Zakir Husain, 20 February 1935, *CWG*, Vol. LX, p. 244.

[132]*Bombay Chronicle*, 2 March 1935.

[133]Ibid., 23 April 1935.

[134]Ibid., 6 April 1935, for editorial comment.

[135]To Zakir Husain, 12 May 1936, Ansari Papers (Miscellaneous files), JMI.

10

The Legacy

> Dr Ansari has passed away and the nation of which he was a shining ornament and of our national movement of which he was so long a pillar and guide, feels desolate and shaken. We remember afresh his brilliant gifts and his services to the nation and his sacrifices for the cause of freedom [Jawaharlal].
>
> *Bombay Chronicle*, 11 May 1936.

ANSARI WAS BURIED in Jamia. The funeral was intended to be private, but the immense popular interest turned it into a public, even a national event. In areas where his name was so firmly associated with the freedom struggle and the cause of communal unity, there was spontaneous expression of grief at his premature death. *Dar-us-Salam*, a familiar landmark in Delhi's political history, was thronged with mourners. Public meetings were held in the capital where, for nearly a quarter of a century, Ansari survived the kicks and buffetings of political life and came to symbolize the composite cultural ethos of the Indo-Gangetic region. He had given a tone to public life that promoted goodwill and had smoothed away the harsher discords of politics. Elsewhere he was remembered as a Congress stalwart, a freedom fighter and an apostle of Hindu-Muslim unity. Wrote the *Bombay Chronicle*: 'While the spectre of communalism stalked the land and many a nationalist even among the Congressmen fell victim to it, Dr Ansari remained unshaken in his faith in democratic nationalism.... His nationalism was pure, unadulterated and undefiled.'[1]

Ansari was with his gentle manner a most attractive person, with an endearing streak of sometimes childlike simplicity. Kindness came naturally to him and he was thoughtful and considerate even to those who were not his personal friends or political comrades. Those to whom he was personally attached

[1] *Bombay Chronicle*, 11 May 1936.

always found him ready to involve himself sympathetically in their affairs. His Congress comrades held him in esteem for his devotion to nationalist causes, his humanity, generosity and kindness.[2] Gandhi and the Nehrus treated him with respect and deference. He was their friend and confidant and, after Mohamed Ali's estrangement from the Congress, the most important front rank leader they could rely on for rallying the Muslims around the Congress banner. From 1924-5 to 1935 he occupied the same position in Congress that Azad enjoyed in the 1940s. During this period, he was a man of action in the best sense: what he had learnt from his practical experience he used to exhort, advise and implore. He led a life of almost ceaseless endeavour and commitment, sustained by a vision of an independent India free from communal antagonism and proved himself in the most searching of political tests.

Outside the Congress circles he got on well with the Liberals. He was not in sympathy with their political creed and was impatient with their limited political objectives. But he had much in common with Sapru whom he had known since 1915 and often acted in unison to bridge the Hindu-Muslim divide. He invited the Liberal leader to preside over the lecture of Husain Rauf Bey, first president of the Angora National Assembly, at the Jamia Millia Islamia,[3] backed his move to resolve the communal deadlock[4] and appreciated his firm advocacy of India's constitutional rights. 'Although it has not been possible for Congressmen during the last 14 or 15 years to see eye to eye,' Ansari told Sapru, 'there have been more occasions than one when your cooperation on critical junctures such as, for instance, the Gandhi-Irwin negotiations, has proved of considerable value.'[5] Sapru, in turn, endorsed Ansari's stand on major political issues, especially on civil disobedience, the Communal Award and the revival of the Swaraj Party, and admired his 'genuine type of nationalism'.[6] In his final tribute to Ansari, he wrote:

There was scarcely any man in the public life of the country

[2]Gandhi wrote that Ansari 'can't refuse anybody, rich or poor. He was once visited by a woman out to rob him, and he emptied his purse into the fold of her sari'. Gandhi to V.J. Patel, 8 April 1935, *CWG*, Vol. LX, p. 400.

[3]To Sapru, 26 February 1933, Hasan (ed.), *Muslims and the Congress*, p. 135.

[4]To Sapru, 25 March 1933, ibid., p. 137.

[5]To Sapru, 28 April 1934, ibid., p. 152.

[6]Sapru to Ansari, 23 April 1934, ibid., pp. 147–50.

> for whom I had greater respect and for whom personally, if I may say so, greater affection. In these days, when it is a fashion for so many to claim to be nationalists, there was no man among the Hindus or the Muslims to whose real feelings of nationalism I felt more drawn than those of Ansari. Whatever else he may or may not have been, he was, in my humble opinion, *a very true, a very selfless and a very earnest nationalist* [italics added]. We have lost in him not only a great patriot, a great nationalist, a great doctor, but what is more, a great gentleman.[7]

Of all his friendships, perhaps that with Hakim Ajmal Khan had been the closest; in fact rarely in Muslim political affairs had such a partnership persisted, so intimate and so loyal. But the hakim died in 1927 and thereafter Ansari was increasingly dependent on Sherwani,[8] Khaliquzzaman, Abdul Majid Khwaja, Abdur Rahman Siddiqi and Shuaib Qureshi. Some like Azad, Syed Mahmud Rafi Ahmad Kidwai, Ghaffar Khan, Mujibur Rahman, Brelvi, Kitchlew and Hasrat Mohani sympathized with him on certain issues; but none could remotely be described as belonging to his personal following. His protege, Khaliquzzaman, also did not act closely with him. For much of the period after 1929-30, indeed, he was on the other side searching for a role outside the Congress. He exuded insincerity to some and seemed at times to embody the popular image of a cynical politician. In fact Ansari complained of Khaliquzzaman's cold and indifferent treatment. He was pained to discover that he had stood for the Assembly elections and had not bothered to inform him about it. 'But I must not forget my place. Who am I to grumble, what am I to take offence to such things?'[9]

What Ansari could not prophesy was that his political legacy

[7]Sapru to Asaf Ali, 12 May 1936, Sapru Papers.

[8]He died on 22 March 1932. Wrote Jawaharlal in his prison diary: 'We had been arrested together on Dec. 26, 1931, and had spent a month together in barrack No. 6. That month and the preceding months during the strenuous true period we had a great deal to do with each other and my liking for him had progressively grown. When he went to Europe with Ansari in the summer of 1934 for treatment he wrote to me to prison almost an apologetic letter for leaving the country at that juncture. A brave man, true man, rather limited in outlook as all of us are, but not to be frightened or bullied.' 24 March 1935, *SWJ*, Vol. 6, p. 337.

[9]Ansari to Khaliquzzaman, 24 February 1923, Hasan (ed.), *Muslims and the Congress*, p. 107.

would be carried forth and made into an integral part of the nationalist movement. Admittedly, he was not as influential as Mohamed Ali was in the years 1918 to 1922; in comparison, he was also lacking in charisma, personal dynamism and popular appeal. But what inspired an entire generation of young Muslims was his consistent defiance of colonial rule,[10] his unassailable loyalty to the Congress movement and its ideals, his contribution to fostering communal amity and harmony and his attractive personality which was free from rancour and bitterness and untouched by any personal or political scandal. Many Muslims who gathered around Jawaharlal in the 1930s were friends and followers of Ansari, a fact which has gone unnoticed in most historical accounts. Many who organized the Muslim Mass Contact Campaign, launched in August 1937,[11] had learnt their political lessons at the feet of Ansari. And many who assembled in Delhi at the Azad Muslim Conference in April 1940 were members of the All India Nationalist Muslim Party, an organization founded by Ansari in July 1929. Equally, various isolated, though ineffectual, endeavours in the 1940s to stem the Muslim League tide were inspired by the example of Ansari.

Ansari's political message was simple and straightforward. The destiny of the Indian Muslims was inextricably linked with their fellow countrymen with whom they had everything in common except religion. The Congress, according to him, was engaged in a historic struggle against a colonial power and it was therefore incumbent upon all sections of the society to rally round such an organization. The debate whether a Muslim was loyal to the country first or to his faith was a sterile one and had no relevance, for Islam and nationalism were compatible in the Indian, as indeed in any other situation. Indian nationalism represented the true and genuine aspirations of the Indian people generally; so the Hindus and the Muslims, who shared common historical experiences and a common destiny, must endeavour to forge a united front in the attainment of independence and harness their energies in the creation of a secular

[10]It is interesting to note that Ansari used professional bodies, such as the All-India Medical Conference, to voice his anti-colonial views. See *IQR*, 1933, Vol. 2, pp. 23–4. I was told by the Maharajkumar of Mahmudabad that Ansari insisted on prescribing medicines produced in India to his patients.

[11]Mushirul Hasan, 'The Muslim Mass Contact Campaign: An attempt at Political Mobilization', *South Asia*, New Series, Vol. vii, No. 1, June 1984.

and democratic polity. Existing differences between them, created and fostered by the British, could be amicably settled through pacts, agreements and unity conferences. The Congress offered, so Ansari argued, an adequate and appropriate framework for the resolution of communal disputes.

Some of these formulations were fairly simplistic, for Ansari took no account of the larger historical processes created largely by a complex interplay of socio-economic forces, which engendered communal conflicts. That is why he exaggerated the ease with which unity could be achieved and assumed, somewhat naively, that unity conferences and frequent negotiations between leaders would put an end to communal discord. When these failed, he complained that Gandhi and Motilal had not shown sufficient interest in the matter. He was right in his perception, but he was wrong in assuming that their influence was so pervasive that any agreement on the communal issue could be pushed through without taking care of the interests, fears and aspirations of their other constituent groups. Moreover, Ansari could not fully discern a shift in the order of priorities. The resolution of communal differences was no doubt a vital part of the Congress programme in the early 1930s, but it was conveniently deferred until the attainment of swaraj. This was as much an admission of failure as a tactical move to divert the attention of the people to the anti-colonial struggle, launched in the form of civil disobedience. Ansari was unable to come to terms with this reality; hence his outburst in February-March 1930 when he distanced himself from the civil disobedience movement. His resignation from the Congress bodies in early 1930 was a step reluctantly taken. It was feared that he might become the leader of a revolt, but he made no such attempt and resisted the considerable pressure placed upon him to align himself with the Muslim League. In the months that followed his resignation he spoke rarely in public or Congress meetings. When he did speak his main theme was the need for national unity and in developing his argument he did little to disturb the unity of the Congress party. He remained loyal and in so doing won the respect among all sections of the Congress.

This was not all. Men with lesser convictions wavered in their loyalty and succumbed to communal pressures. But not Ansari. He sensed the drift in Congress policies but refused to change course. He realized that his own efforts to bring about an overall communal agreement had come to nothing. Yet he did not despair. He persisted in his search for a consensus, continued to champion Hindu-Muslim unity and, in the end, represented the best traditions of Indian nationalism. 'We are not likely to see the like of Dr Ansari again,' concluded Mahadev Desai in his tribute.[12]

[12] Mahadev Desai to Birla, 12 May 1936, *Bapu*, Vol. 2, p. 235.

APPENDIX I

*Names of Muslims elected from Muslim Constituencies to the Assembly with the name of the Party to which they belonged **

Congress—

T. A. K. Sherwani.
Mohd. Ahmad Kazmi (also nominated by Unity Board).

Unity Board—

Maulana Shaukat Ali (also Khilafat and *Jamiyat al-ulama*).
Azhar Ali (also nominated by Oudh National Agriculturists) (also Congress).

Red Shirt—

Dr. Khan Sahib.

Abrar—

K. L. Gauba.

League Conference—
Bombay—

M. A. Jinnah.
Ibrahim Jaffer.

Sind—

Seth Haji Abdulla Haroon.
Bhutto.

Punjab—

Syed Ghulam Bhik Nairang.
Makhdum Syed Rajan Buksh.

Nawab Sir Mehr Shah.
Hafiz Mohammad Abdullah
Sheikh Fazli Haq Piracha.

United Provinces—

Maulvi Sir Mohammad Yaqub.
Dr. Ziauddin Ahmad.

Bengal—

A. H. Ghaznavi.
A. K. Fazlul Haq.
Anwar-ul-Azim.
Sir Abdulla Suhrawardy.
Abdulyahel Baqi (also nominated by the Congress).

Bihar and Orissa—

Maulvi Shafee Daoodi.
Maulvi Badiuzzaman.
Maulvi Mohammad Noman.

Madras—

Umar Ali Shah.

Central Provinces—

Khan Sahib Siddique Ali Khan.

Assam—

Abdul Matin Chaudhri.

Independents.

Madras—

Maulvi Murtaza Sahib (also supported by League Conference).
Haji Abdul Sattar (also supported by League Conference).
Umar Ali Shah (also supported by League Conference).

Assam—

Abdul Matin Chaudhri (also supported by League Conference).

C. P.—

Khan Sahib Siddique Ali Khan. Independent.

Muslims elected from other Constituencies.

From General Constituency—

Asaf Ali (Congress).

From Landholders' Constituency—

1. *Sind.—Sir Ghulam Husain Hidayatullah* (League Conference).
2. *Punjab.*—Ghiasuddin.

*Home Poll. F. No. 150/1934, NAI.

APPENDIX II

*Muslim Organizations in India, 1906–1947**

Serial No.	Name of Organization	When established	Constitution	Aims and Objects	Remarks
1	All-India Muslim League, Delhi.	1906	*President.*—M. A. Jinnah *Secretary.*—Hafiz Hidayat Hosain. *Joint Secretaries*— 1. K. B. S. M. Abdulla 2. Mr. Anwar-ul-Azim, M.L.A. 3. Shah Masood Ahmad, M.L.A.	To protect the religious and political rights of the Muslims in India.	This is the oldest of all the prominent Muslim organizations in India. The scope of the activities of the League is limited and unlike the C. Khilafat Committee it seldom dabbles in affairs relating to foreign countries. About 1928-29 the League was split into two rival sections, one led by M. A. Jinnah and the other by the late Sir Mohd. Shafi. Both of these groups continued to work separately till the beginning of this year when they were amalgamated under the presidentship of M. A. Jinnah through the efforts of H. H. the Aga Khan. The League is now working hand-in-hand with the A.I.M.C.
2	*Jomiyat al-ulama-i Hind*, Delhi.	1919	*President.*—M. Kifayatullah. *Secretary.*—Ahmad Said. *Treasurer.*—Haji Abdul Ghaffar.	*Original* 1. To safeguard the Khilafat. 2. To preach Islam. *Subsequent to the abolition of the Khilafat.*	This organization is mainly composed of *Ulama*. It was established in 1919 through the efforts of Kifayatullah and Ahmad Said of Delhi. Took an active part in Khilafat agitation and after the abolition of the Khilafat turned its attention towards the Hejaz and Arabia—stressing upon the freedom of these countries from non-Muslim influence. Thereafter the *Jamiyat* took some interest in the Riffian struggle and when the latter was over it devoted itself entirely to preaching unity among Muslims and protecting Islam. In 1929 the *Jamiyat* was

Serial No.	Name of Organization	When established	Constitution	Aims and Objects	Remarks
				1. To work for the restoration of the Khilafat. 2. To preach Islam. *Present Aims and Objects.* 1. To preach Islam. 2. To prepare the Muslims for the Congress creed.	split into two sections—*viz.*, Delhi and Kanpur—the former led by Kifayatullah and the latter by the Ali brothers. The Delhi section took an active part in the Civil Disobedience Movement in 1930 in support of the Congress by which it was well supplied with funds
3	*Jamiyat al-ulama-i Hind*. Kanpur.	1929	*President*— Shah Mohd. Sulaiman of Phulwari. *Vice-President.*—Abdul Qadir of Budaun. *Working Secretary.*—M. Mazharuddin of Delhi. *Financial Secretary.*—Kh. Ghulam-us-Sibtain, B.A.	Aims and objects as regards the propagation of Islam are identical with those of the Delhi *Jamiyat* but it is opposed to Congress creed.	Was founded in 1929 by the Ali Brothers with the main object of widening the narrow circle of the *ulama* by including those who though ignorant of Arabic were well informed of the Muslim religion and further to include in the definition of religious *ulama*, all *ulama* and *Mujtahids* of all sects. This *Jamiyat* was backed by the *ulama* of Firangi Mahal, Badaun and M. Mazharuddin of Delhi. When M. Shaukat Ali and his party consisting of M. Inayatullah of Firangi Mahal went over to the Delhi *Jamiyat* the Kanpur *Jamiyat* issued a disclaimer severing its connection with them. The latter body is in full agreement with the A.I.M.C. and the A.I.M. League.
4.	All-India Central Khilafat Committee. Bombay.	1919	*President.*—Abdul Majid Sindhi M.L.A. *Vice-Presidents*— 1. Haji Abdulla Haroon. 2. Maulvi Shafee Daoodi. *Secretaries*— 1. Shaukat Ali. 2. Allah Bukhsh Usafi. 3. H. S. Suhrawardy. 4. Mohiuddin of Ajmer. 5. Mohd. Irfan. 6. Ghulam Rasul 'Mehr'. *Honorary Treasurer.*— Umarbhai Chaudibhai.	1. To secure the solution of the Khilafat question strictly in accordance with the *Sharia*. 2. To launch a comprehensive programme for the moral, political and educational uplift of the Muslims of India. 3. To establish brotherly relations with Muslims of other countries.	Was founded during the Great War by the Ali Brothers and Maulaňa Abdul Bari to safeguard the Khilafat and to watch over the safety and integrity of the Holy Places of Islam but since the disclaimer of Mustafa Kamal Pasha and the termination of the Khilafat the aims and objects of the organization are now confined to (2) and (3) mentioned in previous column only. Is a political body with anti-British aims and propaganda. It is now anti-Congress and wields influence over those Muslims who have communal tendencies. The Central Khilafat Committee has its headquarters at Bombay and affiliated to it are the Provincial and District committee's in all parts of India.

Appendix II (*contd.*)

Serial No.	Name of Organization	When established	Constitution	Aims and Objects	Remarks
5	All-India Majlis-i-Ahrar-i-Islam, Punjab, Amritsar.	May 1931	*President.*—M. Habibur Rahman. *Vice-President.*—Chaudhri Afzal Haq., M.L.C. *Secretaries*— M. Daud Ghaznavi. Mazhar Ali Azhar. *Treasurer.*—Dr. Abdul Qadir.	1. To work for the economic, educational and social uplift of the Muslims. 2. to awaken political consciousness and infuse the spirit of Islam among Muslims. 3. To strive for the freedom of the country by peaceful methods.	Was started by the pro-Congress Muslims with the main object of maintaining the position of the Muslims in the Congress itself and to secure seats in the Working Committee. The Congress formula regarding the settlement of communal question was found to be unacceptable and was consequently rejected by the *Majlis* which thereafter turned its attention towards the Kashmir agitation. The *Majlis* carried on an intense propaganda in the form of a press campaign, meetings, processions of Kashmiri labourers and the celebration of a 'Kashmir Day,' against the State. It also sent *jathas* of volunteers to Kashmir in defiance of the orders passed by the State authorities forbidding their entry in Kashmir. The arrest of prominent leaders and lack of funds and volunteers owing to great distrust of the leaders served to decrease the enthusiasm for the Kashmir agitation and as a result the *Majlis* was forced to change their programme and turn their attention towards the alleged Government excesses in the N.W.F.P. but the agitation was shortlived. The agitation in Kapurthala and Jind States evoked considerable interest among the Ahrars who contemplated to stir the Muslim masses in the same way as was done in the case of Kashmir but fortunately the movement died a natural death. Of late the Ahrar Party in order to enlist fresh support has been carrying on a tirade against the Ahmadiya community. The *Majlis* still wields a considerable influence in the Punjab and has branches in almost all the big cities in that Province.

Serial No.	Name of Organization	When established	Constitution	Aims and Objects	Remarks
6	Anjuman-i Khaksaran, Lahore.	1931	*Executive Committee*— 1. Inayatullah Khan Mashriqi. 2. Mufti Sahib, Mozang Lahore. 3. Masud Ahmad Khan, B.Sc., of Lahore. 4. M. A. Majid of Lahore. 5. Hakim Mohd. Din of Lahore.	Social service and political advancement. To unite all Islamic powers and to achieve independence for India.	The founder of the *Anjuman* is Inayatullah Khan, Mashriqi, of the "Tazkira" fame who was employed in the N.W.F.P. Educational service. He is reported to be eccentric and an ardent pan-Islamist. The *Anjuman* has branches in various cities in the Punjab and one in Peshawar. In July 1933 the Lahore *Anjuman* despatched, by way of advertisement, a *jatha* of 9 volunteers for pilgrimage to Mecca. The movement has made no further progress as Inayatullah has incurred the hostility of the Ahrars.
	Red Shirts (Khudai Khidmatgars or Afghan Jirga) Utmanzai-Charsada.	1929	....	To propagate the congress creed and to carry on the Civil Disobedience Movement.	It commanded great influence over the rural populace in the District through the medium of Khan Abdul Ghaffar Khan. Has been declared unlawful since 1931. Some unimportant persons are now carrying on the organization secretly.
	All-India Muslim Conference.	1929	*President*— Nawab Ahmad Said Khan of Chhatari. *Vice-Presidents.*— Sir Mohd. Iqbal. Dr. Shafaat Ahmad Khan. Shafee Daoodi. *Secretary.*—Seth Abdullah Haroon. *Working Secretary*— Khan Bahadur Haji Rahim Baksh. *Joint Secretaries*— K. B. Syed Abdul Hafiz, Husain	(1) To safeguard and promote the rights and interests of the Indian Muslims at all stages of constitutional advance towards full responsible Government in India. (2) To organize the Indian Muslims and to co-ordinate the existing Muslim organizations having an All-India character for the purpose of giving expression to Muslim opinion on	Was founded early in 1929 on the occasion of H.H. the Aga Khan's visit to Delhi. It passed unanimously the famous 14 points of Mr. Jinnah which represented the Muslim demands in the new Constitution. The Conference firmly stood by these demands (including separate electorates) during the Civil Disobedience Movement from which it remained quite aloof. After the C.D. Movement discussions crept in with the result that the constitution of the conference was re-shaped early in 1934 through the efforts of its promoter, *viz.*, H.H. the Aga Khan. In conjunction with the A.I.M.L. the conference decided in August 1934 to form a Parliamentary Majlis

Appendix II (*contd.*)

Serial No.	Name of Organization	When established	Constitution	Aims and Objects	Remarks
8	All-India Muslim Conference—*contd.*		Imam, A. H. Ghaznavi, Mohd. Moazzam and Zahur Ahmad.	questions affecting the Indian Muslims without interfering with the special features which distinguish such organizations.	with a view to contest seats in the Assembly in direct opposition to the efforts made by the Unity Board formed by the rival organization, *viz.*, the A.P.M.C. to send their own candidates to the Assembly.
9	All Parties Muslim Unity Conference, Lucknow.	1930	Constitution of the Unity Board:— *President*— Nawab Mohd. Ismail Khan. *Working Committee*.—Consisting of 21 members.— *Secretaries*.— 1. Shaukat Ali. 2. Shah Masood Ahmad. 3. Syed Zakir Ali.	1. To create a sense of duty and love for Islam. 2. To organize all Muslims in order to enable them to take their proper share in struggle for freedom. 3. To unite the various sects of Muslims and to strive for unity with other communities. 4. To improve the condition of peasants and zamindars and to fight against unemployment.	This conference was organized at Lucknow at the close of 1933 by Muslims of a nationalist turn of mind who were anxious to save their reputation by bringing about unity among the Muslim ranks. It is composed of members belonging to the nationalist school of thought, of the Delhi group of the *Jamiyat al-ulama*, a section of the *Jamiyat al-ulama-i Hind*, Kanpur, some members of the old C.K.C. and the A.I.M.L., the Shia community and more particularly by Shaukat Ali and his coterie, formerly enthusiastic workers of the A.I.M.C. The conference formed a Unity Board consisting of 21 members with the object of contesting seats in the Assembly elections in opposition to the efforts of the Parliamentary Majlis formed by the rival organization, *viz.*, the A.I.M.C. At its meeting held at Lucknow in May 1934 the Muslim Unity Majlis endorsed the Congress programme regarding the revival of the Swaraj Party and deprecated all agitation to get the Communal Award modified by the British Government in the absence of an agreed settlement among the various communities. The results of the election clearly show that the Unity Board has attained a position of influence and importance slightly better than that held by its rival organization, *viz.*, the

Serial No.	Name of Organization	When established	Constitution	Aims and Objects	Remarks
					A.I.M.C. Judging by the results of the elections the influence of the A.I.M.C. appears to be declining.
10	All-India Shia Conference, Lucknow.	1910	*President*.—Prince Mirza Mohd. Akram of Calcutta. *General Secretary*.—Mojez Husain (of Amroho?).	To safeguard the religious and political rights of the Shia community.	The Conference was affiliated to the All-India Muslim Unity Majlis about the middle of 1934. The latter is in favour of the institution of separate electorates.
11	*Jamiyat Shabbanul Muslimin*, Delhi.	1929	*President*.—Mohd. Usman Azad. *Vice-President*.—Shah Abdul Jabbar. *Secretary*.—Dr. Noor Ahmad. *Joint Secretary*.—Mohd. Ibrahim. *Treasurer*.—Sufi Noor Elahi.	Aims and objects are similar to those of *Jamiyat al-ulama-i-Hind*, Delhi, of which it is a branch.	Was founded with the object of enlisting support of the Muslim youths for the *Jamiyat al-ulama* of Delhi and to induce them to take part in the Civil Disobedience Movement. There are branches (or similar organizations) of the *Jamiyat al-ulama-i Hind* in Lahore and Bombay but they are practically inactive.

*Home Poll. F. No. 150/1934, NAI.

Bibliography

PRIVATE PAPERS

Aligarh Muslim University Archives, Aligarh (AMUA)
Papers relating to the Non-cooperation movement at M.A.O. College, Aligarh.

India Office Library, London (IOL)
Chelmsford Papers.
Fazl-i-Husain Papers.
Harcourt Butler Papers.
James Meston Papers.

National Archives of India, New Delhi (NAI)
M.R. Jayakar Papers.
Rajendra Prasad Papers.

National Library, Calcutta (NLC)
B.S. Moonje Papers.
T.B. Sapru Papers.

Nehru Memorial Museum & Library, New Delhi (NMML)
Abdul Majid Khwaja Papers.
Abdullah Brelvi Papers.
All-India Congress Committee (AICC) Papers.
B.C. Roy Papers.
Habibur Rahman Ludhianvi Papers.
Haroon Khan Sherwani Papers.
Jawaharlal Nehru Papers.
M.A. Ansari Collection.
M.C. Chagla Papers.
Motilal Nehru Papers.
Raja of Mahmudabad Papers.
Sri Prakasa Papers.

Oral History Transcripts, (NMML)
K.G. Saiyidain.
Mohammad Mujeeb.
Zohra Ansari.

University Library, Cambridge (CUL)
Hardinge Papers.

Jamia Millia Islamia, New Delhi (JMI)
M.A. Ansari Papers.
K.G. Saiyidain Collection.
Mohammad Ali Papers.
Mohammad Mujeeb Collection.

Centre of South Asian Studies, Cambridge
J.C. Curry Papers.

Government Records

National Archives of India, New Delhi (NAI)
Records of the Home Department of the Government of India. Home Political files are divided into A, B and D (Deposit) categories.

The Uttar Pradesh State Archives, Lucknow (UPSA)
Records of the UP government in the General Administration (GAD), Reform and Police departments.

Delhi State Archives, Delhi
Records relating to the Police Department.

Newspapers and Journals

Aaj Kal (Delhi), Ansari number, January 1981.
Bombay Chronicle (Bombay).
Comrade (Calcutta and Delhi)
Hamdard (Delhi).
Indian Annual Register, 1922-1936, published as the *Indian Quarterly Register*, 1924-1929.
Jamia (Delhi), Ansari number, July 1981.
Leader (Allahabad).
Modern Asian Studies (Cambridge).
Modern Review (Calcutta).
Mussalman (Calcutta).
New Era (Lucknow).
Naqush (Lahore), Iqbal number, September 1977.
Report on the Native Newspapers of Bengal, Punjab and the United Provinces.
Tribune (Lahore).
Young India (Ahmedabad).

Official Publications

District Gazetteer of the United Provinces of Agra & Oudh, vol. XXIX, Ghazipur (Allahabad, 1909).
Ghazipur. Supplementary notes and Statistics to volume XXXIX of the District Gazetteer of the United Provinces of Agra and Oudh (Allahabad, 1915).
Government of India, *India in 1917-18 to India in 1933-36*, reports prepared annually for presentation to Parliament.

Indian Round Table Conference 12th November 1930-19th January 1931. Proceedings of Sub-Committees (Part II).

Proceedings of Sub-Committees (7 September-1 December 1931) (London, 1932).

Report of the Working of the System of Government, United Provinces of Agra and Oudh (3 vols., Allahabad, 1925).

Report on Indian Constitutional Reforms (1918). Cmd. 9109.

Report of the Indian Statutory Commission, vol 1, *Survey* (1930). Cmd. 3568.

The Disorders Enquiry Committee, vol. I, Delhi (Calcutta, 1920).

Materials Published by Indian Political Organizations

Annual Reports of the All-India Muslim League.

Annual Reports of the Indian National Congress.

Aziz, K.K. (ed.), *All-India Muslim Conference 1928-35: A documentary record* (Karachi, 1972).

Pirzada, S.S. (ed.), *Foundations of Pakistan: All-India Muslim League documents, 1906-47* (2 vols. Karachi, 1970).

Proceedings of the All-Parties National Convention (Allahabad, 1929).

Published Works, Articles and Unpublished Theses

Abbas, K.A. *I am not an Island: An Experiment in Autobiography* (Delhi, 1977).

Abbot, F. *Islam and Pakistan* (New York, 1968).

Abdullah, S.M. *New Kashmir* (New Delhi, n.d.).

Ahmad, A. *Islamic Modernism in India and Pakistan 1857-1946* (London, 1967).

———. *Studies in Islamic Culture in the Indian Environment* (Oxford, 1964).

Ahmad, W. (ed.), *Letters of Mian Fazl-i-Husain* (Lahore, 1976).

———. *Diary and Notes of Mian Fazl-i-Husain* (Lahore, 1976).

Adhikari, G. *Documents of the History of the Communist Party of India*, vol. III-B, (Delhi, 1979).

Amin, M. 'Aadaa-i Shabab', Malik Ram (ed.), *Nazr-i Hameed* (Delhi, 1981).

Andrews, C.F. *Zakaullah of Delhi* (Cambridge, n.d.).

———. 'Hakim Ajmal Khan', in *Eminent Mussalmans* (Madras, 1926).

Ansari K.H. 'The Emergence of Muslim Socialists and their ideas in India between 1917 and 1947' (Ph.D. thesis, University of London, 1985).

Ansari, S. 'Dr Ansari Ki Kitaab: Regeneration of Man', *Jamia*, July 1981.

Ansari, Shaukatullah. *Pakistan The Problem of India* (Lahore, 1944).

Ansari, Z. 'Shamsunnisa awr Dr Ansari', *Aaj Kal*, January 1981.

Azad, A.K. *India Wins Freedom: An Autobiographical Narrative* (Bombay, 1959).

Baird, R.D. (ed.), *Religion in Modern India* (Delhi, 1981).

Bamford, P.C. *Histories of the Khilafat and Non-cooperation Movements* (Delhi, 1975, reprint).

Bamzai, P.N.K. *A History of Kashmir* (Delhi, 1962).

Barkatullah, M. *The Khilafat* (London, 1924).

Barni, Z.A. *Azmat-i Rafta* (Karachi, 1961).

Bayly, C.A. *The Local Roots of Indian Politics—Allahabad, 1880-1920* (Oxford, 1975).

Bedar, A.R. *Mata-i Faqir* (Delhi, 1969).

Begum Nazli. *Sair-i Europe* (London, n.d.).

Bengal Anti-Communal Award Movement: A Report (Calcutta, 1939).

Bijnori, A.L. *Latif Ki Kahani* (Bijnor, 1967).

Birla, G.D. *In the Shadow of the Mahatma* (Calcutta, 1953).

———. *Bapu: A Unique Association*, vol. 1 (Delhi, 1977).

Blunt, W.S. *India Under Ripon: A Private Diary* (London, 1909).

Bose, M. *The Aga Khans* (London, 1984).

Brass, P. *Language, Religion and Politics in North India* (Cambridge, 1974).

Brown, J.M. *Gandhi's Rise to Power: Indian Politics 1915-1922* (Cambridge, 1972).

———. *Gandhi and Civil Disobedience: The Mahatma in Indian Politics 1928-34* (Cambridge, 1977).

———. *Modern India: The Origins of an Asian Democracy* (Delhi, 1984).

Chandra, J. *Gandhiji and Haryana* (Delhi, 1977).

Chatterjee, B. *Aspects of Bengal Politics in the early Nineteen thirties* (Calcutta, 1969).

Choudhary, V. (ed.), *Rajendra Prasad Correspondence and Select Documents*, vol. 1 (Delhi, 1984).

Coatman J. *Years of Destiny—India, 1926-1932* (London, 1932).

Cotton, H. 'India Old and New', *Asiatic Review*, July 1914.

Coupland, R. *The Indian Problem 1833-1935* (Oxford, 1952).

———. *India: A Re-statement* (Oxford, 1945).

Das, D. *India from Curzon to Nehru and After* (London, 1969).

Datta, V.N. & Cleghorn, B.E. (eds.) *A Nationalist Muslim and Indian Politics* (Delhi, 1974).

Desai, M. *Day-to-Day with Gandhi* (Varanasi, 1968).

Edib, H. *Inside India* (London, 1936).

———. *The Turkish Ordeal* (London, 1928).

———. *Conflict of East and West in Turkey* (Delhi, 1935).

Ellisson, G. *An Englishwoman in Angora* (London, 1923).

———. *Turkey To-day* (London, 1928).

Faruqi, Z. *The Deoband School and the Demand for Pakistan* (London, 1963).

Fil Badiya Khutba-i Sadarat (Lahore, n.d.).

Furbank, P.N. *E.M. Forster: A Life: The Growth of the Novelist 1879-1914* (London, 1978).

Fyzee, A. *Iqbal* (Bombay, 1947).

Gallagher, J. 'Congress in Decline: Bengal 1930 to 1939,' *Modern Asian Studies*, vol. 7, 3, July 1973.

Gandhi, M.K. *The Collected Works of Mahatma Gandhi* (Delhi, in process of publication).

Ghaffar, A. *Hayat-i Ajmal* (Delhi, 1950).

———. *Jamaluddin Afghani* (Delhi, 1941).

Gilbert, I.A. 'Autonomy and Consensus under the Raj: Presidency (Calcutta); Muir (Allahabad); M.A.O. (Aligarh)', S.H. Rudolph and L.I. Rudolph (eds.), *Education and Politics in India: Studies in Organization, Society and Policy* (Delhi, 1972).

Gopal, S. *Jawaharlal Nehru A Biography*, vol. 1: 1889-1947 (Delhi, 1975).

Gopal, S. (ed.), *Selected Works of Jawaharlal Nehru* (Delhi, in process of publication).

Gupta, N. *Delhi Between Two Empires 1803-1931: Society, Government and Urban Growth* (Delhi, 1981).

Halil Halid. *The Diary of a Turk* (London, 1903).

Hamied, K.A. *An Autobiography: A Life to Remember* (Bombay, 1972).

Hardy, P. *The Muslims of British India* (Cambridge, 1972).

———. *Partners in Freedom—and True Muslims: The Political Thought of Some Muslim Scholars in British India, 1912-1947* (Scandinavian Institute of Asian Studies, 1971).

Hasan, Mohibbul. 'Mahatma Gandhi and the Indian Muslims', S.C. Biswas (ed.), *Gandhi Theory and Practice: Social Impact and Contemporary Relevance* (Simla, 1969).

Hasan, Mushirul. *Nationalism and Communal Politics in India 1916-1928* (Delhi, 1979).

———. *Mohamed Ali Ideology and Politics* (Delhi, 1981).

———. (ed.), *Communal and Pan-Islamic Trends in Colonial India* (Delhi, 1985).

———. (ed.), *Muslims and the Congress: Select Correspondence of Dr M.A. Ansari 1912-1935* (Delhi, 1979).

———. (ed.), *Mohamed Ali in Indian Politics: Select Writings*, vol. 1 (Delhi, 1982).

———. (ed.), *Mohamed Ali in Indian Politics: Select Writings*, vol. 2 (Delhi, 1983).

Haq, M. *Muslim Politics in Modern India 1857–1947* (Meerut, 1970).

Hayat, Abul. *Mussalmans of Bengai* (Calcutta, 1966).

Holt, P.M. *et al. The Cambridge History of Islam: The Central Islamic Lands*, vol. 1 (Cambridge, 1970)

Hourani, A. *Arabic Thought in the Liberal Age, 1798–1939* (Oxford, 1970).

Husain, A. *Fazl-i Husain: A Political Biography* (Bombay, 1916).

Husain, M.A. *Kashmir aur Dogra Raj, 1848–1931* (Delhi, 1970 edn.).

Iqbal, A. (ed.), *My Life a Fragment: An Autobiographical Sketch of Maulana Mohamed Ali*, Reprint of 1942 edn. (Lahore, 1966).

———. *Life and Times of Mohamed Ali* (Delhi, 1978 reprint).

———. (ed.), *Selected Speeches and Writings of Maulana Mohamed Ali* (Lahore, 1944).

Jafri, R.A. *Karawan-i Gumgushta* (Karachi, 1971).

Jamia Millia Islamia: Some Appreciations (Aligarh Millia Press, 1923).

Jalal, A. & Seal, A. 'Alternative to Partition: Muslim Politics Between the Wars', *Modern Asian Studies*, vol. 15, 3, 1981.

Jalal, A. *The Sole Spokesman: Jinnah, the Muslim League and the Demand for Pakistan* (Cambridge, 1985).

Jamiyat-i Markaziya Tanzim Ka Mujawaza Dasturul Amal (Amritsar, 1925).

Kabir, H. *Muslim Politics 1906–47 and other essays* (Calcutta, 1969).

Kaura, U. *Muslims and Indian Nationalism: The emergence of the demand for India's Partition 1928–1940* (Delhi, 1977).

Keddie, N.R. *Sayyid Jamal-ad-Din "al-Afghani": A Political Biography* (Los Angeles, 1972).

———. *Islamic Response to Imperialism: Political and Religious Writings of Sayyid Jamal ad-Din "al-Afghani"* (California, 1968).

Kedourie, E. *Afghani and Abduh: An Essay on Religious Unbelief and Political Activism in Modern Islam* (London, 1966).

Khaliquzzaman, C. *Pathway to Pakistan* (Lahore, 1961).

Khan, A.A. 'Tehrik-i Aazadi ka ek Khamosh Kaarkun' *Jung* (Rawalpindi, 9 June 1944).

Khan, Aga. *The Memoirs of Aga Khan: World Enough and Time* (London, 1956).

Khan, M.I. *Perspectives on Kashmir: Historical Dimensions* (Srinagar, 1983).

Khan, R.A. *Hayat-i Ajmal* (Delhi, 1931).

Kozlowski, G.C. 'The Power of Language and the Language of Power: A Study of Mawlana Muhammad Ali's Political Rhetoric', *South Asia*, vol. 5, 1, June 1982.

Kidwai, A. *Aazaadi Ki Chaaon me* (Delhi, 1980).

Kumar, K. *Peasants in Revolt: Tenants, Landlords, Congress and the Raj in Oudh* (Delhi, 1984).

Kumar, R. (ed.), *Essays on Gandhian Politics: The Rowlatt Satyagraha of 1919* (London, 1971).

———. *Essays in the Social History of Modern India* (Delhi, 1983).

———. & Panigrahi, D.N. (eds.), *Selected Works of Motilal Nehru*, vol. 3 (Delhi, 1984).

Lewis, B. *The Emergence of Modern Turkey* (London, 1961).

Lewis, G.L. *Turkey* (London, 1955).

Laird, M.A. (ed.), *Bishop Heber in Northern India. Selection from Heber's Journal* (Cambridge, 1971), p. 126.

Lago, M. and Furbank, P.N. *Selected Letters of E.M. Forster, 1879-1920*, vol. 1 (London, 1983).

Low, D.A. (ed.), *Soundings in Modern South Asian History* (University of California Press, 1968).

———. (ed.), *Congress and the Raj: Facets of the Indian Struggle 1917-1947* (London, 1977).

Lytton, Earl of, *Pundits and Elephants: Being the Experience of five years as Governor of an Indian Province* (London, 1942).

Malik, H. (ed.), *Iqbal: Poet, Philosopher of Pakistan* (New York, 1971).

Madani, H.A. *Naqsh-i Hayat: Khudnawisht Sawaanah* (Karachi, 1979 edn.).

Malhotra, S.L. *From Civil Disobedience to Quit India* (Chandigarh, 1979).

Masani, M. *Bliss was it in that Dawn: A Political Memoir upto Independence* (Bombay, 1977).

Mathur, V.S. (ed.), *Zakir Husain: Educationist and Teacher* (Delhi, 1969).

Mcpherson, K. *The Muslim Microcosm: Calcutta, 1918 to 1935* (Heidelberg, 1974).

Metcalf, B.D. 'Nationalist Muslims in British India', *Modern Asian Studies*, vol. 19, 1, 1985.

Millat-i Islamia awr Jamia Millia Islamia, Delhi (Calcutta, 1941).

Minault, G. *The Khilafat Movement: Religious Symbolism and Political Mobilization in India* (Delhi, 1982).

Misra, B.B. *The Indian Political Parties* (Delhi, 1976).

Moazzam, A. *Jamal al-Din al-Afghani: A Muslim Intellectual* (Delhi, 1983).

Mudholi, A.G. *Jamia Ki Kahani* (Delhi, 1965) in 2 volumes.

Mujeeb, M. *The Indian Muslims* (London, 1967).

———. *Dr Zakir Husain: A Biography* (Delhi, 1970).

———. 'Dr Ansari: Chand Yaaden baaten', *Aaj Kal*, January 1981.

Munshi, K.M. *Pilgrimage to Freedom*, Vol. 1 (Bombay, 1967).

Moore, R.J. *The Crisis of Indian Unity 1917-1940* (Delhi, 1974), p. 101.

Nairang, S.G.B. *Jamiyat-i Markaziya Tabligh al-Islam Ambala Shehar ki Satarsala Khidmat Ka Khulasa* (Ambala, 1940).

Namboodiripad, E.M.S. *How I became a Communist* (Trivandrum, 1976).

Nanda, B.R. *Mahatma Gandhi: A Biography* (London, 1958).

Nehru, J. *An Autobiography: With musings on recent events in India* (London, 1936).

———. (ed.), *A Bunch of Old Letters*, 2nd edn. (Bombay, 1966).

Nizami, H. *Tark-i Gayekushi* (Delhi, 1920).

———. *Government awr Khilafat* (Gurdaspur, 1922 edn.)

Nomani, S. *Safarnamah-i Misro-o Shaam* (Agra, 1894).

Noorani, A.G. *President Zakir Husain: A Quest for Excellence* (Bombay, 1967).

Page, D. *Prelude to Partition: The Indian Muslims and the Imperial System of Control 1920-1932* (Oxford, 1982).

Pandey, B.N. *Nehru* (London, 1976).

———. (ed.), *The Indian Nationalist Movement 1885-1947: Select Documents* (London, 1979).

Pandey, G. *The Ascendancy of the Congress in Uttar Pradesh 1926-1934* (Delhi, 1978).

Poynter, M.A. *When Turkey was Turkey: in and around Cons-tantinople* (London, 1921).

Prasad, B. *Gandhi, Nehru and J.P: Studies in Leadership* (Delhi, 1985).

Prasad, R. *India Divided.*(Bombay, 1946).

Qadiri, K.H. *Hasrat Mohani* (Delhi, 1985).

Rahman, F. *Islam* (London, 1966).

Ram, M. (ed.). *Nazr-i Hameed* (Delhi, 1981).

Robinson, F. *Separatism Among Indian Muslims: The Politics of United Provinces' Muslims, 1860-1923* (Cambridge, 1974).

Sadiq, M. *The Turkish Revolution and the Indian Freedom Movement* (Delhi, 1983).

Sayeed, K.B. *Pakistan: The Formative Phase 1857-1948* (Karachi, 1968 edn.).

Schimmel, A. *Gabriel's Wing: A Study into the Religious Ideas of Sir Muhammad Iqbal* (London, 1963).

Shraddhanand, S. *Inside Congress* (Bombay, 1946).

Siddiqi, M.H. *Agrarian Unrest in North India: The United Province 1918-22* (Delhi, 1978).

Smith, W.C. *Modern Islam in India* (Lahore, 1943).

Smith, W.R. *Nationalism and Reforms in India* (Yale University Press, 1938).

Tendulkar, D.G. *Abdul Ghaffar Khan* (Varanasi, 1969).

———. *Mahatma,* vol. 3 (Delhi, 1951).

Thursby, G.R. *Hindu-Muslim Relations in British India* (Leiden, 1975).

Tomlinson, B.R. *The Indian National Congress and the Raj 1929-42. The Penultimate Phase* (London, 1976).

Watson, W.J. 'Muhammad Ali and the Khilafat Movement' (unpublished M.A. thesis, 1955, McGill University).

Wolpert, S. *Jinnah of Pakistan* (Oxford University Press, New York, 1984).

Zaidi, A.Z. (ed.), *The Evolution of Muslim Political Thought in India,* vol. 4 (Delhi, 1980).

Index

Islam in the Subcontinent

Muslims in a Plural Society

MUSHIRUL HASAN

In Memory of

SARVEPALLI GOPAL

زندگی کیا ہے عناصر میں ظہورِ ترتیب
موت کیا ہے انھیں اجزاء کا پریشاں ہونا

Contents

PART IV

PART V

APPENDICES

Tables

Appendix

Acknowledgements

I have substantially revised and updated all the papers in this volume. Some have even been rewritten to make them accessible to the reader. The introduction is based on some of my earlier writings. The next essay 'Resistance and Acquiescence in North India: Muslim Responses to the West' is a substantially revised and enlarged version of my paper published in Mushirul Hasan and Narayani Gupta (eds.), *India's Colonial Encounter: Essays in Memory of Eric Stokes*, New Delhi, 1993. Since then, Gulfishan Khan has published *Indian Muslim Perception of the West During the Eighteenth Century*, Karachi, 1998, a well-researched monograph. I have also made use of the unpublished paper 'Eroticizing Europe' by Mohammad Tavakoli-Targhi, an Iranian scholar based in the US. Rosie Llewellyn-Jones, *Engaging Scoundrels: True Tales of Old Lucknow*, New Delhi, 2001, has interesting references to Abu Talib and his work.

- 'The Myth of Unity: Colonial and National Narratives' was originally published in David Ludden (ed.), *Contesting the Nation: Religion, Community and the Politics of Democracy in India*, Philadelphia, 1996.

- Versions of my paper 'Traditional Rites and Contested Meanings: Sectarian Strife in Colonial Lucknow' have appeared in *The Indian Economic and Social History Review*, Vol. 27, 2, 1990; Violette Graff (ed.), *Lucknow: Memories of a City*, New Delhi, 1996, pp. 114-35; Mushirul Hasan (ed.), *Islam, Communities and the Nation: Muslim Identities in South Asia and Beyond*, New Delhi, 1999, pp. 341-66.

- Two of my papers that were originally published in Mushirul Hasan (ed.), *Communal and Pan-Islamic Trends in Colonial India*, New Delhi, 1985, have been combined into one, and appear under the title 'Mediating the External: Pan-Islamism and Nationalist Renewal'. By far the most analytical study of the khilafat movement is by Gail Minault, *Religious*

Symbolism and Political Mobilization in India, New York, 1982; M. Naeem Qureshi, *Pan-Islam in British Indian Politics: A Study of the Khilafat Movement, 1918-1924*, Leiden, 1999, is a massive researched work. Though Francis Robinson has plotted the trajectory of the movement in the United Provinces, our knowledge of developments in other regions is still inadequate. The part played by the ulama of Firangi Mahal and the Barelwi school are discussed in Usha Sanyal, *Devotional Islam and Politics in British India: Ahmad Riza Khan Barelwi and his Movement, 1870-1920*, New Delhi, 1996, and Francis Robinson, *The Ulama of Farangi Mahall and Islamic Culture in South Asia*, New Delhi, 2001. *My Life: A Fragment: An Autobiographical Sketch of Maulana Mohamed Ali*, edited and annotated by me, is quite instructive. So are the essays in Mushirul Hasan (ed.), *Islam, Communities and the Nation: Muslim Identities in South Asia and Beyond*.

- '*My Life: A Fragment*: Mohamed Ali's Quest for Identity in Colonial India' was originally published in *Islam, Communities and the Nation: Muslim Identities in South Asia and Beyond*, New Delhi, 1999, pp. 57-96.

- 'Representations of Indian Nationalism: Ideology and Praxis of Azad and Mohamed Ali' was originally published in Mushirul Hasan (ed.), *Islam and Indian Nationalism: Reflections on Abul Kalam Azad*, New Delhi, 2001 rpt., pp. 77-99. Some sections of this chapter have been substantially modified.

- 'Congress Muslims and Indian Nationalism, Dilemma and Decline, *c*. 1928-1934' was originally published in Jim Masselos (ed.), *Struggling and Ruling: Indian National Congress 1885-1947*, New Delhi, 1986.

- 'Religion, Politics and Partition' was my Introduction to the volume *India's Partition: Process, Strategy and Mobilization*, New Delhi, 2001 rpt. I have introduced substantial stylistic changes without, of course, tampering with the overall thrust of my argument. I have also provided some additional information.

- 'The Muslim Mass Contact Campaign: a Strategy of Political Mobilization' was originally published in Richard Sisson and Stanley Wolpert (eds.) *Congress and Indian Nationalism: The Pre-Independence Phase*, Berkeley, 1988, pp. 198-222.

• 'The Local Roots of the Pakistan Movement: The Aligarh Muslim University' is a revised and enlarged version of the paper originally published in A.K. Gupta (ed.), *Myth and Reality: The Struggle for Freedom in India, 1945-47*, New Delhi, 1987. This version is close to what appeared in Mushirul Hasan (ed.), *Knowledge, Power and Politics: Educational Institutions in India*, New Delhi, 1999.

• 'Memories of a Fragmented Nation: Rewriting the Histories of India's Partition', was originally published in Mushirul Hasan (ed.), *Inventing Boundaries: Gender, Polities and the Partition of India*, New Delhi, 2000, pp. 26-46, and reprinted in Amrik Singh (ed.), *The Partition in Retrospect*, New Delhi, 2000, pp. 339-60; *The Annual of Urdu Studies*, University of Wisconsin-Madison, No. 15, Part I, 2000, pp. 263-86; S. Settar and Indira B. Gupta (eds.), *Pangs of Partition: The Human Dimension*, New Delhi, 2002, pp. 171-90. The essay does not cover the historical writings on the Bengal province, especially Bangladesh where the histories of Partition are being written differently since 1971. For a recent insight and references to other works, see Willem van Schendel and Erik Jan Znrcher (eds.), *Opting Out of the Nation: Identity Politics in Central, South and West Asia*, London, 1998.

• A slightly modified version of the paper 'Divided Nationhood: India's Partition Revisited' was published in K.N. Panikkar, Terence J. Bryce and Utsa Patnaik (eds.), *The Making of History: Essays Presented to Irfan Habib*, New Delhi, 2000, pp. 550-7. An enlarged version appeared in Mushirul Hasan (ed.), *Inventing Boundaries*, pp. 1-25.

• 'Moradabad Riots, 1980: Causes and Meanings' was jointly written with Satish Saberwal. It was originally published in A.A. Engineer (ed.), *Communal Riots in Post-Independence India*, Bombay, 1984. We visited Moradabad on 8-10 January; and then again on 29-31 January 1981.

• 'Competing Symbols and Shared Codes: Inter-Community Relations in Modern India' was originally published in Sarvepalli Gopal (ed.), *Anatomy of a Confrontation: The Babri Masjid-Ramjanmabhumi Issue*, New Delhi, 1990. A number of major works have appeared since then. For example, Gyan Pandey (ed.), *Hindus and Others: The Question of Identity in India Today*, New Delhi, 1990; Nilanjan Mukhopadhyay, *The Demolition: India at the Crossroads*, New Delhi, 1994; A. Nandy, S. Trivedi, S. Mayaram and A. Yagnik, *Creating a nationality—the*

Ramjanmabhumi movement and fear of the self, New Delhi, 1995; Rajeshwari Ghose, *In Quest of a Secular Symbol: Ayodhya and After*, Hong Kong, 1996. Both *South Asia*, Vol. 17, 1994, and *Asian Survey*, Vol. 33, No. 7, July 1993, brought out special issues on the Ayodhya tangle and its aftermath. Furthermore, the demolition of Babri Masjid generated lively debates on Hindu nationalism, and on secularism and its future in India. For example, Tapan Basu, Pradip Dutta, Sumit Sarkar, Tanika Sarkar and S. Sen, *Khaki Short and Saffron Flags: A Critique of the Hindu Right*, New Delhi, 1993; Peter van der Veer, *Religious Nationalism: Hindus and Muslims in India*, Berkeley, 1994; David Ludden (ed.), *Contesting the Nation: Religion, Community, and the Politics of Democracy in India*, Philadelphia, 1996; Christophe Jaffrelot, *The Hindu Nationalist Movement and Indian Politics 1925 to the 1990s*, London, 1996, is by far the most authoritative work on the subject; Gerald James Larson, *India's Agony over Religion*, New Delhi, 1997; Achin Vanaik, *Communalism Contested: Religion, Modernity and Secularisation*, New Delhi, 1997; Rajeev Bhargava (ed.), *Secularism and its Critics*, New Delhi, 1999, and Rajeev Bhargava, A.K. Bagchi and R. Sudarshan (eds.), *Multiculturalism, Liberalism and Democracy*, New Delhi, 1999.

- 'The Changing Position of the Muslims and the Political Future of Secularism in India, *c.* 1947-1986' was originally published in T.V. Sathyamurthy (ed.), *Region, Religion, Caste, Gender, and Culture in Contemporary India*, New Delhi, 1996, Vol. 3, pp. 200-28. Some additional information is included in this version. In January 2001, the Planning Commission constituted a Working Group on 'Empowering the Minorities' under my chairmanship. I have appended excerpts from that report as Appendix II to update some of the points discussed in this paper.

- 'India and Pakistan: Why the Difference?' was originally published in Mushirul Hasan and Nariaki Nakazato (eds.), *India's Unfinished Agenda: Nation-Building in South Asia*, New Delhi, 2001, pp. 309-44. I wrote this paper during my stay at the University of Virginia, Charlottesville, from January to May 2000. I am grateful to Walter Hauser for his intellectual support and to Douglas Verney for his comments.

For his painstaking editing and indulgence, I am beholden to B.N. Varma and to Ramesh Jain, as always, for his support and understanding.

15 August 2002 MUSHIRUL HASAN

PART I

1

Introduction

When the American historian David Lelyveld started researching at Aligarh in 1967 I, an undergraduate at the university's History department, dutifully attended lectures on medieval India. Here a whole new world was being opened up by scholars with exceptional skills. But unfortunately, we were not acquainted with late-nineteenth-century trends in north India, some of which left an indelible stamp on Aligarh's Muhammadan Anglo-Oriental College. There was no mention of its founder, Saiyid Ahmad Khan, or the intellectual activities of his companions at Aligarh and Delhi. Shibli Numani, Altaf Husain Hali and maulvi Zakaullah were distant figures: they did not figure in an otherwise elaborate curriculum. We read the *Babur-Nama* but not the *Asar ul-Sanadid*. Hindi poets—Kabir, Rahim and Raskhan—were introduced but not Mir Taqi Mir, Sauda and Mirza Asadullah Khan Ghalib. Stocked with numerous scholarly monographs authored by members of the department, the seminar library had few books on Aligarh's more recent history. Nobody had even tried to replicate, in the context of the Aligarh movement, Susobhan Sarkar's seminal work on the Bengal renaissance. I wondered why this was so. I did not ask. I merely sensed that the history of Islam in India during the colonial period was forbidden territory. At the beginning of the present millennium it is probably much the same at the Aligarh Muslim University, though social and cultural histories are being written elsewhere in India (Sumit Sarkar, *Writing Social History*, New Delhi 1997).

Joining Delhi's Jamia Millia Islamia in 1978, I found that the private papers of its two illustrious founders—Mohamed Ali and M.A. Ansari—had been retrieved from a damp basement by my father, Professor Mohibbul Hasan, just a few years ago. I also discovered that a serious history of the institution, described by free India's first prime minister as 'a lusty child of the Non-Co-operation [Movement]', did not exist. Nor did there exist a scholarly assessment of those 'self-sacrificing workers' who were, in the words of Gandhi, 'staunch Muslims and equally staunch nationalists'. Mohamed Ali's long-winded speeches and writings were first compiled, somewhat indifferently, by a retired diplomat and published in Lahore. The Turkish author Halide Edib (who lived in the Ansari household in 1935 and delivered lectures at the Jamia Millia Islamia), wrote the only readable accounts of Dr. M.A. Ansari. So did Jawaharlal Nehru in his autobiography, published in 1936.

This scholarly inertia has also gripped traditional centres of learning. The fortunes of Lucknow's Firangi Mahal, once home to several erudite religious thinkers of Awadh, have not improved since Independence and Partition. And though the Dar al-ulum remains a major theological seminary with a powerful ideological base and an extensive network of schools and colleges in South Asia, scholars at Deoband have yet to produce a scholarly history of an institution that has, for well over a century, influenced the intellectual and religious currents in the subcontinent. The same is true of Lucknow's Nadwat al-ulama. Though the Germany-based scholar Jamal Malik has recently produced a weighty account of Nadwas' history, the late Saiyid Abul Hasan Ali Nadwi almost single-handedly interpreted the political, intellectual and religious trends among Muslims in north India.

Scholars must be alerted to the neglect of an important component of north India's past. It is equally important to remind them that scholarly interventions are essential in order to unfold the variety and diversity in Indian Islam, examine the mixed experiences of its adherents, and reveal the deep internal divides and schisms, as well as tangible areas of interaction with castes and communities. Such researches will, doubtless, remove many misleading and stereotyped ideas associated with the nature and character of Islam and the structure of Muslim communities in South Asia.

The task is an awesome one for several reasons. For one, India's Partition had a curiously mixed intellectual impact. In an attempt to highlight their contribution to the freedom struggle, scores of writers connected with formal groups and organizations, notably the Dar al-ulum at Deoband and the Jamiyat al-ulama, dwell on their nationalist past. But serious scholars are reluctant to study the lives of 'defeated' men and 'lost' causes. The ideals and activities of 'nationalist Muslims' are either not taken into account or submerged within the rationalizations of the 'victors'. Saiyid Ahmad Khan—whose contribution to education and reform matched the intellectual stride of Bengal's early reformers and their contemporaries in Egypt and Syria—is an embarrassment because of his image as the progenitor of Muslim nationalism. The movement he generated among 'Aligarh's First Generation' is virtually written off for having stimulated communitarian ('communal' in common parlance) and pan-Islamic consciousness. The khilafat upsurge is regarded as a mere pan-Islamic outburst reinforcing the image of a 'community' with extra-territorial loyalties, while Muslim 'separatism' and the clamour for a separate Muslim nation are underlined to illustrate a specifically 'Muslim tendency' to organize separately as an exclusive religious entity.

The intellectual milieu after Independence has influenced the choice of, and preference for, certain themes. A number of historians, mostly Marxists, produced seminal works on the colonial economy, on economic nationalism, and on peasant as well as working-class movements. On the other hand, the dominant historiographical trends until the 1970s allowed little space for research on religion, culture, and intellectual life. Such themes, especially those perceived as being outside the framework of 'medieval India', were not seen as a part of the historian's agenda. This may explain why Kunwar Muhammad Ashraf, though endowed with a sharp analytical mind, failed to complete his projected study on Indian Muslims, or that a generation of scholars, especially at Aligarh and Allahabad, studied the economic, agrarian and institutional histories of medieval India to the exclusion of other themes. Professors Khaliq Ahmad Nizami and Saiyid Athar Abbas Rizvi were notable exceptions, but their writings were overshadowed by the Marxist writers.

India's Partition raised the most fundamental historical and sociological issues, but these have not been adequately analysed within studies on nationalism. Aziz Ahmad, Abid Husain, A.A.A. Fyzee, K.A. Nizami, Saiyid Athar Abbas Rizvi, and Muhammad Mujeeb opened up, for the first time after Independence, new areas of research on law, religion and politics and on the histories of ideas and movements. Yet, academic circles in India were neither prepared nor intellectually equipped (most have no knowledge of Persian and Urdu) for a serious engagement on those issues they underlined in their writings.

The result is for everybody to see. The intellectual advance has taken place in the West but not in South Asia. Islam in the subcontinent and its dynamic interaction with local, indigenous traditions remains a peripheral area of research in the country, and outside the college or university curriculum. One turns to David Lelyveld and C.W. Troll to renew acquaintance with 'Aligarh's First Generation'; to Barbara Metcalf,

Francis Robinson (*The Ulama of Farangi Mahall and Islamic Culture*, New Delhi, 2001, and his *Islam and Muslim History in South Asia*, New Delhi, 2000) and Usha Sanyal to uncover the histories of Deoband, Firangi Mahal, and the Barelwi 'schools'; and to Gail Minault for highlighting reformist trends and movements among north Indian Muslims towards the end of the nineteenth century, and, recently, documenting the history of women's education. Rafiuddin Ahmed, Claudia Liebeskind (*Piety on Its Knees: Three Sufi Traditions in South Asia in Modern Times*, New Delhi, 1998), Susan Bayly, Paul Brass, Stephen Dale, Sandria B. Freitag, David Gilmartin, Ayesha Jalal, Jamal Malik, Asim Roy, Ian Talbot—all based in universities outside India—have explored a number of significant areas and added depth to our understanding of Islam in South Asia. David Lelyveld's research, for one, resulted in the finely crafted, broadly erudite and innovative work: yet, not a single scholar at the Aligarh Muslim University has pursued the themes he outlined more than two decades ago.

II

Lelyveld's principal concern—one that commands wide assent nowadays—was to understand what it meant to be a Muslim in the nineteenth-century, how that cultural/social identity changed meaning in colonial India, and how it was articulated in that context. The Aligarh College is his focal point as a formally organized, self-consciously created social establishment, founded 'with the defined goal of carrying out transitions of identity and loyalty suitable to the special circumstances of British India'. But much more than this, *Aligarh's First Generation*: *Muslim Solidarity in British India* (1978) analyses an important group whose role in the nationalist movement has been condemned instead of being understood.

Lelyveld's book—that can still open up new vistas of research—is firmly rooted in history and sociology. Social history is his chief interest, though political themes are also skilfully integrated in his narrative. Not all his conclusions command equal assent; nor is his delineation of situations and problems free from the obscurities of sociological jargon. Yet, readers will find major aspects of his area of study better explained than ever before. Many writers have followed his methodology and framework of analysis; many study the same issues in other contexts; some acknowledge their debt to him; some do not. But discerning readers are likely to be impressed by Lelyveld's contribution to the ongoing debates, some of which have been underlined—though from different perspectives—in recent writings.

To what extent have such writings led to a reappraisal of existing approaches and interpretations? In other words, where does one situate them within the corpus of historical and sociological literature? Or, is it still the case that India's Muslims are treated as a special category for historical exploration?

I have argued elsewhere that social science scholarship and historiography since the 1980s have generated new approaches into different aspects of Indian society: change, variety, and difference have been highlighted in researches conducted under Marxist, post-modernist and subaltern approaches. But research on Muslims is still mired within traditional frameworks, and still dominated by widely accepted stereotypes. (Such trends will be accentuated by the 11 September 2001 terrorist assault on the World Trade Center and the Pentagon.) Colonial categories of knowledge, as applied to the Muslim communities, have been questioned but not changed. Consequently, ideas and movements associated with them are categorized as revivalist rather than reformist, communal rather than secular, separatist rather than nationalist, and finally, reactionary rather than progressive. In this scheme, the ideas and actions of Saiyid Ahmad Khan and his associates are placed within the same binary opposition. The stereotypical figure of the Saiyid as the architect of Muslim separatism, mesmerized by the British, remains unaffected by the knowledge of his reformist endeavours and his role in introducing rationalist ideas and English education in the last quarter of the nineteenth-century.

Similarly, men like Altaf Husain Hali, maulvi Nazir Ahmad and Sheikh Abdullah—all engaged in the project of 'reforming' Muslim women—find little mention in either conventional or unconventional histories and critiques of nationalism and separatism. The old explanations are presumed to unravel and delineate their conduct; it is all too readily assumed that they were imbued with 'reactionary' or 'communal' ideas. There is still talk of a 'Muslim mind', a 'Muslim outlook', and an inclination to construe a 'Muslim identity' around Islam, which is invariably on the wrong side of the binary divide. A sense of Otherness is, consequently, conveyed in such images and polarities.

Notice, for example, how the expression—'nationalist Muslims'—is widely in vogue to describe the activities of those Muslims who were wedded to a broadly secular polity and to the ideal of composite nationality. Its inappropriateness lies in the majoritarian view, a view that ascribes patriotism/nationalism to the vast majority of non-Muslims and not to others. If others share the sentiment, this is grudgingly recognized as an exception rather than the rule. Thus, the 'nationalist Muslims' are treated not only as exceptional individuals, but placed within a separate domain of enquiry and often outside the so-called nationalist discourse. When the Indian state commemorates their memory to advertise its secular credentials, the intellectual resources of specifically Muslim organizations and institutions are pressed into service to organize seminars and conferences. In this way the partition of the nation's heritage proceeds uninterruptedly.

The question is this: if, for example, Ajmal Khan, Ansari and Maulana Azad were 'nationalist Muslims', surely Gandhi, Jawaharlal Nehru and Vallabhbhai Patel were 'nationalist Hindus' by much the same logic. If religion is the criterion for categorizing an individual or a group, then how does one define the identity of a kisan or a trade union leader? Was Muzaffar Ahmad, founder of the Communist Party of India, a 'nationalist Muslim', and P.C. Joshi, also a leading figure in the communist movement, a 'nationalist Hindu'?

There are other widely-held beliefs and assumptions: for instance, the oft-repeated view that orthodoxy represents 'true' Islam, whereas liberal and modernist currents are secondary or peripheral to the more dominant separatist, communal, and neo-fundamentalist paradigms. Hence the focus on traditional revival, on religious revivalism, and on fundamentalist stirrings. When it comes to studying the Muslim communities, the dominant orthodox paradigms are ones that tend to get underlined most often. Contrariwise, heterodox trends—which contest the definition of a 'Muslim identity' in purely religious terms (in the context of imperial institutions), and which refute the popular notion that Islamic values and symbols provide a key to the understanding of the 'Muslim world view'—are not.

Consider another area where, despite the wide range of a rich secondary literature, certain views continue to influence popular beliefs and perceptions. Time and again one is reminded of the pervasive impact of Islam on its adherents, their concern to defend values enshrined in the Koran and the *Hadith*, and their trans-national links with a Muslim fraternity. Time and again one is also led to believe that the major preoccupation of a Muslim is praying, going on pilgrimage, and observing other religious rituals. Time and again we are told that Muslims, more than any other religious entity, attach importance and value to their religio-cultural habits and institutions, and therefore they are more prone to paying heed to Islamist ideas and movements.

Doubtless, theologians, publicists and itinerant preachers invoked the solidarity of the *umma* and other Islamic symbols to cultivate pan-islamism, religio-revivalism, and Muslim nationalism. Notice, how small groups of Muslims in Kanpur took to the streets when a portion of a masjid in the city was demolished in 1913. Notice, too, how the ulama and sections of the professional classes stimulated Muslim sentiments over the khilafat and the holy places. Or consider their stout resistance to interference in Muslim family law, exemplified in the opposition to the Sarda Marriage Bill of 1929, and after Independence, to the Indian Supreme Court's judgement on Shah Bano, and to the demolition of the Babri Masjid on 6 December 1992.

Doubtless, these are important facets, but their significance should not be overstated to construct a unified Muslim structure of consciousness or a singular Muslim community acting in unison to achieve common goals. Why is it *exceptional* if some Muslims, falling prey to colonial enumerations and definitions and their own fanciful theories, regarded themselves as an indivisible component of a religious collectivity? Other communities have nurtured similar self-images. Else, how shall we explain the activism of the Hindu Mahasabha, the RSS, and the numerous Hindu caste associations? What does one make of the nineteenth-century movements in Bengal, Maharashtra and Punjab, and their deepening anxieties over the future of, or the evangelical threat to, their 'Hindu identity'? The historian Susobhan Sarkar commented on 'the obsession with Hindu traditions which helped to keep the men of our [Bengal] renaissance aloof from the masses': this requires elaboration.

At the heart of the Arya Samaj's brand of reconstruction and reform was the object of restoring the supposedly pristine purity of Vedic culture and civilization. The 'Tilak school' in Maharashtra and the leading architects of the Swadeshi movement in Bengal, including Aurobindo Ghose and B.C. Pal, were re-thinking their Hindu heritage and meeting the challenges of modern thought by assimilative-creative processes. The Cow question—one that occupied centrality in the Gandhian discourse as well—was nothing but an evocative symbol of Hindu resurgence in northern and western India. The crusade for Hindi *in opposition to Urdu* was as much linked with government employment as with a widely perceived symbol of Hinduized identity. The historian Romila Thapar shows how the emergent national consciousness appropriated an

Orientalist construction of Hinduism as the heritage of Hindu culture. The need for formulating a Hindu community became a requirement for political mobilization, when representation by religious community gave access to political power and economic resources.

Muslim groups, too, appropriated certain elements from Islam to legitimize their claim to a greater share in the existing power structures. In reality, though, communitarian mobilization, though ultimately successful, failed to obliterate internal differentiations among Muslims. Although religious ties endowed them with a semblance of unity, they were none the less remarkably fragile and unable to override other forms of identity. The links binding Muslim groups with other social classes, though occasionally strained, proved in the end to be demonstrably more powerful and enduring. Hindu-Muslim ill-will in the 1940s was exacerbated, yet, traditional cross-communal associations were revived in the aftermath of the Partition. This is, indeed, part of the reason why India's secular fabric has remained intact more than five decades after Independence.

Second, it must be borne in mind that a Muslim, like his counterpart in any other community, has many acts to perform, and many diverse roles to play. He is not genetically or culturally cast in the role of a religious crusader or a relentless defender of the faith. Besides following Islam by birth and training, a Muslim, or for that matter a Hindu or a Sikh, is a peasant or a landlord, an agricultural worker or a landless labourer, a worker or an industrialist, a student or a teacher, a litigant or a lawyer, a Shia or a Sunni, a Deobandi or a Barelwi. Why, then, harp on his Muslim and Islamic identity and ignore the secular terms in which he relates to more immediate socio-economic needs, and his wide-ranging interactions with his class and not just with his brethren? While the depth and nature of this interaction is debatable, they do not justify an absolute Muslim/Islamic consciousness. If, as we are told, centuries of common living and shared experiences could not create composite solidarities, how could a specifically Muslim self-consciousness emerge out of such multiple and diverse experiences?

Muhammad Ali Jinnah believed he had the answers. So did the Jamaat-i Islami. But there were other explanations as well that were boldly constructed around secular and pluralist conceptions and counterposed to an essentialist view of Indian Islam. Though the tenability of some of those theories were critically scrutinized after the Partition, the basic tenor and thrust of liberal-left arguments is validated by serious and objective scholarship. Scholars, artists and creative writers, in particular, continue to contest the two-nation theory; they unfold the past to discover elements of unity, cohesion and integration, and provide historical legitimation for multi-culturalism and religious plurality. Prominent amongst these are people with pronounced liberal, socialist, and Marxist leanings.

Quite a few intellectuals—Muhammad Mujeeb, Muhammad Habib, A.A.A. Fyzee, Saiyid Abid Husain, Humayun Kabir, K.G. Saiyidain—did much the same after the Partition. They carried forth the inconclusive debates of the post-1857 decades when the ulama and the liberal intelligentsia, being confronted with the external political and religio-cultural threat of colonialism, were constrained to sketch out a role for themselves and reflect on the internal weaknesses within a religious tradition that had strong revivalist precedences as well as liberal and reformist tendencies. They did this because certain key aspects in those debates bore contemporary relevance, and pertained to how Muslims situated themselves in a world brutally shattered by the Partition. The nature of this engagement in pre- and post-Independence India must be explored for a rounded view of the political and intellectual currents embracing the Muslim communities. This is attempted in the following chapters.

Any discussion based on scriptures or on the corpus of knowledge inherited from the theologians cannot explain how Islam, or for that matter any other religion, has been historically *experienced* and *observed* by its adherents. The critical issue is not the apologetic defence of Islam and its tenets—a project that is at any rate pursued relentlessly by theologians of all hues—but to challenge scholarly attempts to 'essentialize' civilizations. The real task at hand is to draw attention to the enormous diversities and the variety of beliefs and practices, the multiple levels at which a Muslim relates to the temporal and spiritual world in day-to-day living, and the currents of change, reform and innovation influencing the course and direction of quite a few Muslim societies the world over. In a nutshell, the collective experience of Muslim polities and societies, rather than segments of it, needs to be considered in plotting their socio-historical evolution. Isolated and sporadic campaigns of Islamic purification, howsoever significant they may have appeared at a given moment, must be seen in perspective and not invoked to lend credence to misleading theories on Islam and Muslim identity.

It needs to be recognized that Islam is not a static point of reference, its interpretations have changed over time, and powerful pluralist visions have shaped Muslim communities in India and elsewhere. Such an approach enables us to challenge, among other things, the distorted vision of the future offered by scholars like Samuel P. Huntington, the author of *The Clash of Civilizations and the Remaking of World Order*. His central argument, developed around the eternal and essential faultlines between Christian and Islamic civilizations, though influential, stands repudiated in several academic circles. So also his view that the survival of the West depends on Americans 'reaffirming their Western identity and Westerners accepting their civilization as unique not universal, and uniting to renew and preserve it against challenges from non-western societies'. Such views reinforce stereotypes of Islamic revivalism and of Muslims, and predispose the reader to view the relationship of Islam to the West in terms of rage, violence, hatred, and irrationality.

Most of us need to take Muslims into account: an end to the neglect that Barbara Metcalf calls 'too little', and all of us need to build a history that does not make 'Islam' prior to the stereotypical thinking she calls 'too much'. Also, rather than creating difference, we need to draw boundaries around common social and political structures, situating Muslims squarely within the complex world of the opportunities and constraints, motivations and tastes they share with everyone else. (Presidential Address: 'Too Little Too Much. Reflections on Muslims in the History of India', *Journal of Asian Studies*, 54, 1995, pp. 951-67).

Contemporary politics in India is characterized by a preoccupation with communitarian identities, chauvinistic ideologies, and movements that exacerbate religious differences. More attention needs to be given to ideologies and movements that have, in the past or in the present, tried uniting Hindus and Muslims thereby furthering the post-colonial agenda of social transformation. Furthermore, we need to locate the social norms, cultural patterns and political responses of Muslim groups in relation to what Aziz Ahmad described as an 'Indian environment'. Prominent political and religious figures need to be situated within a perspective that would enlarge our appreciation of their role as well as prevent their appropriation by denominational groups. This is surely how the contribution of people like Hakim Ajmal Khan, Ansari, Azad, Rafi Ahmed Kidwai and Khan Abdul Ghaffar Khan can be evaluated. This is surely how a nation, desperately in search of symbols of unity, can pay tribute to those men and women who nursed the vision of a secular and democratic Hindustan.

Our own effort to reflect on the changing and varied portraits of Muslim communities in the subcontinent has been vindicated by the rich harvest of literary material gathered in, *Image and Representation: Stories of Muslim Lives in India*, edited by Mushirul Hasan and M. Asaduddin (New Delhi: Oxford University Press, 2000). We have selected most of the stories on the basis of how best they invoke and construct images of Muslims, chronicle our times, articulate many intimate yet historically unfamiliar points of reference, and represent the lived experiences of Muslims in various regions and socio-economic locations. What these literary representations and the nature of their life reveal is the variety of forms, style, language and symbols adopted by different writers. Neither the forms nor the lives they portray derive from a supposedly homogeneous and unbroken tradition.

2

Resistance and Acquiescence in North India: Muslim Responses to the West

When I reflect on the want of energy and the indolent dispositions of my countrymen, and the many erroneous customs which exist in all Mohammedan countries and among all ranks of Mussulmans, I am fearful that my exertions will be thrown away. . . . It may consequently be concluded, that as they will find no pleasure in reading a book which contains a number of foreign names, treats [*sic*] on uncommon subjects, and alludes to other matters which cannot be understood at the first glance, but require little time for consideration, they will, under pretence of zeal for their religion, entirely abstain and refrain from perusing it.

MIRZA ABU TALIB KHAN, *Travels of Mirza Abu Taleb Khan in Asia, Africa, and Europe during the years 1797 to 1803*

Decadence has brought us to a sorry pass; adversity far and wide lays us low. Our honour has long since vanished from the world, and no hope of revival is in sight. One hope alone sustains us now we are laid low; we live on in the expectation of paradise after death.

Too inept to travel, too spineless to journey, we know nothing of what God's creation holds. The four walls of our home which we see before our eyes are for us the limits of human habitation—like fish in a tank, for whom its limits bound their whole world.

ALTAF HUSAIN HALI, *Mussadas-i maddo-jazr-i Islam (Mussadas-i Hali)*

Any number of scholarly works delineate the responses of the Muslim aristocracy, the ulama and the literati to the first major incursion of a European power into India.[1] The late Aziz Ahmad was the first to dwell on this theme in his seminal study of *Islamic Modernism in India and*

Pakistan. Muhammad Mujeeb, former vice-chancellor of Delhi's Jamia Millia Islamia, added fresh insights through his lucid analysis of, among others, Mirza Abu Talib 'Londony's' *Masir-i Talibi fi Bilad-i Afrangi*, Lutfullah's (b. 1802) *Autobiography*, and Mirza Ihtisamuddin's *Shigurf Nama-i Velayet*.[2] In this paper, my concerns are twofold. First, to shift the focus from 'revivalist' and 'fundamentalist' trends in the first-half of the nineteenth-century—extensively covered in secondary literature—to the presence of alternative currents of thought. This may provide a corrective to the essentialist view, which was part of the colonial stereotype, that Muslims were so steeped in their religion and so firmly anchored in Islamic traditions that anything Western or modern was inimical to their world view. Secondly, I wish to underline both the elements of continuity as well as the variety of responses to the West. This places in perspective the ongoing debates on identity politics in the nineteenth century.

I

Most thinking Muslims of the late nineteenth and early twentieth-centuries looked at the events of the past hundred years as a historical catastrophe for their religion. The notion of *umma*, resting on the utopian concept of a unified belief system and ritualistic structure, lost its validity as the house of Islam stood hopelessly fragmented and doctrinally polarized. As the colonial powers established their political hegemony, the beleagured Ottoman sultan remained the sole surviving symbol of resistance to Western imperialism. Many educated Indian Muslims, swayed by the pan-Islamic ferment, rose to defend the sultan and his empire. By the time their passions cooled, the khilafat bubble had burst, the empire had withered away, and the khalifa/sultan was far removed from Constantinople. '*Chhak kar di Turk-i Nadaan ne khilafat ki Qaba*' (Alas, the naive Turk has cut to pieces the khilafat robe), wrote a distraught Muhammad Iqbal.[3]

The trauma of decline, a recurrent theme in world-wide Islamic literature, was expressed in a variety of ways. In some places it was manifested in militant assertions of Islamic identity, a stricter conformity to the Koran and the *Sunna*, and a call for a return to the pristine Islam of the early days of the orthodox khalifas. In other places, most notably in West and North Africa, there was greater consciousness of the internal degeneration of Muslim society and an awareness of the positive lines of reconstruction through an integration of modern ideas and institutions with the bases of Islam.[4] In advocating such a course, early Islamic modernism encouraged the import of Western thought and educational initiatives, and offered partial justification for the Western intellectual influences that were already there and were bound to come anyway.

In the Indian subcontinent, early reformist trends were either dormant or suffered from ambiguity until Saiyid Ahmad Khan advocated, in the tradition of his Egyptian counterpart Muhammad Abduh, integrating the modern scientific world view with the injunctions of the Koran. The theme of decline mattered to him a great deal, though his own discourse was remarkably free of ceaseless lamentations over the eclipse of Muslim power and the declining Muslim civilization. Others did so with unfailing regularity and with great effect. Altaf Husain Hali, acutely sensitive to the departed glory of Islam and its followers, wrote: 'We have eclipsed,' he bemoaned, 'the fame of our ancestors' name. Wherever we set one foot our countrymen are ashamed of us. We have squandered the high honour that our ancestors won, and have lost the nobility of our Arab forbears.'[5] 'With my unskilful mirrors', he stated in his preface to a book, 'I have built a house of mirrors, in which our people can see their face and form reflected.'

There was, in addition, a good deal of soul-searching, and many earnest attempts to ask what had gone wrong, a question Shah Waliullah had raised amid the ruins of the Mughal empire. Few could claim to have the right answers. And fewer still, when faced with the reality of foreign rule, could decide on how best to cope with the colonial encounter, withstand the ideological assault of the Christian West, and acquire the strength to confront Europe and become part of the modern world. There were varied responses, each one being seriously debated. When the poet Mirza Ghalib reached Delhi in 1810 he found the conflict between the 'traditionalists' in religion and the 'radical' reformers 'raging vigorously'.[6] When maulvi Karimuddin (b. 1821) of Panipat visited Delhi he found 'the fountain of knowledge' flowing in every direction.[7] He referred to the setting up of new printing presses in Delhi. These gave spurt to publications and stimulated interest in contemporary social and political issues.

Early responses to colonial rule were, predictably, mixed. Nineteenth-century historical literature is replete with instances of resistance to and rebellion against the 'infidels'. Some tangible expressions of opposition to the new symbols of authority was the *fatwa* of Shah Abdul Aziz, eldest of Waliullah's son, the adventurist campaigns of the *mujahidins* in the Frontier region, the Faraizi movement of Haji Shariat-Allah in Bengal, and the involvement of some prominent ulama in the 1857 revolt. Islam provided a ready-made conceptual framework for such wide-ranging reactions.

Equally intense was the stubborn resistance to the proselytizing activities of Christian missionaries and their denigration of Islam and its Prophet, to the influx of unorthodox ideas which threatened to undermine religious beliefs, and to what Abu Talib described as 'that overbearing insolence which characterizes the vulgar part of the English in their conduct of Orientals'. There was, moreover, strong and pungent criticism of unabashed British expansionist designs. Like so many others his generation, Ghalib's sense of pride was wounded by the annexation of Awadh. 'Although I am a stranger to Awadh and its affair,' he wrote on 23 February 1857, 'the destruction of the state depressed me all the more, and I maintain that no Indian who was not devoid of all sense of justice could have felt otherwise.'[8] 'No doubt,' observed Saiyid Ahmad a year later, 'men of all classes were irritated at its (Awadh) annexation, all agreed in thinking that the Honourable East India Company had acted in defiance of its treaties, and in contempt of the word which it had pledged.'[9]

Nineteenth-century movements of revivalism and reform symbolized anger and indignation against political subordination and the cultural hegemony of the 'outsiders'. They were grounded in the belief that the Islamic community enjoyed an autonomy of its own requiring no mediation. Thus, Islam in India had to be purged of Hindu accretions, and its followers to be equipped to combat the pernicious influence of the West through the unchanging social and religious codes enunciated in the Koran and the *Hadith*. The conception of community, still in its embryonic form, had to be revitalized and its lost pride restored through a carefully devised educational scheme. Such was the rationale behind the founding of the Dar al-ulum at Deoband. The institution, inspired by the ideas of Waliullahi school and conforming to Hanafi codes, delivered hundreds of rulings (*fatawa*) a year to guide the faithful and maintain a close vigil on their social and religious conduct.[10] On a lesser scale, Lucknow's Firangi Mahal, the seminary founded in Aurangzeb's reign (1658-1707), performed the same role. These interventions were designed to bring about an uniformity of belief and practice, rejuvenate and revitalize the slackening faith of the believers, define the place and status of the Muslims in a Western-dominated cultural and intellectual milieu, and cement the bonds of unity in an otherwise stratified community.

Saiyid Ahmad spurned the 'traditionalist' world view. In his generation, he was among the few to recognize the presence of a powerful colonial force in the subcontinent, and, for that reason, laid stress on *ijtehad* (interpretation) and not *taqlid* (conformity), on innovation, reforms and change rather than on unquestioning adherence to the *Shariat*. Drawing upon the Islamic intellectual heritage and his own reading of the contemporary political scene, he endeavoured to convince the British that the Muslims were loyal subjects. Importantly, he told his co-religionists that they would gain much more by cooperating with the government and learning from them than they would by carrying on with futile resistance or withdrawing into a sulk. They were not to live as the British themselves lived, but to carve out a place for themselves within the establishment. To do this, they were not required to adopt nineteenth-century British liberalism, but only to accept some of its values as at least a second-best substitute for the vanished Muslim glories.[11]

Muslim theologians found this a bitter pill to swallow. Denouncing the Aligarh reformer, they called him a *nechari* and an apostate. But Saiyid Ahmad ignored such blunt criticism and the rude *fatawa*. At the end of the day, the grand old man of Aligarh emerged a clean winner and his message embodied, in large part, the *ijma* (consensus) of succeeding Muslim generations in the subcontinent. His interpretation of Islam became part of the mental frame of educated Muslims, including those trained and tutored in the traditional centres of learning. Those who condemned him had to eat their words. Those who chided him sent their own children to the college he founded at Aligarh, a town (also known as Koil) in western Uttar Pradesh (hereafter UP), situated 79 miles south of Delhi. 'The world has seen,' stated Hali in a moving tribute to his intellectual mentor, 'how one man has aroused a whole land, one man saved a caravan from destruction, and small boats sinking ships to the shore . . . Hidden among the gravel there are pearls to be found; and mingled in the sand are particles of gold.'[12]

As the nineteenth-century wore on, it became increasingly clear that there was little prospect of successful military resistance, and little hope of fulfilling the dream of establishing a *Dar al-Islam*. Just as the collapse of the Mughal empire had upset the uncertainties of the previous era, the coming of the British created eddies of uncertainty in certain circles. Yet, a broad consensus existed in favour of an Anglo-Muslim rapprochement as opposed to the repudiation of everything Western. Much before Saiyid Ahmad, the *sajjada nashin* of certain Sufi shrines in Punjab had assisted the British during the siege of Multan in 1848-9.[13] Nor did the Muslims of Bengal stir, a fact noted by Canning (1812-62), the governor-general at the time of the 1857 upheaval. In Punjab, they joined with Sikhs and the tribesmen of Kohat to form part of the reinforcements for the British troops on the Ridge outside Delhi. In the North-Western Provinces, 'the Mahomedans have, I think, behaved better than might have been expected . . . and that the result, far from bringing to light a chronic Mahomedan conspiracy, has been to show that we have not in that class of our subjects that formidable danger that has been sometimes apprehended'.[14] The historian Eric Stokes explained how the economic and political ties of members of Muslim learned families helped moderate their response to cries for *jihad*. Only in the vicinity of Thana Bhawan, north of Delhi, did the poverty of the petty gentry and a strong ideological impulse from local religious leaders, who later helped set up the Dar al-ulum in Deoband, forge a 'truly' Islamic response.[15] The heroics supposedly performed by the ulama, catalogued in *Ulama-i Hind Ka Shandar Maazi*, was no more than a latter-day idealized construction.[16]

New generations grew up for whom foreign rule was an unchanging fact of life, whether they liked it or not. For some time, since the British perpetuated the administrative patterns of the Mughals, including the use of Persian as official tongue, the presence of a handful of Britishers at the top made relatively little difference in day-to-day routine. In judicial and revenue employ, except in the highest posts, Muslims held their own in Bengal until the middle of nineteenth-century, in the region of modern UP for a generation thereafter. Likewise, while the landed classes proved vulnerable to British-induced changes in some areas, it was not so in others. In Bengal, Muslims did not become as insignificant a proportion of the new landed class as their numbers among the population might suggest. In UP, the 'Islamic gentry' in the *qasbahs* remained well-entrenched in the lower levels of the British service during the early nineteenth-century; the Muslim landlord class exercised an influence and power that persisted well into the next century.[17]

Some Muslims quickly sensed that their community could no longer live in a stable and self-sufficient system of inherited culture: their need was now to generate the strength to survive in a world dominated by 'Others'. A large number of them explained the reasons for the strength of Europe to demonstrate that Muslims could adopt European concepts and methods without being untrue to their belief. Although this realization eventually diluted opposition to and softened hostility towards the British, the earliest signs of change is broadly reflected in the careers of Mirza Abu Talib and Lutfullah (1802-74), the two outstanding representatives of early nineteenth-century north India.

II

Abu Talib spent his early years in Murshidabad at the court of Muzaffar Jung. With the accession of Asaf al-Daula (r. 1775-97) he returned to Awadh as *amildar* of Etawah and other districts. He also served as a revenue official under Colonel Alexander Hanny in Gorakhpur, and spiritedly defended his revenue administration in *Tafzih al-Ghafilin*, a history of Awadh under Asaf al-Daula. Later employed by Nathaniel Middleton, the English Resident (1773-82), and connected with Richard Johnson in managing the confiscated jagirs of the Begums of Awadh, his superiors were impressed with his robust attitude to life, his scholarly disposition, and his sensitivity to the winds of change blowing in the areas under Company rule. A Scotsman, Captain David Richardson, recognized these traits in his personality and arranged for his travel to Europe.[18]

On 7 February 1799, Abu Talib sailed from Calcutta to Europe where he visited England, France, Turkey, and other countries, returning to India in August 1803. He reached London on 21 January 1800, the starting point of his trip to other parts of England. He set out on his return journey on 7 June 1802, travelling through France, Constantinople, Baghdad, Karbala, Najaf and the Persian Gulf to 'describe the curiosities and wonders . . . (and) give some account of the manners and customs of the various nations (he) visited, all of which was little known to the Asiatics'.[19]

The Mirza was received with warmth and courtesy. He had an audience with George III and Queen Charlotte, met the old colonial hands—Warren Hastings (1754-1826), Cornwallis (1738-1805) and Charles Metcalf (1785-1846)—and interacted with literary figures and artists. Known as 'The Persian Prince', the press followed him everywhere. 'I declare', he wrote, 'I never assumed the title; but I was so much better known by it than by my own name, that I found it in vain to contend with my godfather.'[20] He was courted, entertained lavishly, and his wit and repartees were apparently the subject of conversation in the politest circles.[21] He was perfectly at ease in such circles, enjoying 'every luxury my heart could desire', drinking 'exquisite' wines, and visiting operas in the company of 'ladies of quality'. He viewed the visit to playhouses as an 'employment of sensuality', and detailed the arrangement of the stage, seats, spectacles, and spectators. He even drew a blueprint of the playhouse in Dublin. He was taken in by the beauty of the women, and their grace in dancing; his senses 'charmed' by the variety and melody of their music. Exhilarated by the coolness of the climate and devoid of all care, the Mirza wrote about how he 'gave' himself 'up to love and gaiety'.[22] On his return journey home he visited the shrines of the Shia *imams*, Hazrat Ali, Imam Husain, and his son Imam Zainul-Abidin, and sought their forgiveness for his sins in Europe. He also composed two elegies in praise of Ali and his son Imam Hasan.

Returning to Calcutta on 4 August 1803, Abu Talib put together his notes and diaries to write a truly 'monumental assessment' of Anglo-Saxon civilization.[23] Written nearly a quarter of a century before the impressions of the Egyptian scholar-educationist Rifa al-Tahtawi, *The Travels of Mirza Abu Taleb Khan* was one of the first introductions to modern Western civilization. 'I believe this is the first time,' wrote Abu Talib's translator, 'the genuine opinions of an Asiatic, respecting the institutions of Europe, have appeared in the English languages.'[24] Translated by Charles Stewart, Professor of Oriental Languages in the East India Company's college at Hertford, the *Masir-i Talibi fi Bilad-i Afrangi* was published in 1810, in two volumes, by Boxbourne, London. A French translation (*Voyages du Prince Persan Mirza Abul Taleb Khan*) appeared in Paris in 1812, the year when the Persian text was published by his son Mirza Husain Ali; its second version a year later. The same year a German translation was out in Vienna.[25]

Lutfullah, who visited England nearly half a century later,[26] agreed with some of Abu Talib's impressions of the West. Both were struck by the progress in mechanical inventions, the tangible benefits of the industrial revolution, and by the organization and functioning of mills, iron foundries and hydraulic machines. 'On entering one of the extensive manufactories in England,' recorded Abu Talib, 'the mind is at first bewildered by the number and variety of articles displayed therein; but, after recovering from this first impression, and having coolly surveyed all the objects around, every thing appears conducted with so much regularity and precision, that a person is induced to suppose one of the meanest capacity might superintend and direct the whole process.'[27] In fact, the 'sixth excellence' of the English people, according to him, 'is a passion for mechanism, and their numerous contrivances for facilitating labour and industry'.[28] He was fascinated by the fire extinguishing 'machines',[29] and by the art of printing, 'the utility of which may not appear at first sight to be Asiatic'.[30] Likewise, Lutfullah admired the bridges in London:

> The first objects that engaged our attention were the enormous bridges in the city, especially the iron bridge, and the swinging bridge. It astonished us greatly to see large masses of cast iron regularly fixed and nicely cemented together in these useful fabrics. The country, we felt convinced, must have some inexhaustible mines of this metal, which is so necessary for man; for, besides these bridges, iron appears to be used profusely. No house seemed to be without iron railings, iron bars, and some houses are even roofed with iron, and some gardens hedged with iron bars.[31]

Consider, too, Abu Talib's description of Woolwich:

> I there saw several large ships on the stocks; and such stores of timber, iron canvas etc. that had the war (Anglo-French) continued for ten years longer, they would not have required a fresh supply. I was particularly attracted by the mode of

casting the cannon-balls and shells; also by the manner of boring and shaping the exterior surface of the guns at the same time, all done by the motion of a wheel turned by a steam-engine, which so facilitated the work, that an old woman or a child might have performed the rest of the operation.[32]

Clearly, the impact and potentialities of the industrial revolution sensitized Abu Talib to its implications. Attributing Britain's economic superiority over the Napoleanic empire to industrial technology and its military success to the navy, he stated: 'The great perfection to which the English have brought their navy is, doubtless, the chief cause of their prosperity, and the principal source of all their wealth.'[33] Likewise, he attributed Britain's conquest of Egypt and other colonies to 'the prowess of their own arms', and to their being formidable on shore as at sea. In this way he thus recognized the importance of sea-power more than eighty years before the publication of Mahan's classical work on the subject.[34]

Abu Talib attributed Britain's industrial revolution to the system of government, to the country's vibrant social and cultural ethos, and to the 'national character' of its people. He commended the unwritten British constitution underlining its monarchical, aristocratic and democratic character, and the respect for individual freedom protected by the British Law; 'liberty may be considered as the idol or tutelary deity of the English; and I think the common people here enjoy more *freedom* and equality than in any other well-regulated government of the world'.[35]

During his stay he went several times to the Houses of Parliament, and was astonished to discover that this was a legislative assembly, with the duty of enacting laws to regulate both civil and criminal matters. The English, he explained to his readers, unlike the Muslims, did not accept any divinely revealed holy law to guide them and regulate their lives in those matters and were therefore reduced to the pitiable expedient of making their own laws 'in accordance with the exigencies of the time, their own dispositions, and the experience of their judges'.

Abu Talib took great interest in the education of English women and their freedom. He mentioned six spheres where the liberty of the Asian women appeared 'less than that of Europeans', though he also pointed to those spheres where they had more rights. Likewise, Mirza Ihtisamuddin (Mirza Itesa Modeen, *Shigurf namah-i-Valaet*, *or*, *Excellent intelligence concerning Europe*: *being the travels of Mirza Itesa Modeen in Great Britain and France-e Velaet*, translated by James Edward Alexander, London, 1872), who visited England in 1765, praised the status of women, their devotion to education, and their quest for knowledge. 'They are not like the people of this country,' he wrote, 'who repeat Hindi and Persian poems in praise of a mistress's face, or descriptive of the qualities of the wine, of the goblet, and of the cup-bearer, and who pretend to be in love.' He was, moreover, impressed with women unveiled in the public sphere, and attracted to the spectacle of male-female intimacy in public parks. This is how he describes the scenes near the Queen's palace in London:

On Sunday, men, women, and youths, poor and rich, travelers and natives resort here. This park enlivens the heart, and people overcome with sorrow, repairing thither, are entertained in a heavenly manner, and grieved hearts, from seeing that place of amusement, are gladdened against their will. On every side females with silver forms, resembling peacocks, walk about, and at every corner fairy-faced ravishers of hearts move with a thousand blandishments and coquetries; the plain of the earth becomes a paradise from the resplendent foreheads, and heaven (itself) hangs down its head for shame at seeing the beauty of the loves. There lovers meet without fear of the police or of rivals, and gallants obtain a sight of rosy cheeks without restraints. When I viewed this heavenly place I involuntarily exclaimed:

> If there is a paradise on earth,
> It is this, oh! It is this.
>
> (*Gar firdows bur ru-ye zamin ast*
> *hamin ast va hamin ast va hamin ast*)

At the same time, Abu Talib noticed widespread poverty, social inequalities, the disparities between the rich and poor, and the effects of a high cost of living,[36] rates of taxation on the common people, and the enormous national debt.[37] He criticized the unsavoury role of commercial magnates and proprietors of joint stock firms enjoying large extra-constitutional powers. He found, much to his dismay, that the privileged sections of society were 'puffed up with their power and good fortune for the last fifty years',[38] and had no idea of how the 'flame, though . . . smothered by a heap of fuel thrown on it, breaks out in the sequel with the greatest violence'.[39] Concerned that no attempt was being made to alleviate the sufferings of those people in London who had 'assembled in mobs on account of the great increase of taxes and high price of provision, and were nearly in a state of insurrection', he opined that this attitude 'betrays a blind confidence'.[40] Instead of meeting the 'danger' and preventing disaffection, the English people waited for the misfortune to arrive: 'such was the case with the late King of France, who took no step to oppose the Revolution, till it was too late.'[41]

In delineating the features of the British 'national character', both Abu Talib and Lutfullah highlighted their sense of honour and prestige, their concern for and recognition of merit, and their cautious, law-abiding, disciplined, and courteous nature.[42] He mentioned, with implied approval, that instead of rushing ahead with changes the British proceeded slowly and cautiously. Yet, he castigated them for their 'want of chastity',[43] criticized the want of faith in religion,[44] and upbraided the upper classes for being complacent and haughty. Contemptuous of their passion for wealth and their preoccupation with worldly affairs,[45] he disapproved of their insularity, their contempt for the customs of other nations, and the preference they gave to their own.[46] He reminiscenced how

> in London, I was frequently attacked on the apparent unreasonableness and childishness of some of the Mohammedan customs; but as, from my knowledge of the English character, I was convinced it would be a folly to argue the point philosophically with them, I contended myself with parrying the subject. Thus, when they attempted to turn into ridicule the ceremonies used by the pilgrims on their arrival in Mecca, I asked them, why they supposed the ceremony of baptism, by a clergyman, requisite for the salvation of a child, who could not possibly be sensible [*sic*] what he was about. When they reproached us for eating with our hands; I replied, 'There is by this mode no danger of cutting yourself or your neighbours; and it is an old and a true proverb, 'The nearer the bone, the sweeter the meat': but, exclusive of these advantages, a man's own hands are surely cleaner than the feet of a *baker's boy*: for it is well-known, that half the bread in London is kneaded by the feet. By this mode of argument I, completely silenced all my adversaries, and frequently turned the laugh against them, when they expected to have refuted me and made me appear ridiculous.[47]

Although receptive to some of the new ideas, Abu Talib distanced himself philosophically from the West and found much that was of enduring quality in his own intellectual traditions. Rooted in his own soil, he derived inspiration and strength from the values he had inherited and imbibed in late eighteenth-century Awadh society without, of course, sharing the scepticism of some of his own contemporaries towards Western ideas and institutions. He noticed the social transformation taking place in the industrialized nations of Europe, and commented on its world-wide impact.

Abu Talib's religious identity was unassailable; it was a major component of his ideological orientation. But he did not find religious categories of much help when it came to understanding either Awadh society or delineating the contours of Western polities, economy and society. If anything, he attached importance to the diverse economic forces moulding attitudes and shaping the destiny of humankind. Thus, in analysing the ancien régime in France and his contemporary Awadh society, he referred to the growing disparities between various classes and to the widening economic disparaties. Implicit in his narrative is the view that the key factor leading to the collapse of the ancien régime was the exacerbation of class differentiation. He wondered why such an upheaval had not occurred in Awadh in spite of excessive taxation, the tyranny of the landlords, the impoverishment of the peasantry, a fall in production, and in land revenue realization. It is not without significance that he attributed the passivity of the oppressed to the role of religion, and to British policies which buttressed the wazir and averted the immediate collapse of his kingdom.

Abu Talib belonged to a declining aristocracy. But, like so many people of his social background, he tried to make the best of the opportunities available under the Company's dispensation. This was a pointer to his generation of Muslims, as indeed to the generations thereafter, who were faced with an inescapable dilemma *vis-a-vis* British rule. Eschewing a defiant posture towards the colonizers, he acknowledged the inevitability of change and the necessity of softening belligerent attitudes towards foreign rule. For this reason he adhered to his resolve, despite fears of being villified and ridiculed, to inform his countrymen about the political and economic conditions, the industry, and the social and cultural life of the British who had come to preside over India's destiny. He hoped that many of 'the customs, inventions, sciences, and ordinances of Europe, the good effects of which are apparent in their countries, might with great advantage be initiated by Mohammedans'.[48] In this respect, at least, he was a forerunner of the ideas of Saiyid Ahmad Khan, the major catalyst of social and educational reforms among India's Muslims in the last-quarter of the nineteenth-century.

III

Representing the scribal class—those serving the regional and local bureaucracies under the Mughals and their British successors—Abu Talib and Lutfullah were not the only ones favouring rapprochement with the British in India or seeking government patronage. Muhammad Khan of Bilgram joined the foreign department of the governor-general in the early days of Company rule.[49] Ghalib's uncle, Nasrullah Beg Khan, served the Company in the Anglo-Maratha war of 1802-3 as commander of a contingent and received a life jagir from the British commander-in-chief, Lord Lake.[50] The father of nawab Mustafa Khan Shefta (b. 1806), Ghalib's fellow-poet, received estates for resolving the disputes between Lord Lake and the Maratha commanders.[51] In this way, the British continued with the Mughal traditions of granting jagirs and *inam* lands for political loyalty and military services. For thirty years after the Maratha war of 1802-3, the holders of such grants were left relatively undisturbed. For a generation after 1803, a gentlemanly existence in something like the old style was thus possible in upper India for those Muslims who were ready to serve the British as auxiliary cavalry and as subordinate revenue and judicial officers.[52] Bishop Heber's *Narrative* for 15 September 1824 contains a British collector's impression of 'a new order rising from the middling classes' to replace that of 'very many ancient families . . . gone to decay'.[53]

The 'middling classes' were drawn from those enterprising groups who were prepared to make the most of what little there was. They were, to begin with, small in numbers. Yet, they formed a major component of what was, until the last-quarter of the nineteenth-century, the Muslim intelligentsia in north India, the harbinger of reforms and social change. They contributed, as in the case of their counterparts in Bengal and Maharashtra, to the efflorescence of modern learning, which C.F. Andrews described as the 'Delhi Renaissance'.[54] They pioneered the Aligarh movement, where the first generation of students and teachers set the tone and tenor of powerful intellectual ideas in the twentieth century.[55] They were also the first to promote Western education and the learning of sciences among Muslims through organizations—the Anjuman-i Himayat-i Islam in Punjab, the Muhammadan Literary and Scientific Society, and the Central National Mohammedan Association in Bengal. Hali would have had them in mind when he spoke of 'men of feeling', 'men of sympathy', 'men of worth'. 'Amongst these heedless sleepers,' he wrote, 'some are awake'. 'In the taverns are some who are still sober. These are men who are not like the rest of their group. Among the worthless are still some men of worth.'[56]

Education was the key to success, a passport to government service. Though most Muslims defiantly stayed away from British schools and colleges, there were others who acquainted themselves with Western languages and literature, philosophy and science. As early as 1775-6, Mirza Ihtisamuddin, who travelled to Europe in the year of the Treaty of Allahabad between Clive (1724-74) and Shah Alam (1759-1806),[57] visited the laboratories and observatories in London. 'In England,' he wrote, 'it would be extraordinary if the arts and sciences did not flourish (from their being encouraged). Now in India, if a person by a long course of study were to acquire knowledge, so as to excel the world, yet he would remain despised and contemned [*sic*]: he would neither acquire honour nor respect, and in the end misfortune and misery would overtake him.'[58] In 1788, Tipu Sultan (r. 1783-99), the ruler of Mysore, wanted one of his sons to be educated in France. The French authorities approved of the idea, but suggested that the prince should learn to read and write French, learn a little calculus and some arithmetic before leaving for Paris.[59] In 1794, Mirza Ahmad Khan of Broach, a town in Gujarat, reached Paris, learnt French in three months, and translated *The Declaration of the Rights of Man* into Persian. He then presented his work to the Committee of Public Safety, which had it deposited in the *Bibliotheque Nationale*. This translation was the first in any oriental language.[60] Such works were channels through which knowledge of the new world of Europe travelled to India.

Tafazzul Husain Khan (d. 1800), long associated with the Company as well as the Awadh nawabs, compiled important mathematical works, and translated into Persian Newton's *Principia*. Officials in Calcutta commended his command over the English language, and his knowledge of European literature and philosophy.[61] His successor, Saadat Ali Khan (r. 1798-1814), founded an observatory in Lucknow. Both Ghaziuddin Haider (r. 1814-27) and Nasiruddin Haider (r. 1827-37) patronized Western and Oriental philological studies. According to Bishop Heber, the former had 'a strong taste for mechanics and chemistry' and constructed a laboratory in Lucknow.[62] Speaking of a breakfast at the Residency at which Ghaziuddin Haider was present, Heber (who visited Lucknow in 1824) noted that the King talked about steam engines and a new device, invented by an English engineer in his pay, of propelling ships by a spiral wheel at the bottom of the vessel. He also explained his acquaintance with English books read to him in Hindustani by his aides-de-camp.[63] Nasiruddin, inheriting such scientific and artistic tastes, hired an English tutor to make himself at home in English culture. He built an observatory in the charge of an English Astronomer-Royal, a colonel Wilcox.

Finally, the Fort William College in Calcutta encouraged literary and scientific learning all over India. A resident of the city, Mansher Khesumul Riya, wrote to the *Calcutta Journal* on 13 April 1820:

> I am a Mooslem of this city, who by early instruction in the English language, have acquired access to the general literature with which that tongue is adorned, and am enabled to enjoy the numerous publications which advocate the cause of liberty.

Lutfullah wrote his *Autobiography* in English, 'the first (and) almost the best autobiography by an Indian in English'. He had read Gibbon, a Latin book on the customs and institutions of the Turks, and a *Universal History* by some Dr Philip Prince.[64] A lesser known person, Abdur Rahim Dahri (1785-1850), travelled from Gorakhpur in eastern UP to acquire proficiency in English at the Fort William College. He wrote widely, including a pamphlet on the virtue of studying the English language and disseminating Western thought. He insisted, in a memorandum submitted to Warren Hastings, that modern education be introduced through the medium of English. Abdur Rahim spent the last years of an extraordinary career as an English teacher at Fort William College.[65] For him the civilization of the West did not appear wholly alien; Muslims could move towards it without any sense of being untrue to themselves or their faith.

The Madrasa Aliyah flourished in Calcutta. Among its beneficiaries were Saiyid Ameer Ali, author-historian, and Abdur Rahim, a judge turned politician. The Delhi College, an early and significant enterprise in secular education, was established in 1825 with two branches: an English branch where English language and literature and modern European sciences were taught and an Oriental branch in which not only Arabic, Persian and Sanskrit were taught but geography, mathematics and sciences as well.[66] By far the most popular side of the education offered in Old Delhi College was that which dealt with science. Maulvi Zakaullah, in his old age, used to tell C.F. Andrews 'with kindling eyes how eagerly these scientific lectures were followed'.[67] The doctrines of ancient philosophy taught through the medium of Arabic were 'thus cast in the shade before the more reasonable and experimental theories of modern science. The old dogma . . . that the earth is the fixed centre of the universe was generally laughed at by the higher students of the Oriental as well as by those of the English Department of the college.'[68]

The Delhi College was the nucleus of a group which tried re-evaluating inherited doctrines and beliefs. Take maulvi Karimuddin, whose book provided the basis of Farhatullah Beg's modern Urdu classic, *Delhi ki Akhri Shama* (The Last Mushairah of Delhi). He belonged to a family of maulvis, left his home town Panipat to join Delhi College in 1839, and set up a printing press to meet the growing demand of writers trying to express, in Urdu and English, their consciousness of themselves and their place in the modern world.[69] Consider, too, the career of Munshi Shafaqatullah, an English teacher in Bareilly. He translated Chamber's introduction to the sciences, as also a well-known work on astronomy, natural philosophy, geology, and other sciences. It was entitled *Khulsatul-Ulum*.

There was another noticeable trend: influential groups in various regions, especially those needing a fresh imprimatur from each ruling power, made the colonial government work. Thus, many *sajjada nashins* in rural Punjab agreed to be incorporated into the framework of the British administration, often playing leading roles as *ziladars*, honorary magistrates, and district board members. By early twentieth-century, they had become an integral part of the class of rural intermediaries on whom British rule rested in the area.[70] In Sind, the British constructed a political system hinging on the cooperation of landed elites, of whom the pirs made up a sizeable proportion. Sarah Ansari has established how both sides took advantage of the system and how the pirs, in particular, discovered new ways of increasing their power and prestige. The very section of the élite which, in theory, had most to lose from being too closely associated with the administration, found that there was much to gain from maintaining a good working relationship with their new 'infidel' rulers. They managed to retain an aura of spiritual aloofness at the same time as making the most of the benefits of cooperation. In the long run, their willingness to participate in the colonial system helped endow pir families with the resilience needed to cope with British rule.[71]

The British realized, particularly after 1857, that the crucial task in maintaining their rule was to be able to react quickly and sensitively as power flowed from one group to another in response to processes of economic, social, or even ideological change. The imposing edifice of colonial government rested on delicate political relationships with powerful and influential groups in a myriad localities.[72] Though wary and distrustful of the Muslims, the British co-opted some of them into administrative and bureaucratic structures. They were to form the pillar of the raj during the inter-War years during the twentieth century.

Some ulama, following an old established tradition of pliancy and conformism, accepted British rule. Some others were, however, made of sterner stuff, falling into the colonial stereotype of being bigoted, fanatical and intransigent. Shah Abdul Aziz had declared India as *Dar al-harb*; so the Friday and Id prayers could not be performed as congregational prayers. 'From here (Delhi) to Calcutta,' he announced, 'the Christians are in complete control.' This pronouncement sustained Saiyid Ahmad Shaheed's exertions against the British, and legitimized other nineteenth-century movements against their rule, even though the *fatwa*, read in its totality, conveyed different meanings to different people and was, therefore, subject to diverse interpretations. Muhammad Ismail, the nephew of Abdul Aziz, recommended a *modus vivendi* with the British as long as they did not interfere with the religious freedom of the Muslims.

In the early days of Company rule, such positions may well have prompted Fazl-i Rasul Budauni, Mufti Sadruddin, Fazl-i Haq Khayrabadi and a section of the Firangi Mahal family to serve the Company, take up jobs in institutions, and accept government titles. There were many more Muslim divines in the nineteenth-century who held the view that India was *Dar al-aman* (land of peace) as the British allowed the Islamic Personal Law to be applied to the Muslims in cases of inheritance, succession, gifts, *auqaf*, marriage, divorce, parentage, guardianship, and maintenance. They invoked the Koranic verse—'Obey God, obey His Prophet, and obey those in authority over you'—to argue that the duty of obedience to a legitimate authority was not merely one of political expediency but a religious obligation. The ulama availed of the opportunities either left by the British policy of non-interference with religion, or created by the development of communications, printing and the press. This enabled them to propagate their teachings more widely and, with their considerable resources and knowledge of Islamic traditions, confront Christian missionaries and the forces inimical to Islam. Saiyid Ahmad Shaheed's *Siral al-Mustaqim* (The Sacred Path) and Muhammad Ismail's *Taqwiyat al-Iman* (Strengthening the Faith) were printed in lithographic editions thus receiving wider circulation than had hitherto been possible.

Nineteenth-century Indian Islam did not produce scholars like Rifa Badawi, Rafi al-Tahtawi, Khayar al-Din, or Abduh, who reinterpreted the Islamic Law in the direction of conformity with modern needs and endeavoured to adapt the *Shariat* to new circumstances. Yet, India's ulama, while jealously guarding their exclusive right as guardians of a fixed and established tradition, grudgingly came to terms with British rule. In the aftermath of the 1857 revolt, in particular, they acquiesced in rather than repudiated Pax Britannica. Deoband's Dar al-ulum, founded in a spirit of compromise rather than opposition to colonial rule, rested on an unstated principle: if living in the nineteenth-century world demanded changes in the Islamic ways of life, the ulama must try to make them while remaining true to themselves and their faith.

IV

Hali's repeated pleas and exhortations, couched in his *Mussadas*, summed up a major strand in the thinking patterns of the north Indian literate Muslims in the nineteenth century. He wrote:

> No man wishes evil to your faith and religion. No man attacks the Traditions and the Koran. No man seeks to harm the pillars of your community. No man seeks to prohibit you from the commands of the Holy Law. Say your prayers without fear in your places of worship, and let the call to prayer ring out in your mosques.
>
> The roads to travel and trade lie open. None blocks the roads to crafts and industry. The roads to the acquisition of learning are lighted. The roads to the gaining of wealth are made level. . . .

> Know the words of this peace and freedom. For the paths to advancement have been cleared in every direction, and the age is the friend of all who would travel upon them. The cry comes persistently from every side, 'There is no enemy to dread, no highway robber to fear: come out and take the road, for the roads are safe!'
>
> Many caravans have long been on the move. Many more are loading up their burdens. Many are in agitation at the movement all round them. . . . You alone amongst them are still sunk in heedless sleep. Take care, lest in your heedlessness you fail to reach your goal![73]

Ghalib announced the tidings of the dawn and pointed the way to the light of the sun.

> The harp player, when he strikes the chord
> One can see what he is after,
> Happiness lies concealed behind the veil of sorrow,
> Not for wrath does the washerman beat the cloth.[74]

NOTES

1. A. Yusuf Ali, 'Muslim Culture and Religious Thought', in L.S.S. O'Malley (ed.), *Modern India and the West: A Study of the Interaction of their Civilization*, Oxford, 1941; Muhammad Mujeeb, 'First Impressions of Western Culture on Indian Muslims', in H. Rao (ed.), *South Asian Studies I*, New Delhi, 1965; Aziz Ahmad, *Islamic Modernism in India and Pakistan, 1857-1964*, Cambridge, 1967; Muhammad Mujeeb, *The Indian Muslims*, London, 1967; S.A.A. Rizvi, 'The Breakdown of Traditional Society', *The Cambridge History of Islam*, Vol. 2, Cambridge, 1970; Peter Hardy, *The Muslims of British India*, Cambridge, 1972; Mujeeb Ashraf, *Muslim Attitudes towards British Rule and Western Culture*, New Delhi, 1982; Peter Hardy, 'Islam in South Asia', in Raphael Israel (ed.), *The Crescent in the East: Islam in Asia Major*, New Delhi, 1985, rpt.
2. Mujeeb, *Indian Muslims*, pp. 491-501.
3. Mushirul Hasan, *Nationalism and Communal Politics in India, 1885-1930*, Delhi, 1991; Mushirul Hasan, *A Nationalist Conscience: M.A. Ansari, the Congress and the Raj*, New Delhi, 1987.
4. On these themes, Albert Hourani, *A History of the Arab Peoples*, London, 1991; and his *Arabic Thought in the Liberal Age, 1798-1939*, London, 1962; Fazlur Rahman, *Islam*, London, 1966; Deliar Noer, *The Modernist Muslim Movement in Indonesia, 1900-1942*, London, 1973; Wilhelm Halbfass, *India and Europe: An Essay in Understanding*, State University of New York Press, 1990; Edward Mortimore, *Faith and Power: The Politics of Islam*, London, 1982.
5. *Musaddas-i Hali*, pp. 43-4, in Aziz Ahmad and Grunebaum (eds.), *Muslim Self-Statement*, p. 95.

6. Ralph Russell and Khurshidul Islam, *Ghalib 1797-1869*, Vol. I: *Life and Letters*, London, 1969, p. 31.
7. Akhtar Qamber, *The Last Mushairah of Delhi*, New Delhi, 1979, p. 39.
8. Russell and Khurshidul Islam, *Ghalib*, p. 134.
9. Saiyid Ahmad Khan, *History of Bijnor Rebellion*, translated with notes and introduction by Hafeez Malik and Morris Dembo, New Delhi, 1982, p. 15.
10. For Muslim revivalist movements in the nineteenth and early twentieth centuries, see Mohiuddin Ahmad, *Saiyid Ahmad Shahid*, Lucknow, 1975; S.A.A. Rizvi, *Shah Abdul Aziz and his Times*, Australia, 1983; Qeyamuddin Ahmad, *The Wahhabi Movement in India*, revd. edn., New Delhi, 1992; Rafiuddin Ahmed, *Bengal Muslims 1871-1906: A Quest for Identity*, New Delhi, 1981; Asim Roy, *The Islamic Syncretistic Tradition in Bengal*, Princeton, N.J., 1983. For Deoband, see Barbara Daly Metcalf, *Islamic Revival in British India: Deoband, 1860-1900*, Princeton, N.J., 1982.
11. Marshall G.S. Hodgson, *The Venture of Islam: The Gunpowder Empires and Modern Times*, Vol. 3, Chicago, 1974, p. 335, and C.W. Troll, *Sayyid Ahmad Khan: A Reinterpretation of Muslim Theology*, New Delhi, 1978.
12. *Musaddas-i Hali*, pp. 83-5, quoted in Ahmad and Grunebaum (eds.), p. 98.
13. David Gilmartin, *Empire and Islam: Punjab and the Making of Pakistan*, Berkeley, 1988.
14. Hardy, *Muslims of British India*, pp. 67-9.
15. Eric Stokes, *The Peasant Armed: The Indian Rebellion of 1857*, edited by C.A. Bayly, Oxford, 1986, p. 240.
16. Mushir U. Haq, *Muslim Politics in Modern India, 1857-1947*, Meerut, 1970, and Metcalf, *Islamic Revival in British India*, pp. 81-5.
17. Anil Seal, *The Emergence of Indian Nationalism: Competition and Collaboration in the Later Nineteenth Century*, Cambridge, 1968, Chap. 7; Francis Robinson, *Separatism among Indian Muslims: The Politics of United Provinces' Muslims, 1860-1923*, Cambridge, 1975; Hardy, *Muslims of British India*, pp. 36-50; Mushirul Hasan, *Nationalism and Communal Politics*, pp. 12-20; C.A. Bayly, *Rulers, Townsmen and Bazaars: North Indian Society in the Age of British Expansion, 1770-1870*, Cambridge, 1983, pp. 190-1.
18. Abu Talib was the son of Haji Muhammad Beg, who fled from Tabriz in his youth, lived in Isfahan in order to escape the tyrannies of Nadir Shah, and settled in Lucknow. The Haji led a troubled life until his death at Murshidabad in 1768. Misfortune also struck his son who, after some years of service in Etawah and Gorakhpur, became a victim of the machinations of his detractors in the Awadh court. He lost his job and his yearly allowance. From 1787 to 1797 he journeyed to Calcutta thrice and sought the help and intervention of senior Company officials into his affair. He met the governor-general, Cornwallis, and his successor, John Shore. 'During the three years of expectation which I passed in Calcutta', wrote Abu Talib, 'all my dependents and adherents, seeing my distress, left me; and even some of my children, and the

domestics brought up in my father's family, abandoned me'. For biographical information, T.W. Beale, *An Oriental Biographical Dictionary*, London, 1894, p. 32; Colin C. Davies, *Encyclopaedia of Islam*, new edn., p. 152; Mujeeb, *Indian Muslims*, pp. 491-2; Humayun Kabir, *Mirza Abu Talib Khan*, Patna: The Russell Lecture, Patna College, 1961.

19. *Travels*, p. xiv.
20. Ibid., p. 111. Wherever he went, Abu Talib aroused interest and curiosity. Nearly half a century before him, Mirza Ihtisamuddin had similar experiences during his stay in England. People were attracted by his robe and turban, the sash tied around his waist and the dagger in his belt. 'Whenever I attempted to go abroad, crowds accompanied me, and the people in the houses of the bazars thrust their heads out of the windows and gazed at me with wonder.' Mirza Ihtisamuddin, *Shigurf Nama-i Velayet*, translated from the original Persian by James Edward Alexander, London, 1827, p. 40.
21. *Travels*, p. 75.
22. Ibid. Notice his description of a party hosted by the Mayor of London, where he spent 'one of the most delightful nights I ever passed'. He was 'gazing all the time on the angelic charms of Miss Combe, who sat in that assemblage of beauties like the bright moon surrounded with brilliant stars'. Ibid., p. 155.
23. Ahmad, *Islamic Modernism*, pp. 6-7.
24. Charles Stewart, in *Travels*, p. xiii.
25. In 1791, Abu Talib produced an edition of *Diwan-i Hafiz*, and shortly after, a compendium account of ancient and contemporary poets (*Khulasat al-Afkaar*). He was himself a poet and there is a manuscript of his *Diwan* in the Bodleian. His collection of poems were edited and translated into English by George Swinton. It was published in 1807 under the title *Poems of Mirza Abu Talib Khan*. He also composed a *mathnawi*, available in the Edinburgh University Library, a medical treatise (*Miraj al-Tauhid*) on astronomy with a prose commentary, a book entitled *Lubb al-Siyar*, and *Tafzih al-Ghafilin* (English translation by W. Hoey, 1888), a history of Awadh under Asaf al-Daula, an important source for the careers of Hyder Beg and the various English residents.
26. Lutfullah belonged to a distinguished Sufi family of Malwa. But the fortunes of the family dwindled to such an extent that 'we sold all we had, and sometimes starved for a day or so, after which we obtained but some food through our own hard labour'. The family travelled to Baroda, Ujjain, Gwalior, and Agra until it reached Delhi in early 1817. Soon thereafter, Lutfullah found odd jobs in the course of his extensive travels. He developed his reputation as a teacher of Arabic, Persian and some Indian languages, notably Marathi, and was *en rapport* with young Britishers of the ICS. In March 1844, he accompanied Mir Jafar Ali Khan, son-in-law of the nawab of Surat, to England. His *Autobiography*, acclaimed in England, was written in 1854 and dedicated to colonel W.H. Sykes. It was later edited by Edward B. Eastwick and published in London, in 1857.

His first reaction on reaching London was:

Here (7, Sloane Street) we settled after our long voyage from the middle of the globe to the end of the world, where the sun appears, far to the south, as weak as the moon, and the polar star nearly vertical; where the country all over is fertile, and the people ingenious, civil and active; where the language, customs, and manners are entirely different from our own; where, in fine, the destiny of our sweet native land lies in the hand of some twenty-five great men (Directors of the East India Company). It cannot be, I am sure, without the will of that one Supreme Being that this island, which seems on the globe like a mole on the body of a man, should command the greater part of the world, and keep the rest in awe.

Autobiography, p. 406. Reprinted in India under the title *Autobiography of Lutfullah: An Indian's Perception of the West*, with an introduction by S.A.I. Tirmizi (Delhi, 1985).

Equally interesting is his comment on a dissection taking place at the St. George's Hospital. He wrote:

Here I became convinced that a great part of what I had studied in 'Galen's Anatomy' in Persian and Arabic was founded upon fancy and conjecture, and that it was impossible for anybody to acquire a thorough knowledge of this most useful study for mankind, without the practical course of dissection.

Autobiography, p. 415.

27. *Travels*, p. 121.
28. Ibid., p. 182.
29. Ibid., p. 184.
30. Ibid., p. 110.
31. *Autobiography*, p. 407.
32. *Travels*, pp. 114-15.
33. Ibid., p. 112.
34. Mujeeb, *Indian Muslims*, p. 498; Kabir, *Mirza Abu Talib*, pp. 10, 24.
35. *Travels*, p. 129.
36. Abu Talib found that 'living is very expensive in England; and a good appetite is a serious evil to a poor man'. He listed the prices of meat and bread to illustrate his point. Ibid., p. 112.
37. It is remarkable that a man of his background and his limited experience of Awadh recognized the 'evil' of National Debt. 'Let the creditors of Government be assembled', he proposed, 'in the presence of the Parliament; and let the Minister, clearly and dispassionately, explain to them, that the state of affairs is arrived at such a crisis, that is impossible the nation can continue longer to pay the amount of the enormous taxes which oppress them; that a revolution is to be apprehended; that the first act of the leaders of the revolution certainly will be *to cancel the national debt*, and that the rich may consider themselves fortunate if left in possession of their real wealth; that the national

debt, being thus cancelled, they, the creditors, will lose *the whole* of their property invested in the funds; and therefore it will be much wiser to enter into an immediate compromise, and relinquish a part'. Ibid., pp. 165-6.

38. Ibid., p. 168.
39. Ibid., p. 179.
40. Ibid., p. 168.
41. Ibid., p. 169.
42. Ibid., p. 181. Also, Lutfullah's comment, *Autobiography*, p. 433.
43. *Travels*, p. 175.
44. Ibid., p. 178.
45. Ibid., p. 169.
46. Ibid., p. 177.
47. Ibid., p. 178.
48. Ibid., p. xv.
49. Bayly, *Rulers, Townsmen and Bazaars*, p. 356.
50. Peter Hardy, 'Ghalib and the British', in Ralph Russell (ed.), *Ghalib: the poet and his age*, London, 1972, p. 56.
51. Russell and Khurshidul Islam, *Ghalib*, p. 67.
52. In an interesting observation, Andrews recorded that the intrusion of the West did not make much difference to maulvi Zakaullah's lifestyle. 'None of his outward manners and customs had been changed, and he remained outwardly the most conservative man in Delhi. His dress, his habits, his domestic life, his religious life—all that he valued most dearly—remained unalterably eastern.' C.F. Andrews, *Maulvi Zakaullah of Delhi*, New Delhi, 1928 edn., p. 118.
53. Hardy, 'Ghalib and the British', p. 55.
54. Andrews, *Zakaullah of Delhi*.
55. David Lelyveld, *Aligarh's First Generation: Muslim Solidarity in British India*, Princeton, N.J., 1978.
56. *Musaddas*, pp. 83-5, in Ahmad and Grunebaum (eds.), p. 100.
57. He travelled to Europe as a representative of Shah Alam, who wanted a British protective force at Allahabad. The identity of his companion, Captain 'S', is not known. Nor is there much information on Mirza Ihtisamuddin. What we know is that the sea voyage took them to Mauritius, and around the Cape of Good Hope to Europe where the Mirza stopped briefly in France. The book—*Shigurf Nama-i Velayet*—is a commentary on his travels and impression of England and Scotland written after his return to India. It was translated from Persian into English by James Edward Alexander and published in London in 1827.
58. *Shigurf Nama-i Velayet*, p. 70.
59. Mohibbul Hasan, *History of Tipu Sultan*, Calcutta, 1971, 2nd revd. and enlarged edn.
60. Mohibbul Hasan, 'An Indian Prince and the French Revolution', *Iran Society Silver Jubilee Souvenir*, 1968.

61. Michael H. Fisher, *A Clash of Cultures: Awadh, The British and the Mughals*, New Delhi, 1987, p. 70.
62. Yusuf Ali, 'Muslim Culture and Religious Thought', p. 391. See also Fisher, *A Clash of Cultures*, pp. 172-3.
63. Ibid., p. 397.
64. Mujeeb, *Indian Muslims*, p. 497.
65. For details of Abdur Rahim Dahri's life and career, see Ashraf, *Muslim Attitudes Towards British Rule*, pp. 190, 261.
66. Barbara Metcalf, *The Islamic Revival*, pp. 72-3.
67. Andrews, *Zakaullah of Delhi*, p. 42.
68. Ibid., pp. 38-40.
69. *The Last Mushairah*, pp. 39-40.
70. Francis Robinson, 'Ulama, Sufis and Colonial Rule in North India and Indonesia', in C.A. Bayly and D.H.A. Kolff (eds.), *Two Colonial Empires: Comparative Essays on the History of Indonesia in the Nineteenth-Century*, Dordrecht, 1986, p. 19.
71. Sarah F.D. Ansari, *Sufi Saints and State Power: The Pirs of Sindh, 1843-1947*, Cambridge, 1992, pp. 53-6.
72. Robinson, *Separatism Among Muslims*.
73. *Musaddas*, pp. 43-4, in Ahmad and Grunebaum (eds.), p. 96.
74. K.M. Ashraf, 'Ghalib and the Revolt of 1857', *Rebellion 1857: A Symposium*, New Delhi, 1957, p. 256.

3

The Myth of Unity: Colonial and National Narratives

> Of all the great religions . . . Islam alone was borne forth into the world on a great wave of forceful conquest. . . . There was seldom a pause in the consolidation of Mahomedan power, seldom a break in the long-drawn tale of plunder and carnage, cruelty and lust, unfolded in the history of the earlier dynasties that ruled India.
>
> VALENTINE CHIROL, *India Old and New*

> You never ceased proclaiming that Islam spread by the sword.
> You have not deigned to tell us what it is the gun has spread.
>
> AKBAR ALLAHABADI in Ralph Russell, *The Pursuit of Urdu Literature: A Select History*

> Hinduism, with its love of images and symbols, and its polytheism, and Islam, with its strict Unitarian faith and its strong iconoclastic principles, are at opposite poles.
>
> REGINALD CRADDOCK, *The Dilemma in India*

A disquieting feature of the *Hindutva* wave was not just the demolition of the Babri Masjid but the way Hindu propagandists conjured up the image of a community outside the 'national mainstream'. Muslims were depicted as aggressive fundamentalists and demonized as descendants of depraved and tyrannical medieval rulers who demolished temples and forcibly converted Hindus to Islam. They were portrayed as 'fifth columnists' tied to the world of Islam, held responsible for the country's vivisection in August 1947, and depicted as proceeding hand in glove with the Congress and left-wing formations in a concerted endeavour to undermine Indian/Hindu culture and civilization.

The reading of what Muslims are and the vain hope of how they ought to have been is echoed with unfailing regularity. Equally familiar are images of the Muslims and the reconstruction of their history. What is less clear is how certain images and constructions, having gained currency during the second half of the nineteenth-century, continue to enjoy widespread appeal and acceptance. How is it that the image of the Other has not altered or modified over time? Why did alternative ideologies fail to construct a different paradigm? Does the explanation lie in the Muslim intelligentsia's own assertion of a unity of interest and ideals, and in its conviction that all Muslims were part of an indivisible community with a monolithic mind? Or is it simply that they were logical victims of their own myth-making, claiming for themselves an alien culture, if not origin, and being so regarded by others? I am inclined to agree with the last point, though the critical issue is how the colonial government fostered the growth of such ideas and helped sections of the Muslim intelligentsia to etch a certain image of themselves. I also believe that the etching of 'nationalistic' images of India's Muslims was just as important as the colonial framework that defined and categorized 'Indian Muslim society'.

Any number of scholarly studies, Edward Said's *Orientalism* included, are replete with instances of Islam's representation as a hostile and aggressive force, of Muslim societies being caricatured as rigid, authoritarian, and uncreative.[1] Quite a few British writers in India, some occupying government positions, perpetuated a repertoire of such images, construing Indian Islam as an emblem of repellent Otherness, 'the faith of a body of savage marauders and conquerors, who swept over the land . . . in a series of cruel raids, bringing rapine and destruction in their train'.[2] The sultans of Delhi and their Ottoman counterparts in Constantinople suffered much the same fate at the hands of several writers. Projected as the great iconoclasts, they were considered tokens of evil and scapegoats for issues with which they had no connection. Bishop Heber, who stayed in India from 1823 to 1826, wanted Hindus to be constantly reminded 'that we did not conquer them, but found them conquered, that their previous rulers were as much strangers to their blood and to their religion as we are, and that they were notoriously far more oppressive masters than we have ever shown ourselves'. Valentine Chirol, in charge of the foreign department of the *Times* (London) from 1908 to 1912, observed that 'with the monumental wreckage of those early Mohamedan dynasties, steeped in treachery and bloodshed, the plain of Delhi is still strewn'.[3]

Travellers, missionaries, administrators, and ethnographers[4] transposed the same imagery to Victorian India. According to their images, Islam was static and dogmatic, its adherents conservative, haughtily contemptuous of things 'modern', and under the influence of an obsolete system of education.[5] The Earl of Ronaldshay opined that, 'a candid Muhammadan would probably admit that the most powerful factors in keeping the majority of Moslems aloof from the educational movement of the day were pride of race, a memory of bygone superiority, religious fears, and a not unnatural attachment to the learning of Islam'. Major-general Stockley Warren, who retired in 1885, reminisced in these terms on his reaction to a Muslim 'coolie' who would not have brandy for medicinal purposes: 'These men I presume we shall ultimately civilize, make them Christians and drunkards, and lead them to liberty' (British Library).[6] The civil servant E.C. Bayley told the viceroy Northbrook in 1864 that the standard of 'Muslim morality' was not pitched very high, and that the 'corruptions' in their manners and social habits preceded their contact with the Europeans.[7]

A 'community' steeped in religious obscurantism was prone to treat the government with contempt and hostility. Recollecting the 1857 days in north India, Arthur Owen added a stereotype to those of the 'wily Mahratta' and the 'crafty Brahman', reporting that the 'sensual Mohammadan' fanatically believed that 'if one of their creed falls in battle against the infidels, Christians in particular, he is immediately translated to the garden of paradise'.[8] Nearly half a century after 1857, Bampfylde Fuller, the first lieutenant-governor of the new province of East Bengal and Assam, discovered an undertone of Muslim hostility to their Christian rulers: 'Of such men it may be truly said that at heart they are disloyal, and probably await their opportunity for manifesting their feelings in hostile acts.'[9]

Owen, Fuller, and other British functionaries believed that Islam in the subcontinent was indelibly stamped by its early history, particularly by its original social carriers, and that Islamic values, inherently hostile to the West, caused Muslim estrangement from the government. The call to wreak a special vengeance upon Muslims in the wake of the so-called Wahhabi movement and the 1857 revolt manifested how things 'Islamic' were constructed, located, categorized, and connected in British India.

Another common belief was that the British presence irked Muslims on account of the latter's close identification with the erstwhile ruling classes. They preserved in their blood the pride of a conquering race and cherished hopes of re-establishing their rule. 'Most Indian Mussulmans', commented one writer, 'cherished in their hearts some memory of the days when their fathers were the masters of India, and they believe, rightly or wrongly, that if ever the English power were shaken they would regain their old dominance'. A closer look reveals that the evidence in support of such contentions was thin. Most Muslims had no cause to be enthused by the glory of the Mughal era or to mourn its end. The fact that a Shah Waliullah or a Mirza Ghalib bemoaned its decline should not be treated lightly, but it should also not be construed as a generalized or undifferentiated 'Muslim response'. Similarly, it was patently hollow for Harcourt Butler, governor of UP (1918-20) during the high noon of British imperialism, to raise the spectre of a Muslim 'conspiracy' to overthrow the British with the aid of their 'virile' co-religionists in India and overseas.[10]

Doubtless, some Muslims at the turn of the century nursed such illusions. There were, likewise, isolated instances of elites or their interlocutors seeking an external Muslim imperium for help in re-consolidating their local or regional authority. In 1759, Shah Waliullah turned to Ahmad Shah Durrani (Abdali) to rescue India for Islam; later, Saiyid Ahmad of Rae Bareli corresponded with Central Asian rulers to recognize his khilafat. In general, however, British officials knew from their long administrative experience that most Muslims were prepared to make the colonial government work and gain benefits from its structures. Yet, colonial mentalities stuck to inherited frameworks, conjuring the image of a belligerent community with extra-territorial loyalties. 'The world is full of groups relying on their connection with some dominant "race" elsewhere', commented G.T. Garrat. 'The claim is natural enough, but the English, in accepting this picture of the Moslems as a race apart, seem to have been misled by a writer of genius (Rudyard Kipling), who had, however, a journalist's flair for the picturesque, and who always saw the Peninsula in terms of the Punjab.'[11]

The generalities extended to an appraisal of Indian Islam, the structure of the Muslim 'community', and the nature of its interaction with the Hindus. Some Britishers found it easy to get on with the Muslims at a social level as opposed to 'the Hindu, with his glib tongue, his pliant brain and back, his fantastic social rites, and his incomprehensible religion'.[12] They also found it easy to comprehend the essentials of their faith, 'built on Jewish foundations and devoid of the crudities and subtleties of Brahminism'.[13] But most were ill-informed and crude in their exposition. They believed, for example, that Islam south of the Himalayas remained, to all intents and purposes, the same as in other parts of the world, and that its adherents were a well-knit religious entity, acting as a monolith and keeping the desert faith pure in the land of 'idolaters'.[14] Muslims were, for this reason, endowed with 'cultural coherence', a real sense of unity transcending considerations of race, class, language, and region, and 'an essential community of thought and point of view that on occasion is able to speak with authority through its representative bodies'.[15] 'The solidarity of Islam was a hard fact against which it was futile to run one's head.'[16] The governor of Bengal, the province where most Muslims lived in British India, illustrated the strength of the call of Islam—'a call which rings insistently in the ears of the devout Muslims, whether of India or elsewhere, drowning the call of country and all else'. He put forward the official view, unchanged for nearly a century, that

> the ethnic pageant which passes across one's vision as one travels over India is made up of many tableaux. There is one such tableau which at once arrests attention because of the many points of contrast which it provides with the rest of the procession. . . . It is a tableau in which we see represented a religion, a civilization and culture, and an outlook differing profoundly in all material respects from those of Hinduism.[17]

Such a view hardly conformed to the reality. Islam in its Persian-Arabic attire had never made much sense to the masses. That is why its 'cultural mediators' were constrained to make the Islamic traditions more meaningful to the converts in syncretic and symbolic forms.[18] In the process, the pristine purity of dogmas and tenets, which the Faraizis in Bengal and the *mujahidins* in the north-west tried in vain to restore, was tailored to suit the people's spiritual and material urges. Local customs and heterodox traditions found a place in the corpus of beliefs and religious practices. This was reflected in the diversity of religio-cultural observances, as also in the variety of political and economic experiences. The medieval sultans may have wanted to erect a uniform religio-cultural system and impose religious authority from 'great' or 'middle' traditions, but geographic distances and particularistic localism inhibited them. In the end, the 'Islamic little tradition' developed, with its roots firmly anchored in Indian soil and autonomous from all centralized political control.[19] The itinerant preachers imposed their will sporadically in certain pockets, as in rural Bengal, but their impact was transient.

Charles Alfred Elliot reported from Unnao, close to Lucknow in UP, that there was a strong tendency among Muslims to assimilate in all externals with their Hindu neighbours. He found them wearing dhotis and using '*Ram Ram*' as the mode of salutation.[20] Fuller, likewise, wrote on Hindu influences among Muslims: in purely agricultural districts, he commented, the people not 'only understood each other's systems, but the systems often seem to overlap'. Hindus and Muslims cheerfully attended each other's festivals and sang each other's songs.[21] Lytton, Bengal's governor in the 1920s, commented on the rank and file of the communities in the province getting on well with each other in all daily business of life.[22] O.M. Martin, having served in Bengal from 1915 to 1926, emphatically stated that Hindu-Muslim mutual dependence and friendship were an old and cherished tradition.[23]

Such knowledge and understanding were neither reflected in concrete political decisions nor translated into constitutional decrees. In the constitutional plans, which broadly reflected the colonial assumptions about Indian society, the Mapilla Muslim appeared indistinguishable from Kipling's sturdy Pathan; the landed élite of Awadh was no different from the Tamil-speaking Muslim merchant; E.M. Forster's Cambridge buddy Saiyid Ross Masood was cast in the same mould as a *karkhandar* (artisan) in Delhi's old city; Shias and Sunnis, Bohras and Khojas, the Barelwis and the Deobandis were all part of pan-Indian Islam; even though politically, as Bishop Heber noted from long experience in central India, the Bohras were 'agreeing far better with Jains and Rajpoots than their Sunnite rivals'.[24]

It is true that conventional wisdom about Muslims and established theories about their role in the 1857 revolt were questioned by George Campbell, second-in-command to James Outram after the capture of Lucknow, W.W. Hunter, the Bengal civilian, and W.S. Blunt, an old-fashioned patriot shocked by the vulgarity of new imperialism.[25] But according to the viceroy, Dufferin, the followers of Islam were still 'a nation of 50 million, with their monotheism, their iconoclastic fanaticism, their animal sacrifices, their social equality and their remembrance of the days when, enthroned at Delhi, they reigned supreme from the Himalayas to Cape Cormorin'.[26] A decade after Dufferin wrote this, Anthony Macdonnell, lieutenant-governor of UP, treated Muslims with the same degree of suspicion and hostility. He found theological seminaries, such as Lucknow's Nadwat al-ulama, promoting disaffection and sedition. His pronounced belief that all Muslims were loyal to the Ottoman khalifa added fuel to the wild notions already present about pan-Islamism and its pervasive appeal the world over. What Macdonnell failed to grasp was that pan-Islamic sensibilities were heightened by the colonial government to bolster its imperial interests in the Balkans, and that there were any number of influential Muslims who denied the Turkish sultan's claim to be a khalifa. Political rights, Saiyid Ahmad Khan had said, 'were more important than religious traditions, and so long as the Muslims lived freely under British rule they would remain good subjects'. He agreed with maulvi Zakaullah that the Muslims should not look to foreign countries for guidance, since 'for a thousand years, our own religion of Islam had been intimately bound up with India; and in India, Islam has won some of its greatest triumphs, for its own popular form of civilization'.[27] Saiyid Mehdi Ali (nawab Mohsinul Mulk), Saiyid Ahmad's close friend and principal of the Aligarh College, made clear that Turkey's sultan could not exercise any of the powers and prerogatives of the khalifa over India's Muslims, who were in no way bound by their religion to obey him.[28]

Though British functionaries perpetuated the myth of the pervasive influence of pan-Islamism, overseas writers visiting India, including the Turkish author Halide Edib, thought differently. She insisted that Muslim allegiance to England during World War I

> demolished a strong historical myth—it showed that political pan-Islamism was a mere bogey. The attachment of the Indian Muslim to the interests of his country was a greater reality than his solidarity with Muslims outside India. *It may be useful for Western powers with Muslim colonies to realize that there is a distinct sense of nationhood separate from their religious life.* The Indian Muslim would resent an Afghan-Muslim domination and fight it; the Arab-Muslim would resent a Muslim-Turkish domination and fight it as much as he would any non-Muslim domination, if he ever got his independence.[29] (italics mine)

The direction and flow of 'Muslim politics', guided first by Saiyid Ahmad and later by the Muslim League, went towards compromise and accommodation with the government. Most modern and traditionally educated Muslims, for whom the Faraizi or the Barelwi adventures were faint memories, recognized the need to change attitudes and generate the strength to survive in a world dominated by colonialism. The ulama, many of whom were harshly treated as arch enemies of the British, made it clear after 1857 that adjustment with rather than repudiation of the raj was their main plank.

In his views on pan-Islamism, Macdonnell was out of sympathy with the official line, which had grudgingly veered around two sets of convictions. One was based on the bizarre belief that the Muslims had to be won over because they were so terrible and fear-inspiring.[30] The other rested on pragmatic imperial considerations. How could so many Muslims, some wielding power and influence in certain areas, be alienated for so long? They had to be enlisted 'as allies and auxiliaries',[31] courted to thwart nationalist aspirations, and encouraged to counter rabble-rousers in the

Indian National Congress. Viceroy Lord Northbrook was told by the colonial office to remove any 'just cause of [Muslim] complaint, because, in the event of any action against Russia, our allies must be the Mohametans of Central Asia, Afghanistan, and of Russia'. Viceroy Lord Mayo's note of 26 June 1871 on Muslim education indicated a change in imperial policy in this direction;[32] and Mayo's successor, Northbrook, received kudos for 'doing great good in directing attention to the long and grievously neglected subject of Mussalman education'.[33] After the 1857 difficulties with Muslim policy in India, Mayo began to fill the cup of reconciliation, Northbrook held it out.

The Simla deputation of October 1906—masterminded by the Aligarh College principal W.A.J. Archbold—paved the way for establishing the Muslim League. It was seen, for this reason, as a decisive break with the silent policy of the earlier decades. The reforms of 1909 established separate electorates for Muslims, along with reservations and weightages, and thus gave birth to a religio-political community, sections of which began to see themselves in the colonial image of being unified, cohesive, and segregated from the Hindus. Separate electorates put a formal seal of approval on the institutionalized conception of Muslim political identity and contributed to the forging of communitarian identities that were, both in conception and articulation, profoundly divisive and inherently conflict-oriented. An otherwise diverse community was thus homogenized, like a 'caste' or a 'tribe', so that it could be suitably accommodated within political schemes and bureaucratic designs. The self-styled Muslim leaders could thus stake their claims to be represent an 'objectively' defined community and contend with others for government patronage, employment, and political assignments. In this way, the ideological contours of the future Pakistan were delineated by British opinion and policymakers long before Jinnah expounded his two-nation theory.

The same process extended to the formation of caste-cluster consciousness and caste politics. By viewing caste categories as units of patronage and proscription, the government forced a predictable response: those seeking patronage or protesting proscription had to speak in the name of the bureaucratically recognized category. In such circumstances, the emergence of 'caste' publicists, spokesmen, and associations say more about the manner in which the foreign rulers viewed Indian society and sought to come to terms with it and the agility of the Indian response than it does about the ubiquity of 'caste' sentiment.[34]

The Montagu-Chelmsford Reforms (1919) projected the same colonial assumptions. The Act of 1935 held out the prospect of a divided nation and implicitly endorsed the hitherto hazy notion of an incipient Muslim nation. Indeed, if the British were to incline overmuch towards the Muslim League in the early 1940s, it was in part because their own political framework left them with little choice except to depend on League leaders. They had, after all, laid the foundations of a state-support realm enabling influential Muslims to define their 'community' on their own terms and to extract statutory concessions and guarantees almost at will. The structures of governance offered them much greater space for articulating sectional interests.

The Muslims in the Congress were put in an awkward position. The official, colonial definition of a community ran contrary to secular, territorial nationalism and undermined their moral authority. They were greatly constrained and unable to operate from a position of strength, because their conception of nationhood had no place in the constitutional blueprint. The overall thrust of British policies, especially after 1909, led to their political isolation. A man of Ansari's stature was virtually prevented from attending the Round Table Conferences in London. Rank communalists, on the other hand, were feted, and welcomed with open arms.[35] Congress Muslims like Azad were 'the wrecking horse', just because Jinnah, whose own status was far from assured, insisted on their exclusion from the Simla conference and from the interim government.[36] Jinnah's plea, which did not go unheeded in official quarters, was that no one but a Muslim Leaguer could represent the 'Muslim interests'. This moment in history must have been relished by the surviving architects of the 1909, 1919, and 1935 constitutions.

In the final analysis, the British bequeathed the Indian republic a truncated nation, a distorted perspective, a series of blurred images, and a number of vague and undifferentiated categories. These need to be challenged, contested, and refuted vigorously and consistently. If the history of intercommunity relations is to be rewritten, it has to steer clear of colonial paradigms, and freed from the stranglehold of an intellectual tradition, orientalist or otherwise.

II

A good number of educated Muslims in the last quarter of the nineteenth-century longed for an 'objective' assessment of their history and sociology and a rigorously argued repudiation of certain popular notions about their community and their creed. Who could they turn to? Not the theologians or the formal body of ulama, many of whom explicitly challenged the ideological tenets of the modern age. They were no doubt trained to debate and defend matters of faith but were ill-equipped, on account of their limited concerns, training, and religious orientation, to match orientalist scholarship. The intervention of scholars based in Aligarh, Delhi, Patna, and Calcutta was far more impressive and in tune with Western intellectual pursuits. The Aligarh College, for one, was a visible embodiment of the victory of forward-looking forces. It was here that movements of reform were consummated. A typically Aligarh version of reformed Islam, based on nineteenth-century liberalism and humanism, grew up in opposition both to the orthodox stream and to the popular syncretism of the masses.

Yet, the intellectual energy released by Saiyid Ahmad, Shibli Nomani, Hali, Zakaullah lost momentum once the reformist trends became increasingly intertwined with political controversies. The ambition of an average student, drawn from the landed class and the upper crust of the bourgeoisie, was government service. His pride was soothed, thanks to early pan-Islamic stirrings, on his being reminded that he was a unit in the great democracy of Islam, and in testament to this brotherhood, he jauntily wore the Turkish fez on his head.[37] Aligarh produced, for the most part, cautious pedagogues instead of a few thinkers of surpassing boldness. There appeared a cloud, to borrow Clifford Geertz's expression, of not terribly distinguished and usually rather unoriginal academicians.[38] This was also true of other centres of learning. Once the newly emergent Muslim bourgeoisie developed a vested interest in the power structures, the initial thrust given to reformist ideas was considerably diluted.

The few who stayed out of the charmed circle of government servants and addressed themselves to issues of reform and innovation were unable to correct colonial stereotypes or stir a debate comparable, in depth and vigour, to what occurred in Turkey under the aegis of the Young Turks. Part of the reason was their self-image of being part of a community—a monolith *umma*—that remained, or was normatively expected to remain, the same across spatial divisions and temporal boundaries. Time and again, this theme was powerfully expressed across a number of élite scholastic factions, especially of Sunni Islam, for which Sufi and syncretic practices and Shi'ism in general were just so many deviations from the norm. Time and again, the theme of eternal and unmitigated Hindu-Muslim hostility was echoed. So also the view that 'internal' differences among groups of Hindus and/or Muslims were secondary and irrelevant to the more fundamental religious cleavage. If Muslim intellectuals had examined such convictions in the light of their normal way of living, they would have discovered ample evidence of great 'internal' political, moral, and social tensions and their disruptive effects. In this way, they would have understood themselves better and made their cultural anxieties and political concerns intelligible to others.

What about nationalist writers, historians, social reformers, and political activists? Did they conceptualize the Indian social reality differently? Or question the Muslim élite's highly exaggerated and romanticized assessment of its historic role and destiny? Did they refute colonial stereo-types and set right the image of a static community, sunk in torpid medievalism, insulated from the winds of change, influenced by the diktat of the mullahs, tied to the Islamic community, susceptible to pan-Islamic influences, and organized, despite internal differentiations, on a pan-Indian basis?

Sections of the intelligentsia were expected to redefine the terms of the debate, not so much on Muslims or on Indian Islam, but on inter-community relations. They were required to harness their intellectual resources to demonstrate that the Muslims, both in their historical and contemporary settings, were part of and not separate from the Indian reality, and that the colonial stereotypes were constructed on false premises. This was a necessary pre-condition for establishing their all-India credentials, as also to hasten the process of nation-building with Muslims as co-partners. They had to contend, moreover, with a problem summed up by Gulshan and Chandra, the two fictional characters in Firoz Khan Noon's novel *Scented Dust* (1942), and to bridge the gulf separating the followers of Islam and Hinduism. 'Do not carry away the idea', Gulshan told Chandra,

> that I think ill of you for your ignorance, because there are thousands of us Hindus, men and women, who are as ignorant of the great Muslim religion and its philosophy as you are of ours. You will meet millions amongst us, who know no more about Islam than that it introduced into India loose trousers and a spouted pot for ablutions. There are also millions amongst us who know no more about the Hindu culture than what is represented by *langoti* (jockstrap dress) and *dal-roti* (lentil and bread/vegetarian diet). It is only the irascible, fiery and short-tempered who speak evil of other people's religions.[39]

III

There are numerous tracts and treatises on Hindu-Muslim intermingling, on social and cultural fusion, and on the commonality of intercommunity interests. There was, likewise, an enlightened conception of state and society grounded in the values of tolerance, syncretism, and fraternal living. One can also discern a wide range of liberal, eclectic, and radical ideas and movements from Raja Rammohun Roy to Jawaharlal Nehru that transcended communitarian barriers and fostered intercommunity linkages. Some were creatively expressed in the poetry of Rabindranath Tagore and the young Muhammad Iqbal. There were serious initiatives, such as the one taken by C.R. Das in Bengal, to resolve the communal deadlock.

Broadly speaking, however, a tentative survey of the vast and amorphous 'nationalist' literature reveals the uncritical acceptance of colonial constructions, their political legitimation through pacts, accords, 'unity' conferences, and the inner religio-cultural tensions within the nationalist paradigm. As a result, subcontinental themes on communal peace and understanding, shorn of their rhetorical value, ceased to be a major reference point in creating or articulating a truly national consciousness. This requires elaboration.

First and foremost, the intellectual understanding of the evolution of Islam in India and its followers was sketchy, superficial, and marred by a majoritarian perspective. The upper castes, who were convinced of their own superiority in the realm of ideas and thought, considered Islam a rather crude approach to the problems of philosophy and metaphysics.[40] There were, consequently, no serious interpreters of Islam, no counterparts of Al-Beruni, Amir Khusro, Malik Muhammad Jaisi, Abul Fazl, Raskhan, Rahim, or Dara Shikoh. M.N. Roy, the Marxist activist, expressed surprise that Hindus and Muslims, having lived together for so many centuries did not appreciate each other's culture and religion; that the Muslims, even after living in the country for many centuries, were 'generally considered to be an extraneous element'; and that educated Hindus were blissfully ignorant of 'the immense revolutionary significance of Islam'. He concluded that a radical change in mutual attitudes 'would shock the Hindus out of their arrogant self-satisfaction, and cure the narrow-mindedness of the Muslims of our day by bringing them face to face with the true spirit of the faith they profess'.[41]

Nineteenth-century writers and reformers, many of whom grudgingly came to terms with the Muslim presence, accepted the 'knowledge' derived from the medieval chroniclers and translated by British historians. Thus, they treated the Muslim intrusion as an aberration or a break in the continuity of Brahmanic traditions; equated Indian culture with Vedic culture; Indian philosophy with Vedic, Puranic, and the Upanishadic; and Indian religion with Hinduism.[42] Most accounts focused on the Muslim ruling élites, their military exploits and glittering durbars, and ignored the subtle fusion of 'little traditions' at the Sufi shrines in particular and in the rural hinterland generally. Islam had no Max Mueller to detail how its dogmas and tenets were gradually incorporated into regional and local belief structures and rituals; how Muslims—most converted to Muhammad's religion at different points of time—and for different reasons, were integrated with the rest of the population through a tangible and clearly identifiable historical process. Islam was mistakenly viewed as part of the 'great tradition'—codified, rigid, unchanging, insular, and close to external influences. Its followers, whether converted or not, were cast in a specifically Muslim/Islamic mould. Regardless of economic status, caste, language, or regional affinity, their identity was understood, defined, and described in strictly textual terms.

K.M. Panikkar, otherwise identified with the liberal stream, commented that 'the organization of Islam in India was . . . frankly communal, and its outlook was governed by the single fact of ensuring to the Islamic nation in India its independence and authority'. Muslims constituted a society everywhere and were much more than a religious minority. Their culture and way of life was different from the Hindus and other communities around them. 'Unlike the Christians who, though they profess a different religion, are not in their way of life different from the Hindus, the Muslims, whether in the south of Kerala or in Kashmir, represent a culture of their own.'[43]

Islam's militancy and inflexible doctrinal structure was a theme in and a major component of the Arya Samaj movement. Its founder, Swami Dayanand Saraswati, was a relentless critic of Islam and his celebrated text, *Satyarth Prakash*, inspired anti-Islamic polemics in much of Punjab. 'The Quoran, the Quoranic God and the Muslims', according to him, 'are full of bigotry and ignorance.'[44] Pandit Lekh Ram, Swami Shraddhanand, and Lala Lajpat Rai carried forward the Swami's polemics, subjected the Koran to severe criticism, depicted Muhammad as a man of dubious sexual ethics, and interpreted Islam as a religion sanctifying war and the slaughter of non-believers.[45] 'When I considered how devoted a Muslim is to his religion', wrote Lajpat Rai, whose father turned Muslim for a while, 'how he regards the propagation of Islam as a bounden duty and how he believes that the highest reward is attached to converting a man to Islam, I can well imagine what great pressure must my father's Muslim friends have brought to bear upon him . . . and how often they must have tried to induce him to become a Mussalman openly.'[46]

Such views correspond to the oft-repeated colonial axiom that orthodoxy rather than heterodoxy had a more direct and profound impact on the Muslims, and that they were deeply committed to fulfilling their

Islamic obligations. What distinguished them from others was their crusading zeal, their inclination to wage *jihad* against non-believers, and their abiding commitment to spreading their faith.

Invoking the past lent credence to such a reconstruction by major literary writers, though by no means all, who contrasted the glory of pre-medieval India with the oppressive character of 'Muslim dynasties'. Quite a few Marathi writers were, thus, concerned with the overall degradation of Hindus during Muslim rule, and with Islam's pernicious influence on their social customs. Gopal Ganesh Agarkar (1856-95), Gopal Hari Deshmukh (1823-92) and Vishnushastri Chiplunkar (1850-82) thought that Muslims were bullies and fanatics, because violence and aggression was the essence of their civilization.[47] Bal Gangadhar Tilak, the fiery politician-writer, sought to build a Maratha identity through a conscious choice of historical figures and symbols that evoked memories of Muslim oppression and exploitation. His essentialist endeavour to define Muslims through constant references to Mahmud of Ghazni, Alauddin Khilji, Timur, Aurangzeb, and Ahmad Shah Abdali created a major religious divide in Maharashtra society and provided ideological coherence to the Hindu Mahasabha and the RSS, two of the most militant Hindu organizations in the 1930s and 1940s.

Noted Hindi writers like Bharatendu Harishchandra (1850-85), Pratap Narain Misra (1856-94), Radha Charan Goswami (1859-1923), and Kisorilal Goswami (1866-1932) portrayed medieval rule as a chronicle of rape and abduction of Hindu women, the slaughter of sacred cows, and the defilement of temples. Bharatendu referred to the 'wounds in the heart' kept fresh by the sight of Aurangzeb's mosque that stood beside the sacred Vishwanath temple in Varanasi.[48] Two closely related themes figure in his and some of his contemporaries' works: the downtrodden, long-suffering Hindu, and the dominant, oppressive Muslim. In his play *Nildevi*, Muslim characters display cruelty, cowardice, treachery, bigotry, and debauchery, while Hindus, though sometimes portrayed as meek and submissive, demonstrate courage, honour, and fidelity.[49]

Kisorilal, following some notable British historians, described in his novel *Tara* (1902) the depraved conditions at the court of Shahjahan in Agra: intrigues, scenes of illicit love, murder among Muslims.[50] Misra and Radha Charan chastised Muslims as the 'abominably impure mlecchas' and damned them as rank outsiders. Both denounced the medieval rulers—'those mad elephants'—who 'trampled to destruction the flourishing lotus-garden of India', slaughtered cows with impunity, and prevented Hindu religious processions.[51]

Bankim Chandra Chattopadhyay looked upon medieval India as a period of bondage, and interpreted the Hindu chieftain's resistance to the Mughals as a form of national resistance. Muslim rule brought neither material nor spiritual improvement to India. Instead, he saw in Islam a quest for power and glory, devoid of spiritual and ethical qualities, irrational, bigoted, devious, sensual, and immoral, and a complete antithesis of his 'ideal' religion.[52] Bhudev Mukhopadhyaya (1827-94), on the other hand, questioned this version and described it as a mischievous fabrication of British historians. In his view, the Delhi sultans contributed significantly to the emergence of an inchoate consciousness of community among Indians. Emphasizing the ties that bound Muslims with the rest of the population, he underlined that Islam in the subcontinent was quite different from Islam elsewhere both in doctrine and in internal social practices.[53] Romesh Chandra Dutt, who wrote a major denunciation of British economic policies, avoided the familiar portrayal of Muslims as innately wicked and bloodthirsty. In *The Lake of Palms*, an English translation of the Bengali text, he avoided, generally, the more or less brazen confrontation of Hindus and Muslims and the attendant display of an anti-Muslim bias that provided the staple for his historical novels;[54] nevertheless, the picture of Muslims as alien emerges strongly in his novels and fiction. Muslims were not quite 'one of us', but enemies of 'our' country and religion.[55]

The Bengali intelligentsia of Nirad C. Chaudhuri's generation absorbed the spirit of such writings. 'Nothing was more natural for us', commented Chaudhuri, 'than to feel about the Muslims in the way we did'. They were told, even before they could read, that the Muslims had ruled and oppressed the Hindus, spread their religion with the Koran in one hand and a sword in the other, abducted Hindu women, destroyed temples, and polluted sacred places. 'As we grew older we read about the wars of the Rajputs, the Marathas, and the Sikhs against Muslims, and of the intolerance and oppression of Aurangzeb.'[56] On the other hand, the pukka sahib nurtured in the Victorian traditions believed in the benevolence of the British intentions and lamented, in no uncertain terms, the eclipse of the empire. The British empire in India was and 'remains one of the central facts of universal history and the concrete evidence that the British people have discharged one of their primary roles in history. They could not disinterest themselves in it without abrogating their historical mission and eliminating themselves from one of the primary strands of human evolution.'

Bengali thinkers, according to Chaudhuri, based their lifework on the formula of a synthesis of Hindu and European currents. Islamic trends and 'Muslim sensitivities' did not touch the arc of their consciousness. They stood outside as an 'external proletariat'.[57] If they wanted to enter the Bengali cultural world, they could do so 'only after giving up all their Islamic values and traditions'. In this way, the new Indian/Bengali culture of the nineteenth-century built a perimeter of its own and put specifically Muslim influences and aspirations beyond the pale.[58]

Nirad Chaudhuri was no different. Intellectually, the European mind was outraged by the Hindus precisely in those three principles which were fundamental to its approach to life, and which it has been applying with ever greater strictness since the Renaissance: that of reason, that of order, and that of measure. Discussing E.M. Forster's *A Passage to India*, his main criticism was that the major Indian character, Aziz, and most of the supporting Indians were Muslims. Nirad Babu believed that Forster did this because he shared the liking the British in India had for the Muslims, and the corresponding dislike for the Hindus. So that Dr Godbole, the chief Hindu character in the novel, was not an exponent of Hinduism but a clown.

Though a self-proclaimed liberal humanist, Chaudhuri nursed an arrogant contempt for and deep-seated hostility towards the Muslims in Calcutta, where he spent most of his life.[59] It was just the same in Kishoreganj, now in Bangladesh. He became conscious of a new kind of hatred for the Muslims during the Swadeshi movement. A cold dislike for them 'settled down in our heart, putting an end to all real intimacy of relationship'.[60] He rejoiced at Italy's attack on Tripoli in 1911. He was pleased—'so that the Muslims would be taught a lesson'—when Turkey joined the German side at the end of 1914.[61] 'Strongly anti-Muslim in 1920' owing to the khalifat upsurge, Chaudhuri was uneasy with the 'menacing assertiveness' of the Bengali Muslims and 'repelled' by the thought of living in a province where Muslims would be a dominant social and cultural entity.[62] His verdict: Muslims constituted a society of their own with a distinctive culture and could not be absorbed into a unified nation. For this reason, 'no historical argument was too false or too foolish to be trotted out by the Hindus to contest the demand of the Indian Muslims to have their own way of life'.[63] Chaudhuri declared, 'When I see the gigantic catastrophe of Hindu-Muslim discord of these days I am not surprised, because we as children held the tiny mustard in our hands and sowed it very diligently. In fact, this conflict was implicit in the very unfolding of our history, and could hardly be avoided'.[64] Whenever he saw a burqa-clad person, he apostrophized her mentally: 'Sister! You are the symbol of your community in India.' The entire body of the Muslims, according to him, was under a black veil. And his advice to them was to immigrate to Pakistan. 'There is something unnatural in the continued presence of the Muslims in India and of the Hindus in Pakistan, as if both went against a natural cultural ecology.'

The following description, which must not be conveniently dismissed as an illustration of Nirad Chaudhuri's 'eccentricity', sharply reflects the images of Muslims:

> One day I saw a procession of Muslim divines trooping into Sarat Babu's house. I was quite familiar with the modern Muslim dress, but had no idea that these learned Muslims wore different clothes. They did, for they had green gowns on and big turbans on their heads. . . . We, the educated and urban Bengalis . . . did not even imagine that such persons existed in Bengal. I with my knowledge of Islamic painting could only assume when I saw them that they were crude incarnations of the Muslim divines I had seen portrayed in Persian or Mughal miniatures. . . . Their faces were grave, and even stern. One face struck me very forcibly. It was pinched and peevish, but of an incredible ferocity. The eyes were large, black, and burning, and in that emaciated face they looked even blacker and larger. . . . He looked like an ill-dressed Robespierre, the sea-green Incorruptible. Sarat Babu's house was not only crowded for the occasion with these survivals of Islam, but even reeked of them.[65]

Such representations of Muslims did not augur well for the nationalist agenda of welding various communities, along with castes, regions, and linguistic units, into a unified nation. The rise of the Congress movement, in particular, imposed serious demands on its leaders to define the contours of multiculturalism and religious pluralism so as to keep intact the fragile social fabric that was being steadily undermined by British policies, as well as by the Hindu-Muslim revitalization campaigns. Otherwise, the Congress project of creating a composite nationality on liberal and secular values was bound to run into serious difficulties. Nehru rightly emphasized that 'only by thinking in terms of a different political framework—and even more so a different social framework—can we build up a stable foundation for joint action'.[66]

IV

Nehru's perspective was influenced by his cosmopolitan family background, his education in England, his social and cultural ambience in Allahabad, his long-standing friendship and political camaraderie with Ansari, Azad, Saiyid Mahmud, Khaliquzzaman, Tassaduq Ahmad Khan

Sherwani, and Abdul Majid Khwaja. He was a product of, and his sensibilities were influenced by, the cultural norms and intellectual ambience of the Urdu-speaking élites of the Indo-Gangetic belt. As a student at Trinity College, Cambridge, he was in close touch with Fabian socialists in London. Such interactions widened his intellectual horizon and enriched his appreciation of political and social transformative processes around the globe. He could thus place in perspective the rapid changes taking place in Muslim countries like Egypt, Turkey, and Iran. Discussions with Azad and other Muslim scholars helped him understand Indian Islam and medieval Indian history better. In *The Discovery of India* (1946), he analysed late-nineteenth-century reformist currents among Muslims in a manner no other nationalist leader did during his lifetime, appreciated Saiyid Ahmad Khan's initiatives, commented on the nationalist stir among the young Muslim intelligentsia of north India, noted the 'sensation' created by Azad—'this very youthful writer and journalist'—and assessed Iqbal's impact on the younger generation of Muslims.[67]

More than anything else, Nehru was aware that the social, educational, and economic backwardness of most Muslims was not because of any innate failing, but because of historical and sociological factors.[68] He knew, so he said, more about their hunger and poverty than those who talked in terms of percentages and seats in councils. That is because he claimed to be in greater touch with them than most Muslim leaders. How could he then accept the League's pretentious claims? How could he recognize Jinnah as the 'sole spokesman'? The League leadership at the top deliberately sought refuge in the name of religion to avoid discussing problems of the common man.

A simple fact that eluded most of Nehru's comrades was that Indian society was at no stage structured around religious solidarities or polarized along 'communal' lines. Nehru's exceptionally eclectic mind grasped this reality. He believed that intercommunity conflicts, as and when they occurred, were counterpoised to the quiet, commonplace routines in which communities intermingled. Cross-community linkages rather than religious ties influenced the direction in which patronage, authority, and economic relations flowed into everyday life. Consequently, he recognized the need to reinforce traditional linkages through 'mass contact' and a radical socio-economic blueprint. He recognized, moreover, the importance of reducing class disparities, creating opportunities for upward mobility, and making the masses aware of their mutual interdependence, their shared historical experiences, and their common concerns, interests, and destiny.

The impulse behind Nehru's brainchild, the Muslim Mass Contact Campaign, launched in March 1937, was to approach the Muslims not as a collective fraternity but as a segment of an otherwise impoverished population. The principal motivation was to convince them that they did not constitute a 'nation', and that their fortunes were not tied to their Muslim brethren per se, but with fellow artisans, peasants, and workers in other communities. Nehru dialogued with Jinnah on these lines, questioned the rationale of 'Muslim nationalism' in a society traditionally anchored in cultural and religious pluralism, and criticized the construct of a 'Muslim identity' in religious terms. He tried in vain to delink issues of proportion and percentages of seats with the more basic and fundamental contradictions between nationalism and colonialism. He expected Jinnah to draw his constituency into this just and legitimate struggle as co-citizens and not as a preferential religio-political 'community'. The two-nation idea made no sense; it was not more than a reversion to some medieval theory.

> Why only two I do not know, for if nationality was based on religion, then there were many nations in India. Of two brothers one may be a Hindu, another a Moslem; they would belong to two different nations. These two nations existed in varying proportions in most of the villages in India. They were nations which had no boundaries; they overlapped. A Bengali Moslem and a Bengali Hindu, living together, speaking the same language and having much the same traditions and customs belonged to a different nation.[69]

There was much ambiguity and fuzziness in nationalist thinking about the corporate identity of the Muslims. Nehru removed some of it. He made clear: 'when we enter the political plane, the solidarity is national, not communal; when we enter the economic plane, the solidarity is economic'.[70] In what way, he asked, were the interests of the Muslim peasant different from those of the Hindu peasant? Or those of a Muslim labourer from those of his Hindu prototypes? The ties that bound people were common economic interest and, in the case of a subject country especially, a common national interest.[71] If the country began to think and act on these lines, the 'myth' of communalism would disappear along with the pseudo-religious mentality.[72] Communalism was not the power it was made out to be: it was a mere creation of educated classes in search of office and employment. The 'communal question' was essentially one of protecting their interests. Religion was just a useful stalking-horse for this purpose.[73] 'The real conflict,' according to Nehru, 'had nothing to do with religion, though religion often masked the issue, but was essentially between those who stood for a nationalist—democratic—socially revolutionary policy and those who were concerned with preserving the relics of a feudal regime. In a crisis, the latter inevitably depend upon foreign support which is interested in preserving the status quo.'[74]

The basic premise of Nehru's argument was valid. He was right in arguing that religious solidarity should not be the basis for political activism or that religious symbols of disunity should be shunned in Congress mobilization campaigns. The alternative strategy, worked out by Tilak in Maharashtra or the Swadeshi leaders in Bengal, had created fissures in the liberation struggle, alienated Muslims in these regions, and weakened the appeal of secular nationalism. Though not the only fervent champion of secular nationalism, Nehru raised the standard of debate on the subject not on the strength of abstract principles of Western democracy, which is a commonly leveled charge against him, but in relation to his perception of and insights into wider social and political processes. There is no reason to believe that his perceptions were flawed or to find fault in his vision. There is no reason to doubt his motives or intentions.

Nehru's ideas ran contrary to Jinnah's two-nation theory, just as they conflicted with the protagonists of a Hindu nation. Some of his own Congress colleagues were, consequently, uncomfortable with his 'pro-Muslim' proclivities. Haunted by the bogey of pan-Islamism, they insisted that the fortunes of the Islamic world counted far more with Muslims than did their country's political regeneration. They harped on Muslims' aggressive instincts and the militancy of their faith. When they agreed to the Lucknow pact (December 1916) and similar accords, they did so on the assumption that Muslims were, after all, a separate religious and political entity.[75] In this way, they quietly legitimized what were later derided as 'separatist' and 'communal' demands. In so doing, they jettisoned their own moral authority to challenge the colonial assumptions outlined in the Acts of 1919 and 1935, and created the space, sometimes unwittingly but mostly consciously, for certain strident sectional claims to be accommodated in the Congress political agenda. The political language in which such accommodation was expressed and the energy derived from recognizing the Muslims as a distinct political unit implied that the basic terms of reference precluded any lasting solution of the communal tangle.

The Congress was sensitized to this reality after the Muslim outcry over certain policies adopted by its ministries in UP, Bihar, and Bombay. But it was too late to retrace its steps. With the political currents flowing in different directions, the Congress agenda could not be written afresh in the post-War years without the Muslim League, the votaries of a Hindu nation, and the British who still held the scales. There were not just 'two parties', as Nehru had mistakenly announced in 1937, but as many as four parties who had jumped into the fray. Nehru and his socialist comrades swallowed this bitter pill when they helplessly witnessed the collapse of the Muslim Mass Contact Campaign.

I do not intend to portray the image of an always liberal, enlightened, largely innocent Muslim community—'sinned against' but hardly ever 'sinning'. Nor is it intended to suggest that their fortunes or misfortunes could be explained solely in terms of the unremitting, overwhelming power and prejudice of the British and 'Hindu' intelligentsia. Sections of the Muslim intelligentsia have made their own history at least as much as others have made it for them—that they have not made it very well should engage social scientists.

It is therefore important to examine the depth, vigour, and variety of Muslim revivalism, to consider why the idea of a singular community appears in Muslim writings, to explore how Islamic ideas moulded élite perceptions, and to analyse why Islamic symbols of disunity were sometimes preferred to Indian historical symbols of unity. We need to acquaint ourselves more fully with the Muslim educational system, 'the master institution', in the words of Clifford Geertz, in the perpetuation of an Islamic tradition, and in the creation of an Islamic vision.[76] In this context, the part played by the itinerant preachers and the ulama requires detailed investigation, not just as models of 'Islamic conduct' or as interpreters of the *Shariat* but also as leaders of a political 'community' in the making. We need to delineate, just as Saiyid Ahmad, Hali, Iqbal, and Azad did, the implications of their social conservatism in a society that was rapidly changing under colonial rule, and also the consequences of their resistance to innovation and change and their suppression of dissent and interpretation (*ijtehad*). The issue, which sometimes escapes notice in some writings on Muslims in Western scholarship, is of considerable significance to the citizens of South Asia generally and to the Muslim communities in particular.

Finally, it is necessary to deconstruct the language of minorityism and uncover the motives of those who practiced modern-day politics in the name of the *millat* they purported to represent, but whose main aim was to wield political power and to use Islam and communitarian solidarity as a shield to cover their designs. The general implication of this idea was summed up by Chandra in her conversation with her lifelong friend Gulshan. 'You see, my dear,' she said, 'a man will use any old argument to achieve his object in all walks of life, and this communal discord is a very useful and good stick with which our men-folk can beat the old India goat—her political progress'. Troubled by the communal cleavage, she remarked angrily: 'This Hindu-Muslim discord only exists because it pays our men-folk to keep it going.'[77]

What we ideally need is a triangular narrative in which the Muslim is not a privileged victim but as much an actor as the others. The main thrust of this discussion is to identify points of convergence between the colonial and nationalist discourses and to argue that, despite various constraints, it was still possible to challenge Hindu majoritarianism and Muslim nationalism. Surely, there was a wide range of options available. If one were to evolve, in the spirit of Ghalib's quintessential message,[78] as an independent/autonomous discourse, this would have entailed discarding the communal categories created by the raj and also ignoring the Muslim élite's own image and representation of itself. There were, objectively speaking, profound historical and sociological reasons for doing so. The fact that this was not done in a concerted and systematic manner weakened the cause of eclectic and secular ideologies.

ہم موحد ہیں ہمارا کیش ہے ترک رسوم
ملتیں جب مٹ گئیں اجزائے ایماں ہو گئیں

My creed is oneness, my belief is abandonment of rituals.
Let all communities dissolve and constitute a faith.

MIRZA GHALIB

NOTES

1. Edward W. Said, *Orientalism*, London, 1978; Normal Daniel, *Islam and the West: The Making of an Image*, Edinburgh, 1960; Aziz Al-Azmeh, *Islams and Modernities*, London, 1993.
2. W. Crooke, *The North-Western Provinces of India: Their History, Ethnology, and Administration*, New Delhi, 1897, 1975 rpt., pp. 258-9.
3. M.A. Laird (ed.), *Bishop Heber in Northern India: Selection from Heber's Journal*, Cambridge, 1971, p. 64. 'With the monumental wreckage of those early Mahomedan dynasties, steeped in treachery and bloodshed', commented Valentine Chirol (1852-1929), journalist in charge of the foreign department of *The Times* (1908-12), 'the plain of Delhi is still strewn'. *India Old and New*, p. 3.

4. The literature on the subject is vast, though its fuller analysis is awaited. For clues and insights see Daniel, *Islam and the West*, pp. 266-85; A.J. Greenberger, *The British Image of India: A Study on the Literature of Imperialism 1880-1960*, London, 1969; Hardy, *Muslims of British India*, pp. 1-2, 62-91; Robinson, *Separatism Among Muslims*, pp. 164-73; Lelyveld, *Aligarh's First Generation*; Gyanendra Pandey, *The Construction of Communalism in Colonial India*, New Delhi, 1990; Clinton Bennet, *Victorian Images of Islam*, London, 1992; Carol A. Breckenridge and Peter van der Veer (eds.), *Orientalism and the Postcolonial Predicament*, New Delhi, 1994; David Ludden (ed.), *Contesting the Nation: Religion, Community and the Politics of Democracy in India*, Philadelphia, 1996; P.K. Datta, *Carving Blocs: Communal Ideology in Early Twentieth Century Bengal*, New Delhi, 1999; Michael R. Anderson, 'Islamic Law and the Colonial Encounter in British India', in Chibli Mallat and Jane Connors (eds.), *Islamic Family Law*, London, 1990; Avril Powell, *Muslims and Missionaries in Pre-Mutiny India*, London, 1993); Lucy Carrol, 'Colonial Perceptions of Indian Society and the Emergence of Caste(s) Associations', *Journal of Asian Studies*, Vol. 27, 2, February 1978; and Kenneth Jones, 'Religious Identity and the Census', in N.G. Barrier (ed.), *The Census in British India*, Delhi, 1981, pp. 83-5.
5. Sidney Low, *A Vision of India*, London, 1911, p. 281. Low was an eminent journalist and writer. His book was well received by *The Times* in London, and by Curzon and Morley. And the comment of the Earl of Ronaldshay, Bengal governor (1917-22): 'A candid Muhammadan would probably admit that the most powerful factors in keeping the majority of Moslems aloof from the educational movement of the day were pride of race, a memory of bygone superiority, religious fears, and a not unnatural attachment to the learning of Islam.' *India: A Bird's-Eye View*, London, 1924, p. 235.
6. Reminiscences (typescript), Mss. Eur. C-607, India Office Library and Oriental Collection, London (hereafter BL). The Major retired from service in 1885.
7. E.C. Bayley to Northbrook, 10 July 1874, Northbrook papers, Mss. Eur. C-144/17, BL.
8. Arthur Owen, 'Recollections of a Veteran of the Days of the Great Indian Mutiny of 1857', Lahore, 1915, 2nd edn., Mss. Eur. 239/120, BL.
9. Bampfylde Fuller, *India The Land and Its People*, pp. 41 and 124, and his *The Empire of India*, London, 1913. And the view that 'the Mahomedan star is not in the ascendant, and his position wars with his religion. That enjoins conversion by the sword if need be, and an almost fierce intolerance of the idolater. His whole entourage therefore is galling.' Low, *Vision of India*, p. 281; also, Flora Annie Steel, *India*, London, 1905, p. 180.
10. Harcourt Butler, 'The Country, Peoples, Language and Creeds' in John Cumming (ed.), *Modern India: A Co-operative Survey*, Delhi, 1932, p. 15; G.T. Garrat, *An Indian Commentary*, London, 1929, p. 172, basing his assessment on the dubious testimony of the Khoja spiritual leader, the Aga

Khan; Low, *Vision of India*, p. 281; *Speeches, by Harcourt Butler delivered at the M.A.O. College, Aligarh, on 25 November 1919*, Allahabad, 1921, pp. 140-1; and his *India Insistent*, London, 1931, p. 38; and Lelyveld, *Aligarh's First Generation*, pp. 9-10.

11. Garrat, *Indian Commentary*, p. 173.
12. As opposed to 'the Hindu, with his glib tongue, his pliant brain and back, his fantastic social rites, and his incomprehensible religion. . . .' Low, *Vision of India*, p. 281.
13. George Lumley to Linlithgow, 14 December 1939, L/P&J/8/645, BL.
14. Bampfylde Fuller, *Studies of Indian Life and Sentiments*, London, 1910, p. 125. The unifying force of Islam, commented Fuller, 'has checked schism, and religious divisions are few in number'. See also W.W. Titus, 'The Reaction of Muslim India to Western Islam' in John R. Mott (ed.), *The Muslim World Today*, London, 1925, p. 93; Claude H. Hill, 'Religion and Caste in India', in *India and the Durbar*, London, 1911, p. 210. He was editor of *The Times*.
15. Henry Whitehead, *Indian Problems in Religion, Education, Politics*, London, 1924. He was Bishop of Madras before becoming a Fellow of Trinity College, Cambridge; Garrat, *Indian Commentary*, p. 172.
16. Lawrence, second Marquess of Zetland, *Essays*, London, 1956, p. 119. See also T.W. Holderness, *Peoples and Problems of India*, London, 1911, p. 127.
17. Ronaldshay, *India: A Bird's-Eye View*, p. 214.
18. Asim Roy, *The Islamic Syncretistic Tradition in Bengal*, p. 249.
19. The argument is based on Frank C. Darling, *The Westernization of Asia: A Comparative Political Analysis*, Boston, 1939, pp. 21-9.
20. C.A. Elliot, *Laborious Days*, Calcutta, 1892, p. 28.
21. Fuller, *Studies*, pp. 130-1; Edward Thompson, *The Reconstruction of India*, London, 1930, p. 234.
22. Earl of Lytton, *Pundits and Elephants: Being the Experiences of Five Years as Governor of an Indian Province*, London, 1942, p. 172; Garrat, *Indian Commentary*, pp. 175-6, 181.
23. Memoirs of O.M. Martin (typescript), Centre for South Asian Studies, Cambridge (hereafter CSAS).
24. Bishop Heber first came in contact with the Bohras—'by far the wealthier and more industrious party'—in Rajasthan. He found them to be 'peaeable and orderly merchants and tradesmen' with considerable 'influence and privileges' in Central India. His other interesting observation was that the Bohras were 'agreeing far better with both Jains and Rajpoots than their Sunnite rivals'. *Bishop Heber in Northern India*, p. 282.
25. James Outram, *Memoirs of my Indian Career*, London, 1893, p. 397. He emphatically denied that there was a Muslim insurrection or that Muslims were a formidable danger to the government. He was unhappy at their 'exclusion' and 'degradation'. He insisted that 'each section of people in each district must be judged by their acts, and not otherwise; and that they

should be fairly judged—not by a foregone prejudice, but with an equal mind'. W.W. Hunter, *Indian Mussalman: Are they Bound in Conscience to Rebel against the Queen*?, Calcutta, 1945 edn., p. 123. Unlike the great majority of his compatriots, Blunt studied Islam and followed the fortunes of Muslim societies with an open mind. Of his book *The Future of Islam*, he wrote: 'In it I committed myself without reserve to the Cause of Islam as essentially the "Cause of God" over an immense portion of the world, and to be encouraged, not repressed, by all who cared for the welfare of mankind.' His sympathy for Islam eventually led him to champion the Arab cause against European intervention and Ottoman injustices. Rana Kabbani, *Europe's Myths of Oriental Devise and Rule*, London, 1986, pp. 96-7.

26. Dufferin's Minute of Nov. 1988, quoted in Hardy, *Muslims of British India*.
27. Annemarie Schimmel, *Islam in the Indian Subcontinent*, Leiden, 1980, p. 197.
28. *Eminent Mussalmans*, Madras, n.d., p. 91.
29. Halide Edib, *Inside India*, London, 1937, pp. 317-18.
30. Edward Thompson to Wedgewood Benn, 31 Dec. 1930, L/PO/6/74 (ii), BL.
31. Alfred Lyall to Morley, 4 Feb. 1909, quoted in Robinson, *Separatism Among Muslims*, p. 170. This view could sometimes get mixed up with the articulation of worldwide imperial interests. For example, in the 1870s, the viceroy was told by the colonial office to remove any 'just cause of [Muslim] complaint, because, in the event of any action against Russia, our allies must be the Mahometans of Central Asia, Afghanistan, and of Russia'. To Northbrook, 21 Feb. 1873, Northbrook papers, Mss. Eur. C-144/21 (1) BL. Similar views were expressed during the First World War.
32. Hardy, *Muslims of British India*, p. 90; and Lelyveld, *Aligarh's First Generation*, p. 12.
33. Rev. J. Long to Northbrook, 19 July 1873, Northbrook papers, Mss. Eur. C-144/21 (1). The secretary of state told the viceroy on 23 October 1882: 'If there be any real special grievances which affect the Muslim population which we can fairly remove, by all means let it be done.'
34. Lucy Carroll, 'Colonial Perceptions of Indian Society', p. 249. For the implications of separate electorates and the claims of Muslims as 'an objectively-defined Muslim community', Farzana Shaikh, *Community and Consensus in Islam*, pp. 90, 157-9; and David Gilmartin, 'Democracy, Nationalism and the Public: A Speculation on Colonial Muslim Politics', *South Asia*, 14, 1, 1991, p. 125.
35. Hasan, *A Nationalist Conscience*.
36. Pethick-Lawrence to Cripps, 30 Sept. 1939, in Nicholas Mansergh (ed.), *The Transfer of Power, 1942-7*, London, 1969, Vol. 1, p. 629. See also my edited volume, *Islam and Indian Nationalism: Reflections on Abul Kalam Azad*, Delhi, 1992, pp. 93-4. The Simla conference was convened by the viceroy, Wavell, to resolve the political issues at the end of war in Europe, but it broke down. 'So my efforts to bring better understanding between the parties have

failed and have shown how wide is the gulf', noted the viceroy.

37. Jawaharlal Nehru, *An Autobiography*, London, 1936, p. 464; Hardy, *Muslims of British-India*, pp. 103-4. Rafiq Zakaria, *Rise of the Muslims in Indian Politics: An Analysis of Developments from 1885 to 1906*, Bombay, 1970, p. 351, quoted in Asma Barlas, *Democracy, Nationalism and Communalism: The Colonial Legacy in South Asia*, Boulder, CO, 1995, p. 148.
38. Nehru and M.N. Roy were in substantial agreement over Aligarh's role after the death of Saiyid Ahmad Khan. I am fascinated by M.N. Roy's reflections, the more so because he arrived at certain important conclusions without any close contact with the university or its scholars. The communist leader pointed out that Aligarh failed to produce youthful elements holding social and political ideas similar to the Hindu intellectuals who conceived of a political nationalism as expressed in the Congress. While the early generation of the Hindu intelligentsia imbibed progressive social and political views, the Aligarh alumni belonged to the landed aristocracy with social and political tendencies that were predominantly feudal. Roy concluded that 'the absence of a class cohesion was responsible for the political divergence between the Hindus and Muslims. . . . Elements so diverse socially could not unite in a national movement.' M.N. Roy, *India in Transition*, Bombay, 1971 rpt., p. 222.
39. Firoz Khan Noon, *Scented Dust*, Lahore, 1941, p. 293. This novel was written at the request of an English friend to acquaint him with some of the con-temporary themes in Indian politics and society. A leading landlord of Punjab, the author played a key part in the Muslim League.
40. Jawaharlal Nehru, *The Discovery of India*, Calcutta, 1946 rpt., p. 225.
41. M.N. Roy, *The Historical Role of Islam*, Delhi, 1981 rpt. This book was first published in 1939 but written in jail in the early 1930s. It was translated into Hindi as *Islam ki etihasik bhoomika* by Chandrodaya Dixit, Bikaner, 1988. A devout follower of Jainism wrote: 'To ascertain the truth about the teaching of Islam, and to separate its valuable gems from valueless stones as also from glittering pebbles, so that its beauty may be brought in the limelight of public notice.' Champat Rai Jain, *The Lifting of the Veil or the Gems of Islam*, Bijnor, 1931.
42. K.M. Panikkar, *The Foundations of New India*, London, 1963, p. 56. Such views were endorsed by quite a number of liberal and secular scholars as well as politicians before and after independence—for example, the contention that 'the great principles of Islam did not afect Hinduism as a whole' or that the 'social structure of Hinduism remained almost unaffected by 700 years of association with Islam'. K.M. Pannikar, *Asia and Western Dominance*, London, 1953, p. 240. In fact, '700 years of Islamic authority over the Indo-Gangetic plain . . . had left Hinduism in a state of depression. It was the religion of a subject race, looked down upon with contempt by the Muslims as idolatry.' *The India We Served*, p. 127, and the Early of Ronaldshay, *The Heart of Aryavarta: A Study of the Psychology of Indian*

Unrest, London, 1925, p. 2. Likewise, it was common to identify India with Hinduism and with 'Hindu culture' and 'Hindu civilization'. This was a classic British theory reinforced by Indologists of different intellectual pedigrees. 'To me', wrote Walter Roper Lawrence, 'India is Hindu, and whatever the picture of "India Reformed" may have been in the minds of the imaginative men who made the rough sketch, in the finished work the Brahman will be the central and the striking figure.'

43. Panikkar, *Foundations*, pp. 55, 60; see S. Radhakrishnan, *Eastern Religions and Western Thought*, London, 1940 edn., p. 339; and the comment of a senior Congress leader: 'The Muslims are an all-India community. Whether organised in one overall organisations or not, it often feels the identity of the interests of its members and acts unitedly where its minority rights are concerned.' J.B. Kripalani, *Minorities in India*, Calcutta, n.d., p. 40.
44. J.T.F. Jordens, *Dayananda Saraswati: His Life and Ideas*, Delhi, 1978, p. 268.
45. K.W. Jones, *Arya Dharma: Hindu Consciousness in 19th-Century Punjab*, Berkeley, 1976, pp. 145, 150; J.E. Llwellyn, *The Arya Samaj as a Fundamentalist Movement: A Study in Comparative Fundamentalism*, New Delhi, 1993, pp. 104-8.
46. V.C. Joshi (ed.), *Lajpat Rai: Autobiographical Writings*, New Delhi, 1965, p. 14.
47. B.G. Gokhale, 'Hindu Responses to the Muslim Presence in Maharashtra', in Yohanan Friedmann (ed.), *Islam in Asia*, Vol. 1: *South Asia*, Jerusalem, 1984, pp. 162-7.
48. Sudhir Chandra, 'Communal Consciousness in Late 19th Century Hindi Literature', in Mushirul Hasan (ed.), *Communal and Pan-Islamic Trends in Colonial India*, New Delhi, 1987, pp. 180-95.
49. Christopher R. King, 'Hindu Nationalism in the Nineteenth Century U.P.', in Dhirendra K. Vajpeyi (ed.), *Boeings and Bullock-Carts: Essays in Honour of K. Ishwaran*, New Delhi, 1990, pp. 187, 191; see also Yogendra Malik, 'Reflections of Inter-Communal Relations through Hindi Fiction', in Vajpeyi (ed.), *Boeings and Bullock-Carts*, Chap. 9; R.S. McGregor, 'A Hindu Writer's Views of Social, Political and Language Issues of his Time: Attitude of Harischandra of Banaras (1850-1885)', *Modern Asian Studies*, Vol. 25, 1, 1991, pp. 91-100.
50. P. Gaeffke, *Hindi Literatue in the Twentieth Century*, Wiesbaden, 1978, p. 27.
51. Sudhir Chandra, *The Oppressive Present: Literature and Social Consciousness in Colonial India*, New Delhi, 1992, p. 120.
52. Partha Chatterjee, *Nationalist Thought and the Colonial World: A Derivative Discourse*, New Delhi, 1980, p. 77; Tapan Raychaudhuri, *Europe Reconsidered: Perceptions of the West in the Nineteenth Century World*, New Delhi, 1988, pp. 188-9; Tanika Sarkar, 'Imagining Hindurashtra: The Hindu and the Muslim in Bankim Chandra's Writings', in Ludden (ed.), *Contesting*

the Nation, pp. 162-84. For a different interpretation, see Sisir Kumar Das, *The Artist in Chains: The Life of Bankim Chandra Chatterjee*, New Delhi, 1984, Appendix C: 'A Muslim Baiter?'

53. Sudipta Kaviraj, 'The Reversal of Orientalism: Bhudev Mukhopadhyay and the Project of Indigenist Social Theory'. Vasudha Dalmia and H. von Stietencron (eds.), *Representing Hinduism: The Construction of Religious Traditions and National Identity*, New Delhi, 1995, pp. 253-82; Raychaudhuri, *Europe Reconsidered*, pp. 41-3.
54. Sudhir Chandra, 'Towards an Integrated Understanding of early Indian Nationalism', in Alok Bhalla and Sudhir Chandra (eds.), *Indian Responses to Colonialism in the 19th Century*, New Delhi, 1993, p. 18.
55. Sudhir Chandra, 'The Lengthening Shadow: Secular and Communal Consciousness', in Bidyut Chakrabarty (ed.), *Secularism and Indian Polity*, New Delhi, 1990.
56. Nirad C. Chaudhuri, *The Autobiography of an Unknown Indian*, New York, 1951, p. 227.
57. It has been noted that the peasants, most of whom were Muslims, never entered Bankim's fictional mind. While commenting on the present in polemical prose, Bankim could see the Hindus and the Muslims both as sections of the oppressed masses but in his historical novels the Muslim was always perceived as the alien. Meenakshi Mukherji, 'Rhetoric Identity: History and Fiction in Nineteenth Century India', in Bhalla and Chandra (eds.), op. cit., p. 35. See also Pradip Kumar Datta, 'Dying Hindus: Production of Hindu communal common sense in early 20th century Bengal', *EPW*, 19 June 1993, pp. 1305-25; and Tanika Sarkar, 'Imagining Hindu Rashtra', op. cit.
58. Chaudhuri, *Autobiography*, pp. 226-7.
59. Ibid., p. 228.
60. Ibid., p. 232.
61. Nirad C. Chaudhuri, *Thy Hand, Great Anarch! India, 1921-1952*, Delhi, 1987, p. 37.
62. Ibid., p. 466.
63. Ibid., p. 39.
64. Chaudhuri, *Autobiography*, p. 225.
65. Chaudhuri, *Thy Hand, Great Anarch!*, p. 469.
66. Nehru, *Autobiography*, p. 137.
67. Nehru, *Discovery of India*, pp. 297-305.
68. Ibid., p. 340.
69. Nehru, *Discovery of India*, pp. 341-2.
70. To Mohammad Ismail Khan, 26 Dec. 1927, S. Gopal (ed.), *Selected Works of Jawaharlal Nehru* (hereafter *SWJN*), Delhi, 1976, Vol. 8, p. 203.
71. Statement to the press, 10 Jan. 1937, ibid., Vol. 8, p. 12.
72. Presidential Address at Punjab National Conference, Amritsar, 11 Apr. 1928, ibid., Vol. 3, pp. 225-6.

73. Ibid., Vol. 8, p. 120.
74. Nehru, *Discovery of India*, p. 343.
75. Hasan, *Nationalism and Communal Politics*, pp. 102-3.
76. Clifford Geertz, 'Modernization in a Muslim Society: The Indonesian Case', in Robert N. Bellah (ed.), *Religion and Progress in Modern Asia*, New York, 1965, p. 95.
77. Noon, *Scented Dust*, p. 282.
78. Russell, *Pursuit of Urdu Literature*, p. 71.

4

Traditional Rites and Contested Meanings: Sectarian Strife in Colonial Lucknow

> The truth is that in those days the whole year was spent waiting for Muharram. . . . After the goat sacrifices of Baqr Id the preparations for Muharram began. Dadda, my father's mother, started to softly chant elegies about the martyrs. Mother set about sewing black clothes for all of us; and my sister took out the notebooks of laments . . . and began to practice them to new airs. In those days film music had not taken grip of *nauha* melodies. They were simple and at the same time deep, like the folk-music of villages and small towns, and when my sister, mother, or an aunt wore black clothes and stood up to recite,
>
> Sleeping spoke out the dreaming Sakina,
> The lord's breast's no more, so no more Sakina . . .
>
> the wrists supporting the book of *nauhas* were immediately transformed. It seemed to the listeners as if the lament was issuing straight from the jail in Damascus where Imam Husain's sister Zainab was trying to comfort his beloved daughter Sakina in a subterranean dungeon. . . . I don't know about Lucknow—I don't even know about Ghazipur—but I certainly do know that among the Saiyid families of Gangauli, Muharram was nothing less than a spiritual celebration.
>
> RAHI MASOOM REZA, *The Feuding Families of Village Gangauli*

As darkness descended on Lucknow, once a prized city of Awadh, some people huddled together in a cafe or on the terraces with their eyes fixed on the distant horizon. After a long and anxious wait, the city comes alive: the moon is sighted in the middle of dark clouds hovering over the Gomti river. The deafening sound of crackers from Nakhaas and the loud and clear call for prayers from Shah Najaf mark the beginning of the holy month of Muharram. Lakhnavis would observe the next ten days with solemnity. They would, moreover, reaffirm their unflinching devotion to those Islamic principles for which Imam Husain, grandson of the Prophet of Islam, and his companions laid down their lives on the banks of the river Euphrates in AD 680. Once more, they would, in their imagination, rally round those gallant men and women at Karbala who kept the Islamic flag flying without capitulating before the evil and tyrannical forces. They would once again desire to share in their *karb* (pain) and *bala* (trial). The ritual recreation of Karbala creates an environment that, in Clifford Geertz's terms, can 'establish powerful, pervasive, and long-lasting moods and motivations in men by formulating conceptions of a general order of existence and clothing those conceptions with such an aura of factuality that the moods and motivations seem uniquely realistic'.

Come day one of Muharram and life in Lucknow comes to a standstill. Perfume and tobacco shops wear a deserted look. Trade is no longer brisk. Business has slackened. The busy and noisy bazaars of Aminabad and Nakhaas are subdued. The city is robbed of its buoyancy and festive look. Meer Hasan Ali, an English lady married to a Shia and living in Lucknow in the 1820s, contrasted the profound stillness of an extensively populated city with the incessant bustle usual at all other times.[1]

The change is also manifested in other ways. Women, including the newly-wed, remove their jewellery, their bangles and flashy clothes; 'the hair is unloosed . . . and allowed to flow in disorder about the person; the coloured pyjamahs (loose trousers) and duppattas (long scarf) are removed, with every other articles of their usual costume, for a suit that, with them, constitutes mourning—some choose black, others grey, slate, or green'.[2] Comfort, luxury and convenience are set aside. The *pallung*, the *charpoy* (the two descriptions of beds) and the *musnad* are removed. Instead, women of all classes use a date mat or simply sleep on a matted floor.[3] Men are equally abstemious, sporting white *angarkhas* (a combination of the *jama*, a collarless shirt and *balabar*) or *achkans* (knee-length tunics) in dark shades. Poets, accustomed to regaling large audiences with *ghazals*, switch to writing *marsiyas* (elegies) and *soz* (dirges). Their chief patrons, the rajas and nawabs, abandon their favourite pastimes to lead a life of piety. Their palaces, *havelis* and forts bear a sombre look during Muharram.

Courtesans and their retinue in the Chowk area put away their musical instruments, their *ghungrus*, *payals* and the *tabla*. Umrao Jan Ada's 'Khanum' commemorated Husain's martyrdom on a more elaborate scale than any other courtesan in Lucknow, decorating the place of mourning with banners, buntings, chandeliers and globes. She was herself an accomplished *soz-khwan* (reciter of dirges). The most celebrated professionals dared not perform in her presence.[4] Her account finds resonances in Attia Hosain's description of her visit down 'the forbidden street whose balconies during the first days of Muharram were empty of painted, bejewelled women when visitors climbed the narrow stairs only to hear religious songs of mourning'.[5] There was the glass *tazia,* the miniature domed tomb, shining, gleaming, reflecting the light of many crystal lamps.

The city's black clad men and women set aside their daily chores to sorrow for the martyred Imam and his loyal and courageous companions. They marched through the lanes and bylanes in fervent lamentation chanting 'Ya-Husain, Ya-Husain', rhythmically beating their chests, self-flagellating, carrying replicas (*tazia*) of Husain's tomb, his coffin (*taboot*), his standards and insignia (*alam* and *panja*) and his horse (*dul-dul*). One of the most impressive religious spectacles, commented William Crooke, was the long procession of *tazias* and flags streaming along the streets with a vast crowd of mourners, who 'scream out their lamentations and beat their breasts till the blood flows or they sink fainting in an ecstasy of sorrow'.[6] Notice, the following description:

> The sun was high above the church steeple when we heard the distant chanting, 'Hasan! Husain! Hasan! Husain! Haider!' It came nearer and the measured sound of bare hands striking bare breasts, the monotonous beat of drums and cymbals made my heart beat with a strange excitement. Then the barefooted, bareheaded men came in view following the *tazias* carried shoulder-high. There were *tazias* of peacock's feathers, of glass, of sugar, of bright-coloured paper, intricate, beautiful arched domed, some as high as telegraph poles, others from poor homes so small that they could be held on one man's head, all hurrying to join the main procession at the allotted time, for burial or, consecration.[7]

Such devotional activities in public were just a small part of Muharram ceremonies. The imambaras (literally, the house of Imam), symbolizing Lucknow's Shia past and present, served as central organizing spaces, physical statements uniting the populace of the city,[8] symbols of communitarian solidarity, and as platforms for articulating individual and collective experiences. Here the gatherings (*majlis*) were structured, adhering to a pattern laid down by the Shia nawabs of Awadh. Beginning with *soz-khwani* (recitation without the aid of musical instruments), a *majlis* would be followed by a sermon or *marsiya-khwani* (reading of elegy), a style of rendering inspired by the legendary Lucknow poet, Mir Anis (1802-75) and conclude with short dirges. 'As soon as the impressive and heart-rendering notes of dirges were chanted by Mir Ali Hasan and Mir Bandey Hasan', wrote the essayist-novelist Abdul Halim Sharar (1860-1926),

> hundreds of men from élite families began to sing them, and then the women of noble Shia families also intoned them with their matchless voices. Matters have now reached the stage that during Muharram and on most days of mourning, heart-rending sounds of lamentation and the melodious chanting of dirges can be heard from every house in every lane in old Lucknow. In every alley one will hear beautiful voices and melodies which one will never forget.[9]

The sermon is an elegiac account of the episodes in the Karbala story, a moving narrative of the pain, anguish, and agony of Husain and his companions. Year after year speakers detail the sequence of events, retaining the order in which individual members of Husain's family were killed. Thus the sixth of Muharram is connected with Husain's young nephew, the seventh with his 18-year old son, the eighth with the brave and devoted brother Abbas, the ninth with the 6-month old son Ali Asghar, and the tenth with Imam Husain's own martyrdom. Qasim, Ali Akbar, Abbas, Ali Asghar and Husain himself exemplified the enormity of the tragedy; so that days linked with their martyrdom convey deep meanings, special attachments, and associations. Their experiences, narrated by an *alim* or a *mujtahid*, move audiences (*azadars*) to mourn, wail and lament, beat their chests (*matam*), and, in this way, share in the sufferings of the martyrs by self-deprivation and mortification. Again, the novelist Attia Hosain captures the mood in Lucknow:

> It was the ninth night of Muharram. On the horizon there was a glow as of a forgetful sun rising before moonset. The glow of a million lamps from the illuminated Imambaras where *tazias* and banners were laid to rest, lit the sky, and the city was alive, crowds forgetful in that bright beauty of the month of mourning . . . . When he (Asad) read of the agonies of thirst of the children of the Prophet, cut off from the river by their enemies, the women sobbed softy. Ustaniji began beating her breast, saying 'Hassan-Husain' softly, with a slow rhythm. Ramzano stared at her strangely and joined in. The others still sobbed softly.[10]

Ten days of mourning ceremonies culminate on *Yaum-i Ashura* with the *Majlis-i Sham-i Ghariban* at the famous Ghufkramab Imambara, the final mournful tribute to the *Saiyid-ash-Shuhada* (Lord of the Martyrs). The final curtain is drawn on Chehlum, the fortieth day. Sharar described a procession of women carrying *tazias* at the Talkatora Karbala. All were bareheaded and their hair hung loose. In the centre a woman carried a candle. By its light a beautiful, delicately formed girl read from some sheets of paper. She chanted a dirge along with other women. Moved by the 'stillness, the moonlight, those bareheaded beauties and the soul-rending notes of their sad melody', he heard the following lament as the group passed through the gates of the shrine:

> When the caravan of Medina, having lost all
> Arrived in captivity in the vicinity of Sham
> Foremost came the head of Husain, borne aloft on a spear
> And in its wake, a band of women, with heads bared.[11]

II

Muharram, Husain and Karbala signified different things to different sections of Lucknow society. Some saw in the observances the potential for political mobilization. The khilafat leadership and the votaries of Pakistan could therefore employ the paradigm of Karbala and harness the most evocative themes of Shi'ism to provide depth to their movements.[12] Husain's martyrdom also served, to the Shias of all times and in all places, as an everlasting exhortation to guard their separate identity, and to brave their numerical inferiority in the face of firmly established and sometimes oppressive majorities. It made sense, according to Hamid Enayat, on two other levels: first, in terms of a soteriology not dissimilar to the one invoked in the case of Christ's crucifixion—just as Christ sacrificed himself at the altar of the cross to redeem humanity, so did Husain allow himself to be killed on the plains of Karbala to purify the Muslim community of sins; and second, as an active factor vindicating the Shia cause, contributing to its ultimate triumph. When one adds to all this the cathartic effect of weeping as a means of releasing pent-up grief over not only personal misfortune but also the agonies of a long-suffering minority, then the reasons for the popular appeal of Muharram ceremonies become apparent.[13]

Husain stirred the passions and sensitivities of several groups. On the night of ninth Muharram, groups of women, largely Hindus, moved about the villages wailing and reciting, mostly improvised lyrics, on the epic tragedy. Urban and rural Hindus venerated Husain, incorporated his cult into their rituals,[14] offered flowers and sweets at local Karbalas, participated in processions, decorated and kept *tazias*, and sought Husain's intercession to cure the diseased, avert calamities, procure children for the childless or improve the circumstances of the dead. The Imam's trial and tribulations inspired faith in a universal nemesis ensuring justice for the oppressed souls. In popular belief and mythology he was the Ram of

Ayodhya carrying his crusade into the wilderness; his brother Abbas personified Lakshman—devoted, energetic and brave; his sister Zainab and wife Um-i Kulsoom, the surviving witnesses to the slaughter at Karbala, were cast in the image of Sita, caring, dutiful and spirited. Yazid, the Umayyad ruler and Husain's persecutor, was Ravana, greedy, corrupt, ambitious, cruel, and ruthless.

W.H. Sleeman found Hindu princes in central and southern India, 'even of the brahmin caste', commemorating Muharram with 'illuminations and processions . . . brilliant and costly'. In Gwalior, a Hindu state, Muharram was observed with splendid pomp. So also in Baroda, where the ruler sent an exquisite prayer carpet of pearls to Mecca.[15] Travellers discovered Hindus clothed in green garments and assuming the guise of faqirs.[16] So did Jafar Sharif.[17] A Hindi newspaper reported in July 1895 that Muharram had passed off peacefully in Banaras. 'When it is Hindus who mostly celebrate [*sic*] this festival, what fear can there be?'[18] In Lucknow, 'thousands of Hindus chanted *dohas* along with the Shias and Sunnis'.[19] Shiva Prasad kept a *tazia* in a specially prepared shed. On the tenth of the month, the elaborate man-high tomb made of bright-coloured paper and tinsel was carried to its burial in procession. The Muslim servants recited dirges, while Shiva Prasad and his sons followed in barefooted, bareheaded respect.[20]

This was not all. Munshi Faizuddin's reminiscences, published in 1885, described Muharram rites in the court of the last two Mughal emperors.[21] So does Saiyid Ahmad Dehlawi's (b. 1946) *Rusum-i Dehli* (Rituals and Traditions of Delhi), written some decades later.[22] The Sunni raja of Nanpara had Shia ulama read to him elegies for Husain.[23] In Allahabad, Sunnis took out 122 of the 220 *tazias*.[24] Rural Muslims, Crooke declared in 1897, joined the Muharram observance 'almost without distinction of sect'.[25] A Western scholar of Indian Islam was struck by the Shia influences on 'the length and breadth of the Sunni community'.[26] In a small north Indian princely state, a British civil servant found every Muslim guild—the painters, the masons, the carpenters, the weavers—having their own *tazias* and their own troupes of actors and mourners who reproduced scenes of the struggle at Karbala.[27] Here and elsewhere, Shia-Sunni relations were not structured around sectarian lines. Regardless of the polemics of the ulama and the itinerant preachers, bonds of friendship and understanding remained intact among Shias and Sunnis of all classes. Most shared a language and literature and a cultural heritage. This is probably why Sharar declared that no one in Lucknow ever noticed who was a Sunni and who a Shia.[28]

Lucknow was, both before and during the nawabi rule, relatively free of religious insularity or sectarian bigotry. The Shia nawabs took their cue from their Sunni overlords in Delhi to create a broad-based polity and a cosmopolitan cultural and intellectual ethos. They adhered to the policy of *sulh-i kul* (peace with all), pioneered by the Mughal emperor Akbar. Wajid Ali Shah is reported to have said that 'of my two eyes, one is a Shia and the other is a Sunni'. Sunni officials occupied important positions in the middle and lower echelons of government department. The highest officials in Wajid Ali Shah's court, including the vazir and paymaster, were Sunnis. Sunni officers also managed the Sibtainabad Imambara and the *baitul buka* (house of lamentation).[29] Generally speaking, the Awadh rulers provided both a liminal cultural glue and a set of structural lines of schism along which conflict could be routed.[30]

Shia-Sunni controversies did not plague most princely states. Several Shia families from Awadh, such as the Saiyids of Bilgram, sought and secured lucrative positions in Hyderabad. Shia-Sunni marriages were commonly contracted in princely states like Rampur, as also in *taluqdari* families. Shias and Sunnis forged a common front in literary and political associations, acted in unison during the Urdu agitation against the April 1900 Nagri resolution of the government in UP, and shared the Muslim League platform. They were one in agitating over the Kanpur mosque, the Aligarh Muslim University issue, and, much to everybody's surprise, on the khilafat question. The raja of Mahmudabad, a devout Shia, kept these causes alive. He patronized the 'young party', funded their newspapers and their agitations. James Meston, lieutenant-governor of UP, reported that a 'clique of noisy and aggressive Muslims of the young party made the raja's house their headquarters and lived and agitated at his expense'.[31]

Urdu prose and poetry, too, offers no clue to polarized Shia-Sunni sentiments. The writings of Saiyid Ahmad Khan, Hali, Shibli, maulvi Zakaullah, maulvi Nazir Ahmad and Abdul Halim Sharar were free of sectarian claptrap. In 1889, Sharar wrote *Hasan aur Anjalina*; Shia-Sunni relations was its theme. The great Urdu poet Asadullah Khan Ghalib wore no sectarian badge, no sectarian colour. He was 'a pure unitarian and true believer'. Suspected by some to be a Shia and by others as a *tafzili* (one who, though a Shia, acknowledges the pre-eminence of Ali), Ghalib revelled in the ambivalence. In fact, there was some confusion at his death as to whether his funeral rites should follow Shia or Sunni rituals.

Dakhni and modern Urdu poetry were both rich in *manqabat*, poems in praise of Ali, and in *marsiyas*, authored by both Shias and Sunnis. Husain is everybody's hero, the embodiment of Islamic virtues of piety, courage and commitment. He laid down his life but did not compromise with a bloody-minded tyrant presiding over a degenerate political and social order. His exemplary courage inspired Mohamed Ali, the volatile khilafat leader, to observe that while Yazid won on the bank of Euphrates it was Husain who 'reigned and still reigns over the hearts of a faith of God's human creation, while the soul of humankind in its entirety applauds the victory and final triumph of the victims of Karbala and shall continue to do so. . . .'[32]

> *Qatl-i Husain asl me marg-i Yazid hai*
> *Islam zinda hota hai har Karbala be baad.*
>
> Husain's assassination, in reality, symbolizes the death of Yazid.
> Islam is revived in the wake of every Karbala.

Iqbal echoed similar sentiments: 'Strange and simple and colourful is the story of Kaaba; its end is Husain, its beginning Ismail.' Husain was a model of the Perfect Man who becomes a martyr in his strife for God's unity against the rulers of the world. Every age brings forth a new Yazid, but resistance to tyranny, as evident in Husain's legendary example, is incumbent upon every believer.[33] Employing the paradigms of Husain and Karbala, Iqbal sent forth the message:

> *Nikal kar khanqahon se ada kar rasm-i Shabbiri.*
>
> Emerge from the confines of the Khanqahs and,
> re-enact the example set by Husain.

All of this underlined the importance of Husain, Muharram and Karbala as living and vibrant symbols of India's composite cultural interaction, the intermixing of religio-cultural strands, and the fusion of religious beliefs and practices. Yet, by the end of the nineteenth century, such representations of unity gradually gave way to symbols of discord. They served, in the hands of the politician-priest combine, to heighten sectarian consciousness, assert judicial and political rights, and widen areas of competition and disharmony. Each side came to nurse profound grievances about the other based on mutually exclusive interpretations of history.

The first ominous sign surfaced around 1906, when some Sunni zealots constructed their own local Karbala at Phoolkatora on the north-eastern edge of Lucknow, opposite the existing one in Talkatora. The fires of sectarian unrest were then stoked by the public praise (*madhe sahaba*) of the three khalifas—Abu Bakr, Umar and Usman—whom the Shias regarded as 'usurpers' of Ali's claim to be the successor of the Prophet.

The Shias retaliated with a vilification (*tabarra*) campaign. Sunni preachers, on the other hand, declared Muharram observances as acts of *biddat* (heresy). They exhorted their followers to avoid them scrupulously.[34] Zafarul Mulk, secretary of the Lucknow Madhe Sahaba Committee, declared *taziadari* 'deleterious to the spiritual and temporal well-being of the Muslims'.[35] The nature of the Shia-Sunni engagement inevitably led to the appropriation of certain symbols and the rejection of others.

The writing on the wall was clear; Muharram was no longer a common symbol of veneration but an exclusively Shia concern both in its format as well as in the composition of the participants.[36] By the 1930s, its popular appeal had considerably diminished, though less so in the rural hinterland.[37] A powerful symbol of unity was transformed into a potent vehicle for sectarian mobilization; in consequence, Shia-Sunni strife became much more common in certain north Indian towns than Hindu-Muslim riots. Shia-Sunni frictions were sparked off in Lucknow in the 1880s and 1890s and 1907-8. 'The feeling of tension between the Sunnis and Shias of Lucknow had reached its climax', reported the *Gauhar-i Shahwar* in April 1907.[38] Allahabad, Banaras and Jaunpur witnessed widespread violence. What began as small-scale skirmishes during the last quarter of the nineteenth century (many went unnoticed in official despatches because they were listed in the category of 'Native Societies and Religious and Social Matters' in the 'Selections from the Native Newspapers') escalated into bloody feuds involving scores of people and turning several areas, including Lucknow and its adjoining districts, into a cauldron of sectarian animus.

The lines of cleavage were sharply demarcated by the mushroom growth of sectarian organizations, such as the Anjuman-i Sadr-us Sudoor, floated by maulana Saiyid Agha Husain in 1901, and the Anjuman-i Jafariya, established by the Saiyids of Barha four years later. A Shia conference was set up in October-December 1907, some months after the Muslim League came into being. There was much talk of 'Shias of light' leading the way and mitigating the economic and educational backwardness of their community. Some conveyed their grievances to the British government, including the viceroy.[39]

The depth of sectarian feelings surfaced at the first Shia Conference in 1907. Delegates delivered fiery and intemperate speeches against the Sunnis. The atmosphere was so vitiated that Gulam-us Saqlain, editor of *Asr-i Jadid*, left the meeting in disgust. The hardliners seized the initiative in renaming the organization as the Shia Political Conference, petitioned the government in December 1909 to enumerate the Shia population separately in the census, and insisted on their separate and distinct identity.[40] The conference, initially formed to foster cultural and educational goals, turned into a powerful vehicle for articulating sectional political goals.

In the mid-1930s, the Shia Political Conference, now firmly controlled by Saiyid Wazir Hasan, the architect of the Congress-League scheme of December 1916, rallied round the Congress and supported the Muslim Mass Contact Campaign, Jawaharlal Nehru's brainchild. At the same time, it continued to clamour for separate representation in the legislative councils, a demand spurred by the defeat of two Shia candidates in the 1937 elections. The *Sarfaraz*, a Shia weekly from Lucknow, attributed their defeat to the 'venomous' Sunni propaganda and called for safeguarding Shia 'national and political rights'.[41] The Anjuman-i Tanzimul Muminin expressed lack of faith in the Muslim League, a body controlled by the 'Sunni Junta'. So did Saiyid Ali of the Shia Students' Conference. The Majlis-i Ulama, held at Lucknow on 5 July 1945, endorsed the memorandum sent by Hosseinbhoy A. Laljee to Wavell as well as the Congress High Command. The Shia Federation threatened to organize strikes, boycotts and demonstrations if its demands were not fulfilled.[42]

These were empty threats. Although sections in the Congress sympathized with Shia aspirations, they were not willing to raise the 'Shia case' in negotiating with the British and the League. Likewise, the government had no reason or compulsion to recognize the Shias as a major political force. 'We cannot give them special help' was how an official reacted. 'We cannot contemplate', commented a senior member in the Home department, 'treating religious sub-division of Muslims as a new minority'. Inevitably, the future editors of the transfer of power documents ignored Shia petitions in their compilation. 'Not wanted: I don't think we need bother at all with those cables from the Shias.'[43]

III

Lucknow was the scene of violent Shia-Sunni riots in 1938-9. These were a sequel to a protest movement, launched in May 1935, against an official suggestion to forbid *madhe sahaba* on certain days.[44] The agitation gained intensity a year later. It turned violent in May-June 1937, with frenzied mobs in Lucknow and Ghazipur going on a rampage. Trouble in Ghazipur was instigated by some Sunnis from Jaunpur. Enraged mobs burnt and looted property, and killed at will. The summer of discontent rumbled on. Sectarian strife, hitherto dormant, became a common occurrence in the daily lives of Lakhnavis.[45]

More trouble was fuelled during the next two years against a committee's ruling against *madhe sahaba* in Lucknow.[46] Husain Ahmad Madani, principal of the Deoband seminary, along with some other Jamiyat al-ulama leaders, advocated civil disobedience. Thousands courted arrest. Although a fervent advocate of secular nationalism and a principled critic of the 'two-nation theory', the Maulana stirred sectarian passions. He spoke at a public meeting in Lucknow on 17 March 1938, sharing the platform with the firebrand Maulvi Abdul Shakoor, head of the Dar al-Muballighin, and Maulana Zafarul Mulk, the chief exponent of *madhe sahaba* in Lucknow.[47] Elsewhere, the Ahrars and the Khaksars developed common cause with the Jamiyat al-ulama. The mercurial Khaksar leader, Allama Mashriqi, mobilized his followers from different places, although police vigilance made sure that not many sneaked into the city's municipal limits.[48] The Ahrars, fresh from their successful agitation against the maharaja of Kashmir, organized bands of volunteers (*jatha*) in Lucknow. They came from neighbouring Malihabad, Kanpur, Delhi, Meerut, and from as far as Peshawar. By the end of March 1939, hundreds were arrested. 'Tension in the city', wrote Lucknow's deputy-commissioner, 'has increased and is now nearing breaking point.'[49]

On 30 March, the Congress ministry bowed to such pressures and allowed *madhe sahaba* on *Barawafat*, the Prophet's birthday. While Sunni leaders promptly called off civil disobedience and organized a 30,000 strong *Barawafat* procession to register their victory, the Shia confidence in the Congress ministry was jolted. The *Sarfaraz* chided G.B. Pant and his ministerial colleagues for their capitulation.[50] An impression gained credence that the Congress had played a 'double game' by contravening established conventions in Lucknow, sowed the seeds of Shia-Sunni dissension, and stoked the fires of sectarian unrest to weaken the Muslim League's claim to represent the Muslim community. This was not an uncommon occurence. C.A. Bayly's study has shown how the Muslim leadership in Allahabad, poorly integrated into both the formal and informal system of power, had become an object of attention for political orators to exploit sectarian fissures.[51]

The Shias responded angrily to the ministerial decree. A large crowd assembled a day after at the imposing Asaf ud-Daula Imambara, indulged in *tabarra*, and excitedly climbed the upper stories of the gateway. Some rushed towards the nearby Tila Mosque, though the police blocked their onward march. Pandemonium prevailed; others set fire to nearby shops. A free exchange of brickbats ensued, and people waved weapons they had acquired from the *shamianas* and palisades. The police opened fire, dispersed the mob, and imposed curfew.[52] The scholar S. Khuda Bukhsh (b. 1842) was anguished to see a posse of police with glistening bayonets in Lucknow. 'Well might we heave a deep sigh at sight such as this? Has time turned its (Islamic) precepts of brotherly love and fraternal unity into sad, mocking derision? These were the mournful thoughts as my carriage glided down the road.' He was sorry that . . . the fabric of Islam is torn by dissensions, fierce and bitter; and that nobody was trying to restore peace, concord and harmony among Muslim. What a noble sight it is to see the police officers interfere at Muharram between the followers of the Prophet to prevent a breach of peace.[53]

Harry Haig, lieutenant-governor of UP, felt that sanctioning *madhe sahaba* set up among Shias conditions of intense emotional hysteria and stiffened their resolve to indulge in *tabarra*.[54] As he had foreseen, Shias assembled each day at the Asafi Imambara, recited *tabarra* on the Husainabad Road, and then courted arrest chanting '*Ya Ali*', '*Ya Ali*'. Tension mounted each day. 'No one knows', wrote an exasperated official in March 1939, 'from hour to hour—let alone from day to day—what will happen next.'[55]

There were other outward signs of protest. The Shia *mujtahid*, Maulana Nasir Husain, threatened to court arrest. So did the wife of Wazir Hasan, member of an influential family, and their son Saiyid Ali Zaheer.[56] Trouble spread to other areas as well. Volunteers from Agra, Kanpur, Fyzabad, Bara Banki and Rampur sneaked into Lucknow in early April to assist their beleaguered brethren. Plans were set afoot in Rae Bareli to congregate in Lucknow on *Barawafat* and participate in the planned *tabarra* agitation.[57] A batch of burqa-clad women from Rae Bareli turned up at Kazimain, a predominantly Shia locality, to court arrest, though the Shia *mujtahid* ultimately dissuaded them from doing so.[58] In August, Shias of Kanpur observed hartal against the police firing in Lucknow, wore badges on their arms, and fluttered black flags on their houses. Riots also broke out in Banaras.[59] A report published in August 1941 suggested that the 'attempt to find a solution to the Shia-Sunni dispute in Lucknow appears to have been abandoned'.[60]

Nehru, having spent some time in Lucknow trying to resolve the Shia-Sunni deadlock, commenting on the tactlessness of his colleagues in dealing with the disputes. 'I fear there has been much bungling about this issue', he wrote to Maulana Azad, who was not consulted before the UP ministry executed a volte-face. The matter was decided, he told the Maulana, 'without full consideration of the consequences'.[61] Rajendra Prasad, having been closely associated with some leading Shias of Bihar, such as Ali Imam, Husain Imam and Sultan Ahmad, was equally wary of the consequences. He observed:

> I presume the Shias will continue civil disobedience and will be courting jail. . . . It must be very distressing to put nine thousand people in jail who are apparently not opposed to the government and many amongst whom are widely respected for one reason or the other. What troubles me even more is the propaganda which is gaining ground that the Congress stands to create division amongst Musalmans and what I apprehend is that after a time both will be more united against the Congress than they have ever been before.

Rajendra Prasad added that the Shias were ardent nationalists and the Shia Political Conference had consistently acted in unison with the Congress. For these reasons, the ministry should not have allowed anti-Congress sentiments 'to grow in any community and more so in a community sympathetically inclined'.[62]

IV

The Shias were few in number, not exceeding 4 per cent in any of the provinces in British India (Tables 4.1-2). They were most numerous in Lucknow and the satellite townships. Here, the imambaras and mosques stood as reminders of Shia domination under the nawabs. Elsewhere in UP, they were unevenly distributed in Jaunpur where the Sharqis once held sway, in Machhlishahar,[63] Bilgram, Sandila, Allahabad, Jalali in Aligarh district,[64] Jansath in Muzaffarnagar, Moradabad, Amroha, Sambhal, Budaun, and Rampur.[65] The nawab of Rampur and the raja of Mahmudabad and his kinsmen in Bilehra and Bhatwamau were Shias. Successful professional men were few, although some like Hamid Ali Khan, a Lucknow lawyer, Saiyid Raza Ali, Saiyid Ghulam-us-Saqlain, Saiyid Wazir Hasan and his son, Ali Zaheer, Saiyid Hyder Mehdi, Congressman and chairman of the Allahabad Improvement Trust, occupied prominent positions in public life. Some achieved fame as writers and poets in the early 1940s or thereafter, notably Saiyid Ehtesham Husain of Lucknow; Khwaja Ahmad Abbas, a descendant of Hali; Saiyid Sajjad Zaheer, son of Wazir Hasan and co-founder of the Progressive Writers' Movement; Ali Sardar Jafri of Balrampur state, an Aligarh student expelled from the university in the mid-1930s for his radical activities; and the poet Kaifi Azmi, who spent years in Bombay in the company of socialists and communists.

Yet, the success of such men does not reflect the condition of their Shia brethren, many of whom lagged far behind their Sunni counterparts. They were few in the professions, and fewer still in trade and commerce. The

Table 4.1: Shia and Sunni Population in India, 1921

Provinces and princely states	Muslim population	Shias	Sunnis
		(percentage)	
Assam	2,219,947	Nil	100
Baluchistan	773,477	1	96
Bengal	25,486,144	1	99
Bihar and Orissa	3,706,277	1	99
Bombay	4,660,828	3	88
CP and Berar	528,032	2	98
Madras	2,865,285	2	94
NWFP	2,084,123	4	95
Punjab and Delhi	12,955,141	2	97
Baroda	162,328	10	88
Kashmir	2,548,514	5	95
Rajputana and Ajmer	1,002,117	2	98

Source: *Census of India*, 1921, Vol. 1, p. 120.
Note: Figures for Bombay, Baroda and Rajputana and Ajmer include Khojas, Bohras, and in some cases, even Memons.

Table 4.2: Distribution of Shia and Sunni Population in UP, 1882

Division	Percentage of total Muslim population	
	Shias	Sunnis
Agra	1.5	98.5
Allahabad	5.3	94.7
Banaras	2.0	98.0
Faizabad	3.6	96.4
Jhansi	0.8	99.2
Lucknow	10.7	89.3
Meerut	2.3	97.7
Rae Bareli	1.8	98.2
Rohilkhand	1.6	98.4
Sitapur	1.7	98.3

Source: *Census of India*, NWFP and Oudh, 1882, Vol. 1, p. 74.

substantial group of poverty-stricken *wasiqadars* clung to the crumbling remains of their ancestral environs. In ghettos, or in the narrow lanes and alleys of Lucknow and Allahabad. In 1913, there were 1,661 *wasiqadars* in Lucknow, many living very much in the past. Some held durbars till as late as the early 1920s.[66] Their condition symbolized the decline of a class which owed its survival to nawabi patronage. Other Shia groups were not able to move up the ladder because they were poorly equipped to seize the opportunities in trade, business, professions and government service. Meston commented that the Shias were 'a community backward beyond all normal degrees of backwardness'.[67]

There can be no doubt that Shia-Sunni estrangement was related to the decline of the Shia aristocracy in the second half of the nineteenth century, the impoverishment of their less privileged brethren, and the relative prosperity of some Sunni groups which deepened Shia anxieties about their future.[68] They were estranged from a world dominated by the 'Other'. The British contributed to this process insofar as they gave legal definition to the Shia-Sunni divide. The approval or ban of religious commemorations, arbitration of disputes, and regulating religious procession routes transformed latent doctrinal differences into public, political and legal issues.[69] An even more powerful current at work towards the end of the nineteenth century appeared in the form of religio-revivalism, affecting the structure of both inter-as well as intra-community relations. Therefore, it is necessary to locate the Shia-Sunni schism in Lucknow, notwithstanding its local specificity, in the context of the countrywide religio-revivalist trends and tendencies.

It is widely known that the cow-protection societies, the Hindi Pracharni Sabhas and the Arya Samaj movement were designed to homogenize Hindu society with the aid of common cultural and religious and symbols. Similar currents, some in response to the intellectual and cultural hegemony of the West but most in reaction to Hindu revitalization campaigns, began to influence the Muslim educated classes as well. Towards the end of the nineteenth century, in particular, the notion of a sharply defined communitarian identity, distinct and separate from others, had acquired some degree of legitimacy among the *ashraf* Muslims. In the political and educational domain, Saiyid Ahmad Khan, despite his eclectic world view, plotted his trajectory within a communitarian framework. The Aligarh College, the All-India Muhammadan Educational Conference, the Urdu Defence Associations, and the Muslim League were concerned to create a Muslim identity in the public and private spaces.

Such concerns were matched by a concerted drive to create an ordered, unified, and cohesive religious community within the Islamic paradigm. Such was the goal of the founders of the Dar al-ulum at Deoband and the Nadwat al-ulama in Lucknow. Asserting their role as interpreters and guardians, they insisted, through sheafs of *fatawa*, on imposing a moral and religious code consistent with Koranic injunctions and free of accretions and interpolations. Not surprisingly, over 200 books listed in London's British Library catalogue, compiled by J.M. Blumhardt in 1900, dealt with ceremonial religious observances and includes compendia of religious duties, treatises on lawful and unlawful actions and collections of religious precepts. In a nutshell, the growth of the printing press, the proliferation of vernacular newspapers, and the expanding educational networks served as powerful instruments for restructuring an ideal community that would conform to and reflect the Islamic ethos that prevailed during the days of the Prophet and his immediate successors, the first four Khalifas.

Initially confined to north India, the Islamic resurgence spread to other areas rapidly. Religious revivalism, conducted under the aegis of the *faraizis*, had already swept the rural Muslims in the Bengal countryside. The dominant strain of the Islamization drive there and elsewhere was to reject composite and syncretic tendencies and to create, instead, a pan-Islamic or a specifically pan-Indian Muslim identity. Rafiuddin Ahmed has shown how religious preachers prompted the masses to look beyond the borders of Bengal in quest of their supposed Islamic past and attach greater importance to their 'Muslim' as opposed to their local or regional identity. This new emphasis proved crucial to the subsequent emergence of a measure of social cohesion in a diversified and even culturally polarized community.[70]

In relation to the Hindu 'Other', the meaning of being a Muslim was translated through late nineteenth-century religious and political idioms. Shias and Sunnis, on the other hand, discovered new symbols of identity in the form of separate graveyards, separate mosques, separate schools, and separate religious and charitable endowments.[71] These institutions defined the boundaries within which Shias and Sunnis were required to stay apart. They were to live as separate entities in a world fashioned primarily by the religio-political leadership. Attempts to disturb the status quo encountered strong resistance.

Sunni Islam was just as much 'corrupted' by the incorporation of Hindu beliefs and customs, as by the adoption of Shia practices. So a campaign was mounted, at the turn of the nineteenth century, to question shared cultural, religious and intellectual paradigms and revive those controversies that had been dormant for long. The *madhe sahaba* processions were, for example, organized with much greater fanfare in Fatehpur, where Maulana Saiyid Abid Husain first started the practice in 1901, and in Lucknow around 1908-9 with the backing of Maulana Saiyid Ainul Qazat, tutor of both the Firangi *alim* Maulana Abdul Bari and Maulvi Abdul Shakoor, one of the chief architects of the Sunni agitation in Lucknow.[72]

There was, in addition, a concerted move to discourage Shia-Sunni marriage, to portray Shias as promiscuous heretics, and as traitors to the country and to Islam. Frequently singled out as traitors were Mir Sadiq, diwan of Tipu Sultan, Mir Alam, diwan of Hyderabad, Mir Jafar, diwan of Siraj ud-Daula, and the Bilgrami family.[73] 'Among the people classed as Muslim', observed Zafarul Mulk,

> the Shias and the Ahmadis are the two sects which have basic differences with Muslims and are a constant source of internecine trouble and discord. . . . *It would be a real gain to the health of the body politic of Islam if these two sects were lopped off and treated as separate minorities*.[74] (italics mine)

The central theme, underlined years later by an *alim* of Nadwat al-ulama, was the impropriety of giving 'vent to one's feeling of sorrow through wailings and lamentation' and crying over a past event.[75] Around 1933-9, considerable polemical literature surfaced against *azadari*.[76] *Taziadari* was denounced as *bida* and *haram*.[77] In February 1939, the Tahaffuz-i Millat sought permission to take out small processions to dissuade Sunnis, by word of mouth, from *taziadari*.[78] Sharar, who bemoaned Shia-Sunni differences, observed how Abdul Shakoor perfected the art of public debates (*munazirah*) with his Shia counterparts.[79]

The indictment of Muharram rites was by no means a new development; on the other hand, the severity with which it was done in Lucknow during the 1930s had few historical precedents. It is true that orthodox Sunni treatises were critical of the Shias and averse to their practices. In the sixteenth century, Shaikh Ahmad Sirhindi, the chief exponent of the Naqshbandi *silsilah* in India, began his career by writing a pamphlet against them. Shah Waliullah, one of the foremost original thinkers in the history of Indian Islam, discussed the question of whether Shias were *Kuffar*, apostates, or just immoral. Shah Abdul Aziz wrote a highly polemical book in 1889 to prevent 'Sunnis from straying away from their faith in polemics with the Shias'. Deoband's Dar al-ulum, inspired by Waliullah and his disciples, was antithetical to Shia beliefs and practices. Saiyid Ahmad's invitation to Deoband's founders met with an emphatic refusal: they would not associate with a college that had room for Shias.[80] One of its foremost ulama, Husain Ahmad Madani, shared this antipathy, though he was, at the same time, a major proponent of secular nationalism. Yet, the diktat of an *alim* here or a theologian there did not undermine those values and customs that people had shared for generations. There were other schools of thought in Sunni Islam advocating reconciliation and rapprochement. In fact, many of the Shia *mujtahids*, including the renowned Maulvi Dildar Ali, were products of the Firangi Mahal in Lucknow, and there were, moreover, forces within Sufi Islam that cemented unity and integration.

Sectarianism in the 1930s, however, was of a distinct nature. The debates were no longer restricted to the khilafat. Nor were the age-old controversies confined to the learned and holy men. The energy released during the decade, spurred by newly-started organizations wedded to separate Sunni and Shia world views, substantially altered the structure of social relations. They imposed severe strains on the overall consensus that had been achieved through long-standing social cultural and economic networks. People were encouraged to transgress traditional codes of conduct and behaviour and organize themselves as a separate entity in opposition to the 'Other'. The emotional charge deepened the intensity and depth of sectarian conflicts, competition, and rivalries.

The Shias were not far behind in fortifying their claims. They tried, first of all, to rejuvenate their educational institutions which had virtually collapsed in the absence of nawabi patronage. They regarded the college at Aligarh as a 'Sunni' institution, though Saiyid Ahmad had, in recognition of Shia-Sunni differences; made a provision for teaching Shia theology. They had no theological seminary of their own. And because entry to Deoband or Nadwa was restricted to Sunni students, those Shias aspiring to become religious leaders received education not in India but in Iran and Iraq. Thus Saiyid Abdul Qasim Rizvi (d. 1906) studied in Lucknow and Najaf in Iraq. Back in Lahore, he promoted Usuli Shi'ism in the second half of the nineteenth century, founded congregational prayer mosques in the city and further north in Peshawar, built edifices for commemorating Husain's martyrdom, and establishing an *imami* seminary in Lahore with the backing of nawab Ali Raza Khan Qizilbash, a wealthy Shia landowner of Iranian origin.[81] Maulana Saiyid Ali Naqi (1903-88), a descendant of the learned Ghuframab family, also studied in Iraq. He returned to Lucknow in 1932, founded the Imamia Mission, and launched a weekly magazine *Payam-i Islam*. Many of his writings in the mid-1930s were in defence of *azadari*.[82]

The establishment of the Nadwat al-ulama led to the founding of a Shia school in Lucknow. The scheme of a Shia college, floated in March 1914, was the brainchild of Fateh Ali Khan Qizilbash, a landowner of Lahore with large estates in eastern UP, but was backed by nawab Hamid Ali Khan of Rampur and the UP government. The idea caught on fast. By mid-June 1916, Rs. 3,17,410 was raised. Because contributions came mainly from UP, there were demands to locate the college in the same province. The Syeds of Jansath in Muzaffarnagar district preferred Meerut. So did Rampur's nawab, though his preference for a city so far removed from his own area of influence is incomprehensible. Some suggested Agra, so that students 'do not imbibe political ideas in tender age and may cause inconvenience and trouble to the government'. But most settled for Lucknow, where the college gates were opened in 1917.[83]

Shia societies mushroomed in every quarter of Lucknow, the hub of Shia intellectual and cultural life. Prominent amongst them were the Madrasatul-Waizeen, organized on the lines of the Shibli Academy at Azamgarh and funded by the raja of Mahmudabad; the Imamia Mission, set up by Maulana Ali Naqi; and the Tanzimul-Muminin, the Shia answer to the Tahafuzz-i Millat, which was patronized by affluent manufacturers of tobacco and perfumes like Muhammad Umar and Asghar Ali, Muhammad Ali. These bodies were backed by an aggressive Shia-owned press—the *Sarfaraz*, an organ of the Shia Political Conference, *Shia*, printed in Lahore, and *Asad*, *Nazzara*, and the *Akhbar-i Imamia*, published fortnightly.[84]

With the country heading towards greater Hindu-Muslim friction, sectarian competition began to resemble inter-community conflicts. Not surprisingly, the process structuring sectarian conflict paralleled that of Hindu-Muslim friction in other urban centres of UP. This was, in part, because Sunnis and Shias of Lucknow could draw on the reservoir of experiences and models developed in the subcontinent during that period. That is, the nationwide impetus to defining one's community in relation to the other provided material that could be used by both groups of Muslims.[85] In general, such tendencies were not countered by a parallel ideological crusade, though individuals like Azad tried in vain to cement the divide, heal the wounds, and keep the recalcitrant parties in check.[86]

The Congress in UP also tried to defuse the mounting sectarian tensions in Lucknow, though most settled for a 'divide and rule' policy doling out concessions first to Shias and then to Sunnis. This strategy worked for a while. Shia leaders, having rallied round the Congress in the past, expected to be rewarded for their loyalty. The bulk of Sunni leaders were, on the other hand, enthused by Pant's gesture on 30 March 1939. They stayed put in the Congress. But their support, having been tied to short-term communitarian interests, was rapidly eroded when the Muslim League raised new hopes and expectations in the early 1940s.

Both the context and the reference point of the Shia and Sunni leaders were rapidly eroded by the powerful drive for a separate 'Muslim nation'. The forces of an overriding and hegemonic 'Muslim nationalism' subsumed sectarian allegiances. A British official had urged the Shias in 1946 'to sink their fortunes with the Sunnis and be treated as Muslims'.[87] So they did. Once the creation of Pakistan became imminent, the Shias and Sunnis hitched their fortunes to the Muslim League bandwagon, and undertook their long trek towards the promised *Dar al-Islam* (Land of Islam). They emerged from the ruptures of history to find that their strength lay in forging ahead, and exploring new options in the future homeland. They were tantalized by this new ideal, exemplified by a new leader. The ideological conflicts were, however, carried over to the new nation, where the inconclusive debates resumed with the same intensity and fervour.

NOTES

1. Meer Hasan Ali, *Observations on the Mussalmans of India*, New Delhi, 1982 rpt., p. 30.
2. Ibid., p. 46.
3. Ibid., p. 43.
4. Mirza Muhammad Hadi Ruswa, *Umrao Jan Ada*, translated by Khushwant Singh and M.A. Husain, Hyderabad, 1982, p. 48.
5. Attia Hosain, *Sunlight on a Broken Column*, New Delhi, 1992, p. 64.
6. W. Crooke, *The North-Western Provinces of India: Their History, Ethnology, and Administration*, New Delhi, 1975 rpt., p. 263.
7. Attia Hosain, *Sunlight on a Broken Column*, p. 72.
8. J.R.I. Cole, *Roots of North Indian Shi'ism in Iran and Iraq: Religion and State in Awadh 1772-1859*, Berkeley and Los Angeles, 1988, p. 98; and Freitag, *Collective Action and Community*, p. 237.
9. A.H. Sharar, *Lucknow: The Last Phase of an Oriental Culture,* translated and edited by E.S. Harcourt and Fakhir Hussain, London, 1975, p. 149.
10. Attia Hosain, *Sunlight on a Broken Column*, p. 68.
11. Sharar, *Lucknow: The Last Phase*, pp. 149-50.
12. See Hasan, *Nationalism and Communal Politics*, and my *Legacy of a Divided Nation*.
13. Hamid Enayat, *Modern Islamic Political Thought*, London, 1982, p. 20; and V.J. Schubel, 'Karbala as Sacred Space among North American Shia', in Barbara Daly Metcalf (ed.), *Making Muslim Space in North America and Europe*, Berkeley, 1996, pp. 186-204; Farnk Korom, 'Identity on the Move: A Trinidadian Shia Ritual in Transnational Perspective', unpublished

paper presented at North Carolina State University, Raleigh, 22-5 May 1997.
14. Cole, *Roots of North Indian Shi'ism*, pp. 116-17.
15. P.D. Reeves (ed.), *Sleeman in Oudh: An Abridgement of W.H. Sleeman's Journey Through the Kingdom of Oude in 1949-50*, Cambridge, 1971, pp. 158-9; Walter Roper Lawrence, *The India We Served*, London, 1928, pp. 292-3; Fuller, *Studies on Indian Life and Sentiment*, pp. 125-6; W.S. Blunt, *India Under Ripon: A Private Diary*, London, 1909, p. 72.
16. Freitag, *Collective Action and Community*, p. 259.
17. Jaffur Shureef, *Qanoon-e-Islam*, translated by G.A. Herklots, Madras, 1863, p. 123; see also Omar Khalidi, 'The Shias of the Deccan: An Introduction', in *Hamdard Islamicus*, Vol. 15, No. 4, 1992.
18. Nita Kumar, *The Artisans of Banaras: Popular Culture and Identity 1880-1986*, Princeton, N.J., 1988, p. 216.
19. Sharar, *Lucknow: The Last Phase*, p. 149.
20. Attia Hosain, *Phoenix Fled*, New Delhi, 1993, p. 176.
21. Munshi Faizuddin, *Bazm-i Akhir*, New Delhi, 1986, pp. 63-6.
22. Saiyid Ahmad Dehlawi, *Rusoom-i Delhi*, New Delhi, 1986, pp. 178-80.
23. Cole, *Roots of North Indian Shi'ism*, p. 105.
24. C.A. Bayly, *The Local Roots of Indian Politics—Allahabad 1880-1920*, Oxford, 1975, p. 81; for Bilgram, Saiyid Athar Raza Bilgrami, 'Bilgram Ki Azadari', in *Islam aur Asr-i Jadid*, Delhi, Vol. 25, No. 2, April 1993. For a brilliant description, Rahi Masoom Reza, *The Feuding Families of Ganguli*, trs. from Hindi by Gillian Wright, New Delhi, 1994.
25. Crooke, *The North-West Provinces of India*, p. 263.
26. Murray T. Titus, *Indian Islam*, Oxford, 1930.
27. Penderel Moon, *Strangers in India*, London, 1943, pp. 86-7.
28. Sharar, *Lucknow: The Last Phase*, pp. 74-5.
29. Ibid. This is not to suggest that the Awadh rulers did not express their solidarity with the Shias or that the Shias were not given preference in appointments. Fisher, *A Clash of Cultures*, pp. 65-6.
30. Ibid., p. 250.
31. Meston to Chelmsford 20 Aug. 1917, Meston papers (1), BL.
32. Mohamed Ali to A.A. Bukhari, 19 Nov. 1916, in Mushirul Hasan (ed.), *Mohamed Ali in Indian Politics: Select Writings 1906-1916*, Vol. 1, New Delhi, 1985, p. 301.
33. Quoted in A. Schimmel, *Gabriel's Wing: A Study into the Religious Ideas of Sir Muhammad Iqbal*, Leiden, 1963, p. 167.
34. Selection from Native Newspaper Reports UP (hereafter SNNR), for the week ending 19 Dec. 1936, and 20 Mar. 1937.
35. Zafarul Mulk, *Shia Sunni Dispute: Its Causes and Cure*, Servants of Islam Society Publication No. 3, n.d., p. 1.
36. The process was not confined to Lucknow; for Bombay, see Jim Masselos,

'Change and Custom in the Format of the Bombay Muharram during the 19th and 20th Centuries', *South Asia*, Australia, Dec. 1982, p. 61; and for Banaras, see Nita Kumar, *The Artisans of Banaras*, p. 216.

37. C. Khaliquzzaman, *Pathway to Pakistan*, p. 149. Referring to Bakhshu's *tazia* procession in Lucknow, Sharar commented: 'Nowadays, because of the quarrels between Shias and Sunnis, this procession lost its original form', Sharar, *Lucknow: The Last Phase*, p. 151.
38. April 1907, SNNR, UP, 1907.
39. *Surma-i Rozgar*, 1 Feb. 1907.
40. *Asr-i Jadid*, Meerut, Oct.-Dec. 1907.
41. *Sarfaraz*, 6, 7 and 13 May 1939.
42. Saiyid Ali to Jawaharlal Nehru, 6 Dec. 1945, Jawaharlal Nehru papers, Vol. 4, NMML; Hosseinbhoy A. Laljee's Cablegram to Wavell, 6 Apr. 1945, in *Shia Muslim's Case*, Bombay, n.d., pp. 1-2, 6-96; L/P and J/8, 693; Transfer of Power papers, L/P and J, 10/64, BL.
43. 18 Feb. and 16 Dec. 1946, 16 Dec. 1974, ibid., L/P7/J, 10, 64.
44. Note by the Intelligence Department on the Shia-Sunni controversy in Lucknow, Home Poll. D., File No. 75/6, NAI.
45. Shia-Sunni riots broke out in May-June 1937. The provincial government believed that the Shias provoked them to indicate that any change introduced in their past practices would be resisted. Harry Haig to Linlithgow, 7 Jun. and 4 Jul. 1937, 2-4 Jun. 1938, 10 and 23 Oct. 1939, L/PJ/5/264-6.
46. The government appointed the Piggot Committee (1907) to regulate Muharram observances. This was followed by the Justice Allsop Committee recommendations of 15 Jun. 1937. The high court judge endorsed the Piggot Committee's report on *madhe sahaba*. Government Gazette of the UP, Extraordinary, 28 Mar. 1939, L/P and J/ File No. 265, pp. 139-50, BL.
47. G.M. Harper to Jasbir Singh, 18 Mar. 1939, General Administration Department (GAD), File No. 65, Box 607, UP State Archives, Lucknow. Harry Haig reported that Madani insisted that the Sunnis should be allowed to assert their right to recite *madhe sahaba*. To Linlithgow, 23 Oct. 1939, L/P/266.
48. Haig to Linlithgow, 6 Sept. 1939, L/P and J/5/26.
49. Jasbir Singh to Harper, 24 Mar. 1939, UPSA.
50. *Sarfaraz*, 30 Mar. 1939.
51. Bayly, *Local Roots*, p. 130.
52. Harper to chief secretary, 16 Mar. 1939, GAD, File No. 65, Box No. 607, UPSA.
53. *Essays: Indian and Islamic*, London, 1912, pp. 215 and 273-4.
54. Haig to Linlithgow, 18 Apr. 1939, Linlithgow papers (microfilm), New Delhi.
55. Jasbir Singh to Harper, 13 Mar. 1939, UPSA.
56. Wazir Hasan's wife was chairman of the All-India Shia Women's Association.
57. Harper to chief secretary, 16 Mar. 1939, UPSA.

58. Ibid.
59. *Pioneer*, 24 Aug. 1939, Kanpur's superintendent of police reported a Shia-Sunni riot and the impending threat of the Ahrars to take out a *madhe sahaba* procession defying government orders, 10 Jun. 1939, Diaries, Harold Charles Mitchell papers, BL. For Banaras, Charles Allen (ed.), *Plain Tales from the raj*, London, 1981, pp. 246-7.
60. L/P and J/5/272. See also fortnightly report, second half of Mar. 1940, L/P and J/5/270. In 1943, Sunnis in Lucknow tried to revive the *madhe sahaba* agitation and defy the ban on the *Barawafat* procession which fell about the middle of March. This led to the externment of some Sunni leaders from Lucknow. Fortnightly report, second half of Jan. 1943, L/PJ/5/272.
61. Nehru to Azad, 17 Apr. 1939, *SWJN*, Vol. 9, pp. 334-5.
62. To Nehru, 16 May 1939, Valmiki Choudhary (ed.), *Dr Rajendra Prasad: Correspondence and Select Documents*, Vol. 3, New Delhi, 1984, p. 77.
63. 'Many of the respectable Mussalmans of Jaunpur and the town Machhlishahar belong to this (Shia) denominaton.' *District Gazetteer* (*DG*), UP of Agra and Oudh, Vol. 28, Allahabad, 1908, p. 85.
64. For Syeds of Jalali, see Saiyid Muhammad Kamaluddin Husian Hamadani, *Siraj-i Manir*, Aligarh, 1978.
65. *DG*, Muzaffarnagar, Vol. 3, pp. 114-15; *DG*, Sitapur, Vol. 11, pp. 105-6.
66. Sarojini Ganju, 'The Muslims of Lucknow, 1919-39', in K. Ballhatchet and J. Harrison (eds.), *The City in South Asia: Pre-Modern and Modern*, London, 1980, p. 286.
67. UP Govt. (Education Department), File No. 398, 1926, UPSA.
68. Imtiaz Ahmad, 'The Shia-Sunni Dispute in Lucknow', in Milton Israel and N.K. Wagle (eds.), *Islamic Society and Culture: Essays in Honour of Professor Aziz Ahmad*, New Delhi, 1983; Ganju, 'The Muslims of Lucknow', pp. 290, 292.
69. Keith Hjortshoj, 'Shi'i Identity and the Significance of Muharram in Lucknow India', in Martin Kramer (ed.), *Shi'ism: Resistance and Revolution*, London, 1987, p. 291.
70. Ahmed, *The Bengali Muslims*, p. 184.
71. As early as 1871, Shias and Sunnis, in separate formal representations, demanded 'distinct and separate burial grounds'. V.T. Oldenburg, *The Making of Colonial Lucknow 1856-1877*, Princeton, N.J., 1984.
72. Zafarul Mulk, *Shia-Sunni Dispute*, op. cit., p. 11.
73. Omar Khalidi, op. cit., pp. 39-40.
74. Zafarul Mulk, op. cit.
75. S. Abul Hasan Ali Nadwi, *The Mussalman*, Lucknow, 1974 edn., p. 65.
76. See, for example, Proscribed Publications (Urdu), 52, 9[illegible], 139, BL.
77. SNNR, UP for the week ending, 19 Dec. 1936, and 20 Mar. 1937.
78. Jasbir Singh to Harper, 10 Feb. 1939, UPSA.
79. Sharar, *Lucknow: The Last Phase*, p. 95.
80. Lelyveld, *Aligarh's First Generation*, p. 134; see also, [illegible].A.A. Rizvi, *Shah Abd*

Al-Aziz, p. 256. For Deoband, Metcalf, *Islamic Revival in British India*, and Sharar, *Lucknow: The Last Phase*, p. 95, for a brief history of public debates in Lucknow.

81. See 'Introduction', in J.R.I. Cole and Nikkie R. Keddie (eds.), *Shi'ism and Social Protest*, New Haven, 1986, pp. 66-7; Cole, op. cit., pp. 288-9, and Freitag, op. cit., p. 263, for the contribution of Maqbul Ahmad to reformist tendencies among Shias.
82. This information is based on Salamat Rizvi, *Saiyid al-ulama; Hayat aur Karnamen*, Lucknow, 1988.
83. 'Establishment of a Shia college at Lucknow', 25 Oct. 1917, UP Govt. (Education), File No. 398, 1926, UPSA; Fateh Ali Khan to Meston, 21 Oct. 1915, File No. 136/15, Meston papers. The raja of Mahmudabad and Saiyid Wazir Hasan were the only two prominent Shias who initially opposed the Shia college. They believed it would weaken the Aligarh Muslim University movement, and accentuate Shia-Sunni differences.
84. For a summary of 'Shia Awakening', Rizvi, *A Socio-Intellectual History*, Chap. 5.
85. Freitag, *Collective Action and Community*, p. 249.
86. Azad was deputed by the Congress High Command to resolve the impasse. His personal stature aided the process of reconciliation. The Shia ulama, in particular, agreed to suspend the *tabarra* agitation at his instance.
87. 16 Dec. L/P and J/8/693, 1946.

PART II

5

Mediating the External: Pan-Islamism and Nationalist Renewal

خاک وطن کا مجھکو ہر ذرّہ دیوتا ہے

Every grain of the dust of my country is a god to me.

MUHAMMAD IQBAL

It is widely known, though scarcely recognized that sections of the Indian Muslim intelligentsia have been sensitive to their fraternal links with their co-religionists in other countries, following their history, detailing their accomplishments, and, at the same time, lamenting their decline. And when Islam fell on evil days owing to the convergence of European powers on the heartland of the Muslim world in the nineteenth-century, the heritage of the past—expressed in Hali lamenting the 'ebb' of Islam, in Shibli's pan-Islamic anguish, and in Iqbal's nostalgic ode to once-Arab Sicily—stood forth as a symbol of community pride.

Interest in Turkey's welfare continued: each time it was involved in a war—the Russo-Turkish war of 1877-8 or the Graeco-Turkish war of 1897—Indian Muslim groups launched fund drives, reaffirmed their loyalty to the sultan of Turkey, and offered prayers for his well-being. 'If the Muhammadans of the world were compared to the human body', wrote the *Akhbar-i Am*, 'the Sultan would be the heart and brain.'[1] Anthony Macdonnell, lieutenant-governor of UP, noted the 'great sympathy with Turkey partly due to incitement from outside India and partly spontaneous, and I think it has been growing for some time and is fostered in Mohammedan schools'. Agra's commissioner told him that many more people than formerly had taken to wearing the Turkish fez, indicating how the wind was beginning to blow.[2]

The 'incitement from outside' came from two distinct sources. In the first place, the British government exploited pro-Turkish feelings to secure Indian Muslim loyalty, as in 1857, and to bolster 'the sick man of Europe', as they did from the Crimean war of 1853-6 onwards, in order to thwart Russian encroachments. Then, Turkey's sultan, Abdul Hamid II (1842-1918), sent his agents to India, as to other lands, to rally Muslim support and enthusiasm for his feeble regime which was threatened by external aggression and internal strife.

Saiyid Ahmad Khan disputed Hamid's claim to the khilafat. The pan-Islamic surge threatened to destroy his effort to strengthen the Anglo-Muslim alliance; so he spoke against the Turcophilia among his Muslim brethren, arguing that they were legally bound to obey the writ not of an external Muslim khalifa but of the British government. Such exhortations fell on inattentive ears, for the sympathy in favour of Turkey was fairly widespread in parts of northern India. When nawab Mohsinul Mulk, one of Saiyid Ahmad's successors at the Aligarh College, opposed the holding of pan-Islamic meetings on the campus a section of the press castigated him as a 'downright sycophant'.[3]

The most bitter criticism came from an unexpected quarter—from that celebrated roving reformer, teacher and political agitator, Jamaluddin al-Asadabadi 'al-Afghani'.[4] He regarded the Aligarh reformer's religious views and his educational programme as ancillaries to his political servitude to British interests, and chided him for relying on the British instead of joining hands with the nationalists. Afghani considered Saiyid Ahmad as his main adversary in India, opposed to pan-Islamism, isolating India's Muslims from the rest of *Dar al-Islam*, especially from the Turks, and hostile to the conception of a universal Muslim khilafat.

Afghani spent the greater part of his life travelling from one country to the other propagating the doctrine of political unification of the Muslim world, known as pan-Islamism. His life, one of endless wanderings, touched and deeply affected Muslims in the last quarter of the nineteenth century. His pan-Islamic views inspired various activist groups in different lands and lives on patiently, if amorphously, in the aspirations of many Muslims.[5] It is also curious that the only instance where his political programme of combined radicalism, modernism, nationalism and pan-Islamism ever became a serious political programme of an active opposition was in the khilafat agitation in India, years after his death.[6]

The power of Afghani's appeal was felt in the first decade of the twentieth-century. Among those who came under his spell was Shibli who visited Istanbul in 1893, received a medal from the khalifa, and established contacts with Afghani's co-worker and disciple, Muhammad Abduh.[7]

His pan-Islamic ideas were echoed in Hali's *Musaddas*, and his strong advocacy of the co-existence of diverse religious faiths was in accord with Mohamed Ali's idea, expressed in 1923, of the 'Federation of Faiths'. Ansari developed his view of a natural solidarity beyond the nation: that which binds together all the peoples of the east threatened by the west.[8] At the khilafat conference held on 27 December 1922, he referred to the need for an Asiatic Federation to promote solidarity among the peoples and countries of Asia with a view to rescuing them from the political and economic bondage of Europe.[9] Afghani had advocated this idea more than two decades earlier.

Afghani also influenced lqbal and Azad. The former was attracted most of all by his endeavour to find in Islam a means of unity for resisting the domination of the West, and shared his desire to express unity on the religious basis of Muslims as a supra class and a supranational unity. On the eve of and during World War I, he tied his hopes for liberation from colonial dependency to pan-Islamic solidarity. This was reflected in his poem *Shama awr Shair* (The Candle and the Poet), written in 1912.[10] In his reply to the *Shikwa* (Complaint of God) he strikes the same note:

> The trouble that is raging in the Balkans
> Is a message of awakening to the forgetful
> Thou may'st think it the means of vexing thy heart
> But in reality it is a test of thy self-sacrifice and self-reliance.

Afghani's influence on Azad can be seen from the time of his stay in Constantinople and Cairo, and his close relations with the Al-Manar group of Syrian and Egyptian scholars. Azad developed the anti-imperialist thrust in his writings in the *Al-Hilal*, a paper inspired by the *Urwat al-wuthqa* (The Indissoluble Link), an anti-imperialist journal Afghani published in collaboration with Abduh. He, too, bitterly attacked Saiyid Ahmad Khan's attitude to the khilafat, and argued on the authority of the Koran that *jihad* was obligatory against those who had occupied even a part of the *Dar al-Islam.* Political loyalty was due to the Ottoman khalifa and obedience to the *khilafat-i mulki* (monarchial khilafat) was therefore binding on the Muslims.[11]

Azad provided greater ideological coherence to those Muslim activists who were beginning to come to terms with Indian nationalism and its anti-colonial strain. He stood strongly for inter-communal harmony citing the Prophet Muhammad's covenant with some Jews as a valid historical precedent for an integrated alliance with the Hindus. He argued that joining in common action with one category of non-Muslims, the Hindus, against another category of non-Muslims, the British, was obligatory. In a similar vein, Ansari quoted the *Sura-i Mumtahanah* (60: 8-9) from the Koran to argue that Indian Muslims should behave 'righteously, affectionately and in a friendly manner towards all those non-Muslims who are neither at war with Muslims nor are they assailants intending to invade or occupy their territories'.[12]

Views on a peaceful *modus vivendi* with the Hindus were representative of Afghani's position that a religious link did not exclude national links with men of different faiths. In fact, he had urged his Muslim audience to cooperate with the Hindus and cultivate 'good relations and harmony in what pertains to national interest'.[13] In his article published in the Hyderabad journal, *Muallim-i Shafiq*, he invoked not only the universal Islamic but also national sentiments with special emphasis on Hindu-Muslim unity. And just as he helped awaken Egyptian nationalism by appeals to the ancient glories of the past, so in India, even when talking to a primarily Muslim audience, he invoked the glory of the Indian Hindu past.[14] This appeal to take pride in a Hindu past was no different from Afghani's earlier appeal to Egyptian Muslims to derive inspiration from pre-Islamic Egyptian greatness. In both cases he wanted to create an effective basis for solidarity against the colonizers.[15]

The message was taken serious note of and found echoes in the political activism of the khilafatists. Various theories were worked out to remove the widespread notion that the pan-Islamic idea implied a break with nationalism. Admittedly, the term nationalism had different, though allied, shades of meaning. But the ideologues of the khilafat movement did not find an inherent inconsistency between their pan-Islamic creed and territorial nationalism. They argued, instead, that their objective of independence from foreign rule—central to the pan-Islamic ideology—had an obvious nationalist dimension. In fact the idea itself was bound to the concept of an emerging Indian nation. They pointed out that, in spite of their pan-Islamic ambition, they always had their own Indian community most clearly in mind and were not oblivious to its trials and tribulations. The emblem used on the khilafat delegation stationery—made up of overlapping twin circles of equal size, with the word 'khilafat' on one and the word 'India' on the other—symbolized their loyalty to the nationalist cause, their vision of a free India, and the Muslim countries liberation from foreign domination. Ansari was able to establish a link between British colonial policies in India and the larger interests of the Western nations in exploiting the weaker nations of the East and in perpetuating 'the bondage and slavery of Asiatic people'. 'It is, therefore, not only a question of India's honour and freedom', he said in December 1920, 'but of a great struggle for the emancipation of all the enslaved Asiatic people from the thraldom of the West.'[16]

The relationship between the Indians and the Turks was in the nature of a compact, because both were subjected to colonial rule. For this reason, Azad observed that the problem of the khalifa was part of the larger issue of British imperialism. Khilafat workers must win India's liberty by means of non-cooperation; only then would they be able to save the khalifa.[17] Mohamed Ali offered the same advice: Muslims must fight for swaraj by plunging into the non-cooperation campaign with their non-Muslim brethren, for only in this way would it be possible to achieve the khilafat aim.[18]

Mohamed Ali made the most passionate attempt to demonstrate that pan-Islamism and nationalism were compatible.[19] His intention was to prove that, objectively speaking, Muslim reactions to events in Turkey deepened their involvement in the anti-colonial struggle in India and brought them closer to the Congress movement under Gandhi's leadership. He argued, furthermore, that they had a pre-eminent sense of community in their *Weltanschaung*, and especially so in India, where their adherence to Islam made them unique and gave them their 'communal consciousness'. He did not, however, believe that being a Muslim he was any less Indian. His religious beliefs, as indeed his commitment to nationalism, never appeared to him to be incompatibles.[20] He could—and must—be true to both Islam and India. To further prove that his loyalty to Islam and to his country was compatible, he explained that 'where India is concerned, where India's freedom is concerned, where the welfare of India is concerned, I am an Indian first, an Indian second, and nothing but an Indian'.[21] Doubtless, individuals, if not groups, were able to easily swing back and forth between pan-Islamic and local nationalist appeals, depending upon which was a more appropriate anti-imperialist weapon in a specific Indian situation.

The khilafat movement has often been denounced on the grounds that its emphasis on Muslim values and extra-Indian loyalties stood in the way of genuine Hindu-Muslim unity. It is also pointed out that those Muslims who accepted Gandhi's leadership were motivated by religious consideration, and their alliance with nationalist forces was of an ephemeral and opportunistic nature. The roots of this assumption lay in the unexpressed postulate that Muslims were unpatriotic because they were moved only by loyalty to the invisible theocracy of which God was the ruler, and that they had developed a nationalism of their own which was Islamic in tone and content. 'Under the circumstances', observed the Congress and Hindu Mahasabha leader, B.S. Moonje, 'how can peace and amity now grow between the Hindus and the Muslims unless either the Hindus surrender and become a consenting party to the Islamic Mission or if they are equally determined to preserve their essentially scientific identity separate from the one-sided Nationalism of the Muslims.'[22]

Setting aside the theological debate centred round the supposed contradiction between Indian nationalism and 'Islamic nationalism', what deserves consideration is the process that enabled the khilafat movement to merge itself into a general political struggle that far outstripped its pan-Islamic limitations.

This is exemplified in the composition and the shared concerns of the khilafat committees, local Congress bodies, kisan sabhas, and Home Rule leagues. 'There is nothing to choose locally,' commented an official, 'between a gathering under the auspices of the kisan sabha or of the khilafat committee. Both movements appear to have been completely captured by the non-cooperation party.'[23] This was not just a joyful demonstration of the newly-found sense of solidarity, but an awareness of the 'extraordinary stiffening-up' of a demoralized, backward, and broken-up people taking part in disciplined, joint action on a countrywide scale.[24]

In several areas, peasant unrest was not just tagged on to the khilafat and non-cooperation programme, but the khilafat committees and the kisan sabhas provided a tangible sign of acting in unison in attacking their common identifiable enemy—the landlord—who was perceived as an ally of the government. Here lay the danger in government's assessment, a fact referred to when the secretary of the Rae Bareli khilafat committee spoke at a kisan sabha meeting on 6 February. 'What might have been in its way a harmful and beneficent movement', observed an official, 'is in danger of being rapidly perverted into a vehicle for virulent abuse of and violent agitation against the government.'[25] Evidence of the potentially dangerous alliance came from other areas as well. A kisan sabha rally at Faizabad, held on 20-1 December 1920, was probably organized by khilafat workers.[26] Local khilafat activists—Lal Muhammad and Maulvi Riasat Husain—addressed a similar gathering at village Salethu in Maharajganj on 2 February 1921. Amid Saiyid, a local khilafat agitator, organized a meeting at village Balla in the same police station a week earlier.

A notable feature of such meetings were the common demands of the kisans and the khilafatists, on the one hand, and the attainment of the swaraj ideal, on the other. Words like 'khilafat', 'kisan ekta', 'swaraj', 'Gandhi' conjured up in the minds of the people a picture of bringing about a better world under the direction of better leaders.[27] Thus maulvi

Salamatullah of Firangi Mahal stated at a kisan sabha meeting that peasant interests would be protected only after the khalifa's dignity and prestige was restored. Kamaluddin Jafri, the Allahabad-based lawyer, linked the redressal of peasant grievances with the attainment of swaraj under the Congress directive. He moved a resolution at a kisan sabha conference at Akbarpur in Faizabad district; it had the support of Hafiz Alam and Muhammad Nabi of Tanda, important activists of eastern UP.[28]

In assessing the historical significance of the khilafat movement, it is equally important to reckon with the Congress-khilafat-League alliance at the national level as well as the bonds of friendship forged at other levels of society. All three organizations met in the same city and around the same time; both the khilafat and the League bodies took their political cue from the Congress, and mostly endorsed its decisions. The 1918 League session echoed the Congress demands, and, as in the Congress so in the League, wrote an intelligence officer, 'the moderates have lost all control'.[29] The same spirit prevailed a year later. Anti-British spirit, emphasized a government report, reigned supreme.[30] In July 1920, the League insisted on the Congress holding its session first so that it could decide 'the course of action which it should recommend to the Muslims of this country'.[31]

Such demonstrations of political unity were matched by spontaneous expressions of communal harmony. In Delhi and Punjab, Prem Sabhas and the Anjuman-i Islam worked strenuously to ensure the peaceful observance of religious festivals.[32] Zafar Ali Khan captured the spirit of the time in the verse:

Aai hain Aasman se chal kar woh quwaten
Jo Muslim-o-Hunood ko sheer-o-shakar karen

Heavenly forces have helped to forge the bonds of friendship between the Hindus and the Muslims.

Or by Agha Hashr:

Ho gaeen bikhri hui einten baham tamir ki
Mil gaee har ek kari tooti hui zanjir ki
But-shikan wahdat-parast ek jism ek jaan ho gaye
Ghul hua duniya me phir kafir Musalman ho gaye

The disjointed pieces have been put in order again
The links of the broken chain have been discerned
The idol-worshippers and the iconoclast have joined hands
There is a dinning clamour that the kafirs have again embraced Islam.

Finally, Akbar Allahabadi wrote:

Na Maulana me laghzish hai na sazish ki hai Gaṇdhi ne
Hilaya ek rukh unko faqat maghrib ki andhi ne

Maulana has not blundered, nor has Gandhi hatched conspiracies;
What blows them on the same course is the gale of Western policies.

Short-lived as this unity was, the fact that it was accomplished indicated the strength and fervour of the nationalistic spirit of which it was the outward expression. 'The scenes that were enacted before my eyes', wrote the secretary of the Bengal khilafat committee, 'made me feel that the artificial barriers that had long been preventing the two major communities of the country to come together, had been miraculously swept away by the onrush of the all-embracing non-cooperation movement.'[33]

II

Ae barq aaj shola-fishan kyon nahin hai tu
Ae raad aaj garm fughan kyon nahin hai tu
Ae abr aaj girya kunan kyon nahin hai tu
Darya-I qahr aaj rawan kyon nahin hai tu
Islam aaj kufr ke narghe men aa gaya
Badal siyah rang ka Kaaba pe chha gaya.

O the thunderbolt why don't you scatter flames?
O the lightning why thou wailest not?
O the clouds why weepest not thou?
Why is it that the river of curse is a frozen puddle and flows not?
Islam has been swamped and overwhelmed by the unbelief
And the Kaaba has been engulfed by darkness.

Proscribed Publications (8), British Library, London.
Also, see 142, 152, 153

It will not do to treat the outburst of religious and nationalistic fervour as an artifact.[34] Its explanation must take into account the importance of the unifying powers of religious symbols in Indian Islam,[35] and the ability of the ulama of Firangi Mahal, Deoband and the Nadwat al-ulama to press them into service.[36] They were, indeed, at the heart of Muslim concern over Turkey and the holy places. From their *madaris* and mosques, they emerged on the national scene to dominate the khilafat agitation, and provided the much needed legitimacy to a cause which had little chance of being sustained by the Western-educated Muslims.

Who were the ulama? Where did they come from? What made them an important group in Muslim society? We must examine these questions in order to understand the significance of their participation in the khilafat movement.

Islam did not provide for a priesthood or a comparable religious institution. Gradually, however, a body of men developed with specialized religious functions—chiefly readers and reciters of the Koran, and also experts in recording the sayings and doings (*Hadith*) of the Prophet. These were the ulama—literally those who possess knowledge (*ilm*). They were not a separate class, but a body of people belonging to every social level. They formed 'an unnumbered aggregate of academicians of all degrees of learning and intelligence', with special interest in and knowledge of the Koranic exegesis (*tafsir*), the science of Prophetic tradition (*ilm-i Hadith*), jurisprudence (*fiqh*) and theology (*ilm-i kalam*). Indeed the hallmark of an alim was his learning in these subjects. According to Fakhr-i Mudabbir, a fourteenth century chronicler at the Delhi court, the ulama owed their special status to their knowledge. He observed:

> All people know that after the apostles and prophets rank the truthful persons (*siddiqin*), martyrs (*shahidin*) and scholars (*aliman*). The scholars are included in the category of siddiqis and have preference over the martyrs. The Prophet has said: 'The *ulama* are the heirs of the prophets'. The world exists on account of the piety of the learned. The laws of *sharia'a* . . . are enforced by them . . . and things illegal and not sanctioned by the *sharia'a* are suppressed by them.[37]

Such a glorified image was not entirely a product of Fakhr-i-Mudabbir's fantasy but was, indeed, grounded in Muslim ethics; it helps to explain the special position occupied by the ulama in Muslim society.

The ulama dominated the upper echelons of religious hierarchy, manned the judicial and ecclesiastical services, and wherever there was a mosque—and every Muslim locality had one—the *imam*, the *khatib*, the *muhtasib* and the *muftis* represented an interest which received state recognition. Some were actually an integral part of the medieval Indian state and shared in the control of the vast revenues of the land; they were consulted and used for foreign negotiations, and took part in the politics and revolutions of the palace. The ulama established matrimonial alliances with the ruling houses, purchased property, and emulated the nobles (*amirs*) in lavish expenditure. Tradition classified them as *ulama-i duniya* as opposed to the *ulama-i akhrat* who led an abstemious life of pious devotion to religious learning and eschewed entanglement in materialistic pursuits and political affairs. The *ulama-i duniya*, on the other hand, were totally mundane in their outlook, aspired for wealth and worldly prestige, and mixed freely with the ruling élite.[38] Their relationship with the sultans was generally harmonious, not least because ties of mutual self-interest bound them together.

The ulama were indispensable allies of the Delhi sultans, for they secured for them the one important element of authority which force alone could not achieve—legitimacy. The sultans needed sanction for their monarchical and despotic rule and expected the ulama to give a favourable ruling in the light of the *Shariat.* The ulama, in turn, seemed to agree that it was far more important to preserve Muslim society and its distinctive way of life than to endanger the unity of that community and the ordered practice of religious duties by encouraging resistance against an impious ruler. For this reason, some taught the faithful a dull stagnation in matters of belief and the acceptance of political autocracy, knowing all the time that almost everything the sultans did as persons and as rulers violated the *Shariat.*[39] To protect their interests and to retain their social status, they chose to become the creatures of the state.[40]

The establishment of British supremacy, however, turned the ulama world topsy-turvy. Educational reforms, the reorganization of law courts, the growth of local governments, the spread of secular ideas, and, above all, the separation of religion and government, steadily reduced their influence in Muslim society. In his address to the first Congress of Nadwat al-ulama in April 1895, Shibli lamented:

> Gentlemen! In the days of the Muslim rule the worldly as well as the religious affairs of the Muslims were in the hands of the *ulama* . . . the reins of the affairs of the community relating to both this and the next world were in the hands of the *ulama.* Now that things have changed , and worldly affairs have come under the authority of (the British) government, we have to see what relationship the *ulama* have with community. . . .[41]

Strongly opposed to the government's encroachment upon Muslim educational institutions and its interference with the Islamic personal law, the ulama asserted the pre-eminent position of the *Shariat* and claimed for themselves the sole right to interpret its meaning for all groups and classes. They submitted memoranda, sent deputations to the government on this point,[42] set up centres of learning to prevent the influx of subversive ideas from the religiously alien and 'morally inferior' British, and took tangible steps to put a premium on unorthodox thought and learning, which was calculated to undermine the position of the ulama. Thus the Nadwat al-ulama aimed to defend Islam against 'contemporary times'.[43] To maintain uniformity in belief and practice, it sought to determine what was true or desirable in the light of the Koran and *Hadith.*

Traditionally, the *madaris* were the basis of Muslim education. Their curriculum, which remained largely unchanged over the centuries, included Arabic and Persian languages and literature, logic, philosophy, Islamic Law, *Hadith*, and commentaries on the Koran. Aurangzeb reprimanded his former teacher for having taught him Arabic, grammar and philosophy rather than subjects more practical for a future ruler, but his criticism had little effect. In the eighteenth century, Mulla Nizamuddin Sihalawi introduced the *Dars-i Nizamia*,[44] the standard syllabus and the basis for instruction in many institutions. Regarded as the most comprehensive form of orthodox education, the *Dars-i Nizamia* was adopted by some of the famous *madaris* in the eighteenth century. These functioned essentially as schools of theology and as strongholds of orthodoxy. With their traditionalist course of studies, the curriculum was confined to purely religious sciences (*maqulat*) with a bit of grammar and literature. Along with *Hadith*, *fiqh*, *kalam* and *tafsir*, the Koran has remained at the heart of the curriculum and its memorization the highest scholastic attainment.

The *makatib*—smaller institutions than the *madaris*—were usually of two kinds: the first of a purely religious character in which the rituals and the tenets of Islam were taught, and the second of a more secular type in which some Persian literature was also introduced. The most important of the first type was established at Deoband soon after 1857. Conforming to the doctrines of the Hanafi school, its goal was to train well-educated ulama who, as prayer-leaders, writers, preachers and teachers, would maintain religious identity and cultural homogeneity. The Nadwat al-ulama, founded as a middle of the road institution between the extremes of Aligarh's 'secularism' and Deoband's rigid conservatism, adhered to the *Dars-i Nizamia*; it failed to combine both religious and secular types of education.[45] The institution developed conservative contours, and its students became generally indistinguishable from those of Deoband in their theological and intellectual outlook.

The Dar al-ulum and the Nadwa endeavoured to make Muslims aware of their Islamic identity, maintain the charismatic or divinely-instituted structure of the community, and preserve the special field of religious interpretation and instruction.[46] Over the years, the ulama resisted the secularizing tendencies. They continued wearing the medieval attire, and their turbans and flowing gowns made them stand out as symbols of conservatism in a society that was becoming less Islamic and more secular. Most still clung desperately to the vestiges of their religious identity, jealously guarding their theological strongholds. Obsessed with significant minutiae of ritual and engaged in fruitless disputations, they excelled in denouncing each other, and dubbing the adherents of other schools of thought as ignorant, irreligious and atheistic.[47]

Yet, they continued to make their presence felt through mosques and shrines, *makatib* and *madaris*. Above all, as guardians, transmitters and authorized interpreteres of the *Shariat*—which comprehends Muslim beliefs, rituals, public and personal law—they played a variety of roles. When, in doubt, the believers turned to them for the definition of controversial points of the doctrine, and their opinion was sought on a wide variety of subjects, ranging from divorce and inheritance to disputes over property. Rashid Ahmad Gangohi, for example, gave rulings on request that it was lawful to learn English if there was no danger to religion, that it was unlawful to take interest from a Christian, and to use money-orders and bills of exchange which contain the element of interest. He also declared the wearing of a cross or a *topi* to be sinful.[48] Such rulings were rarely flouted—at least not openly.

Given their role in regulating religious and social life, it is not surprising that, in small towns and villages where the Muslim population was more susceptible to religious exhortations through local mosques and *madaris*, the ulama provided the inspiration behind a burst of khilafat activity. They succeeded in doing so because of their dominant religious hegemony which transcended class and caste divisions and enabled them to develop an extensive network of social connections ranging from the Awadh *taluqdar* to the impoverished Muslim peasant in East Bengal. It is true that they were frequently attacked for their conservatism, and just as often blamed for the backwardness of the Muslim peoples, but their support was regularly sought by politicians who realized their value, even if it was in the negative sense, of preventing them from showing active opposition or from making adverse religious pronouncements.[49] The promoters of the Aligarh Muslim University, for instance, adopted a conciliatory attitude towards the Muslim divines in order to allay their fears about the future character of the institution; their support was necessary to convince the government that the university movement was backed by influential Muslim groups. Likewise, professional men who dominated the Muslim League after 1911, needed the ulama to rally public opinion around their brand of agitational politics;[50] so they wooed the ulama and allayed their fears about the League's *la-dini* (religion-less) character. This enabled the dividing line between the Western-educated and the orthodox to be blurred, and with it were buried their doctrinal feuds and personal animus. The younger Muslims, observed UP's lieutenant-governor, 'try to work with the priests, hoping through them to influence the mob. For the time being, however, it would be idle to deny that they have attained success'.[51] Other developments, some to be covered in the following two chapters, added thrust to the converging courses in politics of the modern and the traditionally-educated.[52]

The ulama responded favourably to these overtures mainly because they were politically unorganized and unaccustomed to political life. Moreover, their bitter doctrinal disputes created fissures in the apparent solid phalanx of orthodoxy, and prevented them from moving in unison to defend their interests.[53] By 1911, however, they were rudely awakened by the growing threat to Islam, an awakening which coincided with, and was also to a certain extent caused by, the political upheaval in Turkey. They were conscious that they must now be active in addressing themselves to the current anxieties, political, social and religious, of Indian Muslims, or else watch true Islam as they understood it, and their own claims to guide the community, get diluted by default. Such a realization led some to assiduously cultivate the Western-educated Muslim intelligentsia—college students, lawyers, journalists and teachers—who had some experience of conducting constitutional politics, and, in the words of Mohamed Ali, 'to pocket their pride and in a way even accept the lead of men whom they had but a generation ago finally consigned to perdition'.[54]

An early move was initiated by Maulana Mahmud Hasan, an alim convinced of the need to further greater fraternity between the alumni of Deoband and Aligarh.[55] The Jalsa-i Dastarbandi, convened in 1910 and attended by a delegation from Aligarh led by Aftab Ahmad Khan, and the Jamiat al-Ansar, founded by Ubaid-Allah Sindhi, a Sikh convert to Islam, was the fruition of such early efforts. These initiatives were followed by the establishment of the Anjuman-i Khuddam-i Kaaba in May 1912. This was the beginning of the generality of the ulama's formal participation in Indian politics in their capacity as religious leaders. The Anjuman provided, after all, the basis for an alliance between leading ulama of all shades of opinion and the modern educated, and illustrated that, on purely religious issues, the alim and the modernized Muslim could strive together for common ends. The orthodox and the anglicized 'were drawn together and as in a flash of lightning, saw that after all they were not so unlike each other as they had imagined'.[56] 'Once more', observed Mohamed Ali:

> Muslim society in India presented a level of uniformity and the bitterest opponents of a generation ago stood shoulder to shoulder. . . . If even a decade previously anyone had ventured to foretell such a result, he would have been laughed at for such a fantastic prophesy. . . .[57]

The men of 'New Light' or *Nai Raushani* began using the existing networks of religious organizations and institutions for propagating pan-Islamism. In March 1914, Mohamed Ali, Ajmal Khan and Ghulam us-Saqlain (d. 1915), editor of *Asr-i Jadid,* served on the committee to enquire into the affairs of Nadwat al-ulama. M.A. Ansari was elected president of the Anjuman-i Islamia, Ghazipur, a position mostly occupied by the local maulvis. In December 1918, Ansari and Shuaib Qureshi, son-in-law of Mohamed Ali, addressed a meeting at Delhi's Jama Masjid in support of the Muslim League. In return for such concessions, the League began airing the specific religious demands of the ulama.[58] At the same time, Firangi Mahal's leading alim, Abdul Bari, rallied around Gandhi during the Rowlatt satyagraha, lent support to the passive resistance movement, and submitted to his leadership during the khilafat agitation. Writing to Gandhi in 1919, he observed: 'Thanks are due to your kind special attention for the success of the Day of Prayer and Hindu-Muslim unity. Your personality and behaviour are deeply affecting Muslims in general and religious sections in particular. A group of ulama have written to me specially to pay their homage to you.'[59] In November 1920, he again declared: 'I have accepted his (Gandhi) support in getting our aims fulfilled and for that purpose I think it is necessary to follow his advice. . . . *I know that the strength of Islam lies in association with him*' (italics mine).[60]

Although such a subservient posture irked some ulama, particularly Saiyid Ahmad Raza Khan of Bareilly and the Bahr al-ulum ulama of Firangi Mahal, such men were few and wielded limited influence at least during the popular pan-Islamic upsurge. Most favoured accommodation with the Congress, and welcomed Gandhi as their political guide and benefactor.

III

During the first decade of the twentieth-century, Shibli and Azad strongly challenged the notion of separating religion from politics, arguing that 'a very large part of the national life is in the ulama right of ownership and they alone have or can have absolute sway over it'.[61] Addressing the first Congress of Nadwat al-ulama, Shibli berated the ulama for being lackadaisical, and urged them to combine and organize themselves to offer an enlightened interpretation of religion, reorganize Arabic and Persian studies, exert pressure on the government to revise its legal policy, and control and efficiently administer *wakfs*.[62] All this entailed an active and vigorous involvement in politics. In 1912, his disciple, Azad, guided the ulama with the following advice:

> The question whether political discussion should be separated from religious education is very important. But you must know that this is the foundation on which we intend to build the whole edifice of *Al-Hilal*. If you say that the arch is not beautiful we may try to alter its shape, but if you wish that the key-stone

should be removed, then we cannot accede to your wishes. *There will be nothing left with us if we separate politics from religion.*[63] (italics mine)

This was common talk in the early 1920s. Maulana Sajjad suggested to Abdul Bari that the ulama should 'take the reins of politics in their own hands and cross their voices with those in authority' in order to establish their religious supremacy, and fulfil their higher aim of protecting Islam from Western imperialism.[64] Maulvi Kifayatullah of Delhi echoed similar sentiments at the Muslim League meeting in December 1918. He declared, '. . . in Islam religion and politics are not two separate things. For a long time they were together, but probably those who have received modern education think that they are separate from one another. This, however, is a wrong concept: they think that they should monopolize politics and leave religion for the ulama.'[65]

Words were soon translated into deeds. The ulama thronged to the League session to assert the voice of orthodoxy, assumed leadership of the khilafat agitation, and contributed to its ever more radical development. Soon after, they called upon the believers to wage *jihad* against the government, boycott foreign goods, and migrate (*hijrat*) to the *dar al-Islam*. They exercised their right to issue *fatwa* freely using the Koran and *Hadith* as powerful weapons to gain the adherence of the masses who accepted them as infallible. Abdul Bari endorsed the *fatwa* on non-cooperation. So did Azad: he also authored the *fatwa* on *hijrat*. The maulvis of Sukkur in Sind, inspired by Abdul Bari's *istifta* (questionnaire) of January 1919, declared the Jazirat al-Arab as a sacred place 'wherein non-Muslims cannot rule or remain in possession'.[66] In Bengal, a *fatwa* forbade Muslim participation in peace celebrations.[67] Doubtless, the *Muttaffiqa fatwa*, which made non-cooperation mandatory on all Muslims, was opposed by Maulana Ashraf Ali Thanwi, Ahmad Raza Khan and the Bahr al-ulum party of Firangi Mahal. But their opposition, often inspired by cynical government officials, failed to stem the pan-Islamic tide.[68]

The ulama were not content with sheafs of *fatawa,* but travelled extensively enjoining the faithful to wage *jihad*.[69] The Majlis-i Ulama of Madras toured the presidency to incite Muslim emotions on the khilafat issue and, in May 1920, the United Provinces' Ulama Association despatched students to preach *jihad* in the *mofussil*. A few months earlier, Abdul Bari and Shaukat Ali toured Gujarat together preaching the sanctity of the khilafat; later Azad joined them on a tour of Sind.[70] In the N.W.F.P., they established *Shariat* tribunals in a few places and a national school at Utmanzai.[71] In Bengal, the ulama, having held aloof from politics, were eventually drawn into the boycott movement'.[72] In UP, educational centres became the main foci of agitations. Nadwat al-ulama and the Dar al-Musaniffin at Azamgarh were amongst them.

The Nadwa came under suspicion during the Graeco-Turkish war.[73] Pan-Islamic activity was intensified during the Balkan wars and the khilafat and non-cooperation movements.[74] In November 1920, students urged the trustees to refuse the government grant sanctioned by J.P. Hewett, lieutenant-governor of UP from 1907 to 1912. From December 1920 to March 1921, they raised money for the khilafat fund and formed volunteer corps in the towns of Bihar and the UP.

The Dar al-Musaniffin, founded by Shibli in 1913 to promote the publication and translation of historical, religious, and scientific works, also turned into a pan-Islamic stronghold. This was mainly due to Saiyid Sulaiman Nadwi, one of Shibli's pupils at Nadwa. In April 1920 he spoke at Kanpur urging Muslims to give up their lives for protecting the holy places. In 1920, he joined the khilafat delegation to London. He wrote to Abdul Bari that, if Muslims wanted to liberate Kaaba, they would have to liberate India first: 'The political emancipation of India', he noted, 'was a religious duty.'[75]

Masud Ali Nadwi, too, turned the Dar al-Musaniffin into 'an extremist political institution', and a centre for political activism in Azamgarh district.[76] His influence extended to many small towns in the region, such as Mau, Sarai Mir, and Pharuja. Mau was predominantly inhabited by Muslim weavers who, under the leadership of Abdul Aziz, a barber, Maulvi Muhammad Sabir, the *imam* of the local mosque, Maulvi Abdullah, and Maulvi Zamir, were in the forefront of the non-cooperation drive. They pressed honorary magistrates in the area to resign and the local Islamia College to renounce its government aid. In Sarai Mir, on the other hand, khilafat activities were centred around the Arabic school. Here the managers, the staff and the students campaigned enthusiastically in the neighbouring villages to explain the significance of the *fatwa* issued by Abdul Bari and Azad.[77]

IV

قیامت تک وہ سرداری کے قابل ہو نہیں سکتے

Doomsday will come before they are fit to lead.

AKBAR ALLAHABADI

'Take great care', the *Independent* of Allahabad warned its readers on 3 June 1920, 'that the control of the khilafat movement does not fall entirely within the hands of theologians and divines.'[78] Others apprehended that the presence of Muslim divines was fraught with danger.[79]

By early 1921, the warning signals were proving to be prophetic. At the Meerut All-India Khilafat Conference in April 1921 some ulama objected to Hindus being involved in the khilafat movement, and demanded, moreover, the widening of its scope in accordance with the *Shariat*.[80] This was followed by Abdul Bari's warning that Muslims were ready to desert Gandhi and adopt violent methods for redressing their grievances.[81] In May 1921, Darul Qaza courts (House of Justice) mushroomed in parts of Bihar and the N.W.F.P., and the call for *jihad* against the British was heard loud and clear in the countryside.[82] In March, the Jamiyat-i-ulama-i-Hind, founded in November 1919, declared that it was *haram* (sinful) for a Muslim soldier to serve in the army.[83] The Karachi Khilafat Conference on 8-10 July simply endorsed this resolution, introduced by Maulana Husain Ahmad Madani and supported by the Ali brothers, Pir Ghulam Mujaddid, a Sindhi follower of Abdul Bari, and Maulana Nisar Ahmad of Deoband.[84]

Gandhi did not sympathize with this radical strain, fearing that militancy would lead to violence and consequently destroy the credibility of his technique of non-violent non-cooperation. Aware of the signs of discontent amongst Hindu Congressmen following the Moplah riots in August 1921, he was anxious that the khilafat leaders should not alienate them. But men like Abdul Majid Budauni (d. 1931), Ghafoor Ahmad and Nisar Ahmad did not buy his argument. On 21-2 December, their followers demanded an immediate adoption of civil disobedience. Considerable friction occurred before Ansari, Azad, and Ajmal Khan persuaded them to grudgingly accept that Gandhi, 'the recognized leader of all Indians considered that the time was not yet ripe for civil disobedience'.[85]

The showdown came in December 1921 when Hasrat Mohani proposed that the Congress and the Muslim League should strive to attain 'complete independence', and that, if martial law was imposed, Muslims would either have to abandon non-cooperation or face the bullets and bayonets. In the latter event, violence was the natural course to adopt in self-defence. This epitomized the tension between Gandhi's ideal of satyagraha and the khilafatists adoption of it as a political technique. Gandhi himself created this tension, despite his laments about Muslim motives, by making non-violence the pre-condition of his support for the movement.

Gandhi argued that complete independence could not be incorporated in the Congress creed without Hindu-Muslim unity being accomplished. The Congress backed Gandhi rather than Hasrat, as did the League's Subjects Committee on 30 December. 'If Gandhi does not favour complete independence', stated Maulana Abdul Majid, 'we would advise him to join the illustrious group *of jee-huzoors* who would welcome him with open arms.'[86] These were harsh words reflecting the growing rift between

Gandhi and the Muslim priests. With the Ali brothers still in prison, there seemed little hope of a reconciliation. The Moplah riots along the Malabar coast of south India was the last straw.

In the midst of the heated controversy generated by the Moplah riot, Gandhi suspended civil disobedience on 5 February 1922. 'The whole conception of civil disobedience', he informed the Congress Working Committee (CWC), 'is based upon the assumption that it works in and through its non-violent character. . . . I personally can never be a party to a movement half violent and half non-violent.' Three other reasons influenced him to call off civil disobedience; firstly, the patchy success of the movement, second, the resolutions passed at the Karachi Khilafat Conference in July 1921 and the violent and xenophobic speeches made by the ulama; finally, the growing feeling in Congress circles that the party should extricate itself from the travail of non-cooperation. In such a climate, the suspension of civil disobedience suddenly became a political necessity.

Gandhi's decision took the sting out of the khilafat agitation. Hasrat Mohani rejected the Bardoli programme on the ground that, if religion enjoined violence, a policy of non-violence could not be adopted.[87] At the Jamiyat al-ulama conference held in Ajmer, Abdul Bari assailed the Mahatma and the Bardoli resolution.[88] Such attacks continued even after Gandhi's arrest on 10 March 1922. When he returned from prison in February 1924, his interest—whatever little was left—in the khilafat movement had evaporated. When asked to nominate a Hindu to join a khilafat deputation to Angora, the Mahatma pointed out that it would be 'out of place' for any Hindu to do so.[89] How ironical that less than five years earlier he had urged his co-religionists to support the 'just cause of the Muslims', and said: 'for the Hindu not to support them (Muslims) to the utmost would be a cowardly breach of brotherhood'.[90]

The khilafatists had yet another surprise in store. On 21 November 1922, the Turkish National Assembly at Ankara separated the khilafat from the sultanate. And since the maintenance of the khalifa's temporal power was one of the main objects of their movement, this action by a purely Muslim body completely took the wind out of its sails. In March 1924, Mustafa Kamal Pasha burst the khilafat bubble. Its immediate result was the disruption of the khilafat party. From 1918 to 1922, religious zeal and the overwhelming anti-British bias had united various groups, but once the initial euphoria had worn thin the inherent contradictions in the alliance revealed the division among the ranks of the ulama, as also among the other Muslim groups. The Jamiyat al-ulama split, with Nisar Ahmad of Kanpur and Abdul Majid Budauni joining the *tanzim* movement; they also founded a parallel organization of Jamiyat-i-ulama-i-Hind in Kanpur.[91]

The rapprochement between the political and religious wings of the khilafat movement also collapsed in part because international developments had undermined its *raison d'être*, and, in part, because there was no sound basis for a permanent adjustment of diverse and, in some cases, conflicting interests.[92]

Soon enough, the Muslim divines disappeared from the national arena. Having once mobilized new groups, roused their religious fervour, and articulated their grievances, they were now like a contrary jack-in-the-box refusing to retire, to seek new outlets for their energy, and to build something positive out of their experience. Some doggedly kept the khilafat movement gasping, but most, including the ulama of Deoband, entered the arena of religious controversies and organized the *tabligh* and *tanzim* societies as a counterpart to *shuddhi* and *sangathan*.

The khilafat agitation had provided the ulama with a distinct enemy and goals; when the enemy and goals proved elusive other whipping boys and solutions were found. Much of their interests, geared to religious goals, remained, because they seemed to be the hope for their vision of the Muslim community. In consequence, they reverted to their former religious preoccupations. The Jamiyat al-ulama, despite its nationalist sympathies, concerned itself with securing safeguards against interference with the *Shariat* and guarantees for its propagation and implementation.[93] The ulama of Firangi Mahal, too, failed to adapt themselves to the changing realities of Indian politics, leading to Abdul Bari's estrangement from the Congress. In August 1923, he complained: 'The position of the Muslims has been rendered very awkward. Those who pretended to be our friends at one time and made a catspaw of the ulama now seem anxious to get rid of them.'[94] Abdul Bari was right. In the aftermath of civil disobedience, the issues concerning the leaders were of a political nature; so the services of the ulama were no longer required. They were bluntly told not to dabble in politics. The poet Akbar Allahabadi would have said:

اگر مذہب خلل انداز ہے ملکی مقاصد میں
تو شیخ و برہمن پنہاں رہیں دیر و مساجد میں

If religion hinders in pursuing the country's goals
Then the Shaikhs and Brahmans should remain confined
in temples and mosques.

Khaliquzzaman summed up the widespread confusion in the ranks of various influential Muslim groups in the following words:

The history of the next sixteen years of Muslim India is a mass of confusion and a chapter of political benightedness. The disruption of the khilafat organisation was like a breach in the embankment of the flowing stream of Muslim mass emotion, which diverted it into several petty streams, some leading to desert lands there to dry up, some flowing by zig-zag routes to meet the original bed in their headlong march and some others rushing towards the mighty ocean to drown themselves. To try to find any consistency, sound reasoning or logical method in Muslim politics during that period would be utterly fertile. We were divided between ourselves. . . .[95]

NOTES

1. *Akhbar-i Am*, 14 Mar. 1895, Punjab Native Newspaper Reports.
2. Quoted in Hardy, *Muslims of British India*, p. 177. W.S. Blunt (1840-1922) was told on the eve of his visit to India that he should not say anything against the sultan of Turkey because his name 'was now venerated in India as it has not formerly been'. Blunt, *India Under Ripon*, p. 13.
3. *Jasus* (Agra), 14 July 1906; *Al-Aziz* (Agra), 28 July 1906, UPNNR.
4. Afghani was in India from 1857 to 1865. He came again in 1879 to spend three years in Bombay, Hyderabad, Bhopal and Calcutta. The purpose of his visit was to 'meet with all the *navvabs* and princes and ulama and grandees of that land and to explain to them one by one the results that are manifested from unity and solidarity in the whole world and the injuries that have appeared from division and disunity; and to caress their ears with the mystery of the *hadith*, the faithful are brothers; and to express inspiring and prudent words and to attract the friendship and cooperation of the learned and the eloquent; and to breathe into them the new spirit of love of nationality and to rend the curtain of their neglect to explain to them the place of the luminous Sultanate in the world of Islam; and to reveal and make manifest to this group the fact that the perpetuation of religion depends on the perpetuation of this government. And in all the mosques of the famous cities I shall light a flame in their inner hearth by means of appealing sermons and *hadiths* of the Best of the Prophets, and I shall together burn out their patience and long-suffering.'

   Nikkie R. Keddie, *Sayyid Jamal al-Din 'al-Afghani': A Political Biography*, Los Angeles, 1972, pp. 134-5.
5. Aziz Ahmad, *Studies in Islamic Culture in the Indian Environment*, London, 1964, pp. 55-6; Keddie, *Sayyid Jamal al-Din*, p. 167.
6. Fazlur Rahman, *Islam*, London, 1966, p. 227.
7. Keddie, *Sayyid Jamal al-Din*, p. 26. It is not right to argue, as Elie Kedourie has, that Afghani's reputation and influence was to a large extent posthumous and was the work of disciples, or else of academic writers and publicists 'eager to discover trends and precursors' to magnify the importance of their subjects. Elie Kedourie, *Afghani and Abduh: An Essay on Religious Unbelief and Political*

Activism in Modern Islam, London, 1966, p. 3. There is adequate evidence to indicate his influence on his contemporaries, and greater evidence of his impact on subsequent political and intellectual movements in Muslim countries. Aziz Ahmad and Keddie, too, write of Afghani's limited influence. According to them, the people he met exercised no political or religious influence among Muslims, and his articles, published in an obscure journal of Hyderabad, did not cause any stir at the time. But their own evidence does not warrant this conclusion; in fact, the works of W.C. Blunt point to Afghani's influence. Kedourie's cynical view of Afghani becoming a 'British agent' is typical of his attempt to denigrate him and to underplay the role of ideology in politics.

8. Ahmad, *Islamic Modernism in India and Pakistan*, p. 129.
9. Hourani, *Arabic Thought*, pp. 118-19.
10. H.N. Mitra (ed.), *The Indian Annual Register* (*IAR*), 1923, Vol. I, p. 921.
11. L.R. Gordon-Polonskya, 'Ideology of Muslim Nationalism', Hafeez Malik (ed.), *Iqbal: Poet Philosopher of Pakistan*, New York, 1971, pp. 115-16.
12. Ahmad, *Studies in Islamic Culture*, p. 67. For Afghani's influence on one of Azad's devoted followers, see Abdul Ghaffar, *Jamaluddin Afghani*, in Urdu, New Delhi, 1941. Afghani's stay in India is referred to on pp. 12-13, 16-17, 35-7. Also, Schimmel, *Gabriel's Wing*, p. 21.
13. S.S. Pirzada (ed.), *Foundations of Pakistan*, Vol. I, p. 547.
14. Hourani, *Arabic Thought*, p. 118.
15. Keddie, *Sayyid Jamal al-Din*, pp. 155, 159-60.
16. Ibid., p. 160.
17. Pirzada (ed.), *Foundations of Pakistan*, Vol. 1, pp. 545-6.
18. W.J. Watson, 'Muhammad Ali and the Khilafat Movement' (unpublished MA thesis, 1955, McGill University), p. 64.
19. Muhammad Ali, *His Life, Service and Trial*, Madras, n.d., p. 151.
20. *IAR*, 1923, Vol. 2. p. 30.
21. Hasan, *Mohamed Ali: Ideology and Politics*, p. 115.
22. Ibid., p. 115.
23. 7 Aug. 1926, Moonje Dossier, Pad No. 35, National Library, Calcutta.
24. GAD, File No. 50, 1921, Box No. 135, UPSA. All subsequent references, unless otherwise stated, are drawn from the same file.
25. Nehru, *An Autobiography*, p. 76.
26. Note on Rae Bareli disturbances, op. cit.
27. M.H. Siddiqi, *Agrarian Unrest in North India: The United Provinces 1918-22*, New Delhi, 1978, p. 149; Kapil Kumar, *Peasants in Revolt: Tenants, Landlords, Congress and the raj in Oudh*, New Delhi, 1984, pp. 146-65.
28. This idea was beautifully summed up in the verse of Mohmamad Haider, a school teacher in Pilibhit. He wrote:

   Jama do qaum ka sikka baja do deen ka danka
   Mohamed, Shaukat-o-Gandhi ke Pairokaar ho jao

Swadeshi se karo raghbat bidesi se karo nafrat
Ki jis se muflisi ho door aur zardaar ho jao

Let the respect for the nation be restored
  and the trumpet of the faith heralded
Follow Mohamed (Ali), Shaukat and Gandhi
Adopt all that is swadeshi and shun that which is from outside
So that you may remove poverty and achieve self-reliance.

PROSCRIBED PUBLICATIONS (43)

Also, see the collection of poems in *Bulbulan-i Hurriyat* in Proscribed Publications (47). The collection was published by the khilafat committee in Jaunpur.

29. Police Dept., File No. 51-N, 1921, UPSA. Note by Lakhte Husain and Jagannath, 28 Jan. 1921, op. cit.
30. Home Poll. B, Jan. 1919, 160-3, NAI.
31. WRDI (Jan. 1920), Home Poll. Deposit, Feb. 1920, 52, NAI.
32. *Tribune*, 13 Oct. 1919; *Fateh* (Delhi), 1 July 1920; Swami Shraddhanand, *Inside Congress*, Bombay, 1946, pp. 68-70.
33. Abul Hayat, *Mussalmans of Bengal*, Calcutta, 1966, p. 37.
34. Robinson has argued that the professional Muslim groups exploited the khilafat issue to promote their personal and political interests. '. . . the professional politicians', he insists, 'had continually to manufacture issues and to whip up agitations to keep their newspapers going, their organisations active and their coffers full. . . . The issues were religious, usually pan-Islamic: these were the only sure sources of the money they needed.' Robinson, *Separatism Among Muslims*, p. 354.
35. For an elaboration of this argument, Hasan, *Nationalism and Communal Politics*.
36. The standard works on the role of the ulama are by I.H. Qureshi, Peter Hardy, W.C. Smith, Leonard Binder, Z.H. Faruqi and Mushir U. Haq. The most detailed account, however, is that of Qureshi, *Ulema in Politics*, Karachi, 1974 edn.
37. Quoted in K.A. Nizami, *Some Aspects of Religion and Politics in India during the Thirteenth Century*, Bombay, 1961, p. 150.
38. Ibid., p. 152.
39. For a useful critique of the role of the ulama in early medieval India, see Mujeeb, *The Indian Muslims*. For a useful assessment of their activities in Pakistan, see L. Binder, *Religion and Politics in Pakistan*, California, Berkeley, 1963.
40. In the nineteenth century, the traditional idea of a partnership between ruler and ulama was brought up to date by, among others, Rafi al-Tahtawi (1801-73) of Egypt. Hourani, *Arabic Thought*, p. 76.
41. Robinson, *Separatism Among Muslims*, p. 275.
42. The ulama of Firangi Mahal asked for special treatment in judicial matters by the establishment of special courts presided over by Muslim officials. Note

by W.S. Marris, 17.11.1918, Montagu papers, Mss. Eur. 523 (34), BL.

43. *Makatib-i Shibli*, Azamgarh, 1928, Vol. 1, p. 329.
44. Mujeeb, *Indian Muslims*, pp. 407-8.
45. This was the time when scholars like Rafi al-Tahtawi in Egypt and Khayr al-Din (1810-89) in Tunis urged the ulama to come to terms with the new learning and be in touch with the spirit of the times. Hourani, *Arabic Thought*, pp. 92-3.
46. Shibli argued that the Muslim community could only develop if the ulama exercised control over its secular and spiritual existence. S.M. Ikram, *Mauj-i-Kawsar*, Lahore, 1970 edn., p. 233.
47. M. Manzar and R.A. Khan, *Deoband awr Bareilly ke ikhtilaf wa Naza par faisla kun munazara*, Sambhal, 1966.
48. Hardy, *Muslims of British India*, p. 171; Ahmad, *Islamic Modernism*, p. 105.
49. For example, there were vigorous attempts by the Congress leaders to enlist the support of the ulama during the civil disobedience movement in 1930-1. Note by D. Gladding, Officiating Deputy-Secretary to Government of India, 3 July 1931, Home Poll. A, Aug. 1931, 189, NAI. The Government of India, on the other hand, was anxious to counter the efforts of the Congress leaders. The services of the Muslim landowners were utilized to keep the ulama 'straight'. In Apr. 1930, the nawab of Chhatari went on a mission to Deoband 'in order to use his own influence to keep them (*ulama*) going astray'. This loyal servant of the raj was obviously acting on the advice of his master. Hailey to Cunningham, 26 Apr. 1930, Mss. Eur. C. 152, Irwin papers (24), BL.
50. In March 1915, Meston analysed how the professional men and the ulama came to terms with each other. According to him, 'the young educated Muslim is restless and dissatisfied with everybody. His quest is for a cause, a call, something that he can be proud of, something which at small cost will retrieve his self-esteem and restore the glories of his race. This he finds in his religion. It gives him a link with great traditions. It may not be an ethical bond, but it is a militant bond; *in hoc signo vinces*. . . . At this point he comes in contact with the priest. Hence arises pan-Islamism.' Meston to Hardinge, 25 Mar. 1915, Hardinge papers (89). The *Nai Roshni* of Allahabad, edited by Wahid Yar Khan, emphasized the importance of cooperating with the ulama in the struggle against the government's repressive policies. Similarly, the *Mohammadi* of Calcutta suggested that the task of rousing the Muslim masses to the impending danger to the Islamic world should be undertaken by the ulama. It observed: 'Let the *alim*, betake themselves to work. Let the first steps in this great national work be begun in the mofussil, and let it be explained from each village mosque. *Nai Roshni*, 23 Dec. 1917 UPNNR 1917; *Mohammadi*, 23 Apr. 1920, BENNR 1917; *Intikhab* (Gujranwala), 10 Jan. 1920, PUNNR 1920.
51. Meston to Hardinge, 25 Mar. 1915, Hardinge papers (89).
52. See *Nationalism and Communal Politics* (1979), Chap. 2.

53. For an insight into the nature of differences, see Robinson, *Separatism Among Muslims*, pp. 268-71. For personal and rivalries amongst the ulama in Deoband, see Gail Minault, *The Khilafat Movement*. A number of leading ulama kept aloof from the khilafat and non-cooperation movements and criticized their fellow divines for associating with the Hindus. Maulana Ahmad Raza Khan of Bareilly was one of them. In 1921, he formed the Jama'at-i-Ansar-ul-Islam to counter pan-Islamism and convened a conference for that purpose. The first conference of the Jama'at was addressed by Maulana Mohammed Miyan (1892-1956) of *Khanqah-i Barkatia* in Marehra, a small town in Etah district of UP. The Maulana vigorously opposed the khilafat agitation, advocated cooperation with the British and denounced the khilafatists, including Abdul Bari, for associating with Gandhi and other Hindu Congressmen. In Sind, the pirs were equally divided. The pir of Kingri, for instance, not only opposed non-cooperation, but also advised his *murids* to remain loyal to the government. Pir Rashidullah, another influential Muslim divine, held aloof from the movement because it was 'initiated and controlled by Hindus'. WR (Sind), 9 Apr. 1921, J.C. Curry papers, CSAS, Cambridge.
54. Mushirul Hasan (ed.), *Mohamed Ali—My Life: A Fragment*, p. 84.
55. Faruqi, *The Deoband School and the Demand for Pakistan*, London, 1963, pp. 56-7.
56. *My Life: A Fragment*, p. 85.
57. Ibid., p. 84.
58. See, for instance, Maulvi Muhammad Ahmad to Sheweth, 30 Oct. 1917, Meston papers Mss. Eur. F. 136 (19).
59. Abdul Bari to Gandhi, n.d., Firangi Mahal papers (FM), Lucknow.
60. Statement of Abdul Bari, n.d., ibid. (From internal evidence it must refer to the Jamiyat i-ulama session in Oct. 1920.)
61. *Khutbat-i Shibli*, pp. 29-33, quoted in S.M. Ikram, *Modern Muslim India and the Birth of Pakistan, 1858-1951*, Lahore, 1965 edn.
62. Ahmad, *Islamic Modernism*, pp. 109-10; Smith, *Modern Islam in India*, p. 39.
63. *Al-Hilal*, 8 Sept. 1912, quoted in Mushir U. Haq, *Muslim Politics in Modern India, 1857-1947*, Meerut, 1970, p. 72.
64. A.M.M. Sajjad to Abdul Bari, 4 Dec. 1918, *Naqqush*, Lahore, p. 91.
65. Cited in Qazi Abdul Ghaffar, *Hayat-i-Ajmal*, Aligarh, 1950, p. 185.
66. *Tribune*, Lahore, 21 Mar. 1919.
67. *Mohammadi*, Calcutta, 12 Dec. 1919, Bengal Native Newspaper Reports, 1919.
68. Qureshi, *Ulema in Politics*, p. 271.
69. Diary of the Earl of Ronaldshay, 16 May 1919, Ronaldshay papers, Mss. Eur. D. 609(l), BL.
70. For details, P.C. Bamford, *Histories of the Khilafat and Non-cooperation Movements*, Delhi, 1974, rpt.; Brown, *Gandhi's Rise to Power*.
71. Bamford, *Histories*, p. 151.

72. FR (Bengal), Nov. 1921, Home Poll. Deposit, Dec. 1921, 18, NAI.
73. Fears that the *Nadwa* had a pan-Islamic influence helped to deny Shibli a C.I.E. in 1911.
74. J.P. Hewett to Dunlop Smith, 27 Jan. 1908, and C.P. Della Fosse to O'Donnell, 8 Feb. 1914, GAD, 1908, File No. 79, UPSA.
75. Gracey to Lambert, 8 Jan. 1926, GAD, 1921, File No. 1074, ibid.
76. Ibid.
77. Note by R.W. Bigg, 7 Dec. 1920, ibid.
78. Robinson, *Separatism Among Muslims*, p. 316.
79. Some writers, particularly in Pakistan, have argued that it was a mistake to involve the ulama in the khilafat movement. For example, Abdul Hamid, *Muslim Separatism in India: A Brief Survey, 1858-1947*, Lahore, 1971, rpt., pp. 151-2, and M. Noman, *Rise and Growth of the All-India Muslim League*, Allahabad, 1942, pp. 213-14.
80. WRDCI, 11 Apr. 1921, Home Poll. Deposit, June 1921, 54, NAI.
81. Abdul Bari said in June 1921 that his community held non-violent non-cooperation as 'a useful weapon to get our grievances redressed, but we never committed ourselves to always adhere to this principle'. Home Poll. 1921, 45, NAI.
82. Bamford, *Histories,* pp. 168-9.
83. Ibid., p. 165.
84. Weekly Report (Sind), 8 Oct. 1921, J.C. Curry papers.
85. Bamford, *Histories*, p. 177.
86. *Zul Qarnain,* 20 Jan. 1922, UPNNR, 1922.
87. Home Poll. Feb. 1922, 18, NAI.
88. Home Poll. 1922, 501, NAI.
89. Mahadev Desai, *Day-to-Day, with Gandhi*, Varanasi, 1968, Vol. 4, p. 22.
90. *CWMG*, Vol. 17, p. 350.
91. Qureshi, *Ulema in Politics*, p. 302.
92. Faruqi, *Deoband School*, p. 36.
93. See Peter Hardy, *Partners in Freedom—and True Muslims: The Political Thought of some Muslim Scholars in British India, 1912-1947*, Lund, 1971.
94. Statement to the Press, 20 Aug. 1923, Abdul Bari papers.
95. Khaliquzzaman, *Pathway to Pakistan*, p. 76.

6

My Life: A Fragment
Mohamed Ali's Quest for Identity in Colonial India

Mohamed Ali was a controversial figure for his contemporaries and for posterity. Government officials associated him with the 'extreme faction of the Muslim community', the 'Advanced Party' and the 'hot headed Nationalist Party'.[1] He led a clique of noisy and aggressive Muslims of the 'young party', who made the raja's house (raja of Mahmudabad) their headquarters and lived and agitated at his expense.[2] He fomented trouble wherever he went, reported the viceroy. He persuaded some students at the Lahore Medical College to raise the tribes against the government in Afghanistan, and caused 'discontent' at Aligarh's M.A.O. College. That is why he and brother Shaukat Ali were prevented from entering Punjab and UP.[3]

In recent years some historians have seen in Mohamed Ali a charmer and nothing more; a politician greedy for power, an irresponsible declaimer who drove himself and his followers from one disaster to another. He is charged with inspiring the 'Young Party' Muslims to manufacture issues and whip up agitations to keep their newspapers going, their organizations active, and their coffers full.[4]

There are other images as well: the image of an energetic, talented and charismatic figure devoted to Islamic resurgence the world over. Writers in India stress Mohamed Ali's commitment to Hindu-Muslim unity, his adherence to the Congress movement, his passion for the country's freedom.[5] Scholars in Pakistan, on the other hand, eulogize him as one who contributed 'to the march of the Muslim nation on the way to its final destination'.[6] They romanticize the story of his life and extol his achievements, some real but mostly imaginary. Schools, colleges and streets in Karachi and Lahore are named, as in Delhi, Aligarh and Bombay, after him. Indeed, Maulana Mohamed Ali 'Jauhar', the *Rais al-Ahrar* (Leader of the Free Peoples), is one of the most popular and venerated figures in Pakistan.

What lends credence to such images is the construction of a community's identity around leaders who had the energy, drive and the skills to articulate the Muslim/Islamic world-view from public platforms.[7] Therefore, Mohamed Ali, more than Saiyid Ahmad Khan or Maulana Azad, is commonly perceived to be more sensitive than others to the predicaments of the Islamic world and more stridently committed to its well-being.[8] He attracts greater notice also because he possessed to the full the resources of traditional oratory—its repertoire of tricks. Few orators or political journalists had his combination of qualities: his range of articulate emotions, his capacity for analytical argument, his pathos, fantasy and wit, and his power to marshall all these towards ends clearly discerned and passionately desired. His considerable poetic talent, which combined with his fervour and the desperate situation in which Turkey found herself after the First World War, created in him a feeling of impending martyrdom.[9] 'Such sufferings and privations as ours', he wrote, 'have only too often been the lot of mankind, in all ages and climes.'[10]

1.

سکھایا تھا تمھیں نے قوم کو یہ شور و شر سارا
جو اسکی انتہا ہم ہیں تو اسکی ابتدا تم ہو

It is you (Saiyid Ahmad Khan) that had
taught the community its mischiefs;
If we are its culmination;
you are its commencement.

MOHAMED ALI, in 1923

Mohamed Ali was born on 10 December 1878 in Rampur where his grandfather Sheikh Ali Baksh served as a petty official in the court of nawab Muhammad Yusuf Khan. He aided the British in quelling the disturbances at Bareilly and Moradabad in 1857, and received a *khilat* two years later and a *muafi* or a rent-free land with an annual income of Rs. 13,000. The family reaped the rewards of loyalty even after Ali Baksh's death in 1867. Abdul Ali (1848-80), his son, enjoyed the patronage of Rampur's nawab. But he died of cholera in 1880 leaving Abadi Bano

Begum, then only 28 years of age, the responsibility of bringing up her five sons and a daughter. The begum's family—in direct succession to a number of nobles connected with the Mughals—had suffered in 1857. Her father changed his name and lived for several years as a refugee in the Rampur state territory. The British confiscated much of the family's property.[11]

Abadi Bano was undeterred by the family's limited resources and the heavy debt incurred by a spend-thrift husband. When approached by Azimuddin Khan, general of Rampur forces, she agreed to send her eldest son to Bareilly.[12] Mohamed Ali recalled:

> How she managed to bring up her six little children and how she, an uneducated *purdah* lady, as education is understood in these days, managed to educate us better than our educated and richer uncles educated their own children, is a remarkable story which it is not through egotism that I would like to relate. . . . This miracle was not accomplished without personal privations that would do credit to a hermit living in a cave. It is not, therefore, egotism that has suggested this tribute to a mother's memory, but the sense of a heavy debt that can never be paid off. . . .[13]

In the graph of Mohamed Ali's life, the steep arc of youth is missing; we see only the flattened curve of maturity. We see him studying a few Persian classics, reading the Koran in Arabic, and observing the religious rituals in a Sunni home. While in Aligarh (1890-8), he is found writing for the college magazine, sharing Shaukat Ali's love for 'the noble and manly game of cricket', and nursing the ambition of securing 'a nomination for the post of Subordinate Magistrate or Land Revenue Collector'.[14] The 'Big Brother' was impressed with his 'unexpected success' at the BA examinations and arranged for his education in England. In Mohamed Ali's own words, 'So before the proverbial nine days of wonder were over, I was on the high seas in the Indian Ocean in the teeth of a raging monsoon, bound for England. . . .'[15]

Within weeks of his arrival in September 1898, Mohamed Ali made his way into English middle class society with the help of the family of T.W. Arnold, who had taught philosophy at the Aligarh College, and its controversial principal, Theodore Beck. Fazl-i Husain, also in England, found him to be 'a jolly good fellow, very quick in making friends'. They spent 'exceedingly pleasant evenings' discussing literary, philosophical and political issues.[16]

Mohamed Ali reached Oxford on 11 October to study modern history at Lincoln College. He matriculated a year later and secured a second in 1902, missing a first in history by a narrow margin.[17] He impressed his tutors with his vigour, common sense and resourcefulness.[18] James Williams, his guru in Roman and English law, noticed his 'great capacity for acquiring and remembering information'.[19] His paper on *Macbeth* was written by 'a man of ability, capable of thinking for himself'. Yet these skills did not equip him to qualify the civil service examination, 'thanks to an English spring, and a youngman's more or less foolish fancy'.[20] Success eluded him even after returning to India in 1902. Having failed to secure a teaching position at Aligarh owing to sordid manipulations, he opted for the Education department in Rampur, a position for which his tutors in Oxford had found him suitable. But his brief and inglorious innings ended in November 1902, when he sought refuge in Baroda.

Gaekwad Sayaji Rao, the ruler, regarded the new recruit as one on whose shoulders he could place the burden of administrative work, the man who got papers drawn up, orders sent out, correspondence carried on and records kept. But colleagues in Baroda, as in Rampur, resented his initiative, drive, and his proximity to the Gaekwad. Though Mohamed Ali kept himself in the public eye by writing and speaking at conferences, he was set to leave for Bhopal by the end of 1906.[21] Dunlop Smith, private secretary to the viceroy, urged him to stay: 'I quite understand that your surroundings are not always congenial, but after all whose are in every respect.'[22] Around this time Mohamed Ali printed the *Thoughts on the Present Discontent*: it was based on articles published in the *Times of India* and the *Indian Spectator*. He despatched a copy to the viceroy, hoping that it 'would meet with the sympathy and encouragement which India has learnt to associate now with the name of Edward the Peace-Maker'. The viceroy endorsed its contents and wished the book the wide circulation it deserved.[23]

Mohamed Ali stayed in Baroda until 1910, though his heart was not at rest.[24] Activity and companionship were the drugs he craved for. The drab and routine work in the Opium department offered no solace to his buoyant and exuberant spirit. He yearned for the *mehfils* where he could transmit the flame of his intellectual excitement to others. 'I am fed up with this state . . . (and) tired of this job', he told his Aligarh friend Saiyid Mahfuz Ali.[25] He was conceited about his Oxford degree, and contemptuous of those who sported degrees from Indian universities. He submitted, as he did with monotonous regularity during his internment a few years later, long representations to his superiors commending his own abilities, demanding higher pay, and criticizing those placed above him. 'In spite of being an Indian and having received a very similar education to the rest of the Baroda officials,' he complained to the Gaekwad, 'I found that

I differ from them in almost everything, and that it was difficult if not impossible for me to be received by them as one of their own number.'[26] Shaukat Ali, himself a civil servant in the Opium department, felt that his younger brother had crossed the limits of discretion; he admonished him 'to curb yourself a little—you have to work with certain people and you cannot always have your way. If I was your boss, I would strongly object to your correspondence. It borders on insubordination.'[27]

For the time being Dunlop Smith and Harold A. Stuart, the home member, held out the prospect of a government job. But hopes were soon turned into despair when told that 'the expenses of an Indian private secretary would (not) be justified at present', and that Mohamed Ali's lack of experience of detective work was a bar for a posting in the Home department.[28] Though Michael O'Dwyer, later governor of Punjab, recommended him to the nawab of Jaora, this small princely state could hardly assuage Mohamed Ali's thirst for participation in great events, even in a subordinate capacity.[29]

A career in journalism was the only option, the only avenue through which Mohamed Ali could prove to be of 'any appreciable use to it (Muslim community), while still earning a livelihood'.[30] His journalistic ventures, beginning with the *Comrade* on 14 January 1911, were successful. His articles were laced with long and tedious quotations, and tended to be verbose and repetitive. Yet he created for himself a broad-based readership because he wrote, just as he spoke, passionately. The *Comrade*, manned by some of his friends and protégés from Aligarh, grew in size; its circulation shot up to 8,500 copies. Its office in Kucha-i Chelan in the old city became a political salon after the paper moved from Calcutta to Delhi, the new capital of British India. 'No paper has so much influence with the students as the *Comrade*, and no individual has the authority over them which is exercised by Mohamed Ali', reported the UP government in 1914.[31] When he wanted to stop publishing the *Hamdard* at the beginning of his internment, Wilayat Ali, the well-known columnist, begged him not to do so: 'I do not approve of your decision and I do not think many will. . . . You cannot imagine what the loss of *Hamdard* will mean to us—the Musalmans.'[32] Wilayat Ali recognized, as did others, that the *Comrade* and *Hamdard* contributed to a general awakening of educated Muslims who read and financially supported them.[33]

The *Comrade*, more than the *Hamdard*, voiced some of Mohamed Ali's main concerns; for example, the promotion of the Aligarh College, his alma mater. He wanted the college to serve as a common centre where Muslims from all over the world would congregate and energize a common

Islamic consciousness to uphold Muslim interests in India and overseas.[34] Thus, his maiden speech in 1908 on the subject, modelled on the style of Edmund Burke and with quotations from Latin, Arabic, Persian, Urdu and English literature, proved to be the swan song of the first phase of the Muslim University movement.[35]

Mohamed Ali supported—some said fomented—a students' strike in 1907. His involvement in college affairs, a story detailed by David Lelyveld, Gail Minault and Francis Robinson, made him the *bete noire* of the board of trustees. The British staff complained to the English novelist E.M. Forster, then visiting India, that they were neither 'trusted to give the help they had hoped nor could they make some way with the students—not much, owing to the influence of the *Comrade*, a forward Islamic newspaper'. The Muslims 'had an air of desperation, which may be habitual, but was impressive'.[36] The college was transformed into a hot-bed of 'sedition'; officials wondered if anything could be done to prevent its students from 'being tampered with' by Mohamed Ali who, for all his professions of loyalty, was 'a dangerous malcontent', 'an element of strife'.[37]

2.

جورِ گلچیں یاد رکھ، قیدِ قفس کا غم نہ کر!
چین کب اے بلبلِ ناداں تجھے گلشن میں تھا

Grieve not over imprisonment in the cage, but
do not forget the actions of the plucker of the rose.
Oh foolish nightingale! When free in the garden,
When did you ever find repose?

MOHAMED ALI

I have elsewhere traced the breakup of the Anglo-Muslim *entente cordiale*, the growth of political radicalism among some Muslims, and their stridency in areas where colonial policies disturbed the *status quo* most. So have other historians. Some have examined how the anti-Muslim bias of Anthony Macdonnell, the reunification of Bengal (1911), the rejection of the Muslim University scheme (1912), and the fracas over the Kanpur mosque (1913) convinced Muslim political activists that radical self-help was a better solution than mendicancy. Much secondary literature also delineates the role of the men of *Nai Raushni* and the representatives of 'new ideals' and 'new force', many of whom endorsed the Congress policies and programme. Mohamed Ali emerged as the rallying point for such 'younger men', for he himself held the opinion that the Congress, then dominated by the 'moderates', embodied the 'genuine and vigorous aspirations which move educated India for a well-organized and common national life'.[38] He emphasized, as did Azad with greater rigour and consistency, the need for Hindu-Muslim amity and understanding. Without mutual cooperation Hindus and Muslims would 'not only fail but fail ignominiously'. He talked of a 'concordat like that of Canada' and '*a marriage de convenance* [*sic*], honourably contracted and honourably maintained'.[39] In another article—'The Communal Patriot'—he maintained that the two communities, despite their differences, should be mutually tolerant and respectful, and that eventually education and the 'levelling, liberalizing tendencies of the times' would create political individuality out of diverse creeds and races. He compared the Congress and the Muslim League to two trees growing on either side of a road:

> Their trunks stood apart, but their roots were fixed in the same soil, drawing nourishment from the same source. The branches were bound to meet when the stems had reached full stature. . . . The soil was British, the nutriment was common patriotism, the trunks were the two political bodies, and the road was the highway of peaceful progress.[40]

Such views were being aired in many quarters. Still, Mohamed Ali's fame spread far and wide only after he and Shaukat Ali were gaoled on 15 May 1915 for an article entitled 'The Choice of the Turks'.[41] On that day thousands congregated to offer their Friday prayers at Delhi's Juma Masjid and 'to bid adieu to the two patriots who had done all they could to promote their cause'.[42] They were first interned at Mehrauli, then transferred to Lansdowne and, finally, to Chhindwara where they arrived on 23 November 1915 wearing 'grey astrakhan cap with large Turkish half moons in the front, also Khuddam-i Kaaba badges'. Located 'a considerable distance from their friends' and 'far removed from centres of Muhammadan feeling', Chhindwara was chosen because 'pan-Islamism is faintest' and 'the journey there from the United Provinces as regards visitors is exceedingly tedious'.[43]

The Ali brothers were well on their way towards martyrdom, with various organizations vying with each other to record their 'noble services rendered at the most psychological moment in the history of the community'. Their fame was kept fresh through many protest meetings, and also through the incident of the government's conditional offer of their release in 1917. They refused to sign the undertaking suggested by the government; instead, they signed another, adding the qualification: 'Without prejudice to our allegiance to Islam'. Leading Congressmen, especially Gandhi, also courted them and pressed for their release. The

Mahatma, having met the Ali brothers in Aligarh and Delhi in 1915 and early in 1916, assured Bi Amman—'Mataji'—that he was 'leaving no stone unturned' to secure their immediate and honourable release.[44]

Having made Hindu-Muslim unity an essential part of his mission in India since his return from Africa in 1915, Gandhi assumed that Mohamed Ali was an ideal instrument in his hand for creating a Hindu-Muslim alliance with the aim of obtaining swaraj. He was valuable to Gandhi both as an issue on which to cement a communal concordat, and also because he considered him to be a splendid example of that mingling of Hindu and Muslim cultures in the Indo-Gangetic belt.[45] His interest in Mohamed Ali's release was 'quite selfish':[46] 'we have a common goal, and I want to utilize your services to the uttermost in order to reach that goal. In the proper solution of the Mohammedan question lies the realization of Swaraj.'[47]

Gandhi's initiatives made him popular among north India's Muslims, many of whom participated in the *hartal* organized on 6 April 1919 against the Rowlatt Bills. Ansari extolled him as the 'intrepid leader of India . . . who has . . . endeared him as much to the Musalman as to the Hindu'. Mohamed Ali's younger colleagues regarded the Mahatma as a 'Tolstoy and Buddha combined', and they endorsed his non-violent programme. Satyagraha, according to Maulana Abdul Bari, was consistent with the Islamic principles.[48]

Around this time the portrayal of Mohamed Ali as a fiery and relentless anti-colonial crusader was based on the strength of his involvement in nationalist as well as pan-Islamic causes. This image is sustained in much of the secondary literature produced in India and Pakistan. In reality, however, Mohamed Ali's utterances and his frequent references to the good that was to accrue from the 'beneficent contact' with Western culture and civilization explode the myth of his being consistently hostile to the colonial government.[49] Notice, for example, how he assured Meston, whose advice he followed in shifting the *Comrade* from Calcutta to Delhi, of his 'anxious desire' to cooperate with him and other well-wishers of his country and community,[50] and pleaded, on another occasion, for 'some pegs' on which to hang his moderate stance on the annulment of Bengal's partition. He insisted that 'well-merited concessions wisely made at a suitable moment' would curb an agitation far more effectively than the strenuous efforts of Muslim leaders.[51] He even suggested that the presence of the British monarch in India should be utilized to bind still more firmly the seventy million Muslims of India to the Empire.[52] No wonder, high-ranking British officers subscribed to the *Comrade* when it began publication in Calcutta. No wonder, the viceroy Hardinge allowed Mohamed Ali to collect and advance a loan to Turkey, patronized the Delhi Crescent Society, and supported Ansari's medical mission to Constantinople.[53]

Even when officials rebuffed Mohamed Ali in London during his stay from September to 1 December 1913, he declared his loyalty and appreciated the manifold blessings of British rule in India.[54] When the war with Germany broke out, he was on the side of the British, urging India's Muslims to place their services at the disposal of the government. The article 'The Choice of the Turks' proclaimed the hope that the khalifa would stay out of the war and save his Muslim countrymen from a conflict of loyalties. Talking to Abdul Majid, the CID officer, Mohamed Ali defined his position thus:

> His quarrel (Abdul Majid recorded) was not at all with the British Government. He was certainly not so advanced as Messrs. Mazharul Haq, M.A. Jinnah and Lajpat Rai. He believed that is was necessary for Muhammedans that the British Government should and would remain in India much longer than the nationalists desired. . . . The Government did not know its real enemies. They will receive in audience Lajpat Rai and other nationalists, . . . but they would consider Mohamed Ali as their enemy.[55]

Mohamed Ali's antipathy towards Pax Britannica may well have developed during his trip to Europe in 1913, though it was still not explicitly articulated. Meeting writers, journalists and civil servants enabled him to see Turkey from the outside, to observe the strife of the peninsula magnified into the terms of international politics, to watch and appraise the forces remoulding, sometimes deliberately, sometimes almost casually, the destiny of the Ottoman empire. His exchanges convinced him, perhaps for the first time in his public career, that the British were insensitive to Muslim feelings over the khilafat, and their ignorance of conditions back home was 'driving them fast to the brink of the precipice'. Hence his indignation at being denied access to senior officials of the Indian House. 'If we are unable to see even His Lordship', Mohamed Ali told John Morley, 'what could we say to our people on our return except that because some local officials were desirous that we and our co-religionists and many others in our country should be misjudged by our superiors.'[56] Furious at the lack of sensitivity, he was drawn into a kind of *egoisme a deux* in defying their stuffiness. He commented that the government, having taken Muslim loyalty and support for granted, undermined the temporal power of Islam with scant regard for Muslim religious susceptibilities.[57]

Mohamed Ali's internment was the last proverbial straw. Ziauddin Ahmad Barni, a sub-editor of *Hamdard*, traced his mentor's anti-government stance to his confinement in Chhindwara.[58] From here, as also from Lansdowne and Betul, Mohamed Ali expounded on the government's repressive measures, targeting the ICS in particular, 'a political party perpetually in office (with) the power to crush its political opponents with all the resources of the State'.[59] He told Delhi's chief commissioner, Malcolm Hailey, that he understood 'how hateful must be a man of my character to officials of a certain type'. He recognized the implications of the Defence of India Act, 'which makes even the Archangel Gabriel liable to internment by local governments on the secret testimony of Beelzebub'.[60] In June 1915, he announced that the law under which he was interned was 'tyrannous and unjust'.[61] No government was expected in the twentieth century to claim, even by implication, the right to force a man's conscience. He dwelt on 'the spirit of tyranny', the 'gag of prodigious proportions' prepared 'for silencing more than three hundred million of God's articulate creatures'. The Rowlatt Act 'has ended the reign of law, and substituted a reign of terror in its place'.[62] As a symbol of his protest, Mohamed Ali wore half-moons in his grey cap and Khuddam-i Kaaba badge, compared with his European style of dress in previous years.

The enforced leisure made Mohamed Ali more profoundly religious, enabling him to steep himself afresh in his Islamic heritage and turn to the study of Islam—charting out an unfamiliar subject, getting at its rudiments, and exploring its nuances. In *My Life*, a document of deep religious feelings, he laments not having had access to the traditional Muslim learning. 'It is not without a feeling of deep shame that I have to confess, we boys and girls born and bred in Muslim households were taught far less of our religion than most English boys and girls of our age and position.' He bemoaned that Aligarh 'furnished' students with 'little equipment in the matter of knowledge of faith'. Though he attended Shibli Numani's lectures and referred to the elation of sitting in the principal's hall attending these lectures with all the dignity of a quasi-'Undergrad', the Koran practically remained a closed book, and the traditions of the Prophet were no more than a name. In the seclusion of his internment at Mehrauli, however, he found in Maulvi Nazir Ahmad's translation of the Koran 'the consolation and contentment that was denied to us outside its pages'.[63] He discovered, after years of ignorance of his Islamic heritage, that the Koran was a 'perennial of truth' and offered a 'complete scheme of life, a perfect code of conduct and a comprehensive social policy . . .'. As a result, the main tenets of Islam, which were earlier 'little more than a bundle of doctrines and commandments', acquired 'a new coherence and, as it were, fell suddenly into place, creating an effect of units such as

I had never realized before'. *Tauhid* grew upon him as a personal reality, man in the dignity of his 'service' as viceregent of God, and himself as part of this great strength. This was Mohamed Ali's 'unique discovery in that small volume revealed some thirteen centuries ago to an Arab of the desert whose name I bore'.[64]

Mohamed Ali read the *Sihah-i Sittah*, a compilation of the Prophet's traditions (*Hadith*), the works of Imam Ghazali, Arnold, Shibli, the person who made the symbols of Islam a living reality for the Aligarh students, and the poems of Jalaluddin Rumi and Iqbal. He experienced 'an exquisite thrill of delight' reading *Asrar-i Khudi* (Secrets of Self), especially because its author Iqbal expressed 'the same basic truth of Islam, which I had in a blundering sort of way discovered for myself'.[65] Studying Islamic history enabled him to see its great men as figures to whom he could talk, and its crises as guides to action in current affairs.[66] Studying Islam was conventional enough for men like Saiyid Ahmad Khan, Shibli and Azad who did so with greater scholarship, but none with a greater personal need. Mohamed Ali recollected: 'Since I first commenced the study of the Koran I have read a fair amount about Islam from the point of view of Muslims and also of their critics; *but nothing that I have read has altered the significance of Islam for me to which I had stumbled in the first few months of our internment eight years ago*'[67] (italics mine). To Gandhi, he wrote:

> Whatever else my internment may or may not have done, it has I believe set the soul free, and that compensates me for so many items on the wrong side of the account. What I could dimly perceive before I now realize with distinctness, and it is this, that the whole aim and end of life is to serve God and obey His commandments. . . . I confess I had never before grasped this truth in all its fullness. . . . *Internment made us seek refuge in the Holy Koran, and for the first time, I have to confess it, I read it through and with new eyes.*[68] (italics mine)

In Mohamed Ali's view there was just one world of Islam regardless of caste, class, linguistic and regional variations, one vast brotherhood stretching across the continents. This was summed up by the *Comrade* on 18 January 1916.

> It is not only one God, one Prophet and one Kaaba that the Muslims of the world have in common, but in every degree of longitude and latitude they hold the same views of the relations of husband and wife, of parent and child, of master and slave and of neighbour and neighbour. . . . They follow among all races the same laws of marriage, divorce and succession. And they do this in the twentieth century of the Christian era exactly as they did in the sixth and hope to do so to the last syllable of recorded time. . . . There is still the one God to worship and the one

Prophet to follow . . . , always one unaltered and unalterable Book to soothe and to stimulate, and the one Kaaba to act as the magnetic pole for all true believers from all points of the compass.

Underlining the primacy of religious loyalty, Mohamed Ali argued that Muslims have had a pre-eminent sense of community in their *Weltanschauung*, and especially so in India, where their adherence to Islam made them unique and gave them their 'communal consciousness'. 'I have a culture, a polity, an outlook on life—a complete synthesis which is Islam', he stated in his magisterial style at the London Round Table Conference in 1930. 'Where God commands', he added, 'I am a Muslim first, a Muslim second, a Muslim last, and nothing but a Muslim. If you ask me to enter into your Empire or into your nation by leaving that synthesis, that polity, that culture, that ethics, I will not do it.'[69] He did not believe that by being a Muslim he was any less an Indian. His religious beliefs and nationality never appeared to him to be incompatible. He could—and must—be true to both Islam and India. He explained thus: 'Where India is concerned, where India's freedom is concerned, where the welfare of India is concerned, I am an Indian first, and Indian second, an Indian last, and nothing but an Indian.' On another occasion he spelt out his position in the following words:

> I am a Muslim first and everything else afterwards. As a Muslim, I must be free and subject to no autocrat who demands from me obedience to his orders in defence of those of God. . . . Faith is my motive of conduct in every act . . . and my faith demands freedom. That Swaraj will give me, but it does not demand the subjugation of the Hindu or any one else differing from me in faith. . . . My own freedom and not the enslavement of any other is my creed.[70]

In sum, whereas Mohamed Ali's earlier activities had been directed by 'communal loyalty', his motivation after his religious experiences was Islamic duty. This is not to suggest that he held his community in any lesser esteem or that its mundane welfare was less important to him. On the contrary, his awakening confirmed the rightness of what he had done in the past and made it necessary for him to intensify his endeavours along similar lines.[71]

3. مت سہل ہمے جانو پھرتا ہے فلک برسوں
تب خاک کے پردہ سے انسان نکلتا ہے

Don't think us cheap: the heavens revolve for years
To bring forth man out of the veil of dust.

Mohamed Ali's emotional disposition in religious matters had much to do with the nature and with the promptness of his response to events in Turkey. In this context his concerns cannot be doubted: the opinion that it was all feigned or that he was simply playing the pan-Islamic role cannot be defended. He passionately believed that the basis of Islamic sympathy was not a common domicile or common parentage but a shared outlook on life and culture, and that the khilafat stood as 'the embodiment of that culture'. He endorsed Azad's description of a 'political centre' (*siyasi markaz*), and designated the khalifa as the 'personal centre' of Islam and the *Jazirat al-Arab* as its 'local centre'. For these reasons he warned the government that,

> there should be no attempt to remove, whether directly or indirectly, from the independent, indivisible and inalienable sovereignty of the khalifa, who is the recognized servant of the holy places and warden of the Holy Shrines, any portion of the territories in which such holy places and shrines are situated. . . . Nor should there be any such attempt to dismember and parcel out even among Muslim Governments, or in any other manner weaken the Khalifa's Empire with the object of weakening the temporal power of Islam, and thereby make it liable to suffer, without adequate power to prevent, the curtailment of its spiritual influence through the temporal power of other creeds.[72]

Again, he stated in London:

> Well, so long as there are your Bryces and your 'Big Sticks', we, too must have some sort of stick for the defence of our faith. . . . If you think you can please the Muslims of India by allowing the Turks to retain Constantinople in such a way that the khalifa is worst than the Pope . . . for he would in fact be the prisoner of people of an alien race and faith, then, ladies and gentlemen, you know very little of Islam and the Muslims, or of India and the Indians. [*Cheers*] That affront shall never be tolerated, and if you think you can make out that all this 'agitation' is 'fictitious' and 'factitious', then you will be compelling the Indian Muslim soldiery to disprove this lie in a manner that will be far too unambiguous for your tastes or for ours. Beware, beware.[73]

Mohamed Ali envisioned a renascent Islamic world in which all Muslim peoples were united in a strong Islamic world—'the super-natural Sangathan of Muslims in Five Continents'—built around the khalifa and supporting each other through that institution whenever Muslim security was threatened.[74] The new khalifa, judged from his views at the Mecca Conference in 1928, was to be based on a democratic, elective rather than a dynastic institution like the *khilafat-i rashida.* And the person chosen would be virtuous and faithful to Islam. The Muslims of the world would direct the government and be responsible for its welfare, while his brethren in India—the largest single community—would lead the fight to emancipate Islam.[75]

Mohamed Ali infused vigour into the central khilafat committee and its provincial and local units to realize the ideal of a renascent Islam. The *Hamdard* was started on 13 June 1913 to reach out to the Urdu readers. The Ali brothers travelled widely, delivered lectures, organized mass meetings, and galvanized the ulama at the Dar al-ulum in Deoband, the Firangi Mahal and the Nadwat al-ulama in Lucknow. Henceforth, they decided to play to Mohamed Ali's tune and 'to pocket their pride and in a way even accept the lead of men whom they had but a generation ago finally consigned to perdiction'. The orthodox and the anglicized were drawn together. The 'temporal misfortunes' of Islam had such a profound impact that 'the wedge that Western education had seemed to insert between the ranks of the religious, and of the men of the "New Light" vanished as if by magic'. A general levelling took place 'without any dependence on the use of force or external authority'.

Mohamed Ali strengthened these ties following his release on 28 December 1919. He reached Amritsar where, in keeping with the practice that had developed during the War years, the Congress and the League held simultaneous meetings. He had been imprisoned, Mohamed Ali told the Congress, for denouncing the injustices perpetrated on India and on Islam by the British, and now he must denounce them still, even if it meant returning to prison. He expressed his readiness to sacrifice everything he had, including his life, for the sake of Allah and Islam. He made clear that Muslims were subjects of Allah and not of Great Britain. He echoed similar views in London as a member of the khilafat delegation.

The delegation, having arrived in England at the end of February 1920. For six months, it maintained an exhausting pace, spurred on by Mohamed Ali. He was the debonair gentleman, perfectly dressed, dispensing political wisdom, epigrams, jokes and anecdotes to representative audiences, impressing everyone except the British newspapers and Lloyd George—the man who mattered most.[76] He lived well 'in a nice flat with heaps of good food, taxis to go about',[77] set up meetings with British leaders, spoke at length to various bodies, and organized the publication of the *Moslem Outlook* in England and the *Echo de l'Islam* in Paris. Reaching Bombay on 4 October 1920, nearly a month after the Calcutta Congress had adopted the non-cooperation resolution, he advised Muslims to plunge into the campaign with their non-Muslim brethren to achieve the khilafat aims.

Words were soon translated into deeds. Mohamed Ali redoubled his efforts, along with Gandhi, Azad and Ansari, to induce the trustees of the

Aligarh College to give up the government grant-in-aid. When the demand was rejected, quite a few students set up a break-away national university. This is how the Jamia Millia Islamia was founded. To begin with, Mohamed Ali devoted some time to giving the Jamia a solid Islamic footing, reviving Shibli's discourses on the Koran and ensuring that 'our day began with a full hour devoted to the rapid exegesis of the Koran'. But his project in life extended far beyond the confines of a campus. Jamia was too small and too quiet a place for someone accustomed to the humdrum of national politics.[78] Predictably, he virtually abandoned the institution he had himself founded, and headed for Nagpur to address the Congress, Muslim League and the khilafat committee meetings.

Mohamed Ali was among the busiest men in India, speaking before crowds and local committees. He travelled to eastern and western India from January to February 1921. His presence at the Erode session of the Majlis-al Ulama in March heightened the khilafat euphoria, as did his presence in April at Madras where he attracted huge crowds of Hindus and Muslims. His fiery speech at Erode nearly got him into trouble again; only an apology and an assurance that violence in every form would be eschewed led the government to withdraw the prosecution. From April to August, he spoke in Meerut (9 April), Bulandshahar (12 April), Lucknow (1 May and 7 August), Moradabad (26 July and 6 August), Pilibhit and Sitapur (7 August), and Allahabad (10 August). He was joined by his mother who threw off the veil, appeared before the public and began addressing vast audiences. Her journeys brought hundreds of thousands of rupees to the khilafat fund. The whole of India was astir. A popular song of the era reflected the spirit:

بولی امّاں محمد علی کی
جان بیٹا خلافت پہ دے دو

So spoke the mother of Mohamed Ali
Give your life, my son, for the khilafat.

During this tumultuous period, Mohamed Ali had an ambivalent relationship with Gandhi. Though moved by the Mahatma's interest in his release, he could neither grasp the significance of his political message nor his vision of a new social and moral order. And yet Gandhi hoped that 'on seeing the success of my experiment in non-violence, (they) will come to realize its excellence and beauty later on'. In May 1920, he referred to a distinct understanding with the Ali brothers that violence would not be allowed to go on side-by-side with non-violence.[79] Mohamed Ali confirmed in December 1923 that he would not use force even for self-defence.[80] In fact, he and other khilafat leaders chose the path of non-violent non-cooperation to 'secure the interests of their country and their faith'. From Paris, he wrote: 'I only wish that I had a Musheer (adviser) here, and if possible Fazlul Haq, though of course the best man to have is Gandhiji himself.'[81] When accused of being a Gandhiphile, he replied: 'I cannot find in any community—Jewish, Christian or any other a man who has as noble a character as Mahatma Gandhi. My *pir* and *murshid* is Abdul Bari whom I greatly respect. Yet I can say that I have not found anyone superior to Mahatma Gandhi.'[82] 'After the Prophet, on whom be peace,' he said, 'I consider it my duty to carry out the commands of Gandhiji.'[83]

While Mohamed Ali was reaffirming his loyalty to Gandhi, the khilafat conference at Karachi had earlier declared that serving in the army or police was *haram* for the Muslims. The expected happened. Mohamed Ali, the chairman, was arrested two months later. On 26 October 1922 began the trial where he made the famous statement: 'The trial is not "Mohamed Ali and six others *versus* the Crown", but "God *versus* man". The case was therefore between God and man. The whole question was "Shall God dominate over man or shall man dominate over God?".' The jury listened to his rousing speech but were impressed. He and five other Muslim leaders were sentenced to two years' rigorous imprisonment on 1 November.

4. خاک کا پتلا ہے آدم جو کوئی اچھا کہے
عالمِ خاک میں برسوں تئیں وہ بات رہے

> Man was first made of clay, and if the song you sing is good
> This world of clay for years to come will listen to your voice.

Mohamed Ali was released on 29 August 1923, and in his first public address spoke of his gloom at finding on his shoulders the burden of freeing Islam and India. He said that he came out 'from a smaller prison to a large one', and that every executive member of the Congress must sign a pledge of readiness to sacrifice life itself for independence. Non-cooperation was still the main plank of his politics: 'if cooperation was "haram" according to the Islamic law two years ago, it cannot become "halal" today'. He criticized the Swaraj party and its leader, Motilal Nehru, for starting chamber practice in defiance of the Congress decision to boycott British law courts.[84] But three weeks later he himself proposed the compromise resolution at the Delhi Congress, permitting 'such Congressmen as have no religious or other conscientious objections against entering the legislatures . . . to stand as candidates', and calling for 'united endeavours to achieve Swaraj at the earliest moment'. He was concerned, as he wrote to Jawaharlal Nehru who was induced to accept against his will the Congress secretaryship in Mohamed Ali's year of presidentship,[85] to resolve the differences among Congressmen and to unite the factions. Appealing for unity, he stated:

Let the Provincial Congress [UP] assembly send for the sacred soil of Kashi itself the message of the greater and more solid *sangathan*, the *sangathan* of the National Congress. And let us go forth from this Conference truly *shuddh*, purged of all narrowness, bigotry and intolerance in order to free our country from the most cramping slavery—the slavery not only of the body but also of the soul. . . . If there is anything of the old world spirituality in Kashi, let us recommence the work of our great chief, Gandhiji, in the spirit of religious devotion and utter unworldiness.[86]

Whatever the reasons, Mohamed Ali's teaming up with the swarajists enraged the ulama, whose *fatwa* against council entry was being repudiated by one of their own spokesman. The 'no-changers', too, accused their idol of having betrayed the Mahatma's heritage. The front-rank Communist leader, M.N. Roy, summed up his resentment:

Much was expected of Mohamed Ali. . . . The hope had been dashed to the ground. The idol showed its clay feet in such a hurry that the admirers were staggered. Mohamed Ali has failed to give the leadership which was expected of him. His pronouncements since he came out of jail are full of mere platitudes and hopeless contradictions. No constructive programme, no positive suggestion as to the future of the movement is to be found in them. He authorises the removal of the ban on the councils, but holds up the edict of the ulemas [*sic*] on the question. He professes to be the standard-bearer of pure Gandhism, but sets his face positively against civil disobedience, without which the political programme of non-cooperation becomes meaningless. He indulges in fearful threats against the government, but finds the demand for the separation from the British empire 'childish and petulant'. He deplores the Hindu-Moslem feuds, but still insists on khilafat propaganda, which contributed not a little to the success of the enemies of national freedom in creating communal dissensions. . . . In political questions, he has absolutely no programme to suggest. He harps on the threadbare 'constructive programme' which constructs naught but inaction. Such is the record with which Mohamed Ali goes to Kakinada to furnish the nationalist forces with a new direction.[87]

The main tenor of Mohamed Ali's address at Kakinada was that Hindu-Muslim unity was still necessary if Indians hoped to realize their aims.

Similarly, non-cooperation was not outmoded even if one were to grant (only for the sake of argument) that it had failed. He also spoke of his long-standing dream of a 'Federation of Faiths', a 'United Faiths of India'. India's millions were so hopelessly divided into communities and sects that providence had created for the country the mission to solve a unique problem and work out a new synthesis, which was nothing less than a 'Federation of Faiths'. The synthesis was to be of a federal type, for the lines of cleavage were too deep to allow for any other sort of union. He added:

> For more than twenty years I have dreamed the dream of a federation, grander, nobler and infinitely more spiritual than the United States of America, and today when many a political Cassandra prophesies a return to the bad old days of Hindu-Muslim dissensions, I still dream of 'United Faiths of India'. It was in order to translate this dream into reality that I had launched my weekly newspaper, and had significantly called it the *Comrade*—'Comrade of all and partisan of none'.[88]

The motives for India's Muslim efforts towards achieving swaraj were dual. They aimed at freeing India and freeing Islam. The relationship between Indians and the Turks was in the nature of a compact between countries oppressed by the same imperialism. Once India was free and her forces could not be driven to fight against the Turks, the two countries would be safe. Mohamed Ali contended that the Turks would have fought for the freedom of their co-religionists, including India's Muslims, and hence India, if they had not been so weakened. His lack of realism in assessing Turkish aims did not stop here. He pictured them fighting for an ideal khalifa, even though the Kemalist bandwagon rolled on in Turkey. He believed that once the Turks were free from their 'distractions' they would revive the glories of Umayyad or Abbasid dynasties and the pristine purity of the *khilafat-i rashida.*

Mohamed Ali's elevation to the Congress presidentship legitimized his position in nationalist circles. But within months of his exhortations at Kakinada, he began drifting away from the Congress, or, perhaps, as he would have put it, the Congress drifted away from him. This had a great deal to do with worsening Hindu-Muslim relations and the feeling in some Muslim circles that the Congress nurtured the vision of a 'Hindu Raj'. Mohamed Ali developed a point of view from which everything said or done by any Hindu was linked to the Hindu Mahasabha's influence. He saw its evil hand everywhere and its tainted mark on every forehead. Indeed, his new mentality recognized only two divisions in India, Hindu and Muslim, and not nationalist and reactionary or non-cooperating.[89] Nehru could not understand, how a Hindu or a Moslem can have any political or economic rights as Hindu or Moslem. And I cannot conceive why Moslems or Sikhs or Hindus should lay stress on any such rights. No minority should be unjustly treated. But Maulana Mohamed Ali is well aware that minorities get on well enough as a rule. It is the great majority which requires protection. A handful of foreigners rule India and exploit her millions. A handful of India's rich men exploit her vast peasantry and her workers. It is this great majority of the exploited that demands justice and is likely to have it sooner than many people imagine. I wish Maulana Mohamed Ali would become a champion of this majority and demand political and economic rights for them. But this majority does not consist of Hindus only or Moslems only or Sikhs only. It consists of Hindus and Moslems and Sikhs and others. And if he works for this majority, I am sure he will come to the conclusion that he need attach little importance to the imaginary rights of individuals or groups based on adherence to a religious creed.

Mohamed Ali's main grievance was that Gandhi, whom he had only just described as 'the most Christ-like man of our times', gave a free hand to the 'Lala-Malaviya gang'. The Congress, according to him, was no longer a national party but a Hindu one, unprepared to condemn Hindu fanatics, and unprepared to work towards the creation of a secular society. His anxieties were heightened by growing fissures in the Hindu-Muslim alliance in Bengal and Punjab, and the rapid progress of the Arya Samaj, the Hindu Mahasabha, and the *shuddhi* and *sangathan* movements. Commenting on the Delhi riot of July 1924 specifically, and on the deteriorating communal situation generally, he wrote: 'And pray Mahatmaji forgive a pang of sorrow, the cry of a well-nigh broken heart, the credit of it all goes, in the first instance, to the misguided spirit of the *sangathan* movement, and the superfluous boastings of the *shuddhi* leaders. . . . I feel sick, positively sick of it all.'[90] At the same time, the 'pseudo-nationalists', he wrote in the *Comrade* on 17 July 1924,

talk and write as nationalists and run down communals; but only in the use of counters and catchwords of nationalism are they nationalists for their hearts are narrow and they can conceive of no future for India except it be one of Hindu dominance and the existence of the Musalmans as a minority living on the sufferance of the Hindu majority, forgetting that such ill-concealed dreams can have but one interpretation, the existence of the Hindu majority itself on the sufferance of the British masters of India. It is my sad conviction that not one of these pseudo-nationalists would have talked so glibly of nationalism, majority rule and mixed electorates, if his own community had not been in the safe position of an overwhelming majority. It is they who are real culprits as narrow communalists, but since the position of their community is safe enough they mouth all the fine phrases of.nationalism and parade themselves as nationalists. The Cow question provides the best topic for the exposure of their pseudo-nationalism, for in the name of nationalism they make demands on their fellow-countrymen so absurd that none has ever heard of them in any other country or nation in the world, and it is time that their nationalism was fully exposed.

The Nehru report (Appendix I) set in motion the avalanche of Mohamed Ali's eloquence against Gandhi and the Congress. Soon after returning to India from Europe in October, he described the provision of dominion status in the report as being 'inconsistent with the independent spirit of Islam'. Its implication was that the creation was God's, the country was the viceroy's or of the parliament's, and the rule was Hindu Mahasabha's.[91] 'Today', he said on 25 December 1928, 'Mahatma Gandhi and Sir Ali Imam would be sitting under our flag and over them would fly the flag of the Union Jack. The Nehru report in its preamble has admitted the bondage of servitude.' He was equally outraged that Muslim representation in the central legislature was fixed at 25 and not 33 per cent, while separate electorates and weightages were done away with.[92] In his view, separate electorates guaranteed that a small minority was not swamped by an overwhelming majority, while weightages ensured that this majority would not establish 'a legalized tyranny of numbers'.[93]

Such views mostly mirrored the fears of government servants and landowners who, having gained political leverage through separate electorates and government nomination, faced the cheerless prospect of being eased out of legislative bodies. Equally, they were alarmed by the proposal for adult suffrage. The enfranchisement of over fifteen million voters, mainly tenants, was certain to oust the landlords from the general constituencies as well. Not surprisingly, they resisted all forms of provincial advance, and insisted on having separate electorates, weightages, and 'effective' Muslim representation on autonomous institutions created by the legislatures.

Mohamed Ali, now identified with such elements, did his best to turn the tables against his detractors. The first opportunity arose on 21 December 1928. The Ali brothers, in league with some others, disrupted a meeting which was tilted in favour of the Nehru report. When similar tactics were employed elsewhere, several delegates resigned and decided to boycott the forthcoming All India Khilafat Conference that was to be chaired by Mohamed Ali. A few days later Mohamed Ali did not need to stifle opposition at the All-Parties Muslim Conference in Delhi, for this assembly of loyalists had been converted to the idea that the Nehru report had jettisoned their interests.

Mohamed Ali's presence at the Delhi conference was described as 'a tragedy of Indian public life'. *The Servants of India* commented: 'One's heart sinks at the thought that the Ali brothers should have been among the staunchest supporters of the conference.'[94] Ansari, once his comrade-in-arms, was anguished by his parleys with the 'Aga Khan and Co.' He wrote:

> Ever since the Lucknow Convention many of us have been making ceaseless efforts to come to an understanding with the Ali brothers and their friends. . . . They gradually but surely went on receding from us until at last they found themselves in the company of the Aga Khan and Sir Muhammad Shafi in January last. The willingness with which they associated themselves with people whose only distinction is that they have always been reactionary in regard both to Indian and Muslim affairs was surprising. . . . Indeed the differences that in their origin concerned a few provisions of the Nehru Report have now grown into a conflict of the very outlook. This to my mind explained why the Ali brothers are adopting an irreconcilable attitude although they know very well that they are thereby strengthening the government as well as the communalists, both Hindu and Muslim. . . .[95]

A striking feature of the conference was that Mohamed Ali sat beside Muhammad Shafi who he had so often derided as a government stooge, and that the Aga Khan was cheered by Azad Sobhani whose vitriolic speeches at Kanpur in 1913 had forced the Khoja leader to quit the Muslim League. Mohamed Ali actually seconded the resolution proposed by Shafi. Likewise, leaders like Jinnah, Shafi and the Ali brothers, who had not shared a platform before, signed the 'Delhi Manifesto' on 9 March 1929 in order to persuade Muslims to stay away from the Congress meetings and processions. Nehru reacted angrily to Mohamed Ali's signing the 'Delhi Manifesto', declaring it a 'treason' against the Congress by one who had served as its president:

> The ex-Presidents of the National Congress are certainly a mixed lot and not always amenable to discipline. Like the king they appear to be above the law. I had ventured to criticize a statement made by one of them forgetful of this truism in Indian politics because of my high regard for this gallant leader in the cause of Indian freedom. He has made history and, if he but will, can do so again. But just when India is stretching her limbs for another and a stiffer struggle, when drooping spirits are reviving, he cries 'halt' and calls back his regiments and battalions. And have not many of those with whom he consorts in this endeavour been the strongest bulwarks of British rule in India and the antagonists of those who strive for freedom?

In his sharp rebuttal, Mohamed Ali condemned the Congress leaders who had defied the party's decisions on non-cooperation, non-violence,

Hindu-Muslim unity, and untouchability. As a price of his cooperation, Malaviya 'wanted to place a revolver in the hands of every Hindu lady, no doubt as a token of non-violence, and of course all the Hindu-Muslim riots in which he has never said a word against Hindus are in full conformity with the Congress precepts of Hindu-Muslim unity'. He accused Motilal Nehru of 'killing non-cooperation just as he is killing the Congress today and merging it into the Hindu Mahasabha in spite of his well-known lack of Hindu orthodoxy',[96] and deplored Gandhi's endorsement of the Nehru report. Quoting from his writings of 1924 and 1925 to show that the Mahatma was converted to a different creed and striving for different goals, he pointed out:

> Gandhi has defeated all Muslim attempts for a compromise. He is giving free rein to the communalism of the majority. The Nehru constitution is the legalized tyranny of numbers and is the way to rift and not peace. It recognizes the rank communalism of the majority as nationalism. The safeguards proposed to limit the high-handedness of the majority are branded as communal.[97]

Gandhi conceded that the Ali brothers 'had a fairly heavy list of complaints', and that he could not make an impression on them.[98] 'Whatever Maulana Mohamed Ali may think of me, I have nothing but kindly feelings about him. And I feel sure that time will remove misunderstandings. Having no feeling either against Islam or Mussalmans, I feel absolutely at ease', he wrote from the Yeravda Central Prison. He hoped in vain that 'if truth is in me, the brothers must capitulate'.[99] Some months earlier, Mohamed Ali had already lambasted Gandhi for 'fighting for the supremacy of Hinduism [and] the submergence of Muslims'. He refused to join 'Mr. Gandhi' not only because his civil disobedience movement was 'for making the seventy millions of Indian Muslims dependent on the Hindu Mahasabha',[100] but also doubted whether he would stick to his own programme:

> Doubtless man who could suddenly call of the non-cooperation campaign at Bardoli in 1922 with the same astonishing about-face can inaugurate a civil disobedience movement in 1930. But what surety is there that he would not again order suspension, just as he did eight years ago, only a few days after serving an ultimatum to the viceroy?[101]

Moreover the country was unprepared for civil disobedience: it lacked unity, discipline, and self-control. He warned Nehru: 'Your present colleagues will desert you. They will leave you in the lurch in a crisis. Your own Congressman will send you to the gallows.'[102]

Mohamed Ali's appeal to Muslims to send delegations to London symbolized the collapse of the old alliance on which Gandhi had built the non-cooperation movement. He himself joined a delegation, led by the Aga Khan, with the conviction that critical collaboration with the British at the Round Table Conference would bring greater political benefits than 'sedition' in Congress company. But his departure was marked by gloom, for he knew that his mission was condemned as smacking of treachery by those very people with whom he had worked in the past. In fact, the Maulana felt in London that, 'his real place was in the fight in India, not in the futile conference chamber in London'.[103] In Oxford, his alma mater, he addressed students in their tail coats, talked cricket, and made them laugh. But he 'made little or no impression and quite failed to put across the case for the Muslims to a youthful but intelligent audience who were to provide a fair number of the nation's political leaders in later years'.[104] His speech at the Round Table Conference, which turned out to be his last sermon, appeared to be the raving of a man isolated, inconsolably bereaved, dying. 'I want to go back to my country', Mohamed Ali declared, 'with the substance of freedom in my hand. Otherwise I will not go back to a slave country. I would even prefer to die in a foreign country so long as it is a free country, and if you do not give me freedom in India you will have to give me a grave here.' In Mujeeb's view, Mohamed Ali's appeal to the British to give India her freedom or else he would not return alive was no more than a pathetic admission of his failure.[105]

A chronic patient of diabetes, Mohamed Ali died in London on 3 January 1931 and was buried in Jerusalem. Gandhi, whom he derided with such vehemence during the years 1928-30, had this to say at his death: 'In him I have lost one whom I rejoiced to call brother and friend and the nation has lost a fearless patriot. We had differences of opinion between us, but love that cannot stand the strain of differences is like "a sounding brass and thinking cymbal".' Nehru was equally charitable. Reflecting on his role, he observed: 'It was a misfortune for India that he (Mohamed Ali) left the country for Europe in the summer of 1928. A great effort was then made to solve the communal problem. If Mohamed Ali had been here then, it is just conceivable that matters would have shaped differently.' Nehru added:

> For whatever the differences on the communal question might have been, there were very few differences on the political issue. He was devoted to the idea of Indian independence. And because of the common political outlook, it was always possible to come to some mutually satisfactory arrangement with him on the communal issue. There was nothing in common between him and the reactionaries who pose as the champions of communal interests.[106]

5. مجھ کو شاعر نہ کہو میرؔ کہ صاحب میں نے
درد و غم کتنے کیے جمع تو دیوان کیا

Don't think me a poet—no, my verse
Is made of pain and grief for than you know.

Mohamed Ali was blessed with the supreme gift of expression, but he was not one to be identified with any great principle or order, or even a big idea. He relished the trappings of power, the drama of great debates, the high-sounding titles, his name echoing through history. He was too outspoken to be a good manager of people. He excelled at exposing the follies of others but had little to advocate himself; his own thinking was ruthless—he spared nothing and nobody. He had a nimble wit, but sometimes his devastating sarcasm hurt, and he lost many friends.[107] He and his brother Shaukat were 'splendid agitators and very little more'. 'They certainly are not the type of men in whom we would have much faith, were they placed to rule over us', commented Abbas Tyabji, one of Gandhi's lieutenants in Bombay.[108] Edwin Montagu, the secretary of state who had not approved of Mohamed Ali's internment, found him to be 'a quite typical specimen, full of incurable vanity'.[109]

Mohamed Ali was a passionate man, strong in his resentments as in his affections. He left a strong although not wholly pleasant impression on people who knew him, of a man devoted to his convictions. At the same time, he was obstinate, impatient in temper, and choleric in disposition; quick to anger when honour or religion was touched; wild and untameable. He was the man for the people: impetuous, dashing, irrepressible, demanding sympathy by laying his heart open, crying and raising laughter, and believing in God and God's mercy with an intensity that made him at times completely irresponsible.[110] Though he advocated a strikingly wide range of ideas, some grossly contradicted each another, some complemented one another, and some appear to have been floated simply to guage public reaction before being discarded. The Urdu scholar Maulvi Abdul Haq found Mohamed Ali ruthless and dictatorial in his public and private conduct. He had an hysterical streak in his personality, lacked consideration for friends, and was, for these reasons, incapable of carrying through his numerous enterprises. Abdul Haq's final judgement was that Mohamed Ali, although a brilliant writer and orator, 'failed' to enhance his stature and reputation in public life.[111]

In his enthusiastic, unrealistic moods, which were frequent enough, he regarded himself as a link not only between Indian Muslims and the Turks, but also between the Turks and the rest of the world.[112] He was insensitive to the implications of the Turkish revolution, which was directed against the tyrannical rule of the sultan as well as against Western imperialism. Similarly, he was unfamiliar with scholars like Ziya Gökalp, the intellectual leader of that period, who had dismissed the idea of uniting Muslim nations under one ruler as a messianic hope. That is why when Muslims elsewhere were establishing national states independent of external ties of domination, Mohamed Ali was striving to recreate the khilafat of the classical theorists.

Inviting the amir of Afghanistan to liberate India from British imperialism was an indiscrete act. On such matters Mohamed Ali seemed to be wanting to forget, as often as he could, the need to be tactful, in order that he might assert with ever greater vehemence the fact that he was a sincere believer in Islam.[113] His endorsement of the idea of Muslim migration (*hijrat*) to Afghanistan was unrealistic and politically inexpedient. His credibility suffered, moreover, on account of the scandal over the 'misuse' of the khilafat funds and his frequent outbursts that caused a breach between the khilafatists and their liberal and socialist allies in the Congress.[114] The *Comrade* was revived in November 1924, but ceased publication in January 1926. 'Poverty is pestering me', Mohamed wrote. He considered restarting the paper 'and see if I can wipe off the deficit due to those two journals [*Comrade* and *Hamdard*] or I shall retire from public life, and earn 50 rupees from tuitions'.[115] The Ali brothers, having spent more than their means, were in dire financial straits. Delhi's chief commissioner informed the viceroy that Mohamed Ali was 'thoroughly discredited and almost penniless'. He went cap in hand to his former associates and colleagues (the Karachi merchant Haji Abdullah Haroon had already donated Rs. 10,000 to revive the *Comrade*), and having failed in almost all quarters he finally secured a grant of Rs. 6,000 from the deposed maharaja of Nabha.[116] Some years later, the raja of Alwar bore his travel and treatment expenses in London. Even if these are not illustrations of Mohamed Ali's loss of credibility with his own community, they clearly reveal the gradual reversal of his fortunes.

The Congress gradually deserted Mohamed Ali;[117] yet, he clung to the much-maligned khilafat committees. His defence of Ibn Saud, who had demolished numerous sepulchers held sacred by Muslims, alienated him from his spiritual mentor, Abdul Bari, and other friends. But he was not impressed. During his visit to the Arab lands in June 1926 he discovered the squalor of Mecca and Medina, the barrenness of the surrounding land, the degeneracy of the social conditions, and the mismanagement of the *haj* traffic. Yet, he continued to insist that the khilafat committees were destined to bring about a truly Islamic rule in the Holy Land. He wanted India's Muslims to form a party around the nucleus of the khilafat group, persuade other Islamic people to their way of thinking, and ultimately achieve a united Muslim voice. He wanted them to contribute money, time, technical assistance and moral support to the Hijaz, devote themselves wholeheartedly to the reformation of the Centre of Islam, and thus earn the good requital in both worlds. He was confident of resisting Ibn Saud's arrogation of control of the Holy Land and re-establishing a genuine Islamic rule.[118]

Mohamed Ali paid scant regard to his own comrades who had followed his lead in the past but were no longer prepared to pursue his mission. His protégés in UP—Khaliquzzaman and Shuaib Qureshi—opposed his plan of sending three deputations to the Middle East.[119] In neighbouring Delhi, Ansari resigned from the khilafat committees in July 1926, stating that as an Indian owing allegiance first to the motherland he had decided to sever his ties with communal and sectional organizations.[120] In Punjab, after their success in the 1924 elections, the Muslim swarajists took less interest in the khilafat committee; the main opposition to the Ali brothers came from the khilafatists under the leadership of Saifuddin Kitchlew. Iqbal believed that the khilafat movement, in its dying moments, unfolded aspects in which 'no sincere Muslim could join for a single minute'. Turkey, he pointed out, was the first Muslim country to shake off the fetters of medieval mentality and found a way of life of her own.[121]

'Muslim identity' in a plural society had to be defined not in relation to the Islamic world but in response to the specific historical and contemporary experiences of the Muslim communities in the subcontinent. This fact, underlined in Saiyid Ahmad Khan's rejection of pan-Islamism towards the end of the nineteenth century, was creatively expressed by Azad, Ajmal Khan and Ansari. But Mohamed Ali was swayed by his own religious/Islamic rhetoric without reflecting on the wider implications of the khilafat movement on inter-community relations. He even refused to accept that his co-religionists in Turkey themselves had played the final part in destroying what he was almost single-handedly fighting to maintain. As he once put it, he had 'an inherent and almost ineradicable tendency towards diffusion and a fatal attraction for tangents'.[122] He could not build the bridges for retreat, because he did not possess the skill to do so. Instead, he aimed 'to destroy all that did not conform to his ideal, even though he could not reconstruct what he had destroyed'.[123] Although popular with those who thought it a point of honour to wear Islam on their sleeves, he ultimately undermined his own position and damaged the very causes he aspired to serve.[124]

Note on Mohamed Ali's My Life: A Fragment

Since its publication in January 1942, Mohamed Ali's *My Life: A Fragment* has been widely read in academic circles in India and Pakistan. Afzal Iqbal, the editor, secured the 'manuscript' from Mohamed Mujeeb, the vice-chancellor of Delhi's Jamia Millia Islamia, and published this 'autobiographical sketch'.

Mohamed Ali was a prolific writer; yet, he did not consider writing a book until his internment in 1923, following the famous Karachi trial. This is what he told Abdul Majid Daryabadi in 1916 while in Chhindwara, then a small town in the Central Provinces (now Madhya Pradesh):

> You suggest to me that I should write some book during my enforced leisure, and that our people expect one from me. If that is so, I am afraid they don't know me. Firstly, I have not the patient perseverance nor the temper of the researcher. Secondly, my emotions are much too strong to permit what intellect I may possess to be exerted in the writing of a book. . . . No, my friend, my brain is far too busy (and so is my heart) to allow of any leisure for such 'pastimes' as authorship.[125]

He did, however, write a great deal more than many of his contemporaries. He contributed to his own newspapers, and wrote hundreds of routine letters as an editor. Besides writing *My Life*, he wrote poems to fill a not-so-slim volume, and miscellaneous historical, literary and political pieces to fill another.[126] During his internment and his trips to Europe, he corresponded with his friends and family members.[127] These letters constitute a major corpus of pan-Islamic literature in India. They uncover major themes that concerned his generation of educated Muslims who turned to him for political inspiration and leadership.

The tone in his correspondence constantly varies from boredom and depression, on the one hand, to exhilaration and conviction on the other, now relaxed and desultory, now indulging in flights of fantasy or burlesque. A flair for the dramatic, coupled with a wry self-awareness, helped foster a temperament that allowed the fullest reins to intellectual enthusiasm while never really realizing personal ones. This complexity, not rare but fascinating in Mohamed Ali's case, is also noticeable in his speeches.

My Life is much more reflective and analytical than any of Mohamed Ali's other published writings. It is an important personal statement on how some educated Muslims lived through the turbulent decades of the early twentieth century. It is an individual's intellectual and spiritual journey, and his engagement with a society and polity that was undergoing rapid changes. 'Experts often write for experts,' commented Mohamed Ali, 'but I am, so to speak, "the man-in-the-street", and I write for "the man in the street". The individual experience which I relate will make this clear, and being typical of the history of so many Muslim lives of my generation, it will not, I trust, be altogether lacking in interest.'

At the same time, *My Life* reflects the collective experiences of large numbers of people who shared the author's commitment to and his passion for 'rejuvenating' the Muslim communities in the subcontinent. It is no doubt inadequate in many ways—verbose, incoherent, repetitive and full of digressions. Besides, as Afzal Iqbal pointed out, of the four parts Mohamed Ali planned to write, only the first is complete. The second part—included by Iqbal as an appendix—is incomplete. Yet, *My Life* is a document of considerable significance for students of modern Islam in South Asia, its historical value enhanced by the absence of a similar text written by any of the leading Muslim actors of the period. Maulana Abul Kalam Azad, for one, did not write much besides his commentary on the Koran; he expressed himself instead in the literary form of his letters, published as *Ghubar-i Khatir.* In fact, Jawaharlal Nehru commented in his prison diary: 'Free thinker and magnificent writer as he is, he should have turned out a host of splendid books. Yet his record is a very limited one.'[128]

At a time when scholars are attempting to delineate the contours of 'Muslim identity' in South Asia, Mohamed Ali's *My Life* enables us to understand how some Muslims constructed their identity in British India. For this reason this book invites comparison with other texts written around the same time in other countries by Muslim scholars and publicists. At a time when 'communalism' and 'separatism' are rearing their heads again, *My Life* reveals, more than any other contemporary account, the anxieties and aspirations of several Muslim groups in a colonial society that was being gradually transformed as a result of far-reaching political, administrative and bureaucratic changes.

NOTES

1. Sydenham to Hardinge, 18 Mar. 1913, Hardinge papers.
2. Meston to Chelmsford, 20 Aug. 1917, File No. 136 (1).
3. Quoted in Afzal Iqbal, *Life and Times of Mohamed Ali*, p. 113. In May 1915, the Ali brothers were asked to remain in Mehrauli and abstain from political

meetings. They were described by Richard Burn (writing for Meston) as 'disseminators of mischief and would-be-traitors', who 'have done any amount of evil at Aligarh. They have tried to stir up trouble in Lucknow and their message is mischievous wherever they go.' Home Poll. D, Proceedings, May 1915, 36, NAI.

4. Robinson, *Separatism Among Muslims*, pp. 178-9; and Brown, *Gandhi's Rise to Power*, pp. 139-40.
5. Moin Shakir, *Khilafat to Partition*, New Delhi, 1972, pp. 70, 74, 86; S.M. Hadi, *Ali Biradaran aur Unka Zamana*, New Delhi, 1978; Shan Muhammad, *Freedom Movement in India—The Role of Ali Brothers*, New Delhi, 1978; *Aaj Kal*, New Delhi, 1978; *Jamia*, New Delhi, 'Mohamed Ali Number', Apr. 1979, Jan.-Feb. 1980.
6. Moinul Haq (ed.), *Mohamed Ali: Life and Work*, Karachi, 1978, p. 41; *Nigar*, Nov.-Dec. 1976; *Maulana Mohamed Ali Jauhar Sadi Conference*, Karachi, 1978, and for the view that the 'two-nation theory' had been forecasted by Mohamed Ali, see Ahmad, *Islamic Modernism*, p. 162.
7. Thus, an address presented to Mohamed Ali following his release from internment, stated: 'It would require a volume to enumerate in detail your services in regard to the M.A.O. College, the Muslim University, the galvanizing of the Muslim community through your brilliant newspapers, the *Comrade* and the *Hamdard* . . . the raising of funds for Muslim victims in the Balkan War, the organizing of a competent and well-equipped medical mission for the Turkish wounded. Your restoration to liberty is a mark of profound rejoicing to us. . . . Your presence in our midst will stimulate our community into the solidarity seriously imperilled during the last five years of agonizing ordeal.' *Leader* (Allahabad), 12 and 15 Jan. 1917.
8. Mazharul Haq and Ansari to Hony. Secy., Muslim League, 3 Sept. 1917; and Ansari to A.M. Khwaja, 3 Sept. 1917, in Hasan (ed.), *Muslims and the Congress*, pp. 9-10.
9. Mohamed Ali, *Kalam-i Jauhar*, New Delhi, 1938; A. Rauf (ed.), *Mohamed Ali aur Unki Shairi*, Karachi, 1963; Nur-ur Rahman (ed.), *Divan-i Jauhar*, Karachi, 1962.
10. Mohamed Ali to James DuBoulay, 18 Feb. 1919, in Hasan (ed.), *Mohamed Ali in Indian Politics*, Vol. 2, pp. 192-3.
11. The best source for Mohamed Ali's life and career is his own 'autobiography' and his articles published in the *Comrade* on 21 and 28 Nov. 1924. Much additional information is available in the works of Afzal Iqbal, Rais Ahmad Jafri, Shan Muhammad and Abu Salman Shahjahanpuri.
12. 'People wondered why any mother should be so lacking in love for her children as to send them away from home while they are still so young.' *Comrade*, 5 Dec. 1924.
13. Ibid., 21 Nov. 1924.
14. Hasan (ed.), *My Life*, p. 69.

15. Ibid., p. 70.
16. Azim Husain, *Fazl-i-Husain: A Political Biography*, Bombay, 1936, p. 20; Iqbal, *Life and Times*, pp. 31-2.
17. Mohamed Ali to Dewan Tek Chand, n.d., Mohamed Ali papers [hereafter MAP], Jamia Millia Islamia, New Delhi.
18. Testimonial of Rector, Lincoln College, 19 Oct. 1901, ibid.
19. Testimonial of James Williams, 14 Oct. 1901, ibid.
20. Hasan (ed.), *My Life*, p. 73.
21. This is revealed in his exchanges with Saiyid Mahfuz Ali. It is, however, clear that he took a keen interest in political developments. Although exaggerated claims are made about his influence on the Muslim League deliberations in Dec. 1906, he was regarded as a potentially bright recruit. In Feb. 1907, he lectured in Allahabad. A month later he prepared a text of the Muslim League proceedings which was published as 'Green Book No. 1'. This prompted an explanation from an official. 'I sent in a reply,' wrote Mohamed Ali, 'before the Council. In response, a general confidential circular was issued to government servants. They were told not to contribute articles which were likely to create communal animosity.' Mohamed Ali to Mahfuz Ali, 14 Jan. 1910, M. Sarwar (ed.), *Khutut-i Mohamed Ali*, New Delhi, 1940, pp. 252-4. For Mohamed Ali's speeches, see Home Poll. B, 149, 1913, NAI.
22. Dunlop Smith to Mohamed Ali, 31 Jan. 1907, MAP.
23. To Dunlop Smith, 5 Dec. 1907, ibid.; and G.K. Gokhale, 8 Feb. 1908, Gokhale papers (341), NAI.
24. To Mahfuz Ali, 14 Jan. 1910, *Khutut*, pp. 252-4.
25. Ibid.
26. To the Gaekwad of Baroda, n.d., MAP.
27. Shaukat Ali to Mohamed Ali, 4 Jul. 1909, ibid.
28. G.S. Clark to Mohamed Ali, 2 Nov. 1909; Dunlop Smith to Mohamed Ali, 30 Oct. 1909; H.A. Stuart to Mohamed Ali, 10 Dec. 1909, ibid.
29. *My Life*, pp. 33-4, and Mohamed Ali to the nawab of Jaora, 23 Nov. 1910, ibid.
30. Ibid., p. 34.
31. Home Poll. D., Dec. 1914, 31, NAI.
32. To Mohamed Ali, 20 Aug. 1915, MAP. See, Abu Salman Shahjahanpuri, *Maulana Mohamed Ali aur Unki Sahafat* (Maulana Mohamed Ali and his Journalism), Karachi, 1983.
33. For the influence of *Comrade*, see K.M. Ashraf, 'Aligarh ki Siyasi Zindagi', in *Aligarh Magazine*, 1953-5, p. 164. 'Throughout the country, only one voice was heard by the people of the north and the south, the east and the west, by the educated and the illiterate, the ulama and the ignorant. . . .' Abdul Majid Daryabadi, *Maqalat-i Majid*, Bombay, n.d., pp. 233-4.
34. *Comrade*, 28 Jan. 1991.
35. Gail Minault and David Lelyveld, 'The Campaign for a Muslim University',

MAS, Vol. 8, 1974, p. 145; David Lelyveld, 'Three Aligarh Students: Aftab Ahmad Khan, Ziauddin Ahmad and Mohamed Ali', *MAS*, Vol. 9, 1975, pp. 103-16, and his *Aligarh's First Generation*, pp. 330-6.

36. Quoted in P.N. Furbank, *E.M. Forster: A Life: The Growth of the Novelist, 1879-1914*, London, 1978, p. 227.
37. Hardinge to Meston, 14 Nov. 1912; Hardinge to Butler, 29 Oct. 1912; Butler to Hardinge, 3 Nov. 1912, Hardinge papers. Malcolm Hailey, chief commissioner of Delhi, described Mohamed Ali as 'the centre and inspiration of the Pan-Islamic movement'. To H.H. Wheeler, 1 May 1915, Home Poll. D, May 1915, 36, NAI.
38. *Comrade*, 30 Dec. 1911.
39. Ibid.
40. Minault, *The Khilafat Movement*, p. 19.
41. The article gave the government 'ample justification for suppressing such writings'. An official note stated on 6 Oct. 1914: 'I do not see how anyone can read the article except as a direct incitement to Turkey to go to war, and practically what it says is that if this does bring them up against Russia and France, they have no cause to love these Powers and it does not matter much. England is practically threatened if she does not evacuate Egypt, and Germany is extolled. If this is not attacking our allies and siding with our enemies it is difficult to know what it is?' Home Poll. A., Oct. 1913, pp. 142-9, NAI. The Ali brothers maintained that they were interned because they freely expressed their allegiance demanded by their Islamic faith. To viceroy, 24 Apr. 1919, MAP.
42. *Leader*, 12 and 15 Jan. 1920.
43. Home Poll. D, Proceedings, Oct. and Dec. 1915, NAI.
44. Mahadev Desai (ed.), *Day-to-Day with Gandhi* (Varanasi, 1968), Vol. 1, pp. 93, 211.
45. Brown, *Gandhi's Rise to Power*, p. 152.
46. After arriving in India, Gandhi told a khilafat meeting that he began to find out 'good Mohammedan leaders'. He was satisfied when he reached Delhi and met the Ali brothers. 'It was a question of love at first sight between us.' Speech at Bombay, 9 May 1919, *The Collected Works of Mahatma Gandhi* (*CWMG*), Vol. 15, p. 295.
47. Gandhi to Mohamed Ali, 18 Nov. 1918, ibid., p. 64.
48. Hasan (ed.), *Muslims and the Congress*, Appendix 1; Abdur Rahman Siddiqi to Mohamed Ali, 24 Mar. 1919, MAP; WRDCI, Mar. 1919, Home Poll. B, Apr. 1919, pp. 148-52, NAI; A.M. Daryabadi, *Mohamed Ali: Zaati Diary ke Chand Auraq*, Hyderabad, 1943, p. 20.
49. W.J. Watson, 'Mohamed Ali and the Khilafat Movement' (unpublished MA thesis, McGill University, 1955), p. 14.
50. To Meston, 19 Feb. 1913, MAP.
51. To James DuBoulay, 3 Jan. 1912, ibid.

52. To F.H. Lucas, 3 Jan. 1912, ibid.
53. For correspondence with the viceroy on these issues, see Hardinge papers (84); Iqbal, *Life and Times,* pp. 77-8.
54. *Comrade*, 13 Sept. 1913; and Mohamed Ali to James Le Touche, 4 Nov. 1913, MAP.
55. Quoted in B.R. Nanda, *Gandhi, Pan-Islamism, Imperialism and Nationalism*, Bombay, 1989, p. 138.
56. To John Morley, 2 Nov. 1913, MAP.
57. To Chelmsford, 24 Apr. 1919, ibid.
58. 'Maulana Mohamed Ali Jauhar', *Naqqush (Shakhsiat Number),* Oct. 1956, p. 1161.
59. To Chelmsford, 24 Apr. 1919, MAP.
60. To Malcolm Hailey, 24 May 1915, ibid.
61. Ibid., 2 June 1915.
62. To Chelmsford, 24 May 1919, ibid.
63. Hasan (ed.), *My Life*, pp. 63-4.
64. Ibid., p. 122; and Iqbal (ed.), *Selected Writings*, p. 170.
65. Ibid., p. 127.
66. A.M. Daryabadi, *Zaati Diary*, p. 14; to A.M. Daryabadi, 22 May and 25 July 1916, in Hasan (ed.), *Mohamed Ali in Indian Politics*, Vol. 1, pp. 269-76.
67. Daryabadi, ibid., p. 14; Mohamed Ali to Daryabadi, 22 May and 25 July 1916 (Urdu), Daryabadi papers, NMML.
68. To Gandhi, 20 Feb. 1918, MAP.
69. Afzal Iqbal, *Select Writings*, p. 405.
70. *Mussalman* (Calcutta), 13 May 1921.
71. Mohamed Ali's loyalty to Islam was expressed in the days before the Turko-Italian war as loyalty to the Indian Muslim community rather than to an abstract way to Allah. His communal consciousness, as he said, was far more secular than religious: his decision to take to journalism was dictated by the 'secular affairs of my country' rather than by a 'religious call'. Then, in the seclusion of his internment, he read through the Koran. Islam possessed him and he discovered the dogmas and ethical codes of his religion. After this experience, argues Watson, his motivation was 'Islamic duty' rather than 'communal loyalty'.
72. To Chelmsford, 24 Apr. 1919; Hasan (ed.), *Mohamed Ali in Indian Politics*, Vol. 2, p. 236 ; also, speech in London on 22 Apr. 1920; Iqbal (ed.), *Selected Writings*, pp. 183-93.
73. Speech delivered in London on 23 Mar. 1920, in *Selected Writings*, Vol. 2, pp. 20-1.
74. 'Islam united Muslims by offering a set of common ideals and offered the only rational basis for unity and cooperation among its followers. The sympathies of a Muslim are co-extensive with his religion because they have been bred into him by the inspiring spirit of his creed.' *Comrade*, 12 Apr. 1913.

75. Watson, op. cit., p. 55.
76. Mujeeb, *The Indian Muslims*, p. 537.
77. Mohamed Ali to Shaukat Ali, 15 May 1920, MAP.
78. Hasan, *A Nationalist Conscience*, p. 104. Mohamed Ali is reported to have said in Sept. 1923: 'I never conceived of the Jamia's growth and permanence at all. The Jamia's existence today is rather like that of the refugees and the Prophet's helpers at Medina who were lying in wait for the conquest of Mecca. Our real objective is Aligarh which some day we shall conquer.' Quoted in A.G. Noorani, *President, Zakir Husain: A Quest for Excellence*, Bombay, 1967, p. 25. On this point, see Mujeeb, 'Oral History transcript' (407), p. 35, NMML.
79. Brown, *Gandhi's Rise to Power*, p. 331, fn. 2; *Day-to-Day*, Vol. 2, p. 238.
80. Brown, *Gandhi's Rise to Power*, pp. 330-1.
81. To Shaukat Ali, 15 May 1920, MAP.
82. To Swami Shraddhanand, 26 Mar. 1924, ibid.
83. Quoted in Rajmohan Gandhi, *The Good Boatman: A Portrait of Gandhi*, New Delhi, 1995, p. 104; and speech at Lahore, in *Bombay Chronicle*, 26 May 1924.
84. In September 1923 he complained that the swarajists have 'completely gone back on the entire creed and policy of Gandhi'. 'I have been realizing every day that the leaders of the Swaraj Party want to throw Gandhism overboard without some of them having the courage to confess,' he wrote to his khilafat comrade, Saifuddin Kitchlew. He wanted him to be a peacemaker between him and the 'Gujarati friends', although he advised 'caution and restraint'. Mohamed Ali to Kitchlew, 30 Sept. 1923, Hailey papers, Mss. Eur. 220 (7-A), BL.
85. Nehru, *An Autobiography*, p. 99. 'I have just received your letter, and must "protest most indignantly" once more against your misplaced modesty. My dear Jawahar! it is just because some members of the Working Committee distrust and dislike your presence as Secretary that I like it.' Mohamed Ali to Nehru, 15 Jan. 1924, MAP.
86. Mohamed Ali to Nehru, n.d., 1923, in *A Bunch of Old Letters*, pp. 30-1.
87. G. Adhikari (ed.), *Documents of the History of the Communist Party of India*, Vol. 2, p. 181.
88. Iqbal (ed.), *Selected Writings*, p. 256.
89. Ansari to Mazharul Haq, 7 Sept. 1929; Hasan (ed.), *Muslims and the Congress*, pp. 86-7.
90. Mohamed Ali to Gandhi, 21 July 1924, MAP.
91. 'You make compromises in your constitution everyday with false doctrines, immoral conceptions and wrong ideas, but you make no compromise with our communalists—with separate electorates and reserve seats. Twenty-five per cent is our proportion of the population and yet you will not give us 33 per cent in the Assembly. You are a Jew, a Bania.' See Hasan, *Nationalism and Communal Politics* (1979 edn.), pp. 287-8.

92. Ibid.
93. In the very first issue of the *Comrade*, he had declared separate electorates to be necessary because of 'the distinct and well-defined Hindu and Muslim standpoints in regard to the common, immediate and everyday affairs of Indian life'. *Comrade*, 11 and 28 Jan. 1911, 29 Mar. 1913, 19 Jan. and 6 Feb. 1925.
94. *Servants of India*, 10 Jan. 1929.
95. Ansari to Mazharul Haq, 7 Sept. 1929, Hasan (ed.), *Muslims and the Congress*, pp. 86-7.
96. *Nigarishat-i Mohamed Ali*, quoted in Abdul Hamid, *Muslim Separatism in India*, p. 201.
97. *Times of India*, 5 Mar. 1929.
98. Gandhi to Motilal Nehru, 12 Aug. 1929, Motilal Nehru papers (G-1), NMML; see also Gandhi to Shaukat Ali, 17 Apr. 1930, *CWMG*, Vol. 43, p. 280.
99. Gandhi to Horace G. Alexander, 23 Dec. 1930, *CWMG*, Vol. 45, p. 26; *Young India*, 3 Apr. 1930, *CWMG*, Vol. 43, p. 126.
100. Quoted in Reginald Coupland, *The Constitutional Problem in India*, Oxford, 1944, pt. 3, p. 111. The position of the 'Nationalist Muslims', on the other hand, was different. This was explained by Ansari to the raja of Mahmudabad: 'Whilst, on the one hand, we consider the policy and programme of the Congress entirely ill-conceived and detrimental to the larger interests of the country today, we do not consider the campaign of civil disobedience conceived in the spirit of antagonism to the Muslims.' To the raja of Mahmudabad, 11 May 1930, Hasan (ed.), *Muslims and the Congress*, p. 121.
101. Jafri (ed.), *Nigarishat-i Mohamed Ali*, pp. 237-72.
102. Nehru, *An Autobiography*, p. 120.
103. Ibid.,
104. Benthall papers (2), CSAS, Cambridge.
105. Mujeeb, *Indian Muslims*, p. 539.
106. *CWMG*, Vol. 45, p. 203; Nehru, *An Autobiography*, p. 120.
107. Nehru, *An Autobiography*, p. 117.
108. Brown, *Gandhi's Rise to Power*, p. 276. This opinion was shared by others. One of them wrote to Tej Bahadur Sapru: 'Frankly, I am not very much interested in the Ali brothers. I do not believe in them, and to the extent that they are doing right, it is because they are either attracted by Gandhi's glamour, or they feel that they can work more effectively under the kudos of his name.' S.L. Polak to Sapru, 8 July 1981, Sapru papers, Vol. 17, p. 241. Percival Spear, who met Mohamed Ali at Delhi's St. Stephen's College in 1924, wrote: 'He was a handsome bearded man with striking eyes and clothed in flowing robes. His speech was easy, his manner ingratiating, that of a willing sufferer for a noble cause. To me he seemed to be too suave to be sincere and too insincere to be noble. In fact I took an instant dislike to

him.' Percival and Margaret Spear, *India Remembered*, New Delhi, 1981, p. 15.

109. To Chelmsford, 23 June 1920, File No. 6, Chelmsford papers. 'Why we should intern Mohamed Ali for pan-Mohammedanism', Montagu recorded in his diary on 11 Nov. 1917, 'when we encourage pan-Judaism, I cannot for the life of me understand.' S.D. Waley, *Edwin Montagu: A Memoir and an Account of his Visits to India*, Bombay, 1964, p. 141.
110. Mujeeb, *Indian Muslims*, p. 536.
111. Abdul Haq, *Chand Humasr*, Karachi, 1952 edn., p. 164. Muhammad Sadiq had described this sketch of Mohamed Ali as 'vitriolic'. *Twentieth Century Urdu Literature*, Karachi, 1983, p. 368.
112. Mujeeb, *Indian Muslims*, p. 538.
113. Azad stated that 'whatever Mohamed Ali said was quite compatible with the teaching of Islam'. Home Poll., 1921, 45, NAI. Later, of course, Mohamed Ali clarified his position in order to remove the misunderstandings in many quarters. See his presidential address, Allahabad district conference, May 1921, Home Poll., 1921, 10, NAI.
114. The Urdu poet, Brij Narain 'Chakbast' was convinced that the political turmoil in India was fomented to strengthen Islam and create conditions which would give Afghanistan the excuse to invade the country. He did not think that Muslims could be converted to Indian nationalism because of their extra-territorial loyalties. According to him, Mohamed Ali, a pan-Islamist, was not a friend of the Hindus, and that the Ali brothers used Gandhi to save their own ends. Chakbast to Sapru, 28 Apr. 1921 (in Urdu), Sapru papers. In an 'Open letter to the Maulana Sahebs', the editor of *Bharatwasi* took exception to the khilafatists designating themselves as 'Khadim-i Kaaba' (Servants of Kaaba) and not as 'Khadim-i Hind' (Servants of India). He told the Ali brothers: 'For you swarajya for India is not the first duty. You build the whole edifice on religion, while we build the entire edifice on patriotic considerations.' P. Parasram to Ali brothers, 8 July 1921, MAP.
115. *Searchlight*, 17 Apr. 1927.
116. Page, *Prelude to Partition*, pp. 104-5.
117. One of his former colleagues, Arif Husain Hasvi, resigned from the *Hamdard* because of his communal posture. *Searchlight*, 14 May 1926. Page, *Prelude to Partition*, pp. 100-1.
118. Watson, 'Mohamed Ali and the Khilafat Movement', p. 87; Ahmad, *Islamic Modernism*, p. 139; Rais Ahmad Jafri, *Karawan-i Gumgushta*, Karachi, 1971, pp. 16-18.
119. Page, *Prelude to Partition*, p. 502.
120. Ansari to Shaukat Ali, 16 July 1926, Hasan (ed.), *Muslims and the Congress*, p. 19.
121. Page, *Prelude to Partition*, pp. 503-4. For Iqbal, Schimmel, *Gabriel's Wings*, p. 47.

122. Quoted in Nanda, *Gandhi, Pan-Islamism*, p. 201.
123. Khaliquzzaman, *Pathway to Pakistan*, p. 69.
124. Mujeeb, *Indian Muslims*, p. 538.
125. 25 July 1916, Abdul Majid Daryabadi papers, NMML.
126. Rais Ahmed Jafri (ed.), *Selections from Mohamed Ali's Comrade*, Lahore, 1965, and his *Ifadat-i Mohamed Ali*, Hyderabad, n.d.; Mohammed Sarwar (ed.), *Mazameen-i Mohamed Ali*, New Delhi, 1938, 2 vols.
127. Hasan (ed.), *Mohamed Ali in Indian Politics*, 3 vols.; Shan Muhammed (ed.), *Unpublished Letters of the Ali Brothers*, New Delhi, 1979; Abu Salman Shahjahanpuri (ed.), *Siyasi Maktubat Rais al-Ahrar*, Karachi, 1978; Muhammad Sarwar, *Maulana Mohamed Ali ka Europe ka Safar*, Lahore, 1941.
128. Christmas Day—1942, S. Gopal (ed.), *SWJN*, Vol. 13, p. 39.

7

Representations of Indian Nationalism: Ideology and Praxis of Azad and Mohamed Ali

Maulana Abul Kalam Azad's ideological discourse was influenced by his knowledge of and interaction with Islamic societies, while his political praxis was determined by the specificity of India's colonial experience. At the same time, he was not swayed by a unified stream of thought or monolithic ideology. Though Islam was central to his world view, he took great pains to scrutinize and evaluate existing theories and established notions. 'There is no conviction in my heart', he wrote, 'which the thorns of doubt have failed to pierce: there is no faith in my soul which has not been subjected to all the conspiracy, of disbelief.'[1] Allegiance to his intellectual mentors was not constant as the Maulana traversed the rough terrain of religion, politics and philosophy. 'I am under no obligation', he claimed, 'for guidance to any man's hand or tongue, nor to any syllabus of education. All the guidance I have received has been from the Divine Throne.'[2] In the end, he emerged from the darkness of his inner strivings as an independent man.

The same spirit of independence was the hallmark of his public life. He was nobody's follower, not even Gandhi's. Even though religion and moral fervour bound the Mahatma and the Maulana in a common quest for swaraj, they did not share a common perspective on socio-political issues. Azad's relationship with other front-rank Congress leaders was ambivalent. This was because his political survival was not dependent on his loyalty to a Gandhi or a Jawaharlal Nehru or his alignment with or opposition to any of the Congress factions. His stature and charismatic appeal rested on his quality of mind, his unassailable loyalty to the Congress, his deep commitment to India's independence and his firm opposition to communal forces. In the words of Muhammad Mujeeb: 'He was too aloof to concern himself with persons, too intellectual to relish political small talk, too proud to think in terms of alliance, affiliation or opposition. . . . He had to be taken for what he was, with no credentials than his personality.'[3]

This chapter reflects on Azad's relationship with Mohamed Ali, a leading and popular figure who rose like a firmament on the Indian political scene. Both burst on the national stage around the same time, achieving success and prominence through their powerful writings. They voiced their community's anguish over the Balkan issue, the Kanpur mosque, the future of the university at Aligarh, and spearheaded the massive pan-Islamic upsurge. While Azad worked laboriously over sheafs of *fatawa*,[4] Mohamed Ali reached out to the common people to disseminate his ideas on a wide range of contemporary issues relating to Indian nationalism, the future of Islam, and of Indian Muslims. And when the British government put them in gaol time and time again, both reflected on their role with a sense of pride and satisfaction and derived comfort from the fact of occupying centre-stage and influencing the course of history. Azad saw himself in the same role as Jesus, a victim of unjust courts: 'At all events, how strange and glorious a place is this prisoners deck where both the greatest and the best of men are made to stand. For even so great a being as He, this was no inappropriate place.'[5]

I

The first decade of the twentieth-century witnessed the rise of a new generation of young Muslims—the men of *Nai Raushni*—with an ideology and outlook on contemporary social and political issues which was different from Aligarh's first generation. Men like Hasrat Mohani, Zafar Ali Khan, Raja Ghulam Husain, the Ali brothers and Wilayat Ali 'Bambooque' repudiated Aligarh's political legacy by acting in unison with the nationalist forces. All were graduates of the Aligarh College, where they had once learnt the lessons of loyalty at the feet of their mentor, Saiyid Ahmad Khan.

The person who did not belong to UP and was not educated in Western schools and colleges was Mohuiddin Ahmad, better known as Abul Kalam Azad. He studied at Mecca and, in 1898, when the family returned to India, he was tutored by his father Maulana Khairuddin Ahmad in the Islamic sciences. Later, he came into contact with Shibli Numani, and was exposed to the liberal, reformist writings of Egyptian scholars, Muhammad

Abduh and Rashid Rida. With his enriched intellectual experiences, he commented on contemporary issues with sensitivity in his first major journalistic venture, the *Al-Hilal*, launched in 1912, which took educated Muslims by storm with its eloquence and fervour. 'The Muslims were set on fire by his passionate words', recalled Saiyid Sulaiman Nadwi, who worked with him on the staff of *Al-Hilal* for a time in 1913.[6]

Azad strayed into the political arena in Calcutta, then in the throes of the Swadeshi agitation. Impressed by the revolutionaries,[7] he regarded their anti-imperialism parallel to similar movements in other Muslim lands: he claimed that the *Al-Hilal* was founded to propagate his nationalistic, anti-imperialistic stand. From1912-13 until his imprisonment in 1921, he was connected with several agitations for which he was often sent to gaol. He toiled in and out of prison over a monumental *Tarjuman al-Koran* (the first volume was published in 1931), putting forward the view of the transcendental oneness of all faiths and the theology of multi-religious cooperation. He was looked upon, in spite of his youthful years, as one of the elders in the Congress, whose advice both in national and political matters as well as in regard to the communal and minority questions was highly valued. In the final phase of his life, he returned to the front rank of politics as the Congress president from 1939 to 1946, and as the symbol of those Muslims who worked for a united India. He opposed the Partition heart and soul—almost alone among the Congress stalwarts to do so. His speeches echoed the themes of his earlier life and writings: communal harmony, religious broad-mindedness, and cultural cosmopolitanism.

Mohamed Ali's career followed a familiar graph—degrees obtained at Aligarh and Oxford, followed by jobs in the princely states of Rampur and Baroda. While in service, he wrote and lectured on the contemporary political scene and took part in the foundation of the Muslim League. By the time the *Comrade* was launched, Mohamed Ali (yet to acquire the prefix 'Maulana' before his name) had gained a substantial following in his alumni, the college at Aligarh. Around this time, Azad was busy planning his journalistic assault in Calcutta, a city where the echoes of the Swadeshi movement continued to reverberate in many circles.

When the *Comrade* and *Al-Hilal* appeared, they bore the unmistakable style of their editors. Azad was not much of a stylist, but wrote authoritatively. His discourse was subtle, complex, and incisive; his style fierce, combative, and akin to the Egyptian journal *Urwat al wuthqa*. He invoked scriptural and rational arguments assaulting the position of his opponents effectively, pausing only to regret occasionally the necessity of dealing with noisome adversaries. He spoke in the language of a 'high-souled prophet', appealed to religious passions, awakened dormant spirits by invoking Islamic symbols, and urged the ulama to alter the language and tenor of their discourses. At first, he envisaged leading the Muslims at the head of a 'Party of God' (*Hizbullah*) to Indians in ousting the British. He, then, founded the Dar al-Irshad to reform the teaching methods used in religious institutions, encourage independent thinking, and to make plain to students the social applicability of their curriculum. Such activities were a necessary preliminary to Azad's emergence as a powerful political force. They were, moreover, designed to change the intellectual and political climate created by the Aligarh school.

Mohamed Ali had an equally meteoric rise, though without being an ideologue or a theorist like Azad. He was a crusader—one who sought to undo the 'wrongs' done to his community by the forces inimical to Islam. That is why he took to journalism, 'the only avenue through which I could reach a place in which I could prove of any appreciable use to it . . .'. His style was verbose, pedestrian, rambling and repetitive; yet, he had a profound influence in moulding public opinion. The Muslim intelligentsia throughout the country responded with warmth and enthusiasm to his writings.

Islam, as expressed in his life, was different from Islam as expressed in Azad's life. Yet, it was the chief source of intellectual inspiration. Mohamed Ali's early religious training involved a superficial acquaintance with the rudiments of Islam and the concomitant ritual. The family influences, too, do not appear to have been such as to have either inclined him in favour of dogmatic theology, or fostered in him independence of thought and a spirit of rebellion against the prevailing religious beliefs. His mother's gentle influence, to which Mohamed Ali owed so much in life, was exerted more in the direction of promoting his educational career than in creating around him a religious atmosphere.

The enforced leisure at Chhindwara, Lansdowne and Betul jails enabled him to steep himself afresh in his Islamic heritage and turn to the study of his religion—charting out an unfamiliar subject, getting at its rudiments, and exploring its nuances. The experience was, in some ways, similar to that of Azad. His three-and-a-half year internment in Ranchi kindled his Islam into warmth and fervour. He began writing the *Tarjuman al-Koran*, with his commentary on the opening *Surah Fatihah*, and its themes—Divine Providence, benevolence, justice, unity and guidance, *rabubiyah*, *rahma*, *adala*, *tawhid*, and *hidaya*.

Azad and Mohamed Ali asserted the transcendental truth of Islam, 'a way of life, a moral code and social polity', a complete set of rules (*qanun-i falah*), as Azad put it. They were convinced of the rightness of the Islamic ideals that offered a complete way of life for an organized community living out Allah's plan under the kind of government which had prevailed in the days of the Prophet. They were equally convinced of the compatibility of the Islamic principles with reason or science. This was Mohamed Ali's central argument in 'The Future of Islam', and of Azad's essays published in the first three issues of *Al-Hilal.* Alone among his contemporaries, Azad conceived for Islam a vital socio-political role that went against the apparently triumphant secularizing tendencies of the age, and conveyed, first to his associates and pupils and then to Indian society, the large the vibrant and comprehensive Islamic vision that had first animated his being in youth. In April 1913, he wrote in *Al-Hilal*:

> Islam does not commend narrow-mindedness and racial and religious prejudice. It does not make the recognition of merit and virtue, of human benevolence, mercy and love dependent upon and subject to distinctions of religion and race. It teaches us to respect every man who is good, whatever be his religion, to let ourselves be drawn towards merits and virtues, whatever the religion or the race of the person who possesses them. . . . But above and beyond this law of universal goodwill, and I do not hesitate to own it even in this age of hypothetical impartiality, is the *jehad* of helping the cause of justice, worshiping Allah and establishing right-mindedness and justice. Islam teaches us that the purpose of the creation of man is that he should represent God on earth, keep burning the torch of truth and light.[8]

Azad's rationalism was not merely an element in his modernist, intellectual explorations, but an integral part of his traditional scholastic training. Mohamed Ali was a vigorous proponent of neo-intellectual modernism, deriving his ideas from Saiyid Ahmad in his appeal for cultivating scientific disciplines and rejecting *taqlid*. 'I have as much right to interpret God's message as any other man', he declared. Formal renunciation of a 'mildewed scholasticism' will set Islam 'right with itself'.[9] Azad echoed similar views. 'The shopkeepers of religion have given the name of religion to ignorance and *taqlid*, to prejudice and indulgence', he wrote in *Al-Hilal*. Years later, he commented:

> The greatest hindrance to human intellectual progress is unquestioning acceptance of traditional beliefs . . . the first thorn of doubt which pricked my heart was against his very *taqlid*. . . . If the foundation of belief should be knowledge, why on *taqlid* and inheritance.[10]

The rationalist strain enabled Azad and Mohamed Ali to reconcile their passionate attachment to pan-Islamism with the ideological underpinnings of Indian nationalism. They viewed pan-Islamism and nationalism as compatible ideologies; so they sought to establish that their community's anguish over Turkey's future deepened their involvement in the anti-colonial struggle and brought them closer to the Congress. Azad, more than Mohamed Ali, invoked the Koran and *Hadith* to strengthen the case for non-cooperation against the British. Following closely the views of Abduh who, in his answer to inquiries from India, had endorsed inter-religious cooperation, Azad reiterated, with all the religious fervour at his command, that Muslims should be up in front, fighting for freedom. Mohamed Ali offered the same advice: Muslims must fight for swaraj with their non-Muslims brethren, for only in this way would it be possible to achieve the khilafat aim. 'If you want to release the khilafat from slavery', he stated, 'there is only one course for you and that is that you should side with the Hindus and first secure the freedom of your own country. You cannot save Islam from danger so long as you do not rule your own country.' This conviction, shared by many Muslims, enabled them to easily swing back and forth between pan-Islamic and local nationalist appeals, depending upon which was a more appropriate anti-imperialist weapon.

Mohamed Ali's first editorial pleaded for Hindu-Muslim friendship. He believed that, 'if the Muslims or the Hindus attempt to achieve success in opposition to or even without the co-operation of one another, they will not only fail, but fail ignominiously'.[11] And the *Comrade* intended to prepare Muslims to 'contribute' to territorial patriotism without compromising on their extra-territorial sympathies which is the quintessence of Islam'.[12] His misgivings about the Congress were removed in Chhindwara when he reflected on the role of Tilak,[13] and came into contact with Gandhi at Aligarh in 1915.[14] He told Saifuddin Kitchlew: 'It is Gandhi, Gandhi, Gandhi, that has got to be dinned into the people's ear, because he means Hindu-Muslim unity, non-co-operation, *swadharma* and *swaraja*, while the rest are after petty communal or local bodies, most of them tinged with personal ambitions.'[15]

Mohamed Ali's emotional disposition in religious matters had surely much to do with the nature and with the promptness of his response to events in Turkey. In this context there is no reason at all to doubt the sincerity of his indignation, aroused by the machinations of some European Powers, and his genuinely-felt emotional concern for the safety of the holy places. The opinion, presented by Francis Robinson and others, that it was all feigned, that he was simply playing the pan-Islamist, cannot be seriously defended. Calculation comes in, not in pretending an emotion which is not there, but in deciding how much of genuinely-felt emotion to release publicly; how far to let oneself go. Similarly, it is difficult to sustain the charge, rendered plausible by Mohamed Ali's complicated financial situation, that he lived off the khilafat funds.

Mohamed Ali's pan-Islamism was both instinctive and the outcome of much thought and deliberation. Central to his belief was the view, based on the concept of *umma*, that 'the basis of Islamic sympathy is not a common domicile or common parentage, but a common outlook on life and common culture', and that 'the embodiment of that culture is the khilafat'. Inspired by Azad's description of a 'political centre' (*siyasi markaz*), Mohamed Ali argued that the 'personal centre' of Islam was the khalifa and the 'local centre' was the 'Island of Arabia', the *Jazirat al-Arab*.

It was not ceremonial piety that motivated Mohamed Ali and other khilafatists to rally under the khilafat banner. The khalifa, according to the classical theorists, defended the faith, and wielded the authority to ensure that Muslims follow the *Shariat*. For this reason, the khilafat was 'the most essential institution of the Muslim community'; hence its defence a sacred duty.[16] Mohamed Ali gave the need for preserving in the institution a utilitarian quality when he told a London audience:

> Well, so long as there are your Bryces and your 'Big sticks', we, too, must have some sort of stick for the defence of our faith, and to jeopardize at least the dominance of those that jeopardize the freedom of our conscience. That, and that alone is the *rationale* of our main claim that the khilafat should be preserved with adequate temporal power.[17]

He explained that Muslims were not concerned with political dominance, because the 'spiritual force of Islam' did not depend on political supremacy. What concerned them most was the erosion of Islam's temporal power to the extent that it might become 'liable to suffer, without adequate power to prevent, the curtailment of its spiritual influence through the pressures of the temporal power of rival creeds'.[18]

The defence of the khalifa and holy places was seen as the method of assuring that the *Ummat-i-Islamia* had the freedom to conform to its religious precepts. The khilafatists envisioned a renascent Islamic world, in which all Muslim peoples were united—'the supernatural sangathan of Muslims in five continents'[19]—built around the khalifa and supporting each other through that institution. The new khalifa, judged from the views expressed by Mohamed Ali at the Mecca Conference in 1928, would be based on the pattern of *khilafat-i rashida*. It would be an elective institution rather than a dynastic one, and the holder of the office would be chosen by virtue of his godliness, and his devotion to Islam. All the Muslims of the world would have a part in the direction of the government, all responsible for its welfare. Mohamed Ali was not one to recognize the dramatic changes in the 'Islamic world', the emergence of nationalism as a force, and the rejection of pan-Islamism in most countries, including Turkey. He continued to picture a new Muslim world—unified by common religious symbols and experiences—which would present a single force to whatever power attempted to jeopardize the rights of any Muslim nation.

II

So long as Islam occupied centrality in the concerns of Azad and Mohamed Ali and religious symbols retained their primacy in mass mobilization campaigns, Azad and Mohamed Ali spoke from a common platform, acted in unison, and voiced shared concerns. But once Gandhi called off civil disobedience and the Turks burst the khilafat bubble, they began to see the world around them differently.

It is, at first, hard to understand why this was so, for their differences were not so fundamental as they are sometimes portrayed in historical accounts. Admittedly, their experiences in public life were not always the same, especially in the aftermath of the non-cooperation movement. Yet, they were both engaged in a common endeavour: to define the position and status of their community in a free, composite, and plural society. In addition, they continued to play a part in Congress affairs and were engaged in resolving the communal impasse, though sometimes from a different standpoint. Mohamed Ali's views were, for example, often at odds with the Congress, but his enthusiasm for that organization was not dampened until the publication of the Nehru report in August 1928. Likewise, though engaged in verbal feuds with Gandhi and Jawaharlal Nehru, his loyalty to them never slackened. He and the younger Nehru were tied to each other by 'a bond of affection and mutual appreciation . . .'.[20] About the Mahatma, he announced in 1925 that he had identical views 'with regard to the way in which India can win her freedom'. 'I am proud to regard (him) as my chief', he had declared.[21]

Azad shared the same sense of loyalty, though it was much less pronounced in his public utterances. In the post-khilafat era, he was inspired by Gandhi, Nehru and Das, rather than by Afghani and Abduh. His writings and speeches echoed his life-long passion and yearning for India's political liberation, unity, and inter-religious understanding. At Ramgarh, the Maulana said he was prepared to accept Independence whenever available whether during war or peace; his sole object was the attainment of real Independence of Hindustan.

Why, then, the drift, or the 'parting of ways'? Was it because Azad and Mohamed Ali competed with each other to wrest the community's leadership? Were they different in temperament and style? Or, was their divide symptomatic of the ideological polarization during the post-khilafat days? There are no simple answers, though the genesis of their rift can be traced to the collapse of the khilafat and non-cooperation campaigns.

For the men of religion, the demise of the khilafat could only be explained within the legal categories of orthodox Islam. Azad set out to do so: in Islam, he pointed out, spiritual leadership was the due of God and his Prophet alone. So obedience to the khilafat was binding on all Muslims, though not in the same degree as submission to God and his Prophet. In his articles to the *Zamindar*, published in the spring of 1924, Azad opined that by abolishing the khilafat of the Ottoman dynasty, the Turkish government had merely rectified the unsatisfactory division of spiritual and temporal powers which had existed since 1922. By down-playing the importance of Turkey's action, he tried to redirect the energies of the khilafat committees into work for education, social reform and the economic progress of India's Muslims.[22]

Though traumatized by the collapse of the khilafat, there was no break in the essential continuity of Azad's political ideology: he merely adapted himself well to the changed political climate. The shift, if any, was in his framework of analysis. The Koran, the *Hadith* and the traditions of Islam had moulded his political views during the *Al-Hilal* years. Not so afterwards. He now learned to 'eliminate irrelevant religious considerations when thinking of or discussing purely political issues', and his arguments were no longer couched in theological terms but based on his understanding of social realities, and the dynamics of and his commitment to a secular polity. 'It is one of the greatest frauds on the people to suggest', he reaffirmed after Independence, 'that religious affinity can unite areas which are geographically, economically, linguistically and culturally different.' With an insight rare for those from his background, Azad argued: 'The problems of the country were economic, not communal. The differences related to classes, not to communities.'[23]

III

Azad plotted a course strewn with obstacles and difficulties. Seeking refuge in platitudinous statements was one thing, but coping with the ideological assault of the communalists was an hazardous exercise. And yet his Ramgarh speech—perhaps the most eloquent exposition of Indian nationalism ever made from a Congress platform—reaffirmed his secular vision and rebutted the two-nation theory. It could well have served as a political manifesto for those Congress Muslims who were, after Ansari's death in May 1936, in search of a leader and a programme to steer their ship through the rough currents of communalism.

In April 1940, Azad placed proposals for overcoming the constitutional deadlock and, at the same time, challenged the League's claim to be the sole representative of the Muslims. The conference resolution included a declaration beginning: 'India, with its geographical and political boundaries, is an indivisible whole and as such it is the common homeland of all citizens, irrespective of race or religion, who are joint owners of its resources'.[24]

As the Congress president, a position he had already occupied in 1923, Azad sought to narrow down the ever-increasing gulf separating the Congress and the League. He also conducted negotiations with Stafford Cripps and the viceroy, Wavell, and again, after the War, with the cabinet mission. It was a role he enjoyed most. Cripps and Wavell thought well of him and counted on his support for their plans and proposals. The former thanked Azad for his help and friendship and the 'really marvellous way in which you stuck to your guns'. He was 'absolutely convinced' that, but for the Maulana, 'no arrangement would have been come to'.[25] Wavell found Azad 'very moderate and friendly'. He added: 'I have a great respect for him, and if all these politicians were of the same quality matters would be comparatively easy'.[26] Azad reciprocated these sentiments. Complimenting Cripps for his 'courtesy, tact and resourcefulness', he referred to his own part in the negotiations. 'I may tell you', he wrote on 22 July 1946:

> that my attitude was throughout governed by two considerations. I regard the advent of the Labour Party to power an event of historic importance. For the first time in history, there is the prospect of a peaceful transition to a Socialist order. I also feel that the Labour Government have on the whole been following a policy of democracy and freedom, and working for peace and stability in the modern world. I therefore felt it my duty to do everything possible to help it towards a peaceful settlement of the Indian problem.[27]

On the other hand, sections of the Congress leadership doubted Azad's negotiating skills; in fact, Nehru's election as Congress president in 1946 is said to have been an expression of lack of confidence in Azad's ability to follow the dictates of the Congress Working Committee.[28] The judgement is unfair. Azad was, as Alan Campbell-Johnson recorded on

21 December 1947, just a 'titular head of the movement during the vital negotiations with both the Cripps and the Cabinet Missions'.[29] Others like Gandhi and Nehru, backed by Patel, Rajagopalachari and Rajendra Prasad, called the shots, though Azad could bring round the AICC and the CWC to his point of view on a few issues, including the formation of a coalition government composed of both Congress and the League.[30] But, in general, Azad was expected to perform a subservient role. His own initiatives were not welcomed. On occasions, they were thwarted.[31]

In a sense, Azad's position was similar to that of his Congress Muslim comrades who held positions of authority but were rarely allowed to influence major policy decisions. This was so in 1930 when Gandhi ignored the wishes of Ansari and his Nationalist Muslim Party in launching the civil disobedience movement. Again, the Congress in general, and Nehru in particular, ignored the views of Azad on the formation of a Congress-League coalition ministry in UP. On reflection, Azad concluded that 'if the League's offer of co-operation had been accepted the Muslim League party would for all practical purposes merge with the Congress, Jawaharlal's action gave the League in UP a new lease of life'.[32] Azad may not have been right in his assessment, but he, at least implicity, gave vent to the feeling that the upper echelon of the Congress leadership paid no heed to the 'Nationalist Muslim' perspective.

Dealing with the Muslim League posed an added problem: the stout refusal of its diehards to recognize the position and status of the Congress Muslims. The Aligarh students and teachers, who had once idolized the Maulana when their pan-Islamic passions were heightened, turned against Azad. The Barelwi ulama, averse to the Jamiyat al-ulama-Congress alliance, were his sworn critics. And Jinnah, of course, refused to meet him and showed no sympathy for his viewpoint. 'Cannot you realize', he told Azad in July 1940, 'you are making a Muslim show-boy Congress president to give it colour that is national.'[33] In this way, recorded Campbell-Johnson:

> Maulana Azad, a great scholar and a man of retiring disposition, has during the past ten years been a central figure of controversy. He embodied in his position and person perhaps the most important symbol of the Congress aspiration to be a nationalist as against a communal party. His status was thus the focal point of Gandhi's clash with Jinnah, who always maintained that politically no one but a member of the Muslim League could represent Muslim interests.[34]

Jinnah displayed lack of realism in insisting that the League solely represented the Muslim community. How could it be in the light of the poor performance of his party in the 1937 elections? Besides, as Wavell pointed out candidly, 'after all, there is a Congress Ministry in the Province (Bombay) with the greatest proportion of Muslims, and 1 million votes were cast *against the Muslim League at the recent election as compared with about 6 million for the League*'[35] (italics mine). Jinnah was on an equally weak turf in demanding the exclusion of the Congress Muslims from the interim government. They may not have been, in Nehru's description, the 'soul of the Congress', but they had occupied an important enough position in the country's liberation struggle. They may not have always played a pivotal role, but they remained a priceless asset to the Congress movement. Their presence vindicated the Congress stand of representing the Indian nation rather than a segment of it. How could the Congress, then, forsake its close allies for the illusory prospect of an accord with the League? How could Gandhi and Nehru, in particular, sacrifice personal friends and political expediency? 'It has now become clear', wrote the viceroy on 1 October 1946, 'that Congress are unwilling to give way on the Nationalist Muslim issue.'[36] The problem, he told Pethick-Lawrence, 'is an extraordinary intractable one'.[37] This was so because of Jinnah's obstinacy, and his refusal to give way.

Sensing the mood in the Congress circles, Cripps and Wavell urged Jinnah to give way on the question, and, in exchange, secure his other points.[38] Wavell went to the extent of explaining that the Congress would not, in fact, appoint a 'Nationalist' Muslim in the end, if Jinnah conceded their right to do so. The Congress had not given any such assurance.[39]

Azad and his Muslim comrades may have been comforted by the Congress stand, but not by the vicious communal atmosphere that gripped the country. The League campaign gathered momentum day after day, and the country was, consequently, caught up in a bitter and violent confrontation. With their limited constituency, which had steadily shrunk over the years, Azad and his followers could do little to influence the course of events. The inexorable march towards the vivisection of the Indian nation could neither be halted by an individual or a group. Nor could the communal tide be stemmed by the Mahatma or the Maulana. Besides, once the Congress agreed to the Partition Plan, the tide turned against the Congress Muslims. Ghaffar Khan protested loudly and passionately; others did so quietly. Azad maintained his studious silence and aristocratic poise at the Congress Working Committee meeting on 2 June 1947, when the Mountbatten plan for the Partition was ratified. He could do little at the time to prevent this 'abject surrender', particularly after Gandhi and Nehru dithered in the face of the communal onslaught.[40] Dispirited, defeated and detached from the humdrum of political happenings, Campbell-Johnson recorded the details of a meeting on 16 September 1947. 'Throughout this long meeting, Maulana Azad, the Moslem elder statesman in the Congress, sat silent and impassive, as he always does, looking, with his pointed beard, just like Cardinal Richelieu.'[41]

The dawn of freedom had arrived. But 'the sad face of Maulana Azad, to whom the occasion was something of a tragedy, sticking out from the sea of happy faces like a gaunt and ravaged rock'.[42] Azad could well have recalled his own passage from *Ghubar-i Khatir* which summed up the story of his life.

> In religion, in literature, in politics, in everyday thought, wherever I have to go, I have to go alone. On no path can I go with the caravans of the day. . . . Whichever way I walk, I get so far ahead of the (caravan) that when I turn to look back, I see nothing, but the dust of the way, and even that is the dust raised by the speed of my own passage.

NOTES

1. Kenneth Cragg, *Counsels in Contemporary Islam*, Edinburgh, 1965, pp. 132-3, and Ian Henderson Douglas, *Abul Kalam Azad: An Intellectual and Religious Biography*, eds. Gail Minault and Christian W. Troll, New Delhi, 1998, p. 29; Abdur Razzaq Malihabadi, *Zikr-i Azad*, Calcutta, 1965, pp. 132-3. See the collection of articles in Rasheeduddin Khan (ed.), *Abul Kalam Azad: Ek Hamageer Shaksiat*, New Delhi, 1989.
2. Cragg, *Counsels*, p. 134.
3. Mujeeb, *The Indian Muslims*, p. 302.
4. For example, the *fatwa* on the boycott of government-aided educational institutions. *Khilafat*, 1 Nov. 1920.
5. Douglas, *Abul Kalam Azad*, p. 180.
6. Ibid.
7. For Azad's early political life, Rajat K. Ray, 'Revolutionaries, Pan-Islamists and Bolsheviks: Maulana Abul Kalam Azad and Political Underworld in Calcutta, 1905-1925', Hasan (ed.), *Communal and Pan-Islamic Trends in Colonial India*, pp. 101-24.
8. *Al-Hilal*, 23 Oct. 1912.
9. Mohamed Ali, *My Life*, pp. 163-4.
10. Douglas, *Abul Kalam Azad*, p. 76.
11. *Comrade* (Calcutta), 14 Jan. 1911.
12. Mohamed Ali, *My Life*, p. 46.
13. To Tilak, 12 Nov. 1916, *Mohamed Ali in Indian Politics*, Vol.1, p. 292.
14. Hasan, *Mohamed Ali: Ideology and Politics*, pp. 28-9.

15. Iqbal, *Life and Times of Mohamed Ali*, p. 308.
16. 'India's Message to France', Iqbal (ed.), *Writings and Speeches*, p. 158; *Comrade*, 13 May 1913.
17. 'A People's Right to Live', ibid., p. 171.
18. Mohamed Ali to Chelmsford, 24 Apr. 1919, MAP.
19. Mohamed Ali observed: 'Islam united Muslims by offering a set of common ideals and offered the only rational basis for unity and co-operation among its followers. The sympathies of a Muslim are co-extensive with his religion because they have been bred into him by the inspiring spirit of his creed.' *Comrade*, 12 Apr. 1913.
20. Nehru, *An Autobiography*, p. 117.
21. *Comrade*, 16 Oct. 1925; Afzal Iqbal (ed.), *Select Speeches*, pp. 331-2, 337.
22. Douglas, *Abul Kalam Azad*, p. 223.
23. Abul Kalam Azad, *India Wins Freedom: the complete version*, New Delhi, 1988, p. 248.
24. Nicholas Mansergh (ed.), *The Transfer of Power* (hereafter *TP*), 1942-7 (London: His Majesty's Stationery Office), Vol. 1, p. 293. For an account of the Conference, Humayun Kabir, *Muslim Politics, 1906-42*, Calcutta, 1944.
25. *TP*, Vol. 8, p. 103.
26. Wavell to J. Colville, 8/9 July 1946, and Note by Wavell, 19 Aug. 1946, ibid., p. 23; Datta, *Maulana Azad*, p. 171.
27. To S. Cripps, 22 July 1946, ibid., Vol. 8, pp. 102-3.
28. Sarvepalli Gopal, *Jawaharlal Nehru: A Biography 1889-1947*, Vol. 1, New Delhi, 1975, p. 326.
29. Alan Campbell-Johnson, *Mission with Mountbatten*, London, 1951, p. 254.
30. To Wavell, 9 July 1946, *TP*, Vol. 8, p. 24.
31. On differences between the Mahatma and the Maulana, first over the Quit India movement, and later over the conduct of the negotiations with the cabinet missions, see Datta, *Maulana Azad*, pp. 168, 174, 175, 176. For Gandhi's unfavourable response to Azad's proposal for alleviating Muslim fears, see Jenkins to Abell, 28 Aug. 1945, reporting on an intercepted letter from Gandhi to Azad, *TP*, Vol. 6, p. 76. Azad's own version of his differences with Nehru is quite revealing. For a refutation of the Maulana's thesis, see Gopal, *Jawaharlal Nehru*, Vol. 1, pp. 227-9, and S.R. Mehrotra, 'Nehru and the Partition of India, 1935-47', in Philips and Wainwright (eds.), *The Partition of India*, pp. 178-9.
32. *India Wins Freedom*, p. 170.
33. Datta, *Maulana Azad*, pp. 164,171; Douglas, *Abul Kalam Azad*, p. 295.
34. Campbell Johnson, *Mission with Mountbatten*, p. 254.
35. Wavell to A. Clow (Bombay), 7 Oct. 1946, TP, Vol. 8, p. 675.
36. To Pethick-Lawrence, 1 Oct. 1946, ibid., p. 634.
37. To Pethick-Lawrence, 1 Oct. 1946, ibid., p. 636.

38. Wavell to Abell, 1 Oct. 1946, ibid., p. 631.
39. Wavell to Pethick-Lawrence, 29 Sept. 1946, ibid., p. 625.
40. Pethick-Lawrence to Cripps, 30 Sept. 1939, ibid., p. 629.
41. Campbell-Johnson, *Mission with Mountbatten*, p. 194.
42. Douglas, *Abul Kalam Azad*, pp. 232-3 and 238.

8

'Congress Muslims' and Indian Nationalism, Dilemma and Decline *c.* 1928-1934

In the aftermath of the Nehru report controversy, the Congress had to reckon with Jinnah's 'Fourteen Points'. Gandhi tried to soothe suspicions with the assurance that swaraj did not mean Hindu raj, and engaged with him in February and August 1929 to explore possible avenues to peace. But Lajpat Rai, Malaviya, Jayakar, B.S. Moonje, working president of the Hindu Mahasabha (1927-35), and N.C. Kelkar, urged him not to reach a solution outside the terms of the Nehru report.[1] Lajpat Rai refused to accept any modification,[2] while Jayakar pressured Gandhi not to yield on the ground that the government, as in 1919, would deliberately make any concessions part of a constitution.[3] Gandhi wrote to Motilal Nehru in anguish: 'How that can be done [resolving the communal deadlock] or whether it should be done, you know best. My mind is in a whirl in this matter. The atmosphere is too foggy for me to see clearly.'[4]

With the failure of the Gandhi-Jinnah talks and the crusade against the Nehru report gathering momentum, the Lahore Congress let the report lapse, and decided not to accept any solution of the communal problem without the concurrence of the minorities.[5] Gandhi hoped the declaration of complete independence and the launching of civil disobedience would enable leaders of various shades of opinion to draw their followers into the anti-colonial struggle. He wrote in *Navajivan*: 'If we have true freedom we will shed communal fear. Hindus and Muslims will cease to fear one another.'[6]

But soothing Muslim feelings was not enough. The issue at stake was to arrest their growing alienation from the Congress. The process, having begun soon after the khilafat movement came to a halt, was attributed to a wide range of factors, including the failure of the Congress to curb assertive and militant expressions of Hindu nationalism. Such had been the burden of Abdur Rahim's speech at the 1925 Muslim League session. He argued that the Congress would jettison Muslim interests in any future scheme of swaraj, and that their 'salvation' lay in either forging an alliance with the government or in pursuing independent political action.[7] Such views, echoed both in Bengal and Punjab, struck a favourable chord in certain Muslim circles and led to, here and in other provinces of British India, a steady decline in Muslim participation at annual Congress sessions and in national, provincial, and district committees.

Table 8.1 indicates the attendance of Muslim delegates at Congress sessions from 1918 to 1923. Clearly, the number of Muslims gradually dwindled from a few hundred to less than a score. Muslim representation in the AICC was impressive, showing an increase from 11.1 per cent in 1919 to 24.5 per cent in 1923 (Table 8.2). In 1922-3, 84 of the 338 AICC members were Muslims. By 1928, however, their number was reduced to 54 out of 332.[8] Provincial and district committees also had very few Muslim members. In UP, only 7 Muslims served on various district committees: 1 each in Gonda, Allahabad, Jhansi, Moradabad, Faizabad, Azamgarh, and 2 in Bara Banki.[9]

In 1922-3, Motilal Nehru built his support among an influential group of Lucknow and Allahabad based professional men: T.A.K. Sherwani, Rafi Ahmed Kidwai, Khaliquzzaman and M.H. Kidwai.[10] In Bengal, C.R. Das lured the khilafatists into supporting the Swaraj party by offering a set of extravagant concessions. In consequence, his party swept the November 1923 polls, capturing an overall majority of seats, including half the Muslim seats. Muslim backing was strongest in the eastern division of Chittagong and the northern division of Rajshahi, the storm centres of the khilafat movement in Bengal. Likewise, the swarajists won 10 of the

Table 8.1: Attendance of Muslim delegates at the Congress sessions, 1918-23

Year	Total no. of delegates	No. of Muslim delegates
1918	3,975	205
1919	6,717	314
1920	13,532	1,050
1921	4,201	521
1922	NA	NA
1923	1,550	111

Table 8.2: Composition of AICC, 1919-23

Religion	1919 (161 Members)	1920 (163 Members)	1921	1922 (338 Members)	1923
Hindus	139	133	124	242	248
Muslims	18	21	33	84	83
Sikhs	-	2	2	9	8
Parsees	3	4	2	-	-
Christians	1	2	2	3	3

Source: Gopal Krishna, 'The Indian National Congress, 1918-1923', D. Phil. thesis, Oxford, 1960, p. 747.

15 Muslim seats in the Calcutta Corporation elections. The Muslim vote was strongest in the city's central mercantile wards with its up-country Urdu-speaking merchants, property owners and artisans who had formed the backbone of the khilafat movement.[11]

This support was eroded once the Bengal Congress repudiated the Das pact. There were 15 Muslim swarajists in 1923; there were none in 1926. The *Mussalman* rejected the Swaraj party 'as the party which turned out to be inimically disposed towards the Mussalmans,'[12] while Husayn Suhrawardy and Abdul Karim, leading negotiators of the Das pact, led their followers in Calcutta deeper into the labyrinth of distinctly communal politics.[13] The picture was not very different in UP.[14] As against 11 Muslims nominated and 4 elected in 1923, 6 were renominated in 1926 and only 1 returned. Of the 8 swarajist Muslims returned in 1923 to the Central Assembly, only 3 were elected in 1926. Irked by Motilal Nehru's attitude towards reforms in the N.W.F.P., Saiyid Murtaza, a swarajist from Madras, accused him of sacrificing the Frontier Muslims in order to woo Lajpat Rai on the eve of the 1926 elections.[16] Muhammad Shafee Daoodi's indictment was equally harsh: 'Temporary success in your political endeavours has got greater value for you than the more enduring rapprochement of the two great communities of India.' He charged that the Congress, having gradually drifted towards the Mahasabha since 1923, had reduced itself to being its tool.[17] Both Murtaza and Daoodi quit the Swaraj party in 1926. The feeling of insecurity was so widespread that some Muslims, who had in the recent past contributed to Congress's popularity, were now arrayed among its enemies.[18]

Yet, political activity among Muslims was sporadic and fragmented. Conflicting regional, local and class interests—a consequence of the uneven development of the Muslim communities—deepened conflicts and divisions only to expose the hollowness of the leader's claim to represent all Muslims. This was reflected in the formal split between the Jinnah and the Shafi factions in the Muslim League. Any new party, whether cobbled together by the khilafatists or the Leaguers, promised to be a rickety, splintered structure that could collapse at any moment. Such was the fate of the All-Parties Muslim Conference after 1932. The organizers, like the Dutch army, were all generals but no soldiers. Members of the land-owning class, none of them was prepared to spreadhead the movement or to follow the other.[18]

Similarly, Jinnah's brave attempts to infuse some life into the Muslim League were poorly rewarded; its total membership rose from a mere 1,093 in 1922 to 1,330 in 1927.[19] 'We are disgusted', wrote the *Mussalman*, 'with the Muslim League on account of its culpable inactivity. . . . The provincial Leagues have imbibed the inactivity and the character of the parent body.'[20]

Within the Congress ranks were, however, a number of groups, who were described as 'Nationalist Muslims'. Most had been associated with the party from the days of the Rowlatt satyagraha, though the distinction between them and their detractors—the Ali brothers, Muhammad Shafi and the other organizers of the All-Parties Muslim Conference—gained currency in the mid-1920s. 'They are men', said Ansari, the principal spokesman of the Congress Muslim, 'to whom the freedom of the country from alien rule comes merely as a bad second to communal privileges.'[21]

Though the label 'Nationalist Muslim' communicates the ideology and politics of those wedded to Indian nationalist aspirations, its exclusive application to Muslims, as discussed in the introduction to this book, conjures up the false image of a community largely communally-oriented with only a handful integrated with the dominant nationalist trend. Such a label also does not account for the subtle but extremely important differences between a professed nationalist and a so-called communalist. It is thus not easy to place Mohamed Ali in this supposed dichotomous framework. Though a critic of the Congress and the Nehru report, he remained committed to swaraj. Ansari conceded that, in spite of being led into the 'camp of national reaction', the Ali brothers had not 'surrendered their loyalty to the fundamental principle of Indian politics, freedom from foreign domination'.[22]

How, then, does one describe the many Muslim groups connected with the Congress movement at various levels? It is convenient, for descriptive purposes, to identify them as Congress Muslims, though the term does not quite embrace the range of their activities in the social and education spheres. And, yet, it indicates the overall thrust of their political concerns in relation to the community, the region and the nation at large. Some like Azad and Husain Ahmad Madani, head of the Dar al-ulum at Deoband, interpreted Islam as a religion of freedom and equality, of justice, and of cooperation with and respect for all mankind.[23] Thus Madani defended full and individual Muslim participation in a struggle for India's freedom by advancing a theory of territorial nationhood for India rather than by appealing to concepts of safeguards and community confederation. He expressed his ideas in a public controversy with Iqbal shortly before the latter's death in 1938.[24]

For those trained and tutored at the Aligarh College or the institutions in Allahabad, Patna and Calcutta, the Congress expressed the popular yearning for political freedom and independence. 'If I were asked why I have such an abiding faith in Indian nationalism,' stated the Bihar lawyer-politician Ali Imam, 'my answer is that without that India's freedom is an impossibility.'[25] Such men accepted the Congress as a viable vehicle for social change rather than the communal organizations. By joining it in large numbers, observed Maulvi Mujibur Rahman at the Bakarganj District Muslim Conference in May 1931, the Bengali Muslims would take a greater part in the freedom struggle.[26] Khan Abdul Ghaffar Khan announced at a public meeting in December 1931 that the Congress party alone would free the country, feed the hungry, and clothe the naked.[27] The *Jirgah* of India, he reaffirmed, was called Congress—a common *Jirgah* of all the communities of India. Justifying his alliance with Congress he said: 'In order to save himself from the enemies did not the Holy Prophet make alliance with the Jews and the Politheists [*sic*]?'[28] His audience beamed approvingly.

Such individuals and groups spanned several provinces of British India. The Khudai Khidmatgars headed a nationalist and socially progressive movement in the frontier province. Within two years of its creation they were 2,00,000 strong.[29] Quotations from the Koran against slavery served as rallying points for nationalist enthusiasm, and the struggle to liberate the country from foreign rule became the rallying cry. 'No section of India', observed W.C. Smith, the historian of Indian Islam, 'has been more thoroughly nationalist.'[30] During civil disobedience in 1930-1 Khudai Khidmatgar activism was linked with the Congress—the connection was strengthened in August 1931 when the Afghan *Jirgah* merged with the provincial Congress committee. The local *Jirgahs* became the local Congress committees, while 'Red Shirt' volunteers merged with the Congress bodies at various levels. The whole movement was conducted in accordance with the Congress constitution, and the flag used was the Congress flag. The 'Frontier Gandhi' explained:

People complain against me for having joined the Congress by selling my nation. The Congress is a national and not a Hindu body. It is a jirga composed of Hindus, Jews, Sikhs, Parsis, and Muslims. The Congress as a body is working against the British. The British nation is the enemy of the Congress and of the Pathans. I have therefore joined it and made common cause with the Congress to get rid of the British.[31]

The intensity of civil disobedience was reflected in the number of prosecutions and convictions. Until September 1932, the figure was 5,557 in a total population of 25 lakhs. In neighbouring Punjab, the number was 1,620, though the population was more than eight times that of the N.W.F.P.[32] Convictions were also higher than the Bombay presidency (see Table 8.3). Ghaffar Khan's motto: 'We are Pakhtuns but until we attain freedom we do not deserve to be called Pakhtuns'[33] remained the rallying slogan of his followers.

The Majlis-i Ahrar-i Islam, organized in 1929 by a group of Muslims in Punjab, had its base amongst the well-to-do peasantry and the lower-middle classes. The Ahrars combined economic grievances and religious passions to formulate their militant policies,[34] thus expressing something of the old khilafat movement tradition: an ardent and explicit enthusiasm for freedom. And like the Khudai Khidmatgars, the Ahraris steadily and fervently went to jail in large numbers.[35] In Delhi, they combined with the Jamiyat al-ulama activists to organize processions, public meetings, and picket liquor shops. Clashes with the police on 11-13 March 1932 led to the arrest of Azad and Maulvi Kifayatullah and twenty-five other Muslims. Reminiscent of scenes during the Rowlatt satyagraha was a mammoth meeting at the Fatehpuri Masjid, where 4,500-5,000 Muslims endorsed Gandhi's civil disobedience movement.[36]

Table 8.3: Convictions in Bombay and the N.W.F.P.

	Conviction in January-February 1932	Convictions in March-September 1932	Total
Bombay	5,165	6,311	11,476
N.W.F.P.	4,318	1,239	5,557

Source: Home Poll. File No. 5/72, 1932, NAI.

The Ahrar party, also active in Kashmir, agitated against the Dogra ruler, maharaja Hari Singh, seeking redressal of the grievances of the Muslim subjects.[37] These were set out in the memorial submitted to the maharaja on 19 October 1931,[38] and taken note of by B.J. Glancy, chairman of a commission to enquire into the demands of the memorialists.[39] Led by Mazhar Ali, Habibur Rahman of Ludhiana, Abdur Rahman Ghazi, and Ataullah Shah Bukhari, the Ahrars sent *jathas* of red-uniformed *razakaars* (volunteers) from parts of Punjab, especially Sialkot, to Kashmir to bear pressure on the maharaja to meet their demands.[40] Large-scale rioting in Jammu on 2 November 1931, and violent clashes at Mirpur between the *jathas* and state forces, followed. British troops were deployed to quell the disturbances.

The spurt in political activity profoundly influenced Kashmir's future history. With the Ahrar agitation petering out, the Jammu and Kashmir Muslim Conference, founded in 1932, wrested the political initiative. The conference, stated its founder Shaikh Muhammad Abdullah, though Muslim in name, was 'in spirit national and concerned with the welfare of all communities.'[41] He declared in 1931 and, again, in 1935, that the country's progress depended on harmonious communal relations,[42] and that he fought for the country's emancipation. 'Let us all rise above petty communal bickerings and work jointly for the welfare of the masses,' he said.[43] In the years to come, the Muslim Conference formulated a radical 'New Kashmir' plan, and spurned the rising tide of Muslim nationalism.

In Bombay, Saiyid Abdullah Brelvi, editor of the *Bombay Chronicle*, launched the Congress Muslim Party on 8 July 1929 to induce Muslims to join the Congress.[44] His chief support lay among the urban-based politicians, such as Yusuf Meharally, editor of the English weekly *Vanguard*, Abbas Tyabji, a lawyer with a long-standing association with the Congress movement, and M.C. Chagla, also a lawyer who came to the forefront as a vociferous champion of the Nehru report. Gandhi blessed the party with the message: 'If it is fully supported and does not go to sleep, it may prove a tower of strength to the Congress and an instrument of real service to India generally and to Mussalmans in particular.'[45]

The Congress Muslim Party, though assailed by Shaukat Ali and his followers among the Urdu-speaking Muslims, garnered a fair measure of support for civil disobedience: thus, Brelvi, backed by several Muslim mercantile associations, led a mile-long procession on 2 June 1930 and chaired a meeting of about 10,000, including Hindus.[46] 'Conspicuous amongst organizers of procession and speakers at meeting', noted a government report, 'were certain Maulanas and Muslim propagandists from other provinces. To this extent, [the] procession must be regarded as success of Congress propaganda and it must be admitted that during the last *fortnight many Muhammadans have been gathered into the Congress fold*'[47] (italics mine). This is not to deny that, compared to 1920-1, Muslim enthusiasm in Bombay and elsewhere was much less. But, then, the religious passion stirred by the khilafat question was out of the extraordinary: no such issue in the early 1930s evinced the same degree of fervour.

II

The All-India Nationalist Muslim Party was formed on 27-8 July 1929. This was a sequel to the AICC meeting at Allahabad where delegates, reflecting on the political struggle being weakened by inter-communal conflicts and the attempts being made in to wean Muslims away from political activities, resolved to form themselves into a group.[48] They attributed the 'disruption' among politically-minded Muslims and their consequent apathy to a 'confused appreciation of the political obligations implicit in the fact of the community being a part of the Indian nation. Muslim political activity is now confined under the auspices of the existing Muslim institutions, to winning political responsibility as the main objective, and with freedom for the country as merely incidental thereto. Hence the need for the new party.' The NMP set out to develop a mentality above communalism, inspire into the Muslim communities greater confidence in nationalistic ideas, and create harmonious Hindu-Muslim relations.[49]

Khaliquzzaman claimed to be the founder of the NMP,[50] though existing historical evidence points to Ansari as its architect. Others closely associated with him were Rafi Ahmed Kidwai, Sherwani, Azad, Ghaffar Khan, Brelvi, Abdul Majid Khwaja, Mujibur Rahman, Saifuddin Kitchlew, and Abdul Bari of Bihar. Maulvis Kifayatullah, Muhammad Sajjad and Ahmad Said represented the Jamiyat al-ulama, while Maulana Qutubddin Wali belonged to Firangi Mahal.[51]

At its first meeting held at Sherwani's home in Allahabad on 27 July 1929, a central body was constituted: 28 members were elected from Bengal, 27 from Punjab, 3 from the N.W.F.P., 24 from UP. Committees were set up in Lucknow, Rae Bareli, Allahabad, Banaras, Faizabad, Hardoi, Bijnor, Saharanpur, Bareilly, Mahoba, Meerut, Aligarh, and Shahajahanpur.[52] In Punjab, NMP committees functioned in eight districts. There were ten in Bihar, and at least four in Bengal—Calcutta, Dacca, Bogra and Faridpur. Shamsul Huda and Ghulam Qadri headed the Dacca committee;

Mujibur Rahman, Akram Khan, K. Nooruddin and Abdur Razzack (the latter two were Calcutta Corporation Councillors) the Calcutta branch. Local branches in Bogra and Faridpur were controlled by a scattering of others who had been active in the khilafat and non-cooperation movements.[53]

On the strength of this network, the NMP claimed to represent the 'entire Muslim intelligentsia'.[54] Ansari scoffed at the League, pointing out that it had long ceased to be a reality, while the khilafat committee, once so powerful, 'was now but a shadow of its former self'. He concluded his party as the 'real representative group of the Musalmans of India today'.[55]

Such claims were exaggerated, and yet the NMP had the potential of emerging as a powerful force.[56] Hence, Ansari and his comrades staked their claim to represent the Muslims at the Round Table Conference in London. Gandhi insisted on demonstrating Congress's representative position,[57] and told the viceroy that without Ansari he would be 'perfectly helpless' in conducting Hindu-Muslim negotiations.[58] But the viceroy did not acquiesce. The Mahatma said in London that, whoever prevented Ansari from being selected as a delegate, committed a 'fatal blunder'.[59]

Actually, it was Fazl-i Husain, member of the viceroy's council, who vetoed Ansari's participation. Backed by the Muslim Conference and a section of the Urdu press, the Punjabi leader questioned the NMP's claim to represent the Muslims. 'The Muslim press has already stated', he wrote in July 1931, 'that Ali Imam and Ansari should not go as representatives of Muslims. This is the right line to take, and if it is right, there is no reason why it should not succeed.' He admired Ansari, adding, however, how 'during the last few weeks he [Ansari] seems to have done his best to convince all his friends and admirers that [his] partisanship of the Congress has deprived him of any sense of fair-play and propriety'.[60] Fazl-i Husain reserved his harsh comments for Gandhi. 'To confuse the issues, to indulge in irrelevance and to begin to talk of Muslim demands, and then talk of Congress Muslims of Dr. Ansari and so on', he wrote to friends in October 1931,

> all are devices with which Hindus as well as Muslims are quite familiar . . . Gandhi's insistence upon Dr. Ansari's inclusion and his parading readiness for complete surrender in case complete unity is forthcoming have nothing new about them. They are the very old devices which the Congress, Gandhi and the Indian Hindus have been condemning in the British Government and the British statesmen. They are doing now exactly what they alleged Lord Birkenhead was doing—asking for complete unanimity and resorting to the well known principle of Divide and Rule; but Gandhi should know that the people are not so unsophisticated

today as they used to be and that the game he is now indulging in is one which has been played out for some time.[61]

Ansari hated being drawn into the controversy. Gandhi, he wrote on 28 September, 'is harking back on me and wanting me even at this eleventh hour to be invited. . . . It is like a baby crying for his wetnurse'. Convinced that the government would keep the NMP unrepresented,[62] he stated:

I am positive that the government has deliberately left the Nationalist Muslim Party unrepresented . . . because they do not want the Hindu-Muslim question to be settled without their intervention. And they know that if there is any party in India which can bring about Hindu-Muslim unity it is the Nationalist Muslim Party. It is, therefore, against their interest to have the representatives of that party at the Round Table Conference, for they would be able to cement the unity of the various parties in India and thus deprive the government from playing their trump card against the representatives of India who are pressing hard for complete freedom from the British tutelage.[63]

He felt that Gandhi should not insist on his inclusion, but Jawaharlal Nehru dissuaded him not to be 'so rash as to cable him to do what he chooses'.[64] In early October, Gandhi changed gear, arguing that Ansari will be of no use unless the Muslim delegation endorsed his selection as a delegate.[65]

Meanwhile, the NMP secured the adherence of influential Muslims who had built their reputation through years of selfless political work. Its meetings at Lucknow (18-19 April 1931), Faridpur (27-8 June 1931) and Lahore (24 October 1931) were well-attended, and its policies conveyed some sense in the N.W.F.P., Punjab, UP and Bombay.[66] 'One of the most gratifying signs of the times', commented the *Leader*, 'is the rapid growth of nationalism among Indian Muslims. . . . The impressive gathering of the nationalist Muslims at Lucknow from all parts of the country tells its own tale.'[67] The editor of the *Indian Annual Register* expressed similar views.[68]

Ansari worked feverishly to weld together the various Muslim factions and persuade them to accept the NMP's proposals. They were mainly two: joint electorates and adult suffrage;[69] on other issues there was no fundamental difference between Jinnah's 'Fourteen Points' and the NMP resolution adopted in Lucknow on 18-19 April 1931.[70] Political problems, argued the Bihar lawyer Ali Imam, were a reflex of social forces. 'If you erect an iron wall between community and community in their politics, you destroy the social fabric. . . . Nationalism can never evolve from division and dissension.'[71] Ansari, too, refused to countenance separate electorates. He wanted the measure and method of representation in the federal and provincial legislatures to be settled on the basis of joint electorates and adult suffrage,[72] and suggested a round table conference of Muslim organizations to iron out differences.[73]

Ansari's statement set the stage for the real business at hand: ongoing talks between representatives of the NMP and the Muslim Conference. On 10-12 May they met at Bhopal, discussing the vexed issue of joint *versus* separate electorates. Ansari proposed joint electorates for the first ten years with a provision for a referendum thereafter. Alternatively, 50 per cent of the seats were to be contested on the basis of joint, and the other half on the basis of separate electorates in the first general election. The arrangement was to change in the second election with two-thirds of the seats to be contested by joint electorates. Thereafter, joint electorates with adult suffrage, as proposed in the Nehru report, were to be introduced. On the other hand, Iqbal, Shafi, and Shaukat Ali insisted on joint electorates and adult suffrage after ten years, though they could be introduced earlier if a majority of legislators so desired. Their other proposal provided for five years of separate electorates with a referendum on joint electorates at the beginning of the fifth year.[74]

These discussions, announced Ansari with characteristic over-optimism, raised the prospect of a working agreement.[75] But his hopes were soon belied by the intransigence of delegates from both sides,[76] and by Fazl-i-Husain's stout refusal to endorse a compromise.[77] When talks resumed at Simla on 21 June 1931, the Punjab leader demanded separate electorates and reservation of seats for the Muslim majorities in Bengal and Punjab.[78] Ansari found the atmosphere 'very inauspicious'.[79] Hence the Simla conference accomplished little more than restating a daunting agenda of continuing problems and differences.

The blame for the failure of such meetings was placed on Ansari and his colleagues.[80] Their policies, stated the Allahabad historian and publicist Shafaat Ahmad Khan, were 'like the bloom on the peach; you touch it, and it is gone. Where is the party now? Nowhere! The exact minute and detailed account of its branches and activities may be found in the secretariat of the Indian National Congress, but so far as Muslims of India are concerned they exist only on paper.'[81] Shafee Daoodi repeated the charge: Rafi Ahmed Kidwai replied that the number of Muslims in Congress exceeded the combined strength of the provincial Leagues and khilafat committees.[82] Others excoriated the NMP for selling out the community's interest as well as the interest of Islam.[83] Ansari stoutly refuted the allegation: 'We are surely not worse Musalmans because we refuse to turn our faith into a greedy superstition or an ignoble exercise in political hide and seek. . . . Our nationalism is part of our loyalty to our faith and not a betrayal or an infidelity.'[84] Shaukat Ali, who had no pretensions to detachment and only the flimsiest to moderation, told Saiyid Mahmud: 'I consider you all to be weak men and renegades, and, yielding to the open threats of the Hindus, (to) have chosen to live at their mercy',[85] an ill-chosen way to dramatize his contention that the Congress Muslims had 'sold out' to the 'Hindus'. Ansari was unswerving in his resolve to respond to Shaukat Ali. His underlying theme was simple: religion and faith were private matters, not symbols to be exploited by partisan politicians.

The Hindu Mahasabha, too, charged that some Muslims, masquerading as nationalists, had infiltrated the Congress in large numbers in order to exert pressure from within.[86] In substance, B.S. Moonje said, there was no difference between the demands of the communalist and the nationalist Muslim.[87] C. Vijaraghavachariar, the Mahasabha president in 1931, believed that the NMP resolutions adopted at Faridpur, were 'subject to all the infirmities of the proposals of the other section of Moslems to which Mr. Jinnah's fourteen points give expression'.[88] In short, the Mahasabha's strategy was to prevent the NMP activists from extracting concessions from the Congress. This was evident during the Gandhi-Jinnah talks in 1929, and later when Tej Bahadur Sapru tried negotiating with various non-Congress groups. Moonje was morbidly apprehensive of any move to conciliate the Muslims; Jayakar insisted that the Liberals must declare themselves on the communal question, stating the limits beyond which they would not go in their engagement with the Muslims.[89]

In July 1931, Ansari, Malaviya and Sardar Sardul Singh recommended, and the Congress Working Committee adopted, a scheme purportedly based on 'undiluted communalism and undiluted nationalism'.[90] Its main features were: joint electorates and adult suffrage, with reservation for minorities of less than 25 per cent. The N.W.F.P. and Baluchistan would have the same form of government and administration as the other provinces, Sind would form a separate province provided its people bore the financial burden, and residuary powers would rest with the provinces. While Gandhi agreed, the Muslim Conference stuck to its guns.[91] The Mahasabha's rejection was equally unequivocal.[92] The Bengal Provincial Hindu Conference acted likewise.[93]

Ansari reacted angrily. The Mahasabha's nationalism, he argued, cloaked its aggressive communalism. Even with the issue squarely placed in the context of the country's interest—which is where Ansari thought it ought to be—the Mahasabha was anything but enthusiastic. He also criticized some fellow-Congressmen. Malaviya, having formed a breakaway group on the issue of the Communal Award, was one of them. Ansari poured out his anger and frustration in a stream of letters to friends.

As if this was not enough. When Ansari returned to India in January 1933 after a four-month stay in Europe, he found the NMP in disarray. Khaliquzzaman had signed its death warrant in UP by founding the Muslim Unity Board.[94] In Punjab, Fazl-i Husain and the Unionists, and in Bengal Fazlul Haq and the United Muslim Party guided the course of Muslim politics leaving the NMP member crying in the wilderness. Abdur Rahman Siddiqi, one of the founders of the New Muslim Majlis, joined hands with Husayn Suhrawardy, while Mujibur Rahman, a fervent nationalist, failed to cope with the confusing plethora of Muslim factions.[95]

By 1934, the Congress Muslims stood 'divested of every shred of principle or practice on the basis of which they formed their group, and which they had proudly nailed to their masthead—of everything, all, except their name!'[96] Their party lived in the newspapers all right but beyond that it had no positive existence. Khaliquzzaman's idea that the NMP would discipline 'Nationalist Muslims' did not materialize because the remedy, he wrote, was not potent enough to eradicate the 'evil'.[97]

III

Explanations for the NMP's decline already exist.[98] Jawaharlal Nehru attributed it to the upper middle class background of its members, the absence of 'dynamic personalities' amongst them, and their method of drawing-room meetings, mutual arrangements, and pacts. At this game, the communal leaders

> drove the Nationalist Muslims from one position to another, made them give up one by one, the principles for which they stood. Always the Nationalist Muslims tried to ward off further retreat and to consolidate their position by adopting the policy of the 'lesser evil', but always this led to another retreat and another choice of the 'lesser evil'. There came a time when they had nothing left to call their own, no fundamental principle on which they stood except one, and that had been the very sheet-anchor of their group: joint electorates. But again the policy of the lesser evil presented the fatal choice to them, and they emerged from the ordeal minus that sheet-anchor.[99]

To Jawaharlal's explanation, one must add the combined and sustained opposition of the Mahasabha, the Muslim Conference, and certain powerful local and regional formations in Punjab and Bengal. Sure enough, the NMP served as a platform to the Jamiyat al-ulama, the Khudai Khidmatgars, the All-India Momin Conference, and the Ahrars, but it could not present itself as a viable alternative to either the Muslim Conference or the League. It was, consequently, reduced to arbitrating between the Congress and the communally-inclined Muslim parties—a role Ansari played in the early 1930s.

The image of men like Ansari got indissolubly linked with the Hindus, and they were, therefore, pictured as 'renegades' and accused of a 'sell out'. Attempts to remove this impression were, at best, feeble. Ansari persevered doggedly, for he had a greater awareness of the need to respond to the pressures for change than a great many of his Muslim contemporaries. He also had the courage and the conviction to assert his political will, and face the daunting challenge posed by his critics. He met criticism, and at times bitter attacks, but he did not hesitate to fight it out with them. Yet, his lieutenants lacked motivation, and the determination to solve their problems of tactics, coordination or leadership; in fact, Ansari soon became aware of how wayward the elements he was seeking to fuse into one were. Used to playing second-fiddle—first to Mohamed Ali and later to Ansari—several NMP members succumbed to communal pressures; other sturned defensive, sulking when faced with the combined opposition of their detractors. This was true of Saiyid Mahmud, Khaliquzzaman, Shuaib Qureshi, and A.R. Siddiqi, all bound to Ansari by personal rather than political loyalty. Jawaharlal's experience with such leaders led him to observe in April 1937:

> Our experience of the Nationalist Muslim Party in the past was not a happy one. Such half-way groupings confuse the issue and the masses are perplexed. . . . Those who agree (with the Congress) should not stand on the doorstep; they should enter the nation's chamber and take full share in shaping the nation's policy.[100]

The NMP was composed of a small number of professional men—lawyers, doctors, and journalists—who did not operate in politics from a position they could claim their own. They mainly depended on the goodwill of leading Congressmen, who encouraged them to counter the League and patronized them to lend credence to their claims of representing all Indians. This was not good enough. What was also not good enough was the preoccupation of the NMP leaders with constitutional issues. Thus, Ansari was closely associated with the All-Parties Conference; Shuaib Qureshi served as a member of the Nehru Committee; and Khaliquzzaman, Saiyid Mahmud, Sherwani and Khwaja were enmeshed in constitutional controversies which raged from the time of the first Round Table Conference and culminated in the squabbles over the Communal Award. Ultimately, however, such preoccupations led to no tangible results: such men mostly operated on the fringes of politics and were made, in the words of Shaukat Ali, a cat's paw by their Congress co-workers. Their fate was similar to that of the Liberals.

Admittedly, they formed a constituency the Congress assiduously courted in the 1920s to deepen its support. Gandhi did so during the khilafat campaign: Ansari and Ajmal Khan were adroitly used to follow a middle-of-the road policy to restrain the militant khilafatists. Later, Ansari and his associates formed valuable allies in dealing with estranged communal relations, projecting Congress policies among Muslims, and securing their electoral support.[101] Motilal Nehru tried to woo Ansari, Shuaib Qureshi, and Khaliquzzaman in the making of the Nehru report. Gandhi did the same, referring to their commitment to inter-communal harmony and insisting on Ansari's presence in London at the Round Table Conference.

Such symbolic gestures did not, however, empower the Congress Muslims to counter their detractors. Faced with the verbal assault of the Mahasabha and the Muslim Conference, they required strong ideological sustenance and political backing. This was not forthcoming. Though used on occasions, given decorative positions in the Congress hierarchy, and loudly proclaimed as devoted leaders, they were wilfully ignored during the critical negotiations in the 1930s and 1940s. Often, their viewpoint was treated with undeserved contempt.[102] This was so at the Lahore Congress in 1929. 'We found the atmosphere', wrote Khaliquzzaman,

> very secretive, and when in private talks the leading Congressmen decided to throw the Nehru report into the Ravi, even Dr. Ansari was not consulted . . . Dr. Ansari, Tasadduq and myself were leaving Lahore in the evening for our destinations, humbled, disappointed and angry. . . . At the station we had enough time to decide between ourselves that the Nehru report having been drowned in the Ravi, we could not take the responsibility of shouldering the burden of fighting for the independence of India, for the Muslims were bound to consider it to be a purely Hindu fight.[103]

The self perception of the Congress Muslims was that they were, at best, bargaining counters; when not so, they were stored in the deep freeze.[104] Thus when Gandhi agreed to compromise with the Muslim leaders on separate electorates, Abdul Majid Khwaja reacted angrily. 'It means', he wrote indignantly, 'that you are prepared to surrender the Congress Muslims who have fought the battles of the country side by side with you to those Mussalmans who have done nothing except for themselves, their seats, their posts, their salaries and their lunches and dinners at the Government Houses.' Khwaja opposed both separate electorate and communal representation. The 'salvation of the Muslims', he felt, 'lies in the salvation of the motherland and the salvation of the motherland in its turn lies in the mutual trust and goodwill of the two great communities'.[105]

Ansari's exchanges with Gandhi and Motilal Nehru in 1930 illustrates his ambivalences as well as his disenchantment with the Congress. Soon after Gandhi and Motilal turned a blind eye to his criticism of the Lahore resolutions, Ansari summed up the guidelines of his political conduct:

> We must not leave the Congress, nor must we do anything to weaken the Congress. After all the will of the majority must prevail, that is the only guide for any democratic institution. . . . To leave the Congress would be a crime. Therefore we must remain in the Congress and let those who believe in the present policy and programme carry on.

Again,

> As . . . for joining the Liberals or the communalists it is unthinkable for you and me. The Liberals will never do anything, even though they are kicked out of the Round Table Conference . . . As regards the Muslim communalists, we have . . . extricated ourselves from them. We have formed the 'Nationalist Muslim Party' and it would be the height of unwisdom to leave that party or to cease working for its object. *To my mind, that is the only avenue left for our political activities*. We must put all our mind to it and carry on a vigorous campaign to wean the Muslims away from the influence of communalists and reactionary leaders and think and act in terms of 'nationalism'. *That is the only channel left for out political activities.*[106] (italics mine)

It is perhaps surprising to find such a straightforward, commonsense approach in a man who combined strict standards of political honesty and obligation with a passionate emotional involvement in what he was doing. This is not to argue that Ansari was right—that is an opinion which every historian of Indian nationalism will answer for himself. Still, it would not be an exaggeration to say that in opposing the Mahatma, Ansari and others who shared his views acted from conviction and, in their own opinion, would have been false to the principles which brought them into the Congress movement if they had acted otherwise.

NOTES

1. Jayakar to Gandhi, 23 Aug. 1929, Jayakar papers (437), NAI. In his reply, Gandhi assured Jayakar that he had not 'bound anybody' because he had no representative capacity. 'I simply listened to Mr. Jinnah's exposition of his position. Similarly with the Ali brothers too, I heard what they had to say. With the latter the talk turned upon their grievance against me for my reticence.' Gandhi to Jayakar, 24 Aug. 1929, *CWMG*, Vol. XLI, pp. 319 and 289.

2. Lajpat Rai to Motilal Nehru, n.d., File No. 108 (Suppl.), AICC papers. Moonje to Malaviya, 31 July 1928, Moonje to Gandhi, 5 Aug. 1929, Jayakar papers (437).
3. Quoted in Uma Kaura, *Muslims and Indian Nationalism: The Emergence of the Demand for India's Partition*, New Delhi, 1977, p. 50.
4. Ibid., p. 51.
5. CWC resolution on the communal problem, July 1931, File No. G-37/1931, AICC papers; *IQR*, July-Dec. 1929, pp. 310-11; *India in 1929-30*, p. 95.
6. 9 Jan. 1930, *CWMG*, Vol. XLVII, p. 381.
7. S. Pirzada (ed.), *Foundations of Pakistan*, Vol. 2, pp. 42-4.
8. File No. G-59, 1928, AICC papers.
9. File No. 11, 1926, ibid.
10. Motilal was a patron of such men, as indeed of other Muslims, whom he helped to find jobs. See, for instance, the case of Hakim Wali who was recommended for the post of executive officer in Banaras municipality. Motilal Nehru to T.A.K. Sherwani, 29 July 1928, File No. 60 (Suppl.), 1925-6, ibid. Motilal also ensured that the PCC's find Muslims of Congress and swarajist views to elect candidates for elections. In a directive to the Sind PCC he insisted that 'the PCC even though constituted wholly by Hindus must rise above communalism and show that it makes no distinction between Nationalists whether they are Hindus or Muslims'. File No. 76 (Suppl.), 1928, ibid.
11. Kenneth McPherson, *The Muslim Microcosm: Calcutta, 1918 to 1935*, Wiesbaden, 1974, p. 80.
12. *Mussalman*, 27 Apr. 1926. Report on Native Newspapers, Bengal, Jan.-Dec. 1927, pp. 127, 204, 271.
13. McPherson, *The Muslim Microcosm*, sections 5 and 6 in Chap. 5.
14. B.N. Pandey, *Nehru*, London, 1976.
15. Idem, p. 145.
16. Page, *Prelude to Partition*, pp. 132-3.
17. Shafee Daoodi to Motilal Nehru, 26 Mar. 1929, File No. 96, Motilal Nehru papers. *The Frontier Question in the Assembly, being the statements of Pandit Motilal Nehru, MLA, Maulvi Shafi Daudi, MLA, and Saiyid Murtaza, MLA*, New Delhi, 1926.
18. Khaliquzzaman, *Pathway to Pakistan*, p. 117.
19. The membership of the All-India Muslim League was 1,093 in 1922, 1,097 in 1923, and 1,184 in 1924. *Annual Report of the All-India Muslim League*, Lucknow, n.d., Chagla papers, NMML.
20. *Mussalman*, 3 July 1930. The League, according to the 1931 annual report, was unable to perform its functions effectively because of the Muslim Conference 'which has divided our energies and caused a great deal of harm to the All-India Muslim League'. The situation remained unchanged in 1932-3 when the joint secretary warned that 'a little oversight or a little expression of inactivity on the part of Muslims today means lifelong suffering and bondage'. In order to gain members, the annual subscription was reduced from Rs. 6 to Re. 1 and the admission fee was abolished. *Annual Report of the All-India*

Muslim League for the year 1931, New Delhi, n.d., pp. 1, 4; *Annual Report of the All-India Muslim League for the years 1932 and 1933 (upto November)*, New Delhi, n.d., pp. 2, 3.
21. *Modern Review*, July 1929, p. 103.
22. Idem.
23. Smith, *Modern Islam in India*, p. 251; Faruqi, *Deoband School*, pp. 70-1.
24. Hardy, *Partners in Freedom*, p. 37.
25. *Mussalman*, 16 Apr. 1931.
26. *Liberty*, 1 June 1931, quoted in Bhola Chatterji, *Aspects of Bengal Politics in the early Nineteen Thirties*, Calcutta, 1969; pp. 14-15.
27. Home Poll. File No. 5/72, 1932, NAI.
28. Home Poll. File No. 5/54, 1932, NAI.
29. D.G. Tendulkar, *Abdul Ghaffar Khan*, Bombay, 1967, p. 116.
30. Smith, *Modern Islam in India*, pp. 266-7.
31. Home Poll. File No. 5/54, 1932, NAI.
32. Home Poll. File No. 5/62, 1932, NAI.
33. Home Poll, File No. 5/54, 1932, NAI.
34. Humayun Kabir, *Muslim Politics 1905-47 and other Essays*, Calcutta, 1969, p. 22.
35. Smith, *Modern Islam in India*, pp. 270-1.
36. Home Poll. File No. 5/46, 1932, NAI.
37. Malik Afzal Husain, *Kashmir awr Dogra raj, 1848-1931*, New Delhi, 1970 edn.
38. Among the demands listed were representation in ministries and in all grades of services in proportion to the Muslim population, religious freedom, the right to hold public meetings, and the freedom of speech and press. In other areas such as Mirpur *tahsil*, Major General R.G. Finlayson took note of the common grievance relating to high grazing tax and high rent assessments which were double of what they were in neighbouring Punjab, inadequate representation in civil administration, insufficient resources being spent on the development of the *tahsil*, and rampant corruption, inefficiency, and maladministration. Home Poll. File No. 10/28, 1932; Home Poll. File No. 5/2, 1933, NAI.
39. P.N.K. Bamzai, *A History of Kashmir*, New Delhi, 1962, pp. 660-1.
40. Home Poll. File No. 13/23, 1931, NAI.
41. Foreword by S.M. Abdullah in *New Kashmir*, New Delhi, n.d., p. 6.
42. Cited in Bamzai, p. 661: M. Ishaq Khan, *Perspectives on Kashmir: Historical Dimensions*, Srinagar, 1983, pp. 146-7.
43. *New Kashmir*, p. 6.
44. *IQR*, Jul.-Dec. 1929, pp. 350-1.
45. Ibid., p. 351.
46. Brown, op. cit., p. 137.
47. Viceroy to secretary of state, 18 Jan. 1930, Home Poll. File No. 257/V, 1930, NAI.

48. Khaliquzzaman, *Pathway to Pakistan*, p. 102.
49. *IQR*, Jul.-Dec. 1928, Vol. 2, p. 350.
50. Khaliquzzaman, *Pathway to Pakistan*, p. 102.
51. For list of those present at the Allahabad Conference, see *IQR*, Jul.-Dec. 1929; for Jamiyat al-ulama, see *Leader*, 19 Apr. 1931.
52. Funds for their support came from several sources, including the raja of Mahmudabad. He was much active in nationalist campaigns, leading the boycott of the Simon commission in Lucknow, presiding over the all-parties conference in Lucknow in September 1928, and lending his name to the list of those who endorsed the Nehru report. He also proposed launching a newspaper and invited Saiyid Abdullah Brelvi to join as editor. 'In view of the importance of the political situation and also in view of the Nehru Committee Report it is most necessary to start propaganada in right earnest to educate the people and get the report ratified by all recognized institutions.' To Brelvi, 8 Sept. 1928, Saiyid Abdullah Brelvi papers, NMML. Earlier, the raja had supported similar journalistic ventures in support of nationalist causes. The *Comrade*, the *New Era* (Lucknow), and the *Hamdam* (Lucknow) were among them. Both James Meston and Harcourt Butler tried unsuccessfully to persuade the raja to withdraw his patronage from such 'extremists' papers. Butler to the raja of Mahmudabad, 4 Sept. 1920, Mahmudabad papers, NMML.
53. *Mussalman*, 21 Mar. 1931; For Punjab, *Bombay Chronicle*, 4 July 1931.
54. Ibid., 27 June 1931; For Saiyid Mahmud's claims, *Bombay Chronicle*, 20 Apr. 1931.
55. *Modern Review*, May 1931, p. 611; A.Z. Zaidi (ed.), *The Evolution of Muslim Political Thought in India*, New Delhi, 1980, Vol. 4, p. 476. Gandhi's interview to *New Leader*, 25 Nov. 1931, *CWMG*, Vol. XLVIII, p. 333.
56. Letter to the Editor, 15 Apr. 1931, *Leader*, 19 Apr. 1931.
57. Gandhi to Irwin (tel.), 20 July 1931, *CWMG*, Vol. XLVIII, p. 158.
58. Gandhi to viceroy, 29 Aug. 1931, ibid., p. 382.
59. Interview to *Bombay Chronicle*, 14 Sept. 1931, p. 12; Gandhi to Ansari (cable), 14 Oct. 1931, *CWMG*, Vol. XLVIII, p. 148.
60. To Shafaat Ahmad Khan, 28 July 1931, 'Indian Muslims do not believe that Gandhi is serious in the matter of Muslim rights. His desire to have Ansari in London is only a continuation of his tactics at Delhi to demonstrate the existence of cleavage in Muslim opinion, while, as a matter of fact, it does not exist.' Waheed Ahmad (ed.), *Diary and Notes of Mian Fazl-i-Husain*, Lahore, 1977, pp. 213-14.
61. Ibid., p. 228.
62. To Shaukatullah Ansari, 28 Sept. 1931 (ed.), *Muslims and the Congress*, p. 129.
64. Statement to Press, 14 Sept. 1931, *CWMG*, Vol. XLVIII, p. 150; Devdas Gandhi to Jawaharlal, 2 Sept. 1931, *SWJN*, Vol. 5, p. 48, f.n. 3.
65. To Ansari, 4 Oct. 1931, *SWJN*, Vol. 5, p. 98.

66. Draft note on the success of Punjab Nationalist Muslim, n.d., Brelvi papers; 'Lucknow seldom had a bigger gathering of Mussalmans than one seen yesterday in connection with Muslim Nationalists' Conference', reported the *Tribune* of 23 July 1930, and *Indian Daily Mail*, 24 July 1930, Ansari papers.
67. Note on the Press, UP, for the week ending 23 Apr. 1931.
68. *IAR*, Jan.-June 1931, Vol. 2, p. 80.
69. For resolutions adopted at the meetings on 15-17 Apr., *Leader*, 19 Apr. 1931; *Mussalman*, 16 Apr. 1931.
70. *Mussalman*, 23 Apr. 1931.
71. Ibid., 16 Apr. 1931.
72. *Bombay Chronicle*, 27 Apr. 1931.
73. *Leader*, 19, 20, 22, and 23 Apr. 1931, Page, *Prelude to Partition*, p. 238.
74. Brelvi papers; Iqbal to Fazl-i Husain, 14 May 1931, *Letters of Mian Fazl-i-Husain*, p. 143.
75. *IQR*, Jan.-June 1931, Vol. I, p. 304.
76. Saiyid Mahmud to Nehru, 27 June 1931, Datta and Cleghorn (eds.), *A Nationalist Muslim*, pp. 115-16.
77. *IQR*, op. cit., pp. 303-6; K.K. Aziz (ed.), *The All-India Muslim Conference 1928-1935*, Karachi, 1972, pp. 75-6.
78. *Mussalman*, 25 June 1931; Page, *Prelude to Partition*, pp. 238-40; R.J. Moore, *The Crisis of Indian Unity 1917-1940*, New Delhi, 1974, p. 190; Fazl-i-Husain to Shafee Daoodi, 16 May 1931, *Letters of Mian Fazl-i-Husain*, pp. 144-8; *Bombay Chronicle*, 23 June 1931.
79. *Mussalman*, 25 June 1931; *Bombay Chronicle*, 24 June 1931.
80. The nawab of Chhatari to Fazl-i Husain, 3 July 1931, *Letters of Mian Fazl-i-Husain*, p. 158. Fazl-i Husain, who did much to undermine the possibility of a settlement, wrote that there were no Muslims in the Congress strong enough to persuade that body to act in a 'just' and 'righteous' manner. To Umar Hayat Khan Tiwana, 20 June, ibid., p. 152.
81. *IQR*, July-Dec. 1931, Vol. 2, p. 225.
82. *Leader*, 19 Apr. 1931. For Ansari's response, *Bombay Chronicle*, 6 July 1931.
83. Speech of Shaukat Ali at the UP Muslim Conference, 8 Aug. 1931, *IQR*, July-Dec. 1931, Vol. 2, p. 228.
84. *Bombay Chronicle*, 21 Apr. 1931.
85. 26 Apr. 1929, Datta and Cleghorn (eds.), *A Nationalist Muslim*, p. 94.
86. 22 Aug. 1929, Moonje Diaries, National Library, Calcutta: Moonje to Jayakar, 31 July 1926, Jayakar papers (437).
87. Speech at the Bengal Provincial Hindu Conference, *IQR*, Jul.-Dec. 1931, Vol. 2, pp. 260-1.
88. Speech at Akola, 8 Aug. 1931, *IQR*, ibid., pp. 252-3.
89. Moore, *The Crisis of Indian Unity*, p. 105.
90. *Young India*, 16 July 1931, *CWMG*, Vol. XLVII, p. 141; *Bombay Chronicle*, 13 July 1931.
91. For details, Page, *Prelude to Partition*, pp. 241-2.

92. *IQR*, Jul.-Dec. 1931, Vol. 2, p. 254.
93. Ibid., p. 261.
94. Khaliquzzaman, *Pathway to Pakistan*, pp. 119-20.
95. McPherson, *The Muslim Microcosm*, pp. 111, 121-2.
96. Nehru, *An Autobiography*, p. 139.
97. Khaliquzzaman, *Pathway to Pakistan*, p. 102.
98. K.M. Munshi, *Pilgrimage to Freedom*, Bombay, 1967, Vol. 1, p. 29.
99. Nehru, *An Autobiography*, p. 139.
100. *SWJN*, vol. 8, p. 128.
101. Thus in 1926 Ansari, Ajmal Khan, Azad, Mazharul Haq, and Shafee Daoodi appealed to the Muslim electorate of the Madras Presidency 'to stand by the Congress and to vote solidly for the Muslim candidates who stand under the banner of the Congress which is the sole common national organisation of India'. File No. G-66, 1926, AICC papers.
102. Notice Shaukat Ali's comment at the UP Muslim Conference, Allahabad. *IQR*, Jul.-Dec. 1931, Vol. 2, p. 228.
103. Khaliquzzaman, *Pathway to Pakistan*, p. 104.
104. Chatterji, *Aspects of Bengal Politics*, p. 73.
105. Khwaja to Gandhi, 12 Mar. 1931, A.M. Khwaja papers, NMML.
106. Ansari to Sherwani, 6 Jan. 1930, Hasan (ed.), *Muslims and the Congress*, pp. 90-1, and Ansari to Brelvi, 2 Apr. 1930, Brelvi papers.

PART III

9

Religion, Politics and Partition[1]

صبح آزادی

اگست ۱۹۴۷

یہ داغ داغ اُجالا، یہ شب گزیدہ سحر
وہ انتظار تھا جس کا، یہ وہ سحر تو نہیں
یہ وہ سحر تو نہیں جس کی آرزو لے کر
چلے تھے یار کہ مل جائے گی کہیں نہ کہیں

Dawn of Freedom (August 1947)

This stain-covered daybreak, this night-bitten dawn,
This is not that dawn of which there was expectation;
This is not that dawn with longing for which
The friends set out, (convinced) that somewhere
there would be met with.

فلک کے دشت میں تاروں کی آخری منزل
کہیں تو ہوگا شبِ سُست مَوج کا ساحل
کہیں تو جا کے رُکے گا سفینۂ غمِ دل

In the desert of the sky, the final destination of the stars,
Somewhere there would be the shore of the sluggish wave of night,
Somewhere would go and halt the boat of the grief of pain.

جواں لہو کی پُراسرار شاہراہوں سے
چلے جو یار تو دامن پہ کتنے ہاتھ پڑے
دیارِ حسن کی بے صبر خواب گاہوں سے
پکارتی رہیں باہیں، بدن بُلاتے رہے
بہت عزیز تھی لیکن رُخِ سحر کی لگن
بہت قریں تھا حسینانِ نور کا دامن
سُبک سُبک تھی تمنا، دبی دبی تھی تھکن
سُنا ہے ہو بھی چُکا ہے فراقِ ظلمت و نور
سُنا ہے ہو بھی چکا ہے وِصالِ منزل و گام

By the mysterious highroads of youthful blood
When (we) friends set out, how many hands were laid on our skirts;
From impatient sleeping-chambers of the dwellings of beauty
Arms kept crying out, bodies kept calling;
But very dear was the passion for the face of dawn,
Very close the robe of the sylphs of light:
The longing was very buoyant, the weariness was very slight.
—It is heard that the separation of darkness and light
has been fully completed,
It is heard that the union of goal and step has been fully completed;

بدل چکا ہے بہت اہلِ درد کا دستور
نشاطِ وصل حلال و عذابِ ہجر حرام

The manners of the people of suffering (leaders)
have changed very much,
Joy of union is lawful, anguish for separation forbidden.

جگر کی آگ نظر کی اُمنگ، دل کی جلن
کسی پہ چارۂ ہجراں کا کچھ اثر ہی نہیں
کہاں سے آئی نگارِ صبا کدھر کو گئی
ابھی چراغِ سرِ رہ کو کچھ خبر ہی نہیں
ابھی گرانیِ شب میں کمی نہیں آئی
نجاتِ دیدہ و دل کی گھڑی نہیں آئی
چلے چلو کہ وہ منزل ابھی نہیں آئی

The fire of the liver, the tumult of the eye, burning of the heart—
There is no effect on any of them of (this) cure for separation.

> Whence came that darling of a morning breeze, whither has it gone?
> The lamp beside the road has still no knowledge of it;
> In the heaviness of night there has still come no lessening.
> The hour of the deliverance of eye and heart has not arrived.
> Come, come on, for that goal has still not arrived.

In 1970, a volume edited by C.H. Philips and M.D. Wainwright elaborated certain major themes relating to the genesis and growth of the Pakistan movement.[2] Today, 'specialists' and 'non-specialists' alike continue to grapple with much the same issues that were once a historian's delight but are now a nightmare. A case in point was the lively debate sparked off by the release of Maulana Azad's 'thirty pages' in 1989. Newspapers splashed stories on the inept handling of the 'communal' tangle by the Congress, on Jinnah's 'motives' and his use of Pakistan as a bargaining counter to extract concessions from an obdurate Congress leadership. Cryptic comments appeared on the machinations of the colonial government, specially its last representative, Mountbatten, who hastened India's Partition. The baldly stated conclusions in much of the literature that has appeared since the publication of the 'Complete Version' of *India Wins Freedom* are that Partition could have been averted if the Gandhi-Nehru leadership had been magnanimous towards the Muslim League demands, if Mountbatten's predecessors—Linlithgow and Wavell—had shown greater enterprise in devising political initiatives, and if Jinnah had been less intransigent during his dialogues with the Congress high command.

This debate—often conducted polemically and acrimoniously—goes on ceaselessly as more and more information comes to light and as individual and collective memories are revived time and time again through the medium of the vast Indian television network and its screening of popular 'serials' like *Buniyad* and *Tamas.* These are memories of broken homes and families, the wounds inflicted by Partition generally, the 'unequalled mistrust, acerbity and frenzied warfare',[3] and the 'general sense of gloom and despondency that pervaded the subcontinent'.[4]

It is tempting, even more than five decades after Independence and Partition, to reflect on the agony so many experienced, review part of the literature afresh, and explore themes for future research. The story told in the following pages leaves out many vital areas, not because I do not recognize their importance, but because they are explored elsewhere. The colonial government's policies, so central to the evolution of 'separatist' politics, is more than adequately analysed and documented.[5] Similarly, a number of studies have delineated those ideological and social forces that aided 'separatist' politics around shared values and symbols.[6] Discussed in section IV, they illustrate the different frameworks for studying communalism.

I neither detail the history of Hindu-Muslim strife,[7] though some aspects of inter-community relations are analysed,[8] nor the tortuous course of Congress-League-British negotiations leading to Independence and Partition. The Simla conference, the Cripps mission, the cabinet mission, and the Mountbatten plan do not figure in the discussion. I focus instead on the years 1937-40. I see these years as crucial to the legitimization of the League as a powerful political force and as the spokesman of an aggrieved and beleaguered 'community' which gradually distanced itself from secular nationalism, the rallying cry of the Congress, to create a separate Muslim/Islamic nation state. Fears and apprehensions generated during these critical years offered Jinnah and the League a constituency which they had not managed to secure for so long. In the months following the resignation of the Congress ministries they pressed home the political advantage thus secured.

I

The decade preceding Partition frequently escapes historical scrutiny. Part of the reason is that the genesis of Pakistan is traced, quite mistakenly, to the activities of Saiyid Ahmad Khan and his comrades at the M.A.O. College in Aligarh. They are identified as the only vocal group to raise the spectre of Hindu domination, and the first to introduce the language of minorityism. Backed by the Muslim élites of upper India, they turned to 'separatist' politics to safeguard their interests which had come under threat from British educational policies, bureaucratic reforms, and powerful Hindu revivalist campaigns. Muslim government servants and landowners, in particular, whose power was most obviously reduced by the pressure of change in the late nineteenth century, organized the Simla deputation (1 October 1906) and founded the Muslim League (December 1906).[9] Their insistence on separate electorates and reservations, coupled with their concern to defend deeply-cherished religio-cultural symbols, which were being gradually drawn into the public arena and contested by Arya Samajists and Hindu Mahasabhites, was designed to create the space for a distinct Muslim identity in politics. Colonial policies, which began tilting in favour of the Muslims from the days of Mayo (1822-72) and Dufferin (1826-1902), legitimized such initiatives through an accommodation of sectional interests in the Act of 1909 and thereafter.[10]

This is a familiar story told in several different ways—the story of the pressure placed on the Islamic gentry by the rise of monied men and the resurgence of Hindu landholding communities;[11] the dreaded fear of majority rule, vividly described by Saiyid Ahmad in his 1883 speech on a local self-government bill for the Central Provinces;[12] and the apprehensions caused by Hindu resurgence.[13] These factors, together with the theories and institutions for separatism developed by the religious and political leadership in the last decade of the nineteenth-century, point to the heightening of communitarian consciousness. But this process in itself was a slow and tardy one, and impeded by the differentiated structure of the 'community', its regional and local diversities, and by deep-rooted sectarian and doctrinal disputes. No amount of pious exhortation could bridge the wide gulf separating, say, a Muslim peasant in Mymensingh from a Muslim *taluqdar* in Awadh. Nor could religious leaders, who began playing an important role in public affairs from early twentieth century, settle their theological differences. The Barelwis and the Deobandis had little in common. The Ahmadiyas and the Ahl-i Hadith were engaged in a running battle over doctrinal matters. And the Shias and the Sunnis were estranged, especially in Lucknow, both jealously guarding their separate mosques, religious endowments and educational establishments. The lines of cleavage in north India were more sharply drawn between the Sunnis and the Shias than between Hindus and Muslims.

Thus the initiative towards the creation of a separate Muslim homeland, though spurred by the anxieties expressed by Saiyid Ahmad, had its own contextual and ideological specificity. It was the outcome of a particular scenario on the eve of and during the Second World War which altered the tenor of political discourse in India and created the space for Jinnah's manoeuvrings. A beleaguered war-time government, having refused to deal with him in the past, now turned to Jinnah for political and moral support and, in the process, legitimized his critique of the Congress claim to represent all the communities of India. The inglorious breakdown of cross-community alliances and the accompanying collapse of the coalition governments in Punjab and Bengal—the last bastions of resistance to the League—helped turn Jinnah's dream into a reality.[14] That this would happen on the midnight of 14 August 1947 was unthinkable a decade before that date.

In the 1930s, there was no blueprint of a future Pakistan, no Islamic flag, no common platform, no shared goals and objectives. Rehmat Ali's scheme, nurtured in Cambridge, was an illustration of obscurantist political eccentricity. Having caused much political embarrassment back home, it was dismissed as 'chimerical' and 'impracticable'. Iqbal's blueprint, outlined three years earlier, did not envisage a *separate* Muslim state. He did, however, make out a case for provincial autonomy in Punjab, the North-West Frontier Province, Sind and Baluchistan *within the body-politic of India* for much the same reason that had prompted the Nehru report to recommend the separation of Sind from the Bombay Presidency and to constitute the N.W.F.P. into an 'independent' administrative unit. In the same speech, Iqbal, whose patriotic poems continued to be recited and sung in schools and colleges all over India, referred to autonomous states being formed, obviously not all-Muslim, based on the unity of languages, race, history, religion and identity of common interests. He did so in the context of '*India where we are destined to live*' (italics mine). This was surely not the swan-song of the Pakistan movement.

If Pakistan was still a pipe-dream, the League was little more than a paper organization. Having been in the wilderness during the khilafat agitation, its membership had plummeted to 1,330 in 1927. The branch in Bombay, Jinnah's homeground, could only boast of 71 members.[15] The 1929 session was adjourned for lack of quorum. When Iqbal spoke at Allahabad in 1930, the meeting failed to muster the required quorum of 75 members.[16] The organizers of the 1933 session in Delhi had a busy time filling up the hall with students of the Anglo-Arabic College. The League's income that year was Rs. 1,318, with 92 out of the 300 council members under notice to pay their arrears of membership.[17] Halide Edib commented, in 1935, that no one talked of the League as an arbiter of Muslim destiny.[18]

The leadership was fragmented, battered and bruised by frequent splits caused by factional feuds. Nawabzada Liaquat Ali Khan, credited with having persuaded Jinnah to return to India in 1934, set his eyes on securing the High Commissionership in London.[19] Khaliquzzaman was placed uneasily because of his loyalty to the Nehru household in Allahabad and his ambition to carve out his own sphere of influence in UP politics.[20] Nawab Muhammad Yusuf Khan solicited Malcolm Hailey's help in securing a knighthood or a place in the viceroy's executive council. His credentials were: 'I have neither spared money nor energy in creating a mentality among the landholders, the Muslims and other stable elements that their only salvation did lay in throwing their lot with the Government.'[21] The Aga Khan, mellowed after his hectic lobbying at the Round Table Conferences in London, was busy promoting the idea of a Vatican City in the territory of a protected ruler either in India or in the Persian Gulf.[22] And Jinnah, crestfallen after the rebuff he received at the national convention in December 1928, nursed his political wounds at his Hampstead home.[23] In 1934, the year he returned to Bombay, Hailey commented that Muslims had 'too many third-class leaders. There was no solidarity in the community, more so after the Communal Award which removed the sense of danger and prevents reunion under a strong leadership.'[24]

Some signs of revival followed Jinnah's return, and some endeavours to refurbish the League's image and rescue it from the political wilderness came to light. Yet, there was no evidence to indicate that the League had emerged as a political adversary or a force powerful enough to challenge the hegemony of the Congress. When the raja of Mahmudabad, a close friend of Sarojini Naidu, Tej Bahadur Sapru and the Nehrus, joined the League in 1936, he believed that the Congress and the League 'were like two parts of the same army fighting a common enemy on two fronts'.[25]

The raja's belief was grounded in hard facts. The Congress and the League had berated the Act of 1935. They shared, despite the perceived clash of ideologies, a perspective on political and agrarian issues. The League manifesto, minus its rhetoric, endorsed major Congress policies: the manifesto showed as much awareness of the people's needs as that of the Congress. In UP, the League and the Congress even put up Muslim candidates for the elections. Jinnah hoped that the Congress and the League, together in partnership, could inspire their followers by demonstrating that even the most intractable problem could be solved through dialogue and understanding. So, Jinnah talked of a 'united front' when the Congress accepted office in March 1937. There was no difference, he proclaimed on 18 September 1937, between the ideals of the Muslim League and of the Congress.[26]

Jinnah's own political conduct was above reproach. Liberal, eclectic and secular to the core in private and public life, he generally acted in unison with the Congress and initiated and backed proposals to break the communal impasse. 'If out of 80 million Muslims', he observed on 20 October 1936, 'I can produce a patriotic and liberal-minded nationalist block, who will be able to march hand in hand with the progressive elements in other communities, I will have rendered great service to my community.'[27] What India required, he stated a year later, was a united front. 'And then by whatever name you call your government is a matter of no consequence so long as it is a government of the people, by the people, for the people.'[28] That should explain why the viceroy thought of Jinnah as 'more Congress than the Congress', and why others regarded him as an 'arch enemy' of colonialism and a rallying symbol of secular forces.[29] Nobody expected him to foist the flag of Islam on an area supposedly defined by Iqbal and Rehmat Ali. India's unity was an ideal Jinnah still cherished.

In the face of such evidence, it is hard to make sense of Jinnah's subsequent crusade against the Congress and his repudiation of the principles he himself espoused for nearly three decades. It is much less easy to explain why, in the mid-1930s, the League was seen in some quarters as Congress' *bete noire* out on a mission to destroy India's liberation struggle. It was right to expose the League's semi-feudal orientation, but it was equally important to marry this perspective with the fact that not everybody in the League was feudal, obscurantist or religious-minded. People like Liaquat Ali Khan, the raja of Mahmudabad and Khaliquzzaman, for whom Nehru had a 'warm corner' in his heart,[30] were constantly 'torn between two loyalties'[31] but not necessarily imbued with an anti-Congress spirit or swayed by the League's religious claptrap.[32]

In 1936, Haig felt that the 'great majority of UP Muslims' had serious reservations about the Muslim League and opposed the policy of 'running a communal party'. That is why they were keen to wrest control of the provincial League, 'so as to render the All India Muslim League nugatory'. Three years later, Haig commented, despite the crucial changes in the political scenario during the intervening years, that, except for the Muslim landlords in UP, all others in the Muslim League were 'in general outlook much nearer the Congress'. 'For these reasons', he pointed out, 'if the right wing in the Congress found it necessary to strengthen themselves in this Province, they might do so by a coalition with the Muslim League rather than with landlords as such.' Read in the proper sequence of events, these observations reflect a powerful strand in UP 'Muslim politics'—a strand overlooked by other political commentators. It has also not figured in the discourses on Partition and 'communalism'.

Was it not possible to draw estranged comrades back into the Congress fold and assuage their feelings? Nehru would have said 'no' at the time. Rajendra Prasad, on the other hand, felt otherwise. Referring to the large number of 'Congress sympathizers' among the successful Muslim candidates in the 1937 elections who were willing to arrive at some settlement with Azad, he argued that 'if the proposed agreement between the Independent Muslims and the Congress had materialized, the communal animosity which the Muslim League whipped up later might never have been brought about'.[33]

Rajendra Prasad reflected on such events a decade after Independence and Partition. Jinnah did not. He had pleaded with Nehru and with Rajendra Prasad, even at the risk of being rebuffed yet again, that there was no serious difference between him and the Congress, except that he stood for safeguarding 'Muslim rights' against Hindu majoritarianism. Nehru concurred. He told Meerut's nawab Muhammad Ismail Khan in November 1937: 'I do not quite know what our differences are in politics. I had imagined that they were not great.'[34] If this was so it was an error of judgement to treat the League as a counter-force and an adversary. Instead of making clear its own terms of secular and composite nationhood, the Congress leaders, including the secular-minded amongst them, settled for a soft option—one that Jinnah mentioned in his March 1940 speech at Lahore. The 'terms' were, of course, not made explicitly clear, for they ranged from Gandhi's 'Ram-Rahim' approach to the Malaviya-Lajpat Rai vision of 'Hindu India'. 'Indian' nationalism was so often seen as a manifestation of a more 'genuine' expression—'Hindu nationalism'. In 1939, Ashraf, who headed the Muslim Mass Contact Campaign, lamented that 'the Congress position regarding communal organizations and the communal activities of the Congress members has been dangerously vague until now'.[35]

The Congress truculence over a coalition ministry was, in its historical sequence, a political miscalculation. This is an oft-repeated argument, perhaps a bit worn out. Yet, its validity is yet to be questioned with any degree of conviction. Hence its mention is not out of place in tracing the broad sequence of events.

To carry the story forward, it needs to be stressed that, as champion of national unity and as a mediator between rival groups and warring factions, a role performed by the Congress with such adroitness since its inception in 1885, its leaders had two clear-cut options. These were to reach out to the Muslim masses who, in Nehru's reckoning, had rallied round the Congress flag in large numbers, and weaning away those Leaguers who felt dispirited after the party's poor showing in the elections. But nothing of this kind happened. The Muslim Mass Contact Campaign, launched amid much fanfare, petered out owing to the opposition of the Congress right-wing, which feared an influx of Muslim activists and their critical and unacceptable influence on party policy. The prospect of a Congress-League coalition was, on the other hand, dimmed for reasons that had very little to do with principles, more so because the Congress had not just concluded pacts and agreements with the Muslim League, as in December 1916, but also with the Akalis in Punjab.

Both Nehru and Prasad explained the 'breach of faith' in terms of the unexpectedly large Congress majority secured in the elections. This, according to their political calculation, made all talk of a coalition indefensible. In addition, Nehru referred to the feeling in Congress circles that without the League they would be freer to quarrel with Harry Haig, UP's governor, and break with him on their own terms.[36]

Nehru should have added that the Congress strategy was moulded by two conflicting forces, though each aimed to achieve a common goal—jettisoning all hopes of a Congress-League *entente*. There was, first of all, the stranglehold of the Hindu Mahasabha and other Hindu militant bodies opposed to a Congress-League rapprochement. Though acting purposefully and effectively on the strength of their following, their effectiveness derived, in large measure, from their patrons in the Congress. B.S. Moonje, the architect of the Hindu Mahasabha, stated that Vallabhbhai Patel and other right-wing Congressmen constantly urged him to 'stand firm on a variety of points in the interest of Hinduism'.[37]

The Congress strategy was, moreover, influenced by the perceptions of Congress Muslims. Wary of losing their secure and privileged position in the Congress hierarchy, they opposed, despite Azad's assertion to the contrary,[38] the idea of a coalition government in UP. Their instinct of political survival may have prompted them to do so. The socialist K.M. Ashraf, a relatively new arrival on the political stage, disapproved of 'the old methods of coalition, of pacts with Jinnah and others'.[39] The more experienced politician-journalist, Saiyid Abdullah Brelvi, berated élite forms of compromise-hatching.[40] Noble thought, yes, but quite out of tune with the realities of power politics and not quite consistent with Congress' own track record. Besides, how could Congress Muslims advocate a 'principled' posture only in relation to the League when so many of their party stalwarts paid allegiance to the Mahasabha and the RSS creed? This thought weighed heavily on their secular-nationalist conscience. Yet, they were unable to articulate it in the way Ansari had done in his indignant note of protest against Gandhi's decision to launch civil disobedience in 1930.[41] Without bothering to assess the situation independently, they accepted Nehru's harsh and ill-considered verdict on the League.

The Congress decision in the summer of 1937 created the space for the League's revival and offered Jinnah the chance to establish his hold in UP, a province that had spurned his initial overtures. With Khaliquzzaman and nawab Ismail Khan losing face and the National Agriculturist Party in disarray, Jinnah tasted victory in the erstwhile capital of the nawabs of Awadh. It was his finest hour. Appearing belligerent and impatient with his numerous detractors in the N.W.F.P., Punjab, Sind and Bengal, he lost no time humbling the recalcitrant elements. A mass contact campaign, launched under the aegis of the League, was his antidote to the Congress-sponsored programme. The person who consistently opposed the mixing of religion with politics and, for that reason, remained on the fringes during the khilafat upsurge, pressed the ulama into service, cultivated two of Deoband's renowned theologians—Shabbir Ahmad Usmani and Ashraf Ali Thanwi—and created fissures in the ranks of the ulama. The university at Aligarh turned out to be his prized trophy. What had once been a politically benign campus came to be described as the 'arsenal of Muslim India' by Jinnah.

Unwittingly, the Congress bolstered Jinnah's claim to be 'Muslim India's' sole spokesman, and aided the League to cultivate its image as a beleaguered organization, a victim of Congress machinations. Writing to the viceroy on 3 June 1939, UP's governor commented that 'Muslim solidarity would soon have been undermined' had the Congress agreed to a coalition. He added:

> There are bound to be differences between Muslims on the main agrarian and economic issues. The Muslims in office would have to make themselves responsible for definite policies in regard to these matters; they would have received the support of some Muslims and aroused the opposition of others. Nothing seems to be so effective in disintegrating a party as the taking of office.[42]

Harry Haig stated an old axiom of British policy in India, which lay at the heart of the principle of dyarchy detailed in the Montagu-Chelmsford Reforms of 1919. The reckless course adopted by the Congress would have been averted had the party learnt from its own experiences with dyarchy. Bringing the League into government may well have given rise to inter-party feuds. At the same time, rejecting its representatives had the effect of creating a far broader unity among the League factions and greatly hardening their stance thereafter.

II

The coalition issue cast an ugly shadow over the Congress ministry in UP and elsewhere. There was talk of overt manifestations of aggressive Hindu nationalism, of the tyranny of a Hindu brute 'majority' over the Muslim 'minority', and a reiteration of the fear—expressed by Saiyid Ahmad Khan in the 1880s, by the Simla deputationists of 1906, and by Mohamed Ali at the Round Table Conference in 1930—that a non-Muslim majority would use its powers under democratic institutions to undermine 'Muslim interests' and offend cultural sensitivities and religious susceptibilities.

Complaints ranged from the general to the specific. There were pointed references to Hindu Mahasabhites 'in the garb of Congressites', and to 'Hindu Congress Cabinets' paying only lip service to nationalism and religious impartiality: 'The elephant tusks are only for display but it uses its real teeth for chewing its food.'[43] Reports from certain districts spoke of the 'arrogance and oppression of Hindu officials', and the coming of 'Hindu raj'.[44] In UP, Haig noticed cases against Muslim police officers being sent to the anti-corruption department. He intervened to protect Muslim officials from unjust treatment.[45] In Bombay, Roger Lumley was impatient with the arrogance of the Congress leaders in general, and with the rank and file in the districts, in particular. What, in his view, angered the Muslim leadership were the tales of woe that came up to them from Muslims in villages and towns 'where the local Congress boss has made it apparent that in his eyes Congress rule meant that he now wielded local power and that he had every intention of making things uncomfortable for the Muslim minority'.[46] Finally, the scale of Hindu-Muslim rioting led Muslim publicists to conclude: 'Never before in India's history did riots take a heavier toll of life and property within such a short space of time than during the two and a half years of Congress administration in some of the Provinces of India.'[47]

There were added grievances, mostly either localized or specific to a region—for example, the anti-Muslim bias of a welfare officer in the Delhi Cloth Mills, or the declining strength of Muslim wholesale foodgrain dealers in Delhi.[48] On the other hand, contentious issues of a general nature, such as the form of electorates, representation in services and professions, and the future of Urdu, did not bother Muslims everywhere. What irked them in Meerut was the ill-advised policy of the food control authorities causing hardship to Muslim traders in rice,[49] the punitive police tax in Budaun,[50] and the Congress alliance with textile-owners and the Mazdoor Sabha in Kanpur, an alliance forged to weaken the large Muslim working force.[51] Again, in Kanpur, they were concerned with the municipal board fanning the fires of Hindu-Muslim violence and, to add insult to injury, doling out services, contracts and scholarships to its Hindu benefactors.[52] Here and elsewhere, Muslims were aggrieved at being outside the patronage network. Finally, ill-will was sometimes engendered by incidents that could have taken place anywhere and in any other period of history—from offering prayers within the school compound, or Muslim boarders at the Etah Government High School being prevented from cooking beef and being told to participate in games during Ramzan.[53]

In Bihar and the Central Provinces, the Wardha and Vidya Mandir schemes of education, the singing of *Vande Mataram*, and the hoisting of the Congress flag were major contentious issues. Added to these were local grievances: inadequate Muslim representation in certain branches of administration,[54] dissatisfaction with the housing schemes of the Improvement Trust,[55] discrimination in disbursing loans and educational grants, and minor but incredibly trivial issues such as withdrawal of the Jabalpur riot cases of 1938, the arrest of 15 Muslims in the Chandur-Biswa murder case, and the release of a convicted Hindu in the Hoshangabad *paan* (betel) poisoning case.[56] Such incidents, even when unrelated to the policies or actions of the Congress governments, highlighted their 'tyranny'.

The Bombay ministry was held responsible for the discharge of Muslim employees in some Ahmedabad mills. But the fact of the case was that the millowners, some of whom were decidedly not free of communal prejudices and hostility towards the Muslim working force, dismissed 7,000 to 10,000 Muslim workers so as to avoid the risk of having communal trouble inside the mills.[57] They did so despite loud protests from the ministry. Likewise, the UP administration was placed in the dock for fomenting Hindu-Muslim riots in, say, Kanpur and Marehra, a small town in Etah district. As for Kanpur, aggressive action by a rowdy Muslim crowd started the chain of events leading to a bloody feud. In Marehra, ill-feeling was caused through a Congress flagpole having been bent by a *tazia*, perhaps accidentally. This led to brick throwing on the procession. All hell broke loose. Several Hindus were killed, their shops looted, and a temple desecrated. Whatever the provocation, the Muslims were undoubtedly the aggressors.[58]

So many of the grievances catalogued in the Pirpur and Shareef reports and in Dr. Ziauddin's tale of woes were by no means specific to the years of Congress rule. Riots occurred from 1893 onwards, though their frequency and intensity increased only in the aftermath of the khilafat movement. Nor was there any novelty in issues connected with the representation and form of electorates. These were advanced time and time again in Punjab, UP and Bengal, and were contested with equal vehemence. Notice the hue and cry following the Lucknow pact, or the indictment of the Swarajist party in Bengal, the relentless crusade against Fazl-i Husain's ministry in Punjab, and the denunciation of the Nehru report by the Ali brothers and the so-called 'All-India' Muslim Conference.[59]

In the mid-1930s, however, many of the old fears gained an altogether new kind of intensity because of a significant, though less visible, shift in the structural situation. What lent a sharp edge to the debate then was how power and authority, which flowed directly out of the Act of 1935, was going to heighten competition and enlarge arenas of conflict, and how social classes and communities, whose interests were delicately safeguarded by the colonial authority in the constitutional arrangement, were pitted against each other in an uneasy and sometimes antagonistic relationship. Increasingly, local bodies were embroiled in this unlovely struggle. In UP, where the number of municipalities had increased steadily along with the representation of non-official Indians, there were unmistakable signs of a bitter contest to command resources in order to reinforce patronage networks. Thus a report on municipal administration for the year 1937-8 noted: 'The year's working was disfigured by the same unhealthy party action and intrigue, the same interminable wrangles about motions of no confidence, the same jobbery and injustice in connexion with appointments, the same reckless irresponsibility in the financial sphere.'[60] The same report pointed to 'communal dissensions exerting a sinister influence on account of appointments, transfers and postings. A year later the administration of over 30 municipalities was tarnished by communal dissensions, party strife, and intrigue. Boards of Farrukhabad, Fatehpur, Soron, Mainpuri, Mussoorie, Barant, Chandausi and Moradabad were the worst offenders.[61]

At the same time, such dissensions were not always between Hindus and Muslims *per se*. Haig commented on how the 'general political criticisms are the stock in trade of opposition, voiced by non-Congress Hindus just as much as by Muslims'. Thus vocal Muslim groups of his province indicted the G.B. Pant cabinet only for the reason that they did not have the same degree of pull and influence enjoyed by the supporters of the ministry. In essence, therefore, their grievance was not a religious one, though it assumed an intensely communal form.[62]

The conduct of some Muslim *zamindars* illustrates how class issues could so easily degenerate into religious squabbles, and how particularistic concerns were so drawn into the public arena and identified with the fortunes of an entire 'community'. Both the *taluqdars* of Awadh and the *zamindars* of eastern and western UP raised the bogey of Islam to denounce the Congress agrarian programme, including the UP Tenancy Bill, even though they knew full well that the party in power was committed to land reforms well before the ministry was formed, and that the Bill, piloted by Rafi Ahmad Kidwai, was directed against an exploiting class and not specially against the Muslim *zamindars*. Muslim landlords were a target of attack not *qua* Muslims but *qua* opponents of the Congress and its land reforms.[63]

Similarly, when the Bombay ministry levied property tax to pay for prohibition on *all* the urban property owners in the city, it was construed as an anti-Islamic measure on the grounds that Muslims invested savings in property rather than in stocks and shares and that they possessed a large number of religious endowments. In reality, their main grouse was against Brabourne, governor of Bombay, who had not insisted on a Muslim League minister being included in the cabinet. From that moment, the League publicists put the worst possible construction on everything the ministry did.[64]

What about the perception of those Muslims who regarded the ministry as a 'Hindu' administration, the ministers as 'renegades', and the Congress as a 'Hindu' party? It is true that the Congress record was not without blemish. The Wardha and Vidya Mandir schemes of education were ill-conceived.[65] The neglect of Urdu in UP and Bihar, notwithstanding the pro-Urdu sentiments of Gandhi and Nehru, was deliberate.[66] So was the systematic exclusion of Muslims from district and provincial Congress committees. The presence of Hindu militants in the ranks of the Congress was not unusual, but their overbearing attitude was a major irritant and a source of considerable discord. Ramgopal Gupta, secretary of the district Congress committee in Mahoba, Hamirpur, reported:

> The other day the Education Committee of the District Board elected a Hindu Chairman as a result of coalition among the Hindu members on the cry of danger to Hinduism. The defeat of the Muslim candidate through Hindu communalism has angered the Muslim public who cannot distinguish between a Mahasabhite Hindu and a Congressite Hindu.[67]

Ashraf highlighted some other irritants as well. He pointed out how the Congress ignored 'the Muslim sentiment in matters of detail and permitted a number of things to happen which gave the [Congress] annual session a distinctly Hindu appearance'. The League papers emphasized that there were no Urdu posters or Urdu signposts to guide the delegates, no gates and arches named after Muslim leaders, and finally, that propaganda for cow-protection and Hindi was conducted in Congress Nagar. Ashraf regarded these as 'trifles' but conceded the need to make the right gestures. 'Considering its psychological effect on the Muslim visitors,' he observed, 'and particularly in view of the fact that a number of Muslim papers have made it a point to exaggerate to a willing audience, we must take every precaution that the Congress session in Mahakoshal meets all possible susceptibilities.'[68]

In the light of the League's charges, it is an awesome task to prepare a balance sheet of the ministry's performance. Yet, it is worth the effort so as to place the League's Congress-baiting in perspective and uncover the motives behind its well-orchestrated campaign.

It is an undeniable fact, often ignored in secondary literature, that the Congress and its allied partners embarked upon an ambitious programme of legislation, especially to protect the interests of the cultivating class.[69] In the N.W.F.P., *naubat chaukidari* was done away with. The Agricultural Debtors' Relief Act limited the rate of interest realized by moneylenders and cancelled interest due to creditors on 1 October 1937.[70] In UP, the Tenancy Bill was a significant piece of legislation and a forerunner of the abolition of *zamindari* in 1952. In CP and Berar, the Relief of Indebtedness Act, the CP Revision of Land Revenue of Estates Act, and the CP Tenancy (Amendment) Act were examples of radical legislation. The governor of the province admitted that 'there was much of value in the Congress programme and undoubtedly the Congress as a body was striving towards the objective of a better India'.[71] In Orissa, efforts were made to place the tenant in a position of independence, free him from his contract with the landlord, and provide credit and relief from debt.[72] And finally, in Bombay the Agricultural Debtor's Relief Act turned out to be the 'most important legacy left by the legislatures'. The governor's impression was that the ministry was 'inspired by a real ideal of service to the public', and that its performance 'was certainly not bad. And when one takes into account the strange circumstance of . . . the fact that the Ministers, and most legislators, had practically no previous experience of their tasks . . . it was remarkably good and held out promise for the future.'[73]

UP's governor believed—and there is little reason to doubt his opinion—that the provincial ministry had performed admirably in communal matters, and that some of its policies, such as the Rural Development Scheme, benefited the Muslims.[74] They fared well in public services, occupying 39.6 per cent of the posts in the Provincial Executive Service, 25 per cent in the Judicial Service, and 24.4 per cent of Class I positions in the UP Agricultural Service (Table 9.1). Not surprisingly, the governor did not have to use his special powers to protect the 'beleaguered' Muslims. The story was no different in CP, Bihar, and Bombay. The CP Muslims 'have hitherto suffered little, if any, serious injustice at the hands of the Congress Ministry'. The governors of Bihar and Bombay sent out similar reports,[75] observing that the ministers were usually anxious to err on the side of generosity wherever 'Muslim interests' were affected. The Bombay ministry withdrew the textbooks prescribed by the Jamia Millia Islamia and its vice-chancellor Zakir Husain. It also refused to ban cow-slaughter. The CP government allowed Muslim donors to finance Urdu schools for Muslim boys on lines similar to those of Vidya Mandirs and

Table 9.1: Hindu and Muslim Representation in UP Public Services

Services	Hindus		Muslims	
	Number	Percentage	Number	Percentage
Civil				
Executive Service	175	52.5	132	39.6
Tahsildars	106	54.99	84	43.6
Naib Tahsildars	117	55.9	87	44.1
Agricultural Service				
Class I	9	64.2	3	24.4
Class II	32	76.0	5	12.0
Subordinate	401	73.3	137	25.0
Police				
DSP	28	56.0	14	28.0
Inspectors	105	46.4	68	30.0
Sub-Inspectors	1,029	54.2	832	43.8
Head Constables	898	35.2	1,638	64.4
Naiks	884	51.5	883	47.9
Constables	14,063	53.00	12,289	46.4
Educational Service				
Class I	11	73.3	4	26.7
Class II	78	73.6	14	13.2
Subordinate Service:				
Teaching branch	1,062	69.0	372	24.2
Inspecting branch	169	64.0	85	32.2
Judicial Service	159	72.0	55	25.0
Medical Service				
Civil Surgeons	25	83.3	4	13.3
Medical Officers	78	75.0	21	20.1
Assistants	271	80.4	61	18.1
Service of Engineers				
Class I	3	60.00	1	20.0
Class II	21	72.4	3	10.4
Subordinate	104	91.0	8	7.0
Income Tax Department				
Class I and II	24	61.5	12	30.7
Forest Service	12	57.0	4	19.0
Rangers	87	80.5	20	18.5
Deputy-Rangers	175	74.4	59	25.1
Co-operative Societies				
Gazetted Officers	5	62.5	3	37.5
Subordinate	120	77.0	36	22.9

Source: Address by G.B. Pant to members of the UP Press Consultative Committee, 11 January 1939, L/P&J/8/686, BL.

Note: Grants made to Muslim institutions by the Education Department (excluding grants made by local boards) for 1938-9 amounted Rs. 3,83,201. This included a special grant Rs. 48,396 made out to Arabic *madrasas*.

extended official support to such schools (*Bait al-Islam*).[76]

All said and done, however, there is no denying the fact that Muslim grievances existed, and that it was exceedingly difficult to dissipate these by any process of reasoning. After two and a half years of Congress rule, they were embittered by instances (very difficult for the most part to prove, but nevertheless symptomatic of the atmosphere that prevailed) of their oppression. Side by side was the growing realization of the importance, from their point of view, of the Congress claim to be the sole mouthpiece of Indian opinion and the sole party to negotiate with the raj, and an anxiety to secure their own position before their bargaining capacity with Pax Britannica deteriorated further. The result was, of course, seen in the League's consolidation, and the pitching of its demands on a very much higher level.

The demands were that future constitutional arrangements should be made not on the basis of population but on the basis of communities, that the Muslims be treated on complete equality with the Hindus, and that no constitutional change be made without the approval of the two communities. In basing demands on communities rather than parties, the League drew mileage from the Hindu Mahasabha contesting the Congress claims, and the scheduled castes demanding to be treated separately. This was the first tangible step towards delineating the contours of the Pakistan demand. It was very much the outcome of the Congress ministries. The League's only success was in making this perception look *real*.

III

Jinnah raised the war cry at Lahore, the city with a glorious history of cultural synthesis and integration. The mild, moderate statesman, tutored in the liberal traditions of Dadabhai Naoroji, spoke angrily and defiantly, sending out alarm signals all around. Much to the consternation of the Congress Muslims, including Azad who had only just set out his political agenda for his co-religionists at Ramgarh, Jinnah talked of 'two nations', and of Muslims having 'their homelands, their territory and their state'. Refuting the theory of a plural, composite nationhood, he argued that it was a 'dream' for Hindus and Muslims to evolve a common nationality. They belonged to two different civilizations which were based on conflicting ideas and conceptions. Yoking together two such 'nations' under a single State 'would lead to growing discontent, and the final destruction of any fabric that may be so built up for the government of such a State'.

These were ominous remarks; yet, they did not lower the final curtain on the prospect for a united India. Although the crusade against 'Hindu India' had been launched amid cries of '*Allah-o-Akbar*', the syntax and import of the phrases used in the 'Pakistan Resolution' were obscure. The silver lining was that Jinnah had, albeit consciously, refused to define his nation and had thereby left his scheme open to diverse interpretations. The viceroy regarded it as 'very largely in the nature of a bargaining. . . . Half the strength of his [Jinnah's] position is that he has refused to define it and I am quite certain that he would refuse to define it now if asked to. . . .'[77] E.J. Benthall, president of the Bengal Chamber of Commerce and an astute political observer, commented in March 1940 that Jinnah did not want to be dragged into the details of the Pakistan scheme in order to avoid being tangled up in interminable discussions, possibly to the disadvantage of his own case. After an hour-long conversation with him, Jinnah refused to be pinned down to future constitutional proposals: 'his main interest was to keep Congress out while he builds up power and influence.'[78] Resignation of the Congress ministries, combined with the domestic and global compulsions of the British government during the World War, enabled the future Quaid to play his 'Pakistan' card to out-manoeuvre his opponents and detractors. Having been rebuffed and rejected by the Congress leadership for well over a decade, he had at long last earned his moral right and established his political claim to be heard as the chief, if not the sole, spokesman of 'Muslim India'.

Yet, initial reactions to the 'Pakistan Resolution' did not bring much comfort to the League diehards. Sikander Hyat Khan, averse to Jinnah's intrusion into his political territory, was disturbed, as the resolution drafted by him at Lahore provided for definite links with the Centre so as to preserve India's national unity.[79] In Bombay, Muslim leaders saw little in Jinnah's scheme to bolster their self-confidence: 'the best that any Muslim has said . . . is that Jinnah is using it [Pakistan] as a bargaining weapon',[80] an impression not easy to dispel in other quarters as well. As late as the spring of 1946 when Mirza Ismail, the knighted dewan of Mysore, was asked if Jinnah was serious about Pakistan, he said: 'no, it was a move in the political game'.[81] In UP, too, the Pakistan idea was long held to be a bargaining move, 'a counter demand to that of the Congress'.[82] The nawab of Chhatari, architect of the UP National Agriculturist Party, was unsure how the Lahore resolution would protect Muslims in 'Hindu-majority provinces'.[83] Many Muslims in such areas were decidedly unhappy at the prospect of Partition.[84] Their fears were confirmed when they discovered that Jinnah's Pakistan simply provided a homeland for those living in majority areas but not elsewhere.[85]

There were still others—the socialists, the Congress Muslims of Azad's generation, the ulama in the Jamiyat al-ulama, the Ahrars, the Shias, the Khudai Khidmatgars and the Momins—who doggedly adhered to their vision of a united India.[86] The All-India Ahrar Conferences, held in 1943 and 1945 and attended by maulana Ataullah Shah Bukhari and Mazhar Ali Azhar, denounced Jinnah's plan to divide the country. The Momin Conference, convened in September 1945 by its charismatic leader, Abdul Qayyum Ansari, took a similar stand. The slogan of Pakistan, stated Ansari, was 'invented' by well-to-do Muslims to grind down their impoverished co-religionists. The nationalist concerns of the Jamiyat al-ulama, which had already declared complete independence as its goal in 1939,[87] was reflected in the activities of learned and distinguished men like maulanas Husain Ahmad Madani, Ahmad Said, and Kifayatullah. They were insulted, rebuffed and violently attacked,[88] but refused to capitulate to the forces of political reaction and religious fanaticism. Their role must not be written off or relegated to a historian's footnote. In the evolution of a composite, nationalist ideology, the turbaned men with flowing gowns had as much role to play as their counterparts among the Western-educated intelligentsia.

Finally, some of Jinnah's own close associates quibbled and hesitated. Ismail Khan and the nawab of Chhatari, friends of the Nehrus, decided to stay put in India. Khaliquzzaman and the raja of Mahmudabad, brought up in the liberal and composite ethos of Lucknow and Allahabad, dithered for long. But when the reality, so to speak, dawned on them, they journeyed to Pakistan with a sense of unease and remorse. Like so many of their generation, they were pained to bid adieu to the symbols of their faith—the great Imambaras of Lucknow and Matiya Burj, the sacred shrines at Ajmer and Delhi, and the *dargahs* at Bansa-*Sharif*, Rudauli, Kakori and Dewa-*Sharif* in Awadh. They were agonized, as reflected in their diaries and memories, to snap their ties with Lucknow and Delhi, the cities of Mir Anis and Ghalib, or the *qasbahs* in Awadh which served as centres of cultural and intellectual life.

There were, indeed, memories on both sides of the fence, memories of living side by side for generations with a shared heritage, memories of friends and of long-standing associations. The birth of Pakistan severed cultural ties and fragmented an intellectual tradition which was neither 'Hindu' nor 'Muslim' but, in its essence, Hindustani. Quratulain Hyder's Urdu novel *Mere Bhi Sanamkhane* ('My Temples Too'), published in 1947, captured the anguish of a group in Lucknow whose dream of a united India was shattered by the grim and tragic happenings in 1946-7. What was there for them to celebrate at the fateful midnight hour or at the dawn of Independence? Which country did an author like Saadat Hasan Manto belong to? India or Pakistan? When he sat down to write he tried in vain to 'separate India from Pakistan and Pakistan from India'. He would repeatedly ask himself: 'to whom will now belong what had been written in undivided India? Will that be partitioned too?' Other Urdu writers and poets, too, conveyed their agony and experiences in their own inimitable styles. Khwaja Ahmad Abbas, a key figure in the Progressive Writers' Movement, bemoaned the 'death' of one's country. 'Who killed India?' he asked indignantly: '. . . that an imperialist power planned the dismemberment of our country is not surprising. The wonder and the tragedy is that India should have been killed by the children of India.'[89]

IV

So, why did a Pakistan come about which served the interests of most Muslims so poorly? Why did an ill-defined and vague concept sway the masses in such large numbers? What enabled Jinnah to create and popularize the symbol of a separate Muslim nation? Why did the Congress, having championed national unity with such gusto, capitulate without offering much resistance to the two-nation theory? Was it a case of 'betrayal', as Azad pointed out retrospectively, or an implied recognition of the failure of secular nationalism? Or should we search for clues in two of Nehru's statements?—one made in April 1940 when he told Malcolm Darling, a civil servant, that he would accept Pakistan rather than not have freedom,[90] and the other in 1960 when he confessed to the author, Leonard Mosley: 'The truth is that we were tired men and we were getting on in years . . . the plan for partition offered a way out and we took it. . . .'[91] Or, perhaps, in a highly suggestive post-facto justification of Congress acquiescence to the country's vivisection: in an appeal to the Indian electorate on the eve of the first general election in 1952 it was stated:

> The price of freedom was Partition. The Congress and its leaders resisted the idea of Partition till the last moment and they yielded only when they realized that the alternative was indefinite perpetuation of foreign rule or civil war or both. The short experiment of coalition government with the Muslim League in 1946-7 demonstrated that no real co-operation was possible between the secular nationalism of the Congress and the narrow communalism and the two-nation theory of the Muslim League. *A strong and stable Central Government could be established by peaceful means only through Partition. . . . It should not be forgotten that without Partition there might have been no transfer of power at all, or the whole of India might have been involved in a civil war the consequences of*

which would have been *infinitely more tragic than the sad events of the latter half of 1947.*[92] (italics mine)

Some of these questions, as indeed the clues offered by the election appeal of 1952, have been tackled from a wide range of perspectives. There are, first, those who see Muslim nationalism linked with the demand of a nationality apprehensive of its future in a Hindu-dominated federal structure, and who regard secular nationalism out of place in a society where the 'divisive forces have proved much more dynamic than the cohesive ones'.[93] They find Hindu-Muslim antagonism 'embedded in the historical logic of India'. Farzana Shaikh argues that the call to Partition was driven by a long history of ideas that saw the Muslims as an exclusive political entity separate from others, an 'awareness of the ideal of Muslim brotherhood, a belief in the superiority of Muslim culture, and a recognition of the belief that Muslims ought to live under Muslim governments'.[94]

Such an interpretation, coupled with crude expositions of the two-nation idea, are grounded in the mistaken belief that the ideologues of Muslim nationalism had shared paradigms or a common Islamic framework for determining the place and status of Islam and of Muslims in the subcontinent. Did Mohamed Ali and Ansari share the same world view? Did Muzaffar Ahmad, one of the founders of the communist movement in India, and Fazlul Haq have a common discourse? Was Azad's secular vision and Jinnah's two-nation idea compatible? Was there no difference in the perspectives of the ulama of Deoband, Nadwat al-ulama, and Firangi Mahal? Moreover, even if one were to recognize, for the sake of argument, a common theme across the political spectrum, what place does one assign to the Ahrars, the Khaksars, the Khudai Khidmatgars, of the Momin Conference, the Shia Political Conference and the Jamiyat al-ulama?[95] Their presence communicates forcefully the message that Indian Muslims had a strong secular and nationalist tradition as well which ought not to be forgotten, and that their perspective should not be submerged beneath the rationalizations of the 'victors', the founders of Pakistan.[96]

Furthermore, the two-nation theory is grounded in the mistaken belief that Hindus and Muslims constitute exclusive, autonomous entities, with no common points of contact and association, and that religious loyalty gains precedence over bonds of relationship based on inter-social connections, cross-cultural exchanges, and shared material interests. A corrective to an approach that underlines the primacy of religion is required in order to understand the movement towards Partition in its specific context and not as a 'logical' sequel to developments dating back to the pre-colonial era.

'Communalism' or 'separatism', both in their latent and overt forms, only touched limited groups in certain areas. Their impact was, moreover, transient, for groups embroiled in inter-religious feuds at a given moment could be seen living harmoniously at other times. The governor of Bengal, where Hindu-Muslim conflicts were almost endemic, commented on the rank and file of the two communities co-existing peacefully. 'Only at rare intervals', he added, 'when religious feelings became inflamed, that they treat each other as enemies and clashes occur.'[97] Recent studies reveal the fusion of Hindu and Muslim 'folk' worship, with the practices and teachings of the high or 'orthodox' Islamic tradition and the participation, as in the case of the Muslim weavers of Banaras, in public ceremonials relating to particular Hindu figures.[98] There are also instances, such as the one from Bahraich in eastern UP where the outbreak of cholera in 1930 prompted Muslims to join in great force to worship the goddess Bhawani to induce her to remove the pestilence, which illustrate that religious barriers could be transcended and strict codes of behaviour transgressed.[99] Or the way Islamic ceremonies relating to birth, marriage and death were observed in many areas, though the 'outer labels' were sometimes discarded to make the rituals and practices look 'Islamic'.[100] 'The rigidity of intolerance on view', stated the 1921 Census report, 'which is a marked feature of the religion of Islam in its purer form, does not extend to the masses, who are quite willing to recognize and assist the efforts of their neighbours to keep on peaceful terms with unknown powers'.[101]

Much work needs to be done on the historical development of Islam and of the various Muslim communities scattered across the subcontinent. On the basis of existing studies, we can safely trace the strength of composite and syncretistic tendencies, though their growth and progress were neither unilinear nor unimpeded. Islam in Kashmir developed a resilient tradition of its own, incorporating many social and cultural practices of pre-Islamic origin.[102] Islam in Punjab provided a repertoire of concepts and styles of authority which served to encompass potentially competing values, including the values of tribal kinship, within a common Islamic idiom.[103] Islam took many forms in Bengal and assimilated values and symbols not always in conformity with Koranic ideals and precepts. The cultural idioms, rooted in the Koran and the *Hadith* (traditions), underwent a rapid transformation, giving birth to a set of popular beliefs and practices which, in essence, represented the popular culture of rural Bengal rooted in the pre-Islamic past.[104] Finally, Islam in south India evolved a tradition of worship marked by a striking capacity to accommodate itself to indigenous patterns of faith and worship. Islam gained a foothold because of its capacity to forge links with the religions and peoples of the wider society, and to offer a form of access to the divine which could be grasped and built upon through means already present within these societies. This interpenetration was neither 'degenerate' nor a product of superficial accretions from Hinduism. The sharing of belief and practice was, in fact, built up into a dynamic and expensive religious system.[105]

Nationalist writers in the 1940s and thereafter were wedded to the concept of composite nationality, a quintessential feature of India's liberation struggle, and laid stress on cultural assimilation and social intermingling between Hindus and Muslims. Perhaps they painted an idyllic picture, and disregarded elements of discord and disharmony. Still, the essential thrust of their argument—that the followers of different religious creeds had co-existed peacefully even in turbulent times—was profoundly true. Nehru's reflections in Ahmednagar jail and Azad's introspection at Ramgarh are as relevant today as they were in the 1940s. India's Partition did not make their perspective any less relevant.

In his book published in 1971, Anil Seal, the doyen of the 'Cambridge School', questioned the common assumption which marred historical narratives of previous decades, that the Indian Muslim 'community' formed a bloc of peoples whose conditions were generally equal, whose interests were generally the same, and whose solidarity was generally firm. Unevenness of socio-economic development, he argued, produced disparities between Muslims in different provinces and between Muslims in the same province, just as it was doing between Hindus. In 'so shapeless, so jumbled a bundle of societies, there were not two nations, there was not one nation, there was no nation at all, what was India?—a graveyard of nationalities and the mother of new nationalisms struggling to be born'.[106]

Following the same framework, Paul Brass argued that the ideology of Muslim separateness did not flow out of the objective differences between Hindus and Muslims but out of the use made of those differences through a conscious process of symbol selection. Nor was it the consequence of the objective circumstances of Muslims in UP, who were better placed than Hindus in urbanization, literacy, English education, social communications and government employment.[107] Francis Robinson arrived at similar conclusions; the threat of becoming backward, rather than backwardness itself, encouraged UP Muslims to organize themselves separately. Their influence in the province helped them to do so with much effect.[108] More recently though, Robinson has sought to establish a 'fundamental' connection between Islamic traditions and 'political separatism'.[109]

Until the 1980s, UP was seen as the heartland of Hindu and Muslim revitalization movements, and the chief arena where competing elites devised and followed their political trajectory within communitarian frameworks. Historians have since turned to regions outside the Indo-Gangetic belt to explore the terrain of elite politics within formal imperial structures. David Page detailed the profoundly divisive effects of the Montagu-Chelmsford Reforms in Bengal and Punjab. His story is about how Hindu-Muslim antagonism became a permanent feature of provincial politics, how 'communal' interests were consolidated around 'communal' issues, and how 'Muslim attitudes' were formed towards the emergence of provincial autonomy and the eventual withdrawal of imperial control.[110] Ian Talbot and David Gilmartin carry the story further to trace the roots of Partition in Punjab. In Talbot's analysis, the 'decisive shift' takes place as late in the day as the 1946 provincial elections, when landholders tilted the balance in favour of the League.[111] Gilmartin, on the other hand, examines the evolution of support for the Pakistan movement in terms of a search for ideological identity amid the severe contradictions established by colonial rule. The Pakistan movement remains essentially a paradox to Gilmartin: millennarian tendencies and Islamic revivalism on the one hand; political objectives shaped by the structures of the colonial state on the other. Yet, many of the political pressures that produced Pakistan—and led to Punjab's partition—originated outside the province. The events of 1947 in Punjab owed much to the broader currents that brought the decline of the British empire, the rise of the Congress, and the rapid progress of the League in other parts of India. Indeed, Jinnah's political ascendancy, which in its beginnings owed little to Punjab, ultimately shaped events there deeply. But in the end the Punjabi Muslims decided their own future, for the creation of Pakistan could not be denied.[112]

Studies of this nature lay bare the main contours of political 'separatism' in the critical regions of British India, establish the linkages between provincial and national leaders, and trace the strength of social/cultural inter-connections as instruments of mobilization. The appeal of ideology—nationalist or otherwise—is best mirrored in the specific context of a region. So also its use by the political and religious leadership.

Regional studies do not, in any way, diminish the value of other works that concentrate on all-India leaders and organizations, and unfold the happenings at the apex. For example, Anita Inder Singh manages to fill in some of the gaps in our knowledge of the interplay of British, Congress and Muslim League strategies. She assesses, with much sensitivity, the attitudes and tactics of the three parties in the negotiations for the transfer of power and the factors that induced the Congress and the British to accept the idea of Pakistan.[113] It is not very often that the story of such negotiations is told with such clarity and objectivity.

R.J. Moore provides useful insights into the official mind in Delhi and Whitehall. *The Crisis of Indian Unity* deals with the problems of wresting freedom from the British and keeping the country united in the wake of the Pakistan demand. *Churchill, Cripps and India* and *Escape from Empire* trace the evolution of the Labour party's policies to solve the many-sided Indian problem.[114] Read together with the earlier versions and interpretations of Leonard Mosley, Penderel Moon, V.P. Menon, H.V. Hodson and P.S. Gupta,[115] Moore's researches cover important aspects of British policy and strategy towards Independence and Partition.

Many of the themes delineated in their writings figure in a work of outstanding merit—Ayesha Jalal's *The Sole Spokesman: Jinnah, the Muslim League and the Demand for Pakistan.* It is by far the most refined statement on this cataclysmic and violent event. Raising the standard of debate, she underlines the importance of Jinnah's cleverly disguised manoeuvres and the significance of keeping the terms of the Lahore Resolution vague and amorphous. The critical importance of her work lies in presenting the resolution as a tactical manoeuvre and in her success in elevating this interpretation basically from the realm of doubts and speculations and giving it academic authenticity and credibility.[116] Equally important is the way in which she uncovers the provincial world of Bengal and Punjab to argue that behind the simple cry of Pakistan lay a host of complex and conflicting interests, some of which had very little to do with the shape Pakistan was going to assume in Jinnah's guarded exposition in March 1940 or thereafter. Finally, her summation of Mountbatten's role is a powerful indictment of a man who made such tall claims for so modest a 'feat'—conducting an administrative operation that left hundreds of thousands dead and rendered millions homeless. His 'great operation' was an ignominious scuttle enabling the British to extricate themselves from the awkward responsibility of presiding over India's 'communal madness'.

There are, however, notable gaps in an otherwise fascinating exposition. Part of the reason why this is so is because Jalal's perspective is based on high politics and diplomacy. Jinnah occupies centrestage in her narrative, with provincial leaders rather than interest groups extracting their price for supporting the Quaid. That is why the sense of a growing movement, drawing its constituents from different regions and social classes at various stages of its progress and development, is missing. Also missing is a perspective on the ideological content of the movement, on the social base of the League, its mobilization techniques, and its ability to use Islam as a rallying symbol with such great effect. Both Talbot and Gilmartin have argued how the linking of Islamic appeals to social and economic grievances and their transmission through the all-important rural idiom of *biradari* and Sufi networks succeeded in transmitting the League's message from its strongholds in the towns to the countryside, which had the bulk of the voters.

Jalal's version of the Congress' part in the making of Pakistan is one-sided, because her book is almost solely based on official sources, on League records, and on Jinnah's private collection. While it is possible to argue, as Asim Roy does, that the Congress steadily and deliberately worked itself up to a position where Jinnah was forced to take his 'Pakistan' and leave the scene for good,[117] the nature of its political intervention still awaits careful historical scrutiny.

While Jalal marshals an array of facts to establish Jinnah's popularity and the League's acceptability, she does not mention that Pakistan was not everybody's dream and Jinnah not everybody's Quaid. It is a lesser known fact that, in terms of the actual number of votes secured and against the background of the tremendous build up to Pakistan, 'nationalist Muslim' groups did not fare too poorly in the 1946 elections (Table 9.2). Their performance in some UP constituencies, such as Bahraich (south), Meerut (east), Gorakhpur (east) and Pilibhit was, in fact, comforting.

Table 9.2: Votes Polled in the Muslim Constituencies

Parties	Seats contested	Votes polled	Percentage
Muslim League	64	5,15,229	64.70
Congress	29	1,07,877	13.54
Nationalist Muslims	32	1,14,686	14.39
Ahrars	2	10,154	1.27
Sunni Board	1	11,188	1.40
Shia Conference	2	5,847	0.73
Khaksars	3	176	0.02
Independents	30	31,491	3.95

Sources: L/PJ/8/478 and L/PJ/8/483, British Library, London.

Though Congress stalwarts like Rafi Ahmad Kidwai lost in Rae Bareli, success came to Nisar Ahmad Khan Sherwani in Mainpuri and Etah, Bashir Ahmad in Bijnor south-east, and Hafiz Muhammad Ibrahim in Garhwal and Bijnor north-west. Some additional gains were possible had the Congress put up Muslim candidates in the general urban and rural constituencies, and if its nominees were chosen with care. It was a mistake, for example, to pit Abdul Aleem of the Aligarh Muslim University against Haji Muhammad Shakoor in the Jaunpur-Gorakhpur constituency. Similarly, Aftab Ali was too weak a candidate to be pitted against Jamshed Ali Khan, the nawab of Baghpat and a recent convert to the League creed. A more formidable rival could have performed better at the hustings.

In any case, asking people to sit on judgement on the partition plan, which had already been thrashed out during the prolonged confabulations at the viceregal lodge, was an act of deception, a monumental fraud. The die was cast, more so after the 1946 elections which were held under a restricted franchise but were treated as the people's final verdict. The predictable collapse of the interim government and the fire of violence in Bihar and Bengal, which nobody tried to extinguish,[118] offered to every party an opportunity and an excuse to hammer out the modalities of transferring power to two separate nations. Never before in South Asian history did so few decide the fate of so many. And rarely did so few ignore the sentiments of so many in the subcontinent. A distraught eye witness to the trauma of 1946-7 recalled on the eve of her departure from Rajshahi: 'Tears began to flow, I realized for the first time that the part of Bengal which had been my home was no longer my home. It was a foreign land. . . . The underlying feeling was that we were being driven from our own country. . . . We were angry with both Nehru and Jinnah for not handling the situation properly.'[119] Such impressions need to be reflected in our historical discourse. Only then will it become clear that, in the ultimate analysis, it does not matter whether, in the penultimate phase of the League crusade, Jinnah bargained for a separate nation or not. What mattered was his articulation of the two-nation idea and his successful mobilization strategies. The whims and personal idiosyncrasies of individuals do not give birth to new nations. The conjunction of forces and circumstances do. For many of us in the subcontinent, still confronted with and troubled by the bitter legacy of Pakistan, the critical and unresolved issue is how Jinnah and the League secured the support of so many Muslims in so short a time.

Does the explanation lie in UP society and polity? In the evolution of ideas, reinforced by colonial policies, from the days of Saiyid Ahmad Khan? In the unequal contest between Hindu and Muslim revitalization movements? In the conflict between the symbols of Kaaba and Kashi? In the self-perception of a minority community placed in a disadvantageous position in relation to the power structures? In the manipulation of religious and cultural symbols by competing elites? Jalal does not address herself to these possibilities. In any event, she does not think, though it is nowhere explicitly stated in her book, that in making Jinnah the 'sole spokesman' of 'Muslim India' the part played by the UP Muslims was of any consequence. She does not attach much importance to the role of Muslim landlords, the students and teachers of the university at Aligarh, described by Jinnah as the 'arsenal of Muslim India', a section of the Deobandi ulama, and the leading priests of the Barelwi school who had much following amongst the weavers, artisans, and other entrepreneurial groups in the *qasbahs*. Did Jinnah not have such groups in mind when he spoke of those 'who spread the light when there was darkness in the majority provinces. It is they who . . . suffered for you in the majority provinces, for your sake, for your benefit and for your advantage.'[120] These were comforting remarks, though one cannot help concluding with a not-so-comforting thought—never before in South Asian history did so few divide so many, so needlessly.

NOTES

1. The use of the expression 'secular nationalism' in this chapter in the context of India's nationalist struggle may be contested on the grounds that nationalism and its secular dimension was associated with an amalgam which ranged all the way from Gandhi to V.D. Savarkar. I have consciously used the expression because, in theory at least, the Congress and its allies in the left parties and groups subscribed to secular values and were committed to the building of a secular society, a legacy bequeathed to the makers of India's constitution. It is of course arguable that Jinnah tried to fashion a particular variant of secular nationalism for the Indian Muslims, in the perspective of 'modern' ideas of ethno-territorial nationhood and self-determination. I am inclined not to agree with this view for reasons made clear in this introduction.
2. *The Partition of India: Policies and Perspectives, 1935-1937*, London, 1970.
3. G.D. Khosla, *Stern Reckoning: A survey of the events leading up to and following the partition of India*, New Delhi, 1989, p. vii.
4. K.A. Abbas, *I Am Not an Island: An Experiment in Autobiography*, New Delhi, 1987; A.K. Gupta (ed.), *Myth and Reality: The Struggle for Freedom in India, 1945-7*, New Delhi, 1987.

5. Robinson, *Separatism Among Muslims*; Bipan Chandra, *Communalism in Modern India*, New Delhi, 1984; Gyanendra Pandey, *The Construction of Communalism in Colonial North India*, New Delhi, 1990; Freitag, *Collective Action and Community*.
6. Hardy, *Muslims of British India*; Robinson, *Separatism Among Muslims*; S. Gopal (ed.), *Anatomy of a Confrontation: The Babri Masjid-Ramjanambhumi Issue*, New Delhi, 1991; K.N. Panikkar (ed.), *Communalism in India: History, Politics and Culture*, New Delhi, 1991.
7. Suranjan Das, *Communal Riots in Bengal, 1905-1947*, New Delhi, 1991, and Gyanendra Pandey, 'In Defence of the Fragment: Writing about Hindu-Muslim Riots in India Today', *EPW*, Annual Number, 1991.
8. I have discussed this aspect in detail in 'Competing Symbols and Shared Codes: Inter-Community Relations in Modern India', below.
9. Robinson, *Separatism Among Muslims.*
10. Hasan, *Nationalism and Communal Politics.*
11. Bayly, *Rulers, Townsmen and Bazaars*, pp. 456-7.
12. For an extract of the speech, Philips (ed.), *The Evolution of India and Pakistan*, p. 185.
13. A substantial monograph on Hindu revivalist movements is still awaited, though some of the aspects are adequately covered in J.R. McLane, *Indian Nationalism and the Early Congress*, Princeton, N.J., 1987 (for an excellent account of the cow-protection movement); Kenneth W. Jones, *Arya Dharm: Hindu Consciousness in 19th-Century Punjab*, California, 1976 and J.T.F. Jordens, *Dayananda Sarasvati: His Life and Ideas*, New Delhi, 1978, for the Arya Samaj movement; Robinson, *Separatism Among Muslims*, pp. 66-82, for Hindu nationalism; D.A. Low (ed.), *The Indian National Congress: Centenary Hindsights*, New Delhi, 1985. And Gyanendra Pandey, 'Hindus and Others: the Militant Hindu Construction', *EPW*, 28 Dec. 1991.
14. It is a comment on fluctuating loyalties that Fazlul Haq, who was so virulent in denouncing the Congress ministries, had this to say after his fallout with Jinnah. He wrote that the Muslim League had roused Muslim passions against the Congress and the Hindus through ceaseless propaganda and 'clever distortion of facts'. Muslims were 'naturally drawn towards the Muslim League as the only organized political body among the Muslims and their only heaven [*sic*] of refuge against Hindu oppression'. British imperialist policy favoured such a development as it 'expected to be able to set off the Muslim League against the political ascendancy of the Congress'. The result 'is that the Muslim League has now got a foothold in the land which is not justified by the extent to which it can truly claim to be representative of Muslim interests'. A.K. Fazlul Haq, *Bengal Today*, Calcutta, Dec. 1944, p. 46.

    It is equally significant that Fazlul Haq, the champion of 'Muslim interests', was prepared to forego this role and fill the vacancy in the viceroy's council created by the death of Sir Akbar Hydari. He wanted the viceroy to give him a chance 'to serve my king and my country in a position of much greater responsibility than that I have yet occupied in my activities in the provincial sphere'. To Linlithgow, 12 Jan. 1942, Linlithgow papers (125/124), BL.

15. The membership was 1,093 in 1922, 1,097 in 1923, and 1,184 in 1924. *Annual Report of the All India Muslim League*, Lucknow, n.d. Khaliquzzaman recalled how the League merely lived on paper during the khilafat days and how afterwards a 'new set of Nawabs' wrested control of the body. 'They merely attended the annual sessions and received praise from their equally honourable hosts for having undertaken the journey in a first-class compartment at great inconvenience to themselves, and their staying as guests in good, well-decorated buildings with the most delicious dishes to devour and plenty of pans (betels) and cigarettes to chew and smoke.' The proceedings were duly sent to the Press, though long before the British officials received from their own inner sources news of every word spoken at the meeting. 'The end of the session was the end of the organization for the year and no one took notice of what had been said except in the critical record of the Government of India.' *Pathway to Partition*, pp. 137-8.
16. I have cited an eyewitness account of the session in 'Congress Muslims and Indian Nationalism, Dilemma and Decline 1928-34', below.
17. Sayeed, *Pakistan: The Formation Phase*, p. 176.
18. Halide Edib, *Inside India*, p. 348.
19. Liaquat Ali Khan to Willingdon, 14 Sep. 1934, Samuel Hoare papers (4), BL.
20. Harry Haig took special note of the factional struggles in the UP Muslim League and keenly followed the moves of Khaliquzzaman, 'an extremely astute and ambitious man'. Haig to Linlithgow, 2 Dec. 1936, Harry Haig papers (microfilm), NMML.
21. Malcolm Hailey to Melville, 14 Mar. 1934, Hailey papers (E 220/27B), BL.
22. Hoare to Willingdon, 8 Mar. 1935, Samuel Hoare papers (4).
23. Jinnah's stay in London from 1930 to 1934 is covered in Wolpert, *Jinnah of Pakistan*, pp. 119-33.
24. To the nawab of Chhatari, 15 Feb. 1934, Hailey papers (27-A), and Haig to Linlithgow, 29 Oct. and 2 Dec. 1936, Jan. 1937, Haig papers.
25. Raja of Mahmudabad, 'Some Memories', in Philips and Wainwright (eds.), *The Partition of India*, p. 387.
26. Quoted in Mujahid, pp. 230-1, and Zaidi, 'Aspects of Muslim League Policy', pp. 290-1. Some writers do not share such a view. Notice the observation that in 1936-7 a clash between Congress and the League, spearheaded by Nehru and Jinnah, lay in the logic of history'. Bimal Prasad, 'Congress versus the Muslim League 1935-1937', in Sisson and Wolpert (eds.), *Congress and Indian Nationalism*, p. 309.
27. *Civil and Military Gazette*, March 1936, quoted in Zaidi, 'Aspects', p. 230.
28. Pirzada (ed.), *Foundations of Pakistan*, Vol. 2, p. 267.
29. See raja of Mahmudabad, 'Some Memories', in Philips and Wainwright (eds.), *The Partition of India*, p. 384, and the impressions of some prominent

individuals associated with Jinnah. For example, M.R.A. Baig, *In Different Saddles*, Bombay, 1967 and M.C. Chagla, *Roses in December: An Autobiography*, Bombay, 1977; Kanji Dwarkadas, *India's Fight for Freedom, 1913-1937*, Bombay, 1966, and his *Ten Years to Freedom*, Bombay, 1968.

30. Nehru hoped that Khaliq would some day break from 'the reactionaries who surround him'. To Abdul Wali, 30 Mar. 1937, AICC papers (G-5, K.W. i, 1937).
31. Khaliquzzaman to Nehru, 29 June 1937, AICC papers (G-61, 1937).
32. To Linlithgow, 21 May 1936, Linlithgow papers (11-B), Haig to Linlithgow, 10 June 1939, Haig papers.
33. Rajendra Prasad, *Autobiography*, New Delhi, 1957, p. 446.
34. Cited in Zaidi, 'Aspects', p. 256.
35. To Mohanlal Saxena, 5 Sept. 1939, AICC papers (Misc. 30, 1937).
36. Linlithgow to Zetland, 29 Mar. 1940, L/PJ/8/50-B, BL; Rajendra Prasad put forth the same reasons in his *Autobiography*, pp. 446-7.
37. B.S. Moonje, quoted in Linlithgow to Zetland, 17 Sept. 1940, L/PJ/8/507.
38. A.K. Azad, *India Wins Freedom: The Complete Version*, New Delhi, 1988, p. 170. For a different version, S. Gopal, *Jawaharlal Nehru: A Biography 1889-1947*, Vol. 1, New Delhi, 1975, p. 22.
39. To Brelvi, 5 May 1937, AICC papers (G-67/1937).
40. To Ashraf, 5 May 1937, ibid. Also, Abdul Wali (of Bara Banki in UP) to Nehru, 28 March 1937, AICC papers (G-5, K.W. i, 1937).
41. See Hasan, A *Nationalist Conscience*.
42. Draft letter in enclosure: Haig to Linlithgow, 3 June 1939, Haig papers.
43. *Haqiqat* (Lucknow), *Hamdam* (Lucknow), UPNNR, week ending 4 Sept. 1939.
44. *Hamdam*, UPNNR, week ending 18 Dec. 1937.
45. Haig to Linlithgow, 6 Dec. 1939, L/PJ/8/645.
46. F.V. Wylie to Linlithgow, 14 Dec. 1939, L/PJ/8/645.
47. There was a marked deterioration in communal relations, affecting large parts of the north and centre of India. There was rioting in CP on the occasion of Dussehra (Oct. 1937) and at Jabalpur on Holi (Mar. 1938). This was followed by a whole series of riots spreading from the south-west corner of Berar, right across the Jabalpur district in the extreme north-east of CP. In UP there were riots at the Dadri fair in Ballia (20 November 1937), Banaras (15 Mar. 1938), Tanda (25 Aug. 1939), Allahabad (17 Mar. 1938) and at Kanpur (7-15 Feb. 1939). The casualties in the Banaras and Kanpur riots were high. See *It Shall Never Happen Again* (Department of Publicity & Information, All-India Muslim League, New Delhi, 1946). This is a collection of articles published in *Dawn*, with a foreword by Qazi Muhammad Isa, president of the Baluchistan Muslim League. Riots in UP and Bihar are described in Ashiq Husain Butalwi, *Hamari Qaumi Jaddo-Jehad* (*Our National Struggle*): *January 1939 se December 1939 tak*, Lahore, 1968; Maulana Basituqqal Ghori, *Meri Sarguzasht ya Congress ka Raaz*, Unnao, 1938. Publications like

Uriyaan-e Muraqqa, Budaun, 1939 described the riots in Bareilly and Budaun districts.

48. All-India Muslim League papers (hereafter AIML papers) (12), History of the Freedom Movement Archives, University of Karachi.
49. The lead was taken by the district Muslim League in Saharanpur, one of the largest centres of rice industry in UP.
50. L/P&J/8/86.
51. *Al-Bashir* (Etawah), UPNNR, week ending 4 Dec. 1939.
52. *Hamari Awaaz*, UPNNR, week ending 20 Nov. 1937; *Sarguzasht* and *Asia*, UPNNR, week ending 4 Dec. 1937; *Haq*, UPNNR, week ending 11 Dec. 1937..
53. *Hamdam*, UPNNR, week ending 18 Dec. 1939.
54. F.V. Wylie to Linlithgow, 24 Dec. 1939, L/P&J/8/645; Saiyid Iftikhar Ali, *Working of the C.P. Congress Ministry* (Nagpur, n.d.).
55. Hallet to Brabourne, 6 Sept. 1938, Linlithgow papers (126/1010).
56. Wylie to Linlithgow, 2 Dec. 1939, L/P&J/8/645.
57. Roger Lumley to Linlithgow, 23 Jan. 1940, L/P&J/8/686.
58. Haig to Linlithgow, 10 May 1939, Haig papers.
59. See Hasan, *Nationalism and Communal Politics*, Chap. 5.
60. *Report on the Municipal Administration and Finances in the UP of the Year 1937-38*, Allahabad, 1940, p. 9.
61. Ibid., 1938-9, p. 9.
62. To Linlithgow, 10 May 1939, Haig papers.
63. Ibid.
64. Lumley to Linlithgow, 14 Dec. 1939, Linlithgow papers (107).
65. Ashraf to Saiyid Mahmud, 14 June 1938, and Ashraf to Azad, 3 Sept. 1938, AICC papers (Misc. 30/1937).
66. Aftab Ahmad (from Calcutta) to Azad, n.d., ibid.
67. Ramgopal Gupta to Ashraf, 3 July 1937, AICC papers (38/1938). Such unholy alliances were quite common. This made it difficult for Muslim Congressmen to secure a position in the Congress hierarchy at the provincial and district levels. Cases from Nagpur, the stronghold of the RSS and the Hindu Mahasabha, were reported by Manzar Rizvi to the secretary, Nagpur PCC, 24 June 1938, ibid. Ashraf was greatly upset with the outcome of a by-election in a Muslim constituency in Amritsar. The Congress candidate was defeated owing to an alliance between the party bosses and the Hindu Mahasabha. 'I could go on multiplying instances', wrote Ashraf, 'to prove that the Congress machinery is fast disintegrating and our provincial and district Congress committees are more or less confident that no direction will come from the Centre and in any case they will be left free to do what they please in a given situation.' To Narsinh, 4 June 1938, ibid. Fida Ḥusain Sherwani, cousin of the Congress stalwart, T.A.K. Sherwani, commenting on the lack of preparedness on the eve of the election, shared his anguish with Nehru: 'I have all the time been feeling that my enthusiasm for the Congress is second to none

including yourself and Mahatma Gandhi but this heartless neglect of us by the so-called socialist party in power has made me believe for the last three days that a Mussalman has no place in the Congress and that a good and true Mussalman like myself has no alternative but to commit suicide.' To Nehru, 30 June 1937, AICC papers (G-61/1937).

68. Ashraf to the secretary, reception committee, Mahakoshal sessions, Jabalpur, 25 July 1938, AICC papers (Misc. 30/1937).
69. This is not to deny the inadequacy of some legislative enactments or implementation. Many Congress supporters were, in general, quite dissatisfied with the performance of the ministries in certain spheres. There are many reasons why this was so. But in the case of one UP minister, Sampurnanand, the predicament was succinctly expressed. 'We have to work', he wrote in *Congress Socialist*, 'within the four walls of the Government of India Act, against which we revolt with every fibre of our being. It is not easy. We feel like kicking over the traces. Believe me, not one of the ministers I know does not, immersed in his files, pine for the old days. We live in an atmosphere of unreality. There are many of us who would like to get out of it. But there we are. To my knowledge, there is no historical parallel to the circumstances in which we accepted office. A people struggling for national Independence, meaning to continue to fight for it, stop half-way to accept administrative responsibility! This is a contradiction in our position which creates difficulties.' Quoted in J.C. Donaldson to Puckle, 16 Sept. 1938, Linlithgow papers (101).
70. George Cunningham to Linlithgow, 19 Nov. 1941, ibid. (109).
71. Henry Twynam to Linlithgow, 10 Mar. 1941, ibid.
72. Hawthorne to Linlithgow, 6 Jan. 1942, ibid.
73. Roger Lumley to Linlithgow, 11 Apr. 1942, ibid. See Rani Dhavan Shankardass, *The First Congress Raj*, New Delhi, 1982, for the Bombay ministry.
74. In Sitapur, the Rural Development movement was of help to Muslim weavers as well as the Hindu cultivators. Besides, out of the 789 rural development organizers 20 per cent were Muslims recruited from rural areas. Considering that the Muslim population in UP was largely concentrated in the towns this was by no means a low percentage. Haig to Linlithgow, 10 May 1939, Haig papers; Hallet to Linlithgow, I Jan. 1940, Linlithgow papers (125/103).
75. Wylie to Linlithgow, 18 Apr. 1939, Hallet to Linlithgow, 8 May 1939, L/P&J/8/686. *The Central Provinces and Berar Government at Work*, Nagpur, 1939.
76. Wylie to Linlithgow, 24 Dec. 1939, L/P&J/8/645.
77. Linlithgow to Amery, 2 May 1943, L/P7J/8/512 (part 2).
78. E.J. Benthall papers, File Nos. 12 & 19, CSAS, Cambridge.
79. Malcolm Darling to Linlithgow, 25 Apr. 1940, L/P&J/8/506 (part B). Also, the anguish of Khizar Hyat Khan who felt that Pakistan, deeply tinged as it was with religious prejudice, was getting at a point at which it could not be resisted. He wanted the British government to define 'Pakistan' and to reject

the idea if found unreasonable. But Linlithgow did not agree. The government's response, in his view, would convey to the League and the Hindu Mahasabha the mistaken impression of its bias in favour of either position. He told the secretary of state for India: 'I fear Khizar and his friends will have trouble with the Muslim League, and Khizar may be . . . much less qualified to deal with it than Sikander.' Linlithgow to Amery, 2/4 May 1943, L/P&J/8/512 (part 2).

80. Governor of Bombay to Linlithgow, 30 Mar. 1940, ibid.
81. 'Punjab Memories 1910-1941' (typescript, 1971), James Penney papers, CSAS.
82. Enclosure 2 in: governor of UP to governor-general (telegram), 31 Mar. 1940, Linlithgow papers (125/108). The viceroy referred to the 'uncertainty of the Muslims and the leaders as to where they stand and what policy they are to pursue'. Linlithgow to Haig, 17 Apr. 1939, Linlithgow papers (125/102).
83. To Jinnah, n.d. (probably written in early Jan. 1940), L/P&J/8/507. The role of the nawab of Chhatari illustrates how personal or class interests rather than ideology dictated political preferences. In August 1934 he suggested the revival of the defunct All-India Muslim Conference. In April 1936 he broke away from the League Parliamentary Board to revive a 'mixed Party in preference to a Muslim communal Organisation'. But his subsequent experiences compelled him to re-think his position *vis-a-vis* the National Agriculturist Party and the League. Chhatari to Linlithgow, 4 Aug. 1936, Linlithgow papers (125/11B); Chhatari to Hailey, 28 Oct. 1936, Hailey papers (220/28C).
84. Linlithgow to Amery, 6 April 1940, L/P&J/B/506 (B).
85. In an anonymous letter to *Dawn* dated 19 Jan. 1948, a correspondent who styled himself 'A Musulman' enquired from the newspaper's readers whether or not refugees from India such as himself had been cleverly duped by the creation of Pakistan: the country was surely meant not for them but rather for the people of Punjab, Sind, Baluchistan and Bengal alone. Quoted in Sarah Ansari, *MAS*, Vol. 24, 4, 1990, p. 819.
86. The Haripura session of the Congress in February 1938 took special note of the growth in anti-imperialist feelings among the Muslims. In November 1939, Nehru listed a large number of Muslim organizations which had rallied round the Congress. 'So you will see', he informed Krishna Menon, 'that it is quite absurd to talk of the Congress facing the Muslims. I am quite sure that as matters develop, large numbers of Muslims will be with us.' Report of the Indian National Congress, Haripura, Feb. 1938, p. 7; Nehru to Krishna Menon, 8 Nov. 1939, *SWJN*, Vol. 10, pp. 230-2.
87. Statement of the Working Committee of the Jamiyat al-ulama. Home Dept. (Political), File No. 37/1939, NAI.
88. The League rowdies insulted and, in some cases, physically assaulted leaders of the Jamiyat al-ulama and the Central Muslim Parliamentary Board. Azad was ill-treated in Delhi and Aligarh. His friend, Abdur Razzaq Malihabadi, editor of *Hind*, was attacked in Calcutta. Maulanas Muhammad Quddus and

Muhammad Ismail escaped a murderous assault in Gaya. And in Saidpur (Bengal), the police and a handful of volunteers prevented Husain Ahmad Madani, president of the Jamiyat, from being lynched by an angry mob.

89. Abbas, *I Am Not an Island,* p. 280.
90. Darling to Linlithgow, 25 Apr. 1940, L/P&J/8506 (B).
91. Leonard Mosley, *The Last Days of the British Raj*, London, 1961, p. 77.
92. *Vote Congress—Congress and the Welfare State* (published by the Central Publicity Board, New Delhi, n.d.).
93. Ahmad, *Islamic Culture*, p. 74.
94. Farzana Shaikh, *Community and Consensus in Islam: Muslim Representation in Colonial India, 1860-1947*, Cambridge, 1989, p. 230.
95. For an elucidation of the role of some of these groups, see my *A Nationalist Conscience*, and my introduction to *Islam and Indian Nationalism: Reflections on Abul Kalam Azad*, New Delhi, 1992.
96. See the reviews of *A Nationalist Conscience* by Francis Robinson, *Modern Asian Studies*, 1989, pp. 609-19, and by P.G. Robb, *Bulletin of the School of Oriental and African Studies*, Vol. 1, 1991, pp. 104-25.
97. Earl of Lytton, *Pundit and Elephants: Being the Experiences of Five Years as Governor of an Indian Province*, London, 1942.
98. Judy F. Pugh, 'Divination and Ideology in the Banaras Muslim Community', in K.P. Ewing (ed.), *Shariat and Ambiquity in South Asian Islam*, New Delhi, 1988; Sandria Freitag (ed.), *Culture and Power in Banaras: Community, Performance and Environment 1800-1980*, New Delhi, 1989.
99. *Census of India*, 1931, p. 515.
100. Rafiuddin Ahmed, 'Conflicts, and Contradictions in Bengali Islam', in Ewing (ed.), *Shariat and Ambiguity*, p. 134, and the excellent study of Asim Roy, *The Islamic Syncretistic Tradition in Bengal*, Princeton, N.J., 1983.
101. *Census of India*, 1921, p. 115.
102. M. Ishaq Khan, 'Islam in Kashmir: Historical Analysis of its Distinctive Features', in C.W. Troll (ed.), *Islam in India: Studies and Commentaries*, New Delhi, 1985, and his 'The Significance of the Dargah of Hazratbal in the Socio-Religious and Political life of Kashmiri Muslims', in C.W. Troll (ed.), *Muslim Shrines in India: Their Character and Significance*, New Delhi, 1989.
103. David Gilmartin, 'Customary Law and Shariat in Punjab', in Ewing (ed.), *Shariat and Ambiguity,* p. 44.
104. Rafiuddin Ahmed, 'Conflicts and Contradictions in Bengal Islam', in ibid., p. 115.
105. Susan Bayly, *Saints, Goddesses and Kings: Muslims and Christians in South Indian Society 1700-1900*, Cambridge, 1990, pp. 13-14.
106. Seal, *The Emergence of Indian Nationalism*, p. 339.
107. Brass, *Language, Religion and Politics in North India*, pp. 178ff.
108. Robinson, *Separatism Among Muslims*, Chap. 1.
109. Francis Robinson, 'Nation Formation: The Brass Thesis and Muslim

Separatism', and reply by Paul Brass, *Journal of Commonwealth and Comparative Politics*, Vol. 15, 3, pp. 215-34.

110. Page, *Prelude to Partition.*
111. Ian Talbot, *Punjab and the Raj and Provincial Politics and the Pakistan Movement, 1849-1947*, New Delhi, 1988.
112. David Gilmartin, *Empire and Islam: Punjab and the Making of Pakistan*, London, 1988, and its review by Sarah Ansari, *Modern Asian Studies*, Vol. 24, 4, 1990.
113. *The Origins of the Partition of India 1936-1947*, New Delhi, 1987.
114. *The Crisis of Indian Unity 1917-1947*, Oxford, 1974; *Churchill, Cripps and India 1939-1945*, Oxford, 1979, *Escape from Empire: The Attlee Government and the Indian Problem*, Oxford, 1989.
115. For a useful bibliographical survey, see A.K. Majumdar, 'Writings on the Transfer of Power', in B.R. Nanda (ed.), *Essays in Modern Indian History*, New Delhi, 1980.
116. Asim Roy, 'The High Politics of India's Partition: The Revisionist Perspective', in Hasan (ed.), *India's Partition.*
117. Ibid., p. 123.
118. Commenting on the massacre of August 1946 in Calcutta, Leonard Mosley remarked: 'A few weeks later, however, you would have found it difficult to believe that anyone (with the possible exception of Mahatma Gandhi) had taken any notice of them at all. Not the Hindus. Not the Muslims. Not the British.' Mosley, *The Last Days of the British raj*, p. 40. I believe one should attach some weight to Azad's judgement that 'the people of India had not accepted Partition. In fact their heart and soul rebelled against the very idea. I have said that the Muslim League enjoyed the support of many Indian Muslims but there was a large section in the community which had always opposed the League. They were naturally deeply cut by the decision to divide the country. As for the Hindus and Sikhs, they were to a man opposed to Partition. . . .' *India Wins Freedom*, p. 224. At the same time, it must be said that the Maulana, like everybody else, readily agreed to the Partition plan. In the crucial meeting of the Congress Working Committee held on 2 June 1947, he, according to Ram Manohar Lohia, a special invitee to the meeting, 'sat in a chair throughout the two days of the meeting in a corner of the very small room which packed us all, puffed away at his endless cigarettes and spoke not a word'. According to Lohia, barring four persons—himself, Jayaprakash Narayan, Ghaffar Khan and Gandhi—'none spoke a word in opposition of Partition'. And though the Mahatma 'turned to Mr. Nehru and Sardar Patel in mild complaint that they had not informed him of the scheme of Partition before committing themselves to it', he stopped well short of obstructing 'a leadership united for acceptance'. Quoted in Rajmohan Gandhi, *Patel: A Life*, Ahmedabad, 1992, p. 402.
119. H. Ghoshal, 'The Memsahib I could never be', CSAS, p. 8.
120. Pirzada (ed.), *Foundations of Pakistan*, Vol. 2, p. 224.

10

The Muslim Mass Contact Campaign: A Strategy of Political Mobilization

From the days of the Lucknow Pact (1916), the Congress leadership expressed eagerness to negotiate with a handful of Muslim politicians in order to arrive at a consensus on major political and constitutional issues. The logic of such negotiations stemmed from the belief that India's Muslims were entitled to certain concessions and safeguards because of their distinct political identity and because their interests were different from those of other groups in society. As I have discussed earlier, the political language within which such accommodation was expressed and the energy that derived from a recognition of this conception of society necessarily implied that the very terms of reference precluded any lasting solution to the communal tangle. At the same time, by negotiating with Muslim politicians whose organizational base and political stature were by no means assured, Congress perpetuated its legitimacy as spokesperson of the whole community—a recognition that flowed largely from the organizational and political structures within which the Congress leadership was itself elaborated. Rather than forcing these so-called leaders into a situation where they had, as it were, to demonstrate their implied support, Congress consistently refused to draw out the conditions for such a confrontation, from an apparent desire not to weaken the integral and unified nature of the national movement. It also feared that the consequences of such a confrontation would reveal a divide too profound to remedy. Since national integrity was Congress' cardinal political assumption, such a confrontation had to be avoided.

The collapse of the Congress-khilafat alliance in 1922-3, the revival of communal bodies, and the recrudescence of widespread Hindu-Muslim riots exposed the limitations of Congress' approach. Some contemporary commentators believed that the Hindu-Muslim alliance was artificially cemented on the 'unreliable foundations of religious sentimentalism'. 'The present debacle,' noted the Communist Party of India manifesto, 'was a foregone conclusion of such ill-starred movement.' 'The Congress programme,' observed another manifesto, 'has to be denuded of all sentimental trimmings.... The object for which the Indian people will fight should not be looked for somewhere in the unknown region of Mesopotamia or Arabia or Constantinople, it should be found in their immediate surroundings—in their huts, on the land, in the factory. Hungry mortals cannot be expected to fight indefinitely for an abstract ideal.'[1]

Later attempts to revive the spirit of the khilafat days through widely publicized unity conferences and hastily concluded pacts failed to resolve the communal deadlock: such was the fate of the so-called Indian National Pact (1923), the Das Pact (1923), and the Nehru report (1928).[2] Likewise, Gandhi's 'Ram-Rahim' approach and his initiatives in the form of fasts, such as the one undertaken during the bloody Kohat riots of 1924, did not improve deteriorating communal relations.[3]

The problem of attracting Muslim support became an issue within Congress as well. Writing to Ansari, whose own efforts to bring about communal rapprochement were noteworthy, Gandhi conceded in early 1930 that the Hindu-Muslim problem was to be approached 'in a different manner from the one we have hitherto adopted—not, as at present, by adjustment of the political power but by one or the other acting on the square under all circumstances'.[4] In a more candid recognition of Congress' failure, Motilal Nehru observed that 'no amount of formulae based upon mutual concessions . . . will bring us any nearer Hindu-Muslim unity than we are at present'. 'It is my firm conviction,' he continued, 'that Hindu-Muslim unity cannot be achieved by preaching it. We have to bring it about in a manner which will accomplish it without either Hindus or Muslims realizing that they are working for unity. *This can only be done on an economic basis and in the course of the fight for freedom from the* usurper'.[5] (italics mine)

Motilal's formulation was close to that of his son, Jawaharlal, but did not reflect the thinking of most Congress leaders, who persisted with the belief that the surest and perhaps the easiest way of coming to terms with the Muslim communities was to settle the controversy over the issue of joint versus separate electorates, reservation of seats in legislatures, especially in the Muslim-majority provinces of Bengal and Punjab, weightage to Muslims in provinces where they were in a minority, separation of Sind from the Bombay Presidency, and the introduction of reforms in the N.W.F.P. Resolution of the controversies centred around these demands was not easy, as became evident from the deliberations of the All-Parties National Convention and the Round Table Conferences in London. A new approach was thus called for to resolve the communal impasse, to draw Muslims into the Congress fold, and to reach over the heads of Muslim politicians to the rank-and-file Muslim voter. The lead was given by the CWC meeting, held at Wardha on 27-8 February 1937, to discuss the plan of Muslim mass contacts. Nehru took the initiative and, on 31 March 1937, urged provincial Congress committees:

> to make a special effort to enrol Muslim Congress members, so that our struggle for freedom may become even more broad-based than it is, and the Muslim masses should take the prominent part in it which is their due. Indeed when we look at the vital problem of independence and of the removal of poverty and unemployment, there is no difference between the Muslim masses and the Hindu or Sikh or Christian masses in the country. Differences only come to the surface when we think in terms of the handful of upper class people.[6]

The October 1937 session of Congress approved Nehru's plan, pointing out that its aim was to protect the religious, linguistic, and cultural rights of the minorities in order to ensure their participation in the political, economic, and cultural life of the nation.[7]

Organization of the Mass Contacts Campaign

The plan of Muslim mass contacts was in some ways different from previous mobilization campaigns. To begin with, it was based on a series of fresh assumptions that questioned the efficacy of negotiating with a handful of Muslim politicians for short-term political gains. 'We have too long thought in terms of pacts and compromises with communal leaders, and neglected the people behind them', observed Nehru. He called it a 'discredited policy' and hoped that Congress would not revert to it.[8] He also rejected the earlier religio-political initiatives, such as Congress' support to the khilafat cause, in favour of establishing direct contact with the Muslim masses. On the basis of an optimistic—some may say misleading—assessment of the outcome of the 1937 elections, the high command felt that if the party could obtain support from a great majority of Hindus, it could also win over Muslims. Experience during the election campaign reinforced this optimism. Both Rajendra Prasad and Nehru were convinced that in many provinces Muslims appreciated Congress policies.[9] Constrained by various factors, however, Congress could not realize their latent sympathy and take advantage of the 'new interest and awakening'.[10] The remedy, then, was to explain and project its programme, to impress on poor Muslim villagers that they would not lose under the Congress dispensation as their interests were identical with those of the Hindu poorer classes, and to convey the message that their real champions were not the landlords and lawyers of the Muslim League. With a degree of persistence it could thus wean the masses away from the League and draw them into the Congress fold.

On 31 March 1937, Nehru set out his ideas on 'The need for greater contacts with Muslims', directed Congress committees to concentrate on enrolling Muslims, and suggested taking in hand the work of increasing contacts with Muslim masses living in rural and urban areas.[11] The AICC set up a cell to control and direct activities relating to propagate Congress' programme through newspaper articles and pamphlets, and to counteract anti-Congress propaganda. Kunwar Muhammad Ashraf, one of Nehru's most trusted lieutenants, headed the cell. Impressed with Nehru's 'language of Marxism', Ashraf felt that 'we were on the threshold of a fresh mass struggle'. He seemed convinced that 'any honest and consistent anti-imperialist struggle led by the Congress would wean away the Muslim masses from the growing influence of Jinnah and the revived Muslim League'.[12]

The campaign was launched amid much fanfare. Ashraf went on a countrywide tour, addressing innumerable meetings at which he referred to the mass contact programme as a 'decisive state' in Congress' history—'the state of revolutionary mass action'.[13] He exhorted Congressmen to form ward and *mohalla* committees to take up the day-to-day struggle of the masses and advised them to organize peasants, industrial workers, and the unemployed on the basis of Congress' programme.[14] He challenged the notion of a Muslim community with an exclusive and distinct political and social personality; the fundamental contradiction, according to him, was between the class interests of Muslim leaders and the political and economic demands of the Muslim masses; the 'religious outlook' obscured this fundamental division in Indian Muslim society.[15] Using Marxist phraseology, Ashraf tried to dispel the notion that Indian Muslims could achieve freedom on their own. Political experience, in his opinion, demonstrated that the Muslims could build their own strength through the national struggle and not by organizing themselves on a communal basis. Politics was dictated essentially by class interests, and efforts to obscure class differentiation led to the suppression of the exploited elements.[16] The anti-imperialist struggle of the exploited and poor masses in India was 'essentially one and indivisible' and could not be carried out 'on the basis of separate political organizations working within a particular community'. Indian Muslims should join this struggle by participating in the Congress—'the only joint organization of the Indian exploited masses which interprets and organizes this struggle'.[17]

Ashraf's strenuous efforts were backed by Nehru, who, with his usual flair and aplomb, set out to combat League propaganda, and extended support to the launching of an Urdu periodical 'to give the Urdu-knowing public the ideological message of the Congress to fight all sectarian tendencies'.[18] He rebutted Jinnah's charge that the policy of mass contact was fraught with grave consequences.[19] To boost the campaign, he turned to the Jhansi-Jalaun-Hamirpur by-election where Nisar Ahmad Khan Sherwani was pitted against his League rival, Rafiuddin Ahmad. He attached significance to this election because Sherwani's victory would give a 'tremendous fillip' to its crusade against communalism. 'I want to tell you,' he wrote to Sherwani on 30 June 1937, 'that we regard your election campaign as a most important one and I hope that you and all Congressmen in Bundelkhand will realize this fact and do their utmost in it.'[20] Words were matched with action. Nehru placed Rafi Ahmed Kidwai in charge of the election campaign and mobilized friends and political comrades to take part in electioneering, urging them to 'work in earnest' and give 'all your great energy to this election'.[21] Nehru's own energy, drive, and resourcefulness was truly remarkable.

Although Sherwani lost and the League rejoiced at its unexpected victory, Nehru referred to some positive gains that enhanced Congress' prestige and strength: the party contested a Muslim seat after many years; its candidate secured the majority of votes in Orai and Jhansi, which formed two of the three districts in the constituency; and the rural votes of peasants were almost entirely cast for Congress. For these reasons the Bundelkhand election was 'one of the most encouraging sign of times. It points to the inevitable growth of the Congress among the masses, both Hindu and Muslim.'[22] Gandhi shared Nehru's optimism, pointing out that the election gave rise to the hope that 'if we plod away we can effectively take the Congress message to the Mussalmans'.[23]

The outcome of the election, some prophesied, would place the mass contact programme in jeopardy. Such fears were unwarranted. Reports from some parts of the country indicated an unexpectedly favourable response, leading Nehru to announce that the Congress efforts to increase our contact with the Muslim masses proved rewarding.[24] What pleased him and surprised many was the enthusiasm of newly mobilized groups such as the Ahrars,[25] the Khudai Khidmatgars, and the socialists. They spearheaded the mass contact campaign in N.W.F.P. and Punjab with the active backing of leaders who wielded considerable influence in certain areas and were known for their involvement in nationalist politics. They included Ghaffar Khan and his brother Khan Saheb, Saifuddin Kitchlew of Rowlatt satyagraha fame, the socialist Mian Iftikharuddin, Muhammad Alam, Fazal Din, and Babu Muhammad Din. They attended a meeting in early May 1937 when mass contact committees were first formed in Punjab.[26] A series of conferences held in the following month and addressed by Ashraf and Sajjad Zaheer also had a 'favourable impact on many Muslims'. Impressed by the success of one such gathering in Lahore, the Punjab PCC decided to hold a number of such meetings in the province to attract Muslims to the Congress.[27] Such organized activity spelt danger to the Punjab Unionist Party and the Muslim League. They combined to launch a counter-offensive in order to keep their political base intact.[28] Their fierce reaction reflected a recognition of the growing strength and popularity of the mass contact programme in the N.W.F.P. and Punjab.

In UP, the mass contact programme appealed to Muslims in places such as Aligarh, Lucknow, Allahabad, Budaun, Pratapgarh, Ghazipur, and Shamli in Muzaffarnagar district, while in Jaunpur, for instance, 'the fresh wave is not being passed unobserved and we are sure that the Congress would open a way to us in approaching the masses'.[29] Equally noticeable was the favourable impression on the students of Aligarh Muslim University; the ulama of Deoband; the Shias of Lucknow, Jaunpur, and Amroha; and the Ansaris of Ghazipur and Mirzapur connected with the All-India Momin Conference.[30] Here, too, the Muslim League sensed danger, and Harry Haig, who succeeded Malcolm Hailey as UP's governor, noted that its leaders were 'alarmed at the Congress attempts on the Muslim masses' because they 'feel very strongly that if the community is to retain its individuality, no efforts must be spared in resisting the attempts of the Congress to absorb them'.[31] The raja of Mahmudabad informed his political mentor, Jinnah, that Congress was exploring all avenues of approaching the Muslim masses, and would intensify its efforts in that direction; so 'it was essential that we have funds so that we may try to put up an organization analogous to the very efficient and aggressive organization of the Congress'.[32]

In other parts of the country the drive to enroll Muslims met with success. In neighbouring Delhi the groundwork for the prosecution of the mass contact campaign was prepared by Congress socialists such as Faridul Haq Ansari and Asaf Ali, and Muslim divines such as maulvis Abdul Majid and Ahmad Said, both associated with Congress from the time of the Rowlatt satyagraha. 'There has been a marked change in the attitude of Muslim masses,' stated a Congress report, 'and primary membership among them has also increased.'[33] An 'Enrolment Week' observed in Bombay resulted in 500 Muslims joining Congress.[34] In Bihar the efforts were equally rewarding, especially in Patna, Champaran, and Purnea. Here Kisan Sabhas, the Students' Federation, the Muslim Independent Party, and the Jamiyat al-Momineen were in the forefront of the mass contact campaign.[35] Finally, the *mohalla* and city mass contact committees in Calcutta, Burdwan, and Comilla—all in Bengal—fared well. By May 1937 over 1,000 Muslims joined the Congress in the suburbs of Calcutta.[36]

Several organizations, representing a wide range of provincial, local, sectional, and religious interests, supported the mass contact programme to express their solidarity with Congress. This was true of the Jamiyat al-ulama, dominated by the pro-Congress faction of Husain Ahmad Madani and Kifayatullah; the Shia Political Conference, founded in 1929 with a strong base among the small but influential Shias of Lucknow, Amroha, Bilgram, and Jaunpur; the All-India Ahl-i Hadis League;[37] and regional parties and groups, such as the Khudai Khidmatgars, the Ahrars in UP and Punjab, and the Momin Conference in parts of UP and Bihar. Rallying the Shias, made possible by two important *fatawa* issued by their *mujtahids* in Lucknow and Jaunpur, was the handiwork of a Shia, Wazir Hasan, who took advantage of estranged Shia-Sunni relations in UP to draw the Shias into the Congress movement.[38] Estranged from the Sunni-dominated Muslim League and irked by the violent outbursts over the *madhe sahaba* controversy in 1935-6, the Shias hoped to receive a better deal from UP's Congress ministry.[39]

The Allahabad conference, held on 15-16 May 1937, brought some of these groups on a common platform. Thus Abdul Majid Khwaja, Nehru's contemporary at Cambridge, as well as Wazir Hasan, who had chaired the Muslim League session in May 1936 and had since returned to the Congress fold, appeared alongside Muslim divines such as maulanas Hifzur Rahman and Ahmad Said, and avowed socialists and communists such as Sajjad Zaheer, Mian Muhammad Iftikharuddin, Z.A. Ahmad, and Ashraf. There was much patriotic fervour, reminiscent of the early 1930s when conferences of the Nationalist Muslim Party were held in different parts of the country. There was talk of extending 'unconditional support' to Congress, and speeches made on the theme of inter-communal unity elicited much interest. Reference was made to the League's unrepresentative character, and its leadership—'these upper class gentlemen'—were castigated for their reactionary policies and their 'theories of inactivity and cowardice'.[40] This conference, masterminded by Ashraf and Azad, was a notable feat, the like of which was accomplished only once during the khilafat movement; it was also a significant one in terms of being the first organized expression of Muslim support for Congress in the 1930s.

Leadership and Representation

Lack of adequate evidence makes it difficult to relate the protagonists of the mass contact campaign to their social, occupational, and political backgrounds. A rough survey, however, indicates that they were mostly urban based and drawn largely from the professional classes: lawyers, students, and teachers sharing socialist and Marxist ideas; journalists such as Saiyid Ali Ahmad, editor of a leading Patna-based weekly *Itehad*; Saiyid Abdullah Brelvi and Muhammad Nazir, editors of the *Bombay Chronicle* and *Mussawir*, respectively; Mujibur Rahman, founder and editor of the leading Calcutta newspaper *Mussalman*; Hayatullah Ansari, editor of the *Hindustan Weekly*, published first from Lucknow and later from Delhi; and Muhammad Ismail and Muhammad Jafri, editors of the Delhi papers *Daily Qaumi Akhbar* and *Millat.* Some sections of the mass contact leadership had been associated with Congress from the khilafat days and were connected with the Nationalist Muslim Party and the Congress Muslim Party, organizations founded in early 1929 to canvas support for the Nehru report; others were drawn during the 1930-2 civil disobedience movement.

Among the most vociferous mass contact campaigners in UP were young and brilliant lawyers, journalists, teachers, poets, and writers. Most of them were educated either in Aligarh or in British universities. Having been tutored in Marxism-Leninism, they shared a common commitment to the revolutionary transformation of society through an alliance with radical elements in Congress. They brought a Marxist perspective to communalism that was markedly different from both the religious-oriented approach of the khilafatists and that of the Congress Muslims of Ansari's generation, whose efforts to achieve Hindu-Muslim reconciliation found fruition merely in unity conferences, pacts, and short-term agreements. They rejected communal categories that they believed had been superimposed by the British to create fissures in the mass struggle, and regarded any rapprochement with the self-styled Muslim leaders as counter-productive. The Congress, they argued, deserved support because it favoured abolition of the *taluqdari* system and liquidation of rural indebtedness and insisted on relief for the landless and the unemployed. The League, in contrast, was allied with the British government and engaged in promoting the interests of the privileged classes; thus, its real contradiction, according to Ashraf, 'lies in the fact that a few landlords and reactionaries want to exploit the backward Muslim masses for the redemption of their privileges and a fundamentally reactionary political outlook'.[41] In sum, then, their emphasis was not so much on 'mere honeyed phrases and appeals couched in eloquent and winsome phraseology to the communities to live in amity and grace', but rather on the unity and solidarity of the peasants and workers in their struggle against the British government and its collaborators.

Those Muslims who advocated this position represented a powerful ideological strand among the Muslim intelligentsia. Prominent amongst them were Ashraf, who rose to political prominence in the 1930s as a member of the Congress Socialist Party (CSP) in charge of the minorities cell in the Congress; Z.A. Ahmad, an Aligarh graduate who joined the Economic Information Department of the AICC as secretary (1936-7) and was a member of the National Executive of the CSP from 1937 to 1940; Faridul Haq Ansari, cousin of M.A. Ansari, one of the founder members of the CSP and convener of the Mass Contact Committee in Delhi; Hayatullah Ansari of Firangi Mahal in Lucknow, a graduate of the Aligarh Muslim University and editor of the pro-Congress *Hindustan Weekly* from 1937 to 1942; Ansar Harvani, also an Aligarh graduate with the distinction of being both the founder and general secretary of the All-Indian Students' Federation (1936-9); Husain Zaheer, son of Wazir Hasan, educated in Lucknow, Oxford, and Heidelberg; and Husain's brother, Sajjad Zaheer, and young poets and writers such as Kaifi Azmi, Khwaja Ahmad Abbas, and Ali Sardar Jafri, who was expelled from Aligarh University for organizing a political strike in 1936. The support of such men gave the mass contact campaign in UP an ideological thrust that was lacking in earlier Congress efforts at popular mobilization.[42]

Equally vital was the part played by the Jamiyat al-ulama. Founded in the wake of the khilafat agitation in December 1919, its alliance with Congress, although strained in the aftermath of non-cooperation, remained largely intact. This was evident in 1930-2, when the Jamiyat favoured 'Muslims working shoulder to shoulder with their brethren in the fight for freedom' and its leaders such as Husain Ahmad Madani, Ahmad Said, Ataullah Shah Bukhari, Hifzur Rahman, and Moinuddin joined the ranks of satyagrahis. In June 1937 some of them worked for the Congress candidate in the crucial Bundelkhand election and toured various parts of UP to promote the Mass Contacts campaign.

In August 1937 Husain Ahmad Madani, president of the Jamiyat al-ulama, appealed to his community to join Congress in the fight for freedom'[43] and a year later propounded his theory of composite nationalism in *Mutahhidah qaumiyat awr Islam* (composite nationalism and Islam). In his letters to Iqbal he argued that the word *quam* could be applied to any collective group regardless of whether its common characteristics were religion, common habitat, race, colour, or craft. It should be distinguished from *millat*, which refers to a collectivity with a *Shariat* or *din*. Indian Muslims were fellow nationals with other communities and groups in India, although separate from them in religion. At present, he said, nations are made by homelands, as England, for instance, where members of different faiths constitute one nation. Madani argued that freedom from British rule was necessary for the welfare of Islam, so that Muslim religious duties could be properly performed. The Muslims were not strong enough to win this freedom for themselves, but needed the help of non-Muslim communities. He wanted independence for India so that Muslims could freely express their religious personality, enjoy a truly Islamic system of education, and remove corruption from their social life by abolishing British-made laws.[44] On 3-6 March 1939, the Jamiyat called for cooperation with Congress 'according to Islamic principles and dictates of wisdom and foresight', and urged Indian Muslims to enlist as primary members of Congress and participate in its activities—'as it is the only constitutional way to reach the goal of independence and achievement and protection of religious and national rights of Mussalmans'.[45]

Madani's sympathy for the Congress and his advocacy of Indian nationalism represented a trend set by maulana Mahmud Hasan, principal of the Dar al-ulum at Deoband. In the mid-1930s, however, these views were vigorously challenged by Madani's two distinguished colleagues, Ashraf Ali Thanvi and Shabbir Ahmad Usmani, and by the theologian-politician, maulana Abul Ala Mawdudi. In a series of articles in the monthly journal, *Tarjuman al-Koran*, Mawdudi first related the history of the Muslims in India, debunking Congress secularism, and showing the unsuitability of India for democratic rule. In the *Tahrik-i Azadi-i Hind awr Mussalman* (1939), he concluded that the Muslims and the Congress movement had absolutely nothing in common, and indicted the Jamiyat for its acquiescence in the mass contact campaign—a campaign directed toward the 'total disintegration' of the Muslim community and intended to convert the Muslim masses to Marxism.[46]

While Mawdudi and his ilk viewed the idea as a challenge to the traditional Muslim belief that Islam pervaded every sphere of human activity, and Congress advocated secular politics, Jinnah, who was averse to mass politics, viewed mass contact as a deliberate attempt to divide the Muslims and break the League by 'falsely representing that the Congress alone has the monopoly to champion and fight for the freedom of India'.[47] The Leaguers saw in the Congress campaign a threat to their very existence and felt that, unless they organized themselves like the Congress and won over the Muslim masses, they might find that, Congress had walked away with their flock. For this reason the UP Muslim Parliamentary Board chalked out its own plan to enroll 25 per cent of the adult population of the province in just three months.[48] In September 1937, the raja of Mahmudabad suggested a plan of action to be worked out by men 'with determination and consciousness'.[49] Although Congress and the League had existed as separate organizations for a long time, never before was there such a rivalry between them for association with the Muslim masses.[50]

The importance of the ulama-League protest and the significance of their counter-offensive cannot be ignored or dismissed; nevertheless, it is crucial to take note of the ascendancy of the pro-Congress elements in the Jamiyat, forcing men such as Ashraf Ali Thanvi and Shabbir Usmani to resign from that body to fall in line with the Muslim League. Madani and Kifayatullah guided the affairs of the Jamiyat; others merely followed their lead. Also, the progress of the mass contact campaign was not greatly hampered by the virulent propaganda of Jinnah and his newly found allies among the ulama. By mid-1938, as Table 10.1 indicates, a hundred thousand Muslims were enrolled as primary members of the Congress outside UP, Bengal, and the N.W.F.P.[51] Of these, 25,000 were from Bihar, 15,000 from Madras, and 13,995 from Punjab.

Table 10.1: Enrolment of Muslim Primary Members by 1938

Ajmer	477
Andhra	2,832
Assam	425
Bihar	25,000
Bombay	1,346
Delhi	1,114
Gujarat	1,600
Kerala	2,574
Maharashtra	3,894
Punjab	13,995
Sind	1,000
Madras	15,000

The Failure of Peasant Mobilization

It is a mistake to argue, a view held by writers in Pakistan and uncritically accepted by historians of Indian nationalism, that the Muslim community rejected the mass contact campaign unequivocally. The evidence marshalled herein demonstrates that, despite vigorous opposition from certain quarters, the campaign enjoyed success in some parts of UP, Bihar, Bengal, and Punjab. It failed, however, to have much of an impact in rural areas. This was due not to a resolute or determined Muslim opposition; it reflected the limited nature of Congress mobilization. Significantly, Muslim peasants and other underprivileged groups in the countryside, the very sections supposedly mobilized on a massive scale, were largely ignored, with efforts concentrated instead on enlisting urban-based ulama and the professional classes.[52]

What Nisar Ahmad, an advocate from Bahawalpur, observed on 31 March 1937, remained largely true of Congress' strategy in the years to come. Congress, he complained, had not reached the masses—'the backbone of the community' who, besides being familiar with the names of Gandhi and Mohamed Ali, were ignorant of 'everything else'.[53] Ashraf, too, conceded in mid-1938 that the mass contacts work in various provinces was 'totally unorganized' and that no '*substantial effort was made to come in direct contact with the Muslim masses in large numbers*'[54] (italics mine). The pattern was thus similar to that from 1930 to 1932, when the Congress leaders minimized civil disobedience propaganda in areas with a high proportion of Muslims in the population in order to avoid igniting communal passions.[55] They did the same in the mid-1930s, although for different reasons and with far more serious implications.

Another important conclusion that emerges from our analysis is not only strikingly different from standard accounts of the mid-1930s but is also inconsistent with the popular belief that, by 1937-8, most Muslims were arrayed against the Congress and had rallied around the League banner. This is not to say that Hindu-Muslim antagonism was not fairly widespread nor to deny Jinnah's success in capitalizing on the 'wrongs' done by the Congress ministries, but to underline that in 1937-8 neither did there exist a sharp communal political solidarity among Muslims. In Bengal, Punjab, and UP, a common Muslim political identity had yet to crystallize, and the League struggled to acquire legitimacy. The Krishak Praja Party in Bengal and the Punjab Unionist Party, organized essentially on cross-communal lines, maintained their ascendancy well until the mid-1940s, thwarting Jinnah's attempts to undermine their linkages. Likewise, there was no clear sign of a complete polarization in UP, and little evidence of the so-called Muslim drift into the League. Hindu and Muslim landlords, although torn by personal feuds and jealousies, continued to act in unison to protect their landed interests against the UP Tenancy Bill; in fact, the Hindu-Muslim landlord combination works reasonably well in the National Agriculturist Party. Powerful landlords—the nawab of Chhatari, nawab Jamshed Ali Khan of Bagpat, and nawab Muhammad Yusuf of Jaunpur were more concerned to protect their class interests, represented by landlords' organizations, than their communal interests, represented by the League.

Doubtless, the ulama of the Barelvi and Firangi Mahal schools hitched their fortunes to the League bandwagon, and yet most Deobandi ulama joined forces with the Congress. The Jamiyat sponsored, in April 1940, an Azad Muslim Conference which, in opposition to the demand for a separate Muslim state, declared India as 'the common homeland of all its citizens irrespective of race and religion'. Representing at that time a substantial number of Muslims, the conference protested against the Pakistan idea and against the use made of the Muslims by the British government and others as an excuse for political inaction. Allah Bux Soomro, premier of Sind and president of the conference, stated that to regard 'Muslims as a separate nation in India on the basis of their religion was un-Islamic'.[56]

The Muslim University at Aligarh mirrored some trends. K.G. Saiyadain, who joined the institution in 1919 and was on the staff of the Teachers' Training College from 1926 to 1938, recalled his participation in the 'great Jubilee debate in 1926 when the students of the university endorsed with great acclaim a policy of united nationalism'. Campus politics in the 1930s remained unchanged, with men such as T.A.K. Sherwani, Khaliquzzaman, Shuaib Qureshi, and A.M. Khwaja—all graduates of Aligarh and closely associated with Nehru and the Congress movement in UP—enjoying a greater following than leaders with communal proclivities. Most office-bearers of the influential Students' Union belonged to the radical alumni circles, anti-British and pro-Congress; the 1936 students' strike against the university's repression of nationalist activities as well as the opposition to a move initiated in the Students' Union in the same year to form an All-India Muslim Students' Federation, was organized in Aligarh; the widely circulated *Aligarh Magazine* retained its pro-Congress bias; and the theme of national unity and communal harmony—central to Mirza Samiullah Beg's (nawab Mirza Yar Jung Bahadur) Convocation Address of December 1938—continued to evoke a ready response in Aligarh. The mass contact campaign also struck a favourable chord in wider Aligarh circles. Its chief protagonists in UP, Bihar, and the N.W.F.P. were Ghaffar Khan, A.M. Khwaja, Saiyid Mahmud, N.A.K. Sherwani, Zakir Husain, Ashraf, Ansar Harvani, Hayatullah Ansari, and Sardar Jafri—all either educated at or closely connected with Aligarh.[57]

The political climate in the country in general, and in UP in particular, was thus no less conducive for the success of the mass contact campaign than in 1930-1, when Congress launched civil disobedience. True, there was now much evidence of mounting communal pressures and increased communal strife. It is also true that the 'highhandedness' of the Congress ministries was bitterly attacked; so was the singing of *Vande Mataram*, the hoisting of the tricolor flag, the introduction of Wardha and the Vidya Mandir schemes of education, which implied a Hindu orientation, the exclusion of Muslims from local bodies, the imposition of Hindi at the expense of Urdu, and the recurrence of communal riots. Yet, Congress was still able to count on the support of several powerful Muslim groups in the N.W.F.P., UP, and Bihar, a fact that explains why the progress of mass contact work caused panic in League circles and led Jinnah to launch a counter-offensive.

The Collapse of the Campaign

Ashrafuddin Chowdhury, editor of the Comilla newspaper *Naya Bangla* and an associate of Subhas Chandra Bose, wanted to know whether the 'Congress Secretariat' would take up the mass contact work seriously and earnestly or whether it would remain 'a mere paper propaganda'.[58] He should have known better. Within two years of its launching, the mass contact campaign ran into serious trouble, not so much due to the League's opposition or the lack of Muslim support, but because of Congress' own reluctance to pursue it with any vigour or sense of purpose. In the early summer of 1939, mass contact committees were scrapped, signifying the unhappy ending of a campaign that was started amid much hope and enthusiasm.

Why did this happen? Some suggest that the programme, devoid of any social and economic content, offered 'too little too late';[59] others argue that it remained largely on paper, and secularist, and radical rhetoric in the end alarmed Muslim vested interests without winning over the Muslim masses.[60]

Part of the explanation must reckon with the fact that the idea was Nehru's brainchild, and he alone, along with some of his trusted comrades, pressed it relentlessly until it formed part of the Congress agenda. Few Congress members shared his enthusiasm. Gandhi disapproved and preferred to proceed cautiously through constructive work among the Muslim masses by both Hindu and Muslim workers.[61] Nehru's socialist allies, too, argued that their concern was with the masses, not as Hindus or Muslims but as peasants and workers of all communities.[62] The idea of a separate mass contact campaign for the Muslims, however, was consistent with the structure of Congress politics and its strategy of mobilization; in fact, it was a logical consequence of the approach followed from the time of the Lucknow Pact when the Congress leaders, in effect, recognized the distinct political identity of the Muslims.

The most bitter criticism came from the Congress right wing. Their opposition was symptomatic of the ideological rift with the socialist Nehru, and based on the fear that the success of mass contact would further bolster Nehru's image and provide him, as in the case of Gandhi during the khilafat days, with a solid Muslim base. They girded themselves to resist the campaign that threatened their political dominance and raised the chances of Nehru's Muslim, socialist, and communist allies dominating the Congress. G.B. Pant, chief minister of UP, thus argued that it was 'not necessary to lay emphasis on the Muslim mass contact' and advised Nehru that Congress should stick to its old policy and creed of representing the 'masses of India regardless of caste or creed'.[63] At the same time, he explained that he was busy securing the 'goodwill and cooperation' of the Muslims by appointing them to high government positions. 'Two of the six Hon'ble Ministers and three out of the twelve Parliamentary Secretaries,' announced a government report, 'have been appointed from the Muslims'.[64] Likewise, J.B. Kripalani, general secretary of Congress, brusquely chided Riyazul Mustafa of Bulandshahar for having 'subscribed yourself as the secretary of the Muslim Mass Contacts Committee . . . as there are no such things in the Congress', and directed the UP PCC to ensure that 'such committees are disbanded'.[65] More discreet critics such as Morarji Desai pointed out that it was neither 'expedient' nor 'prudent' to implement the scheme in Gujarat on the false plea that there were no Muslim workers through whom the work could be done. 'If non-Muslims take up the work,' he wrote, 'it will meet with no response and will perhaps give rise to a dangerous counter-propaganda.'[66]

These were not exceptional or isolated instances. In several parts of UP, such as Agra, Bareilly, and Meerut, there were complaints of inactivity and 'idleness' on the part of mass contact committees; in some cases their activities were hampered by shortage of funds and lack of any organized or coordinated line of action.[67] 'What is being done by the local Congress for mass contact?' asked an agitated secretary of the Young Muslim Party in Meerut. 'How many leaders have been called to Meerut for this object? How many Muslims have been enrolled here as Congress members? *So far I think the Congress diary is nearly blank.*'[68] The Bombay-based socialist Yusuf Meharally was equally disappointed with the indifference of the Congress committees, while a number of Calcutta Muslim leaders were dismayed by the Bengal PCC's reluctance to pursue the campaign and enroll Muslims.[69] They sought the intervention of Nehru, the leader whose integrated secular outlook inspired them most.

The drive to enroll Muslims did not make much headway also because several leading Congressmen had unpleasant memories of the khilafat and non-cooperation days when the Mahatma pandered to the religious sentiments of the Muslims and allowed them to dictate Congress policies. With mass contact making rapid progress, they were now faced with the cheerless prospect of yet another Muslim 'influx'.[70] Fearful that with Nehru's backing and Gandhi's grudging support Muslims would wrest major concessions, the Congress right wing, in alliance with the Hindu Mahasabha, fiercely attacked the mass contact programme in an attempt to thwart its success. Part of their strategy was to starve mass contact committees of funds, to fill them with their trusted lieutenants, and to ensure that Muslims were kept out of provincial and district Congress committees.[71] In Aligarh, for instance, Nehru got wind of the plan to exclude the only two Muslims who filed their nominations out of the fifty DCC seats. He intervened to set matters right. In Budaun, there was quite a furore when Idris Khan Lodi, associated with Congress for nearly two decades, was not allowed to contest a PCC seat. Lodi resigned in disgust, along with seventy-five other Muslims. In Mahoba and Hamirpur, the Hindu members forged a coalition on the cry of danger to Hinduism to defeat a Muslim candidate from being elected to the Education Committee of the district board. 'The defeat of the Muslim candidate through Hindu communalism,' wrote Ramgopal Gupta, secretary of the DCC, 'has angered the Muslim public who cannot distinguish between a Mahasabhite Hindu and a Congressite Hindu.' Finally, in the vital Bundelkhand and Amritsar by-election the Congress right wing worked against two Congressmen of long standing—Nisar Ahmad Khan Sherwani and Saifuddin Kitchlew—and contributed to their defeat. Such belligerence could hardly inspire confidence among the Congress Muslims, who braved the fierce and bitter attacks of the League, resisting pressures to desert the Congress camp and becoming part of the communal front.[72]

The success of the mass contact campaigns—as, indeed, of any such initiative—depended on the active backing of provincial and district Congress committees. This was not easily forthcoming. One of the reasons—one that constantly figured in the Muslim-owned Urdu press—was that these bodies were often controlled by men with close links with the Hindu Mahasabha and other overtly communal organizations.[73] In Gorakhpur a Holi procession, with spears, swords, and sticks on display, was led by senior office-bearers of the DCC 'reacting very badly on the position of the Congress Muslims and on the prospect of Congress work in general'.[74] In Budaun and Bareilly, districts with large Muslim populations, local Congressmen exacerbated communal tensions, while in Dehradun an indignant Khushi Lal, chairman of the municipal board, warned Nehru of serious consequences if Congressmen fomented communal troubles, and 'try to impose a social boycott of all the Muslims for the sins, imaginary or real, of one or two'.[75] Lal was right. The presence of such elements in Congress made the task of drawing Muslims into the nationalist fold difficult and diminished chances of accomplishing Hindu-Muslim amity.

Congress' one and only attempt to isolate the communal elements failed. On 11-16 December 1938, the CWC declared, probably at the initiative of Ashraf and his socialist comrades,[76] the Hindu Mahasabha and the Muslim League as communal organizations and debarred *elected* members of Congress committees from serving on similar committees in the Mahasabha and the League.[77] This decision, adopted somewhat belatedly, elicited much interest, and PCCs and DCCs all over the country wanted to know whether they could exclude the Hindu Mahasabhites. 'In our belief,' wrote the secretary of the Bengal PCC, 'Congress organization will suffer very much in prestige and hold over the masses if Congress members be allowed to be members of the Hindu Mahasabha organizations.'[78] J.B. Kripalani, Congress' general secretary, ignored such views, however, and gave an interpretation that defeated the purpose of the CWC's resolution. He wrote to the secretary of the Bengal PCC:

> You must remember Article V(c) in the constitution refers not to primary members of any communal organization but to members of elected committees. There is therefore nothing in the Congress constitution, even if the working committee named some organizations as communal, in the sense contemplated by Article V(c) to prevent ordinary primary members of such organization from being office holders in the Congress organization.[79]

Inconsistent with the spirit of the CWC resolution, this interpretation gave a free hand to communal groups to move in and out of the Congress with ease and to meddle in its affairs brazenly. Congress' own position regarding communal organizations and the communal activities of its members remained dangerously vague.

Summary

The mass contact campaign was Congress' last serious attempt to mobilize Muslims in a joint struggle against colonial rule. Although based on a set of assumptions that did not adequately take into account the presence of the 'third party', this campaign, conceived at a crucial historical juncture, was a significant move in the right direction. Pursued purposefully, it had the potential of weaning large sections of the Muslim communities away from the Muslim League camp, a point so well made by some contemporary observers.[80] There can be no doubt about the problems that Nehru and other protagonists of mass contacts were confronted with: the stout resistance of Jinnah, the lukewarm support of their own party comrades, and communal animosities manifest in Hindu-Muslim rioting and other forms of antagonism. These problems were not insurmountable, however, as would appear from Nehru's own assessment. The League, after all, was weak, divided, and disorganized, and its leader, Jinnah, did not yet command widespread allegiance in Punjab, UP, and Bengal. Congress, however, enjoyed a fair measure of goodwill, a fact that places Jinnah's outburst against mass contact and the League's endeavors to arrest its progress, in perspective. Its inability to consolidate the gains of the year 1937 to 1938, was a sure case of letting an opportunity slip by. By letting the mass contact campaign peter out, Congress allowed Jinnah, perhaps involuntarily, to take advantage of deteriorating communal relations and rally his community around the symbol of a Muslim homeland; in fact, Ashraf suggested many years later that one reason why the League 'turned overnight into a full-fledged manager' was because Congress abandoned the struggle of mass contact for ministry-making.[81]

NOTES

1. G. Adhikari (ed.), *Documents of the History of the Communist Party of India*, Vol. 1: *1917-1922*, New Delhi, 1971, p. 345; Vol. 2: *1923-1925*, New Delhi, 1974, p. 210.
2. For details see, Hasan, A *Nationalist Conscience*.
3. Hasan, *Nationalism and Communal Politics*.
4. Statement by Gandhi on 16 February 1930, Hasan (ed.), *Muslims and the Congress*, p. 101.

5. Ibid., pp. 103-4.
6. *SWJN*, Vol. 8, p. 123. All references are drawn from this volume.
7. Deepak Pandey, 'Congress-Muslim League Relations 1937-9: "The Parting of the Ways"', *MAS*, Vol. 12 (1978), p. 643.
8. *SWJN*, Vol. 8, p. 128.
9. For Rajendra Prasad statement, *Bombay Chronicle*, 26 Apr. 1937.
10. *SWJN*, Vol. 8, p. 123.
11. Ibid.
12. Horst Kruger (ed.), *Kunwar Muhammad Ashraf: An Indian Scholar and Revolutionary 1903-1962*, Berlin: Academie-Verlag, 1966, pp. 112-13. Ashraf's excitement was shared by his associates. His comrade, Sajjad Zaheer, one of the founders of the Progressive Writers' Movement, recalled: 'As I belonged to the same Allahabad group of young Indians who had then arrived from Europe after finishing their education there, I wish to record here the feeling of hopefulness in and enthusiasm for . . . the success of our revolutionary mission with which we and a large number of young Indian intelligentsia were moved during that time.' Sajjad Zaheer, 'Recent Muslim Politics in India and the Problem of National Unity', in S.T. Lokhandwala (ed.), *India and Contemporary Islam*, Shimla: Indian Institute of Advanced Study, 1971.
13. AICC papers, File No. 30/1937, Misc., p. 15.
14. AICC papers, File No. 48/1937, p. 155; *Hindustan,* 10 Oct. 1937, p. 5.
15. AICC papers, File No. 13/1937, p. 39.
16. To Hassan Habib, editor of *Agra Citizen* (Agra), 15 Jul. 1938, AICC papers, File No. G-67/1938, pp. 17-21.
17. Resolution proposed by Ashraf and Z.A. Ahmad at the 1938 Haripura session of the Congress, AICC papers, File No. G-103/1938.
18. *Bombay Chronicle*, 10 Jul. 1937; *SWJN,* Vol. 8, p. 156.
19. *SWJN*, Vol. 8, 25 Apr. and 23 May 1937, pp. 125, 131-2.
20. Ibid., 30 Jun. 1937, p. 138. Also see letters to R.V. Dhulekar, 30 Jun. 1937, and to Rafi Ahmad Kidwai, 1 Jul. 1937, pp. 139, 146.
21. To A.G. Kher and Manilal Pande, 30 Jun. 1937, *SWJN*, Vol. 8, pp. 140-1.
22. To Rajendra Prasad, 21 Jul. 1937, *SWJN*, p. 167; statement to the press, 25 Jul. 1937, *SWJN,* Vol. 8, p. 171; *Bombay Chronicle*, 27 Jul. 1937.
23. To Nehru, 30 Jul. 1937, *CWMG*, Vol. LXV, p. 445.
24. Circular to PCC's, 10 Jul. 1937, *SWJN,* Vol. 8, p. 156. 'The Mussalmans of UP and Punjab,' reported the *Bombay Chronicle*, 3 Jun. and 1 Nov. 1937, 'are rallying round the Congress in large numbers much to the discomfiture of big landlords and the Muslim Leaguers.'
25. S. Tufail Ahmad Manglori, *Ruh-i Raushan Mustaqbil*, Budaun, 1946, p. 132; M. Rafique Afzal, *Political Parties in Pakistan: 1947-1958*, Islamabad, 1976, pp. 27-8; statement of Anwar Sabri, secretary of the UP Provincial Ahrar Committee, in *Leader*, 8 Apr. 1937; resolution of the Provincial Ahrar

Conference, Lucknow, *Bombay Chronicle*, 19 Apr. 1937. See Smith, *Modern Islam in India*, pp. 270-6.

26. *Leader*, 6 and 12 Jun. 1937.
27. AICC papers, File No. P-24(i)/1937, p. 8.
28. *Bombay Chronicle*, 8 May 1937.
29. Ahmad Khan president DDC to Ashraf, 24 Jul. 1938 (in Urdu); Muhammad Aqil to Ashraf, 30 Apr. 1937 (in Urdu); and Hargovind Singh to Ashraf, 29 Jun. 1937, respectively, in AICC papers, File No. 42(B)/1937, Misc., p. 378, File No. 42(i)/1937, p. 557.
30. Aftab Ahmad Khan to Ashraf, 26 Apr. 1937, AICC papers, File No. 11/1937, Misc., p. 279; Fazalbhoy, editor of the university magazine, in *Bombay Chronicle*, 24 May 1937. The Momin Conference was established in 1926 in order to focus on the separate and distinct interests of the weavers, variously known as Ansari and Momin. The conference, with its headquarters in Kanpur, claimed to have a membership of 2 lakhs with over 500 branches in UP alone. Abdul Qaiyum Ansari to Rajendra Prasad, 9 Oct. 1939, Jawaharlal Nehru papers (hereafter cited as Nehru papers), File No. 136, part 2, NMML. For further details, Manglori, *Ruh-i Raushan Mustaqbil*, pp. 143-4.
31. Haig to Linlithgow, 7 and 24 May 1937, Haig papers.
32. The raja of Mahmudabad to M.A. Jinnah, 8 Aug. 1937. Shamsul Hasan collection, Karachi.
33. Annual Report of the Delhi PCC for 1937, AICC papers, File No. P-25/1937, p. 60. *Leader*, 21 Apr. 1937.
34. Report for the month of Sept. 1937, AICC papers, File No. P-24(i)/1937, p. 13. By Dec. 1937, 3,894 Muslims joined Congress in Maharashtra. Report of the Maharashtra PCC, 8-31 Dec. 1937, AICC papers, File No. P-25/1937, p. 101. 'The Muslim Leaguers of our province', reported Brelvi, editor of the *Bombay Chronicle*, 'are whipping themselves into furious activity. . . . Some local friends are even holding out threats of violence if we go on spreading our contacts with the masses.' To Ashraf, 5 May 1937, AICC papers, G-67/1937, p. 101.
35. Wali Hasan to Ashraf, 20 Jun. 1937; Saiyid Mahmud and Abdul Bari organized meetings, lectures, and conferences; so did Maulvi Nizamuddin, president of the Champaran branch of the Muslim Independent Party. *Bombay Chronicle*, 19 Apr. and 18, 26 Jun. 1936. Significant also was the support extended by the provincial Jamiyat al-Momineen. Hakim Wasi Ahmad to Rajendra Prasad, 12 Mar. 1937 (telegram), Valmiki Chaudhary (ed.), *Dr. Rajendra Prasad Correspondence and Select Documents*, New Delhi, 1984, Vol. 1, p. 30.
36. *Bombay Chronicle*, 18 May 1937. For an optimistic assessment of the work Calcutta Mass Contact Committee, see Manzoor Ahmad to Ashraf, 13 July 1938 (in Urdu), AICC papers, File No. 42/1937 (1), pp. 117-18.
37. *Bombay Chronicle*, 25 Nov. 1937. The Ahl-i Hadis accepted the entire corpus of the Prophet Muhammad's *hadis* (traditions) and rejected the four juristic

schools: Hanafi, Shafai, Maliki, and Hambali. Ahmad, *Islamic Modernism*, pp. 113-22.

38. *Leader*, 25 Apr. and 9 Jun. 1937.
39. *Sarfraz* (Lucknow), 17 Aug. 1937, AICC papers, File No. 49/1937, Misc., p. 160.
40. *Leader*, 18 May 1937; AICC papers, File No. 12/1937, Misc., pp. 43-5. For Jinnah's criticism of the Allahabad conference, *Bombay Chronicle*, 20 Apr. 1937.
41. *Leader*, 15 Apr. 1937; AICC papers, File No. 31/1937, Misc., pp. 39, 207.
42. Leaders of the CSP were strong supporters of a more general mass contacts strategy.
43. *Bombay Chronicle*, 3 June and 16 Aug. 1937; AICC papers, File No. 30/1937, Misc., p. 585.
44. The summary is based on Hardy, *Muslims of British India*, pp. 227-8.
45. *Leader*, 8 Mar. 1939.
46. Qureshi, *Ulema in Politics*, pp. 335-8.
47. *Bombay Chronicle*, 20 Apr. 1937. The Pirpur Report (1938) also charged that the aim of mass contact was 'to destroy Muslim solidarity and create disruption in the community', and to 'lure' Muslims into the Congress fold by following a policy of 'divide and rule'. For Shaukat Ali's outburst, *Bombay Chronicle*, 28 Dec. 1937, and Sayeed, *Pakistan: The Formative Phase*, pp. 89-90.
48. *Bombay Chronicle*, 20 Apr. 1937.
49. The raja of Mahmudabad to Jinnah, 24 Sept. 1937, Shamsul Hasan collection.
50. Khaliquzzaman to Nehru, 29 June 1937; AICC papers, File No. G-1/1937, p. 173.
51. AICC papers, File No. G-22/1938.
52. Some Muslims, such as Fahimuddin Noori, a regular contributor to the Delhi paper, *Alaman,* opposed the ulama being pressed into service. Their intervention in politics, he observed, would eventually prove 'harmful'. To Ashraf, 20 Apr. 1937 (in Urdu); AICC papers, File No. 41/1937, p. 173. For the role of ulama, especially in the Bundelkhand elections, AICC papers, File No. 30/1937, pp. 583-5.
53. AICC papers, File No. 41/1937, p. 27. Abul Hayat, one of Bengal's most consistent nationalists, regretted that the Congress leadership 'persistently neglected to pay heed to the needs and aspirations of the Muslim masses and always tried to come to a settlement with the top leaders of the Muslim League'. Abul Hayat, *Mussalmans of Bengal*, Calcutta, 1966, pp. 65-6.
54. AICC papers, File No. G-22/1938.
55. Pandey, *Ascendancy of the Congress*, p. 149.
56. For his role, *Bombay Chronicle*, 18 and 26 June 1937.
57. The role of the Muslim intelligentsia is the subject of a separate study. See my, 'Nationalist and Separatist Trends in Aligarh, 1915-47', *Indian Economic and Social History Review*, Vol. 22 (1985), pp. 1-33.

58. To Ashraf, 16 Apr. 1937, AICC papers, File No. 26/1937, Misc., p. 9.
59. Pandey, *Ascendancy of the Congress*, p. 151; Deepak Pandey, 'Congress-Muslim League Relations', pp. 643-9; Hardy, *Muslims of British India*, p. 227; Sayeed, *Pakistan*, pp. 89-90.
60. Sumit Sarkar, *Modern India, 1885-1947*, New Delhi: Macmillan, 1983, p. 354; Bipan Chandra, *Communalism in Modern India*, New Delhi, 1984, p. 300.
61. *SWJN*, Vol. 8, p. 225.
62. B.P.L. Bedi, 'Communalism Enters Congress', *Congress Socialist*, 12 June 1937.
63. Nehru papers, Vol. 79, part I, pp. 65-6; V.N. Tiwary to Nehru, 7 Jan. 1939, Nehru papers, quoted in Deepak Pandey, 'Congress-Muslim League Relations', p. 649. For opposition of Mohanlal Gautam, see proceedings of the executive council of the UPPCC held at Allahabad on 20 June 1937, recorded in UPPCC papers (microfilm), Reel No. 2, NMML.
64. AICC papers, File No. 1/1937, p. 41.
65. 7 Jan. 1939, AICC papers, File No. P-20/1938, pp. 329, 341.
66. To Ashraf, 26 June 1937, AICC papers, File No. 49/1937, p. 129. Ashraf's view, however, was that the 'average Mussalman hesitates to join the Congress not because he has any inherent dislike but because he is ignorant of what the Congress stands for'. To Morarji Desai, 5 June 1937, p. 133.
67. Manzer Siddiqi, editor of *Asia*, to Ashraf, 10 Sept. 1938, AICC papers, File No. 30/1937, Misc., p. 179; Damodar Swarup Seth to Ashraf, 20 Aug. 1937, AICC papers, File No. 42/1937 (2), p. 381; and Shamsul Huda, secretary, Barabazar Congress Committee, to Ashraf, AICC papers, 48/1937, Misc., p. 73. A.K. Azad's pamphlet *Congress and Mussalmans* could not be distributed for lack of funds; AICC papers, File No. 11/1937, p. 65.
68. AICC papers, File No. 47/1937, p. 62 (italics mine).
69. Yusuf Meharally, 'Non-Congress Ministries in the Melting Pot', *Congress Socialist*, 26 Mar. 1938, p. 223; S.M. Ahmad to Ashraf, 19 Aug. 1937 (in Urdu), AICC papers, File No. 47/1937, p. 85.
70. In anticipation of Congress' electoral victory in Bijnor and the expected Muslim entry into the party in large numbers, B.S. Moonje proposed to Bhai Parmanand and raja Narendranath that all the Hindu Mahasabhites should join Congress to counteract the effect of such an influx. See *Bombay Chronicle*, 9 Nov. 1937. Notice the comment of the Urdu daily *Hind*:, 'Responsible Congressmen,' wrote the Calcutta paper, 'have never countenanced the entry of Muslims in the Congress and they have in fact encouraged communalism.' Nehru to president, Bengal PCC, 10 Apr. 1937, AICC papers, File No. 49/1937, Misc., p. 251.
71. Manzar Rizvi of the Political and Economic Information department brought this complaint to the notice of the secretary, Nagpur PCC. Such reports also reached the AICC office from Jabalpur, Hamirpur, and Bulandshahar. For

relevant information, see AICC papers, File No. 30/1937, Misc., pp. 63, 429; File No. 38/1938, p. 99. For Aligarh, see File Nos. P-20(2)/1938-9, p. 276; for Budaun see, Ashraf to K.D. Malaviya, 12 Jan. 1939, AICC papers, File No. 30/1937, Misc., p. 81, and Mahoba and Hamipur, 3 July 1937, AICC papers, File No. 38/1938, p. 99.

72. Fida Ahmad Khan Sherwani attributed the defeat of his brother Nisar to the 'ruthless' neglect of Congress and reached the conclusion that 'a Mussalman has no place in the Congress'. To Nehru, 30 June 1937, AICC papers, File No. G-61/1937, pp. 197-9. See K.C. Nigam to Ashraf, 26 July 1937, AICC papers, File No. 42(2)/1937, p. 391.
73. Ashraf was posted with such news. The president of the Jessore Hindu Sabha, he was informed, was also a prominent member of the provincial, district, and town Congress committee. There were reports of an alliance between V.D. Savarkar, one of the founders of the Hindu Mahasabha, and the speaker of the Central Provinces Assembly. The links of many UP Congressmen, such as Malaviya, with Hindu communal and revivalist causes is fairly well known. This was, incidentally, the strain of many editorial comments. See *Din Duniya Weekly* (New Delhi), in Urdu, 11 Feb. 1937; AICC papers, File No. 41/1937, Misc., p. 107; Saiyid Hasan Baqai, editor of *Peshwa*, an Urdu monthly, to Ashraf, 5 Aug. 1937, in Urdu, AICC papers, File No. 47/1937, Misc., p. 123; *Hilal* (Bombay), AICC papers, File No. 47/1937, Misc., p. 81. Abbas Husain, editor of *Akhbar Qaum wa Risala-i Tamaddun*, to Nehru, 19 Apr. 1937, AICC papers, File No. 41/1937, Misc., p. 169. Also, references in Ashraf to Azad, 3 Sept. 1938, AICC papers, File No. 30/1937, Misc., p. 213, and M. Umar Khan to Ashraf, 8 May 1937, AICC papers, File No. P-5/1948, pp. 77-81.
74. To A.K. Azad, 27 June 1938, AICC papers, File No. 30/1937, Misc., p. 399.
75. Ashraf to Lal Bahadur Shastri, 5 Apr. 1939, AICC papers, File Nos. 6(1)/1937, P-20(2)/1938-9, pp. 273-7 and 193.
76. Ashraf to Mohanlal Saxena, 3 Sept. 1938, AICC papers, File No. 30/1937, Misc., pp. 209-10.
77. Resolution of the CWC, Wardha, 11-16 Dec. 1938, AICC papers, File No. P-1/1938.
78. Ashrafuddin Chowdhury to Kripalani, 16 Aug. and 20 Sept. 1938, AICC papers, File No. P-5/1938.
79. To Chowdhury, 6 Oct. 1938, AICC papers, File No. P-5/1938, p. 101.
80. Dube Rai to Ashraf, 19 Dec. 1937, AICC papers, File No. 54/1937, Misc., p. 399; Faridul Haq Ansari, 'Communalism Clarified', *Congress Socialist*, 19 Feb. 1938, pp. 122-3; Hayat, *Mussalmans of Bengal*, p. 65.
81. Kruger, *Kunwar Muhammad Ashraf*, pp. 413-14.

11

The Local Roots of the Pakistan Movement: The Aligarh Muslim University

> One of the author's earliest memories is of the arrival in our ancestral village in northern India of three young men carrying the Muslim League flag—the Islamic crescent and star on a deep green background. The three were students from Aligarh University. They planted the flag in the village square and a crowd of little boys gathered around them. . . . Within an hour our quiet village had been turned into a 'Pakistan Village'. . . . Every piece of green material our mother could find was made into Muslim League flags. . . . A few months later they [parents] all walked in their bare feet and some carried their aged and sick parents on the backs to the polling booth four miles away to vote for the Muslim League and Pakistan. This was repeated all over India. Seldom in History have so few inspired so many with so little effort.
>
> KALIM SIDDIQUI, *Conflict, Crisis & War in Pakistan*

This chapter seeks to examine, with the aid of hitherto unexplored materials from the Sir Saiyid Archives at Aligarh and the Shamsul Hasan collection in Karachi, how and why the Pakistan idea caught the imagination of people who were far removed from the mutual bickering at the national scene. By focusing on the Aligarh Muslim University, I endeavour to analyse how and why an important centre of nationalist activity during the khilafat and non-cooperation days was so quickly transformed into the 'arsenal' of 'Muslim India' and the 'emotional centre' of the Pakistan demand.

The choice of the university is dictated by its critical role in creating a Muslim intelligentsia in north India and its overall impact on their intellectual and political activities. The M.A.O. College, founded by Saiyid Ahmad Khan in 1886, headquartered the Muhammadan Educational Conference and hosted five of its eleven sessions. It was the arena in which Muslim opinion was created and in which the Muslim leadership in UP assembled. The agitation against the Nagri resolution of 18 April 1900 was led, organized and dominated by the Aligarh Muslims, while the Simla deputation of October 1906, a catalyst for the formation of the Muslim League in December that year, was also an act of the Aligarh elders. Just before its elevation to the status of a university in 1920, the college was in the forefront of the great post-War agitation on behalf of the Turkish khalifa. Finally, it attained new heights of practical and symbolic prominence in the 1940s as a centre for mobilizing a powerful Muslim response to the Pakistan movement. In the words of the Aga Khan,

> often in civilized history a university has supplied the springboard for a nation's intellectual and spiritual renaissance. . . . Aligarh is no exception to this rule. But we may claim with pride that Aligarh was the product of our own efforts and of no outside benevolence, and surely it may also be claimed that the independent, sovereign nation of Pakistan was born in the Muslim University of Aligarh.[1]

II

The foundation of the college marked the fulfilment of Saiyid Ahmad Khan's dream to equip his co-religionists for government employment and to make them 'worthy and useful subjects of Crown'. But soon after his death in 1898, this most 'benighted' and conservative of institutions responded to the political currents prevailing in the country. The agitation against the Nagri resolution, followed by the students' strike of February 1907, confronted the British with serious dissidence and a trend to steer the Muslim communities on a course different from the one chartered by the Saiyid. The Aligarh students, sensitized to the political upheaval in the wake of Bengal's partition, were beginning to throw to the winds all the caution that had been enjoined upon them by their mentor.

Political activity on the campus was heightened during and after World War I. Funds were raised for the beleaguered Turkey, and prayer meetings organized for the Turkish armies and the Anjuman-i Khuddam-i Kaaba.[2] Four Aligarh graduates joined Ansari's medical mission to Constantinople. At least one Aligarh Old Boy—Mahendra Pratap—was involved in the 'Silk Letter Conspiracy' and headed the provisional government in Kabul.[3] In September-October 1920, Gandhi and his khilafat partners chose Aligarh to garner support for non-cooperation.[4] The Mahatma reached the campus on 12 October and, according to an eye-witness account, spoke to the students haltingly in Hindustani. He tried to find the right words, but 'his accent seemed droll to his "pseudo-sophisticated" audience who did not agree with him, for their political and economic background and affiliations did not predispose them to accept his radical new doctrine of non-cooperation'.[5] The first shot misfired. He then appealed to the trustees:

> to decline any further Government grant, disaffiliate the great institution of which you are the trustees and reject the charter of the Moslem University. The least that the Aligarh boys can do, if you fail to respond to the call of Islam and India, is to wash their hands clean of an institution acknowledging the aegis of Government that has forfeited all title to the allegiance of Islam and India and to bring into being, a larger, nobler and purer Aligarh that would carry out the most cherished wishes of its great founder.[6]

Brought up in the tradition of sturdy loyalty to Pax Britannica, the trustees paid no heed to his plea. They had already decided, much before receiving Gandhi's letter of 24 October, to run their college on 'old established lines' and make their Muslim brethren 'worthy and useful subjects of the British Crown'.[7] For once, they had their taste of revenge. Having failed to curb Mohamed Ali's influence in Aligarh during the past few years, they drew satisfaction from his isolation. Most trustees rallied round the principal, Dr Ziauddin Ahmad, and agreed with his decision to use the big stick to isolate the pan-Islamists and the Anjuman-i Khuddam-i Kaaba, co-founded by Abdul Bari and Shaukat Ali.[8]

The khilafat contingent, led by Ansari, Azad Subhani, Azad, and the Ali brothers, returned to Aligarh on 23 October and addressed numerous meetings. On this occasion, there was a change of heart. A graduate student wrote to Ziauddin that his doubts had been 'removed within the last four or five days', and that he would continue his studies only if the college was 'nationalised' [*sic*]. Otherwise, he was 'ready to face the doom awaiting my non-cooperating brothers'.[9] Another student from Azamgarh, impressed by the speeches of Azad and Azad Subhani, decided to join the non-cooperators.[10] Amidst fiery and passionate speeches, resolutions, promises and assurances, many more responded—estimates range from 200 to 700[11]—to the call of non-cooperation and enrolled themselves with the newly-founded Jamia Millia Islamia.

This mood remained unchanged until the mid-1930s despite the escalation of Hindu-Muslim violence and the growing rift between the Congress and the League. In general, campus politics was not marred by religious polarization. K.G. Saiyadain, who joined the university as a lecturer in

1925, participated in the Jubilee debate where his fellow-students spoke in favour of Indian nationalism.[12] He himself argued, in the presence of luminaries like the Aga Khan, Jinnah and Ali Imam, that his community should not organize themselves on communal lines but must work together with the nationalist forces for the country's freedom and progress.[13] In 1931, Tofail Ahmad Manglori, a distinguished Aligarh alumni, critiqued the Muslim demand for separate electorate, arguing that the real cause for the communal tangle was the recognition of special interests 'which appears to have dimmed the national outlook'. He proposed a constitution that would safeguard minority rights by 'correct redistribution of India with compact homogeneous zones, autonomous in character and with as few central subjects as circumstances permit'.[14] Most office-bearers of the influential students' union belonged to the radical alumni circles, anti-British and pro-Congress; the *Aligarh Magazine* retained its pro-Congress stance until its charge was handed over to Muhammad Noman Zuberi, a law student with League sympathies.[15] In 1930, the vice-president of the union exhorted his audience to

> turn ourselves into the biggest, the most disciplined, the most educated and the most united army that India possesses, to fight against the evils that have made India the laughing stock of the world and let nobody say that Aligarh lagged behind anybody in India's battle of freedom. . . . To be indifferent towards anything that happens in a depressed country like India is criminal. To be ignorant of one's own political status is far worse than death. And not to think of and dream of a brilliant future for one's own country is a state which will reduce one to a lifeless mass of flesh.[16]

Support for nationalism combined comfortably with socialist commitments. The themes of capitalist exploitation, class conflict, and of revolt against imperialism, figured in the writings of former Aligarh graduates like Hasrat Mohani, Sajjad Hyder Yaldaram, Wilayat Ali 'Bambooque', Qazi Abdul Ghaffar, and Abdur Rahman Bijnori.[17] The younger generation often turned to Marxist writers and poets for political and intellectual inspiration. Saiyid Muhammad Tonki, who later turned to 'Islamic socialism' under the influence of Hasrat Mohani, received M.N. Roy's writings 'which discussed the Russian revolution, the reality of the socialist system, and the weakening of big empires as a result of capitalist and imperialist exploitation'. He and Ashraf often discussed 'what a socialist system might achieve in India'.[18] Nasim Ansari of Firangi Mahal in Lucknow and an intermediate class student in 1947 recalled how socialism 'carried the same poetic and romantic appeal as the poetic blasphemy in the work of Hafiz, Ghalib and Hasrat Mohani'.[19] Finally, the Progressive Writers' Association, formed in the mid-1930s, represented the continuation and development of the literary and political trends set by many writers connected with Aligarh. Their writings gave Urdu literature a vital stimulus, a new vigour, and a liberating consciousness.[20]

Political debates were conducted in and around the hostels. The revolutionary poems of Josh Malihabadi, Asrarul Haq 'Majaz' and other younger poets filled the Aftab Hall, the focal point of much radical activism and the venue of public lectures delivered by local Congress stalwarts like Maulvi Abu Bakr Muhammad Shish (d. 1941), chairman of the Sunni theology department from 1925 to 1940. He caused a furore by chairing a Congress meeting in Jaunpur.[21] The 1936 students' strike against the suppression of nationalist activities was triggered in Aftab Hall,[22] as also the moves to prevent the All-India Muslim Students' Federation (AIMSF) from forming its branch in Aligarh.[23] In December 1937, one of its residents declared support for the All India Students' Federation (AISF) and his stout opposition to the setting up of a Muslim organization in the university.[24]

Just a few later, however, campus politics was in the throes of a dramatic change. Emboldened by the spate of successfully organized League conferences in Delhi and the neighbouring districts,[25] the AIMSF[26] arrived on the scene with its strident demand for removing teachers holding 'socialistic' and 'atheistic' ideas. As a result, a few radical teachers were dismissed, some were told to fall in line; others were eased out of administrative positions and replaced by the Leaguers. 'Dangerous' books, like those of James Harvey Robinson on rationalism and Freud's on religion, were removed from the Lytton Library, *purdah* was reintroduced in an institution which had once led the crusade for the emancipation of women,[27] and the students' union platform was denied to the communists. K.M. Ashraf was, for instance, ridiculed when he intervened in a meeting addressed by Zafar Ali Khan, the editor of the Lahore newspaper *Zamindar*. 'The treatment meted out to Dr. Ashraf', stated the vice-president of the union, 'must serve as a warning to the Communists and the unscrupulous nationalists who may venture to speak on this platform, for the students are ever prepared to vindicate the honour of their religion, community and Alma Mater.'[28] Criticism of the League was suppressed with an iron hand. Thus an article by Khwaja Ahmad Abbas, a law student, was not published. A.B.A. Haleem, the pro-vice-chancellor, stated that 'Pakistan has been adopted as a creed by the great bulk of the Muslim community in India and the publication of the article in the *Aligarh Magazine* was sure to be exploited by the critics of the University and the opponents of the movement'.[29] Clearly, young students poured 'their idealistic zeal into the emotionalism of Pakistan and discussed rational arguments with the contentment of religious authoritarianism, and its scorn'.[30]

The Lahore resolution, followed by the lectures of Jinnah and Liaquat Ali Khan delivered at Aligarh in the summer of 1940,[31] generated fresh hopes and excitement. The students' body promptly endorsed the resolution as its official creed;[32] in this way, the Aligarh boys' adolescent pride in their institutional identity got easily and temporarily merged with the League's politically-oriented search for a collective identity.[33] They soon started claiming that the Pakistan scheme was itself shaped and crystallized by them, and that they were privileged to express 'the hidden feelings of the Muslim nation'.[34] Their new fervour led to a flurry of activity. Associations and debating societies, including a Buchha Muslim League to train children, mushroomed;[35] the University City League, established in 1937 and controlled by Saiyid Abdus Sattar Kheiri, a professor of German, gained a new lease of life; the 'Duty Society' was revived;[36] the AIMSF launched a quarterly journal—*Awakening* in English and its Urdu version *Bedaari*; the *Aligarh Magazine* carried scores of articles in support of Pakistan and Jinnah.[37] Indeed, the Quaid's visits to Aligarh were celebrated with much fanfare. Large crowds gathered at the otherwise sleepy railway station and crackers were laid on the track so that when the engine of the Kalka Mail passed over them, it seemed that a gun salute had been fired to welcome him.[38] His leadership 'created a spirit of obedience to the command of our Leader', for he was not just the voice of a 'Muslim Nation' but also personified its sense of 'persecution' by the 'Hindu-dominated' Congress.[39] 'The walls of the Strachey Hall', commented an AIMSF activist, 'had echoed with the voices of great men right from the days of Sir Saiyid. These voices were now silent. A new voice had begun to be heard there in the later nineteen-thirties, and during the last decade before independence it was the only political voice that mattered at Aligarh: it was the voice of Muhammad Ali Jinnah.'[40]

The reasons for gravitating towards the League had much to do with the League's refurbished image, its widening financial and recruitment base, the frustration and anger caused by the Congress rebuff to the League on the coalition issue,[41] and the resentment triggered by the Congress ministry in UP. There was talk of overt manifestations of aggressive Hindu nationalism, of the tyranny of Hindu brute majority, and of how the Congress policies jarred upon Muslim sensibilities. The ministry, headed by G.B. Pant, was accused of forcing cow-protection upon the Muslims, pushing the use of Hindi, interfering with Muslim worship, and fanning the fires of communal violence.[42]

Jinnah drew political mileage from these trends, as also from the pan-Islamic ferment in the early 1920s that had heightened religious consciousness, reinforced the community's perception of being unified and cohesive, and made it susceptible to religious appeals. When the going was tough, the Aligarh-based scholars, many having invoked the theme of a separate Muslim identity in their polemical defence of the khilafat cause, found it intellectually convenient to defend the two-nation theory.[43] Likewise, the 'communal consciousness' of the students which 'was far more secular than religious' when Mohamed Ali was a student,[44] expressed itself in a vigorous movement of Muslim nationalism.

In retrospect, it was an error of judgement to mobilize a highly stratified and differentiated community around pan-islamic symbols that mattered so little to the Muslim communities. No wonder, the khilafat issue faded in their memory after a few years. No wonder, they parted company with their erstwhile allies after civil disobedience was called off and the khilafat was abolished in Turkey.[45] The structure of Hindu-Muslim unity, so assiduously built by Gandhi, also crumbled. This was foreseen by, among others, the early communist movement. It was argued then and later that the basis of Hindu-Muslim unity, built on the 'unreliable foundations of religious sentiment', was artificial.[46] Attributing the root cause of Hindu-Muslim antagonism to religion, it was observed:

> it may be comparatively easy to fire politically backward people with religious fanaticism; but it is impossible, even dangerous, to base a political movement on such unreliable grounds. . . . If the hostility against British imperialism is made a religious issue, the hostility thus aroused can at any moment turn into antagonism among the two great Indian communities as they do not profess the same religion. It is precisely what happened now.[47]

Finally, Jinnah's own endeavours to gain a foothold in the university yielded immediate rewards. He sedulously cultivated Ziauddin, maintained regular contacts with the AIMSF,[48] offered funds to the Muslim University City League, made frequent visits to Aligarh,[49] and won over the tall poppies in the Aligarh Old Boys' Association. Khaliquzzaman was his prized trophy in UP. Though associated with the Congress and the Nehru household for nearly a decade, in the early 1930s he began flirting with the League for advancing his political career.[50] In June 1937, Nehru chided him for working against the Congress candidate in the Bundelkhand election.[51] 'Is it not strange,' he wrote, 'that in this conflict men like Wazir

Hasan and Husain Ahmad [Madani] should be ranged on the progressive side and that you should be on the side of the reactionaries.'[52] A few months later Khaliquzzaman tried to justify his stand when he visited Aligarh. 'I was feeling a little nervous', he wrote,

> because the students had known me as a khilafatist and a Congressman and they might not appreciate the circumstances in which I had undertaken the opposition to [the] Congress. I began slowly narrating to them step by step the negotiations carried on by me with the Congress, resulting ultimately in the terms and conditions imposed by the Congress for a coalition with the Muslim League and finally took out a copy of the document which had been handed over to me by Maulana Abul Kalam Azad. While reading it I could see the effect on the boys. By the time I had finished I felt that I had won the day.[53]

For Jinnah's project to succeed, it was equally vital to secure the adherence of the leading Muslim landlords of Aligarh and the neighbouring Bulandshahar district, many of whom had a voice in local and provincial affairs. Influential men like the nawab of Chhatari, Haji Muhammad Ismail Khan, nawab Muzammilullah Khan and the nawab of Pahasu used the university platform to maintain their predominance, furthered Saiyid Ahmad Khan's dream of an institution with close links with the government, and promoted their own goals as landlords. They thus voiced their anxieties over the implications of the new constitutional reforms. The reforms, they stated in their address,

> will transfer a large measure of power and responsibility to the vote of the majority and it is natural for those who are in the minority to feel anxious about their future. We, as educationists, are concerned with these reforms in so far as we have to train our future generation to enable it to appraise the benefit of good and progressive government, to live as law-abiding citizens and to become, some day, leaders of public opinion.[54]

The rise of Hindu-Muslim antipathies in the mid-1930s created deep fissures in the landlord fraternity; in consequence, many of its tall poppies succumbed to communal pressures.[55] Harry Haig noted this trend in May 1937, though he hoped that the 'non-Congress Hindus' would not be tempted to join the communal organization, namely, the Hindu Mahasabha, and thereby jettison the prospect of the 'non-Congress Muslims and Hindus' acting in unison.[56] The simple fact that eluded the lieutenant-governor was that a number of Hindu *taluqdars* had already taken part in reorganizing the Oudh Liberal League in 1935, a body committed to protecting the 'legitimate Hindu interests'.[57] Likewise, quite a few Muslim *taluqdars*, especially the of Mahmudabad, revived and reorganized the Muslim League.[58] Some did so because of their commitment to the idea of an Islamic republic; others to protect themselves from the anti-landlord policies of the Congress ministries and the socialist rhetoric of Nehru and his comrades. The fears and grievances of such men were summed up by nawab Muhammad Yusuf of Jaunpur who wrote to Jinnah: 'I and Moslem zemindars look up to you to protect our fundamental rights and save them from economic ruination or elimination in U.P.'[59]

III

Admittedly, some demurred at the League movement and a few voices of protest mingled with the jubilant welcome accorded to Jinnah during his visits to Aligarh. Several writers and historians wanted the communal tangle to be resolved within a secular framework,[60] while the two-nation theory remained an anathema to committed Congress, socialist and communist activists.[61] 'The communists have openly come out in the field', reported a Leaguer in early 1943, 'preaching communist doctrines, distributing communist literature and their organ of the People's War, and enrolling members of the League. They have established a regular centre at the house of a professor and some other professors are secretly supporting them.'[62] This was an exaggerated assessment, for opposition to the League was considerably diluted in Aligarh and elsewhere after the Communist Party of India backed the Pakistan demand on the principle of 'national self-determination'.[63] Yet, Jinnah reacted to this 'disturbing' trend in Aligarh: 'I should have thought that Aligarh is now strong, well-knit and organized enough to resist any mischief that may be created against us.' He told friends 'to face any attempt to disrupt the Aligarh solidarity'.[64]

Soon thereafter, the League machine got rapidly into gear. Liaquat Ali Khan, Aligarh's Old Boy and president of the UP Muslim League, set up fourteen libraries in various hostels to propagate his party's message;[65] the University League published pamphlets on the Pakistan movement;[66] and an army of National Guards demonstrated Aligarh's solidarity with the 'Muslim cause'.[67] This burst of activity was not all hot air and uncoordinated action. In May 1944, a blistering attack was launched on the pro-Congress Nationalist Muslim Majlis started by Abdul Majid Khwaja and Shaukatullah Ansari, Dr Ansari's son-in-law. They were challenged to speak at the university, 'representing the cream of Muslim intelligentsia of India'.[68] A League camp, organized in October 1944, was the raja of Mahmudabad's brainchild. The *Aligarh Magazine* published a 'Pakistan Number' in 1945 to silence its detractors,[69] while the

AIMSF conference condemned the Sergeant Scheme of Education, and backed the proposal of Muslim emigration from Bengal to Assam.[70]

Such initiatives contributed to the League's ascendancy in Aligarh. The two-nation theory, with its emphasis on division and conflict in Hindu and Muslim 'cultures' and 'civilizations', began to make greater sense than the painstaking researches of historians underlining multiculturalism in medieval India.[71] An undergraduate student declared that 'Hindus and Muslims represented two different cultures and civilizations—one rooted in Islam and the other being the synthesis of the Central Asian and Indian traditions'.[72] In 1945, Abdus Sattar Kheiri argued that no other 'nation' possessed so many factors and attributes which constituted a Muslim nation in India, and that India's Muslims had no 'natural bonds of affection' with the Hindus. 'They will achieve Pakistan,' he wrote, 'and the independence of India for themselves, for the Hindus, and for all those to whom the independence of India is dear.'[73] A.B.A. Haleem and Moinul Haq in Aligarh and Ishtiaq Husain Qureshi in the Delhi University reinforced such ideas through their researches. Haleem launched the Historical Research Association in 1940 to collect material for bringing out a 'reliable history of India relating to the Muhammadan period'.[74]

By all accounts, the Aligarh students played a critical role in the 1945-6 elections to the central and provincial legislative assemblies. The election was, as is well-known, 'a kind of rehearsal for the bigger fight later on',[75] while Jinnah had to vindicate his claim as the 'sole spokesman' of 'Muslim India'. Haunted by the electoral debacle in 1937, he and his comrades left nothing to chance. They organized fund-raising missions, launched many newspapers, and enlisted the support of the ulama, the pirs of Sind and Punjab, and a large body of students and teachers to broaden their base.[76]

Aligarh's response to the elections—'a matter of life and death—'[77] was impressive. Elaborate plans were put in place to mobilize Muslims in the countryside and equip young students for campaigning.[78] Those touring Punjab during December 1945 attended such a camp and heard lectures on Islam, Islamic history, the League, and the religious background to the demand for a separate Muslim nation.[79] Omar Ali Siddiqi, who headed the Aligarh group in Punjab, raised the spectre of a bloody civil strife in the land of the five rivers, reminiscent of the battle of Karbala, and urged his audience to rally round the League to save the imminent destruction of the 'Muslim Nation'.[80] In other areas, the Aligarh students harped on familiar themes to make public the wrongs, real or trivial, suffered by the Muslims under the Congress governments in UP and Bihar. Exaggerated accounts of Hindu atrocities, based on the Pirpur and Shareef reports, were disseminated. Reference was made to Muslim children being made to sing the *Vande Mataram*, to the exaltation of Hindi and the accompanying attack upon Urdu, for many UP Muslims the heart and soul of their culture, the exclusion of Muslims from local bodies and government service, and the loss of Muslim lives in communal riots.[81] The whole campaign was marked by instinctive hostility towards Hindus and towards the idea that there should be any reconciliation with them except, on the terms laid down by Jinnah. Its scale and intensity, comparable only with the khilafat agitation, was aided by a large contingent from Aligarh.[82] By the end of 1945, 225 students canvassed in Punjab, 75 in UP, 25 in the N.W.F.P., and 7 in Bengal.[83] In early 1946, an additional 250 students campaigned in Assam, Sind, and Punjab.[84] An ebullient M.B. Mirza, dean of the science faculty, declared: 'So far all the students [are] united and working under one Leader, one Party and one Flag.'[85]

The intervention of the Aligarh boys tilted the balance in several constituencies.[86] In Hardoi, the League candidate secured 'a walk-over by hundreds over the Nationalist candidate due to the selfless work of the Muslim university students';[87] in Meerut, some 500 students made a difference.[88] Liaquat Ali Khan conceded that they had 'contributed largely towards the success which we have achieved in the elections'.[89] The final tribute came from Jinnah himself. 'I have been following the wonderful work that the Aligarh boys have done,' he wrote, 'you have proved what I said, that Aligarh is the arsenal of Muslim India.'[90]

IV

Students alone did not form the arsenal of the League. Jinnah was also backed by the university administration, headed by Ziauddin and his two influential colleagues: A.B.A. Haleem, chairman of the History department and pro-vice-chancellor since February 1935, and Obaidur Rahman Khan Sherwani, member of the UP legislative assembly and the university treasurer.[91] Ziauddin ruled Aligarh with an iron hand, organized factions, stifled dissent, and employed coercive methods to curb Congress activists.[92] Allied with the colonial government whose interests he served in public life, the Cambridge-educated administrator had been a relentless critic of the non-cooperation campaign in Aligarh.[93] In the 1930s, he sought the moral support of Fazl-i-Husain and the Aga Khan to isolate the AISF and the Congress activists.[94] The Aga Khan concurred. 'I have never looked upon Aligarh or UP', wrote the Khoja leader, 'as the leadership [*sic*] of Islam but I do understand here with its geographical position midway between Pakistan and Bengal how important it is that the Congress should not capture our Centre.'[95] In 1936, Ziauddin denied admission to the organizers of a students' strike, led by Ali Sardar Jafri, Jalil Abbasi, Khalilul Rab and Zamir Siddiqi, for his mission was to 'suppress their feelings of nationalism and patriotism'.[96] A similar fate awaited other students 'with progressive social and political views'.[97] In September 1938, one of them was found guilty of agitating against the authorities and for publishing a pamphlet against a provost and some staff members.[98] He could thus boast that the Congress was lying low in Aligarh, and that he had advised students 'to boycott every person who misleads the Mussalmans'.[99] He reaffirmed his loyalty to Jinnah in August 1947, claiming that he had been working for him for nearly a decade and that he would cheerfully follow his command. To serve the 'national cause', he offered to resign the vice-chancellorship and the legislative assembly membership.[100] But his offer came a bit late in the day. A massive student agitation, led by a group of militant Leaguers who accused the vice-chancellor for disrupting their activities and turning the university into a 'hot-bed of intrigues',[101] led to his resignation on 26 December 1946. Having used students on many previous occasions to consolidate his own personal gains, Ziauddin eventually paid a price for his own machinations. His reinstatement, the honorary secretary of the students' union told Jinnah, 'will be a great betrayal of this university and the Muslim youth'.[102]

Closely allied with Ziauddin were teachers like Jamiluddin Ahmad, lecturer in English and convenor of the committee of writers of the League; M.B. Mirza, a zoologist with a D. Phil. from Frankfurt (1927-8), provost of Aftab Hall (1942-4), and dean of the science faculty;[103] Abdus Sattar Kheiri, who headed the pro-German group in Aligarh;[104] and Muhammad Afzal Husain Qadri, a Cambridge graduate, member of the League and the Aligarh-based education sub-committees.[105] Qadri was involved in making proposals for 'a whole-hearted and more effective struggle' in realizing the ideal of Pakistan.[106] Education was his main concern. 'You have given them [Muslims] the lead to become a consolidated nation,' he wrote to Jinnah, 'and to struggle for an independent national existence. It is for you now, Sir, to give them the lead for their future being and advancement also, viz., Muslims should have throughout their own system of education, and they should have their own separate institutions, *so far as possible*.'[107]

The insistence on a new education policy was designed to counter the Wardha scheme of basic education, devised by Zakir Husain and blessed by Gandhi. Though the idea was to combine manual work with mental training and shift the emphasis from mere literary to vocational efficiency, the League propagandists dubbed the scheme as a diabolical plot designed to 'de-Islamize the Muslim nation',[108] destroy Muslim culture, and impose the domination of the Congress. So that Qadri, who published an alternative scheme for primary Muslim education in 1940,[109] claimed to have succeeded in establishing its 'evil effects' and, at the same time, persuading Muslims to plan and run their own system of education.[110]

Around the same time, some Aligarh scholars mooted several schemes of Muslim autonomy within the Indian federation and of independent Muslim states. In August 1939, Qadri and Zafarul Hasan, the philosophy professor, came up with an extraordinarily naive and unrealistic proposal for the Indian Muslims—'a nation by themselves'—who faced the cheerless prospect of being enslaved into a single all-India federation with an overwhelming Hindu majority at the Centre. They demanded a repartition of India 'on the only fundamental and valid principle of division, viz., Nationality, and to get India divided into Muslim India and Hindu India'. They proposed three sovereign states in British India: north-west or Pakistan, Bengal, and Hindustan. The principalities within these states or exclusively on the frontier of one of them would be attached automatically, while those adjoining more than one state had to choose their attachment. But Hyderabad must recover Berar and Karnatak, and with its restored territories, become a fourth sovereign state, 'the southern wing of Muslim India'. Pakistan would include the four north-western provinces, Kashmir and other adjacent states, Bengal would embrace the existing province, including the districts of Purnea and Sylhet but excluding the districts of Howrah, Midnapur, and Darjeeling. Both Pakistan and Bengal would be Muslim states. Hindustan would compromise the rest of India but within it two new autonomous provinces—Delhi and Malabar—should be formed, with strong Muslim minorities. The three states would have separate treaties of alliance with Britain and a joint court of arbitration to settle dispute between themselves or between them and the Crown.[111]

The Hasan-Qadri scheme (Appendices 11.1 and 11.2) was endorsed by ten Aligarh professors, who felt that it 'offered the right outline on which the future India must be reconstituted', and satisfied the 'just claims of the two nations inhabiting India'. 'It appears', they continued, 'as if Providence has in His mercy offered an opportunity to Muslims of India to launch a reasonable plan of political partition—*political partition* which is the only solution of their problem. *It is our bounden duty to fight for it to a man.*' A few months later, two of them—Zakiuddin and Burhan Ahmad—joined Zafarul Hasan and Ubaidullah Durrani, leaders of the Khaksar organization in Aligarh, in repudiating Gandhi's criticism of the two-nation theory. In their statement, they pointed out that neither the fear of British bayonets nor the prospect of a bloody civil war would weaken their determination to achieve 'free Muslim states' in Muslim-majority areas. It is noteworthy that Jinnah relied upon this Aligarh petition for selecting the rhetoric of his classic exposition of the two-nation theory.[112]

In the wake of India's Partition, Zafarul Hasan, Qadri, Haleem, Noman, and Jamiluddin Ahmed, who had voted for the creation of a state whose constitution and political life would be Islamic, joined hundreds of Aligarh students on the long trek to Pakistan. With their goal accomplished, they could draw comfort from their own part in its making.

V

After Independence and Partition, the university at Aligarh was left rudderless with some of its well-known teachers rushing to Karachi in search of greener pastures. The number of students dropped from 2,497 in 1946-7 to 1,753 a year later.[113] Those who stayed behind in India had a rough time, for it was not easy to disentangle the institution from its Muslim League past. They were harassed and harangued, and called upon to prove their loyalty. For years, wild rumours were afloat of Pakistani officials recruiting students to the army, of arms and ammunition being stored on the campus, and of bombs being recovered from the hostels. Demands were also made in the UP assembly and parliament to close down the university. But Nehru, India's first prime minister, and Azad, the education minister, resisted the Hindu communalist onslaught. In 1948, Nehru persuaded Zakir Husain to quit the Jamia Millia Islamia and join the Aligarh University as its vice-chancellor. This was a smart move, for Zakir Husain proved to be extremely successful in fulfilling the demands of his new assignment. He worked imaginatively and creatively, revived the dampened spirits of teachers and students alike, isolated the last remnants of the Muslim League ideology, and placed the university on a sound footing.

In 1947, Aligarh had four faculties and twenty-one departments; in 1964, there were seven faculties and 5,000 students. Today, the number of students has risen to well over 17,200 with a teaching faculty strength of 1,209, seventy-six departments and four colleges, including those for medicine and engineering. The non-plan expenditure exceeds Rs. 6,048 lakh.

There is little doubt that the university has surged ahead, despite many setbacks, in its quest to establish its distinct identity and meet the educational needs of the Muslim communities. Though its overall academic performance has been patchy in many areas and violence and discipline have marred campus life in recent decades, the institution has expanded vastly since Independence. Aligarh graduates, who were once tempted to seek employment in neighbouring Pakistan, are now comfortably placed in business, industry and the professions in India and elsewhere. Go to a district town in UP and you see the familiar sight of BA (Alig.). Travel to Birmingham in England or Cleveland in the United States and you will find the Aligarh Old Boys' Association listed in the telephone directory. Here and elsewhere, far removed from the humdrum of campus life, the 'Aligarians' regard themselves as a closely-knit community. Whether in Sydney or in Toronto, they congregate every year on 17 October to celebrate 'Sir Saiyid Day', fraternize with each other wearing the black *achkan* (*sherwani*) with the university monogram, recall the festive occasion brought by the annual exhibition held in the civil lines in close proximity to the district jail, revive memories of the years spent in Sir Saiyid, Viqarul Mulk or the Mohsinul Mulk Hall, and take much pride in being part of the Old Boy network.

Aligarh has so far negotiated with its past and succeeded in creating a niche for itself in the country's academic structures. And yet, it faces the uphill task of preparing the fraternity of teachers and students to meet the challenges of the next millennium. It needs to complete Saiyid Ahmad's unfinished agenda of fostering liberal and modernist ideas and take the lead, once and for all, in debating issues of education, social reforms and gender justice. It needs to interpret Islam afresh in the light of world-wide intellectual currents, respond to the winds of change just as the Saiyid had done, guide the 120 million Muslims, and equip them to cope with the harsh realities of life. This is what the great visionary Saiyid Ahmad would have expected it to do. With the Jamia Millia Islamia, its closest counterpart, unable to rise to the occasion during its lazy existence since Independence, the university can no longer shirk its responsibilities.

abhi manazil-i dasht-o-daman kuch aur bhi hain

NOTES

1. *The Memoirs of Aga Khan: World Enough and Time*, London, 1954, pp. 34-5; see also, *A History of the Freedom Movement*, Karachi, 1970, Vol. 4, pp. 249-99.
2. For accounts of politics in Aligarh during these years, see K.M. Ashraf, 'Aligarh ki siyasi zindagi', *Aligarh Magazine* (Special issue: Aligarh Number), 1953-4–1954-5, pp. 163-6; Khaliquzzaman, *Pathway to Pakistan*, pp. 17, 21; Hasan, *Mohamed Ali: Ideology and Politics*, pp. 17-20; R.A. Siddiqui; *Ashufta Bayani*

Meri, New Delhi, 1977 edn.; Mukhtar Zaman, *Students' Role in the Freedom Movement*, Karachi, 1978; Hasan (ed.), *Mohamed Ali in Indian Politics*, Vol. 1.

3. A sum of Rs. 6,000 was raised by January 1920 and handed over to the Central Khilafat Committee. Mushtaq Husain to principal, 17 Jan. 1920, File No. 62-B, Sir Saiyid Academy (hereafter SSA), Aligarh Muslim University, Aligarh.
4. For the impact of the non-cooperation, see S.Y. Shah, *Higher Education and Politics in Colonial India*, New Delhi, 1996, pp. 256-9.
5. K.G. Saiyadain, *Gandhian Idea on Education: Their Relevance to our Times*, New Delhi, n.d., pp. 6-7; S.M. Tonki, *Aligarh and Jamia: Fight for National Education*, New Delhi, 1983, p. 50.
6. *CWMG*, Vol. 18, p. 369.
7. Proceedings of the Syndicate meeting, 10 Oct. 1920, File No. I/1, 1920-1, SSA.
8. D. Lelyveld, 'Three Aligarh Students: Aftab Ahmad Khan, Ziauddin Ahmad and Muhammad Ali', *MAS*, Vol. 9, 2, 1975, p. 238.
9. M.A. Husain to Ziauddin, 24 Oct. 1920, SSA.
10. Nurul Hasan to Ziauddin, n.d., ibid.
11. Home Poll. A. Dec. 1920, 210-16 and K.W., NAI. According to Sheikh Muhammad Abdullah, a strong critic of the non-cooperation movement, 700 students left the college. *Mushahidaat wa Tasuraat*, Aligarh, 1969, p. 295. On 27 Oct., 14 graduates, 37 4th year, 21 3rd year, 52 2nd year and 35 1st year students wrote to the principal as 'firm adherents of the non-cooperation movement'. Tonki, *Aligarh and Jamia*, p. 72.
12. K.G. Saiyadain, 'Aligarh—A Retrospect and a Prospect', in Saiyid Muhammad (ed.), *The Aftabs' Memoirs Special*, Aligarh, 1975-6, p. 55.
13. Abbas, *I am not on Island*, pp. 50-1.
14. Tofail Ahmad, *The Solution of the Indian Communal Problem*, Aligarh, 1931, p. 2. Notice that Tofail Ahmad also wrote the *Mussalmanon ka Raushan Mustaqbil*, published in 1937, which was a sympathetic exposition of the principles of Indian nationalism.
15. He was appointed editor for the session 1937-8. A notification to this effect was issued by the pro-vice-chancellor after much deliberation. File No. 7/18, 1937-8 (Academic), SSA.
16. *Aligarh Magazine* (English), Jan.-Aug. 1930, pp. 56-7; Abbas, *I am not an Island*, pp. 59, 66.
17. K.R. Azmi, 'Urdu Shair wa Adab me Aligarh ka hissa', in Naseem Qureshi, *Aligarh Tehrik: Aghaaz ta Imroz*, Aligarh, 1960, pp. 313-53. Note that Majaz wrote poems like *Inqilab* (Revolution), *Sarmayadari* (Capitalism), *Khwab-i Sehar* (Dream of Tomorrow) which echoed the political trends in Aligarh. Ehtisham Husain, 'Majaz: Fikro-o-fan ke chand pahlu', *Aligarh Magazine 1955*, in A.K. Ķasimi (ed.), *Intikhab Number 1975-76*.
18. Saiyid Muhammad Tonki, in Horst Kruger (ed.), *Kunwar Muhammad Ashraf: An Indian Scholar and Revolutionary 1903-1962*, Berlin, 1966, p. 344.

19. Nasim Ansari, 'Aligarh Muslim University, 1935-1947: Recollections of a Student', in Parshotam Mehra, Narayani Gupta and Rajiv Lochan (eds.), *Society, Religion and the State: Identity Crisis in Indian History*, New Delhi, n.d., p. 94.
20. Ibid., pp. 94, 98.
21. M.A. Zuberi, *Ziya-i Hayat*, Karachi, n.d., p. 160.
22. As 'ring-leaders' of the strike Ali Sardar Jafri and Jalil Abbasi were refused admission in 1937. The latter, according to the pro-vice-chancellor, was 'guilty of repeated acts of indiscipline, and was repeatedly reprimanded, warned and forgiven'. A.B.A. Haleem to K.M. Ashraf, 5 Oct. 1937, File No. 12, 1937, AICC papers. Jafri eventually completed his degree at the Lucknow University.
23. Its founder at Aligarh were Muhammad Noman, Abul Lais Siddiqui, and Ali Jawaad. The AIMSF was formed to counter the activities of the Congress and the AISF, and to 'create a common platform for the Muslim students of the universities and colleges in all the provinces of the country with a view to bringing about closer social contact, better cultural, political, economic and religious understanding, and a deeper sense of common relationship'.
24. *Indian Annual Register*, July-Dec. 1937, Vol. 2, p. 466. The first session of the AIMSF was held in Calcutta on 27-8 Dec. 1937. Jinnah presided.
25. The UP League conference was held in Gorakhpur on 18 Mar. 1939 with nawab Muhammad Ismail Khan as president. A month later, the Meerut division of the League held its conference chaired by Jinnah. On 8 Apr., the raja of Mahmudabad chaired the Delhi provincial Muslim League conference. See *IAR*, Jan.-Mar. 1938, Vol. 1, p. 372.
26. The number of students in Mar. 1940 was 1,717. Registrar to Director of Public Instruction, UP, 24 Sept. 1940, File No. 8/2, 1940-1, SSA.
27. Smith, *Modern Islam in India*, pp. 181-2.
28. Statement by M.M. Sayeed, 16 Nov. 1937, File No. 7/5, 1937-8 (Academic), SSA.
29. Haleem to F.J. Fielden, 29 Aug. 1941 and 29 Nov. 1941, File No. 7/18, 1941-2 (Academic), SSA.
30. Smith, *Modern Islam in India*, pp. 181-2.
31. Jinnah and Liaquat Ali Khan were invited by the Students' Union in Apr. 1940. Their visit was followed by that of Zafar Ali Khan, Rizwanullah, secretary of the UP Provincial League, and other Muslim League leaders. Report by Muhammad Mohsin Siddiqui, honorary secretary, students' union, 2 Dec. 1940, File No. 51, 1940-1 (Executive), SSA.
32. Zaman, *Students' Role in the Pakistan Movement*, p. 49.
33. Masoodul Hasan, 'Some Glimpses of the University in the Forties', Saiyid Muhammad (ed.), *The Aftabs' Memoirs Special*, p. 69.
34. Zaman, *Students' Role in the Freedom Movement*, p. 49.
35. Fasihuddin Ahmad to Jinnah, 5 Dec. 1942, Jinnah to Fasihuddin, 9 Dec. 1942, *The Quaid-e-Azam Papers*, Lahore, 1976, p. 247.

36. The membership of the University Muslim League rose to 1600 in 1944. Freedom Movement Archives, University of Karachi, Vol. 356, part xiii. M. Mukhtar Azad to Jinnah, 23 Sept. 1942, ibid., p. 241.
37. For instance, Saiyid Hamid, 'Iqbal and Politics', *Aligarh Magazine* (English), Special Number, 1939-40, 48, 1, p. 305; Ashkar Husain, 'Hindustan ke siyasi ikhtilaf ka haal', Mar. 1944, 22, 1, p. 60; Muhammad Afzal Mahmood, 'Pakistan ka iqtisadi wa siyasi pahlu', pp. 70-1, 79, ibid.; Jamiluddin Ahmad, *Indian Constitutional Tangle*, Lahore, 1941; *Is India one Nation?*, Aligarh, 1939; Muhammad Noman, *Muslim India: Rise and Growth of the All India Muslim League*, Allahabad, 1942.
38. Nasim Ansari, op. cit., p. 95.
39. *Aligarh Magazine* (English), 1943-4, 52, p. i.
40. Zaman, *Students' Role in the Freedom Movement*, p. 48.
41. Khaliquzzaman, *Pathway to Pakistan*, p. 195.
42. *Aligarh Magazine* (in Urdu), Mar. 1939, 17, 1, p. 6; *History of the Freedom Movement*, Vol. IV, pp. 1-50.
43. Muhammad Noman, *Whither India?* Serial No. 1, n.d.
44. Mohamed Ali, *My Life: A Fragment*, p. 22.
45. *Nationalism and Communal Politics in India*, Chap. Six.
46. Adhikari (ed.), *Documents of the History of the Communist Party of India*, Vol. 2, p. 210.
47. Ibid., p. 211.
48. In a message to the Aligarh MSF, Jinnah referred to his speech in which he appealed to the Muslim intelligentsia to 'take off your coats' and 'sacrifice all that you can and work selflessly, earnestly and sincerely' for the Muslim community. To S.A.M. Naqshbandi, 6 Dec. 1941, Sharifuddin Pirzada (ed.), *Quaid-e-Azam Correspondence*, Karachi, 1977, Vol. 2, p. 182.
49. According to Athar Parvez, then a student at Aligarh, Jinnah was worshipped (*parastish*) in Aligarh around 1941. At that time there were just a few nationalists among students, none enlisted among teachers. *Aligarh se Aligarh tak*, New Delhi, 1977, pp. 28, 31. In April 1942, the University Court decided to confer upon Jinnah the Honorary Degree of Doctor of Law. Jinnah, however, refused to accept the honour of the plea 'that I have lived as plain Mr Jinnah and I hope to die as plain Mr Jinnah. I am very much verse to and title or honours and I will be more happy if there was no prefix to my name.' Jinnah to Ziauddin Ahmad, 4 Oct. 1942, Shamsul Hasan Collection (hereafter SHC), Karachi University Archives, Karachi.
50. Harry Haig spoke of Khaliquzzaman's 'manoeuvres' in his correspondence with the viceroy, especially on the eve of Ministry-making in UP. To Linlithgow, 7 May 1937, Haig papers.
51. Nehru to Khaliquzzaman, 27 June 1937, S. Gopal (ed.), *SWJN*, Vol. 8, pp. 135, 142.
52. Ibid., 1 July 1937, p. 144.
53. Khaliquzzaman, *Pathway to Pakistan*, p. 195.

54. Address presented to Harry Haig, 27 Jan. 1937, *Addresses and Speeches relating to Aligarh Muslim University, Aligarh, from January 1920 to June 1937*, Aligarh, 1937, p. 67.
55. P.D. Reeves, 'Landlords and Party Politics in the United Provinces, 1934-7', in Low (ed.), *Soundings in Modern South Asian History*, p. 272.
56. Haig to Linlithgow, 5 May 1937, Haig papers.
57. Reeves, op. cit., p. 273.
58. Ibid.
59. To Jinnah, 14 Jan. 1946, SHC.
60. The writer Rasheed Ahmad Siddiqi, for example, was unhappy at the deterioration in Hindu-Muslim relations. In his reminiscences (*Apni Yaaden*), published in the *Aligarh Magazine* of March 1944, he regretted that the two communities asserted their communal rights as opposed to the national interests.
61. Ashraf listed a number of writers, poets, and political activists who belonged to Congress, Socialist and Communist circles. Ashraf, 'Aligarh awr Siyasat-i Hind', op. cit., p. 191. See also Ansari, op. cit., p. 102.
62. Jamiluddin Ahmad to Jinnah, 1 Jan. 1943, SHC.
63. Hasan, *Legacy of a Divided Nation*, pp. 112-3.
64. Jinnah to Jamiluddin Ahmad, 9 Jan. 1943, ibid.
65. *Aligarh Magazine*, 1943-4, p. 109.
66. The two well-known pamphleteers were Muhammad Numan and Jamiluddin Ahmad.
67. For instance, sixty 'National Guards' were raised at Aligarh to attend the Karachi session of the Muslim League in 1943. *Aligarh Magazine*, 1943-4, p. iv.
68. Statement by Jamiluddin Ahmad, n.d., SHC.
69. Zaman, *Students' Role in the Freedom Movement*, p. 45.
70. Ibid., p. 46.
71. Muhammad Habib, 'An Introduction to the Study of Medieval India, 1000-1400 A.D.', *Aligarh Magazine*, Jan.-Mar. 1931, pp. 5-20.
72. Ibid., Mar. 1944, p. 60.
73. *National States and National Minorities* (Pakistan Literature Series No. 1, Lahore, 1945).
74. *Minutes of the Annual Meeting of the University Court*, 7 Apr. 1940, p. 20.
75. Ziauddin also wrote pamphlets dealing with the administration of railways, financial and economic policies, and the development of industries in the Pakistan area. Ziauddin to Jinnah, 17 Aug. 1946, SHC. The election committee consisted of M.B. Mirza, chairman, Ubaidur Rahman Khan Sherwani, Manzar-i Alam, president of the Muslim University Muslim League, and Jamiluddin Ahmad, convenor.
76. For details of the mobilization campaign, see *Legacy of a Divided Nation: India's Muslims Since Independence*, Chap. 3.

77. Iqbal Masud to Jinnah, 24 Sept. 1945; M.A. Humayun to Jinnah, 16 Aug. 1946, SHC.
78. Ziauddin also wrote pamphlets dealing with the administration of railways, financial and economic policies, and the development of industries in the Pakistan area. Ziauddin to Jinnah, 17 Aug. 1946, SHC. The election committee consisted of M.B. Mirza, chairman, Obaidur Rahman Khan Sherwani, Manzar-i Alam, president of the Muslim University Muslim League, and Jamiluddin Ahmad, convenor.
79. I.A. Talbot, 'Deserted Collaborators: Political Background to the Rise and Fall of the Punjab Unionist Party, 1923-1947', *The Journal of Imperial and Commonwealth History*, Oct. 1982, Vol. XI, 1, f.n. 44, p. 93.
80. *Dawn*, 19 Dec. 1945.
81. Ibid.
82. Jamiluddin Ahmad to Jinnah, 1 Dec. 1945, SHC. An activist claimed: 'We have gone into the mohallas, villages, and even to the houses and have left some abiding impressions.' Qadir to Jinnah, 28 Nov. 1945, SHC.
83. Manzar-i Alam to Jinnah, 17 Dec. 1945, ibid.
84. Manzar-i Alam to Jinnah, 16 Jan. 1946, ibid.
85. Baber Mirza to Jinnah, 8 Feb. 1946, ibid.
86. For detailed reports of electioneering conducted by Aligarh students and teachers, see *Dawn*, 1, 9, 11, 12, 22, 27, 30, 31 Dec. 1945.
87. Ibid., 3 Dec. 1945.
88. Ali Ahmad Faziel to Jinnah, 2 Dec. 1945, SHC.
89. Liaquat Ali Khan to Manzar-i Alam, 2 Dec. 1945; K.R. Khan, offg. secy., UP, Muslim League Parliamentary Board, to Manzar-i Alam, 28 Nov. 1945, ibid.
90. Jinnah to Zahid Husain, 5 Dec. 1945, ibid.
91. As the acting vice-chancellor, he asked Jinnah to lay the foundation stone of the proposed medical college and hospital. To Jinnah, 23 Feb. 1947, in Zaidi (ed.), p. 71.
92. He was in constant touch with the lieutenant-governor's and kept them posted with the developments on the campus. His role in the university affairs was far from exemplary. As the pro-vice-chancellor, he led a faction against Aftab Ahmad Khan, the vice-chancellor (1924-9). In a pamphlet circulated in December 1926, Aftab Ahmad Khan observed: 'I tried my best to work with him [Ziauddin] but bitter experience has opened my eyes as it has shown me the other side of his personality.' *Aligarh Mail*, 19 Feb. 1927; *The Aligarh of Today*, Aligarh, n.d., pp. 4, 64. The Rahimtoola Enquiry Committee (1927) also indicted Ziauddin and referred to his use of Aligarh as a 'stepping stone to political advancement'. The root cause of the 'Present Discontent', according to the committee, was the personal differences between Aftab Ahmad Khan and Ziauddin, irregularities and disregard of the Act, Statutes and Regulations prompted by the 'interests of petty faction and intrigue' and the appointment of 'a large proportion of men of insufficient academic qualifications'. *Report of the AMU Enquiry Committee*, Oct. 1927, Aligarh, n.d. This

led to Ziauddin's resignation in Apr. 1925. But he turned to Aligarh to continue his intrigues against the new vice-chancellor S.R. Masood (1929-32). A severe indictment of Ziauddin was made by Faiyaz Khan, member of the University Court and the UP legislative council. In his letter of resignation from the University Court, he stated: 'I have been watching with concern the affairs of the Aligarh Muslim University since the days of the Rahimtoola Committee, which put its finder on the right spot, when it diagnosed that the main cause of the decadence of Aligarh was the factious spirit which you, as pro-vice-chancellor, were largely responsible for creating in the life of the University.' To Ziauddin, 5 Sept. 1942, Freedom Movement Archives, University of Karachi.

93. Hasan, *Nationalism and Communal Politics in India*, pp. 182-3.
94. Zuberi, *Ziya-i Hayat*, p. 170.
95. The Aga Khan to Fazl-i-Husain, 14 Jan. 1936, Waheed Ahmad (ed.), *Letters of Mian Fazl-i-Husain*, Lahore, 1976, p. 481.
96. 'Appeal' (Printed), p. 19, File No. 13, 1937, AICC papers.
97. Ashraf to A.B.A. Haleem, 26 July 1937. Ashraf tried to raise the issue in the legislative assembly through his friend, Husain Zaheer. Ashraf to Husain Zaheer, 3 Aug. 1937, ibid. The extent to which the authorities were sensitive to the Congress movement is evident from the fact that they kept a close watch on the contents of books distributed by the students' union as prizes for debating competitions. Note by S.M. Ahsan, registrar, 25 May 1939, File No. 7/5, 1939-40 (Academic), SSA.
98. A.B.A. Haleem to M.A. Ghani, 30 Sept. 1938, File No. 1/4, 1938-9, ibid.
99. Ziauddin to Jinnah, 30 Nov. 1945, SHC.
100. Ziauddin to Jinnah, 17 Aug. 1946, ibid.
101. Ghayurul Islam to Jinnah, n.d., ibid., and Abid Ahmedali to Jinnah, 20 February 1947, in Z.H. Zaidi (ed.), *Quaid-i Azam Muhammad Ali Jinnah Papers: Prelude to Pakistan*, Vol. 1, part 1, Islamabad, 1993, pp. 4-6.
102. 22 Feb. 1947, ibid., p. 42.
103. Baber Mirza, married to a German lady, was suspected to be the chief link in the Nazi-Khaksar connection. According to the intelligence department, he gave a pro-Nazi lecture in Aligarh after returning from Germany in December 1938. This was published as 'Modern Germany—A Lesson to India' in the Muslim University League Publication Series. Towards the end of March 1939, he stated that Germany would soon be the liberator of India. Home Poll. File No. 21/65, 1939, NAI; Home Poll. File No. 111, 1940, NAI.
104. The 'red-hot' Nazi in Aligarh was Abdus Sattar Kheiri. He was involved in pro-German propaganda for which he received funds and literature through the Allianz and Stuttgarter Insurance Bank and other agencies. He launched *The Spirit of Time* in June 1938, which was 'anti-Communist, pro-Muslim and pro-Nazi in tone'. Home Poll. File No. 21/65, 1939, NAI. Sattar and his German wife, Fatima, were detained in Sept. 1940. The League pressed for their release; so did Jinnah who wrote to Maurice Mallet, lieutenant-

governor of UP, on 12 Oct. and 28 Nov. 1943. The Kheiris were released in Oct. 1944. See Saiyid Shamsul Hasan, *Plain Mr Jinnah*, Karachi, 1976, pp. 266-7.

105. Qadri, a resident of Budaun, was educated in Aligarh. He joined the University of Cambridge in 1936 and wrote a thesis on 'The Development of Locusts and Allied Insects' in May 1938 with the distinguished scientist, I.D. Imms. His research work at the Cavendish Laboratory was highly commended.
106. Qadri to Jinnah, 4 Feb. 1943, ibid.
107. Qadri to Jinnah, 5 Dec. 1943, ibid.
108. Qadri to Jinnah, 22 Nov. 1943, *Quaid-e-Azam papers*, p. 161.
109. Ibid.
110. Qadri to Jinnah, 28 Apr. 1943, SHC.
111. This summary is based on R.J. Moore, 'Jinnah and the Pakistan Demand', *MAS*, July 1982, Vol. 17, 4, Oct. 1983, pp. 541-2.
112. Ibid., p. 546.
113. *Report of the AMU Enquiry Committee*, Aligarh, 1961, p. 13.

APPENDIX 11.1

CONFIDENTIAL

DR AFZAL H. QADRI'S SCHEME

The Problem of Indian Muslims and Its Solution

The Government of India Act of 1935 and therein the proposed All India Federation as well as the partial working out of it in the form of Provincial Autonomy have brought the Muslims of India face to face with the gravest danger, viz., the annihilation of their specific national identity.

There is little need of explaining at length what this Act means. It hurls down the 90 million Muslims of India under the heels of the perpetual domination of a Hindu majority at the Centre, reduces the Muslim majority provinces to the status of mere vassals and leaves the Muslim minority provinces entirely at the mercy of the Hindu majority. Its fundamental fault is that it does not recognize the undeniable fact that the Muslims of India are a Nation distinct from Hindus, vitally opposed to the latter in their outlook and aspirations and incapable of being merged into any other so-called nation, Hindu or no Hindu.

The London Times (India No., 1 April 1937) commenting on the Government of India Act of 1935 wrote that undoubtedly the difference between Muslims and Hindus is not merely that of religion in the strict sense of the word, but also that of law and culture—that they may be said indeed to represent two entirely distinct and separate civilizations; however in the course of time the superstitions will die out and India will be moulded into a single nation. To this homily of the *London Times* one cannot but demur, for the 'superstitions' that shall have to die out are exactly the characteristic features of the Islamic culture and the contributions of Islam to India; without the shadow of a doubt the All India Federation will, within the space of a generation, bring about total annihilation of the specific Islamic outlook, culture, and language and will mould the Muslims after the will of the Hindus. Unequivocal signs of this are making themselves felt in the Muslim Mass-Contact programme of the Indian National Congress as well as the various educational schemes like the Vidya Mandir and the Wardha schemes, the drive for Hindi, and other

* A.H. Qadri collection, Vol. I, Box No. 25, Freedom Movement Archives, Karachi, University of Karachi.

urban and rural movements recently inaugurated under the auspices of that nationally-minded [*sic*] body.

Therefore, it is absolutely obligatory on us, the Muslims, that we must do our utmost to save our national identity in India and to safeguard our interests. We must win independence and equality for Muslims and should in no case acquiesce in their subjugation, whether planned by Hindus or the British, or even if agreed to by certain Hinduized anti-British Muslims.

To realize this great object I beg to offer, in the following, a scheme for your careful consideration. But before coming to it I must state the principles on which it is based. I am convinced that we Muslims of India must insist persistently and strenuously on them, namely,

1. That the Muslims of India are a nation by themselves—they have a distinct national entity wholly different from the Hindus and other non-Muslim groups; indeed, they are more different from the Hindus than the Sudetan Germans were from the Czechs;
2. That the Muslims of India have got a separate national future and their own contribution to make to the betterment of the world;
3. That the future of the Muslims of India lies in complete freedom from the domination of the Hindus, the British, or for the matter of that, any other people;
4. That the Muslim majority provinces cannot be permitted to be enslaved into a single All India Federation with an overwhelming Hindu majority in the Centre; and
5. That the Muslims in the minority provinces shall not be allowed to be deprived of their separate religious, cultural and political identity, and that they shall be given full and effective support by the Muslim majority provinces.

Now, in order to save the Muslim Nation in India we have to demand a repartition of India on the only fundamental and valid principle of division, viz., Nationality, and to get India divided into Muslim India and Hindu India further we must do all we can to safeguard the interests of our nationals living in Hindu India. On this principle British India must be divided into three wholly independent and sovereign states.

1. North-West India, including the Punjab, the N.W.F. Province, Sindh, and Baluchistan;
2. Bengal, including the adjacent district of Purnea (Bihar) and the Sylhet Division (Assam), but excluding the south-western districts of Howrah

and Midnapore (Burdwan) and the north-western district of Darjilling; and

3. Hindustan, comprehending the rest of British India. Inside Hindustan there must be formed two new autonomous provinces;

   (a) Delhi Province, including Delhi, Meerut Division, Rohilkhand Division and the district of Aligarh (Agra Division); and
   (b) Malabar Province, consisting of Malabar Coast. Further, all the *Towns* of Hindustan with a population of 50,000 or more shall have the status of a Borough or Free City.

Also, in Hindustan Muslims in *villages* shall have to live together in considerable numbers.

The Indian States: The Indian or native states included inside the boundaries of any of the above three proposed States or exclusively on the frontier of one of them, ought to be attached to that State.

Those bordering on more than one of the three States should have the option of joining any of the adjoining States.

Hyderabad with its old dominions Berar and Karnatik to be at sovereign state.

A map is herewith attached in which the proposed division of India is visualized. Some explanatory remarks may be added.

North-West India will include several native states, e.g. Qalat, Jammu and Kashmir, Bahawalpur, Khairpur, Patiala, Jhind, Nabha, Kapurthala, Malerkotla, Faridkot, and the Simla Hills States. With the inclusion of Kashmir it may well be called 'Pakistan' as it has been for some years past.

The Pakistan Federation will be a Muslim state. It will include about 25 millions of Muslims, i.e. more than 60 per cent of the total population. It is a self-sufficient unit on the basis of geographical, economical and political considerations. The realization of this federation will open a new and living future for the Muslims of India and will have a far-reaching effect on the whole of the Islamic world. The Pakistan will form the north-western wing of Muslim India.

The Hindus and Sikhs are the two non-Muslim minorities in Pakistan. They will have the same cultural, religious and political safeguards granted to them as the Muslims will have in Hindustan. It will be of greater advantage for the Sikhs to be in this State than in an All India Federation as envisaged by the Government of India Act of 1935, for they will be relatively in much larger proportion in their province and in the Centre.

The claim of Pakistan to form a separate federation cannot be challenged by any one on any reasonable ground; and if not conceded, the Muslims of these provinces will leave no stone unturned and will carry on the struggle by all means at their disposal until their goal is achieved.

The new Bengal will again be a Muslim State. It will contain more than 30 million Muslims, i.e. 57 per cent of the whole population. New Bengal can be entirely self-sufficient on account of its natural wealth and agricultural richness. It will be equal to France in area as well as in population. Because of having no component provinces, it will be no Federation. However, it will be a Sovereign State, having a status analogous to Burma, and will be the eastern wing of Muslim India.

Hindustan will be a Hindu State. It will have a population of 245 millions. It will include about 23 million Muslims, forming a minority of 10 per cent. It is our duty to safeguard their interests politically as far as it is at present possible. We must consequently insist on the formation of two new provinces inside Hindustan, one in the north and the other in the south, viz., Delhi and Malabar respectively.

In the newly constituted province of Delhi there will be more than 3.5 millions of Muslims, forming about 38 per cent of the total population. Indeed they will still be a minority. However they will be such an important minority as cannot easily be swept aside by the Hindu majority. Being highly cultured and educated as the Muslims of these parts are, and having their boundaries close to the Muslim Federation of Pakistan, they will be in a much stronger position to guard their interests than otherwise. Aligarh, the centre of Muslim education, must be included in this province, for we cannot afford to leave it unprotected inside the remaining portion of the U.P. which will be overwhelmingly Hindu.

The southern or Malabar province will comprise the southern part of Madras presidency especially that lying adjacent to Malabar Coast. This part is well populated by Muslims. There are about 1.4 million Muslims in it, forming about 27 per cent of the total population. They have large trading interests in this province and possess an eminent cultural position. Moreover, they are a virile race and being such an important minority can look after their interests far better than they can at present.

In Hindustan the Muslims largely live in cities and in considerable numbers, we cannot afford to leave them entirely at the mercy of the Hindu government. Therefore, it is necessary to protect their interests. Left to themselves they can fight their battle with the Hindus of those towns. All that can be done for them at present is to eliminate the undue interference of the provincial and central Hindu governments. This can well be done by giving the status of Free Cities or Boroughs to large towns of a population of 50,000 and more. They shall have their own police and magistracy, and they may have powers to legislate and execute on local manners to a large extent. In this way the interests of about 1.25 millions of Muslims of Hindustan can be protected.

The Muslims in the rural area of Hindustan must be persuaded not to remain scattered in neglegible minorities, as they do at present, in different villages. They must be induced to aggregate in villages with a preponderant Muslim population. In this way alone can their cultural as well as economical interests be protected. A number of useful and constructive programmes for social, educational and economical improvement may at once be launched in rural areas of Hindustan for the sake of this object as well as for the immediate amelioration of the conditions of Muslims residing therein.

The afore-mentioned three states of Pakistan, Bengal and Hindustan should enter into a defensive and offensive alliance on the following bases:

1. Mutual recognition and reciprocity.
2. That Pakistan and Bengal be recognized as the homelands of Muslims, and Hindustan as the homeland of Hindus, to which they can migrate respectively, if and when they want to do so.
3. In Hindustan the Muslims are to be recognized as a nation in minority and part of a larger nation inhabiting Pakistan and Bengal.
4. The Muslim minority in Hindustan and non-Muslim minorities in Pakistan and Bengal will have (i) representation according to population; and (ii) separate electorates and representations at every state, together with effective religious, cultural and political safeguards guaranteed by all the three states.

Note: Separate representation according to population may be granted to all considerable minorities in the three States, e.g. Sikhs, non-caste Hindus, etc.

5. The All India Muslim League will be the sole official representative body of the Muslims in Hindustan.

Each of these three independent states, Pakistan, Hindustan and Bengal will have separate treaties of alliance with the Great Britain and separate Crown Representatives, if any. They will have a joint Court of Arbitration to settle any dispute that may arise between themselves or between them and the Crown.

Hyderabad commands a position which is exclusive amongst Indian States. It is even now recognized as an ally by the British Government, and its Ruler addressed by the distinctive title of His Exalted Highness. In truth it is a sovereign state by treaties. Berar and Karnatik were taken from it by the British for administrative reasons. Now, when the British are giving the control of India to its rightful owners, they must return to Hyderabad its territories, and recognize Hyderabad expressly as a sovereign state, at least as sovereign as Nepal. Karnatik will restore a sea coast to Hyderabad, and Hyderabad will naturally become the southern wing of Muslim India.

Muslim University, Aligarh.

MOHD. AFZAL HUSAIN QADRI, M.Sc., Ph.D. (Alig.), Ph.D. (Cantab).

APPENDIX 11.2

Muslim University,
Aligarh.
.... September 1939

Dear Sir,

We beg to place before you our proposals about the problem of Indian Muslims and its solution. It is needless to assure you that they are the outcome of our most earnest efforts and extremely serious deliberations lasting over a number of years. The proposals mentioned below rest on the following fundamental theses, which we strongly believe admit of no alteration, if a just and honourable solution of the Hindu-Muslim problem is at all to be sought:

1. That the 90 millions Muslim of India constitute a distinct nation by themselves and as such must possess complete independence and the right of self-determination.
2. That the Muslim majority provinces are the embodiments of the hope and future of Muslims in India, and as such cannot be permitted to be enslaved in an All-India Federation under the perpetual domination of a Hindu majority in the centre.

*A.H. Qadri collection. The typescript of this representation includes the names of Abdus Sattar Kheiri and Syed Zafarul Hasan.

For permission to include these documents, I am obliged to the Director of the Freedom Movement Archives at the University of Karachi, Karachi.

3. That the future of Muslims in the minority provinces lies in their own determination to guard their separate political and cultural entity and the support they receive from their brethren in the majority provinces.
4. That the Hyderabad State represents the symbol of a thousand years old empire of Muslims in India. It is a sovereign State on the basis of every historical, political and constitutional consideration. The Muslims of India, therefore, cannot tolerate any attempt to undermine the sovereignty of H.E.H. the Nizam of Hyderabad.

We sincerely believe that our proposals will meet your approval and will enlist your fullest support and sympathy for the cause of our national future.

Your faithfullies,
The Authors.

We have carefully considered the 'Aligarh Scheme' as drafted by Professor Dr. Syed Zafarul Hasan and Dr. Afzal Husain Qadri, and fully discussed it with them in principle and in detail. We are convinced that it offers the right outline on which the future India must be reconstituted. It goes to satisfy as much the just claims of the two nations inhabiting India, viz., Muslims and Hindus, as seems to be apparently possible.

We have also studied the Scheme of Dr. Abdul Latif with sympathy and with care. However, we are afraid that Scheme does not satisfy the essential requirements of such a Scheme. Dr. Abdul Latif conceives of the whole of India as one political entity. That will necessarily give the Hindus overwhelming majority at the Centre and, therefore, effective sovereignty of the whole country. In one India, the Muslims, who shall be in a minority of 25 per cent scattered throughout the country, must but live as a subject nation. This cuts at the very root of all hope for Indian Muslims. They must in no case agree to it.

Further, Dr. Abdul Latif would create so many cultural zones and corridors by means of large scale migrations and thereby save Muslim culture. The idea is a pleasing one, but we do not think that such large scale migrations are practical politics. Moreover, to contemplate, in course of time, total denudation of Hindustan from Islamic influences by wholesale migration of Muslims, would contravene the very mission of Islam in this world and its spirit of expansion. However, the Aligarh Scheme does not exclude migration, if necessary; nor the creation of cultural zones, if feasible. It has room for and absorbs in itself this aspect of Dr. Abdul Latif's Scheme.

The Aligarh Scheme gives complete independence to 25 million Muslims in the north west, and 30 million Muslims in the east; while it provides semi-independence to 5 million Muslims in Malabar and around Delhi. Moreover, it procures respectable existence in Hindustan for about 13 lakhs of Muslims living in smaller towns. And for the remaining 22 million Muslims living in smaller towns and villages of Hindustan, the Scheme urges reasonable rights and safeguards which are calculated to make their existence self inside the ocean of Hindu population.

Now when the question of the constitution of India is most likely to be reopened the time is propitious for a new Scheme. It appears as if Providence has in His mercy offered an opportunity to Muslims of India to launch a reasonable plan of Political Partition—Political Partition which is the only solution of their problem. It is our bounden duty to fight for it to a Man.

The Aligarh Scheme seems to us to present the best solution of the problem, and we offer ourselves as the whole-hearted supporters of it.

Amiruddin Kedwaii,
B.A., L.L.B. (Alig.),
Hony Secretary,
All India Muslim Conference.

Dr. Zaki Uddin,
M.Sc. (Cantab), Ph.D. (Alig.),
Dr. Phil. (Bon.).

Umar Uddin
M.A., B.T. (Alig.).

Dr. Burhan Ahmad Faruqi,
M.A., Ph.D. (Alig.).

Zafar Ahmad Siddiqi,
M.A. (Alig.).

Jamil-uddin Ahmad,
M.A. (Alig.).

Masud Makhdum,
M.A. (Alig.).

Muddassir Ali Shamsee,
M.A., LL.B. (Alig.).

12

Memories of a Fragmented Nation: Rewriting the Histories of India's Partition

> Today I am asking Waris Shah to speak from the grave,
> To turn the page of the book of love.
> Once the daughter of the Punjab wept, and you wrote endlessly.
> Today Lakhs [1,00,000] of daughters are weeping
> and they are imploring you Waris Shah
> Get up, you who sympathise with our grief, get up and see your Punjab.
> Today there are corpses everywhere, and the Chenab is filled with blood.
> Somebody has mixed poison in all the five rivers,
> The rivers we use to water our fields. . . .

> When I think of Lahore, I go back to the days of my youth
> just before the Partition.
> Life then was so romantic, slow, deep and beautiful.
> Really, they were good times, they were great times.[1]

> I hope that one day . . . displaced families on both sides of the fence will at least be able to freely cross the borders and show their grandchildren where their grand parents had once lived and belonged. The day such a change comes about, I shall be the first to cross the Wagah or Hussainiwallah border posts to take my grand-daughter to Lahore, and show her the home of my youthful dreams – 91, Garden Town.[2]

The countdown to 15 August 1997, India's fiftieth year of Independence, generated an extraordinary interest in plotting the history of Partition.[3] One wonders why painful memories and traumatic experiences were revived on such an occasion, why the nostalgia, why the celebration of the dead?[4] Was it because there was not much to celebrate? Or did the occasion itself finally sensitize us to the painful legacy of a brutal past.

Amrita Pritam, the noted Punjabi writer who lived in Lahore before moving to Delhi in 1947 and whose celebrated poem quoted in the epigraph became one of the most influential and representative works of Partition, recalled: 'What I am against is religion—the Partition saw to that. Everything I had been taught—about morals, values and the importance of religion—was shattered. I saw, heard and read about so many atrocities committed in the name of religion that it turned me against any kind of religion. . . .'[5]

Sure enough, a common refrain in popular and scholarly writings was that the country's division was a colossal tragedy, and a man-made catastrophe brought about by hot-headed and cynical politicians who failed to grasp the implications of division along religious lines.[6] For a change, the focus was on the popular experiences of violence and displacement,[7] on the impact of Partition on the lives of hundreds of millions, including the trauma of women,[8] and the great variety of meanings they attached to the upheaval in and around their homes, fields and factories.[9] Indeed, the inclination to sideline the tall poppies in the debates expressed the growing disillusionment with high politics and its post-colonial practitioners.

The mood reflected in popular literature was decisively against the leaders and their inability to resolve their perennial disputes over power-sharing. Doubtless, the colonial government's role in heightening Hindu-Muslim rivalries and the implications of Bengal's partition in 1906 were recounted. So also the political blunders committed by Wavell (1883-1950) during his inglorious years in the viceregal lodge, the impetuousness of Mountbatten who revelled in his role as arbiter, the destiny of millions sitting light on him, the collapse of the law and order machinery which was kept in a state of readiness to protect the Europeans but not the hapless victims of a civil war, and, finally, the demarcation of the border by a British jurist who had neither been to India nor shown interest in Indian affairs.[10] 'Nothing could illustrate', commented the senior journalist Ajit Bhattacharjea, 'the callous haste with which Partition was pushed through more strikingly than the last-minute arrangements to demarcate the border.'[11]

According to the same writer, the onus nonetheless rested on the Indian leaders, many of whom ensured that the transfer of power was not delayed and were therefore 'unaware and uncaring of the human cost of cutting a border through the heart of populous provinces'.[12] Illustrating Nehru's 'lack of touch with grassroots reality' and his 'self-delusion' that Pakistan would be compelled by its limitations to return to the greater Indian fold,[13] Bhattacharjea recalled what Nehru told the author Leonard

Mosley. 'We were tired men', India's first prime minister said in 1960,

> and we were getting on in years too. Few of us could stand the prospect of going to prison again—and if we had stood out for a united India as we wished it, prison obviously awaited us. We saw the fires burning in the Punjab and heard of the killings. The plan of Partition offered a way out and we took it. . . . We expected that Partition would be temporary, that Pakistan was bound to come back to us.[14]

With the focus on high politics, the same old story does the rounds with unfailing regularity. The engagement continues to be with the 'major' political actors, who conducted their deliberations lazily in cosy surroundings and presided over the destiny of millions without their mandate. One is still encumbered with the details of what went wrong and who said what from the time the first Round Table Conference was held in London in 1930. Thanks to the publication of the voluminous transfer of power documents and the works of Gandhi, Nehru, Jinnah, Patel and Rajendra Prasad, the spotlight remains on the 'mystery' behind the protracted and tortuous negotiations triggered by the Cripps offer and the cabinet mission.[15] The bitter and acrimonious exchanges thereafter, which have all along dominated the historiography on nationalism, 'communalism' and 'Muslim separatism', continue to haunt present-day writers. The search for the 'guilty men', based on personal reflections/memories or the blunt testimony of the socialist leader Ram Manohar Lohia and the guarded 'revelations' of Maulana Azad, goes on relentlessly.[16] As a result, the historians' history of partition 'is not a history of the lives and experiences of the people who lived through that time, of the way in which the events of the 1940s were constructed in their minds, of the identities and uncertainties that partition created or reinforced'.[17]

These concerns are not so widely reflected in Pakistan, where the 'Partition issue', so to speak, was resolved well before 1947 by the weight of the two-nation theory.[18] The result is for everybody to see. Although Jinnah of Pakistan has been elevated to a high pedestal, he would remain, unless rescued from his uncritical admirers, a lonely figure in the pages of history and in the gallery of nation-builders. If the desire is to come to terms with his political engagement and explain his extraordinary success, it is not at all helpful to press him into service to establish Pakistan's identity as an Islamic State. Likewise, the use of religious symbols, long forsaken by that country's bureaucracy and military establishment, can hardly serve as the starting point for a meaningful dialogue on Partition.

The engagement of several writers in India, though sometimes marred by a majoritarian perspective, centres around secular nationalism, the main inspiration behind much of liberal-left activism from the 1920s onwards. Their chief concern, though nowadays pooh-poohed in the 'post-modernist' discourse, is to examine why the secular elites and their ideologues, whose presence is grudgingly recognized across the ideological divide, failed to mediate between those warring factions/groups who used religion as a cover to pursue their worldly goals and ambitions. While detailing the cynical games played out on the Indian turf by the British, the League, and the self-proclaimed 'nationalists' of every variety, they do not spare the Congress stalwarts, Gandhi, Nehru and Patel included, for failing to guide the movements they initiated away from the forces of reactionary communalism.[19] They marshal a wide array of sources to comment on Hindu communalists preventing the national movement from becoming truly inclusive. They also point to Gandhi's role in introducing religion into politics, the anti-Muslim proclivities of the Hindu right, led by Patel in the 1940s, the *Hindutva* agenda of the Hindu Mahasabha, the Arya Samaj, and the Rashtriya Swayam Sewak Sangh (RSS), and Nehru's arrogance and haughtiness in dealing with Jinnah and the Muslim League. At a time when the League was flexing its muscles, India's first prime minister is said to have jettisoned the plan for a Congress-League coalition in 1937 and dimmed the prospect of an enduring Hindu-Muslim coalition in Indian politics. The mainstay of the argument is that the country's vivisection could have been avoided had Nehru acted judiciously at such critical junctures in the 1940s.[20]

Though such impressions rest on questionable assumptions, they cannot be brushed aside.[21] The real difficulty lies with the grand narrative itself and the tendency to generalize on the basis of the actions of a few. While the grand narrative illuminates several facets of the Pakistan story, it fails to take into account the complexities and subtleties of institutional and structural changes introduced by the colonial government, as also the impact of socio-economic processes on caste, class, and religion-based alignments. One does not, moreover, get a sense of why the two-nation theory was floated in March 1940 and not earlier, why and how different forms of identities and consciousness got translated into a powerful campaign for a separate Muslim homeland, why Partition created ten million refugees, led to the death of over a million people, and resulted in sexual savagery, including the rape and abduction of 75,000 women.

Finally, the grand narrative does not reveal how the momentous happenings in August-September 1947 affected millions, uprooted from home and field and driven by sheer fear of death to seek safety across a line they had neither drawn nor desired. Clearly, the issue is not whether a million or more died or whether only 33 per cent of the country's population was affected by the communal eruption. The essential facts, as pointed out by the chief of the governor-general's staff, were that 'there is human misery on a colossal scale all around and millions are bereaved, destitute, homeless, hungry, thirst—and worst of all desperately anxious and almost hopeless about their future'.

In order to probe those areas which directly or indirectly impinged on the sudden and total breakdown of long-standing inter-community networks and alliances, it is necessary to locate the Partition debates outside the conference chambers. Without being swayed by the paradigms set by the two-nation theory or the rhetoric of Indian nationalism, it is important to examine why most people, who had so much in common and had lived together for generations, could turn against their neighbours, friends and members of the same caste and class within hours and days.

Such tragedies have taken place in the former state of Yugoslavia, but it is unclear why they have gone unnoticed at research centres in the subcontinent, especially in areas worst affected by gruesome violence and migration. Is it because the ghosts of Partition should be put to rest and not exhumed for frequent post-morterms? Or, is scholarship on the subject itself is so woefully inadequate and contentious that it fails to excite the imagination of young graduates?

Perspectives and attitudes on such vexed matters are bound to differ, though scholars in Pakistan tenaciously adhere to the belief that the creation of a Muslim nation marked the culmination of a historical process. Perhaps, it is hazardous to contest such inherited wisdom in a society where nationality is still defined, often clumsily, in purely Islamic terms, and religious minorities, Hindus and Ahmadiyas (Qadianis) included, are left to stew in their own juice. Perhaps, Partition does not convey the same meanings in Lahore and Islamabad as it does to some people living in Delhi, Lucknow, Calcutta, and Dacca. It is not bemoaned, for understandable reasons, as an epic tragedy but celebrated as a spectacular triumph of Islamic nationalism. After all, why should people inhabiting the fertile districts of western Punjab or the rugged Frontier region mourn the break-up of India's fragile unity or lament the collapse of a common cultural and intellectual inheritance? Some beleaguered *muhajirs* may still want to recall their friendships and associations in Hindustan (*guzashta bada-paraston ki yaadgar koi*), trace their intellectual and cultural links with Lucknow or Delhi, and occasionally revive memories of a bygone era by dipping into the writings of Manto, Ahmed Ali, Josh Malihabadi, Quratulain Hyder and Intizar Husain.[22] Yet, the nostalgia for what has already become an imaginary homeland or the identification with Lucknow's grand *imambaras* or with the sufi shrines of Khwaja Muinuddin Chishti at Ajmer and Nizamuddin Auliya in Delhi is gradually fading away with the passage of time and the passing of a generation. The Badshahi mosque, standing majestically as a symbol of India's secular dream, is as distant and remote as the Masjid-i Qartaba, the theme of Iqbal's melodious poem. Aminabad in Lucknow or Ballimaran in Old Delhi are far removed from the imagination of a generation nurtured in a different social and cultural milieu.

The differences in approaches and perspectives should not, however, stand in the way of developing a common reference point for rewriting the *histories* of an event that cast its shadow over many aspects of state and society in the subcontinent. Despite decades of mutual suspicions and antipathies leading to a mindless arms build up and contributing to the backwardness and appalling poverty of the region, it is still possible for the peoples, rather than the governments, to make sense of the poignant writings of creative writers and poets and to reflect on how and why a generation was caught up in the crossfire of religious bigotry, intolerance and sectarianism. Such an exercise can be undertaken without calling into question the legitimacy of one or the other varieties of nationalism.

For the initiative to get off the ground, it may be useful to revisit the old-fashioned theories on the syncretic and composite trajectory of Indian society, and detail, as the writer Krishna Sobti did in an interview, the shared values and traditions that had enabled diverse communities to live harmoniously for centuries.[23] It is not necessary to be swayed by the 'nationalist' historians who portray an idyllic picture of Hindu-Muslim relations during the pre-colonial days in order to strengthen inter-community ties during the liberation struggle. It is nonetheless important to underline the fusion and integration of the Hindu communities at different levels and the value they attached to religious tolerance and pluralism in their day-to-day living.[24] In so doing, one can put to rest those speculative theories that lend respectability to British colonialism and offer a corrective to the distorted Islamist or the *Hindutva* world views which have, in equal measure, created widespread confusion in the minds of the common people and, in the process, caused incalculable damage to state and civil society.

The conclusions flowing from such formulations are bound to differ, yet the urgency to underline the commonality of interests amongst large segments of the population must be felt in India where *Hindutva* could well be the new *mantra* of civil society in the foreseeable future, and in neighbouring Pakistan, where ethnic and sectarian strife, combined with deep-seated regional and linguistic cleavages, reveal the limits of an agenda tied to wild and imaginary notions of Muslim/Islamic brotherhood or solidarity.

II

The following three impressions are drawn from a period when Hindu-Muslim relations had reached their lowest watermark. The first is of Malcolm Darling, a civil servant in Punjab for many years. During his travel in 1945-6, he found much similarity between the Hindu and Muslim communities in the tract between the Beas and Sutlej and the Chenab and Ravi rivers. He noticed, something he would have done on numerous occasions during his long career as a British civil servant, how often Hindus, Muslims and Sikhs had a common ancestor in a village, how a Hindu from Karnal proudly announced that the Muslim inhabitants of the fifty neighbouring villages belonged to his clan and were prepared to return to the Hindu fold on the one condition that the Hindus would give them their daughters in marriage. Although the condition was refused, Hindus and Muslims of the area continued to interchange civilities at marriage, inviting the mullah or the Brahman, to share in the feasting. Malcolm Darling wondered how Pakistan was to be fitted into these conditions. 'What a hash politics threatens to make of this tract', he observed, 'where Hindu, Muslim and Sikh arc as mixed up as the ingredients of a well-made pilau (rice cooked with fowl or meat).'[25]

Muhammad Mujeeb, the vice-chancellor of Delhi's Jamia Millia Islamia, had a similar experience in Bihar soon after the orgy of violence had taken a heavy toll of human lives. While visiting the grave of a sufi saint on the bank of the river Ganga, he found that the Muslims living in the shrine had already abandoned the place. But soon a group of Hindu women appeared. They performed the same rituals that their ancestors had observed for generations. It appeared 'as if nothing had happened that affected their sentiments of veneration for the tomb of a Muslim saint'.[26]

Finally, consider the reports of Phillips Talbot, written for the Institute of Current World Affairs in New York on the eve of Independence and published recently in the daily newspaper, *The Hindu*. For one thing, Talbot was struck by the countrywide expression of Hindu-Muslim cordiality during the Independence celebrations.

For twenty long and bloody weeks after 16 August 1946, Hindus avoided entering Muslim neighbourhoods and *vice versa*. Communal clashes and deaths were daily occurrences. Yet at the climax of Independence celebrations this week, Hindus and Muslims mixed together freely. Many Hindus visited mosques on the 18th and distributed sweets to Muslims who were observing their Id festival. . . . It was a spectacular truce, if not a peace treaty, between the two communities. Similarly, in Delhi and Bombay I saw Hindus and Muslims playing hand in hand. Reports of the same nature came from most places except the still-troubled Punjab.[27]

Talbot's own explanation was that the political parties desired peace and friendship between the communities, though he laid greater stress on 'the popular revulsion against the constant dislocation and actual fear of life during the last year'. 'Terror', he added,

is an enervating emotion. I've seen neighbourhoods so distraught by the medieval lack of personal security that they could not think of nothing else. I think that people everywhere used the excitement of the celebrations to try to break the vicious cycle of communal attacks and retaliations. How permanent the change may be is yet to be seen.[28]

Such impressions need to be drawn into the discussions on Partition so that the past is not judged through our recent encounters with Hindu-Muslim violence in India. It is just as important to delineate the multiple strands in the Muslim League movement, underline its complexity, assess its ideological orientation afresh, and explore the mobilization strategies adopted by Jinnah after he returned from his home in Hampstead to plunge into the humdrum of Indian politics. In addition to having greater access to source materials, this is an opportune moment, fifty years after Independence, to revise and reconsider established theories on Partition, introduce a more nuanced discourse, and stay clear of the conventional wisdom that we, the generation born after Independence, have inherited on the theme of 'communal' politics generally, and the Pakistan movement, in particular. As 'old orthodoxies recede before the flood of fresh historical evidence and earlier certitudes are overturned by newly detected contradiction', this is the time to heal 'the multiple fractures which turned the promised dawn of freedom into a painful moment of separation'.[29]

For example, one of the points adequately documented, though not sufficiently considered in secondary literature, is that not everyone who raised or rallied around the green flag was uniformly wedded to or inspired by a shared ideal of creating an Islamic society. The reality is that many were pushed into taking religious/Islamic positions, while many others, especially the landed classes in Punjab and UP, used the Muslim League as a vehicle to articulate, defend, and promote their material interests. In fact, the intensity of emotions expressed in the 1940s, which is so often invoked in the subcontinent to create popular myths and stereotypical images, had more to do with the political and economic anxieties of various social classes than with a profound urge to create a *Shariat*-based society. Today, the issue is not the legitimacy of a movement but to place in perspective the dynamics of power-politics in a colonial context. In fact, a rounded picture of the Pakistan movement is possible only if we are able to contest the exaggerated claims made in the name of Islam, then and now, by the Islamists and the proponents of the two-nation theory.

In sum, the clamour for a separate nation, though pressed vigorously in the post-War years with much popular backing and enthusiasm, was raised not so much by the Muslim divines, many of whom were waiting on the fringes of Indian politics to intervene on behalf of Islam, but by the vociferous professional groups in UP, Bihar, the princely state of Hyderabad, and the small but upcoming trading and banking communities in Gujarat, Bombay, and Calcutta. Interestingly enough, the Muslim landlords of UP were the first to raise the banner of revolt against the League; in fact, the nawab of Chhatari and nawab Muhammad Yusuf of Jaunpur broke away from the Muslim League Parliamentary Board in April 1936 in order to revive 'a mixed party in preference to a Muslim communal organization'.[30] They changed course once the Congress ministry adopted the UP Tenancy Bill and Nehru and his comrades became more and more strident in their socialistic pronouncements. These men were not concerned to defend the Koranic injunctions which they probably flouted every day of their life. Nor were they interested in the welfare of poor Muslims, victims of their oppression and exploitation. Their chief goal was to defend their landholdings, orchards, havelis, palaces and, above all, the nawabi paraphernalia built through the courtesy of their British benefactors. Notice the following conversation between Saleem and his father Hamid in Attia Hosain's (died in January 1998) celebrated novel *Sunlight on a Broken Column*:

> Saleem was saying, 'In the final analysis, what you are facing is the struggle for power by the bourgeoisie. It is not really a peasant's movement, but when it comes to a division of spoils even class interests are forgotten. For example the four hundred or so Taluqdars insisted the British should give them higher representation than the thousands of other landlords.'
>
> 'It is not a question of numbers alone', protested Uncle Hamid, sitting up and waving his pipe in negation. 'We Taluqdars have ancient rights and privileges, given by a special charter, which we have to safeguard. . . .'
>
> 'Yes, yes, of course. One respects tradition. One fights for one's self, one's interests. But you cannot expect the tenants to love you for it.'
>
> 'That is because so-called reforms are destroying the personal ties between landlord and peasant. Surely a Government and its changing officers cannot have personal relations or traditional ties with the tenants? With whom are the

people in constant touch? Their landlords or local political leaders?. . .'

'How can landlords but be uneasy at the thought of such reserves of power being vested in officials at a time when it is uncertain what class of persons will obtain political power?. . .' (Uncle Hamid)

Saleem could not let an argument die an unnatural death. He began, 'What you said, father, about the landlords' fear of abolition is the crux of the matter. This fear for their existence is the basis for the formation of a new parry which is interested in keeping the status quo intact, that is favoured by the British and is fundamentally opposed to progressive, national movements. . . .'

'Words? Theories! Irresponsible talk!' Uncle Hamid burst out. 'I am a part of feudalism, and proud to be. I shall fight for it. It is my heritage—and yours. Let me remind you of that. And that you enjoy its 'reactionary' advantages. You talk very glibly of its destruction, but you live by its existence. It is, in fact, your only livelihood.'[31]

No wonder, the landed elements in UP, as also the Jamaat-i Islami and some sections of the ulama connected with the Barelwi 'school', Nadwat al-ulama, Firangi Mahal and Deoband, hitched their fortunes with the Muslim League at different points of time and for different reasons. Their overall strategy, one that suited the raj during and after World War II, was to masquerade their hidden agenda and project the Congress, their main rival in the political world, as a 'Hindu' party inimical to Islam. Once the League bandwagon rolled on, other aggrieved groups, especially those who had failed to secure employment, contracts or seats on regional and local bodies, jumped into the fray as the defenders of the faith.

Still, Pakistan was not everybody's dream. Nor was Jinnah everyone's Quaid (leader).[32] In this respect, one should not, as is generally the case with both the Hindu and Muslim majoritarian discourses, lose sight of the perspectives of those who were intellectually committed to secular nationalism or were actively engaged in repudiating the two-nation theory. Their voices, which have been stifled by 'secular' as well 'communal' histories, should not be relegated to a historian's footnote. Indeed, the part played by those Muslims, who are patronizingly described as 'Nationalist Muslims', the Khudai Khidmatgars in the N.W.F.P., who were eventually let down by the dispirited Congress leadership on the eve of Independence, the ulama of Deoband and the Momins in Bihar, should not be submerged beneath the rationalization of the 'victors'. Their main contribution, exemplified by Azad's exemplary conduct and performance,[33] lay in keeping alive the vision of a secular India. These 'marginal' voices should be recovered to rewrite the histories of Partition.[34]

For these and other reasons, it would be appropriate to ask if the Muslim League movement was as cohesive and unified as it is made out to be by some writers in India and Pakistan. If the Congress was faction-ridden and ideologically fragmented, so was the League.[35] This is illustrated by the depth and intensity of jealousies and internal discord in the organization, the regional groupings, the *Ajlaf-Ashraf* divide, the Shia-Sunni strife in many places, and the unending doctrinal disputes between the theologians, especially the followers of the Barelwi and the Deobandi 'schools'. Such differences, though conveniently overlooked in the histories of the freedom movement in Pakistan, were real and not imaginary. If so, it will not do to portray the Muslim Leaguers as earnest and self-sacrificing crusaders or equate them with the *muhajirs* or *ansars* of the Prophet Muhammad. What is perhaps challenging, as indeed intellectually rewarding, is to probe those critical areas where the 'faithful', despite having projected themselves as a community acting in unison, were themselves so hopelessly split. Such an exercise, far from reducing or tarnishing the reputation of historic figures, will enrich our knowledge and understanding of a complex phenomena. Arguably, if we know our leaders better and question their reading of the authentic and vibrant histories of shared memories and experiences, we may not repeat their mistakes and errors of judgement which cost the nation dearly at the stroke of the midnight hour on 14-15 August 1947.

III

> The decision about the creation of Pakistan had just been announced and people were indulging in all kinds of surmises about the pattern of life that would emerge. But no one's imagination could go very far. The sardarji sitting in front of me repeatedly asked me whether I thought Mr. Jinnah would continue to live in Bombay after the creation of Pakistan or whether he would resettle in Pakistan. Each time my answer would be the same, 'Why should he leave Bombay? I think he'll continue to live in Bombay and continue visiting Pakistan.' Similar guesses were being made about the towns of Lahore and Gurdaspur too, and no one knew which town would fall to the share of India and which to Pakistan.[36]

In the specific context of the Pakistan movement, the professed ideology of the nation state itself, though celebrated on both sides of the border, had no significant impact on or relevance to the millions living in India or Pakistan. Contrary to the exaggerated claims made in both countries, most people were either indifferent to or unconcerned with the national borders or the newly-created geographical entities that were being laboriously created. National borders were political constructs, and imagined projections of territorial power. Although they appeared in deceptively precise forms, they reflected, at leat initially, merely the mental images of politicians, lawyers, and intellectuals. Their practical consequences for most people were quite different.[37] Rajinder Sachar, jurist and human rights activist who has spent a lifetime struggling with his memories of Lahore, recalled: 'One day I ran into a Muslim villager who had come to Lahore all the way from Sargodha looking for my grandfather, a well-known criminal lawyer. Poor chap he didn't realize that Partition had taken place and that the Hindus had left. It just shows how long it took for the implications of Partition to sink in.'[38] Indeed, though such people were repeatedly fed with ill-informed and biased views, they were neither committed to the land of *Aryavarta* nor the *Dar al-Islam*. They had no destination to reach, no mirage to follow. Even though the trains had started carrying people to their death-traps, they were unclear whether Lahore, with its splendid Mughal monuments, beautiful gardens and boulevards, would be part of India or Pakistan. They did not know whether Delhi, the city of Mir Taqi Mir and Mirza Ghalib, would remain in Gandhi's India or Jinnah's Pakistan. Manto captures the mood in his brilliant story 'Toba Tek Singh', a character from the lunatic asylum. This is what he writes:

> As to where Pakistan was located, the inmates knew nothing. That was why both the mad and the partially mad were unable to decide whether they were now in India or in Pakistan. If they were in India where on earth was Pakistan? And if they were in Pakistan, then how come that until only the other day it was India?. . .
>
> Those who had tried to solve this mystery had become utterly confused when told that Sialkot, which used to be in India, was now in Pakistan. It was anybody's guess what was going to happen to Lahore, which was currently in Pakistan, but could slide into India any moments. It was still possible that the entire subcontinent of India might become Pakistan. And who could say if both India and Pakistan might not entirely vanish from the map of the world one day? . . .
>
> Just before sunrise, Bisham Singh, the man who had stood on his legs for fifteen years, screamed and as officials from the two sides rushed towards him, he collapsed on the ground.
>
> There, behind barbed wire, on one side, lay India and behind more barbed wire, on the other side, lay Pakistan. In between, on a bit of earth which had no name, lay Toba Tek Singh.

The paradox of how borders simultaneously separate and unite is discussed elsewhere.[39] The significance of Manto's description lies in describing an existentialist reality—the separation of people living on both sides who had a long history of cultural and social contact—and the pradoxical character of borders being a metaphor of the ambiguities of nation building.[40] He, in essence, offered a way of correcting the distortions inherent in state-centred national histories. Finally, 'India' or 'Pakistan' were mere territorial abstractions to most people who were ignorant of how Mountbatten's plan or the Radcliffe Award would change their destinies and tear them apart from their social and cultural moorings. In their world view, there was no nationalism, religious or composite. They were blissfully unaware that their fate, which had rested in the hands of the exploiting classes for centuries, would be settled after Mountbatten's three days of 'diplomacy' leading to the 3 June Plan, and that the frontiers would be decided by Cyril Radcliffe in just seven weeks and 'a continent for better or worse divided'.[41] They had no clue whatsoever that these vain, insensitive and conceited representatives of the Crown, having received the mandate from Clement Atlee's Labour government to preside over the liquidation of the most important imperial possession of all time, would abandon them in mid-ocean 'with a fire in the deck and ammunition in the hold'. Nobody had warned them how Mountbatten's mentor Winston Churchill had, likewise, sat with T.E. Lawrence and the Emir Faisal in Cairo as colonial secretary in 1922 drawing nation states on the map of what had previously been the Ottoman empire. But, then, how were they to know that the colonial powers divide people and territories when in ascendancy, as also in retreat.

IV

For a long time I refused to accept the consequences of the revolution, which was set off by the Partition of the country. I still feel the same way; but I suppose, in the end, I came to accept this nightmarish reality without self-pity or despair. In the process I tried to retrieve from this man-made sea of blood, pearls of a rare hue, by writing about the single-minded dedication with which men had killed men, about the remorse felt by some of them, about the tears shed by murders who could not understand why they still had some human feelings left. All this and more, I put in my book *Siyah Hashye*. (Saadat Hasan Manto)[42]

Everytime I visited Amritsar, I felt captivated. But the city this time presented the look of a cremation ghat, eerie and stinking. . . . The silence was so perfect that even the faint hiss of steam from the stationary engine sounded a shriek. . . . The brief stoppage seemed to have lingered into eternity till the engine whistled and gave a gentle pull. . . . We left Chheharta behind and then Atari and when we entered Wagah and then Harbanspura everyone in the train felt uplifted. A journey through a virtual valley of destruction has ended when finally the train came to a halt at Platform No. 2—Lahore, the moment was as gratifying as the consummation of a dream.[43]

Scores of writers reveal the other face of freedom, the woes of divided families, the agony and trauma of abducted women, the plight of migrants and the harrowing experiences of countless people who boarded the train that was supposed to take them to the realization of their dream, but of whom not a man, woman or child survived the journey. A Zahid in Attia Hosain's *Sunlight on a Broken Column* or a Saddan in Masoom Reza Rahi's *Aadha Gaon* (Half-a-Village) offer a vivid and powerful portrayal of a fragmented and wounded society.[44] What political debate will never fully do—and the reason we so badly need the literature—is defeat the urge to lay blame, which keeps animosity alive. Only such a literature can truly evoke of the sufferings of the innocent, whose pain is more universal, and ultimately a vehicle of more honest reconciliation than political discourse.[45]

Board the *Peshawar Express* or the *Train to Pakistan* to discover the implications of what happened before and after the fateful, midnight hour. Consider the exchanges between Choudhry Muhammad Ali, a well-known landlord of Rudauli in Barabanki district (UP) and his daughter who left her father to settle in Karachi, or the correspondence of Brahm Nath Dutt, father of the historian V.N. Datta, to capture the poignancy of the moment. Turn to Rahi's Gangauli village—a world where people are seen to be wrestling to come to terms with competing ideologies—in order to uncover how the intricate and almost imperceptible way in which the politics of Partition worked its way into the interstices of people's consciousness.[46] Read Attia Hosain's *Sunlight on a Broken Column* or *Phoenix Fled* to discover how the Pakistan movement split families on ideological lines and created fears and uncertainties in the minds of people. To read her novel and collection of short stories is, 'as if one had parted a curtain, or opened a door, and strayed into the past'.[47]

Indeed, if the *histories* of Partition are to be rewritten, there are several reasons why we must judiciously draw upon the intellectual resources made available to us by such creative writers. They expose the inadequacy of numerous narratives on Independence and Partition, compel us to explore fresh themes and adopt new approaches that have eluded the grasp of social scientists, and provide a foundation for developing an alternative discourse to current expositions of a general theory on inter-community relations. Their strength lies in representing a grim and sordid contemporary reality without drawing on religion or a particular community as the principal reference point. In their stories, the experiences of each community distinctly mirror one another, indeed reach out to and clutch at one another. No crime, no despair, no grief in exile belongs uniquely to anyone.[48] In the words of Krishna Sobti, whose best-known Hindi writings on Partition are *Sikka Badal Gaya* and *Zindaginama*, the fiction written about that cataclysmic event preserved 'essential human values'.[49] That is probably why we emerge from the literature with a mistrust toward group solidarity of an oppositional bent. If so we must emerge at the same time, paradoxically, with a conviction to oppose such mistrust with trust in the goodness of the human life-urge wherever we find it. Indeed,

> we emerge from the literature as searchers of such trust. If we find it in the solitary dissidence of even a singly person, we feel obliged to offer him or her our companionship. And if we find it stitched into whole communities, we come away not necessarily more pious, but inspired. The literature as a whole seeds pathos for the suffering and inhumanity of the Partition, and related instances of cultural chauvinism, but not merely so. It also sprouts a countervailing protest, a voice of justice that must be the surging of our humanity itself—something greater than our bestiality—within us. In this sense the literature does what religious leaders in each community failed to do: to make communities forces for the affirmation of humanity broadly. . . . If religious politics worked nefariously in favour of Partition, it was because an ecumenical religious politics never de-veloped. We are in a different position than the men and women of August, 1947. Our choices are not limited to exile, death or resignation. . . .[50]

In other words, if creative writings on Partition can still stir the individual and collective imagination of sensitive readers in the subcontinent, there is no reason why people on both sides of the Wagah border cannot share the anguish of Faiz Ahmad Faiz[51] and, at the same time, echo the optimism and plea of Ali Sardar Jafri expressed in the following lines:

> *Tum aao Gulshan-i Lahore se chaman bardosh,*
> *hum ayen subha Banaras ki raushni lekar,*
> *Himalaya ki hawaon ki taazgi lekar,*
> *Phir uske baad ye puchen ke kaun dushman hai?*
>
> You come covered with flowers from the Garden of Lahore
> We bring to you the light and radiance of the morning of Banaras,
> the freshness of the winds of the Himalayas,
> And then we ask who the enemy is?

NOTES

1. Krishna Sobti, in conversation with Alok Bhalla, in Geeti Sen (ed.), *Crossing Boundaries*, New Delhi, 1997, p. 78.
2. N.N. Vohra, '91, Garden Town', ibid., p. 54.

3. Some years ago, the historian Gyanendra Pandey complained that the history of violence accompanying Partition had not been written. Ashis Nandy bemoans that the finest creative minds of India had maintained a profound, almost cultivated silence about Partition and the bloodbath. *Times of India*, 20 July 1997. See, Urvashi Butalia on the 'Official Silence', *Hindu*, 21 Sept. 1997. My principal interest in this essay centres around articles published in newspapers, magazines and journals during the fiftieth year of Independence. I have, however, used scholarly writings, mostly published in 1996-7, to comment on the theme of Partition.

   The Delhi-based weekly newsmagazine, *Outlook*, brought out a special issue on 28 May 1997. *The Asian Age*, edited by M.J. Akbar, published extracts from books on Partition, personal memories, recollections and interviews. See, for example, the reports of the Reuters correspondent Don Campbell who arrived in India in March 1947 and spent the next 15 months in Delhi. The coverage in the newspaper *The Hindu* (Delhi) was also quite extensive. The impressions of Phillips Talbot, an American, were particularly interesting.
4. For example, Urvashi Butalia, 'Blood', Granta (London), Mar. 1997; Sunil Mehra, 'Sufferers and Survivors', *Outlook*, 28 May 1997, pp. 32-3; 'Bridging a Great Divide', *India Today*, 18 Aug. 1997; Anita Mukhopadhya, 'The Last Journey', *The Hindu*, 31 Aug. 1997; Ajeet Cour, 'I've seen rootless trees wobbling and walking', *Hindustan Times*, 4 Jan. 1998; C.M. Naim, 'Pakistan or Hindustan', *Communalism Combat*, Sept. 1997; 'India's unforgettable divide', *Guardian* (London), 30 July 1997; Iqbal Masud, 'Dream Merchants, Politicians & Partition: Memoirs of an Indian Muslim', New Delhi, 1997.
5. *Femina* (Bombay), 1 Aug. 1997.
6. For example, Patrick French, *Liberty or Death: India's Journey to Independence and Division*, London, 1997.
7. See, for example, Gyanendra Pandey, 'Community and Violence', *EPW*, 9 Aug. 1997, and his 'Partition and Independence in Delhi: 1947-48', *EPW*, 6 Sept. 1997; also, Azhar Abbas, 'The Twice Displaced', *Outlook*, 28 May 1997, p. 66. For insights into ethnic violence in Sri Lanka in 1983 that had many features in common with the Hindu-Muslim riots before and after Independence, S.J. Tambiah, *Ethnic Fratricide and the Dismantling of Democracy*, Chicago, 1986.
8. Urvashi Butalia, *The Other Side of Silence: Voices from the Partition of India*, New Delhi, 1998; Ritu Menon and Kamla Bhasin, *Borders & Boundaries: Women in India's Partition*, New Delhi, 1998.
9. Hasan, *Legacy of a Divided Nation*, and *India Partitioned: The Other Face of Freedom*, New Delhi, 1997, 2nd rev. edn.
10. For a critique of Mountbatten, see N.N. Vohra, '91, Garden Town' and F.S. Aijazuddin 'Same to Same' from a different perspective, in Sen (ed.), *Crossing Boundaries*.
11. *Outlook*, 28 May 1997. Notice the following letter of Cyrill Radcliffe to his

son: 'I thought you would like to get a letter from India with a crown on the envelope. After tomorrow evening nobody will ever again be allowed to use such stationery and after 150 years British rule will be over in India. . . . I am going to see Mountbatten sworn as the first governor-general of the Indian Union . . . and then I station myself firmly on the Delhi airport until an aeroplane from England comes along. Nobody in India will love me for the award about the Punjab and Bengal and there will be roughly 80 million people with a grievance who will begin looking for me. I do not want them to find me. I have worked and travelled and sweated—oh I have sweated the whole time.' Quoted in Sunil Khilnani, *The Idea of India*, London, 1997, p. 201.

12. Ajit Bhattacharjea, 'Cyril's Scalpel', *Outlook*, 23 July 1997, p. 8.
13. Thus the following view: 'Looking back 50 years, the haste and self-delusion of Congress and Muslim leaders that contributed to the bloodiest religious cleansing in history emerges with disturbing clarity.' *Outlook*, 28 May 1997.
14. Mosley, *The Last Days of the Raj*, p. 77.
15. For example, the presidential address delivered by Professor V.N. Datta at the Indian History Congress held in Madras, 1996.
16. Kuldip Nayar, 'Was Pakistan Necessary?', *Indian Express*, 15 Aug. 1997, and his 'Partition: An Inevitability', *The Hindu* (Special Issue on 'India!'), Aug. 1997. For earlier accounts of 'who is to blame?', see Chimanlal Setalvad, *India Divided*, Bombay, n.d., pp. 4-7.
17. Gyanendra Pandey, 'The Prose of Otherness', David Arnold and David Hardiman (ed.), *Subaltern Studies VIII: Essays in Honour of Ranajit Guha*, New Delhi, 1994, p. 194.
18. This is the common refrain in the writings of Ayesha Jalal and Farzana Shaikh. For his critique of Jalal's work, see Pandey, 'The Prose of Otherness', pp. 209-10. And for her response, see 'Secularists, subalterns and the stigma of "Communalism": Partition historiography revisited', *The Indian Economic and Social History Review*, Vol. 33 (1), 1996, pp. 93-103. The tendency to exaggerate the difference in perspectives and to castigate each other for that reason is the hallmark of recent historiography on South Asia. Young and upcoming social scientists, many of whom have not even written their doctoral dissertations, are engaged in polemical writings. They regard this as a shortcut to establishing their scholarly reputation in the West. Ayesha Jalal's critique of my introduction to *India's Partition: Process Strategy and Mobilization*, is based on a misunderstanding of my overall argument. Yet, I respect her views and her understanding of a highly complex phenomena which should not, incidentally, be reduced to polemical exchanges among fellow-historians.
19. In a perceptive article, Aijaz Ahmad has offered a powerful critique of 'the Congress-inspired mythology'. His analysis suggests: (a) that the politics of caste and communalism was inherent in the structure of the colonial society itself; (b) that the reform movements usually contributed to solidifying such identities rather than weakening them in favour of ecumenical culture and a non-denominational politics; and (c) that the national movement itself, includ-

ing the majority of the Congress under Gandhi, was deeply 'complicit in a transactional mode of politics which involved bargaining among the elites and a conception of secularism which was little more than an accommodation of the self-enclosed orthodoxies. Given the immensity of this historical weight, the wonder is not that there was a partition but that there was one.' *The Hindu*, 'India' (Special Number), p. 28.

20. The judgement is harsh, although many contemporary observers believed that Jinnah may not have had the space to press his campaign in the United Provinces if the coalition issue was amicably resolved. The governor of UP felt that way. Harry Haig to Linlithgow, 3 June 1939, File No. 115/6, BL. See also, my introduction to *India's Partition*, pp. 12-15.
21. There is unmistakable evidence to suggest that talks for a Congress-Muslim League alliance were initiated some time in Mar.-Apr. 1937. Although Nehru had opposed 'all pacts and coalitions with small groups at the top'. (To Abul Wali, 30 Mar. 1937, AICC papers, G-5, K.W. i, 1937. Abdul Wali of Bara Banki (UP) referred to a scheme 'being hatched with the help of Pantji [G.B. Pant] and Mohanlal [Saxena] to bring about coalition between the Congress and League parties in the Assembly'. To Nehru, 28 Mar. 1937, AICC papers. The governor of UP reported on 7 Apr. that the League was looking forward to an alliance with the Congress and felt that 'at present it looks as if the new government will gradually attract to itself a fair number of the Muslim Leaguers'.
22. See Masud Hasan Shahab Dehlavi, in Mushirul Hasan (ed.), *India Partitioned*, Vol. 2, pp. 184-95.
23. Interview with Alok Bhalla, in Sen (ed.), *Crossing Boundaries*, p. 66. And the comment of J.S. Butalia, a retired journalist: 'I was born and brought up in a predominantly Muslim village, Butala. There were 300 Muslim families and only 10 or 15 Hindu homes but we lived in such close harmony that it was difficult to make out who was who. A Hindu-Muslim conflict was something we had not imagined even in our worst dreams. It is with a sense of horror and shame that I look back . . . but, finally, I am overwhelmed by nostalgia'. *The Hindu*, 'India' (Special Number), 15 Aug. 1997, p. 32. For Bengal, see Mukhopadhaya, 'The Last Journey', *The Hindu*, 31 Aug. 1997.
24. See the contributions of Rakshat Puri, Muchkund Dubey and Sumanta Banerjea, in Sen (ed.), *Crossing Boundaries*, op. cit.
25. This is quoted in full in my, *Legacy of a Divided Nation*, p. 168.
26. See Hasan, *India's Partition*, p. 405. For Punjab, see Sobti, pp. 67, 69-70. For Bengal, see Samaddar (ed.), *Reflections on Partition in the East*, and its review by Sumanta Banerjee in *Biblio*, New Delhi, Jul.-Aug. 1997, pp. 40-1; and Peter van der Veer, 'Playing or Praying: A Suf Saint's Day in Surat', *The Journal of Asian Studies*, Vol. 51, 3, Aug. 1992, pp. 545-64.
27. Phillips Talbot, 'Thus Independence came to India', *The Hindu*, 4 and 24 Aug. 1997.
28. Talbot filed this report on 10 Aug. 1947.

29. I have borrowed these lines from Ayesha Jalal, 'Secularists, Subalterns and the Stigma of "Communalism"', p. 1.
30. Nawab of Chhatari to Hailey, 28 Oct. 1936, Malcolm Hailey papers, File No. 28c.
31. Attia Hosain, *Sunlight on a Broken Column*, New Delhi, 1992 edn., pp. 231-3, 234.
32. In this respect, my reading of the Pakistan movement is different from that of Ayesha Jalal.
33. The following impression of Azad by Kanji Dwarkadas is interesting. 'Abul Kalam Azad,' he wrote, 'is dignified and level-headed, but his health is giving way. Jinnah dislikes him heartily and a few years ago he called him the "show boy" of the Congress and in private conversations Jinnah says much worse things about Abul Kalam Azad.' 'India—April 1944 to Nov. 1945: What Next', 28 Nov. 1945 (typescript), George Lumley papers, BL.
34. Pandey, 'The Prose of Otherness', p. 214.
35. In fact, Jinnah exhorted various regional groups and other factions to overcome their differences and rival claims so that the Muslim League could concentrate all its energies towards the achievement of Pakistan. 'We shall have time to quarrel ourselves,' he said, 'and we shall have time when these differences will have to be remedied. We shall have time for domestic programmes and politics, but first get the Government. This is a nation without any territory or any government.' Quoted in Sayeed, *Pakistan: The Formative Phase*, p. 297.
36. Bhisham Sahni, 'We have Arrived in Amritsar', Stephen Alter and Vimal Dissanayake (eds.), *The Penguin Book of Modern Short Stories*, pp. 180-7.
37. These lines are based on Michiel Baud and Willem van Schendel, 'Towards a Comparative History of Borderlands', in *Journal of World History*, Vol. 8, 2, 1997, pp. 211-42.
38. Quoted in *The Hindu*, 'India' (Special Number), 15 Aug. 1947, p. 28.
39. Baud and Schendel, 'Towards a Comparative History of Borderlands', p. 242.
40. Benedict Anderson, *Imagined Communities: Reflections on the Origin and Spread of Nationalism* (1983; rpt., New York, 1991); E.J. Hobsbawm and Terence Ranger (eds.), *The Invention of Tradition*, Cambridge, 1983.
41. This is a line from W.H. Auden. See Khilnani, op. cit., p. 200.
42. For my translation of *Siyah Hashye* ('Black Margins'), see my (ed.), *India Partitioned*, Vol. 1, pp. 88-101.
43. Muhammad Saeed, *Lahore: A Memoir*, Lahore, 1989, p. 94.
44. On *Aadha Gaon*, see Sudhir Chandra, 'The Harvest of Fear: A Retrospective Critique of Hindu-Muslim Relations in Two Hindi Novels', in T.V. Sathyamurthy, *Region, Religion, Caste, Gender and Culture in Contemporary India*, Vol. 3, New Delhi, 1996.
45. Jason Francisco, 'In the Heat of Fratricide: The Literature of India's Partition Burning Freshly (A Review Article)', *The Annual of Urdu Studies*, No. 2, Madison, 1996, p. 250.

46. Chandra, 'The Harvest of Fear', p. 195.
47. Anita Desai, 'Introduction', *Phoenix Fled*, New Delhi, 1988, p. viii.
48. Jason Francisco, op. cit., p. 250.
49. Geeti Sen (ed.), *Crossing Boundaries*, p. 77; and Alok Bhalla (ed.), *Stories about the Partition of India*, 3 vols., New Delhi, 1994.
50. Francisco, op. cit., p. 250.
51. This leprous daybreak, dawn night's fangs have mangled—
    This is not that long-looked-for break of that day,
    Not that clear dawn in quest of which those comrades
    Set out, believing that in heaven's wide void
    Somewhere must be the stars' last halting place,
    Somewhere the verge of night's slow-washing tide,
    Somewhere an anchorage for the ship of heartache.

13

Divided Nationhood: India's Partition Revisited

> Ghalib died long ago, but I still remember
> his constant questioning.
> To everything he would counter
> *had it been this way*, what would have been?

Theories of nationalism have traditionally been divided into two main categories, instrumentalist and primoridialist. The former conceived nationalism as a product of élite manipulation and contend that nations can be fabricated, if not invented. The latter see nationalism as a spontaneous process stemming from a naturally given sense of nationhood. Locating India's Partition in this debate is a daunting task. In addition to the die-hards who regard the 'event' as imminent and inevitable, one has to contend with writers who have lazily settled for the two-nation theory, articulated not just by the Muslim League but also by the Hindu right.[1] Similarly, while the government's part in stoking the fires of communalism is underscored, its 'divide and rule' policy is readily invoked, rhetorically, to explain 'Muslim separatism' rather than the overt manifestations of Hindu communalism.[2]

But the more fundamental difficulty lies elsewhere—in the overall direction and orientation of research on the Muslim communities that is still mired within traditional frameworks. Though some new voices are being heard, most academic exchanges involve a range of intellectual suppositions that still rest on the belief that Muslims are an exclusive category, with a shared world view, a common outlook, and a structure of consciousness in accord with the fundamental tenets of Islam.[3] This approach underlines the primacy of culture and ideology, assigns a privileged place to Islam, and portrays the image of a community acting in unison. In other words, the emphasis is on a monolithic conception of Islamic ideology and practice or a teleology dictating the actions of the Muslims or a general acquiescence in the actions of a few. The mere fact of people being Muslim in some general sense is usually conflated with their adherence to beliefs and practices that are strictly described as 'Islamist' or 'separatist'.[4]

By now, the continued harping on such views has perpetuated the mistaken belief that the roots of the Partition lie not in the 1930s on early 1940s but in the late-nineteenth century 'Neo-Muslim modernist and separatist' tradition of Aligarh's modernism and its spokesperson Saiyid Ahmad Khan.[5]

What also plagues the Partition studies is the misplaced emphasis on, what Anthony D. Smith calls *ethno* history—the tendency to extol the heroic deeds of past national leaders and to provide a legitimizing historical perspective as the basis of the project. Hence the use, in the writings of some Pakistani scholars, of Saladin as a metaphor, a cultural construct, to compare him with Jinnah. The oddity of the comparison is apparent in the comment: 'Both Saladin and Jinnah took on the most renowned opponents of their age, almost mythical in stature. Saladin fought against Richard the Lionheart and Jinnah challenged Mounbatten, Gandhi and Nehru.'[6] Yet, this is how the writings on Partition are dignified as an academic speciality not because it contains demonstrably special features, but because they allow the historian to identify with his heroes and 'his' event.[7]

Though the adulation of Jinnah is by no means exceptional in Pakistan, historians of all hues have painstakingly profiled national parties and their leaders for decades to construct the grand narrative of India's vivisection. This exercise cannot be decried or considered unimportant: the Congress and the Muslim League were, undeniably, the key players in the decade preceding the transfer of power. Introducing a volume in 1993, I referred to the complexities of the years 1937 to 1940 embodied in the three paradoxes—the League's being catapulted to prominence after years of political wilderness; Jinnah's transformation from a secular politician to an ideologue of Muslim nationalism; and the Congress acceptance of the Partition plan with seeming alacrity, thus relinquishing its vaunted principles of national unity. Pointing to the intricacies of the conjuncture, I analysed the performance of the 1937-9 Congress ministries, including the interaction between class and communal tensions, in influencing the timing of the emergence of the Pakistan demand. I revisited the debates over the Congress truculence over a coalition ministry in UP, examined the failure of the Muslim mass contact campaign, and mapped out the political consequences of the Congress, refusal to join the war effort in 1939.[8] 'It was the war', wrote the historian Eric Hobsbawm, 'that broke India in two. In one sense it was the last great triumph of the raj—and at the same time its last exhausted gasp.'[9]

I have since argued that concentrating only on the British-Congress-League negotiations cannot unravel the complex nature of the Partition story. Similarly, individual pronouncements, party resolutions and manifestos, though a pointer to various crucial turn of events in politics and society, are not good enough. For one, they convey the impression that the subcontinental leaders occupied an unassailable place in deciding the nation's destiny on the eve of the transfer of power. The reality, obscured by dense official papers and documents, was profoundly different. 'Major' players in the high politics of the 1940s, though influential, were by no means free agents able to pursue their own or their party's agenda. Some, if not all, of their initiatives were severely curbed by those sections of their following who were embroiled in communal campaigns and affected by changing political alignments in UP, Punjab and Bengal, the eventual storm-centres of the Pakistan movement. This explains, at least in part, why Nehru's brainchild, the Muslim mass contact campaign, petered out long before the Lahore resolution was adopted amid cries of *Allah-o-Akbar*: it ran into serious trouble because district Congress committees, often dominated by Hindu Mahasabhites, girded themselves to ward off the 'Muslim influx' into the organization. Likewise, in a different context but an equally important milestone in polarizing communal sentiments, local units of the League and their ulama collaborators, imbued with a misguided zeal to expose the 'wrongs' of the Congress ministries, mounted ceaseless pressure on central leaders to celebrate 'Deliverance Day'. Amid the exuberant rejoicing and by the general expression of loathing for Congress, they demanded their pound of flesh for their 'sufferings' under a 'Hindu Raj'. 'The Deliverance Day', wrote one of Jinnah's admirers in Lucknow, 'was such a success that it was even celebrated in those quarters where the League is looked upon as a vile disease. . . . You have laid the foundation of a self-respecting nationhood for the Muslims. It (Deliverance Day) is the first concrete step that shows [*sic*] without ambiguity that there are not one but several nations in India.'[10]

Much the same energy was released, in a communally-polarized climate, whenever the prospect of a Congress-League rapprochement brightened up. Local Hindu, Muslim and later the Sikh bodies, infused with religious fanaticism and sensitive to escalating communal violence, sent out loud and clear signals to the Congress, League and Akali Dal representatives, many of whom were obliged to dispel the impression of a 'sell out'. 'So ends the second Simla Conference', the viceroy wrote in his *Journal* on 12 May 1946, 'with much the same fate as the first. I was always very doubtful about it, I have never attached the same importance as the (Cabinet) Mission to Congress and the League reaching agreement, as I was pretty sure that they never would.'[11] In the months following the Simla conference, the lonely figure of the Mahatma, forsaken by his Congress lieutenants and wilfully targeted by the Hindu right for 'appeasing' Muslims and helping to destroy Hindus and Hinduism, Gandhi wrote in October 1946: 'I know that mine is today a voice in the wilderness.' As the 'vivisection of India' became imminent, his own sense of impotence increased. 'My writ runs no more. . . . No one listens to me any more. . . . I am crying in the wilderness.'[12]

Another instance is how, to begin with, both Nehru and Liaquat Ali Khan had set their faces against any wholesale transfer of populations, but how events, rapidly becoming too large for them, dictated the course of their policy.[13]

Although the pressure on national leaders came from various quarters, the constraints on their capacity to act freely and independently need to be probed in the context of the direction, thrust, and modus operandi of the mobilization campaigns. Whether it was the Congress or the League, their initiatives often generated new fears and uncertainties in many regions though in significantly different ways. They also enlarged, thanks to the colonial structures, areas of conflict and competition. This paved the way for religious and cultural bodies, some founded in the last-quarter of the nineteenth century, to assume the mantle of community leadership and intervene stridently in national affairs. Although every single step in the process of devolution of authority, commencing with the Morley-Minto Reforms (1909) onwards, legitimized their operations, a good many 'reformist' movements, notably the Arya Samaj in Punjab or the *tabligh* and *tanzim* societies in the Indo-Gangetic belt, developed their ideas and support base outside institutional structures, colonial policies, and 'external' influences. They derived sustenance from their own complex repertoire of ideas and concepts, from their own self-image and self-representation, from their apprehension of the intrusive influences responsible for contemporary decadence, and from their overall comprehension of where they stood in a world, they believed, was dominated by the Other.

We need to know how and why this occurred; in fact, making sense of the occurrences outside the national and regional spheres requires delineating the local roots of Hindu and Muslim nationalisms. That is how we can perhaps establish how local interests, operating within sharply-demarcated religious boundaries and using their linkages with *Hindutva* or Islamist movements, mounted pressure on all-India leaders to safeguard their special claims; also, how they opposed, sometimes violently, the occasional concession being offered to their adversaries as a price for reconciliation. Their profile, location and linkages serve to explain the reasons why they occupied a vantage point in Indian politics in the mid-1940s, and why they were able to (mostly in doubt in earlier decades) prepare the groundwork for Partition well before the Union Jack was lowered in Delhi and Karachi.

Two 'conflicting forms of urban solidarity' in eighteenth and nineteenth century north India served as the foundation for nationalism and religious communalism, which so dramatically affected events in the twentieth century.[14] Sumit Sarkar noted, more explicitly, that 'the decisions and actions of [the] leaders cannot really be understood without the counterpoint provided by pressures from below'.[15] This is corroborated by the pattern of communal violence between 1905 and 1947: a transition from a phase of rioting which was relatively unorganized, less related to institutional politics and with a strong class orientation, to outbreaks connected with organized politics, exhibiting a higher degree of organization and overt communalism.[16] Sarkar has delineated, moreover, the process by which Hindu-Muslim divisions in Bengal became elaborated in the 1920s. As a result, the masses 'outstrip[ped] their leaders', while the 'specific features and collective mentalities' of the subaltern groups involved became sharply defined in relation to 'the domain of the elite politicians'. Popular notions began to define community not by a shared Bengali culture but by religious identity.[17] Much the same process is discernible among the Urdu-speaking elites of UP in the last-quarter of the nineteenth century,[18] the Sikhs in Punjab,[19] and the Jats in rural south-east Punjab in the 1920s and 1930s.[20]

It is true that localities often mirrored the regional and all-India setting, hence the argument that the political pressures leading to the partition of Punjab and Bengal originated outside the province.[21] Yet the complex and intricate processes of the formation of community-based solidarities and how, these spread their tentacles upwards, can be delineated in the 'public arena', the arena of public performance and of 'collective activities in public spaces'.[22] So it may be that the untold story lies in the dusty lanes and by-lanes of towns and cities and not only or always in the faceless metropolitan centres; in and around the bustling vernacular newspaper offices, district courts, *thanas*, municipalities; or in the seemingly benign *madaris*, *pathshalas*, mosques, temples and Sufi shrines, the focal point of mobilization in Sind and Punjab;[23] and in the highly charged and volatile precincts of *shuddhi* and Gauraksha Sabhas, the Anjuman-i Islamia's, and the *tabligh* and *tanzim* outfits. These were, undeniably, the sites where myths, memories and divisive religious symbols got invented and propagated to heighten communitarian consciousness and perpetuate the image of the Other. They were also the arenas where wide-ranging issues—some having breached the citadel of inter-community harmony towards the end of the nineteenth century—were passionately contested. Public discussions over cow-slaughter and music in front of mosques, conducted in the columns of newspapers and in printed tracts, pamphlets, journals and books, all added fuel to controversies of one kind or another.

The intricate nature of such processes can be traced to urban centres—Lucknow, Aligarh, Allahabad and Banaras—in late-nineteenth and early twentieth centuries, as also to the rough and rugged rural south-east Punjab where the Jats, having been converted to the Arya Samaj, became the votaries of *shuddhi*, Hindi and cow-slaughter.[24] The urban-rural divide, having been partially bridged by the pan-Indian ideology of re-vitalization movements, involved the separation from and rejection of earlier symbols of joint Hindu-Muslim culture, the definition and affirmation of newer communal symbols,[25] and the invention of a tradition which Christophe Jaffrelot describes, in the context of Hindu nationalism, as 'the strategy of stigmatization and emulation'.[26] This was a new and, from the liberal-left perspective, an ominous development. There had after all, been, common traditions and common reference points in the pre-colonial past, but they had not necessarily developed into the consolidated solidarities which 'Islam' or 'Hinduism' in late-nineteenth and early-twentieth century came to signify.[27] Christopher Bayly thus argued, quite rightly, that prior to 1860 there was perhaps no identifiable 'Muslim', 'Sikh' or 'Hindu' identity that could be abstracted from the particular circumstances of individual events or specific societies.[28] Accordingly, in her work on the interaction between Muslim, Hindu and Christian traditions in the south, Susan Bayly identifies a borrowing of symbols and ideas, a frequently shared vocabulary, and an interweaving of motifs within a common sacred landscape.[29]

Whatever the debate on the nature and depth of such interactions, it must be recognized that Islamization or the 'Nationalization' of Hindu traditions was triggered by factors that not only converged, but also gained salience, at a particular historical conjuncture. It is therefore imperative to properly contextualize these trends rather than read them in the light of dubious theories on the long-standing, irreconcilable Hindu-Muslim differences.

I have no common ground with those who celebrate religious nationalism or contest the pluralist/composite heritage in what has been one the most multicultural societies in the world; on the contrary, the weight of evidence, some of it assembled by British historians and ethnographers, points to a flourishing plural and synthetic civilization providing a hospitable framework within which different communities, cultures and religions have lived side by side and made their distinctive contribution.[30] Within the paradigms of secular historiography—nurtured by the liberal-left strands in Indian nationalism—my own concerns—far removed from the post-modernist discourses and the 'New' histories—are simple enough: why do a people, with a long-standing history of shared living, respond to symbols of discord and disunity at a particular historical juncture? Why was the innocence of the mind, in the words of a common man at Sakhua village in Mymensingh district, 'banished after so many days of living together? Why did the structure of the human mind change overnight?' 'How could that land become somebody else's forever', asked his/her counterpart in Bimyapher village! 'Just one line drawn on the map, and my home becomes a foreign country!'[31] Surely, 'India belongs to all of us, and we have to live and die here. But why this Partition and the exchange of population.'[32] Why did a society with its splendidly plural heritage, become the site of one of the most divisive event of the twentieth century? And last but not the least, if the nineteenth century Urdu poet Mirza Ghalib had been alive, he would have asked in his inimitable style:

> When all is You, and nought exists but You
> Tell me, O Lord, why all this turmoil too?

Despite the recent breakthrough in scholarship on nations and nationalism initiated by Benedict Anderson's *Imagined Communities: Reflections on the Origin and Spread of Nationalism* (1983), these questions (as pertinent today as they were at the time of Independence) need to be analysed afresh with the aid of historical and sociological insights,[33] and in the light of fresh source materials now available in the libraries and archives of India, Pakistan, and the United Kingdom.

To do so, it is important, first of all, not to read the present into the past; in other words, to shed our present-day prejudices and preconceived notions about communalism, and not be guided by the nature of inter-community relations in post-colonial India. Scholarship, although stimulated by preoccupations stemming from the present, is never sufficient in itself to modify the conceptualization of a problem or an event. For this and other reasons, it is necessary to challenge commonly-held assumptions on Islam and the Muslims, a point repeatedly underlined in my writings, delineate the multiple ideological strands amongst them, and trace the *evolution* of a Muslim political personality not in doctrinaire terms, but in the context of colonial policies and the exertions of powerful *Hindutva* and Islamist forces. Their profound impact needs to be explored, as was fruitfully done by the 'Cambridge School' in studies on Indian nationalism, in the regions and localities.

Islam, for one, can no longer be treated as a static point of reference. Contemporary scholarship has drawn attention to changing interpretations over time and the powerful pluralist visions that have shaped the Muslim (not *Islamic*) communities in India and elsewhere. Indeed, as historians and anthropologists have noted, the Islamic tradition has produced a repertoire of concepts that have been employed to validate and explain a wide variety of political, social and intellectual ideas and movements.[34] No longer can we assume, despite the rhetoric of the theologians and the publicists, the existence of a single, inalienable Muslim identity. 'I am against the identities built on religion', stated Nawal El Sadwi, the Egyptian novelist,

> because the history of religion was written in the endless rivers of blood flowing in the name of God. . . . I am an Arab woman. But in my body run the rivers of Africa that flow through Africa from Jinja and Tana. I am African and Arab and Egyptian because my genes were drawn from all these, because my history goes back in Egypt for seven thousand years, to Isis and Ma'at and Noon.[35]

Much the same sentiment was expressed, though contextualized differently, by Azad. In his presidential address at the Ramgarh Congress in 1940, he declared:

> I am a Muslim and profoundly conscious of the fact that I have inherited Islam's glorious traditions of the last thirteen hundred years. I am not prepared to lose even a small part of that legacy. . . . As a Muslim I have a special identity within the field of religion and culture and I cannot tolerate any undue interference with it. But, with all these feelings, I have another equally deep realisation, born out of my life's experience, which is strengthened and not hindered by the spirit of Islam. I am equally proud of the fact that I am an Indian, an essential part of the indivisible unity of Indian nationhood, a vital factor in its total make-up without which this noble edifice will remain incomplete. I can never give up this sincere claim.[36]

Generally speaking, identities in South Asian history and politics have seldom been unified; in colonial India they were increasingly fragmented and fractured. Indeed, they were not singular but multiple, and thus difficult to capture on a single axis. Constructed across different, intersecting and antagonistic sites, discourses, and practices, they are subject to a radical historicization, and are constantly in the process of making and unmaking.[37] Thus Nita Kumar focuses on the existential experiences, of the Hindu and Muslim masses based on their culture of everyday life to argue that 'identity in Banaras has not been communal in the past nor is it progressively becoming so. It is based rather on occupation, social class, and a city's tradition.'[38] An interesting insight into the community of weavers in Banaras is also provided in the following comment in Abdul Bismillah's much acclaimed Hindi novel, *Jhini Jhini Bini Chadaria*: 'There is a community of the world. There is a community of India. There is a community of Hindus. There is a community of Muslims. There is also a community of the weavers in Banaras. *This community is in many different ways different from other communities in the world*'[39] (italics mine).

III

> I thought we would stay by our land, by out stock, by our Mussalman neighbours. No one can touch us, I thought. The riots will pass us by. But a man attacked our village—Oh, the screams of the women, I can hear them still. . . . I had a twenty-year-old brother, tall and strong as a mountain, a match for any five of them. This is what they did: they tied one of his legs to one jeep, the other to another jeep—and then they drove the jeeps apart. . . .
>
> Mola Singh stands quite still. The men look away despite the dark. Their indignation flares into rage.
>
> 'God give our arms strength,' one of them shouts, and in a sudden movement, knives glimmer. Their cry, 'Bole so Nihal, Sat Siri Akal', swells into the ferocious chant: 'Vengeance! Vengeance! Vengeance!' The old Sikh sinks to his knees.
>
> BAPSI SIDHWA, *The Pakistani Bride*

Interest in Partition has grown by leaps and bounds over the last few years: its legacy looms larger than ever before, the scars having proven to be deeper than the healing touch of freedom from colonial rule.[40] This revival of interest in India, according to the novelist Shama Futehally, began with the Babri Masjid dispute, which 'made it impossible, so to speak, to keep the lid on partition any more'.[41] Thereafter, social scientists began recognizing, after having neglected the subject for decades, that Partition is, indeed, the defining moment for understanding India's modern history and specially the current turmoil over religion.[42] Some even wonder 'why we didn't set up a museum to preserve the memory of partition', why 'we chose to live with communal hatred, rather than to objectify it'.[43]

The author Urvashi Butalia bemoaned a few years ago that 'the human history of Partition has a lesser status than the political history'.[44] This is no longer so. Her own book, based on oral narratives and testimonies, illuminates the 'underside' of Partition history.[45] In fact, the disconnection between the rarefied decisions leading to Partition, and the searing consequences in individual lives, remains one of the most powerful tropes that has been carried from Partition fiction into the work of historians and other social scientists.[46] So that, in part a response to the growing interest in 'history of beneath', the task of restoring a human dimension to the partition has received serious attention.[47] Alok Bhalla, editor of an anthology on Partition stories, painfully wonders why religious conflicts destroyed the subcontinent's communal life. The stories he puts together reveal how '*we* fell out of a human world of languages, customs, rituals and prayers into a bestial world of hatred, rage, self-interest and frenzy'.[48]

My own writings recount the trauma of those caught up in the politics of hate and violence, the anguish of the silent majority which was invisible in national or provincial arenas of formal and institutional politics.[49] Moving further away from the meta-narratives of nationalism and communalism, I endeavoured to give a voice to the 'feelings and interests' of 'ordinary folks'. My aim was to emphasize the different meanings and perceptions of Partition, a theme that to the best of my knowledge had not been explored before, and to underline the pluralist view in which religious community is just one and not the sole source of identity. In particular, the two-volume anthology of short stories, poems, diaries, excerpts from autobiographical accounts, and interviews, serves as a reminder of how Partition cruelly displaced millions, divided India's past, wrecked its civilizational rhythm and unity, and left behind a fractured legacy.[50]

Elsewhere, my concern, which I share with my colleague M. Asaduddin, has been to examine how the stories invoke and construct images of Muslims, articulate many intimate yet historically unfamiliar points of reference, and represent the lived experiences of Muslim communities in different regions and socio-economic locations. It has been comforting to discover that, unlike so many historical accounts, the literary representations of Muslims and the nature of their life reveal a wide variety of forms, style, language and symbol adopted by different writers. Neither the forms nor the lives they portray derive from a supposedly homogeneous and unbroken tradition.[51] Sadly, this simple but important fact is lost sight of in constructing the Partition story.

Let me conclude this section with three axioms that have guided my research for nearly two decades. The first relates to the League's rhetoric, mouthed by the Jamaat-i Islami and a section of the Deobandi ulama, on Islam, the *Muslim* nation, and the birth of an *Islamic* society. Their battle-cry, though spurred by some leading Muslim intellectuals—notably Iqbal—and the resurgence of militant Hindu nationalism in certain spheres, had more to do with the political and economic anxieties of various social classes than with a profound urge to carve out an Islamic society and society.[52] This explains the conduct of, and the reasons why, Muslim landlords and professional groups in UP, Bihar and the princely state of Hyderabad, together with the small but upcoming trading and banking communities in western India, hitched their fortunes to the Pakistan demand. Muslim landlords of UP, having had no truck with the League until the 1930s and allied with their Hindu counterparts in their last-ditch battle against the Congress,[53] changed course once the Congress ministry, with its refurbished radical image, adopted the UP Tenancy Bill. Although they continued speaking in the name of Islam, their chief goal was to defend their landholdings, orchards, *havelis*, palaces, and the nawabi paraphernalia built through the courtesy of their British benefactors. Their counterparts in Punjab, many of whom had been staunch supporters of Punjab's Unionist Party—a unique and successful experiment in class-based combination—also sensed the winds of change. They abandoned their erstwhile allies and adopted, by the end of 1945 and *not* before, the safe course of joining the League. Their strategy, one that suited the raj during and after World War II, was to project the Congress and the Unionists, their perceived rivals in the political world, as a *Hindu* party inimical to Islam. In a nutshell, the discordance between the League and the Congress politics in the final decade of the raj was caused by 'the sense of exclusion from the dominant sentiment of Indian nationalism, and not religious zeal, devoid of all temporal considerations'.[54] In the words of the historian Muhammad Mujeeb, whose family split in 1947, 'the needs which found political expression were not the needs of the community as a whole but those of a class, which consisted of big and small landlords, and the lawyers, doctors, government servants who belonged to the families of these landlords'.[55] Once the League bandwagon rolled on, other aggrieved groups, such as the *jotedars* in Bengal and peasant proprietors of the eastern and the ex-servicemen of its north-western districts in Punjab,[56] jumped into the fray as defenders of the faith. In neighbouring Sind, the influential pirs, having received assurances that their social and economic interests would be protected, flocked to the League: it was primarily their position as local leaders that drew them into party politics.[57]

My second axiom, though obvious enough, is scarcely recognized in nationalistic historiography. Pakistan was neither everybody's dream nor was Jinnah the Quaid of the socialists and Marxists,[58] the Khudai Khidmatgars, the ulama of Deoband, the Momins,[59] the Shias connected with the Shia Political Conference,[60] and scores of Muslim groups pushed to the periphery and surviving uneasily on the margins of mainstream national and provincial politics. Yet the standpoint of those, patronizingly referred to as 'Nationalist Muslims',[61] is wilfully ignored because of certain misplaced assumptions about Islam and nationalism and the insistence on projecting the so-called monolithic world view of the Muslim communities. Represented as weak and ineffective by religious and political orthodoxies, their voices, which were by no means inconsequential, have been stifled by 'imperial', 'secular' and 'communal' histories written before and after Independence. Thanks to active state patronage, we celebrate and valorize Muslim/Islam-baiters and rank Hindu communalists, but relegate secular and liberal-minded Muslims—from Badruddin Tyabji's generation to that of Rafi Ahmad Kidwai's—to a historian's footnote. I have been arguing for years that the historian of twentieth century Indian nationalism should foreground the so-called marginal voices among Muslims to rewrite the histories of nationalism, communalism, and Partition.[62]

There is, finally, the need to come to terms with the fact that most 'Hindus', 'Muslims' and 'Sikhs' had no feelings for national borders or the newly created geographical entities that were being laboriously created in 1947; the cartographic and political divisions constituted by Partition are 'the shadow lines' that the novelist Amitav Ghosh seeks to repudiate.[63] National borders, as argued elsewhere, were political constructs, and imagined projections of territorial power. Although they appeared in deceptively precise forms, they reflected, at least initially, merely the mental images of politicians, lawyers, and intellectuals.[64] Their practical consequences, which worked out so differently in various regions and for different classes, must be disaggregated from state-centred academic historiography.[65] Even though the trains had started carrying people to their death traps, large numbers of people, uprooted from their homes in search of a safe haven, were unclear whether Lahore would be part of India or Pakistan, or whether Delhi, the erstwhile imperial capital of the

Mughals and the British, would remain in Gandhi's India or Jinnah's 'moth-eaten' Pakistan. As the novelist Bapsi Sidhwa describes:

Hysteria mounted when the fertile, hot lands of the Punjab were suddenly ripped into two territories—Hindu and Muslim, India and Pakistan. Until the last moment no one was sure how the land would be divided. Lahore, which everyone expected to go to India because so many wealthy Hindus lived in it, went instead to Pakistan. Jullundur, a Sikh stronghold, was allocated to India. . . .[66]

Such descriptions point to an existentialist reality—the separation of people living on both sides who had a long history of cultural and social contact—and the paradoxical character of borders being a metaphor for the ambiguities of nation-building.[67] A lesser known but a highly gifted writer Fikr Taunsvi (1918-87) has poignantly captured this theme in one of his stories. It reads:

A few astrologers in 1947 made the heavenly bodies revolve in such a scientific manner that instead of having one border between them, India and Pakistan had two. Actually the word 'two' had befuddled their minds in such a way that now neither the stars moved in an orderly manner nor did their predictions come true. Exasperated by this very 'two' and swayed by their animosity to 'one' they became oblivious of the fact that the new unit they were trying to create was itself a derivative of one. . . .

The most interesting feature of the Wagah border was the shops set up for the organised sale of religion. A bearded Maulvi sat there with a huge pile of books, including the Vedas, Shastras, Granthas, Gitas and Upanishads . . . Sitting next to him was a Sardarji who sold copies of the Koran, *Fiqh* and *Hadith* and dozens of other writings in Arabic. All those books were a part of the loot that the two gentlemen had brought to sell. Otherwise, they would have been at each other's throats by now. But at Wagah they were selling their books peacefully. . . . If by selling religion one could have two square meals everyday, what could be better. . . .

I quietly took the army sentinel aside and asked: 'Well sir, a tree stood on the bank of the Wagah canal. Can you tell me whether it has been felled and thrown away or…?'

The sentry pointed his bayonet at me and staring at me said: 'Who are you to interfere in this business that concerns the two governments?'

And in the core of my heart I said: 'Listen good man, after all I am a branch of the same tree.'[68]

Saadat Hasan Manto's stories, on the other hand, question the intellectual underpinnings of state-centred national histories: most of his characters, especially Toba Tek Singh, are not reconciled to borders being drawn and people being uprooted from their social and cultural milieu. They remind us time and again that, regardless of religious passions being heightened by the politics of hate and separation and of the fragile nature of inter-community relations in the 1940s, most people had no clue whatsoever that their fate would be settled after Mountbatten's three days of 'diplomacy'; that a man called Cyril Radcliffe—whose credentials as an eminent British jurist is invoked to compensate for his lack of knowledge and experience of the subcontinent—would descend on Indian soil on a hot and sultry summer day and decide the frontiers in just seven weeks. Though diehard apologists of the raj—H.V. Hodson, the Reform Commissioner in 1941, Philip Ziegler, biographer of Mounbatten, & Co.—and their intellectual allies in the subcontinent have a different tale to tell, a creative writer, writing in the early 1980s, portrays the brutal consequences of a reckless though calculated imperial design:

> Now that it was decided they would leave, the British were in a hurry to wind up. . . . Preoccupied with misgiving and the arrangements attendant on relocating themselves in their native land, by the agony of separation from regiments, Imperial trappings and servants, the rulers of the Empire were entirely too busy to bother overmuch with how India was divided. It was only one of the thousand and one chores they faced.
>
> The earth is not easy to carve up. India required a deft and sensitive surgeon, but the British, steeped in domestic preoccupation, hastily and carelessly butchered it. They were not deliberately mischievous—only cruelly negligent! A million Indian died. The earth sealed its clumsy new boundaries in blood as town by town, farm by farm, the border was defined. Trains carrying refugees sped through the darkness of night—Hindus going one way and Muslims the other. They left at odd hours to try to dodge mobs bent on their destruction. Yet trains were ambushed and looted and their fleeing occupants slaughtered.[69]

Anguished by the communal riots, Nehru wrote in June 1947: 'It is curious that when tragedy affects an individual we feel the full force of it, but when that individual is multiplied a thousand-fold, our senses are dulled and we become insensitive.'[70] This was certainly not true of creative writers, many of whom reveal the other face of freedom, the 'freedom drenched in blood and gore'.[71] They bring to light, in a way that official chronicles do not, the plight of migrants, the woes of divided families and the trauma of raped and abducted women. Numerous texts, retrieve from the silence untold stories of women, stories that have died unspoken on the lips of their hapless protagonists.[72] Locating women at the centre (rather than the periphery) of discussions around Partition, argues Ritu Menon, casts a rather different light on the event and its consequences. In an engaging discussion of government policy on the recovery of abducted women by India and Pakistan, she explores the relationship of women to community identity and to the state and citizenship. Adult women, according to Menon, were forcibly 'recovered' purely on the basis of religious identity and in violation of all rights of citizens in a secular state.[73]

All said and done, literary narratives, whether in Hindi, Urdu, Bengali or Punjabi, are an eloquent witness to 'an unspeakable and inarticulatable history'.[74] Evoking the sufferings of the innocent, whose pain is more universal and ultimately a vehicle of more honest reconciliation than political discourse,[75] they provide a framework for developing an alternative discourse on inter-community relations. What lends greater credence to their creative imagination is their ability to unfold certain critically important dimensions without religion or community as the principal reference points. This is illustrated in Manto's literary vignettes, *Siyah Hashye* (Black Margins):

PRAISE BE TO THE LORD

The dancing session was over. The clients went away. That is when *Ustadji* said, having lost everything (during Partition) we came to this city. Praise is to Allah *Miyan* for having showered us with these riches in just a few days.

DOUBLE CROSS

Look buddy, you sold me petrol at black-market prices and not a single shop could be set on fire.

WHO ARE YOU?

The rioters wrestled hard with the landlord to drag him out of the house. He stood up, brushed his clothes and told them. 'Kill me for all I care. But I warn you not to touch my money—not a paisa.'

IV

Where do we go from here? asks the writer Bhisham Sahni.

Should people organize themselves on the basis of caste and community and fight collectively for their rightful demands? Or, should they ignore caste and community and fight on the basis of the deprived against the privileged, for there are both rich and poor among castes and communities? 'I believe the second course is still the right one, for it cuts across caste and community loyalties, and thereby weakens their stranglehold, and in consequence strengthens, in its own way, the pluralistic character of our polity. We certainly have a very long way to go.[76]

Today the historiography of Partition is hampered by mental laziness and pious rehashing even more than political ideology. Surely, it is time to strip it of the elementary significations it has bequeathed to its heirs, and to restore to it another *primum movens* of the historian, namely, intellectual curiosity and the free search for knowledge about the past.[77]

NOTES

1. It is common to connect the two-nation theory with the Aligarh reformer, Saiyid Ahmad Khan, and not his contemporary Dayanand Saraswati, the high priest of the Arya Samaj. The former appears to me to be far more tolerant, eclectic and broad-minded in his orientation and outlook than the latter. Beginning with the Arya Samaj movement and culminating in the writings of Veer Savarkar and Guru Golwalkar, the relentless search for a 'Hindu nation' and a 'Hindu identity' provided the underpinnings of the two-nation theory. Long before Jinnah appeared on the scene, Lala Har Dayal stated in 1925: 'I declare that the future of the Hindu race, of Hindustan and of the Punjab, rest on four pillars: (1) Hindu Sangathan, (2) Hindu raj, (3) *Shuddhi* of Moslems, and (4) Conquest and *Shuddhi* of Afghanistan and the frontiers. . . . The Hindu race has but one history and its institutions are homogeneous. But the Mussalmans and Christians are far removed from the confines of Hinduism, for their religions are alien and they love Persian, Arab and European institutions. Thus, just as one removes foreign matter from the eye, *Shuddhi* must be made of these two religions.' Quoted in Emily C. Brown, *Har Dayal: Hindu Revolutionary and Rationalist*, New Delhi, 1975, p. 233. This characterization of Christianity and Islam led Savarkar to write that, 'when the Muslims penetrated India, the conflict of life and death began'.
2. Adding a fresh dimension to the debate, Sumit Sarkar points out that constructions of Indian nationalism, Hindu unity and *Hindutva* were partly related, though in different ways, to efforts to respond to counter 'pressures from below' in the form of lower-caste aspirations. Sumit Sarkar, *Writing Social History*, Chap. 9.
3. Increasingly, this view is being challenged by regional and local studies. For example, Tazeen M. Murshid, *The Sacred and the Secular: Bengal Muslim Discourses, 1871-1977*, Calcutta, 1995, and the collection of essays in Mushirul Hasan (ed.), *Islam, Communities and the Nation*.
4. I have discussed this point at length in *Legacy of a Divided Nation*.
5. Larson, *India's Agony Over Religion*, pp. 183-4.
6. Akbar S. Ahmed, *Jinnah, Pakistan and Islamic Identity: The Search for Saladin*, Karachi, 1997, p. xviii. Notice, too, his comment: 'When a leader who commands respect in the Muslim community appears, and can focus on a cause, Muslims are capable of moving mountains', p. xxi.

7. I have borrowed this idea from Furet, *Interpreting the French Revolution*, p. 10.
8. Hasan (ed.), *India's Partition: Process, Strategy and Mobilization*.
9. Eric Hobsbawm, *Age of Extremes: The Short Twentieth Century 1914-1991*, London: 1994, pp. 219-20. Ian Talbot has examined the Punjabi Muslims support to the Muslims in the context of the War. *Punjab and the Raj, 1849-1947*, while Anita Inder Singh argues that the outbreak of War 'saved' the League and made it a representative Muslim body. Her contention is that the British deliberately built up Jinnah's prestige at the all India level for their war purposes, though at the provincial level they subordinated this objective to the prime necessity of operating the war machine with maximum efficiency. *The Origins of the Partition of India*, pp. 238, 241-2. The provincial scene is best surveyed in Jalal, *The Sole Spokesmen*.
10. Muhammad Amir Ahmad (brother of the raja of Mahmudabad) to Jinnah, 29 Nov. 1939, Shamsul Hasan Collection, Karachi.
11. Moon (ed.), *The Viceroy's Journal*, p. 267.
12. Quoted in Brown, *Gandhi: Prisoner of Hope*, p. 369.
13. 21 Sept. 1947, Alan Campbell-Johnson, *Mission with Mountbatten*, p. 201.
14. Bayly, *Rulers, Townsmen and Bazaars: North Indian Society in the Age of British Expansion*.
15. Sumit Sarkar, *A Critique of Colonial India*, Calcutta, 1985, p. 116.
16. Das, *Communal Riots in Bengal*, p. 207.
17. Sumit Sarkar, 'The Conditions and Nature of Subaltern Militancy: Bengal from Swadeshi to Non-Cooperation, c. 1905-22', in Ranajit Guha (ed.), *Subaltern Studies*, Vol. 3, New Delhi, 1984, p. 272. Rafiuddin Ahmed has shown how religious preachers prompted the masses to look beyond the borders of Bengal in quest of their supposed Bengali Islamic past and attach greater importance to their 'Muslim' as opposed to their local or regional identity. This new emphasis, according to him, proved crucial to the subsequent emergence of a measure of social cohesion in a diversified and even culturally polarised society. Ahmed, *The Bengal Muslims*, p. 184.
18. Robinson, *Separatism Among Indian Muslims*, Chap. 1.
19. The emergence of a corporate Sikh identity, according to Harjot Oberoi, was 'a sort of dialectical process', a response to what was happening to the Hindus and Muslims in terms of 'imagination, experience and cultural organization'. Historically, 'it is more precise to speak in terms of a simultaneity of religious identities rather than distinct, universal, religious collectivities'. *The Construction of Religious Boundaries: Culture, Identity and Diversity in the Sikh Tradition*, New Delhi, 1994, pp. 418, 424.
20. Nonica Datta's incisive study traces the emergence of Jat identity within the cultural context of rural southeast Punjab, arguing that identities are not just products of colonial institutions and economic changes but created by communities on the strength of inherited cultural resources as well as invented

traditions. So that the Jats were active participants in the construction of their own identity. *Forming an Identity: A Social History of the Jats*, New Delhi, 1999.

21. For Punjab, Gilmartin, *Empire and Islam*, p. 225.
22. Freitag, *Collective Action and Community*.
23. Ansari, *Sufi Saints and State Power: The Pirs of Sind, 1843-1947*, and Gilmartin, *Empire and Islam*, op. cit.
24. Datta, *Forming an Identity*, and her 'The "Subalternity" of Education: Gurukuls in Rural Southeast Punjab', in Hasan (ed.), *Knowledge, Power and Politics*; Kenneth W. Jones, *Socio-Religious Reform Movements in British India*, Delhi, 1994, and his *Arya Dharm: Hindu Consciousness in 19th century Punjab*, Berkeley, 1976.
25. See, for example, Christopher R. King, 'The Hindi movement in Banaras, 1868-1914', in Freitag (ed.), *Culture and Power in Banaras*.
26. Christophe Jaffrelot, *The Hindu Nationalist Movement and Indian Politics 1925 to the 1990s*, London, 1997, p. 6.
27. For Hinduism, Vasudha Dalmia, *The Nationalization of Hindu Traditions: Bharatendu Harischandrra and Nineteenth-century Banaras*, New Delhi, 1997, p. 1.
28. C.A. Bayly, 'The Pre-history of "Communalism"? Religious Conflict in India, 1700-1860', *MAS*, Vol. 19, 2, 1985, p. 202.
29. Bayly, *Saint, Goddesses and Kings*, and, Kate Brittlebank, *Tipu Sultan's Search for Legitimacy: Islam and Kingship in a Hindu Domain*, New Delhi, 1995.
30. For an incisive analysis of Gandhi's views, also in the context of the Partition, Bhiku Parekh, *Gandhi's Political Philosophy: A Critical Examination*, London, 1989.
31. Chakrabarty: 'Remembered Villages' in Low and Brasted (eds.), *Freedom, Trauma, Continuities*.
32. Anis Kidwai, 'In the Shadow of Freedom', in Hasan (ed.), *India Partitioned*, Vol. 2, p. 161.
33. For example, essays in T.N. Madan (ed.), *Muslim Communities of South Asia: Culture, Society, and Power*, New Delhi, rev. and enlarged edn., 2000, and his *Modern Myths, Locked Minds: Secularism and Fundamentalism in India*, New Delhi, 1997. Peter van der Veer, *Religious Nationalism: Hindus and Muslims in India*, Berkeley, 1994.
34. Introduction to Imtiaz Ahmad (ed.), *Ritual and Religion Among Muslims in India*, New Delhi, 1981, pp. 18-19; Barbara Daly Metcalf (ed.), *Moral Conduct and Authority: The Place of Adab in South Asian Islam*, Berkeley, 1984, p. 15.
35. *The Nawal El Saadwi Reader*, London, 1997, p. 127.
36. Quoted in Syeda Saiyidain Hameed (ed.), *India's Maulana: Abul Kalam Azad*, Vol. 2, New Delhi, 1990, and p. 161.
37. Hasan (ed.), *Islam, Communities and the Nation*.
38. Nita Kumar, *The Artisans of Banaras: Popular Culture and Identity, 1880-1986*, Princeton, N.J., 1988, p. 227.

39. Cited in Sudhir Kumar, 'Reconstructing the Nation: Image of the Nation in the Fiction of Muslim Writers', in *Studies in Humanities and Social Sciences* (Shimla), Vol. 1, Nov. 1994, p. 125.
40. Sugata Bose and Ayesha Jalal, *Modern South Asia: History, Culture, Political Economy*, New Delhi, 1998, p. 191.
41. *Indian Book Review* (New Delhi), Oct. 1993, p. 19.
42. Larson, *India's Agony Over Religion*, p. 183. Historians, in particular have taken the lead in challenging the old shibboleths dominating partition studies. As a result, we now have a better sense of, in the context of the transfer of power, the 'contradictions and structural peculiarities of Indian society and politics in late colonial India', 'the history that Partition creates' and the impact and representation of Partition violence. Some of the interesting works are by: Pandey, 'The Prose of Otherness', Arnold and Hardiman (eds.), *Subaltern Studies VII*; Shail Mayaram, 'Speech, Silence and the Making of Partition', in Shahid Amin and Dipesh Chakrabarty (eds.), *Subaltern Studies IX: Writings on South Asian History and Society*, New Delhi, 1996; Ranabir Samaddar (ed.), *Reflections on Partition in the East*, New Delhi, 1997.
43. Krishna Kumar, *Times of India* (Delhi), 10 Feb. 1999.
44. *Seminar* (Delhi), Aug. 1994.
45. Urvashi Butalia, *The Other Side of Silence: Voices from the Partition of India*, New Delhi, 1998, p. 10.
46. David Gilmartin, 'Partition, Pakistan and South Asian History: In Search of a Narrative', *The Journal of Asian Studies*, Vol. 57, No. 4, Nov. 1998, p. 1069.
47. See, for example, Ian Talbot, *Freedom's City: The Popular Dimension in the Pakistan Movement and Partition Experience in North-West India*, Karachi, 1996.
48. Alok Bhalla (ed.), *Stories About the Partition of India*, Vol. 1, New Delhi, 1994, pp. xxxii-xxxiii.
49. *Legacy of a Divided Nation*, Chap. 4.
50. Hasan (ed.), *India Partitioned.*
51. See Mushirul Hasan and M. Asaduddin (eds.), *Images and Representation: Stories of Muslim Lives in India*, New Delhi, 2000.
52. Brass, *Language, Religion and Politics in North India*, argued that Muslims of UP had a larger share of government jobs than their 14 per cent of the population warranted, and that Muslim politicians created the myth of 'Muslim backwardness' to protect their privileges and then selected divisive symbols to mobilise support for their own drive to power. Focussing on the landowning class, the economic mainstay of the Muslim elite, Lance Brennan demonstrated that, 'by mid-1939 the Muslim elite of UP had lost their illusion: the foundation they had fought so hard to build were shown to be straw. It was from this time that they began to embrace a new separatism. . . . Previously, they had aimed at striking a set of bargains with the Hindus in the province—now their objective was complete separation from the Hindus.' 'The Illusion of Security: The Background of Muslim Separatism in the United Provinces', Hasan (ed.), *India's Partition*, p. 360. Partha Chatterjee has, on

the other hand, argued that Muslim politics in Bengal in the period 1937-47 had a great deal to do with the structures and processes of the colonial state machinery. 'Bengal Politics and the Muslim Masses, 1920-47', in *India's Partition*, pp. 174-5.

53. Peter Reeves, 'Adjusting to Congress Dominance: The UP Landlords, 1937-1947', Sisson and Wolpert (eds.), Congress *and Indian Nationalism*, pp. 160-9.
54. Ayesha Jalal, 'Ideology and the Struggle for Democratic Institutions', Victoria Schofield (ed.), *Old Roads New Highways: Fifty Years of Pakistan*, Karachi, 1997, pp. 129-30.
55. M. Mujeeb, 'The Partition of India in Retrospect', in Philips and Wainwright (eds.), *The Partition of India*, p. 410.
56. Talbot, *Punjab and the raj*, p. 208.
57. Ansari, *Sufi Saints*, p. 122.
58. K.H. Ansari, *The Emergence of Socialist Thought Among North Indian Muslims 1917-1947*, Lahore, 1990.
59. Papiya Ghosh 'Partition's Biharis', in Hasan (ed.), *Islam, Communities and the Nation*, pp. 229-64.
60. Mushirul Hasan, 'Traditional Sites and Contested Meanings: Sectarian Strife in Colonial Lucknow', see above.
61. I have argued against the use of this expression in *A Nationalist Conscience*.
62. 'Those who got the worse of it, both in India and Pakistan', commented a well-known Urdu writer, 'were the honest, sincere Nationalist Muslims who, in the eyes of Hindus, were Muslims, and *vice versa*. Their sacrifices were reduced to ashes. Their personal integrity and loyalty were derided. Their morale was shattered like a disintegrating star; their lives lost meaning. Like the crumbling pillars of a mosque they could neither be saved nor used. India, for whose independence they had fought the British, refused to offer them refuge. So much so that they incurred the wrath of their own community. They were like that distant thunder which rises in the desert and then descends and disappears into the sand dumes. . . . For them the special day of independence was unusual, spent in the seclusion of the four walls of their homes. The League had made them untouchables to their fellow-Indians; they were reduced to the status of harijans in India.' Shorish Kashmiri, *Boo-i gul Naala-i dil Dood-i Chiragh-i Mehfil*, cited in Hasan (ed.), *India Partitioned*, Vol. 2, p. 145.
63. The reference to the novel *Shadow Lines* (Delhi, 1988) is drawn from Priya Kumar, 'Testimonies of Loss and Memory: Partition and the Haunting of a Nation', *Interventions*, 1999, p. 204.
64. Michiel Baud and Willem van Schendel, 'Towards a Comparative History of Borderlands', in *Journal of World History*, Vol. 8, 2, 1997, pp. 211-42.
65. See my 'Memories of a Fragmented Nation: Rewriting the Histories of Partition' above, and Ritu Menon, 'Cartographies of Nations and Identities: A Post-Partition Predicament', *Interventions*, London: Routledge, Vol. 1, 2, 1999.

66. Sidhwa, *The Pakistan Bride*, p. 4.
67. These lines are based on Baud and Schendel, 'Towards a Comparative History of Borderlands', pp. 211-42.
68. 'The Wagah Canal', in Hasan (ed.), *India Partitioned*, Vol. 1, pp. 250, 253, 255.
69. Sidhwa, *The Pakistan Bride*, pp. 17-18.
70. *SWJN*, Vol. 3, second series, p. 180.
71. Anis Kidwai, 'In the Shadow of Freedom', in Hasan (ed.), *India Partitioned*, Vol. 2, p. 161.
72. Deepika Bahri, 'Telling Tales: Women and the Trauma of Partition in Sidhwa's Cracking India', *Interventions*, 1999, p. 219.
73. Menon and Bhasin, *Borders & Boundaries*, and Veena Das, 'National Honour and Practical Kinship: Of Unwanted Women and Children', *Critical Events: An Anthropological Perspective on Contemporary India*, New Delhi, 1995, pp. 55-83.
74. Kumar, 'Testimonies', *Interventions*, 1999, p. 202.
75. Francisco, 'In the Heat of Fratricide', p. 250.
76. Bhisham Sahni, 'Images of Communities: Reflections of a Writer', *Studies in Humanities and Social Sciences*, Vol. 1, Nov. 1994, p. 5.
77. Francois Furet's plea to the historians of the French Revolution makes very good sense in the context of partition studies. See *Interpreting the French Revolution*, Cambridge, 1981, pp. 10-11.

PART IV

14

Moradabad Riots, 1980: Causes and Meanings

Between mid-August and early November 1980, Muslims in Moradabad experienced the most bloody orgy of violence.[1] Officially verified deaths, for which the government paid 'compensation' ran to about 400; a careful, responsible Muslim group estimated deaths at 2,500; other observers put the number between 1,500 and 2,000. This sustained, frenzied aggression was unmistakably engineered by the city policemen in uniform. The events were no less shattering for anyone who cares about the state of society in present and future India.

Various studies have revealed that these events were not so strange as to defy belief; previous riots from Ahmedabad to Pune and Sholapur presaged most of the themes.[2] Notable only are the intensity of the frenzy, the depth of official complicity, and the wholly unjustified confidence of the mass media—with but a few exceptions—in the official version of events. What happened in Moradabad has to be seen, however, in its historical setting, both in India as a whole and in the city of Moradabad. These pages seek to bring the events alive again, and reviewing the attitudes and actions in Moradabad might cause some of us to assess our own attitudes.

It is not, however, intended to provide an expose of events in Moradabad—although that is needed—but to illustrate several facets of contemporary Indian society. We wish to comment on the position of Muslims in north Indian society generally; we wish to advance a more candid examination of the tenor of Hindu-Muslim relationships in our past and our present; and finally, we wish to take notice of a chilling case of administrative regression, one that happens to illustrate more general tendencies around us too.

II

We begin with the general position of Muslims in north Indian society. There are enclaves of professional groups where one could almost forget whether one is a Muslim or a Hindu. We also know of areas like Chandni Chowk in Delhi where mutual understanding and exchange of services is widespread, if only because Muslim craftsmen have to rely heavily on the predominant Hindu trading community in the locality. To live apart—'within one's community', meaning kin or caste—is an old Indian pattern; but recent decades have seen a great deal of intermingling, especially in the new urban areas. Yet, one would not easily find many Muslims among the tenants or houseowners in the mixed, privately-owned urban localities. In part, as this reflects the Muslims' general economic position, observations on this are not out of place.

The weakness of the Muslims' economic position, particularly in north India, is partly due to the fragmentation of the community in the wake of Partition, and the exodus of certain powerful professional groups, traders and bankers to the newly-born country. This is evident in their sparse representation in the upper echelons of commerce, industry, administration, or the professions in India. Recent figures indicate that the percentage of Muslims in the Indian Administrative Service is less than half their percentage in the total population; while barely 2 per cent of government officials at the highest levels and less than 0.5 per cent of government clerks and peons are Muslims (Table 14.1).

Table 14.1: Muslims in the combined gradation list of IAS Officers 1948-74

Years	All	Muslims	Percentage
1948-52	149	1	0.67
1953-7	242	5	2.06
1958-62	361	5	1.38
1963-7	596	10	1.67
1968-72	500	9	1.80
1973-7	689	21	3.04
Total	2,537	51	2.01

Source: A.R. Shervani, 'Muslims in Indian Administrative Service, *Journal of Rabitat Al-Alam Al-Islami*, p. 33.

Precise figures are not available for the army, but they are usually said to be about the same as for the police. The figure commonly provided is that Muslims account for about 3 per cent of the total Indian police force. In the Provincial Armed Constabulory (PAC), notorious for its anti-Muslim venom, there are only 300 Muslims out of a force of 2 lakhs.

Politics is a rather special domain but if we ignore the decorative offices of president and vice-president, the 'Sarkari Muslims' who help the powers-that-be in sidestepping the major crises facing the country and concern ourselves with the substantative issues facing the Muslims, their weak base in politics would be plain. The same pattern is apparent in academia. Apart from institutions like Aligarh Muslim University,[3] and limited fields like Urdu and medieval Indian history, there is very little to cheer the Muslims. More distressing perhaps is the mushroom growth of *Dini Talim* schools—6,000 in UP with an enrolment of 6,00,000 students[4]—where the pupils are lulled into an illusion of education with Islamic texts.[5] The importance of such blockages goes far beyond statistics or particular persons' incomes. At stake are the informal access to certain kinds of information, the orientation to the wider social order commonly transmitted in the informal social relationships, and the sense of efficacy and competence that comes from knowing those who know and who can help put the 'official' seal of approval upon things happening the way you would like them to happen.

We realize, of course, the difficulty with categories like Hindu and Muslim in such matters: differentiation and inequalities within the categories may well be much greater than between the categories. If we choose, nevertheless, to employ these categories, this reflects our judgement that during the past three decades the Muslims in north India at different levels have had to cope with considerable hostile prejudices. Given the background to, and the fact of, Partition, the existence of some antagonism is not unexpected. What we need to recognize, however, is the co-existence of widespread public and private denial that any prejudice exists and the fact of its even more widespread, informal, active operation. To be sure, Muslims are not excluded from opportunity completely. It is merely that this happens often enough to make all the difference.

This difference is magnified by the rules by which we play the game. These rules are permissive enough for our competitive situations often permit assertive aggression without limits, with no holds barred. In such situations, a Muslim always has to reckon with the possibility that his religious identity might be thrown at him, publicly or privately, in a threatening manner. He would have grown up knowing the pain and the humiliation of being so insulted. More often than not, he chooses to withdraw, or at least not to press things to a point where the communal card would be played against him. The combination of active antagonism and this inclination to withdraw acts cumulatively to depress ambitions, especially in the generation which has been taught to take a constructive view of the prospects in the immediate milieu. As one Muslim observer pointed out: 'The demoralizing effect of such perceptions is that people give up the struggle to improve their competence. Consequently, whenever opportunity is available, they are left behind. Thus, the "self-fulfilling prophecy" comes true.'

The same point may be made from another angle. Economic weakness is by no means unique to the Muslims in north India. There are the scheduled castes and tribes, but the compensatory programmes have been useful at least in certain pockets within these categories; there are no counterparts to these for the Muslims, nor are any likely. Yet, other categories in the north Indian population—Kurmi, Yadav, Gujar—have been economically weak and have not had access to compensatory programmes; but they have in some measures sought to neutralize their weakness through mobilization in the political domain, using their numbers and voting strength to secure attention. To be sure, such mobilization, when it seeks politically allocated resources by way of job quotas, etc., has generated violent contentiousness in Bihar and elsewhere; but the magnitude of this contentiousness is small compared to the consequences that await Muslims when they seek to assert themselves, politically or otherwise. And this brings us to the general question of relations between Hindus and Muslims in these parts.

Concerning this relationship, various interpretations are abroad, often argued with intense passion. We have space here only to indicate our own understanding of tne relationship in its historical context. We judge the relationship to have been highly ambivalent. The two traditions build upon widely divergent ideals concerning the nature of human beings and their relationship to the supernatural and to each other. In a milieu where the weight of religious orthodoxy has been variable, but always considerable, with religious precepts and observances influencing much in daily life, these divergent premises have inevitably led the two traditions to grate upon each other. Yet, most people have a large stake in the smooth flow of their daily life, and therefore, the appropriate accommodations, sometimes extending into syncretic sects, have generally been forthcoming.

It is nevertheless difficult to deny that considerable antagonism has resided in this relationship over the decades. To account for it, serious consideration should be given to Ratna Naidu's point that there is a history of mutual humiliation between those anchored in the two traditions in India. The urge to humiliate an adversary may be unusually strong and widespread in our society; whether this is so, and if so why, are questions worthy of enquiry. Insofar as this proclivity is expressed through attacks on religious symbols, one would imagine that the religious specialists of the affected side would interpret political attacks in religious terms and their interpretations would be handed down in myth and legend.

When myths and legends identify certain adversaries as posing grave threats to crucial social identities, the basis is laid for neurotic fears and anxieties such as would foist apocalyptic intentions upon the most ordinary of acts. It is necessary to posit some such mechanism in order to account for the heady rumours which invariably take wing during communal tension. Two examples will suffice. During the Ahmedabad riots in 1969, a widely circulated evening daily carried on its front-page lurid, though totally imaginary, details about the molestation of Hindu women in the Lal Mill area, and the All India Radio broadcast a false rumour about the poisoning of the city's milk supply in that communally charged atmosphere. In Moradabad in 1980, some activity on moving two *madaris* to more spacious grounds, and some talk of starting a third, led to the inference, published in a pamphlet, *Burning Moradabad*, that the Muslims were planning to turn the city into a fortress, in order to lay the basis for another Pakistan. Also, 'a college built with foreign money (reference to petro-dollars from Saudi Arabia and some Gulf States, in particular) will be (an) abode of foreign powers; one day this may even place our capital Delhi in jeopardy. . . . Though there is no objection to (the) spread of religious education . . . there is valid objection in setting up of religious forces convertible into armies.'[6]

Such fantasies are no monopoly of the Hindus: similar fears and anxieties lay behind the demand for a separate homeland in the 1940s, and, in more recent times, are served up by the Muslim communalist press, such as the *Dawat* daily and the *Radiance* weekly. We wish merely to stress that these anxieties and fantasies are often pathological. As with individuals so with societies, such complexes, to be resolved satisfactorily, need to be brought into our consciousness and tested against the probabilities in real life, not suppressed into the unconscious—as is often done by *both* communalists *and* secularists—for that merely makes their resolution that much more difficult.

To account for the particular course of events in Moradabad recounted below, one more element—the city administration—has to be kept in mind.

To expect to find a Solomon in every seat of local authority may be foolish. If communal fears are as deeply ingrained as the foregoing has suggested, one may take it for granted that these percolate in some measure into officialdom—which, as we have suggested, is invariably largely Hindu. We know that elsewhere the local officials and the guardians of law and order have often acted brutally towards the Muslims, for example in Aligarh. In Jamshedpur in April 1979, lapses on the part of the local officials, combined with the Bihar Military Force actively participating in the riot on the side of the Hindus, helped turn a minor fracas into the worst communal carnage since 1964 in that industrial metropolis (Singh 1979). Likewise Moradabad. The city's police, for long weeks, acted rather like a force organized to beat, loot, and kill the Muslims. The PAC, in particular, collaborated with communal elements and *goondas* in one community to bring about an open clash between Hindus and Muslims.[7] The PAC, reported a *Patriot* correspondent on 27 August 1980, 'has . . . earned for itself the rather dubious distinction of being the most hated organization in Moradabad'. This is not all. The various organs of administration including, alas, the judiciary appeared to act in a way supportive to the activities of the local police and the PAC.

We proceed now to consider the social setting in Moradabad and to recount the specific developments between August and November 1980.

III

The earliest known communal riot in Moradabad, once an administrative part of Rohilkhand division, occurred in 1848 on the occasion of the Muharram procession, followed by a more serious outburst in 1872. Similar riots in later years flowed from the structure of municipalities which were gradually being turned into arenas of intense communal battles. Tension arose in the 1980s over frequent reports of Muslims manipulating the electoral machinery to their advantage, leading the vice-chairman of the municipal board to complain that: 'Ever since the introduction of the principle of local self-government, the Hindus in Moradabad have had no share in Municipal administration, and are really worse off than they would have been if local self-government had never been granted to Moradabad.'

The result of such complaints, combined with the redrawing of ward boundaries that followed the 1900 Municipalities Act, destroyed the Muslim majority, a trend also noticeable in other Rohilkhand towns, such as Budaun and Chandpur. Such losses mattered a great deal, for the victorious community often used its dominance to assert its religious interests.

For instance, after the Hindus gained the upper hand in Moradabad, they compelled Muslim butchers to dry their hides outside the city; in Chandpur, they forbade cow-slaughter. Such pressure, often reinforced by the communal proclivities of national and provincial leaders, contributed to the growing communal animosity in Moradabad.[8]

In the late 1930s, the Muslim League gained a strong foothold in Moradabad; in 1946, it captured a majority of Muslim seats in the provincial elections. This astonishing success of an organization which had been so effectively displaced by the Congress in the 1937 elections reflected the widespread Muslim disillusionment with the Congress movement (Brennan 1977: 476). It also indicated the momentum gained by the League electoral machinery, which was geared up for the occasion by nawabzada Liaquat Ali Khan, and Khaliquzzaman, a 'deserter' from the Congress camp. In Moradabad, the initiative was wrested by Qazi Taslim Husain, a lawyer, who operated from the Muslim *Musafir Khana*—now frequented by the migrant Bihari workers and enthusiasts of the Tablighi Jamaat. Indeed, the *Musafir Khana*, located across the railway station in a predominantly Muslim area, was the focal point of Muslim 'separatist' politics in Moradabad.

Hindu communal groups, organized under the aegis of the RSS and the Arya Samaj, carried on their campaign against Muslims in general, and the Muslim League in particular. Raising the spectre of Muslim dominance, they organized *akharas* in the 1930s and revived the *shuddhi* and *sangathan* movements. Among those who joined such activities were traders, wealthy merchants, and some professional men who resented Muslim dominance in the law courts, in medicine, and in education. Following the Calcutta killing in 1946, such elements launched themselves with renewed vigour. After Partition, their growth was markedly enhanced and, in early January 1948, there occurred widespread riots.

During the August-November 1980 riots, the propaganda machinery made special reference to the 'Muslim atrocities' in the past in order to justify the killings in the present. Today, Moradabad is reached in a little over three hours by a fast train from Delhi; a fast bus takes an hour longer. Physically, the city offers a marked contrast between the Civil Lines, with its cluster of courts, administrative offices and neatly laid out residences, and the wealthy Punjabi exporters' new residences off Station Road and showrooms on Station Road (an area built after 1950) on the one hand, and the more crowded bulk of residential areas on the other. In many of these areas, little bits of industrial activity—a furnace here, a grinder there—are virtually part of family life; a cluster of lathes may be located in a separate room. It appears that in areas like Katgarh where the bulk of small-scale industrial work gets done—and where the population happens to be predominantly Muslim—civic neglect is the greatest; nearly every crossing has its mound of nightsoil and other rubbish, awaiting leisurely removal. In many of these areas, drainage was bad even during a dry January; during the monsoons we heard that some of these streets become open sewers, heavy with acid and other industrial waste from the workshops. Given these conditions, it is not surprising that some of the new wealth in Muslim hands, which we discuss later, should have sought to flow into new housing colonies, or that these colonies should have been given Muslim sounding names. The beginnings of a few such neighbourhoods set alarm bells ringing. Says the pamphlet *Burning Moradabad*: 'They have a dream of creating a Muslim State within UP, constituted of (the) western districts. . . . So they are creating the same conditions of panic and disorder for bending the knees of Hindus as they did in 1945, 1946 and 1947.'

Where does Moradabad's wealth come from? The city used to be a centre for making brass kitchenware in small scale units. After Partition, a number of Punjabi families, displaced from their ancestral homes in Pakistan, settled in Moradabad and, over the years, reoriented the industrial apparatus into producing decorative brassware—inlaid with other metals, wood, shell, and so forth—principally for export. The annual output, according to the *Patriot* (29 August 1980) is in the range of Rs. 100 crore, with about half exported. In recent years, the indigenous Muslims have been moving into this export business on a growing scale, attracting workers to the tune of 75,000 from different parts of UP and Bihar and providing employment to Muslims from the neighbouring towns of Sambhal, Chandausi and Budaun. But their offices tend to be located in their homes, usually alongside some production facility. The workshops are virtually all small-scale, each concentrating on one or another of the scores of manufacturing stages in the production of the intricate designs. At each stage the partly-finished goods move to a different locale.

The district population according to the 1971 Census was 24,28,971, while Moradabad city had a population of 2,72,355 in the same year. Moradabad has no elective municipal body.[9] Lying next to Rampur, a state formerly ruled by a Muslim prince, Moradabad district has long had a concentration of Muslims who, in pre-1947 days, congregated in towns as absentee landlords, officials, traders, artisans and weavers, and who played an important part in the life of most Rohilkhand towns. In the city, Muslims represented nearly 60 per cent of the population. In the district, they held

42 per cent of the land. Indeed, Muslims were more powerful in Moradabad than in any other district of UP. But this is no longer the case. Muslims have gradually lost out to the enterprising Punjabis, selling off their land and property. Many of the houses now lined up in Adarsh Nagar, Kothi Bal Nagar and the Civil Lines were purchased from depressed, absentee Muslim landlords who, under force of circumstances, have withdrawn into the countryside to guard their limited landholdings.

The Muslims of Moradabad have lagged behind in education. Except for a few families who insist on sending their children to the Aligarh Muslim University, the majority have stayed away from both government and privately-managed institutions, a fact noted by Mr Lawrence, vice-principal of Parker Intermediate College. Most of them flock to the five or six well known *madaris* which impart instruction in traditional Islamic learning. They are pathetically under represented in the degree colleges. Discrimination against Muslims in admission, combined with their own indifference to Western education, has caused much concern amongst the admittedly small Muslim intelligentsia. The answer, we were told, lay in imparting modern scientific-oriented education that would ensure Muslim representation in government service and the professions. Such words are expressed by, among others, the *Nazim* of Anjuman-i Madaris-i Arabia.[10]

The proportion of Muslims in the city appears to have been growing somewhat in recent years. The city's articulate Hindu opinion sees in this the Muslims' unrestrained fertility. How much of the growth is in fact due to immigration, to a preference for more children common to poor workers in the unorganized sector generally, and to a genuine fertility differential between Hindus and Muslims—this question we are unable to answer. Were elections to be held to municipal institutions, Muslims would probably be in a majority among those elected. The probability that in such a situation their political weight, however modest, might favour the Muslim exporters probably gives the Punjabi merchants an uneasy feeling. We shall discuss this matter later.

Since manufacturing in Moradabad is organized on a small-scale, and in subcontracting units, there are obvious difficulties in organizing the working class. We could not investigate the matter in depth, but we suspect that the exporters corner the lion's share of the surplus value, while the subcontracting workshop owner may often be a direct producer himself, sharing the worker's religious identity in a milieu seen to be hostile. When an active trade union organization has no clear focus, tensions of class conflict, may, therefore, often be felt as between Punjabi Hindu exporters and the local Muslim producers. There are Muslim exporters too; but these tensions, due to the reasons stated earlier, tend to be articulated through communal terms rather than class terms. In the elections to the state legislature in May 1980, for example, the principal contest was between a Congress(I) Muslim candidate and a RSS backed Punjabi candidate of the Bharatiya Janata Party, which drew political and financial sustenance from the rich brass merchants and grain traders of Moradabad, Sambhal and Chandausi.[11] The contest was turned by the Congress(I) organizations into one between the locals (of all religions) and the Punjabi outsiders, with somewhat menacing undertones of chasing the latter out of town. The Punjabis' connection with the RSS is said to be generally strong; they took the threat seriously.

These identities—Punjabi *versus* local, Hindu *versus* Muslim—are spacious enough to absorb varied other tensions too, e.g. those arising due to the substantial dent the Muslim traders are making by exporting to West Asia on their own account. In this 'free enterprise' economy, such ups and downs are routine—the Mahishyas in Howrah's small engineering sector outcompete the Brahmins and Kayasthas; Ramgarhia and other Sikhs in Punjab far outpace the Hindu Khatris in industry; Syrian Christians in Kerala buy up lands for plantations from the Nairs; aggressive Marwaris and Gujaratis often get the better of Parsis. But if the Muslims in Moradabad—or a handful among them—come into a measure of affluence, their rivals are quick to point to foreign money (a foreignness invisible in the Punjabi exporter's wealth), and to whip up communal frenzy resulting in large scale destruction of property and the migration of people from one area to another. A senior police official has rightly observed that 'adventurism can succeed best only in chaos and confusion, and the political and economic adventure knows that the best form of confusion, instability and panic can be generated only by a communal riot' (*Sunday* 17 May 1981).

If social consciousness in Moradabad is organized strongly along religious lines, this is not unconnected with the strong Islamic religious presence in town. There are two long established *madaris*, providing religious instruction for the future maulvis and other religious workers. Given the town's composition, there is a large number of mosques, and the calls to prayer go out on loudspeakers regularly. Our stay in Moradabad was too brief for us to judge the specifics of communal organization, Hindu or Muslim; but given the long history of communal conflict, with public force often poised against them in recent years, it would be surprising if the Muslims did not feel the need to secure for themselves a considerable measure of armed protection.

These engines of religious or communal consciousness are not much countered by secular institutions. We have noted the lack of elective municipal bodies and the weakness of trade union activity. There are a great many schools and a dozen colleges, these latter controlled largely by their Hindu patrons. We often heard of the damaging consequences of many kinds of commercialization for the content of education and for teachers' status. With a minor exception or two, these institutions are *not* neutral ground for discussing conflict or for mediating in disturbed situations. One meets articulate college teachers, but often hears only a communal view from them. We met only a handful of individuals able to view their social milieu critically, and to act upon it with disinterested passion.

IV

The bare bones of the events on Ramzan Id day, 13 August 1980, in Moradabad are fairly well known, but we recount them briefly to establish the context, relying largely upon the report in *Sunday* (24 August 1980) by the weekly's editor, M.J. Akbar, who reached the city on 15 August.

Some 80,000 Muslims had gathered at the Idgah, and the Id prayers were in progress. A pig wandered in, violating the Muslim sense of cleanliness appropriate to the sanctity of prayer. Some people asked the attending policemen why the pig had been let in, and were told that guarding pigs was not the job of the police. An altercation followed, and escalated so rapidly as to make any precise sequence difficult to establish.

Brickbatting from the crowd, firing by the police, an injured police officer, and scores of *namazis* shot dead, all these took place within about five minutes while the prayer drew to a close. 'The tragedy of Moradabad', declared an aggrieved Saiyid Shahabuddin in Parliament, 'is nothing but Jallianwala Bagh re-enacted. Both happened on a day of rejoicing. Both occurred in a closed place, and the firing in both instances took place, from the only exit and the point of entry that was there, against the people congregated there.'

A stampede followed the police firing, in which 50 more people lost their lives. The furious crowd surging out of the Idgah roughed up policemen in different localities. Later in the evening, a Muslim mob attacked the Gulshahid police *chowki*, killing two policemen, burning a portion of the *chowki*, and stealing two rifles. Nothing on that day can be construed as an attack by Muslims upon Hindus; it was rather the gross over-reaction of the police to the altercation at the Idgah, leading to Muslim fury, which in turn invited grotesquely brutal, escalatory reprisals by the police upon them, including in areas adjoining the police outpost of Gulshahid.

Before proceeding further, we may pause and wonder at the swift pace at which violence grew. Communal tension did not spring up overnight; the climate for its growth had been assiduously, if thoughtlessly, nurtured over the months with the knowledge and often silent consent of the district administration.[12] Our probes into such prior antagonisms between the Muslims and police brought mentions of various incidents a month or a year or two prior to this particular one on 13 August. Beyond that there is the petty tyranny of the neighbourhood policemen, which the ordinary Muslim is normally too weak to resist, but whose memory festers to prepare the ground for the ultimate explosion. Such an explosion is, in turn, immensely punitive and, after a while one returns to the workaday life. Normalcy appears to be restored at least on the surface.

To return to the aftermath of 13 August. The disturbances in the city were usually long drawn out, with fresh outbreaks beginning on 10 September and 20 October. The particular events touching these latter half are inconsequential. Important throughout is the immensely punitive stance taken by the city police and the PAC towards the Muslims. Hundreds of men were dragged out of their homes, beaten, and locked up.[13] Scores of men had their arms, knuckles, legs, and ankles broken by the police in cold blood. Except on the last occasion, curfew was enforced only against the Muslims; Hindus were free to roam at will.

M.J. Akbar's report and all other accounts agree that on 13 August and for several days after, there was no conflict between the Hindus—other than policemen—and the Muslims. The magnitude of police violence, however, had widespread repercussions in several towns in north India on 15 August; and the Moradabad police force appears to have been under pressure to divert attention from itself. It sought to do this by inciting Hindus to attack the Muslims, as in Barbaran *mohalla*, to simulate a communal riot. In this enterprise it may have received help from the group which had lost in the May 1980 elections; to have the socio-political boundaries reinforced in Hindu-Muslim terms would suit them too.

The police efforts succeeded. Several Hindus told us that policemen went around taunting Hindus to attack the Muslims, and, at least in one instance the PAC allowed students of K.G.K. College to launch an organized assault on the Muslims of Pul Paar Colony. Students of the same college are reported to have led a mob to Ram Talaiya, a village across the railway lines, and burnt alive 15 men, women and children (*Patriot* 29 August 1980).

To generate the requisite fire among the Hindus, diverse rumours were planted. The Hindu principal of a major college told us that he received a phone call, by someone who declined to identify himself, that the city's water supply had been poisoned; there were numerous such phone calls. A rumour announced that the Shiva temple next to the cremation ground had been demolished and its priest killed; in retaliation, Muslims living in the *line-paar* area lost their lives and a mosque in the neighbourhood was demolished.[14] In fact, neither the temple nor the priest had been touched.

The rumour on 14 August that a certain PAC platoon had been wiped out by the Muslims persuaded other PAC jawans to kill ten men who had been brought into the Kotwali by the police, by beating them to death with sticks. A leading advocate in the town told us that when on 16 August, in Patparsarai there was a rumour that Muslims were going to attack the area, Hindus assembled with whatever weapon they could lay their hands on. A police jeep came and shot a Hindu down. The advocate and some others who later asked the police the reason for their action were told that Muslims in police uniform, roaming around in a jeep, had done the killing! The victim's family was given Rs. 5,000 in compensation.

Another rumour was floated that a man, Sunil—no further detail—and a girl had been taken off a rickshaw; the listener could draw his own inferences. The (Muslim) MLA was rumoured to be distributing arms from a white Ambassador car. Muslims were credited with large arsenals, gathered in preparation for an uprising. Hindu *goondas* enjoyed immunity; they took Muslims off buses coming into the city bus-stand and killed them in broad daylight on Grand Trunk (GT) Road. The evidence of the frenzy among the Hindus being whipped up by the police is overwhelming. This is how communal frenzy is created.

During at least the first two bouts beginning 13 August and 10 September, curfew was enforced for Muslims alone. The police are reported to have made deals with Hindu *goondas* over sharing the spoils from the looting of Muslim shops. Some Hindu looters were arrested too, but charged with the light offence of merely breaking the curfew. The same advocate told us that a senior police official is reported to have said that some Hindus too had to be arrested in order to fill in the quota. Judicial action on the granting of bail and the like was generally such as to let the Hindus off lightly and to come down hard on the Muslims.

Clearly the Muslims were up against not only the police but also the judiciary. This applied to the news media too. Akbar's report in the *Sunday* (24 August 1980) is quite exceptional. Most reports were filed by newsmen who stayed away from Muslim areas, believing the administration's warning that their lives would not be safe there. These reports tended to reflect the police and the Hindu-communal view of what was happening in the city.

V

The events of Moradabad bear witness to the regression of a society and of its political, administrative, and judicial organs to a depth where one may no longer speak of the norms of a minimally civilized community. Within the city, to be sure, a few Hindus continued to help Muslims throughout the terror—among them Kishen Sharma, a trade unionist, and Umesh Caerey, a city journalist. They retained the Muslims' confidence throughout, and their good offices enabled us to reach a wide range of Muslims as well as Hindus during our brief visits. Such exceptions apart, what is striking about this bustling, 'prosperous' city is its woeful poverty in matters of head and heart, its lack of thought and effort over the manner in which life in the city might be organized, its lack of any feeling for a community of interests at any level.

How is it, one asks in despair, that the children of two great religious traditions, citizens of a country that lays claim to being a world leader, can be so inept and often so brutal in their mutual relations? Communal killings at Moradabad and elsewhere are discussed extensively, charges are traded, guilt proclaimed without any investigation, scapegoats sought, and appeals made for communal harmony. These shallow echoes of the poverty of thought, feeling, and effort noted earlier bespeak too profound a social crisis in Indian society, a crisis whose depths and dimensions we cannot consider here. It is evident, however, that even 'prosperous' urban centres like Moradabad lack the intellectual and moral resources needed to use what is available for creating a halfway civilized round of life for their inhabitants. We are persuaded that, if those of us who pride ourselves on our rational, secular world views are unable, or unwilling, to find ways to reach such centres, the malignancies being fostered there will, in quick time, come to engulf our metropolitan islands too.

NOTES

1. Since the publication of this article, the Moradabad riots have been extensively researched.
2. Some of the notable studies on communal riots are: Ratna Naidu, *Communal Edges to Plural Societies: India and Pakistan*, New Delhi, 1980; G.S. Bhargava, 'Structure of a Riot', *Seminar*, Jan. 1970.

3. Rasheeduddin Khan notes that the total number of Muslim students in the university is just about 5,000 out of a total enrolment of approximately 8,000. 'This should be indicative', he observes, 'of the fact that Aligarh is but an oasis in the vast desert-land of Muslim illiteracy. Its importance, in terms of the challenging task of spreading higher education for the Muslim masses is more symbolic than substantive.' 'Minority segments in Indian polity: Muslim situation and plight for Urdu', *EPW*, 2 Sept. 1978.
4. These figures are quoted in the articles by A.R. Sherwani in *Radiance* (Delhi) and *Mainstream* (Delhi). The articles provide interesting clues to the state of Muslim education in northern India.
5. For a survey of this literature see Satish Saberwal, 'Elements of Communalism', *Mainstream*, 28 Mar. 1981.
6. The pamphlet was reported to have been written by a group of Hindu lawyers.
7. This account was corroborated by our respondents.
8. Instances of communal squabbles in the municipalities of Rohilkhand can be found in Mushirul Hasan, *Nationalism and Communal Politics in India, 1916-1928*, New Delhi, 1977.
9. Uttar Pradesh is one of the several states where 'all civic bodies stand suspended, most of them for several years with no prospect of fresh elections being held' (*Indian Express*, 1981).
10. Interviews with Maulana Kalzum Ansari and S. Najmul Hasan, advocate. Most Muslims we interviewed were aware of the importance of *Angrezi talim* (Western education) and regretted that, in spite of the efforts of Sir Saiyid Ahmad Khan, the community was educationally backward.
11. We have not dealt with the role of the RSS because it was difficult to ascertain some of the facts pointing to its 'complicity' in the events leading to the communal outbreak in August. Some of the leading Congressmen were, however, closely associated with RSS activities. These included Vinod Gupta, a close associate of N.D. Tewari, Dinesh Rastogi, Mahesh Rastogi, a former MLA from Sambhal and Dayanand Gupta, president of the city congress committee. Professor B.S. Verma of K.G.K. College, Moradabad, told us that the RSS activitists published posters commending the role of the PAC and the CRP.
12. The background is provided in the *Sunday* (1981) and, more perceptively in the articles published in the *Patriot* (1980).
13. Such were the varied experiences of Babu Nabi Husain, Akhtar Jahan, Jamil Ahmad (his brother-in-law was murdered on 18 Oct. near the Katghar *thana*), Muhammad Hasan and Sadiq Hussain.
14. Interview with Fakir Chand, an activist of the Students' Federation of India.

15

Competing Symbols and Shared Codes: Inter-Community Relations in Modern India

I'll tell you truth, oh Brahmin, if I may make so bold!
These idols in your temples—these idols have grown old;
To hate your fellow-mortals is all they teach you, while
Our God too sets his preachers to scold and to revile;
Sickened, from both your temple and our shrine I have run,
Alike our preachers' sermons and your fond myths I shun.
—In every graven image you fancied God: I see
In each speck of my country's poor dust, divinity.
Come, let us lift suspicion's thick curtains once again,
Unite once more the sundered, wipe clean division's stain.
Too long has lain deserted the heart's warm habitation—
Come, build here in our homeland an altar's new foundation,
And raise a spire more lofty than any of this globe,
With high pinnacles touching the hem of heaven's robe!
And there at every sunrise let our sweet chanting move
The hearts of all who worship, pouring them wine of love:
Firm strength, calm peace, shall blend in the hymns the votary sings—
For from love comes salvation to all earth's living things.[1]

MUHAMMAD IQBAL

The controversy over the Babri Masjid-Ramjanmabhumi issue did not just arouse deep religious passions but raised the fundamental issue of how best to allow competing religious symbols to co-exist in a society committed to the secular ideal. Admittedly, the pressing need is to resolve conflicting claims over the masjid at Ayodhya. But, in the long, run, all concerned citizens will need to marshal their intellectual resources so as to evolve a mechanism and, at the same time, define social codes for resolving controversies of this nature. Otherwise, the initiative, as always, will rest with those who manipulate both political institutions and processes to create and widen arenas of conflict.

It is not surprising that the flare-up, centred around the masjid in Ayodhya, caused such deep concern. After all, no other issue since India's Independence generated such violent passions, led to such widespread riots (Table 15.1),[2] gripped the people with panic, fear and anger, and threatened to destroy the democratic, secular consensus envisaged by the architects of the Indian Constitution. Sentiments were polarized to such an extent that two successive governments collapsed in the course of just a year, with the BJP succeeding in placing the mandir issue on the national agenda.[3] As the *Times of India* commented on 17 October 1989, 'Jettisoning once and for all its mumbo-jumbo about Gandhian values, the BJP, under Mr L.K. Advani's spirited leadership, has gone on the offensive with a strategy clearly designed to polarize life in the country along antagonistic religious lines.'

For the first time, religious zealots, bolstered by politically articulate groups, found both a cause and an opportunity to create a bonding among their divided and stratified constituency. In the *shilanyas* ceremonies, the Vishwa Hindu Parishad (VHP), backed by the BJP and the RSS, found a unifying symbol which had, for centuries, eluded Hindu reformers and

Table 15.1: Communal Riots from 1 September to 20 November 1990

State	No. of places	No. of deaths
Andhra Pradesh	4	27
Assam	1	7
Bihar	8	19
Delhi	–	8
Gujarat	26	99
Karnataka	22	88
Kerala	2	3
Madhya Pradesh	5	21
Maharashtra	3	4
Rajasthan	13	52
Tamil Nadu	1	6
Tripura	1	–
Uttar Pradesh	28	227
West Bengal	2	6
Total	116	567

preachers.[4] Through flamboyant demonstrations of religious worship and mindless retaliatory acts, these groups succeeded in stoking the fires of communal unrest.

On the other side of the spectrum, members of the Babri Masjid Action Committee (BMAC) acquired much political legitimacy and support. Some of its members, having tasted success over the Shah Bano case, reached out to the Muslim population, aired their long-standing grievances, and extracted concessions from political parties on the eve of the 1989 general elections. Given their capacity to mobilize Muslim opinion, especially in UP and Bihar, it was neither possible nor expedient to ignore the powerful imam of the Jama Masjid in Delhi or the renowned head of the prestigious Nadwat al-ulama. They represented a Muslim consensus which had been achieved only once in the history of Indian Islam, i.e. during the khilafat movement in the early 1920s.

Many contemporary aspects of the Babri Masjid-Ramjanmabhumi dispute remain shrouded in mystery. For example, why was a district judge in Ayodhya allowed to disturb the *status quo*? Was it to court the so-called Hindu constituency? Or, to mollify enraged feelings over the government's 'surrender' over the Shah Bano case? Even if these explanations are seemingly valid, it is still not clear why the VHP and their allies enjoyed the freedom to make political capital out of the judgement and launch a massive countrywide agitation which, in an extremely surcharged atmosphere, could only exacerbate tensions among the rival contestants? It would appear that the ruling party, already riven with dissension over the handling of the *shilanyas* ceremonies, lost the initiative to the VHP and failed to keep its leaders on a tight leash. Soon, the concern was not just confined to Rama's birthplace in Ayodhya. Amid the chanting of Vedic hymns and the ringing of temple bells, a general clamour was raised for 'recovering' other mosques, such as the ones in Varanasi and Mathura. Though such demands are being unabashedly voiced on public platforms and expressed in ominous terms,[5] they are also being contested with equal fervour by members of the BMAC and their vociferous supporters.

It is not uncommon to find scapegoats in history—to place the blame on the medieval sultans of Delhi who defiled and destroyed temples—and to attribute Muslim intransigence to the policies of the British government and its successor, the Congress party.[6] It is pointed out that the colonial rulers courted the Muslims by granting them privileges and special concessions in order to create their separate and distinct identity in Indian politics. It is also argued that the Congress succumbed to the League pressures in agreeing to the Partition of the country. After Independence, the Congress leadership continued to placate the Muslims and pandered to their sentiments for electoral reasons. In this way, secularism has merely served the interests of the minorities, especially the Muslims. The Hindus, on the other hand, have been at the receiving end. While their co-religionists in neighbouring Pakistan and Bangladesh have been relegated to the status of second-class citizens, Indian Muslims have been allowed to retain their personal law, conduct their proselytizing activities, and preach and practise their religion without inhibition.[7] This was the essence of the BJP's advertisements published in the national newspapers from 30 October to 1 November 1991.

Such generalized and simplistic formulations are backed by perspectives which dwell on the separateness and inherently contradictory nature of the Hindu and Muslim traditions and their estrangement, both in colonial and pre-colonial days. Thus the contest over the Babri Masjid-Ramjanmabhumi issue is seen as part of a recurring theme of conflict and tension in Indian history.

This is not the place to refute such ill-conceived theories. My main aim is to highlight certain broad aspects of Hindu-Muslim relations during the last decade of the nineteenth and the early decades of the twentieth centuries. In the final section, I focus on Faizabad/Ayodhya, a district with a long and chequered history, in order to outline the broad contours of local politics and to see if political linkages and socio-economic relations transcended religious cleavages or not.

II

Both as an ideology and as a movement, communalism derives ideological sustenance from the view, popularized by Henry Elliot and other colonial writers, that Islam and Hinduism, as indeed their followers, co-existed uneasily in India, and that religious conflicts rather than harmonious living was the hallmark of the medieval Indian ethos. In fact, the dominant images of the Muslim presence, nurtured by publicists and major literary writers, were concerned with the degradation of the Hindus through forcible conversions, imposition of the *jizya* (tax levied on non-Muslims to guarantee their safety and protection), strict application of the *Shariat*, and the desecration of Hindu temples.[8]

Admittedly, there existed a fragmented and differentiated form of religious consciousness which may have led the sultans and their ideologues to offend religious sensibilities. But religious solidarity was not the basis of collective socio-economic experiences. The ideology of the state, trimmed to suit the interests of the ruling elites, accommodated religious concerns. Yet, it did not rest on the notion of a unified 'community' with identifiable interests, which forms the main pillar of modern day 'communalism'. Moreover, while there were stray, localized and sporadic incidents of conflicts over religious symbols, integrative and syncretic forces were also at work amongst the elites as well as the common people. The dominant picture of the seventeenth and eighteenth centuries is not of the Hindus and the Muslims forming exclusive and antagonistic categories but of their cooperating in cultural life and social affairs.[9]

This scenario, however, gradually changed with the coming of the British. For the first time, signs of Hindu-Muslim friction surfaced in some areas and amongst certain groups. Now, the terms of dispute were articulated differently. The language and vocabulary of discourse changed. Muted expressions were replaced with angry exchanges. Mild protests took the form of violent outbursts. The reasons for this were quite numerous, ranging from the introduction of Western-style institutions to the emergence of religio-revivalist trends stimulated by powerful reform movements in Bengal, Punjab, and Maharashtra.

No summing up of late-nineteenth century trends can be complete without reference to the activities of the Arya Samaj, the spurt in cow-protection activity, and the vigorous campaign in support of the Nagri script and its use in government and law courts. These were not isolated assertions of militant, religio-revivalist tendencies, but manifestations of the new and burgeoning Hindu consciousness.[10]

Among the Muslims, the Graeco-Turkish war of 1897 stimulated pan-Islamic feelings. Islamization in Bengal and parts of northern India, inspired by Shah Waliullah and his successors and bolstered by the faraizis in Bengal, was an equally potent force. Insistence on a revitalized consciousness and identity, with its corresponding denigration of Islam's local roots, began to erode syncretistic traditions and undermine religious peace and understanding.[11] The massive communal rioting in 1893, preceded by sporadic but violent altercations, illustrated that the fabric of Hindu-Muslim unity was too fragile to withstand the onslaught of various revitalization movements. 'If the smouldering fire of religious enmity is not put out', warned an observer, 'it will before long be kindled into a mighty flame and destroy the noble edifice which the Congress has built with so much pains.'[12]

The prophecy did not come true. Though relations between certain sections of Hindus and Muslims were sometimes strained, their deterioration was neither deep nor irreversible. 'Nothing strikes the intelligent traveller in India more forcibly', observed a senior police official in 1894, 'than the friendly peaceable attitude of all castes and classes towards each other.'[13] He was right. Friction between religious groups was not ordinarily a major source of disturbance in the last quarter of the nineteenth-century.[14] During 1889-94, there was no violence in Bengal, except once in Calcutta and its suburbs.[15]

Such sporadic outbursts did not signify, as some writers are wont to suggest, the fragmentation of society along communal lines. Inter-community tensions and disputes were counterbalanced by the quiet, commonplace routines in which Hindus and Muslims intermingled without notice or incident and they could still be found involved in a range of 'religiously promiscuous' practices. In 1909, the *Imperial Gazetteer of India* stated that it was the regular practice of 'low-class Muhammadans' to join in the Durga Puja and other Hindu festivals; it mentioned Muslim consultation of Hindu almanacs, worship of Sithala and Manasa, use of vermilion and joint offerings to village deities before the sowing or transplanting of rice seedlings.[16] Another inspiring legitimation of the more mundane expressions of peaceful co-existence came daily in the sounds of Muslim *shehnai* players joining in the *arti* at Hindu temples, including the *arti* of the Vishwanath temple in Banaras.[17] Sandria Freitag and Nita Kumar have shown how in this holy city of the Hindus, Muslim weavers actively participated in public ceremonials expressing a shared Banarasi culture, including 'the marriage of the Laut' (Bhairava), *Bharat Milap* and the day-today observances related to particular figures and shrines.[18]

Contemporary writings took note of the ongoing process of social and cultural fusion. The poet Iqbal shared the vision of a united India—one that was free of both alien domination and inner dissension. He called his land of birth a garden where the people inhabiting it were members of a *qaum* (nation), with the two circles of Islam and *watan* intersecting and at several places coalescing into a coherent whole. *Himala,* the first poem in *Baang-i Dara*, was inspired by the beauty of his land of birth. *Hindustani Bachhon ka Qaumi Geet* (National Anthem of Indian Children) and the *Tarana-i Hind* (The Song of India) were refined, and buoyant expressions of patriotic sentiments. In *Naya Shiwala* (New Temple), Iqbal chided both Hindus and Muslims for their narrow mentality and appealed to the keepers of the temple and the mosque to foster mutual goodwill and understanding.[19]

Akbar Allahabadi, a merciless satirist equipped with an irrepressible sense of humour, had similar concerns. He subjected to ridicule, to scathing criticism or damning exposure the social and political strategy of imperialism and Saiyid Ahmad Khan's policy of loyal cooperation with the government. And, like Iqbal, he championed Hindu-Muslim unity. Both Hindus and Muslims, he wrote, have to bear the blows of those who wield the rod of worldly power, but they should respond by being like water on which the blows of a rod have only a momentary effect.[20]

Iqbal and Akbar stated the obvious. They recognized, as indeed did the others, that the direction in which patronage, economic welfare and authority flowed in everyday life indicated the continuing importance of cross-communal networks.[21] The Saiyid's Aligarh project was backed by the Hindus and Muslims alike. He encouraged, despite his misgivings over the Nagri resolution of 1900 (which sparked off a Hindu-Urdu controversy), a Hindu-Muslim *entente* in cultural and religious matters. His contemporary, Ajudhia Nath Kunzru, owed his fortunes as much to the wealthy Muslim landholders as to his extensive banking and commission agencies.[22] In east UP and Awadh generally, the dominant factor in the politics of the towns tended to be an Urdu-speaking élite connection based on landed interests. Communal considerations did not necessarily foul the path of politics.[23]

The competing units in early municipal politics were multi-factions, not antagonistic groups. In the composition of early municipal factions, caste and communal considerations played a secondary role to personal rivalries, family linkages, and economic ties. The lawyer, Maulvi Sirajul Islam, was elected from Chittagong to the Bengal legislative council largely on the strength of the 'Hindu vote'. Surendranath Banerjea, on the other hand, was backed by Muslims for a seat in the prestigious Calcutta corporation. Around the same time the Congress backed Hamid Ali Khan for a seat in the UP council.

Nor did communal divisions last long after they had been politicized. Soon after the violent eruptions in 1893, tempers began to cool everywhere and there was much display of 'mutual love and affection' in the riot-torn cities of UP.[24] Public statements and newspaper editorials on national unity and the commonality of Hindu-Muslim interests were matched by strenuous efforts of local reconciliation committees to resolve and defuse tensions.[25] When asked how the 'upper classes' of the two communities behaved when the riots occurred, the assistant magistrate of Gorakhpur replied: 'By taking leading Hindus and Muslims into confidence, matters are satisfactorily arranged. . . . In Aligarh, we left the whole matter to leading Hindus and Mussalmans and everything went off without hitch.'[26]

Such was the pattern everywhere. By the end of the nineteenth century, there was no sign of the Hindus and the Muslims going their separate ways. If anything, the lines of cleavage in north India were more sharply drawn between the Shias and the Sunnis rather than the Hindus and the Muslims.[27] Though expressed in exaggerated terms, there is merit in the observations of W.S. Blunt and Henry Cotton that the Hindu-Muslim animus was accentuated only after the government translated the principle of divide and rule into formal constitutional arrangements.[28]

With the onset of the twentieth-century, there was a tendency towards the use of religious solidarity as a basis of political action. It started with the Nagri resolution of April 1900 which created fissures among the professional classes in UP. The prospect of reforms and of a greater share in the expanding administrative and bureaucratic machinery triggered the Simla deputation and the establishment of the Muslim League in December 1906, while widespread religio-revivalist movements aided the growth of Defence Leagues, Anjumans, and Sabhas. The Turko-Italian war fanned pan-Islamic passions leading to intense religious activity.

Many of the controversies, both political and religious, subsided during the khilafat and non-cooperation movements when Gandhi cemented an extraordinary alliance between different segments of society.[29] But not long afterwards, the edifice of inter-communal unity, so passionately built by the Mahatma, began to crumble. The khilafat movement itself got bogged down in religious issues instead of concentrating on the consolidation and integration of anti-colonial forces. Consequently, a popular political movement, a gift of history, was a great opportunity absurdly wasted.

Still, it would be wrong to either conclude that the gulf separating the Hindus and Muslims was unbridgeable or that they were hopelessly polarized after Gandhi called off the non-cooperation campaign in February 1922. Most people, especially in the countryside, were unruffled by communal controversies and continued to live, as they had done in the past, in peace and harmony. This was so because of the bonds of socio-economic interests, centuries of common experiences, and shared memories. The governor of Bengal commented on the 'rank and file' of the two major communities in his province cooperating with each other in all 'daily business of life'; it was 'only at rare intervals, when religious feelings become inflamed, that they treat each other as enemies and clashes occur'. O.M. Martin, who served in the same province from 1915 to 1926, made similar observations. Hindu-Muslim unity, he added, was not a temporary occurrence but an old and cherished tradition.[30]

The pan-Islamic euphoria, which had caused so much excitement in the subcontinent, did not take much time to disappear as the Turkish nationalists began to rewrite their political agenda without a khalifa/

sultan. Faced with this reality, unpleasant though it was to committed pan-Islamists, there was an unmistakable reordering of priorities.[31] From then onwards, Islam was once more firmly rooted in the Indian subcontinent and the interests of its followers were much more closely linked with their country and their countrymen. That is why the ulama, based at Deoband and connected with the Jamiyat al-ulama, emerged as powerful advocates of composite nationalism and rejected the two-nation theory. Their arguments in defence of their position was backed by the theological weight of Islam.

It is assumed that the perspective of the Deobandi ulama, with its emphasis on composite nationhood, was rejected by the Muslim community and that the creation of Pakistan validated Jinnah's two-nation theory. These are questionable assumptions. The League's success neither vindicates nor legitimizes the ideological underpinnings of the two-nation theory, for the birth of Pakistan in that summer of discontent in August 1947 was neither imminent nor historically inevitable. It symbolized, more than anything else, Jinnah's personal triumph, his answer to the obdurate Gandhi-Nehru-Patel leadership which had persistently refused to treat him on equal terms or discuss with him the blueprint of a free and united India. Sadly, Indian nationalists of all shades, including the socialists and communists, failed to grasp this reality. As a result, they bowed to the mounting pressure of the League and acquiesced in India's partition, though for different reasons.

One final point. In the debates that preceded and followed the birth of Pakistan, communal rivalries alone were projected as *the* stark Indian reality. It is necessary to provide a corrective to this approach, for there still existed, despite the trauma and agony that accompanied the vivisection of the country, large areas of Hindu-Muslim cooperation and tangible expressions of cultural fusion and religious syncretism. Most people, Hindus and Muslims alike, clung to their inherited ideas, traditions and customs. This was so in the case of, for example, the Meos, the Malkana Rajputs, the Khojas, Bohras and Memons in western India and the Mappilas in Malabar.[32] Given their long, uninterrupted history of social mingling and cultural fusion, it is hard to conceive of a different scenario. Similar trends, syncretic and composite, were at work elsewhere.

True, the rise of communal and 'separatist' politics diminished the importance of certain religio-cultural symbols which had, in the past, transcended caste and community distinctions. Yet, one could still find Hindus observing Muharram—which marks the martyrdom of Prophet Muhammad's grandson and his seventy-two companions.[33] Thousands continued to gather around shrines of the Sufis and other venerated men and sought their intercession to avert calamities, cure diseases, procure children for the childless, or even improve the circumstances of the dead.[34] Frederick Graham Cracknell, magistrate and collector of Etawah and Kanpur, reported that the *mela* commemorating Shah Madaar, who settled at Makanpur in Bilaur *tahsil* in the fifteenth-century, was attended by 50,000 people, mostly Hindus. Unmoved by a Hindu-Muslim fracas in the area in 1931, Hindus and Muslims flocked to his shrine in equal numbers. The pattern was largely the same elsewhere.[35]

Faizabad district in UP, once the capital of the Awadh nawabs and an important Muslim centre, mirrored national and provincial trends in large measure. The Muslim population was relatively small—11.11 per cent in 1901. Most of them belonged to the weaving community, followed by the Sheikhs who held considerable land in Mangalsi, Haveli, Awadh and Khandansa, and the Saiyids whose vast estates lay in Pirpur, Samanpur, and Bhadarsa. In fact, Faizabad was among those districts of UP where a large proportion of land was held by Muslims. There were 2,051 separate estates at the beginning of 1905. Of these, 1,115 were owned by Rajputs, 366 by Brahmins, and 286 by Muslims.

In general, Faizabad and its adjoining areas, including Ayodhya, were no different from other places in UP: they were equally affected by religious and revivalist currents. The militancy of the cow-protection agitation, which led to widespread rioting in 1893 in Azamgarh and the neighbouring districts of Bihar, also caused much excitement in Faizabad. Yet, there was no outbreak of violence. When the 'cow-question' surfaced in 1906 it was amicably settled by local leaders. During 1910-12, however, the consensus broke down largely in reaction to extensive cow-riots in certain areas of eastern and western UP.[36] Although a 'snowball plan', based on the 'heavenly voice' heard at Hanumangarhi in Ayodhya, circulated in Faizabad district,[37] its impact was blunted by alert district officials. Backed by the UP government, local and provincial leaders, including the raja of Mahmudabad, were able to soothe frayed tempers. By September-October 1915, the provincial government, headed by James Meston, evolved a compromise formula acceptable to various contending groups.[38]

Hindu-Muslim relations in Faizabad were only marginally soured by the cow-protection movement and the great 'communal' debates that started with Saiyid Ahmad Khan's crusade against the Congress and culminated in the Lahore resolution of 1940. A major source of irritation was the mosque at Ayodhya which was allegedly built on the site of an ancient temple raised on the actual spot of Rama's birth. Evidence on the destruction of the temple is disputed.[39] Most historians at the Centre for Historical Studies, Jawaharlal Nehru University, point out that neither Abul Fazl, the sixteenth-century author of *Ain-i Akbari*, nor Tulsidas, a celebrated devotee of Rama, mention the demolition of a temple at the site of Rama's birthplace. They conclude, 'It is in the nineteenth century that the story circulates and enters official records. These records were then cited by others as valid historical evidence on the issue.'[40] H.R. Neville, who compiled the *District Gazetteer of Fyzabad*, recorded a view widely shared by British civil servants. He observed:

> The materials of the old structure were largely employed, and many of the columns are in good preservation; they are of close-grained black stone, called . . . *basauti*, and carved with various devices. Their length is from seven to eight feet, and the shape square at the base, centre and capital, the rest being round or octagonal. The mosque has two inscriptions, one on the outside and the other on the pulpit; both are in Persian and bear the date 935 Hijri. Of the authenticity of the inscription there can be no doubt, but no record of (Babur's) visit to Ajodhya is to be found in the Musalman historians.[41]

What is perhaps not in dispute is that Ayodhya was, well before the sixteenth-century, a centre of pilgrimage for the Buddhists, the Jains, and the Hindus. It is known that Hindu worship remained possible in the compound of the Babri Masjid and the activities of the Brahmin *pandas* of Ayodhya are recorded by the first European visitor to the place, William Finch, between 1608 and 1611.[42] When Ayodhya first became an important pilgrimage centre in the eighteenth-century it was as much due to the activities of the Ramanandi sadhus as to the patronage of the nawabi court. The diwan of nawab Safdarjang, raja Naval Rai, built and repaired several temples in Ayodhya, while Safdarjang himself gave land for building a temple on what is known as the Hanuman's hill. Asaf ud-Daula's diwan, Tikayat Ray, supported the building of the important temple-fortress Hanumangarhi on this land. Peter van der Veer refers to documents indicating that Muslim officials of the nawabi court gave away gifts for rituals performed by the *pandas*,[43] i.e. Hindu priests on the site of pilgrimage centres.[44]

Peter van der Veer observes that, when the power of the nawabs gradually eroded due to the influence of the British in Awadh politics, the peaceful co-existence of Hindus and Muslims in Ayodhya came to be threatened.[45] Michael H. Fisher and J.R.I. Cole have shown how the changes in the configuration of forces under Wajid Ali Shah deepened religious conflicts and, in 1833 and 1855, nearly exploded into civil war.[46]

Though the last nawab of Awadh dealt with the recalcitrant forces, headed by Amir Ali, he did not emerge unscathed from the incident. His power and authority, already clipped by the British, waned as the firebrand agitators chose the reckless course of waging a holy war against each other. The British intervention in the mandir-masjid fracas was decisive. Hence, an ambivalent nawab was goaded into taking action. At the same time, it sealed his fate and gave the British an excuse to annex the kingdom of Awadh.

The confrontation in 1855 was serious, bitter and violent. But it did not take long for the wounds to be healed. Apart from litigation between 1883 and 1886,[47] the mandir-masjid dispute remained dormant until 1934 when a communal riot near Ayodhya, triggered by cow-slaughter, inflamed passions. Again, between 1950 and 1984 there was no movement to demand the occupation of Rama's birthplace, except for legal actions destined to remain endlessly unfruitful.

There can be no doubt that the Ayodhya mosque was a powerful symbol of communal mobilization in UP. Yet, it was not strong enough to polarize sentiments to a degree where Hindus and Muslims in the province or in the locality would be arrayed against each other. Even when religious sentiments ran amok in the towns of UP from 1 February 1986 onwards, Ayodhya remained unaffected by communal frenzy. 'It is remarkable', reported a newspaper correspondent, 'that while the controversy surrounding the Babri Masjid-Ramjanmabhumi has aroused religious passions elsewhere, Ayodhya and its surrounding areas have been able to maintain communal peace.'[48]

This was not an uncommon feature in Ayodhya. For nearly a century, most Hindus and Muslims in the area did not allow their daily lives to be influenced by the mandir-masjid controversy. They conducted their affairs and performed their usual chores without being swayed by religious passions. Their political life was not moulded by religious considerations alone. In the 1989 elections, for example, the majority of voters voted for the Communist Party of India (CPI) candidate who opposed the communalization of Faizabad polity and society by 'outside' forces. In this way communal groups and parties were humbled soon after the *shilanyas* ceremony. This was an extraordinary development, especially in the light of the fact that the then ruling party capitulated on that occasion and, in the process, legitimized the activities of the VHP, the RSS, and the Shiv Sena.

Generally speaking, political affairs in Faizabad were conducted on a supra-communal network. Before Independence, this process was aided by professional ties, cultural links and common landed interests that bound the Urdu-speaking élites and helped create a strong and powerful composite cultural tradition. More often, caste loyalties rather than religious affiliation moulded public life. This is illustrated by the strong links between the Kayasthas, who occupied one-quarter, and the Muslims, who held two-fifths, of the municipal board seats in the last quarter of the nineteenth-century.[49] Between 1905 and 1911, Muslims, in general, were attracted to Balak Ram and his Kayastha party whose *taluqdari* links gave it a class dimension, a more cosmopolitan, and a cross-communal image.[50] Until after the first general elections in 1952, municipal bodies in Faizabad-*cum*-Ayodhya remained in control of the Kayastha party and its Muslim allies.[51]

In the late 1930s and 1940s, however, there were visible strains in such cross-communal alliances. This was largely due to the failure of the Congress to thwart the communal forces. It allowed the Muslim League to wrest the initiative, as in the 1937 elections to the Faizabad-Sitapur-Bahraich urban constituency, when the Congress literally surrendered the seat to its adversary. What happened in the 1946 elections is a different story altogether. Like the rest of the country, Faizabad district was communally polarized. Here, as elsewhere, the success League's was a foregone conclusion.

Harold Gould has shown how, after Independence, the district became the focal point of a political showdown between Acharya Narendra Deva, the socialist leader, and his Congress rival Baba Raghava Das. In the course of the by-election campaign in 1948, Pandit Govind Ballabh Pant visited Ayodhya and declared that the Acharya did not believe in the divinity of Rama as proven by the fact that he did not wear the *choti* (topknot), displayed by all devout, genuine Hindus. Baba Raghava Das, for his part, moved among his followers distributing *tulsi* leaves to emphasize the spiritual difference between him and his socialist adversary. Ayodhya voted overwhelmingly for the Baba. This is how, concludes Gould, the 'Ayodhya strategy' had worked to perfection.[52]

It is easy to establish the connection between this election campaign and the event on the night of 22 and 23 December 1949 when an idol of Rama suddenly appeared in the Babri Masjid, which had been guarded by a posse of policemen. Baba Raghava Das and his Congress patrons in Lucknow not only revived but exploited the mandir-masjid issue which had remained dormant for decades. They pressed into service the Bairagis and the Mahants who, in subsequent years, headed a vigorous movement to 'liberate' the mosque at Ayodhya. In this way, the Congress introduced a discordant note in an otherwise harmonious society of Faizabad.

The 'Ayodhya strategy' was also used in a different context but with similar results. In May 1986, Rajiv Gandhi capitulated to the strident clamourings of some Muslim groups by introducing the retrograde Muslim Women (Protection of Rights on Divorce) Bill.[53] The motive was simple: the rising tide of anger over the Shah Bano verdict had to be stemmed to retain Muslim votes which, in the wake of the momentous Supreme Court judgement, had tipped the balance in favour of the opposition parties.[54] At the same time, the growing Hindu sentiment over the Ayodhya mosque, voiced by the VHP, the Bajrang Dal, the Shiv Sena and the RSS, had to be assuaged. Rajiv Gandhi's former associate and ministerial colleague, whose own conduct in the murky happenings on 1 February 1986 is not beyond reproach, is reported to have stated the following:

> In early 1986 the Muslim Women's Bill was passed to play the Muslim card; and then came the decision on Ayodhya to play the Hindu card. It was supposed to be a package deal. I knew it was a dangerous thing to do and I did not agree. . . . When I asked Mr. Rajiv Gandhi who is showing the worship in the disputed shrine at Ayodhya on Doordarshan two days after it was unlocked, he did not reply; he merely smiled and observed it was tit for tat for the Muslim Women's Bill.[55]

The 'Ayodhya strategy' worked in 1948, but not in 1989. The Congress gained a prestigious seat in a constituency then but was thrown out of office in 1989. The goodwill of the Muslims, achieved in 1986 through cynical means, was frittered away by a reckless act. 'The alienation of the Muslims', commented a newspaper editorial, 'will undoubtedly rank as the most grievous lapse of the Rajiv Gandhi government.' The paper added:

> In retrospect the laying of the foundation stone of the Rama temple in Ayodhya on November 9 can be seen to be a dangerous turning point in the history of independent India. The seeds for a disintegration of the secular vision of the country were sown on that day. History cannot easily pardon the Congress for its direct and indirect contribution to the spectacular growth of Hindu chauvinist forces today and for the tightening hold of the fundamentalists on the Muslim community.[56]

The use of the 'Hindu card' by a party that laid claims to the secular legacy of Gandhi and Nehru proved counterproductive. The BJP rather than the Congress benefitted from an ill-conceived and ill-advised electoral plan.[57] Communal mobilization not only divides people but often devours its own protagonists.

Competing symbols supposedly cause friction and create cleavages. Not so in Faizabad, where the people, with some exceptions, have withstood the communal onslaught for well over a century. There is much room for optimism that they will be able to weather the present storm. The people of Faizabad have done so in the not so distant past; there is no reason why they cannot do so now.

The real issue is not the future of the Babri Masjid or of Rama's birthplace; in fact, the seemingly endless debate among scholars over the existence of a temple on the present site of the mosque or the actual birthplace of Rama is not even of much academic interest. The main concern of the people of Faizabad and their brethren in other parts of the country must be to create an ethos and a social order in which competing symbols can be blended into a harmonious whole. Individuals and groups have quite successfully done so in the past, and there is no reason why it cannot be done in our times.

All said and done, India's hope lies in areas like Faizabad where shared memories and common historical experiences should slowly but steadily promote consensus and accommodation between different segments of society.[58] Even though strewn with obstacles and difficulties, it is worth fighting for the realization of such an ideal.

NOTES

1. Mujeeb, *Indian Muslims*, p. 485.
2. The official count of the deaths due to communal riots in 1990 put the number at 831. A report compiled by the Delhi unit of People's Unit for Democratic Rights (PUDR) lists 116 places where riots took place in the wake of the *rath-yatra*. An agonized journalist commented, 'The 831 or 1,662 or more deaths due to the mandir-masjid row were not due to material causes, and the dead did not belong to an alien land. Think in the way poets think, and you are hit by the indicting realization that Indians as a nation are not growing, but diminishing.... The only way we can grow, individually and nationally, is by struggling to stop this *tandava nritya* (devil's dance) of communal violence.' Sudheendra Kulkarni, 'India Brutalised', *Sunday Observer*, New Delhi, 30 Dec. 1990. Also, see editorial comments, 'Bestiality in Bhagalpur', *Sunday Observer*, 5 Nov. 1989; 'Stop the Carnage'; *Times of India*, 17 Oct. 1989; 'Anguished India'; *Times of India*, 31 Oct. 1990.
3. Rajiv Gandhi conceded that '*shilanyas* played a crucial role in the (Congress) debacle', *Times of India*, 30 Nov. 1989 and 15 Dec. 1989 for analysis of the UP elections where seven of the nine Muslim candidates elected to the Lok Sabha belonged to the Janata Dal. Zafar Agha, 'UP Muslims Desert Congress-I', ibid., 26 Nov. 1989.
4. This view has found much support and is echoed in the writings of leading journalists like Chandan Mitra, then editor of the *Sunday Observer*, and

Swapan Dasgupta, then assistant editor of the *Times of India*. Dasgupta has argued that the fragmentation of India can only be arrested by creating alternative focal points of national consolidation. For this reason, he backs the 'movement in Ayodhya', pointing out that the defeat of the BJP on this issue 'will, in one important sense only aggravate the crisis of Indian nationalism'. 'Nationalist Disarray: Renewed Importance of Ayodhya', *Times of India*, 10 Sept. 1990. Also, 'Journey to Ayodhya: Hindu Nationalism Comes of Age', ibid., 23 Oct. 1989. However, the views of Swapan Dasgupta have been effectively challenged in the columns of the *Times of India* itself. For example, Arvind N. Das, 'Pathology of Uncivil Society: Ritualism United Mandal-Mandir Moves', 5 Oct. 1990; Praful Bidwai, 'BJP in a Clef Stick: Yatra's Success is a Liability', 12 Oct. 1990; Harish Khare, 'Sparring with Communalism: Why Sadhus are Setting National Agenda', 20 Oct. 1990; H.M. Seervai, 'NF-BJP Divorce: Hinduism Not Above the Constitution', 2 Nov. 1990.

5. The Jagatguru Shankaracharya of Dwarka Peeth announced that, 'as long as the three sacred places, which the Muslims had destroyed to build mosques, are not restored to the Hindus, no peace or communal harmony is possible'. *Times of India*, 9 Sept. 1990. L.K. Advani, president of the BJP, and his colleagues have also made similar statements. While announcing his plan of undertaking the *rath-yatra* from the Somnath temple to Ayodhya, the BJP president declared, 'So far as the question of the birthplace of Lord Rama in Ayodhya and Lord Krishna in Mathura and the Kashi Vishwanath temple is concerned, the Hindu community cannot compromise'. Ibid., 13 Sept. 1990.
6. See the collection of essays in, *Hindu Temples: What Happened to Them*, New Delhi, 1990.
7. Balraj Madhok, 'Persecuted or Pampered', *Illustrated Weekly of India*, 9 Jan. 1983. The thrust of this article is that Indian Muslims 'have no legal or moral claim or right on [*sic*] this country'.
8. Hasan, *Nationalism and Communal Politics*, Chap. 8.
9. Satish Chandra, *Parties and Politics at the Mughal Court 1707-1740*, New Delhi, 1972, pp. 261-6.
10. McLane, *Indian Nationalism and the Early Congress*, pp. 271-331 (for an insightful account of the cow-protection movement). Robinson, *Separatism Among Indian Muslims*, pp. 66-78, for a sensitive analysis of revivalist tendencies, including the development of the Hindi-Urdu conflict and the campaign for Hindi.
11. Roy, *The Islamic Syncretistic Tradition in Bengal*, p. 251; and Rafiuddin Ahmed, *Bengal Muslims*, 1981, p. 184.
12. *Al Waqt*, Gorakhpur, 21/26 February 1894, Selections from Native Newspapers, UP.
13. T.C. Arthur, *Reminiscences of an Indian Police Official*, London, 1894, p. 145. Both British and Indian witnesses before the Public Service Commission testified to the harmonious relations between the Hindus and Muslims

and took note of the cross-communal links. See *Public Service Commission*, NWP & O Sub-Commission, Calcutta, 1888, pp. 15, 23, 26.

14. McLane, *India Nationalism*, p. 318.
15. Rajat Kanta Ray, *Social Conflict and Political Unrest in Bengal 1875-1927*, New Delhi, 1984, p. 121. The commissioner of Dacca noted the 'extraordinary fact' that in five years 'not a single riot of any description should have occurred'.
16. *Imperial Gazetteer of India*, pp. 48-9.
17. Judy F. Pugh, 'Divination and Ideology in the Banaras Muslim Community', Ewing (ed.), *Shariat and Ambiquity in South Asian Islam*, p. 289.
18. Freitag (ed.), *Culture and Power in Banaras*, pp. 13-14, 168-9.
19. See the collection of essays in Hafeez Malik (ed.), *Iqbal: Poet-Philosopher of Pakistan*, New York, 1971.
20. Ralph Russell and Khurshidul Islam, 'The Satirical Verse of Akbar Allahabadi (1846-1921)', *MAS*, 1974, Vol. 8, 1, pp. 44-6.
21. Notice the comment on Banaras: 'It should be explained that in Benaras the Mahomedan population is nearly entirely dependent upon the Hindus. With the exception of a few members of the old Mahomedan aristocracy, who are now in straitened circumstances, the entire community lives a hand to mouth existence. . . . The weavers are without exception dependent on the goodwill of their Hindu employers. The two communities are therefore closely bound to each other by economic ties.' Quoted in Freitag, *Culture and Power in Banaras*, p. 13. Nita Kumar has argued that what seems more influential in promoting harmony is the fact that Hindus and Muslims of 'lower classes' share a similar lifestyle and ideology of work, leisure and public activity. 'Work and Leisure in the Formation of Identity: Muslim Weavers in a Hindu City', in Freitag, *Culture and Power*, p. 169.
22. Henry Sender, *The Kashmiri Pandits: A Study of Cultural Choice in North India*, New Delhi, 1988, p. 244.
23. Robinson, *Separatism Among Muslims*, p. 79.
24. Hasan, *Nationalism and Communal Politics*, p. 50.
25. Ibid., pp. 50-1.
26. *Public Service Commission*, NWP & O, Evidence, p. 158.
27. Mushirul Hasan, 'Sectarianism in Indian Islam: The Shia-Sunni Divide in the United Provinces', *The Indian Economic and Social History Review*, Vol. 27, No. 2, Apr.-June 1990.
28. Henry Cotton, *India and Home Memoirs*, London, 1911; Blunt, *India Under Ripon*, p. 94.
29. See the collection of essays in *Communal and Pan-Islamic Trends in Colonial India*, New Delhi, 1985.
30. Earl of Lytton, *Pundits and Elephants*, p. 172; 'Memoirs of O.M. Martin' (typescript), CSAS.
31. Hasan, *A Nationalist Conscience*, 1987, Chap. 6.
32. Mujeeb, *Indian Muslims*, pp. 10-20; and the collection of essays in Imtiaz Ahmad (ed.), *Caste and Social Stratification Among the Muslims*, New Delhi, 1984.

33. *Census of India*, 1931, United Provinces of Agra and Awadh, Vol. 1, Appendix E, p. 515.
34. See, for example, P.M. Currie, *The Shrine and Cult of Muin-al-din Chishti of Ajmer*, New Delhi, 1989.
35. Cracknell papers, CSAS.
36. Home (Political), B, File No. 109-14, April 1913, NAI.
37. Home (Political), A, File No. 1-4, Dec. 1913, NAI.
38. Home (Political), A, File No. 258-9, Oct. 1915, NAI.
39. R.S. Sharma, *Communal History and Rama's Ayodhya*, New Delhi, 1990. Asghar Ali Engineer (ed.), *Babri Masjid-Ramjanmabhoomi Controversy*, New Delhi, 1990.
40. The document was generally appreciated. 'All those', wrote a leading journalist, 'who have given up neither their belief in secularism nor the hope that Indians will one day stop killing one another should be grateful to Professors S. Gopal, Romila Thapar, Bipan Chandra and other historians of Jawaharlal Nehru University.' Praful Bidwai, 'Appeasing Hindu Bigotry', *Times of India*, 20 Nov. 1989. But there was adverse criticism as well, much of which, quite predictably, coming from the ideologues of the BJP and the RSS. The debate was conducted in the letters to the editor column of the *Times of India* (15, 21, 23 Dec. 1989), as well as in the *Indian Express.* Within the Centre for Historical Studies, Majid H. Siddiqi alone struck a discordant note with the view that 'it is not for historians to "prove" or "disprove" as right or wrong every instance of an assertion made by a political or cultural group as social winds blow this way or that'. Siddiqi, who did not sign the document, concluded with the exhortation: 'Historians must discard their personae as historians if they are to intervene in the dispute without at the same time endangering the very basis of their intellectual stand. They must exhibit intellectual self-confidence in their discipline and determine their own agenda in terms of their own questions and not allow the existence of communalism in this society . . . to force its agenda upon them.' 'Ramjanmabhoomi-Babri Masjid Dispute: The Question of History', *EPW*, 13 Jan. 1990.
41. *District Gazetteer of the United Provinces of Agra and Oudh, Fyzabad*, Vol. XLIII, Allahabad, 1905, pp. 173-4.
42. Peter van der Veer, 'God must be Liberated! A Hindu Liberation Movement in Ayodhya', *MAS*, Vol. 21, No. 2, 1987, p. 287.
43. For their importance in Ayodhya, see Peter van der Veer, 'The Concept of the Ideal Brahmin as an Ideological Construct', Günther-D. Sontheimer and Hermann Kulke (eds.), *Hinduism Reconsidered*, New Delhi, 1989, pp. 71-7.
44. Peter van der Veer, 'God must be Liberated', p. 288.
45. Ibid.
46. Fisher, *A Clash of Two Cultures*, pp. 228-36; Cole, *Roots of North Indian Shiism*, pp. 244-9.
47. S.K. Tripati, 'One Hundred Years of Litigation', in Engineer (ed.), op. cit., pp. 15-27.

48. Kuldip Kumar, 'Ayodhya Ready for Compromise', ibid., p. 106. Likewise, several neighbouring areas, such as Akbarpur in Sultanpur district, remained undisturbed. Suneet Chopra, 'Akbarpur: An Island of Communal Unity', *Times of India*, 3 Nov. 1989.
49. Robinson, *Separatism Among Muslims*, p. 64.
50. Harold A. Gould, *Politics and Caste*, Vol. 3, New Delhi, 1990, p. 49.
51. Ibid., pp. 48-9.
52. Ibid., pp. 76-7.
53. See Zoya Hasan, 'Minority Identity, Muslim Women Bill Campaign and the Political Process', *EPW*, 7 Jan. 1989.
54. Mushirul Hasan, 'Indian Muslims Since Independence: In Search of Integration and Identity', *Third World Quarterly*, London, Vol. 10, No. 2, Apr. 1988.
55. Arun Nehru quoted in A.G. Noorani, 'The Babri Masjid-Ramjanamabhoomi Question', in Engineer (ed.), op. cit., p. 57.
56. *Times of India*, 28 Nov. 1989.
57. Harish Khare, 'Rise of the BJP: Reemergence of the Right', *Times of India*, 6 Dec. 1989. Notice that in Maharashtra the BJP-Shiv Sena won fourteen seats and emerged as the only credible opposition to the Congress. *Sunday Observer*, 3 Dec. 1989.
58. 'Patient and sustained efforts of right thinking writers, researchers and educators can foil the communalist attempt to use the past as a wedge to divide the people into warring camps.' R.S. Sharma, 'Communal History and Rama's Ayodhya', op. cit., p. 32.

16

The Changing Position of the Muslims and the Political Future of Secularism in India, *c.* 1947-1986

> The scenes will return, like deranged ghosts, to haunt those of us who were at the graveside to witness the burial of a secular dream. The screams of exultation with each blow of a pickaxe, each thrust of a rod, each dome that came crashing down. If there were no implements, the frenzied hordes would have used their bare hands to the same effect, so powerful was the poison that coursed through their veins in those few hours of madness.
>
> AWASTHI, 1992: 15

> Something . . . basic took place at Ayodhya—a massive assault on the very foundations of Indian culture and civilization, its very identity, its *sanskriti*, the very tradition and inheritance that these *kar sevaks* and their political leaders thought they were upholding. . . . How India will survive this dual onslaught remains to be seen . . . I, for one, doubt if it can. Not the India we have known.
>
> KOTHARI, 1992: 26

> Hindutva, once an abstract article of faith of a handful of determined crusaders on the margins of political life, is on the verge of becoming the new *mantra* of civil society . . . [The] impossible has almost happened and that Hindutva has succeeded in linking the past, present and future, and the individual, family, community and nation into a powerful expression for change.
>
> DASGUPTA, 1993: 8

What lies behind the Ayodhya catastrophe? Does it mark the end of India's tryst with destiny; a snapping of ties with its secular past? Will the votaries of *Hindutva* rewrite the nation's agenda, foist a Hindu *rashtra*, and reduce religious minorities to the status of second-class citizens? If so, what is in store for the secular and democratic forces which are already in a state of disarray?

What accounts for the politics of *Hindutva* and its extraordinary appeal in the Hindi heartland? Explanations are sought in the weakening of secular forces, and the Congress turning away from its own 'unique institutional and ideological enterprise'. Some writers question the wisdom of the enterprise itself, palpably based on mistaken assumptions and on a distorted Western-orientated version of secularism. There is, furthermore, talk of a 'Hindu backlash' in reaction to 'Muslim appeasement', the political nurturing of the minority vote-bank, and the dogged refusal of Muslims to join the 'national mainstream'. Finally, the *Hindutva* movement, spearheaded by the BJP, is seen as an expression of cultural nationalism and Hindu awakening, hitherto stifled by 'pseudo-secularists' and by the politics of minorityism. These formulations are no longer of academic interest alone. They have acquired new meaning and relevance, especially to those who have a stake in preserving India's democratic and secular fabric.

The votaries of *Hindutva* are, moreover, haunted by the presence of a ramshackle coalition of Muslim bodies acting as conscience-keepers and guardians of the community, and by the fact that Muslims possess a strong impulse to act as a separate, monolithic entity and advance their interests through religious networks and their representatives in parliament and state legislatures. I have tried to examine these propositions in relation to the political trajectory plotted by influential Muslim groups in the first decade after Independence, the nature of their interaction with the community and the nation, and their responses to the evolution of democracy and secularism. This is followed by a discussion of how Nehru's endeavour to lend a secular thrust to government policies was thwarted by his own party's ambivalence towards the very conception of civil society based on secularism. It is necessary to understand the nature of this ambivalence owing to its implication for the general communal situation and for the Congress party's own long-standing commitment to secularism.

The Future of Secularism

For well over a decade now, social scientists and political commentators have introduced a discordant note in the discourse on secularism, equating secularism with either Western liberalism or minority appeasement. It is often argued that the Western concept of state and civil society is intrinsically out of place in India where primordial loyalties, reinforced by the colonial experience of well over two centuries and the bitter legacy bequeathed by Partition in August 1947, exercise a pervasive influence in the public and private domain, and where religion is not just recognized as a mediating force in political and social affairs but legitimized through private and state intervention. That is why the secularizing forces, which conventional wisdom associates with literacy, urban growth, and industrial expansion, are said to have only touched the fringes of urban life.

Thus, Ashis Nandy (1990a: 69) challenges 'the hegemonic language of secularism popularized by the westernized intellectuals and middle classes exposed to the globally dominant language of the nation-state'. As an avowed 'anti-secularist', he believes that both the ideology and politics of secularism 'have more or less exhausted their possibilities and . . . we may now have to work a different conceptual frame which is already vaguely visible at the borders of Indian political culture' (Nandy 1990a: 73).

He has also written that 'modern India has a lot to answer for. So have the cosmopolitan intellectuals in this part of the world. They have failed to be respectful to the traditions of tolerance in Indian society. These traditions may have become creaky but so is, it is now pretty dear, the ideology of secularism itself' (Nandy 1990a: 85). In such writings, secularism tends to be dismissed as an import from the West grafted on a traditional society. It is written-off because of its limited appeal among the Western-educated élite. If one were to follow this intrinsically flawed logic, should India repudiate nationalism, parliamentary democracy, and free speech? The central issue is not the Western provenance of an idea but its place and relevance in a plural society.

The essence of the secular idea, flowing from the historical experiences of Western societies in the era following the French revolution, lies in drawing a sharp distinction between the symbols of a modern state and the Church, and of keeping the public domain free from religious interference. The inspiration behind this exercise, as also the impulse for creating a secular polity, rested on a refined conception of civil society, on restructuring community relations without reference to scriptures or religious texts, and on developing a scientific temper without being encumbered by the weight of scholasticism and religious traditionalism. In this schema, religious tolerance and religious neutrality undoubtedly occupied a central place, but many more inputs were required to lend meaning and weight to secularism.

It is possible to trace the roots of the 'secular' idea to the ancient Hindu and Buddhist texts, the Bhakti movement, and the religio-cultural syncretism evolved by Akbar, the sixteenth-century ruler, and Dara Shikoh, the Mughal prince. Still, it is perhaps inappropriate to equate those undifferentiated and undefined ideas and trends with the modern concept of secularism. *Sarva dharma sambhava* is a laudable notion, as it probably encapsulates the trajectory plotted by the state and society in precolonial India. At the same time, while *sarva dharma sambhava* forcefully conveys the spirit of religious tolerance, it does not imply a disjunction between the state and religion. Rooted in religion and spirituality and sustained by the ecumenical traditions of Hinduism, *sarva dharma sambhava* exuded the 'low-born', the *mlechhas* or those who were outside the *varna* system.

The chief ideologues of the nationalist movement generally refrained from adopting *sarva dharma sambhava* as their motto. Most of them, seeking refuge in the Western variant of secular nationalism, designed their mobilization campaigns accordingly. After Independence, too, India adopted, by and large, the Western model of secularism. It gave itself a secular constitution, one based on a broad national consensus.

The architects of the secular constitution were not always drawn from a particular intellectual ethos, designated as 'Western' in the recent trendy social science literature, but came from mixed and diverse traditions. Some were rooted in the soil, so to speak, and had powerful 'indigenous' cultural moorings. Aware of traversing the path of secularism, they believed it to be the only viable and acceptable course open to them. They knew full well, notwithstanding their ideological predilections, that a secular state was the surest way of preserving national unity and containing centrifugal tendencies that threatened to undermine, in the aftermath of a bloody Partition, an already fractured social structure.

No wonder secularism, along with democratic socialism, occupied a central place in their discourse. It also constituted, at least in public pronouncements and party manifestos, a key item on their agenda. Invoking secular symbols and slogans drew the political support of the trade union movement and the growing urban intelligentsia. To be non-secular, on the other hand, carried a stigma. To adopt 'non-secular' postures was considered an act of political blasphemy, an unforgivable sin. These trends conveyed the impression that the nation as a whole surged ahead, despite the grumblings of certain political leaders, in its quest for a secular state and society, and that the relevance and utility of the secular experience had gained wide acceptence. It is in this light that the resolution passed by the All India Congress Committee in May 1964 acquires significance. It reiterated that secularism was a priceless heritage and constituted the foundation on which a progressive modern state could be built for the welfare of all.

There is, however, little doubt that the secular ideology has been in a state of steady decline since the demise of Nehru, and that its appeal has diminished even among the 'Westernized intellectuals and middle classes' who are supposed to have popularized the 'hegemonic language of secularism' (Hasan 1991). The prospects for secularism appear to be fairly dim in the light of the events that have jolted Indian society since the demolition of the mosque at Ayodhya. There are other disturbing signs as well—the passive role of the Congress in allowing the anti-secular forces to run amok and seize the initiative in the public domain, the deconstruction of the secular paradigm by overtly communal parties, and the legitimacy accorded to *sadhus*, *mahants* and *mullahs* in the course of feeble efforts to resolve the deadlock aver the Babri Masjid issue. These are indeed ominous signs. Still, it is hard to agree with Nandy's denial of a place for secularism on the nation's political agenda.

The broad survey attempted in this chapter points to certain tangible gains and identifies certain bright spots in the slow progress made by India in its march towards the goal of a secular polity and society. One should, of course, not be wary of working out alternative frameworks preferably rooted in 'indigenous' traditions and tied to the legacy of the nationalist movement. But, in the end, Indian society, the liberal intelligentsia included, will have to restore the democratic, secular consensus of the 1950s and 1960s, and subscribe to the *ideal* of a composite and plural society with secularism as is masthead.

In this scheme of things, Nehru's secular manifesto, an outcome and prized legacy of the anti-colonial struggle, needs to be reiterated. The reason for this lies not in any intrinsic merit secularism may possess, but rather in its role in outlining the contours of India's historical development and providing a *rational ground* for a reconciliation of diverse and conflicting sectarian and communitarian perceptions and goals. The manifesto may bear the imprint of ambiguity; it may well be tailored and trimmed to suit the rapidly changing realities of political life. Yet, the ideological underpinnings of the democratic, secular consensus envisaged by the architects of India's Constitution and so assiduously forged by the country's first prime minister, are as relevant today as they were during the 1950s and 1960s. There may be differences of opinion about the nature of the secular consensus, and on the most effective way of rooting out communalism. One would, however, like to believe that there would be no divergence of views on the imperative of carrying out the secular and democratic provisions of the Constitution itself.

The mainstream of Indian nationalism has a decidedly secular orientation. That is why, when the newly created state of Pakistan was fostering its Islamic image in 1947-8, India was engaged in reconstructing a democratic and secular polity amidst the brutal and bloody violence that accompanied Independence and Partition. After more than four decades of Independence, this secular experiment needs to be reviewed for its implications both for other plural societies endeavouring to tackle their ethnic, regional, and religious problems in Asia and Africa, and for India's Muslims who form the largest minority in the country. My analysis will not lose sight of the obvious fact that the differentiating features that characterize Indian society as a whole are also to be found within the Muslim community. At the same time, my concern is to uncover certain broad trends amongst Muslims, excluding regional, local, and class nuances from the analysis.

During the 1940s, Jinnah led a powerful movement to advance the interests of Muslims after the withdrawal of the colonial power from the subcontinent. But the final outcome of his campaign proved catastrophic to the more than 35 million Muslims who remained in India after Partition. Leading industrial families, trading groups, and practitioners of various professions shifted base to Pakistan in order to improve their fortunes, and left behind a socially fragmented and economically depressed Muslim community. UP and Bihar were the areas most affected by the riots, the exodus to Pakistan, and a considerable 'skimming off' from the professional classes; a process that continued until the early 1960s. As a result, there were hardly any Muslims left in the defence services, in the police force, in universities, law courts and in the vast central secretariat in Delhi (Parthasarathi 1987). Likewise, the urban artisan and entrepreneurial class east and south of Delhi was reduced by riot and migration (Qureshi 1970). In Delhi itself, the *karkhandars*, petty traders, and shopkeepers suffered heavily at the hands of refugees dispossessed of their homeland in west Punjab.

The dissolution of the princely states impoverished a large percentage, if not the majority, of the upper and middle classes. With sources of patronage rapidly disappearing, prospects of securing employment in places such as Rampur, Bhopal, and Hyderabad deteriorated. The abolition of the *zamindari* system reduced the rural influence of the former Muslim landlords even more than that of their Hindu counterparts, because of the smaller number of Muslim peasants in the north and the greater number of urban *rentiers* among the Muslim landlords (Brass 1974; Husain 1965). The smaller landlords, as in the case of the Kidwais in Bara Banki district, lost much of their land to the tenants who acquired legal rights over the land they cultivated. The great *taluqdari* estates of Awadh declined due to families being divided, one branch migrating and the other electing to stay. Such was the fate of the Mahmudabad estate, the second largest *taluqdari* in Awadh after Balrampur. The raja hurried to Pakistan, leaving behind his wife, son, brother, and his vast estates in Bara Banki, Sitapur, and Bahraich districts.

Finally, politics for Muslims as Muslims had no *raison d'être*. With the Muslim League dissolved in the north and its leadership located in Pakistan, the political trajectory of the Muslims had to be defined within the broad democratic and secular framework; a framework that had evolved through a painful and tortuous process and depended on the consensual model that the Congress was attempting to create in the aftermath of Independence and Partition.

Rhetoric of Communal Solidarity: The Politics of the Jamaat

In 1957, W.C. Smith commented on an Indian Muslim community, battered by inward circumstances and gripped inwardly by dismay (Smith 1957). A decade later, Percival Spear tried to assess its 'inner life or soul in the New India' (Spear 1967). In recent years, scholars have defined the distinct ethos of Islam and pointed out how the ideal of the Islamic community shapes their apprehension of what is legitimate, desirable and satisfactory political action (Robinson 1985: 373).

These formulations rest on questionable assumptions. There is, for example, no justification for perpetuating an exclusive political and religious category, created by the raj in its various constitutional arrangements, or to *create* an 'Islamic community' with a self-image and unified self-perception, supposedly its alone. One is even wary of using the expression 'Indian Muslim community', though one does so in this chapter with an implied recognition of socio-economic differentiations, multiple ideological strands, and diverse cross-currents both in the realm of thought and action.

Given their divisions and diversities, Indian Muslims, in general, could neither harness their inner resources to evolve a common vision nor work as a collective group in pursuit of shared goals. After Independence, in particular, the options of exercising 'free will', as it were, diminished. *The*

Destiny of Indian Muslims, the title of Abid Husain's work (1965), had to be defined within established parameters and in relation to newly-created democratic structures. This involved a redefinition of the Islamic community in the Indian environment, a task attempted by Maulana Azad and Rafi Ahmad Kidwai in the political domain, and by Zakir Husain, Mohammad Mujeeb, K.M. Ashraf, Humayun Kabir, K.G. Saiyidain, and Abid Husain in the realm of ideas.

The Congress Muslims of Azad's generation remained wedded to the concept of composite nationalism and pleaded for greater Muslim participation in nation-building (Hasan 1987; 1992). They envisaged a new role for themselves, not as leaders of Muslims but as members of a new political elite. With the disappearance of separate electorates and reserved seats, they were no longer required to woo the Muslim voter. Indeed, with their enlarged constituency, they began to enjoy the trappings of power, oblivious of their vulnerability in a system in which communal considerations continued to mould political life.

The co-option of Congress Muslims in governmental structures restricted their ability to keep up their links with large segments of the Muslim people. This need not have been so. With their vast and rich experience of public life, they were ideally placed to lead the Muslims in a critical phase of transition and prevent their alienation. But they did not take advantage of the opportunity presented to them after Independence. Instead, they settled for a soft option. Having been integrated into the vast Congress party machinery and assured of Nehru's backing, they developed a vested interest in defending the status quo. They eschewed involvement in all issues which were seen to be specifically Muslim and were likely to leave them vulnerable to charges of promoting sectarian causes. In particular, during the first three general elections 'the nomination and election processes work[ed] to put into the legislatures Muslims who [were] inclined to be docile and not raise embarrassing issues too persistently, lest they either not "[got] the ticket" next election or [were] shifted to less safe constituencies' (Wright 1966: 110). Even someone of Azad's stature, though deeply aggrieved by the communal posture of some of his own colleagues, avoided the more public forms of protest.

While the Congress Muslims nursed their political wounds after Independence/Partition, the political initiative was wrested from them by the Jamiyat-i-ulama-i Hind and the Jamaat-i Islami. Though competing for political supremacy, their members had the same high stakes in making the most of the newly created social and political structures. They recognized the need to mould their political strategy and to restore their hold over their followers, which was slackened by the fragmentation of leadership and by deep ideological schisms.

The Jamiyat, founded in 1919 amid the khilafat enthusiasm, plotted a nationalist, anti-colonial course in alliance with the Congress. In the 1940s, the Jamiyat, under Husain Ahmad Madani's leadership, opposed Partition wholeheartedly and identified itself with the forces of composite nationalism. After Independence, the Jamiyat met in April 1948 to 'chalk out the path to be traversed by the community for reconstruction [and to march] shoulder to shoulder with members of other communities inhabiting the country' (Qasimi n.d.: 1).

Its leaders acclaimed the democratic and secular principles of the Constitution, interpreting it as a *muhaadih* (social contract), comparable to the concordat between the Prophet of Islam and the Jewish people in Medina (Qasim n.d.: 2-3).[1] The emphasis, as in the past, was on promoting fraternal links between the two estranged communities, on political cooperation with the Congress under Nehru's secular leadership, and rejection of all previous demands. The latter included separate electorates and reservation of seats, and raised the spectre of 'Muslim separatism'. The Jamiyat expressed the view that Indian Muslims 'should [also] realize that in a country like India it is only this brand of secularism which can provide safeguards for their culture and religious freedom and can give strength to their status as a religious minority. It is, therefore, in their own interest to support the secular ideal envisaged in the Constitution with sincerity and ardour' (Faruqi 1966: 144).

The political manifesto of the Jamiyat was set out by Husain Ahmad Madani in September 1951. Writing to a correspondent who was troubled by the events in the aftermath of Partition, Madani made the following characteristically candid observation:

> My respected friend (*mere muhtaram*)! You [certainly] entertain laudable religious sentiments. But why do you forget where you are and under what circumstances? Would the problems that we are facing today have arisen if the country had not been partitioned? The Muslims would then constitute 37 per cent of the population of the Republic of India. As an influential minority, they would number 100 million. But today they number only 40 million and constitute only 9 or 10 per cent. It is precisely because of such things that the Jam'iyya opposed partition, but our voice was not heard. Communalist (*firma parast*) Hindus wholeheartedly wish that not even one Muslim remain in India and that they may do whatever they please. . . . As you have brought about the partition of the country, what is the reason for your anger? It is an act of generosity on the part of the Hindus that they establish secularism in the country. Failing this, the decisions

and actions of the League and of yourself call for a situation in which the Hindus do in their area of majority whatever they wish without your being able to utter a word. Likewise, in Pakistan you can do whatever you please and nobody can say a word. If you plan to hold a convention and wish the Muslims to leave India if their demands are not conceded—then this is precisely what the Hindus want! And again, are you saying that these 40 million Muslims will migrate from here? Even if you and I and several thousands of people like us will leave—will all follow us? And even if they did—which country will provide them with a permanent home?

What was the migration movement which took place during the khilafat (in comparison with the migration that took place after partition)? What calamity descended upon the Muslims who left the UP, Bihar, East Punjab and other places after the partition of the country and in what calamity do they remain! Not hundreds, not a thousand or two thousand, but hundreds of thousands of Muslims can find no home. . . . As for Afghanistan and the Arab countries—what can they do and what sympathy do they feel towards you or towards the Indian Muslims? Please, look at the situation thoughtfully.

Provincial bigotry (*subajati ta'assub*) of the worst kind is being practised in Sind, Punjab and Bengal against the Muslims of UP, Bihar and other provinces. . . .

This is not *der al-islam*. It was partitioned by our own hands. You and I did it Our forefathers chose to live here in cities, towns and villages before Mahmud of Ghazna [*sic*] and Muhammad b. al-Qasim. To what extent is the situation of that time different from the present one? Yet our forefathers did not make observations such as 'we are one thousand or two thousand, one hundred thousand or two hundred thousand and the country is full of infidels. They are extremely hostile to us. God knows what will happen and when.' But today—looking forward makes you so restless!

When the Muslims became stronger and their armies entered India, at that time they were also a negligible minority. Today you number 40 million. Were the vicissitudes of time (*irqilabat-i-zamana*), which may happen at any time, not taken into consideration by those early Muslims? But today the Muslims fear from such vicissitudes. Were the polytheists at that time their friends, did they not entertain polytheistic sentiments (*mushrikana jadhabat*) or were the vicissitudes of time absent? Granted that they have acquired power, but who could ensure that it would continue? Still, they remained here, propagated Islam and converted millions of people. Today you lose courage and are prepared to leave the country.

My respected friend! When Madina became *dar al-islam* and the [Koranic] verses relating to jihad were revealed and the battles of Badr and Uhud took place—the *sura* of Al' Imran was revealed. At the end of this *sura* there is the following verse: 'Assuredly you will be tried in your property and in your persons and will hear much wrong from those who were given the Scripture before you and from the idolators. But if you persevere and fear God, then that is of the steadfast heart of things.' If at that time the [divine] commandment was to endure, then what import does it have today? To act with fortitude and endurance, perseverance and high-mindedness, to be assiduously engaged in strengthening Islam is our and your duty. . . . (quoted in Friedmann 1971: 177-80)

In general, thus, the Jamiyat acted within a broadly secular framework. Its leaders were closely allied with the Congress which, in turn, helped them to secure seats in parliament and in state assemblies. Prominent amongst them were Maulanas Asaf Madani, Ishaq Sambhali, and Hifzur Rahman. Theodore Wright has indicated that 10 of the 21 traditionally trained men were among the 20 legislators who claimed adherence to the Jamiyat al-ulama in their Who's Who entries (Wright 1964: 259).

The Jamaat-i Islami, on the other hand, was an organization with a difference. It surfaced in 1941, nearly two decades after the birth of the Jamiyat al-ulama, and was founded not by a traditional *akim* but a scholar-journalist. Saiyid Abul Ala Maududi was tutored in the nationalist traditions of the Jamiyat al-ulama before he embarked on a mission to create a righteous group which, in turn, would effect a political and social transformation on an Islamic pattern. Though initially opposed to the aspirations of the Muslim League, Maududi and his spirited band of followers migrated to Pakistan where they mounted a campaign for creating a truly Islamic state. Their argument was that as Pakistan had been fought for and won in the name of the Muslims and their Islamic aspirations, was it not the duty of the leadership to create a state and a society based upon Islamic ideology, following Islamic policies, and actively striving towards an Islamic ideal (Adams 1966: 376).

The Jamaat was barely in its infancy when it was overwhelmed by the trauma of Independence and Partition. Its leadership in India was depleted, the command structures fractured, and the ideological equilibrium, which Maududi had so zealously maintained, was disturbed.[2] Above all, the Jamaat faced the daunting task of reconciling its ideology with the democratic and secular order in India. India was no *Dar al-Islam*, an ideal close to the heart of the undivided Jamaat leadership; but it was neither a *Dar al-harb*. The constitutional provisions, though warily implemented, guaranteed certain basic, fundamental rights to the minorities which were denied to their counterparts in Pakistan.

The Jamaat's early history after 1947 is shrouded in mystery, though there is fragmentary evidence of a debate over democracy, nationalism, and secularism. Maududi regarded nationalism as a Western phenomenon resting on the false philosophy of Western civilization. For this reason, he attacked the ulama of the Jamiyat al-ulama for a nationalism that ran counter to Islam and also, in tactical terms, risked the socio-cultural absorption of Muslims into Hindu society.[3] In May 1947, he published his political manifesto which, in large measure, served as a guide to his devoted band of followers in the subcontinent.

> We are opposed to the 'secular, national, democratic' system. On whichever country or nation this curse falls we will warn all God's creatures living therein to beware of it and avoid it scrupulously. As against those three principles we put forward another three principles, and appeal to the conscience of all men to observe and test for themselves . . . (a) as against secularism is the principle of submission and obedience to God; (b) as opposed to nationalism is humanism; and (c) as against democracy or sovereignty of the masses is the sovereignty of God and the vice-regency [*khilafat*] of the people. (Maududi, n.d.: 25)[4]

The Jamaat has remained, despite its protestations to the contrary, a retrograde and reactionary force, deriving ideological sustenance and financial support from conservative and semi-feudal regimes in West Asia. It is opposed to social reform, enforces strict adherence (*taqlid*) to the tenets of Islam through their vast network of *madaris* and *makatib*, and has stalled Muslim participation in the democratic processes.[5] Though continuing to equate secularism with irreligiousness, the Jamaat leaders have, at the same time, pinned their hopes on the survival of a democratic and secular society. 'In contrast to other totalitarian and fascist modes of government', declared an official Jamaat publication, 'the . . . secular democratic mode of government in India should endure' (Wright 1979: 86).[6]

Muslim Participation in India's Secular Democratic Political Process: 1947-1962

The rhetoric of communal solidarity often obscures the fragmented character of Muslim political formations. Divided on ideological grounds, the Jamiyat al-ulama and the Jamaat-i Islami pursue separate goals and follow independent political trajectories. Though seemingly united on some issues, they have yet to find a meeting ground for common action. This is equally true of the Ittehad al-Muslimeen and the Tamir-i Millat in Hyderabad, and the Shia Political Conference and the Muslim Majlis in Lucknow. The supposedly monolithic structure of the Muslim leadership and organization does not exist either at the national or the local level. This is not to deny the absence of community consciousness or of communal solidarity, but to emphasize that a separate communitarian consciousness was not always translated into any tangible political reality.

The All India Muslim Convention (AIMC), held at Aligarh in October 1953, was ineffective. Likewise, the initiative taken in 1964, leading to the formation of the Majlis-i Mushawarat, petered out after much fanfare. The Majlis, stigmatized as a sinister, incipient revival of the old Muslim League, legitimized Hindu communalism in UP and pushed more votes towards candidates who appealed to Hindu sentiments (Hasan 1988: 824-5).

The message was loud and clear. Political mobilization along communitarian lines carried serious risks, because it hardened communal attitudes among majority segments and deepened insecurity amongst the minorities. The alternative, then, was not to function as a separate political entity but to take advantage of the diverse political formations. In fact, the tendency to assume national party identifications and to lend electoral support to secular-orientated parties pointed to the effectiveness of the democratic forces among large segments of the Muslim population.

Rising Tide of Communalism in India: 1967-1980

Only 15 years after Independence, the communal forces, long kept under check by Nehru's leadership, surged forward, causing serious stress to India's secular fabric. The Jamaat-i Islami and the Ittehad al-Muslimeen gained legitimacy from the wave of communal violence sweeping through much of north India. Spearheaded by the cadre-based RSS and its political wing, the Jana Sangh, Hindu communalism, with its repudiation of secularism and the Congress 'appeasement' of Muslims under the camouflage of secularism, gained considerable support; a fact reflected in the electoral advances made by the Jana Sangh during the period 1952-67 (Baxter 1968).

In the 1962 general election, the party more than doubled its strength in parliament and in the state assemblies. In the general election, the Jana Sangh's share of the total vote was double that in 1952 for the Lok Sabha and nearly 150 per cent for the various state assemblies. In UP and Madhya Pradesh, the Jana Sangh became the second largest party—with 49 seats to the Congress party's 248 in the UP state legislative assembly; and 41 seats to the Congress party's 142 in the Madhya Pradesh state legislative assembly (Smith 1963: 474-5). This upward trend continued, especially in UP where the party polled 21.53 per cent of the total votes and gained 98 seats at the fourth general election (1967). The *Hindustan Times* (12 March 1962) regarded the extension of Jana Sangh's influence to the rural areas as 'the most significant development of this election in Uttar Pradesh'.

Another indication of the rising tide of communal forces was the steady rise in the incidence of Hindu-Muslim rioting. During the 1950s, the number of violent communal disorders fell steadily, reaching a low of 26 in 1960.

The number rose to 92 in 1961; the worst year was when the disappearance of a religious relic from the Hazratbal mosque in Srinagar on 26 December 1963 triggered off extensive riots. There were, moreover, the notorious January (1964) riots in Calcutta which spread to 215 villages around the metropolis, where, according to one estimate, 1,500 Muslims were killed. The worst rioting took place at TELCO—the locomotive and truck factory operated by Tatas in cooperation with Mercedes-Benz. In Rourkela, about 5,000 Muslims were killed (Zinkin 1971).

During the period 1965-7, 515 outbursts of violence were recorded (Brass 1974: 219) in which Muslims suffered at the hands of rampaging communal mobs, headed all too often by RSS volunteers. Nehru declared that, from his own inquiries, it appeared that local Congress leaders had made no attempt whatsoever to calm the communal frenzy which seized Jabalpur and other cities and towns of Madhya Pradesh during the riots of February 1961.[7] They simply sat in their houses like '*purdah* ladies' as the situation deteriorated (*Hindustan Times*, 24 April 1961). The pattern was no different in the communal catastrophe at Ahmedabad in September 1969. Over a thousand people, mostly Muslims, lost their lives.

The communal upsurge during the decade of the 1960s represented a sharpening of existing caste, class, and community cleavages, reflecting the limitations of the secularization process which had been boldly initiated through democratic processes, progressive social legislation, rapid industrialization, and a massive adult literacy campaign. These cleavages were kept under some control during the anti-colonial struggle, but not after Independence. The Congress was no longer at the head of a movement: it was turned overnight into a political party whose principal aim was to exercise control and dominance over the levers of power and authority. Devising electoral strategies became its prime concern, whilst populist slogans, radical rhetoric, and diffused socio-economic policies were its answers to growing caste/class tensions and increased communal animosities. 'The image of Indian unity', warned the *Economic and Political Weekly*, 'cannot be built merely of eye-catching laces and frills: it must also have the supporting "stays" of harder material.'

The Congress was singularly lacking in ideological coherence, as signified by the presence of communal and revivalist elements entrenched in the states and districts, and their uneasy relationship with Nehru who was committed to the destruction of communalism and the establishment of a secular state and society. It surged ahead without isolating such elements,[8] without developing any formal or informal structures to effect social transformation, and without evolving instruments to widen the social basis of secularism and thus assuage the fears of the minorities whilst satisfying the rising aspirations of various social groups. Nehru was no doubt aware of these limitations, but he also prevaricated on vital issues. He either took or failed to take certain steps which contradicted his promotion of secularism.

An easy solution to the communal impasse was to woo sectional and parochial interests and to make occasional friendly gestures towards the minorities, even if it meant heightening their community consciousness. In his keenness to win Muslim confidence, Nehru allowed Muslims a voice in the debate about the provision of equality before the law to all Indian women and the promulgation of a common civil code, thus damaging the prospects of progressive legislation in either of these spheres. He stated in 1954 that he thought a unified civil code was inevitable, but that the time was not ripe to push it through in India. Again, he failed to press his own initiative for the banning of communal parties. The banning of cow-slaughter was also a matter on which Nehru failed to act according to his convictions. Legislation imposing a total ban on cow-slaughter was enacted in UP, Bihar, Madhya Pradesh, and Rajasthan. All these states were ruled by the Congress.

In dealing with communalism, Nehru himself was not proud of his government's record. Rajendra Prasad, his lifelong political comrade and the Indian Republic's first president, was swayed by Hindu reactionary opinion. So were some of his own ministers and chief ministers. Yet, Nehru did little to curb or counteract their influence. He expressed pious sentiments, but his pronouncements were not backed by any administrative action or an ideological cleansing of the party he led with such authority. Many of his ideas and plans could not be translated into practice partly because of his preoccupation with other domestic and international affairs and partly because they were 'hacked into mincemeat' by the hatchet men in the Congress (Tyabji 1971).

In relation to Urdu, Nehru betrayed a marked tendency to compromise with his ideological adversaries. The cause of Urdu was no doubt dear to him and he was much distressed by the hostility of Hindu chauvinists towards a language which, in his view, symbolized the rich and composite traditions of the Indo-Gangetic belt. Yet, he hesitated when it came to implementing electoral promises and constitutional guarantees. It was during his first term as prime minister, when his detractors were few and his position unassailable, that Pant and Sampurnanand launched their assault on Urdu.

Urdu lost its place in UP in 1951, when Hindi was declared the sole official language of the state. Acharya Kripalani performed the final rites in 1961 with his anti-Urdu, anti-minorities, and anti-Muslim report. Nehru remained silent. Sensitive to the communally vitiated atmosphere, he was wary of pressing the case of Urdu and taking the lead in delinking the question of Urdu from communal controversies. He repeatedly said that Urdu was not the language of Muslims alone but was also spoken by Hindus and Sikhs. Yet, he did precious little to promote this idea among the rank and file of his own party (Parthasarathi 1987: 379).[9]

Consider the anti-Urdu campaigns spearheaded by the Hindi Sahitya Sammelan before and after Independence. Its leaders were instinctively hostile to any trace of Muslim/Islamic inheritance, and hence Hindustani, which they saw as a mask for Urdu, was anathema to them. They depicted Urdu as a Muslim language, which it was not, identified it with the Pakistan movement and claimed that its style was distinctly 'unnational', if not anti-national. The position of Hindi was assured after the Constituent Assembly declared it as the national language, Urdu was not its rival. Yet, active and aggressive campaigns were mounted to suppress the language of Mir and Ghalib, spoken by millions of people of all religious creeds and a vital and graceful aspect of a vibrant composite tradition in the Indo-Gangetic belt.

Not much has changed over the last five decades. The establishment-oriented Urdu speakers boast of numerous Urdu academies and translation bureaus, housed in elegant buildings with plenty of funds to dole out to friends and admirers. Some take pride in Urdu being the language of Bollywood; others draw satisfation from awards and scholarships given to literary figures in the glittering halls of the Raj Bhawans and the Rashtrapati Bhawan. Some derive comfort from the mere fact that *mushairas*, where sections of the audience pronounce Ghalib as Galib and applaud poor quality romantic 'poetry', attract larger audiences than the *kavi sammelans*.

In reality, Urdu has been marginalized in the country as a whole. Even the democratic and secular forces have not shown much inclination to defend a language that symbolizes our composite heritage. In UP, the then chief minister, V.P. Singh, after failing to act on repeated promises, finally issued an ordinance in 1982 granting Urdu the status of a 'second language' (not second official language). His government did not convert the ordinance into legislation. Five years later, when the Vidhan Sabha adopted the Official Language (Amendment) Bill in 1989 amid unruly scenes, the BJP MLAs stormed into the well and raised slogans like 'Urdu Bill Murdabad' (Death to the Urdu Bill) and '*Ek Rajya, ek Bhasha, nahi chahiye dusri Bhasha*' (One state, one language, a second language not required).

Urdu survives lazily in the alleys and by-lanes of Muslim localities. It has lost its position in Osmania University, Hyderabad, Delhi's Jamia Millia, and the Aligarh Muslim University. An Urdu university languishes in Aligarh; another one is in the making at Hyderabad. Except for some districts in UP and Bihar, Urdu has ceased to be the language of administration, the judiciary and the police. Even symbolic attempts to promote Urdu have led to a violent backlash. Thus, riots were triggered off when the UP government made Urdu the state's second official language in 1989. Ten-minute Urdu television news bulletin in Bangalore led to riots in October 1994, leaving 30 dead.

Urdu poetry? How can there be Urdu poetry when there is no Urdu language left? It is dead, finished. The defeat of the Mughals by the British threw a noose over its head, and the defeat of the British by the Hindi-wallahs tightened it. So now you see its corpse lying here, waiting to be buried. This is not just the anguish of a living Urdu poet in Anita Desai's novel, but a summation of the grievance of Urdu-speakers all over the country. The story of a weak, gasping poet in *In Custody* is, indeed, the story of Urdu language and poetry.

Nehru's ambivalence is further reflected in his handling of the Kashmir problem, which has been historically linked with the communal question because of the 'third party', namely Pakistan. His understanding, to say the least, was distorted by misleading reports from dubious quarters in the Kashmir valley. That is why he committed the colossal blunder of dismissing Sheikh Abdullah and putting him in jail. The Sheikh was no ordinary politician; it was not for nothing that his people idolized him as 'Sher-i Kashmir'. He was a political giant, his place in history assured by the dogged tenacity with which he led the struggle for the political and social emancipation of his people, Kashmiri Pandits and Muslims alike. Who could have known these facts better than Nehru? Yet, he chose to stifle the voice of the people. It is not important who were the guilty men—Patel, Rafi Ahmad Kidwai, Bakshi Ghulam Mohammad, or D.P. Dhar. The ultimate responsibility for this political blunder rests with Nehru.

Erosion of Secular Democracy and The Economic Decline of Muslims[10]

The last phase of Indira Gandhi's government witnessed an unprecedented intensification of religious fervour, an exacerbation of sectarian feuds, and an increased polarization of Indian society not along class lines, as Nehru had envisaged, but on purely communal grounds. Approximately 4,000 persons were killed in communal riots during the 1980s. This is almost four times the figure for the 1970s, which had witnessed a relative lull after the bloody rioting in Ahmedabad in 1969.[11] The number of districts affected by communal rioting increased from 61 in 1961 to 250 in 1986-7 (out of a total of just over 350 districts). From February 1986 to June 1987, nearly 60 'major' and 'minor' riots broke out in UP alone. Over 200 people were killed and 1,000 injured. Damage to property was estimated in the region of Rs. 15,00,00,000.

Equally significant was the growth of communal organizations with militant overtones. They numbered less than a dozen in 1951; by 1987 there were over 500, with an active membership running into several million. The newly formed Hindu militias were the *trishuldharis* of the Akhil Bharatiya Shiv Shakti Dal (ABSSD) which boasted 3,000 followers and 60 branches between Delhi and Saharanpur; the Hindu Manch (HM), activated after the highly publicized conversions to Islam of a few hundred Harijans in the Tamil Nadu village of Meenakshipuram in 1981, with a following of 20,000 among the lower middle classes; and the Shiv Sena (SS) with strong supporters among the Hindu migrants from Punjab. All these bodies, combined with the VHP and the Virat Hindu Sammelan (VHS) which are at the apex of several right wing organizations, have been vying with each other to emerge as the greatest champion of Hindu communal causes, and are now in the forefront of an aggressive campaign to 'liberate', along with the Babri Masjid, 450 other mosques in north India alone.

Thus the secular consensus, an imprimatur of the Nehru era, was all but discarded by the dominant Congress leadership, eager to accommodate revivalist and obscurantist tendencies in order to isolate and deflect the emergence of alternative political forces surfacing in various parts of the country. This was most certainly the perception of politically sensitive Muslim groups. What angered them most was the systematic neglect of their material interests and the steady decline of economic opportunities. The view that the economic weakness of the Muslims must be seen in the context of the society as a whole, where development is slow, wages are low, and unemployment is on the rise, carries no conviction with most Muslim activist groups who argue that opportunities for economic advancement are specifically blocked for their community which has borne the consequences of official neglect and discrimination.

The causes of the economic decline of the Muslims are debatable. But there is no doubt that they have occupied the lowest rung of the ladder in terms of the basic categories of socio-economic indicators of development (Faridi 1965). In modern industry and trade, except for isolated instances, they have not owned large-scale industry or business. Until 1985, there was not a single Muslim house among 50 industrial groups, whilst at the lower end of the scale most Muslims are poor and backward (Khan 1978). The position remains unchanged at the time of writing.

No benefit has accrued to the Muslims from various government schemes aimed at improving the conditions of disadvantaged sections of society. Of the houses allotted by state governments to lower and middle income groups, until 1985 only 2.86 per cent went to Muslims. Of the licences issued for fair price shops, only 6.9 per cent were awarded to them. Finally, Muslims received just 0.25 per cent of the tangible benefits extended to artisans by the Khadi and Village Industries Commission (KVIC).[12]

The cooperative sectors fared no better. Of the loans advanced by financial institutions, only 3 per cent of those between Rs. 50,000 and 1,00,000 went to Muslims. Of those between Rs. 1,00,000 and 2,00,000, less than 2 per cent was received by Muslims. Of loans between Rs. 2,00,000 and 10,00,000 the figure was under 1 per cent.

In the sphere of employment, Muslims complain that they have been reduced to the position of 'the hewers of wood and the drawers of water'. Muslims settle for discrimination as a convenient explanation, though much of the problem in UP and Bihar has arisen out of the depletion of the Muslim middle classes in the aftermath of Partition and the abolition of Urdu as a language of administration and education, the latter adversely affecting the very section of the middle classes that sought employment at the clerical level, in lower government service, or in educational institutions. Widespread abandonment of Urdu has also made it difficult for a great many Muslim candidates whose mother tongue is Urdu to take competitive examinations for government posts. This accounts for the fact that very few Muslims take the examinations at all; another reason, of course, is a constant fear of discrimination if they do.

The plight of the Muslims is compounded by the occurrence of 'major' communal riots in towns where they have attained a measure of economic success through their traditional artisanal and entrepreneurial skills.[13] Ashutosh Varshney has recently shown that Hindu-Muslim violence has been primarily an urban phenomenon, as also highly locally concentrated. In fact, his study reveals (Table 16.1) that eight cities account for a disproportionate share of communal violence from 1950 to 1995; nearly 46 per cent of all deaths. This is the lesson of Aligarh where Muslims own

Table 16.1: Hindu-Muslim Riots in 28 Indian Cities (1950-95)[a]

Minimum of 15 deaths in 3 riots over 2 five-year periods[b]	Minimum of 20 Deaths in 4 riots over 3 five-year periods[c]	Minimum of 25 deaths in 5 riots over 4 five-year periods[d]	Minimum of 50 deaths in 10 riots over 5 five-year periods[e]	Total deaths 1950-95
Bombay	Bombay	Bombay	Bombay	1,137
Ahmedabad	Ahmedabad	Ahmedabad	Ahmedabad	1,119
Hyderabad	Hyderabad	Hyderabad	Hyderabad	312
Meerut	Meerut	Meerut	Meerut	265
Aligarh	Aligarh	Aligarh	Aligarh	160
Jamshedpur	Jamshedpur	Jamshedpur		198
Bhiwandi	Bhiwandi			194
Surat				194
Moradabad	Moradabad			149
Vadodara	Vadodara	Vadodara	Vadodara	109
Bhopal	Bhopal	Bhopal		108
Delhi	Delhi	Delhi	Delhi	93
Kanpur	Kanpur	Kanpur		81
Calcutta	Calcutta	Calcutta	Calcutta	63
Jabalpur				59
Bangalore	Bangalore	Bangalore		56
Jalgaon	Jalgaon	Jalgaon		49
Sitamarhi				47
Indore	Indore	Indore		45
Varanasi	Varanasi	Varanasi		42
Allahabad	Allahabad	Allahabad		37
Nagpur	Nagpur	Nagpur		37
Jaipur	Jaipur			32
Aurangabad	Aurangabad	Aurangabad		30
Srinagar	Srinagar	Srinagar		30
Ranchi				29
Malegaon	Malegaon			23
Godhra				18

Source: Ashutosh Varshney, 'Ethnic Conflict and Civil Society', *World Politics*, 53, April 2001, 3, 362-89.

Notes: [a] Total number of deaths from riots for all of India, 1950-95 = 7,173, of which 3.57 per cent of deaths took place in rural India.

[b] Total number of deaths from riots in these cities = 4,706. This is approximately 66 per cent of deaths from riots throughout India and 69 per cent of all deaths in urban riots during these periods.

[c] Total number of deaths from riots in these cities = 4,359. This is about 61 per cent of deaths from riots throughout India and 64 per cent of all deaths in urban riots during these periods.

[d] Total number of deaths from riots in these cities = 3,887. This is about 54 per cent of deaths from riots throughout India and 58 per cent of all deaths in urban riots during these periods.

[e] Total number of deaths from riots in these cities = 3,263. This is 45.5 per cent of deaths from riots throughout India and 49 per cent of all deaths in urban riots during these periods.

lock manufacturing industries and have recently moved into producing building materials; Varanasi, where Muslim weavers established their hold over the silk saree trade and tried to obtain ownership of the industry itself; Moradabad, where the industrial apparatus was reorientated into producing decorative brassware for export to rich Arab countries; Bhiwandi in Maharashtra, where Muslims gradually bought up small-scale textile units; Meerut in western Uttar Pradesh, where Muslim weavers became entrepreneurial and have done well in iron foundries, furniture manufacture, scissors-making, and lathe operations; and in the walled city of Delhi, where the traditional Hindu mercantile community resents Muslim intrusion into its commercial enclave. 'Hindus tend to raise their eyebrows at the assertion of an equal status by a community which they have been used to looking down upon as their inferiors in the post-Independence era', concludes a report on the Delhi riots of May 1987 (PUDR 1987: 2).

This 'economic resurgence' is often ascribed to Islamic fundamentalism and to a new sense of confidence among Muslims, now that their co-religionists in the Gulf have acquired wealth and considerable global influence. The connection is at best tenuous, though the Hindu petty bourgeoisie has not hesitated to use this argument to whip up communal sentiments. The motive is to displace the emerging Muslim entrepreneurial class in certain crucial areas of trade and business, and to reduce the possibility of keen competition. This was attempted in Moradabad and Meerut where Muslims witnessed the destruction of their hard-earned capital, invested in small factories.[14] A similar pattern can be seen in Ahmedabad and Bhiwandi (Engineer 1984), important centres of textile manufacturing. Yet, the more bizarre theories in circulation include the suggestion that riots at these centres were fuelled by petro-dollars funnelled through various Muslim organizations.

Communal riots, though by no means uncommon when Nehru was prime minister, were sporadic, localized, and easily controllable. Not so afterwards. Since the communal outburst in Ahmedabad (September 1969), riots have tended to be bloodier and more prolonged, with areas like Aligarh, Ahmedabad, Vadodara, Moradabad, and Meerut in a state of near perpetual tension.

The apathy, negligence, and complicity of local officials has also grown over the years; wherever public authority is compliant to anti-Muslim forces, the administration has offered weak or inadequate protection to the Muslims. This was a crucial variable in Ahmedabad, where the Congress administration delayed a crackdown on rioters for several days. It was the same a decade later in the steel township of Jamshedpur. In UP, on the other hand, the police and the PAC have often acted as if they were a force expressly organized to beat, loot, and kill Muslims (as for example, in Moradabad, and Malliana, a township dose to Meerut city). 'The massacre of Malliana [conducted by the PAC]', wrote an angry journalist, 'will go down in the history of this once-proud city as an unimaginable instance of sadism and brutality'. Amnesty International indicted the PAC for its brutalities in Malliana and in the Hashimpura area of Meerut.

Congress-Muslim Relations and Muslim Interests

The articulation of minority interests is often constrained, even in a democracy, as is illustrated by the case of India's Muslims whose identification with the Muslim League movement in the pre-Independence period has inhibited them from voicing their grievances in a sustained and organized manner. The formation of the All India Muslim Convention (AIMC) and the Majlis-i Mushawarat were bold initiatives, but the strategy of working through the electoral process backfired. The bitter controversy over Urdu, faced by the non-Congress governmental coalitions in Uttar Pradesh and Bihar after 1967, reinforced the proposition that parties identified with minority causes risked alienating their own constituents. Indira Gandhi was quick to learn this lesson when she spoke of a 'Hindu backlash' against any further 'pampering' of the minorities.

Though parliament and the state legislatures have remained important fora, the part played by Muslim legislators has not been seen in a favourable light by most Muslims. Muslim legislators, though often elected from Muslim-populated constituencies and sponsored as minority representatives, have eschewed the more public forms of protest and rebuffed petitions for help on minority causes. As a result, sponsored mobility has improved the political fortunes of a few chosen legislators without advancing the interests of their constituents. Hence, when scholars or publicists prepare impressive lists of the Muslim candidates elected over a number of years, they may contribute to group pride, but they signify not more than a pyrrhic victory (Schermerhorn 1978: 177-8).

Some formal and informal channels of articulation existed because of Nehru's close links with certain sections of the Muslim leadership, especially in the Jamiyat al-ulama, his long-standing association with Muslim nationalists, and his personal commitment to providing equal opportunities to the minorities and ending discrimination against them. Sensitive to the demands of the minorities, he pressed his colleagues to offer adequate representation to Muslims in the armed forces and civil services (*Statesman* 12 May 1958), instructed chief ministers, to submit quarterly reports of official recruitment (Gopal 1979: 206), advocated justice for the Urdu language, and warned that communalism, especially of the majority, was the greatest of all the dangers facing India. He was unsparing in criticizing senior party members who were unfriendly towards Muslims, pulled up Charan Singh for his reported remarks against Muslims, expressed unhappiness over the anti-Muslim bias of Pant, UP's chief minister (who subsequently became home minister of India), and was disappointed that Vallabhbhai Patel, India's first home minister, had lapsed into his old attitude of suspecting the loyalty of Muslims in India. 'All of us', he wrote sadly, 'seem to be getting infested with the refugee mentality or, worse still, the RSS mentality. That is a curious finale to our careers.'[15]

Though Nehru's exhortations went unheeded and the grievances of the minorities remained unredressed, Muslims continued to maintain confidence in his leadership and recognized the Congress as the principal vehicle of their aspirations. The AIMC, revived in June 1961 by Maulana Hifzur Rahman of the Jamiyat al-ulama, acted within the Congress framework and appealed to Muslims to 'stand shoulder to shoulder with their non-Muslim brethren inside secular political and social organizations'. Pro-Congress sentiment was also strong within the Majlis-i Mushawarat. Under the influence of Saiyid Mahmud, Nehru's contemporary at Cambridge, the Bihar unit of the Majlis did not go along with Faridi's anti-Congressism and supported as many as 50 Congress candidates for the 1962 assembly elections (Brass 1974: 251).

After Nehru's death, Congress-Muslim relations strained, and the links that India's first prime minister had established with the minorities were either weakened or altogether severed. Having supported Indira Gandhi in her early years of political dominance, Muslims slowly but steadily drifted away from her to swell the ranks of, for example, the National Conference (JKNC) in Kashmir, the Lok Dal (LD) in UP and Bihar, and the parties constituting the Left Front government in Bengal. The internal Emergency (1975-7) and its accompanying excesses were the last straw. 'The incongruous coalition of traditionalists, secularists, and repentant former Muslim League modernists', who had supported the Congress in previous elections, was broken up by forced sterilization, *jhuggi* clearance, slum removal, police firing on Muslims, and the suspension of civil liberties, which included the banning of the Jamaat-i Islami (Wright 1977).

Indira Gandhi's efforts to win over the Muslims during the 1980 elections were only partially rewarded. In the two crucial states of UP and Bihar, the LD rather than the Congress emerged as a powerful political force. The LD won 12 out of the 23 Muslim constituencies in UP and secured 33.3 per cent of the Muslim vote as against 34.4 per cent gained by the Congress party. Even in Bihar, where the Congress did exceptionally well in Muslim constituencies, the LD did better (23.4 per cent) in the Muslim constituencies than in the state as a whole (16.6 per cent).

Weiner (1984) contests the popular view that Muslims voted for the Congress(I) party. His conclusion is that a substantial number of Muslims who had voted for other parties in 1977 voted for the Congress(I) in 1980, but in no greater proportion than other communities (and except for Bihar and West Bengal, possibly even less).

The Rise of Communal Forces among Muslims?

The gradual weakening of the Congress base amongst Muslims made it possible for the religious-orientated Muslim groups to occupy the political vacuum, while frequent riots and unending discriminatory practices against Muslims legitimized their activities. This is a familiar pattern. During the 1940s, the Muslim League success was, in some measure, linked to Muslim estrangement from the Congress after the Quit India movement of 1942. Capitalizing on the 'wrongs' done by the Congress during the period 1937-9, when it held office in eight provinces, the League persuaded Muslim splinter groups to join it. Nearly three decades later, Muslim organizations of different shades of opinion extended their base of support by dwelling on the Congress failure to stem the communal tide and assuage the fears of the minorities. The rise of the Ittehad-ul Muslimeen in Hyderabad, the political intervention of the Jamaat-i Islami in Kashmir, and the increased support enjoyed by the Muslim League in Kerala must be seen against this background. They remain, as always, the principal force behind Muslim conservatism and political reaction.

It is hard to delineate the principal contours of Muslim conservatism, though its basic aim has remained unchanged since the advent of British rule in India: the preservation of cultural and religious identity within the defined Islamic framework. Its more tangible manifestation has been the resistance to modern education, opposition to the composite and syncretic trends in Indian Islam, and the tendency to thwart reformist initiatives. Thus, Muslim organizations and institutions have led successful mobilization campaigns centering on these issues, and insulated the community from the process of social change and modernization so as to resist the secularizing tendencies generated during and after colonial rule. This phenomenon was unique to Indian Islam, for reformist ideas and movements have not been inconsequential in Muslim countries like Egypt, Turkey, and Iran.

Conservative reaction after Independence has been most pronounced in opposing the demand for a uniform civil code—an issue which unites the three principal organizations in India which are otherwise opposed to each other on fundamental doctrinal matters. These are:

1. Tablighi Jamaat, established by Maulana Muhammad Ilyas to unite all sections of the community and 'make them realize their common bond of religion';
2. Jamaat-i Islami, founded in 1941 by Saiyid Abul Ala Maududi to create a state and a society based upon Islamic ideology, following Islamic policies, and actively striving towards an Islamic ideal; and
3. Jamiyat al-ulama, born in the throes of the massive khilafat upsurge and dominated by the ulama connected with the Dar al-ulum at Deoband.

Though radical in its political orientation, the Jamiyat has regarded 'modernism' as the most dangerous heresy of the day, and its leaders have challenged it vigorously.

The Jamaat-i Islami, which takes the most militant position on the issue of change in the personal law, argues that even a ban on polygamy cannot be accepted, because Muslims are sure it will be only 'the first step in the direction of erasing every symbol of a separate Muslim culture in India' (quoted in Brass 1974: 220). The Jamiyat al-ulama agrees, arguing that any attempt to alter the personal law would be an infringement of the 'covenant' of composite nationalism which binds Muslims to India and its Hindu countrymen. This was echoed at a convention organized in December 1974, and is repeated at every annual session of the Jamiyat (Qasimi, n.d.). Following this convention, an All India Muslim Personal Law Board was set up as a watchdog body to monitor and actively resist any changes in the *Shariat*. Just over a decade later, the AIMPLB spearheaded a campaign which signified a massive fundamentalist upsurge, unprecedented in post-Independence India.

The immediate provocation for this was provided by a Supreme Court judgement (on 23 April 1985) which criticized Islamic law and Koranic concepts in granting maintenance rights to Shah Bano, a 69 year old Muslim woman divorced by her husband after 43 years of marriage.

Several Muslims groups considered this judgement as an assault on the *Shariat* which, in their opinion, makes no such provision in the event of a divorce, and as 'the thin end of the wedge for securing the extinction of the Muslim personal law and its substitution by a common civil code'.[16] They took to the streets to register their protest and accused the Supreme Court of sacrilegious trespass.

The Rajiv Gandhi government capitulated to the strident clamourings of some Muslims by introducing the retrograde Muslim Women (Protection of Rights on Divorce) Bill in May 1986. This was done to stem the rising tide of anger over the Shah Bano verdict which was losing the Congress party its Muslim votes. The electoral defeats of the Congress after the momentous Supreme Court judgement were sharp reminders of this. Assam, Bijnor, and Kishanganj,[17] Bolpur, Kendrapara, and Vadodara were all areas where the Muslim vote tipped the balance in favour of the opposition parties. With Assam, West Bengal, UP, Bihar, Jammu & Kashmir, and Kerala having a substantial Muslim population, the stakes were obviously far too high.

The 'victory' tasted over the Shah Bano issue encouraged Muslim reaction in several different ways. In early January 1987, Saiyid Shahabuddin, editor of *Muslim India* and a member of parliament, called upon Muslims to stay away from the Republic Day celebrations on 26 January. This was followed by a call for an all-India strike (*bandh*) on 1 February 1987, the first anniversary of the day when, by an order of the district magistrate, the gates of the Babri Masjid in Ayodhya were thrown open for Hindus to offer worship in the mosque's inner sanctum.

The same forces which had exerted pressure on Rajiv Gandhi to undo the 'wrong' done by the Supreme Court judgement in the Shah Bano case incited communal frenzy amongst Muslims. As a result, violence spread to several towns of UP and Bihar, culminating in a massive congregation of over 3,00,000 Muslims in Delhi demanding justice and an end to discrimination against their community. The centre stage was once more occupied by, among others, Saiyid Abdullah Bukhari, the mercurial imam of Delhi's Jama Masjid and the 'messiah' of the Muslim backlash during the tumultuous general election of 1977. Organizer of a Muslim militia, Adam Sena, the imam was also the moving spirit behind the widely publicized incident on the night of 14 April 1987, when thousands of Muslims forced their way into several of the protected national monuments in the capital under the charge of the Archaeological Survey of India, to offer prayers on the occasion of Shab-i Baraat, a Muslim festival observed only in the subcontinent.

Such stirrings in the Muslim communities, which are only remotely related to fundamentalist movements in the Islamic world, symbolize their alienation from the wider democratic and secular processes in the country. The Indian people must wake up to the dangers of allowing their alienation to grow. It may be that Nehru's secular model, battered and bruised by India's troubled history after Independence, is still the answer to India's present communal impasse.

NOTES

1. Qasimi rejected the Jamaat-i Islami's slogan of *Hukumat-i Ilahiya* as 'a baseless optimism with which the sentimental sections of Muslims were fooled'.
2. The Jamaat claimed in 1959 to have 183 local units and a membership of 1,318 ('Introducing the Jamaat-e-Islami Hind', quoted in Brass 1974: 241). It owned two papers. *Dawat* (in Urdu) and *Radiance* (though not officially) in English.
3. Such views were echoed in *India after Independence* (Siddiqi 1952; Hasan 1988: 821).
4. This is an oft-quoted extract from Maududi's speech. Research on the Jamaat-i Islami is wanting in many respects, though one can still turn to the researches of Adams, Binder, and Kalim Bahadur for background information. Their writings, however, fail to make full use of the vast corpus of Jamaat literature and provide limited insight into the organizational structures.
5. While giving the Jamaat a clean chit, Wright ignored the fact that ideology and policy positions are as important as 'behaviour', the theme of his paper. In any case, a content analysis of *Dawat*, the Jamaat's organ, is hardly a satisfactory way of arriving at a meaningful conclusion (Wright 1979: 84-5).
6. The Jamaat had categorically stated on several occasions that, under the circumstances prevailing in India, it wanted a secular form of government to continue. Some writers have suggested that the Jamaat's aim of attaining *Hukumat-i Ilahiya* was dropped in 1962 in favour of the 'establishment of deen' (religion). It is not clear why this was done and which individuals or groups were responsible for this significant shift.
7. The Communist Party of India shared this view, especially in relation to the disturbances in western UP in 1961 (*Hindustan Times*, 10 Oct. 1961).
8. Acharya J.B. Kripalani, a senior Congress leader, warned that the Congress authorities will not tolerate the presence in the party's ranks of people who neither believed in socialism nor in secular democracy.
9. For Hindi-Urdu controversy, see Brass (1974: 119-276).
10. The empirical information contained in this section is drawn from national newspapers and periodicals, and not specifically attributed item by item.
11. In May 1979, the minister of state for Home Affairs reported in the Lok Sabha a threefold rise in deaths due to riots since 1977, with UP heading the

casualty list from 10 in 1977 to 65 in 1978 (*Times of India*, 4 May 1979).

12. Only four units were owned by Muslim industrialists, in a group of 2,832 industrial houses owned by large corporate units, each with a minimum annual turnover of Rs. 5,00,00,000.
13. Some would argue that riots tend to occur in medium-sized towns with a relatively large entrepreneurial class competing with and challenging the monopoly of the Hindu trading and business class. This has led them to conclude that communalism is essentially a by-product of competition between rival segments of the petite bourgeoisie in medium-sized towns (Engineer 1983; Alam 1983).
14. It is worth noting that since the riot, Mo radabad has experienced a slump in its traditional trade in brass. Exports dropped from Rs. 720 million in 1980 to Rs. 300 million in 1985 (Chowdhury 1986).
15. This quotation is taken from one of Nehru's letters to Mohanlal Saxena, dated 10 Sept. 1949.
16. Maulana Saiyid Asad Madani delivered the presidential address at the session convened by the Jamiyat al-ulama (Bombay: 14-16 Jan. 1983). See also Nadwi (1969) for a discussion of the Jamiyat's opposition to change and reform.
17. Saiyid Shahabuddin, fighting purely on the strength of his fundamentalist posture, won this constituency by an impressive margin of 73,000 votes.

REFERENCES

Adams, C.J., 1966: 'The Ideology of Maulana Maududi', in D.E. Smith (ed.), *South Asian Politics and Religion*, Princeton, N.J., pp. 371-97.

Alam, J., 1983: 'Dialectics of Capitalist Transformation and National Crystallisation: The Past and Present of National Question in India', *EPW*, 18 (29 Jan.): 5, pp. PE 29-46.

Awasthi, D., 1992: 'Ayodhya December 6, 1992: A Nation's Shame', *India Today* (Special Issue) (31 Dec.), pp. 15-27.

Baxter, C., 1968: *The Jana Sangh: A Biography of an Indian Political Party*, Philadelphia.

Blair, H.W., 1979: *Voting, Caste, Community, Society Explorations in Aggregate Data Analysis in India and Bangladesh*, Delhi.

Brass, P.R., 1974: *Language, Religion and Politics in North India*, Cambridge.

———, 1985: *Caste, Faction and Party in Indian Politics*, New Delhi.

Chowdhury, N., 1986: 'Growing Assertiveness', *Statesman* (19 Apr.).

Das, V. (ed.), 1990: *Mirrors of Violence: Communities, Riots and Survivors in South Asia*, New Delhi.

Das Gupta, S., 1993: 'Right Angles', *Sunday* (28 Feb.-8 Mar.): 8, p. 89.

Engineer, A.A., 1983: 'Socio-economic Basis of Communalism', *Mainstream* 21 (16 Jul.): 45, pp. 15-18.

———, (ed.), 1984: *Communal Riots in Post-independence India*, Hyderabad.

Faridi, S.N., 1965: *Economic Welfare of Indian Muslims*, Agra.
Faruqi, Z.H., 1966: 'Indian Muslims and the Ideology of the Secular State', in Smith (ed.), 1966, pp. 138-49.
Friedmann, Y., 1971: 'The Attitude of the Jamiyyat-i ulama-i Hind to the Indian National Movement and the Establishment of Pakistan', *Asian and African Studies* 7 (Jerusalem): I, pp. 157-80.
Gopal, S., 1975, 1979, 1984: *Jawaharlal Nehru: A Biography* (in 3 vols.), London.
———, 1989: *Jawaharlal Nehru: A Biography* (Abridged Edition), New Delhi.
Gould, H.A., 1966: 'Religion and Politics in a UP Constituency', in Smith (ed.), pp. 51-73.
———, 1990: *Politics and Caste, Volume 3: The Hindu Caste System*, New Delhi.
Hasan, M. (ed.), 1985: *Communal and Pan-Islamic Trends in Colonial India*, New Delhi.
———, 1987: *A Nationalist Conscience: M.A. Ansari, the Congress and the Raj*, New Delhi.
———, 1988: 'In Search of Identity and Integration: Indian Muslims since Independence', *Third World Quarterly*, 10 (Apr.): 2, pp. 818-42.
———, 1991: 'Changing Orientation of the State and the Emergence of Majoritarianism in the 1980s', in Panikkar (ed.), 1991, pp. 142-52.
———, (ed.), 1992: *Islam and Indian Nationalism: Reflections on Abul Kalam Azad*, New Delhi.
Husain, S.A., 1965: The *Destiny of Indian Muslims*, New Delhi.
Khan, R., 1978: 'Minority Segments in Indian Polity: Muslim Situation and Plight of Urdu', *EPW*, 13 (2 Sept.): 35, pp. 1509-15.
Kogekar, S.V. and R.L. Park (eds.), 1956: *Reports on the Indian General Elections 1951-1952*, Bombay.
Kothari, R., 1992: 'Pluralism and Secularism: Lessons of Ayodhya', *EPW*, 27 (19-26 Dec.): 51-2, pp. 2695-8.
Krishna, G., 1967: 'Electoral Participation and Political Integration', *EPW*, 2 (Feb.): 3-5, pp. 179-90.
Madan, T.N., 1987: 'Secularism in its Place', *Journal of Asian Studies* 46 (Nov.): 4, pp. 747-60.
———, 1990: 'Religion in India', *Daedalus* 118 (Fall): 4, pp. 115-46.
Mason, P. (ed.), 1967: *India and Ceylon: Unity and Diversity*, London.
Maududi, A.A. (n.d.): *The Political Theory of Islam*, Pathankot.
Nadwi, Maulana Abul Hasan Ali, 1969: *Western Civilisation: Islam and Muslims* (transl. from Urdu: M.A. Kidwai), Lucknow.
Nandy, A., 1990: 'The Political Culture of the Indian State', *Daedalus* 118 (Fall): 4, pp. 1-26.
———, 1990a: 'The Politics of Secularism and the Recovery of Religious Tolerance', in Das (ed.), 1990, pp. 69-93.
Panikkar, K.N. (ed.), 1991: *Communalism in India: History Politics and Culture*, New Delhi.

Parthasarathi, G. (ed.), 1987: *Jawaharlal Nehru: Letters to Chief Ministers: 1947-1964*, Vol. 3, New Delhi.

People's Union For Democratic Rights (PUDR), 1987: *Walled City Riots: A Report on the Police and Communal Violence in Delhi, 19-24 May 1987*, New Delhi.

Philips, C.H. and M.D. Wainwright (eds.), 1970: *The Partition of India Policies and Perspectives, 1935-1947*, London.

Qasimi, M.A.H. (n.d.): *The Community in Retrospect*, New Delhi.

Qureshi, I.H., 1970: 'A Case Study of the Social Relations Between the Muslims and the Hindus, 1935-1947', in Philips and Wainwright (eds.), 1970, pp. 360-8.

Robinson, F., 1985: 'Islam and Muslim Separatism', in Hasan (ed.), 1985, pp. 344-81.

Schermerhorn, R.A., 1978: *Ethnic Plurality in India*, Tucson.

Siddiqi, M.M., 1952: *After Secularism, What*?, Rampur, Maktaba-i Jamaat-i Islami Hind.

Smith, D.E., 1953: *India as a Secular State*, Princeton, N.J.

———, (ed.), 1966: *South Asian Politics and Religion*, Princeton, N.J.

Smith, W.C., 1957: *Islam in Modern History*, Princeton, N.J.

Spear, P., 1967: 'The Position of the Muslims, Before and After Partition', in Mason (ed.), pp. 30-50.

Tyabji, B., 1971: *The Self in Secularism*, New Delhi.

Weiner, M., 1984: *India at the Polls 1980: A Study of the Parliamentary Elections*, New Delhi.

Varshney, A., 2001: 'Ethnic Conflict and Civil Society: India and Beyond', *World Politics* 53 (Apr.): 3, pp. 362-89.

Wright (Jr.), T.P., 1964: 'Muslim Legislators in India: Profile of a Minority Elite', *Journal of Asian Studies*, 23 (Feb.): 2, pp. 253-67.

———, 1966: 'The Effectiveness of Muslim Representation in India', in Smith (ed.), 1966, pp. 102-37.

———, 1977: 'Muslims and the 1977 Indian Elections: A Watershed?', *Asian Survey*, 17 (Dec.): 12, pp. 1207-20.

———, 1979: 'Inadvertent Modernisation of Indian Muslims by Revivalists', *Journal of the Institute of Muslim Minority Affairs* (Jeddah) 1 (Summer): 1, pp. 80-92.

Zinkin, T., 1971: *Challenges in India*, New York.

PART V

17

India and Pakistan: Why the Difference?

> The irony of history is that the last battle of our war of independence in 1947 was not fought against the foreign rulers . . . but between the two major religious communities living in the subcontinent. . . . In the river of blood which flowed during the twilight days of the British Empire in India, not a drop of foreign masters' blood could be discerned [*sic*]; it was purely South Asian. The Britishers left with all their prestige and goodwill and their colonial legacy intact.
>
> RAO RASHID, *Snobs and Spices: The True Face of Pakistani Politics 1990-1996*

> An elemental force had burst its confines (on the stroke of midnight on August 14, 1947) and swept like a flood across the land. Would it also wash away the cobwebs, the inertia and deadness of centuries? Would it create overnight a brave new country in which everything would be perfect? Anything seemed possible. Next morning, the sun rose in the eastern sky to reveal the same squalor, the staggering poverty and hunger, the deep inequalities as the day before. Myriad of flowers, yellow and orange marigolds and pink rose petals, lay scattered on the ground, stale, scentless, trampled. The municipal sweepers came and swept away the street, and the blossoms mingled in the dust.
>
> KUSUM NAIR, *Blossoms in the Dust*

Three years ago the Human Development Centre in Islamabad described South Asia as the 'poorest, the most illiterate, the most malnourished, the least gender-sensitive—indeed, the most deprived region in the world'.[1] India and Pakistan account for the bulk of South Asia's population. Arguably, these two countries, in varying degrees, fit into the paradigm of soft states proportionate to their respective level of institutional slump, governance crises, and domestic conflicts. Generally speaking, nation states in recent decades have been weaker than ever before. Indeed, the old concept of omnipotent sovereignty is dwindling, and indeed, the ecology of statehood itself has been shifting—sovereignty is no longer The Holy Grail, and state power is migrating to a variety of non-state institutions.[2]

Let me begin with the judgement that Pakistan—with years of half baked or controlled democracy, followed by full-fledged military dictatorships—is less than a nation state on account of its failure to resolve issues of integration and identity.[3] Is this the Pakistan envisaged by Muhammad Ali Jinnah or dreamt of by a people who proclaimed their faith in a partition of their patrimony, asks the columnist Mazhar Ali Khan. 'How can we return to the ideals that inspired the fight for freedom and revive the principles and purposes that the Quaid bequeathed to us?'[4] The task is an awesome one: 'too much time has been lost, and too many resources squandered in the attempt to fashion a nation-state from the social milieu that makes up the country'.[5]

Some had expected that General Zia-ul-Haq, 'one of the three Bonapartes who cast their malign shadows across the national horizon after 1947', to be the last dictator.[6] But General Parvez Musharraf has dashed this hope to the ground.[7] A democratically elected prime minister, whose descent from power proved to be as precipitous and quick as his ascent had been two years earlier, languished in jail, before being exiled to Saudi Arabia. The parliament, where he enjoyed a two-thirds majority, is closed; the Constitution put in cold storage. The fragile nature of democracy is evident from the opposition parties and their followers welcoming the coup in the first flush of excitement. This is how it has always been since October 1958, when Ayub Khan took over as martial law administrator.

Ayesha Jalal, having questioned some of the certitudes about post-Independence states and societies in South Asia, reminds us that Pakistanis have the 'state' if not quite the 'nation' of their collective imaginings. She draws attention to the hollowness of civil society, the weakness of the institutions of the state, and the ideological contradictions in the self-projections and self-perceptions of the Pakistani state. Created on the strength of Muslim solidarity, Pakistan almost immediately gave birth to its own minorities, the Bengalis in East Pakistan (now Bangladesh), the *muhajirs* in Sind, the Baluchis and Pathans in the North West Frontier Province. Each of these collectivities defines its linguistic regions as its homeland. Regional and linguistic diversities have provided through much of Pakistan's turbulent history, the highest common denominator of the multifaceted grievances of the people, denied as most of them have been of democratic rights and of basic rights of citizenship. Declaring the Ahmadiyyas as a 'minority' in the 1970s created a precedent for exclusion, exposing the state's claim of inclusionary nationalism.

Exclusive nationalism, argues Ayesha Jalal, is no substitute for nationalism based on equal citizenship rights, the nation state's main claim to legitimacy. Pointing to the inherited colonial structures that were not realigned with the dominant conceptions that had fired the Muslim struggle for equality, solidarity and freedom, she underlines how, for example, Muhammad Iqbal's lofty equation of Islam and civil society has been lost sight of in the litany of confusion surrounding conceptions of national identity and state sovereignty. Incidentally, in the 1960s, the scholar Fazlur Rahman expressed the view that Iqbal's philosophical legacy had not been followed, partly because of what he had said but largely because he was both misunderstood and misused by his politics-mongering followers.[8]

What has contributed to Pakistan's woes is the absence of a social coalition of the three main segments—the underprivileged, the middle class and the élite. For this, the power élites—professional groups, merchant capitalists and the big landowners drawn mostly from Punjab and Sind—must share the blame. Though repeating *ad nauseam* the rhetoric of Muslim nationalism, they abandoned the Pakistani ship adrift in turbulent waters. They squandered the opportunity to reshape the country, to break the stranglehold of the civil-military oligarchy, and to create a multi-party system that would aggregate and synthesize the interests of many disparate groups. Zulfiqar Ali Bhutto, riding on the crest of an unprecedented popular wave, promised much in his 1970 election manifesto but delivered little. 'The Himalayas will weep, if I am harmed', a beleaguered Bhutto told his prosecutor in jail. But the mountains did not cry when Zia-ul-Haq, who ruled from 1977 to 1988, signed his death warrant.

Benazir Bhutto's legacy was a country torn apart by intense regional rivalries, sectarian animus, and ethnic strife in Karachi. Her successor, Nawaz Sharif, won a landslide victory in February 1997 and declared his intention to keep faith with the people.[9] But he turned out to be a reckless country politician with no sensitivity to the elementary principles of governance. Instead of breaking loose from the military-bureaucracy nexus, the chief cause of the previous crises, he subverted established political institutions. As was the case during the dark days of the Emergency in India (1975-7), the Big Brother arrived with his rabble-rousers, judges and executioners, ready to strike down any one who deviated from the legislated code of conduct. Instead of concentrating on economic discontent and a recession unprecedented in Pakistan's history, he chose to go nuclear. Washington responded angrily; Nawaz Sharif lost face with his people. Instead of diffusing widespread social unrest, he used the rhetoric of Islamization to buy peace. If he had read his country's history, he would have discovered the merit in what Iskander Mirza had said, 'We can't run wild on Islam; it is Pakistan first and last.'[10] He should have sensed, moreover, that Islam offers 'agency' to its adherents in the sense that the sociologist Anthony Giddens uses the terms—an individual's or groups capability to intervene, or to refrain from intervening, in a series of events so as to influence their course. But religio-political fundamentalism is different: so often in Pakistan, as indeed in the annals of public life elsewhere, it has devoured its own protagonists.

There are numerous prescriptions, starting with the long forgotten recommendations of the Munir commission (1953) to the bold journalistic and scholarly assertions in recent years.[11] Some scholars call for sustained debates on citizenship rights towards forging a collective ethos as a nation state, and a national dialogue to create the necessary consensus to begin rebuilding anew. Who is to initiate this dialogue is by no means clear. Besides, with the General having ruled out an early return to democracy (a referendum is being held at the time of finalizing this draft for publication) and the former prime minister in exile, it may not be easy to achieve such goals. The writer Feroz Ahmad pleads for rejecting 'legalistic shibboleths' and 'unsubstantiated hypotheses' in order to 'get down to the nitty gritty of how to materially transform this country into a voluntary association of equal, prosperous and happy peoples'.[12] While this concern is widely felt, the main issue is whether or not the current wave of ethnic and religious movements will be partially outgrown, partially domesticated, and partially mediated by the political process in the near future. 'Much may be lost,' comments a concerned Pakistani citizen, 'but the situation is not irretrievable.'[13]

Some of these concerns, if not all, are relevant to India as well. The rise of Hindu nationalism poses a major threat to pluralism and multiculturalism. Violence against religious minorities,[14] intolerance towards dissenters,[15] saffronization of education, exemplified in rewriting of history textbooks[16] and the appointment of the BJP-RSS ideologues to prestigious centres of learning,[17] and the review of the Constitution constitute a frightening trend. Reviewing certain aspects of the Constitution may not, after all, be such a bad thing, yet attempts to tinker with state structures, according to the noted columnist Harish Khare,

> . . . would be tantamount to an assault from above on the legitimacy of the Indian

state. Simply put, the Vajpayee regime does not have the credentials to review the Constitution because it lacks the legitimacy that accrues to a leadership either on account of participation in a nationalist struggle, or from an overwhelming popular acceptance, or from demonstrated outstanding performance and competence. After all, the efficacious exercise of any constitutional authority is to be negotiated through the democratic idiom. Only through a vigorous democratic engagement can we temper our constitutional arrangement against political expediencies. The clamour for a Constitution review is a subterfuge from non-democratic temptations; but this authoritarian project will also fail because it is intended to bypass the egalitarian assertiveness from below.[18]

Already, the new RSS chief K.S. Sudarshan has launched a diatribe against conversions and the 'Anglicization' of Indian society.[19] He favours a new code of conduct (*dharma*) based on Hindu philosophy and a 'Hindu way of development'. In an interview to the RSS mouthpiece *Organiser*, he described Bharat as a *Hindu rashtra*, based on *dharma*. Its identity, according to him, lies in one motherland, one *sanskriti* (culture), common ancestry and heritage. 'It is these three that constitute the national culture.' Pointing to 1989 as a milestone, he said that the situation had undergone a 'total metamorphosis'. While the Berlin wall was being dismantled brick by brick, Bharat was witnessing the *shilanyas* at Ramjanmabhumi, 'which in a sense was a symbol of the nation as an edifice'. The incident, stated Sudarshan, instilled a new-found self-confidence in Hindus, though some anti-*Hindutva* elements had ganged up in total disregard of 'this sublimation of society'. But, prophesied the RSS chief, 'it is going to be the last gasp of those haunted by the spectre of defeat. . . . There is yet another epic war between Hindus and anti-Hindus, a veritable *Mahabharat* in which sometimes Abhimanyu will fall, sometimes Ghatotkacha or it may be Jayadratha's turn yet another day.'[20]

II

> Churchill [Winston] said that India wasn't a nation, just an 'abstraction'. John Kenneth Galbraith, more affectionately and more memorably, described it as 'functioning anarchy'. Both of them, in my view, underestimated the strength of the India-idea. It may be the most innovative national philosophy to have emerged in the postcolonial period. It deserves to be celebrated—because it is an idea that has enemies, within India as well as outside her frontiers, and to celebrate it is also to defend it against its foes.
>
> SALMAN RUSHDIE, *Time*, 11 August 1997

Watching the Republic Day parade in 1955, India's first prime minister had a sense of fulfilment 'in the air and of confidence in our future destiny'. Two years later, Nehru told the chief ministers: 'If we look about to various countries which have recently attained freedom . . . India compares favourably with them, both in regard to our stability and the progress we have made in these last 10 years. The record is a creditable one, and this is increasingly recognized by other countries of the world.' Recent commentators echo the same optimism. According to an editorial comment,

> At fifty, the crisis of the sovereign Republic of India cannot be purely biological. No mid-life crisis this, for fifty years in the life of a nation is an occasion to worry about the cellular stability of nationhood. And India this morning shows no signs of 'the state withering away'. Rather, the Republic is seemingly confident, not irredeemably subordinated to tradition, and it is not looking back with nostalgia. The popular will still continues to drive national destiny. No singular man's paranoia or fantasy has succeeded in repudiating that will. Democracy, with all its chaos and anarchy, has not only survived. It has thrived beyond the limits of an average Indian's expectation.[21]

Likewise, *The Hindustan Times* observed on Republic Day:

> The first Republic Day of the Year 2000 sees India emerging in a far more confident frame of mind than in the recent past. Once again the country has recovered the mood of marching ahead with great elan as it did in the period immediately after Independence. The difference is that, this time, it is based less on hope and surmise than on a realistic assessment of what is possible. . . . India is poised to take a great leap forward as its economy is unshackled and the burden of a false ideology is abandoned. In the process, the country is also bound to emerge as a centre of stability—and modernity—in an area where military, communist, one-party and medieval fundamentalist regimes thrive, fostering indiscriminate terror, and vicious civil wars that drag on indefinitely. In contrast to its neighbours, India's normality stands out like a beacon.

If this were the whole story it would be hard to explain the mounting unrest in Kashmir and the north-east, the growing socio-economic inequities, the escalation of social tensions, and the violence against Dalits, minorities and women. More than 50 years after Independence, more than 40 per cent of the rural households are either landless or own less than 0.2 hectare of land. Less than 1 (0.8) per cent of the households own 14 per cent of the land.[22] There has been an increase in the number of people below the poverty line—from 305.87 million in 1987-8 to 314.66 million in 1993-4—an increase by an average of 1.76 million a year.[23] Poverty alleviation programmes are underfunded and insufficiently implemented; thus public food distribution has poor rural coverage. Funding for primary education, an aspect Amartya Sen has ever so often repeated,[24] declined from 56 per cent of all education expenditures in the First Five Year Plan (1951-6) to 29 per cent in the Seventh Five Year Plan (1985-90).[25] In short, traditional faultlines of social deprivation—based on class, caste and gender—continue to characterize patterns of social deprivation. A Constitution may indicate the direction in which we are to move, but the social structure will decide how far we are able to move and at what pace.[26]

No wonder, on the eve of the Golden Jubilee of the Republic, president K.R. Narayanan called for an 'honest self-analysis and self-questioning about where we, as a people and a society, are headed?' Drawing attention to the sullen resentment among the masses against their condition, often erupting in violence, he cautioned that these voices of resentment should not go unheard.

> Violence in society has bared a hundred fangs as advertisement-driven consumerism is unleashing frustrations and tensions in our society. The unabashed, vulgar indulgence in conspicuous consumption by the nouveau riche has left the underclass seething in frustration. One half of our society guzzles aerated beverages while the other half has to make do with palmfuls of muddied water. Our three-way fast lane of liberalization, privatization and globalization must provide safe pedestrian crossings for the unempowered India also.

The president talked of the raw deal given to women—'our greatest national shame'—and the indifference towards Dalits. There were signs, he added, that the privileged classes were getting tired of the affirmative action provided by the Constitution.[27] On the eve of Independence Day on 14 August 2000, the president spoke yet again of the 'dark clouds of prejudice and callous unconcern' over the problem of rape and atrocities against women and suggested rewriting of laws to deter such crimes.

Few will deny the enormous gains of the last 50 years,[28] a point underscored by the president. Political power has moved downward. A democratic empowerment of the lower castes, the chief catalyst for what has been described as the second democratic upsurge, has made India's democracy more inclusive and participatory. Writing a decade ago, Paul Brass concluded that, despite the evident decay over time, the performance of India's political institutions compares favourably in many respects with those of its neighbours or with most other post-colonial societies. Indeed, the Indian political regime is one of the most democratic in the world by most conventional measures of political participation, electoral and party competition, and persistence of parliamentary institutions.[29]

These developments need to be located in the context of, though not always as a sequel to, the larger political processes at work. After all, scholars and generalists alike have commented on the decline of the Congress[30] and its decimation in UP, the most populous state,[31] the crisis of governability,[32] the unreconstructed bureaucracy,[33] the political decay,[34] and the many institutions associated with liberal democracy looking messy, worn out and frayed at the edges.[35] The failure to assure substantive democracy and equitable development for significant segments of civil society has resulted in the discrediting and delegitimization of state-sponsored nationalism.[36] Analysts have pointed out the changes taking place in the familiar world of modern politics after Nehru's death and the passing away of the leadership of the national movement.[37] Sometimes they bemoan the absence of strong political and social actors; on other occasions, they invoke the names of Gandhi, Jawaharlal Nehru, Vallabhbhai Patel, B.R. Ambedkar, Jinnah and Sheikh Mujibur Rahman to contrast their spirited role with the decline in public standards and the poor quality of leadership. 'Where are the heirs to the great political tradition bequeathed by them' (Jinnah, Maulana Azad, Abdul Ghaffar Khan and Mian Iftikhar-ud-Din), asks a leading Pakistani columnist. Lamenting that 'the mantle of leadership lies neglected, tattered and torn, frequently defiled by unworthy hands', he asks, 'who will pick up the banner, cleanse it to its pristine purity, and then raise it aloft so that the people can recognise it as the symbol of their redemption and follow it to bring the country to its salvation?'[38]

Analysts question the efficacy and the appropriateness of focusing on high politics, and yet they cannot deny that the electorate in South Asia continues to repose confidence in its leaders, many of whom have inherited the political and intellectual legacy of the anti-colonial struggles.[39] True, leaders have mostly failed to deliver; yet their followers pin their hopes on their ability to deliver.[40] This is not surprising. Compared to the Pakistani élite, the Indian élite, largely connected with the Congress movement, represented a much wider range of interests, and its social composition and political aims were far more heterogeneous than what the British or some historians dominated by the official mind have argued.[41] Undeniably, members of this élite jockeyed for positions in the colonial structures, captured important positions in the post-colonial state, jealously safeguarded their political interests, and made the most of the economic opportunities that came their way. At the same time, they developed over a period of time an agenda setting out national goals and aspirations and guided some of the more important social and political movements. Thus, the limited repertoire of the early Congress was enlarged in the aftermath of the Swadeshi agitation. With the Mahatma energizing the rural poor in places like Champaran and Kheda, the party gradually developed an organizational structure starting with village and taluqa units at the bottom and then, in ascending order, district, provincial and all-India committees, each elected by the lower units. The Rowlatt satyagraha (1919) and the khilafat and non-cooperation movements (1919-22) deepened Congress' support in urban and rural areas, and led to a partial radicalization of its politics. It was at Nagpur (December 1920), wrote the kisan leader Swami Sahajanand, 'that the Congress forsook the time-honoured procedure of begging for something . . . and instead took to the path of self-respect'.[42] Starting with its feeble demand for dominion status, the party began to clamour, as in 1921 and 1929, for complete independence (*purna swaraj*). 'When the resolution on full and complete Independence was passed,' noted Sahajanand, 'it seemed as though a new world had come into being.'[43] 'No one can describe the great enthusiasm which pervaded the Congress,' Sahajanand was to write, 'wave after wave of enthusiasm was visible.' As he listened to the Mahatma with rapt attention, he noticed that 'every word that came out of his mouth was like a thunderbolt against the government. It seemed that Shiva, the God of Destruction, was raging and that soon the great deluge would follow.'[44] 'Quit India', Gandhi's final cry in August 1942, laid to rest the lingering doubts over the timing of the British withdrawal from Delhi's viceregal lodge.

The estrangement of many Muslims and the disillusionment of the underclasses marred the ascendancy of the Congress. But the energy generated by some of its leaders had its glorious moments as well. In 1920, for instance, when Gandhi's personal charisma, rhetoric and mobilization strategies heightened countrywide excitement. Again, when the same frail man, aged 60 years, accompanied by his 78 followers, walked 241 miles from his Sabarmati Ashram to the shores of Dandi. This was nationalism, pure and simple, on the move. Rabindranath Tagore commented that the influence emanating from Gandhi's personality was ineffable, like music, like beauty. Its claim upon others was great because of its revelations of a spontaneous self-giving. Not only did the Mahatma awaken the villages to a sense of their power, but also his novel conception of motion, exemplified in the Dandi March, shot across the changeless horizon.[45] One of his British followers remarked that this march was 'the beginning of a revolution'.[46] It was not. Yet, the Dandi March set Indian nationalism on a new course. Nehru noticed the extraordinary enthusiasm of the people during a frenetic 130 days tour in 1937. As he moved about, 'often in remote parts of the country, addressing enormous audiences everywhere . . . and probably covered over fifty thousand miles by railway train, motor car and aeroplane', he found himself addressing as many as a dozen meetings and upwards of 1,00,000 people a day, and at the end reckoned he had addressed something like 10 million people all told.[47] No wonder, the Congress won overall majorities in the provincial elections in 5 of the 11 provinces of India (Madras, Bihar, Orissa, CP, and UP): it had after all, claimed the general secretary, Acharya Kripalani, the biggest individual membership that any organization had, the world over.[48] An elated Nehru told Strafford Cripps:

> As a whole India is wide awake and expectant. . . . My extensive touring has been a revelation to me of the suppressed energy of the people and of their passionate desire to be rid of their burdens. The Congress is supreme today so far as the masses and the lower middle classes are concerned. . . . It has hardly ever been in such a strong position.[49]

From 1937 to 1939 their supporters and detractors subjected the Congress ministries to critical scrutiny. They were justified in doing so; in fact, satyagraha campaigns were mounted in some districts of Bihar against the ministry, resulting in the arrest of a number of kisan sabha volunteers. Yet, it is undeniable that the ministries, having performed poorly in some areas, brought about some major shifts in the political, social and economic spheres. Doubtless, they diluted or tailored policies and programmes, as in the case of the 1939 UP Tenancy Act, to meet political exigencies.[50] But this was not unexpected in the case of a party that had no pretension of heralding a socialistic era. The critical issue is that the leadership, though riven with dissension and lacking in internal cohesion on policy matters, endeavoured to build a consensual base for itself, a fact that has been crucial for its own survival. Social engineering was a daunting prospect, but at least some political actors, both at the national, regional and local levels, willy-nilly brought together a cross-section of intellectuals and activists, all of whom contributed in varying degrees to the formulation of its agenda. Men like Baba Ramchandra and Swami Sahajanand had worked, however uneasily, with the Congress before the parting of ways took place. Walter Hauser's thesis hints—in his discussion of the charisma of the Swami—at the ideological link between nationalist leaders and peasants.[51] The young socialists, fiery and idealistic, drafted the Fundamental Rights Resolution as well as the Congress party's 1936 agrarian programme. They, too, drifted apart in due course. The efforts of the Communist Party resulted, at least in some periods, in the wider participation of the trade unions, peasant and other organizations. This arrangement was also short-lived.

Navigating between the demands of political incumbency and the dictates of economic development, the post-colonial Congress governments tried implementing, though not without considerable conflicts of principle and tussle of interests, the unfinished agenda of the ministries. The Constituent Assembly, with an abundant faith in the common man and the ultimate success of democratic rule, sought to breakdown the provincialism of local loyalties through the provision for direct election by adult suffrage.[52] To many, these urges and the initial moves towards their fulfilment captured the spirit and essence of nationalism.[53] Arguing for the moral value and legitimacy of nationalism in a form compatible with liberal democratic principles and institutions, Nehru underlined in 1951 that India had infinite variety and there was absolutely no reason why anybody should regiment it after a single pattern. In this context, a written constitution turned out to be

> the first-ever attempt in the last 2,000 years of our collective civilizational existence to put in place a quintessentially egalitarian polity and a pluralistic social order. It is this promise of egalitarianism that garnered for the Indian state a modicum of democratic legitimacy and popular acceptance, despite all the aberrations and anti-poor biases in the ruling and governing classes.[54]

True, the notion that loyalty to the people came before loyalty to the party or government—in the nineteenth century European sense where nationalism was associated with the idea of popular sovereignty—did not find favour in India. Yet, the urge to clear the debris of the raj and to fashion a dynamic nation state was central to the post-colonial project. Democracy bestowed an aura of legitimacy on modern political life: laws, rules and policies appeared justified when they were democratic. Leaders differed in intellectual outlook and leadership style; yet, they shared a single vision of the system of rule that was to guide the new nation. It was a parliamentary system, and its leaders answerable to the people through elections.[55] That is why, in what can be called a gentle rap on the knuckles for the ruling BJP-led government which has been clamouring for reviewing the Constitution, president Narayanan saluted the 'far-sighted vision and arduous labours' of the Constitution's founding fathers. Reminding the nation that 'Republic' meant 'supreme power is exercised not by some remote monarch, but by the people', Narayanan wanted the nation to use the occasion of the Golden Jubilee to hail that proclamation and commitment. He subtly rebuffed all those who wanted to free the 'Executive' from the rigours of accountability.

A qualitative agrarian transformation took place during the Nehruvian era. Morris-Jones commented, in the early 1970s, on the vast social and economic changes being accomplished and being accommodated and digested by and within a political structure which was successfully flexible, and 'politically multi-lingual'.[56] Though ravaged by the effects of Partition, Punjab made rapid strides in the consolidation of landholdings. This contributed to the progress in agricultural productivity.[57] In 1948, the government of Madras moved to under-cut communist support among the Andhra peasants by passing the Madras Estate Abolition and Conversion into Ryotwari Act. The legislation abolished all *zamindari* and *inamdari* estates and gave the *ryot* the *pattas* of their lands over 30 per cent of the areas in the Andhra district.[58] The communist government in Kerala adopted the Agrarian Relations Bill on 10 June 1959, only a few days before the Centre imposed presidential rule.[59] Nehru was able to push through legislation abolishing *zamindari* in UP and Bihar, though the Zamindari Abolition Act did little to alleviate the suffering of the former tenants; equally, the goals set in the First Five Year Plan for pursuing land reforms were not accomplished.[60] In Punjab, legislation was enacted but too late to prevent landlords from taking the necessary precautionary measures.[61] In Bihar, a land of villages with nearly 85 per cent of its population living in about 67,000 villages, the feudal classes jettisoned land reforms.

On balance, the economic and political power of the *zamindars* was curtailed in some states where the very structure of power in the countryside was redesigned by reforms of land tenure and credit.[62] Besides, the state took up on itself the responsibility for transforming the economy,[63] and sought to deliver new services, education, public health, sophisticated agricultural technology and cooperative marketing to half a million villages. The initiatives, though sometimes ill conceived and poorly coordinated, produced results in some areas, but not everywhere. Despite two Five Year Plans, the economy of UP, with its 74 million people in 1961, was characterized by agricultural stagnation and industrial decline.[64] According to the Planning Commission estimates for 1960-1—after the first decade of planning—50 to 60 per cent of the rural population, or approximately 211 million people, could not afford minimum levels of consumption, calculated primarily in terms of calorie intake necessary to avoid the onset of malnutrition.[65] Here and elsewhere, the basic malaise was that the colonial apparatus of governmental administration was not even tinkered with. Likewise, the basic structure of civil and criminal law remained largely unchanged.[66] Clearly, there were many contested visions of nationhood and alternative frameworks for its realization. This meant two things: the absence of structural transformation and the lack of a composite long-term vision. Yet, the overarching authority of the state and the goods and services it was able to provide consolidated unity and the democratic tradition. A weaker or a more disengaged state may not have been able to motivate the people to have faith in the country or to participate in its political dynamic.[67] This requires elaboration.

Unlike Pakistan, the Indian national movement bequeathed a leadership that was somewhat better equipped to cope with the changes ushered in by the upheaval caused by Partition. In this respect, Nehru's leadership made a significant difference. Like Lord Krishna who lured the *gopis* (milkmaids) with his flute, the charismatic Nehru lured India's masses with the magic of his name.[68] Despite his failures and weaknesses, he managed to lead a truncated nation through an extremely difficult phase of nation-building. He failed to put into practice many of his own ideas and proved weak and indecisive in dealing with his ideological adversaries, but he set modern goals for his otherwise ideologically divided party and government. Though all that glittered in the refurbished parliament was not gold, Nehru did not allow regional, linguistic and religious/communal cleavages to get out of hand. While Pakistan moved dangerously close to becoming an Islamic theocracy, Nehru relentlessly pursued, despite the opposition of some comrades, the secular projects. 'For all of us in India', he told the chief ministers in May 1950, 'the issue of communal unity and a secular state must be made perfectly clear. We have played about with this idea sufficiently long and moved away from it far enough. We must go back and go back not secretly or apologetically, but openly and rather aggressively.'

Similarly, while Pakistan's political leadership in the early years searched for secular and unifying symbols, Nehru painstakingly referred to the Mahatma's message of inter-community peace and his courage in extinguishing the flames of religious hatred. In so doing, he tried to settle the issue whether the government and the party were going to adhere to old Congress principles in regard to communalism or whether the country as a whole was going to drift away from them. He did not waver in his belief that religious and caste strife must be fought tooth and nail no matter what the cost or how daunting the opposition; in fact so frequently did he inveigh against communalism, linguism, casteism and the like that the composers of newspaper headlines were hard-pressed to make the theme arresting.[69] In the words of Sarvepalli Gopal: 'To a whole generation of Indians he was not so much a leader as a companion who expressed and made clearer a particular view of the present and vision of the future. The combination of intellectual and moral authority was unique in his time.'[70] The historian Walter Hauser 'followed him more than once in 1957 as he swept out of Anand Bhawan (in Allahabad) in his black, convertible Buick, moving swiftly to one of the neighbouring villages to engage the peasants about the meanings of the new India. It was always a magnetic moment to be sure, and that Nehru did it on some regular basis in the eight or nine months I was in Allahabad was in itself impressive, but the encounter always had for the peasants certainly, something of a *darshan* quality. *Which in itself told us much about the nature of the relationship, and about the quality of the freedom movement itself at this level of engagement*'[71] (italics mine).

Some fumed and fretted against Nehru's exertion to change the fabric of Hindu society, his lenient policy towards Pakistan, and his undue tenderness for the Muslims, but most recognized that the country's first prime minister enjoyed countrywide support and legitimacy. This was especially true after Vallabhbhai Patel's death in 1950. To Patel goes the remarkable feat of integrating the princely states into the Union. It is to Nehru's credit that the language issue was amicably resolved, whereas it led to riots in East Pakistan in protest against the central government's attempts to impose Urdu as the only official language.[72] The reorganization of states in 1956 along linguistic lines was a masterstroke: if the first prime minister had been a linguistic naivete rather than a linguistic sophisticate like Nehru, then we would have had today not a unified India with a strong government at the Centre but an India weakly divided along linguistic and cultural lines into two or three semi-autonomous regions. The unity of India would be as a faded dream. In creating linguistic states, Nehru provided a vernacular political milieu that was conducive to the flowering of many linguistically rooted cultures and thereby evolved a system, which greatly enriched the cultural life of the nation as a whole.[73]

III

> We are only a four-month-old child. You know somebody would like to overthrow us. I know you would say we have not done such and such thing, but we are only four-month-old.
>
> JINNAH on 14 December 1947

In so many different ways, the first decade of Nehru's government stands in contrast to developments in neighbouring Pakistan. In 1947 India went on to consolidate itself as a democracy; the enthusiastic members of the Constituent Assembly burnt the midnight oil over a period of two years and adopted a constitution on 26 November 1949, which came into force on 26 January 1950. On the other hand, Pakistan's Constituent Assembly took nine years to agree to a constitution. No national elections were held under the 1956 Constitution, however. Two years later, Pakistan fell prey to military rule. The *coup d'etat* was followed by the dissolution of the National Assembly. Parliamentary elections, scheduled for early 1959, were cancelled.[74]

Jinnah died on 11 September 1948. The Muslim League, having led the demand for and achieved a Muslim homeland, declined thereafter. The ideological cement that held it together dissolved once Pakistan was achieved. If the League had institutionalized itself or provided the leadership essential for underwriting stability or democracy, it could well have devised a programme or a mechanism to adjust the conflict of interests that existed between different social and economic classes.[75] But that was not to be. In 1954, the party was routed in provincial elections in East Pakistan. This is where 54 per cent of Pakistan's population lived. The Muslim League was likened to

> a virtuous lady who has fallen into bad times and is forced by circumstances to become a courtesan. As such, she is now ever ready to serve as a concubine of any adventurer who is in a position to pay her the right price. . . . After the death of Quaid one adventurer followed another to claim her hand. Muslim League lost her innocence and became a handmaiden of every charlatan who came to seize the reins of power in Pakistan.[76]

A Hindu fanatic assassinated the Mahatma on 30 January 1948. But the Congress survived not only as a powerful organization but also its pragmatic leadership created a democratic and secular polity, and accommodated, through a policy of conciliation and compromise, diverse social and political forces in its own ranks.[77] The Congress in Bihar, for example, enjoyed a virtual monopoly over two important 'vote banks', that of the scheduled castes and the Muslims. Moreover, the party coopted aspiring politicians from the Yadav and Kurmi caste groups and prevailed upon the leaders of the Bhumihars and the Rajputs to subordinate personal ambitions to party unity.[78] In the south, a relatively peaceful lower caste revolution, pioneered by the Daravida Munnetra Kazhagam (DMK), was well underway.[79]

Elected governments in Pakistan, by contrast, held power at the discretion of what Hamza Alavi has described as the all-powerful military-bureaucratic oligarchy.[80] The problem was further compounded: in an area where religious passions had been heightened to create a Muslim nation, Jinnah's belated plea for a secular society did not strike a favourable chord. Whereas the Hindu Mahasabha and the RSS were discredited and isolated, more so after Gandhi's assassination, the Jamaat-i Islami, a party wedded to Islamic theocracy, was out in the open ready to seize power in order to enforce the *Shariat*. Its leader maulana Abul Ala Maududi began flexing his muscles and made his intentions known during the anti-Ahmaddiya riots that the Jamaat-i Islami instigated. It was the first major blow to the Quaid's dream of a united Pakistan. Meanwhile, in India, the first Backward Classes Commission was appointed on 29 January 1953 under the chairmanship of a former disciple of Gandhi, Kaka Kalelkar. Although Nehru's government rejected its recommendations, the issue of backward caste empowerment soon became the nation's preoccupation.[81]

Why have the experiences of India and Pakistan been so different since their Independence? Various explanations already exist. Ayesha Jalal's emphasis on the structural and ideational features of colonialism in the post-colonial era is valid. But her attempt to obfuscate the dichotomy between democracy in India and military governments in Pakistan and Bangladesh does not carry conviction. Similarly, her attempt to discover the common strand of authoritarianism in the political experiences of India and Pakistan reveals her insensitivity to the important achievements of Indian democracy.[82]

The subaltern historians argue that Indian democracy was not the outcome of a national-popular revolution but a passive one carried out by the Gandhian-led Congress that enabled the bourgeoisie to institute its hegemony over the subaltern groups, but without a formal confrontation with them. Most other writers ascribe Indian democracy to a developed political culture, viable institutions, dedicated élites, unique organizational skills on the part of the Indians, a tradition of compromise and accommodation, the success of the Congress in having institutionalized itself in state and society, and the British role in bequeathing tutelary democracy to India. Conversely, the breakdown of democracy in Pakistan is attributed to a backward political culture, unseasoned or corrupt leaders, ethnic and group frictions, weak institutions debilitated further by stresses arising from the exigencies of nation building in a new state, the incompatibility of Islam and democracy,[83] and the contradictions between the Islamic notions of community and the recently instituted idea of electoral politics.[84]

What these theories fail to sufficiently underline are the differences in the social bases, ideological orientations, and the contrasting styles of leadership in India and Pakistan. Although the structures and social composition of formal political parties mattered substantially, more so in post-colonial societies, the striking contrast between India and Pakistan, as also between military rulers in West Pakistan and the Awami League leaders in East Pakistan (later Bangladesh), was not just the charisma, popular appeal and moral authority of some Congress leaders, notably Nehru and Patel, but their legitimacy across regions, castes and classes. Indeed, they inscribed their preferences in the routinized practices of quotidian politics. That is why, even in so divided and fragmented a society, people sought a resolution of their dilemmas and predicaments in their leader's policies and pronouncements. Unlike Pakistan, where regional parties were weak, the Lucknow, Calcutta or Patna-based actors kept intact their caste, class and community linkages and patronage networks. This gave them considerable leverage in local, regional and, in some cases, national politics. Consequently, Sri Krishna Sinha, who first served as chief minister between 1937 and 1939, ruled as chief minister of Bihar from the formation of the Congress ministry in 1946 until his death in 1961. Such leaders also enjoyed greater latitude in choosing from a menu of institutional options. After Nehru's death in 1964, the influence of the chief ministers increased, though the pattern was already well established during the Nehru era. Some of it was exercised through the National Development Council (formed in 1956), under which all the chief ministers met members of the Planning Commission several times a year to discuss development problems for the country as a whole.[85]

The person who probably made the greatest difference of all was Mohandas Karamchand Gandhi, who, in the words of Nehru, 'was like a powerful current of fresh air that made us stretch ourselves and take deep breaths, like a beam of light that pierced the darkness and removed the scales from our eyes'. To people like Nehru, he did not descend from the top but seemed to emerge from the millions of India. Although assassinated just when the country had tasted the fruits of freedom, his legacy lived on in the hearts and the minds of the people (if not the government), whom he had served with such singular devotion. Many aspects of the Constitution itself bore the imprint of his personality.

There is no denying that Gandhi possessed a sharp and intuitive mind and had the ability to marshal his resources towards ends clearly discerned and goals clearly defined. He was an innovator and synthesizer of diverse political and philosophical traditions. He was therefore able to develop a political theory grounded in the unique experiences and articulated in terms of the indigenous philosophical vocabulary. Sustaining collective action in interaction with powerful opponents marks his movements off from the earliest forms of protest or contention in the late nineteenth and early twentieth centuries. On balance, his engagements developed out of his concern to articulate the interests of different castes, communities and regions. He was a devout Hindu but not a *Hindu* leader, a distinction not recognized by the estranged Muslim leadership in the 1940s. He turned to popular religious traditions, including some Hinduized symbols, to unite and not to divide the fairly broad-based constituency that he had created during the khilafat movement. No wonder, the pan-Islamic leader Mohamed Ali stated in the early 1920s: 'It is Gandhi, Gandhi, Gandhi that has got to be dinned into the peoples ears, because he means Hindu-Muslim unity, non-cooperation, *dharma* and *Swaraj*.' Mohamed Ali became Gandhi's most relentless critic in the late 1920s, but the Mahatma maintained, 'I have nothing but kindly feelings about him.' He continued: 'and I feel that time will remove misunderstandings. Having no feeling either against Islam or Mussulmans, I feel absolutely at ease.'[86]

Jinnah's role should not be interpreted from the lofty heights of majoritarianism. Nor should he be vilified for rejecting the Congress creed or held solely responsible for the vivisection of India. The nationalist rhetoric can no longer obscure the part played by some key Congress and Hindu Mahasabha players in signing united India's death warrant. What is undeniable, however, is Jinnah's self-imposed isolation from the Gandhian-led movements, and his distaste for the socialist programme of the Congress. He did not approve of the *purna swaraj* resolution, adopted by the Lahore Congress in 1929, and blamed Gandhi 'for this sudden outburst of political hysteria'.[87] The civil disobedience movement, according to him, 'has struck the imagination mostly of the inexperienced youth, the ignorant and the illiterate. All this means complete disorganization and chaos.'[88] By the time Gandhi launched the Quit India movement, Jinnah, having descended from the heights of Malabar Hills, was soldiering on to accomplish his mission of creating a Muslim homeland.

Jinnah relished debating, in the traditions of British parliamentary democracy, finer points of law and legal processes and performed with his characteristic élan in Home Rule Leagues and the cozy chambers of the Central Legislative Assembly. He stayed clear of the dusty roads, the villages inhabited by millions of hungry, oppressed and physically emaciated peasants, and the British prison where so many of his countrymen were incarcerated for defying the colonial government. Like Mohamed Ali, he enjoyed the trappings of power. But, unlike the volatile khilafat agitator, he was ill equipped to lead the masses from the front. While Gandhi walked barefoot to break the Salt Law and to galvanize the masses by culturally resonant and action-oriented symbols, a pensive and restless Jinnah waited in London to occupy the commanding heights of political leadership in Delhi. While Gandhi treaded the path fouled by Hindu and Muslim zealots in the riot-stricken areas of Bihar and Bengal, Jinnah was being crowned as the governor-general of Pakistan. For the Mahatma, it was a moment of deep anguish and agony; for the Quaid the fulfilment of his dream.

For much of his public life Jinnah had operated, entirely out of choice, on the periphery of national politics. He made no enemies but cultivated no friends either. But, having finally returned to India in October 1935, he expected a miracle to occur in the 1937 elections. This did not happen. He was dismayed to discover that Gandhi's Congress and not the Muslim League was the people's party. Yet, he was not one to lick his wounds: he launched the League version of the Muslim mass contact campaign, upbraided the Congress ministries for their anti-Muslim bias, and chided Gandhi and Nehru for their intransigence. As a dogged lawyer who had built up a fine reputation in the British-Indian courts, he bounced back, with active British support, to extract major political concessions from a beleaguered wartime government. That was the time when Gandhi, his chief *bete noire*, languished in British jails. His own personal and professional skills were many, but he used them to humble rather than win over his adversaries or potential rivals. He enticed the provincial Muslim bosses in Punjab, Sind and Bengal before destroying their own power base.[89] That is because he liked being on the winning side, even if it meant sacrificing his own cherished principles. Whenever he negotiated with the Congress, he did so not to arrive at a modus vivendi but to vindicate his own stand.[90] With Nehru it was a clash of personalities; with the Mahatma it was a titanic clash of ideologies. 'The two mountains have met,' the viceroy Wavell referred to the Gandhi-Jinnah talks in September 1944, 'and not even a ridiculous mouse has emerged.'[91] Earlier, Jinnah's call to observe 'Deliverance Day' in 1939, or his later appeal for 'Direct Action Day', conformed to Tej Bahadur Sapru's description of him as a 'spoilt child'.[92] In the end, the fruits of freedom were split between the two nations, born in the throes of ugly violence and bloodshed.

Gandhi and Jinnah, brought up in Gujarat and nurtured in British legal schools, should have been able to make sense of each other. In reality, their life-story ran a parallel course. They were distanced from each other long before their acerbic exchanges in the late 1930s. True, the anglicized Jinnah, whose English speech as governor-general of Pakistan to a *Jirgah* of the Pakhtuns in the frontier was translated into Pushtu by the British governor, George Cunningham, was not a devout Muslim or an Islamist.[93]

Somebody accustomed to living in Hampstead and moving in the company of British lawyers and judges could not have felt comfortable before the rustic maulvis or the erudite Muslim theologians, who began to throng the Muslim League sessions after 1940. Yet, he, rather than the ulama of Deoband or Nadwat al-ulama, expounded the idea of a civilizational unity among Muslims and counterpoised it against the heterodox religious and cultural traditions. Having advocated multiculturalism until the mid-1930s for which he earned the title 'Ambassador of Hindu-Muslim unity' from Sarojini Naidu, he authored the two-nation theory in complete disregard of his early conviction.

Grounded in the historical experiences of two mutually incompatible entities engaged in creating their separate destinies, Jinnah questioned, something he had not done before, the very *idea* of unitary nationalism being foisted on different nationalities. For him, the idea of Pakistan, though vaguely defined and interpreted in the early stages, was the only way out of the Muslim predicament. And for the colonial rulers, who had precipitated the Hindu-Muslim divide and had no qualms in seeing the fragmentation of a nation, Jinnah was a trump card to be used against the Congress during the War. He had been ignored and rebuffed on previous occasions, but his newly acquired status in the mid-1940s as the 'sole spokesman' suited imperial designs. While paying lip service to India's unity and bemoaning its imminent division, British policies ensured, particularly in the aftermath of the War, the creation of not one but two nations in 1947.

It was easy to split people and divide territory, but the more challenging task was to *create* a nation out of highly disparate and unevenly developed communities in Pakistan: 'The final truth for man', wrote W.C. Smith in his incisive chapter on Islam, 'lies not in some remote and untarnished utopia, but in the tension and struggle of applying its ideals to the recalcitrant and obstructive stuff of worldly sorrow.'[94] It was easy to project Islam as the cementing bond, a politically motivated exercise that did not find favour with the leading ulama of the period, especially those connected with Deoband and the Jamiyat al-ulama. Realistically speaking, the real task was to initiate new rounds of state building under conditions of intense conflict that divided the élite and militated against compromise, to lay down ground rules for building a state system divorced from the rhetoric of the mullahs, and to accommodate divergent interests in the unreformed bureaucratic and institutional structures. Creating such a system and its long-term effectiveness depended on the capacity of the élites to distance themselves from the theologians, devise an economic strategy to curb the power of the landowning class, and evolve mechanisms to defuse mounting linguistic, sectarian and ethnic tensions.

In other words, instead of attempting to homogenize Pakistan society on the basis of Muslim nationalism, the compelling need was to lay bare the outlines of a pluralist society. That was one way of meeting the various demands of the Bengalis in East Pakistan, the Baluchs and Pathans in the North-West Frontier Province, the Sindhis in Sind, and the *muhajirs* in Karachi, capital of the same province. Mere references to Islamic solidarity, as Jinnah's successor Liaquat Ali Khan discovered the hard way, were no substitute for the hard imperatives of building a new central government machinery for Pakistan's western and eastern wings.[95] As a result, tensions between the dominant and subordinate regions, rather than the purported unities of a common religion, characterized Pakistan's polity for well over two decades.[96] The ruling élites, vying with each other for the pickings, had no intellectual resources to draw upon, and no cadres to translate their nebulous plans into action. The commitment and enthusiasm generated by the Pakistan movement left little of any substantial political value behind on which the post-Jinnah political leadership could rely for support.[97]

The ailing and beleaguered founder of Pakistan had neither the time nor the intellectual reserves to define his long-term agenda. Although he led, organized and conducted powerful mobilization campaigns under the aegis of the Muslim League, he made no attempt to discuss and devise an economic programme. In fact, Nehru noted in 1938 that Jinnah did not show much interest in the economic demands of the masses and the all-important question of poverty and unemployment. During his lifetime, he thwarted even feeble attempts to propose democratic reforms and economic policies. New ideas breaking out among fiery young idealists were nipped in the bud.[98] Those who asked fundamental questions about Pakistan's future trajectory were either told that the time was not appropriate or that they had raised them to pursue partisan interests.[99]

IV

> Have you not heard what happened to Mansur?
> Here, if you speak, they crucify you.
>
> MIR TAQI MIR

Given the historical role of the Congress and Muslim League activists and their contrasting legacies, Pakistan would have probably plotted a predictable course with or without Jinnah. Its fate or destiny was not, however, predetermined. Nor was its survival as a national entity at stake. For Pakistan's ruling classes, the more pressing issue was to negotiate the terms of a post-1947 social contract with the migrants who had moved from their birthplace in search of better opportunities. Given Pakistan's *raison d'être*, this arrangement would have been workable. But the dynamics of power politics, combined with the leadership crisis and the fundamental tension between an autocratic centre and regional interests,[100] belied the expectations raised by Muslim nationalism. The country was unable to work out the four institutionalized arrangements that define the developmental capacity of the state: state-society relations, the nature of the bureaucracy, state fiscal practices, and patterns of state economic intervention.[101] Powerful landlords in Sind and Punjab, having helped Jinnah realize his goal, showed no inclination to share power or agree to land redistribution. There was no Nehru or his socialist comrades to push through land reforms. In 1970, Bhutto's Pakistan People's Party promised to destroy the power of the feudal landowners; but in 1977 the PPP sought to preserve the *status quo*. The Noons and Tiwanas of Sargodha, the Maliks of Mianwali, the Qureshis of Multan, the Hayats of Rawalpindi and Campbellpur, the Legharis and Mazaris of Dera Ghazi Khan were back in the political arena as its candidates.[102]

Similarly, the nascent bourgeoisie, drawn mainly from the migrant entrepreneurs belonging to the ethnic minorities, notably the Memons, Khojas and Bohras, had no stake in democracy. Rather, it relied on the authoritarian state structures to expand and consolidate its position. Finally, the leadership could not rein in the ulama, who demanded a theocratic state. No wonder the ideal of an Islamic state and society, though vaguely defined in the Objectives Resolution in 1952, was ultimately consummated years later during the inglorious regime of Zia-ul-Haq. The contestation between the modernist and traditionalist world views imposed severe strains on a nation that was still trying to find its feet after the untimely death of its founder.[103]

Jinnah, in a broadcast in February 1948, stated: 'Islam and its idealism have taught us democracy. It has taught equality of man, justice and fairplay to everybody. . . . In any case Pakistan is not going to be a theocratic state—to be ruled by priests with a divine mission.' Equally, some leaders and intellectuals talked of 'the nightmare of Pakistan's going back to a rigid, backward, narrow country'. 'For us, the intellectuals, the problem is that Pakistan shall not go back. That it should not become simply an extension of Afghanistan. It is a nightmare for us. The danger of the mullahs coming to power is serious; it would be calamitous. This is the terror.' Yet, the secular project remained dormant, exposing the liberal and secular voices to the fundamentalist fury of the Jamaat-i Islami. The ulama desired the state to be declared Islamic, which the first Constitution, adopted in 1956, declared it to be. Later, they attacked the progressive Muslim Family Laws Ordinance, promulgated by Ayub Khan on 2 March 1961. In the First Amendment Act of 1964, the name of the country was again changed from the Republic of Pakistan to the Islamic Republic of Pakistan.

The PPP fared no better. When Bhutto was caught up in his own quagmire, he resorted to repression. As a practitioner of realpolitik and moving according to the conception of what was most advantageous in the gaining and maintaining of power, he cultivated conservative and religious elements. In 1974, he declared the Ahmadiyas, or Qadianis, a non-Muslim sect, banned alcohol, gambling and night-clubs, and replaced Sunday with Friday as the weekly holiday. Zia-ul-Haq's Islamization programme covered judicial reforms, the introduction of an Islamic penal code, the creation of a federal *Shariat* court, and an educational policy incorporating Islamic tenets. But his main project was the Federal Court, the product of twelve Presidential Ordinances promulgated between 1980 and 1985 and grafted onto the 1973 Constitution.[104] These measures legitimized the power of the ulama, institutionalized theocracy against the wishes of most people, and, in the process, increased the divisions, ruptures and bitterness within an already insecure nation.

The Pakistan scholar Fazlur Rahman, who was exiled from his own country, had pointed out that the slogan, 'in Islam religion and politics are inseparable, is employed to dupe the common man into accepting that, instead of politics or the state serving the long-term objectives of Islam, Islam should come to serve the immediate and myopic objectives of party politics'. Since then, the failure of successive leaderships has led to a deep and justified scepticism on the part of much of Pakistan civil society regarding their leaders, and the political rhetoric behind which they camouflage their failings.

Military dictatorships, even without divine missions, are bad enough. When imbued with the spirit of religious fundamentalism, they suffocate the creative impulses of a society.[105] Though committed to the Islamization Bill after assuming office in February 1997, Nawaz Sharif had no immediate political compulsions, regardless of America's cruise missile attack on Afghanistan, to introduce the Fifteenth Amendment Bill in the Assembly on 28 August 1999. He should have learnt his lesson from his country's bitter experiences in the past. He should have known that the essence of

Table 17.1: Indicators of Development for India and Pakistan

	Year	India	Pakistan	South Asia	All developing countries
Human Development Index (value)	1997	0.545	0.508	0.544	0.637
HDI Rank	1999	132	138	–	–
Real GDP per capita (PPP$)	1997	1670	1560	1803	3240
Female real GDP per capita (PPP$)	1997	902	701	950	2088
Male real GDP per capita (PPP$)	1997	2389	2363	2606	4374
Life Expectancy (value)	1997	0.63	0.65	0.63	0.66
Life Expectancy of Birth (Years)	1997	62.6	64.0	62.7	64.4
Female Life Expectancy at Birth (Years)	1997	62.9	65.1	63.1	66.1
Male Life Expectancy at Birth (Years)	1997	62.3	62.9	62.3	63.0
Education Index (value)	1997	0.54	0.41	0.52	0.67
Adult Literacy Rate (%)	1997	53.5	40.9	52.2	71.4
Female adult literacy rate (%)	1997	39.4	25.4	38.6	62.9
Male adult literacy rate (%)	1997	66.7	55.2	65	80
Female gross enrolement ration (combined [%]	1997	47	28	44	55
Male gross enrolment ration (combined) [%]	1997	62	56	60	64

Gender-related Development Index (value)	1997	0.525	0.472	0.525	0.630
GDI Rank	1997	112	116	–	–
Gender empowerment measure (value)	1997	0.240	0.176	–	–
GEM Rank	1997	95	101	–	–
Seats in Parliament held by women (% of total)	1997	8.3	2.0	6.0	10.0
Human Poverty Index (value) [%]	1997	35.9	42.1	36.6	27.7
HPI Rank	1997	59	71	–	–
Population without safe water	1990-7	19	21	18	28
Population without health services	1981-92	25	15	NA	NA
Population without sanitation	1990-7	71	44	64	57
Real GDP per capita of poorest 20% (PPP$)	1980-4	527	907	–	–
Real GDP per capita of richest 20% (PPP$)	1980-4	2641	4288	–	–
Richest 20% to poorest 20%	1980-4	5.0	4.7	–	–

Source: UNDP, 1999, *Human Development Report 1999*, New York.

a democratic order lies in letting people follow their moral and religious codes, and that state authority should not be used to prescribe, in the light of a religious text, what is right and to forbid what is wrong.

Today, Pakistan can ill-afford to either nurture or acquire the role of a vanguard for a fundamentalist vision of Islam. It may succeed in becoming an Islamic state. Or it may transfer its loyalty to some new ideal. Or it may fail. Each of the alternatives is momentous; and the choice between the people is searching and inexorable.[106] Yet, history is no longer a very effective guide for defining Pakistan's *raison d'être*; too much has happened since 1947. The country is half its original size; culturally, socially, and economically, it is now less a part of South Asia than before. It is in these very changed circumstances that the people of Pakistan will need to find a direction for themselves and for their country,[107] and think in terms of a comprehensive social action—aggregating people with different demands and identities and in different locations in concerted campaigns of collective action. This solution involves, first, mounting collective challenges; second, drawing on social networks, common purposes, and cultural frameworks; and, third, building solidarity through connective structures and collective identities to sustain collective action. These, according to Sidney Tarrow, are the main processes of social movements.[108]

Out of various contradictory tendencies the Pakistanis must find the capacity to create a secularized state and confront the powerful trends towards authoritarianism. If the past is any indication, they have an uphill struggle ahead of them. Yet their case, with all its specificities, will be relevant to other countries trying to cope with daunting external circumstances and beset with internal problems.

NOTES

1. Quoted in *The Economist* (US), 22 May 1999.
2. M. Rashiduzzaman, 'Is Bangladesh Soft State?', *Daily Star*, 2 Feb. 2000.
3. Norman D. Palmer, 'Pakistan: The Long Search for Foreign Policy', in Lawrence Ziring et al. (eds.), *Pakistan: The Long View*, Durham, N.C., 1977, p. 413.
4. 17 Aug. 1989, *Pakistan the Barren Years: The Viewpoint Editorials and Columns of Mazhar Ali Khan, 1775-1992*, Karachi, 1998, p. 63. See also Ghulam Kibria, *A Shattered Dream: Understanding Pakistan's Underdevelopment*, Karachi, 1999.
5. Lawrence Ziring, *Pakistan in the Twentieth Century: A Political History*, London, 1997, p. 614.

6. 6 July 1989, *Pakistan the Barren Years*, p. 730.
7. Iftikhar H. Malik, 'Reconstructing Pakistan: The Way Ahead', *EPW*, 24 Nov. 1999, p. 3277. For the author's optimistic assessment some two years ago, see *State and Civil Society in Pakistan: Politics of Authority, Ideology and Ethnicity*, London, 1997, pp. 259-60.
8. Ayesha Jalal, 'Ideology and the Struggle for Democratic Institutions', in Victoria Schofield (ed.), *Old Roads New Highways*, Karachi, 1997, pp. 135, 136. For Iqbal, see Fazlur Rahman, *Islam*, London, 1966, p. 226. See Feroz Ahmad, *Ethnicity and Politics in Pakistan*, Karachi, 1998, Chap. 10. Notice, too, the lament by Akbar S. Ahmed, a leading Pakistani writer: '. . . Pakistan meant more than just territory, more than a defined area with boundaries. Pakistan meant a culmination of a Muslim movement rooted in history, the quest for a mystical homeland, a Pakistan, a land of the pure. That is why the reality of the violence, corruption, nepotism, mismanagement and materialism of Pakistan in the 1990s is so painful. Mosques are not sacred, public places, private homes, nowhere are safe especially in its main city Karachi.' Akbar S. Ahmed, *Jinnah, Pakistan and Islamic Identity: The Search for Saladin*, Karachi, 1997, p. xviii.
9. Some believed that his electoral support in all the four provinces was a happy augury. 'Upon this support and alliance, trust between provinces and between ethnic groups can be strengthened and governments in the provinces, especially in Sindh, can use the rare opportunity to demonstrate that people of different ethnic backgrounds can work together, narrow their differences, and build a better future together.' Feroz Ahmad, *Ethnicity and Politics in Pakistan*, p. 286. It was also pointed out that his government had the political space and the support of business to give the country a sense of economic direction. 'Early moves suggest a promising start. Much depends on the outcome of this historic opportunity for Nawaz Sharif, perhaps even greater than the opportunity that Z.A. Bhutto had in 1972.' Omar Noman, *Economic and Social Progress in Asia: Why Pakistan did not Become a Tiger*, London, 1997, p. 314.
10. All the constitutions, including the first Constitution of the Islamic Republic of Pakistan in 1956, contain common Islamic elements. For details, see Kemal A. Faruki, 'Pakistan: Islamic Government and Society', in John L. Esposito (ed.), *Islam in Asia: Religion, Politics and Society*, New York, 1987, pp. 55-6. See also Ishtiaq Ahmed, *The Concept of an Islamic State: An Analysis of the Ideological Controversy in Pakistan*, London, 1987.
11. For example, Omar Noman, *Economic and Social Progress*, pp. 297-314; Iftikhar H. Malik, *Islam, Nationalism and the West: Issues of Identity in Pakistan*, Oxford, 1999, p. 145; Ziring, *Pakistan in the Twentieth Century*.
12. Feroz Ahmad, *Ethnicity and Politics in Pakistan*, p. 11.
13. Kibria, *A Shattered Dream*, p. 234.
14. At the time of writing this paper, newspapers report that less than a fortnight after a Christian priest and nun were assaulted in Mathura (UP), a Christian

group from Hyderabad was attacked and Biblical literature was set on fire by Bajrang Dal activists on the outskirts of Agra. *The Hindu* and the *Hindustan Times*, 24 Apr. 2000. Attack on Christians in Agra rocked the Lok Sabha with the opposition demanding the dismissal of the UP government.

15. The orchestrated outcry against the noted painter, M.F. Husain, followed by campaigns against two films—*Fire* and *Water*—exemplify the *Sangh Parivar's* intolerance. The BJP-Shiv Sena government in Maharashtra registered a case against Husain for hurting Hindu sentiments. The basis for the hue and cry against him, according to some, 'is that he happens to be a Muslim and hence the outcry is essentially an attempt to intensify the communal divide', *The Hindu,* 10 Oct. 1996.
16. 'Clearly, what is going on is quiet subversion of the academia through the time-tested method of infiltration and rewriting of textbooks and "fine-tuning" of curricula.' Hasan Suroor, 'The Return of the Thought Police', *The Hindu,* 31 Oct. 1999.
17. 'The only thing that is distinctive about the Sangh Parivar's intervention in the field of education is the speed with which it has moved and its propensity to promote the highest form of mediocrity. That all this has been achieved without the slightest trace of remorse or shame is yet another instance of the narcotic effect a self-important, self-righteous and morally smug ideology can have on its adherents.' Editorial, *Times of India*, 21 Feb. 2000. See also, *Frontline*, 13-26 Nov. 1999.
18. Harish Khare, *The Hindu,* 15 Mar. 2000.
19. *Hindustan Times*, 10 Jan. 2000.
20. *Indian Express*, 15 Mar. 2000.
21. Ibid., 26 Jan. 2000.
22. Kirpa Shankar, 'Tenancy Reforms: Rhetoric and Reality', *EPW*, 20 Nov. 1999, p. 3264.
23. 'Persistent Deprivation', *Frontline* (Special Issue), 9-22 Aug. 1997, and 'New Economy at Work', *Frontline*, 15-28 Aug. 2000.
24. 'How India has fared', *Frontline*, 9-22 Aug. 1997. See also, Myron Weiner, *The Child and the State in India: Child Labour and Education Policy in Perspective*, Princeton, N.J., 1999.
25. See John Echeverri-Gent, *The State and the Poor: Public Policy and Political Development in India and the United States*, Berkeley, 1993, pp. 195-6.
26. Andre Beteille, 'The Backward Classes', p. 1, quoted in Granville Austin, *Working a Democratic Constitution*, New Delhi, 1999, p. 665.
27. Summary based on Harish Khare's report, *The Hindu*, 26 Jan. 2000.
28. Ashutosh Varshney, 'Is India Becoming Democratic?', *The Journal of Asian Studies*, Vol. 39, No. 1, Feb. 2000.
29. Paul R. Brass, *The Politics of India Since Independence*, Cambridge, 1990. For statistical details substantiating these claims, see Ahrar Ahmad, 'The State, Participation, and Constitutionalism: Political Crises and Democracy in India', *Asian Affairs: An American Review*, Vol. 26, Fall 1999.

30. The actual decline of the Congress over the long-term is from a level of 46 per cent (until and excluding 1967) to an average of 42 per cent (from 1967 to 1984) to 39.5 per cent in 1989. The share slipped further to 36.5 per cent in 1991, when a powerful sympathy factor following Rajiv Gandhi's assassination boosted the figure for the second stage of a split contest, and to 29.7 per cent in 1996. Another feature of this decline is the plight of the ruling party at the state level. Of the seven large states, that is, those with more than 35 Lok Sabha seats (UP, Bihar, Maharashtra, West Bengal, Andhra Pradesh, Madhya Pradesh and Tamil Nadu), which make up a total of 350 or nearly two-thirds of the House, the party is in power only in Madhya Pradesh. Its chances of bidding for power in the conceivable future in UP, Bihar, West Bengal and Tamil Nadu are virtually non-existent. Of the five medium sized states, that is, those with 20 to 30 Lok Sabha seats (Karnataka, Gujarat, Rajasthan, Kerala and Orissa), the party is in power only in Karnataka. It has suffered an upset in the smaller northern states (Punjab, Haryana and Jammu & Kashmir) where it shows few signs of recovery. This data stands for the period mentioned earlier. See *Frontline*, 9-22 Aug. 1997. At the end of Nov. 1998 the Congress swept the Assembly elections in Madhya Pradesh, Rajasthan and Delhi.
31. Zoya Hasan, *Quest for Power: Oppositional Movements and Post-Congress Politics in Uttar Pradesh*, New Delhi, 1998.
32. Atul Kohli, *Democracy and Discontent: India's Growing Crisis of Governability*, Cambridge, 1990.
33. Sudipta Kaviraj, 'The Modern State in India', in Martin Doornbos and Sudipta Kaviraj (eds.), *Dynamics of State Formation: India and Europe Considered*, New Delhi, 1997. For Pakistan, see Charles H. Kennedy, *Bureaucracy in Pakistan*, New York, 1987.
34. James Manor, 'Political Regeneration in India', in D.L. Sheth and Ashis Nandy (eds.), *The Multiverse of Democracy: Essays in Honour of Rajni Kothari*, New Delhi, 1996, pp. 231-2.
35. See the çollection of essays in Francine R. Frankel et al. (eds.), *Transforming India: Social and Political Dynamics of Democracy*, New Delhi, 2000.
36. Sugata Bose and Ayesha Jalal (eds.), *Nationalism, Democracy and Development*, New Delhi, 1997, p. 2.
37. Sudipta Kaviraj (ed.), *Politics in India*, New Delhi, 1999, p. 15.
38. 16 Jan. 1992, *Pakistan the Barren Years*, pp. 745-6. In Bangladesh, the coup against Mujibur Rahman 'underscores the quality of leadership as an independent variable in political change'. Talukdar Maniruzzaman, *The Bangladesh Revolution and its Aftermath*, Dhaka, 1980, p. 237.
39. Hence slogans like '*Gharibi-hatao*' or '*Roti-Kapra-Makan*' conjured up the image of a better world fashioned by the leaders at the top. In Pakistan, a populist like Zulfiqar Ali Bhutto, perceived as a worthy successor of Jinnah, acquired the image of a 'saviour' despite his murky role in East Pakistan. Similarly, Indira Gandhi capitalized on her ancestry and her family's contri-

bution to the freedom struggle to harness popular support for abolishing privy purses and nationalizing banks. 'Indian nationalism was, after all, plural at the top, a *dhoti* with endless folds. Its diversity was emblematically incarnated in the gallery of characters who constituted the nationalist pantheon, a pantheon whose unaging, cherub-like faces are still on display, painted with garish affection on calendars and posters or moulded into just recognizable statues and figures, in tea-shops and at cross-roads across the country.' Sunil Khilnani, *The Idea of India*, London, 1997, p. 6.

40. Echoing the views of many, a number of Bangladeshi scholars argued following prolonged periods of instability that the growth and stability of the country was dependent on the performance of president Zia. 'The critical issue . . . is the way in which Zia civilianises his regime and builds up a civilian base of power.' Maniruzzaman, *The Bangladesh Revolution*, p. 239.
41. This is not to suggest that the making of the Indian nation and the development of the nationalist consciousness were exclusively or predominantly élite achievements. Nor do I represent Indian nationalism here, or in any of my previous writings, as 'primarily an idealist venture in which the indigenous élite led the people from subjugation to freedom'. Given my concern in this paper, it will be obvious why I focus on the Congress and not the subalterns. Ranajit Guha has himself written, 'let a hundred flowers blossom and we don't mind even the weeds'.
42. Walter Hauser, 'Swami Sahajanand and the Politics of Social Reform, 1907-1950', *The Indian Historical Review*, Vol. 28, Nos. 1-2, July 1991 and Jan. 1992, p. 72.
43. Cited in Walter Hauser, 'Changing Images of Caste and Politics', *Seminar*, 450, Feb. 1997, p. 49.
44. *Mera Jiwan Sangarsh*, cited in Hauser, 'Swami Sahajanand', p. 72.
45. D. Dalton, *Mahatma Gandhi: Nonviolent Power in Action*, New York, 1993. I am aware of the debate on the Salt Satyagraha, but this is not the place to reflect on it. On balance, however, I agree that, 'whatever one thinks of the amazing event that was the Dandi March, there can be no failure for someone who was doing what he had to do and reminding people that they too should be doing what they had to do—in order to be free'. Thomas Weber, *On the Salt March: The Historiography of Gandhi's March to Dandi*, New Delhi, 1997, p. 481.
46. Horace Alexander, *Gandhi through Western Eyes*, Philadelphia, 1984, p. 62.
47. Cited in D.A. Low, *Britain and Indian Nationalism: The Imprint of Ambiguity*, Cambridge, 1977, p. 260.
48. Quoted in ibid., p. 263 and fn. 49.
49. Ibid., p. 262.
50. Gyanendra Pandey, 'A Rural Base for Congress: The United Provinces 1920-40', in D.A. Low (ed.), *Congress and the Raj: Facets of the Indian Struggle 1917-47*, London, 1997.
51. Hauser, 'Swami Sahajanand', pp. 59-75.

52. Granville Austin, *The Indian Constitution*, New York, 1966, p. 22.
53. Thus, the political scientist Rajeev Bhargava speaks of 'a single vision on the assumption that, despite the absence of a unified collective subject, a loose disjointed, somewhat incoherent vision of India did emerge briefly in the 1950s'. 'Democratic Vision of a Republic, 1950', in Frankel (ed.), *Transforming India*, p. 26.
54. Harish Khare, *The Hindu*, 27 Jan. 2000. There is therefore little reason to endorse Ayesha Jalal's insistence on the formal and not substantive nature of Indian democracy.
55. Harry C. Hart, 'Political Leadership in India: Dimensions and Limits', in Atul Kohli (ed.), *India's Democracy: An Analysis of Changing State-Society Relations*, Princeton, N.J., 1990, pp. 18-19.
56. W.H. Morris Jones, *The Government and Politics of India*, 3rd revd. edn., London, 1971, p. 70.
57. Baldev Raj Nayar, 'Punjab', in Weiner (ed.), *State Politics*, p. 494.
58. G. Ram Reddy, 'The Politics of Accommodation: Caste, Class and Dominance in Andhra Pradesh', in Francine R. Frankel and M.S.A. Rao (eds.), *Dominance and State Power in Modern India*, New Delhi, 1989, p. 280.
59. T.J. Nossiter, *Communism in Kerala: A Study of Political Adaptation*, New Delhi, 1982, pp. 149-53.
60. D. Bandyopadhyay, 'Reflections on Land Reforms in India Since Independence', in T.V. Sathyamurthy (ed.), *Industry and Agriculture in India Since Independence*, New Delhi, 1995, pp. 310-27.
61. Nayar, 'Punjab', in Weiner (ed.), *State Politics*, p. 494.
62. Ibid., p. 21; Zoya Hasan, 'Power and Mobilisation: Pattern of Resilience and Change in Uttar Pradesh Politics', in Frankel (ed.), *Dominance and State Power*, pp. 155-7.
63. Kaviraj, 'The Modern State in India'.
64. Paul R. Brass, 'Uttar Pradesh', ibid., pp. 66-7.
65. Francine R. Frankel, *India's Political Economy, 1947-1979: The Gradual Revolution*, Princeton, N.J., 1978, p. 4. For comparative figures from Pakistan, see Sayeed, *Politics in Pakistan*, pp. 60-1.
66. This point has been emphasized in a number of works, including Sayeed, *Politics in Pakistan*, Chaps. 1-2; Ayesha Jalal, *Democracy and Authoritarianism in South Asia: A Comparative and Historical Perspective*, Cambridge, 1995, Chap. 1; and Kennedy, *Bureaucracy in Pakistan*.
67. Ahrar Ahmad, 'The State, Participation, and Constitutionalism'.
68. Frank Moraes, *Jawaharlal Nehru: A Biography*, New York, 1956, p. 491.
69. Morris-Jones, *Government and Politics*, p. 55.
70. Sarvepalli Gopal, *Jawaharlal Nehru: A Biography, 1956-1964*, Vol. 3, London, 1984, p. 198.
71. Walter Hauser, 'The Life of a Text and its Meanings: Reflections on Sahajanand Saraswati's *Mera Jiwan Sangharsh*', unpublished paper presented at the Conference on South Asian Life-Histories at the School of Oriental and

African Studies, University of London, 15-17 May 2000.

72. Robert D. King, *Nehru and the Language Politics of India*, New Delhi, 1997, p. xv.
73. Ibid., p. xvi. Joseph E. Schwartzberg, 'Factors in the Linguistic Reorganisation of Indian States', in Paul Wallace (ed.), *Region and Nation in India*, New Delhi, 1985, p. 177.
74. During 1950-8, Pakistan had seven prime ministers, whereas India had one.
75. Sayeed, *Pakistan: The Formative Phase*, p. 298, and his *Politics in Pakistan: The Nature and Direction of Change*, New York, 1980, Chap. 2; D.A. Low, *The Political Inheritance of Pakistan*, London, 1991, p. 15; Barlas, *Democracy, Nationalism and Communalism*, p. 189.
76. Rao Rashid, *Snobs and Spices*, p. 29.
77. The Congress held power at the Centre and the states until the 1967 election when the party won control of only half of the state assemblies.
78. Francine R. Frankel, 'Caste, Land and Dominance in Bihar: Breakdown of the Brahmanical Social Order', in Frankel (ed.), *Dominance and State Power*, pp. 82-4.
79. It is therefore argued that 'the rise of lower castes to power between the 1950s and 1960s has a great deal to do with the transformation of South India'. Varshney, 'Is India Becoming more Democratic?', p. 22.
80. Hamza Alavi argued that the bureaucratic-military oligarchy mediated between the competing demands of the three propertied classes—the indigenous bourgeoisie, the neocolonial metropolitan bourgeoisie, and the land-owning classes—and in playing this role the bureaucratic-military oligarchy represented the relative autonomy of the postcolonial state of Pakistan. Hamza Alavi, 'The State in Postcolonial Societies: Pakistan and Bangladesh', in Kathleen Gough and Hari P. Sharma (eds.), *Imperialism and Revolution in South Asia*, New York, 1973, pp. 159-61.
81. For details, see Christophe Jaffrelot, 'The Rise of Backward Classes in the Hindi Belt', *The Journal of Asian Studies*, Feb. 2000.
82. Jalal, *Democracy and Authoritarianism in South Asia*, pp. 249-50.
83. Barlas, *Democracy*, p. 8.
84. Shaikh, *Community and Consensus in Islam*.
85. Myron Weiner (ed.), *State Politics in India*, Princeton, N.J., p. 21.
86. To Horace Alexander, 23 Dec. 1930, in *Gandhi through Western Eyes*, p. 194.
87. Quoted in Wolpert, *Jinnah of Pakistan*, p. 113.
88. Omar Noman, *Pakistan*, p. 23.
89. Wolpert, *Jinnah of Pakistan*, pp. 192-5, 216-17.
90. Ibid., *Jinnah*, pp. 263, 274-5. Wavell's assessment of Jinnah in mid-September 1943 was; 'it is hardly too much to say that Jinnah is the Muslim League. He is a vain, shallow and ambitious man who would probably think twice the present time inopportune for any rapprochement with the Hindus.' Quoted in Wolpert, *Jinnah*, p. 225.

91. Ibid., p. 236.
92. Sapru made this remark at the All-Parties National Convention in Dec. 1928.
93. Sayeed, *Politics in Pakistan*, p. 28.
94. W.C. Smith, *Islam in Modern History*, Princeton, N.J., 1967, p. 241.
95. Ayesha Jalal, *The State of Martial Rule: The Origins of Pakistan's Political Economy of Defence*, Cambridge, 1990, p. 23.
96. Ibid., p. 1.
97. Low, *Political Inheritance of Pakistan*, p. 6. 'Pakistan's early history', observed Shahid Javed Burki, 'is marked by the birth, development and demise of a number of political and economic institutions. None of them took root, not because Pakistani society could function only in an institutional vacuum, but because its various components did not succeed in reaching a state of equilibrium. Although Jinnah had won the partition of British India on the basis of his two-nation theory, deep social and economic fissures continued to run through the Muslim nation that he created.' Shahid Javed Burki, *Pakistan Under Bhutto, 1970-1977*, London, 1980, p. 34.
98. Hasan, *Legacy of a Divided Nation*, p. 81.
99. Sayeed, *Pakistan: The Formative Phase*, p. 206.
100. Yunus Samad, *A Nation in Turmoil: Nationalism and Ethnicity in Pakistan, 1937-1958*, New Delhi, 1995.
101. These are defined in David Waldner, *State Building and Late Development*, Cornell, 1999, p. 2.
102. Burki, *Pakistan under Bhutto*, p. 192.
103. The 'secular' or 'modernist' view is reflected in a number of statements quoted in Noman, *Pakistan*, p. 8. I use the expression modernist in the context of an ideology that separates religion from politics.
104. See Charles H. Kennedy, 'Islam and Constitutionalism in Pakistan, 1979-2000', paper presented at the Conference on 'Islam and Constitutionalism', Harvard University, 7-9 Apr. 2000.
105. Omar Noman, *Pakistan: Political and Economic History Since 1947*, London, 1988, p. 214.
106. Smith, *Islam in Modern History*, p. 208.
107. Shahid Javed Burki, *Pakistan: A Nation in the Making*, Karachi, 1986, p. 207, and Ian Talbot, *Pakistan: A Modern History*, London, 1999, pp. 372-4.
108. Sidney Tarrow, *Power in Movement: Social Movements and Contentious Politics*, Cambridge, 1998, 2nd edn., p. 4.

APPENDICES

Appendix I

Report of the Committee appointed by the All Parties Conference (1928) to determine the principles of the Constitution for India

CHAPTER II

THE COMMUNAL ASPECT

The Problem

The communal problem of India is primarily the Hindu-Muslim problem. Other communities have however latterly taken up an aggressive attitude and have demanded special rights and privileges. The Sikhs in the Punjab are an important and well knit minority which cannot be ignored. Amongst the Hindus themselves there is occasional friction, specially in the south, between non-Brahmans and Brahmans. But essentially the problem is how to adjust the differences between the Hindus and Muslims.

Population Ratios

These two communities indeed form 90 per cent of the total population of India and Burma. The proportions at the 1921 census were:

*A list of those who signed the resolution is given in a note at the end of the report.

Hindus	65.9 per cent
Muslims	24.1 "
Buddhists (chiefly in Burma)	4.6 "
Tribal religions (in hill tracts)	2.8 "
Christians	1.2 "
Sikhs	1.0 "
Jains	.2 "
Others	.2 "
	100.0 "

A study of the figures of previous census reports shows that while Hindus and Jains have been gradually decreasing, all the others have increased their numbers from census to census. The increase in the case of Muslims has not been great but it has been continuous. The following percentages since 1881 will show the relative numbers of the Hindus and Muslims at different periods:

	1881	1891	1901	1911	1912
Hindus	72.0	70.1	68.3	66.9	65.9 = -6.1
Muslims	22.6	22.4	23.2	23.5	24.1 = +1.5

These are the percentages in relation to the whole of India. Taking the Muslims separately we find that they have increased by 3.1 per cent during the last decade. The Hindus have slightly decreased during this period.

The distribution of the Muslim population is such that except in the frontier provinces in the north-west, and in Bengal and Punjab, they form a small minority everywhere. Their highest minority is in the United Provinces but even here it is less than 15 per cent. This 15 per cent in the United Provinces is not spread out all over the province, but is largely concentrated in urban areas, specially in the northern part of the province.

In the Punjab, the Muslims are 55.3 per cent and in Bengal 54.0 per cent. In Sind they are 73.4 per cent and in Baluchistan and the N.W.F. Provinces they are overwhelmingly strong.

Communal Protection

A new corner to India looking at these figures and at the strength of the Muslim community, would probably imagine that it was strong enough to look after itself and required no special protection or spoon feeding. If communal protection was necessary for any group in India it was not for the two major communities—the Hindus and the Muslims. It might have been necessary for the small communities which together form 10% of the total.

LIVE AND LET LIVE

But logic or sense have little to do with communal feeling, and today the whole problem resolves itself into the removal from the minds of each of a baseless fear of the other and of giving a feeling of security to all communities. In looking for this security each party wants to make for itself-or to retain, a dominating position. We note with regret that the spirit animating some of the communal spokesmen, is not one of live and let live. The only methods of giving a feeling of security are safeguards and guarantees and the grant, as far as possible, of cultural autonomy. The clumsy and objectionable methods of separate electorates and reservation of seats do not give this security. They only keep up an armed truce.

The Muslims being in a minority in India as a whole fear that the majority may harass them, and to meet this difficulty they have made a novel suggestion—that they should at least dominate in some parts of India. We do not here criticise their demand. It may have some justification in the present communal atmosphere but we do feel that it has little to do with the premises we started from, unless indeed the best safeguard that one can have is to occupy a position of domination oneself. The Hindus on the other hand although in a great majority all over India are in a minority in Bengal and the Punjab and in Sind, Baluchistan and the N.W.F. Province. In spire of their all India majority they are afraid of the Muslims in these provinces.

We cannot have one community domineering over another. We may not be able to prevent this entirely but the object we should aim at is not to give dominion to one over another but to prevent the harassment and exploitation of any individual or group by another. If the fullest religious liberty is given, and cultural autonomy provided for, the communal problem is in effect solved, although people may not realize it.

COMMUNAL COUNCILS

With this view point before us we have provided several articles in the Declaration of Rights giving the fullest liberty of conscience and religion to each individual. We considered also a proposal to create communal councils to protect the cultural interests of each considerable community. This proposal was that any community being ten lakhs or more in number in any province shall have the right to have a council representing the members of the community for certain purposes which were mentioned. The manner of election of the members of these councils by their respective communities was to be determined by the Provincial Council. Each council was to consist of not more than 25 members. The functions of the communal council were laid down as:

(1) Supervision of primary education, schools, orphanages, dharamshalas, sarais, widows homes, and rescue homes.
(2) Encouragement of scripts and languages.

The communal council could recommend that grants be given to institutions or for scholarships, such grants being made either by the provincial or central government after being submitted to the vote of the House.

These were the main provisions in regards to the communal councils. The idea appealed to us as affording some kind of a substitute for other and worse forms of communalism. But some of our colleagues and several friends whom we consulted were strongly opposed to the creation of these councils, both on communal and administrative grounds. They felt that these councils would help to keep communalism alive. We have therefore rejected the proposal.

The communal problem, so far as its political aspect is concerned, resolves itself now into the question of electorates, the reservation of seats, the separation of Sind, and the form of government in the N.W.F. Province and Baluchistan.

Separate Electorates

It is admitted by most people now that separate electorates are thoroughly bad and must be done away with. We find however that there has been a tendency amongst the Muslims to consider them as a 'valued privilege', although a considerable section are prepared to give them up in consideration for some other things. Everybody knows that separate electorates are bad for the growth of a national spirit, but everybody perhaps does not realize equally well that separate electorates are still worse for a minority community. They make the majority wholly independent of the minority and its votes and usually hostile to it. Under separate electorates therefore the chances are that the minority will always have to face a hostile majority, which can always, by sheer force of numbers, override the wishes of the minority. This effect of having separate electorates has already become obvious, although the presence of the third party confuses the issues. Separate electorates thus benefit the majority community. Extreme communalists flourish thereunder and the majority community, far from suffering, actually benefits by them. Separate electorates must therefore be discarded completely as a condition precedent to any rational system of representation. We can only have joint or mixed electorates.

We find that the Ceylon Reform Enquiry Committee, who have recently made their report, have recommended the abolition of communal electorates throughout the island.

N.W.F.P. and Baluchistan

Regarding the form of government in the N.W.F. Province and in Baluchistan, we are of opinion that the status of these areas must be made the same as that of other provinces. We cannot in justice or in logic deny the right of any part of India to participate in responsible government. The All Parties Conference has already agreed to this and we gather that no considerable group oppose this reasonable demand.

The questions that remain are the separation of Sind from the Bombay presidency and the reservation of seats in the legislatures. These are mixed questions of communal and general importance. We have reserved the question of reservation of seats to be considered both in its communal and general aspects in a subsequent chapter. The communal aspect of the question of the separation of Sind may conveniently be dealt with here and we proceed to consider it.

Sind

Sind has, by a strange succession of events, become a major problem in our politics. It is strange that those who were in favour of its separation from Bombay only a few years ago are now opposed to it, and those who were against separation then now vehemently desire it. All India is exercised about this comparatively trivial matter. This sudden and somewhat inexplicable change of opinion demonstrates how communal considerations warp and twist our better judgement. For the last eight* years, since the National Congress made Sind into a separate province, no voice was raised in protest. We feel that in the conflict of communal allegations and

*Note by Secretary AICC: Sind was constituted into a separate Congress province in 1917, eleven year ago.

counter allegations the only safe course is to try to ignore them and consider the problem as dispassionately as possible. But unhappily it has become a part of the sentiment of the people and sentiment cannot be ignored.

It is stated on behalf of the Hindus in Sind and elsewhere that they are strongly opposed to the creation of 'communal' provinces. We agree that the Muslim demand for the separation of Sind was not put forward in the happiest way. It was based on communalism and it was tacked on irrelevantly to certain other matters with which it had no concern whatever. We can understand the Hindu reaction to this. But the manner of putting it forward does not necessarily weaken the merits of a proposal. There is no question of creating a 'communal' province. We have merely to recognize facts as they are. A long succession of events in history is responsible for the distribution of the population of India as it is today. Sind happens to contain a large majority of Muslims. Whether a new province is created or not Sind must remain a predominantly Muslim area. And if the wishes of this large majority are not acceded to, it would not only be doing violence to the principle of self-determination, but would necessarily result in antagonizing that majority population. No Indian desiring a free India, progressing peacefully and harmoniously, can view this result with equanimity. To say from the larger view point of nationalism that no 'communal' provinces should be created is, in a way, equivalent to saying from the still wider international view point that there should be no separate nations. Both these statements have a measure of truth in them. But the staunchest internationalist recognizes that without the fullest national autonomy it is extraordinarily difficult to create the international state. So also without the fullest cultural autonomy, and communalism in its better aspect is culture, it will be difficult to create a harmonious nation.

We suspect that the real opposition to separation is not due to any high national considerations but to grosser economic considerations; to the fear of the Hindus that their economic position might suffer if Muslims had the charge of affairs in a separated area. We are sure that this fear is baseless. Among all the people of India the Hindus of Sind are perhaps the most enterprising and adventurous. The traveller meets them in the four quarters of the world, carrying on prosperous businesses and enriching their people at home by their earnings abroad. No one can take away this spirit of adventure and enterprise from the Hindus of Sind and so long as they have it their future is assured. It must be remembered also that the powers of a provincial government are limited and there is the central government which has power in all important departments. If however there is still some ground for fear that is a matter for safeguards, not of opposing a just demand.

We are therefore of opinion that even communal grounds justify the separation of Sind. If the Hindus stand to lose thereby and the Muslims stand to gain, of which we see no chance, such risk of loss by the one and the chance of gain by the other community will not, we hope and trust, be allowed by either to endanger the larger cause. We shall deal with the general aspect of the question later. We would note here that our colleague Mr. Aney does not agree with all the above views but agrees with our conclusion.

CHAPTER III

RESERVATION OF SEATS

Alternative Proposals

Coming now to the question of reservation of seats, it was found that each party held strongly to its own opinion and was not prepared to give in. Muslims were insistent on the reservation of seats for the Muslim majorities in the Punjab and Bengal, and the Hindu Maha Sabha and the Sikh League were equally strongly opposed to this. The Committee considered various proposals, among them being:

1. Reservation of seats on population basis for majorities as well as minorities.
2. Part reservation for majorities with freedom to contest other seats.
3. Proportional Representation.
4. Amalgamation of the Punjab and N.W.F. Province, with no reservation of seats.
5. No reservation, but special safeguards in the constitution for educational and economic advance of backward communities.

Before considering these proposals, some of which were new, the Committee was of opinion that representatives of the principal organizations concerned might be consulted. An invitation was therefore sent on June 11th to the Hindu Mahā Sabha, the All India Muslim League and the Sikh League to send one or two representatives to meet the Committee on June 21st. The response to these invitations was not very encouraging. The secretary of the Hindu Maha Sabha wrote to express his inability to send any representative on that date, and the secretary of the Muslim League did not send any answer at all. The Sikh League were prepared to send representatives but as the Maha Sabha and Muslim League were not sending any one, our colleague Sardar Mangal Singh did not think it necessary to trouble the Sikh representative to come. Some others who had been personally invited could not come. We had the privilege however of conferring with Dr. M.A. Ansari, who took the trouble to come and assist us with his advice.

The proposals set out above were discussed at two consecutive sittings at which Dr. Ansari was also present. No agreement could be reached on the first proposal, but decisions were taken on the remaining four. It will be convenient to deal with these latter before taking up the main proposal.

Part Reservation

The suggestion was to have part reservation of the majority community in the Punjab and in Bengal with freedom to contest the other seats. This part reservation was granted to the non-Brahmans in the south and is still continuing. But even in the case of the non-Brahmans it has been found to be wholly unnecessary as they have always, so far as we are aware, captured a far larger number of seats on the strength of their votes and have had no need to invoke the aid of the reservation clause. It is not the case of any one in the Punjab or Bengal that the Muslim majority will not succeed in capturing a large number of seats. What is feared by the Muslims, unreasonably most of us think, is that they may not capture the majority of seats. In any event they will capture enough seats to make them if not a clear majority at least a strong minority just short of a majority. If they are sure of capturing, let us say, 45 per cent of seats the need for part reservation disappears. We are not opposed to part reservation for majorities or minorities, with freedom to contest the remaining seats, but we feel that in the case of Bengal and the Punjab it is unnecessary and does not materially affect the situation either way.

Proportional Representation

The next proposal is that of Proportional Representation. The subcommittee appointed by the All Parties Conference to consider this method of election and representation has presented no report but some individual members have sent their separate notes. Sardar Mangal Singh has supported the proposal, but the others, while favouring the system, are of opinion that under present circumstances in India it will not work. We feel strongly attracted to this method and are of opinion that it offers the only rational and just way of meeting the fears and claims of various communities. There is a place in it for every minority and an automatic adjustment takes place of rival interests. We have no doubt that proportional representation will in future be the solution of our problem.

How far is it immediately practicable? Great stress is laid on its intricacy and of the general illiteracy of the electorate in India. We are told that it is impossible to work this system, desirable as it may be, so long as the electorate is not educated up to understanding its significance. We recognize this difficulty. It is considerable. And yet we feel that it is a little exaggerated. Proportional Representation requires not so much a high standard of intelligence in the voters, as expert knowledge in the returning officers and the people who count and transfer votes from one head to another. There can be no doubt that there is a sufficiency of Indians who are competent enough to do this work of counting of votes satisfactorily. As for the general electorate it is very true that a standard of intelligence is necessary for a proper choice to be made in order of merit. But a certain standard is also necessary to exercise the right of vote even in a single member constituency. It is notorious that even in highly democratic England that standard is lacking and votes are given not for high matters of policy or considerations that are really important, but for trivial matters or even sometimes most objectionable considerations which the exigencies of election times force to the front. A general election has turned in the past on the cry of hanging the ex-Kaiser or on a forged letter, and the men, who were to govern an empire and influence largely world events, have been elected for reasons which make every intelligent person despair of democracy. In India the standard of intelligence of the vote will, to begin with at least, be lower than that of the English voter. But these are reasons against democracy, not so much against Proportional Representation.

We are told that another strong argument against Proportional Representation is that for the illiterate voter it would do away with the secrecy of the ballot. We think that the device of three boxes of the same colour for each candidate with different symbols painted on each box to indicate the first, second and third choice, would remove this objection. But it applies in equal measure to the illiterate voter at most of the ordinary elections today. In Malta, where there is a large majority of illiterate voters, Proportional Representation has been tried with success, but of course we cannot compare the little island of Malta to our enormous country with its millions.

Most of us feel that there are no insuperable difficulties in the way of giving a trial to Proportional Representation in India. There are drawbacks and risks, but no proposal which we have considered is free from objection, and some of these involve a departure from principle which may bring greater difficulties in its train. Some of our colleagues however are not satisfied that Proportional Representation can be introduced at this stage in India. We therefore refrain from recommending it.

Amalgamation of Punjab and N.W.F. Provinces

It was suggested that the N.W.F. province be amalgamated with the Punjab and that there should then be no reservation of seats in this province. We have no objection to this proposal but we do not know how far this will meet the different view points of the parties concerned. If it does meet with their approval, we would gladly recommend it. There is no special principle involved in it. Its acceptance or otherwise depends entirely on whether it is approved or not. Our colleague Sardar Mangal Singh does not approve of the proposal and we understand that some other people also are of his opinion. We therefore make no recommendation in regard to it.

Amalgamation of Punjab N.W.F.P., Sind and Baluchistan

A similar but more far reaching proposal was made to us, namely, that the Punjab, the N.W.F. Province, Baluchistan and Sind should all be amalgamated together and that there should be no reservation of seats, unless the minority desires it, in this area. We were unable to entertain this proposal. It would mean the creation of an unwieldy province sprawling all over the north and north-west.

No Reservation in the Punjab

Another proposal in regard to the Punjab was that there should be no reservation whatever but that special safeguards in the constitution for educational and economic advance of backward communities may be provided. We would cordially welcome such a solution if it was agreed to. But we have to recognize that a unanimous acceptance of this proposal is at present unlikely, otherwise there would have been no communal friction. In our draft constitution we have included many safeguards for minorities and provisions for the educational and economic advance of backward communities. We would gladly add to these safeguards and provisions if thereby we could remove feelings of insecurity in any community and do away with reservation of seats and other communal expedients. It seems unnecessary to pursue the subject any further in the present atmosphere.

Reservation of Seats on Population Basis

We now come to the main question, the reservation of seats on the basis of population, both for majorities and minorities.

General

It was never seriously denied that reservation of seats for communities was as bad in principle as communal electorates, but, for various reasons of expediency, such reservation was recommended for a time to serve as a transitional stage between communal electorates and general mixed electorates without any restrictions. The idea was that during the interval the distrust of one community of the other would be very much lessened if not altogether removed. Similar arguments were used when the Lucknow pact was arranged, but the actual experience of the last 12 years has belied the expectations then formed. Communal electorates might or might not be responsible for the increasing communal tension of recent years but they have certainly failed to pave the way to a better understanding between the communities as was hoped. General reservation of seats for any community whether found in a minority or a majority is a full recognition of communalism and differs little from communal electorates.

Reservation for Majorities

Reservation of seats for majorities has been fiercely opposed—both on grounds of theory and fact. The question arises only in the provinces of the Punjab and Bengal where the Muslims are in a slight majority over all others. It has not been claimed for any other majority in any other province. We have therefore to consider the Punjab and Bengal only in this connection.

We should have thought that of all the provinces of India the Punjab and Bengal were the most fortunate in that the distribution of population was such that there was little chance of one community or group dominating over another or harassing it and preventing its growth in any way. Although one community is in an absolute majority in both of these provinces the others are strong enough to protect their own interests and prevent any oppression.

Reservation for a majority is indefensible in theory. It is in artificial restriction on the growth both of the majority and the minority and must necessarily retard national progress. It is, we feel, specially injurious to the majority itself for it makes it rely on legislative provision to keep up its position and not on its own inherent strength. After a period of reservation such a community is bound to lose in self-reliance and all the qualities that contribute towards building up a people and adding to their creative energy. Ordinarily a majority captures seats in excess of its population strength unless the method of election is by Proportional Representation. This is evident as the majority may be so spread out as to be in a commanding position in each or at any rate most of the constituencies. It is this danger of the majority capturing far more seats than its population strength entitles it to, and thereby encroaching on the limited preserves of the minority, that leads to the protection of minority interests.

A majority reservation or other fixation of seats is incompatible with real representative and responsible government. It obviously interferes with the right of the electors to choose whom they like. Further, it is bound to come in the way of other and more natural groupings in and outside the legislature and it will give a longer lease of life to communalism. Everybody regrets the communal spirit and desires to exorcise it from the body politic. But it is clear that it cannot go merely by talking about unity and indulging in pious platitudes which take us nowhere. Communalism can only go when the attention of the people is directed in other channels, when they begin to take interest in questions which really affect their daily lives rather than in fancied fears based on an artificial division of society. We must therefore try to create this new interest in the people and we must put no barriers in the way of the development of this interest. There can be no doubt that a majority reservation and fixation of seats is such a barrier.

Methods of Reservation

An examination of the methods by which reservation for a majority can be secured will show that it is not only a negation of representative government but is in direct conflict with the principle on which responsible government rests.

The Montagu-Chelmsford Method

One of these methods has been applied in the Madras and parts of the Bombay presidency to secure a partial reservation for the overwhelming majorities of non-Brahmans in those presidencies. This large community which forms over 96 per cent of the population of the Madras presidency succeeded in inducing the government, on the recommendation of the Southborough Committee, to reserve for them 28 seats out of a total of 98 to protect them from the small minority of Brahmans who did not exceed 2½ per cent of the whole population. The manner in which this reservation was secured was that two purely non-Brahman constituencies, each returning a single member, were created and, of the remaining constituencies, 25 were made plural, each returning three or more members, two of whom must be non-Brahmans in Madras City, and one must be a non-Brahman in each of the remaining 24. The rule on the subject is thus stated:

When the counting of the votes has been completed the Returning Officer shall forthwith declare the candidate or candidates as the case may be, to whom the largest number of votes has been given, to be elected: provided that if one or more seats are reserved the Returning Officer shall first declare to be elected the non-Brahman candidate or candidates, as the case may be, to whom the largest number of votes has been given.

To illustrate this rule take the case of Madras City where out of six seats in a mixed electorate two are reserved for non-Brahmans. Assume that no non-Brahman candidate has secured enough votes to be placed among the first six who have polled the largest number of votes and that the only non-Brahman candidates who have secured any votes are to be found somewhere near the bottom of the list. Under the rule just quote two of these non-Brahmans would be at once declared to be duly elected and the 5th and 6th candidates on the list who are not non-Brahmans would have to give place to them. Thus in the case of non-Brahmans the choice of the electorate is wholly set aside even though a majority of their own community voted against them. The question is whom would these two non-Brahmans represent. It is clear that they do not represent the majority of the electorate nor possibly even a majority of non-Brahmans. They have come in by an artificial rule based on no principle whatever. Happily the fears of the non-Brahmans in Madras turned out to be unfounded and we are informed that there never was a single occasion to put the rule into practice.

It is bad enough to have 28 members of this kind in a representative house of 98 members, but when the majority of members are elected in this manner and the ministry is formed from out of them, representative government becomes a farce.

'Sind Pact' Method

Another method of reservation of seats both for the majority and the minority has been suggested by the promoters of what is called the 'Sind Pact'. This method is thus described in clause 5 of the 'Pact':

> In order to make the system of joint electorates truly effective, there shall be one common electoral roll for each constituency and the election of Muslim and non-Muslim representatives should be held separately but on the same day, so that the whole electorate, Muslim and non-Muslim, shall have the right and opportunity to vote at both these elections separately, whereby the members so elected shall have been returned by the entire constituency and not only by the voters of their own communities.

The only merit claimed for this method is that the 'members so elected shall have been returned by the entire constituency and not only by the voters of their own communities'. For this purpose it would not be necessary to hold the elections separately as in a single election also the whole electorate—Muslim and non-Muslim—would have the right and opportunity to vote. The real object of the clause seems to be to avoid competition between the Hindu and Muslim candidates and thus secure to them reservation of seats according to their numbers. Apart from the fact that such competition is essential for the exercise by the elector of his free choice, the method proposed entirely shuts out all opportunity for a Hindu elector to vote for a Muslim candidate in preference to a candidate of his own community and *vice versa*.

It is obvious that the result of two separate ballots for each group of candidates can never be the same as that of a single ballot for both and that there will always be much greater chance at separate elections for the majority community to secure the return of their mandatories from among the minority community by concentrating their votes on them.

Both Methods Unsatisfactory

It will thus be seen that neither of the two methods discussed above is likely to give satisfactory results. The third and the only remaining method of which we are aware is that of separate communal electorates which we have already discussed. The doing away of communal electorates is intended to promote communal unity by making each community more or less dependent on the other at the time of the elections. But reservation for a majority community in a mixed electorate will take away much of the incentive for communal unity, as the majority community as a whole would under all circumstances be assured of its full quota without the help of the other communities. There is no doubt some advantage to be gained by individual candidates of either community having to canvass the other community as against their rivals of the same community but this small advantage will probably not be availed of in times of acute communal tension.

It is absurd to insist on reservation of seats for the majority and claim full responsible government at the same time. Responsible government is understood to mean a government in which the executive is responsible to the legislature and the legislature to the electorate. If the members of the executive with the majority behind them have all got in by reservation and not by the free choice of the electorate there is neither representation of the electorate nor any foundation for responsible government. Reservation of seats for a majority community gives to that community the statutory right to govern the country independently of the wishes of the electorate and is foreign to all conceptions of popular government. It will confine minorities within a ring-fence and leave them no scope for expansion.

Defects of Elections

We have based the foregoing observations on the principles generally applied to representative government. We are aware that those principles have in practice been found far from perfect and that serious objections have been raised in certain quarters against democratic government itself. We can hardly enter into these considerations in this Committee and must at this stage of our evolution accept the principles governing elections in most of the advanced countries of the world. We are also aware that the system of election we have recommended has sometimes failed to establish the rule of the majority, as in the case of the last British elections, which resulted in the return of an overwhelming majority of members who had only the support of a minority of electors. This we believe was mainly due to inequalities in voting strength and the wastage of votes on candidates who did not need them. The only remedy is proportional representation which for the reasons already mentioned we have refrained from recommending at present.

Facts and Figures

We have so far considered the question of reservation for majorities on principle but the strongest argument against such reservation is furnished by the facts as they are. We are indebted to Pandit Jawaharlal Nehru for the figures given in Appendices A and B which he has compiled with great industry from the reports of the last census relating to Bengal and the Punjab—the only two provinces in which the Muslims are in a majority. These figures conclusively show that there is no foundation in fact for the fears entertained by the Muslims in these two provinces, and indeed no occasion for any adventitious aid to secure to them the full benefit of their natural majority. The argument is that Mussalmans will not obtain adequate representation and the slight majority they have will be more than counter-balanced by their educational and economic backwardness in these provinces. The whole force of this argument, which is based on the total population of the two provinces, disappears when we examine in detail the figures relating to the administrative divisions and the districts composing them.

It appears from an analysis of the population figures of the Punjab and Bengal that Muslims can certainly have nothing to fear from a free electorate, without any reservation of seats, in these two provinces. It will be clear from the figures given in the appendices that in both the Punjab and Bengal the distribution of population is such that the Muslim majority in most of the geographical and administrative areas comprising these provinces is much greater than it appears when the whole province is taken as a unit. We find that there are natural areas of reservation for the different communities which ensure the representation of each community far more effectively than any artificial reservation can do.

The Punjab

Thus in the Punjab, we have a Muslim zone in the north and north-west of the province, where the Muslims are overwhelmingly strong and where no other community can encroach on their preserve. We find also a smaller area in the south, the Hindu zone, where the Hindus and Sikhs are equally strong. Between the two there is a third area where the Muslims are predominant, but not overwhelmingly so. This analysis leads us to the conclusion that Muslims are bound to capture over 47 per cent of the total seats in the Punjab from their special zone alone, whilst the Hindus and Sikhs will jointly capture nearly 30 per cent. The remaining 23 per cent of seats will lie in either a predominantly Muslim area or in districts where the Muslims are the strongest single community. Allowing for every contingency we cannot conceive of Muslims not capturing enough seats in this area to give them a clear majority in the provincial legislature.

We have discussed these population figures for each Punjab district in detail in our note attached (Appendix A). We may here however refer to some of these figures.

The population of the Punjab (British territory) at the last 1921 census was as follows:

Muslims	11,444,321	55.3%
Hindus	6,579,260	31.8%
Sikhs	2,294,207	11.1%
Others (mainly Christians)	367,236	1.8%
Total Punjab population	20,685,024	100.0%

There are 29 districts in all. We have divided these into four zones:

I. Fifteen districts in the overwhelmingly Muslim zone. The percentage of Muslims in one district is nearly 91; in nine districts it is between 80 and 90; in two districts it is 71 or over; and in three it is 63.3, 61.9 and 60.7. We have included the last three districts in this zone as, although the Muslim percentage is not so high as in the adjoining districts, it is very high compared to the Hindus and Sikhs combined. Thus in one (Sheikhupura) Muslims are 63.3%, Hindus 16.0% Sikhs are 15.9%; in Sialkot, Muslims are 61.9%, Hindus are 19.5% and Sikhs are 8.0%; in Lyallpur Muslims are 60.7%, Hindus are 18.1% and Sikhs are 16.4%.
It should be remembered that the non-Muslim minority in all these districts consists not of one group but of several communities Hindus, Sikhs, Christians and others.
If we give one member of the legislatures to every 1,00,000 popu-lation as we have suggested elsewhere, we find that 98 members will be returned from this Muslim zone alone. This amounts to 47.3 per cent of the total membership of the legislature.

II. There are two districts (Lahore and Gurdaspur) which might be called the predominantly Muslim zone. Here the Muslims are greater than Hindus and Sikhs combined—in Lahore they are 57.3% of the total—but they are not so many as in zone I. The number of members of the legislature for these two districts are 19½ or 9.4 per cent of the total membership.

III. There are three districts where no community is predominant but even here the Muslims are the strongest single community. The number of members of the legislature for these districts is 27½ that is, 13.3 per cent of the total.

IV. There are nine districts which might be called the overwhelmingly

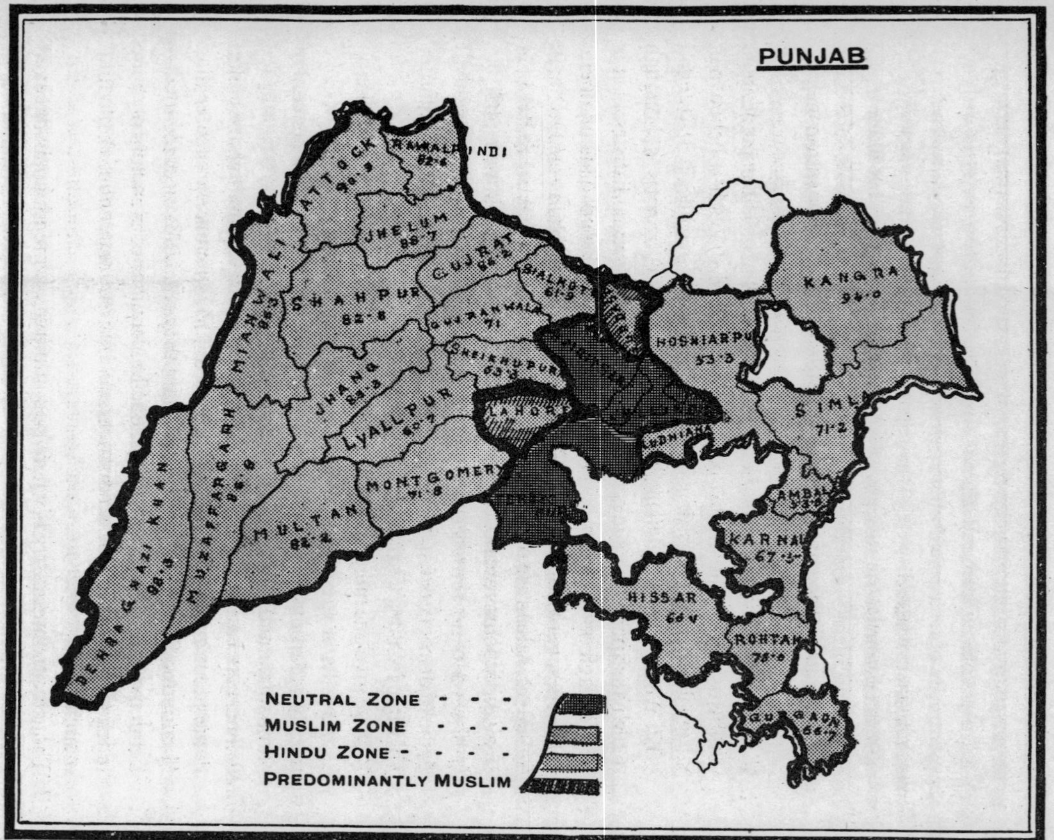
PUNJAB
ATTOCK 90.9
RAWALPINDI 82.6
JHELUM 88.7
GUJRAT 84.2
SIALKOT 61.9
SHAHPUR 82.8
GUJRANWALA 71
SHEIKHUPURA 63.3
JHANG 84.3
LYALLPUR 60.7
LAHORE
MONTGOMERY 71.8
MULTAN 82.4
MUZAFFARGARH 86.6
DERA GHAZI KHAN 88.9
HOSHIARPUR 53.3
LUDHIANA
KANGRA 94.0
SIMLA 71.2
KARNAL 67.5
HISSAR 66.V
ROHTAK 78.6
GURGAON 66.7
NEUTRAL ZONE - - -
MUSLIM ZONE - - -
HINDU ZONE - - - -
PREDOMINANTLY MUSLIM

Hindu-Sikh zone. The number of members for this zone is 61½ or 29.7 per cent of the total.

We thus see that Muslims are certain of 47.3 per cent seats; have a good chance of capturing the majority of at least 9.4 seats; and a fair chance of some seats out of the 13.3 per cent of group III. They are thus, humanly speaking, assured of a clear majority in the legislature.

Bengal

In Bengal the figures are even more illuminating. These are discussed in full detail in the separate note attached (see Appendix B). We give here only a brief summary. The population figures are:

Muslims	25,210,802	54.0%
Hindus	20,203,527	43.3%
Others (chiefly tribal religions and Christians)	1,281,207	2.7%
Total Bengal population (British territory)	46,695,536	100.0%

Here also we find definite zones as in the Punjab.

I. Overwhelmingly Muslim zone. There are 13 districts with 282 members of the legislature or over 60 per cent of the total.
II. Predominantly Muslim zone—two districts with 23 members or 5 per cent of the total.
III. Neutral or predominantly Hindu zone. Four districts with 42 members or 9 per cent of the total.
IV. Overwhelmingly Hindu zone. Nine districts with 118 members or 25 per cent of the total.

Thus in Bengal from the overwhelmingly Muslim zone alone, not taking into consideration the predominantly Muslim zone, Muslims are assured of over 60% seats in the legislature. The Hindu minority, although it is a very big minority, is highly likely to suffer in numbers in an open general election without reservation.

Bengal District Board Elections

This has recently been demonstrated in a remarkable manner by the figures of the last District Board elections in Bengal, printed in Appendix C.

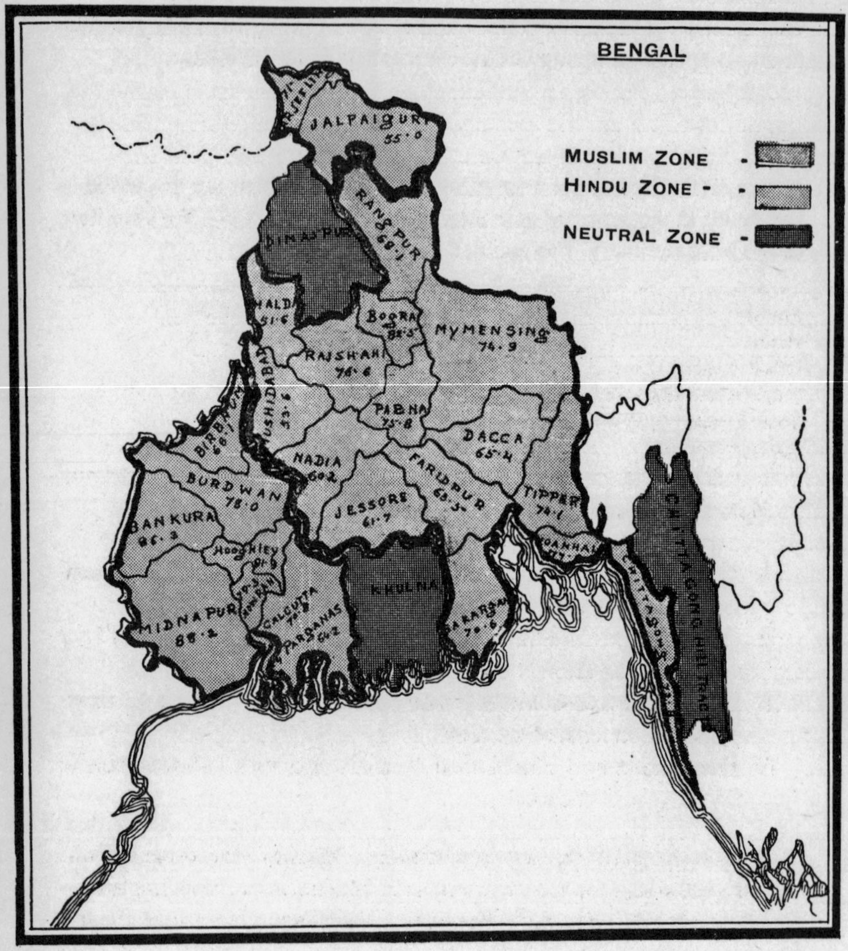
BENGAL
MUSLIM ZONE
HINDU ZONE
NEUTRAL ZONE
JALPAIGURI
55·0
RANGPUR
68·1
DINAJPUR
MALDA
51·6
BOGRA
MYMENSING
74·9
RAJSHAHI
76·6
MURSHIDABAD
53·6
PABNA
75·8
BIRBHUM
66·1
DACCA
65·4
NADIA
60·2
FARIDPUR
63·5
BURDWAN
78·0
JESSORE
61·7
TIPPERA
74·1
BANKURA
86·3
HOOGHLY
KHULNA
MIDNAPUR
88·2
CALCUTTA
PARGANAS
BAKARGANJ
CHITTAGONG
CHITTAGONG HILL TRACTS

The electorates for these boards are mixed Hindu and Muslim, but the electoral roll being based on a property or tax paying franchise does not maintain the population proportions of the two communities. We expect that the voting strength of the Muslims, who are economically weaker than Hindus, is much less than it would be with adult suffrage and yet we find that they made a clean sweep of the Hindu minority in three districts—Mymensingh, Chittagong and Jessore. In the first two of these not a single Hindu was elected though the Hindus are about 24 per cent of the population, and in the third only one Hindu managed to get in though the community forms 38.2 per cent of the population. As against this we find that Muslims, where they are in insignificant minorities of 3 and 4 per cent, have managed to send one to three representatives to the District Board. We have also very interesting examples of what happens when the two communities are found in about equal strength. The cases of Khulna and Dinajpur are in point. In the former the non-Muslims being 50 per cent of the population carried 11 seats as against 5 taken by Muslims who were 49.8 per cent. In the latter the Muslims being 49 per cent of the population carried 14 seats as against 4 of the Hindus who were over 44 per cent. Actual population is not a safe guide in the absence of exact figures showing the voting strength of the two communities, but we think it can safely be inferred that the Muslims in Bengal need no protection from all the non-Muslims put together. The case of Jessore is particularly interesting. As long as the Muslim majority did not take much interest in the local affairs of the district the Hindu minority had it all its own way. Once roused to action the Muslims not only swept the polls but for the first time in the history of their District Board gave it a Muslim chairman and a Muslim vice chairman, both members of the Bengal Council. We are informed that the last elections for the District Boards in Bengal have opened the eyes of both communities and that Muslim opinion is now veering round to mixed electorates. It is one of the tragedies of communal hostility that men shut their eyes to facts and fight against their own best interests. We commend a careful study of the figures we have given in Appendices A, B and C to those who are flooding the country with elaborate manifestos and memoranda in support of communal electorates for the Punjab and Bengal.

Economic and Educational Standards

We find therefore from an analysis of the actual figures that Muslim fears in the Punjab and Bengal are largely imaginary. These fears are based on the superior economic and educational standards of the Hindus and Sikhs.

We have seen that this superiority has not helped the Hindus of Bengal at the District Board elections and we are sure that the result of council elections will be even more strikingly in favour of Muslims. But there is no doubt that Muslims are backward both in education and in wealth, specially in Bengal, as compared to the other communities. There is also no doubt that the power of wealth is great in the modern State. It is so great indeed that it seldom troubles to contest seats in the legislature as it.can pull the strings from behind the scenes. Reservation of seats or separate electorates, or any other device of this kind, cannot materially reduce this power. So long as people think and act in terms of communalism, so long will they not face the real problem. And if they will not face it, they will not solve it.

We are not here called upon to advise on a new structure of society where the economic power is not concentrated in the hands of a few. We take it that the communal organizations which aggressively demand special rights and privileges for their respective communities are not desirous of attacking the basis of the existing structure. If this is admitted then all we can do is to provide safeguards and guarantees for education and economic advancement, specially for all backward groups and communities.

Parties in Free India

We are certain that as soon as India is free and can face her problems unhampered by alien authority and intervention, the minds of her people will turn to the vital problems of the day. How many questions that are likely to be considered by our future legislatures can be of a communal nature? There may possibly be a few now and then, but there can be no doubt that the vast majority of the questions before us will not be communal in the narrow sense. The result will be that parties will be formed in the country and in the legislature on entirely other grounds, chiefly economic we presume. We shall then find Hindus and Muslims and Sikhs in one party acting together and opposing another party which also consists of Hindus and Muslims and Sikhs. This is bound to happen if we once get going.

Hindu and Sikh Minorities

Looking at it purely from the Hindu point of view however, we can well imagine that a reservation of seats for the Muslim majorities in the Punjab and Bengal, may actually benefit the Hindus, and it may be Sikhs also, more than no reservation. The facts and figures we have stated demonstrate that the Muslim position in the Punjab and Bengal is so strong that in all likelihood they will gain in a joint electorate with no reservation more seats than their population warrants. Thus the Hindu and Sikh minorities may find their representation even reduced below their population ratio. This is a possible and indeed a likely contingency. But it is impossible to provide for such contingencies. The safest and most obvious course is to have an open election with such safeguards as we can devise.

Informal Conference

The considerations set out above were fully discussed at the informal conference to which reference has already been made and the following resolution was unanimously adopted, subject to a note by our colleague Sardar Mangal Singh on the second part of the resolution:[1]

> We are unanimously opposed to the reservation of seats in the legislatures either for majorities or minorities and we recommend that no such reservation should be provided for in the constitution. But if this recommendation is not accepted and an agreement can be arrived at only on a reservation of seats on the population basis we recommend that such reservation be made for majorities or minorities without any weightage and with a clear provision that it shall automatically cease at the expiry of ten years or earlier by the consent of the parties concerned.

The note of Sardar Mangal Singh runs as follows:

> I agree with the first part of the above proposition, namely that there shall be no reservation of seats either for majorities or minorities in the legislatures of the country. But I am very strongly opposed to the creation of statutory communal majorities by reservation of seats for majorities on population basis under all circumstances and for any time howsoever short it may be. If the agreement can only be reached by reservation of seats I will recommend that the case of the Sikhs be considered as that of an important minority and adequate and effective representation, far in excess of their numerical strength, be given to them in the Punjab on the basis adopted for Muslim minorities under the Lucknow Pact in Behar and other provinces. And I further suggest that special weightage be given to Sikhs for representation in the central legislature.

It will be seen that the first part of the resolution contains the actual recommendation of the informal conference and the second part deals with a contingency which can happen, if at all, only when that recommendation is rejected in favour of an agreement by all the parties concerned on reservation of seats on the population basis. There has not only been no such agreement among the members of this Committee but they have definitely expressed themselves in the first part of the resolution to be unanimously opposed to reservation. It is highly unlikely that the agreement referred to in the second part of the resolution will be reached in the All Parties Conference. But if by any chance such an agreement is arrived at, it would be binding on all those who join it and in that case all that the second part provides is that it should not be given effect to for more than ten years. We cannot be taken to have recommended what we have expressly opposed. But we recognize the value of a compromise between parties and communities however wrong it may be in principle, and if such a compromise is arrived at in spite of ourselves, we can do no more than try to limit its operation. This is exactly what we have done. As regards the special claim of the Muslims and Sikhs for greater representation than their population would justify, it is enough to say that in the view we have expressed above, no such claim is admissible on the part of any community however important it may consider itself to be.

We shall have to revert to the resolution of the informal conference in considering the question of reservation for minorities to which we now address ourselves.

Reservation for Minorities

Muslims in provinces other than the Punjab and Bengal are in small minorities and in some parts of India almost negligible, though in the total population of India the proportion is over 24 per cent.

Reservation for Muslim Minorities in Proportion to Population

After the resolution of the informal conference referred to above was passed it was pointed out to us that it would work great hardship on the Muslim minority which would in all probability be able to elect no more than 30 or 40 Muslims from the Punjab and Bengal, and perhaps one or two from the U.P. and Behar, to the central legislature of 500 members, and that there was little chance of any of the other provinces with less than 7 per cent of the population returning a single Muslim. The result, it was argued, would be that Muslims, who form nearly one fourth of the total population of British India, would have no more than one tenth of representation in the central legislature. The same reasoning, it was urged, applied to the legislatures of provinces where the Muslims are in small minorities. We recognize the force of this argument and it is here that we feel compelled by force of circumstances to introduce a temporary element of communalism in the electoral system of the country. We are therefore unable to adopt the resolution of the informal conference of the 7th July in its entirely as our recommendation. In provinces other than the Punjab and Bengal we must make an exception in favour of Muslim minorities by permitting reservation of seats, if so desired by them, in proportion to their population both in the central and the provincial legislatures. The retention of communal representation to this extent for some time to come is in our opinion a necessary evil. It will be seen that by making this concession in favour of Muslim minorities we are not introducing the anomalies arising out of reservation for majorities. A minority must remain a minority whether any seats are reserved for it or not and cannot dominate the majority.

Weightage not Permissible

Representation in excess of their proportion in the population fixed for Muslims in a number of provinces under the Lucknow pact, as well as the Montagu-Chelmsford reforms, will disappear under our scheme. Such representation is only possible in separate electorates and has no place in joint or mixed electorates. It is of course not physically impossible to reserve a larger proportion of seats for Muslim minorities than their population would justify but, apart from the obvious injustice of such a course not only to the majorities but to the other minorities as well, it will in our opinion be harmful to the development of Muslims themselves on national lines. We have allowed them their full share on the population basis by reservation and anything over and above that share they must win by their own effort. We do not propose to impose any restrictions on their right to contest a larger number of seats than those reserved for them. The main consideration which has guided us in accepting reservation for their minority is that we are not thereby putting it in a ring-fence beyond which it cannot advance however competent it may be to do so. It is in our opinion more important to secure a free and open field for the expansion of the political activities of all communities large or small than to reserve a maximum number of seats for them even in excess of their numbers. Such reservation will never bring them in open competition with any community other than their own and the inevitable result will be stagnation. It is true that a Muslim candidate will have to canvass non-Muslim votes to defeat his Muslim rival but this is not calculated to advance the Muslim on national lines. It will always be a question of whether Muslim A is better than Muslim B without regard to the fact that non-Muslim C is better or worse than both.

Muslims cannot reasonably claim reservation of seats beyond their strict proportion to population along with the right to contest additional seats, and the question for them to consider is which of the two is likely to be of greater advantage to them. We have no doubt that when they carefully weigh the pros and cons of the reservation of a larger number of seats than they are entitled to on the population basis *without* the right to exceed that number, against the pros and cons of reservation in proportion to their population *with* the right to contest as many more seats as they like, they will find that the latter is by far the better choice. As we have already pointed out, reservation to the fullest extent deprives mixed electorates in a considerable measure of their utility in promoting national unity. Whatever inducement a Muslim candidate may have to approach the non-Muslim voter to defeat his Muslim rival, so far as his community as a whole is concerned, it will have its full quota assured to it with or without the help of the non-Muslim voters, and at times of extreme communal tension it will be easy both for Muslims and non-Muslims to run their elections quite independently of each other without either losing a single seat. It is only by maintaining the interdependence of the two communities that we can hope to minimize their differences.

Muslims in U.P.

Having regard to the actual conditions prevailing in the U.P., where the Muslim minority is the largest, we are convinced that the Muslims stand to gain more seats under our scheme than the number fixed for them under the present system. In several urban areas in the U.P. they are in majorities and in others they have strong and influential minorities. They may perhaps lose a few seats in some other provinces but the net result of a general election in the country as a whole is likely to be fairly satisfactory to all.

Reservation for Muslims in the Central Legislature

So far as the Muslim demand is concerned it only remains for us to deal with that part of it which relates to reservation of one third of the total number of seats in the central legislature for Muslims. This point was not directly raised or discussed at the informal conference, but we think that it is concluded by the general recommendations we have made in regard to reservation of seats. The principle we have adopted is that wherever such reservation has to be made for the Muslim minority it must be in strict proportion to its population. The Muslims are a little less than one fourth of the total population of British India and they cannot be allowed reservation over and above that proportion in the central legislature. It must be remembered that they have the right to contest additional seats both for the central and provincial legislatures in provinces other than the Punjab and Bengal, and that in the two last mentioned provinces their right is unfettered to contest any number of seats they like for both legislatures. In the case of provincial legislatures we have substituted this right for the present weightage they enjoy. In the central legislature the Muslims do not at present enjoy any definite weightage and their numbers to be returned by the provinces are fixed on a more or less arbitrary basis. The actual number of the Muslim members falls short of one third of the total strength of the Assembly. There is thus no foundation for the demand even in existing conditions. A little reflection will show that it is far better to have a free hand than to be tied down to the difference between $^1/_3$ and $^1/_4$. But as we have already observed we cannot depart from the principle we have accepted for the Muslim minorities in the provincial legislature. Besides the question of principle there are practical difficulties in the way. How are we to secure this one third reservation in the central legislature without restricting the Punjab and Bengal majorities to definite numbers of members and allowing weightage in the other provinces all round? And on what principle is the excess in the number of members in the provinces to be allotted to each province? We have given our best consideration to the matter but we regret we are unable to recommend reservation of one third of the total number of seats for Muslims in the central legislature.

Recommendation

For these reasons we recommend reservation of seats, when demanded, for Muslim minorities both in the central and provincial legislatures in strict proportion to their population, with the right to contest additional seats for a fixed period of ten years. We would add, however, that our colleague Mr. Shuaib Qureshi does not agree with some of the arguments and conclusions given above. He is of opinion that the resolution of the informal conference, referred to above, should be adopted in its entirety.

He further desires that one third of the seats in the central legislature should be reserved for Muslims.

Non-Muslim Minorities in N.W.F. and Baluchistan

As regards non-Muslim minorities the only provinces which deserve consideration are the N.W.F. and Baluchistan where they are in much the same position as the Muslim minorities in Madras and the C.P. We recommend that the same concession be made to them as to the Muslims in provinces other than the Punjab and Bengal.

Other non-Muslim Minorities

Turning to the other non-Muslim minorities we find that there is no such sharp cleavage between them and the majorities among whom they live as there unfortunately is between Hindus and Muslims. We do not think that any protection by way of reservation is either necessary or desirable in their case. They will realize that we are recommending such protection to Muslim minorities under very special circumstances and for a limited period only. The latter have sooner or later to stand on their own legs. We shall indeed be glad if they will make up their minds to do without reservation from the beginning.

There is no analogy between the Muslim and non-Muslim minorities in India. The latter are nowhere when the total population of India is considered. Leaving out the case of Buddhists, who are to be found chiefly in Burma and are in a majority there, the percentage of the population of other non-Muslim minorities to the total population of India is as follows:

Christians	1.2%
Sikhs	1.0%
Jains	.2%
Others (besides tribal religions in hill tracts)	.2%

It will thus appear that so far as the central legislature is concerned the reservation of seats for non-Muslim minorities on a population basis will hardly help them to any appreciable extent and that there is no occasion to reserve seats for minorities, other than those in the N.W.F. Province and Baluchistan, even in the provincial legislature. Any attempt to do so will only cause confusion and will in our opinion be a very doubtful advantage to the communities concerned.

We have not mentioned the Hindu minorities in the Punjab and Bengal as by no stretch of the imagination 32 and 45 per cent of the population can be regarded as small minorities.

SIKHS

Among the non-Muslim minorities the Sikhs deserve special consideration. They are concentrated in the Punjab and the position they occupy in that province is very similar to that of the Muslims in the U.P. The latter being about 15% of the population are in fact more numerous in the U.P. than the Sikhs in the Punjab where they are only 11%. Under the existing system they have their separate electorate and are given considerable weightage. We recognize that Sikhs are a distinct and important minority which cannot be ignored and we have, all along, been giving our best consideration to the point of view of the Sikhs as expressed by our colleague Sardar Mangal Singh. It must be said to their credit that they have shown an admirable spirit of self-sacrifice by their decision to give up these communal advantages in the general interest of the country. Throughout the communal controversies that have raged round the question of representation in the legislature during recent years they have taken their stand on joint electorates with no reservation for any community. Our colleague Sardar Mangal Singh has drawn attention to the fact that the Sikhs do not form the majority of the total population of any district in the Punjab, and that the strongest position they occupy is in Ludhiana district where they are the strongest single community. Even in this district they are only 41.5% and are not in a majority. In every other district they are outnumbered either by Muslims or Hindus, and usually by both. It is obvious that situated as the Sikhs are in the Punjab . . . subject to all the disadvantages of a minority in a joint mixed electorate based on the wide adult suffrage we have recommended. In these circumstances they have in the Punjab at least as strong a case for reservation both in the provincial and central legislatures as the Muslims have in the U.P. There is however a third and a very potent factor to be taken into account and that is the presence of the strong Hindu minority side by side with the Muslim majority and the Sikh minority. It is this circumstance in the Punjab which, apart from general considerations has so far defied all attempts at a satisfactory adjustment on the basis of reservation for any community. The Punjab problem has assumed an all India importance and we cannot look at it as an isolated case arising in a single province. The only effective way of avoiding complications and giving full play to the forces of nationalism is to eradicate the virus of communalism from the body politic of the Punjab. Our colleague, Sardar Mangal Singh, who has discussed the matter very fully and frankly with us shares our difficulty. We believe that nothing is farther from the wishes of the Sikh League than to introduce any complications directly or indirectly in the solution of the communal problem. They could, if they had insisted on any special advantage, have caused endless difficulties in the adoption of a uniform rule of representation. They fully realized this and voluntarily gave up all their claims with the sole object, we are assured, of preventing an impasse. We appreciate this spirit and congratulate them on their patriotic resolve.

The Only Alternative

The only alternative to the proposal we have made is to adopt the recommendation of the informal conference and have no reservation for any minorities, including Muslims, in any legislature. But this will cause considerable dissatisfaction to Muslims without conferring any special benefit on non-Muslims. It must be remembered that besides reservation by means of communal electorates the Muslims at present enjoy considerable weightage in every province. We are offering them the right to contest additional seats in lieu of this weightage and we cannot very well do away with reservation in their case. We see no hardship in this to non-Muslim majorities or minorities. Endless complications will arise if we recommend reservation for all minorities. Besides the existing well defined minorities such as Christians, Parsis, Jews, fresh groups from among the Hindu castes and sub-castes will claim the right and it will be a perpetual source of trouble.

The communal question is essentially a Hindu-Muslim question and must be settled on that basis. We shall indeed be doing poor service if in our attempt to settle it we let communalism loose on the country to swallow up communities and sub-communities most of whom have not even dreamt of it.

Non-Brahmans

There remain two important communities included in the Hindu majority—the non-Brahmans and the depressed classes. The sharp division between Brahman and non-Brahman is to be met with only in the south and is unknown in other parts of India. Where the non-Brahmans as such are found, they are either an overwhelming majority as in Madras or a very strong minority as in parts of Bombay. They need no protection in the matter of representation in the legislatures as has been established by the elections held in recent times. Their grievances against Brahmans are all traceable to the ascendency gained by the latter in the political and social life of the country. This is the natural result of their intellectual ascendency which is now seriously threatened by the rapid advance of non-Brahmans.

'Depressed' Classes

The problem of the 'depressed' or 'suppressed' classes has come to the front in recent years and their present condition is put forward as an argument against the political advancement of India. We are certainly of opinion that the Hindus are chiefly responsible for this suppression of a large class, but we are equally clear that the solicitude for this class which the British government has endeavoured to show has its basis on reasons other than humanity or love for this class. This solicitude is of very recent growth. As the national movement has grown in the country, so has the political value of the 'depressed' classes grown in the eyes of the government. It is only since 1917 that their numbers have been separately given in the official reports on education and reference has been made to the educational facilities offered to them. The solicitude of government has so far brought little relief to these classes. It has resulted in giving them some nominated seats in the legislatures and some minor contributions for special schools.

Far more serious and effective attempts have been made by non-official Indian agencies to raise these classes. The Christian missions have also helped in this task. The Congress made the abolition of untouchability one of its principal planks in 1920 and, as is well known, Mahatma Gandhi has thrown himself with all his great powers and energy into the movement. Other political organizations, and we are glad to find even communal organizations, have with equal emphasis declared against untouchability. The practical work done and the considerable results achieved already make it quite clear that these declarations were not mere pious wishes. We realize that there are still conservative elements in the country which are strong enough to put obstacles in the way and retard the progress of the movement. But we are convinced that untouchability is doomed.

In our suggestions for the constitution we have not made any special provision for the representation of the 'depressed' classes in the legislatures. This could only be done by way of special electorates or by nomination. We have dealt fully in another place with the question of special electorates and reservation of seats. We are not prepared to extend this unsound and harmful principle if we can help it, nor do we think that we will do any good to these classes by ensuring some seats for them in this way. We are still more opposed to nomination. This can only result, as it has resulted, in the government of the day nominating some one who will support it through thick and thin, and will not represent anybody.

We feel strongly however that the 'depressed' classes must be abolished or rather that they should be raised socially and economically so that they may take their proper place in the community. The only effective way to do this is to give them educational and other facilities for this advance and to remove all obstacles in the way of this advance. Some of the articles in the Declaration of Rights, which we have recommended, will go a long way to remove the disabilities from which these classes suffer and will give them an opportunity to go ahead. The proposal that we should have adult suffrage will also automatically raise their level and increase their political power. Finally, we have strongly recommended that the education of all backward classes should be a special concern of the state. If all these recommendations are acted upon we are convinced that the 'depressed' classes will rapidly disappear and will be replaced by a self-reliant and progressive group, co-operating with other groups in the welfare of the entire community.

APPENDIX A

AN ANALYSIS OF THE POPULATION FIGURES OF THE PUNJAB ACCORDING TO RELIGION

Being a note on the population figures of the Punjab with special reference to the probable extent of the representation of various religious groups in the legislature

This note is based on the following assumptions:

1. That there is ordinary territorial representation with what are called joint or mixed electorates and without any reservation of seats.
2. That there is adult franchise, or at any rate some franchise which ensures that the numbers of electors of the various communities bear the same ratio to each other as the population figures of those communities.

The figures and calculations in these notes are based entirely on the 1921 census. It may be mentioned however that the ratio of increase of Muslims in the Punjab is slightly greater than that of Hindus. This according to the census report is not due now to conversions but to certain social causes—widow remarriage and a higher marriage age amongst the Muslims. Infantile mortality is greater amongst the Hindus owing to early marriages. Hence it is probable that the Muslim population in the Punjab today is slightly greater proportionately than is evidenced by the 1921 census figures. The next census may show this increase. This means that the calculations in these notes are conservative figures so far as the Muslims are concerned, and the actuality is more favourable to them.

It is not possible to arrive at any accurate conclusion regarding representation in legislatures on population figures from a census report. A great deal must depend on the grouping of constituencies. It is also by no means certain, and it certainly is most undesirable, that in a joint electorate a Hindu should always vote for a Hindu, and a Muslim for a Muslim. But it is not possible to make allowances for this in these calculations. As the question is being considered in its communal aspect we must presume that as a general rule votes will be cast on communal lines. The constituencies not having been formed the only alternative is to examine the figures for the individual districts. It is likely that either a whole district or a part of it will form a single constituency.

The population of the Punjab (excluding Indian States) in 1921 was 2,06,85,024. This was made up as follows:

Muslims	1,14,44,321	55.3%
Hindus	65,79,260	31.8%
Sikhs	22,94,207	11.1%
Others (mainly Christians)	3,67,236	1.8%
	2,06,85,024	100.0%

Thus the Muslims are in a clear but not a great majority over all others combined. If the distribution of population is more closely examined it will be seen that the Muslims are in an even stronger position than the all Punjab figures might indicate. This is due to the fact that the Hindus and Sikhs are present in large numbers in the southern part of the province—Ambala and Jullundur divisions. Muslims are in a minority in these two divisions but they make up for it by increasing their majorities elsewhere.

The Punjab can be divided roughly into three natural belts or areas (1) the predominantly Muslim area (2) the neutral area but with Muslim majority and (3) the Hindu-Sikh area. If we take the existing divisions as corresponding approximately to these areas we have the following three belts:

I. Rawalpindi and Multan divisions forming the Muslim zone with Muslims in very great majorities (86.9% and 76.9% respectively).
II. Lahore division forming the neutral zone, but Muslims in a majority (57.0%) over all others combined.
III. Ambala and Jullundur divisions forming the Hindu-Sikh zone. Muslims are in a minority (26.3% and 32.8%) respectively.

We can form some rough idea of the representation in the legislature on the basis of these communal zones. Allowing one member for every hundred thousand of population we have:

		Population in thousands	*Members of legislatures*	
Punjab.		20,685	207	
I.	Rawalpindi division	3,461	35	77
	Multan division	4,218	42	
II.	Lahore division	4,997	50	50
III.	Ambala division	3,827	38	80
	Jullundur division	4,182	42	
				207

We may presume that the Muslims will capture all the seats in the Muslim zone and Hindu-Sikhs all the seats in the Hindu-Sikh zone. In the Lahore division there may be a division of the spoils. This of course cannot and should not happen in its entirety. It is not desirable that each division should be represented by one community only. But in making a rough calculation one may presume this much—the seats gained by the Muslims in the Hindu-Sikh area will probably be counter-balanced by the seats gained by the Hindu-Sikhs in the Muslim area. As a matter of fact there is more chance of the Muslims gaining a seat in the Hindu-Sikh area than the reverse, as the Muslim majorities in Rawalpindi and Multan divisions are tremendous (86.0% and 76.9%).

Thus we arrive at the conclusion that the Muslims are bound to get 77 seats in their zone, and the Hindu-Sikhs combined 80 seats in their zone. The third zone—Lahore division—will probably be divided between the two, but the division is likely to be very much in favour of the Muslims. They are 57.0% of the population, the Hindus being 20.7% and the Sikhs 16.2%. Christians, etc., amount to 6.1% but they may be left out of consideration here as presumably they have no special affiliations to the major communities and can certainly not be considered as being anti-Muslim or as belonging to the Hindu-Sikh *bloc*. Hindus and Sikhs together amount to 36.9% as against the 57.0% of the Muslims. The Muslims are thus more than one and a half times stronger than the Hindu-Sikh group. The difference is considerable and the Muslim strength must make itself felt in an election. The Muslim majority in this division should ordinarily gain more seats than it is entitled to on basis of population. But even if it got seats exactly in proportion to its population in the division, it would have 29 seats. This added to the 77 seats in the Muslim belt gives the figure 106 which gives a small but clear majority in the legislature of 207, over all other communities and groups combined. The majority will really be much greater over the Hindu-Sikh *bloc* as the 'others' may also be in the minority.

All this proceeds on the basis that Hindu and Sikh interests are identical and the two groups hang together on all occasions. This of course is not a justifiable presumption and it is more than likely that they may not always act together. In such a contingency each community's hopeless minority in the face of the solid Muslim majority will become even more obvious.

As the Lahore division is likely to be the critical one, it may be examined in greater detail. Out of the 6 districts in this division three districts—Sialkot, Gujranwala and Sheikhupura—have very substantial Muslim majorities. And as 'others' (Christians, etc.) are present in appreciable numbers in these districts the Muslim majorities *vis-a-vis* the Hindu-Sikh *bloc* become even greater and are really overwhelming.

The figures are:

Sialkot district

Muslims	61.9%	9½ seats
Hindus	19.5%	
Sikhs	8.0%	
Others	10.5%	

The Hindu-Sikh *bloc* totals 27.5% as against the 61.9% of the Muslims. The latter thus are considerably more than double the number of the Hindus and Sikhs combined.

Gujranwala district

Muslims	71.0%	6¼ seats
Hindus	15.8%	
Sikhs	8.2%	
Others	5.1%	

The Hindu-Sikh *bloc* totals 24.0% as against the 71.0% of the Muslims. The latter are thus nearly three times the number of Hindus and Sikhs combined.

Sheikhupura district		
Muslims	63.3%	5¼ seats
Hindus	16.0%	
Sikhs	15.9%	
Others	4.8%	

The Hindu-Sikh *bloc* totals 31.9% as against the 63.3% of the Muslims. The latter are thus just double the number of the Hindus and Sikhs combined.

In these three districts the Muslims are in an impregnable position. Indeed they really form part of the Muslim zone and should be considered along with it. These districts will be entitled to send 21 members to the legislature. These can be added to 77 members from the Muslim zone giving the total 98.

In the other districts of Lahore division the position is as follows:

Lahore district		
Muslims	57.3%	11 seats
Hindus	21.5%	
Sikhs	15.9%	
Others	5.3%	

Here the Hindu-Sikh *bloc* totals 37.4% as against the 57.3% of the Muslims. The Muslim majority is not so great as in the northern districts but it is substantial. The Muslims greatly outnumber the Hindus and Sikhs, being over one and a half times their number.

Amritsar district		
Muslims	45.6%	9 seats
Hindus	21.6%	
Sikhs	30.9%	
Others	1.8%	

In this district the Hindus and Sikhs combined amount to 52.5% and are in a fair majority over the 45.6% Muslims.

Gurdaspur district		
Muslims	49.6%	8½ seats
Hindus	26.0%	
Sikhs	16.2%	
Others	8.2%	

Here the Muslims outnumber the Hindus and Sikhs combined—49.6% against 42.2—but the majority is not great. The position in Amritsar district is reversed. There are a fair number of 'others' here.

Thus in these three districts, the Muslim position is strong in Lahore, fair in Gurdaspur and weak in Amritsar. But even in the last mentioned place the Muslims are by far the strongest single community.

It is highly likely that Muslims will capture some seats in these districts, specially in Lahore.

The Lahore division will thus be largely represented by Muslims and this representation added to that from the Muslim zone in the north and west ought to give them a clear majority.

This question can be considered from another point of view. Instead of looking at the divisions as a whole the individual districts may be taken. This will probably give a more accurate idea of the result.

There are 29 districts in the Punjab. These may be divided into four groups (1) overwhelmingly Muslim districts where the Muslim position is impregnable: (2) predominantly Muslim districts, where there is a Muslim majority but not so great as in (1); (3) districts where there is no special predominance of any community; and (4) overwhelmingly or predominantly Hindu-Sikh districts.

I. *Overwhelmingly Muslim districts*

		Percentage of Muslims given after districts	No. of members in legislatures
1.	Gujrat	86.2	8
2.	Shahpur	82.8	7
3.	Jhelum	88.7	5
4.	Rawalpindi	82.6	6
5.	Attock	90.9	5
6.	Mianwali	86.3	4
7.	Montgomery	71.8	7
8.	Lyallpur	60.7	10
9.	Jhang	83.3	6
10.	Multan	82.2	9
11.	Muzaffargarh	86.8	5½

12.	Dera Ghazi Khan	88.3	5
13.	Sialkot	61.9	9½
14.	Gujranwala	71.0	6
15.	Sheikhupura	63.3	5
			98

II. *Predominantly Muslim districts*

1.	Lahore	H.	21.5	
		M.	57.3	11
		S.	15.9	
		O.	5.3	
2.	Gurdaspur	H.	26.0	
		M.	49.6	8½
		S.	16.2	
		O.	8.2	
				19½

III. *Districts with no special predominance of any community*

1.	Jullundur	H.	29.4	
		S.	25.1	8
		M.	44.5	
		O.	1.0	
2.	Ferozepur	H.	27.6	
		S.	27.6	11
		M.	43.9	
		O.	.9	
3.	Amritsar	H.	21.6	
		S.	30.9	
		M.	45.6	9
		O.	1.8	
				28

Even in these three districts the strongest single community is the Muslim.

IV. *Overwhelmingly or predominantly Hindu-Sikh districts*

1.	Hissar	H.	66.1	8
2.	Rohtak	H.	78.0	8
3.	Gurgaon	H.	66.7	7
4.	Karnal	H.	67.5	8
5.	Ambala	H.	53.8	7
6.	Simla	H.	71.2	½
7.	Kangra	H.	94.0	8

8.	Hoshiarpur	H.	53.3	9
9.	Ludhiana	H.	23.6	
		S.	41.5	6
		M.	34.0	
		O.	00.9	
				61½

According to this the Muslims get from their special zone of 15 districts where they are impregnable — 98

The Hindus similarly get from their zone — 61½

Two districts predominantly Muslim return — 19½

Three districts more or less neutral, but Muslims strongest single community in each — 28

Total — 207

104 seats give an absolute majority in the legislature.

The result of the analysis of the figures for the districts leads us to the following conclusions:

1.	From the Muslim zone alone, where the Muslim position is unassailable, the Muslims get 98 seats or	47.3 of the total seats
2.	From the Hindu Sikh belt where the Hindu-Sikh position is very strong the Hindus and Sikhs get 61½ seats or	29.8 -do-
3.	In two districts where Muslims are predominant there are 19½ seats or	9.4 -do-
4.	In 3 districts the strength of the various communities is more or less evenly balanced but Muslims are the strongest single community in each, total 28 seats or	13.5 of the total seats
		100.0

It is exceedingly likely that from group II above, which is predominantly Muslim, the Muslims will get at least 10 out of the 19½ seats. This added to their seats from their particular zone gives them 108 seats which is a clear majority in the legislature. In group III above the Muslims should also get some seats as they are the strongest single community. They might safely count on 12 out of the 28. This raises the Muslim number in the legislature to 120 out of 207 or 58% if the total. Thus on a conservative estimate Muslims are highly likely to have 58% of the seats in the legislature.

PUNJAB (BRITISH TERRITORY)

Detailed population figures

Punjab		
Total population	2,06,85,024	100.0 per cent
Muslims	1,14,44,321	55.3 "
Hindus	65,79,260	31.8 "
Sikhs	22,94,207	11.1 "
Others (mainly Christians)	3,67,236	1.8 "

PUNJAB DIVISIONS

(Population figures in thousands)

Ambala Division	Populations	Percentage	No. of members in legislatures 1 for 100,000
Total	3,827	100	
H.	2,556	66.6	
M.	1,006	26.3	38
S.	158	4.2	
O.	106	2.8	

Jullundur Division			
Total	4128	100	
H.	1893	45.0	
M.	1370	32.8	42
S.	880	21.0	
O.	40	00.9	

Lahore Division			
Total	4997	100	
H.	1033	20.7	
M.	2849	57.0	50
S.	813	16.2	
O.	303	6.1	

Rawalpindi Division

Total	3461	100	35
H.	296	8.5	
M.	2973	86.0	
S.	153	4.4	
O.	38	1.1	

Multan Division

Total	4218	100	42
H.	602	14.3	
M.	3246	76.9	
S.	290	6.9	
O.	80	1.9	

Note: H = Hindu M = Muslim S = Sikh O = Others

PUNJAB DISTRICTS

I. *Overwhelmingly Muslim Districts*

District	Population in Thousands		Percentage	No. of members in legislature
1. Gujrat	T.	824	100	8.2
	H.	59	7.2	
	M.	710	86.2	
	S.	49	6.0	
	O.	6	.7	
2. Shahpur	T.	720	100	7.2
	H.	79	11	
	M.	596	82.8	
	S.	30	4.2	
	O.	15	2.1	
3. Jhelum	T.	477	100	4.8
	H.	33	6.9	
	M.	423	88.7	
	S.	19	4.0	
	O.	2	.4	
4. Rawalpindi	T.	569	100	5.7
	H.	55	9.7	
	M.	470	82.6	
	S.	32	5.6	
	O.	12	2.1	
5. Attock	T.	512	100	5.1
	H.	25.5	5.0	
	M.	465.5	90.9	
	S.	20	3.9	
	O.	1	.2	

District		Number	Per cent	
6. Mianwali	T.	358	100	3.6
	H.	45	12.6	
	M.	309	86.3	
	S.	3	.8	
	O.	1	.3	
7. Montgomery	T.	714	100	7.1
	H.	92	12.9	
	M.	513	71.8	
	S.	96	13.4	
	O.	13	1.8	
8. Lyallpur	T.	980	100	9.8
	H.	177	18.1	
	M.	595	60.7	
	S.	161	16.4	
	O.	47	4.8	
9. Jhang	T.	570	100	5.7
	H.	84	14.7	
	M.	475	83.3	
	S.	9	1.6	
	O.	2	.4	
10. Multan	T.	890	100	8.9
	H.	129	14.5	
	M.	732	82.2	
	S.	18	2.0	
	O.	11	1.2	
11. Muzaffargarh	T.	568	100	5.7
	H.	66	1.6	
	M.	493	86.8	
	S.	5	.9	
	O.	4	.7	
12. Dera Ghazi Khan (including Biloch tract)	T.	496	100	5.0
	H.	54	10.9	
	M.	438	88.3	
	S.	1	00.2	
	O.	3	00.6	
13. Sialkot	T.	938	100	9.4
	H.	183	19.5	
	M.	581	61.9	
	S.	75	8.0	
	O.	99	10.5	
14. Gujranwala	T.	623	100	6.2
	H.	98	15.8	
	M.	443	71	
	S.	51	8.2	
	O.	31	5.1	

15.	Sheikhupura	T.	523	100	
		H.	84	16.0	
		M.	331	63.3	5.2
		S.	83	15.9	
		O.	25	4.8	
15	Districts				97.6

II. *Predominantly Muslims Districts*

(Where Muslims are greater than Hindus and Sikhs combined but are not so many as in I above.)

1.	Lahore	T.	1,131	100	
		H.	243	21.5	
		M.	648	57.3	11.3
		S.	180	15.9	
		O.	60	5.3	
2.	Gurdaspur	T.	852	100	
		H.	222	26.0	
		M.	423	49.6	8.5
		S.	137.5	16.2	
		O.	69.5	8.2	
2	Districts				19.8

III. *Districts in which there is no special predominance of any community but Muslim community strongest single group*

1.	Jullundur	T.	822.5	100	
		H.	242	29.4	
		M.	366.5	44.5	8.2
		S.	206	25.1	
		O.	8	1.0	
2.	Ferozepur	T.	1098	100	
		H.	303	27.6	
		M.	482	43.9	11
		S.	303	27.6	
			O.	10	.9
3.	Amritsar	T.	929	100	
		H.	201	21.6	
		M.	424	45.6	9.3
		S.	287	30.9	
		O.	17	1.8	
3	Districts				28.5

IV. *Overwhelmingly or predominantly Hindu-Sikh Districts*

1.	Hissar	T.	817	100	
		H.	540	66.1	
		M.	216	26.4	8.2
		S.	46	5.6	
		O.	15	1.8	

2.	Rohtak	T.	772	100	
		H.	602	78.0	
		M.	125	16.2	7.7
		S.	1	.1	
		O.	44	5.7	
3.	Gurgaon	T.	682	100	
		H.	455	66.7	
		M.	217	31.8	6.8
		S.	1	.1	
		O.	9	1.3	
4.	Karnal	T.	829	100	
		H.	560	67.5	
		M.	236	28.5	8.3
		S.	12	1.4	
		O.	21	2.6	
5.	Ambala	T.	682	100	
		H.	367	53.8	
		M.	206	30.2	6.8
		S.	98	14.4	
		O.	11	1.6	
6.	Simla	T.	45	100	
		H.	32	71.2	
		M.	7	15.5	0.4
		S.	1	2.2	
		O.	5	11.1	
7.	Kangra	T.	766	100	
		H.	722.3	94.0	
		M.	38.3	5.0	7.7
		S.	2	.3	
		O.	3.4	.7	
8.	Hoshiarpur	T.	927	100	
		H.	494	53.3	
		M.	289	31.2	9.3
		S.	133	14.3	
		O.	11	1.2	
9.	Ludhiana	T.	568	100	
		H.	134	23.6	
		M.	193	34.0	5.7
		S.	236	41.5	
		O.	5	.9	
9	Districts				60.9

These figures demonstrate that quite apart from any artificial reservation of seats there is a natural reservation in more than three-fourths of the Punjab. In less than one-fourth there is some chance of free play. The distribution of population favours the majority community, Muslims, considerably.

Appendix II

Report of the Working Group on 'Empowering the Minorities' constituted by the Planning Commission in the context of formulation of the Tenth Five Year Plan (2002-2007) 10 May 2001

CHAPTER I

BACKGROUND

The Central Government notified Muslims, Christians, Sikhs, Buddhists and Parsis as religious minorities for the purpose of the National Commission for Minorities Act, 1992. These communities constitute about 17% of the country's total population numbering about 14.5 crore as per the 1991 census. Community-wise population is estimated as Muslims—12%, Christians—2.3%, Sikhs—2%, Buddhists—0.77% of the population of country while the Parsis are about 1.0 lakh in number. 41 Minority Concentration Districts (MCDs) spanning 11 States have been identified based on significant minority population.

1.2 India has the third largest Muslim population next only to Indonesia and Pakistan. Muslims constitute a majority in the Union Territory of

*In December 2000, the Planning Commission constituted a Working Group on 'Empowering the Minorities' under the Chairmanship of Prof. Mushirul Hasan. The Working Group in its first meeting held on 30 January 2001 decided to constitute Sub-Groups in order to examine the issues in detail and provide necessary inputs for the report of the Working Group. This edited version is based on their findings and recommendations.

Lakshadweep (94.31%) and in Jammu & Kashmir (64%). In three other States their population is much above the national level average, viz., Assam (28.43%), West Bengal (23.61%) and Kerala (23.32%). The States having the sizeable Muslim population are Uttar Pradesh (2.50 crore), West Bengal (1.80 crore) and Bihar (1.30 crore). The total Muslim population of the country is approximately 11 crore. . . .

ECONOMIC STATUS

1.8 An analysis has been carried out by Prof. Abusaleh Shariff, Principal Economist, National Council of Applied Economic Research (NCAER), on the relative position in economic, educational and health areas according to poverty line classification between the majority community, the SCs, STs and the Muslims. The study has been carried out on the basis of the survey of 33,000 nationally representative rural sample on household income and a range of human development parameters (comparative data is given in Table II.1). The study reveals that:

(i) SC/ST (including Buddhists in the context of the minorities) are the most poverty-stricken group and the Muslims are next only to them compared with all India average.

Table II.1: Comparison of various Parameters among Different Groups

	STs	SCs	Hindus	Muslims	All
Household Income (Rs.)	19,556.0	17,465.0	25,713.0	22,807.0	25,653.0
Per Capita Income (Rs.)	3,504.0	3,237.0	4,514.0	3,678.0	4,485.0
Work Male	51.6.0	52.8	52.3	48.0	51.9
Participation Ratio Female	27.7	23.0	19.3	9.6	18.4
Source of Agriculture	55.6	37.7	56.1	44.1	55.0
Income Artisanship	2.7	5.7	4.3	8.3	4.5
Salaried	14.8	15.2	16.4	14.7	16.5
Land Holding Reporting Household (Acres)	4.3	2.8	4.6	3.6	4.5
% of Kutcha House	74.0	66.6	55.2	65.9	55.4
% of Electric Connection	29.7	30.7	43.2	30.0	42.9
% Protected Water	61.6	72.8	71.1	78.1	72.0
% Piped Water	17.2	22.6	25.3	19.4	24.8
% Having Toilet	12.2	8.3	13.2	26.7	15.3
% Using PDS	37.5	32.1	34.1	21.8	33.2
Poverty Head Count	51.0	50.0	39.0	43.0	39.0
Capacity Poverty %	68.0	60.0	–	56.0	52.0

Source: India Human Development Report of the 1990s.

(ii) SC/STs (including Buddhists in the context of the minorities) and the Muslims can be considered as the economically deprived population groups. However, there is wide gap in the per capita income amongst *the Muslims* because of their larger family size as compared to the other groups.

(iii) The Muslims are largely engaged as artisans and as workers in the industrial sectors. Their involvement in agriculture and allied activities is much lower.

(iv) The Work Participation Rate (WPR) amongst the Muslims is the least, both for male and females, suggesting a relatively higher unemployment rate. WPR amongst the Muslim women is as low as 10% compared with the all-India average of 18%.

Educational Status

1.9 In its report submitted in 1983, a panel, appointed by the Ministry of Home Affairs in 1980 and headed by Dr. Gopal Singh, identified Muslims and Neo-Buddhists as educationally backward at the national level.

1.10 As per the National Family Health Survey (1998-9), incidence of illiteracy, female illiteracy among Muslims continues to be significantly high (Table II.2).

Table II.2: Educational Status of Women (15-49 years)

Religious community	Educational Level	
	Illiteracy (%age)	Higher Secondary & above (%age)
Hindus	59.3	6.8
Muslims	60.5	3.5
Christians	32.9	16.7
Sikhs	38.9	13.8
Jains	6.8	30.4
Buddhists/Neo-Buddhists	44.7	7.9
Others	70.3	2.1
No religion	51.2	8.0
Overall	58.2	6.8

Source: National Family Health Survey 1998-9 (89, 199 women respondents).

Table II.3: Fertility Rate, Infant Mortality Rate and Current use of Family Planning Methods

Religious community	Total fertility rate	infant morality rate	Using FP methods
Hindus	2.78	77.1	49.20
Muslims	3.59	58.8	37.00
Christians	2.44	49.2	52.40
Sikhs	2.26	53.3	65.20
Jains	1.90	(46.7)	65.10
Buddhists/Neo-Buddhist	2.13	53.6	64.70
Others	2.33	80.3	48.60
No Religion	3.91	(77.6)	30.10
Overall	2.85	73.0	48.20

Source: National Family Health Survey 1998-9 (89, 199 women respondents).

Health and Social Status

1.11 The effects of low literacy level are also reflected in terms of poor health, large families, high fertility rates leading to socio-economic backwardness as evident from the National Family Health Survey (1998-9) (important health indicators for various communities are given in Table II.3).

1.12 A document entitled 'Status of Muslim Women in India' brought out by the National Commission for Women stated that, 'Muslim women are the weakest link in the generally disempowered chain of Indian womanhood.'

Employment

1.13 It appears that the Muslims, in particular, have not been able to take advantage of the Government schemes on account of their educational backwardness. In a sample of 73 Public Sector Undertakings, only 1.2% of the Directors were Muslims. The proportion of Muslim Directors in private corporate sector appears to be even lower. Likewise, the percentage of Muslims employed in the executive, supervisory or worker cadres is extremely low. In addition to the low representation of Muslims in employment, particularly at the decision making or decision influencing levels, Muslims as a community lag behind others in self-employed categories of activity (*Source*: *Study on Muslim Potential In India* by Sh. K.M. Arif, President United Economic Forum, Mumbai).

Perception of Isolation and Insecurity

1.14 Despite the constitutional safeguards, the minorities feel insecure and suffer from a sense of isolation and deprivation. With this background, the Minorities Commission was set up in 1978. In May 1992, the National Commission for Minorities Act, 1992, was enacted giving statutory status to the erstwhile Minorities Commission. . . .

1.16 Realizing the need for instilling security and for ensuring the rapid socio-economic development of the minorities, a special 15-point programme was proclaimed by the then Prime Minister in May 1983. The 15-point programme was based on a 3-pronged approach, viz. (i) to tackle the situation arising out of communal riots and prevent communal riots, (ii) ensuring adequate representation of the minority communities in employment under Central and State Governments as well as Public Sector Undertakings and (iii) introducing other measures, such as under various development programmes, maintenance and development of religious places, Wakf properties, and redressal of minority grievances.

CHAPTER II

REVIEW OF ACTION TAKEN IN THE PREVIOUS PLANS, SUCCESS, LIMITATIONS AND THE PRESENT SCENARIO

The Ninth Plan was committed to empowering the minorities as the agents of socio-economic change and development. It suggested a fresh approach envisaging efforts to create an enabling environment that would be conducive for their welfare, progress and prosperity.

Education Sector

2.2 Education, being the most effective instrument of empowerment, received serious attention. It was envisaged that all-out efforts be initiated to improve the educational status of these groups, especially women and the girl child, through the universalization of primary education by the year 2005. In brief, the Planning Commission suggested the following strategies for removing educational backwardness among the minorities:

- (i) Universalization of primary education by 2005;
- (ii) Strengthening of the Maulana Azad Educational Foundation;
- (iii) Provision of additional facilities to minority schools, colleges and hostels;

(iv) Remedial coaching for under-achieving students;
(v) Upgrading the existing institutions and networking with vocational and technical education;
(vi) Provisions for *scholarships/fellowships*;
(vii) Provision of educational facilities with appropriate infrastructural support in those areas where educationally backward Muslims, particularly women, are concentrated;
(viii) Modernization of existing traditional institutions, such as the Madarsas;
(ix) Expansion of pre-examination coaching centres in minority concentrated districts;
(x) Promotion of the minority languages and protection of their cultural identity. Also, safeguarding and promoting the linguistic and cultural identity of the Muslims.

2.3 The following interventions already existed at the commencement of the Ninth Plan:

(i) The Maulana Azad Education Foundation was set up in 1989, under the aegis of the Ministry of Welfare, to promote education amongst the educationally backward minorities, especially Muslims;
(ii) An Area intensive scheme was under implementation at the block level in all the 41 Minorities Concentration Districts to provide basic education and related infrastructural facilities under the Department of Education;
(iii) Community Polytechnics were set up in 41 Minorities Concentration Districts to impart technical skills to eligible persons belonging to Minority communities under the Department of Education.
(iv) The Ministry of Labour set up Industrial Training Institutes in 19 out of the 41 districts and introduced trades relevant for the minority artisans and workers;
(v) Pre-examination Coaching Centres in 21 Universities and 32 Colleges by the University Grants Commission;
(vi) A special scheme of pre-examination coaching was launched by the Ministry of Welfare in 1992-3. Under this scheme, 1,888 institutions provided coaching to 9,480 candidates for competitive examinations. . . .

2.5 The major programmes for the educational upliftment of the minorities are reviewed in the following paragraphs.

AREA INTENSIVE PROGRAMME FOR
EDUCATIONALLY BACKWARD MINORITIES

2.6 This Central scheme was the direct outcome of the action points contained in the Programme of Action as part of the revisions in the strategies for implementation. It was launched in May 1993, to provide basic infrastructure and facilities in areas where educationally backward minorities were concentrated, which do not have provision for elementary and secondary education. Under the scheme, 100 per cent financial assistance is provided to State Governments and the voluntary organization for the following programmes:

(i) Establishment of new primary/upper primary schools, non-formal education centres where such a need is felt and viability established on the basis of a school mapping exercise.
(ii) Strengthening of educational infrastructure and physical facilities in the primary/upper primary schools.
(iii) Opening of multi-stream residential Higher Secondary Schools for girls to impart studies in Sciences, Commerce, humanities and vocational courses.

2.7 Since the inception of the scheme, i.e. from 1993-4, financial assistance of Rs. 6068.80 lakh has been released. The scheme has so far been implemented in 12 States, though the number of blocks covered in each district varies. The State-wise break-up of the grant released so far under the scheme is given in Table II.4.

2.8 On analysis of various aspects of implementation of the scheme, the Working Group observed the following:

(i) School Mapping exercise was not carried out to determine the needs for schools, though this was an underlying condition for the opening of new schools.
(ii) Substantial amount of financial assistance with the State Governments has not been utilized.
(iii) No time schedule has been fixed by the State Governments to complete the projects.
(iv) Often, sanctions for grant-in-aid were given almost at the close of the financial year, and the State Governments were expected to seek permission to carry over the grants to the next financial year.

Table II.4: Scheme of Area Intensive Programme for Educationally Backward Minorities–Grant released during the period 1993-4 to 2000-1 State-wise

(*in Rs. lakh as on 31.12.2000*)

Name of State/Trust	1993-4	1994-5	1995-6	1996-7	1997-8	1998-9	1999-2000	2000-1
Andhra Pradesh	–	–	–	–	42.91	–	42.9062	–
Assam	–	–	–	–	37.50	21.00	29.35	–
Bihar	–	–	–	–	–	–	439.64	–
Gujarat	–	4.30	–	–	–	–	–	–
Haryana	2.08	–	–	–	15.015	22.275	2.08	45.90
Karnataka	68.42	9.00	–	69.03	76.765	9.265	58.50	38.32
Kerala	–	105.48	–	–	17.98	–	–	–
Madhya Pradesh	20.88	15.30	–	–	9.30	17.32	6.00	20.36
Rajasthan	65.62	12.71	27.64	112.305	55.60	–	–	–
Tamilnadu	–	–	–	–	–	72.81	–	–
Uttar Pradesh	45.00	83.71	173.06	38.665	597.87	855.74	551.43	1371.85
West Bengal	13.00	6.70	19.30	–	146.00	354.51	12.00	194.25
R.A. Kidwai Trust	–	5.00	–	–	–	–	–	–
Total	215.00	242.00	220.00	220.00	1099.00	1352.00	1142.90	1670.00

(v) The schools have not been recognized by the State Governments. This has given rise to a number of problems such as:

(a) Merit scholarships and special scholarships given to girl students are also denied to them.
(b) Transfer Certificates issued by the schools are not considered valid.
(c) Teachers of these schools are not included in the DPEP programmes.
(d) Students of these schools are also not included in the common programmes of the departments, such as the Youth Festival, sports and games, science festival, etc.
(e) These schools have been instructed by the State Governments not to collect any fees.
(f) The teaching and non-teaching staff of these schools are qualified but are unpaid. Their services are not counted because the schools are not recognized.
(g) The mid-day meal is also denied.
(h) There has been little effort on the part of the State Governments to monitor the scheme at the gross-root level.
(i) Some States have poorly responded to the scheme.

Scheme for the Modernization of Madrasas

2.9 The other major scheme of the Department of Education is Modernization of Madrasas, initiated in 1993-4 to introduce Science, Mathematics, Social Studies, Hindi and English. The basic objective was to improve the standard of Madrasa education at par with the general education so that Muslim children studying in Madrasas may obtain education that will equip them to compete in every walk of life. Under the scheme, 100 per cent financial assistance is provided to State Governments/Union Territories and voluntary organization for the following programmes:

(i) Financial assistance to the extent of 100% for appointing qualified teachers for the teaching of Sciences, Mathematics, Social Studies, and Languages.
(ii) Assistance for establishment of Book Banks and strengthening of libraries in the Madrasas for these subjects.
(iii) Provision of Science kits, mathematics kits, essential equipment, etc.

Table II.5: Details of year-wise Outlay and Expenditure under Scheme of Modernization of Madrasas during the Ninth Five Year Plan

(in Rs. crore)

1997-8		1998-9		1999-2000		2000-1		2001-2	
Out-lay	Actual Exp.	Out-lay	Actual Exp.	Out-lay	Actual Exp.	Out-lay	Actual Exp.	Out-lay	Actual Exp.
7.00	1.73	7.00	6.74	10.00	4.61	12.00	6.61	12.00	–

2.10 During the Ninth Five Year Plan, Rs. 48 crore was earmarked out of which only Rs. 19.69 crore has been released in the first four years. The Year-wise breakup of the outlay and actual expenditure during the Ninth Five Year Plan is given in Table II.5.

2.11 The Working Group on Minorities for the Ninth Five Year Plan had recommended Rs. 91.65 crore in the Ninth Five Year Plan for Madrasa Modernization Scheme. However, only Rs. 48 crore was earmarked in the Ninth Five Year Plan. The scheme has been expanded recently. Its main features are:

(i) Salary to two teachers instead of one Grant of assistance to State Madrasa Education Boards to prepare text books and to organize teachers training programme.
(ii) Increase on time Grant for purchase of Science/Maths kits from Rs. 4,000 to Rs. 7,000.
(iii) One time grant of Rs. 7,000 for books and the strengthening of libraries.

2.12 Analysis of the implementation of the scheme of Modernization of Madarsas indicates the following:

(i) Against Rs. 91.65 crore recommended and Rs. 48 crore provided in the 9th plan, only Rs. 19.69 crore was released in the four years.
(ii) The Madarsas, which have been assisted under the scheme, fall in three categories:

(a) Madarsas affiliated and assisted by Arabic Persian Examination Board in UP/or with other respective Madarsas Education Board by their State Govts.
(b) Madarsas affiliated to the Board but not assisted by it.
(c) Madarsas not affiliated to the Board.

(iii) In Uttar Pradesh, Science and Mathematics kits were issued only in 31 out of 699 Madarsas covered by the scheme, while books and furniture were issued to 109 Madarsas. No effort has been made to train teachers in the utilization of these kits.

(iv) In many cases, the buildings housing the Madarsas are in a dilapidated condition.

(v) Adequate ground work needs to be done to ensure success of the scheme. Detailed guidelines are needed about the modern subjects to be taught and the time to be assigned to each of them in the Timetable. This would avoid wide discrepancies between the different Madarsas and ensure some measure of uniformity of standards.

MAULANA AZAD EDUCATION FOUNDATION

2.13 The Maulana Azad Education Foundation was strengthened during the Ninth Plan by augmenting its Corpus Fund from Rs. 30.01 crore to Rs. 70.01 crore. The interest earned on the corpus is utilized for promoting

Table II.6: Grant-in-aid Sanctioned by MAEF (up to 31.3.2001)

S. No.	State/UTs	Amount sanctioned (Rs.)	No. of NGOs
1.	Andaman	10,00,000	01
2.	Andhra Pradesh	03,37,75,000	23
3.	Assam	01,00,00,000	06
4.	Bihar	04,01,51,800	25
5.	Delhi	1,07,15,500	07
6.	Goa	25,00,000	01
7.	Gujarat	03,22,11,800	17
8.	Haryana	85,00,000	04
9.	Jammu & Kashmir	91,42,000	06
10.	Karnataka	05,10,66,800	32
11.	Kerala	03,38,80,000	17
12.	Madhya Pradesh	61,90,000	06
13.	Maharashtra	02,79,41,800	21
14.	Manipur	19,00,000	01
15.	Orissa	10,32,000	04
16.	Punjab	61,67,000	06
17.	Rajasthan	65,00,000	04
18.	Tamil Nadu	01,06,00,000	05
19.	Uttar Pradesh	17,51,73,740	149
20.	West Bengal	03,00,40,000	20
	Total	49,84,87,440	355

education among the educationally backward minorities by providing grant-in-aid for the establishment/expansion of School/Colleges, Girls Hostel, Residential Schools, opening remedial coaching, upgrading the existing professional and technical institutions.

2.14 Since its inception, the Foundation has sanctioned grant-in-aid amounting to Rs. 49.85 crore to 355 NGOs spread in 20 States/Union Territories. The State-wise breakup of the grant sanctioned and released so far under the scheme is given in Table II.6.

2.15 It is observed that the assistance released to States like West Bengal, Bihar is much less than the proportion of minority population. The Working Group felt that there is a need to popularize the scheme in all States and also to cover all the minority communities under the scheme.

Educational Development Schemes of the Central Wakf Council

2.16 The Central Wakf Council (CWC) is a statutory body established by the Central Government under sub-section (1) of Section 9 of the Wakf Act, 1995. It advises the Government on matters relating to the working of the Wakf Boards and the proper administration of wakfs.

2.17 The Central Wakf Council collects 6% as donation on loan advanced by it to Wakf Institutions under the scheme for the Development of Urban Wakf Properties. The amount thus received is deposited in the 'Education Fund'. The interest earned on the bank deposits, as well as interest accrued from the Revolving Fund, is credited to the Education Fund. This Education Fund is utilized in financing:

(i) Scholarship to students undergoing technical/professional degree course (B. Tech., MBBS, BUMS, B. Pharma, MCA. etc.) @ Rs. 6,000 per annum.

(ii) Ad-hoc grant to the poor and needy students of general degree courses Rs. 3,000.

(iii) Matching grant to State Wakf Boards for scholarships to students of diploma courses in technical education, higher secondary and Madarsa education.

(iv) 50% matching grant to the technical institutes for starting fresh courses or strengthening the existing trade courses.

(v) Financial assistance for vocational training courses.

(vi) Financial assistance to book banks in school libraries and reading rooms.

2.18 For the year 2000-1, budgetary provision of Rs. 210 lakh was earmarked for the educational programmes of the Council out of which Rs. 105.87 lakh had been sanctioned (by December 2000) in respect of programmes like scholarship to students in respect of professional/technical degree courses, ad/hoc grant to students of general degree course, matching grant to State Wakf Boards for educational programmes, 50 per cent matching grant to technical institutes and financial assistance to Library and Vocational Training Centres.

ECONOMIC SECTOR

2.19 The mid-term appraisal of the Ninth Five Year Plan has recognized that the Indian economy has reached a stage where there would be greater demand for skilled manpower rather than for clerical positions in white collar professions. The expansion in government jobs will be limited, as compared to its growth during the last 40 years. More jobs will be created in factories, small business and crafts where minorities and OBCs have an edge over other communities. Therefore, they would do well by taking advantage of the new opportunities that might come their way.

CREDIT AVAILABILITY

2.20 Evaluation studies on the credit flow by the banking sector/financial institutions to minority communities in the minority concentration districts, conducted by the Ministry of Social Justice and Empowerment, reveal the following:

(i) The share of institutional credit has increased considerably in the rural as well as in the urban areas.

(ii) Maximum credit was availed under the general credit scheme of the banks, followed by IRDP, Crop loan scheme, PMRY, Differential rate of Interest scheme, DWACRA, special schemes of the State Govt./ Central Govt. Co-operative banks, Co-operative societies, etc. There is no target fixed for the poor amongst the minority community and the credit available to them is along with other weaker sections under the priority sector lending.

(iii) Persons facing difficulties in accessing loans on account of complicated procedures is much more in the case of commercial banks, regional and rural banks as compared to the co-operative banks and co-operative societies.

(iv) Generally, no rural/urban bias has been observed in extending credit, though some complaints have been reported.

(v) High incidence of poverty, unemployment, big family size, more expenditure, indebtedness were the major factors that compelled the poor, including the members of the minority community, to take institutional or non-institutional credit for generating extra income. .

(vi) Major share of the institutional credit has been cornered by the upper strata in rural areas. The poorer section resort to taking credit from non-institutional sources, even though the rate of interest they have to pay is very high.

(vii) Literate beneficiaries have utilized the fund in a better manner than the illiterate beneficiaries.

(viii) Illiterate and low income people engaged in marginal occupations, such as livestock and agricultural labour, have proven to be most vulnerable. Credit utilisation and repayment have been low in the case of such groups.

(ix) Apprehension amongst the poor of losing land and other assets if given as *collateral or mortgaged* against the requirement of bank for security against loan. This restricts the poor from availing bank credit. Source study conducted on credit facilities to minorities in minority concentration district of Rampur (U.P.), Mumbai and Aurangabad (Maharashtra) and Kutch (Gujarat).

Credit from Public Sector Banks

2.21 The priority sector lending schemes of different Ministries/Departments are being implemented through the scheduled banks. These constitute a major portion of credit flowing to the poorer sections of the different communities. The priority sector schemes being implemented through the banks include the PMRY, IRDP, JRY, Swarna Jayanti Gram Swarojgar Yojana. Besides, the banks also provide credit under their normal business. The poorer section of the minority community are also benefited from the credit being extended by the scheduled banks. Compilation of data on the number of persons covered under the bank credit has been started by the Reserve Bank of India at the behest of the National Commission for Minorities, though the banks still do not ask for the religious demonication of the applicant/loanee. The data on the bank credit flow to the minorities is being reported in the half-yearly progress reports by the RBI to National Commission for Minorities. The data pertains to the overall flow of credit to the minorities and does not segregate between the credit extended under priority sector lending or loans given under normal course by the banks. Analysis of data on flow of credit to the minorities, made available by the RBI to the NCM, has been analysed in four separate tables.

2.22 The performance of Nationalized Banks in providing credit to Minorities has been found to vary (Table II.7). The State Bank of India, followed by the Canara Bank and the Punjab National Bank, lead in advancing credit to Minorities. At present, the Nationalized Banks provide credit to the tune of Rs. 11,789 crore through about 64 lakh accounts.

Table II.7: Credit to Minorities by Nationalized Banks in the Country

(in Rs. crore)

S. No.	Name of the Bank	Credit extended during March '99	Credit extended during Sept. '99
1.	State Bank of India	3,014.17	3,134.90
2.	State Bank of Hyderabad	141.11	164.42
3.	State Bank of Bikaner and Jaipur	82.13	93.11
4.	State Bank of Mysore	50.92	50.93
5.	State Bank of Patiala	496.24	411.37
6.	State Bank of Saurashtra	43.44	49.06
7.	State Bank of Travancore	540.62	590.46
8.	State Bank of Indore	30.46	35.72
9.	Andhra Bank	45.59	43.86
10.	Allahabad Bank	169.68	177.75
11.	Bank of India	588.61	604.92
12.	Bank of Baroda	535.63	535.97
13.	Bank of Maharashtra	82.05	87.36
14.	Canara Bank	859.19	923.99
15.	Central Bank of India	351.96	338.93
16.	Corporation Bank	104.99	121.80
17.	Oriental Bank of Commerce	419.05	447.07
18.	Punjab and Sindh Bank	682.24	704.40
19.	Dena Bank	116.23	111.01
20.	Indian Bank	156.37	142.68
21.	Indian Overseas Bank	413.54	402.66
22.	Punjab National Bank	1,161.55	1,160.86
23.	Syndicate Bank	331.57	339.57
24.	Union Bank of India	406.03	474.21
25.	United Bank of India	177.71	178.20
26.	Uco Bank	244.84	244.70
27.	Vijay Bank	195.98	200.14
	Total	11,445.01	11,789.07
	Number of Accounts	6,130,279	6,407,346.00
	Average Credit per Account	18,600	18,400.00

2.23 Table II.8 gives the State-wise position of credit given to minorities compared with percentage of the minority population. In Orissa (5.15%), Arunachal Pradesh (29.82%), Tamil Nadu (11%), Pondicherry (21.57%) and UT of Chandigarh 25.62%), the share of credit flow to the minorities

Table II.8: State-wise Position of % Credit and average amount per Account Extended to Minorities Compared to % of Minority Population

S. No	Name of State/UT	% of Population	March '99 % of Credit	March '99 Avg. amt. per Actt.	September '99 % of Credit	September '99 Avg. amt. per Actt.
1.	Andhra Pradesh	10.8	6.62	9,000	7.6	9,300
2.	Arunachal Pradesh	24.7	16.78	13,000	29.82	13,000
3.	Assam	32.11	11.14	11,000	10.8	11,000
4.	Bihar	15.88	9.19	6,700	8.55	6,300
5.	Delhi	15.31	7.9	1,40,000	6.08	1,29,000
6.	Goa	35.22	25.4	49,000	25.63	48,000
7.	Gujarat	9.31	2.99	21,400	3.48	22,000
8.	Haryana	10.56	8.5	29,000.	8.76	30,000
9.	Himachal Pradesh	4.06	3.64	29,000	3.94	31,000
10.	Jammu & Kashmir	–	29.35	14,000	51.54	36,000
11.	Karnataka	13.73	9.94	21,000	9.04	25,000
12.	Kerala	42.66	37.96	11,000	39.71	11,000
13.	Madhya Pradesh	6.18	5	17,000	4.71	10,000
14.	Maharashtra	17.45	5.33	29,000	5.28	26,000
15.	Manipur	41.49	28.97	20,000	28.59	20,300
16.	Meghalaya	68.35	49	31,700	58.54	29,000
17.	Mizoram	94.27	77.74	98,500	87	85,000
18.	Nagaland	89.28	48.76	30,000	54.35	25,000
19.	Orissa	4.01	4.9	11,000	5.15	13,400
20.	Pondicherry	13.78	20	50,000	21.57	48,000
21.	Punjab	65.36	45.59	39,000	43.33	36,500
22.	Rajasthan	9.61	5.26	20,000	5.23	20,400
23.	Sikkim	31.49	19.05	7,000	23.09	9,300
24.	Tamil Nadu	11.17	10.47	17,500	11	17,000
25.	Tripura	13.49	8.75	7,500	9.09	7,600
26.	Uttar Pradesh	18.12	14.32	18,000	13.53	19,000
27.	West Bengal	25.56	13.34	10,500	12.41	10,500
28.	A. & N. Islands	32.16	5.7	22,000	9.41	26,400
29.	Chandigarh	23.91	12.19	79,000	25.62	72,000
30.	Daman & Diu	–	6.12	36,000	7.22	38,000
31.	Lakshadweep	95.47	41.2	14,000	36.73	12,000
32.	Dadra & Nagar Haveli	–	17.61	5,41,000	11.19	3,46,000
	All India	17.17	12.46	18,600	12.25	18,300

Source: National Commission for Minorities.

is comparable to their percentage population. Whereas in the rest of the States/UTs, the percentage of credit flow to the minorities is less than their percentage of population. At the all India level also the flow of credit to the minorities is 12% of the total credit. Their population percentage, on the other hand, is 17%.

2.24 Table II.9 gives the region-wise position of credit facilities. It is observed that the average amount of credit per account is highest in the

Table II.9: Region-wise Flow of Credit to Minorities in the Country

		March '99		September '99	
Region	State/UTs Region	Amt. in crore	Credit per Actt.	Amt. in crore	Credit per Actt.
North East	Assam, Mizoram Arunachal Pradesh Nagaland, Manipur Sikkim, Tripura	183.18	14,000	182.51	14,000
Eastern	Bihar, West Bengal Orissa and A. & N.	1,088.68	9,000	1,088.09	9,000
Western	Gujarat, Maharashtra, Daman & Diu, Goa, D. & N. Haveli	982.04	28,000	979.64	27,000
Central	UP & MP	1,421.72	18,000	1,505.32	16,200
Southern	Andhra Pradesh Karnataka, Lakshadweep, Tamil Nadu Kerala, Pondicherry	3,576.76	14,000	3,816.03	14,000
Northern	Delhi, Punjab Haryana, Chandigarh J&K, HP, Rajasthan	4,192.62	38,000	4,217.47	38,000
		11,445.00		11,789.06	

Source: National Commission for Minorities.

Northern region at Rs. 38,000 followed by Rs. 27,000 in the case of the western region. Though reasonable also in the north east, central & southern regions, it is quite low in the eastern region at Rs. 9,000.

2.25 Table II.10 gives information on credit offered to minority groups in the 41 Minority Concentration Districts. Percentage of credit to minorities under lending programmes of the scheduled banks is limited to *around 13-14%* of the total credit flow in the minority concentration districts whereas the percentage of minority population in these areas ranges *from 25 to 50%*. Also, in the Minority Concentration Districts the share of

Table II.10: Credit Flow in Minority Concentration Districts

	March '99		September '99	
Communities	Amt. in crore	% to Total	Amt. in crore	% to Total
Muslims	1,392.71	71.69	1,388.18	72.87
Christians	277.03	14.26	274.32	14.40
Sikhs	172.58	8.88	173.58	9.12
Buddhists	62.74	3.23	52.05	2.73
Parsis	37.65	1.94	16.79	0.88
Total	1,942.71	100.00	1,904.92	100.00
All Communities	14,131.86	13,469.49		
% of Minorities to Total Credit flow	13.75	14.14		

Source: National Commission for Minorities.

credit to each minority community as in Sept. 1999, is Muslims (72.87%), Christians (14.40%), Sikhs (9.12%), Buddhists (2.73%) and Parsis (0.88%).

2.26 The above information indicates that the percentage of minority accounts may not be in proportion to their percentage of population. This necessitates capacity building so that more and more persons of the minority community can access bank credit. Per account loaning is also less, as minority groups do not own big business/industries and the quantum of loaning is small.

2.27 Some reference of credit flow to minorities has also come under the financing schemes of Prime Minister Rojgar Yojana (PMRY) under the Ministry of Small Scale Industries. Though no specific targets are fixed, separate data is available about the credit flow to the minorities. This scheme is being implemented in collaboration with the banks. The banks provide 95% of the project cost as loan; the balance of 5% is brought by the beneficiary in his business. The government provides 15% of the funds (subject to a maximum of Rs. 7,500) as subsidy. This is adjusted by the banks against the repayments made by the loanee.

PRIME MINISTER'S ROZGAR YOJANA (PMRY)

2.28 Though in a span of 7 years, the total credit flow under PMRY scheme has been nearly Rs. 9,500 crore, no separate earmarking has been made by either the Govt. or the Banks for capacity-building of the loanees. This adversely affects the loan absorption capacity of the loanees and, with poor recoveries, burdens the banks with non-performing assets. This is reflected in terms of diminishing number of suitable applicants for loans.

2.29 The details of the assistance provided to the minorities under PMRY is given in the following Table II.11.

Table II.11: Assistance to Minorities under PMRY

S. No.	Year	Total	Minorities	% (Col 4/3)	Total	Minorities	% (Col 7/6)
1	2	3	4	5	6	7	8
1.	1993-4	18,673	1,318	7.06	14,001	950	6.79
2.	1994-5	114,846	9,457	8.23	84,565	6,715	7.94
3.	1995-6	281,968	22,334	7.92	201,144	15,419	7.67
4.	1996-7	270,811	22,201	8.20	181,646	14,950	8.23
5.	1997-8	288,316	25,957	9.00	182,472	16,383	8.98
6.	1998-9	299,061	29,140	9.74	178,083	17,581	9.87
7.	1999-2000	255,222	24,692	9.67	152,188	14,435	9.48
Total		1,528,897	135,099	8.84	994,099	86,433	8.69

(a) Sanction and disbursement to the minorities is hovering around 9% of the total credit provided during the period.

(b) Share of credit to the minorities has been found to be *quite low* in Andhra Pradesh, Uttar Pradesh and Kerala. These states have a sizeable minority proportion.

(c) Achievement is satisfactory in those states where the religious minorities have a major share of population, such as Punjab, Jammu & Kashmir, Mizoram, etc.

(d) Special steps need to be initiated to increase the share of the minorities.

(e) Separate data about credit flow to minority groups under other schemes of priority sector lending is not maintained.

National Minorities Development & Finance Corporation (NMDFC)

2.30 Besides the general credit mechanism of the banking sector and the Government, the National Minorities Development & Finance Corporation (NMDFC) extends credit for self-employment to the minorities. NMDFC was set up in 1994 under the Ministry of Social Justice & Empowerment to promote welfare and economic development of the poorer sections amongst them. The paid up share capital of NMDFC so far is Rs. 238 crore, of which the Union Government has contributed Rs. 202 crore and the States/UTs have provided Rs. 36 crore.

2.31 The main focus of NMDFC has been to provide loans for self-employment at concessional rates of interest. These are lower than the bank rates, though other promotional programmes, such as vocational training, skill upgradation and marketing support, are also provided.

2.32 NMDFC operates through a networking with the State Govt. bodies called the State Channelising Agencies (SCAs). These SCAs are the main links in the implementation mechanism of NMDFC, as they identify the applicants and disburse the loans. They are also responsible for the utilization of loans and repayment of funds to NMDFC. Presently, there are 32 SCAs (among them 28 being operational in 21 States and 2 UTs). These include 9 State Minorities Finance Corporations or Backward Classes Financial Corporations or some other Corporations. The maximum amount of loan given by NMDFC is upto Rs. 5 lakh. As most of the borrowers are from the poorer sections, quite often the loans are very small (depending upon the need of the borrowers). NMDFC has been able to disburse loans worth Rs. 296.79 crore to over 86,874 beneficiaries. At the same time, inadequate infrastructure of the SCAs—both administrative and financial—has constrained the implementation of NMDFC's programmes.

2.33 The existing system has not been able to cover the poorest of the poor whose credit needs were small but recurring in nature. These were the poorest men and women in our villages and towns who were mostly illiterate and could not hope to avail of loans from the banks or even the SCAs because of the procedures involved. Their need was an informal and flexible credit delivery mechanism at their doorstep. Also to make credit really a means of empowerment, a more active intervention in their lives was felt necessary. The *micro-financing* scheme itself has been modelled on the credit system of Bangladesh Gramin Bank and the Rashtriya Mahila Kosh, which are the pioneers in this field. This scheme is being implemented as a parallel strategy of NMDFC and is taken up directly through the NGOs, which have proven record in this field. As of now, NMDFC has evolved linkages with 84 NGOs in different parts of the country and has brought nearly 20,000 beneficiaries under its purview. Apart from giving small loans for income generation, support is also given for the promotion and sabilization of SHGs. The concept of Self Help Groups among the minorities is a relatively novel concept.

Credit through Community Based Organizations

2.34 Religious organizations also extend credit to members of the minority community. There are about 200 Islamic credit institutions in India operating (as per the tenets of Koran). They do not charge interest on the loan extended by them. As they do not conform to the rules of conventional banking, they function as societies, trusts, etc. However, they have wide acceptability amongst the minorities and, with a degree of restructuring and development of administrative/infrastructural base, they can play an important role in channelizing funds to the targeted minority groups.

Efficacy of Existing Delivery Mechanism

2.35 The 15-point programme for the minorities emphasizes that care be taken to see that in various development programmes, including the 20-point programme, minorities secure a fair and adequate share of benefits. This has sought to be achieved through the NMDFC. But, on a wider plane, minorities form only a part of the overall target group of the socio-economic developmental schemes being taken up by the government and the banking sector. Unlike the SCs/STs, no specific targets are fixed for the minorities, which consequently results in diluting the focus in ensuring that the benefits reach these segments of society. Even the specific flow of information about the quantum of benefits that have reached the minorities is not always available.

2.36 Credit to the minorities is reaching predominantly through the general banking structure. It also includes the efforts being complemented by specialized agencies such as SIDBI, NABARD, etc. There has not been any evidence of any bias observed in the flow of credit to the minorities. The comparatively lower percentage of credit flowing to the minorities as compared to their population percentage has been mainly on account of illiteracy and lack of capacity to avail loan. Thus capacity building should be made part of the loaning programme targeting the poorer sections including the minorities. A training module should be developed for skill development focussed to the needs of the cluster area/target group with inbuilt flexibilities and involvement of the local community.

2.37 The weaker sections need comparatively smaller loans whereas the conventional systems and attitudes followed by the banks and other financial institutions are more or less the same as for larger quantum of loans. As these systems and procedures are not attuned to the credit needs of the poor small loanees, the same are responsible for adversely affecting the credit flow to them. This also applies to the minorities. Thus what is required is that the system of financing for schemes targeting the vulnerable sections of the society should be made simple and easy to execute, less cumbersome and time consuming, guarantee norms should be made more flexible and compliable.

Traditional Occupations of Minorities and Related Issues

2.38 A sizeable section of the Muslim population, which comprises the predominant group amongst the minorities are good artisans and are involved in handloom and handicraft activities, such as the brass work in Moradabad, glasswork in Firozabad, leather industry in Agra and Kanpur, carpet and banarasi sarees industry in Mau/Varanasi/Bhadohi/Mirzapur, Chikan work in Lucknow, and so on. About 38% of the weavers in the country are Muslims. Buddhists are also engaged in the traditional handicraft and handloom activities. It is a well known fact that the poor artisans are fleeced by middlemen and do not get remunerative prices for their work. In addition, these handloom and handicraft items are being edged out on account of higher prices in areas where they have to compete with articles made by machine and powerlooms. Also due to *poor profit margins*, the working capital has been depleted. As a result, the artisans do not have the wherewithal to carry on further and are gradually moving away from their traditional activities and are looking up for other avenues for their livelihood. Further, the problem of the children engaged in these activities also requires specific attention for ensuring that they are not deprived of education and protection.

2.39 It is felt, that in order to support such artisans, they may be provided with necessary inputs, such as the design developments to match with the current market requirements, introduction of new techniques, infusion of fresh credit in the sector and market tie-up. Socio-economic development of the artisans is given priority on the agenda of a number of financial institutions and Govt. Departments. However, due to lack of co-ordination among these Departments the reach and effectiveness of their programmes is limited. Better co-ordination is required between agencies such as the offices of Development Commissioner Handicraft and Handlooms with the various financial institutions. The services of the good Primary and Apex Handloom Weavers Co-operative Societies and the National Award Winning Master Craftsmen can also be utilized.

Management of Wakfs

2.40 The Institution of Wakf is a striking feature of Islamic jurisprudence. The word 'Wakf' applies to any property movable or immovable, dedicated for purposes recognized by the Muslim Law as religious, pious or charitable. Apart from their religious aspect, the Wakfs are also instruments of socio-economic upliftment. The benefit from the Wakfs flow to the needy persons for their socio-economic, cultural and educational development. Income from Wakfs also plays an important role in providing community services. There are about 3 lakh Wakfs in the country. Improvement in management of Wakfs is crucial not only for the preservation of religious and charitable institutions but also for educational and economic development of the Muslim community. Wakfs constitute a national asset as a very large number of them support schools, colleges, technical institutions, libraries, reading rooms, charitable dispensaries, musafir-khanas, etc., which benefit the general public irrespective of their caste or creed.

2.41 To improve the financial position of the Wakfs and Wakf Boards and to enable them to enlarge the area of their welfare activities, the Central Government has been giving, from 1974-5, annual grants-in-aid under a Non-Plan scheme to the Central Wakf Council. The projects involve construction or reconstruction of commercially viable buildings on Urban Wakf Lands. The budget provision and utilization under the scheme during the Ninth Five Year Plan period (Table II.12) indicate that the utilization of funds under this scheme has been satisfactory.

Table II.12: Development of Urban Wakf Properties

(*in Rs. crore*)

	1997-8	1998-9	1999-2000	2000-1
Budget estimate	1.40	1.49	1.70	2.00
Revised estimate	1.40	1.49	1.70	1.80
Actual expdr.	1.08	1.49	1.70	1.80

CHAPTER III

RECOMMENDATIONS

Strategic Imperatives

During the Tenth Five Year Plan the strategy for empowering the minorities has to be moulded against the backdrop of the emerging social and economic scenario in the country. The 1990s saw a shift from the socialistic pattern of economic development to a policy based on globalization, liberalization, and privatization. The private sector is being consciously promoted to take up the production and commercial activities, while the role of the government and the government-aided sector is getting restricted to core activities. Thus, employment opportunities are likely to come up mainly in the private sector in the coming years.

3.2 Coupled with the changes above, the sectoral composition has also undergone a fundamental change over the years. Agriculture, which used to contribute 55.4% of the national income in 1950-1, accounted for only 25.5% in 1999-2000. On the other hand, the share of the services sector has increased from 31.8% in 1950-1 to 52.4% in 1999-2000. The expansion of the service sector has, thus, created new employment opportunities.

3.3 Following the 73rd and 74th amendments to the Constitution, Panchayati Raj bodies and local bodies have also started playing a major role. Further, various non-government bodies have come up as alternative modes of delivery of services. These institutions are required to be strengthened and actively associated in the implementation of the Plan. Importance of involving the community in the initiatives for their welfare needs to be recognized.

Data on development of the minorities, particularly those belonging to the economically weaker sections, indicates that among the minority communities, those who have taken advantage of the modern education system have been able to achieve greater success in terms of exploiting the employment opportunities both in the government and private sectors. As such, adoption of regular educational curriculum and formal recognition from State Board of Education has to be taken as a major strategy for the upliftment of the educationally backward minorities during the Tenth Five Year Plan. In this context, while the curriculum followed in the religious institutions, such as Madarsas, will continue to be of significant, efforts should be made to also introduce courses that would enable the students to compete for employment in government and the professions. For this reason, the existing programme for modernizing the Madarsa education should be suitably re-oriented.

3.5 Analysis of the general trend of development indicates that States like Kerala which have better human development index in terms of a better literacy rate, better health and nutrition, and higher status of women, etc., have been able to tackle the population growth. In Uttar Pradesh, Bihar and Rajasthan, on the other hand, this is not so owing to the low human development indices. With a view to deal with unemployment and poverty effectively on one hand, and to develop the human resources which is the most important resource in India, making provision of social infrastructure such as education, primary health, sanitation, hygiene, etc., has to be given importance during the Tenth Plan.

3.6 This will be of special significance for the minority communities, whose rate of growth of population impinges adversely on their socio-economic well-being. While the concerned Departments (Ministry of Human Resource Development, Ministry of Health and Family Welfare, and Ministry of Urban Development) would be requested to gear up their activities, these programmes should be suitably supplemented by the Ministry of Social Justice and Empowerment. The Civil society at large, particularly, those of religious background should be actively associated in making various programmes acceptable to the community and ensuring their active participation.

3.7 On account of poor socio-economic condition, at times, children who represent future of the country, are subject to a lot of hardship and are forced to take up manual work. As a result, they are not only deprived of their childhood days but also the benefit of education. Specific efforts have to be made for ensuring that child labour in all forms is prohibited and the children are given full benefit of education along with nutrition and other support.

3.8 Sizeable population of the minority communities is engaged in traditional arts and crafts like handloom, handicraft, leather work, glass work, etc. With globalization, the new opportunities at the national and international level are likely to open up which can be exploited for their economic empowerment. Introduction of appropriate technology, development of entrepreneurship, and formation of self help groups hold the key for enabling the community to produce goods as per the market demand and exploit the market. Tenth Plan should emphasize this strategy for economic empowerment of the artisans belonging to minority community.

3.9 The working group recommends that in the above background, the Tenth Plan will have to envisage implementation of schemes and programmes for welfare of minorities for integrating them with the national mainstream—economically, socially and psychologically. The factors such as the content of the programmes, the quantum of resources allocated to the sector, and their delivery mechanisms are critical to their effective implementation. Based upon the review in the previous Chapters and in the context of the strategic imperatives outlined above, the recommendations of the Group are given below. The presentation has been made sector-wise for the sake of convenience. However there is some overlap between the sectors, which has arisen as no sector can be viewed in isolation.

RECOMMENDATIONS

Educational Sector

3.10 Among all the interventions deemed necessary for empowerment of minorities, the educational sector is the most important one and is required to be given specific attention during the Tenth Plan. Various plan and programmes for provision of education, including those minorities, are implemented by the Ministry of Human Resource Development, which is primarily responsible in this regard. Action taken by the Ministry of Social Justice & Empowerment are supplemental in nature for meeting the specific needs of the educationally backward minorities. In this regard civil society based institutions like the Maulana Azad Education Foundation and the Central Wakf Council assume special significance in view of their acceptance among the minorities.

SCHEMES IMPLEMENTED BY MINISTRY OF HUMAN RESOURCE DEVELOPMENT

Area Intensive Programme for Educationally Backward Minorities

3.11 The Group recommends the continuation of the Area Intensive Programme of the Department of Secondary & Higher Education during the Tenth plan. The Programme as currently being implemented covers only those educationally backward Blocks, where the minorities population is more than 20%. The Working Group recommends that in view of the educational backwardness prevailing among the minorities and its adverse impact on the employability, the basis for identification of blocks should be relaxed to cover all blocks having more than 12.5% of minority population.

3.12 While the precise number such blocks would have to be identified by a fresh District-wise survey in minority concentration areas, the Group has assumed that there are 600 such educationally backward Blocks in the country.

3.13 In addition to the number of the blocks to be covered, certain aspects of the ongoing scheme as indicated below also need revision for making it effective and purposeful. The standard of education also needs to be improved with focus on the quality of education, effective administration and periodic inspections.

(i) The whole purpose of a well intended scheme is lost if recognition is not granted to these schools.
(ii) School mapping exercises are required to be carried out immediately prior to opening of new schools.
(iii) State Governments should give wide publicity to the programme as well as the benefits that the targeted communities are getting from the programme.
(iv) Implementation of proposals under the scheme of Area Intensive Programme in a time bound manner.
(v) State-level Committees should exclusively monitor the implementation of the Area Intensive Programme. This is essential to ensure that the target group is benefited as per the objectives of the Scheme.
(vi) All States need to evolve a system by which to initiate the action as per the provisions of the National Education Policy and maintain an effective monitoring system.
(vii) Only those *NGOs* which have capacity to bear the cost of the expenses will be considered under the scheme. For the rest the assistance will be made available only when the State Govt. agrees to bear the cost of the recurring expenditure.
(viii) State Governments must pursue the implementation of the Scheme more vigorously.

3.14 Taking into account importance of education in empowerment of minorities and the prevailing scenario, the financial requirement for the Area Intensive Programme during the Tenth Plan will be as under:

(i) Construction of Primary and upper Primary Schools: 2,500 nos. at a cost of Rs. 5 lakh each
Total cost: Rs. 12,500 lakh
(ii) Construction of Secondary School buildings: 1,000 nos. at a cost of Rs. 7 lakh each
Total cost: Rs. 7,000 lakh
(iii) Construction of Multi-stream Residential Schools (10+2 level) for girls (boarding facility for atleast 200 girls): 150 nos. at a cost of Rs. 150 lakh each
Total cost: Rs. 22,500 lakh
(iv) Construction of additional classrooms/toilets, etc., for Primary/Upper Primary School: 5,000 nos. at a cost of Rs. 75,000 each
Total cost: Rs. 3,750 lakh

(v) Construction of additional classrooms/toilets for secondary school: 1,000 nos. at a cost of Rs. 1 lakh each

Total cost: Rs. 1,000 lakh

(vi) Upgradation of Primary Schools to Junior High Schools: 2,000 nos. at a cost of Rs. 3.50 lakh each

Total cost: Rs. 7,000 lakh

(vii) Supply of teaching/learning material to primary schools not covered by Operation Black Board : 10,000 nos. at a cost of Rs. 10,000 each

Total cost: Rs. 1,000 lakh

3.15 The total requirement of the Area Intensive Programme for Tenth Plan will be about Rs. 54,750 lakh.

SCHEME FOR THE MODERNIZATION OF MADRASAS

3.16 The Working Group feels that the ongoing scheme of Modernization of Madrasas implemented by the Department of Secondary and Higher Education has served a purpose in educational empowerment of the minorities. However it is required to be revised incorporating the following points for making it more effective:

(i) Considering the varying standards of Science, Humanities and English education in Madrasas, it is necessary that the syllabi followed by the State level recognized boards should be adopted. A Central Madarsa Board may be set up to coordinate with the States and to ensure quality of education in all relevant subjects.

(ii) The task of modernization of Madrasas involves the modernizing teaching methodology and broaden mental horizon of the teachers and managements of these institutions through exposing them to the new trends in the field of education, pedagogy, technology, psychology and educational management which may be relevant to them, and motivating them to make use of this knowledge in the teaching of their own traditional subjects so as to improve the quality of learning of these subjects. The in-service training of madarsa teachers in a modern University setting may be used for the modernization scheme. Such a project should expose madarsa teachers to new developments that have taken place both in the universe of knowledge as well as Indian society. The exposure programme may be *operationalized* either through a programme culminating in a degree like Bachelor in Education (B. Ed.) or basic education diploma, or else it may be a non-formal exposure programme for a lesser duration.

(iii) The teaching of modern subjects appears to be restricted to Class III to Class VIII. It should be extended to the school certificate (10+2) level covering all higher classes.

(iv) Provision of assistance for reconditioning and repair of these buildings are essential and should be provided in Tenth Plan.

(v) The funds under the scheme for modernization of madarsas have not been utilized fully for various reasons. These include lack of dissemination of information, particularly about the usefulness of such modernization, to the community and community leaders, lack of coordination between the Union and State Government agencies, absence of interaction with community leaders, delayed release of funds resulting in non-payment of salaries to teachers and consequent abandonment of the scheme, procedural hindrances like registration and recognition of institutions, non-availability of teachers, etc. Appropriate remedial measures may be taken for overcoming these constraints.

3.17 With a view to achieve the above stated objectives, the Group recommends the following provisions under the Scheme of Modernization of Madrasa Education during the Tenth Plan:

(i) Assistance to 2,500 Madrasas, i.e. @ 500 Madrasas every year for the plan period. The assistance should be based on the provision of an *average three teachers* per Madrasa @ Rs. 48,000 per annum per teacher (i.e. one teacher each for Sciences and Maths, English & Humanities, and Computer education).

Total cost: Rs. 3,600 lakh

(ii) Provision for assistance to State Madrasa Education Board/State Govt. to prepare *text books* during the Tenth Plan.

Total cost: Rs. 500 lakh

(iii) Provision for assistance to State Madrasa Education Board/State Govt. for organization of *teacher training Programme* for 2,000 Madrasa teachers every year @ Rs. 300 lakh per year.

Total cost: Rs. 1,500 lakh

(iv) *Provision of Computers* and accessories on a one time basis to 1,000 Madrasas at cost of Rs. 1.00 lakh per Madrasa covering 200 Madrasas each year.

Total cost: Rs. 1,000 lakh

(v) Provision of *laboratory equipment* at the rate of Rs. 25,000 to each of 500 High School level Madrasas, i.e. 100 Madrasas per year.

Total cost: Rs. 125 lakh

(vi) Supply of *teaching aids/learning material* on an one time basis to 2,500 Madrasas at cost of Rs. 10,000 for the plan period.

Total cost: Rs. 250 lakh

(vii) Priority for assistance to 2,500 Madrasas for reconditioning and repair of building and expansion of existing infrastructure at the rate of Rs. 5 lakh per Madrasa (one-time grant).

Total cost: Rs. 12,500 lakh

3.18 The total cost of the above proposals under the Scheme of Modernization of Madrasa Education during the Tenth Plan works out to Rs. 19,475 lakh.

Scheme of Community Polytechnics

3.19 The scheme of community polytechnics was started in 1978-9 as a Central Sector scheme. Community polytechnic is a wing of an existing polytechnic mandated to undertake rural/community development activities through manpower development, transfer of technology, provision of technical support/services and dissemination of information. Among men, training courses on house wiring, motor winding, repair of electronic consumer durables, repair of agricultural machinery, welding and fabrication, civil construction, vehicle repairing, etc., are popular. Among women, garment making, textile printing, screen printing, embroidery, food processing and secretarial work are popular. More than 500 community polytechnics have been established so far covering most of the 41 identified Minority Concentration Districts.

3.20 The Group recommends that coverage under this Scheme should be extended during the Tenth Plan for covering the remaining 100 other Districts having significant minority population with at least one such community Polytechnic per District and to include new and innovative trades as per the emerging market demand.

3.21 About Rs. 51.25 lakh will be required per polytechnic at the rate of Rs. 10 lakh for purchase of equipment and Rs. 5 lakh for creating infrastructure as one time grant basis and @ Rs. 7.25 lakh per annum for recurring expenditure. The total financial implication on this during the Tenth Plan will be Rs. 5,125 lakh.

Scheme for providing one year Diploma Computer Applications and Multilingual DTP

3.22 The National Council for Promotion of Urdu Language, Ministry of Human Resource Development, Government of India has been conducting a two year course, namely, 'Calligraphy, Introduction to Computer and Desk Top Publishing', using Urdu. First year of the course deals with Urdu Calligraphy and fundamentals of computer and in the second year advance course on computer application and Desk Top Publishing is conducted. During the Ninth Plan Rs. 5.47 crore has been sanctioned for setting up of 160 computer centres and 10,002 students have been covered.

3.23 Keeping in view the emerging potential in the Information Technology sector, the Group feels that this scheme is very promising and has great potential for self-employment. Continuation of the scheme during the Tenth Plan is recommended for establishing 30 computer institutes every year. This will require a provision of Rs. 25 crore during the Tenth Plan.

Scheme of provision of Urdu Teachers

3.24 Taking note of the fact that the Constitution of India seeks to safeguard the right of minorities for conservation of their language and culture, the Group recommends that in the Tenth Plan at least 5,000 schools must be assisted to have Urdu teachers, based on accepted parameters of the number of students wishing to learn the language. This scheme should apply equally to minority and non-minority (including government) educational institutions. The average number of Urdu teachers to be deployed may be 1.5 per school. For covering 5,000 schools during the Tenth Plan under this scheme at a cost of Rs. 26,400 per annum per teacher, the total expenditure for the Tenth Plan comes to Rs. 19.80 crore.

Community Colleges

3.25 The Working Group further recommends that, with a view to enable the minorities to exploit the emerging job opportunities particularly in the services sector, vocationalization of education should be given emphasis by establishment of community colleges in Minorities Concentration Areas as has been envisaged in the Programme of Action of National Policy on Education.

Minority Educational Institutions

3.26 Minority Educational Institutions can play a more positive role in promotion of education among the educationally backward sections among minorities provided their growth is facilitated. Rules guiding recognition of minority educational institutions for starting professional and technical courses should be simplified by the All India Council of Technical Education. Further, the Central and State Governments should grant permission to minorities for opening professional institutions such as Medical Colleges, vocational training institutions and teacher training institutions.

3.27 The State Governments should simplify the procedures *for issuance of recognition* of minority educational institutions. Complaints about delay in, or refusal to, issue Minority Status Certificates have come to notice in some States. Issue of certificate by the State Governments should be expedited. This would be in accordance with the Programme of Action (1992) and enable the enable minority educational institutions to exercise their legitimate rights which have been recognized in the National Policy on Education (1986).

3.28 Special efforts need to be made for the professional development of Managers, Principals and teachers of minority educational institutions including both initial training like B.Ed. and subsequent on the job orientation at regular intervals. Assistance of institutions such as the All India Association for Christian Higher Education, Aligarh Muslim University, Jamia Millia Islamia may be availed for the purpose.

Linguistic Minorities

3.29 In order to eliminate frustration and build a sense of confidence among minorities, it is essential that the State also plays a positive role to maintain cultural pluralism. Towards this purpose the facilities for teaching of minority language and protection of their cultural traditions should be made available outside the areas of their concentration. For example, Sikhs and Punjabis living outside Punjab, particularly in States of Delhi, U.P., Maharashtra, Bihar, Rajasthan, etc., where they are in substantial numbers, need to be provided facilities for Punjabi teaching in Schools. For this purpose schools, may be provided assistance for appointing teachers under the plan scheme. Also, creation and strengthening of cultural academies, like Urdu, Punjabi and Sindhi academies in Delhi may be considered in various States in due course.

3.30 Recommendations by various committees for instructions up to class V in mother tongue should be implemented for effective fulfillment of the constitutional right conferred upon the linguistic minorities under Article 350(A). For this, the greatest challenge is to develop curriculum and material in minority languages particularly in States other than minority concentration population.

3.31 Necessary arrangements for teaching of minority languages are also lacking. For example, it was brought to the notice the Group that in Leh district of Ladakh, Bhoti language has been introduced from 1971 in 272 Government Schools but only 37 Bhoti teachers posts have been created so far. Such glaring contradictions need to be attended urgently.

Scheme of Remedial Coaching

3.32 The Remedial Coaching scheme has been under operation for enabling the minorities student to overcome their difficulties in specific subjects. This scheme is operated through UGC. The Group recommends that it should be continued in the Tenth Plan. The UGC scheme assists students at higher secondary level and above. At least 1,60,000 students may be assisted under the scheme during the Tenth Plan through 500 Institutes (@ 320 candidates per institute) at the rate of 100 Institutes per year. The cost of assisting 500 Institutes (at a rate of Rs. 7,65,200 per institute) will come to Rs. 3,826 lakh.

SCHEMES IMPLEMENTED BY MINISTRY OF SOCIAL JUSTICE & EMPOWERMENT

Maulana Azad Education Foundation

3.33 According to the National Policy on Education 1986 (modified in 1992) the minority groups which are educationally deprived or backward need special interventions. For accelerated growth, intensive investment is required in the field of education, vocational training and upgradation of skills. There is an urgent need of additional focus in girl child and women empowerment.

3.34 The Maulana Azad Education Foundation has made considerable contribution towards this cause during the Ninth Plan so far, by sanctioning over Rs. 41 crore to 287 NGOs as grant-in-aid for establishment/expansion of schools/colleges, girls' hostels, residential schools, remedial coaching (for students at secondary level) and upgradation of the existing professional and technical institutions. The scheme has been received well as is evident from the large number of proposals (worth

Rs. 195 crore) pending with the Foundation for consideration.

3.35 As the impact of the scheme is substantial, the *Corpus Fund* of the Foundation may be *raised* from Rs. 70 crore to Rs. 200 crore. Thus the provision for this purpose required during the Tenth Plan would be Rs. 130 crore.

Merit Linked Scholarship

3.36 With a view to ensure that the meritorious students among the minorities are able to pursue education at higher level at par with others, the Group feels it is necessary to introduce a *merit linked scholarship* scheme for students belonging to minorities at the earliest, as envisaged by the Ministry of Social Justice & Empowerment to formulate. The scholarship is conceived as a special intervention to improve the educational standards of educationally backward minorities to bring them at par with the rest of the community as they are not able to avail of the opportunities for higher and technical education. 10,000 scholarships are proposed to be given annually at a cost of Rs. 17 crore. The Tenth Five Year Plan outlay works out to Rs. 85 crore.

Scheme of Hostels for Minorities Students

3.37 The Working Group felt the need for having adequate hostel facility for enabling the minority students to pursue education at matric and post matric level in general and for the girl students, in particular. Ministry of Social Justice & Empowerment has been implementing schemes for construction of hostels for SC and OBC students. However there is no scheme for construction of hostel for the minorities. It was learnt that a proposal for merger of the two ongoing schemes for hostel for SC and OBC students and also the inclusion of minorities is under consideration. The proposed 'Centrally Sponsored Scheme of Sangati Hostels for students (Boys and Girls) belonging to Scheduled Castes, Minorities and Other Backward Classes' aims at integrating the weaker sections with the mainstream. The Group endorsed the proposal.

3.38 The Group recommends that, in the Tenth Plan period, a conscious effort be made to have *one hostel each for minorities boys and girls* (*capacity of 50 students each*) in the sub-divisional headquarters of all the 41 Minority Concentration Districts. At an estimated cost of Rs. 30 lakh per hostel (5 sub-divisions per district), the total cost works out to

Rs. 41 x 5 x 2 x 30 lakh or Rs. 12,300 lakh. Under this Centrally assisted scheme, State Governments/UT Administration as well as the Voluntary Organizations may be assisted for setting up hostels. Operation and maintenance cost should, however, be borne by the agency concerned. It may be stated that, as far as possible, the hostels should not be exclusive—that is—they should cater to all sections of the society; the minorities can be allotted a certain proportion of the seats available as envisaged under the proposed scheme of 'Sangati hostels'.

Scheme for Coaching

3.39 The Group considered the progress, problems and potential of the scheme of Coaching Classes for competitive examinations operated by the University Grants Commission through selected Universities/Colleges and came to the conclusion that the scheme *should be continued in the Tenth Plan and specific efforts should be made for increasing the success rate* so as to ensure that the minority communities are adequately represented in the government services.

3.40 The *Ministry of Social Justice & Empowerment* also operates a pre-examination coaching scheme for weaker sections including minorities under which assistance is given to national and State-level NGOs of repute. During the Ninth Five Year Plan the Rs. 9.50 crore has been sanctioned to 222 institutions covering 17,750 beneficiaries under this scheme. It was learnt that the Ministry of Social Justice & Empowerment is contemplating to formulate a common coaching scheme for students belonging to Scheduled Castes, Other Backward Classes and Weaker Sections including Minorities and for widening the scope of the scheme for meeting the requirement of government as well as private sectors. The Group supports this initiative in view of the need for supporting students appearing for Professional courses. A provision of Rs. 50 crore, i.e. Rs. 10 crore per year may be made for the Tenth Plan.

Educational Development Schemes of the Central Wakf Council

3.41 The Central Wakf Council is at present implementing a scheme through the network of wakf institutions, for helping the minority students for pursuing education. The working group feels that the wakf organization has enormous potential in empowering the minority community educationally and recommends that the efforts of the Central

Wakf Council should be supplemented by the government during the tenth plan. The Council should be assisted for focusing on the elementary education, particularly on the girls education for achieving total literacy during the Tenth Plan with particular stress on common health and hygiene, sanitation, mother and child health, etc. A provision of Rs. 25 crore during the Tenth Plan @ Rs. 5 crore per annum is recommended for this new scheme.

Vocational Training Sector

3.42 The Ministry of Labour (Directorate General of Employment Training) have been operating a scheme for upgrading Industrial Training Institutes (*ITIs*) in minority concentration areas under which 41 Minorities Concentration Districts have been covered so far. In view of the peculiar nature of problems faced by the minorities, the Working Group recommends the expansion of this scheme to 100 more Districts, having significant minority population, during the Tenth Plan. This would require a provision Rs. 1,000 lakh during the Tenth Plan assuming at the rate of Rs. 10 lakh per ITI.

ECONOMIC SECTOR

Empowerment of Women

3.43 Women are the weakest link amongst the minorities. With one of the lowest literacy and enrolment rates, burden of bearing large number of children leading to poor health and lowest Work Participation Rate (WPR), they need maximum focus. The most effective strategy to reach women and empower them economically should be through (i) organizing them to form Self Help Groups (SHGs) support; (ii) capacity building through increased income generation skills and, (iii) provide them micro-financing/ term loan for running micro enterprises/setting up production based activities suitable to women.

3.44 Considering inherent constraints of the conventional banking system in reaching the poor women, the financing institutions need to place a special thrust on micro-financing scheme. Besides allowing small loans for income generation, active support for promotion and stabilization of SHGs would be needed. To ensure grassroot level reach a networking of Governmental agencies and programmes with accredited organizations in the voluntary sector seems imperative. While involvement of Government agencies such as DRDA in DWACRA schemes has shown that if such agencies are decentralized and have flexible procedures they can play an important role, the main agents for micro-financing would have to be non-Governmental organizations. Such organizations can be encouraged by providing financial support by way of revolving funds or some specific project based activities. Considering the low level of skills and entrepreneurship qualities available among the women, it would also help them to encourage more and more production based activities by various NGOs/ Governmental organizations, which would ensure assured wage employment to them. While provisions for revolving funds can be a part of the normal credit operations by various organizations, special support can be provided by the Government to encourage training activities among the minority women.

3.45 The Working Group recommends a provision of Rs. 1,000 lakh for the Tenth Five Year Plan for making a breakthrough in this by assisting at least 100 NGOs of repute for organizing self-help groups, orientation and training.

3.46 For the enhancement of income generation skills of women, the ITIs and community polytechnics can play an important role. However, it has been observed that participation of women of minority communities in the polytechnics and the ITIs is negligible. The main reason is their inherent hesitation to study in co-educational institutions. Keeping in view this practical problem, the group recommends holding of separate vocational training course exclusively for women in the existing ITIs and community polytechnics in trades suited to them, to be started in the 41 minority concentration districts in the first phase during the Tenth Plan. For this purpose an amount of Rs. 205 lakh is envisaged at the rate of Rs. 5 lakh for district.

Empowerment of Artisans

3.47 The Handloom and Handicraft sector is the biggest sector after agriculture in terms of employment. Sizeable population of the minorities are engaged in these activities for earning their livelihood. Thus this is the second most important area of focus for empowerment of the minorities.

3.48 As the needs of craft-persons are multifaceted, such as relating to design development, marketing, working capital, etc., promotional schemes should be integrated in nature with an in built element of flexibility. This would mean a change from the existing system in which several schemes are implemented by promotional agencies in a parallel manner with little coordination between different schemes of the same agency, not to speak of different ones. Steps in this direction have already been initiated by recent introduction of 'Deen Dayal Hatkargha Protsahan Yojana' and Baba Saheb Ambedkar Hastshilp Vikas Yojana respectively by the Development Commissioner (Handlooms) and Development Commissioner (Handicrafts).

3.49 A cluster based integrated project dovetailed with the promotional schemes and credit programmes of financial institutions would be more suitable to need of the artisans.

3.50 Due to its uniqueness the handlooms sector should be encouraged to concentrate in such project range and markets, which are not covered, by the powerloom and the mill sector. The elite section of the society and the export market should be targeted for higher returns. To tap this market fresh designs and adequate marketing facilities will be needed.

3.51 Growth centres with required forward and backward linkages for ensuring design development, bulk processing, quality control and export based production may be set up which will facilitate design development for marketable designs, processing, finishing, and quality control for meeting the requirement of domestic market as well as exports. Training on product diversification will also be imparted there. The Group recommends an outlay of Rs. 30 crore for setting up 200 such Growth Centres in the first phase the rate of Rs. 15 lakh per centre. This may be dovetailed with the programmes of the NMDFC and other financing institutions.

3.52 To meet the working capital needs of the artisans, *credit cards* on the lines of the cards for the farmers need to be started.

3.53 It is extremely important to provide permanent marketing outlays to the craft-persons, specially targeting the higher income group customers both domestic and foreign tourists. It is recommended to open Minority Craft Bazaars at selected places, similar to 'Dilli Haat'. To begin with in the Tenth Five Year Plan, three such craft bazaars are recommended to be opened at three centres on the 'Golden Tourist Cresent' on the roads leading from Delhi to Agra, Agra to Jaipur, and Jaipur to Delhi. The scheme could be implemented by the Ministry of Social Justice & Empowerment through the National Minorities Development & Finance Corporation with tie-up with the Development Commissioner (Handicrafts) and the Ministry of Tourism. The outlays for each craft bazaar are given below:

Cost of land	:	Rs. 1.00 crore
Cost of building	:	Rs. 2.00 crore
Common facilities	:	Rs. 1.00 crore
Total	:	Rs. 4.00 crore

Thus for three outlets an outlay of Rs. 12.00 crore would be required.

CAPACITY BUILDING THROUGH SKILL DEVELOPMENT TRAINING PROGRAMMES

3.54 It has been observed that the ventures of the beneficiaries often fail on account of lack of proper training required for the trade or their skills have become outdated and do not match with the current market needs. The current financing schemes of most of the financing institutions/banks, departmental schemes either do not have provision for capacity building or lack adequate allocation. It has also been observed that it is difficult for the financing institutions to find good training institutes where quality training could be imparted to those who can be considered for financing. On the other hand, there are Government Departments/Institutions which have been created to provide training and whose infrastructure is not utilized fully as sufficient avenues are not available for fruitful absorption of the trainees. Thus, there is need for better co-ordination between the financial institutions desirous of capacity building of their prospective beneficiaries and the training institutes. Also the infrastructure of the training institutes such as the ITIs needs to be upgraded, especially in the minority concentration districts. The norms of general vocational trades may be revised by DGET and those trades that are more popular with the minorities should be included in the course curriculum of these ITIs. Capacity building should be made part of the loaning programme targeting the poorer sections including the minorities. A training module should be developed for skill development focussed on the needs of the cluster area/target group with inbuilt flexibilities and involvement of the local community.

NETWORKING WITH NGOs

3.55 Lack of awareness and information have been found to be the major handicaps in the empowerment of the minorities, particularly the poorer sections of the community. Civil society, including the religious/charitable institutions, can play a vital role in disseminating information and educating the community about various welfare schemes of the Government. Assistance of such institutions should be availed fully in identification of beneficiaries, monitoring and recovery of dues, etc.

3.56 Women, especially belonging to the minority community, are particularly vulnerable and are often subject to immense hardship. Civil society can play an active role in organizing these women into Self-Help Groups (SHGs) and providing them required skill, entrepreneurial ability, credit, etc. Success achieved by the SEWA, Ahmedabad, the SEWA,

Bhopal Development Credit Bank, and the Annapurna Mahila Mandal indicates that the involvement of *Community Based Organisations* (CBOs) in developmental programmes has led to an effective implementation of self-employment schemes. The Working Group recommends that formation of SHGs with help of the civil society should be taken as a major plank of the strategy for empowerment of women belonging to the minorities during the Tenth Plan.

National Minorities Development & Finance Corporation (NMDFC)

3.57 The group recommends that National Minorities Development & Finance Corporation (NMDFC) should be adequately strengthened during the Tenth Plan. For the purpose, the authorised share capital of the corporation should be increased from Rs. 500 crore to Rs. 1,000 crore. The Central Government is expected to contribute almost its entire earmarked share of Rs. 300 crore by the end of Ninth Five Year Plan. The capital structure of NMDFC is such that it requires the contribution of the State Govt. and the interested groups in the equity of NMDFC. NMDFC has been trying to obtain contribution from the groups/individuals/institutions. However, no success has been achieved so far. As the contribution from this group is not likely to increase substantially, the group recommends that the capital structure of NMDFC should be revised with the share of Central Govt. being 75% and that of the State Govt./UT administration being 25% in the equity of NMDFC.

3.58 By the end of the Ninth Plan period, NMDFC would have extended loans of nearly Rs. 300 crore to about 1.30 lakh families. This is a small proportion of the approximately 1.20 crore minority families targeted to be assisted. Thus there is every need to increase the quantum as well as the pace of financing. It is proposed to double the level of financing during the 10th Five Year Plan period to Rs. 600 crore to cover 2.50 lakh families under the SCA programme. The achievements under the NGO programme have been very modest during the 9th Plan period as it has taken some time to gain sufficient expertise and stabilize. However, during the 10th Five Year Plan the Corporation can be expected to provide micro-credit of about Rs. 100 crore to over 2 lakh families. Thus the financing programme of NMDFC is expected to be of the order of Rs. 600 crore under the SCA programme and another Rs. 100 crore under the NGO programme. The total financing programme is expected to be of Rs. 700 crore. During the 9th Five Year Plan period, an amount of nearly Rs. 300 crore is expected to be disbursed by NMDFC against the paid-up capital of Rs. 235.44 crore. Funds are disbursed by NMDFC for a maximum period of 5 years. It is expected that the disbursement of Rs. 300 crore made during 9th Plan will be recovered during the 10th Five Year Plan period. This NMDFC shall have Rs. 300 crore available with it for ploughing it back for further financing as per the projections of 10th Five Year Plan period. It may however, be seen that there will be a shortfall of Rs. 400 crore which shall have to be met primarily through contribution by the Central Govt. Thus the outlay for contribution towards the equity of NMDFC during the Tenth Five Year Plan is proposed at Rs. 300 crore (Rs. 60 crore per year) and the balance Rs. 100 crore will be contributed by the State Governments.

Thrust areas in Credit Delivery Mechanism

3.59 In various credit programmes of the banks as well as Government specific targets for the minorities should be fixed and monitored at various levels. This would help to ensure that necessary benefits reach the minorities as part of the general programmes.

3.60 To have a wider reach and acceptability among the minorities, it is recommended that the financing institutions are encouraged to network with the financial institutions of the minorities. This would include the institutions which have been registered as Trusts or Societies and are taking up grass root activities among the beneficiaries specially those relating to income generation and credit, as well as traditional financial institutions like cooperative banks and cooperative societies of the minorities.

3.61 Poor people need a personalized approach. Owing to their illiteracy or low literacy, there is a special need to making the channels of communication effective and transparent. The need for proper motivation and mobilization is foremost. Financial institutions would do well to opt for cluster based personalized approach to ensure that selected beneficiaries are not discouraged by cumbersome procedures and running around various Government offices/Banks for different purposes. The approach would also include the post disbursement follow up including timely recoveries. Involving local persons in various kinds of enquiry and scrutiny can prove to be extremely effective.

3.62 Closer coordination between the promotional organizations like the Development Commissioner (Handlooms), Development Commissioner (Handicrafts) and financing institutions is required.

Social Sector

3.63 In the social sector the importance of religious and social institutions such as Churches, Mosques, Gurudwaras, Wakfs has to be recognized and their cooperation elicited for reaching out to the target groups in a more effective manner.

Delivery of Health Services

3.64 It has to be ensured that health services including family welfare schemes provided by the Government reach out effectively to the minorities, especially the poor in both quality service and timely delivery. To achieve this objective, community involvement appears to be of critical importance in the strategy for delivery of health services to minorities as it will not only smoothens reach but also facilitate acceptance. Cooperation of religious and other social institutions among the minorities may be elicited for the effective implementation of the Information, Education and Communication (IEC) component in the health sector. The cooperation of institutions like the Central Wakf Council and the State Wakf Boards can also be obtained. It is felt that representation of the target communities among the implementing staff would improve delivery of services.

3.65 The Working Group appreciates the importance of the Indian Systems of Medicine and Homeopathy and recommends that the benefits of Ayurveda, Unani, Homeopathy, etc., systems may be availed of along with the greater involvement of the community for helping the minorities more effectively.

3.66 . . . The Working Group recommends that the NGOs should be encouraged to spread their activities in the areas/villages inhabited by educationally and economically backward minority communities for improving the delivery of health services as well as promotion of the small family norms.

Management of Wakfs

3.67 As noted in Chapter-II, improvement in management of Wakfs is crucial not only for the preservation of religious and charitable institutions but also for the educational and economic development of the minority community. Since 1974-5 the Central Government has been giving grant-in-aid to the Central Wakf Council for the development of Urban Wakf Properties. The Council extends loan to Wakf institutions and charges 6% donation on the outstanding amount of loan repayable which is used to fund its programmes for educational development. The amount received as repayment of loan forms a revolving fund, which is used to fund minor development projects up to Rs. 20 lakh. Sizeable number of proposals are pending from State Wakf Boards and individual Wakf management for development of respective Wakf properties, which could not be processed due to inadequate fund. There is enormous potential for commercial development of wakf properties. The increased income can be utilized for the purposes of taking measures to protect the Wakf land/properties and construction of boundary walls around graveyards, Idgah (Prayer grounds), etc., instead of looking for government assistance.

3.68 In view of the procedure followed for availing bank loan and the legal aspects of management of wakf properties, the group recommends that the Non-Plan scheme of grant to the Central Wakf Council for *Development of Urban Wakf Properties* may be brought under the Plan and Rs. 25 crore may be provided during the Plan period.

3.69 The National Foundation for Communal Harmony (NFCH) was set up in 1992 under the aegis of Ministry of Home Affairs to undertake programmes for assisting children of families affected by communal violence, particularly for their physical and psychological rehabilitation including their education/vocational training, and for their assimilation into the mainstream. This scheme needs to be given wide publicity and the provision enhanced suitably. A corpus also needs to be established with all the State Governments and particularly the major riot-prone States, so as to enable them to make payment to the families of the victims as compensation for the loss of life and property.

Building up of Data Base on Minorities

3.70 It is observed that the data relating to demographic and socio-economic characteristics of the minorities is collected during the censuses but it is not collated. This has resulted in a significant information gap limiting the effectiveness of Government interventions. It is felt, for example, that State-wise and district-wise literacy figures for men and women among the minorities can be a useful pointer for prioritizing flow of assistance within these areas. The Registrar General & Census Commissioner of India may be requested to collate and publish the data on the basis of religion. In case it is not possible to do so for the entire country, the same needs to be done at least for the identified Minority Concentration Districts in the country.

Abstract of Financial Outlays Proposed

3.72 . . . The abstract of outlays proposed under various schemes during the Tenth Plan for empowering the minorities is given in the following Table:

Abstract of Outlays proposed in Tenth Five Year Plan

S. No.	Details of the Scheme	Page No.	Para No.	Ministry/ Deptt.	Outlay (Rs. Lakh)
1.	Area Intensive Programme	39	3.15	HRD	54,750
2	Modernization of Madrasa Education	41	3.18	HRD	19,475
3.	Community Polytechnics	42	3.21	HRD	5,125
4.	Diploma Computer Applications and Multilingual DTP	42-3	3.23	HRD	2,500
5.	Provision of Urdu Teachers	43	3.24	HRD	1,980
6.	Remedial Coaching	45	3.32	HRD	3,826
7.	Maulana Azad Education Foundation	46	3.35	SJ & E	13,000
8.	Merit linked scholarship	46	3.36	SJ & E	8,500
9.	Scheme for Hostels	47	3.38	SJ & E	12,300
10.	Scheme for coaching	47-8	3.40	SJ & E	5,000
11.	Educational Schemes of the Central Wakf Council	48	3.41	SJ & E	2,500
12.	Vocational Training for Women	48	3.42	Lab./HRD	1,000
13.	Training for capacity building	50	3.45	SJ & E	1,000
14.	Vocational Training for Women	50	3.46	Lab./HRD	205
15.	Growth Centres for support to Craft-persons	51	3.51	SJ & E	3,000
16.	Craft Bazaars	51-2	3.53	SJ & E	1,200
17.	Equity support to NMDFC	54	3.58	SJ & E	30,000
18.	Development of Urban Wakf Properties	57	3.68	SJ & E	2,500
					Total Rs. 1,67,861 lakh or (say) Rs. 1,679 crore

Conclusion

The strategy for the empowerment of the minorities during the Tenth Five Year will be multi-faceted in nature and would involve effective interventions by the Central Government, State Governments, Panchayati Raj institutions, local bodies, and also the various minority institutions and religious bodies. Involvement of the civil society at large including NGOs, in particular, would play an important role in this strategy. It is through the wider interaction between the government, the institutions, and the community, and their combined efforts, that the goal of empowering the minorities and their mainstreaming can be achieved.

Index

Note: Some full names (with titles) which were difficult to insert into the text in the proof stage have been included in the index.